D0206289

THE DISSENTERS

II

THE DISSENTERS

Volume II
The Expansion of Evangelical Nonconformity

Michael R. Watts

CLARENDON PRESS · OXFORD
1995

LIBRARY
SCHOOL OF LAW
IN SOUTH ASIA

Oxford University Press, Walton Street, Oxford OX2 6DP

Oxford New York
Athens Auckland Bangkok Bombay
Calcutta Cape Town Dar es Salaam Delhi
Florence Hong Kong Istanbul Karachi
Kuala Lumpur Madras Madrid Melbourne
Mexico City Nairobi Paris Singapore
Taipei Tokyo Toronto
and associated companies in
Berlin Ibadan

Oxford is a trade mark of Oxford University Press

Published in the United States
by Oxford University Press Inc., New York

© *Michael Watts 1995*

First published 1995

All rights reserved. No part of this publication may be reproduced,
stored in a retrieval system, or transmitted, in any form or by any means,
without the prior permission in writing of Oxford University Press.
Within the UK, exceptions are allowed in respect of any fair dealing for the
purpose of research or private study, or criticism or review, as permitted
under the Copyright, Designs and Patents Act, 1988, or in the case of
reprographic reproduction in accordance with the terms of the licences
issued by the Copyright Licensing Agency. Enquiries concerning
reproduction outside these terms and in other countries should be
sent to the Rights Department, Oxford University Press,
at the address above

British Library Cataloguing in Publication Data
Data available

Library of Congress Cataloging in Publication Data
Watts, Michael R.
The dissenters.
Includes index.
Bibliography: v. 2, p. [511]–514.
Contents: v. 2. From the Reformation to the French Revolution.
1. Dissenters, Religious—England—History.
2. England—Church history. I. Title.
BX5203.2.W37 280'.4'0941 77–30144

ISBN 0–19–822968–2

1 3 5 7 9 10 8 6 4 2

Typeset by Jayvee, Trivandrum, India
Printed in Great Britain
on acid-free paper by
Biddles Ltd., Guildford and King's Lynn

**LIBRARY
ALMA COLLEGE
ALMA, MICHIGAN**

For Linda

LIBRARY
ALMA COLLEGE
ALMA, MICHIGAN

Preface

I MUST begin this, the second volume of *The Dissenters*, with an apology for the length of time it has taken to reach the public. My excuse is simple: I have tried to apply the same research techniques to the first half of the nineteenth century that I applied to the seventeenth and eighteenth centuries and the vast quantity of material available has all but overwhelmed me. The two major sources for plotting the numerical strength and geographic distribution of Dissent are the list compiled by Dr John Evans between 1715 and 1718, and now in Dr Williams's Library, and the religious census of 1851 conducted by Horace Mann. Whereas the Evans manuscript lists some 1,100 Dissenting congregations scattered among 52 counties, the published report of the 1851 religious census reveals the existence of nearly 20,000 Nonconformist congregations dispersed throughout 624 registration districts. This published report has provided the basis for many of the calculations and for the maps in this volume, but is itself merely the digest of the original manuscript returns in the Public Record Office. I have examined these original returns for Nottinghamshire and for a selection of other districts, but the exploration of all 19,478 would be beyond the capacity of a single historian. A crucial source for an understanding of the social and economic status of Dissent are the non-parochial birth and baptismal registers for the period before 1837 which are also lodged in the Public Record Office. But whereas only some hundred or so Dissenting registers have survived from the early eighteenth century, and few of these contain evidence of the occupations of the fathers who had their children baptized in Dissenting meeting-houses, nearly 4,000 have survived from the first four decades of the nineteenth century, and nearly half of these provide evidence of parental occupation. All the registers in the Public Record Office for the period covered by this book have been examined; in addition registers in seventeen County Record Offices have been researched for the post-1837 period; and all the information derived from these registers has been analysed to determine the social structure of the chapels concerned. Finally there is the most important source of all for the study of nineteenth-century Nonconformity: the periodical press. In the mid-eighteenth century there was not a single Nonconformist periodical in existence: the first periodical to be edited by a Dissenter was Joseph Priestley's *Theological Repository* which made its appearance in 1769.[1] By 1850 at least thirty-nine Nonconformist periodicals were being published[2] and in addition scores of secular newspapers were being published and edited by Dissenters. All these periodicals reported Nonconformist activities, provided evidence of Nonconformist growth, and reflected Nonconformist opinion. It is impossible for a single researcher to do more than sample a tiny proportion of this enormous output and I can only hope that what I have looked at is representative of what I have not.

It is pleasant to turn from apologies to thanks. The enormous task of transcribing fathers' occupations, together with their names, from nearly 2,000 birth and baptismal registers became almost a family business, involving my wife Linda, my daughter Rosemary, and my cousin Christine Jakeman. Analysing the material thus collected was an even more formidable undertaking for which I received the help of Linda, Rita Holt, Freda Duckitt, and Stephen Wallwork. But the greater part of the burden both of transcribing and of analysing was borne by Rachel Pardoe, an enthusiastic, supremely efficient, and seemingly tireless research assistant. Funding for the project was provided by the British Academy and support at a crucial point was offered by Professor Patrick Collinson and by Emeritus Professor W. R. Fryer. To all I am deeply grateful.

The University of Nottingham provided funds for the subsequent investigation of post-1837 baptismal registers in a selection of County Record Offices and also for the drawing of the maps at the end of this volume. The maps were drawn by Chris Lewis and Elaine Watts of the Nottingham University Geography department with their usual exemplary skill. Much of the work for this book was done in the splendid surroundings of Dr Williams's Library in London and I am indebted to the trustees and librarians of that magnificent institution for providing a haven of peace, sanity, and scholarship in an increasingly crazy academic world. In particular I must once again express my gratitude to Janet Barnes for her unfailing courtesy, kindness, and efficiency, even when carrying the heaviest tomes of the *Patriot* or the *Nonconformist* to my table. My frequent visits to London have been made all the more pleasant by the kind hospitality provided by Angeline and Leon Paget and by my daughter and son-in-law Rosemary and James

[1] J. L. Altholz, *The Religious Press in Britain, 1760–1900* (Westport, Connecticut, 1989), 10.
[2] Ibid., *passim*.

Sawyer. The wonderful Jewish–Baptist household presided over by Leon and Angeline provided me with love and solace at a traumatic juncture of my life, and Alan Paget on numerous occasions willingly surrendered his bed to me.

I am grateful for the help afforded me by the staffs of the British Library, the Friends House library, the Public Record Office, and the John Rylands Library, Manchester, and by the archivists of the Bedford, Birmingham, Bradford, Chelmsford, Colchester, Greater London, Halifax, Huddersfield, Leeds, Leicester, Maidstone, Matlock, Northampton, Nottingham, Sheffield, Wakefield, and Warwick Record Offices. I am particularly indebted to the numerous scholars who have allowed me to read and cite information from their unpublished theses, and to the librarians to whose care such theses are entrusted. The librarians of Nottingham University have fought a valiant battle, confronted by rising student numbers and limited funds, to keep up with my demands, and in particular I must thank Patricia Hargreaves, Barbara Rogers, and Elizabeth Le Marchant Brock for the efficiency with which they have operated the Nottingham end of the interlibrary loan service on my behalf. Of my colleagues at Nottingham Dr Alan Booth, Professor Stanley Chapman, Julian Robinson, and Professor Chris Wrigley have all lent books, exchanged ideas, and listened patiently to my constant expositions of the history of Dissent; Stephen Wallwork confirmed the correlation between areas of high Nonconformist support and of high rates of illiteracy on his computer; and a former student, Debra Lewis, provided me with translations from Welsh. Finally I must thank my typist Barbara Andrews, without whose efficiency, speed, and good humour this book would have taken even longer to produce, and my wife Linda, without whose love, tolerance, and constant support it might never have appeared at all.

MICHAEL WATTS

Lowdham,
Nottinghamshire,
The feast of St Stephen,
1993

Contents

List of Illustrations

FIGURE

MAPS

List of Tables

List of Abbreviations

BMS	Baptist Missionary Society
DNB	*Dictionary of National Biography*
DWB	*Dictionary of Welsh Biography*
DWL	Dr Williams's Library, London
HMC	R. Davies, A. R. George, and G. Rupp (eds.), *A History of the Methodist Church in Great Britain*, 4 vols. (1965–88)
JFHS	*Journal of the Friends Historical Society*
LMS	London Missionary Society
PRO	Public Record Office
PWHS	*Proceedings of the Wesley Historical Society*
TBHS	*Transactions of the Baptist Historical Society*
TCHS	*Transactions of the Congregational Historical Society*
TUHS	*Transactions of the Unitarian Historical Society*
WYAS	West Yorkshire Archive Service

All works referred to in the footnotes were published in London unless otherwise stated.

Introduction

ENGLISH, and still more Welsh, society in the nineteenth century was profoundly influenced by religion. For millions of English men and women, and for tens of thousands of Welsh men and women, religion determined their choice of marriage partners, conditioned the upbringing of their children, and moulded their family life. Religion pervaded education, shaped morals, motivated philanthropy, controlled leisure, permeated literature, inspired poetry, stimulated music, reduced crime, inhibited class conflict, moderated industrial strife, decided political loyalties, and on occasion influenced foreign and imperial policy. The chief characteristic of nineteenth-century religion was Evangelicalism, the belief that every man and woman was heir to the sin of Adam and destined to spend eternity in hell unless justified by faith, through the personal experience called conversion, in the sacrifice which Christ had made on his or her behalf on the cross at Calvary. Instead of being damned to suffer eternal torment in the fires of hell, those men and women who experienced conversion believed that they would, after death, enjoy everlasting bliss in heaven. A substantial minority of Anglicans subscribed to the Evangelical version of Christianity in the first half of the nineteenth century, but the influence of Evangelicalism on the lives of the English and Welsh peoples was mediated primarily through the channels of the Baptists, the Congregationalists, and the Methodists: the Dissenters.

The Congregationalists, alternatively known as Independents, traced their ancestry back to the Separatists of the reign of Queen Elizabeth and believed in the independence of the local Christian congregation to conduct its own affairs under God's guidance, without interference from bishop, synod, or the State. In theology the Congregationalists were officially followers of the sixteenth-century reformer John Calvin, believing that a man's eternal destiny to either enduring happiness or everlasting punishment was predetermined by the decrees of a sovereign God, but in the course of the eighteenth century such views were modified in a way which permitted the preaching of the Gospel to all and which thus enabled the Congregationalists to benefit from the explosion of Evangelical enthusiasm in the second half of the century. The majority of Baptists agreed with Congregationalists on questions of church government and on theology and because of their adherence to the tenets of Calvinism were known as Particular Baptists. The Particular Baptists differed from the Congregationalists only in their insistence on administering baptism not to infants but to converted believers. But though claiming that salvation was particular to the elect rather than general to all men the Particular Baptists, too, were moderating their Calvinism to the extent of agreeing with one of their leading preachers, the elder Robert Hall, that the way to Jesus was 'open for everyone who chooses to come to him'. A minority of Baptists, the General Baptists, had always rejected the Calvinist belief that some men were predestined to eternal damnation but by the late eighteenth century were themselves divided into a literalist section which was moving towards Unitarianism and an Evangelical section which formed themselves into the New Connexion of General Baptists in 1770. Rejection of Calvinism was also one of the central tenets of those Methodists who followed the lead of John Wesley. Wesley named his monthly periodical, the *Arminian Magazine*, after the Dutch sixteenth-century opponent of Calvin, Jacob Arminius. But other Methodists, including the main body of Methodists in Wales and the followers of George Whitefield and the Countess of Huntingdon in England, adhered, like the Congregationalists, to the central Calvinist tenet of the sovereignty of God without it in any way impeding their evangelistic zeal. Both the Arminian Methodists in England and the Calvinistic Methodists in Wales had begun as revivalist movements within the Church of England, but by the time of Wesley's death in 1791 many of his followers had only tenuous links with the established church and the Calvinistic Methodists of Wales severed their connections with the Church of England in 1810–11.

Not all Dissenters were Evangelicals. By the late eighteenth century many Presbyterians, who traced their ancestry back to the clergymen who were ejected from their livings in 1662 for refusing their 'unfeigned assent and consent' to everything in the Prayer Book, had rejected the Trinity in favour of belief in the unity of God and were seeking to apply rational criteria to traditional Christian teaching. Doyen of these rational Dissenters was the scientist, philosopher, and historian Joseph Priestley, the destruction of whose home and meeting-house at the hands of the Birmingham mob in 1791 brought to an end the first volume of this work. A substantial number of Quakers, the followers of the seventeenth-century seer George Fox, also rejected Evangelicalism. By the end of the eighteenth century the Quakers had lost much of their earlier missionary zeal in favour of obedience to the inner light and a passive waiting on God which was known as quietism. Unitarian rationalism and Quaker quietism alike impeded church growth, and Nonconformity was increasingly dominated by the three great Evangelical movements of Congregationalism, Methodism, and the Baptists.

The extent of popular support for Evangelical Nonconformity was made evident by the unique religious census of 1851. The census revealed that some 40 per cent of the population of England and Wales were present at a place of worship on Sunday, 30 March 1851, and that nearly half that 40 per cent were Protestant Nonconformists. It was a measure of the hold that religion had over the leaders of opinion in early Victorian England that that figure of 40 per cent was regarded as appallingly low. Contemporaries had no knowledge of the low levels of religious observance in England in previous centuries and were not to know of the collapse in attendance at public worship that was to come in the twentieth century. Viewed in the light of historical perspective, what was remarkable about the level of religious practice in 1851 was not that it was so low, but that it was so high. If one views religion, as did the Dissenters, as a matter of individual conscience and personal profession rather than outward obedience to the constable or the magistrate, then there can have been few, if any, periods of history when the English and the Welsh nations were as deeply religious as they were in the early decades of Queen Victoria's reign.

Evangelical Christianity was not just the preoccupation of ministers of religion and itinerant evangelists, it was not the motivating force merely of public figures such as William Wilberforce and Lord Shaftesbury, it affected the lives, the loves, the hopes, and the fears of millions of ordinary men and women. If the appeal of rational Dissent was often to the prosperous, the well-educated, and the cultured, Evangelical Nonconformity found its main support among the poor, the ignorant, and the unsophisticated. In its impact on the lives of working-class men and women the influence of Evangelical Nonconformity was behind only that of the population explosion, the industrial revolution, and possibly that of its great rival, the public house. The Nonconformist chapel touched the lives of far more working-class people in the first half of the nineteenth century than did either political radicalism or trade unionism. The adherents of Evangelical Dissent vastly outnumbered those of Owenism, Socialism, or even Chartism. The history of late Georgian and Victorian England and Wales cannot be understood without a knowledge of Nonconformity.

I

'Expect Great Things from God...'
The Expansion of Dissent, 1791–1851

1. 'THE KNOWLEDGE OF THE LORD SHALL COVER
THE WHOLE EARTH': COKE, CAREY,
AND MISSIONARY ENTERPRISE

The French Revolution was a divide in British as well as in French history. It revived memories of the constitutional struggles of the seventeenth century, it fostered new political alignments, it gave fresh meaning to the old terms Whig and Tory, and it aroused hopes of the dawning of a new age of civil liberty and spiritual awakening. To those Whigs who followed Charles James Fox and to those radical Dissenters who shared the views of Joseph Priestley and Richard Price, the revolution in Paris was a belated recognition by their continental neighbours of the principle that Englishmen had asserted in 1688: that an oppressed people has the right to depose a tyrannical ruler. To Tories who found a new apostle in Edmund Burke and to Anglicans who discovered a novel sympathy with French Roman Catholics, the execution of Louis XVI was a hideous reminder of the death of Charles I, a blasphemous crime against a man anointed by God to preserve the fabric of society against anarchy. But to Methodists and Evangelical Dissenters the overthrow of the Roman Catholic church in France presented a new field for missionary enterprise, and perhaps the beginning of the days prophesied by Isaiah, when 'the earth shall be full of the knowledge of the Lord, as the waters cover the sea'.[1]

The contrasting attitudes of rational Dissenters and Evangelical Nonconformists were exemplified by the differing purposes of two of their

---

[1] Isaiah 11: 9.

representatives who journeyed to France in the early years of the revolution. In the spring of 1790 William Taylor, the future literary critic, German scholar, and friend of Robert Southey, was a twenty-four-year-old member of Norwich's Unitarian Octagon meeting. His father, also named William Taylor, was a wealthy Unitarian textile manufacturer and secretary of Norwich's Revolution Society. On 7 May 1790 the younger Taylor sailed to France with letters of introduction from Richard Price to the Duc de la Rochefoucauld and with the intention of listening to the debates in the National Assembly. On landing at Calais Taylor 'kissed the earth on the land of liberty', and four days later rejoiced at his arrival in Paris 'within these dazzling precincts of freedom'.[2] Sixteen months later, in September 1791, the Anglican clergyman and Methodist preacher Thomas Coke also crossed the English Channel. His purpose was not to celebrate the cause of liberty or to take fraternal greetings to the National Assembly, but to take advantage of the discomfiture of the Roman Catholic church to establish a Methodist mission in France. He ordained two French-speaking evangelists from Jersey and Guernsey for service in France and was able to establish a class of thirty Methodists in Caen. But he found Paris less congenial than William Taylor. Having purchased a disused church for £120 he was able to attract a congregation of only six; he was threatened with being strung up from a lamppost if he stayed; and he had to admit that 'our success in that dissolute city was not equal to our expectations'.[3]

Eight months after Coke's journey to France, on Tuesday, 29 May 1792, ministers and representatives of the churches of the Northamptonshire Particular Baptist Association, churches extending from St Albans in Hertfordshire to Sutton-in-Ashfield in Nottinghamshire, met at the Baptist meeting-house in Friar Lane, Nottingham, for three days of prayer, sermons, and business. The assembled delegates had in their hands a recently published pamphlet by William Carey, the minister of the Harvey Lane Baptist church in Leicester, a pamphlet entitled *An Enquiry into the Obligation of Christians to use Means for the Conversion of the Heathen*. The burden of Carey's message was that Christians should not only pray for the coming of Christ's kingdom, but should 'use every lawful method to spread the knowledge of his name'.[4] This, too, was the theme of the sermon which he preached on the second day of the proceedings at Nottingham, based on Isaiah 54: 2, 3, 'Enlarge the place of thy tent, and let them stretch forth the curtains of thy

   [2] J. W. Robberds, *A Memoir of the Life and Writings of the late William Taylor* (1843), i. 67–8.

   [3] J. Vickers, *Thomas Coke, Apostle of Methodism* (1969), 312–13.

   [4] W. Carey, *An Enquiry into the Obligation of Christians to use Means for the Conversion of the Heathen* (1934, facsimile of the 1st edn., Leicester, 1792), 3.

habitations'. The combined effect of Carey's pamphlet and sermon was seen on the following day, 31 May, when the ministers and church representatives, after voting that five guineas be forwarded to the committee 'for procuring the abolition of the inhuman and ungodly trade in the persons of men', resolved that 'a plan be prepared against the next ministers' meeting at Kettering, for forming a Baptist society for propagating the Gospel among the heathens'.[5] The delegates returned to their homes and churches with Carey's message ringing in their ears, 'Expect great things from God, attempt great things for God'.[6]

Carey's choice of words was significant, for his sermon and Coke's visit to France were symptomatic of the sense of expectancy with which Dissenters and Methodists waited for the opening of the nineteenth century, a sense of expectancy borne up by the continuing impetus of the Evangelical revival, fed by the study of biblical prophesies, encouraged by the events in France, and given scope by the expansion of British influence throughout the world. The apocalyptic hopes expressed by Dissenters in the 1790s recalled those of their millenarian forefathers a century and a half earlier.[7] The deacons of the Maze Pond Particular Baptist church in London saw the French Revolution as a link 'in that great chain of events foretold in Scripture which will finally issue in [Christ's] glory and the happiness of mankind'.[8] For Thomas Coke, writing in 1790, the Lord was 'hastening apace the great millennium, when Christ shall reign with his ancients gloriously a thousand years'.[9] The younger Robert Hall, just embarking on his career as pastor of the Baptist church in Cambridge, wrote in his *Christianity consistent with a Love of Freedom* in 1791 that 'the scenes of Providence thicken upon us so fast . . . as if the great drama of the world were drawing to a close'.[10] The younger John Ryland, taking the chair at the Nottingham meeting of the Northamptonshire Baptist Association in May 1792, declared that 'circumstances were conspiring towards the fulfilment of great prophecies'.[11] The Congregationalist David Bogue told a London meeting of the Society in

---

[5] *Godly Zeal, described and recommended in a Circular Letter, from the Baptist Ministers and Messengers Assembled in Nottingham* (1792).

[6] E. A. Payne, in the *Baptist Quarterly*, 22 (1967–8), 326–7, argued that Carey's words were 'Expect great things; attempt great things', but the fuller version passed into Baptist folklore and in this form it has been repeated continually for two centuries.

[7] For the connection between millenarian expectations and the missionary movement see J. A. De Jong, *As the Waters Cover the Sea, 1640–1810* (Kampen, Netherlands, 1970), *passim*.

[8] *Baptist Quarterly*, 8 (1936–7), 216.

[9] D. Hempton and M. Hill, *Evangelical Protestantism in Ulster Society* (1992), 29.

[10] R. Hall, *Christianity consistent with a Love of Freedom* (1791), 76.

[11] S. P. Carey, *William Carey* (1923), 80.

Scotland for Propagating Christian Knowledge that just as Satan had used the tyrannical government of Louis XIV to banish the Protestant religion from France, so 'the present zeal for liberty [was] designed by the great Governor of the world as a preparatory step to the extending of the Redeemer's kingdom'.[12] The Baptist James Bicheno identified Louis XVI with the beast of Revelation 13: 11 and saw the fall of the French monarchy as the prelude to the coming of the millennium in 1864.[13] Even the sober Joseph Priestley saw the destruction of the temporal power of the Roman church in France as partial fulfilment of the destruction of 'the mystical Babylon' foretold in the Revelation of John, and expected 'the late wonderful extension of navigation' to be the means of carrying knowledge of the Gospel to every nation of the world, the necessary prelude to the return of Christ.[14] And when Calvinist ministers of various paedobaptist persuasions came together at the end of 1794 to emulate their Baptist brethren and take steps which led to the formation of the London Missionary Society, their first circular letter referred to 'the recent "shaking of nations" ' which had 'led not a few pious minds to anticipate those glorious days, when "the knowledge of the Lord shall cover the whole earth" '.[15]

Though apocalyptic expectations quickened the interest of their fellow countrymen in missionary enterprises, the concern of Coke and Carey went back longer and deeper. The two men were drawn from different backgrounds and were of contrasting personality. Thomas Coke, born in 1747 to the wife of a successful Brecon apothecary, was educated at Jesus College, Oxford, and later obtained from his university a doctorate in Civil Law. He was ordained to the Anglican ministry and served as a curate to the Somerset parish of South Petherton until 1776 when, having come under Evangelical influences, he tried to replace the singing of the Psalms with the hymns of Charles Wesley and was dismissed. Coke met John Wesley for the first time in August 1776, he threw in his lot with the Methodists, and, as an Anglican clergyman without parochial duties or family responsibilities, soon rose to prominence in the Methodist movement. Wesley himself came to regard Coke as his 'right hand', to the resentment of Methodist preachers of longer service.[16] By comparison William Carey's parentage was humble and his

[12] D. Bogue, *A Sermon Preached at Salters Hall, 30 March 1792, before the Correspondent Board in London of the Society in Scotland for Propagating Christian Knowledge* (1793), 46–8.

[13] De Jong, *As the Waters Cover the Sea*, 163.

[14] *Theological and Miscellaneous Works of Joseph Priestley*, ed. J. T. Rutt (1817–31), xv. 544–5, 548.

[15] J. Morison, *The Fathers and Founders of the London Missionary Society* (1844), p. xvi.

[16] Vickers, *Thomas Coke*, 34–5, 43.

schooling limited. He was born in the village of Paulers Pury in Northamptonshire in 1761, his father earning his living as a hand-loom weaver until he became master of the village school which was to provide all that William had by way of formal education. Carey's parents, like Coke's, were Anglicans, but when William was apprenticed to a shoemaker at the age of fourteen he was thrown into the company of a fellow apprentice, John Warr, a Congregationalist who was the instrument of his conversion and of his secession to Dissent. In 1781 Carey joined a newly formed Congregational church at Hackleton, but two years later he embraced Baptist views and was baptized in the River Nene at Northampton by the younger John Ryland. Having moved to the village of Moulton in 1785 to take up the post of village schoolmaster, Carey accepted an invitation to become pastor of the local Particular Baptist church in the following year. Since his annual stipend was only £10— supplemented by five guineas from the Particular Baptist Fund—he continued to teach and to cobble, and even carried on his trade after moving to the better-paid pastorate of the Harvey Lane church in Leicester in 1789.[17] When, in later years, a pompous critic sought to demean his character, he referred to him by the term which had been used of an earlier pastor-cobbler, Samuel How, that of 'tub-preacher'.[18]

The characters of Coke and Carey befitted their parentage and upbringing. Coke was a rotund, fresh-faced, handsome, impetuous Welshman, perhaps a little too full of his own importance, the man who, appointed superintendent of American Methodism, accepted to Wesley's horror the title of bishop of the Methodist Episcopal Church, the man who, when comparing Wesley to Elijah, did not scruple to reserve the role of Elisha to himself.[19] By contrast Carey was a man of slight build, of pleasing but undistinguished features, looking older than his years as a result of premature baldness, a man of deep humility who, notwithstanding his considerable achievements, was dogged by a sense of his own guilt and unworthiness.[20]

Yet, despite their wide differences of upbringing and personality, Coke and Carey shared a common concern for the salvation of the heathen. In the case neither of the Methodist Coke nor of the Baptist Carey did their views find easy favour among their co-religionists. As early as 1778, only two years after he had joined the Wesleyans, Coke had circulated Methodist preachers

[17] Carey, *William Carey*, 1–61.

[18] Ibid. 308. The critic was Charles Marsh, MP for East Retford. For Samuel How see M. R. Watts, *The Dissenters* (Oxford, 1978), i. 69–79.

[19] Vickers, *Thomas Coke*, 47, 118.

[20] E. A. Payne, 'Carey and his Biographers', *Baptist Quarterly*, 19 (1961–2), 10; E. D. Potts, *British Baptist Missionaries in India* (Cambridge, 1967), 18.

with an appeal for volunteers to take the Gospel to West Africa, but the Methodist Conference declined to take any action. 'You have nothing to do at present in Africa,' wrote Wesley to one who did volunteer, 'Convert the heathen in Scotland.' Five years later, in 1783, Coke issued a *Plan of the Society for the Establishment of Missions among the Heathens*, and although a subscription list was opened nothing else was done. Coke had set his heart on sending missionaries to Bengal, yet again Wesley tempered the Welsh-man's enthusiasm, thinking it 'imprudent to hazard at present the lives of any of our preachers, by sending them to so great a distance, and amidst so many uncertainties and difficulties'. But Wesley was prepared to support the dispatch of missionaries to what was left of British North America and to the West Indies, and in 1786 Coke opened a second subscription list with Wesley's approval.[21] There were already 1,100 negro Methodists on the island of Antigua: Methodism had been introduced in 1759 by Nathaniel Gilbert, the son of a wealthy planter, and his work had been continued after his death by John Baxter, a shipwright who settled in the island in 1778. And now, in 1786, the Methodist Conference appointed a missionary, William Warrener, to assist Baxter in Antigua and two other preachers for New-foundland. They set sail, in company with Coke, in September 1786, intend-ing to make their landfall at Halifax, but the ship was blown off course and they made straight for the West Indies, landing on Antigua on the morning of Christmas day. Coke visited six of the islands, settled missionaries on St Vincent and St Christopher as well as on Antigua, and came again in 1788–9, 1790, and 1792–3. By 1814 Methodist membership in the Caribbean had increased to 17,000.[22]

As long as he lived Coke shouldered, almost alone, the burden of organiz-ing and financing Methodist missionary work. A large part of the fortune he inherited from his father was devoted to missions; so, too, was much of the wealth of the woman whom he married in 1805, the daughter of a prosperous solicitor. When he was not in the United States or the West Indies he was touring Britain to raise money for the missions and when, in 1793, the deficit on missionary work rose to £2,167, Coke himself gave £917 to help to wipe off the debt. Although the Methodist Conference authorized an annual collec-tion for missionary work in all congregations from 1798 onwards, it was not until 1813 that the first local Methodist Missionary Society was founded—in Leeds—and it was not until 1818 that the local societies were united in the General Wesleyan Methodist Missionary Society. By that time Coke had been dead four years.[23] In 1811 the Conference had empowered Coke to plan

---

[21] Vickers, *Thomas Coke*, 132–7.   [22] Ibid. 149–72.   [23] Ibid. 262–8, 353–4.

the realization of his long-cherished dream: a mission to the East. Ceylon, under direct British rule since 1795, rather than India, under the control of the unsympathetic East India Company, was the chosen field, and Coke and eight companions embarked on 30 December 1813. During the voyage Coke set himself the task of learning Portuguese, but the strain of studying in a stuffy cabin in a tropical climate proved too much for his sixty-seven years: he died on 3 May 1814 and his body was committed to the waves of the Indian Ocean. Three weeks later his companions landed in Bombay to launch the Wesleyan mission to Asia.[24]

In 1786 Coke had dreamed of Bengal and had been diverted to the West Indies; seven years later William Carey, who had dreamed of Tahiti, sailed to Bengal. In the mid-1780s Carey had read the *Journal of Captain Cook's Last Voyage*, a book which had fired his imagination with stories of adventure in the South Seas, yet had challenged his conscience with its accounts of the savagery and idolatry of the natives. As village schoolmaster at Moulton Carey put his skill in shoemaking to pedagogic use by stitching together a leather globe of the world, and he collected information concerning the size, population, and religion of foreign countries and entered his findings on a handmade map which hung on the wall of his schoolroom. In later years he used this information in his *Enquiry*, to calculate that, of the 731 million people in the world, 431 million were pagan and a further 130 million Muslims.[25] But Carey's concern for the 'vast portion of the sons of Adam . . . who yet remain in the most deplorable state of heathen darkness' was not at first shared by his fellow Baptists. The story is told that when Carey raised the question of a mission to the heathen at a meeting of the Northamptonshire ministers in 1786, the elder John Ryland silenced Carey with the words, 'Young man, sit down: when God pleases to convert the heathen, he will do it without your aid or mine.'[26] The younger Ryland later denied that his father could have uttered such High Calvinist sentiments, but some such confrontation appears to have taken place. And even Andrew Fuller, minister of the Kettering Baptist church, whose attempt to reconcile evangelism with Calvinism in *The Gospel Worthy of All Acceptation* had been published in the previous year, shied away from the magnitude of the task.[27] But ever since 1784 the churches of the Northamptonshire Association had been holding monthly prayer meetings for 'the spread of the Gospel to the most distant

---

[24] Ibid. 357–66.   [25] Carey, *Enquiry*, 62.

[26] J. C. Marshman, *The Story of Carey, Marshman, and Ward* (1864), 7.

[27] J. Ryland, *Life and Death of the Rev. Andrew Fuller* (1833), 175; Carey, *William Carey*, 50; F. D. Walker, *William Carey* (1926), 63. For Andrew Fuller see Watts, *The Dissenters*, i. 459–60.

parts of the habitable globe',[28] and Carey's entreaties and the promptings of their own consciences could not be resisted for ever. By 1791 Andrew Fuller had been won round to Carey's point of view and at the meeting of the Northamptonshire Association at Clipstone he attacked the 'procrastinating spirit' which was 'of great detriment to the work of God'. 'We pray for the conversion of the world', complained Fuller, 'yet we neglect the ordinary means by which it can be brought about.'[29] And when the Baptist ministers gathered at Nottingham in the following year seemed inclined to postpone action on Carey's proposition yet again, it was Fuller who seized the initiative and moved the resolution which led at Kettering in October to the founding of the Particular Baptist Society for the Propagation of the Gospel amongst the Heathen.[30] Fuller went on to serve the missionary society as its first secretary, and despite a paralytic stroke he suffered in 1793 and a series of domestic tragedies, he proved to be a tower of strength to the mission for the last twenty-odd years of his life. For several years he spent a quarter of his time collecting money for the mission, travelling throughout England and visiting Scotland five times and Ireland once. Initially 'he was so grieved with the want of greater zeal for the cause of God, that he sometimes retired from the more public streets of London into the back lanes, that he might not be seen by other passengers to weep for his having so little success'.[31] He died in 1815, at the age of sixty-one, worn out in the service of the mission.

When Carey thought of sending missionaries to the heathen, he thought first of Captain Cook's voyages and of Tahiti, but in January 1793 he received a letter from John Thomas, a Baptist who was trying to raise money for a mission to Bengal. Thomas was an impetuous, restless, thriftless, impractical, exasperating yet lovable man who had run away from his Fairford home in his early teens and had acquired medical training at Westminster Hospital. He became a surgeon in the navy but could not stand the sea, opened a medical practice in London but could not make a living, and then returned to sea in the service of the East India Company. Having paid two visits to Bengal he decided to settle in the country as a missionary, and for five years lived among the Bengalis, learning their language and ministering to their needs without winning any permanent converts.[32] He returned to England in 1792 in search of money and assistance and found the answer to his prayers in William Carey. Carey agreed to accompany Thomas back to Bengal, and since the East India Company was opposed to missionary work for fear it

[28] Watts, *The Dissenters*, i. 460–1.   [29] Walker, *William Carey*, 75–6.
[30] Carey, *William Carey*, 84–5.   [31] Ryland, *Life of Andrew Fuller*, 247–50.
[32] E. A. Payne, *The First Generation: Early Leaders of the Baptist Missionary Society* (1936), 68–71.

would provoke the Indians to rebellion, it was on a Danish ship that Thomas, Carey, and his family embarked on 13 June 1793. They landed in Calcutta five months later.

Carey's first years in India were unhappy: John Thomas's lack of financial ability was a continual source of worry as their money dwindled and debts mounted; dysentery struck both Carey's five-year-old son, Peter, who died after a fever, and his wife Dorothy, whose mind became permanently unhinged; and for seven years Carey and Thomas did not make a single Indian convert. Yet Carey had the faith and resilience to overcome his early trials. Thomas redeemed his other lapses by obtaining for Carey a post as manager of an indigo factory owned by an English planter, and Carey devoted himself to the study of Bengali and started translating the New Testament into the language. Towards the end of 1799 the persistence of the two men began to be rewarded. They received valuable new recruits in William Ward, a printer and former newspaper editor who was to set up the printing works on which Carey's translations were to be printed, and John Marshman, who organized the mission's schools. Since the East India Company refused to admit Ward and Marshman to British India, Carey and his family moved to the Danish settlement of Serampore, sixteen miles from Calcutta. And in December 1800 John Thomas, shortly before he died at the age of forty-four, had the satisfaction of winning the mission's first convert, Krishna Pal, whom Carey baptized in the Ganges.

Carey himself lived to be seventy-two, never returning to England and dying at Serampore in June 1834, his last year gladdened by the news of the ending of slavery in the West Indies. In the course of those last thirty-odd years British Baptists in India baptized over a thousand converts; the Serampore College was founded in 1819 to train Indians for evangelism, though opened to Christians and non-Christians alike; Carey and the missionaries initiated the campaign which led in 1829 to the outlawing of sati— the practice of burning widows alive with the bodies of their husbands; and Carey, with the assistance of Indian pandits, translated the whole Bible into six Indian languages, and parts of it into a further twenty-nine. The number of Carey's converts may have been infinitesimal when compared with Bengal's total population, and the quality of some of his translations has been severely criticized, but his achievements were, none the less, very considerable for a largely self-educated Northamptonshire shoemaker.[33]

Coke and Carey were not the first Protestant British missionaries: Coke had been preceded to Antigua by Nathaniel Gilbert, Carey to Bengal by

[33] Potts, *Baptist Missionaries, passim.*

John Thomas. Carey held up to the eyes of his fellow Baptists the example of John Eliot, a Cambridge graduate who for more than forty years from 1646 had preached and settled churches among the Red Indians of Massachusetts, and of David Brainerd who from 1743 to 1747 had laboured with some success among the Indians of New Jersey and Delaware until he died from consumption at the age of twenty-nine.[34] Quakers in the 1650s and 1660s had ventured to Egypt, Jerusalem, and the Turkish court, and eighteenth-century Friends such as Thomas Chalkley travelled widely in the West Indies, the Netherlands, and Germany.[35] Chaplains of the Anglican Society for the Propagation of the Gospel, founded in 1701, also worked among the Indians of North America and the negroes of the West Indies, although their main concern was for English colonists in these countries and the missionaries were withdrawn from the American colonies when they became independent.

The work of Carey did, however, mark a radical new departure in missionary history: the Particular Baptist Society for the Propagation of the Gospel was the first of the modern British missionary societies, having as its primary concern the conversion of the heathen, and deriving its support from local organizations at home—known as auxiliaries—which were responsible for collecting funds, stimulating interest in missions, and praying for their success. The example of the Particular Baptists was followed in 1795 by a group of paedobaptist Calvinists—Congregationalists, Presbyterians, Calvinistic Methodists, and Evangelical Anglicans—who came together to form the London Missionary Society. The society dispatched its first group of thirty missionaries to Tahiti, Tongatabu, and the Marquesas Islands in 1796, John Vanderkemp was sent to South Africa in 1798, six missionaries started work in Ceylon and Travancore in 1804, Robert Morrison arrived in Canton in 1807, John Wray settled in Demerara in 1808, Robert Milne founded a mission at Malacca in 1815, and three years later David Jones arrived in Madagascar and Edward Stallybrass and Cornelius Rahmn crossed Siberia by sledge to take the Gospel to the Mongol tribe of Buriats.[36] Similar non-denominational missionary societies were founded in Edinburgh and Glasgow in 1796, and in 1799 Evangelical Anglicans founded what was to become the Church Missionary Society. The Wesleyan Methodist Missionary Society, organized between 1813 and 1818, supported missionaries in Sierra Leone, where George Warren had started work in 1811,

---

[34] Carey, *Enquiry*, 367; E. A. Payne, *The Growth of the World Church* (1955), 22–3.
[35] R. M. Jones, *The Later Periods of Quakerism* (1921), i. 18.
[36] C. S. Horne, *The Story of the LMS* (1895), *passim*.

Namaqualand (1816), Madras (1818), the Gambia (1821), among the Maoris of New Zealand (1822), Tonga (1822), the Gold Coast (1835), and Fiji (1836).[37] A General Baptist Missionary Society was founded in 1816 and five years later sent its first missionaries to Cuttack in Orissa; the Bible Christians sent missionaries to Prince Edward Island in 1831 and to Canada in 1833; the first Welsh Calvinistic Methodist missionaries went to Bengal and to Brittany in 1840; the Primitive Methodists sent missionaries to New Zealand and to South Africa in 1844; the first missionaries of the Methodist New Connexion arrived in Tientsin in 1860; and the Quakers, in this as in other matters experiencing the full force of the Evangelical revival half a century after the other Dissenters, sent their first modern missionary to India in 1866.[38]

The devotion, courage, and self-sacrifice with which these men and women went out to save their fellow men is a testimony to the quality of the lives of nineteenth-century Nonconformists, and of nineteenth-century Britons, at their very best. They gave up not only homes and comfort, but frequently life itself, in their efforts to do good to others. Tropical climates and natural disasters took a heavy toll of missionary lives. One of the first Wesleyan missionaries to the West Indies, the Irishman William M'Cornock, died a few months after landing on Dominica in 1788; George Warren lived less than twelve months after his arrival in Sierra Leone in 1811; the Baptist John Chamberlain, the first English missionary to preach in Delhi, lost two wives and three children in India; John Rowe, the first English Baptist missionary to Jamaica, lived only two and a half years after his arrival in 1813; Felix Carey, the son of the Baptist pioneer, saw his wife and two children drown in the Irrawaddy in 1814; James Chater, who started Baptist work in Ceylon in 1812, lost two sons in 1815 when the ship in which they were sailing sank off South Africa; when the London Missionary Society landed its first missionaries on Madagascar in 1818—Thomas Bevan, David Jones, their wives and two children—within a few weeks five of the six were dead; five Wesleyan missionaries were drowned in a shipwreck off the coast of Antigua in 1825; and by 1850 more than fifty Wesleyan missionaries had died in West Africa. But the gaps caused by death were always filled by new and eager volunteers. When twenty-three-year-old Thomas Knibb died in Jamaica in 1823 after

[37] G. C. and M. G. Findlay, *Wesley's World Parish* (1913), *passim*.

[38] A. C. Underwood, *A History of the English Baptists* (1947), 154–5; F. W. Bourne, *The Bible Christians* (1905), 204–14; W. Williams, *Welsh Calvinistic Methodism* (1872), 214; H. B. Kendall, *The Origin and History of the Primitive Methodist Church* (n.d.), ii. 426; G. Parker (ed.), *The Centenary of the Methodist New Connexion 1797–1897* (1897), 125–7; E. Isichei, *Victorian Quakers* (Oxford, 1970), 13.

three months on the island, his younger brother William immediately offered to take his place, to become a leading opponent of slavery and the most celebrated Baptist missionary to the West Indies.[39] During his twenty years in Jamaica William Knibb mourned the deaths of five of his seven children, and he himself died on the island at the age of forty-two.

To the natural hazards of missionary enterprise was added the hostility of unsympathetic men. Opposition came both from colonial authorities and European settlers on the one hand and from native governments and pagan tribes on the other. The suspicious attitude of the East India Company, which had compelled Baptist missionaries to sail in Danish ships and obliged Carey to move from Calcutta to Danish Serampore, continued to trouble the mission at periodic intervals. Baptist missionaries were allowed back to Calcutta in 1800, but a mutiny among the East India Company's sepoy troops in 1806, and the missionaries' publication of a tactless pamphlet describing Islam as a 'lying religion' in 1807, led to orders forbidding missionaries to preach in British India. A Baptist missionary, William Johns, who arrived in Bengal without a licence in 1812 was expelled.[40] But this was the last occasion on which officials of the East India Company were able to harry the Baptist missionaries. When the company's charter came up for renewal in 1813 a strenuous campaign organized outside Parliament by Andrew Fuller and led in the Commons by Wilberforce resulted in the opening of the company's territory to missionary work. The campaign exhausted Fuller and shortened his life.

In the West Indies, as in India, opposition to missionary work was rooted in the fear that it would lead to insurrection. The governor of the Dutch island of St Eustatius ordered that any negro found praying should receive thirty-nine lashes of the whip; the assembly of British St Vincent prohibited preaching without a licence, and one Wesleyan missionary, Robert Gamble, was murdered by a gang of whites in 1791, while another, Matthew Lumb, was thrown into prison; the assembly of Jamaica tried to prevent Nonconformists from preaching to negroes, and after a slave insurrection on the island in 1831 William Knibb and his colleagues were imprisoned, while Baptist and Methodist chapels were destroyed by white mobs. But it was in British Guiana that tension between white planters and missionaries led to the most serious consequences. John Wray had started work in Demerara in 1808 under the auspices of the LMS, but three years later Governor Bentinck attempted to prevent him from influencing the colony's negroes by forbid-

---

[39] J. H. Hinton, *Memoir of William Knibb* (1847), 25.
[40] Potts, *Baptist Missionaries*, 177, 185, 197.

ding slaves from gathering together before sunrise or after sunset, and Wray had to sail back to England, on a round trip which took six months, in order to get the order revoked. By 1817 Wray had moved on to New Amsterdam and his original station at Le Resouvenir was taken over by John Smith, a twenty-seven-year-old member of the Tonbridge chapel. When, in 1823, rumour that Governor Murray was withholding an emancipation edict provoked a slave insurrection Smith was arrested, kept in close confinement in an insanitary prison for seven weeks, sentenced to death in defiance of the evidence of his innocence, and died in prison before the sentence could be carried out.

British missionaries in India and the British West Indies could at least appeal to Parliament against the intolerance of white planters and local administrators, and such appeals were ultimately successful, but missionaries in Africa, most of Asia, Polynesia, and in territories controlled by other European powers, had no such recourse. Wesleyan missionaries were expelled from Haiti in 1808 and from Spain in the 1830s; the Russian tsar, after admitting the LMS missionaries to Siberia in 1818, forced them to leave in 1841; and until 1842 the Chinese government refused to admit foreigners into the country except for trade, thus obliging the lonely Morrison, toiling at his Chinese grammars and dictionaries, to obtain employment as translator to the East India Company. Less civilized peoples had more summary methods of ridding themselves of unwanted intruders: three of the first LMS missionaries to Tongatabu were murdered in 1798, the missionaries on Tahiti lived among continual tribal warfare and eleven fled to Australia, also in 1798, and in 1839 John Williams, a former ironmonger's apprentice from Moorfields Tabernacle who had evangelized Rarotonga and Samoa, was clubbed to death on the island of Erromanga in the New Hebrides. The worst persecution of all was suffered by the converts of the LMS missionaries on Madagascar. In 1835 Queen Ranavolona, who had secured power on the death of her husband by murdering seven of her nearest rivals, initiated a reign of terror against Christians which continued until the queen's death in 1861 and led to the death of some two hundred Malagasy Christians, the flogging, imprisonment, and fining of two or three thousand more, and to the retirement of the last missionaries from the island in 1836.

But perhaps the heaviest cross the missionaries had to bear was the initial lack of response from those they had gone out to save. Carey was in India seven years, Morrison in China seven years, and Robert Moffat laboured among the Bechuanas for eight years, before they were able to baptize their first converts; LMS missionaries worked in Vizagapatnam on the east coast of India for thirty years before claiming their first convert;

and nineteenth-century Wesleyans, like seventeenth-century Quakers, failed to make any impression on the Catholics of Malta or the Muslims of Alexandria. When the missionaries did appear eventually to win converts, their devotion to Christianity all too often proved to be superficial and short-lived. John Thomas believed he had won a handful of converts during his first years in Bengal, but they all subsequently relapsed into Hinduism, and in Jamaica many of the negroes who joined Christian churches after emancipation reverted to the practice of African spirit-religions in the depressed economic circumstances of the late 1840s.[41]

The missionaries complained, with justice, that the men who ran the missionary societies at home did not always appreciate the problems which faced the men and women in the field. In India Carey and his colleagues endeavoured to make themselves financially independent of home support by their indigo business and by their printing press, and in 1801 Carey accepted a post as tutor in Bengali at Fort William College. They sought moreover to understand Hindu culture, translated Sanskrit writings into English, and admitted non-Christians to Serampore College to study secular subjects. All this suggested to some members of the missionary committee at home that the Serampore leaders were being diverted from the task for which they had gone to India. As long as Fuller remained secretary of the Baptist Missionary Society no attempt was made to interfere in the running of the mission, but after Fuller's death in 1815 relations became strained until, in 1827, Joshua Marshman refused to give the society an account of the way Serampore spent BMS money and the missionaries broke away from the parent body. For the next ten years, until both Carey and Marshman were dead, the Serampore mission maintained an independent existence.[42]

Yet, despite such frustrations and disappointments, by 1850 the Nonconformist missionaries had notable achievements to their credit. Success came more quickly among primitive peoples with a debased form of religion than among the devotees of Buddha, Allah, or Vishnu. In Polynesia LMS and Wesleyan missionaries brought about the spectacular conversion of heathen chieftains: King Pomare of Tahiti in 1812; King Taufa-ahau of Haabai in the Tonga group in 1830; the cannibal King Thakombau of Mbau in Fiji in 1854. The LMS established institutions to train native preachers on Rarotonga in 1839 and on Upolu in the Samoan Islands in 1844, and preachers

---

[41] F. A. Cox, *History of the Baptist Missionary Society* (1842), i. 25–6, 93–4; D. A. Ryall, 'Organisation of Missionary Societies . . . and the role of missionaries in the diffusion of British culture in Jamaica, 1834–65', Ph.D. thesis (London, 1959), 6.

[42] Carey, *William Carey*, 164, 314–16, 330–2; Potts, *Baptist Missionaries*, 112, 133–4; Cox, *History of the BMS*, i. 291–6.

from these islands played a crucial and heroic role in the evangelization of the Sandwich Islands, the New Hebrides, and the Loyalty Islands in the 1840s and the 1850s. Similarly in the West Indies a good deal of missionary work was undertaken by negro preachers: Methodism was introduced into St Eustatius and Demerara by negroes; the establishment of Wesleyanism in the Bahamas was largely the work of a coloured man, William Turton; and the first Baptist in Jamaica, George Liele, was a freed slave from Georgia who arrived in the island in 1783, thirty years before the first BMS missionary. Baptist membership in Jamaica trebled in the 1830s, so that by 1842 the Jamaican Baptists felt strong enough to become independent of the BMS. In the following year they established Calabar College for the training of negro ministers and sent a contingent of negro missionaries to Fernando Po in the hope that they would be able to evangelize West Africa.[43]

By 1850 the Wesleyan Missionary Society had 432 missionaries and native preachers, 104,235 members, and an annual income of £104,661. The London Missionary Society, which by mid-century had become largely Congregational, had 170 missionaries, 700 native teachers, 16,000 members, and an annual income of £51,509. And the Baptist Missionary Society had 40 missionaries, 118 native preachers, and 5,013 members, while the now independent Jamaica Baptist Union had a further 20,000 members. The three main Nonconformist missionary societies thus claimed to have a total of 1,460 missionaries and native teachers and 125,248 members, which compared favourably with the Anglican Church Missionary Society which had 1,918 missionaries and native teachers but only 17,000 communicants.[44]

Today it is fashionable, even in Christian circles, to denigrate the nineteenth-century missionary movement. Alec Vidler has criticized the movement on account of its association with imperialism, the political quietism of its leaders, its lack of sympathy with non-Christian religions, and its failure to appreciate the importance of training native church leaders.[45] Much of this criticism is inapplicable to the Dissenting and Wesleyan missionary pioneers: in India and the West Indies colonial authorities were a hindrance rather than a help to their work; the Serampore missionaries in India, the Baptists and Wesleyans in the West Indies, the LMS missionaries in Polynesia all recognized the crucial importance of training and using native preachers; and while all Nonconformist missionaries were sent abroad with orders to avoid political controversy, the experiences of men like John Smith of Demerara

---

[43] Ryall, 'Organisation of Missionary Societies', 132–4.
[44] *Census of Great Britain 1851. Religious Worship. England and Wales* (1853), pp. xliii, lvii–lviii, lxii; J. Telford, *Short History of Wesleyan Methodist Foreign Missions* (c.1905), 276.
[45] A. R. Vidler, *The Church in an Age of Revolution* (1961), 251–3.

and William Knibb of Jamaica with the exploitation of coloured peoples transformed them into political activists. It is true that the missionaries saw their chief task, in the words of John Love, the first secretary of the LMS, as the rescuing of heathens who were 'perishing in the blood, gall, and wormwood of a Christless state, and ... hastening to eternity in guilt, pollution, and darkness'.[46] But the incidental blessings they brought to the lands in which they worked were not inconsiderable: the abolition of sati in India, the ending of infanticide and cannibalism in Polynesia, the amelioration and then the abolition of slavery in the West Indies. And to these must be added the influence which the missionaries had on the Hindu reform movement of Rammohun Roy, the part they played in easing the path to freedom of emancipated slaves in Jamaica by arbitrating in wages disputes and setting up villages of independent freeholders, the reduction of scores of languages to writing for the first time, and the pioneer educational work done by the missionaries in three continents and two oceans.[47] It was one of the paradoxes of the Evangelical movement that the men who had their eyes fixed most firmly on eternity did far more than their contemporaries to improve the temporal existence of their fellow men here on earth.

The influence of the missionary movement did not end on the mission field: it helped, in its turn, to stimulate the expansion of Dissent at home. Men set up local auxiliaries to pray and collect money for missionaries overseas, ladies met in sewing classes to make goods to sell for missionary funds, young men and young women were stirred by the stories they read of the heroic exploits of John Williams and Robert and Mary Moffat, children collected farthings in jam jars to assist in the conversion of the heathen, and whole churches were periodically enthralled to listen to the first-hand experiences of missionaries home on furlough from Barbados, Bechuanaland, or Bangalore.[48] In December 1841 Wesleyan chapels in the Cambridgeshire Fens were packed to capacity for missionary meetings for which 'Mr Bond has got a great idol from Ceylon, which we take from place to place'.[49] In March 1842 Exeter Hall was filled to overflowing for a meeting of children and young people organized by the London Missionary Society. Robert Moffat introduced a Bechuana girl whom he had taken 'from the grave to which her mother and other relatives had consigned her when she was but a

[46] Morison, *Fathers and Founders of the LMS*, p. xv.

[47] For India see Potts, *Baptist Missionaries*, 226–43. For Jamaica see Ryall, 'Organisation of Missionary Societies', 222–30.

[48] For an account of the involvement of the local churches in the missionary cause see Ryall, 'Organisation of Missionary Societies', 75–80.

[49] J. E. Coulson, *The Peasant Preacher: Memorials of Mr Charles Richardson* (2nd edn., 1866), 106.

month old'; he produced a young man whom he had rescued, when an infant, from the field of battle on which his father had been killed; and the Revd G. Pritchard showed his audience an idol, from Mangaia near Rarotonga, to which human sacrifices had been offered.[50]

Some Dissenters complained that the financial demands of the mission field syphoned off funds that were desperately needed at home, and certainly the overseas missionary societies, with their exotic appeal, attracted considerably greater sums of money than the home mission societies.[51] But the challenge of the overseas missionary movement, at least initially, had an invigorating effect on the churches in England and caused them to be increasingly conscious of the missionary needs of their own immediate neighbourhoods. In 1796 Daniel Bowell of the Ipswich Congregational church left for service in Polynesia, where two years later he was to meet a martyr's death on Tongatabu; in 1797 members of the Ipswich church 'went out for the first time into the villages around, to instruct such as they could find disposed to receive them'.[52] The formation of both the Baptist and the London Missionary Societies led Evangelical Dissenters to the conclusion that if they could organize themselves for the evangelization of the heathen abroad they should organize themselves for the evangelization of the heathen at home. In 1795 part of the Baptist Missionary Society's funds were set aside for missionary work at home; as a result William Steadman of Broughton in Hampshire and John Saffery of Salisbury went on a preaching tour of Cornwall in 1796; and in 1797 the 'Baptist Society in London for the Encouragement and Support of Itinerant and Village Preaching' was established.[53] The foundation of the London Missionary Society inspired the establishment of Congregational societies for the evangelization of Hampshire in 1797 and of Essex in 1798, and led to the formation, in 1797, of the most successful of all the Calvinist agencies for village preaching, the interdenominational Bedfordshire Union of Christians.[54] The example of the Bedfordshire Evangelicals was in turn emulated by their brethren in Warwickshire, and in both the east Midlands and Yorkshire the formation of LMS auxiliaries led to the establishment, in 1815 and 1819, of itinerant home

---

[50] *Evangelical Magazine*, NS 20 (1842), 246–8.

[51] B. Semmel, *The Methodist Revolution* (1974), 168–9; G. A. Weston, 'The Baptists of North-West England, 1750–1850', Ph.D. thesis (Sheffield, 1969), 168–9.

[52] J. Browne, *History of Congregationalism in Norfolk and Suffolk* (1877), 384.

[53] K. R. Manley, 'John Rippon and the Particular Baptists', D.Phil. thesis (Oxford, 1967), 370–1; D. W. Lovegrove, *Established Church, Sectarian People* (Cambridge, 1988), 25.

[54] J. Wilson, *Memoir of Thomas Wilson* (1849), 149–50, citing *Memoirs of Dr Bogue*, 203; Lovegrove, *Established Church, Sectarian People*, 16–17; J. Brown, *Centenary Celebration of the Bedfordshire Union of Christians* (1896), 13–16.

missionary societies.[55] Andrew Fuller, writing in his diary in 1791, noted that 'towards the latter end of this summer, I heard of some revival of religion about Walgrave and Guilsborough; and that the means of it were their setting apart days for fasting and prayer'. 'We had long been praying for the revival of God's cause, and the spread of the Gospel among the heathen', he added, but 'perhaps God would begin with us at home first.'[56]

2. NUMBERING THE PEOPLE: THE RELIGIOUS CENSUS OF 1851

The expansion of English Nonconformity overseas was thus both a cause and a consequence of the expansion of Dissent at home. The extent of that expansion can be seen from comparing the list of Dissenting congregations drawn up by Dr John Evans in the years 1715–18, and the two subsequent lists compiled by the Baptist pastor Josiah Thompson in 1772–3, with the findings of the religious census of 1851.[57] While Thompson's purpose was partly political, to remedy the lack of organization evident in 1772 when an abortive attempt had been made to exempt Dissenting ministers from subscription to the Thirty-nine Articles,[58] the 1851 census was a unique attempt by the State to make an impartial assessment of the extent of religious observance in England and Wales and of the relative strengths of denominational allegiance. Its conduct and the interpretation of its findings were entrusted to a London barrister, Horace Mann, who sought to discover how many places of worship were in existence in England and Wales on Sunday, 30 March 1851, how many sittings were provided by such places, and how many of those sittings were occupied at morning, afternoon, and evening services.

The two Thompson lists, which differ slightly in their details, are less satisfactory than either the Evans list or the 1851 census as a basis from which to estimate the strength of Dissent. Except in the cases of London and Monmouthshire, Thompson made no attempt to distinguish between Presbyterian and Independent congregations and lumped them together under the general heading of 'paedobaptist'; for the most part he did not differentiate between General and Particular Baptists; and, unlike Dr Evans, he

[55] W. R. Ward, *Religion and Society in England, 1790–1850* (1972), 48–9; Minutes of the Castle Gate Congregational Church, Nottingham, University of Nottingham Library, 128; J. G. Miall, *Congregationalism in Yorkshire* (1868), 178.

[56] Ryland, *Life of Andrew Fuller*, 192.

[57] For the Evans list see Watts, *The Dissenters*, i. 267–89, 491–510.

[58] Josiah Thompson, List of Dissenting Congregations, 1715 and 1773, DWL MS 34.5, 6.

made little attempt to compile estimates for the number of 'hearers' who attended Dissenting services. But he did provide a list of Dissenting meetings throughout England and Wales, and by supplementing his evidence with information gleaned from the Quaker 'Index to Meetings for Church Affairs' in the Friends House library[59] it is possible to compare the number of Nonconformist congregations in the reigns of George I, George III, and Queen Victoria (Table I).

TABLE I. *Number of Nonconformist congregations, 1715–1718, 1773, and 1851*

	1715–1718	1773	1851
ENGLAND (including Monmouthshire)			
Presbyterian	637		142
Unitarian	—	741	202
Independent	203		2,604
Particular Baptist	206		
General Baptist	122	378	2,347
Seventh-day Baptist	5	3	2
Quaker	672	563	363
Wesleyan Methodist	—	—	6,151
Other Arminian Methodist	—	—	4,323
Other Nonconformist	—	—	885
TOTALS	1,845	1,685	17,019
WALES			
Presbyterian	25		—
Unitarian	—	91	27
Independent	26		640
Baptist	14	21	440
Quaker	24	14	8
Calvinistic Methodist	—	—	780
Wesleyan Methodist	—	—	428
Other Arminian Methodist	—	—	105
Other Nonconformist	—	—	31
TOTALS	89	126	2,459

The Thompson survey of 1773 had on the whole presented a pessimistic view of the state of Dissent: the Baptists had 55 more congregations in 1773

---

[59] It is not always possible to compare the number of Quaker meetings in existence in 1773 with the number at the beginning of the century, but direct comparison is possible in 29 English counties, and in these counties the number of Quaker meetings had fallen from 457 around 1715 to 373 in 1773, a drop of 16.2%. By applying this reduction of 16.2% to the estimate for the total number of Quaker meetings in the early 18th cent. arrived at in Vol. I of *The Dissenters* (672), one arrives at an estimate of 563 Quaker meetings in England in 1773. The number of Quaker meetings in Wales had fallen from 24 around 1715 to 14 in 1773.

than half a century earlier—and indeed had 130 more than Dr Evans's incomplete total—but the number of paedobaptist congregations in England had fallen by a hundred and the Quakers had suffered a similar decline. Josiah Thompson's correspondents had reported Dissenting losses in Derbyshire, Devon, Kent, Somerset, Surrey, and Sussex, and although more optimistic reports came from Lancashire and Yorkshire it was the Baptist rather than the paedobaptist congregations which were multiplying, and Independent increases had been counterbalanced by Presbyterian losses. Only in Wales had paedobaptist Dissent made solid progress since the reign of George I, the Independents already benefiting from the Evangelical revival and from secessions from the Calvinistic Methodists.

By 1851 the situation had been radically transformed. While the population of England and Wales had increased from perhaps 7 million people in 1773 to 17.9 million in 1851, an increase of 155 per cent, the number of Nonconformist congregations had increased by 975 per cent. Not only had the number of Nonconformist congregations increased tenfold between 1773 and 1851, but the religious census showed that they outnumbered Anglican places of worship by 5,420. Admittedly more than half the Nonconformist congregations were Methodist, and although Horace Mann had no scruples about classifying the Wesleyan Methodists as Nonconformists, the Wesleyan leaders themselves were anxious to distance themselves from the older Dissenting bodies. But more than 40 per cent of the Arminian Methodist congregations of 1851 owed no allegiance to the Wesleyan Conference, and these non-Wesleyan Methodists did not share the objections of the parent Connexion to their classification as Dissenters. And the 1851 census revealed not only the vast proliferation of Methodist chapels that had taken place in the first half of the nineteenth century, it also revealed massive increases in the number of Independent and Baptist congregations. Whereas there had been perhaps 300 Independent congregations in 1773, the religious census revealed 3,244 Congregational places of worship, and whereas Josiah Thompson had listed 402 Baptist congregations, Horace Mann listed 2,789. Both the Friends and the Presbyterians, however, suffered considerable losses between 1773 and 1851: the number of Quaker particular meetings appears to have fallen by some 200, and whereas the Presbyterians probably had over 500 congregations in 1773, by 1851 their forces were divided between the Unitarians (229 places of worship), the orthodox Presbyterian Church in England (76 places of worship), and the United Presbyterian Church (66 places of worship). Even these figures disguise the extent of Presbyterian decline, for the two latter denominations consisted very largely of Scottish immigrants: when the Presbyterian Church in England was founded in 1839 it emphasized it was 'in connexion with the Church of Scotland', and the United Presbyterian Church was the result of the union, in 1847, of the churches of two Scottish dissenting denominations, the United Secession and the Relief churches.[60]

Horace Mann not only collected information about the number of places of worship in existence in 1851, he also attempted to estimate the strength of the churches, and it was this aspect of the census which proved to be the most controversial to contemporaries and to historians alike. In order to obtain data on which to base his calculations Mann decided to count the number of worshippers at each church and chapel on census Sunday rather than to ask people for their religious affiliations. He argued, quite properly, that 'the outward conduct of persons furnishes a better guide to their religious state than can be gained merely by vague professions',[61] but since an expression of 'vague professions' would have been to the advantage of the established church many Anglicans were opposed to the census from the start. The task of counting the worshippers was entrusted to the clergyman or minister of the place of worship concerned, but many Anglican clergymen refused to co-operate and Mann was left without an attendance figure for 939 out of a total of 14,077 Anglican churches.[62] Dissenting ministers were more willing to co-operate with the census officers, indeed far too willing in the view of some Anglicans who alleged that they had packed their chapels and exaggerated their numbers. Mann rushed to the defence of the probity of Dissenting ministers, claimed that the ministers' returns were checked by the census officers, and pointed out that Anglicans and Dissenters had roughly the same proportion of worshippers to seats. He admitted, however, that some informants may have given over-optimistic estimates of the size of their congregations, and in Nottinghamshire at least Anglican clergymen appear to have been more culpable in this respect than Dissenting ministers.[63] On the other hand some ministers of religion, when giving the actual size of their congregations, were anxious to point out that these were smaller than usual on census Sunday because of peculiar seasonal or local factors: 30 March was Mothering Sunday and it was claimed in many parts of the country that the

---

[60] O. Chadwick, *The Victorian Church* (1970), i. 399; J. M. McKerrow, *Memoir of William McKerrow* (1881), 86. The Presbyterian Church in England severed its connection with the Church of Scotland in 1844, following the latter's disruption in 1843. It is therefore legitimate to classify the churches and members of the Presbyterian Church in England as Nonconformists, but I have not treated churches and members of the Church of Scotland as Nonconformists.

[61] *Religious Census*, p. cxix.   [62] Ibid., p. clxxxii.

[63] H. Mann, 'On the Statistical Position of Religious Bodies in England and Wales', *Journal of the Statistical Society of London*, 18 (1855), 142–4; M. R. Watts, *Religion in Victorian Nottinghamshire* (Nottingham, 1988), i, p. x.

custom of visiting relatives on that day reduced attendance at church or chapel. In parts of Nottinghamshire and Lincolnshire a violent thunderstorm just before the evening service kept some people at home, and others were said to have been absent because it was the lambing season.[64] In Wales the day of the census was 'very wet and stormy' and in some districts roads 'were almost impassable'.[65]

The use of the census for estimating the relative strength of the denominations was further complicated by the continuing practice, especially in some rural areas, of people attending both their parish church and their Wesleyan or Calvinistic Methodist chapel when services were held at different times of the day.[66] A question mark was also placed over the reliability of the census by the failure of many ministers and clergy to distinguish clearly between Sunday school children and the general congregation, despite instructions so to do. Mann decided, when compiling his results, to include Sunday scholars in his totals except in cases where Sunday schools met at a time when there was no service for the adult congregation.[67] His assumption appears to have been that Sunday scholars who met at the same time as the general congregation were more likely to participate in worship than scholars who did not, and although he failed to justify such a proposition it did have the unintended merit of preventing the double counting of many Sunday scholars who met for more than one Sunday session. Yet despite the various objections which have been raised against the reliability of the religious census, it appears on the whole to have been conducted honestly and conscientiously, and where the returns from individual Nonconformist churches can be compared with their membership figures the census statistics seem plausible.[68]

It was in attempting to convert his statistics for attendances into estimates of the number of actual people worshipping on census Sunday that Mann left himself most open to criticism. He based his calculations on the assumption that half the people attending afternoon services had not been present in the morning, and that a third of those attending evening services had not been at

[64] PRO HO 129/435.2.10.16. 436.1.1.5. 436.2.1.1. R. W. Ambler, *Lincolnshire Returns of the Census of Religious Worship, 1851*, Lincolnshire Record Society, 72 (1979), pp. xxviii–xxx.

[65] I. G. Jones (ed.), *The Religious Census of 1851: A Calendar of Returns Relating to Wales* (Cardiff, 1981), ii. *North Wales*, 51, 65, 123, 126.

[66] Ambler, *Lincolnshire Returns*, pp. xxiv, 172; W. T. Morgan, 'The Diocese of St David's in the Nineteenth Century', *Journal of the Historical Society of the Church in Wales*, 22 (1972), 34–5; Jones, *Religious Census, North Wales*, 338.

[67] *Religious Census*, p. clxxi.

[68] W. Leary, *Methodism in the City of Lincoln* (Lincoln, 1969), 47, 76; D. M. Thompson, 'The Churches and Society in Leicestershire, 1851–81', Ph.D. thesis (Cambridge, 1969), 355; B. J. Biggs, *The Story of the Methodists of Retford and District* (Retford, 1970), 15; Watts, *Religion in Victorian Nottinghamshire*, i, p. ix.

any previous service. But he produced no evidence to justify these assumptions and his formula, as he later admitted, was unfair to the majority of Dissenting denominations whose best-attended services were usually in the evening.[69] It is, however, possible to devise a more satisfactory formula for translating Mann's attendance figures into worshippers, and I have done so by using the totals for the best-attended services for each denomination in each of the 624 registration districts in England and Wales, and by adding a third of the total attendances at other services. This formula can be justified by what is known about the frequency of church attendance in the nineteenth century, and produces results which are consonant with what information we have about church membership.[70] The detailed results of these calculations are given in Table XIV at the end of this volume and summaries are provided in Table II.

The estimates suggest that 7,198,647 people out of a total population in England and Wales of 17,927,604 attended church or chapel on census Sunday, 1851, a proportion of 40.15 per cent. Of these nearly half, 3,338,885, were Protestant Nonconformists, a proportion of the total of 18.62 per cent, figures which were only slightly behind the Church of England's total of 3,528,535, a proportion of 19.68 per cent. The massive increase in Nonconformist strength which had taken place in the late eighteenth and first half of the nineteenth centuries can be seen, in Table III, from comparing the estimates for 1851 with those produced in the first volume of this work on the basis of the Evans list.[71] Between the second decade of the eighteenth century and the middle of the nineteenth century the number of Nonconformists in England in proportion to the total population increased nearly threefold; in Wales the proportion increased eightfold.

Among the old Dissenters both the Independents and the Baptists roughly trebled their share of the total population of England between the reigns of George I and Victoria, while in Wales the Independents increased their share fivefold and the Baptists sevenfold. By contrast both the Quakers, and the orthodox Presbyterians and Unitarians combined, were less than half as numerous—in absolute, not proportionate, terms—in 1851 as they had been in 1715–18. Indeed, the denominations which traced their ancestry back to the seventeenth century or earlier accounted for less than half the total number of Nonconformists in either England or Wales in 1851, and in England the tenfold expansion of the Independents and Baptists had, in

---

[69] Mann, 'Statistical Position of Religious Bodies', 147.
[70] For further discussion of these points, see Appendix I.
[71] Watts, *The Dissenters*, i. 269–70.

relation to the total population, done little more than make good the losses of the Presbyterians and Friends. It was the denominations which had been founded as a result of the Evangelical revival—the Wesleyan and other

TABLE II. *Estimates of church and chapel attendance, 30 March 1851: denominational totals*

	England		Wales	
	Numbers	% of population	Numbers	% of population
Independents	655,935	3.88	132,629	13.11
Baptists	499,604	2.95	92,344	9.13
Quakers	16,783	0.10	115	0.01
Unitarians	34,110	0.20	2,901	0.29
Presbyterian Church in England	28,263	0.17	—	—
United Presbyterian Church	21,817	0.13	—	—
Wesleyan Methodists	924,140	5.46	58,138	5.75
Methodist New Connexion	61,937	0.37	954	0.09
Primitive Methodists	329,867	1.95	5,791	0.57
Bible Christians	48,015	0.28	120	0.01
Wesleyan Methodist Association	61,527	0.36	1,052	0.10
Wesleyan Reformers	62,164	0.37	435	0.04
Independent Methodists	1,544	0.01	—	—
Calvinistic Methodists	19,270	0.11	160,671	15.88
Lady Huntingdon's Connexion	21,942	0.13	750	0.07
Moravians	7,212	0.04	—	—
New Church	7,503	0.04	—	—
Brethren	6,894	0.04	203	0.02
Other Protestant Non-conformists	70,016	0.41	4,239	0.42
All Nonconformists	2,878,543	17.02	460,342	45.50
Church of England	3,415,861	20.19	112,674	11.14
Church of Scotland	8,692	0.05	—	—
Roman Catholics	288,305	1.70	3,725	0.37
Catholic and Apostolic Church	4,908	0.03	—	—
Mormons	19,792	0.12	3,368	0.33
Other Christians	2,437	0.01	—	—
Totals	6,618,538	39.13	580,109	57.34
Population Totals	16,915,820		1,011,784	

Arminian Methodists, the Calvinistic Methodists, Lady Huntingdon's Connexion, and the Moravians—which accounted for the contrast between the
statistics of Horace Mann and those of Dr John Evans. In 1851 these denominations claimed 53.42 per cent of all Nonconformist worshippers in England
and 49.51 of all Nonconformist worshippers in Wales.[72] It was they who had
transformed the religious scene of both countries.

TABLE III. *Nonconformists as a percentage of the total population:*
1715–1718 and 1851

	1715–1718		1851	
	Estimated numbers	% of population	Estimated numbers	% of population
ENGLAND (including Monmouthshire)				
Independents	59,940	1.10	655,935	3.88
Baptists	59,320	1.09	499,604	2.95
Quakers	39,510	0.73	16,783	0.10
Presbyterians and Unitarians	179,350	3.30	84,190	0.50
Arminian Methodists	—	—	1,489,194	8.80
Calvinistic Methodists	—	—	19,270	0.11
Lady Huntingdon's Connexion	—	—	21,942	0.13
Moravians	—	—	7,212	0.04
Others	—	—	84,413	0.50
Nonconformist Totals	338,120	6.21	2,878,543	17.02
Population Totals	5,442,670		16,915,820	
WALES				
Independents	7,640	2.47	132,629	13.11
Baptists	4,050	1.31	92,344	9.13
Presbyterians and Unitarians	6,080	1.96	2,901	0.29
Arminian Methodists	—	—	66,490	6.57
Calvinistic Methodists	—	—	160,671	15.88
Lady Huntingdon's Connexion	—	—	750	0.07
Others	—	—	4,557	0.45
Nonconformist Totals	17,770	5.74	460,342	45.50
Population Totals	309,750		1,011,784	

[72] The New Connexion of General Baptists also originated in part from the Evangelical
revival, but many of the returns from Baptist chapels in 1851 failed to specify whether they were
Particular, Strict, Old Connexion General Baptist, or New Connexion General Baptist, and the
published returns for the registration districts, on which my calculations are based, did not distinguish between the varieties of Baptists.

3. 'A SYSTEM WHICH FOSTERS THE POPULAR ELEMENT': THE VARIETIES OF METHODISM

By 1851 the Arminian Methodists were no longer joined together in the single Connexion that John Wesley had left behind sixty years earlier. Wesley himself had always regarded his Connexion as a personal network of itinerant preachers with himself at the hub, and long after his death Wesleyan Methodism continued to reflect the fact that its founder had been a High Churchman who had experienced an Evangelical conversion, the consequences of which had pushed him half-way towards Dissent. The tension between Wesley's own wish to 'live and die' a member of the Church of England and the desire of many of his followers to achieve independence as Nonconformists was kept in check, up to a point, by loyalty to Wesley himself during his own lifetime.[73] There were numerous local and individual secessions from Wesleyan Methodism to Dissent in the second half of the eighteenth century, but it was not until after Wesley's death that impatience with the order and discipline of the Wesleyan Connexion led to mass expulsions and secessions and to the founding of rival Arminian Methodist denominations.

Wesley had provided for the continuance of his organization by means of a Deed of Declaration, which had been enrolled in the Court of Chancery in 1784, whereby legal control over the Connexion was entrusted to a hundred itinerant preachers whom he named in the document. Wesley's decision to select a hundred out of the 192 preachers then engaged in the itinerant ministry was both arbitrary and unwise: it caused resentment among the excluded preachers and nearly thirty of them sooner or later left the Connexion.[74] But in practice the 'legal hundred' came to share their power with all the itinerant preachers who attended the annual Wesleyan Conference. That Conference, immediately after Wesley's death, asserted its collective power by frustrating the ambitions of Thomas Coke and Alexander Mather to be appointed Wesley's successor. They chose in his stead, as president of the Conference for 1791, the innocuous William Thompson and stipulated that his power should end when Conference ceased to meet. An attempt to curtail the authority of Conference was similarly frustrated three years later. An attempt by eight leading preachers, meeting in secret conclave in Lichfield, to launch a scheme to provide Methodism with bishops was defeated by the

---

[73] On relations between Methodism and the Church of England and between Methodism and Dissent before 1791 see Watts, *The Dissenters*, i. 434–52.

[74] L. Tyerman, *The Life and Times of the Rev. John Wesley* (2nd edn., 1872), iii. 418–25.

combined fury of those who wished to remain within the Church of England and of those who already regarded themselves as Dissenters.[75] Instead of appointing bishops, Conference in 1792 divided Methodism into districts under chairmen who would hold office for one year only and whose task would be the implementation of Conference decisions and the government of the Connexion between Conferences.

Consequently, once Wesley was dead, Conference exercised supreme legislative power over the Connexion. It was always Wesley's intention that Methodism should avoid the drift towards heterodoxy he had witnessed in Old Dissent by denying both chapel trustees and society members control over the appointment of preachers.[76] Instead, the admission of new preachers to the itinerant ministry, the stationing of preachers in circuits, and the appointment of the chairmen of District Meetings were all controlled by Conference. And it was the District Meetings which in their turn chose preachers to attend Conference, a privilege which was confined exclusively to the itinerant preachers.[77] Whereas in Wesley's day the itinerant ministry had been composed largely of laymen with a sprinkling of Anglican clergymen, in the decades after his death it developed into a separate clerical order. In 1793 Conference dropped the distinction between ordained and unordained itinerant preachers; in 1795 superintendents of circuits and preachers appointed by them were allowed to administer the Lord's Supper in chapels where the trustees and leaders would give their consent; in 1818 preachers on the committee of the Wesleyan Missionary Society were designated by the title 'Reverend'; and in 1836 the Conference recommended that ministers be ordained by the laying on of hands.

While on the one hand the Wesleyan preachers were setting themselves up as a clerical caste apart from their lay followers and were, for the most part, intent on keeping the government of the Connexion in their own hands, on the other hand changes were taking place within both Methodism and society at large which alienated successive waves of Methodists from the Connexion's leadership. Between 1791 and 1850 the membership of Wesleyan Methodism in England and Wales increased from 57,139 to 354,178, and as the membership of the Wesleyan Connexion expanded so it drew an increasing proportion of its followers from the more humble sections of society, from semi-skilled and unskilled workers.[78] At the same time it became increasingly dependent on laymen to pay for the erection of chapels

---

[75] A. Kilham, *Life of Alexander Kilham* (Nottingham, 1799), p. xi; J. Macdonald, *Memoirs of the Rev. Joseph Benson* (1822), 262.

[76] *The Letters of the Rev. John Wesley*, ed. J. Telford (1931), vii. 205.

[77] J. C. Bowmer, *Pastor and People* (1975), 68–9.   [78] See below, Ch. II, sect. 9.

and the maintenance of the ministry, and to serve as chapel stewards and trustees, class leaders, local preachers, and Sunday school teachers. All this was happening at a time when the demand for popular representation in both Parliament and local government was becoming increasingly vociferous. The divisions of Methodism, wrote James Stacey, were the consequence of 'a system which fosters the popular element . . . training it to every sphere of religious activity up to the very highest, yet denying it all share in those legislative acts for which in this very training a certain preparation is given'.[79]

In the sixty years after Wesley's death the Wesleyan leadership was faced with challenges to its authority both in the field of evangelism and in the sphere of connexional government. In the years following the French Revolution religious liberty was at times threatened by Anglicans and Tories who equated religious deviance with political rebellion, unlicensed preachers were liable to prosecution under the Conventicle Act, and the Wesleyan hierarchy was anxious both to prove its loyalty to the State and to demonstrate its respectability to the country's establishment. Wesleyanism, which in the eighteenth century had been accused of enthusiasm, indiscipline, and fanaticism, came in the nineteenth century to censure such faults when they appeared among its own followers. In 1796 an attempt by official Wesleyanism to suppress cottage meetings in Warrington, where worshippers believed they could manage without the oversight and expense of an itinerant minister, led to the secession of a group of Methodists who came under the leadership of a chair-maker named Peter Phillips.[80] Since Phillips and his followers rejected a paid ministry, were joined by a number of former Friends, and adopted Quaker speech and dress, they were known initially as 'Quaker Methodists'. In 1805–6 they united with other disgruntled Methodists, including John Broadhurst's Band Room Methodists in Manchester and the Christian Revivalists of Macclesfield, to form the small Independent Methodist denomination.[81] The Independent Methodists were assisted in their early years by the American evangelist Lorenzo Dow, who was also a major influence on the much more significant revivalist movement which broke out on the borders of Cheshire and Staffordshire in the first decade of the nineteenth century. Under Dow's inspiration camp-meetings—daylong open-air gatherings—were held on the slopes of the Pennine spur of Mow Cop, near the headwaters of the River Trent, in 1807. The camp-meetings were denounced by the Wesleyan Conference and their chief instigator, the carpenter Hugh Bourne, was expelled in 1808. Three years later

[79] J. Stacey, *A Prince in Israel, or, Sketches of the Life of John Ridgway* (1862), 99.
[80] A. Mounfield, *A Short History of Independent Methodism* (Warrington, 1905), 5.
[81] J. Vickers, *History of Independent Methodism* (1920), 8–13.

Bourne and his followers issued their first class tickets, drew up their first preaching plans, and in 1812 they took the name of Primitive Methodist. In the later 1810s and 1820s the movement spread down the Trent valley to Derbyshire, Nottinghamshire, Leicestershire, and Lincolnshire and thence to the East and North Ridings of Yorkshire, Durham, and Norfolk. By 1851 the Primitive Methodists constituted the second largest Methodist body in England, with 106,074 members and nearly 330,000 estimated worshippers on census Sunday.[82] Movements akin to Primitive Methodism were launched in Cornwall in 1801 by William O'Bryan, a farmer from Luxulyan, and in the Bristol area in 1814 by two Wesleyan local preachers, George Pocock and John Pyer. Pocock and Pyer carried out their evangelistic campaigns in large tents without the permission of the Wesleyan itinerants in the circuits concerned and as a result they were expelled in 1820. The Tent Methodists, as they called themselves, went on to issue their own class tickets but by the end of the decade they had ceased to exist as a separate denomination.[83] William O'Bryan's movement endured longer. As in the cases of Bourne and Pocock his refusal to restrict his itinerant labours to the confines of the Wesleyan circuit system led to his expulsion and to the formation, in 1815, of the Bible Christian denomination. By 1851 the Bible Christians had 13,324 members and 48,000 estimated worshippers, concentrated largely in Cornwall, Devon, and the Isle of Wight.

While the Independent Methodists, the Primitive Methodists, the Tent Methodists, and the Bible Christians all owed their origins to lay evangelistic activity which would not accept the constraints of Wesleyan order, a second group of Methodist denominations arose in the late eighteenth and second quarter of the nineteenth centuries whose origins lay primarily in protest movements against Wesleyan church government, and whose support derived not so much from evangelistic activity as from secessions from Wesleyan Methodism. The leader of the first major secession was Alexander Kilham, an itinerant preacher who came from Wesley's native village of Epworth. From 1792 to 1795 Kilham had served in Aberdeen, and while in Scotland he had come to admire the Presbyterian system of church government, an experience which prompted him to launch a campaign for lay representation in the Wesleyan Conference. The demand, and the intemperate language in which he voiced it, led to Kilham's expulsion in 1796 and to the formation, in 1797, of the Methodist New Connexion, which made

---

[82] The membership figure of 106,074 is for Great Britain but nearly all Primitive Methodist societies were in England. For Primitive Methodist expansion see below, Ch. I, sect. 9.

[83] J. Vickers, 'Methodism and Society in Central Southern England, 1740–1851', Ph.D. thesis (Southampton, 1987), 274–7.

modest inroads into Wesleyan congregations in Nottinghamshire, Staffordshire, and the West Riding of Yorkshire. At the time of the religious census the New Connexion had 16,962 members and nearly 62,000 estimated worshippers.[84]

Dissatisfaction with the government of the Wesleyan Connexion intensified in the second quarter of the nineteenth century as the annual Conference appeared to be using its power in an increasingly arbitrary and partisan spirit, and resentment focused on the dominant character of Jabez Bunting, who came to exercise something of the personal control over the Connexion that had once been wielded by John Wesley. In 1827 a proposal by the trustees of the Brunswick chapel in Leeds to install an organ led to the secession of nine hundred members when the opposition to the organ by the local preachers and many of the society's leaders, supported by the District Meeting, was overturned by the Wesleyan Conference which decided in favour of the trustees. The seceders came to be known as the Protestant Methodists.[85] Four years later a group of Wesleyan local preachers in Anglesey and Caernarfonshire led a secession in protest against the domination of the itinerant preachers and constituted themselves as Y Wesle Bach, the Minor Wesleyan Methodists.[86] And in 1832 what were claimed to be the 'despotic acts of superintendents' led over five hundred Wesleyans in Derby to break away from the parent organization and form the Arminian Methodist Connexion.[87] The Leeds Protestant Methodists, Y Wesle Bach, and the Derby Arminian Methodists all later joined forces with the Wesleyan Methodist Association, the occasion of whose formation in 1835 was a dispute over a proposal to establish a theological institution for the education of ministers with the omnipresent Jabez Bunting as both president and tutor.[88] The Association's chief areas of support were in Cornwall and parts of Lancashire and by 1851 it claimed 20,577 members with an estimated 61,000 worshippers.

The most serious of all the secessions from Wesleyanism, that of 1849, was a consequence both of growing opposition to the conservative and pro-Anglican stance of the Wesleyan hierarchy under Bunting's leadership, and of frustration with the Wesleyan Conference's opposition to the revivalist techniques of the American evangelist James Caughey. The controversy centred on a series of anonymous pamphlets, *Fly Sheets from the Private*

---

[84] For the origin of the Methodist New Connexion see below, Ch. III, sect. 2.
[85] See below, Ch. III, sect. 7.
[86] A. H. Williams, *Welsh Wesleyan Methodists* (Bangor, 1935), 221.
[87] R. C. Swift, *Lively People: Methodism in Nottingham, 1740–1939* (Nottingham, 1982), 71.
[88] See below, Ch. IV, sect. 2.

Correspondents, which pilloried the Wesleyan leadership in general and Bunting in particular. The expulsion of James Everett, who was suspected of writing the *Fly Sheets*, and of Samuel Dunn and William Griffith, who had both criticized the Wesleyan leadership openly in the press, was the signal for massive expulsions and secessions which in five years reduced the membership of the Wesleyan Connexion in England by 95,322, a loss of 28.5 per cent.[89] According to estimates based on the 1851 census, the Wesleyan Reformers had some 62,000 worshippers in England, slightly more than the Wesleyan Association. In 1857 rather less than half the Reformers joined with the Association to constitute the United Methodist Free Churches, with a membership of 38,767.

   Estimates based on the 1851 census show that the total number of worshippers in the chapels of the revivalist and secessionist Arminian Methodist denominations amounted to over 573,000—nearly 37 per cent of all Arminian Methodists in England and Wales. And what was most significant about these new Methodist denominations was that, unlike the leaders of the original Wesleyan Connexion, they had no doubt that they were Nonconformists. By institutionalizing the revolt against the Tory and pro-Anglican leadership of the Wesleyans in the first half of the nineteenth century, the newer Methodist denominations made their own distinctive contribution to the expansion of Dissent.

4. 'THE LAND WHICH JOSHUA GAVE TO THE TRIBES OF ISRAEL':[90] THE GEOGRAPHY OF DISSENT

The 1851 religious census not only revealed the bewildering variety of denominations competing for the attention of prospective worshippers, it also exposed an even more bewildering pattern of regional and local variations of religious observance. The calculations based on Horace Mann's figures for attendances in each of the 624 registration districts, which have been used above to provide an estimate for the total number of worshippers for each denomination in 1851, can also be used to plot the geographic distribution of religious observance and of denominational strengths and weaknesses, and they provide a more detailed and accurate picture than would be revealed by using the county totals alone.

---

[89] See below, Ch. V, sect. 3.   [90] Joshua 12: 7.

Table XIV and the maps at the end of this volume, showing the distribution of the combined totals of worshippers, reveal the extent to which religious practice varied from one part of the country to another. Three areas stand out as having a level of religious observance well above the national average: an area centred on Bedfordshire and Huntingdonshire but extending into Northamptonshire, Buckinghamshire, south Cambridgeshire, north Hertfordshire, north Essex, and parts of Suffolk; a second area centred on Wiltshire and stretching into south Gloucestershire and north Dorset; and north and west Wales. In many of the districts in these areas more than 60 per cent of the population attended a place of worship on census Sunday, and the estimates of attendance exceed 70 per cent for Bedford (70.5), Royston in Hertfordshire (71.8), St Ives in Huntingdonshire (70.9), Risbridge and Stow in Suffolk (73.1 and 71.4), and Melksham in Wiltshire (70.1). But the highest estimated percentages of all were recorded in certain Welsh districts: Aberystwyth 78.6, Machynlleth 75.4, Bangor 73.3, Aberayron 72.3, Conway 72.2, and Cardigan 71.4.

As one moves away from these three centres of very high religious observance so attendance in 1851 declined step by step. Immediately adjoining the areas of high attendance were districts whose level of attendance, though lower, still exceeded 50 per cent of the total population: much of Leicestershire, north Oxfordshire, much of Norfolk, west Berkshire, west and northern Hampshire, east Somerset, south Dorset, parts of Devon and Cornwall, and south Wales. But in most of Sussex, Kent, Hertfordshire, and Middlesex, in most of the east Midlands (apart from Leicestershire), in north Gloucestershire and in mid-Devon and mid-Somerset, Warwickshire, and in the East and North Ridings of Yorkshire attendance fell below 50 per cent. And in the next band of districts—London, Surrey, west Kent, south Essex, most of the west Midlands, the industrial areas of the West Riding, and in most of northern and north-west England—fewer than 40 per cent of the population attended a place of worship.

The lowest levels of attendance were recorded in two very different types of area: the poorer parts of large cities, where crowded living conditions and poverty proved to be inimical to religion, and, at the other extreme, sparsely populated mountainous border regions. The correlation between prosperity and religious observance was especially noticeable in London. Four districts in the East End had estimated percentages of worshippers of less than 20 per cent—Shoreditch (15.3), St George-in-the-East (16.1), Bethnal Green (18.7), Poplar (19.5), whereas prosperous low-density areas produced estimates two or three times as great: Hampstead 48.9 per cent, Wandsworth 45.2, Hackney 39.7. Low levels of religious practice were not, however, confined to the poorer districts of commercial and industrial towns. The lowest percentage of worshippers in the whole of England and Wales was to be found in rural Cumberland—Longtown (12.7)—and other rural districts in Cumberland and Northumberland had very low levels of attendance: Brampton (17.2), Haltwhistle (17.2), and Wigton (19.3). Low levels of attendance were also recorded in a group of adjoining districts in Herefordshire and Radnorshire: Knighton (25.9), Leominster (26.8), and Bromyard (28.4).

The low level of religious observance in districts such as Longtown and Knighton is sufficient evidence that industrialization and population density were not the only factors keeping substantial proportions of the English people out of church or chapel, and it is clear that some of the factors determining the level of attendance at public worship in 1851 were present long before the nineteenth century. Hugh McLeod suggests that 'the national pattern of churchgoing closely resembled the Anglican pattern', and to explain the Anglican pattern he uses Dorothy Sylvester's concept of a 'parish line', separating an area of large parishes containing several townships from an area of small parishes which were coterminous with townships.[91] To the north of the 'parish line' were north and north-west England, the West and North Ridings of Yorkshire, Staffordshire, Derbyshire, Shropshire, and north-east Wales, for the most part a highland region which, when parishes were settled in the tenth and eleventh centuries, had a sparse population. In most of the registration districts of this region, apart from north-east Wales, fewer than half the population attended a place of worship on census Sunday 1851, whereas nearly all the districts with an attendance level of more than 50 per cent were to the south of the 'parish line'.

There is thus some evidence to suggest that the level of religious observance in 1851 was determined by the strengths and weaknesses of the Anglican parish system. Bedfordshire, Northamptonshire, Suffolk, and Wiltshire were all counties of high overall religious practice, of small parishes, and of high Anglican attendance. But equally there were areas where Anglican attendance was comparatively high but overall observance was low: Surrey, east Hampshire, south Sussex, and parts of Warwickshire, Worcestershire, Shropshire, and Herefordshire. And throughout much of south-east England, the Midlands, and Wales the general pattern of religious observance corresponded much more closely to the Nonconformist pattern than to the Anglican pattern. In most registration districts in central and

---

[91] H. McLeod, 'Class, Community, and Region: The Religious Geography of Nineteenth-Century England', in M. Hill (ed.), *A Sociological Yearbook of Religion in Britain*, vi (1973), 31–2; D. Sylvester, *The Rural Landscape of the Welsh Borderland* (1969), 165–78.

southern England outside London, the Church of England could count on
the steady support of 20 or 30 per cent of the population, but whether the
overall religious practice of the district was above or below the national
average would frequently depend on the strength or weakness of Nonconformity in the area. It was the weakness of Dissent that accounted for the low
level of religious attendance in Herefordshire, though the county was rural,
lay to the south of the 'parish line', and had an Anglican attendance of
nearly 25 per cent. Conversely it was the strength of Nonconformity which
explains the high level of religious observance in every district in which more
than 70 per cent of the population attended a place of worship on 30 March
1851. In Bedford it was the three main Nonconformist denominations—
the Independents, Baptists, and Wesleyans in nearly equal strength—who
largely accounted for the fact that 39.0 per cent of the district's population
attended a Nonconformist place of worship, out of a total worshipping
percentage of 70.5. At Royston in Hertfordshire it was the Independents,
who constituted 29.1 per cent of the population, who helped to push the
Nonconformist total for the district to 38 per cent and the total percentage of
worshippers to 71.8. Similarly the Baptists of the Melksham district of
Wiltshire, who numbered 26.5 per cent of the population, were the major element in producing a Nonconformist percentage of 47.5 and a total percentage of worshippers of 70.1. It was the strength of the Independents (22.3 per
cent) which distinguished Risbridge, and the combined strengths of the
Independents and Baptists (14.8 per cent each) which distinguished Stow,
from their neighbouring Suffolk districts. And in Wales the very high attendance figures for Aberystwyth were due largely to the Calvinistic Methodists
(41.1 per cent), for Machynlleth to the Calvinistic Methodists (24.8 per cent),
the Independents (18.1 per cent), and the Wesleyans (16 per cent), and for
Bangor again to the Calvinistic Methodists (31.5 per cent).

But the fact that, throughout much of England and most of Wales, it was
the presence or absence of Nonconformity, rather than of Anglicanism,
which accounted for the differences in the levels of religious observance in
1851 does not itself invalidate the proposition that explanations for those differences should be sought deep in the roots of English and Welsh history,
long before the industrial revolution. We are thus faced with the question of
whether Nonconformity expanded so rapidly in the late eighteenth and early
nineteenth centuries by taking advantage of the failure of the Church of
England to adapt its parochial machinery to the demographic changes that
were taking place, and so evangelizing people who would otherwise have
been neglected by the established church; or whether Methodism and
Dissent flourished in areas where the ground had already been prepared by

the Church of England, and were winning over men and women from the established church rather than rescuing them from unbelief.

Robert Currie suggests that one's answer to the question will depend on whether one is looking at Old Dissent or at Methodism. He writes that whereas Old Dissent 'generally grew strong where the Church of England was strong, deriving (at least historically) much of its membership directly from the Church of England, Methodism grew strong where the Church of England was weak, and recruited from those sections of the population that Anglicanism failed to reach'.[92] There is some evidence to support Currie's generalization, but in the cases both of Old Dissent and of Methodism it must be qualified. It is true that as far as the Congregationalists and Baptists were concerned the areas in which both denominations had their largest following, apart from Wales, were rural counties in which the Church of England was also strong. The Congregationalists commanded the support of 11 per cent of the population of Essex and 8 per cent of the population of Suffolk, and they also had a considerable following in east Hertfordshire and in much of Northamptonshire and south Leicestershire, in parts of south Hampshire and the Isle of Wight, and in east Dorset, west Wiltshire, and south Gloucestershire. In some registration districts the Independents had the support of over 20 per cent of the population: Braintree, Dunmow, and Halstead in Essex; Risbridge in Suffolk; Royston in Hertfordshire; Catherington and Christchurch in Hampshire; and Dursley in Gloucestershire. These were all registration districts in which the Church of England also had a respectable following. However the area of greatest Congregationalist strength was Wales, and especially south Wales, where the Church of England was particularly weak. The Independents attracted the support of over 20 per cent of the population of Carmarthenshire and over 15 per cent of the population of Breconshire, Cardiganshire, and Glamorgan, and in all these counties Independents outnumbered Anglicans. What best explains the geographic distribution of Congregationalism in 1851 is not its relationship to the Church of England but its descent from the Independency of the Interregnum: the areas of Independent strength in 1851 were areas of Independent strength in the 1650s and 1710s. The Congregationalists flourished in the nineteenth century, as in the seventeenth century, in parts of eastern England and the south Midlands which had lain safely behind the parliamentary lines for most of the Civil War and where Puritans had been able to afford the luxury of disputes about church government, and in south

---

[92] R. Currie, 'A Micro-Theory of Methodist Growth', *Proceedings of the Wesley Historical Society*, 36 (1967), 68.

Wales where the Congregational message had been spread by Vavasor Powell and the 'propagators of the Gospel in Wales'.[93] The chief differences between the geographic distribution of Independency in 1851 and 1715 were the new concentrations of strength in Dorset, Wiltshire, and to an extent Carmarthenshire, where the Congregationalists had inherited that part of the Presbyterian tradition that had remained loyal to Calvinism.[94]

The religious census did not distinguish with sufficient clarity between the General and the Particular Baptists to enable us to produce separate statistics for the two denominations, but the geographical distribution of the Baptists as a whole can also be best explained by reference to their distribution in the seventeenth and early eighteenth centuries. The Baptists in 1851 attracted the support of more than 10 per cent of the population of Huntingdonshire, Bedfordshire, Cambridgeshire, Monmouthshire, Glamorgan, Carmarthenshire, Pembrokeshire, Cardiganshire, and Breconshire. There were also pockets of Baptist support in Buckinghamshire, north Essex, Hertfordshire, Leicestershire, Northamptonshire, Suffolk, east Sussex, and west Wiltshire. Apart from Cardiganshire, Leicestershire, and Suffolk these were all counties in which Baptist strength had been concentrated in 1715.[95] Baptists constituted over 20 per cent of the population of the registration districts of Berkhamsted in Hertfordshire, Amersham in Buckinghamshire, St Ives in Huntingdonshire, Chesterton in Cambridgeshire, and Melksham and Westbury in Wiltshire. The St Ives registration district included the village of Fenstanton whose Baptist church had been founded by the General Baptist Henry Denne in 1645 and which had served as a base for the evangelization of the surrounding villages of Huntingdonshire and Cambridgeshire.[96] The Baptist strength in Amersham and Berkhamsted registration districts in 1851 can be traced back to the concentration of General Baptists in the Chilterns in the early eighteenth century and before that to the Lollards. The same thread linking fifteenth-century Lollards, seventeenth- and eighteenth-century General Baptists, and areas of Baptist strength in 1851 is evident in northern Essex and the Weald of Sussex.[97] And the concentration of Baptists in the Melksham and Westbury districts of Wiltshire is traceable back to areas of Particular Baptist strength at least a century and a half earlier.[98] There was also a concentration of Baptists in the Pennine valleys of the Todmorden and Haslingden districts of the West Riding and Lancashire, a legacy of the evangelization of William Mitchell and David Crossley in the 1690s.[99] One of the few significant areas of Baptist strength which cannot be

---

[93] Watts, *The Dissenters*, i. 273, 281–2.   [94] Ibid. 468–9.   [95] Ibid. 274–5, 509–10.
[96] Ibid. 206, 287.   [97] Ibid. 14, 284.   [98] Ibid. 283.   [99] Ibid. 389.

traced back to the seventeenth or earlier centuries is Leicestershire. In the districts of Loughborough, Market Bosworth, and Leicester itself, the churches founded as a result of the Leicestershire revival of the mid-eighteenth century, and which later joined the New Connexion of General Baptists, pushed the Baptist proportion of the total population above 10 per cent.[100] In both the Leicester and Loughborough districts in 1851 the Church of England commanded the support of less than 20 per cent of the population, but in so far as the New Connexion of General Baptists was a manifestation of New rather than Old Dissent, its strength in Leicestershire is evidence in support of Currie's thesis.

Currie's argument that Old Dissent flourished in areas where the Church of England was strong does, however, collapse in the case of the Presbyterians. The Presbyterians constituted the largest Nonconformist denomination in the early eighteenth century and among their major areas of influence were Cheshire, Lancashire, Northumberland, and the West Riding of Yorkshire where, even at the turn of the seventeenth and eighteenth centuries, they were compensating for the inadequate parochial machinery of the established church.[101] It was primarily the subsequent decline of Presbyterianism which enabled Currie to draw the conclusion that the strength of Old Dissent lay in the same areas as did that of the Church of England. By the time of the religious census only Northumberland retained a strong orthodox Presbyterian presence, with around 20 per cent of the population of its northernmost districts worshipping in Presbyterian chapels. Those Presbyterian meetings which had become Unitarian enjoyed the support of a statistically significant proportion of the population only in middle-class areas of London such as Hackney and Hampstead and in their historic strongholds Birmingham, Bristol, Exeter, and Nottingham. Even in these towns the Unitarians constituted only about 1 per cent of the total population, and the only areas in which their support rose much above this level were the Lampeter, Aberayron, and Newcastle Emlyn districts of Cardiganshire and Carmarthenshire.

Currie's contention that, in contrast to Old Dissent, Methodism flourished where the Church of England was weak can be supported by the strength of Calvinistic Methodism throughout the Welsh-speaking districts of north and west Wales; by the support for Wesleyanism in Cornwall, Lincolnshire, Nottinghamshire, much of Derbyshire, most of Yorkshire, and in north and central Wales; by the strength of the Bible Christians in Cornwall and west Devon; and by the support for Primitive Methodism in north Lincolnshire

---

[100] Ibid. 454–6.   [101] Ibid. 277–80.

and west Durham. The Calvinistic Methodists attracted the support of around a third of the people of Anglesey, Caernarfonshire, and Merioneth, and nearly a quarter of those of Cardiganshire. The Wesleyans enjoyed the adherence of nearly 20 per cent of the people of Cornwall, and of more than 10 per cent of those of Lincolnshire, the North and East Ridings, Flintshire, and Montgomeryshire. The Primitive Methodists had the adherence of over 16 per cent of the inhabitants of Alston in Cumberland and of over 10 per cent of those in Weardale in Durham and in Gainsborough and Glanford-Brigg in Lincolnshire. The Bible Christians attracted over 16 per cent of the population of the Scilly Isles, of Camelford in Cornwall, and of Holsworthy in Devon. Apart from the Scilly Isles, these areas of Methodist strength were all districts in which the Church of England was significantly weak.

The relationship between Methodist strength and Anglican weakness, and conversely between Anglican strength and Methodist weakness, can be further illustrated by reference to the maps for the south Midlands, the eastern counties, south-west England, and the east Midlands. A glance at Maps 16, 20, 23, 27, 31, 35, 48, and 52 will show that in these regions the districts of greatest Wesleyan strength, and the districts which showed the greatest loyalty to the established church, fit together like the interlocking pieces of a jigsaw puzzle. To take the example of the south Midlands, Maps 16 and 20 show that the districts in which the Church of England could command the support of more than 40 per cent of the population—Linton, Brackley, and Hendon—were districts in which Wesleyan Methodism was noticeably weak, and, conversely, that the districts in which the Wesleyans had the adherence of more than 15 per cent of the people—North Witchford, Wellingborough, Leighton Buzzard, and Luton—were areas of particular Anglican weakness. But some of the areas in which the districts of greatest Wesleyan strength and the areas of greatest Anglican strength form an interlocking pattern—Bedfordshire, Northamptonshire, Hertfordshire, Cambridgeshire, Suffolk, Somerset, Dorset, Devon, and Cornwall—were also counties in which the overall level of religious observance in 1851 was well above the national average. This raises the possibility that Methodism had expanded not only by moving into those areas such as Durham in which the Church of England was inadequately prepared to cope with the changes brought about by the industrial revolution, but also by challenging the Church of England in counties such as Bedfordshire where both Anglicanism and Old Dissent were already well entrenched, and in which a high proportion of the population was consequently well disposed towards religion. In such counties in the south Midlands and the West Country it is likely that Methodism grew as much by winning converts from the existing churches as it did by evangelizing those whose religion was purely nominal before they came into contact with Methodism.

One of the difficulties involved in any attempt to explain the geographic distribution of Nonconformity in 1851 lies in the fact that we have no precise knowledge of the geographic distribution of Anglican worshippers before that date. But we do know how many Anglican churches existing in the mid-nineteenth century had been built before 1801, we know that the number of new parish churches built in the course of the eighteenth century was not statistically significant, and we do have a fairly accurate idea of the size of the population in each English county and in Wales in both 1700 and 1801.[102] It is thus possible to see whether there was any correlation between inadequate Anglican provision for the people at the beginning and end of the eighteenth century and the areas of Nonconformist strength in the mid-nineteenth century.

Table IV suggests that there was a connection between inadequate Anglican provision and the growth of Methodism in Cheshire, Cornwall, Derbyshire, Durham, Staffordshire, and the West Riding of Yorkshire. These were all counties which had seen significant industrial development and population growth in the course of the eighteenth century. It was the misfortune of the Church of England that the areas in which conditions were favourable to the growth of industry—upland areas with a plentiful supply of water and timber and mineral resources—were precisely the areas which had been unfavourable for arable farming and hence for settlement in the early middle ages when the parochial organization of the established church had taken shape. Such factors had already assisted the survival of Presbyterianism in the woollen towns of the West Riding and the shipbuilding and coal-producing areas of the north-east after 1660,[103] and they continued to work to the advantage of the Methodists in the late eighteenth and early nineteenth centuries. Methodism flourished in communities of tin- and copper-miners in Cornwall, nailers in the Black Country, and coalminers in Durham which had grown up in areas in which the Church of England was especially weak. In such districts the Methodists did fill a gap left by the failure of the Church of England to adapt quickly enough to population movement. 'We were not Dissenters,' said a miners' leader in later years, 'there was nothing to dissent from.'[104]

---

[102] *Religious Census*, pp. ccxxxix–cl; Watts, *The Dissenters*, i. 507–10; P. Deane and W. Cole, *British Economic Growth, 1688–1959* (Cambridge, 1962), 103.

[103] Watts, *The Dissenters*, i. 277–8.

[104] H. H. Henderson, *Retrospect of an Unimportant Life* (1943), ii. 80.

TABLE IV. *Relationship between Anglican accommodation in the eighteenth century and religious observance in 1851*

	Anglican churches built before 1801	Number of people per Anglican church		Percentage of population in church or chapel, 1851			
		1700	1801	Church of England	Old Dissent	Methodists	Total
Bedfordshire	107	511.8	611.4	26.0	17.1	18.8	65.6
Berkshire	141	541.0	799.3	31.3	8.0	8.3	48.5
Buckinghamshire	161	518.1	688.7	29.4	14.5	10.6	55.5
Cambridgeshire	122	663.5	755.7	24.6	13.2	11.1	51.0
Cheshire	130	859.2	1,522.1	16.8	4.6	10.8	35.2
Cornwall	150	779.8	1,295.2	13.7	2.8	30.6	47.7
Cumberland	125	541.8	967.8	15.2	3.7	6.2	27.4
Derbyshire	156	664.9	1065.9	16.0	6.0	16.7	40.5
Devon	341	742.4	1038.0	27.7	8.3	8.4	47.0
Dorset	221	405.2	538.5	33.9	8.8	9.0	53.1
Durham	76	1,125.0	2,177.4	11.3	3.8	13.4	31.1
Essex	320	529.9	730.2	30.5	15.3	4.0	51.2
Gloucestershire	294	564.5	880.3	27.2	11.2	5.6	47.6
Hampshire	286	435.9	792.5	27.3	10.0	6.5	45.3
Herefordshire	203	351.9	453.4	24.9	3.8	5.6	35.4
Hertfordshire	113	678.1	891.1	28.7	15.6	5.9	51.3
Huntingdonshire	79	485.1	490.7	29.1	18.5	12.3	64.0
Kent	341	566.9	930.9	25.6	6.3	5.9	40.3
Lancashire	218	899.6	3,184.4	14.4	5.0	6.1	32.4
Leicestershire	205	429.7	654.8	24.8	12.3	10.3	49.4
Lincolnshire	495	389.1	434.8	20.0	3.9	19.3	43.9
Middlesex and London	162	3,587.5	5,211.4	16.2	6.6	2.1	27.5
Monmouthshire	106	275.5	443.7	12.7	20.0	13.8	49.0
Norfolk	611	382.1	461.7	24.8	6.0	12.8	44.8
Northamptonshire	237	490.9	573.7	29.9	14.3	9.6	54.9

Northumberland	99	1,228.9	1,637.5	11.7	8.7	7.2	31.0
Nottinghamshire	186	427.9	778.7	16.7	5.9	14.6	39.2
Oxfordshire	181	480.3	625.0	30.6	6.9	9.1	47.4
Rutland	42	371.0	401.9	31.7	9.4	8.1	50.3
Shropshire	222	514.4	779.2	25.9	4.3	9.8	41.7
Somerset	417	482.2	677.4	28.8	8.8	8.7	47.9
Staffordshire	172	654.4	1,434.8	15.5	3.9	12.4	34.1
Suffolk	443	416.2	490.2	33.0	17.0	5.3	55.8
Surrey and Southwark	113	1,489.9	2,456.9	19.8	6.7	2.2	30.7
Sussex	241	420.0	682.1	27.4	7.4	3.1	40.0
Warwickshire	177	567.9	1,213.8	18.9	7.3	4.2	33.6
Westmorland	63	471.1	681.7	24.0	2.5	7.6	36.9
Wiltshire	241	508.9	792.6	30.4	15.2	9.7	57.0
Worcestershire	198	512.2	726.2	22.9	4.0	7.0	36.0
Yorkshire, East Riding	205	⎫	681.5	16.6	4.4	18.0	41.5
Yorkshire, North Riding	206	⎬ 712.9	792.6	19.1	3.8	19.9	44.7
Yorkshire, West Riding	292	⎭	1,997.7	12.8	6.2	14.2	35.3
North Wales	272	524.6	954.9	10.9	15.1	32.8	59.2
South Wales	497	336.1	601.7	11.3	28.0	16.3	56.1
TOTALS	9,667	595.0	917.9	19.7	8.3	9.7	40.1

On the other hand Table IV also suggests that in many parts of the country there was no obvious connection between the success of Methodism and of Old Dissent and inadequate provision by the Church of England. Most of the areas in which more than a quarter of the population attended a Non-conformist place of worship in 1851—Bedfordshire, Buckinghamshire, Huntingdonshire, Monmouthshire, Wiltshire, and south Wales—were areas in which Anglican provision was considerably better than the national aver-age in both 1700 and 1801. Only Cambridgeshire (in 1700), north Wales (in 1801), and Cornwall are exceptions. Indeed in the county which had most parish churches per head of population in 1700—Monmouthshire—the Baptists and Congregationalists between them accounted for 20 per cent of all worshippers in 1851, and the Methodists for another 13.8 per cent. And it was not only the presence of Old Dissent that enabled Nonconformity to flourish in areas where Anglican provision for worshippers was a good deal better than average. After Cornwall, Lincolnshire was the most strongly Methodist county in England, and in 1851 there were almost as many Methodists as there were Anglicans in Wesley's native county. But in 1801 Lincolnshire had a more favourable ratio of parish churches to population than any other county apart from Rutland. The level of Methodist support in Bedfordshire was almost as high as in Lincolnshire, and here again the provi-sion of Anglican parish churches was well above the national average. In the West Riding of Yorkshire the Methodists benefited, as had the Presbyterians before them, from the fact that the proportion of parish churches to popula-tion was one of the worst in the country. But Methodism did even better in the East and North Ridings where the provision of parish churches was far more adequate. If Methodism gained from the weakness of the Church of England in the West Riding, it appeared to gain more from its strengths in the East and North Ridings. In Nottinghamshire Methodism flourished not in the larger industrial towns where the Church of England was being outpaced by population growth, but in medium-sized villages of between 400 and 600 inhabitants where the established church was also holding its own.[105]

All this suggests that throughout much of central England and Wales in particular, Methodism and Dissent grew so rapidly in the late eighteenth and early nineteenth centuries not because the Church of England was failing to provide churches in which their people could worship, but because the estab-lished church had in fact sown the seed for the Evangelical revival which swept through England and Wales, leaving the Methodists and Dissenters to reap the harvest. There may be no correlation between adequate Anglican

---

[105] Watts, *Religion in Victorian Nottinghamshire*, i, p. xxx.

provision in the eighteenth century and Anglican attendance in 1851, but Table IV shows that in many counties there *was* a correlation between Anglican provision in the previous century and overall religious observance in 1851. Of the 26 English counties in which church attendance was above the national average in 1851, 22 had a better-than-average number of parish churches per head of population in 1801. Of the 15 counties in which attendance was below the national average in 1851, 10 had a lower-than-average number of parish churches per head of population in 1801. The figures for Wales provide some support for Currie's thesis that Old Dissent flourished where the Church of England was strong whereas Methodism grew where it was weak. Anglican provision was far more adequate in south than in north Wales and Old Dissent was the dominant religious force in south Wales whereas in north Wales Calvinistic Methodism was in the ascendant. But even in north Wales Ieuan Gwynedd Jones's detailed study of Caernarfonshire has shown that the Church of England suffered little from pluralism, lay impropriation, or language problems, and he concludes that the Church lost ground to Nonconformity not in places 'where it was weak but where it was strong'.[106] When industrialization came to south Wales the Anglican church found that many of its buildings were situated at some distance from the new centres of population—on the tops of hills instead of in the valleys[107]—but in the eighteenth century south Wales was, compared with most of England, well provided with parish churches. Yet by 1851 south Wales had very low levels of Anglican support and exceptionally high overall levels of religious observance. All this adds substance to the thesis advanced in Volume I of this work, that the foundations of the Evangelical revival and of the subsequent growth of Nonconformity in Wales were laid by the Church of England and by its educational agencies.[108]

Conversely, the failure of the Church of England to provide adequately for the people of London, Lancashire, Durham, Northumberland, and the industrial regions of the West Riding even at the end of the seventeenth century was reflected in some of the lowest overall attendance figures in the country a century and a half later. Only by the Presbyterians in Northumberland and by the Wesleyans and Primitive Methodists in Durham were the deficiencies of the established church compensated for in a limited way by the Nonconformists. In London the Congregationalists had an important following in the middle-class suburb of Hackney, and in Lancashire and

[106] I. G. Jones, *Explorations and Explanations: Essays in the Social History of Victorian Wales* (Llandysul, 1981), 34–5.
[107] E. T. Davies, *Religion in the Industrial Revolution in South Wales* (Cardiff, 1965), 24.
[108] Watts, *The Dissenters*, i. 424–5, 437–8.

the West Riding both the Baptists and the Wesleyans had a significant impact on the adjoining Pennine districts of Haslingden and Todmorden. But in general those areas which were worst served by the established church in the eighteenth century did not respond to the Evangelical message of the Methodists, Baptists, and Congregationalists in the nineteenth. The Church of England had lost—perhaps had never had - the loyalty of the mass of the people in the poorer parts of London, the industrial towns of Lancashire and the West Riding, and of the more remote parts of Cumberland and Northumberland. Nonconformity was never able to make good that loss.

The conclusion of this discussion of the geographic distribution of Nonconformity is that both Old Dissent and Methodism did to some extent benefit from the failure of the Church of England to adapt its machinery to the shifts in population brought about by the demographic and industrial revolutions, but that both Old Dissent and Methodism also grew in areas where the ground had already been prepared by the Church of England. The overall pattern of religious observance in 1851 does not coincide with the pattern of Anglican support, but it does reflect the success of the Church of England and its agencies in preserving vestigial remains of Christian belief throughout much of Wales, the south Midlands, East Anglia, and the West Country, its failure to cater for the rapid rise in the population of the London area, and its centuries-old weakness throughout most of England north of the Trent. Nonconformity expanded in the late eighteenth century and early nineteenth century both by moving into areas which were being inadequately served by the Church of England, and by converting men and women who had derived what knowledge of Christianity they had from that same established church. To that extent the expansion of Evangelical Nonconformity in England and Wales paralleled the similar growth of Evangelical Christianity in the United States. In both countries the upsurge of aggressively evangelistic religion was made possible by the rapid growth and movement of a population that was favourably disposed towards Christianity but whose needs were ill-served by conventional ecclesiastical structures. The explanation for the phenomenal growth of Nonconformity in England and Wales is thus to be found in the psychology of those who experienced Evangelical conversion, in the social conditions that disposed men and women to see a need for religion and yet alienated them from the established church, and in the dynamic evangelistic activity and ecclesiastical organization of the Methodists, Baptists, and Congregationalists. Such activity and organization guaranteed that when men and women experienced Evangelical conversion they would, for the most part, find their spiritual homes not in their parish churches but in Nonconformist meeting-houses and chapels.

5. 'FUEL FOR THE EVERLASTING BURNING':
THE PSYCHOLOGY OF CONVERSION

The way in which the Church of England prepared the ground for the expansion of Evangelical Nonconformity in the late eighteenth and early nineteenth centuries is nowhere better illustrated than in the *Memoirs of Mr Thomas Tatham* who, for nearly forty years, was a Wesleyan local preacher and a pillar of Wesleyan Methodism in Nottingham. Tatham's experience typified that of a generation of men and women who were raised in the Church of England and who found their spiritual home in Methodism. Tatham was born in Malham in Craven, in the West Riding, in 1761 of Anglican parents who, to use his own words, 'were not privileged with an evangelical ministry', and yet who brought up their son 'to fear God' and to suffer the terrors of a guilt-ridden conscience. 'I had such a sense of God's omniscience', wrote Tatham, 'that I feared to commit evil, yet notwithstanding I often transgressed, which brought great sorrow and anguish upon my mind for a considerable time after.'[109]

At the age of thirteen Tatham moved to Nottingham, was apprenticed to a grocer in the market-place, and worshipped at St Mary's parish church with his parents. When he looked back through Wesleyan eyes at the Anglican preaching he heard in his youth he concluded that it 'was little better than heathen-morality'. In particular it did nothing either to assuage the guilt that stemmed from his teenage sexual frustration or to calm the fear of hell that he knew to be its penalty. In a clear reference to masturbation he wrote that he was 'filled with terror unspeakable; for though I had an outward show of goodness, I was living in the commission of a most easily besetting sin unknown to any being except God and myself'. He described the agony he suffered in terms similar to those used by William Perkins in the sixteenth century, by John Bunyan in the seventeenth century, and by thousands of other men who claimed, in their youth, to have had a conversion experience.[110] Because he could not conquer his 'one besetting sin' he believed that he was 'a transgressor against the whole law'.

Justice demanded satisfaction; but I knew not where to find it, nor how to fly from the wrath of an avenging God . . . The arrows of death stuck fast in me, and the pains of hell got hold of me, insomuch that my appetite failed, sleep departed, and nothing but eternal destruction was presented to my view. When I retired to rest in the evening, I expected I should wake in hell before morning. If I walked out in fields, I feared lest

---

[109] S. Dunn, *Memoirs of Mr. Thomas Tatham* (1847), 25.
[110] For a discussion of conversion experiences in earlier periods see Watts, *The Dissenters*, i. 172–9, 200–4, 240–1, 409–28.

the earth should open and swallow me up . . . Often did I wish that I had been a dog, or anything inanimate, rather than what I was.

Like many other future Methodists he read *The Whole Duty of Man* and tried to perform the religious duties it prescribed only to find they did not bring the peace he sought.[111] Salvation came in the summer of 1782 when Tatham, consumed with guilt at attending a race meeting on a Sunday afternoon, and too ashamed to attend his parish church, made for the Wesleyans' Octagon Tabernacle in the centre of Nottingham. There he heard the aged George Snowden preach a sermon 'in which he so exactly described my miserable condition, that I thought someone must have told him everything about me'. While listening to Snowden, Tatham later recalled, 'the Lord suddenly spoke peace to my troubled soul, and in a moment my mourning was turned into joy'.[112]

   All the ingredients of an Evangelical conversion are present in Tatham's account: the religious upbringing; the attempt to adhere to a strict moral code; the guilt, usually following the onset of puberty, induced by the failure to live up to that moral code; and the consequent fear that eternal punishment would be the price of that failure until persuaded that acceptance of the salvation offered by Christ could remove the danger of hell. The extent to which Tatham's experience was typical of the Evangelicals of his generation is revealed by an analysis I have made of the religious experience of 670 English and Welsh Methodists and Dissenters whose conversions took place after 1780 and who were active in Nonconformity between 1790 and 1850. The 670 conversion accounts have been taken from the biographies and autobiographies of Nonconformist personalities, and in particular from memoirs and notices of religious experience published in the denominational periodicals. The selection has been determined by the availability and quality of the material and cannot claim to be a scientific cross-section of the Nonconformists of the first half of the nineteenth century. Arminians who believed that a man's eternal destiny was determined by his personal response to the Gospel were much more likely to regard dramatic, instantaneous conversions as the crucial element in religious experience than were Calvinists who believed that a person's future fate was pre-ordained by the eternal decrees of God. It was more usual to read in Calvinist than in Arminian biographies that the subject of the memoir, brought up in a religious home, had 'known no sudden transition with respect to my religious views, no particular event or admonition which led me to see the value of real

---

[111]   For the influence of *The Whole Duty of Man*, see ibid. 425–7.
[112]   Dunn, *Memoirs of Tatham*, 27–31.

vital Christianity; but gradually and imperceptibly have I been convinced of the evil and danger attending sin [and] of the necessity of a change of heart'.[113] Consequently memoirs which reveal something of the motives which prompted conversion are much less plentiful in the *Congregational* and *Baptist Magazines* than in the *Arminian, Methodist,* and *Wesleyan Methodist Magazines*, and are most common of all in the *Primitive Methodist Magazine*.[114] My sample of 670 conversion experiences thus includes 362 Wesleyans and 232 Primitive Methodists, but only 55 Baptists and 13 Congregationalists. Moreover many of the memoirs were more concerned to relate the 'happy deaths' of their subjects rather than reveal details of their formative years, and accounts which tell us nothing about their subjects' upbringing or the process of their conversion have been discarded. Accounts of conversion experiences tended to become increasingly stereotyped as the years went by and to reflect the peculiar characteristics of the denomination to which the subject belonged. Memoirs in the *Baptist Magazine* were more often concerned to give the date of a person's baptism than reveal the details of his or her conversion, while explanations of conversion in the *Primitive Methodist Magazine* were frequently subsumed in the phrase 'it pleased the Lord to send Primitive Methodist missionaries' to the place where the convert lived. The subjects of the Baptist, Congregational, and Wesleyan memoirs were for the most part prominent in denominational life and one cannot be certain that their experiences were typical: the mere fact that their subjects were literate—and in the case of the Congregationalists male—cuts them off from a substantial section of their fellow believers. On the other hand, my selection of conversion experiences contains a disproportionate number of Primitive Methodists (34.6 per cent), and the fact that the memoirs in the *Primitive Methodist Magazine* included those of a much higher proportion of humble men and women than the memoirs in the other denominational periodicals helps to counter the balance towards denominational leaders in the Congregational, Baptist, and Wesleyan magazines. And for this very reason the Primitive Methodists in my sample are likely to be more representative of Nonconformity as a whole than are the samples from the other denominations. Despite the necessarily unscientific nature of the

[113] *Baptist Magazine*, 13 (1821), 345. See also ibid. 9 (1817), 223; G. Redford and J. A. James (eds.), *The Autobiography of the Rev. William Jay* (1855), 21–3; R. W. Dale, *The Life and Letters of John Angell James* (1861), 34; E. R. Conder, *Josiah Conder, A Memoir* (1857), 63–4; W. H. Stowell, *Memoir of the Life of Richard Winter Hamilton* (1850), 51, 80.

[114] The *Arminian Magazine* was renamed the *Methodist Magazine* in 1798 and the *Wesleyan Methodist Magazine* in 1821. To avoid confusion in their numbering I have treated the magazines as a single series.

sample, the fact remains that the experiences which these memoirs describe are so similar, and the conclusions to which they point are so overwhelming, that they must constitute a major source for an understanding of the expansion of Methodism and of Dissent in the late eighteenth and first half of the nineteenth centuries.

The first and most obvious characteristic of those Methodists and Dissenters who experienced an Evangelical conversion between 1780 and 1850 was that 89.9 per cent claimed to have had a religious upbringing. In 596 of the 670 cases I have examined we have evidence of the influences on their early lives and in only 63 of those cases do their subjects claim to have had an irreligious childhood. And it is particularly significant that of the 326 Wesleyan Methodists whose biographies provide evidence of their upbringing, 123 were raised by practising members of the Church of England, another 103 were brought up in Wesleyan homes, 20 were raised by Dissenters, while a further 61 asserted that they had benefited from early religious training without specifying the denomination to which they were indebted. In other words, if the sample I have consulted is in any way typical, a third of the third and fourth generation of Wesleyans who were converted during the great age of Methodist expansion between 1780 and 1850 were brought up by parents who were loyal members of the Church of England. And if we exclude those converts who were themselves raised within the Methodist tradition, at least 55 per cent of the converts won over to Wesleyanism were won from the Church of England, whereas only 18 (8 per cent) were converted from an irreligious background. The Primitive Methodists were more successful in winning converts from an irreligious background, but even they won over only 38 out of a total of 201 converts of whose early life we have knowledge. Forty-nine of those 201 Primitive Methodist converts had an Anglican upbringing, 42 were raised by the Wesleyans, 10 were brought up by the Primitive Methodists themselves, 11 by the Dissenters, and a further 50 were stated to have had a religious upbringing without specifying the denomination to which they were affiliated. All this substantiates the point made in the discussion of the geographic distribution of Nonconformity, that Methodism in general and Wesleyanism in particular flourished among people whose willingness to embrace Evangelical religion was the result of the preparatory work done by the Church of England.

The typical Wesleyan comment on an Anglican childhood was that of John Barnett who said that his parents were 'very moral in their conduct, but strangers to that change of heart which the Gospel requires'.[115] Similarly the

---

[115] *Methodist Magazine*, 41 (1818), 763.

biographer of Henry Dudeney wrote that while his mother and father were 'strictly moral in their conduct . . . their views of the method of personal salvation by our Lord Jesus Christ were exceedingly obscure'.[116] The Wesleyan children of Anglican parents were grateful for the religious atmosphere in which they were raised, but sad that their parents and their parents' church were unable to give them assurance of salvation. Those Methodists and Dissenters who were born of parents who were themselves converted were naturally more appreciative of their early religious upbringing. For many of the leading Nonconformists of the nineteenth century it was the early influence of their mothers that was the decisive influence on their lives. Such was the case of two of the most prominent Congregational ministers of the century, Robert William Dale and Newman Hall. Dale's mother, who early lost four of her five children, lavished on him the devotion she could not give to her dead children: from 'his birth she gave him to God . . . and watched over him with earnest prayer', and 'prayed incessantly' that he should live to become 'a minister of the Gospel of Jesus Christ'.[117] Newman Hall's earliest memory of his mother was of her teaching him to repeat 'God so loved the world, that He gave His only begotten Son, that whosoever believeth in Him should not perish but have everlasting life'. 'I know what love meant by the love of my mother', was his comment.[118] In the case of the young Charles Haddon Spurgeon, who was to become the most popular Baptist preacher of the nineteenth century, it was his mother's fears for his eternal salvation that most impressed him. She sought to persuade God that, if her children did end up in hell, it would be through no fault of hers. 'Lord, if my children go on in their sins', he remembered her praying, 'it will not be from ignorance that they perish, and my soul must bear a swift witness against them at the day of judgement if they lay not hold of Christ.'[119] It is perhaps not surprising that the child who heard his mother pray thus was to become one of the most terrifying preachers of the century.

Some converts were products of homes in which the religious aspirations of the mother clashed with the vices of the father. Such were the experiences of the two leading early Primitive Methodist preachers Hugh Bourne and William Clowes, and of a revivalist preacher of the next generation, Richard Weaver. While Hugh Bourne's father was fond of drink and was a man of violent temper 'and wrathful passions', his mother devoted herself to 'training her children to fear God' and in 'inculcating sobriety, industry, and the proper

---

[116] *Wesleyan Methodist Magazine*, 69 (1846), 943–4.
[117] A. W. W. Dale, *Life of R. W. Dale of Birmingham* (2nd edn., 1899), 4.
[118] Newman Hall, *An Autobiography* (1901), 2–3.
[119] *C. H. Spurgeon's Autobiography* (1897–1900), i. 68.

method of husbanding time'.[120] William Clowes's father was 'wild and dissipated', his mother of 'blameless' morals and a regular attender at her parish church.[121] Richard Weaver's childhood was marred by conflict between his 'ungodly, drinking' father and his pious mother. 'Many a time have I clung to my mother', he later recalled, 'and cried to my drunken father, "Don't kill my mother".'[122] In all three cases the influence of the religious mother prevailed over that of the irreligious father.

Those Nonconformists who looked back on their childhood years as periods devoid of serious religious impressions were very much in a minority. There were few later converts like William Hervey of Lewknor in Oxfordshire who was born of poor parents who were 'ignorant of things moral and divine'. Hervey grew up unable to read, 'was led into abandoned company', and neglected his home and abused his wife until, in 1834, he was converted by a Primitive Methodist missionary.[123] But even in the case of those few Dissenters and Methodists who claimed to have had irreligious childhoods, the seeds of their later conversions were often being sown. William Booth, the founder of the Salvation Army, had an unhappy childhood and claimed that he learnt nothing of religion, but he also reveals that although his father never entered a place of worship, he insisted on his children's attendance at church.[124] And Christmas Evans, who for more than forty years was the most celebrated Baptist preacher in Wales, was from the age of nine brought up by a drunken uncle and did not learn to read until he reached the age of seventeen, but he records that on one occasion his mother, of whom next to nothing is otherwise known, warned him to think of his 'eternal welfare'.[125]

The role of religious women was thus crucial in the expansion of Dissent. Their influence was increased paradoxically by the secondary role to which they were relegated by society at large and by the churches—both Anglican and Nonconformist—in particular. In the increased competition for jobs which followed the population explosion of the late eighteenth and early nineteenth centuries women were among the major casualties. As men found it increasingly difficult to find work women were denied employment opportunities which had been open to them earlier in the eighteenth century in both agriculture and industry; when women were able to find work it was at

[120] J. Walford, *Memoirs of the Life and Labours of the late Venerable Hugh Bourne* (1855), i. 2–3.

[121] J. T. Wilkinson, *William Clowes, 1780–1851* (1951), 15.

[122] R. C. Morgan, *Life of Richard Weaver* (1906), 6.

[123] *Primitive Methodist Magazine*, 2nd ser. 8 (1838), 62.

[124] W. Begbie, *Life of William Booth* (1920), i. 26–7, 40.

[125] D. M. Evans, *Christmas Evans: A Memoir* (1863), 3.

rates of pay far below the levels commanded by men; and there developed an increasingly rigid sexual division of labour in which women were under pressure to marry earlier and, once married, to stay at home and devote themselves entirely to the care of their husbands and the upbringing of their children.[126] It became one of the marks of a 'respectable' family that the wife should not undertake paid work, and indeed in the most prosperous families she was relieved even of household chores by the assistance of servants. Similarly in the churches women were compelled to occupy a subservient position. The women preachers whose appearance had so shocked conservative pamphleteers in the 1640s did not become a permanent feature of the life of the older Dissenting denominations apart from the Quakers, and although women preachers made an important contribution to Wesleyan revivalism in the 1790s, this was frowned upon by the Wesleyan leadership and effectively stopped by a decision of the Methodist Conference in 1803. Women still occupied an important role among Wesleyans as class leaders and Sunday school teachers, and neither the Primitive Methodists nor the Bible Christians shared the inhibitions of the older Connexion about women preachers. But the number of female preachers among the Primitive Methodists had declined by the mid-nineteenth century, and again with the partial exception of the Quakers, all the leading and visible roles throughout Nonconformity, as of course in the established church, were occupied by men. In the words of David Barker of the Methodist New Connexion, females might 'be useful in leading classes, visiting the afflicted, teaching the young, and exhibiting lovely examples of domestic piety', but they were not to be 'introduced into stations of authority and publicity'.[127]

Such attitudes prevailed at a time when the emotional appeal of Evangelical Christianity had a much greater impact on women than it had on men, and when the Methodist chapel and Nonconformist meeting-house had a social value as an escape from the home which was far greater for women (whether they were wives or domestic servants) than it was for men. C. D. Field has recently conducted a detailed analysis of Wesleyan, Baptist, and Congregational membership lists for the late eighteenth and early nineteenth centuries and has found that of a sample of 63,235 Wesleyans for the period 1751–1825 57.2 per cent were females; of 11,398 Baptists for the years 1801–50 64.6 per cent were women; and of 3,623 Congregationalists for the same half-century 59.8 per cent were women.[128] With many of the avenues for

[126] K. D. M. Snell, *Annals of the Labouring Poor* (Cambridge, 1985), 45–66, 312, 348–9.

[127] J. S. Werner, *The Primitive Methodist Connexion* (Madison, Wisc., 1984), 218–19.

[128] C. D. Field, 'Adam and Eve: Gender in the English Free Church Constituency', *Journal of Ecclesiastical History*, 44 (1993), 63.

service, in both society and the church, closed to them, women inevitably saw their families as the focus—and in many cases the only focus—of their Christian endeavours. The Anglican household in which the future Wesleyan preacher William Dawson was raised was typical of religious households in the reigns of the last three Hanoverians and of Queen Victoria: 'Mrs Dawson took upon herself the momentous charge of the children as to religion and morals . . . she prayed with them, read the Holy Scriptures to them and enforced many of her remarks by select portions from the *Practice of Piety*.'[129]

The family, in its religious aspect usually dominated by the mother, was not only of decisive importance in preparing the ground for future conversion, it was often the means by which that conversion was brought about. Of all the pressures that were brought to bear on men and women to experience an Evangelical conversion in the period under review, the pressures that were hardest to resist were pressures from members of one's own family. Hugh McLeod has found that missionaries of the London City Mission received their most hostile reception in the late nineteenth century among communities of men cut off from the civilizing influence of women and home: 'among sailors, railway navvies, brickmakers, residents of common lodging-houses'.[130] Conversely, the pleadings of a mother or father, brother or sister, son or daughter, that not only was one's eternal destiny at stake, but that in a future state one might be separated totally from one's loved ones, were instrumental in numerous conversions. A revival among the sons of Wesleyan preachers at Woodhouse Grove school near Leeds in 1833–4 was prompted by a sermon of Robert Aitken in which he pointed to 'their fathers' success in the salvation of others, and the terrible final severance of parents and sons which must be the result of a neglect of "so great salvation" '.[131] William Hill, a coalminer, danced and drank heavily and scorned his mother's concern for his salvation, but he was converted after his mother was 'found on her knees, by the bed-side, and her soul had departed'.[132] Robert Robinson, of Coningsby in Lincolnshire, was converted at the age of sixteen and 'feeling the power of religion in his soul, he earnestly prayed that his parents, brothers, and sisters might experience the same blessing', and within the next three years the whole family was converted.[133] Thomas Tatham's family joined the Wesleyans after the deathbed conversion and the 'tri-

---

[129] J. Everett, *Memoirs of the Life, Character, and Ministry of William Dawson* (1842), 7–8.
[130] H. McLeod, *Class and Religion in the Late Victorian City* (1974), 55.
[131] B. Gregory, *Autobiographical Recollections* (1903), 108–9.
[132] *Primitive Methodist Magazine*, 2nd ser. 2 (1832), 145–6.
[133] *Methodist Magazine*, 24 (1801), 68.

umphant death' of his youngest sister at the age of seventeen: his father commented how 'he had lived so long as to be taught his duty to God by his children'.[134] A Mrs Aspden attended the services of the Church of England regularly until she was over fifty years old, but her son was a Methodist, and one evening in the late 1780s when she was boasting of her attachment to the established church her son retorted that 'if she did not take care, her props would deceive her, and that she would fall into hell'. Her son's remark disturbed her, she began to wonder why he was more concerned about the fate of her soul that she was herself, and she was converted during family worship at her son's house the following evening.[135]

The age at which Mrs Aspden was converted was unusual. Of the 670 conversion experiences I have analysed the age of conversion was given in 607 cases (361 men and 246 women) and these ranged from eight to eighty. But half the conversions (52.4 per cent of the men and 48.0 per cent of the women) occurred between the ages of fourteen and twenty, and 74.2 per cent of the men and 74.8 per cent of the women were converted before the age of twenty-six. These figures strongly suggest a connection between conversion and the arousal of sexual feelings at puberty. It was suggested in the first volume of this work that the awakening of sexual desires and the guilt which such feelings induced played an important part in the religious development of both seventeenth-century Puritans and eighteenth-century Methodists,[136] and although there is less direct evidence from the conversion accounts of the period 1780–1850, the very age at which most conversions occurred suggests a link between sexual guilt and repression and religious experience. William Bramwell, who after John Wesley himself was the most effective Wesleyan preacher of the late eighteenth century, certainly saw the need to emphasize the importance of sexual restraint to recent and potential converts. After his appointment to the Kent circuit in 1785 'many young people were added to the society' and Bramwell 'guarded them against the temptations peculiar to their age, and to give greater effect to his exhortations, he addressed the two sexes separately'.[137] Very few of the post-1780 conversion accounts, however, suggest that their subjects had ever committed sexual offences. The *Baptist Magazine* for 1809 gave an account of the conversion of the inappropriately named Temperance Pascoe of Penzance, a notorious drunkard, who was converted when dying from consumption at the age of fifty-one, and there is a hint in her memoir that she had been a prostitute.[138] The conversion experiences

[134] Dunn, *Memoirs of Thomas Tatham*, 37–8.
[135] *Methodist Magazine*, 34 (1811), 943.   [136] Watts, *The Dissenters*, i. 187, 418–21.
[137] J. Sigston, *Memoir of the Venerable William Bramwell* (Halifax, 1860), 22.
[138] *Baptist Magazine*, 1 (1809), 302.

of young men sometimes suggest that their subjects, like Thomas Tatham, were oppressed by remorse at being unable to give up the habit of masturbation. The Wesleyan John Sugden Smith was convinced 'he had provoked the anger of God by personal crimes', and the Baptist Charles Barraclough, removed from his father's house at the age of fourteen, looked forward to being freed from parental restraint that he might have 'my fill of sin . . . though I committed it not openly'.[139] The fact that such references are rare is, however, not surprising given the blanket of silence which descended on the discussions of sexuality following the Evangelical revival. Except for a handful of oblique references, those Nonconformists who wrote their autobiographies and those Wesleyans and Primitive Methodists whose experiences were recorded in the denominational magazines appear to have committed, in Evangelical eyes, every youthful transgression apart from those connected with sex. Boys confessed to drunkenness, swearing, playing cards, attending horse-races, visiting the theatre, and breaking the Sabbath. Unregenerate girls read novels, were 'much given to society and fashion', and were 'fond of dress, dancing, [and] card-parties'.[140] But offences against the Evangelical sexual code were clearly too shocking to be admitted in print.

If, indeed, most Nonconformists and Wesleyans were converted while they were teenagers one might expect an important role to have been played by the Sunday schools. The practice of teaching the children of the poor to read on Sundays had begun at least as early as the 1760s on the initiative of individual clergymen and of lay men and women, but it was after Robert Raikes publicized the success of the Sunday schools in Gloucestershire in 1783 that the movement spread rapidly throughout the country.[141] The object of the Sunday schools, wrote one of their Methodist supporters, 'was not only to teach the children of poor people to read and write, but to instruct, in the most important practical principles of religion, all the children either poor or rich who were sent to them'.[142] This attempt to make children religious by means of education was not new, and it was argued in the first volume of this work that the charity-school movement in England and the circulating schools in Wales played an important part in preparing the way for the Methodist revival.[143] The Sunday school movement was in effect a continuation of the charity-school movement, adapted to the changed circumstances of Britain of the industrial revolution: Sunday schools had the tremendous

---

[139] *Methodist Magazine*, 49 (1826), 73; *Baptist Magazine*, 13 (1821), 481.
[140] *Methodist Magazine*, 36 (1813), 758.
[141] P. B. Cliff, *The Rise and Development of the Sunday School Movement in England, 1780–1980* (Redhill, Surrey, 1986), 20–9.
[142] *Methodist Magazine*, 28 (1805), 6.   [143] Watts, *The Dissenters*, i. 423–6.

advantage over charity day-schools that their teachers were part-time and consequently did not require payment, and with the increasing employment of children in industry they were often left with only one day in which they could receive some elementary schooling. Robert Raikes was moved to start his school in Gloucester by the knowledge that on Sundays the streets in the poorest areas of the city were filled by 'children wretchedly ragged' who, 'released on the day from their employment, spent their time in noise and riot and playing at chuck, and cursing and swearing in a manner so horrid, as to convey to any serious mind an idea of hell'.[144]

Such was the popularity of the Sunday schools that the numbers of children in England who were enrolled increased from 200,000 at the beginning of the century to over 2,000,000 in 1851. By the 1840s half the children in England between the ages of five and fifteen were enrolled in a Sunday school, and Thomas Laqueur comments that 'the magnitude of enrolment was such that very few working-class children after 1830 could have escaped at least a few years in Sunday school'.[145] But the extent to which the Sunday schools were successful either in providing the rudiments of a secular education or in preparing children for future church membership is far from clear. Laqueur, in the most exhaustive study of Sunday schools that has yet appeared, concluded that in general the schools 'were a failure as recruitment agencies for church and chapel'. He even adds that in towns and cities with populations of over 10,000 people in 1851 there was 'a strong negative correlation between church attendance and Sunday school enrolment . . . suggesting that in certain urban areas, particularly in the north, Sunday schools replaced church or chapel as the focus of working-class religious life'.[146] Sunday schools often had a rapid turnover of pupils and a high wastage rate: the Wesleyan Red Hill Sunday school in Sheffield, with over a thousand children on its books in 1832, claimed that there was virtually 'an entire change of boys in less than two years'.[147] In some Sunday schools critics complained that religious teaching was neglected in favour of secular instruction: the Wesleyan Sunday school at Burslem in the Potteries had 1,400 children on its roll in 1834, but the school had 'no direct connexion with the worship of Almighty God'.[148] And in others the use of the Bible as a textbook produced a hostility to scripture that was to last a lifetime.[149]

---

[144] T. W. Laqueur, *Religion and Respectability: Sunday Schools and Working-class Culture, 1780–1850* (New Haven, Conn., 1976), 21–5.

[145] Ibid. 44–5. [146] Ibid. 160, 59.

[147] E. R. Wickham, *Church and People in an Industrial City* (1957), 155.

[148] W. R. Ward, *Early Victorian Methodism: The Correspondence of Jabez Bunting, 1830–1858* (Oxford, 1976), 43.

[149] Cliff, *Sunday School Movement*, 125.

Church leaders frequently bemoaned the fact that the time and effort devoted to educating the young did not yield the expected benefits in terms of church membership. Andrew Reed of the Wycliffe Independent church in East London wrote in 1840 that the Sunday schools had 'brought us far less fruit than, for the culture bestowed and the blessing promised, might reasonably be expected.[150] In the fifty years from 1810 to 1860 1,800 scholars passed through the school attached to the Kettering Congregational church, but of that 1,800 only 150 became members of that church.[151] The Fish Street Congregational church in Hull had an even worse return: of the 10,000 scholars who attended the church's Sunday school between 1815 and 1877 only about 500 went on to join the Fish Street church.[152] Figures from the Halifax, Hull, and Nottingham Sunday School Unions show that less than 1 per cent of their pupils joined their respective churches annually.[153] The statistics, commented a Wesleyan in 1854, demonstrated 'that vast multitudes of children are incessantly passing through our Sunday schools and then becoming ... utterly alienated from our religious fellowship'.[154]

On the other hand some historians are convinced that Sunday schools played an important part in church expansion, and they can cite contemporary evidence to support their contention. Richard Carwardine argues that a large proportion of converts in the revivals of the 1830s and 1840s 'were drawn from Bible classes and Sunday schools', and notes that during the mission to England of the Irish American evangelist James Caughey between 1857 and 1859 up to 50 per cent of his converts were under the age of twenty. Caughey's converts, Carwardine argues, were drawn 'disproportionately from the young and the Sunday schools'.[155] Tudur Jones claims that in England 'the Sunday schools became a most efficient recruiting agency for the Nonconformist churches' and cites the opinion of R. W. Dale that 'between 1860 and 1890 many Congregational churches derived a third, and in some cases even a half, of their members from their Sunday schools'.[156] D. G. Evans similarly argues from his study of the Swansea valley that 'Sunday schools lay at the centre of the whole Nonconformist mechanism of growth'. 'When a Nonconformist cause was set up it was usually the Sunday school room that was established first, or if a church decided to send an off-shoot branch to a far corner of the valley, the schoolroom was the probing satel-

---

[150] A. Reed, *The Revival of Religion* (1840), 26. I owe this reference to Veronica Goodwin.
[151] F. C. Goodman, *The Great Meeting: The Story of Toller Congregational Church, Kettering* (1902), 37–40.
[152] C. E. Darwent, *The Story of Fish Street Church, Hull* (Hull, 1899), 176.
[153] Laqueur, *Religion and Respectability*, 80.   [154] *HMC*, ii. 104.
[155] R. Carwardine, *Transatlantic Revivalism* (Westport, Conn., 1978), 80, 193.
[156] R. T. Jones, *Congregationalism in England* (1962), 164.

lite.'[157] Similarly in England the Baptist churches at Burnley, Alletroyds, Enfield, Church, and Waterfoot in Lancashire, the Particular Baptist church at Blaby in Leicestershire, and the Congregational church at Pendleton in Manchester all evolved out of Sunday schools.[158] Contemporaries often noted that religious revivals began in Sunday schools. The revival which started in Beddgelert at the end of 1817, and which was to transform Caernarfonshire into a stronghold of Calvinistic Methodism, began among a class of Sunday school girls, and the 1,500 people who were added to the Calvinistic Methodist churches of the same county in the revival of 1832 were also said to have come mainly from the Sunday schools.[159] Sunday schools in Wales were not confined to children, and the fact that at least half the members of some Sunday schools were adults may explain why such schools appear to have played a larger part in church recruitment in Wales than in England.[160] But revivals in England also on occasion started with the conversion of Sunday school children: for example, that among the Wesleyan Methodists at Northdelph in Norfolk in 1832, and that among the Primitive Methodists at Danegree near Dewsbury in 1833.[161] There were also Nonconformist churches that claimed that a high proportion of their membership was made up of present or former Sunday school pupils. The Wesleyan society at Bolton estimated in 1820 that a third of its membership consisted of Sunday scholars, and the Primitive Methodist church at Driffield in the East Riding claimed in 1889 that its 264 members were 'largely recruited from the Sunday school'.[162] And while fewer than 10 per cent of the Sunday scholars attached to the Kettering Congregational church may have become members of that church, some children who attended that Sunday school did become members of other churches, not least the future Baptist missionaries Thomas and William Knibb. William Knibb's own conversion was precipitated by an address given by his Sunday school superintendent when he was teaching in the Broadmead Baptist Sunday school in Bristol: Knibb was

[157] D. G. Evans, 'The Growth and Development of Organized Religion in the Swansea Valley, 1820–1890', Ph.D. thesis (University of Wales, 1978), 347.

[158] Weston, 'The Baptists of North-West England', 490; G. Jackson, 'The Evangelical Work of Baptists in Leicestershire', MA thesis (London, 1955), 71; *Congregational Year Book* (1847), 167.

[159] W. Williams, *Welsh Calvinistic Methodism* (2nd edn., 1884), 156–62; *Evangelical Magazine*, NS 10 (1832), 568.

[160] I. G. Jones and D. Williams, *The Religious Census of 1851: A Calendar of Returns relating to Wales*, i. *South Wales* (Cardiff, 1976), p. xxvii.

[161] *Wesleyan Methodist Magazine*, 55 (1832), 747; *Primitive Methodist Magazine*, 2nd ser. 4 (1834), 314.

[162] Ward, *Religion and Society in England*, 136; H. Woodcock, *Piety Among the Peasantry: Being Sketches of Primitive Methodism on the Yorkshire Wolds* (1889), 88, 90.

ashamed that, as a teacher, 'the address should be as suitable to me as to the children'.[163]

Some light can be thrown on the issue of the contribution that the Sunday schools made to church expansion by my analysis of 670 conversion accounts. At first sight the evidence seems to support Laqueur's contention that the schools largely failed as recruiting agencies for the churches. In only 58 of the 670 conversion experiences I have analysed (a mere 8.7 per cent) was Sunday school mentioned as having played a part in a young person's religious development. A breakdown of the figures on a denominational basis does, however, reveal a rather different picture. Of the 58 converts whose conversion accounts mention attendance at Sunday school, no less than 42 ultimately became Primitive Methodists. Whereas only 10 out of 362 Wesleyan conversion accounts mention Sunday school attendance (2.8 per cent), in 42 out of 232 Primitive Methodist memoirs (18 per cent) Sunday school was thought worth mentioning as part of their subjects' spiritual pilgrimage. And of those 42 Primitive Methodists who attended Sunday schools, at least 16 attended Wesleyan Sunday schools. If my sample of converts is at all representative, this means that the Wesleyan Sunday schools were more effective in preparing converts for the Primitive Methodists than for their own Connexion! A much more likely explanation, however, is the point already mentioned, that because the conversion accounts printed in the *Primitive Methodist Magazine* recorded the experiences of humble men and women rather than those of denominational luminaries or even chapel stalwarts, they are likely to be much more representative of the experience of the average Nonconformist church member than those recorded in the *Wesleyan Methodist Magazine* or in Baptist or Congregational biographies. The Primitive Methodists did, admittedly, have a higher proportion of working-class members than did the other Nonconformist denominations, and the Sunday schools were, at least initially, directed at those children whose parents could not afford to provide them with full-time education. But, as will be argued later, the working-class constituency of the other Evangelical Nonconformist denominations has been seriously underestimated by most historians: the Wesleyans, Baptists, and even Congregationalists contained a much larger working-class element than has been usually assumed. If, as seems likely, my sample of Primitive Methodist converts is much more typical of Nonconformity as a whole than the Wesleyan, Baptist, or Congregational samples, this suggests that by 1850 up to 20 per cent of Nonconformist converts had passed through a Sunday school.

[163] Hinton, *Memoir of William Knibb*, 8–9.

There is, moreover, a good deal of evidence which suggests that the influence of the Sunday schools increased as the nineteenth century progressed (at least until the 1870 Education Act), and that the religious component in their teaching also increased. The proportion of children between the ages of five and fifteen who were enrolled in English Sunday schools increased from 10 per cent at the beginning of the century to over 50 per cent by 1851,[164] and at the same time the churches made a determined effort to guarantee that the religious objectives of the schools should not be lost sight of in the working-class quest for secular instruction. In 1817 the Wesleyan Conference urged that Sunday schools 'should be connected as closely as possible with the Church of Christ', and that school hours should be arranged so that they did not prevent 'the punctual attendance, both of teachers and children, on [the] ordinances of public worship'.[165] In 1827 the Conference tried to forbid the teaching of writing in Wesleyan Sunday schools on the ground that writing was an aid to secular rather than spiritual advancement. And in 1829 the Primitive Methodist Conference drew up rules which stated that since the chief object of Sunday schools was 'to promote the eternal salvation of the children', pupils should 'attend divine worship in the chapel'.[166] Alan Gilbert argues that this growing preoccupation with the Sunday schools as a nursery for future church members was in fact a sign of weakness. From the 1830s, he contends, Nonconformists ceased to recruit adults 'from the wider society of early industrial England' and increasingly came to rely on the recruitment of young people who had been raised in chapel Sunday schools.[167] But the evidence produced above shows that even at the turn of the eighteenth and nineteenth centuries Methodists and Dissenters were recruiting teenagers as much as they were recruiting adults, and that when they were converting members of 'the wider society' outside the chapel communities, these were usually young people who had been brought up in the Church of England. The Sunday schools may not have assisted the churches in making major inroads into completely irreligious families, but they were an additional factor in predisposing children from religious homes towards Evangelical conversion. In this way they occupied a role analogous to that of the charity and circulating schools of the early eighteenth century.

The way in which the Sunday schools replaced the charity schools in preparing children for conversion can be seen in the career of Thomas Charles of Bala, the leading Welsh Calvinistic Methodist at the turn of the

[164] Laqueur, *Religion and Respectability*, 44.
[165] *Minutes of the Methodist Conferences*, 4 (1817), 337.
[166] *Primitive Methodist Magazine*, 2nd ser. 3 (1833), 217.
[167] A. Gilbert, *Religion and Society in Industrial England* (1976), 57, 200–2.

century. The circulating schools founded by Griffith Jones between 1737 and his death in 1761 closed down in the 1780s when the will of the lady to whom he had entrusted their care, Mrs Bridget Bevan of Laugharne, was challenged by one of her executors. But around 1785 Thomas Charles revived the idea of circulating schools and by 1794 he was employing twenty schoolmasters covering five counties. Each schoolmaster, wrote Charles, was paid £10 a year and 'stays but half or three-quarters of a year in the same place, then we move him to another neighbourhood; by these means we are able to teach the whole country with no great expense'. The children were taught 'to read their *native* language correctly, and were instructed in the principles of Christianity, and *nothing more*, as the salvation of their souls is the only point we have in view'.[168]

According to Charles, it was his circulating schools which provided many of the converts in the revival which occurred in Bala in the autumn of 1791. At the close of Charles's evening service on the last Sunday of October people began to shout out, 'What must I do to be saved', and 'God be merciful to me a sinner'. 'About nine or ten o'clock at night, there was nothing to be heard from one end of the town to the other, but the cries and groans of people in distress of soul . . . there was hardly a young person in the neighbourhood but began to enquiry, "What will become of me?" ' A similar revival took place in Caernarfonshire in the spring of 1793 and here, as at Bala, most of the converts were 'children and young people, from eight or ten to thirty' years of age.[169] Initially Charles believed that 'in our wild country children are too much scattered for Sunday schools', and there was some opposition to Sunday schools in north Wales on the ground that they were a violation of the Sabbath.[170] But Charles subsequently came to the view that Sunday schools were necessary for people who were 'too much engaged or too poor to avail themselves of the day schools', and from the late 1790s he devoted his energies to the founding of Sunday schools.[171] He was soon attributing to the Sunday schools the role that he had hitherto ascribed to his circulating schools in preparing children for conversion: revivals in Aberystwyth in 1805, in Merioneth in 1811, in south Wales in 1812, and in Caernarfonshire in 1813 were all in 'great measure . . . the happy fruit of our Sunday schools'.[172]

The terms in which Thomas Charles described the revivals in Bala in 1791 and in Caernarfonshire in 1793 are very like those used by Wesleyan

---

[168] D. E. Jenkins, *Life of Thomas Charles of Bala* (Denbigh, 1908), i. 562–3, 566; ii. 29, 101.
[169] Ibid. ii. 89–90, 100–1.   [170] Ibid. 30, 144.
[171] D. Evans, *The Sunday Schools of Wales* (1883), 171, 173; Jenkins, *Life of Thomas Charles*, ii. 180–4.
[172] Jenkins, *Life of Thomas Charles*, iii. 114, 413, 420, 492.

Methodists to describe the revival which swept through Yorkshire from 1792 to 1796. The revival seems to have begun with the arrival in July 1791 of the charismatic preacher William Bramwell in the Dewsbury circuit. Bramwell, who was born in 1759 of strict Anglican parents and was converted 'while receiving the sacred elements from the hands of the Rev. Mr Wilson, a pious clergyman at Preston', had become a Wesleyan itinerant preacher in 1785. With his powerful preaching voice, his dark, piercing, eyes, his strong commitment to prayer (so that his breeches were threadbare at the knees), his spiritual perception (so that contemporaries believed that he had the gift of 'discerning of spirits'), his precognitive dreams, and his claims to have effected cures of blindness and whooping cough, there was much about Bramwell that was reminiscent of the Quaker pioneer George Fox. He had a powerful impact on people who met and heard him and in the 1790s and early 1800s his appointment to successive Wesleyan circuits—Dewsbury (1791–3), Birstall (1793–5), Sheffield (1795–8), Nottingham (1798–1800), and Hull (1804–6)—was followed by revival and a large increase in Methodist membership.[173] The memory of the power and spirituality of Bramwell's preaching long remained fresh. He had been dead thirty-seven years when another revivalist, the founder of the Salvation Army, William Booth, named his eldest son after him.[174]

Bramwell was a convinced believer in Wesley's doctrine of 'entire sanctification',[175] but when he got to Dewsbury he found that the Methodist society had been torn apart by a dispute over Wesley's claim to appoint preachers in opposition to the chapel's trustees, that the chapel had been lost to the Connexion, and that not one person had 'experienced sanctification'. To remedy the situation he started prayer-meetings at five o'clock in the morning and was joined in Dewsbury by one of his converts, Ann Cutler, otherwise known as 'Praying Nanny' since 'an amazing power of God' attended her prayers. When Joseph Entwisle preached at Dewsbury in April 1792 he found 'a considerable increase of the power of godliness in this neighbourhood, through the labours of Mr Bramwell'.[176] But Bramwell himself modestly attributed the start of the revival to the prayers of Ann Cutler in the autumn of 1792. 'Under Nanny Cutler's prayers, one soul received a clean heart'; the same week four more people 'found peace with God'; and soon

---

[173] Sigston, *Memoir of Bramwell, passim*; J. Baxter, 'The Great Yorkshire Revival, 1792–6', in M. Hill (ed.), *A Sociological Yearbook of Religion in Britain* (1974); Swift, *Lively People*, 43–6; G. Smith, *History of Wesleyan Methodism* (1863), ii. 408–9.

[174] F. de L. Booth-Tucker, *The Life of Catherine Booth* (1892), i. 174.

[175] See Watts, *The Dissenters*, i. 432–4.

[176] T. Entwisle, *Memoir of the Rev. Joseph Entwisle* (1867), 77.

'sixty persons in and around Dewsbury received sanctification . . . our love feasts began to be crowded, and people from every neighbouring circuit visited us'.[177]

According to Bramwell's own account, Ann Cutler was instrumental in spreading the revival to the Birstall, Leeds, and Bradford circuits and thence to Lancashire. In one week in the Oldham circuit 'there was near a hundred souls brought to God' and similar success was claimed in Manchester.[178] But Praying Nanny's constant labours and frugal diet—'she lived chiefly upon milk and herb-tea'—took their toll and she died in Macclesfield in December 1794, aged thirty-five, praying at the end 'Dear Jesus, take me for thy bride . . . how I long to be with Thee in heaven!'[179]

By the time of Ann Cutler's death the revival she had helped to initiate was gathering momentum. In June 1793 Methodists from the Bradford circuit attended a love-feast at Greetland near Halifax and so inspired the Halifax Methodists with their accounts of the Bradford revival that prayer-meetings or class-meetings were held every night of the week. At such prayer-meetings 'frequently ten, fifteen, or twenty souls were either justified or fully sanctified'. Some 'cried aloud for mercy', 'many were much agitated in their bodies, and even fainted away', and others 'remained in distress for several hours, till they were sensibly delivered from their misery'. Seven hundred people joined the Wesleyan societies in the Halifax circuit in 1793–4, and in May 1794 the itinerant preacher Robert Lomas reported that 'the young converts had stood their ground much better than we expected'.[180] Meanwhile Bramwell had been appointed to the Birstall circuit in 1793, and at a love-feast on Christmas day 'not less than fifty obtained salvation through faith in Christ'. At Gomersal 'young persons only ten years of age were awakened and savingly converted', and 'this had such an effect upon their parents that many of them were also converted'.[181] A year after Bramwell's arrival in Birstall membership in the circuit had increased from 820 to 1,300.[182]

The revival reached Hull in March 1794 and thence spread to Beverley, Riversbridge, and Gilbersdyke where many of the converts were said to be under fourteen years of age.[183] Similarly in the Otley circuit many of those converted were 'young persons of twelve and fourteen years of age', and in some places there was 'a considerable degree of irregularity and confusion in the meetings', but within a year more than 600 people had joined the

[177] W. Bramwell, *A Short Account of the Life and Death of Ann Cutler* (Sheffield 1796), 20–2.
[178] Ibid. 21–3.   [179] Ibid. 16, 33.
[180] J. U. Walker, *A History of Wesleyan Methodism in Halifax* (Halifax, 1836), 192–6.
[181] Sigston, *Memoir of Bramwell*, 36.   [182] Baxter, 'The Great Yorkshire Revival', 69.
[183] *Arminian Magazine*, 17 (1794), 603–4, 651–3.

Wesleyan societies in the circuit.[184] In Leeds Joseph Entwisle believed that the revival 'got beyond all bounds of decency' with much screaming and bawling, confusion and uproar.[185] But here again Wesleyan membership increased by 1,280 between 1793 and 1794, and once more the converts were predominantly young. John Allen wrote that in one evening he had admitted eighty to the society at Bramley of whom about sixty were unmarried, and on one occasion at Armley he had admitted sixty, of whom 'fifty seemed to be under twenty years of age'. He confessed that 'at many places the work has been attended with much noise and apparent confusion', but believed that conversions effected more quietly had proved more durable.[186]

In Sheffield the full impact of the revival was felt in June 1794. At a love-feast a local preacher who was praying 'was carried out of himself with holy fervour so that spirit of God came as a mighty rushing wind . . . and over-whelmed every individual by its powerful influence'. 'A few who did not understand it, and resisted it, were confounded and in their terror escaped as if for their lives', but over a hundred others were converted.[187] The following year Sheffield Methodists pleaded with the Wesleyan Conference to appoint Bramwell to their circuit, and in his first year in Sheffield Wesleyan member-ship increased from 1,750 to 3,000.[188] The enthusiasm generated by the Sheffield revival in its turn inspired a revival in Nottingham in 1796, and as in the case of Sheffield revivalism in Nottingham was reinforced by the appoint-ment of Bramwell to the circuit in 1798.[189] Between 1798 and 1800 Wesleyan membership in the Nottingham circuit doubled from 1,100 to 2,200.

Wesleyan membership in all the Yorkshire circuits increased by 6,048 in 1793–4 and was the major factor in giving the Connexion in that year the highest growth rate in its history: membership in England and Wales rose by 8,498, an increase of 14.4 per cent.[190] To Methodists the revival of the 1790s was God's answer to the continued outpourings of prayer, and it is by no means easy to explain the revival in secular terms. Robert Currie, Alan Gilbert, and Lee Horsley have suggested that the high level of Wesleyan growth in 1793–4 was the result of 'political excitement attendant on war with France'.[191] According to Thomas Pearson, a Wesleyan class leader in Gomersal, the revival in his village dated from a prayer-meeting held in his house on the day appointed by the government for fasting and prayer at the

[184] Ibid. 18 (1795), 475–8.   [185] Entwisle, *Memoir of Joseph Entwisle*, 111.
[186] *Methodist Magazine*, 35 (1812), 86–7.
[187] Baxter, 'The Great Yorkshire Revival', 56.   [188] Sigston, *Memoir of Bramwell*, 47.
[189] Werner, *Primitive Methodist Connexion*, 41–2.
[190] R. Currie, A. Gilbert, and L. Horsley, *Churches and Churchgoers* (Oxford, 1977), 139.
[191] Ibid. 42.

outbreak of the war.[192] Although this is the only contemporary reference I have seen which connects the revival to the war, apocalyptic hopes aroused by the French Revolution and which helped to fire the missionary enthusiasm of the 1790s did find an echo in Yorkshire. John Allen wrote of the revival in Leeds that some were 'alarmed by dreams and visions, and often by seeing people going to hear preaching, thinking it indicated the near approach of the day of judgement'.[193] And John Moon, a preacher in the Sheffield circuit, wrote in August 1794 that the Yorkshire revival was preparing the way 'for the grand millennial reign of our redeeming God'.[194] I have not, however, found a single reference to apocalyptic hopes or fears in any of the many conversion experiences from the 1790s I have examined. It has been suggested by John Baxter that the Methodists provided a refuge for radicals whose political aspirations were frustrated by the repressive policies embarked on by the government after the outbreak of war, and he cites a few individual examples to illustrate his point.[195] But it is highly unlikely that the response to Evangelical preaching of the mainly young people who were converted in 1793–4, and of the predominantly female membership of the Wesleyan societies, was determined by political considerations. Baxter recognizes that 'evidence relating to the most politically active does not have to be representative of mass behaviour', and it seems probable that the Wesleyans were drawing their converts from the most apolitical sections of society. It was not the political implications of the French Revolution that provided the secular impetus to the Methodist expansion of the 1790s, but the economic and social consequences of the outbreak of war between Britain and revolutionary France. The resulting inflation and economic dislocation, coupled with a series of bad harvests, and the consequent fall in living standards for many families led some to take refuge in the warmth, comparative security, and excitement of Methodist meetings. The Yorkshire revival coincided with an increase in unemployment in the Sheffield cutlery trade and a rise in poor law expenditure in West Riding parishes. In Wakefield poor law expenditure increased from £1,827 to £2,545 in 1794–5, and Wesleyan membership in the Wakefield circuit rose from 1,080 to 1,500 in 1795–6. In Sheffield poor law expenditure rose from £5,691 to £8,688 per annum between 1793–4 and 1795–6 while Wesleyan membership in the same period jumped from 1,370 to 3,000.[196]

In Lancashire in 1793 the Wesleyan society in Bolton established a Benevolent Society for the relief of the poor, and one of the first people

---

[192] Baxter, 'The Great Yorkshire Revival', 49, 52.
[193] *Methodist Magazine*, 35 (1812), 86.   [194] Baxter, 'The Great Yorkshire Revival', 46.
[195] Ibid. 67.   [196] Ibid. 69–71.

assisted was a recently bereaved widow named Dorothy Cellars, the mother of three small children. Since Mrs Cellars had been born in Chorley, and since parishes often denied poor relief to people born or married outside their bounds, the Bolton parish had refused her request for relief, and it is possible that one of the contributory factors in the expansion of Methodism and Dissent during the industrial revolution lay in the way in which chapel benevolent societies and Methodist Strangers' Friend societies helped to fill the gaps left by the poor law. The Bolton Wesleyans were surprised by the number of cases of hardship they discovered in the winter of 1795. 'Some were destitute of both food and fire; and several without beds, or even straw to lie upon, having only a few shavings for their bed. Among them were many poor women and children, whose husbands or fathers were gone for soldiers, and had left them to starve.' Dorothy Cellars herself was converted during a revival in Bolton in June 1794, and the Methodist preacher Thomas Taylor added that several other people in the town had been 'brought out of misery' as a result of assistance from the Benevolent Society and were 'also in a hopeful way of being eternally saved'.[197] Cases similar to that of Dorothy Cellars were recorded by the *Primitive Methodist Magazine* and by the Independent Methodists' *Free Gospel Magazine*. In Halifax at Christmas 1823 Ann Cliff's husband died 'leaving her a widow with two small children, without any means to support them', and they suffered hunger and starvation until they were visited by a Primitive Methodist woman who gave them 'one shilling and six pence and some other relief'. Ann Cliff was so certain that the help had come from God that 'for the first time' she 'bowed her knees in sincerity to the Lord' and was soon afterwards converted.[198] Ann Hill of Oldham was similarly reduced to poverty after she and her children left her husband because of his 'abandoned life', and when the death of one of her children reduced her to despair she took refuge in the comfort and security of an Independent Methodist class-meeting.[199] There may have been a connection between the spectacular growth of the Cambridge Baptist church during Robert Robinson's ministry and the assistance the church offered to the poor. Membership more than trebled in the fifteen years after his induction to the pastorate in 1759, and by 1774 of eighty male members twenty-four were recorded as being in receipt of poor relief from the church.[200] Seventy

---

[197] *Arminian Magazine*, 20 (1797), 225–6.
[198] *Primitive Methodist Magazine*, 2nd ser. 4 (1834), 265–6.
[199] D. Valenze, 'Prophetic Sons and Daughters: Popular Religion and Social Change in England, 1780–1850', Ph.D. thesis (Brandeis, 1982), 250–1.
[200] J. E. Bradley, 'Religion and Reform at the Polls: Nonconformity in Cambridge Politics, 1774–1784', *Journal of British Studies*, 23 (1984), 61.

years later the Primitive Methodist minister John Petty claimed that a recession in the coal and iron industries of the Black Country had led to a religious revival. An attempt by coal-owners and ironmasters to impose a cut in wages had led to a strike and to ironworks being shut down in the early months of 1848. But those Methodist workers who thus found themselves out of work resolved that 'as they could not follow their usual employment, they would work the more for God', with the result that Primitive Methodist membership in the Darlaston circuit increased by 368 in the first half of 1848.[201]

But there is no clear-cut connection between economic distress and church expansion and contemporaries were often quick to blame unemployment and bad trade for slow rates of church growth. The Wesleyan Conference saw a connection between economic depression and a temporary fall in membership figures in 1819–20: 'commercial embarrassment, and consequent distress, have largely prevailed, and especially in those districts where usually we have had the greatest success'.[202] During the depression in the cloth trade between 1837 and 1841 sixty-eight members of the Shortwood Baptist church at Nailsworth in Gloucestershire emigrated to Australia, and the membership of the Penuel Calvinistic Methodist church in Ebbw Vale was 'reduced very considerably' by emigration to the United States.[203] The Mansfield Primitive Methodist circuit reported in 1838 that depression in the hosiery industry was 'so intolerably bad' that many workers had been reduced 'to a morsel of bread', that this had had a disastrous effect on circuit finances, and that 'eighty members have been removed from our class-books'.[204] Membership of the Wesleyan Methodist Association fell by 146 between 1841 and 1842 and the Association attributed their loss to the current 'commercial distress' which had caused many members to absent themselves 'from their classes and from public worship in consequence of their extreme poverty and inability to obtain decent clothing'.[205] The Wesleyans of Leeds also ascribed their fall in membership in 1842 to the depressed state of the economy: many members had moved 'in order to obtain more readily the means of subsistence in other parts of the country' and others had given up 'meeting in class in consequence of inability to keep up their regular contri-

---

[201] R. Leese, 'The Impact of Methodism on Black Country Society', Ph.D. thesis (Manchester, 1972), 244.

[202] *Minutes of the Methodist Conferences*, 4 (1817), 161.

[203] A. M. Urdank, 'Dissenting Community: Religion, Economy, and Society in the Vale of Nailsworth, Gloucestershire', Ph.D. thesis (Columbia, 1983), 426; E. Price, *History of the Penuel Calvinistic Methodist Church, Ebbw Vale* (Wrexham, 1925), 53.

[204] *Primitive Methodist Magazine*, 2nd ser. 8 (1838), 334–5.

[205] O. A. Beckerlegge, *The United Methodist Free Churches* (1957), 27–8.

butions'.[206] In 1851 the ministers of the Baptist churches at Trevethin and Tal-y-Waun in Monmouthshire reported that the attendances at their services were down by a hundred or so as a result of a depression in the iron industry and the closure of four blast furnaces at the Abersychan ironworks.[207] And during the cotton famine of 1863–4 membership of the Stalybridge Primitive Methodist circuit fell by 20 per cent, some members having moved from the area and others having 'stayed away from their class meeting because they could not afford their class pence'.[208]

Historians are divided on the relationship between the trade cycle and church growth. Elie Halévy tried to link the birth of Methodism with a commercial crisis in 1738, though he provided not a shred of evidence to support his thesis.[209] Julia Werner has maintained that in the Yorkshire revival of 1792–6, in the Nottingham revival of 1798–1800, and in the Primitive Methodist revival in the east Midlands in 1816–17, 'economic distress was an especially powerful goad to revivalism'.[210] Richard Carwardine has argued that both in the United States and in Great Britain economic depression drove men and women into the churches, and cites as examples the financial crisis of 1837, the depression of 1842–3, and the panic of 1857–8 in the United States, and the depression of 1839–41 in England and Wales.[211] Carwardine quotes the opinion of Whitney Cross that in the United States 'the revival cycle had long been inclined to an inverse conformity with the business cycle', but W. R. Ward says exactly the opposite of England: 'Bad years for business were almost always bad or indifferent years for Methodism'.[212] R. B. Walker has suggested 'that economic depression, if not too severe, favoured a revival, but that boom conditions were inimical', and cites in support local revivals of Wesleyanism in Lancashire during the cotton famine of 1861–4 and in Sheffield during the times of depression in 1874 and 1877. The membership of the Preston and Chorley circuits rose by 38.6 per cent between 1861 and 1864, whereas that of the Wesleyan Connexion as a whole rose by only 3.09 per cent.[213]

In an attempt to resolve the issue I have, in the accompanying graph, Fig. 1, attempted to show the relationship between the growth rate of the

[206] B. Greaves, 'Methodism in Yorkshire, 1740–1851', Ph.D. thesis (Liverpool, 1968), 112.
[207] Jones and Williams, *Religious Census, South Wales*, 75, 80.
[208] E. A. Rose, *Methodism in Ashton-under-Lyne* (Ashton, 1968), ii. 82.
[209] E. Halévy, *The Birth of Methodism in England*, ed. B. Semmel (Chicago, 1971), 65–8.
[210] Werner, *Primitive Methodist Connexion*, 43, 89.
[211] Carwardine, *Transatlantic Revivalism*, 41–2, 82.
[212] W. R. Cross, *The Burned-Over District* (Ithaca, NY, 1950), 268–9; Ward in *HMC*, ii. 45.
[213] R. B. Walker, 'The Growth of Wesleyan Methodism in Victorian England and Wales', *Journal of Ecclesiastical History*, 24 (1974), 269–71.

membership of all the Arminian Methodist churches in Great Britain between 1767 and 1860 and the movement in real wages.[214] The graph suggests that although the Methodists may have benefited from economic hardship in the mid-1790s and again around 1804–6, in most years from 1796 onwards the growth of Methodism tended to ebb and flow with the fall and rise of living standards. The year in which the real-wage index dipped to its lowest point—1800–1—was also a year in which membership totals of the Wesleyan and New Connexion churches fell by 1.8 per cent. The years in which the real-wage index made its most impressive advance—1848–50— were years in which the Methodists made solid gains before the Wesleyans tore themselves apart in the *Fly Sheets* controversy. If any conclusion can be drawn from this discussion of the relationship between the growth of Methodism and the state of the economy, it is that at a time of distress, especially at the turn of the eighteenth and nineteenth centuries, the poor and the unemployed may well have been induced to seek consolation and comfort in revivalist religion, but that once chapels had been established the Methodists found bad trade and unemployment an obstacle rather than a help to continued growth. If distress aided revivalism, it hindered settled religious life.[215]

The most important factor which induced men and women to attend chapel, which prompted them to seek salvation, which secured their conversions, and which thus guaranteed the expansion of Nonconformity, has yet to be discussed. It was fear: fear of disease, fear of death, fear of judgement, fear above all of eternal punishment in the torments of hell. Of the 670 Methodists and Dissenters whose spiritual experiences I have analysed, 58 ascribed their conversion to fear of death, 75 revealed that conversion had been prompted by a serious illness or the approach of death, and 83 mentioned the death of a relative, friend, or acquaintance as being the factor which turned his or her thoughts towards religion. Most significant of all, 128 made clear that it was fear of judgement, future punishment, and an eternity spent in hell which had been the major instrument of their conversion.

---

[214] I have calculated the Methodist growth rate from the statistics provided in Currie, Gilbert, and Horsley, *Churches and Churchgoers*, 139–41, 161–2. I have not used the figure given for 1857 as this omits those Wesleyan Reformers who declined to join the United Methodist Free Church and it should be noted that the extent of the growth in 1836–7 is probably exaggerated by the inclusion in the aggregate statistics for the first time of 21,262 members of the Wesleyan Methodist Association. For real wages I have used the index printed by E. A. Wrigley and R. S. Schofield in *The Population History of England 1541–1871* (1981), 643–4, and based on the work of E. H. Phelps Brown and S. V. Hopkins.

[215] Evidence collected by Julia Werner in her *Primitive Methodist Connexion*, 171, points to the same conclusion. It is safe to assume that the growth rates of the other Evangelical Nonconformist denominations fluctuated in the same way as those of the Wesleyans. Deryck Lovegrove, in his analysis of the baptismal records of the Northamptonshire, Midland, and

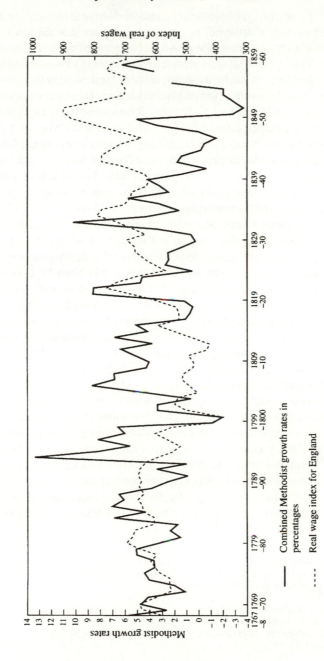

FIG. 1. The relationship between combined Methodist growth rates and the index of real wages

Some of the warnings of mortality came in dramatic fashion. In May 1787 John Kershaw was employed as a surgeon on board a ship in Greenland waters when 'a tremendous gale arose, accompanied with snow and intense frost . . . and our principal sails were blown to strips'. He wanted to pray to God but knew that ' "God heareth not sinners" unless they be penitent', and the incident laid the foundation of his conversion later in the same year.[216] A similar experience befell Joseph Russell, who sailed from Liverpool for the West Indies in a merchantman in 1799, and during the voyage he was first seized by yellow fever and then attacked by a French privateer. The engagement lasted three hours during which time Russell was brought face to face with the prospect of death and the pains of hell. The attack of yellow fever prompted him to promise God that, if he were spared, he would give himself 'up to his service', and he was converted in the following year.[217] Other disasters occurred nearer home. Mary Shepherd's mother was killed while she was collecting fruit and the rung of the ladder on which she was standing snapped under her. 'The Lord', in the words of the *Methodist Magazine*, 'by this extraordinary mean' alarmed the fears of Mary and her two younger sisters and all three were converted.[218] The suddenness with which disease could strike an individual and a family was a potent force for conversion. Jane Stanley's fiancé died from a fever shortly before they were to be married, and his death 'so powerfully impressed her mind with a sense of the instability of every earthly joy that, from this time, she sought that happiness which the vicissitudes of life cannot destroy'.[219] Peter Haslam was converted in 1790 at the age of sixteen, following 'an epidemic fever [which] raged in the neighbourhood where I resided, and in a little time swept away a considerable number'. Peter looked upon 'the distemper as a messenger of divine vengeance, sent from heaven to consign my body to the grave, and my soul to perdition'.[220] Other converts were confronted with the brevity of life by means of thunderstorms and dreams. Thomas Geeke's favourite pastime was wrestling, and he 'was in almost every contest the victor', until, at the age of twenty-three, 'he was greatly alarmed by a tremendous thunder-storm' which broke over one of his wrestling bouts. 'The horrors of guilt and the fear

---

Western Particular Baptist Associations, concludes that 'the most rapid church growth occurred between 1795 and 1798, and from 1805 to 1817'. Lovegrove did not continue his analysis beyond 1830 (*Established Church, Sectarian People*, 146).

[216] *Methodist Magazine*, 25 (1802), 180.
[217] *Wesleyan Methodist Magazine*, 64 (1841), 627–9.
[218] *Methodist Magazine*, 27 (1804), 467–8.   [219] Ibid. 29 (1806), 227.
[220] Ibid. 28 (1805), 49.

of death seized upon his mind; and . . . he resolved on the spot that if God would in mercy spare his life, he would entirely relinquish those sinful pleasures.'[221]

The Calvinistic, Wesleyan, and Primitive Methodists all found a ready hearing among communities of miners and fishermen where the breadwinner was exposed to constant danger and the risk of sudden death. A colliery explosion at Llansamlet in Glamorgan in 1787 which killed nineteen people was regarded as a token of divine displeasure and prompted scores of people to join the local Calvinistic Methodist society.[222] In the late 1790s the *Methodist Magazine* recorded numerous deaths of Methodist colliers from pit accidents, and after a mining disaster at Hebburn colliery in County Durham in 1805 in which thirty-two men died the Methodist preacher John Stephens reminded the colliers that they were 'particularly exposed to accidental death' which 'often sends numbers of you into eternity in a moment'.[223] The Primitive Methodist Nathaniel West similarly used the opportunity of a pit explosion at Colliery Row in Durham in 1823, in which sixty people were killed, to urge unconverted colliers to heed the warning of the 'mangled, burned, and suffocated bodies', and to remember that there is a 'burning hell, and a sin-avenging God, who will by no means clear the guilty'.[224] A revival among the Wesleyans of the Wellington circuit in Shropshire in 1835 was the result of a fatal pit accident in which a Wesleyan collier was killed.[225] The Christian belief in a life after death gave men and women in such communities the resilience with which to face disaster. During a ferocious storm off the Yorkshire coast in October 1869 the Primitive Methodist fishermen, Richard, Frank, and Matthew Haxby insisted on being lashed to the tillers of their respective boats while their fellow crewmen sought comparative safety below deck. Richard Haxby explained that their colleagues were 'not ready for another world', but the Methodists were 'insured for eternal life'.[226]

Of all the 'acts of God' which led men and women to worry about their eternal destiny and respond to the Evangelical appeals of the Methodists and Nonconformists the best documented is the cholera epidemic of 1831–2. In the late 1820s the disease spread from Bengal across central Asia to Russia, in August 1831 it reached Sunderland from the Baltic port of Riga and

---

[221] *Wesleyan Methodist Magazine*, 61 (1838), 561.

[222] Evans, 'Religion in the Swansea Valley', 57.

[223] *Arminian Magazine*, 20 (1797), 556; *Methodist Magazine*, 22 (1799), 489; 23 (1800), 43; E. P. Stigant, 'Methodism and the Working Class', Ph.D. thesis (Manchester, 1972), 105, citing J. Stephens, *Meditations on Death* (1805), 10–11.

[224] *Primitive Methodist Magazine*, 5 (1824), 40–3.

[225] *Methodist Magazine*, 58 (1835), 378.

[226] H. B. Kendall, *The Origin and History of the Primitive Methodist Church* (n.d.), ii. 107.

Hamburg, and by February 1832 it had been carried by east coast coal ships to London.[227] Some 32,000 people were killed by the epidemic in Britain, every victim, according to the *Wesleyan Methodist Magazine*, 'selected by infinite wisdom, acting under the direction of mercy or justice, according to the character of the person whose days are numbered'.[228] Among those ultimately struck down were the Wesleyan scholar Adam Clarke and the preachers John Storey and Joseph Sanders, but initially the Methodists claimed that the cholera attacked chiefly 'those persons whose constitutions have been debilitated by prolonged habits of dissipation and debauchery'.[229] In Gateshead one of the worst-reputed streets 'parallel with the Tyne, was said to be swept of confirmed drunkards from one end to the other': as a result 'drunkenness has greatly diminished, and places of religious worship of every denomination are thronged with deeply attentive hearers'.[230] In Sunderland the Primitive Methodists claimed that their preachers 'ran to the chambers of the sick, heedless of the contagious effluvia that was arising from the dead and the dying', and that 'they had but to announce that they were going to preach or hold a prayer meeting in any of the narrow lanes, and the houses would be immediately crowded to excess'.[231] In the five Wesleyan circuits of Newcastle, Gateshead, Shields, Sunderland, and Durham, over 2,200 people were admitted on trial in the first quarter of 1832; in four Primitive Methodist circuits in the same area membership jumped from 1,583 in 1831 to 4,110 a year later.[232]

In July 1832 the epidemic hit the Black Country with devastating consequences: more than 2,500 people died in the area, 750 in Bilston and over 400 in Tipton.[233] In both towns the Wesleyans claimed that the disease had 'appeared in connection with the revelry and dissipation' associated with local 'wakes', and in both towns the Methodist chapels were crowded every night of the week, 'many groaned under a sense of their sin and guilt, sought mercy with cries and tears, and would hardly leave the chapel at a late hour'.[234] At Darlaston the Primitive Methodist Thomas Baynton reported that a man who heard him preach 'was so affected that he cut off a cock's head which he had trained for fighting, and drowned a bull-dog he had trained

[227] R. J. Morris, *Cholera 1832* (1976), 22–3, 40, 70.   [228] Ibid. 132.
[229] *Primitive Methodist Magazine*, 2nd ser. 2 (1832), 75; G. Smith, *History of Wesleyan Methodism* (1864), iii. 172–4, 177.
[230] *Wesleyan Methodist Magazine*, 55 (1832), 203, 275.
[231] *Primitive Methodist Magazine*, 2nd ser. 2 (1832), 76.
[232] *Wesleyan Methodist Magazine*, 55 (1832), 450; *Primitive Methodist Magazine*, 2nd ser. 2 (1832), 386–7.
[233] Morris, *Cholera*, 145.   [234] *Wesleyan Methodist Magazine*, 55 (1832), 662, 748.

for baiting', and during one week in August 'about sixty were saved'.[235] Membership of the Darlaston and Dudley Primitive Methodist circuits increased by 719 between 1832 and 1833; membership of the Wednesbury and Dudley Wesleyan circuits rose from 3,315 in 1832 to 5,382 the following year.[236] By October 1832 the cholera had reached Somerset and Wesleyans in the village of Paulton reported that 'whilst eighty and upwards have been swept away by the dreadful malady, a similar number have come forward to offer themselves as candidates for admission into our society'. In fifteen months membership of the Midsomer Norton Wesleyan circuit increased by 361, with another 301 on trial, many of them coalminers and their families.[237] The Arminian Methodist churches in England and Wales recorded a net increase of 32,867 members in 1832–3, an increase of 10.54 per cent: apart from 1794 this was the highest annual growth rate in the history of English Methodism.[238]

In 1849 the cholera returned to stimulate another wave of revivalism in south Wales and the Black Country. At a Congregational association meeting at Beaufort in Monmouthshire David Rees of Llanelli preached in a field to an audience of over 10,000 on Matthew 23: 33, 'How can ye escape the damnation of hell?'. Such was the power of his message that thousands were said to have 'cried out in agony for mercy'.[239] On two successive Sundays in August William Robert Davies, minister of the Caersalem Baptist church in Dowlais, baptized a total of 150 converts, but by the third Sunday he too had died of cholera.[240] Over 11,000 new members were added to the Independent churches of Monmouthshire, Glamorgan, Breconshire, and Carmarthenshire, and another 9,000 were added to the Baptist churches in Wales.[241] In the Black Country membership of the Dudley circuit of the Methodist New Connexion increased by 700. At Gornal Wood membership of the New Connexion society jumped from thirty to 200, some of the converts being 'the worst and most desperate characters in the neighbourhood'.[242] In the wake of the 1849 cholera epidemic the Primitive Methodists achieved the highest net increase in membership in their history, 8,878.[243] Not all the conversions

---

[235] *Primitive Methodist Magazine*, 2nd ser. 3 (1833), 52.
[236] Ibid. 336; Walker, 'Growth of Wesleyan Methodism', 271.
[237] *Wesleyan Methodist Magazine*, 56 (1833), 217; PRO RG 4. 1732.
[238] Currie, Gilbert, and Horsley, *Churches and Churchgoers*, 140.
[239] T. Rees, *History of Protestant Nonconformity in Wales* (2nd edn., 1883), 474–5.
[240] J. R. and G. Williams, *History of Caersalem, Dowlais, Welsh Baptist Church* (Llandysul, 1967), 35.
[241] T. Rees, *Miscellaneous Papers on Subjects relating to Wales* (1867), 94–5; T. M. Bassett, *The Welsh Baptists* (Swansea, 1977), 211.
[242] Leese, 'Impact of Methodism on Black Country Society', 204.
[243] Currie, Gilbert, and Horsley, *Churches and Churchgoers*, 141.

induced by the epidemics proved to be enduring. In 1833 the membership of the Sunderland, Newcastle, North Shields, and South Shields Primitive Methodist circuits, which had risen to 4,110 in the previous year, fell back to 3,576, though this was in part attributed to a strike in the coal industry.[244] Two years later the Darlaston Primitive Methodist circuit in the Black Country reported that 'we have had to put about 300 out of society, the greater part of whom joined us during the cholera'.[245] None the less the Arminian Methodist churches in England and Wales increased their combined membership from 298,145 in 1830 to 447,793 in 1840, a rise of 50.2 per cent and the most dramatic decennial increase in their history.[246] And a year after the south Wales revival of 1849 Thomas Rees, the Independent minister at Beaufort, was able to write that 'the thousands of young converts, with comparatively rare exceptions, are walking worthy of their profession'.[247]

The fear mentioned most frequently by my sample of 670 Nonconformist converts was that of hell. Every child brought up in a religious household knew that after death his or her immortal soul would either enjoy eternal happiness in heaven or be damned to everlasting torment in the fires of hell. Thomas Edman remembered hearing, when he was thirteen years old, a member of Lady Huntingdon's Connexion tell his parents 'that as soon as children begin to know good from evil, if they do that which they know to be sinful, they then begin to be in danger', and that night young Thomas felt 'the sentence of death in my soul'.[248] The Congregational Sunday school at Dursley in Gloucestershire gave its scholars, in the late eighteenth century, copies of James Janeway's *A Token for Children*, first published in 1709, and the book was sometimes mentioned in conversion experiences as an important factor in provoking fears of hell.[249] Janeway reminded his young readers that little children often died, and that when they did so those that had lied, spoken 'naughty words', and broken the Sabbath would go 'to their father the Devil into everlasting burning'. Hell, he warned, 'is a terrible place, that's worse a thousand times than a whipping'.[250] John Bezer recalled how his Whitechapel Sunday school teacher in the 1820s talked 'to us about hell-fire and eternal brimstone, and how wicked we was, and if we didn't believe all he

[244] *Primitive Methodist Magazine*, 2nd ser. 3 (1833), 377.
[245] Leese, 'Impact of Methodism on Black Country Society', 240.
[246] Currie, Gilbert, and Horsley, *Churches and Churchgoers*, 140–1.
[247] Rees, *Miscellaneous Papers*, 95.
[248] *Methodist Magazine*, 23 (1800), 149.
[249] D. E. Evans, *As Mad as a Hatter! Puritans and Whitefieldites in the History of Dursley and Cam* (Gloucester, 1982), 92; *Methodist Magazine*, 58 (1835), 401–2.
[250] J. Janeway, *A Token for Children* (1709), preface.

said to us, we should be burnt for ever and ever'.[251] James Baldwin Brown, writing in 1875, said that his pages would be 'read by many who can remember that in the days of their childhood their hands were held to scorch before the fire as a key to hell torments'.[252]

The way to avoid hell and to attain salvation was the theme of a much reprinted book, *The Anxious Inquirer*, by John Angell James, minister of the Carr's Lane Congregational church in Birmingham. 'You are an immortal creature, a being born for eternity, a creature that will never go out of existence,' James warned his reader. 'Millions of ages, as numerous as the sands upon the shore, and the drops of the ocean, and the leaves of all the forests on the globe, will not shorten the duration of your being', and 'every day brings you nearer to everlasting torments or felicity.' Because every man was a sinner, every man was 'under the curse of the Almighty', and that curse condemned the human spirit to the 'lake that burneth with fire and brimstone'. To escape hell it was essential to repent of one's sins, to have faith in Christ, and to be 'born again'. 'Never forget that nothing short of the new birth will save you. . . . The very nature must be changed. . . . There must be a superhuman, a Divine, a total alteration of disposition.'[253]

Such was the message impressed on successive generations of young men and women from scores of books, hundreds of tracts, thousands of pulpits, and millions of sermons. The avoidance of hell was the *raison d'être* of Evangelical preaching. Thomas Charles, while still an Anglican curate, ransacked 'the livid flames of hell' and exposed 'to view the glories of heaven, to terrify (if possible) soreless sinners by the one, and allure them by the other'.[254] John Leifchild, minister of the Craven Congregational chapel in London, was said to depict the torments of hell as realistically 'as the sufferings of a convict stretched on a rack by a human torturer'. His son claimed that his 'descriptions of the terrors of outer darkness affected himself quite as much as his hearers', so that he was reduced to emotional and physical exhaustion after preaching.[255] Christmas Evans, the most effective Welsh Baptist preacher of the early nineteenth century, addressed his congregation as 'withered and fallen trees, fuel for the everlasting burning, ready to ignite

---

[251] D. Vincent (ed.), *Testaments of Radicalism: Memoirs of Working Class Politicians, 1790–1885* (1977), 158.

[252] J. B. Brown, *The Doctrine of Annihilation in the Light of the Gospel of Love* (1875), 39. Wesley recorded that this was common practice in the 18th cent. (Watts, *The Dissenters*, i. 415).

[253] J. A. James, *The Anxious Inquirer after Salvation Directed and Encouraged* (1838), 2–3, 66, 85–6, 105.

[254] Jenkins, *Life of Thomas Charles*, i. 132.

[255] J. R. Leifchild, *John Leifchild, His Public Ministry, Private Usefulness, and Personal Characteristics* (1863), 57–8, 189.

at the first spark of vengeance'.[256] Charles Richardson, the Wesleyan lay preacher known as the 'Lincolnshire thrasher' and one of the most popular Methodist preachers of the mid-nineteenth century, asked his hearers to imagine that they could 'smell the stench and smoke, hear the heart-rending cries and groans coming from the burning-gulf, and ... see lost souls agonizing in horrible distress'.[257]

Of all the factors inducing Evangelical conversion, this was the most important. When Henry Spencer was trapped and injured by the collapse of a colliery roof at Ighton Hill near Burnley in January 1822, his conscience was awakened 'to a sense of the horrible feelings which the damned in hell experience'. 'All his sins stood as in battle array against him'; he thought he was dying and that 'hell from beneath was moving to meet him at his coming'; but he was freed by his fellow workers and converted later that year.[258] Robert Knight was converted after a drinking bout during which he and his companions burned their hats: looking into the fire Knight exclaimed, 'If we do not repent, we shall burn in hell!'[259] Billy Bray, having strayed from the Methodism in which he was reared and having taken to drink, was converted after reading Bunyan's *Visions of Heaven and Hell* with its description of 'two lost souls in hell cursing each other for being the author of each other's misery'. Billy Bray had a close friend with whom he worked, went to the alehouse, and got drunk. 'The arrow that pierced his heart was the thought, "Shall S. Coad and I, who like each other so much, torment each other in hell?"'[260]

Not every conversion fits into this pattern. It was said of Mary Pilling that 'during the period between conviction and conversion, she did not experience those distressing fears and terrors common to persons in that state, but was gradually drawn by the cords of love'.[261] But the very terms in which her conversion is described indicate that her experience was exceptional.

---

[256] E. Paxton Hood, *Christmas Evans: The Preacher of Wild Wales* (1881), 406.
[257] Coulson, *The Peasant Preacher*, 380.
[258] *Primitive Methodist Magazine*, 10 (1829), 337–8.
[259] Bourne, *The Bible Christians*, 712.
[260] F. W. Bourne, *The King's Son, or a Memoir of Billy Bray* (31st edn., 1893), 5.
[261] *Arminian Magazine*, 19 (1796), 497–8.

6. 'NOTHING THAT ALARMS THE CONSCIENCE': THE UNITARIAN AND QUAKER EXCEPTIONS

That it was fear of the eternal torments of hell that filled Methodist, Baptist, and Congregational chapels in the first half of the nineteenth century is further suggested by the history of those Nonconformist denominations which did not insist that an Evangelical conversion was essential to salvation: the Unitarians, the Quakers, the old General Baptists, and the Swedenborgians.

The religious census of 1851 revealed that there were only 202 Unitarian congregations and only 363 Quaker meetings in England, with a further 27 Unitarian congregations and a mere 8 Quaker meetings in Wales. In England the Unitarians had only an estimated 34,110 attenders on census Sunday, and the Quakers only 16,783, 0.2 and 0.1 per cent of the total population respectively. The extent of the Unitarian and Quaker failure to benefit from the Evangelical revival can be gauged from a comparison with figures for the early eighteenth century. Around 1715 the Presbyterians, from whom the nineteenth-century Unitarians claimed direct descent, had nearly 180,000 adherents, constituting 3.3 per cent of the total population of England, while the Quakers had nearly 40,000 adherents. And the Quakers, at the beginning of the eighteenth century, had 696 meetings throughout England and Wales, 34 more than the Presbyterians, and more than the Independents, Particular Baptists, and General Baptists combined.[262] While the population of England had trebled between 1715 and 1851, the number of Quaker adherents had more than halved.

The decline of the old General Baptists was even more precipitate. Around 1715 the General Baptists had some 18,800 adherents in 122 congregations. By 1800, thirty years after the founding of the New Connexion of General Baptists had syphoned off the denomination's Evangelical churches, there were only 24 churches still in connection with the old General Assembly with at most 2,000 members. Forty years later three of those 24 churches had joined the New Connexion, another three had ceased to be Baptist, three more had ministers who were not Baptists, four were extinct, and the membership of most of the rest had slumped.[263] Theologically the old General Baptists were torn between the Evangelicalism of the New Connexion with which they had historic ties, and the Unitarianism of the former Presbyterian congregations with which they often had doctrinal sympathies. Despite the energetic activities of Joseph Calrow Means, who was secretary of the

---

[262] Watts, *The Dissenters*, i. 269–70.
[263] White's Alley Church Book, iv. 618, Guildhall Library, London.

General Baptist Assembly in the early 1830s and again from 1847 to 1870, the Old Connexion found it increasingly difficult to preserve a distinctive denominational witness.[264] Means himself ascribed the Old Connexion's decline to its abandonment of the doctrine of atonement and the 'decay of piety which ... has been consequent on the prevalence of the ordinary system of Unitarianism', but few of his fellow Baptists sympathized with his attempt to 'combine the doctrine of atonement with that of the divine unity'.[265] More Old Connexion churches died in the 1850s and 1860s, and it was symptomatic of the denomination's decline that the pastor of its Godalming church used the chapel's disused baptistry for storing his potatoes.[266]

The Swedenborgians were followers of the eighteenth-century Swedish mystic and scientist Emanuel Swedenborg who, having experienced two visions of Christ in 1744 and 1745, claimed that Christ had returned to earth to set up the church of the New Jerusalem in 1757.[267] Swedenborg died in London in 1772 leaving behind a small group of like-minded mystics, but the centre of the movement was in Lancashire where John Clowes, the rector of St John's, Deansgate, Manchester, taught Swedenborg's doctrines from 1773 until his death in 1831. The tacit support of Bishop Porteous of Chester enabled Clowes to retain his living in Manchester while at the same time taking his message to surrounding industrial villages where Swedenborgian groups were formed. In combining itinerant evangelism with continuing membership of the Anglican church Clowes resembled the early Methodists, but in doctrine the two movements were polls apart.[268] Swedenborgians argued that the Bible should be interpreted in a spiritual, not a literal sense; they rejected the Trinity; and they ridiculed the doctrine of the atonement as teaching that 'God had killed his son so that any evil person could go to heaven'.[269] The Swedenborgians won support in a few predominantly working-class communities in Lancashire and Yorkshire, but like other denominations which abandoned the Trinity they lacked mass appeal. By 1850 they had only 2,559 members in 36 societies with an estimated attendance, on census Sunday, of 7,503.[270]

More rationalist and even less successful than the Swedenborgians was a small group which broke away from them under the leadership of William Cowherd in 1800 to found Christ Church, King Street, Salford. Cowherd's church, which imposed vegetarianism and abstinence from alcohol as quali-

---

[264] I. Sellers, 'The Old General Baptists, 1811–1915', *Baptist Quarterly*, 24 (1971), 30–8, 74–85.
[265] White's Alley Church Book, iv. 619.   [266] Sellers, 'The Old General Baptists', 76.
[267] The best study of the Swedenborgians is P. J. Lineham, 'The English Swedenborgians, 1770–1840', D.Phil. thesis (Sussex, 1978), on which the following account is based.
[268] Ibid. 94, 101, 107–8, 121.   [269] Ibid. 127.   [270] Ibid. 379.

fications for membership, became in 1809 the nucleus of the tiny denomination of Bible Christians.[271] They had nothing to do with the Bryanites of Devon and Cornwall and although they founded a few churches in the Manchester area only one appears to have survived to be included in the religious census of 1851. This is hardly surprising in view of the attitude of one of their ministers, James Scholefield, who was pastor of a church in Ancoats. On his deathbed he is reputed to have told his daughters to 'make what use you can of the chapel'. 'Use it for a circus if you can—after all, it's round. It's served its term as a chapel.'[272]

Whereas the old General Baptists, the Swedenborgians of Lancashire, and the Cowherdite Bible Christians were composed very largely of poor people, the Unitarians and Quakers drew their membership disproportionately from the commercial and intellectual élite of the manufacturing towns. And although their theology, their organization, and their discipline were very different, Quakers and Unitarians shared the same civilized reluctance to consign those who disagreed with them to the eternal flames of hell.

Unitarian thinking at the turn of the eighteenth and nineteenth centuries was dominated by the influence of Joseph Priestley, and Priestley's materialism had as a necessary corollary the denial of the immortality of the soul and a reassertion of what Priestley claimed to be the true New Testament teaching of the resurrection of the body.[273] Priestley's emphasis on the resurrection of the body was echoed by other Unitarian writers in the first half of the nineteenth century,[274] and his rejection of the immortality of the soul made it possible for some Unitarians to conclude that the souls of the wicked would not suffer everlasting punishment but would be annihilated, that the wages of sin would be, literally, death.[275] An even more radical departure from orthodox eschatology was provided by the Universalist views of Elhanan Winchester. Winchester, who had ministered to a congregation of Calvinist Baptists in South Carolina in the 1770s, was converted to a belief in the universal salvation of all men in 1781, and six years later went to England as a Universalist missionary. He won over to his views William Vidler, a stonemason who was minister of the Particular Baptist church in Battle, Sussex, and in 1793 formed a Universalist congregation which met in a former

---

[271] W. E. Axon, *A History of the Bible Christian Church, Salford, 1809–1909* (Manchester, 1909), 21–2, 42; P. J. Lineham, 'The Bible Christians of Salford', in W. J. Sheils (ed.), *The Church and Healing* (Oxford, 1982), 209–10.

[272] Lineham, 'English Swedenborgians', 318.   [273] Watts, *The Dissenters*, i. 475.

[274] R. Wright, *An Essay on Future Punishment* (1808), 16–17; G. Rowell, *Hell and the Victorians* (Oxford, 1974), 40–1.

[275] R. B. Aspland, *Memoir of the Life, Works, and Correspondence of the Rev. Robert Aspland* (1850), 218.

General Baptist meeting-house in Parliament Court, Artillery Lane, in the City of London. When Winchester returned to the United States in 1784 Vidler succeeded him as pastor of the Parliament Court church, and three years later Vidler launched a monthly magazine entitled the *Universalists' Miscellany* as 'an antidote against the anti-Christian doctrine of endless misery'. In 1802 Vidler was converted to Unitarianism and changed the name of his periodical to the *Universal Theological Magazine*. It was the decision of the General Baptist Assembly to admit Vidler's church to membership in that year that led to the final rupture between the Old and New Connexions of General Baptists.[276]

The reaction of Vidler's congregation to his frequent changes of views suggests that Universalism was more popular than Unitarianism. When he informed his Particular Baptist church in Battle of his conversion to Universalist opinions in 1792, 153 out of 168 members voted that he should remain as pastor of the church, but when he told his Universalist church of his conversion to Socinian views ten years later three-quarters of his hearers left and his salary fell from £250 to £30 a year.[277] In the United States the Universalists had more than twice as many churches as the Unitarians by 1850,[278] and in England most Unitarians came to embrace Universalist views. Priestley himself appears to have accepted Winchester's teaching during his last years in America, and on one occasion preached in the Universalist's pulpit in Philadelphia.[279] A debate between the rival advocates of the destruction of the wicked and universal restoration which took place in Price's and Priestley's old church at the Gravel Pit, Hackney, in 1807 resulted in a victory for the Universalists, and the church's new minister, Robert Aspland, after initial hesitation, accepted the doctrine of universal salvation.[280] But both sides in the argument were agreed in rejecting eternal punishment, and the Unitarians' abhorrence of the doctrine was the major attraction which Unitarianism had for liberal Christians who could not accept the teaching of the orthodox churches. Richard Wright, who travelled throughout Great Britain as a Unitarian missionary from 1806 to 1822, found people readier to renounce eternal punishment than to give up the Trinity.[281] This, too, was the experience of James Martineau, the most distinguished Unitarian minister of

---

[276] G. Rowell, 'The Origins and History of Universalist Societies in Britain 1750–1850', *Journal of Ecclesiastical History*, 22 (1971), 38–42; Watts, *The Dissenters*, i. 456.

[277] F. W. Butt Thompson, 'William Vidler', *Baptist Quarterly*, 17 (1957–8), 1–9.

[278] W. S. Hudson, *Religion in America* (New York, 1965), 162.   [279] *DNB*.

[280] Aspland, *Memoir of Robert Aspland*, 120–1, 218, 498.

[281] R. Wright, *A Review of the Missionary Life and Labors* [sic] *of Richard Wright* (1824), 69–70, 75.

the nineteenth century. In 1865 he quoted the opinion of 'a once orthodox friend' that 'when we begin our approaches to you heretics, the first doctrine that loses hold on us is that of eternal punishment'.[282]

The issue was much debated between Unitarians and orthodox Christians in the late eighteenth and early nineteenth centuries. When Andrew Fuller heard of Vidler's conversion to Universalist views he wrote to his fellow Baptist warning him against 'raising the hopes of the ungodly'.[283] The letter was published in the *Evangelical Magazine* in 1795 and led to a lengthy exchange of views which appeared in Vidler's *Universalists' Miscellany* and was subsequently reprinted in pamphlet form. Both parties to the controversy claimed to base their arguments on the teaching of the Bible. Vidler maintained 'that the words which the scriptures use . . . to express the duration of future misery, do not necessarily mean endless, for they are all of them applied to things that have ended, or must end'. 'The *everlasting* covenant of circumcision', for example, 'is, in the New Testament, declared to be abrogated.' 'The writers of the New Testament do not use the word αιων to convey the idea of eternity, because there are *different aions* spoken of, and one *aion* is represented as succeeding another.'[284]

The chief argument, however, in favour of universal restoration, in the eyes of its advocates, was that it best agreed with the concept of a God of justice and of love. 'It is not . . . contended that the final restitution of all mankind is so clearly revealed in the scriptures as to be capable of being supported otherwise than by inference and deduction', admitted Richard Wright, but 'it is presumed to be a fair deduction from the character and known perfections of God.'[285] The Universalists did not deny that the wicked would be punished: what they maintained was that their punishment would be 'limited and corrective' rather than endless and vindictive, and would 'terminate in their recovery to purity and happiness'.[286] Whereas 'the doctrine of annihilation gives indiscriminate and endless death to all the wicked', wrote Vidler, 'and the doctrine of endless misery seems to confound all degrees of punishment in giving infinite punishment to them all', the doctrine of universal restoration makes possible discrimination between one sinner and another, how one may have *few* stripes and another *many*'.[287] By contrast the doctrine of endless misery 'is contrary to all the benevolent feelings of every renewed heart, and . . . must be much more so to the benevolence of God'.[288]

[282] J. E. Carpenter, *James Martineau* (1905), 449.
[283] A. Fuller, *Letters to Mr. Vidler* (1802), 9.
[284] W. Vidler, *Letters to Mr Fuller on the Universal Restoration* (1803), 13–14, 112.
[285] Wright, *Future Punishment*, 32–3.   [286] Ibid. 22, 36.
[287] Vidler, *Letters to Fuller*, 19–20.   [288] Ibid. 66.

Richard Wright took up the same theme, that the concept of eternal punishment placed God's moral code on a lower plane than that of men. 'Paul exhorts, "Be not overcome of evil, but overcome evil with good" ', but if God, throughout eternity, will 'render evil for evil, how can he command his creatures not to render evil for evil to any man?'[289]

The point was made most forcibly by Henry Giles, minister of the Unitarian church in Toxteth Park, Liverpool, who contributed to a series of lectures entitled *Unitarianism Defended* given in the town in 1839 in response to an attack by the Evangelical vicar of Christ Church, Fielding Ould. Giles contrasted the compassion of the best human beings with the cruelty attributed by orthodox Christians to God. 'We tread not knowingly on the crawling worm . . . and yet many of us who would not look unmoved on the last spasms of an expiring dog, can believe that God regards with ruthless sternness the eternal tortures of numberless eternal spirits.' 'Fear is the parent of cruelty', he argued, and claimed 'that no mere worldly wickedness has ever cursed mankind with so many sufferings as the belief' in endless punishment. To it he ascribed wars of religion and 'the most horrible religious persecutions'. 'If reverence to God demand us to believe that the smoke of eternal torment from the depths of an unfathomable hell is an incense well pleasing in his sight, or an evil which he must endure but has no power to remove, then that is an honour we do not and cannot give: that is not the God we worship: that is not the God we can love.'[290]

While the Unitarians had the best of the moral argument in the controversy, the orthodox had the best of the argument from Scripture. The notion of universal salvation, claimed Andrew Fuller, is contradicted by 'every other sentiment in the Bible', and to prove the point he gave four pages of texts in which the happiness of the saved is contrasted with the misery of the damned, two pages of texts in support of the doctrine of endless punishment, and a further two pages to show 'that a change of heart, and a preparedness for heaven, are confined to the present life'.[291] The orthodox regarded the twenty-fifth chapter of Matthew as especially conclusive. Another Baptist, Francis Cox, used the forty-sixth verse in confrontation with Robert Aspland, recorded in the *Baptist Magazine* in 1809. In that verse the wicked are promised 'everlasting punishment', the righteous 'life eternal'. The epithets 'everlasting or eternal' are applied to the conditions both of the saved and of the damned, and 'consequently the felicity of the one and the misery of the other must be

[289] R. Wright, *An Essay on the Universal Restoration* (1816), 22.

[290] H. Giles, 'The Christian View of Retribution Hereafter', in H. Giles, J. Martineau, and J. Thom, *Unitarianism Defended* (Liverpool, 1839), 4, 6–7, 45–6.

[291] Fuller, *Letters to Vidler*, 7, 44–8, 51–2, 55–6.

equally final and interminable'.[292] No one asked whether the Unitarians' all-loving God could in fact be found in the Bible.

Throughout the period 1791–1851 the Unitarians attracted a steady stream of converts from the other Nonconformist denominations, though surprisingly few from the Church of England.[293] The Unitarian church in Brighton dates from the point in 1793 when nineteen members of the town's Particular Baptist church were excommunicated for rejecting eternal punishment, and Northampton's Unitarian church was founded after the secession, in 1827, of members from the Castle Hill Congregational church. When the Baptist Association of south-west Wales tried to stem the growth of Arminianism in 1799 by insisting that its member churches conform to the Calvinist Confession of 1689, ten congregations withdrew and of these five ultimately became Unitarian.[294] Some of the most distinguished Unitarian ministers of the early nineteenth century came from other denominations. From the Particular Baptists they acquired, in addition to William Vidler, Daniel Jones, James Lyons, Thomas Southwood Smith, John Gisburne, and Robert Aspland. Daniel Jones was pastor of the Back Lane Calvinist church in Swansea in the 1790s until he was converted to Unitarianism, and from 1800 was minister of the Unitarian (formerly Particular Baptist) church at Trowbridge in Wiltshire.[295] James Lyons ministered to a Baptist church in Hull until 1807 when he embraced Unitarian views after reading some of Wright's pamphlets and subsequently became, like Wright, a Unitarian missionary.[296] Thomas Southwood Smith also left the Baptists in 1807 when he was a student at the Bristol Baptist College and went on to read medicine at Edinburgh University. From 1816 to 1820 he combined a medical practice at Yeovil with the pastorate of the town's Unitarian congregation and in 1820 was appointed physician to the London Fever Hospital which position

---

[292] *Baptist Magazine*, 1 (1809), 97.

[293] William Frend, one-time fellow of Jesus College, Cambridge, was, after Theophilus Lindsey, the most celebrated convert to Unitarianism from the established church. He announced his change of opinion in 1788 (F. Mineka, *The Dissidence of Dissent: The Monthly Repository (1806–38)* (Chapel Hill, NC, 1944), 148–9). Most Anglican clergymen who sympathized with Unitarian theology—including two bishops—either stayed within the Church of England or gave up the ministry altogether (J. Seed, 'The Role of Unitarianism in the Formation of Liberal Culture, 1775–1851', Ph.D. thesis (Hull, 1981), 30, 34–6).

[294] J. Rowland, 'Christ Church (Unitarian), New Road, Brighton', *TUHS*, 10 (1951–4), 148; T. Coleman, *Memorials of the Independent Churches in Northamptonshire* (1853), 33; D. D. J. Morgan, 'The Development of the Baptist Movement in Wales between 1715 and 1815', D.Phil. thesis (Oxford, 1986), 231–3, 240.

[295] *Minutes of the General Assembly of the General Baptist Churches in England*, ed. W. T. Whitley, ii (1910), 287; *DWB*.

[296] Aspland, *Memoir of Aspland*, 287–8; *Monthly Repository*, 3 (1808), 166.

launched him on his career as a public health reformer.[297] John Gisburne was minister of the Baptist church at Soham in Cambridgeshire until 1808 when he too announced his adoption of Unitarian views. The defections of Gisburne and Aspland were particularly galling to Andrew Fuller, for Aspland had been brought up in the Soham church of which Gisburne later became pastor, and this was the church in which Fuller himself had been brought up and of which he had also been pastor from 1775 to 1782. Moreover, Gisburne had been Fuller's assistant at Kettering for six months around 1803 before going to Soham.[298]

Aspland's break with Calvinism came while, at the age of seventeen, he was studying at the University of Aberdeen. Having been excommunicated from the Devonshire Square Particular Baptist church in London, he was invited to the pastorate of the Old General Baptist church in Newport in the Isle of Wight in 1801, and four years later succeeded Thomas Belsham at the Gravel Pit meeting, Hackney. Aspland was one of the most attractive, energetic, and warm-hearted of Unitarian ministers. At the end of 1805 he bought Vidler's *Universal Theological Magazine* and changed its name to the *Monthly Repository of Theology and General Literature* with the intention of making 'theology rational and literature popular'. Aspland edited it for the next twenty-one years, establishing it as the most outspoken and courageous voice of rational Dissent and himself as a leader of the Unitarian denomination.[299] He also edited the *Christian Reformer* from 1815 until 1844, a more popular and less controversial version of the *Repository*, was secretary of the Unitarian Fund from 1806 until 1818, and secretary of the newly founded British and Foreign Unitarian Society from 1825 to 1830.

William Johnson Fox, who succeeded Aspland, after a brief interregnum, as editor of the *Repository* in 1828 and as owner in 1831, came to the Unitarians from the Independents. After studying at the rigidly Calvinist Homerton academy in Hackney he became minister of the Congregational church at Fareham in Hampshire in 1809, but he soon came to have doubts about the Trinity, taking 'books on the Unitarian controversy to bed with me' and reading them 'for hours with the candle on my pillows'. In 1812 he became minister of a Unitarian church in Chichester and four years later accepted an invitation to the pastorate of the Parliament Court church on the death of William Vidler.[300] Richard Wright was also initially an Independent, and having rejected Calvinism at the age of nineteen was excommunicated

[297] G. Lewes, *Dr Southwood Smith* (1898), 7–9, 15–16.
[298] Aspland, *Memoir of Aspland*, 207–8.
[299] For the *Monthly Repository* under Aspland's editorship see Mineka, *Dissidence of Dissent*.
[300] Ibid. 172–9, 186.

by the Congregational church of which he was a member. He embraced the Sabellian view that the three persons of the Trinity are merely aspects of one God and was briefly pastor of a General Baptist church in Norwich but was again 'excommunicated as a heretic and a blasphemer'. By 1794 he was virtually a Unitarian and when in that year he accepted an invitation to the pastorate of a once Particular Baptist church at Wisbech in Cambridgeshire which had also adopted Sabellian views, he set about converting his new congregation to Unitarianism.[301] The Quakers also provided a number of converts to Unitarianism. William Rathbone, the fourth of the Liverpool dynasty of merchants and philanthropists to bear that name, joined the Unitarian Book Society in 1792 and in 1805 was disowned by Friends for publishing a pamphlet expressing sympathy for a Unitarian movement among the Quakers of Ireland.[302] Rathbone in his turn introduced Thomas Foster to the Unitarian Book Society, and he too was disowned by the Quakers in 1812 for helping to disseminate Unitarian views.[303]

Even the Methodists provided recruits for the Unitarians. William Tate, who moved with some speed from the Wesleyans to the Particular Baptists to the Methodist New Connexion, was converted to Unitarianism after reading an account of the trial of Edward Elwall, a Sabbatarian Baptist who had been prosecuted for blasphemy at the Stafford assize in 1726. Tate was subsequently minister of the Unitarian church at Chorley in Lancashire from 1799 to 1836.[304] Joseph Cooke, a popular Wesleyan preacher in Rochdale, was expelled by the Methodist Conference in 1806 for publishing sermons in which he had cast doubt on the Wesleyan teaching on assurance: his heresy was to contend that whenever 'a sinner returns to God . . . God accepts that sinner, whether he has any comfortable persuasion of it in his mind or not'. Cooke was followed out of the Connexion by sympathizers in Rochdale and in Newchurch-in-Rossendale, and after his early death in 1811 his followers, under the leadership of the woollen manufacturer John Ashworth, adopted Unitarian views and organized a circuit of Methodist Unitarian preachers.[305] Another Wesleyan minister who ultimately became a Unitarian was John Gordon, who in 1834 resigned in protest at the action of the Methodist Conference in suspending Joseph Rayner Stephens for advocating the disestablishment of the Church of England. Returning to his native Dudley to run

[301] Wright, *Missionary Life and Labors*, 23–4, 37–45, 259.
[302] I. Sellers, 'Liverpool Nonconformity', Ph.D. thesis (Keele, 1969), 205; Isichei, *Victorian Quakers*, 26.
[303] Aspland, *Memoir of Aspland*, 234 n.
[304] A. Gordon, *Historical Account of Dukinfield Chapel* (1896), 63–4. For Elwall see *DNB*.
[305] H. McLachlan, *The Methodist Unitarian Movement* (Manchester, 1919), 7–38.

the family wine business, Gordon played a leading part in the disputes which rocked the Wesleyan Connexion in 1834–5 and, too radical for the Wesleyan Methodist Association, he took a large part of the Wesleyan membership in Dudley and Stourbridge into the Methodist New Connexion in 1836. But within a year Gordon announced his conversion, under the influence of the American William Ellery Channing and the Birmingham minister John Kentish, to Unitarianism. He became minister of the Unitarian church in Coseley in 1838, and his son Alexander was to become a distinguished historian of Unitarianism.[306]

The conversions of liberal Baptists such as Aspland and of maverick Methodists like Gordon could not, though, disguise the fact that Unitarianism did not have the popular appeal of either orthodox Dissent or of Methodism. Both critical Unitarians and their opponents maintained that the doctrines preached in Unitarian chapels were too intellectual and too cold to move the hearts of most Englishmen (and, perhaps, more importantly, of Englishwomen).[307] Unitarian sermons, observed the Evangelical Anglican Charles Jerram, 'were mere moral essays, philosophical disquisitions, and refined in style'. They contained 'no appeal to conscience; no instruction for the poor, if such had constituted part of their assembly; no consolation for the afflicted'.[308] Richard Wright denied that the Unitarians were lacking in zeal or that their version of Christianity was unsuited to the 'poor and unlearned', and it was to refute such charges that he accepted an invitation to become an itinerant missionary in 1806 and continued in this role under the auspices of the Unitarian Fund until 1822. But Wright's enthusiasm was exceptional: some Unitarians regarded the Fund with suspicion, as putting Unitarians 'on a level with the Methodists'; Wright's own proposal that the Unitarians adopt a modest version of the Methodist circuit system was never taken up; and the results of his own strenuous activities were limited.[309] From his base at Wisbech Wright devoted much time to Lincolnshire,[310] but the Unitarians had, according to my calculations, only 285 adherents in the whole of that county in 1851. He regarded Cornwall as one of his most important mission fields: he visited the duchy in 1811, 1815, and in 1819, other Unitarian missionaries followed in his wake, and he established churches at Falmouth and Flushing.[311] But on census Sunday, 1851, there were but eight Unitarian worshippers in the whole of Cornwall in the morning, and in the evening a mere twenty-three.

---

[306] Leese, 'The Impact of Methodism on Black Country Society', 150–97.
[307] Mineka, *Dissidence of Dissent*, 218.   [308] Rowell, *Hell and the Victorians*, 50.
[309] Wright, *Missionary Life and Labors*, pp. viii, 443; Aspland, *Memoir of Aspland*, 198.
[310] Wright, *Missionary Life and Labors*, 61–8, 163–74.   [311] Ibid. 382–401.

One suspects that the chief effect of the hundreds of sermons preached, and of the thousands of tracts distributed, by Wright and his fellow missionaries was to unsettle the faith of the orthodox without converting them to active participation in Unitarian church life. It was a frequent accusation levelled against the Unitarians that their faith was but a staging post on the road from orthodoxy to infidelity, and there is some evidence to support the contention. Arthur Aikin, descended from three generations of Dissenting ministers and assistant pastor at the Unitarian meeting-house in Shrewsbury, renounced Christianity for Deism in 1795, and resigned from the ministry in order to devote himself to literature and science.[312] Thomas Martin, minister of the once Congregational but now Unitarian Old Meeting in Great Yarmouth, rejected the miraculous elements in Christianity, resigned his pastorate in 1797, and went on to burn his Bible and his other theological books.[313] In the previous year John Hollis had resigned from membership of Theophilus Lindsey's Essex Street chapel and published his apologia in *Sober and Serious Reasons for Scepticism*.[314] The younger William Taylor, the Norwich Unitarian with whose trip to France this volume opened, is said to have become by middle life 'a Deist, or perhaps an agnostic'.[315] Another product of Norwich Unitarianism, Harriet Martineau, the daughter of a bombazine manufacturer and sister of James, who in her youth had hung a portrait of Joseph Priestley from her bookshelves, had by the age of forty-five abandoned belief in a personal God and in life after death.[316] In 1840 a Mr Kendall, minister of the Unitarian church at Devonport, retired from his pulpit and the ministry because he no longer believed in the resurrection of Christ.[317] William Johnson Fox, who in early life had moved from Calvinism to Unitarianism, in his middle years moved from Unitarianism to a secularized version of Christianity which foreshadowed the social gospel of the later nineteenth century. Under his ownership the *Monthly Repository* devoted more and more space to literary and political subjects until religion almost disappeared from its pages.[318] After Fox's church moved from Parliament Court to South Place chapel in Finsbury in 1824 its services became distinguished for their musical rather than for their religious content.[319] The final

---

[312] B. Rodgers, *Georgian Chronicle* (1958), 163.

[313] Browne, *Congregationalism in Norfolk and Suffolk*, 251; G. M. Ditchfield, 'Some Aspects of Unitarianism and Radicalism, 1760–1810', Ph.D. thesis (Cambridge, 1968), 327; Seed, 'Unitarianism and Liberal Culture', 179.

[314] Ditchfield, 'Unitarianism and Radicalism', 92.

[315] D. Roper, *Reviewing before the 'Edinburgh', 1788–1902* (1978), 260.

[316] R. K. Webb, *Harriet Martineau, a Radical Victorian* (1960), 85, 285, 292.

[317] H. Solly, *These Eighty Years* (1893), i. 322.   [318] Mineka, *Dissidence of Dissent*, 250.

[319] Ibid. 197.

break with Unitarianism came in 1835 when it became known that Fox had ended an unhappy marriage by separating from his wife and setting up house with a lady seventeen years his junior. Fox offered to resign his pastorate, and though a majority of the congregation at South Place voted that he be asked to stay, he was expelled from the association of Presbyterian ministers in London.[320] Fox was elected to Parliament for Oldham in 1847 and effectively ended his ministry at South Place in 1850. Under his eventual successor, the American Moncure Conway, the chapel's metamorphosis from Unitarianism to humanism was complete.[321]

Once she had abandoned Unitarianism Harriet Martineau dismissed it as 'a mere clinging, from association and habit, to the old privilege of faith in a divine revelation, under an actual forfeiture of all its essential conditions'.[322] It was the belief that the Unitarians had abandoned the essentials of Christianity, and were thus endangering men's souls, that explains the ferocity with which they were assailed by Evangelicals. As one of Charles Wesley's hymns put it:

> Stretch out thine arm, thou Triune God!
> The Unitarian fiend expel,
> And chase his doctrines back to Hell![323]

It was not just a war of words. The bitter struggle between orthodox and heterodox for the control of Dissenting meeting-houses which had begun at Exeter in 1718 and erupted periodically throughout the second half of the eighteenth century reached its climax in the first half of the nineteenth.[324] Early in the century there was an unseemly struggle between Calvinists and Unitarians for possession of Walmsley chapel near Bolton which manifested itself in a race between the two contending parties to conduct a funeral service. John Holland, the Unitarian minister in Bolton, got to the pulpit first and conducted the service, but while he was out at the graveside the Calvinists attempted to gain control of the chapel and were only induced to leave when the chapel keeper threatened to lock them in for the night.[325] The conversion of John Gisburne to Unitarianism in 1808 resulted in a bitter contest for control of the Particular Baptist meeting-house in Soham. A major-

---

[320] Ibid. 188–95; R. Garnett, *The Life of W. J. Fox* (1910), 163–4.
[321] For Conway see Warren S. Smith, *The London Heretics* (1967), 106–24.
[322] H. Martineau, *Autobiography* (1877), i. 40.
[323] Mineka, *Dissidence of Dissent*, 19. The lines are part of a hymn attacking Mohammed, but Islam is obviously not the only target (B. L. Manning, *The Hymns of Wesley and Watts* (1940), 17).
[324] Watts, *The Dissenters*, i. 374–6, 468–71.
[325] F. Kenworthy, 'The Story of Walmsley Unitarian Chapel', *TUHS* 9 (1947–50), 63–4.

ity of the church membership wished Gisburne to retain his pastorate, but the orthodox minority interrupted Gisburne's services and locked him out of the meeting-house, and when a window was forced open to enable the pastor to conduct a Sunday afternoon service, he was arrested and prosecuted on the basis of the penal laws against Unitarians. The prosecution failed, but Gisburne agreed to restore the meeting-house to the Calvinists in return for a sum of money to enable the Unitarians to build their own chapel in Soham.[326]

The most far-reaching dispute of all was that for the control of the John Street Presbyterian meeting-house in Wolverhampton. Between 1759 and 1781 the congregation had been ministered to by John Cole who seems to have preached with sufficient circumspection to satisfy both the Unitarians and Trinitarians among his hearers. But on Cole's retirement in 1781 Benjamin Mander and three other trustees invited a Trinitarian, William Jameson, to occupy the pulpit. Six other trustees, who held heterodox opinions on the Trinity, replied by locking the doors of the meeting-house against Jameson, and Jameson and his followers went off to found an Independent church. John Street settled down to a succession of Unitarian pastorates, but in 1816 their minister, John Steward, renounced Unitarianism for Trinitarianism, and tried to retain the use of the meeting-house with the help of Benjamin Mander, who was still one of the trustees. This time it was the Unitarians who left the chapel, and Mander and Steward started a long and costly legal battle to prevent the trustees from ejecting Steward from the John Street pulpit.

Mander and Steward's case rested on the grounds that since Unitarianism was proscribed by law at the time of the erection of the meeting-house in 1701 Unitarians could not be the lawful owners of the property, and that despite the Unitarian Toleration Act of 1813, which extended to Unitarians the benefits of the Toleration Act of 1689, Unitarianism was still illegal at common law which again prevented its advocates from legally holding property. The case initially went against the Unitarians, they appealed, and the final decision was not given until 1842, again against the Unitarians, by which time the Trinitarians had had to close the John Street meeting-house through lack of support and the legal costs had swallowed up the whole value of the property.[327]

---

[326] Aspland, *Memoir of Aspland*, 208–10.
[327] A. G. Cumberland, 'Protestant Nonconformity in the Black Country', MA thesis (Birmingham, 1951), 104–6; Aspland, *Memoir of Aspland*, 378–80.

The Wolverhampton chapel case threatened the Unitarian denomination with financial ruin: if Calvinists could reclaim all meeting-houses which had a Presbyterian ancestry the Unitarians would be dispossessed of most of their property. In 1824 a dinner held in Manchester in honour of John Grundy, who was leaving the Cross Street Unitarian chapel, Manchester, for Paradise Street chapel, Liverpool, provided George Harris of Bolton with an opportunity to contrast the 'light and liberty and joy' of Unitarianism with the 'slavish, mean, cruel, and vindictive' spirit of orthodoxy. A Congregationalist solicitor, George Hadfield, was stung to reply, in a series of letters published as *The Manchester Socinian Controversy*, that the Unitarians' claim to moral superiority came ill from a denomination which occupied chapels and enjoyed endowments which had been founded for the propagation of quite different doctrines. Of 223 Unitarian chapels whose origin Hadfield investigated, 178 had been founded by Calvinists.[328]

The issue came to a head in the Lady Hewley case. Lady Sarah Hewley, a devout Presbyterian and wife of Sir John Hewley, lawyer and MP for York from 1676 to 1678, had in 1704 founded a trust for 'poor and godly preachers . . . of Christ's holy Gospel', for 'the education of young men designed for the ministry', and for the support of an almshouse.[329] While Lady Hewley's theological opinions were Trinitarian, by the beginning of the nineteenth century the fund was being administered by trustees who had advanced from Calvinist Presbyterianism to Unitarianism, and in 1829 thirty-nine of the 237 ministers who were being supported by the fund were Unitarians, including a Methodist Unitarian who could hardly claim a lineal descent from the Presbyterians of the early eighteenth century.[330] In 1830 a group of Independents led by George Hadfield took legal action against the trustees of Lady Hewley's Fund on the ground that its proceeds were being used to support the propagation of views abhorrent to the fund's founder. Three years later Sir Lancelot Shadwell gave his verdict that 'no persons who denied the doctrine of our Saviour's divine person and the doctrine of original sin were entitled to participate in Lady Hewley's charities', and after a further nine years of appeals and legal costs amounting to over £18,000, in 1842 the House of Lords upheld the original decision and disqualified the Unitarian trustees from managing the fund.[331]

---

[328] B. Manning, *The Protestant Dissenting Deputies* (Cambridge, 1952), 65; H. L. Short in C. G. Bolam *et al.*, *The English Presbyterians* (1968), 246.

[329] J. G. Miall, *Congregationalism in Yorkshire* (1868), 116–18.

[330] H. L. Short in *The English Presbyterians*, 247; McLachlan, *Methodist Unitarian Movement*, 39.

[331] Miall, *Congregationalism in Yorkshire*, 189–90; Manning, *Protestant Dissenting Deputies*, 84; Carpenter, *James Martineau*, 233.

For Unitarians the decisions in the Wolverhampton chapel case and in the Lady Hewley's Fund case were potentially disastrous. They raised the possibility of at least two hundred bitter legal actions in which the Unitarians risked losing three-quarters of their meeting-houses. Unitarian congregations petitioned Parliament to prove their direct descent from Presbyterian congregations existing at the turn of the seventeenth and eighteenth centuries and even from congregations of the Interregnum.[332] Congregationalists and Particular Baptists petitioned to show with equal justice that the theology of those congregations was Calvinist. The Wesleyans, anxious to keep their chapels out of the hands of the numerous secessionist Methodist bodies, joined in the fray on the side of the orthodox.[333] Peel's government resolved the issue by pushing through Parliament, in 1844, the Dissenters' Chapels Act which guaranteed to congregations the title to their property if they had held possession of it for twenty-five years.

The Dissenters' Chapels Act settled the dispute to the satisfaction of the Unitarians and to celebrate their victory they built University Hall in London's Gordon Square, the present home of Dr Williams's Library.[334] But the controversy did much damage to their cause. As relations between Unitarians and Trinitarians worsened so the latter made attempts to exclude the former from positions of influence which they occupied as legatees of the eighteenth-century Presbyterians. An attempt in 1829 by the Particular Baptist historian Joseph Ivimey to expel Unitarians from the administration of Dr Williams's Trust, which, if successful, would have had disastrous results for scholarship (and for the writing of this book), was fortunately frustrated.[335] But the orthodox were more successful in securing, in 1835, the rejection of Thomas Rees as secretary of the Committee of the Three Denominations (Presbyterian, Congregational, and Baptist) which had been set up in 1792 to protect Dissenting interests, and which Rees had served as secretary for seven years. The Unitarians replied by seceding both from the ministerial Committee of the Three Denominations and from the lay Protestant Dissenting Deputies.[336]

More serious was the uncertainty which for twenty years or more hung over the future of most Unitarian meeting-houses. The Bowl Alley Lane Unitarian church in Hull delayed building a schoolroom for its Sunday school from 1833 to 1850 because of the doubts about the legality of its title to its property, and a trustee of the Dean Row Unitarian chapel at Wilmslow

[332] Carpenter, *James Martineau*, 235.　　　[333] Ward, *Religion and Society in England*, 204.
[334] F. Hankinson, 'The Dissenters' Chapels Act, 1844', *TUHS* 8 (1943–6), 56.
[335] Aspland, *Memoir of Aspland*, 494.
[336] Ibid. 531–2, 537–8; Manning, *Dissenting Deputies*, 72–8.

in Cheshire explained in 1845 that the delay in restoring the building was the result of the 'intentions of certain orthodox parties, who proposed to let the Unitarians repair it and then take possession of it for themselves'.[337] Uncertainty of another kind plagued a denomination many of whose churches still insisted that if their services could not be conducted by an educated minister, they should be not conducted at all. In 1791 Priestley had pointed to the insistence on a learned ministry as one of the reasons for the decline of rational Dissent, and it was a factor which continued to undermine Unitarian churches in the nineteenth century as it had helped to destroy Presbyterian congregations in the eighteenth.[338] The diary of the Unitarian farmer, Samuel Mason, reveals that even in Stand chapel near Manchester, which was often helped out by one of Cross Street's two ministers, there was 'no preaching' on one Sunday in 1812, on two in 1813, on four in 1815, and on three in 1817. When he moved to Preston in 1819 he found the situation much worse: from the end of May to the middle of August 1828 only one Sunday service was held in the chapel, and Mason saw it would 'do great injury to have the chapel so long shut up'.[339]

Richard Wright, like Joseph Priestley, believed that one of the answers to the Unitarians' problems was to follow the Methodists in recruiting a vast army of local preachers.[340] But the recruits were not available in any number, and the reason they were not available was that the liberal gospel preached by the Unitarians could never have either the compelling power or the motivating force of the Evangelical gospel which taught that acceptance or rejection issued in either eternal joy or everlasting misery. At the ordination of Robert Gore in Cross Street, Manchester, in 1779 William Enfield declared that their business as Christian ministers was 'to stop the progress of ignorance and error; to discourage superstition; to promote useful knowledge; to reprove the vices of the age in which we live', but not a word did he say about the saving of souls.[341] The Unitarians, declared Priestley in 1782, 'do not consider the holding of [their principles] to be at all necessary to salvation', and consequently 'take much less pains to make proselytes' than do other Christians 'and are less concerned to inculcate their principles upon their children'.[342] Eighty years later Charles Berry, former minister of the

---

[337] W. Whitaker, *Bowl Alley Lane Chapel, Hull* (1910), 135–6; W. H. Burgess, *The Story of Dean Row Chapel* (Wilmslow, 1924), 68.

[338] Watts, *The Dissenters*, i. 385–6, 487, 489–90.

[339] J. M. Bass, 'A Farmer's Chapel-going, 1812–29', *TUHS* 9 (1947–50), 211–17.

[340] Wright, *Missionary Life and Labors*, 445.

[341] T. Baker, *Memorials of a Dissenting Chapel* (1884), 41–2.

[342] *Priestley's Works*, xv. 46.

Unitarian Great Meeting in Leicester, similarly explained the Unitarians' lack of popular appeal by reference to their inability to present their views 'as necessary to salvation'. 'I believe honest men and women of all creeds are safe in the hands of a merciful Creator,' said Berry; 'I cannot think that they will any of them be consigned to everlasting torments.' But in taking so optimistic a view of the fate of their fellow men Unitarians deprived themselves 'of a great power of moving the public mind'.[343] Andrew Fuller made the same point: there was nothing in either the Arian or the Socinian systems, he wrote, 'that alarms the conscience'.[344]

Much the same was true of the Quakers. The Quakers were not Unitarians: when Thomas Foster was disowned in 1812 for subscribing to the Unitarian Book Society the leading Evangelical Friend Joseph John Gurney recalled with delight that Foster's final appeal to the London Yearly Meeting was rejected unanimously by 1,200 male Quakers.[345] Nor did the Quakers deny officially the doctrine of eternal punishment. The Society of Friends' *Rules of Discipline*, revised and republished in 1834, continued to carry the words of George Fox, that Christ saves us 'from hell and the wrath to come'.[346] Gurney believed 'the doctrine of eternal rewards and punishments' to be 'far too explicitly stated in Scripture to admit of any refutation', and devoted ten pages of his *Essays on . . . Christianity* to its defence.[347] But even Gurney confessed that the question caused him 'some powerful exercise of mind', and for the most part nineteenth-century Quakers were much too humane to threaten their fellow men and women with the eternal fires of hell. Edward Ash was, like Gurney, an Evangelical, so Evangelical that he even looked with favour on predestination, a doctrine which to Quakers had always been anathema.[348] But when he came to deal with the fate of those who stood 'apart from the knowledge and belief of the gospel of Christ', he did so with arguments familiar to Unitarian advocates of universal restoration. There is much in Scripture, argued Ash, 'which justifies the conclusion that some way of deliverance is accessible to all mankind . . . so that all who finally perish will be lost by their neglect or refusal to hear it'. He cited 'the general consideration of the divine goodness and mercy . . . conveying to us the assurance that "the Lord is good to all" '; the declaration 'that God willeth

---

[343] C. G. Bolam, 'Presbyterianism in the Counties of Derby, Leicester, and Nottingham', MA thesis (Nottingham, 1957), 560–1.

[344] A. Fuller, *The Calvinistic and Socinian Systems Examined and Compared* (1794), 52.

[345] J. B. Braithwaite, *Memoirs of Joseph John Gurney* (Norwich, 1854), i. 98–100.

[346] *Rules of Discipline of the Religious Society of Friends* (3rd edn., 1834), p. viii.

[347] *Memoirs of J. J. Gurney*, i. 257–8; J. J. Gurney, *Essays on the Evidence, Doctrines, and Practical Operation of Christianity* (1825), 198–208.

[348] Isichei, *Victorian Quakers*, 8.

not the death of any . . . but that all should repent and live'; and 'the great truth so often . . . declared in Scripture, that Christ "died for all" '. 'We are justified', concluded Ash, 'not only in strenuously rejecting every dogma which would consign to inevitable perdition those who are destitute of the privileges we ourselves enjoy, but even in concluding that a way of life and salvation is opened to all mankind without exception, so that the destruction of those who perish is wholly of themselves.'[349]

Ash's argument is significant, for it illustrates the reluctance to divide mankind into saved sheep and lost goats which was shared by other Quakers. It also reveals that even at the height of Evangelical influence on the Society of Friends there was much in the Quaker tradition that was resistant to Evangelical theology.[350] These phenomena were alluded to by several writers, both Quaker and non-Quaker, who submitted contributions to an essay competition sponsored in 1858 by an anonymous 'gentleman who laments that, notwithstanding the population of the United Kingdom has more than doubled in the last fifty years, the Society of Friends is less in num-ber than at the beginning of the century'. He offered a prize of a hundred guineas for the best essay on the subject and the winner of the competition, John Stephenson Rowntree, pointed to 'birth-right membership' as one of the major causes of Quaker decline. Rowntree argued that the adoption of rules of settlement in 1737 in an attempt to resolve disputes concerning responsibility for the relief of poor Quakers led ultimately to 'the children of Friends being registered as members at the time of birth, and being esteemed as such till their names are removed by death, disownment, or resignation, even should they give little or no evidence of personal piety'. In Rowntree's Evangelical eyes the lines of division drawn by birth-right membership were the wrong lines. 'Membership has become virtually hereditary', descending 'from father to son almost like other property', and producing a religious denomination 'containing a number of persons unconverted to God'.[351]

Other contributors to the essay competition made the same point even more forcefully. Samuel Fothergill, who admitted he had leanings towards Wesleyan Methodism, agreed with Rowntree that birth-right membership was one of the major causes of Quaker decline. The result was that the

---

[349] E. Ash, *An Inquiry into some parts of Christian Doctrine and Practice* (1841), 61–2, 67.

[350] For the influence of Evangelicalism on Quakerism see Isichei, *Victorian Quakers*, 3–16; E. Grubb, *The Evangelical Movement and its Impact on the Society of Friends* (Leominster, 1924); and Watts, *The Dissenters*, i. 462–3.

[351] J. S. Rowntree, *Quakerism, Past and Present* (1859), 112. Richard Vann has criticized the significance which Rowntree attributed to the rules of settlement of 1737 (*The Social Development of English Quakerism* (Cambridge, Mass., 1969), 145–53).

Society of Friends contained many who had 'never been influenced by converting grace, are totally ignorant of the divine life, and are either rank hypocrites or mere worldlings', who thus exerted 'a deadening influence upon the whole community', and transformed 'the Society from an Evangelical church into a Society for the most part of mere moralists'.[352] Silent worship, complained Fothergill, encouraged Quakers to neglect the preaching of the Gospel and inhibited them from seeking the conversion of their fellow men. 'For a Friend now to ask his neighbour after the state of his soul, or to take any direct steps to bring about his conversion to God, would be painfully repugnant to his habitual silence on religious subjects.'[353] Robert Macnair, who confessed that when he wrote his essay he did not know 'a single member of the Society of Friends', pointed to the Quaker emphasis on the inner light to explain the contrast between the missionary enthusiasm of the first Quakers and the fact that, by the mid-nineteenth century, 'of all the various churches of Christendom, the least missionary is that of the Quakers'. In his view the Quakers' belief in the inner light, like the Unitarians' belief in universal restoration, inhibited missionary zeal. 'The truth which [the Quakers] possess, they believe to lie in germ in the heart of each man around them; so that, if he attend to the light within, he must arrive at the position which they themselves have attained. . . . they do not recognise themselves as links in the chain which is to connect him with God.'[354]

The High Churchman Thomas Hancock also pointed out that the Quakers no longer regarded their inspiration as unique and their message as essential to salvation. 'The great body of men and women who are looking upon salvation as an escape from physical or metaphysical fire and torment . . . are in constant danger of becoming the prey of any teacher . . . putting forth such an assumption.' In the seventeenth century, argued Hancock, 'Quakerism had plausible things to say to [that] fearful and unsettled body'. 'It claimed to be the one Holy Church, the only Ark of Salvation.'[355] But by the nineteenth century Friends no longer believed that the distinctive Quaker message offered the only escape from the everlasting torments of hell. In that they were at one with the Unitarians; and in that fact lies the explanation of their common decline.

---

[352] S. Fothergill, *Essay on the Society of Friends* (1859), 174, 178–9.
[353] Ibid. 46, 54, 148–9.   [354] R. Macnair, *The Decline of Quakerism* (1860), 38–40, 53.
[355] T. Hancock, *The Peculium* (1859), 186–8, 172–3.

7. THE PRETENDED 'POWER OF LAYING GHOSTS':
THE CONDITIONS OF EXPANSION

The failure of the humane, civilized, and sophisticated versions of Christianity offered by the Unitarians and Quakers to attract a mass following contrasts with the success of the Evangelical version of Christianity in winning wholesale conversions among superstitious and unsophisticated communities, both in England and Wales and throughout the world. Just as Hinduism, Buddhism, and Islam were far more resistant to Christianity than were the primitive faiths of the peoples of the West Indies, central Africa, and Polynesia, so Nonconformity in England and Wales was most popular in its most unsophisticated form and found its readiest converts among the more backward and superstitious sections of the English and Welsh people.

It was suggested in the first volume of this work that the revivalists of the eighteenth century found their most appreciative audiences among unsophisticated communities,[356] and there is strong evidence to indicate that in the nineteenth century Evangelical Nonconformity had its widest appeal in the least educated parts of the country. Following the establishment of the Civil Registry of Births, Marriages, and Deaths in 1836 the registrar-general published figures showing the proportion of men and women who signed the marriage register with a mark rather than with a signature, and the statistics in Table V show that there was a marked correlation between areas of high illiteracy and of strong support for religion in general and for Nonconformity in particular.[357] Of the fourteen counties in which half or more of the men and women married between 1838 and 1841 were unable to sign their names, nine had estimated attendances at a place of worship of 50 per cent or more on census Sunday in 1851, and in seven more than a quarter of the total population attended a Nonconformist chapel. The areas of very high Nonconformist support—Wales, Monmouthshire, Bedfordshire, Huntingdonshire—were all areas with high rates of illiteracy. Only Cornwall and Buckinghamshire had more than 25 per cent of its population in a Nonconformist chapel and more than half of its men and women able to sign their names. On the other hand the areas with the highest literacy levels in 1838–41—London, Cumberland, Westmorland, and Northumberland—all had low levels of religious observance in 1851 and were areas where Nonconformity was particularly weak.

---

[356] Watts, *The Dissenters*, i. 410.

[357] James Obelkevich makes a similar observation in *Religion and Rural Society* (Oxford, 1976), 79 n. 2. Throughout this section I have used 'illiteracy' as a shorthand term denoting 'inability to write one's name' although the term is strictly inaccurate since there is evidence that many people who could not sign their name could in fact read.

TABLE V. *Relationship between illiteracy and religious observance: county totals*

	Mean proportion of men and women signing marriage registers with a mark, 1838–41 %	Estimated proportion of the population attending a Nonconformist chapel in 1851 %	Estimated proportion of the population attending any church or chapel in 1851 %
Bedfordshire	59	39.1	65.6
North Wales	59	47.9	59.2
Monmouthshire	59	34.1	49.0
South Wales	58	43.9	56.1
Hertfordshire	54	22.1	51.3
Worcestershire	54	12.0	36.0
Lancashire	53	12.0	32.4
Staffordshire	52	16.6	34.1
Yorkshire, West Riding	52	21.1	35.3
Cambridgeshire	51	26.1	51.0
Essex	51	20.1	51.2
Huntingdonshire	50	34.8	64.0
Suffolk	50	22.5	55.8
Wiltshire	50	25.9	57.0
Buckinghamshire	49	25.8	55.5
Cheshire	49	16.0	35.2
Shropshire	49	15.0	41.7
Norfolk	47	19.5	44.8
Cornwall	44.5	33.8	47.7
Northamptonshire	44.5	24.7	54.9
Berkshire	44	16.5	48.5
Nottinghamshire	44	21.3	39.2
Leicestershire	42	23.2	49.4
Somerset	42	18.6	47.9
Derbyshire	41	23.1	40.5
Herefordshire	41	9.9	35.4
Lincolnshire	41	23.3	43.9
Warwickshire	41	12.3	33.6
Oxfordshire	40	16.2	47.4
Durham	37	17.3	31.1
Gloucestershire	37	18.8	47.6
Dorset	36.5	18.4	53.1
Sussex	36	12.2	40.0
Hampshire	35	17.1	45.3
Kent	35	14.2	40.3
Devon	34	19.0	47.0
Middlesex	34	10.4	35.6
Surrey	34	7.7	38.3
Yorkshire, North Riding	33	24.0	44.7

TABLE V (cont.): Relationship between illiteracy and religious observance:
county totals

	Mean proportion of men and women signing marriage registers with a mark, 1838–41 %	Estimated proportion of the population attending a Nonconformist chapel in 1851 %	Estimated proportion of the population attending any church or chapel in 1851 %
Rutland	32	18.5	50.3
Yorkshire, East Riding	30	23.1	41.5
Northumberland	29	15.9	31.0
Cumberland	26	10.3	27.4
Westmorland	26	12.0	36.9
London	18	8.9	27.0

That this is more than coincidence is suggested by the more detailed Table XIV at the end of this volume which shows the proportion of men and women who made their marks in marriage registers in 1851 in each registration district alongside the detailed analysis of the 1851 religious census. The table reveals that in many counties there was a significant correlation between districts with a high level of illiteracy and districts with a high level of Nonconformist support.[358] There are exceptions to this rule: the poorer districts of London such as Bethnal Green and Whitechapel and the cotton towns of Lancashire were marked by high rates of illiteracy and low levels of religious observance. Conversely prosperous districts such as Hampstead and St George's, Hanover Square, had the highest rates of literacy in the country and also, for London, high levels of religious observance. But religious observance in such areas was almost entirely Anglican, and Nonconformity had less support in those educated upper-class districts than anywhere else in England.

Outside Lancashire, districts in which more than 50 per cent of men and women were unable to sign their names in the marriage register in 1851 were usually districts with a significantly high attendance at Methodist and Dissenting chapels on census Sunday: Fordingbridge and Whitchurch in Hampshire; Hemel Hempstead and Berkhamsted in Hertfordshire;

---

[358] The correlation coefficient between the percentage of Nonconformists and the percentage of illiterates for 55 English and Welsh counties, based on the marriage registers for 1851, is the highly significant 0.74. The correlation coefficient between the percentage of Nonconformists and the percentage of illiterates for 624 registration districts is the highly significant 0.40. In both cases the probability of the correlation being due to chance is less than 0.001. There is no significant correlation between Anglican attendance and illiteracy in the registration districts.

Wellingborough and Thrapstone in Northamptonshire; Biggleswade, Ampt-
hill, Woburn, and Leighton Buzzard in Bedfordshire; Caston, Linton, and
Ely in Cambridgeshire; Halstead and Dunmow in Essex; Risbridge, Cosford,
Stow, and Hartismere in Suffolk; Tunstead and Aylsham in Norfolk; Melk-
sham in Wiltshire; Redruth in Cornwall; Keynsham in Somerset; Dudley and
Stourbridge on the borders of Worcestershire and Staffordshire; Foleshill in
Warwickshire; Hinckley in Leicestershire; Congleton in Cheshire; Keighley,
Todmorden, and Dewsbury in Yorkshire; Abergavenny and Pontypool in
Monmouthshire; and most of the districts in the Welsh-speaking parts of
Wales. Conversely there were districts with high literacy rates and signifi-
cantly low levels of Nonconformity such as Eton in Buckinghamshire,
Headington in Oxfordshire, West Ham in Essex, St Thomas in Devon, King's
Norton in Worcestershire, Stamford in Lincolnshire, the Wirral in Cheshire,
West Derby in Lancashire, Ecclesall-Bierlow and Richmond in Yorkshire,
Rothbury in Northumberland, and Penrith and Longtown in Cumberland.
The supposition that Evangelical Nonconformity appealed primarily to the
ill-educated is further strengthened by the evidence which suggests that in
many chapels at least half the members were unable to write. Sixty-nine
per cent of the parents who had their children baptized by the Ruddington
Primitive Methodist society in Nottinghamshire between 1828 and 1838
could not sign their names.[359] Half the men and women baptized by the
Accrington Baptist church in Lancashire between 1821 and 1850, and half
those who joined the Ebenezer Baptist church in Bacup in the 1830s, could
not write.[360] In the Black Country a high proportion of the men who approved
chapel trust deeds had to make their mark rather than sign their names: half
the Netherton Baptists in 1746, three-quarters of the Upper Ettingshall
Wesleyans in 1829, nearly half the Old Hill Primitive Methodists in 1851.[361]
And these men were the leaders of their communities, not the rank and
file.

Degrees of superstition cannot be measured in the ways that levels of
literacy can, but there is a great deal of evidence to suggest that Evangelical
Nonconformity flourished in communities in which superstitious beliefs
were particularly prevalent. Methodism, in either its Calvinistic or its Arminian forms, found a ready response in Wales, Yorkshire, and Lincolnshire,
and in all three areas in the early nineteenth century there was a widespread belief in a devil who 'intermeddled in the affairs of men' and who

[359] G. M. Morris, 'Primitive Methodism in Nottinghamshire', Ph.D. thesis (Nottingham, 1967), 204.
[360] Weston, 'Baptists of North-West England', 246, 249.
[361] Cumberland, 'Nonconformity in the Black Country', 124.

appeared in material form to men and women who drank too much or who broke the Sabbath. In all three areas death was surrounded by superstition. In the West Riding boggards were believed to appear in churchyards after a funeral and 'the neighbourhood for a time after was a terrible terror to many'. Children who were naughty were told by their parents that 'there was a black boggard up the chimney, or coming down to fetch them'.[362] 'Ghosts and hob-goblins were nightly visitors' in the Yorkshire Wolds 'and travellers passing a lonely spot between Fimber and Wetwang' used to see a headless woman on a galloping horse.[363] In both Lincolnshire and Wales death was associated with candles. Lincolnshire people thought they could see portents of death in the flame of a candle.[364] The Welsh believed in the existence of 'corpse-candles' which appeared when people were mortally ill, shedding their 'sickly glare on the homes of the dying' and wending their way to the churchyard.[365] A farmer in Ebbw Vale recalled that in the late eighteenth century 'the people's one recreation during the long winter evenings would be to relate weird, superstitious stories of ghosts and goblins, corpse candles, [and] the hounds of hell'.[366] In the 1830s people in the mountains around Merthyr Tydfil were said to be 'serious believers in fairies, ghosts, and spirits'.[367] Even in the 1870s the inhabitants of the Amman valley in Carmarthenshire were reputed to believe in the need for a 'sin-eater' to be summoned to a corpse and to be paid 2s. 6d. to place 'a plate of salt and bread on the breast of the deceased person' to eat his sins.[368]

Superstition was particularly rife in communities of fishermen and miners where men followed hazardous occupations, and such communities were peculiarly responsive to Evangelical religion. David Clark's study of the north Yorkshire fishing village of Staithes in the 1970s, a village in which three-quarters of the population attended a Nonconformist chapel on census Sunday in 1851, reveals characteristics of geographic isolation and lack of sophistication which John Wesley noted in the Isle of Man two centuries earlier.[369] Fishermen believed it was unlucky to refer to land-animals such as foxes and pigs, or to meet a woman on the way to a boat, and these superstitions were transferred from the sea to the land by men who had gone to work

[362] J. Lawson, *Progress in Pudsey* (Firle, Sussex, 1973), 70–1.

[363] Woodcock, *Piety among the Peasantry*, 10.

[364] Obelkevich, *Religion and Rural Society*, 276–9, 295.

[365] Evans, *Christmas Evans*, 24; Hood, *Christmas Evans*, 23; G. Borrow, *Wild Wales* (n.d.), 53–4, 315.

[366] Price, *The History of Penuel Calvinistic Methodist Church, Ebbw Vale*, 12, 13.

[367] Carwardine, *Transatlantic Revivalism*, 88.   [368] Hood, *Christmas Evans*, 23.

[369] D. Clark, *Between Pulpit and Pew* (Cambridge, 1982), 32; Watts, *The Dissenters*, i. 410.

in the ironstone mines in the nineteenth century.[370] Over 30 per cent of the population of Cornwall attended a Methodist chapel on census Sunday, and Cornwall was arguably the most superstitious county in England. The tin and copper miners believed that the mines they worked were inhabited by 'knackers', the spirits of Jews who were reputed to have worked the mines during the Roman occupation and who had to be appeased if good veins of ore were to be found and disaster averted.[371] In both Staithes and Cornwall belief in witchcraft continued well into the nineteenth century. An Anglican clergyman writing in Cornwall in 1826 remembered a time when 'there were conjuring parsons and cunning clerks; every blacksmith was a doctor, every old woman a witch'. 'All nature seemed united—its wells, its plants, its birds, its beasts, its reptiles . . . in predicting or in averting, in relieving or in aggravating misfortunes.'[372]

There is a mass of evidence to suggest that Methodism in particular both reinforced and was itself sustained by such popular superstitions. John Wesley himself had never doubted the existence of witches and ghosts, and in Pudsey in the West Riding in the first half of the nineteenth century both the Bible and Wesley's *Journal* were appealed to as 'proof of the truth of witchcraft' and of the reality of 'boggards'.[373] Joseph Barker, born in Bramley in the West Riding in 1806, was brought up among Wesleyans who believed as firmly in witchcraft, boggards, and fairies as they did in Christianity. One Methodist claimed that he could cure a bewitched person by bleeding him and allowing his blood to run into a fire: 'by this means the witch herself might be burned to death'.[374] In Delph near Saddleworth Methodists used the lines of a hymn to exorcize boggards:

> Jesus the name high over all
> In hell, or earth, or sky,
> Angels and men before it fall
> And devils fear and fly.[375]

The first Wesleyan chapel to be built in Leeds was even known as 'the Boggard chapel'.[376] Some Wesleyan preachers denounced belief in witchcraft but others were prepared to live with it. Geographic isolation and the prevalence

---

[370] Clark, *Between Pulpit and Pew*, 147–56.

[371] J. G. Rule, 'The Labouring Miner in Cornwall', Ph.D. thesis (Warwick, 1971), 247–60.

[372] Ibid. 250, citing R. Polwhale, *Traditions and Recollections* (1826), ii. 605.

[373] Lawson, *Progress in Pudsey*, 69.

[374] J. Barker, *The Life of Joseph Barker, Written by Himself* (1880), 19–22.

[375] M. A. Smith, 'Religion in Industrial Society: the case of Oldham and Saddleworth, 1780–1865', D.Phil. thesis (Oxford, 1987), 476.

[376] D. C. Dews, 'Methodism in Leeds from 1791 to 1861', M.Phil. thesis (Bradford, 1984), 25.

of superstition facilitated the growth of Methodism on the Isle of Portland in Dorset, but when a new minister, Francis Derry, arrived in the circuit in 1816 he was horrified to find how many of the local Wesleyans believed in witch-craft and fifty were expelled. However, the expelled Methodists formed themselves into a separate congregation, met in a chapel at Chesil which became known as the 'Conjuror's Lodge', and were readmitted to the Wesleyan fold ten years later.[377] A rumour went round Manchester at the end of 1816 that during a watchnight service to be held at the Oldham Street Wesleyan chapel at midnight on the last day of the year 'Satan was to be exorcised' and would 'take his departure in visible form'. As a result the 'benches, pews, aisles, orchestra, stairs, and doorways' of the chapel were packed and hundreds of people could not get in.[378]

The Primitive Methodist and Bible Christian movements both origi-nated in communities in which supernatural beliefs were widely held. The Primitive Methodist pioneer William Clowes sought divine protection from the 'Kidsgrove bogget' who was reputed to terrorize an area of north Staffordshire, and he exorcized a devil from a woman in Harriseahead.[379] Clowes and the Primitive Methodist founder Hugh Bourne paid frequent visits to the former Wesleyan local preacher and farm labourer James Crawfoot who held prayer-meetings in his cottage in a remote part of Delamere Forest at which people fell into trances or had visions. Since it was rumoured that Crawfoot and his followers used 'magic or were in league with Satan' they became known as 'Magic Methodists'.[380] While in London in 1810 Bourne and Crawfoot visited the prophetess Joanna Southcott whom Bourne decided was 'in witchcraft', and a few weeks later he commented that a Ramsor woman who was once 'believed to deal in witchcraft' was 'now in a state of grace'.[381] The Primitive Methodist preacher John Oxtoby claimed to have seen the devil—'a little man, with two horns, a long tail, and knee-breeches'—and William O'Bryan, the founder of the Bible Christians, on one occasion believed that he was being followed by Satan 'like a great bear on his hind legs'.[382] A revival in the Primitive Methodist Keighley circuit in the win-

[377] R. Pearce, *Methodism in Portland* (1898), 76–80.

[378] R. Chew, *James Everett* (1875), 121.

[379] Werner, *The Primitive Methodist Connexion*, 70.

[380] G. Herod, *Biographical Sketches of some of those Preachers whose Labours have con-tributed to the Organisation and early Extension of the Primitive Methodist Connexion* (n.d.), 257–9; E. Langton, 'James Crawfoot: The Forest Mystic', *PWHS* 30 (1955), 12–13.

[381] J. Walford, *Memoirs of the Life and Labours of the Late Venerable Hugh Bourne* (1855), i. 290, 296.

[382] Woodcock, *Piety among the Peasantry*, 40; T. Shaw, *The Bible Christians, 1815–1907* (1965), 78 n.

ter of 1825–6 was assisted by stories of the ghost of William Clarkson who was said to have appeared to his friend William Mann at a farm at Kirby Malzeard every night for a month. The ghost pulled William Mann down his bed, stroked his face with a cold hand, and moaned that he was 'lost forever' because he had 'trusted all upon my own good works'.[383]

The ease with which Evangelical Christianity was grafted on to popular superstitious beliefs is in part explained by the Evangelical doctrine of divine providence. The Evangelicals, basing their views on what they regarded as an infallible Bible, saw God as an omnipotent and omnipresent being who was constantly intervening in human affairs to reward the virtuous and to punish the wicked. For them divine providence was, in the words of Jonathan Crowther, 'the conduct and direction of the several parts of the universe, by a superintending and intelligent Being'.[384] To men and women who had always believed in the power of witches and the appearance of ghosts, the daily interventions of an all-seeing God were easily credible. Joseph Lawson recalled how, around 1830, a young man who had been drinking was walking down a lane in Pudsey one dark night when there appeared to him what he took to be the ghost of his Methodist mother who had died when he was but a few weeks old. The incident resulted in the young man's conversion and in his becoming a Methodist local preacher, and was widely regarded 'not only as a direct interposition of divine providence, but as proof of the existence of apparitions'.[385]

Belief in divine providence enabled its holder to share with Paul the conviction that 'all things work together for good to them that love God'.[386] At its best it gave Evangelicals the strength with which to endure and to explain otherwise inexplicable disasters. When Andrew Fuller lost his favourite daughter Sally at the age of six in 1786 he wrote in his diary that her death had been 'decided by an infallible God'.[387] At its worst the idea that God was constantly intervening in human affairs led Christians to pass facile judgements for party purposes on those who suffered misfortune. The *Methodist* and *Evangelical Magazines* were full of accounts of men and women who died suddenly after breaking the Sabbath, dancing on the village green, or playing at cards.[388] When the Primitive Methodist preacher John Hallsworth attempted to address a crowd at Fulbeck in Lincolnshire in 1818 a number of people tried to drown his voice by ringing the bells of the parish church. Two

[383] *Primitive Methodist Magazine*, 7 (1826), 159–62, 246.
[384] *Wesleyan Methodist Magazine*, 58 (1835), 743.
[385] Lawson, *Progress in Pudsey*, 69–70.
[386] Romans 8: 28.   [387] Ryland, *Life of Andrew Fuller*, 128.
[388] M. J. Quinlan, *Victorian Prelude* (New York, 1941), 187–8.

years later he returned to Fulbeck to find that 'the ring-leader of them was gone to the mad-house, and others had had losses in their cattle'. 'God will show himself great all over', was Hallsworth's comment on the misfortunes of his adversaries.[389] In 1832 R. G. Stannard, also a Primitive Methodist, tried to preach to a crowd at Reedham in Norfolk from the top of an upturned wheelbarrow when he was confronted by a man known as 'Flying Tommy'. Tommy placed himself in front of the preacher, stared into his face, and in foul language 'laid various dreadful crimes' to Stannard's charge. The preacher replied: 'There is salvation or damnation for you within three weeks', and three weeks later Tommy attempted to swim across a river when drunk and sank to the bottom.[390] A third Primitive Methodist, William Driffield of St Ives in Cornwall, in 1839 listed in his diary the names of seven opponents who in the previous four years had died, gone mad, or lost money, all 'put down' by God.[391] In October 1812 Hopkin Bevan, one of the first Welsh Calvinistic Methodist preachers to be ordained after the denomination's break with the Church of England in 1810, was reported to have drowned when the boat in which he was believed to be sailing went down in the Bristol Channel. Some High Anglicans regarded this a just punishment for his unepiscopal ordination. But Bevan was not on the boat—at the last minute he had decided to take the coach—and concluded that he had received 'a special deliverance through the providence of the Lord'.[392]

Liberal Anglicans and Unitarians disliked the Evangelical belief in divine providence. Sydney Smith argued that it was dangerous 'to test the merit of an individual by counting his strokes of good fortune or to judge his demerit by the numbers of his misfortunes'.[393] And Evangelicals were all too ready to blame cholera epidemics in England, earthquakes in the Windward Islands, and mining disasters in Cornwall on the 'wicked and abandoned character' of the victims.[394] But at the same time they managed to see God's intervention on behalf of the converted in any situation, no matter how grisly. In 1797 the *Arminian Magazine* recorded the death of a Wesleyan class leader, John Finley, after being injured in an explosion in a coalmine in Lanesley in County Durham. 'His body was dreadfully wounded' and his groans were heard by two boys who called for assistance to men who helped to carry him out of the pit. Had the boys not heard him at that point his cries would have

---

[389] *Primitive Methodist Magazine*, 2 (1821), 45.   [390] Ibid. 2nd ser. 8 (1838), 65–6.
[391] Rule, 'Labouring Miner in Cornwall', 256.
[392] Jenkins, *Life of Thomas Charles*, iii. 305.
[393] Quinlan, *Victorian Prelude*, 188; Mineka, *Dissidence of Dissent*, 223.
[394] Ryall, 'Organisation of Missionary Societies', 365; Rule, 'Labouring Miner in Cornwall', 253.

been drowned by the noise from the engine which was about to pump water out of the pit. The fact that John was brought out of the mine to die in bed the *Arminian Magazine* described as 'remarkably providential'. Why providence had allowed the explosion to occur in the first place was not discussed.[395]

The belief in divine providence thus provided an explanation for natural and personal disasters that was hardly more rational than the Cornish miners' belief in 'knackers'. Keith Thomas, in his *Religion and the Decline of Magic*, speaks of 'the triumph of religion over magic' in the late seventeenth century, and of belief in 'special providences' giving way 'to the notion of a Providence which itself obeyed natural laws accessible to human study'.[396] But it was Newton's physics and Boyle's chemistry, not religion, that destroyed the educated classes' belief in magic, and evidence from the nineteenth century suggests that for the uneducated a belief both in magic and in 'special providences' persisted, and that Christianity and superstition were not in fact mutually exclusive. Many of the developments of the late seventeenth century which Keith Thomas suggests reduced man's dependence on magic—the development of newspapers, improvements in the postal services, the growth of insurance—had little relevance for the farm labourers, fishermen, and miners who flooded into Nonconformist chapels in the first half of the nineteenth century. Such people were almost as dependent for survival on the vagaries of the weather and the fortuitous absence of infectious diseases as were their ancestors. James Obelkevich's observation that Christianity and superstition flourished and declined together seems nearer the truth.[397] There is consequently no contradiction between the conclusion drawn above from the study of the geographic distribution of Dissent, that Nonconformity often flourished in areas where the ground had been prepared by the Church of England, and the conclusion of this section, that Methodism and Dissent found their largest body of supporters in the worst educated and most superstitious parts of England and Wales. Both the teachings of the established church and beliefs inherited from pre-Christian paganism reinforced a frame of mind which accepted the supernatural as normal and which predisposed their holders to accept the Evangelical beliefs in sin, judgement, instantaneous conversion, and heaven and hell. Anglican clergymen in eighteenth-century Cornwall were said to owe their influence over their flocks solely to their pretended 'power of laying ghosts'.[398] In

[395] *Arminian Magazine*, 20 (1797), 556–7.
[396] K. Thomas, *Religion and the Decline of Magic* (1973), 639–40.
[397] Obelkevich, *Religion and Rural Society*, 330.
[398] Rule, 'Labouring Miner in Cornwall', 250.

Cornwall, in Wales, in Lincolnshire, it was this mixture of Anglicanism and superstition that was to prove the most fertile ground for the growth of Methodism.

8. OPEN PARISHES AND INDUSTRIAL VILLAGES: THE PATTERN OF EXPANSION

Dissent, it was suggested above, grew in areas where the soil had been prepared by the Church of England but where the established church had proved incapable of reaping the harvest. Densely populated areas with a high level of poverty in which the mass of the population was already alienated from the Church of England, such as the east end of London and the cotton towns of Lancashire, proved as difficult for the Nonconformist churches as for the Church of England to penetrate in the first half of the nineteenth century. Dissent flourished in areas where the majority of people were still susceptible to the appeal of religion, where they still felt the need to look for help to powers greater than themselves, where a mixture of Christianity and pagan superstition predisposed men and women to believe in the supernatural, yet where the inflexible parochial structure, inadequate pastoral machinery, and unemotional moralistic theology of the Church of England proved inadequate to meet their spiritual needs.

The Church of England of the early nineteenth century was not Catholic, nor was it reformed. In the sixteenth century it had exchanged monarch for pope without changing the essential structure of the Church that had helped to provoke the Protestant Reformation. Three hundred years later the Church of England still retained abuses that would have been familiar to the critics of Cardinal Wolsey. Glaring inequalities in clerical income were as evident in the 1820s as they had been in the 1520s. The practice of clergy holding livings in plurality and so absenting themselves from their cures was even more prevalent in the reign of George IV than it had been in the reign of Henry VIII. The consequent neglect of the souls of men and women in parish after parish was a feature of the English church under Archbishop Manners-Sutton just as it had been under Pope Julius II. In some ways the Reformation had made matters worse. The Church had lost half its land, which had been seized to the benefit not of the poor and the ignorant, but of the king and those nobles and gentlemen to whom he had given or sold vast estates. Moreover, in over 3,840 out of 9,000 parishes tithes had been appropriated by monastic houses in the middle ages and had been sold after the

Reformation to laymen who paid only a proportion—often a small proportion—to the vicar or curate for whom the tithe had been originally levied.[399] In 1851 the perpetual curate of Llanfachreth in Merioneth complained bitterly that of the tithes of his parish, worth between £300 and £400 a year and belonging to the lay impropriator, Sir Richard Williams Vaughan, he received a mere £7, 'at which sum his scullery girl would turn up her nose'.[400] The ensuing poverty of the clergy was used to justify pluralism and non-residence, though it was not the poorest incumbents who benefited from pluralism. In appointing incumbents to benefices patrons frequently followed the dominical precept that 'he that hath, to him shall be given'.[401] Throughout England and Wales there were 3,998 livings worth less than £150 a year in 1810, while the Archbishop of Canterbury and the Bishop of Durham each collected £19,000 a year. Inequalities of clerical income were used to justify incompetence in the performance of clerical duties, though again an adequate income was no guarantee that a parson would devote more time to ministering to the needs of his parishioners than to undermining the welfare of the local fox population. In 1813 out of a total of 10,558 incumbents only 4,183 were resident and another 1,641, though non-resident, were performing their duties. Elsewhere the functions of the incumbents were being performed by curates, but in over a thousand parishes there was resident neither rector, vicar, nor curate to minister to the parishioners of the established church.[402]

In Wales the problems raised in England for the Church by the poverty of its clergy, the incompetence of its administration, and the corruption of its patronage, were compounded by the issue of language. The majority of people in Wales in the first half of the nineteenth century spoke the Welsh language in their daily lives; their rulers, whether they were squires, MPs, or bishops, spoke English. The middle and upper classes which in England provided the recruits for the clergy of the established church did not, in Wales, speak the native language of the majority of the inhabitants. The linguistic divide thus tended to become a class divide and crippled the Church of England in its dealings with the Welsh people. No native Welsh speaker held a bishopric in Wales between the death of John Wynne in 1727 and the elevation of Joshua Hughes in 1870, so that at many confirmations the bishops

---

[399] C. Hill, *Economic Problems of the Church* (Oxford, 1955), 144.
[400] Jones, *Religious Census, North Wales*, 270.
[401] Mark 4: 25; R. Mitchison, 'Pluralities and the Poorer Benefices in Eighteenth Century England', *Historical Journal*, 5 (1962), 188–90; W. T. Morgan, 'The Diocese of St David's in the Nineteenth Century', *Journal of the Historical Society of the Church in Wales*, 21 (1971), 31–3.
[402] W. R. Ward in *HMC*, ii. 40; Gilbert, *Religion and Society*, 7.

and the confirmands understood 'each other as well as the dumb animals exhibited at cattle shows'.[403] Few Welsh-speaking Welshmen could afford to send their sons to university with the result that clergymen who could speak Welsh usually received no more than grammar school education, while clergymen who had been to university could rarely speak Welsh fluently.[404] There was no shortage of candidates for the ministry of the Church in Wales, but there was much criticism of their quality. For conscientious bishops like Edward Copleston of Llandaff the linguistic division of Wales was a nightmare.[405] There were churches where services were conducted in Welsh and English on alternate Sundays, churches where Welsh and English were used for alternate services, churches where every service was conducted in a mixture of both languages. There were parishes where an absentee English incumbent took off with the bulk of the parish's revenue, leaving the cure of souls to a Welsh-speaking curate; there were parishes where an English-speaking clergyman made a valiant effort to preach in Welsh, with results that were often hilarious and sometimes obscene; there were parishes where English clergymen could scarcely communicate with their Welsh-speaking parishioners. Even in the mid-eighteenth century, before the major expansion of Welsh Nonconformity, Griffith Jones had argued that the chief cause of Welshmen dissenting from the established church was the 'want of plain, practical, pressing, and zealous preaching in a language and dialect they understand'. In 1811 Bishop Burgess of St David's claimed that 'the Welsh language is with the sectaries a powerful means of seduction from the Church'.[406]

The Church of England, plundered in the sixteenth century, weakened by Civil War and the loss of Puritan ministers in the seventeenth century, proved incapable of responding to the industrial and demographic revolutions of the eighteenth century. The population of England and Wales doubled between 1700 and 1820, and yet the Church of England entered the nineteenth century with a parochial structure virtually unchanged since the eleventh century. The population of medieval England, and consequently its parish churches, was concentrated in the arable lands of the south-east; the industrial revolution was centred on the upland areas of the Black Country, the West Riding, Lancashire, Durham, and Northumberland where the

---

[403] Morgan, 'Diocese of St David's', *Journal of the Historical Society of the Church in Wales*, 22 (1972), 16; 23 (1973), 18.

[404] D. Walker (ed.), *A History of the Church in Wales* (Penarth, 1976), 116.

[405] Davies, *Religion in the Industrial Revolution*, 116–18.

[406] Morgan, 'Diocese of St David's', *Journal of the Historical Society of the Church in Wales*, 23 (1973), 18–43.

resources of the established church were spread too thinly to meet the needs even of the early eighteenth century.[407] In the reign of Queen Ann Parliament provided for the construction of fifty new churches in London, but only ten were ever built.[408] By the early nineteenth century Norfolk had 731 parishes, Lancashire had 70. Birmingham's five parish churches had room for only 24,000 of its 185,000 people.[409] In London and the most populous parts of Middlesex 'not a tenth part of the Church of England population', complained a group of High Churchmen, could be 'accommodated in our churches and chapels'.[410] Until 1818 it required a special Act of Parliament to create a new Anglican parish and, given the vested interests in undivided parishes, such Acts were rare. A belated attempt was made by Parliament in 1818 to enable the established church to repair the damage when the Additional Churches Act gave £1 million for the building of new churches and facilitated the creation of new parishes. A further £½ million was granted by Parliament in 1824, over £7 million was raised by voluntary contributions, and between 1831 and 1851 2,029 new Anglican churches were built.[411] The effort came too late to recapture the English people for the English church. When the new churches were built, they remained half empty.[412] 'The present rate of church-and-chapel increase', commented Horace Mann on the results of the 1851 census, 'brings before our view the prospect, at no distant period, of a state of things in which there will be small deficiency of structures where to worship, but a lamentable lack of worshippers.'[413]

One must not exaggerate the shortcomings of the Church of England. It was Anglican efforts to revive the religious life of England and Wales that had prepared the way for the Evangelical revival in the eighteenth century, and there is evidence to suggest that a majority of first-generation Methodists had the foundations of their later religious convictions laid by the established church.[414] But the Anglican church at the turn of the eighteenth and nineteenth centuries, with its formal worship, cold sermons, and absence of lay participation, lacked the excitement, the emotional fervour, and the opportunities for involvement provided by Methodist chapels and Nonconformist meeting-houses. Most serious of all, the theology of many of the Church of England clergy, from the bishops downwards, left them without the motivating power of Evangelical Nonconformists. Middle-of-the-road Anglicans, like the Unitarians, lacked the conviction of the Evangelicals

---

[407] Watts, *The Dissenters*, i. 277–80.
[408] R. A. Soloway, *Prelates and People* (1969), 281–2.
[409] Ward in *HMC*, ii. 53, 55.   [410] Soloway, *Prelates and People*, 289.
[411] *Religious Census*, p. xii.   [412] Soloway, *Prelates and People*, 310–12, 441.
[413] *Religious Census*, p. clv.   [414] Watts, *The Dissenters*, i. 422.

that those who ignored their message would burn for ever in the fires of hell. Bishop Porteus of London was more aware than most prelates of the failure of the Church of England to come to grips with the upsurge in population, but even he was concerned principally with the morals of those outside the churches and with the threat they posed to the social order, rather than with their salvation.[415] Despite its glaring defects the eighteenth-century Anglican church educated men and women in the basic tenets of Christianity and taught them to behave justly towards their neighbours and to respect their superiors. It was left to the Methodists and Dissenters to convert them to what they called 'a saving knowledge of Jesus Christ'. A curate in Skegness in Lincolnshire was told by one of his congregation, 'We comes to church in the morning to please you, Sir, and goes to chapel at night to save our souls'.[416]

The Church of England was at its most powerful in the compact nucleated villages in the arable lands of southern and eastern England where parishes were of manageable size and where the land was owned by a single landlord sympathetic to the Church of England. Such was the parish of Nocton in Kesteven in Lincolnshire which was reported, in the episcopal visitation returns of 1844, to belong entirely to the Earl of Ripon, with the consequence that the vicar had 'no complaint of non-attendance on a Sunday morning, the church is well filled, even with some who are known to be regular Dissenters'.[417] Obelkevich's study of south Lindsey in the same county shows that attendances at the services of the established church were highest in small parishes with fewer than 200 people and in which one landlord owned more than half the land, and lowest in parishes with more than 600 people in which land was held by freeholders with less than 40 acres each.[418] My own work on Nottinghamshire points to the same conclusion: support for the Church of England was twice as high in villages of less than 200 people, and in villages where all the land was owned by a single proprietor, as it was in the county at large.[419] And in South Yorkshire D. G. Hey has noted the 'complete absence of any Nonconformity in the history of such estate villages as High Melton or Sprotborough' where 'resident lords such as the Fountaynes and Montagues of Melton and the Copleys of Sprotborough ensured that these villages remained small and wholly agriculture in character'.[420]

---

[415] Soloway, *Prelates and People*, 284.
[416] Obelkevich, *Religion and Rural Society*, 157.
[417] Ambler, *Lincolnshire Returns*, p. lxv.
[418] Obelkevich, *Religion and Rural Society*, 12, 154–5.
[419] Watts, *Religion in Victorian Nottinghamshire*, i, pp. xviii–xix.
[420] D. G. Hey, 'The Pattern of Nonconformity in South Yorkshire, 1660–1851', *Northern History*, 8 (1973), 86.

Landlords who were deeply committed to the established church could and did use their power over their tenants to try to ensure that they did not attend Nonconformist places of worship or, worse still, try to obtain land for the building of Nonconformist chapels. The Wesleyan preacher Thomas Taylor ascribed the small size of Methodist congregations in the York circuit in the 1780s in part to the fact that the farmers were 'in a great bondage to their wealthy landlords, to whom they are a kind of vassals, and in general dread them more abundantly than they do their Maker'.[421] It is impossible to know just how widespread was the landlord practice of enforcing conformity to the established church, but Wesley's *Journal* and the histories of all the Nonconformist denominations are littered with cases of tenant farmers who were evicted from their holdings because they chose to worship in a Dissenting meeting-house or Methodist chapel rather than in their parish church.[422] The Independent William Prichard was ejected from three separate farms in Caernarfonshire and Anglesey on account of his Dissent in the mid-eighteenth century.[423] Robert Llwyd, a Calvinistic Methodist preacher, was driven from his farm at Cilcain near Mold in Flintshire and was only able to find another farm to rent because it was said to be haunted.[424] Edward Parry, evicted from his farm at Llansanan in Denbighshire because he used it for Calvinistic Methodist meetings, told his landlord, 'Your land, Sir, is only temporal, while religion is eternal'.[425] William Carey's sister Ann was evicted from her farm at Cottesbrooke in Northamptonshire on the death of her husband because her late partner had allowed the farmhouse to be used 'for the preaching of the Gospel'.[426] A landlord who was determined to preserve the agricultural nature of a village could destroy a Dissenting presence even where one was already established. The whole village of Widmerpool in Nottinghamshire was owned by the lord of the manor, Frederick Robinson, and in 1855 it was reported that he had 'pulled down the cottages formerly occupied by the Dissenters and had compelled them to seek habitations in neighbouring villages'. As a result the General Baptist chapel was nearly empty and was sold to Robinson three years later for a mere £325.[427]

The Wynn family of Wynnstay Hall near Ruabon in Denbighshire, the most powerful landed family in north Wales, was notoriously intolerant of their Nonconformist tenants for much of the eighteenth and early nineteenth

---

[421] T. Jackson (ed.), *The Lives of Early Methodist Preachers* (3rd edn., 1865), v. 56.

[422] For earlier examples see Watts, *The Dissenters*, i. 286–7, 406.

[423] T. Rees, *History of Protestant Nonconformity in Wales* (2nd edn., 1883), 395–401.

[424] W. T. Owen, *Edward Williams* (Cardiff, 1963), 3.

[425] W. Williams, *Welsh Calvinistic Methodism* (1872), 66.   [426] Carey, *William Carey*, 40.

[427] F. M. W. Harrison, 'The Life and Thought of the Baptists of Nottinghamshire', M.Phil. thesis (Nottingham, 1972), i. 252.

centuries. In the mid-eighteenth century Sir Watkin Williams Wynn fined tenants on his estates £80 for attending Calvinistic Methodist meetings. But, so the Methodists believed, God intervened on their behalf for, having threatened Methodists with eviction from their holdings, in 1749 Wynn fell from his horse while hunting and was killed.[428] John Roberts, minister of the Independent church at Llanbrynmair, Montgomeryshire, was tenant of another Sir Watkin Williams Wynn in the early nineteenth century, and after he had spent £700 on improving his holding Sir Watkin's steward imposed 'an unreasonable increase' in his rent, and when Roberts died in 1834 his widow was subjected to a further increase.[429] By the mid-nineteenth century the squires of Wynnstay Hall had perforce to accept the presence of Nonconformity on their estates and in 1858 the current Sir Watkin even admitted that had it not been 'for the labour of Dissenters in Wales, the great mass of the people would be without religion'. But this did not stop him and another landowner, R. W. Price of Rhiwlas, from evicting eleven tenants in Merioneth who either voted Liberal or abstained in the general election of 1859.[430]

Landlords such as the Wynns could also try to hinder the expansion of Dissent by refusing to let Nonconformists have land on which to build chapels. The Independent chapel at Llanbrynmair was built in the middle of a wood because Sir Watkin would not allow it to be built near the village.[431] The Congregationalists of Llanarthney in Carmarthenshire explained in 1851 that they worshipped in a private house because 'proprietors in the neighbourhood have refused the rent of a spot of ground for the erection of a house of worship'.[432] The Earl of Stamford, who 'owned almost all the land' in Ashton-under-Lyne in Lancashire, refused to allow any of it to be used for Nonconformist chapels.[433] Sir Tatton Sykes would not allow Primitive Methodists to build a chapel at Sledmere in the Yorkshire Wolds and threatened to eject tenants who gave hospitality to Ranter preachers.[434] For half a century Wesleyans at Deighton near York were obliged to walk a mile and a half from their village to the Methodist chapel because Lord Wenlock

[428] R. W. Evans, 'The Eighteenth-Century Welsh Awakening', Ph.D. thesis (Edinburgh, 1956), 138; anon., *The Life and Times of Selina, Countess of Huntingdon* (1839), i. 110; Williams, *Welsh Calvinistic Methodism*, 86.

[429] G. Williams, *Samuel Roberts, Llanbrynmair* (Cardiff, 1950), 51–3.

[430] Jones, *Explorations and Explanations*, 138–9, 303 n. 36.

[431] Aspland, *Memoir of Aspland*, 440.

[432] Jones and Williams, *Religious Census, South Wales*, i. 328–9.

[433] R. Halley, *Lancashire: Its Puritanism and Nonconformity* (1869), ii. 462.

[434] Woodcock, *Piety among the Peasantry*, 129, 134.

refused them permission to build in the village centre until 1880.[435] And at Dyke near Clovelly in north Devon in 1858 the landlord, Sir J. Hamlyn Williams, evicted the Bible Christians from a converted barn in which they had worshipped for more than twenty years.[436]

In Nottinghamshire, where 38 per cent of the land was 'occupied by estates which in aggregate exceeded 10,000 acres' Nonconformists were particularly at the mercy of aristocratic favour.[437] Two of the county's most powerful landowners, the Duke of Newcastle and Lord Middleton, were largely successful in keeping Nonconformist congregations out of the villages in which they were principal proprietors, and when Nonconformist services were held they were usually confined to private houses.[438] On occasion Nottinghamshire's Methodists resorted to ingenious devices to circumvent the problem of finding sites for the chapels in villages in which all the land was owned by unsympathetic landlords. In 1844 the Wesleyans in the Bingham circuit paid a Mr Clifton £60 to construct at Sibthorpe an 'elegant moveable wooden chapel on wheels' with seating for 130 people which could if necessary be towed to other villages in the circuit where all 'the land was the property of noblemen or other landed proprietors'.[439] At nearby Shelford the Earl of Chesterfield was the only landowner and two villagers who allowed their stud and mud cottages to be used by the Primitive Methodists had their homes demolished by the earl's steward. But the Ranters got round the problem by purchasing a boat which had been used as a waterman's chapel in Nottingham. The chapel was floated down the Trent to Shelford and pulled ashore into Matthew Woodward's garden to be used for Primitive Methodist services.[440]

Not all landlords, though, tried to stem the growth of Dissent, and not all were successful when they tried. A few landowners went out of their way to assist in the building of Nonconformist chapels. The lord of the manor of Brompton near Northallerton in the North Riding not only allowed Wesleyans to build a chapel on his land in 1794, but charged no rent for it.[441] In Peterborough in 1833 Earl Fitzwilliam both found the Wesleyans a site for a chapel in a new thoroughfare he was constructing and headed their subscription list with a donation of £25.[442] Although Sir Tatton Sykes had denied

---

[435] B. Greaves, 'An Analysis of the Spread of Methodism in Yorkshire during the Eighteenth and early Nineteenth Centuries', MA thesis (Leeds, 1961), 24.

[436] Bourne, *Life of James Thorne*, 86.

[437] F. M. L. Thompson, *English Landed Society in the Nineteenth Century* (1963), 32.

[438] Watts, *Religion in Victorian Nottinghamshire*, i, p. xviii.

[439] R. C. Swift, 'A Chapel on Wheels', *PWHS* 28 (1952), 122–3.

[440] Herod, *Biographical Sketches*, 347–50 n.

[441] B. Greaves, 'Methodism in Yorkshire', Ph.D. thesis (Liverpool, 1968), 182.

[442] *Wesleyan Methodist Magazine*, 58 (1835), 61.

the Primitive Methodists land for chapels in the villages he owned in the Yorkshire Wolds, after his death in 1863 his son and heir allowed the Ranters to build chapels in Wansford, Wetwang, and Sledmere, commenting that 'if it had not been for the Dissenters the English people would have been heathens'.[443] In Nottinghamshire the hostility which Nonconformists encountered from the Duke of Newcastle was counterbalanced by the tolerance of the Duke of Portland, who not only allowed Methodists to build chapels on his land—including the Wesleyans' chapel-on-wheels at Sibthorpe—but gave permission to the New Connexion Methodists to take all the stone they wanted from his quarry for the building of their chapel at Hucknall.[444] At Retford in the same county the Duke of Norfolk, although a Roman Catholic, gave timber and window frames from Kiveton Hall for inclusion in the Wesleyan chapel.[445] And at Shelford the Earl of Chesterfield lacked either the motivation or the pertinacity of his persecuting steward, for by 1851 Wesleyans and Primitive Methodists in the village outnumbered Anglicans by over a hundred.[446]

A glance at the maps illustrating the distribution of Nonconformists in mid-nineteenth-century Wales will show just how futile was the policy of the Watkin Williams Wynns in trying to stem the growth of Dissent in Merioneth, Montgomeryshire, and Denbighshire: owners of vast estates in upland regions could not control the religious behaviour of their tenants in the same way that resident squires in the south of England could do. And indeed one suspects that the action of landlords like Sir Watkin in making martyrs of Calvinistic Methodist farmers did Nonconformity more good than harm, and that the alliance between the Church of England and the landowning class could on occasion do the established church more harm than good. In Wales the close ties between English-speaking landlords and the Anglican clergy inevitably predisposed the Welsh-speaking tenantry in favour of Dissent. In several parishes in the principality, wrote the Congregationalist Thomas Rees, 'the most convenient part of the Sabbath is chosen by the rector to preach to the *élite* of the parish' in English, 'while an inconveniently early or late hour is allotted to the common people to hear a sermon from the curate' in Welsh. By such methods, commented Rees, 'the clergy of the establishment ... have emptied their churches'.[447]

---

[443] Woodcock, *Piety among the Peasantry*, 135–7, 144.
[444] W. White, *History, Gazetter and Directory of Nottinghamshire* (1853), 573–4; Swift, *Lively People*, 86.
[445] B. J. Biggs, 'Methodism in a Rural Society: North Nottinghamshire, 1740–1851', Ph.D. thesis (Nottingham, 1975), 284.
[446] Watts, *Religion in Victorian Nottinghamshire*, ii. 306.
[447] T. Rees, *Miscellaneous Papers on Subjects Relating to Wales* (1867), 28. Rees's point is sub-

In England the rise in the economic and social status of the parish clergy which followed acts of enclosure and the commutation of tithes for land drove a wedge between the Anglican clergy and their poorer parishioners. Many Anglican incumbents became owners of estates worth more than £100 a year which entitled them to serve as justices of the peace, and by 1831 22 per cent of all magistrates in England and Wales were clergymen, administering game laws designed to prevent the poor from sharing the bounty of the country-side.[448] W. R. Ward has argued that resentment at the new status of the clergy following the exchange of tithes for land assisted the spread of Nonconformity in rural England.[449] No direct evidence, so far as I know, has been produced to sustain this thesis and the example of Yorkshire would seem to contradict it: before 1831 most tithe commutation in the county had occurred in the arable vale of York, the one part of Yorkshire (apart from Sedbergh and Settle) where Anglicans outnumbered Nonconformists in 1851.[450] But the counties which had the highest proportion of clerical magistrates in 1831—Lincolnshire (47 per cent), Cambridgeshire (45 per cent), Bedfordshire (41 per cent), and Northamptonshire (39.5 per cent)—were all counties in which Dissent had the adherence of more than 20 per cent of the population twenty years later.[451] Warwickshire, however, had a high proportion of clerical magistrates (36 per cent), and a very low level of support for Dissent in 1851, and the explanation of the connection between the large number of clergymen serving as justices in the other counties and the strength of Nonconformity may lie in the lack of resident lay landowners rather than in hostility towards the clergy.[452]

Notwithstanding the failure of landlord influence to halt the advance of Nonconformity in Wales, there is ample evidence that elsewhere the absence of a resident landowner was a powerful encouragement to Dissent. D. E. Evans, in his history of Congregationalism in the village of Dursley in Gloucestershire, ascribes the success of Dissent in this Cotswold valley to the fact that 'for hundreds of years there have been no great landowners living here', and that the area had been populated instead by a succession of

---

stantiated by Morgan, 'Diocese of St David's', *Journal of the Historical Society of the Church of Wales*, 23 (1973), 33–6.

[448] E. J. Evans, 'Some Reasons for the Growth of English Rural Anti-clericalism, c.1750–c.1830', *Past and Present*, 66 (1975), 101.

[449] W. R. Ward, 'The Tithe Question in England in the Early Nineteenth Century', *Journal of Ecclesiastical History*, 16 (1965), 74.

[450] Greaves, 'Analysis of the Spread of Methodism', 44.

[451] Evans, 'Rural Anti-clericalism', 104.

[452] This was certainly the case in Lincolnshire (Obelkevich, *Religion and Rural Society*, 31–2).

'independent or semi-independent farmers and woollen cloth workers'.[453] What the absence of a squire could mean to a parish church was recorded by the vicar of Shillington in Bedfordshire in 1851 when he noted on his census return that since all the landowners were non-resident 'little interest' was 'taken in the labouring population' and 'great ignorance' prevails. As a result only 152 adults and 49 Sunday scholars out of a total population of 1,598 attended the parish church's one service on census Sunday and Nonconformist services attracted three times as many worshippers.[454] In Kent, Leicestershire, Northamptonshire, Nottinghamshire, and in the Lindsey division of Lincolnshire, Nonconformist chapels were far more numerous in 'open' villages in which land was owned by a multiplicity of small freeholders than in 'closed' villages in which land was in the hands of a few single landowners. Out of 119 parishes in Leicestershire, Lindsey, and Northamptonshire which were owned by single landowners, Alan Everitt was able to find only three that had a Nonconformist place of worship. In contrast over three-quarters of the 'open' parishes had Nonconformist chapels.[455] In Nottinghamshire support for Nonconformists rose from less than 10 per cent in 'closed' villages to over 30 per cent in villages in which land was either divided among several proprietors or owned by numerous freeholders.[456] The presence of a large number of freeholder villages in the vale of Belvoir more than compensated for the hostility of landowners in closed villages, especially when the population of the freehold villages was on average nearly three times as large as that of the closed villages. The number of freeholders in the vale of Belvoir helps to explain why, in 1851, the Wesleyans and Primitive Methodists in the Bingham district scored their highest percentage attendances in Nottinghamshire and combined to give the highest Nonconformist attendances proportionate to the total population in the whole of the east Midlands. Elsewhere in England Dissent flourished, in the nineteenth as in the previous centuries, in rural areas such as the Fens of Cambridgeshire and Lincolnshire, the Isle of Axholme, and the Chilterns of Buckinghamshire in which small freeholders predominated.[457] The Isle of Ely affords a particularly instructive example of a continuing radical

---

[453] Evans, *As Mad as a Hatter!*, 9.

[454] D. W. Bushby (ed.), 'Bedfordshire Ecclesiastical Census, 1851', *Publications of the Bedfordshire Historical Record Society*, 54 (1975), 149–50.

[455] A. Everitt, *The Pattern of Rural Dissent in the Nineteenth Century* (Leicester, 1972), 20–1. Similar conclusions have been reached by Thompson and Ambler in more detailed studies of Leicestershire and Lincolnshire (D. M. Thompson, 'The Churches and Society in Leicestershire, 1851–1881', Ph.D. thesis (Cambridge, 1969), 40–1; Ambler, *Lincolnshire Returns*, pp. lxvii–lxix).

[456] Watts, *Religion in Victorian Nottinghamshire*, i, p. xviii.

[457] Watts, *The Dissenters*, i. 283–4, 353.

tradition: in the sixteenth century the governments of Elizabeth were troubled by the activities of the Family of Love in the area; in the seventeenth
century the people of the Isle rioted against the drainage and enclosure of the
Fens; in the Civil War the inhabitants of Ely rallied to the parliamentary
cause and its radicalism prompted Thomas Edwards to condemn it as 'the
island of errors and sectaries';[458] in the middle of the nineteenth century north
Cambridgeshire had nearly twice as many Nonconformist worshippers as
Anglicans; in the 1980s the Isle of Ely was one of the few English constituencies to elect a Liberal MP.

One of the reasons for the strength of Dissent in Cambridgeshire and Lincolnshire was the size and shape of the parishes. As land had been reclaimed
from the fens or from the sea it had been added to existing parishes with the
result that many parishes grew into long, narrow shapes, and people living in
the 'new' parts of the parish could find themselves anything up to twelve miles
from their parish church. The vicar of Pinchbeck near Spalding wrote to
the Bishop of Lincoln in 1845 that his parish was 'nine miles in length, by four
in breadth, and the church nearly being at the end of it, renders it a matter
of great difficulty for the inhabitants of the distant parts to attend it, particularly as those inhabitants are generally speaking of the poorer class, who
have no means of conveyance'. The most populous part of the parish, he
added, was 'between two and three miles from the church so that Dissent has
obtained a footing there, for which state of things we can hardly blame the
people'. In 1851 Pinchbeck, with a population of 3,062, had two General
Baptist chapels, two Wesleyan chapels, one Independent chapel, and one
Primitive Methodist chapel with a total estimated attendance of over five
hundred.[459]

The situation in Pinchbeck was repeated in hundreds of parishes in the
mountainous regions of Wales, among the Pennine moorlands of Lancashire
and Yorkshire, in the valleys of Durham. Some of the happiest hunting-
grounds for Nonconformists were on the fringes of large parishes where people were still ready to embrace a supernatural view of the world but where
the Church of England was too remote to cater for their immediate needs.
One reason for the support of Methodism in Cornwall lay in the fact that
many parish churches had been built on sites revered because of their connections with the Irish missionaries who brought Christianity to Cornwall
but which were often remote from their parishioners.[460] The strength of

[458] T. Edwards, *Gangraena* (3rd edn., 1646), part ii, 29.
[459] Ambler, *Lincolnshire Returns*, pp. xxxvi–xxxviii, 18–19.
[460] J. D. Gay, *The Geography of Religion in England* (1971), 159–60.

Methodism in Staithes in the North Riding can in part be explained by the fact that its parish church, at Hinderwell, was a mile from the village and no provision was made for Anglican worship in Staithes itself until 1849.[461] Even where an Anglican church was conveniently situated there was no guarantee that its incumbent would make any effort to retain the loyalty of his parishioners. One of Josiah Thompson's correspondents in 1772 reported of Irthlingborough in Northamptonshire that 'twenty years ago there were not a dozen Dissenters in the place, but there is now a congregation in very flourishing circumstances consisting of upwards of 200 members . . . owing in a great measure to the gradual and now total neglect of divine service in the church'.[462] And even when an Anglican incumbent was an enthusiastic Evangelical there was no certainty that his work would not ultimately benefit Dissent rather than the Church. When the Hon. William Bromley Cadogan, the Evangelical vicar of St Giles, Reading, died in 1797, and his hearers were unable to obtain an Evangelical successor, they seceded to form a separate congregation which was initially served by ministers of Lady Huntingdon's Connexion and in 1836 became a Congregational church.[463] Similar circumstances produced secessions from the parish churches at Farnham in Surrey in 1793, at Longton in Staffordshire, and at Turvey in Bedfordshire, and to the formation of three more Congregational churches.[464] John Thorne, the patriarch of the Devonshire dynasty of Bible Christians, worshipped contentedly at his parish church as long as it had an Evangelical curate, David Evans, but when Evans was removed by the Bishop of Exeter on account of his Evangelical sympathies and replaced by a clergyman whose sermons 'had no Saviour in it', Thorne left the parish church and in 1817, with his son James, resolved to build the first Bible Christian chapel at Lake near Shebbear.[465]

The plight of the Church of England was epitomized in the return of John Jones, vicar of Nevern in Pembrokeshire, to the religious census. The tithe had been commuted for a rent charge, of which £193 a year went to the vicar and £579 to a lay impropriator who contributed 'nothing towards the spiritual wants of the parishioners', save a few bottles of communion wine at Easter.

---

[461] Clark, *Between Pulpit and Pew*, 58.

[462] Josiah Thompson, List of Dissenting Congregations, DWL MS 34.5.6. A similar situation was reported from Hinckley in Leicestershire.

[463] W. H. Summers, *History of the Congregational Churches in the Berkshire, South Oxfordshire, and South Buckinghamshire Association* (Newbury, 1905), 179–84.

[464] A. G. Matthews, *The Congregational Churches of Staffordshire* (1924), 17; A. D. Gilbert, 'The Growth and Decline of Nonconformity in England and Wales', D.Phil. thesis (Oxford, 1973), 244; Brown, *Bedfordshire Union of Christians*, 49.

[465] F. W. Bourne, *The Centenary Life of James Thorne of Shebbear* (1895), 75–7, 175–6.

The parish consisted of 1,642 people scattered over twenty-two square miles, but in a quarter-mile radius from the parish church there were only seventeen cottages, a mill, and a farm. The parish was so extensive, acknowledged the vicar, that 'the distant inhabitants cannot attend their parish church'. 'They would be living as heathens had not the Dissenters built chapels in different parts of the parish, of which there are *six* chapels.' Even those who attended the Nevern parish church in the morning, added Jones, went to a 'chapel in their different localities in the evening'.[466] On census Sunday 236 people attended the parish church. The estimated attendance at the six Dissenting chapels was nearly 1,000.

If that was the state of the Church of England in an entirely agricultural parish in Pembrokeshire, how much more was it its condition in the rapidly industrializing regions of south Wales, the west Midlands, and the West Riding of Yorkshire. It was suggested in the first volume of this work that even in the early eighteenth century the strength of Dissent in places as diverse as Newcastle upon Tyne, Manchester, Nottingham, and Taunton was in part the consequence of the failure of the Church of England to cater for the increased population of those towns.[467] As early as 1736 the vicar of Ecclesfield noted that in Sheffield there were 'a great many who go to the meeting-houses for want of seats' in the parish church, and a great many more who 'go nowhere at all'.[468] And with the industrial revolution comments that trade worked to the disadvantage of the established church and-facilitated the growth of Methodism and Dissent multiplied. The mayor of Liverpool wrote to the Home Office in 1792 pleading for the construction of parish churches in the industrial villages of Lancashire since 'in all these places [there] are nothing but Methodist and other meeting houses, and as the people in the country are in general disposed to go to some place of worship on the Sunday, they go to these because there is no other'.[469] If Thomas Taylor blamed the lack of response to his ministrations in the York circuit in the 1780s in part on the power of the landlords, the other side of the coin was the lack of trade. 'There is but little trade in any part of the circuit; and where there is little trade, there is seldom much increase in religion.'[470] George Eliot noticed in villages in parts of the Midlands that where there were no hand-looms or mines there were no Dissenters: in *Adam Bede* she puts into

---

[466] Jones and Williams, *Religious Census, South Wales*, 462–5.
[467] Watts, *The Dissenters*, i. 277–8.
[468] Greaves, 'Methodism in Yorkshire', 54.
[469] J. L. and B. Hammond, *The Town Labourer* (1925), 270.
[470] Jackson, *Early Methodist Preachers*, v. 56.

Mrs Poyser's mouth the observation that 'It's on'y trades folks as turn Methodists; you niver knew a farmer bitten wi' them maggots'.[471]

Such generalizations are open to serious objection. The maps at the end of this volume show that throughout much of England and Wales Nonconformity, and especially Methodism, commanded the support of a higher proportion of the population in rural than in urban areas. And Tables XV–LXVI show that in numerous counties a substantial proportion of male Dissenters earned their living either as farmers (especially in the case of the Quakers and Calvinistic Methodists) or, more often, as agricultural labourers. But there is no doubt that the growth of industry in the late eighteenth and early nineteenth centuries freed workers from their dependence on the parson and the squire and created conditions in which both Methodism and Dissent might expand. In 1796 the Baptist ministers John Saffery and William Steadman reported of their mission to Cornwall that the inhabitants, 'being either miners or fishermen, are more in a state of independence, and less subject to the influence of superiors, who may be hostile to itinerant preaching, than those counties which depend wholly upon agriculture'.[472] Much the same could have been said of the miners and nailers of the Black Country, the framework knitters of the Trent valley, the quarry workers of north Wales, and the ironworkers of south Wales, all of whom proved to be particularly responsive to the appeal of Evangelical Nonconformity.[473] The rector of Llanddeiniolen in Caernarfonshire reported in 1851 that his church was 'well placed as regards the old agricultural population' of his parish, but that 'the bulk of the present population which has during the past forty years, been drawn together by the working of Mr Assheton Smith's slate quarries, lies at a distance from the church of from three to five miles', and to serve that population thirteen Dissenting chapels had been built.[474] An estimated 3,230 people attended the Nonconformist chapels in Llanddeiniolen on census Sunday—66 per cent of the population of the parish—while the total number of attendants at Anglican worship was just 75. In such circumstances the level of Nonconformist support could sometimes be a good deal higher in industrial areas than in the surrounding countryside. In Monmouthshire the proportion of the total population attending a Nonconformist chapel was much

---

[471] George Eliot, *Felix Holt, the Radical* (Oxford, 1980), 6; ead., *Adam Bede* (Everyman edn., 1960), 185–6.

[472] Gilbert, *Religion and Society*, 108, citing *The Baptist Annual Register*, 2 (1796), 459–64.

[473] E. Hopkins, 'Religious Dissent in Black Country Industrial Villages in the First Half of the Nineteenth Century', *Journal of Ecclesiastical History*, 34 (1983), 419; Gilbert, *Religion and Society*, 109.

[474] Jones, *Religious Census, North Wales*, 324.

higher in the industrial districts of Abergavenny and Pontypool than in the more rural districts of Chepstow and Monmouth; in Worcestershire the heavily industrialized district of Stourbridge had the highest level of Nonconformist support in an otherwise largely agricultural county; and across the county boundary the neighbouring Black Country district of Dudley had by far the largest proportion of the inhabitants of any Staffordshire district in a Nonconformist chapel on census Sunday (nearly 30 per cent), and also the highest overall level of religious observance in the county.[475] It was precisely these overcrowded, poorly paid, and largely illiterate working-class communities of south Wales and the Black Country that were most deeply affected by the religious revival that accompanied the cholera epidemic of 1849.

South Wales provides us with the most extreme example of the way in which industrialization accentuated the existing inadequacies and corruption of the Church of England and provided Dissent with opportunities for spectacular growth. In the south-east corner of Breconshire lay a group of parishes—Llangattock, Llangynidr, Llanelly, Llangenny, Crickhowell, and Cwmdu—all of which were in the gift of the Duke of Beaufort, and all of which apart from Llangynidr were bestowed by the fifth duke on his sixth son, Lord George Henry Somerset. In addition Lord George held the living of Tormarton in Gloucestershire and was a prebendary of the cathedral church of Bristol. He was absent from all his Welsh livings and was said to have preached only twice in Bristol cathedral in twenty-two years. None the less he received a total of £2,818 a year from these sinecures, from which he paid three curates the modest total of £356. Unfortunately for the Church of England, two of the parishes from which Lord George Henry Somerset gained such a large unearned income, Llangattock and Llanelly, had experienced a rapid increase in population as a result of the development of the iron industry in the Ebbw Fawr and Clydach valleys in the late eighteenth century and the construction of the Brecknock and Abergavenny canal.[476] Together with Llangynidr these parishes had a population of 18,305 in 1851, and to serve them the Church of England had four churches (one of which had been opened only in 1850), a licensed lecture room, and a service in the union workhouse. To make matters worse, the parish churches of both

---

[475] Cf. Davies, *Religion in the Industrial Revolution*, 36; G. Robson, 'Between Town and Countryside: Contrasting Patterns of Churchgoing in the Early Victorian Black Country', in D. Baker (ed.), *Studies in Church History*, xvi (1979), 402–3; E. Hopkins, 'Religious Dissent in Black Country Industrial Villages', 411–24.

[476] Morgan, 'Diocese of St David's', *Journal of the Historical Society of the Church in Wales*, 21 (1971), 35–6; 22 (1972), 31–4.

Llangattock and Llangynidr lay some five miles from the bulk of their parish-ioners, and between the people and the churches there straggled 'a large and extensive track of mountain and wild uninhabited country'.[477] While the Church of England had only five places of worship open to the general public on census Sunday, the Nonconformists offered a total of thirty-eight places of worship: thirteen Independent, eleven Particular Baptist, eight Wesleyan Methodist, three Calvinistic Methodist, and three Primitive Methodist. According to estimates based on the census returns 1,104 people attended Anglican services in the three parishes on census Sunday, a mere 6 per cent of the total population. The Nonconformist chapels attracted ten times that number: 11,343, or 62 per cent of the total population of Llangat-tock, Llanelly, and Llangynidr. These three parishes also illustrate the con-nection between illiteracy and Dissent: two-thirds of the male population of the Crickhowell registration district who were married in 1851 were unable to sign the marriage registers.

If industrialization, in its early stages, facilitated the growth of Dissent, large-scale urbanization frustrated it. The social needs which attracted men and women to Nonconformist chapels and the psychological pressures which impelled them to experience Evangelical conversion operated most effec-tively in comparatively small self-contained unsophisticated communities. The fishing villages of Yorkshire and Cornwall, the hosiery villages of the east Midlands, the mining communities of Cornwall and Durham, and the industrial villages of the Black Country and south Wales all responded to the appeals of Evangelical Nonconformity. But in the large urban concentra-tions of London, Birmingham, Liverpool, and Manchester not only were men free from the social and economic pressures of the established church, they were also largely free from the psychological pressures of Methodism and Dissent. Industrialization freed men from the control of the Church, urbanization freed them from the influence of religion.

In the early eighteenth century Nonconformity was proportionately stronger in large towns and cities than it was in the countryside,[478] but by the mid-nineteenth century the growth of Methodism had largely reversed the position. In some parts of England in 1851 Old Dissent was still a predominantly urban phenomenon: in Nottinghamshire the strength of Congregationalism lay in the market towns which had had a significant Nonconformist presence in 1715, and the Baptists were largely concentrated in Nottingham itself and some of its suburbs. But the overwhelming strength

---

[477] Jones and Williams, *Religious Census, South Wales*, 610.
[478] Watts, *The Dissenters*, i. 285–6.

of Methodism in the county lay in villages of between 400 and 1,000 people, with the result that Nonconformity as a whole had the support of 30 per cent of the population in communities between 400 and 5,000 inhabitants and was weaker both in very small and in comparatively large communities.[479] In this respect Nottinghamshire was probably typical of the rest of the country. Nonconformity found some medium-sized towns of around 30,000 to 60,000 people—places such as Dudley, Leicester, Merthyr Tydfil, and Rochdale—conducive to growth. And in a number of towns of between 100,000 and 200,000—Bradford, Bristol, Leeds, Wolverhampton—Nonconformity had the support of around 18 per cent of the total population, a figure slightly above the national average for England.[480] But in the largest English towns—London, Liverpool, Manchester, Birmingham—Nonconformity found almost as much difficulty as the Church of England in coping with the problems posed by the agglomeration of vast numbers of people in a limited space. In all these towns of more than 200,000 people Nonconformists attracted the support of only 10 per cent or less of the population on census Sunday. Table VI gives the strength of Dissent in a number of large and medium-sized towns where a direct comparison is possible between the level of support in the early eighteenth century and in the mid-nineteenth century. While the size of the Dissenting community in proportion to the total population of England nearly trebled between 1715 and 1851—from 6.21 per cent to 17.02 per cent—and in some counties such as Bedfordshire and Cambridgeshire quadrupled, the proportion of Nonconformist support in most of the towns listed in Table VI either did not increase at all or, in some cases, declined. Dissent in Nottingham still retained the allegiance of a quarter of the town's population, although the artificial restriction of the town's boundaries gave an unduly favourable picture of the situation within the limits of the future city; in Leicester Nonconformist support doubled between 1715 and 1851; and the addition of the Methodists had brought Nonconformity as a whole some modest gains in London—although its support in the capital in the mid-nineteenth century still fell short of 10 per cent of the total population. On the other hand, the decline of Presbyterianism in its former strongholds of Manchester and Bolton had resulted in the Nonconformist proportion of the population in those towns nearly halving between 1715 and 1851. But what is remarkable about most of the towns listed

---

[479] Watts, *Religion in Victorian Nottinghamshire*, i, p. xxx.

[480] These calculations are based on the figures for large towns on pp. ccliii–cclxxii of the *Religious Census*, and because the boundaries of the towns did not coincide with those of the registration districts, the figures used in this section are sometimes different from those given in Table XIV.

TABLE VI. *Nonconformists as a percentage of the total population in major towns: 1715–1718 and 1851*

	1715–1718		1851			
	Population	Nonconformists	Population	Old Dissenters[a]	Methodists	Total Nonconformists
Bolton	5,500	19.9	61,171	4.9	5.8	11.6
Bristol	28,170	19.6	137,328	10.2	6.8	18.6
Leicester	6,000	11.3	60,584	14.5	6.7	21.7
Liverpool	12,500	9.3	375,995	3.5	3.9	8.0
London and Middlesex	581,180	5.7	2,512,842	6.6	1.9	9.0
Manchester	8,000	18.9	303,382	5.2	4.6	10.3
Newcastle upon Tyne	18,000	11.1	87,784	6.0	4.9	11.2
Nottingham	8,000	23.3	57,407	11.8	12.6	25.0
Sheffield	10,000	13.6	135,310	4.2	8.0	12.2

[a] I have included the New Connexion of General Baptists under the heading of Old Dissent in order to distinguish them from the Methodists. This helps to explain the unusual strength of 'Old Dissent' in both Leicester and Nottingham.

in Table VI is the way in which the strength of Nonconformity is shown to have been virtually the same at the time of the 1851 religious census as it was at the time of the compilation of the Evans list nearly a century and a half earlier. There were, of course, major shifts of allegiance between the various Nonconformist denominations between the two surveys. In London the Congregationalists, who had quadrupled their support, had replaced the Presbyterians as the largest Nonconformist denomination. In Bristol it was again the Congregationalists who had usurped the leading Dissenting positions occupied in 1715 by the Presbyterians and the Quakers. And in Nottingham it was the Wesleyans and the Baptists who had supplanted the Presbyterians as the strongest of the Nonconformist groups. But the most significant conclusion to be drawn from a comparison of Dissenting strength in large towns in 1715 and 1851 is that while Nonconformity had made enormous gains in the countryside, industrial villages, and smaller towns of England, in the larger urban areas Dissent, even with the addition of the Methodists, was struggling, in the mid-nineteenth century, just to maintain its position of a century and a half earlier. And if one looks at the figures for Old Dissent alone, in most towns the percentage of the total population supporting the Congregationalists, Baptists, Presbyterians, and Quakers together had halved between the compilation of Dr Evans's list and the religious census.

Why did Old Dissent find its proportion of the total population halved and why was Nonconformity as a whole unable to do more than mark time in the large urban concentrations? The answer lies in the absence of those factors that so powerfully aided the advance of Dissent in the countryside and the industrial villages: a residual attachment to Christianity which the Church of England fostered but could not always exploit to its own advantage, a sense of helplessness that derived from man's reliance on the vagaries of the seasons and his exposure to sudden catastrophes such as mine explosions or cholera epidemics, and the geographical and cultural isolation which meant that both superstitious and Evangelical explanations of human fate were widely accepted and not seriously challenged. In the early Christian centuries it was the Christians who were urbanized and 'civilized', it was the pagans who were country dwellers. In the nineteenth century the position was reversed. In the wheat-growing areas of Cambridgeshire and Lincolnshire, on the sheep-farming hills of Wales, in the tin and copper mines of Cornwall, in the fishing villages of the East Riding of Yorkshire, men and women in the reign of Queen Victoria could still feel that their lives were determined by unseen forces infinitely more powerful than themselves. By contrast in London, in Birmingham, in Manchester men were conscious that their housing conditions, working conditions, and expectations of life were determined not by unseen forces but by landlords, employers, poor law guardians, and medical officers of health. William Hale White's 'Mark Rutherford' felt something of this: 'When I was living in the country, the pure sky and the landscape formed a large portion of my existence, so large that much of myself depended on it, and I wondered how men could be anything if they could never see the face of nature.' But when he moved to London he found the contrast between his deep love of nature and the stark reality of urban life deeply depressing: 'Hope, faith, and God seemed impossible amidst the smoke of the streets.'[481]

Some historians have been so impressed by the dislocation experienced by men and women who moved from the countryside to the towns in the first half of the nineteenth century that they have concluded that it was a major factor in the secularization of modern society. K. S. Inglis points out that 'the census of 1851 showed that in all towns (except Leeds) at least half the inhabitants were immigrants from the countryside' and argues that 'among the immigrants were many . . . who had worshipped in their village where religious practice was a familiar part of the weekly round' but who subsequently lost the habit when they found themselves in an urban environment.[482] There is no doubt some truth in this, but it is equally true that men and women took with them to the towns habits—both religious and irreligious—acquired in the countryside. The continuity between rural and urban religious practice was as important as the discontinuity. As Hugh McLeod has emphasized, most migration in the first half of the nineteenth century took place over short distances, and 'the majority of migrants would be no more than a few hours walk from the village or town of their birth'.[483] One of the reasons for the contrast between the comparatively high level of Nonconformist support in Nottingham and Leicester and Nonconformist weakness in Birmingham was that Nottingham and Leicester were attracting immigrants from the villages and small towns of the east Midlands where Dissent was strong while Birmingham was absorbing immigrants from Staffordshire, Worcestershire, and Warwickshire where, on the whole, Nonconformity was weak. One of the contributory factors to the extreme feebleness of Nonconformity in

---

[481] W. H. White, *The Autobiography of Mark Rutherford and Mark Rutherford's Deliverance* (2nd edn., 1888), 149.

[482] K. S. Inglis, *Churches and the Working Classes in Victorian England* (1963), 3–4. For supporting evidence see D. Thompson, 'The Churches and Society in Leicestershire, 1851–1881', Ph.D. thesis (Cambridge, 1969), 333–4.

[483] H. McLeod, 'Class, Community, and Religion: The Religious Geography of Nineteenth Century England', in M. Hill (ed.), *A Sociological Yearbook of Religion in Britain*, vi (1973), 37–8.

Liverpool was the fact that in 1851 nearly 30 per cent of the town's adult population had been born in Ireland. By contrast a major factor in the strength of Dissent in Merthyr Tydfil was the fact that this, the fastest growing and largest town in Wales, was attracting immigrants from rural counties where Nonconformity was predominant. The development of the iron industry increased the town's population from 18,000 in 1821 to 63,080 in 1851, and at the time of the 1851 census only 26 per cent of Merthyr's adult population was native to the town. Fifty-six per cent of Merthyr's men and women had been born elsewhere in south Wales, and rural and predominantly Nonconformist Carmarthenshire contributed far more immigrants (20 per cent of Merthyr's total adult population) than any other Welsh county. All the ragamuffins, thieves, and dregs of a vast population found their way to Merthyr, complained the town's rector, 'as decomposed elements in refuse water all gravitated to the bottom of the basin'.[484] He had cause to be bitter: an absentee predecessor was said to have visited the parish but once in thirty-two years, 'when he came in a post-chaise . . . to vote for a church rate',[485] so that by 1851 fewer than 4 per cent of the town's population worshipped in an Anglican church on census Sunday. But more than half the population of Merthyr attended a Methodist or Dissenting chapel on 30 March 1851: immigrants who had brought with them to the town the devotion to Evangelical religion and to Nonconformist worship that they had learned in the Welsh countryside.

Migration was thus no barrier to church growth, and social immobility was no guarantee of religious prosperity. Over 70 per cent of the inhabitants of Bethnal Green in 1851 had been born in London, and over 80 per cent of Bethnal Green's population avoided religious worship on census Sunday. Their absence from church or chapel was brought about not by recent migration from the countryside, but by attitudes and habits inherited from generations of Londoners going back to at least the Reformation. The anti-clericalism among Londoners provoked by Hunne's case in 1514, the hostility to orthodox religion which surfaced in the parish of St Stephen's, Coleman Street, in the 1640s, and the antipathy to all religion in the east end of London revealed by the religious census, were all part of the same historical process.[486] The growth of London provided a cultural melting-pot into which was poured differing religious and irreligious attitudes, one man's

---

[484] W. Lambert, *Drink and Sobriety in Victorian Wales* (Cardiff, 1983), 54 n. 166.
[485] P. E. Razzell and R. W. Wainwright, *The Victorian Working Class* (1973), 262, citing the *Morning Chronicle*, 15 Apr. 1850.
[486] D. A. Kirby, 'The Parish of St Stephen's, Coleman Street', B.Litt. thesis (Oxford, 1968), *passim*; Watts, *The Dissenters*, i. 69, 82–3, 112, 115, 122 n.

religion became as valid as another's, the freedom to embrace a variety of religious opinions often led to the option to embrace no religion at all, and if religious belief survived it was as a very private matter. Both the social pressures to conform to the Church of England and the psychological pressures to undergo Evangelical conversion were much weaker in London and especially in the East End of London than they were in most other parts of England and Wales.[487] The religious census showed that 15 per cent of the capital's population attended an Anglican church on census Sunday and that 6.5 per cent attended one of the chapels of Old Dissent. This was a slight increase on the level of Nonconformist support in 1715 over a period in which London's population had more than quadrupled, and one must not underestimate the effort by which both the Congregationalists and the Baptists had significantly increased their level of support in the capital. In absolute terms there were as many Nonconformist worshippers in London in 1851 as there were in the Dissenting strongholds of Bedfordshire, Cambridgeshire, Huntingdonshire, and Wiltshire combined. But what was most remarkable about the census returns for London was their revelation of the extraordinary weakness of Methodism. The Wesleyans had the support of only 1.4 per cent of London's population, the Primitive Methodists had made almost no impact on the capital's working class, and all the Methodist denominations together attracted the adherence of less than 2 per cent of the inhabitants of the metropolis. Where the Church of England had failed to sow, the Nonconformists were unable to reap.

9. ITINERANT PREACHERS AND CAMP-MEETINGS: THE AGENCIES OF EXPANSION

The phenomenal expansion of Nonconformity in the first half of the nineteenth century thus took place in the countryside, the industrial villages, and the small and medium-sized towns of England and Wales where either language, the absence of landlord influence, the presence of trade and industry, or its own antiquated parochial structure undermined the influence of the Church of England, but where large-scale urbanization had not yet rendered Christianity either psychologically unnecessary or socially irrelevant. At a time when the population of England and Wales was increasing by around

---

[487] Cf. the view of Lou Wirth on the American city quoted by H. McLeod, 'Religion in the City', *Urban History Yearbook* (1978), 7.

two million people every ten years—and the decade 1811–21 saw the fastest recorded rate of population growth in English history[488]—and in an age when the English were moving around the country to a greater extent than at any time since the Anglo-Saxon invasions, the great advantage which Nonconformity possessed over the Church of England was flexibility. Whereas before 1818 the Church 'required an Act of Parliament, a grant of money, an educated gentleman, and a crop of lawyers' before it could establish a new cause, wrote E. R. Wickham, all the Methodists needed was 'a friendly barn and a zealous preacher'.[489] The Wesleyan Methodists had the most flexible organization of all the Nonconformist denominations in the late eighteenth century, a fact which goes far in explaining why they were the most successful. The most significant characteristic of Wesley's own ministry had been its itinerant nature: the ceaseless journeying from village to town and from town to city in a desperate effort to rescue as many men and women as possible from perdition before death swept them away and destroyed forever the possibility of their salvation. Wesley organized his preachers on the same itinerant basis, except that they were expected to go on the circuit not of the whole of the United Kingdom but of more restricted geographic areas, and were expected to stay in the same circuit for no more than two years. The ideal circuit, in Wesley's view, was one served by at least three preachers and necessitating at least 'four hundred miles riding in four weeks'.[490] As the number of preachers increased so the number of circuits grew—from 7 in England in 1746 to 68 in 1790 and to 336 in England and Wales in 1830[491]—but Wesley was always insistent that his preachers should not become, like so many of the ministers of Old Dissent, tied to one particular chapel. In 1786 he roundly condemned a proposed division of the Hull circuit since it implied that a preacher would stay in the same place for a fortnight. 'No one of our preachers must be still while I live,' he protested.[492] Two years later he made the same point to Hampshire Methodists: 'No preacher ought to stay either at Portsmouth, or Sarum, or any other place a whole week together.'[493] Contemporaries believed that the variety of preaching available from Methodist pulpits was one of the reasons for their appeal. Methodist preachers, wrote an Anglican clergyman in 1804, 'are perpetually changing, and this

---

[488] S. G. Checkland, *The Rise of Industrial Society in England* (1971), 27.
[489] E. R. Wickham, *Church and People in an Industrial City* (1957), 80.
[490] *The Letters of the Rev John Wesley*, ed. J. Telford (1931), viii. 206.
[491] *Minutes of the Methodist Conferences*, i (1821), 40, 224–6; vi (1833), 559–76.
[492] *Letters of John Wesley*, vii. 337.   [493] Ibid. viii. 104.

novelty alone is sufficient to seduce many from the Church who in matters of faith, as in other things, are fond of change'.[494]

The system of Methodist itinerancy was ideally suited to a society of rapidly growing yet widely dispersed settlements, both in England and Wales during the industrial revolution and in the expanding territories of the United States. By 1820 the Methodists had overtaken the Baptists as the largest denomination in America,[495] and by 1851 Arminian Methodist worshippers in England outnumbered all other Nonconformist worshippers put together. It is particularly significant that Methodism (in both its Calvinistic and its Arminian varieties) grew much faster than Old Dissent in predominantly agricultural areas such as northern and central Wales, Norfolk, Lincolnshire, and the North and East Ridings of Yorkshire. Yet Old Dissent had also had its itinerant evangelists in the past—Stephen Hughes in Carmarthenshire, Oliver Heywood in the West Riding, Richard Davis in Northamptonshire[496]— and both the Baptists and the Congregationalists were quick to learn from the Methodist success in the late eighteenth century. What is more, the Particular Baptists from 1792 and the Congregationalists from 1795 had been raising money to send missionaries to India and to the islands of the Pacific, and they were inevitably confronted with the question of why they were organizing themselves to convert foreigners when there were so many men and women nearer home who were going to hell because there were too few preachers to reach them.[497] As we have seen, the example of overseas missionary work was an important inspiration of missionary work in England. The Particular Baptist William Steadman had his interest in missionary work aroused by reading Jonathan Edwards's *Life of David Brainerd* which led him first to support the Baptist Missionary Society and then to advocate missionary work in England. 'Whilst it is readily allowed that the millions of heathens abroad call loudly for our help,' he wrote in 1797, 'do not the hundreds of thousands of little better than heathens at home call for our pity too?' Steadman suggested that Baptist ministers, though pastors of particular churches, should embark on itinerant preaching either by making frequent excursions 'in the villages around them' or by leaving their congregations for a season and making 'a more extensive circle'.[498]

Steadman adopted the second course in 1796 when he accompanied John Saffery on a mission to Cornwall, but the Baptists made little headway in the

[494] Stigant, 'Methodism and the Working Class', 55.
[495] W. S. Hudson, *Religion in America* (New York, 1965), 121.
[496] Watts, *The Dissenters*, i. 280–1, 292–3.
[497] Lovegrove, *Established Church, Sectarian People*, 25.
[498] W. Fancott, 'William Steadman's Hampshire Years', *Baptist Quarterly*, 16 (1955–6), 365.

duchy, and it was by pursuing the first alternative, itinerating from estab-lished centres, that both the Baptists and Congregationalists made the most effective contribution to the expansion of their denominations. Ministers, and more often laymen, went out from existing churches to the surrounding towns and villages, preached either in the open air or in the house of a sym-pathizer, and followed this up by renting a room, barn, or shop in which to hold regular services. Once a viable congregation had been gathered a small chapel would be built.[499] William Roby, who was minister of Lady Hunting-don's chapel in Wigan from 1788 to 1795, paid regular visits to eight neigh-bouring towns and villages, preaching to congregations in houses and barns. When he became minister of the Cannon Street Congregational church in Manchester in 1795 (which moved to Grosvenor Street in 1807) he contin-ued to itinerate and in thirty-five years contributed to the foundation of Congregational churches in Leigh, Hulme, Rochdale, Dukinfield, Oldham, and Salford. In addition, Roby saw the size of his own congregation grow from 150 to 1,200.[500] The Congregational church in Fish Street, Hull, began a mission to Holderness in 1798 and in the next twenty-two years was respon-sible for the gathering of congregations in fourteen towns and villages, eleven of which had their own chapel;[501] after a Particular Baptist church was formed at Grundisburgh in Suffolk in 1798 it became the centre of an evangelistic network which led to the formation of eight other churches;[502] the Congregational Old Meeting in Bedford established meetings in six surrounding villages between 1812 and the 1840s;[503] the Queen Street Con-gregational church in Wolverhampton sent out itinerant preachers to Wom-bourn, Tettenhall Wood, Heath Town, and Swindon between 1810 and 1839 and chapels were subsequently built in each of these places; and the King Street Congregational church in Dudley opened branch chapels in Tipton, Brierley Hill, Woodside, and Netherton between 1830 and 1858.[504] Most remarkable of all was the achievement of the Stoney Street New Connexion General Baptist church in Nottingham which helped in the formation of six-teen other churches in the area between 1775 and 1836, churches by which latter date had a total membership of 1,400.[505]

The Baptists and Congregationalists not only grafted the Methodist prin-ciple of itinerancy on to their own congregational systems, they also began to

[499] Harrison, 'Baptists of Nottinghamshire', i. 92.
[500] W. G. Robinson, *William Roby* (1954), 39–40, 93–7.
[501] Darwent, *The Story of Fish Street Church, Hull*, 128–9.
[502] A. J. Klaiber, *The Story of the Suffolk Baptists* (1931), 67.
[503] H. G. Tibbutt, *Bunyan Meeting, Bedford* (1950), 107–35.
[504] Cumberland, 'Nonconformity in the Black Country', 63.
[505] Harrison, 'Baptists of Nottinghamshire', i. 129.

see virtues in a form of church association which would secure the advantages of the Wesleyan connexional system without sacrificing the independence of the local church. The Particular Baptists had had regional associations as early as the 1650s, and following the Toleration Act associations for the West Country and for Yorkshire and Lancashire had been established.[506] Congregationalists from Nottinghamshire, Derbyshire, and south Yorkshire had formed an association in 1720 to protect Calvinist churches from Arian infiltration and the Independents of Norfolk and Suffolk had formed a regional association in 1751.[507] But it was under the impact of the Evangelical revival that the association movement among both the Particular Baptists and the Congregationalists flourished, and the need to co-operate in the task of evangelism was a major factor in persuading independent churches to come together in county and regional associations. In 1775 the Western Particular Baptist Association was founded 'to encourage evangelizing, or itinerant preaching'; in 1776 a group of Congregationalists, Baptists, and Evangelical Anglicans formed the 'Societas Evangelica' to sponsor itinerant evangelism; in the same year the Particular Baptist Fund and the Welsh Baptist Association financed the journeys of Dafydd Evans and Morgan Evans into Merioneth, Caernarfonshire, Anglesey, and Denbighshire; and in 1779 the Northamptonshire Baptist Association, founded fifteen years earlier, adopted village preaching as one of its aims.[508] Between 1792 and 1830 the Particular Baptists and Congregationalists founded sixty-eight additional associations (twelve Baptist, twenty-one Congregational, and thirty-five interdenominational) for the promotion of itinerant preaching.[509] Initially the funds at the disposal of these local associations were very limited and they could usually support only one or two paid evange lists, but with the formation of the Congregational Home Missionary Society in 1819 and with the reorganization of the Baptist Society in London for the Encouragement and Support of Itinerant and Village Preaching as the Baptist Home Missionary Society in 1821, the wider resources of both denominations could be tapped. By 1830 the Congregational Home Missionary Society was employing fifty-three full-time evangelists and the Baptist Home Missionary Society another thirty-six.[510] But the associations for the

---

[506] Watts, *The Dissenters*, i. 161–2, 166; A. C. Underwood, *A History of the English Baptists* (1947), 130, 172.

[507] A. R. Henderson, *History of the Castle Gate Congregational Church, Nottingham, 1655–1905* (1905), 109–10; Bolam, 'Presbyterianism in the counties of Derby, Leicester, and Nottingham', 535–40; Browne, *Congregationalism in Norfolk and Suffolk*, 188–9.

[508] Lovegrove, *Established Church, Sectarian People*, 32; T. Timpson, *Church History of Kent* (1859), 300; Bassett, *The Welsh Baptists*, 101–4.

[509] Lovegrove, *Established Church, Sectarian People*, 182–4.   [510] Ibid. 52, 200 n. 56.

furtherance of itinerant preaching were most effective when they encouraged the co-operation of local churches in providing preachers, usually laymen, for unevangelized towns and villages on something resembling the Methodist circuit system.[511] Within a year of its foundation in 1797 the interdenominational Bedfordshire Union of Christians was providing 150 lay preachers for nearly a hundred towns and villages in the county, and by 1816 it was giving financial assistance for the maintenance of preaching in at least twenty-seven different places.[512] Bedford's three Particular Baptist churches alone were sending out thirty preachers to the surrounding villages on every Sunday afternoon in 1798.[513] Similarly the Bristol Baptist Itinerant Society, founded in 1824, helped to establish nine new Baptist churches in neighbouring villages over a period of thirty years.[514] By 1827 the Norfolk and Suffolk Baptist Association was providing preachers for eighty-one villages in the two counties, and although the association split over the issue of closed versus open communion two years later, by 1837 the two successor associations were conducting services in 140 different villages.[515]

Bedfordshire and Bristol, though not Norfolk and Suffolk, had been Particular Baptist strongholds since the seventeenth century, and the success of the denomination's village preaching in these areas illustrates one of the limitations of the Particular Baptist and Congregational association method of encouraging itinerant evangelism: it was often most effective in areas of existing denominational strength and least effective where it was most needed. Occasional forays by Baptist itinerants into Cumberland and Westmorland met with no success, and both Baptists and Congregationalists remained weak in the four northern counties and in the North and East Ridings of Yorkshire.[516] In Durham and the East and West Ridings the vacuum left by the failure of Old Dissent was filled first by the Wesleyans and later by the Primitive Methodists.

In the 1790s the enthusiastic, emotional revivalism of William Bramwell and his associates had resulted in the rapid expansion of Wesleyan Methodism in Yorkshire and Nottinghamshire, but by the turn of the century Wesleyan leaders were increasingly worried by what they saw as the noise, confusion, and indiscipline which so often accompanied such revivalist

---

[511] In 1810 the Lancashire Congregational Union used the term 'itinerant circuit' in its annual report (B. Nightingale, *Lancashire Nonconformity* (1890–3), iv. 118).

[512] Brown, *Bedfordshire Union of Christians*, 46; D. W. Lovegrove, 'The Practice of Itinerant Evangelism in English Calvinistic Dissent', Ph.D. thesis (Cambridge, 1980), 258.

[513] Lovegrove, 'Itinerant Evangelism', 64.

[514] A. G. Hamlin, 'Bristol Baptist Itinerant Society', *Baptist Quarterly*, 21 (1965–6), 321–2.

[515] Klaiber, *Suffolk Baptists*, 71.

[516] Lovegrove, *Established Church, Sectarian People*, 50, 152.

movements. Thomas Taylor complained of the Yorkshire revival that 'all discipline was laid aside; sensible people were shocked and disgusted at seeing such irregular and unscriptural proceedings'; and 'many poor men ran themselves out of breath in staying late at nights, and neglected their families, and even their labour, and of course got into debt'.[517] The Wesleyan leadership was concerned, too, by the possible political repercussions of popular revivalism at a time when many of the government's supporters regarded Methodist itinerants as Jacobin incendiaries in disguise.[518] But Wesleyan attempts to impose some sort of control on such revivalism merely resulted in a series of secessions of Methodists who, like John Wesley himself, regarded the saving of souls as of greater importance than ecclesiastical order. It was Wesleyan attempts to suppress cottage meetings that led to the secession of the Quaker Methodists of Warrington in 1796; James Crawfoot's action in preaching to the Quaker Methodists led to Wesleyan criticism and to the secession of the 'Magic Methodists' of the Delamere Forest; John Broadhurst's refusal to restrict attendance at his band meetings in Manchester to Wesleyan ticket holders resulted in the secession of his Band Room Methodists in 1806; William O'Bryan's claim to preach wherever God sent him, notwithstanding Wesleyan preaching plans, led to the formation of the Bible Christians in 1815; and George Pocock's refusal to allow Wesleyan circuits to control his tent mission issued in the short-lived Tent Methodist movement of 1820.[519] William Bramwell himself was on the point of leaving the Wesleyans on at least two occasions: in May 1797, when he met Alexander Kilham, the founder of the New Connexion, at night and in secret at Sheffield,[520] and in 1803 when he was tempted to join the secession of his biographer, James Sigston, and a group of Leeds revivalists known as the 'Kirkgate Screamers'. Bramwell seems to have briefly entertained the idea of uniting the 'Kirkgate Screamers' with the Manchester Band Room Methodists and another secessionist group, the Christian Revivalists of Macclesfield.[521] He was persuaded to stay with the Old Connexion, but he continued to complain of the rich and mighty Wesleyans who 'too frequently usurp improper authority, which damps too much the living flame among the simple'.[522] And the man who was soon to become the embodiment of

---

[517] T. Jackson (ed.), *The Lives of the Early Methodist Preachers* (1866), v. 86.

[518] Thomas Coke was worried by the republican views of Lorenzo Dow during the latter's tour of Ireland in 1799–1801 (Carwardine, *Transatlantic Revivalism*, 104).

[519] Herod, *Biographical Sketches*, 252–3; Werner, *Primitive Methodist Connexion*, 26; Shaw, *Bible Christians*, 6, 11; Vickers, 'Methodism and Society', 274–7.

[520] Kilham, *Life of Alexander Kilham*, 149, 191–2.   [521] Ward, *Religion and Society*, 80–1.

[522] Werner, *Primitive Methodist Connexion*, 25–6, 49.

Wesleyan authority, Jabez Bunting, was sorry that Bramwell had decided not to leave.[523] Bunting wrote of the Macclesfield revivalists that 'Divisions *from* the church, though awful, are perhaps after all less to be dreaded than divisions *in* the church. . . . Revivalism, as of late professed and practised, was [likely if] not checked, to have gradually ruined genuine Methodism'.[524]

Revivalism thus had perforce to find an outlet elsewhere. On Christmas eve, 1805, there arrived at Liverpool the itinerant American evangelist Lorenzo Dow, an advocate of the revivalist techniques that were sweeping the United States in what was to become known as America's 'Second Great Awakening'. Dow, who had been brought up in Connecticut as a Congregationalist and was so terrified by Calvinist doctrine that he was tempted to commit suicide, was converted by a Methodist preacher at the age of thirteen in 1791. He was admitted on trial as a Methodist preacher in 1795 but, like so many of his fellow evangelists in England, disliked the restraints of the Methodist circuit system and took it upon himself to visit Ireland in 1799 and Georgia and Canada in 1802. With piercing brown eyes, hair which reached down to 'the cuff of his coat sleeve', a long beard, and a broad-brimmed Quaker hat, Dow had an eccentric appearance and manners which soon earned him the title 'Crazy Dow'. While in England he preached for Peter Phillips's Quaker Methodists in Warrington, visited the scenes of James Crawfoot's labours in the villages of Delamere Forest, and in April 1807 preached near the Staffordshire and Cheshire border in the Wesleyan chapel at Harriseahead which had recently been built for the colliers of the area under the leadership of the carpenter Hugh Bourne. In the Harriseahead chapel Dow spoke at length of the camp-meetings which from 1797 onwards had brought excitement, drama, and religion to the frontier regions of Kentucky and Tennessee. Dow described how, on a Friday morning, wagons would be brought to a selected site away from a town but near to a trading route, undergrowth cut down and the area fenced in with poles, and tents pitched in rows around a hollow square. Within the square stages were erected and people spent most of the night in prayer for the meeting the following day. On the Saturday morning people flocked in by hundreds, at noon a meeting of prayer and singing was held, and by the evening one could see 'a hundred fires, while candles, lamps, and lanterns are suspended from the

---

[523] Bowmer, *Pastor and People*, 81.

[524] Ward, *Religion and Society*, 80. It is an indication of the extent to which Wesleyan Methodism turned its back on the tradition of William Bramwell that he gets not a single mention in the second volume of the *History of the Methodist Church in Great Britain* (1978). Ward dismisses Bramwell with the ludicrous understatement that he had 'aspirations to be a revivalist' (*Religion and Society*, 81).

boughs of trees'. A trumpet was sounded to announce the start of the evening meeting; at the close 'an invitation is given to mourners to come forward to be prayed for'; and as many souls, claimed Dow, had been 'brought to God at camp-meetings, as at all other meetings put together'.[525]

Lorenzo Dow left Liverpool for the United States on 6 May 1807, but not before he had inspired Hugh Bourne to introduce camp-meetings into England. Bourne had already been persuaded by the writings of the early Quakers and by the example of John Wesley of the importance of open-air preaching, and in 1801 he had overcome his natural shyness (though with 'his left hand before his face—fingers outspread—like one who looks forth from a barred window') to preach in a field on the Cheshire side of Mow Cop, the ridge which divides that county from Staffordshire.[526] It was on this spot, on 31 May 1807, that the first gathering designated as a camp-meeting was held on English soil. The crowds which assembled on Mow Cop were addressed by Wesleyan local preachers, by Independent Methodist preachers, and by preachers who were accredited by no denomination, and the informality and spontaneity of the proceedings led to their denunciation first by the Wesleyan preachers of the Burslem and Macclesfield circuits, and then by the Wesleyan Methodist Conference. Bourne responded by organizing a second camp-meeting at Norton-on-the-Moors near Tunstall in August, and in the following June he was expelled from the Wesleyan Connexion by the Burslem circuit Quarterly Meeting.[527] Bourne issued his first class tickets in May 1811 and his first preaching plan in June. The next year he and his followers took the name of Primitive Methodists.

By adopting the title of Primitive Methodist Bourne and his associates intended to signify a rejection of the respectable, dignified, and restrained Wesleyanism of the nineteenth century and a return to what they regarded as the original zeal of John Wesley and the first Methodist preachers. 'I never knew a Burslem circuit travelling preacher perform what Mr Wesley calls "field-preaching" all the time I was a member', commented Bourne on his experiences as a Wesleyan.[528] When James Crawfoot was arraigned before his Wesleyan Quarterly Meeting for preaching to the Quaker Methodists he reminded his accusers of Wesley's final words to his preachers during his last visit to Chester in 1790: 'Fellow labourer, wherever there is an open door, enter in and preach the Gospel, if it be two or three, under a hedge or tree,

---

[525] Herod, *Biographical Sketches*, 17, 200.
[526] J. T. Wilkinson, *Hugh Bourne, 1772–1852* (1952), 33–4; Kendall, *Primitive Methodist Church*, ii. 34.
[527] Kendall, *Primitive Methodist Church*, i. 63–84.   [528] Ibid. 39.

preach the Gospel.' It was the modern Wesleyans, claimed Crawfoot, who were deviating 'from the old usages'. 'I still remain a primitive Methodist.'[529]

The Primitive Methodists added a new dimension to Nonconformist evangelism. Between 1820 and 1850 total Arminian Methodist membership in England increased by 292,189 and nearly a third of that increase, 94,380, was due to the Primitive Methodists.[530] Some of the growth was, of course, at the expense of the Wesleyans, and one must not underestimate the continuing dynamism of Wesleyan expansion. It is not true, as some writers have claimed,[531] that the momentum of Wesleyan expansion slowed down after 1820 or that the Old Connexion lost contact with the working class: the net increases in Wesleyan membership in the 1820s and 1830s were, in absolute terms, the largest decennial increases in the history of the Connexion. But there can be little doubt that the sheer exuberance and showmanship of the Primitives appealed to a section of the community who might otherwise have remained untouched by the more sedate methods of the Baptists, Congregationalists, and the Wesleyans. The Primitive Methodists were to the first half of the nineteenth century what the original Methodists were to the eighteenth century and what the Quakers were to the seventeenth century. Like the Quakers and the early Methodists they ignored ecclesiastical boundaries, preached in the fields and on the moors, claimed to have effected miraculous cures, and produced shakings, fits, and hysteria among their converts.[532] It was with pride that many Primitive Methodists appropriated to themselves the nickname of 'Ranter' given to them at Belper,[533] just as the Friends had adopted the name of Quaker with which they had been dubbed in nearby Derby a century and a half earlier. Hugh Bourne, like the Independent Methodist leader Peter Phillips and the Bible Christian founder William O'Bryan, was deeply influenced by the Quakers.[534] But for other early nineteenth-century Ranters the inspiration for Primitive Methodism was more recent: it was a return to the 'good old ways of Bramwell'.[535]

Though the Primitive Methodists were not the only British Nonconformists to emulate the American camp-meetings, vast open-air meetings were the

---

[529] Herod, *Biographical Sketches*, 252–3; Langton, 'James Crawfoot', *PWHS* 30 (1955), 12–14.
[530] Calculations based on the figures given in Currie, Gilbert, and Horsley, *Churches and Churchgoers*, 140–1.
[531] e.g. D. Hempton, *Methodism and Politics in British Society, 1750–1850* (1984), 227, 236.
[532] For miraculous healing see Herod, *Biographical Sketches*, 264–5, and J. Walford, *Memoirs of the Life and Labours of the late Venerable Hugh Bourne* (1855), ii. 144–6; for shakings see *Primitive Methodist Magazine*, 6 (1825), 271.
[533] Kendall, *Primitive Methodist Church*, i. 185–7.
[534] Wilkinson, *Hugh Bourne*, 24, 27, 34.
[535] Werner, *Primitive Methodist Connexion*, 174, 199 n. 36.

most distinctive of the Ranters' evangelistic techniques. The Primitive Methodists made a point of holding their camp-meetings at the same times as parish wakes, originally festivals commemorating the dedication of the parish church which, by the nineteenth-century, had become excuses for revelry, drunkenness, and fornication.[536] By timing their camp-meetings to coincide with such occasions the Ranters offered an alternative to what they regarded as the temptations to vice provided by the wakes and also seized the opportunity to maximize their own audiences. The number of people who were attracted to these exuberant celebrations of popular religion were huge, even if one remains sceptical about the claims made for the size of the audiences by their organizers. On the first Sunday in May 1808 a 'vast number' were attracted to a camp-meeting on the summit of the Wrekin in Shropshire on a day traditionally set aside for the celebration of a pagan fertility rite.[537] Twelve thousand people, it was claimed, crowded on to the Forest in Nottingham on Whit Sunday in June 1816 for a camp-meeting.[538] In Holderness on Maudlin Sunday in August 1820 a camp-meeting was held to coincide with the annual football match between the villages of Hedon and Preston, the object of which was to kick the ball through the windows of the public houses in the rival villages.[539] Six huge camp-meetings were also held in 1820 in the Sheffield and Barnsley circuit in the West Riding, of which the largest was held on Mexborough Common in June, attended by a multitude which Hugh Bourne put at 10,000 and a local newspaper at 20,000.[540] But in the eyes of the Primitive Methodists the greatest significance of the camp-meetings lay not in the thousands who attended, but in the individual men and women who were converted. It was in these terms that George Jarrat described a camp-meeting held at Woodhouse, a village three miles south of Loughborough in Leicestershire, in July 1820. The day began with prayer and singing and with a sermon preached from Acts 17: 6, 'These that have turned the world upside down are come hither also'. During the preaching 'many were pricked in their hearts and began to cry for mercy'. The crowd was then divided into praying companies, and in one of these companies 'the cries of the penitents were so affecting' that those engaged in prayer could not be persuaded to attend to the preaching when it recommenced. Instead the Ranters 'succeeded in removing the souls in distress to the distance of about one hundred yards from the preaching stand, and great numbers repaired with them'. What most impressed Jarrat was the case of one back-

---

[536] Kendall, *Primitive Methodist Church*, i. 61.
[537] Werner, *Primitive Methodist Connexion*, 64.   [538] Swift, *Lively People*, 54.
[539] Kendall, *Primitive Methodist Church*, i. 389–90.   [540] Ibid. 489.

slider whose 'pangs of sorrow' were such that 'he appeared as one deeply convulsed, and lay upon the ground for the space of three hours, groaning'. But after this 'long conflict, he obtained pardon and was justified; and such a burst of praise and glory echoed between the surrounding hills as I never heard, and hardly ever expect to hear again'.[541]

The Independent, New Connexion, Association, and Free Methodists all followed the Primitives in using camp-meetings,[542] but apart from the Ranters the denomination which made the most determined attempt to emulate the American camp-meeting were the Calvinistic Methodists. The outdoor meetings held in connection with their Quarterly Associations provided the Calvinistic Methodists, as did the Primitive Methodists' camp-meetings, with opportunities for fellowship with new friends and for renewing acquaintances with old ones, for the excitement, drama, and inspiration of a crowded festival, and, above all, for evangelism.[543] Two years before the historic gathering on Mow Cop, in April 1805, Thomas Charles reported on a meeting held on a common near Aberystwyth during the Association. A stage was erected on the common, and a crowd estimated at over 20,000, hundreds of them children, was caught up in a revival which helped to give the Aberystwyth district the highest level of religious observance in the whole of England and Wales in 1851.[544] At the Llanrwst Association in Denbighshire in 1818 John Elias, the central figure in the revival which had begun at Beddgelert in the previous year, preached to an audience which the local newspaper put at over 5,000. At the end of Elias's address his hearers were said to have 'commenced waving their hats, jumping, shouting, etc., like enthusiastic fanatics'.[545] At Bala in 1835 John Elias electrified a huge audience on the Green when he preached in tears from Isaiah 6: 9, 10, and told his audience that he 'would rather be a common hangman, going from here to London, than that I should come to Bala to make the heart of this people fat, their ears heavy, and their eyes blind'. Men in his audience were said to have been so terrified that they fell 'down dead like logs of wood, their limbs stiffened, their eyes glaring', while others stood 'as if they were statues of stone, with fear depicted upon their countenances'.[546] Both the enthusiasm and the suspect statistical claims of the Calvinistic Methodists were communicated in turn to the Welsh Independents. At an open-air meeting held in 1822 in

---

[541] *Primitive Methodist Magazine*, 1 (1819–20), 241–2.
[542] Smith, 'Religion in Industrial Society', 340–1.
[543] Turner, 'Revivals and Popular Religion in Wales', 6.
[544] Jenkins, *Life of Thomas Charles*, iii. 114.
[545] Turner, 'Revivals and Popular Religion in Wales', 122.
[546] O. Jones, *Some of the Great Preachers of Wales* (1885), 256–8.

connection with their Assembly at Blaen-y-coed near the point at which Caernarfonshire, Denbighshire, and Merioneth met, the Independents claimed that sixty ministers and sixty lay preachers preached to an audience of 27,000.[547]

The camp-meetings were the most characteristic expression of Primitive Methodist revivalism, but what was of equal importance was the new wave of missionary enthusiasm they represented which carried Evangelical Nonconformity into areas hitherto untouched by the Baptists and Congregationalists and not fully exploited by the Wesleyans. A Wesleyan acknowledged in 1860 that the Ranters were 'doing a good and great work amongst the lower orders of our population',[548] and they achieved notable successes among the agricultural labourers of Berkshire, northern Hampshire, Wiltshire, Norfolk, and Lincolnshire, among the fishermen of the North and East Ridings, and among the miners of Durham. The Ranters brought excitement and entertainment to remote and superstitious rural communities and to rough and unsophisticated industrial villages and small towns. 'Their manner of entering a town or village', wrote George Herod, one of their first itinerant preachers, 'produced great excitement.' 'In general the missionary was accompanied with a number of warm-hearted singers, and so soon as they entered the place of their attack they commenced singing down the street, and continued so doing until they arrived' at the village green or town market-place. 'The Spiritual Songs which Lorenzo Dow had brought from America, with the very lively airs to which they were sung, produced a very wonderful effect upon multitudes', and hundreds of people were 'collected together through the novelty of lively singing'.[549] The way in which the Primitive Methodists copied and rivalled the showmanship of popular entertainers was tacitly acknowledged by John Harrison when he described how he and a woman preacher, Sarah Healand, entered the town of Caistor in Lincolnshire in 1819. 'We went to an inn and sent for the bell-man', wrote Harrison, who at their request 'went through the town crying "There will be a Ranters' meeting held this evening in the middle of the market place".' 'The town was all in an uproar; they ran from all quarters, as if they had been coming to a bull-baiting.'[550] What the arrival of a Ranter preacher could mean to a remote rural community was described by William Clowes when he wrote of his visit to Auterley in Bilsdale in the North Riding of Yorkshire in October 1820. After 'a tedious journey across the mountains'

---

[547] R. T. Jones, *Hanes Annibynwyr Cymru* (Abertawe, 1966), 185.
[548] Swift, *Lively People*, 138.
[549] Herod, *Biographical Sketches*, 12.
[550] Ibid. 371. Sarah Healand's surname was also spelt 'Eland'.

Clowes reached his destination at seven o'clock to find 'the congregation waiting, and the house so full I could not get in'. He therefore asked 'the people to come out, and preached by the light of a lantern'. 'There were several hundreds', he claimed, 'and they behaved well.' After his sermon he announced that he 'would pray with a few in the house who were desirous to get their souls at liberty', but immediately the house was so 'crammed full of people that we could not well remove one from another'.[551]

The Primitive Methodists not only offered drama, music, and fellowship to people who had little access to other forms of entertainment, they, along with the other Evangelical Nonconformist denominations, also had one other immeasurable advantage over the Church of England: they required no university degree or college training of the men who preached in barns and market-places or even of those who occupied their pulpits. William Dawson was converted in 1791 at the age of eighteen during a communion service at his parish church at Garforth in the West Riding and started to exhort in prayer-meetings. But he found that the Church of England did not provide scope for his talents and ambitions as a lay evangelist and this contributed to his decision to join the Wesleyans, among whom he was quickly welcomed as a local preacher.[552] Throughout the nineteenth century no academic qualifications or formal training were necessary for a man to secure approval as a Baptist or Congregational lay preacher or as a Methodist local preacher; in the first half of the century a significant proportion of Baptist and Congregational churches welcomed to their pastorates men who had had no college training;[553] and during their great age of expansion neither the Wesleyans, the Calvinistic Methodists, nor the Primitive Methodists required formal qualifications of their itinerant and ordained ministers.[554] What was required of a Nonconformist preacher was evidence of conversion, a passion to save souls, and an ability to communicate the essence of the Gospel message to men and women of his own class, and usually of his own locality, in simple, direct English or Welsh.

Not only did most Nonconformist preachers have no formal training, the overwhelming majority of them were laymen. Until the Wesleyan

---

[551] *Primitive Methodist Magazine*, 2 (1821), 119.

[552] Everett, *Memoirs of William Dawson*, 22–3, 120, 190–1, 204.

[553] In the mid-19th cent. nearly 30% of men entering the Congregational ministry, and over 50% of those entering the Baptist ministry, had had no college training (R. T. Jones, *Congregationalism in England* (1962), 235; K. D. Brown, *A Social History of the Nonconformist Ministry in England and Wales* (Oxford, 1988), 60).

[554] The Calvinistic Methodists required their ordination candidates to pass an examination from 1859 onwards (D. C. Jenkins, *Calvinistic Methodist Holy Orders* (Caernarfon, 1911), 234–6).

Conference adopted ordination in 1836 the essential difference between Methodist preachers was not between those who were ordained and those who were not, but between those who had been admitted to the itinerant ministry and those who remained local preachers. At the end of the eighteenth century the Wesleyans had 330 itinerant ministers and some 2,000 local preachers, so that 70 per cent of Methodist services were being conducted by laymen.[555] The 1851 religious census revealed that with 6,579 Wesleyan congregations in England and Wales there were only 1,024 itinerant preachers to serve them.[556] The proportion of local preachers to itinerant preachers was even greater among the Primitive Methodists, and by 1859, the first year for which national statistics are available, the Ranters had almost exactly twenty times as many local preachers as ministers.[557] In Lincolnshire more than three-quarters of all Primitive Methodist services were conducted by local preachers, and in villages the figure was over 80 per cent.[558] The success of the Methodists encouraged the Baptists in particular to make increasing use of lay preachers, and both the Bristol Particular Baptists and the Stoney Street, Nottingham, General Baptists sent lay preachers out to the surrounding villages on preaching plans copied from the Methodists.[559] The vicar of Harrold in Bedfordshire complained that the preachers sent into the county's villages by the Bedfordshire Union of Christians were largely uneducated men 'destitute of Greek, the language in which the New Testament was originally written'. They included a shoemaker, an upholsterer, a gravestone cutter, a carpenter, and, in his own village, 'a tailor, a watchmaker, a sievemaker, a woodman, and a schoolmaster'.[560] Such men were, no doubt, worthy successors to the cobbler Samuel How.[561]

While Nonconformity in general provided a channel for the preaching ambitions of shopkeepers, tailors, and masons, Primitive Methodism in particular offered an outlet for the religious enthusiasm of the young and of women. The youth of most of the Dissenting and Methodist converts of the early nineteenth century has already been stressed, and once converted the neophyte was expected to pass on the message of salvation to others. William

---

[555] Currie, Gilbert, and Horsley, *Churches and Churchgoers*, 208; W. J. Warner, *The Wesleyan Movement in the Industrial Revolution* (1930), 261–2.

[556] Laqueur, *Religion and Respectability*, 78.

[557] G. Morris, 'Primitive Methodism in Nottinghamshire', Ph.D. thesis (Nottingham, 1967), 110; Currie, Gilbert, and Horsley, *Churches and Churchgoers*, 204.

[558] Obelkevich, *Religion and Rural Society*, 223.

[559] A. G. Hamlin, 'Bristol Baptist Itinerant Society', *Baptist Quarterly*, 21 (1965–6), 323; Harrison, 'Baptists of Nottinghamshire', i. 455–6.

[560] Brown, *Bedfordshire Union of Christians*, 43.

[561] Watts, *The Dissenters*, i. 69–79, 82–3.

Antliff, later editor of the *Primitive Methodist Magazine*, twice president of the Conference, and first principal of that anomaly the Ranters' Theological Institute, became an itinerant preacher at the age of sixteen.[562] John Petty, who also became connexional editor and president of the Conference, started to preach soon after his conversion at the age of sixteen and entered the itinerant ministry two years later.[563] Such was the extreme youthfulness of many Primitive Methodist preachers that the Connexion was sometimes called upon to mourn the deaths of preachers who had not yet attained the age of twenty. Elizabeth Elliot of Oswestry was converted at fourteen, became a local preacher, and at fifteen, when proceeding to a preaching appointment at Llandrinio in Montgomeryshire, was drowned as the boat in which she was crossing the River Vyrnwy capsized.[564] And at Beeford in the East Riding a tombstone marked the death in 1837 of Thomas Watson, Primitive Methodist minister, in 'the 19th year of his age, and the 6th year of his ministry'. His memorial recorded that 'his slender age, deep piety, and extraordinary abilities render his death a subject of deep and lasting regret'.[565]

Women preachers, like boy preachers, had a novelty value which was an added inducement to the curious to hear Methodist evangelists. The Evangelical revival of the late eighteenth century, which shared so many of the characteristics of the eruption of religious enthusiasm which accompanied the Civil War of the 1640s, was characterized by a similar belief in the spiritual equality of men and women and by a consequent demand, in some quarters, that women be allowed to join in preaching the Gospel. But the Evangelical insistence that, if people were perishing through lack of preaching, it was logical to enlist women in the work of evangelism, was countered by Paul's command to the church at Corinth that 'women keep silence in the churches'.[566] John Wesley himself could not make up his mind as to the propriety of women preachers. In 1769 he told Sarah Crosby that she could pray in public and give short exhortations, but that she should never take a text and should 'keep as far from what is called preaching as you can'.[567] Two years later he acknowledged that Mary Bosanquet had what he described as 'an extraordinary call to preach'.[568] In 1780 he ordered John Peacock at Grimsby 'to put a final stop to the preaching of women in his circuit', yet nine

[562] Kendall, *Primitive Methodist Church*, ii. 376.
[563] G. E. Milburn in D. C. Dews (ed.), *From Mow Cop to Peake* (n. p., 1982), 60.
[564] *Primitive Methodist Magazine*, 6 (1825), 410–12.
[565] Kendall, *Primitive Methodist Church*, ii. 96–7.
[566] 2 Corinthians 14: 34.　　[567] *Wesley's Letters*, v. 130.　　[568] Ibid. 257.

years later he rejoiced that opposition to the preaching of Sarah Mallet was declining.[569]

After Wesley's death the issue of women preachers became a major source of contention among his followers. In their favour was the undoubted fact that women preachers were a considerable attraction, especially to male audiences. The reception given to Dinah Morris by the men of Hayslope in George Eliot's *Adam Bede* had plenty of parallels in reality. 'I'll stick up for the pretty women preachin',' says Wiry Ben. 'I know they'd persuade me over a deal sooner than th' ugly men.'[570] William Lovett of Newlyn in Cornwall, the future Chartist leader, was attracted to the Bible Christians by two women preachers, though he left the Connexion when the women were expelled for getting themselves pregnant.[571] Female preachers played an important part in the Yorkshire revival of the 1790s. About 1792 considerable excitement was aroused in the neighbourhood of Bingley by the open-air preaching of Elizabeth Dickinson, as well as by 'the "trances" which she professed to fall into'. She was an attractive nineteen year old and 'thousands flocked to hear her, and many were said to be converted through her instrumentality'.[572] We have already seen William Bramwell's tribute to the role of Ann Cutler in the revivals in the Dewsbury, Birstall, Leeds, Bradford, and Oldham circuits in 1792–4, and it was Ann Cutler's example which inspired a twenty-year-old Lancashire girl named Mary Barritt to undertake itinerant preaching. Mary Barritt went to Nottingham to assist Bramwell in 1799, and in the Nottingham revival of 1799–1800 Bramwell attributed to her a role similar to that played by Ann Cutler in the Yorkshire revival. 'I never knew one man so much blessed as this young woman is in the salvation of souls', was his comment.[573] Bramwell encouraged other women to become preachers, among them a lacemaker named Elizabeth Tomlinson who was the inspiration for George Eliot's Dinah Morris. In 1804 Elizabeth Tomlinson married a Wesleyan local preacher named Samuel Evans who was the younger brother of George Eliot's father. It was Elizabeth Evans who provided her niece with the central theme of *Adam Bede* when she recalled how in 1802, as a Wesleyan preacher in Nottingham, she had visited in a prison cell 'a very ignorant girl who had murdered her child and refused to confess her guilt'. Elizabeth remained with the girl, 'praying through the night' until 'the poor

---

[569] Ibid. vii. 9; viii. 90; L. F. Church, *More About Early Methodist People* (1949), 140–1.

[570] George Eliot, *Adam Bede*, 22.

[571] W. Lovett, *Life and Struggles of William Lovett* (1967), 18.

[572] J. Ward, *Historical Sketches of the Rise and Progress of Methodism in Bingley* (Bingley, 1863), 46.

[573] Dunn, *Memoirs of Thomas Tatham*, 154.

creature at last broke into tears, and confessed her crime', and next day went 'with her in the cart to the place of execution', accompanied by a procession of singing Methodists.[574]

Bramwell's patronage of women preachers did not go unopposed. He could not, he wrote, prevent prejudice against Ann Cutler among 'many of my good elder brethren', and John Pawson, who was president of the Methodist Conference in 1793, wrote of the Leeds revival of 1794 that it was 'uncommonly turbulent' with women as 'the principal mischief makers'.[575] What was barely tolerated by Wesleyan leaders in northern England and the Midlands provoked a major crisis in the south. In 1802 Mary Barritt married a Wesleyan itinerant preacher named Zachariah Taft, and after her husband's appointment to the Dover circuit she continued to preach out of doors as she had done in Nottingham, attracting crowds of 'many hundred'. Mrs Taft's action split the local Wesleyan society, the District chairman ordered her to stop preaching, and in 1803 the Wesleyan Conference resolved the issue by declaring that 'in general' women ought not to preach 'because a vast majority of our people are opposed to it'.[576] Mary Taft and Elizabeth Evans were not completely silenced, and as late as 1833 complaints were still being made at the Methodist Conference about their preaching, but among Wesleyans theirs was a lost cause.[577] The material Zachariah Taft carefully collected for his *Biographical Sketches of the Lives and Ministry of various Holy Women* (1825) was just as carefully excised by Jabez Bunting from the obituaries in the *Wesleyan Methodist Magazine*.[578] The effect of the Wesleyan attitude was to drive would-be female preachers into the arms of the Primitive Methodists and Bible Christians, denominations which had no scruples about using so proven a means of saving souls. Hannah Woolhouse, the wife of a Hull sailcloth manufacturer and a Wesleyan class leader who 'had a great desire to preach' but received no encouragement from the Wesleyans, joined the Ranters and was responsible for inviting the first Primitive Methodist mission to Hull in 1819.[579] By 1818 20 per cent of Primitive Methodist preachers were women and by 1824 30 per cent of Bible

[574] V. Cunningham, *Everywhere Spoken Against: Dissent in the Victorian Novel* (Oxford, 1975), 154; Swift, *Lively People*, 45.

[575] Bramwell, *Life of Ann Cutler*, 22; Dews, *From Mow Cop to Peake*, 17.

[576] Valenze, 'Prophetic Sons and Daughters', 68–70; *Minutes of the Methodist Conferences* (1812), ii. 188.

[577] B. Gregory, *Side Lights on the Conflicts of Methodism* (1898), 127.

[578] Church, *More About Early Methodist People*, 171–2.

[579] Kendall, *Primitive Methodist Church*, i. 102–3, 361–2; Valenze, 'Prophetic Sons and Daughters', 198–202; Dews, *From Mow Cop to Peake*, 19–20.

Christian travelling preachers were women.[580] The Bible Christians' most successful mission outside Devon and Cornwall was to the Isle of Wight, and it was launched in 1823 by a woman, Mary Toms, supported by William O'Bryan's wife Catherine and Eliza Jew.[581] The most successful of the Primitive Methodist women preachers was Sarah Kirkland of Mercaston in Derbyshire who was converted at the age of twenty and in 1816 became the Ranters' first woman travelling preacher at a salary of two guineas a quarter. It was Sarah Kirkland who on Christmas day 1815 launched the Primitive Methodist mission in Nottingham and initiated the revival which culminated in a huge camp-meeting on the Forest on Whit Sunday in the following year.[582]

In 1818 Sarah Kirkland married her fellow Primitive Methodist preacher John Harrison, but the marriage did not end their journeyings nor did it enable them to spend much time together. By November 1819 Harrison, although only twenty-four, was beginning to suffer the ill-effects of two years of itinerant labours and spent a fortnight at his parents' home at Bradley Park near Hulland in Derbyshire to recuperate. On Monday, 15 November, he left Bradley Park on foot, 'although very unwell', with Hull as his ultimate destination. 'I had caught a bad cold', he recorded in his journal, 'and in addition to this, whilst walking to-day my shoes came seam-rent, and I have walked several miles wet-shod; so I have added one cold to another.' None the less that night he preached at Belper; the following day he walked eighteen miles to Nottingham; and the day after he walked twenty miles to Newark. 'It rained much, and although it was nearly seven in the evening before I arrived, and I was very wet and fatigued, the friends would have no nay but I must preach.' On Thursday, 18 November, he walked twenty-five miles to Gainsborough and preached at night, and on the following day took the packet-boat for Hull 'but remained very poorly'. That was the last entry in his diary; he died in July 1821 still only twenty-five years of age.[583]

The privations endured by John Harrison in his brief career as a travelling preacher were not uncommon in the early nineteenth century, nor was his early death unusual. In February 1824 George Wallace, already weakened by his labours as a Primitive Methodist preacher, walked seventeen miles from Wingates to Kirkwhelpington in Northumberland in rain and snow over 'great mountains and crags and burns . . . which nearly exhausted my strength'. He died a month later, aged twenty-three.[584] Northumberland also

---

[580] Werner, *Primitive Methodist Connexion*, 142; Bourne, *The Bible Christians*, 165.
[581] Bourne, *The Bible Christians*, 129–37.   [582] Herod, *Biographical Sketches*, 305–16.
[583] Ibid. 387.   [584] *Primitive Methodist Magazine*, 5 (1824), 225–6.

claimed the life of a young Bible Christian itinerant, Mary Ann Werrey, who was preaching in the Channel Islands when she dreamed she was called to take the Gospel to Scotland. In November 1823 she sailed from Guernsey to Blyth in Northumberland but soon after her arrival she was struck down by illness and disappeared from history, leaving no trace of the place or time of her death.[585]

The distances walked by John Harrison and George Wallace were not unusual in an age when most preachers could not afford horses. Samuel Deacon, the pastor of the New Connexion General Baptist church at Barton-in-Fabis in Leicestershire, 'repeatedly walked from Ratby to Melbourne, a distance of twenty miles, on the Lord's day morning, and returned after evening service, not reaching his humble habitation till two or three o'clock in the morning'.[586] Students at the Congregational academy at Idle near Bradford, as at other Independent and Particular Baptist colleges, were expected to exercise their preaching talents in surrounding villages: in 1817 fifteen students were each walking an average of twenty-two miles a week and six years earlier some had undertaken a round trip of sixty miles on foot to preach at Grassington in Wharfedale.[587] Most romantic of all was the story of how Primitive Methodism was taken to Manchester by a former army officer named Eleazar Hathorn who had lost a leg in battle but none the less walked from Macclesfield and back on his wooden leg, a total of thirty-six miles.[588]

Those preachers who survived to old age took pride in calculating the distances they had covered on their itinerant journeys. William Castledine, a leader of the Independent Primitive Methodists of Bingham in Nottinghamshire who broke away from the Ranters in 1828 in protest at the payment of preachers, 'preached 4,000 times and walked 16,000 miles to preach the Gospel'.[589] Dan Taylor, the founder of the New Connexion of General Baptists, travelled 25,000 miles and preached 20,000 sermons, besides attending 200 conferences and publishing nearly fifty books and pamphlets.[590] John Morton, pastor of the Bucklebury Congregational church in Berkshire, was crippled by illness at the age of thirteen, but none the less despite his lameness walked 34,000 miles in a ministry spanning fifty-five

[585] Bourne, *The Bible Christians*, 139–45.
[586] A. Taylor, *History of the General Baptists* (1818), ii. 61.
[587] Lovegrove, *Established Church, Sectarian People*, 79, 83.
[588] Kendall, *Primitive Methodist Church*, ii. 15–16; Herod, *Biographical Sketches*, 280.
[589] Vickers, *History of Independent Methodism*, 204–5.
[590] Underwood, *History of the English Baptists*, 157.

years.[591] William Garner, a Primitive Methodist minister, claimed in twenty-one years to have walked 44,936 miles and to have preached 6,278 sermons.[592] John Knowles, an agricultural labourer from Lymm in Cheshire, put his total at over 60,000 miles during his career as an Independent Methodist preacher.[593] Ebenezer Richard, the Calvinistic Methodist father of Henry Richard, the future secretary of the Peace Society and Liberal MP, was also said to have travelled 60,000 miles to preach more than 7,000 sermons in the last twenty-two years of his life.[594] Two preachers calculated that the total mileage they had covered in the course of preaching the Gospel came to 80,000 miles: William Sanderson, a Liverpool tailor and Independent Methodist preacher for fifty-six years, and John Plowright, a Nottingham toll-keeper and General Baptist lay preacher for more than fifty years—and Plowright claimed that his journeys were all accomplished on foot.[595] But the claim to be the most travelled preacher of all was made by the Wesleyan Reformer and first president of the United Methodist Free Churches, James Everett. In a ministry spanning sixty-six years Everett calculated that he had travelled 320,000 miles to preach 13,000 sermons. Even in 1866, his eighty-third year, he claimed to have travelled 700 miles to fulfil preaching engagements.[596]

The long distances James Everett claimed to have covered were accomplished despite the fact that he twice resigned from the Wesleyan itinerancy on grounds of ill-health. For many preachers whose labours did not condemn them to an early death, the price extracted for their itinerant journeys was intense suffering. When Thomas Charles was returning to Bala over the Migneint mountain from a preaching tour of Caernarfonshire in the winter of 1799–1800 he suffered from severe frostbite which necessitated the amputation of his left thumb.[597] In the early years of Primitive Methodism Hugh Bourne 'used to walk forty or fifty miles a day', sometimes with his foot in great pain, and he eventually died from gangrene at the age of seventy-nine.[598] Unlike the Primitive Methodists and General Baptists, Wesleyan itinerants usually had allowances sufficient to purchase 'a horse, saddle, bridle, [and] saddle bags', but this did not insulate them against cold garrets and damp beds. When Joseph Entwisle began preaching in the Oxford circuit in 1787 in one of his lodgings his 'bed-chamber was immediately under the roof,

[591] Summers, *Congregational Churches in Berks, South Oxon, and South Bucks*, 104–7.
[592] *HMC* iv. 465–6.   [593] Valenze, 'Prophetic Sons and Daughters', 231.
[594] C. S. Miall, *Henry Richard, MP* (1889), 5.
[595] Harrison, 'Baptists of Nottinghamshire', i. 462; Vickers, *History of Independent Methodism*, 43–5.
[596] R. Chew, *James Everett* (1875), 489.
[597] D. Evans, *The Sunday Schools of Wales* (1883), 315.
[598] Wilkinson, *Hugh Bourne*, 70, 96–7, 179–89.

which was in so dilapidated a state that, in wet weather, the rain came in upon the bed; and on cold, clear frosty nights, he could see the stars through the roof'.[599] It was through sleeping in such places that Joseph Entwisle and William Bramwell were crippled by rheumatism, and that John Petty suffered from disorders of the stomach and liver that were ultimately to kill him.[600]

Not only did Nonconformist preachers in the age of expansion have to endure physical hardship, they were frequently the victims of persecution. The way in which landlords in rural areas on occasion sought to stem the growth of Dissent by depriving tenants of their holdings has already been noted, and the strategy was sometimes extended to include threatening Nonconformists with the loss of their jobs. When the Leicestershire General Baptist Joseph Donisthorpe started preaching, local farmers and tradesmen tried to ruin him by withdrawing their custom from his blacksmith's forge.[601] And when, in 1809, the Methodists at Cotgrave in Nottinghamshire tried to build a Wesleyan chapel, the vicar and his supporters threatened local builders, brickmakers, and joiners with the loss of trade if they took any part in the project.[602] At Iddesleigh and Beaford in Devon people who joined the Bible Christians were threatened with the loss of employment and of parish relief.[603] At Brixton in the Isle of Wight the rector of the parish, the future Bishop of Oxford, Samuel Wilberforce, persuaded farmers to sack labourers who attended Bible Christian meetings and brought pressure to bear on the owner of a barn to eject from it the Bible Christians whom he had allowed to worship there.[604]

More direct methods were frequently used to deter Nonconformist expansion. William Bramwell, in the Blackburn circuit in 1787, had to defend himself with a large stick against bulldogs that were let loose on him whenever he passed a tan-yard.[605] At Epperstone in Nottinghamshire a landowner let a bull out of a field to scatter a Wesleyan open-air gathering; at Shrigley near Macclesfield the local squire ran a large mastiff through a Wesleyan service; and in Lincoln when William Clowes tried to introduce Primitive Methodism into the city opponents chased a goat through his meeting.[606] When a Congregational meeting-house was opened at Farnham in Surrey in 1793

---

[599] Entwisle, *Memoirs of Joseph Entwisle*, 26.

[600] Ibid. 264; Sigston, *Memoirs of Bramwell*, 263; Milburn in Dews, *From Mow Cop to Peake*, 62–3.

[601] Taylor, *History of the General Baptists*, ii. 12–13.   [602] Swift, *Lively People*, 47.

[603] Bourne, *Life of James Thorne*, 48–9.   [604] Bourne, *Bible Christians*, 242.

[605] Sigston, *Memoirs of Bramwell*, 28.

[606] Swift, *Lively People*, 46; Kendall, *Primitive Methodist Church*, i. 463; B. Smith, *Methodism in Macclesfield* (1875), 278.

'the wealthy and overbearing people in the town' encouraged a rabble to stone the worshippers and throw bricks through the meeting-house windows.[607] In 1818 the perpetual curate of Ansty in Wiltshire incited a riot against villagers meeting in a cottage to hear a Baptist preacher.[608] And when in 1817 a Wesleyan local preacher and landowner, William Lockwood, tried to preach in Newark market-place, the vicar ordered the town's chief fireman, who was also a barber, to bring out the fire-engine to drench the preacher with water. The Methodists recorded with grim satisfaction that the next time the fire-engine was called out it was to the barber's shop, for the unfortunate man was also a manufacturer of fireworks which accidentally exploded, blowing him through his shop window and mortally wounding him.[609]

Anglican antipathy to itinerant Nonconformists prompted Lord Sidmouth's attempt to control their activities in 1811,[610] and although Sidmouth's bill was withdrawn this did not stop hostile magistrates from harassing Dissenting preachers for the next twenty years. In 1812 a Wesleyan preacher named McKilrick was arrested while preaching in Tonge in Lancashire and taken to Bolton by 'horse soldiers with drawn swords'.[611] In 1821 the Primitive Methodist Samuel Waller was sentenced at Salford to three months' imprisonment on the ground of obstructing the public highway, and during his time in prison he was seriously ill with a bowel complaint.[612] Two years later when another Ranter, Francis Jersey, attempted to preach at the market cross at Dalton-in-Furness a 'gentleman in the town' hired three men to blow horns to drown his preaching. When this happened a second time those who wanted to hear the preacher 'threw a number of rotten eggs at the horn men, and then drove them off the cross, and a general battle ensued'. Jersey spent two weeks in Lancaster Castle for 'riotous and tumultuous worship' before being freed on bail.[613] In 1824 two Baptist preachers from Raunds, Northamptonshire, who were collecting money for a new chapel, were arrested as vagrants in Buckinghamshire and sentenced to a month's hard labour in Aylesbury gaol.[614] And in 1830 Thomas Russell, at Chaddleworth in Berkshire, was sentenced to three months' hard labour at the treadmill, of which he served one month, ostensibly for selling hymn

---

[607] J. Waddington, *Surrey Congregational History* (1866), 208–9.

[608] Lovegrove, 'Itinerant Evangelism', 194.

[609] Kendall, *Primitive Methodist Church*, i. 268–9.   [610] See Ch. III, sect. 3.

[611] R. F. Wearmouth, *Methodism and the Working-Class Movements of England, 1800–1850* (1937), 35.

[612] *Primitive Methodist Magazine*, 3 (1822), 281–3.

[613] Ibid. 4 (1823), 260–2, 283–4.

[614] R. W. Davis, *Political Change and Continuity, 1760–1885: A Buckinghamshire Study* (Newton Abbot, 1972), 64.

books and the *Primitive Methodist Magazine* without a licence, 'but really because he would persist in preaching the Gospel in the streets'.[615]

Much of this persecution, however, proved to be counterproductive. Jeremiah Gilbert, a Ranter preacher in the Sheffield circuit, was taken 'before the magistrates six or seven times for preaching the Gospel' in 1819–20, but his experiences merely increased the size of his audiences since people 'seemed to pay more attention to me when I was a prisoner than when I was a free man'.[616] Three Primitive Methodist preachers were imprisoned for a week in Worcester in 1820, and on their release 'held a vast meeting on the race ground'. 'Multitudes flocked in to see and hear those who had been in prison … and hundreds were in tears.'[617] When James Bonsor was imprisoned at Shrewsbury in August 1822 he was accompanied to prison by a huge crowd of sympathizers, and the following morning a practical token of their support was provided for him in the form of eight breakfasts.[618]

One of the most dramatic confrontations between itinerant evangelists and would-be persecutors occurred at Car Colston in Nottinghamshire in 1817. The Primitive Methodist evangelist John Benton was seeking to extend the Nottingham revival to the villages of the Trent valley and planned a camp-meeting on the village green at Car Colston near Bingham. The plan was bitterly opposed by some of the local clergy and landowners and half a dozen of them, led by Colonel Hildyard of Flintham Hall, rode up to the camp-meeting and 'commanded the people to disperse'. When the assembly refused to move, Hildyard 'threatened to read the Riot Act'. At this point William Lockwood intervened. Lockwood had been a Wesleyan itinerant preacher but had retired from the ministry in 1803 on marrying a wealthy widow of East Bridgford, and had settled down to farm his wife's estate. However he remained a local preacher and worshipped at the Wesleyan chapel in East Bridgford which had been built at his wife's expense.[619] Benton's arrival in East Bridgford revived Lockwood's interest in evangelism and led, as we have seen, to his confrontation with the fire-engine in Newark market-place. When Hildyard and his fellow gentry tried to disrupt the Car Colston camp-meeting, Lockwood rode up to the preaching stand and demanded by what authority Hildyard and his companions came there, 'to disturb religious worship'. Thus challenged by a fellow landowner Hildyard and company withdrew from the scene, 'disappointed and mortified'. George Herod, who at the time was a boy in East Bridgford, later

[615] Kendall, *Primitive Methodist Church*, ii. 332.
[616] *Primitive Methodist Magazine*, 2 (1821), 155–7, 213–15.   [617] Ibid. 35.
[618] Kendall, *Primitive Methodist Church*, ii. 278.   [619] Ibid. i. 234–7.

commented that 'clerical influence, in the vale of Belvoir, received at this meeting a heavy stroke, from the effects of which it has never recovered'. 'The working-classes, without fear of country squires or parsons, have gone on uninterruptedly in worshipping God according to the dictates of their consciences.'[620] The truth of Herod's observation was amply confirmed by the religious census of 1851.

While relations between Nonconformity and the established church in areas such as the vale of Belvoir were mostly bad, relations between the various Nonconformist denominations were on the whole good. Unitarians were, of course, regarded by most Evangelical Dissenters as heretics who were endangering men's souls, and in Wales the growth of Wesleyan Methodism in the early nineteenth century was looked on with hostility by Calvinist Nonconformists who, from their eighteenth-century experience, saw in Arminianism the first step in the declension towards Unitarianism.[621] And contention between Baptists and Independents over the rival merits of believer's baptism and infant baptism led in 1844 to a two-day public debate from wagons outside the Clarence Hotel in Rhymney, Monmouthshire, which attracted vast crowds and some disorder.[622] But co-operation was more usual than confrontation. Congregationalists preached in Baptist meeting-houses,[623] Baptists preached in Primitive Methodist and Bible Christian chapels,[624] Congregationalists met in Baptist and Wesleyan chapels when their own meeting-houses were being altered,[625] Wesleyans and Baptists co-operated in tract distribution,[626] and Congregationalists, Baptists, Wesleyans, and Primitive Methodists united for open-air meetings.[627] Even relations between the Wesleyans and the revivalist and secessionist Methodist denominations became cordial once the dust of the original schisms had settled. By 1850 it was becoming usual for either Wesleyan or Primitive Methodist chapels to close when special services were being held in the chapel of the other denomination in the same area, and for the pulpits of the one denomination to be occupied by the ministers of the other on such occasions.[628]

Indeed, the tendency towards fragmentation shown by the Methodist denominations in the first half of the nineteenth century, and the similar tendency among the Baptists and Congregationalists for individual congrega-

---

[620] Herod, *Biographical Sketches*, 293–5.
[621] T. Rees, *History of Protestant Nonconformity in Wales* (2nd edn., 1883), 421–2.
[622] Davies, *Religion in the Industrial Revolution*, 51–2.
[623] Harrison, 'Baptists of Nottinghamshire', i. 502.
[624] Morris, 'Primitive Methodism in Nottinghamshire', 348; Bourne, *The Bible Christians*, 241.
[625] Henderson, *History of the Castle Gate Congregational Church, Nottingham*, 165.
[626] Harrison, 'Baptists of Nottinghamshire', i. 499–500.
[627] Morris, 'Primitive Methodism in Nottinghamshire', 355.   [628] Ibid. 320.

tions to split and split again, contributed in no small measure towards the expansion of Dissent. A Primitive Methodist revival at Skelmanthorpe in the West Riding in 1821 encouraged 'holy rivalry' among the Wesleyans and resulted 'in such an outpouring of the Spirit as Skelmanthorpe had never seen'.[629] Unholy arguments were just as likely to promote amoeba-like growth among the Baptists and Congregationalists. Disputes over the election of new ministers and dissatisfaction with established pastors led to splits in existing churches and to the founding of new Congregational churches in Sheffield in 1774 and 1784, in Coventry in 1775, in Talgarth in 1811, in Chorley in 1835, in Southampton in 1844, in Bath in 1853, and of new Particular Baptist churches in Southwark in 1774, in Bacup in 1821, in Trowbridge in 1813 and again in 1821, and in Abergavenny in 1827.[630] Arguments over discipline resulted in the formation of new Congregational church at Warrington in 1811, and a disagreement over the voting rights of women members in Northampton in 1834 led to the foundation of new Particular Baptist church.[631] But it was the Baptists of Nottingham who perfected the policy of expansion by division. In 1816 the Stoney Street General Baptist church appointed a young man named Catton as assistant to their minister Robert Smith. Soon after his arrival it was alleged that Catton, when staying with a Baptist family in Newark, had attempted to kiss a forty-five-year-old woman in her bedroom, and when she had refused had offered her money to keep her quiet. Smith wanted Catton to go; the church voted by a majority of one that Catton should stay; Smith tried to keep Catton out of the pulpit; and after two magistrates and a constable were unable to reinstate Smith in his pulpit he and his supporters seceded to form a new church in Broad Street. Both the new churches flourished: by 1836 Broad Street had 304 members and Stoney Street 635.[632] In 1849 another dispute at Stoney Street between an established minister and a new co-pastor led to a further secession and to the founding of a new church on Mansfield Road.[633] And in

---

[629] Werner, *Primitive Methodist Connexion*, 123.

[630] Wickham, *Church and People in an Industrial City*, 47; J. Sibree and M. Caston, *Independency in Warwickshire* (1855), 67; T. G. Thomas and J. Jones, *Brecon and Radnor Congregationalism* (Merthyr Tydfil, 1912), 91; B. Nightingale, *Lancashire Nonconformity* (1890–3), ii. 17; A. T. Patterson, *A History of Southampton, 1700–1914* (Southampton, 1971), ii. 78; G. Redford and J. A. James, *The Autobiography of the Rev. William Jay* (1855), 233–4; K. R. Manley, 'John Rippon and the Particular Baptists', D.Phil. thesis (Oxford, 1967), 52; F. Overend, *History of the Ebenezer Baptist Church, Bacup* (1912), 190; W. Doel, *Twenty Golden Candlesticks* (1890), 123, 131–2, 149; B. P. Jones, *Sowing Beside all Waters: The Baptist Heritage of Gwent* (Cwmbran, 1985), 66.

[631] Nightingale, *Lancashire Nonconformity*, iv. 242–3; E. A. Payne, *College Street Church, Northampton* (1947), 30.

[632] Harrison, 'Baptists of Nottinghamshire', i. 106–14.   [633] Ibid. 137–40.

1847 dissatisfaction with the pastor of the George Street Particular Baptist church also led to a secession and to the formation of the Derby Road Particular Baptist church.[634] All four churches continued to thrive after the divisions of 1847–9, and although the foundations of the Mansfield Road and the Derby Road churches were occasioned by undignified squabbles, they were fully justified by Nottingham's increasing population.[635] As the seceders from the Back Street Particular Baptist church in Trowbridge maintained in 1821, 'the great increase in the population of this town' provides 'ample room for the establishing of another church, without interfering with such as are at present in this place'.[636]

Nonconformity flourished in an atmosphere of free trade and competition in religion. The multiplication of sects, said Samuel McAll, minister of the Castle Gate Congregational church in Nottingham, 'led to a division of labour in the Church of Christ'.[637] George Herod, the Primitive Methodist, rejoiced that the Church of Jesus Christ was 'divided into numerous sects'. 'It is our opinion,' he wrote in the introduction to his *Biographical Sketches*, 'that if the Church were confined to one particular mode of worship, or form of government, a diminution of usefulness would inevitably follow; and probably mankind would be in danger of sinking into darkness and superstition.' 'The awful state in which the world was placed, with respect to true piety, whilst Popery universally prevailed, and the mighty . . . spread of religion which took place upon the Reformation, exhibit a strong proof of the correctness of this opinion.'[638] George Herod's defence of the divisions of Nonconformity is reminiscent of that of John Robinson, pastor of the Pilgrim Fathers, over two centuries earlier.[639] Robinson's apologia was justified by the liberty that Dissenters helped to bring to seventeenth-century Englishmen. Herod's case was substantiated by the massive expansion of Nonconformity that took place between the death of John Wesley and the religious census of 1851.

---

[634] Ibid. 190–201.   [635] Ibid. 206.   [636] Doel, *Twenty Golden Candlesticks*, 132.
[637] J. C. Weller, 'The Revival of Religion in Nottingham, 1780–1850', B.D. thesis (Nottingham, 1957), 253.
[638] Herod, *Biographical Sketches*, 3.
[639] With which I ended Ch. I of Vol. I of *The Dissenters*.

II
'The Society of God's People'
The Community of Dissent

1. 'THIS PEOPLE SHALL BE MY PEOPLE':
THE CHURCH AND THE FAMILY

The conversion of millions of men and women in England and Wales to Evangelical Nonconformity in the first half of the nineteenth century was the result of the enthusiasm generated by the eighteenth-century revival and by the overseas missionary movement; of the deep reserves of supernatural and Christian belief which the Church of England had helped to conserve but which it was unable to tap in an age of rapid demographic and economic change; of the dedication, zeal, and self-sacrifice of thousands of itinerant ministers, local preachers, Sunday school teachers, and Christian parents; and of their passionate concern to save the souls, both of their loved ones and of total strangers, from what they saw as their imminent danger of everlasting torment in the fires of hell. But why did these millions, once converted, become attached and remain attached to their Dissenting meeting-house or Methodist chapel? For this there were two main reasons: the obligation imposed on every new convert to join in the great crusade to save his or her fellow men; and the fellowship, opportunities for service, and prospect of self-realization offered by the Dissenting community.

The great age of Nonconformist expansion was also a period of profound economic and social change, with the rapid growth of population, the application of revolutionary techniques to manufacturing industry, and the disruption of the traditional ways of the countryside through enclosure, the Speenhamland system, and the replacement of farm servants with day labourers. Alan Gilbert was so impressed by the coincidence of these developments that he put forward the view that one of the reasons for the success of Nonconformity was its role in satisfying the communal needs of people suffering from social disorganization ('anomie') and insecurity at a time when 'technological changes and changes in settlement patterns' were placing 'increasing numbers of people in unfamiliar, unstructured, and largely normless environments in early industrial England'.[1] It is, however, difficult to find evidence of any correlation between social dislocation and the growth of Nonconformity. Just as there is no simple correlation between mobility and a low degree of religious observance to support Inglis's thesis,[2] so there is no obvious connection between mobility and Nonconformist success to sustain Gilbert's case. Dissent flourished both in towns such as Merthyr Tydfil where, in 1851, 74 per cent of the adults were immigrants from outside, and in Lye in the Black Country where in 1851 82 per cent of the town's population had been born there.[3] Conversely Nonconformity was weak both in socially stable Bethnal Green and in highly mobile south Lancashire. There were, as we have seen in the cases of Dorothy Cellars and Ann Cliff, instances in which poor people were attracted to Methodist chapels because they offered relief for their destitution, but if the search for temporal security was a major factor in the growth of Dissent, it was one about which the sources for Nonconformist history are for the most part silent.

What those sources do make clear is that the appeal of the Nonconformist chapel was not so much as a haven for men and women suffering the effects of social dislocation, but as a psychological refuge for young men and women brought up in religious households who sought to return to the standards of their parents after a period of youthful rebellion. The chapel did serve people's communal needs, but so did the pub. And whether one chose the chapel or the pub as the focus of one's communal life depended to a large degree on the example one had been set by one's mother and father. Particularly instructive was the experience of William Robinson who was born at Haslingden in Lancashire in 1789 of Wesleyan parents. During his boyhood his mother took him to her class meetings 'where his tender heart was powerfully wrought upon whilst listening to the statements of the members respecting their religious experience', and had he remained at home, commented his biographer, 'the early impressions he received might more speedily have brought about his conversion'. But his father decided to send him

---

[1] Gilbert, *Religion and Society*, 89. Compare my discussion of Gilbert's thesis as applied to 18th-cent. Methodist preachers in *The Dissenters*, i. 408–9.

[2] See above, Ch. I, sect. 8.

[3] Hopkins, 'Religious Dissent in Black Country Industrial Villages', 420.

away to school and after completing his education he entered a 'mercantile establishment' in London where he was led astray by 'gay' companions. The death of his father not only brought him back to Haslingden, it marked also a return to his mother's values, 'to the society of God's people, and ultimate to a union with the church of Christ'.[4]

William Robinson's experience can be paralleled again and again in the conversion accounts of the late eighteenth and early nineteenth centuries. Alexander Kilham, the future founder of the Methodist New Connexion, resented his father's attempts to force him to 'attend public service and read the Scriptures on the Lord's day': he indulged in 'Sabbath-breaking, gaming, and other wicked habits, which caused my parents to weep and lament over me' until, at the age of eighteen, he was converted and 'returned to my father's home where we rejoiced together for what God had done for our souls'.[5] Robert Lomas, having been brought up at Monyash in Derbyshire by Wesleyan parents whose laws he 'esteemed . . . as binding', went to London at the age of thirteen, neglected both business and worship, and wasted money and associated 'with boys of bad practices' until guilt destroyed his appetite and health and led to his conversion: the immediate consequence was that he 'now earnestly longed to see [his] parents and relations'.[6] John Lawson, sent to London to be apprenticed to a wood-engraver by his Baptist father, for three years neglected his father's advice 'to attend the ministry of the Gospel every Sunday' until illness 'brought with it terror and uneasiness of mind' and sent him back to the Bible and his chapel.[7] William Pike 'was blest with pious parents', and 'to escape from the restraint of parental authority he enlisted as a soldier', but his father pursued him by 'by letters and prayers' which brought about his conversion.[8] Titus Close, sent to boarding-school by his Congregational parents, broke off 'the yoke of parental government' and frequented theatres and went sailing on Sundays until converted in a Wesleyan chapel.[9] In all such cases conversion marked a reversion to type, a return to the womb, the prodigal's home-coming. But in experiencing conversion one not only returned to the values of one's parents, and especially one's mother, one joined a vastly extended family. Thomas Tatham, after his conversion in the Wesleyans' Octagon Tabernacle in Nottingham in 1782, determined that 'This people shall be my people, and their God my God!' 'Their love to each other and to the preachers', he

---

[4] *Wesleyan Methodist Magazine*, 67 (1844), 529.
[5] Kilham, *Life of Alexander Kilham*, 4–5, 12.   [6] *Methodist Magazine*, 34 (1811), 4–8.
[7] *Baptist Magazine*, 18 (1826), 498–9.
[8] *Primitive Methodist Magazine*, 2nd ser. 8 (1838), 104.
[9] *Wesleyan Methodist Magazine*, 58 (1835), 402.

recalled, 'was without dissimulation.' 'I was delighted to see how affection-ately each individual shook hands with the preacher as he passed through the congregation. By the world they were persecuted and despised, which caused them to cleave closer to each other.'[10]

The close interconnection between family and church can be seen in all the Nonconformist denominations. Children were taken to chapel at an early age by Nonconformist parents and, increasingly as the nineteenth century progressed, sent to Sunday school. With the onset of puberty the chapel both fuelled the feelings of guilt which accompanied the development of sexual appetites and offered satisfaction of those appetites by providing marriage partners. Marriage with a member of the same chapel or denomination strengthened one's ties with the chapel community and frequently led to the founding or perpetuation of a dynasty that was to be a pillar of chapel society for generations to come. In 1798 Charlotte Talbot, a member of the Salem Congregational church in Hunslet Lane, Leeds, and herself the descendant of three generations of West Riding Dissenters, married Edward Baines, soon to be the proprietor of the *Leeds Mercury*. Baines himself did not join the Salem church until 1840, when he was sixty-five years old, but in the course of the nineteenth century twenty-nine of their descendants and fourteen of their descendants' marriage partners joined either Salem or its successor, East Parade.[11] The time span of the Talbot–Baines family's con-nection with West Riding Nonconformity thus stretched from the early eight-eenth century to the early twentieth century. Even more fruitful, over a shorter span of time, was the union of John and Jean McFarlan, weavers from Paisley, who joined the Particular Baptist church in Reading in 1782. Over the next hundred years fifty-one of their descendants joined the same church, of whom thirty-five became Sunday school teachers, eleven Sunday school superintendents, four deacons, and three deacons of other churches.[12] For a hundred years the New Connexion of General Baptists was served by a suc-cession of members of the Goadby family as ministers, missionaries, and lay preachers. The founder of the Baptist dynasty, the staymaker Joseph Goadby, joined the original New Connexion church at Barton-in-Fabis in Leicestershire in 1793, married the daughter of a fellow church member, and from 1799 until his death in 1841 served as pastor to the church at Packington and Ashby-de-la-Zouch. His eldest son, also Joseph, was pastor to General Baptist churches at Manchester, Leicester, and Loughborough, for twenty-

[10] Dunn, *Memoirs of Thomas Tatham*, 31.
[11] E. Baines, *Life of Edward Baines* (1851), 30–2, 291; C. Binfield, *So Down to Prayers: Studies in English Nonconformity 1780–1920* (1977), 72–3.
[12] C. A. Davis, *History of the Baptist Church, King's Road, Reading* (Reading, 1891), 47.

eight years was secretary to the General Baptist academy, and for twenty-six years editor of the *General Baptist Repository*. The elder Joseph's second son John went to Orissa as a missionary in 1833 and when ill-health forced him to leave India he moved to the New World and served as pastor to a succession of Free Will Baptist churches in Vermont and Canada. Joseph's third son, James, did not enter the ministry and established a printing business in Ashby, but he served the church of which his father had been pastor as a deacon and on nearly every Sunday for fifty years preached in the surrounding villages. The younger Joseph Goadby's first and sixth sons both became General Baptist ministers; his second son Thomas in 1873 became principal of the General Baptist college at Chilwell near Nottingham; and his third son, John Orissa, born in the year that his uncle went to India, also went to Orissa as a missionary, pioneered work among the animistic tribes of the Kond Hills, and died in India at the age of thirty-five.[13]

Dynasties were similarly established in the various Methodist denominations. H. B. Kendall, writing around 1905, observed that in Chester Primitive Methodism had 'become hereditary in families'. 'Amongst the officers and teachers of the Sunday school', he wrote, 'are children, grandchildren, and great-grandchildren of former superintendents, and there is one scholar who is at once the grandchild of the present superintendent and the fifth in descent from a former superintendent.'[14] The Bible Christian denomination was run virtually as a family concern by the Thorne family from their native village at Shebbear in west Devon. John Thorne, the farmer and patriarch of the family, was one of William O'Bryan's earliest supporters and was responsible for the building of the Bible Christians' first chapel at Lake. After criticism of O'Bryan's autocratic leadership of the denomination led to his resignation in 1829, John's son James became its undisputed leader, holding office either as president or secretary of the Bible Christian Conference between 1819 and 1835, editing the *Bible Christian Magazine* from 1829 to 1869, and serving as book steward from 1837 to 1869 and as a governor of the denominational school, Shebbear College, from 1837 to 1869. James married one of the Bible Christians' first itinerant female evangelists, Catherine Reed, and Catherine's father, William Reed, was himself four times president of the Conference. James Thorne's brother Samuel printed the denominational magazine, books, and tracts on the denominational press, also at Shebbear, and married Mary O'Bryan, the daughter of the denomination's founder.[15] Conversion and church membership, in a spiritual and often in a

---

[13] B. and L. Goadby, *Not Saints but Men* (1906), *passim*.
[14] Kendall, *Primitive Methodist Church*, i. 556.　　[15] Shaw, *Bible Christians*, 33, 52, 73–4.

practical sense, thus both reinforced the bond between child and mother and added to that bond ties that were to last a lifetime and beyond.

The sagas of these Nonconformist dynasties reveal not only the part played by the churches in forging family ties, but also the way in which those churches provided hundreds of thousands of men and women with opportunities for participation, self-expression, and leadership which would have been denied them in any other contemporary setting. In 1836 the *Wesleyan Methodist Magazine* published a 'Portrait of a Wesleyan Layman', a memoir of George Osborn of Rochester, who was clearly regarded as an exemplar of his type. Osborn had been a class leader for forty years, the treasurer to the trustees of the Rochester chapel for twenty-five years, a steward in the Rochester circuit for twenty-one years, and treasurer of three local auxiliaries of the Wesleyan Methodist Missionary Society.[16] Twenty years later the secretary of the London Diocesan Church Building Society told a select committee of the House of Lords that people were more willing to rent pews in Dissenting chapels than in Anglican churches because 'they have more offices in the Dissenting chapels'. 'They have deaconships and visitors, and tract distributors: and in these ways the Dissenting chapels manage to employ their people very much better than the Church in general does. This is an attraction to small shopkeepers and mechanics, who find they are looked upon as somebody in their congregation, and they are not an unheard-of unit as they are in the Church congregations.'[17] Among Methodists, calculated Robert Currie, 'one member in twelve was a local preacher or steward, one in ten a trustee, one in four a Sunday school officer or teacher'.[18] Not only was the member of a Nonconformist church the member of an extended family: he was the member of a family which conferred on him importance and status as an individual.

2. 'REHOBOTH: THE LORD HATH MADE ROOM FOR US': BARNS, OCTAGONS, AND TEMPLES

If the church was an extended family, the chapel was a larger home. In the late eighteenth and early nineteenth centuries many churches and indeed denominations began life as cottage meetings and thereafter graduated to barn and chapel. The Quaker Methodists of Warrington, James Crawfoot's

---

[16] *Wesleyan Methodist Magazine*, 62 (1839), 793.
[17] *Parliamentary Papers* (1857–8), ix. 59.   [18] R. Currie, *Methodism Divided* (1968), 46.

'Magic Methodists' of the Delamere Forest, the Wesleyan prayer-meetings which were the nucleus of the future Primitive Methodist Connexion, all met in cottages. Alan Gilbert has pointed to the coincidence of the growth of domestic industry and of the expansion of Evangelical Nonconformity,[19] and, as we shall see, the Baptists and Primitive Methodists of Leicestershire and the Primitive Methodists and New Connexion Methodists of Nottinghamshire contained a disproportionate number of framework-knitters.[20] Dorothy Valenze has suggested that the growth of cottage-based churches was part of 'the struggle for domestic security' in an increasingly uncertain world.[21] But the connection between domestic industry and the growth of Dissent lay not so much in the 'social disorganization' brought about by industrialization as in the integration of home and work. Nonconformity often flourished in a situation in which work as well as leisure was centred on the hearth. Hugh Bourne learned his religion and his reading from his mother while she was 'spinning at the wheel',[22] and in the Merioneth villages of Llanuwchllyn and Llangywer near Lake Bala religious revival was associated with 'knitting nights' when men and women gathered in each other's homes on winter evenings to knit stockings, to pray, and to discuss 'the doctrines and duties of religion'. Roger Thomas, Ap Fychan, recalled of his childhood in Llanuwchllyn in the early nineteenth century that these 'knitting nights' usually lasted three hours: matters such as 'original sin, the influence of the Holy Ghost, regeneration, justification, [and] the sacrifice of Christ' were discussed in a 'free and independent spirit', a chapter from the Bible was read and a verse sung, and the meeting was concluded with prayer. Such meetings, he observed 'were certain to awake in the minds of the children and young people [thoughts] concerning their eternal happiness'.[23]

Throughout the first half of the nineteenth century cottage meetings both supplemented the more formal services held in chapels and served as an alternative to chapel services for rural churches which were too small or too poor to support a permanent chapel, or which were unable to find a building site in the face of landlord opposition. The Wesleyans of Irby-upon-Humber in Lincolnshire worshipped 'for nearly half-a-century in the thatched cottage near the church occupied by Mrs Todd and her blind son, Frank'; the Baptists of Kirmington in the same county reported in 1851 that they had worshipped

[19] Gilbert, *Religion and Society*, 112–13.
[20] See below, Ch. II, sect. 9, and Tables XXXIV and XL.
[21] Valenze, 'Prophetic Sons and Daughters', 303.
[22] Walford, *Memoirs of Hugh Bourne*, i. 3.
[23] T. M. Owen, 'Chapel and Community in Glan-Llyn', in D. Jenkins *et al.*, *Welsh Rural Communities* (Cardiff, 1960), 206–12.

in a house for some sixty years; and at Appleby, also in Lincolnshire, the Primitive Methodists held services in the home of Richard Keightley for more than fifty years before they were able to build a chapel in 1894.[24]

Such cases were, however, exceptional. It was more usual for infant Nonconformist groups either to outgrow fairly rapidly their original cottage homes and move to a rented barn or shop, or to worship in some such place from the beginning. Nonconformist churches began life in a rich variety of buildings. The Wesleyans of Bradford-on-Avon in Wiltshire met in a room behind the bar of the Cross Keys public house, and in Walsall they met in the George Inn; in Bedford they worshipped over a hog-sty, in Grantham in a room over a smithy, and at Prescot 'in a garret in the tanyard'; at Keighley they gathered in a granary and in Leeds in a barber's shop.[25] The Primitive Methodists in Nottingham worshipped in a disused factory in the Broad Marsh capable of holding a thousand people, and at Woodborough in the same county they met in a 'barn carpeted with straw, [with] planks for seats and lit by candles mounted on a wood wheel'.[26] The Congregationalists at Formby in Lancashire were on occasion led in worship by the well-connected Thomas Raffles, minister of the large Newington Green church in Liverpool and cousin of Sir Stamford Raffles, the founder of Singapore. But they met in a building 'whose walls were mud, the roof straw, the floor bare earth, the pulpit the back of a chair, and the seats an old weaving-loom'.[27] And in Preston the Congregationalists occupied a room over a cockpit which was sometimes used for plays. On one occasion the Congregationalists were trying to worship at the same time that a performance of *Romeo and Juliet* was proceeding below, and the singing of the congregation so disturbed the players that 'Romeo came up and expostulated [and] threatened so violently, and with a drawn sword in his hand', that the Dissenters were obliged to end their service.[28]

Worshipping in barns, public houses, and over cockpits helped to give Nonconformity a sense of purpose, of vitality, and of excitement that it was one day to lose, but it also had obvious disadvantages and it became the ambition of most Nonconformist groups to graduate from their cottages,

---

[24] G. W. Dolbey, *The Architectural Expression of Methodism* (1964), 24; Ambler, *Lincolnshire Returns*, 238, xliv–xlv.

[25] L. F. Church, *The Early Methodist People* (1949), 38; Church, *More about Early Methodist People*, 10; Cumberland, 'Nonconformity in the Black Country', 64; *The Journal of the Rev John Wesley*, ed. N. Curnock (1909–16), ii. 463; Dolbey, *Architectural Expression of Methodism*, 29; Greaves, 'Analysis of the Spread of Methodism', 19.

[26] Kendall, *Primitive Methodist Church*, i. 202; Swift, *Lively People*, 68.

[27] T. S. Raffles, *Memoirs of the Life and Ministry of the Rev Thomas Raffles* (1865), 152.

[28] Nightingale, *Lancashire Nonconformity*, i. 26.

hay-lofts, and factories to their own purpose-built chapel or meeting-house.[29] But it was an ambition that was but slowly realized by many poor rural congregations: before 1800 most Welsh chapels were converted barns or houses, and as late as 1847 the number of rented chapels and rooms the Primitive Methodists were using for services outnumbered their permanent chapels by more than two to one.[30] Horace Mann calculated that in 1851 16 per cent of all Nonconformist places of worship were not permanent and separate buildings devoted solely to religious services.[31]

The older Dissenting denominations did of course have meeting-houses going back to the seventeenth and early eighteenth centuries. But even when these were not converted from cottages or barns and were specifically built for worship they usually looked like domestic buildings from the outside, and inside consisted of dark-stained pews and often a gallery, arranged on three sides of a rectangle facing a pulpit centred on the long wall.[32] Such a plan was adopted for some of the earliest Methodist chapels, such as those at Greetland, near Halifax, and at Colne in Lancashire, both built in 1777.[33] Other chapels were built on a square plan which was believed both to make preaching easier and to be justified by a text from the Book of Revelation, that 'the city of the Lord shall lie foursquare and the breadth shall be no greater than the width'.[34] Both the charming stone Unitarian Underbank chapel at Stannington near Sheffield, built in 1742 'for Protestant Dissenters of the Presbyterian or Congregational denominations', and the brick General Baptist meeting-house built in 1790 at Elim Court, Fetter Lane, London, with galleries round the four sides of building, were erected on a square plan, and again a number of early Methodist chapels followed suit.[35]

---

[29] Wesley called his purpose-built edifices 'preaching-houses' to indicate that they were not intended to rival the services of the established church. His successors used the buildings for the administration of the sacraments and even for liturgical worship and so called them 'chapels'. The Baptists and Congregationalists had always called their buildings 'meeting-houses' until, in the early 19th cent., they borrowed the term 'chapel' from the Methodists. The Quakers, who rejected the sacraments, continued to use the term 'meeting-house'.

[30] A. Jones, *Welsh Chapels* (Cardiff, 1984), 6; Kendall, *Primitive Methodist Church*, ii. 456.

[31] Jones and Williams, *Religious Census, South Wales*, p. xvii.

[32] Eighteenth-century Dissenting meeting-houses are attractively illustrated in K. Lindley, *Chapels and Meeting Houses* (1969), A. Jones, *Welsh Chapels* (Cardiff, 1984), and in the two superb volumes produced for the Royal Commission on Historic Monuments by Christopher Stell, *Nonconformist Chapels and Meeting-Houses in Central England* (1986) and in *South-West England* (1991). These books emphasize that both 18th-cent. meeting-houses and many 19th-cent. chapels are an important part of our architectural heritage and have as much right to conservation as have medieval parish churches.

[33] Dolbey, *Architectural Expression of Methodism*, 85–7.

[34] Revelation 21: 16; Jones, *Welsh Chapels*, 24.

[35] F. T. Wood, *A History of Underbank Chapel, Stannington* (Sheffield, 1944), 44–5;

But the Dissenting meeting-house which most commended itself to Wesley was the Presbyterian, later Unitarian, Octagon chapel in Norwich which he visited in 1757. 'It is eight-square', wrote Wesley, 'built of the finest brick, with sixteen sash-windows below, as many above and eight skylights in the dome, which, indeed, are purely ornamental. The inside is finished in the highest taste, and is as clean as any nobleman's saloon. The communion-table is fine mahogany; the very latches of the pew-doors are polished brass.'[36] The Norwich Octagon was begun in 1754 from plans drawn up for the city's Presbyterians by two local carpenters, Christopher Lee and Thomas Ivory.[37] It cost £5,000 and is dominated by a cupola supported on arches resting on eight fluted Corinthian columns, single tree trunks which rise from the floor to the dome in front of the galleries.[38] Wesley detested the liberal theology which John Taylor preached from the Octagon's pulpit and asked of its elegant interior, 'How can it be thought that the old coarse Gospel should find admission here?'. But this did not prevent him from urging his followers to build their preaching-houses, 'where the ground will permit, in the octagon form' since it was 'best for the voice'.[39] Between 1761 and 1776 eleven Methodist octagons were built in England and another three in Scotland, but their cost was much below that of the Norwich Octagon, ranging from £128. 2s. 6d. in Nottingham to £977. 8s. 9d. in Bradford.[40] When Wesley preached in the Nottingham Octagon in 1766 'in the morning the house contained the congregation; but in the evening many were constrained to go away',[41] and the incident, only two years after the building of the chapel, illustrates the great disadvantage of the octagons: they were incapable of accommodating the vast numbers of people who sought to worship in Methodist chapels in the great age of Nonconformist expansion. The Nottingham Methodists moved to a new, almost square chapel in Hockley in 1783 and the Octagon was sold to the Baptists for £250.[42]

It was because of the need to accommodate rapidly increasing congregations that the most favoured plan for both Methodist and Old Dissenting chapels was neither the octagon nor the square nor the rectangle with the

W. Wilson, *The History and Antiquities of the Dissenting Churches and Meeting Houses in London* (1810), iii. 474; Lindley, *Chapels and Meeting Houses*, 56; Dolbey, *Architectural Expression of Methodism*, 93–6.

[36] *Wesley's Journal*, iv. 244.   [37] F. Jenkins, *Architect and Patron* (1961), 157–9.
[38] H. Davies, *Worship and Theology in England*, iv. *From Newman to Martineau, 1850–1900* (Princeton, NJ, 1962), 62.
[39] Church, *Early Methodist People*, 53.
[40] Dolbey, *Architectural Expression of Methodism*, 103–10.   [41] *Wesley's Journal*, v. 160.
[42] Swift, *Lively People*, 21–2.

pulpit against the long wall, but the auditorium with both pulpit and communion table centred on the short wall of a long rectangle, surrounded on
three sides by galleries. Both the New Room in Bristol, built in 1739 and the
oldest Methodist chapel in the world, and Wesley's chapel in the City Road,
London, begun in 1777 to replace the Foundry as the headquarters of
Methodism, were built on this plan, and they became the model for the thousands of Nonconformist chapels which sprang up in every city and town, and
in many villages, in the late eighteenth and early nineteenth centuries.
Externally the City Road chapel was built in a plain Georgian style with two
semi-circular rounded windows on either side of the entrance and three more
above under a gable-end.[43] A Greek entrance porch was added around 1809
and in this respect, too, the City Road chapel provides an early example of
what was to become a major influence on Nonconformist chapel architecture
for the next half-century: the inspiration of classical Greece. For the increasingly populous and prosperous congregations of the manufacturing and commercial towns of England and Wales the Greek temple became the ideal
external model with which to clothe the inner sanctuary of the Nonconformist chapel. St Mary's Particular Baptist church in Norwich opened a
new meeting-house in 1812 with an 'imposing front of white bricks, with
Grecian portico and an ample flight of stone steps' which no doubt owed
something to the example of the Norwich Octagon; around 1820 the Carr's
Lane chapel in Birmingham became the first Congregational meeting-house
to be built in the Greek style; and the Unitarian chapel in Brighton, built also
in 1820, was modelled on the temple of Theseus with a Doric portico. In the
opinion of the *Royal Brighton Guide* of 1827 the town's new Unitarian
chapel was 'built after the manner of a heathen temple', but for the moment
Dissenters had no qualms about emulating the architectural style of pagan
temples: to the treasurer of the Norwich Baptists the great merit of their new
meeting-house was its freedom 'from all popery and popish adornments of
Gothic within and Gothic without, as well as from all vestiges of popish
canonicals'.[44]

For the Methodists Wesley had laid down that their preaching-houses
should be 'plain and decent but not more expensive than is absolutely necessary'. The interior of the chapels should contain no unnecessary adornments
such as 'Chinese paling' or 'tub-pulpits', and, presumably to deter congregations from falling asleep, there should be 'no pews, and no backs to the seats'
which should be 'parted in the middle, by a rail running all along to divide the

---

[43] Dolbey, *Architectural Expression of Methodism*, 48.
[44] *Baptist Quarterly*, 10 (1940–1), 344: Davies, *Worship and Theology*, iv. 50; J. Rowland,
'Christ Church (Unitarian), New Road, Brighton', *TUHS* 10 (1951–4), 152.

men from the women'.[45] Wesley's insistence that men and women sit apart
provoked some opposition: he was forced to warn Methodist leaders in
Sheffield in 1780 that he would never again set foot in preaching-houses in
which men and women were mixed together, and that he would forbid collections to be made for such places.[46] The rule appears to have been obeyed
in most Methodist preaching-houses during Wesley's own lifetime, as it was
in some Baptist and Congregational meeting-houses, but it proved impossible to insist on the segregation of the sexes as chapels became a focus of
family life and with the increasing reliance on pew rents to sustain chapel
finances. Kenneth Lindley concludes from the evidence of the Wesleyan
chapel at Elvington near York, built in 1810, that since the building has sets
of original hat-pegs along each wall 'by that date it had become customary for
families to sit together without segregation of the sexes'.[47] But even in the
1870s men and women who did not have family pews were kept apart in some
Congregational chapels, and there were separate seating arrangements for
the sexes in the Wesleyan chapel at Hayle in Cornwall as late as 1893.[48]

In the early nineteenth century the interiors of many Baptist and Congregational meeting-houses had remained unchanged for a hundred or a
hundred and fifty years. William Hale White was no doubt recalling the
Bunyan Meeting in Bedford of the 1830s when he described how on Sunday
mornings Mark Rutherford and his fellow scholars were 'marched across the
road' after Sunday school to the chapel, 'a large old-fashioned building dating from the time of Charles II'. 'The floor was covered with high pews. The
roof was supported by three or four tall wooden pillars which ran from the
ground to the ceiling and the galleries by shorter pillars. There was a large
oak pulpit on the side against the wall, and down below, immediately under
the minister, was the "singing pew", where the singers and musicians sat, the
musicians being performers on the clarinet, flute, violin, and violoncello.
Right in front was a long enclosure, called the communion pew, which was
usually occupied by a number of the poorer members of the congregation.'[49]
By 1850 chapel orchestras were being replaced by organs and in the new
auditoriums the pulpit had been moved from the long wall to a central position against the end wall of the long rectangle, but in other respects the
interiors of Dissenting meeting-houses remained as they had been in the

---

  [45] Church, *Early Methodist People*, 53–4.   [46] *Wesley's Letters*, vii. 32.
  [47] Lindley, *Chapels and Meeting Houses*, 37.
  [48] Browne, *Congregationalism in Norfolk and Suffolk*, 240; T. Shaw, *A History of Cornish
  Methodism* (Truro, 1967), 42–3.
  [49] White, *Autobiography of Mark Rutherford*, 5–6. Bedford Old Meeting was in fact built in
  1707 (H. G. Tibutt, *Bunyan Meeting, Bedford* (Bedford, 1950), 24).

eighteenth century and the new Methodist chapels closely resembled them: the dark varnished pews, the galleries supported on columns of wood or stone or cast iron, the high sash-windows, and the dominating pulpit emphasizing that the building's chief function was the preaching of the word of God. The pulpit, writes Anthony Jones, 'was nearly always the most elaborate interior feature of the chapel from which the preacher commanded like a captain on the bridge of a ship'.[50] Despite Wesley's disapproval, in urban Methodist chapels backless forms gave place to more comfortable pews, but in some rural meeting-houses moveable seats without backs were retained until well into the nineteenth century: at Tan-y-Fron in Denbighshire when 'some members asked to be allowed to have proper pews' their 'request was considered to be an extravagant luxury' and was only granted 'after they had agreed to install the pews themselves at their own expense'.[51] The walls of the chapels were usually whitewashed and sometimes decorated with appropriate texts set in embellished scrolls: congregations were reminded that 'God is Love' and urged to 'Repent . . . for the Kingdom of Heaven is at hand'.[52] In Dursley's Old Tabernacle (once part of Whitefield's Rodborough Connexion and after 1784 a Congregational chapel) it was the preacher who was warned by a board fitted to the gallery, 'His blood will I require of the watchman's hand'.[53] In the Independent Primitive Methodist chapel at Lowdham in Nottinghamshire preachers were admonished from a text over the doorway facing the pulpit to 'Preach the Gospel'.

Anglican critics such as Thomas Arnold denounced these late eighteenth- and early nineteenth-century Dissenting chapels for their 'coarseness and deformity', and even the Congregationalist Thomas Rees dismissed them as 'plain, unsightly buildings, more like barns or warehouses than places of worship'.[54] But John Betjeman, in his enthusiastic appraisal of Nonconformist architecture, points out that barns were 'serviceable structures obeying the traditional rules of proportion and solid craftsmanship' and goes on to describe Nonconformist chapels as 'the true architecture of the people'. They were paid for by voluntary contributions, built by local builders and carpenters out of local materials, decorated by local ironmongers anddrapers, polished and cleaned by humble caretakers and chapel ladies: 'not since medieval days had the people clubbed together to adorn a place of worship'.[55] Dan Taylor, the founder of the New Connexion of General Baptists,

---

[50] Jones, *Welsh Chapels*, 66.   [51] Ibid. 21. See also Rees, *Nonconformity in Wales*, 45.

[52] Lindley, *Chapels and Meeting Houses*, 39.   [53] Evans, *As Mad as a Hatter!*, 71–2.

[54] T. Arnold, *Principles of Church Reform* (1833), 69–70, cited by Cunningham, *Everywhere Spoken Against*, 84; Rees, *Nonconformity in Wales*, 45.

[55] J. Betjeman, *First and Last Loves* (1960), 101–3.

quarried the stone for his meeting-house at Wadsworth near Hebden Bridge in 1763, and the popular Bible Christian preacher Billy Bray built the chapel at Kerley Downs in Cornwall with his own hands.[56] Even the very names of the chapels proclaimed their origin as monuments of the people's faith. Some were called Siloam: 'hither men have come blind, and have departed seeing'. Others were named Bethesda: 'in this place a man thirty-eight years in his infirmity was made whole, and arose and walked'. Salem indicated that 'the revolt of rebellious souls has been subdued'; Pisgah was the place from which the children of God looked 'out over the Promised Land'; and Bethel suggested 'the house of God'. In Wales whole communities took their name from Nonconformist chapels such as Ebenezer and Bethesda,[57] and in Nottingham the Primitive Methodists' Canaan chapel gave its name to the street in which it was situated. Most poignant of all was the name used for some Cornish chapels by the Bible Christians, who, 'driven from cottage to cottage and sorely cramped for a meeting-place, found themselves at last with a building all their own, and in their gladness they cry Rehoboth, "for the Lord hath made room for us" '.[58]

3. 'CROWN HIM, LORD OF ALL!': PREACHING AND PRAISE

Just as the meeting-houses of Dissent encompassed not only converted barns and disused factories but also elegant sanctuaries styled on Greek temples, so Nonconformist preaching embraced both the unsophisticated hell-fire sermons of the Primitive Methodists and the cultured rational discourses of the Unitarians, while Nonconformist worship ran the whole gamut from the spontaneous and exuberant revivalist meetings of the Bible Christians through the dignified liturgical services of the Wesleyans to the frequently silent waiting on God of the Quakers.

In their contributions to the essay competition of 1858 both John Stephenson Rowntree and Samuel Fothergill pointed to Quaker worship as one of the reasons for the decline of the Society of Friends. In Rowntree's view the Quaker belief that any Friend who felt moved by the Holy Spirit could rise and speak in his or her meeting had, by the nineteenth century, diminished the number of Quaker preachers. While such a practice might, 'in the first outburst of zeal, increase the number of preachers; yet when that zeal

[56] Underwood, *A History of the English Baptists*, 152; Bourne, *The King's Son*, 59.
[57] Sylvester, *Rural Landscape of the Welsh Borderland*, 187 n. 2.
[58] H. W. Horwill in Bourne, *The Bible Christians*, 62.

cooled, its effect was precisely the reverse; and, instead of having in each congregation many who possessed and exercised the gift and "true liberty of
prophesying", such became even less numerous than in the other churches
... where the ministrations were confined to one person'.[59] Samuel Fothergill
similarly pointed out that the Quaker practice of waiting on the Spirit both
increased the boredom and diminished the amount of Scriptural instruction
in Friends' meetings. He estimated that in the whole of England 'not a quarter of an hour on an average in each meeting of every Sabbath is occupied in
oral communication', while 'many meetings have no minister at all, and generally spend the whole time in silence'.[60] The tedium of many Quaker meetings was recorded with bitterness in the diary of thirteen-year-old Louisa
Gurney, daughter of the prosperous Norwich wool-stapler John Gurney of
Earlham Hall, and sister to the future banker Joseph John Gurney and to
Elizabeth Fry. The Gurney children were compelled by their father to attend
the Quaker meeting-house in Goat's Lane, Norwich, at least once every First
Day and Louisa resented having to spend 'Sunday so disagreeably and use-
lessly'. After spending '*four* hours at Meeting' on Christmas eve, 1797, she
wrote that she 'wished never, never, to see that nasty hole again'. Of John
Gurney's seven daughters only two died as Friends.[61]

The contrast between the near-silent meetings of the Quakers and the
noisy, boisterous, and exciting services of the Primitive Methodists and Bible
Christians goes far to explain the appeal of the latter and the unpopularity
of the former. In an age when respectable opportunities for leisure were limited the services of the revivalist Methodist denominations, and even of the
Wesleyans, Baptists, and Congregationalists, provided people both with the
entertainment of listening to a stirring oratorical performance and with the
exhilaration of participating in an emotional and sometimes inspiring event.
When the Primitive Methodist John Oxtoby was leading a prayer-meeting at
Swinehopeburn in Durham in 1824 a man whom he said 'was going to get his
soul sanctified ... fell down, and tumbled about the floor', three others also
started 'rolling about in the same manner', and half an hour later they 'arose
with uplifted hands, shouting Glory! Glory! Glory!'. Four days later when
Oxtoby preached at Westgate chapel in Weardale men and women again
'began to fall over on all sides, crying "Glory! Glory! Glory!" '. 'Some ran out
of the chapel. One said it was devilism. To some it appeared nothing but confusion; some were praying with mourners, others rejoicing with believers,

---

[59] Rowntree, *Quakerism Past and Present*, 33.
[60] Fothergill, *Essay on the Society of Friends*, 46.
[61] A. J. C. Hare, *The Gurneys of Earlham* (1895), i. 70, 90, 328.

and others were singing.'[62] Bible Christian meetings could be even more uninhibited than those of the Primitive Methodists, and although William Clowes objected to fettering the souls of men 'too much with what [is called] system and order',[63] when he visited Cornwall in 1825 he found that the enthusiasm of the Bible Christians went too far even for his tastes. He preached at Twelve Heads near Redruth and was annoyed by 'several of Mr O'Bryan's people [who] were present who began in the worship to laugh and dance'. When the Bible Christians started to meet at Michaelstow in 1818 a villager complained that his sleep was disturbed because 'the buggers were up chorusing at an early hour' on Sunday mornings. Nine years later the inhabitants of St Columb were said to have been annoyed by the noise engendered by a Bible Christian meeting held in a room above the market-place: 'what with the ravings and shrieks of the preachers and their disciples within, and the shouts and laughter of the crowds without, the place was a perfect Babel'.[64] Even Wesleyan services in Cornwall could be noisy affairs: Charles Richardson visited the Redruth area a quarter of a century after William Clowes and found that 'when a sinner is convicted, the people around him begin to shout . . . [they] appear to think that a penitent is not soundly converted unless they make a great noise'.[65] But even in his native Lincolnshire Richardson could evoke a spontaneous emotional response from his congregations. On one occasion when he was preaching on 'The kingdom of God' 'his audience became very much impressed, and many voices gave loud expression to adoring joy and exultation'. Richardson broke off his sermon and exclaimed, 'Let us crown Him!' and 'sang out in his own rich and ringing tones'

> All hail the power of Jesu's name!
> Let angels prostrate fall,
> Bring forth the royal diadem,
> And crown Him Lord of all!

'The whole of the congregation arose upon their feet and with deep emotion and grand effect joined in the hymnal coronation of their Lord, swelling the chorus, "Crown Him! Crown Him! Lord of all!" '[66]

Noisy, emotional interruptions of worship were, however, frowned upon by many Wesleyans, and especially by ministers. In Leicester a man named Andrews, 'an eccentric character, but a sterling jewel', was said to have 'lost

[62] *Primitive Methodist Magazine*, 6 (1825), 271.
[63] Valenze, 'Prophetic Sons and Daughters', 41, citing W. Clowes, *Journals*, 26, 53.
[64] Shaw, *The Bible Christians*, 85–6; Rule, 'Labouring Miner in Cornwall', 267.
[65] Coulson, *The Peasant Preacher*, 197; see also 203, 205.   [66] Ibid. 362.

his status as a Wesleyan in consequence of breaking out into bursts of praise during the time of service' and as a result joined the Primitives.[67] John Jackson, a Black Country collier, shouted ' "Glory!" whenever he felt so moved', but the wealthier members of his Wesleyan congregation disapproved of such responses and he was 'plain told . . . that persons of culture could not endure such interruptions'.[68] Unlike the Congregationalists and the Presbyterians, the Wesleyans had not broken with the Church of England because they could not give their 'unfeigned assent and consent' to the Book of Common Prayer, and the Wesleyan leadership continued to emphasize 'the value of liturgical solemnity in public and sacramental worship'.[69] For much of the nineteenth century Wesleyans in some areas still attended both their parish church and their Methodist chapel: in Bradford in the West Riding the Wesleyans delayed holding services in 'church-hours' for as long as the parish church was able to contain both the Wesleyan and the Anglican congregations; in 1812 the vicar of Bridgerule in Devon observed that the Methodists in his parish worshipped more regularly in his church than did parishioners who were not Methodists; in 1861 Wesleyan local preachers altered the time of their services at Burton Joyce in Nottinghamshire to avoid clashing with services at the parish church; and as late as 1871 Wesleyans at Spridlington in Lincolnshire were still leaving their chapel 'sufficiently early to go straight to morning service at the parish church'.[70] The Plan of Pacification of 1795 tried to insist that if Wesleyans did hold services at times which conflicted with those of the established church, they should at least use either the Prayer Book or Wesley's abridgement of it, and in London and the large towns the injunction was widely obeyed.[71] When the Wesleyan Brunswick chapel in Liverpool was built in 1811 at a cost of £8,000 Adam Clarke advised its superintendent minister, Joseph Entwisle, to use the Anglican liturgy: 'where we read these prayers, our congregations become better settled, better edified, and put further out of the reach of false doctrine'.[72] Alexander Mather, when reflecting on the Yorkshire revival of 1794, had argued that one of the obstacles to revivalism among the Wesleyans had

---

[67] Kendall, *Primitive Methodist Church*, i. 207.

[68] Leese, 'Impact of Methodism on Black Country Society', 133, citing H. Bunting, *Old Glory: A Story of South Staffordshire Methodism* (n.d.), 841.

[69] *Wesleyan Methodist Magazine*, 64 (1841), pp. i, v.

[70] *Wesleyan Methodist Magazine*, 68 (1844), 95; A. Warne, *Church and Society in Eighteenth Century Devon* (Newton Abbot, 1969), 109; Swift, *Lively People*, 139; Obelkevich, *Religion and Rural Society*, 214.

[71] *Minutes of the Methodist Conferences* (1812–55), i. 322; Church, *More About Early Methodist People*, 223.

[72] Entwisle, *Memoirs of Joseph Entwisle*, 239.

been 'a too anxious attachment to decorum and order, and a strong aversion to loud lamentations and cries, especially in the public congregation'.[73] But, in the nineteenth century, the outbreaks of spontaneous enthusiasm that had characterized the Yorkshire revival were discouraged by the Wesleyan leadership, and in the large urban chapels at least decorum and order reigned.

Though their theology was anathema to the Wesleyans, the Unitarians shared both the aversion of the Wesleyan leadership to unseemly behaviour during worship and their devotion to decorum and order. Just as Primitive Methodists saw in the Wesleyan clinging to the Anglican Prayer Book evidence that their Evangelical enthusiasm was waning, so Congregationalists saw in the Presbyterian hankering after liturgies further evidence of that denomination's departure from its Calvinist heritage. In 1753 *A Specimen of a Liturgy* had been published by an anonymous Dissenting minister who had come to the conclusion that congregations were too inclined to look upon public prayer as the sole business of their minister and to regard his performance as either 'a trial of skill or a test of orthodoxy'.[74] The author of the liturgy had been prevented by the opposition of his congregation from introducing the liturgy in his own meeting-house, but the proposed liturgy found some support among Presbyterians in Liverpool, and in 1763 members of both the Benn's Garden and Kay Street meetings in the city seceded in order to found a third meeting, the Octagon, in which liturgical services could be held. Three liberal Presbyterian ministers, John Seddon of Warrington, Phillip Holland, and Richard Goodwin, composed a liturgy for the new meeting-house, but the experiment was not a success and the Octagon closed in 1776.[75] However the failure of the Liverpool liturgy did not prevent other liberal Presbyterians and Unitarians from trying to emulate the Liverpool experiment. The former Anglican vicar and Unitarian minister Theophilus Lindsey produced a revised liturgy for use in his Essex Street chapel in 1774; Lindsey's liturgy was adopted by the Unitarian meeting in Shrewsbury in 1780; and liturgical orders of service were also adopted by the Mill Hill chapel in Leeds in 1801, by the Old Meeting in Birmingham in 1829 (though dropped again in 1835) and by George's Meeting, Exeter, around 1833.[76] To contemporaries the connection between the adoption of liturgical forms and the waning of religious zeal seemed obvious. Job Orton found 'that the most

---

[73] *Arminian Magazine*, 17 (1794), 603.   [74] *A Specimen of a Liturgy* (1752), 2–4.

[75] A. Holt, *Walking Together, A Study in Liverpool Nonconformity* (1938), 126–7, 134, 146.

[76] T. Belsham, *Memoirs of Theophilus Lindsey* (1820), 75; Ditchfield, 'Unitarianism and Radicalism', 330; W. L. Shroeder, *Mill Hill Chapel, Leeds* (1924), 53; J. Murch, *A History of the Presbyterian and General Baptist Churches in the West of England* (1833), 410; E. Bushrod, 'The History of Unitarianism in Birmingham from the Middle of the 18th Century to 1893', MA thesis (Birmingham, 1954), 76–7.

serious and exemplary Christians are for free prayer', whereas 'those who are lukewarm, though in general sober and virtuous, seem willing to admit forms'.[77] The Congregationalists David Bogue and James Bennett noted with relief that neither the Independents nor the Particular Baptists contemplated the use of liturgies, and poured scorn on the Unitarian claim that the use of liturgies would reconcile 'members of the Church of England to the dissenting worship'. If any Anglicans strayed into a Unitarian meeting, they scoffed, they must have imagined themselves 'in Nova Zembla, when the Presbyterian teacher read the Liverpool liturgy with his frozen lips, and must have fled with shivering and horror from the place'.[78]

That these two Congregationalists should have criticized the Unitarian Presbyterians for 'coldness' is itself a reflection of the change that was coming over services, and especially the sermons, of both the Independents and the Particular Baptists. Dissenting sermons of the eighteenth century, recalled the Congregationalist William Jay, were 'studied, grammatically correct, and methodical; but, with a very few exceptions, pointless, cold, and drawled off from notes'.[79] The sermons of Thomas Toller, who was minister of the Kettering Congregational church from 1776 to 1821, consisted of the minute dissection and exhaustive elucidation of the supposed meaning of biblical passages.[80] The Old General Baptists had retained extempore preaching as a vestige of their tradition of 'liberty of prophesying' and the church at Turner's Hill in Sussex criticized the use of notes 'or writing sermons at full length by the preaching brother' in 1745, but among Congregationalists and Presbyterians the practice of reading sermons had become increasingly common by the mid-eighteenth century.[81] Job Orton, who ministered to a combined congregation of Presbyterians and Independents at Shrewsbury from 1741 to 1765, 'always wrote the whole of his sermons with great care' and regarded it as exceptional and reprehensible that Philip Doddridge preached extempore at Northampton, 'which was very improper before a number of divinity students'.[82]

By the early nineteenth century the Evangelical revival had brought a new style of preaching to the Dissenting pulpit: extempore, emotional, passionate, dramatic, designed to bring the hearer to a pitch of excitement at which he would respond to the call to confess that he was a sinner and that he was in

---

[77] S. Palmer (ed.), *Letters to Dissenting Ministers from the Rev. Mr Job Orton* (1806), i. 21.

[78] D. Bogue and J. Bennett, *History of Dissenters* (1810), iii. 343–6.

[79] G. Redford and J. A. James (eds.), *The Autobiography of the Rev. William Jay* (1855), 141.

[80] Goodman, *The Great Meeting, Kettering*, 44.

[81] W. H. Burgess, 'The Church Book of the General Baptist Church of Turner's Hill and Horsley', *TUHS* 1 (1917–18), 214; Bogue and Bennett, *History of Dissenters*, iii. 339.

[82] Palmer, *Letters to Dissenting Ministers*, i. 1, 4.

need of salvation. Every sermon, wrote Andrew Fuller, 'should have an errand': the 'eternal salvation' of those who heard it.[83] William Jay claimed that some Dissenting ministers were so impressed by the 'strokes of fancy, touches of passion, striking metaphors, plain anecdotes, bold addresses and characteristic applications to the conscience' which distinguished Methodist preaching, that they produced a style of preaching which combined the best features of both Dissenting and Methodist sermonizing.[84] Bogue and Bennett maintained that it was Whitefield who brought his fellow Calvinists back to the traditions of Baxter and set before them the example of 'homely, straight-forward, and pointed address[es] . . . to impenitent sinners to seek the salva-tion of their souls'. By 1812, they claimed, the reading of sermons among Evangelical Dissenting ministers 'has almost gone out of fashion': 'where it is retained instead of procuring, as in the former period, commendation for a display of Dissenting regularity, it is now generally considered as the staff of the feeble, and the crutch of the lame'.[85] The reading of sermons, like the use of liturgies, came to be regarded as a mark of the fall from Evangelical grace: Yorkshire Congregationalists pointedly related the story of Daniel Jones, Presbyterian minister at Mixenden in the 1780s, who one Sunday morning left his congregation to sing hymns 'while he ran nearly half a mile to Sandy-fore to fetch his forgotten sermon'.[86] When Evangelical Dissenters did con-tinue to write out their sermons they tried to hide the fact from their congregations: Thomas Raffles 'so far committed [them] to memory that people were for the most part ignorant that he had his notes in the pulpit'; when John Angell James preached for two hours to the London Missionary Society in 1819 he took the precaution of handing the manuscript of his ser-mon to his brother who, seated by his side, acted as prompter; and John Leifchild even went to the length of writing out his sermons *after* they had been delivered.[87] Bogue and Bennett claimed that the Methodists and the Old Dissenters had influenced each other's preaching styles to their mutual benefit: 'the Dissenter had adopted the more natural address and easy con-versation style of the Methodist; and the Methodist has taken to the more regular divisions and orderly method of the Dissenter'.[88]

[83] O. C. Robison, 'Particular Baptists in England, 1760–1820', D.Phil. thesis (Oxford, 1963), 231, citing A. Fuller, *Works*, iv. 678–82.
[84] Redford and James (eds.), *Autobiography of William Jay*, 142.
[85] Bogue and Bennett, *History of Dissenters*, iv. 313, 346.
[86] Miall, *Congregationalism in Yorkshire*, 319.
[87] Raffles, *Memoirs of Thomas Raffles*, 217; Dale, *John Angell James*, 143; Leifchild, *John Leifchild*, 204.
[88] Bogue and Bennett, *History of Dissenters*, iv. 346.

No greater compliment could be paid to a preacher than that which was said of David Davies, who was ordained pastor of the small Independent church at Drefach near Llangeler in Cardiganshire in 1790 and who in 1795 moved to the co-pastorate of the Congregational churches at Mynyddbach, Morriston, and Sketty near Swansea. Davies remained at Sketty until his death in 1816 and was renowned throughout south-west Wales for his melodious voice, for his eloquent delivery, and for the facility with which he could captivate his audiences and move them to tears. 'Mr Davies's style of preaching', it was said, 'was especially adopted to alarm the unconverted, and to win them to the love of religion.'[89]

The effect which the greatest Welsh Nonconformist preachers strove for was the *hwyl*, the emotional climax of the sermon. Paxton Hood explained to his English readers that '*hwyl* is the Welsh for the canvas of a ship, and probably the derivation of the meaning is from the canvas or sails of a ship filled with a breeze: the word for a breeze, *awel*, is like it, and is used to denote a similar effect'.[90] An example of the way in which the *hwyl* was summoned up is provided by the preaching of Robert Roberts, a Calvinistic Methodist from Clynnog in Caernarfonshire. Robert Roberts, although 'originally a farm labourer of scarcely any education', had 'a powerful voice, retentive memory . . . natural dramatic oratory, and extraordinary fervour and boldness'. The dramatic quality of his preaching was provided by alternating passages of calm and outbursts of exclamation and tears. He would interrupt the flow of his oratory by bowing his head, remaining silent for a moment, and then whispering, 'Hush, hush, hush! What did I hear?' 'Then he would thunder out, till the whole congregation trembled: "Upon the wicked He shall rain snares, fire, and brimstone, and a horrible tempest: this shall be the portion of their cup!" '[91]

Such oratorical devices were not limited to uneducated Welsh Methodists. Reports which have been preserved of the sermons of John Leifchild, the educated Congregational minister of the prosperous Craven chapel in London, suggest a preaching style very similar to that of Robert Roberts. James Baldwin Brown sat under Leifchild as a young man and later recalled how 'he would paint in the most intense and vivid language the tremendous issues which were hanging upon his appeals . . . the joy of the redeemed, the horror of the lost; . . . the anguish of the remembrance, "Too late! too late!" in the abode of eternal pain'. A contributor to the *London Magazine* in 1821 reported hearing Leifchild, 'at the close of a striking description of the alarm

---

[89] Rees, *Nonconformity in Wales*, 434–9. [90] Paxton Hood, *Christmas Evans*, 16.
[91] Evans, *Christmas Evans*, 62–3.

felt by a sinner at the approach of death, exclaim in a wild tone, "His friends rush to him—he is gone!" then with a solemn impressiveness add, "*he is dead!*" and at last, in a voice that came on the ear like low thunder pronounce, "*He is damned!*" The effect was petrifying and withering."[92]

In the eyes of Anglicans the central position which Dissenters accorded to preaching distorted their services and diminished the worship of God: 'Dissenters go to chapel chiefly to hear sermons', commented Charles Kingsley with justice.[93] But although Baptists, Congregationalists, Calvinistic, Primitive, and many Wesleyan Methodist congregations eschewed the formal liturgy of the Church of England, the part which the Prayer Book played in Anglican worship was paralleled in Dissenting worship by the hymn-book.[94] For Nonconformists hymn-singing was both an expression of an individual's religious faith and experience and an act of communal commitment and devotion. Among Old Dissenters (apart from the Quakers and some General Baptists) the war waged by Benjamin Keach and Isaac Watts to secure acceptance of hymn-singing had been largely won by the middle of the eighteenth century,[95] and among Methodists hymn-singing was inseparable from their evangelistic mission. The singing of hymns was an essential part of the excitement and sense of expectation provided by Methodist services, and is one factor which helps to explain the success of Methodism at a time when hymn-singing was still opposed by many Anglican clergymen and condemned by some bishops.[96]

It appears to have been the example of the Moravians which first impressed John Wesley with the contribution that hymn-singing could make to the devotional life of the Christian, and he published his first hymn-book in 1737, the year before his conversion and that of his brother Charles.[97] But it was those transforming experiences that led to the great flowering of Methodist hymnody as both brothers sought to express the intense relief and joy of their conversions in poetic form. In fifty-three years the two brothers published fifty-six books of poetry, the majority of them from the pen of Charles.[98] Charles Wesley's hymns were at once intensely personal and at the same time of such general application that they could be sung by any Christian who had passed through Charles's own evangelical experience. 'O for a thousand tongues to sing' was written on the first anniversary of Charles's conversion, and others followed in a flood as Charles sought to

---

[92] Leifchild, *John Leifchild*, 201–2, 57–8.   [93] Davies, *Worship and Theology*, iv. 217.
[94] This point is made by Bernard Manning in *The Hymns of Wesley and Watts*, 135 n.
[95] Watts, *The Dissenters*, i. 308–12.
[96] S. S. Tamke, *Make a Joyful Noise unto the Lord* (Athens, Ohio, 1978), 27.
[97] L. F. Benson, *The English Hymn* (1915), 223–5.   [98] Ibid. 230.

express his gratitude that Christ had died to ensure his eternal salvation. Charles was the most prolific and most popular hymn-writer in the history of the Christian church. One need mention only the profound 'Jesu, lover of my soul', the beautiful 'Love divine, all loves excelling', and two of the most popular hymns sung at the two main Christian festivals: 'Hark! the herald angels sing!' and 'Christ the Lord is risen today'. Other early Methodists wrote hymns which remained popular into the nineteenth century and beyond: Thomas Olivers who composed 'The God of Abraham praise', Edward Perronet who wrote 'All hail the power of Jesu's name', and above all the Calvinistic Methodist William Williams, Pantycelyn, whose 'Guide me, O thou great Jehovah', is one of the best loved of all Christian hymns. But it was Charles Wesley who towered above all other Methodist hymn-writers, and when his brother John edited the influential *Collection of Hymns for the Use of the People called Methodists*, published in 1780, all but ten of the 525 hymns included were by one of the brothers, the overwhelming majority by Charles.[99] Of the 6,500 hymns written by Charles, some 500 were still in use at the beginning of the twentieth century.[100] The Wesleyan hymn-book, wrote James Martineau, was, 'after the Scriptures . . . the grandest instrument of popular religious culture that Christendom has ever produced'.[101]

The uncompromising Arminianism proclaimed by the Methodist hymns was one of the factors which helped to undermine Calvinism in the first half of the nineteenth century, not least because Charles Wesley's hymns found their way into the hymn-books of hitherto Calvinist denominations. The ascendancy which the hymns of Isaac Watts had enjoyed among the Particular Baptists was first challenged in 1787 when John Rippon published his *Selection of Hymns from the Best Authors* and included twenty-four by the Wesleys.[102] But in addition to borrowing the hymns of Watts and the Wesleys the Baptists themselves contributed to the canon of nineteenth-century hymnody with John Fawcett's 'Blest be the tie that binds', Robert Robinson's 'Come, Thou fount of every blessing', and Robert Keen's 'How firm a foundation'.[103]

It is arguable that the tunes to which hymns were set were more important than their words in arousing the emotional commitment of the singer and in securing that the hymn was remembered long after it had been sung. John Wesley himself recognized that the music accompanying hymns was of crucial importance and published four tune-books to supplement his

[99] Ibid. 236.   [100] Ibid. 245–6.
[101] Ibid. 249 citing *The Life and Letters of James Martineau* (1909), ii. 99.
[102] Manley, 'John Rippon and the Particular Baptists', 156.
[103] Robison, 'Particular Baptists', 255.

hymn-books.[104] He borrowed German tunes from the Moravians, persuaded Handel to compose 'Gopsal' for 'Rejoice, the Lord is King', and obtained tunes from other successful contemporary composers such as John Lampe and Jonathan Battishill.[105] George Herod claimed, as we have seen, that the collection of hymns which Lorenzo Dow brought from America, sung to popular and lively tunes, was a factor in drawing crowds to listen to the first Primitive Methodists.[106] In Ashton-under-Lyne the Ranters processed through the streets singing their hymns to 'common song tunes, such as are sung by factory lads in the street'.[107] In time popular hymns and tunes became inseparable, the music reinforcing the message of the words and thus facilitating their easy recall and enabling them to be sung spontaneously.

These factors were all the more important since churches could not always afford to buy hymn-books, and members of their congregations could not always read. Ever since the seventeenth century the problem had been dealt with by the practice of 'lining out' whereby a precentor, chapel clerk, or minister read out the hymn two lines at a time and the congregation sang after him. The custom obviously impeded both the coherence and the quality of the singing, and in the course of the eighteenth century the practice of lining-out had been discarded by some of the better-educated meetings of Old Dissent. Thomas Reynolds's Presbyterian King's Weigh House abandoned the lining-out of psalms as early as 1714 on the ground that 'there are but few among us but can read, or who, if they would be at the pains, might soon attain it'.[108] And in 1760 the Castle Gate Congregational church in Nottingham resolved 'to sing forward and not give out the lines', and gave members of the congregation a month's notice 'to lay in psalm and hymn books'.[109] But the use of hymn-books in the Baptist chapel in Caernarfon was opposed by Christmas Evans on the ground that lining-out fastened the words of the hymns in the singer's memory,[110] and the practice was retained by poorer and partly illiterate congregations well into the second half of the nineteenth century.[111] An attempt to abandon lining-out in the Halifax Place Wesleyan chapel in Nottingham was successfully opposed in 1860 on the ground that it would be injurious 'to the poorer class of our fellow worshippers'.[112] In 1872, when an illiterate farm worker, George Edwards, was

[104] Benson, *The English Hymn*, 239.
[105] P. A. Scholes, *The Oxford Companion to Music* (9th edn., 1955), 503, 637.
[106] Herod, *Biographical Sketches*, 12.   [107] Rose, *Methodism in Ashton-under-Lyne*, ii. 41.
[108] E. Kaye, *History of the King's Weigh House Church* (1968), 26–7.
[109] Castle Gate minutes, 51.   [110] T. M. Bassett, *The Welsh Baptists* (Swansea, 1977), 185.
[111] Harrison, 'Baptists of Nottinghamshire', i. 438; Morris, 'Primitive Methodism in Nottinghamshire', 120; Shaw, *The Bible Christians*, 87.
[112] Swift, *Lively People*, 139.

appointed to the Aylsham Primitive Methodist preachers' plan in Norfolk, his wife helped him to memorize the words of three hymns before his first service so that he in turn could recite them two lines at a time to his equally illiterate congregation.[113] And hymns were still being lined-out in the Porthleven Wesleyan chapel in Cornwall as late as 1886.[114]

In some chapels the role of precentor was filled by a group of 'singers'. The Baptists of Rossendale in the mid-eighteenth century attracted a group of instrumental musicians and singers known as the 'Deighn Layrocks' (Larks of the Dean Valley). In 1747 their leader, John Nuttall, was baptized by Joseph Picop, the minister of the Bacup Particular Baptist church, and Nuttall went on to serve the Baptist churches at Lumb and Goodshaw successively as minister from 1753 until his death in 1792. In the nineteenth century the 'Deighn Layrocks' included in their number Robert Ashworth, a Baptist lay preacher who composed twenty overtures and fifty psalm tunes.[115] But in other Baptist churches the attempt to improve congregational singing met with opposition. When, in the 1770s, Samuel James, pastor of the Hitchin Baptist church in Hertfordshire, formed a choir and tried to persuade his church to sing Isaac Watts's hymns, a deacon objected that the tunes were 'too light and airy' and Watts's hymns were accepted only on condition that each and every hymn in the book was sung to the same tune, no matter what its metre.[116]

John Wesley disliked the singing of what he called incomprehensible anthems and the Methodist Conference repeatedly opposed anthems, solos, fugueing, musical festivals, and selections of sacred music.[117] Such performances, claimed the Wesleyan Conference in 1805, drew the attention of the worshipper to the singers and the singing rather than to God, and singing by choirs, argued the Bible Christian Conference in 1820, cuts off 'a great part of the congregation from this part of the worship'.[118] The Bible Christians believed that choirs 'have a tendency to beget formality' and it was for this very reason they were more acceptable to Unitarians than to other Nonconformists. The New Meeting in Birmingham introduced a choir in

---

[113] G. Edwards, *From Crow-Scaring to Westminster* (1922), 32–3. Edwards was elected Labour MP for South-West Norfolk in 1920.

[114] Shaw, *Cornish Methodism*, 45.

[115] T. Newbigging, *History of the Forest of Rossendale* (1868), 154, 191-3; Weston, 'Baptists of North-West England', 759–60; Scholes, *Oxford Companion to Music*, 83.

[116] G. E. Evans, *Come Wind, Come Weather: Chronicles of Tilehouse Street Baptist Church* (1969), 21, 28.

[117] *Wesley's Journal*, iv. 112–13, 194; *Minutes of the Methodist Conferences*, i. 350; ii (1799), 27; iii (1805), 290–1.

[118] *HMC*, iv. 380.

1832 and fourteen years later began paying its choristers.[119] George's Meeting in Exeter had a choir in the 1820s led by a man with the splendid name of Noah Flood.[120]

Another reason for the Bible Christians' opposition to choirs was their belief that the best singers were often drawn from 'the unconverted part of the congregation',[121] and it was an observation supported by the experience of members of other denominations. The Wesleyan Samuel Bradburn locked his Wakefield singers out of their gallery because he disliked their unsuitable tunes and because they included 'persons of lax morals'.[122] The leaders of the Wesleyan society in Canterbury resolved in 1816 that no one could be a member of the singers 'who lives in open habitual sin'.[123] And at the Congregational Lower chapel at Heckmondwike the custom whereby the singers celebrated the marriage of members of the congregation by singing a wedding anthem when they appeared at chapel led to a bitter dispute with the minister, Joseph Mather. When he became pastor of the church in 1823 Mather found that it was usual to pay the singers for their services on these occasions, money which they spent on drinking on the following night. When he tried to put a stop to the custom and locked the singers' pew they broke it open, insisted on singing loudly to drown his protests, and finally forced him to leave for another congregation.[124] Thomas Jackson complained that in several Wesleyan chapels 'the choirs had introduced almost every variety of musical instruments', thus 'destroying the simplicity and devotional character of the singing' and for this reason he preferred the singing to be accompanied by organs rather than by choirs.[125]

There was considerable opposition among Nonconformist leaders to the use of musical instruments. The Midland Conference of the New Connexion of General Baptists voted in 1783 that it was unlawful 'to use musical instruments in our congregations'; the Wesleyan Conference of 1805 resolved that 'no instruments of music' should be 'introduced into the singers' seats'; when the Primitive Methodists' Canaan chapel in Nottingham was built in 1825 its trust deed stipulated that 'no choir of singers, musical instruments, or music books be introduced or used in the said chapel except on occasions of anniversary services'; the Synod of the Presbyterian Church in England

[119] Bushrod, 'Unitarianism in Birmingham', 61–2.
[120] A. A. Brockett, *Nonconformity in Exeter* (1962), 174.
[121] Shaw, *The Bible Christians*, 87.
[122] T. Jackson, *Recollections of my own Life and Times* (1873), 48.
[123] D. M. Rosman, *Evangelicals and Culture* (1984), 137–8, citing J. A. Vickers, *The Story of Canterbury Methodism* (1970), 137–8.
[124] Scholes, *Oxford Companion to Music*, 244–5; Miall, *Congregationalism in Yorkshire*, 276.
[125] Jackson, *Recollections*, 133–4.

condemned the use of organs in 1856; and the English Synod of the United Presbyterian Church banned the use of musical instruments until 1872.[126] But these expressions of disapproval by denominational conferences were countered by considerable enthusiasm for musical instruments at chapel level. When the Wesleyan Conference of 1805 tried to ban the use of musical instruments it made an exception of the bass viol and that exception led, in the next two decades, to the development of Wesleyan chapel orchestras.[127] The bass viol, and its successor the violoncello, were also popular in Baptist and Congregational chapels in the first half of the nineteenth century, and by the middle of the century the Baptist church at Hucknall in Nottinghamshire had an orchestra consisting of three fiddles, basso, two tenor horns, ophicleide, cornet, and flute.[128] The playing of such orchestras was, however, more often robust than harmonious: J. C. Browne, the minister of the Stoke Abbott Congregational church in Dorset, on occasion felt obliged to stop his violinist and trumpet players in the middle of hymns and to lecture then on the quality of their playing.[129]

To some Dissenters the solution to the problem of the over-exuberant chapel orchestra was the installation of an organ. However organs were associated with liturgical worship and were widely regarded as adjuncts of popery. Consequently organs, like choirs, were adopted more readily by the Unitarians who were beginning to experiment with liturgies than by Primitive Methodists or Bible Christians who better appreciated spontaneity in worship. Organs were installed in the Mill Hill Unitarian chapel in Leeds in 1794; in the Cross Street chapel in Manchester in 1799; in Leicester's Great Meeting in 1800; and in Norwich's Octagon chapel in 1801.[130] But among orthodox Dissenters organs provoked a good deal more opposition than did other musical instruments. The Congregationalist Thomas Binney opposed the erection of an organ in the King's Weigh House in the forty years that he was minister (1829–69); the Baptists of Upton chapel, Lambeth, would not commit themselves to an organ until 1883; and the Baptists of Felinfoel near

---

[126] *TBHS* 5 (1916–17), 122; *Minutes of the Methodist Conferences*, iv. 290; Swift, *Lively People*, 58; D. G. Cornick, 'The Expansion and Unification of the Presbyterian Church in England, 1836–76', Ph.D. thesis (London, 1989), 311. J. M. Mckerrow, *Memoirs of William Mckerrow* (1881), 214.

[127] Biggs, 'Methodism in a Rural Society', 336.

[128] Harrison, 'Baptists of Nottinghamshire', i. 437.

[129] W. Densham and J. Ogle, *The Story of the Congregational Churches of Dorset* (1899), 292.

[130] Schroeder, *Mill Hill Chapel*, 52; T. Baker, *Memorials of a Dissenting Chapel* (1884), 48; A. H. Thomas, *A History of the Great Meeting Leicester* (Leicester, 1908), 57–8; C. B. Jewson, *The Jacobin City: A Portrait of Norwich, 1788–1802* (1975), 136.

Llanelli kept all instruments out of their chapel until 1922.[131] Elsewhere, however, churches graduated from bass viols and cornets to organs as surely as they moved from converted barns to mock Greek temples. The Fish Street Congregational church in Hull, having voted in 1821 that the singing be accompanied by a violoncello and a bass viol, replaced both instruments with an organ in 1853.[132] The Beeston General Baptist church bought a bass viol and a clarinet in 1838 and changed them for a harmonium in 1854.[133] The Rugeley Congregational church in Staffordshire introduced a violoncello in 1840 when 'a gallery was built for the accommodation of the singers'; ten years later the violoncello was abandoned in favour of a harmonium; and in 1859 the harmonium itself was displaced by an organ.[134] Sadly even the Hucknall General Baptists dispensed with the services of their fiddlers and tenor horns in 1854 in favour of a harmonium.[135]

As so often happened in the nineteenth century, the conflicting arguments surrounding the introduction of organs provoked the most ferocious disputes among the Wesleyan Methodists. The Wesleyan Conference of 1796 laid down that no organs should be installed in Methodist chapels 'till proposed in the Conference' but none the less organs were introduced into some chapels. Conference in 1808 again repeated its refusal to sanction 'the erection of any organ in our chapels', but added that where organs had already been introduced they should not overpower the singing of the congregation.[136] Despite this ruling an organ was installed in the new Wesleyan chapel in Pitt Street, Liverpool, in 1810, and a furious controversy ensued which led its superintendent minister, Joseph Entwisle, to complain that there was 'more talk about the organ than about the presence of Christ in the new chapel'.[137] The Liverpool Quarterly Meeting rejected an application for approval of the organ by 33 votes to 30, but despite this vote the Conference in 1811 gave its sanction both to the Pitt Street organ and to one which was proposed for Liverpool's new Brunswick chapel.[138] By the 1810s organs were clearly seen as a token of the Wesleyan leaders' struggle to secure order and respectability in the Connexion, and in 1820 Conference agreed that organs might be installed in 'some of the larger chapels . . . by special consent of the

[131] Kaye, *King's Weigh House*, 76; S. J. Price, *Upton: The Story of One Hundred and Fifty Years* (1935), 142–3; Bassett, *Welsh Baptists*, 270.
[132] Darwent, *Story of Fish Street Church, Hull*, 182, 186–7.
[133] Harrison, 'Baptists of Nottinghamshire', i. 435.
[134] A. J. Matthews, *The Congregational Churches of Staffordshire* (1924), 208.
[135] Harrison, 'Baptists of Nottinghamshire', i. 437.
[136] Benson, *The English Hymn*, 243; *Minutes of the Methodist Conferences*, i. 350; iii. 31.
[137] Entwisle, *Memoir of Joseph Entwisle*, 236–8.
[138] T. B. Bunting and G. S. Rowe, *Life of Jabez Bunting* (1887), 336, 338.

Conference' provided that the approval of the appropriate District Meeting had first been obtained.[139] The larger the chapel the greater was the difficulty in producing harmony out of unaccompanied singing and in 1827 the trustees of the huge Brunswick chapel in Leeds, opened two years earlier with seating for nearly three thousand people, sought Conference's permission for the installation of an organ. Despite the opposition of many of the society leaders and members, and notwithstanding a vote of the Leeds District Meeting against the organ, Conference sanctioned the introduction of the instrument. The decision led to the secession of over nine hundred Leeds Wesleyans in protest at what they regarded as Conference's breach of its own regulations and to the formation of the denomination which was to become known as the Protestant Methodists.[140] But the dispute did little to halt the erection of organs in Methodist chapels. In 1855 even the successors of the Leeds Protestant Methodists came to the conclusion that singing in their large Lady Lane chapel would be improved by musical accompaniment and they too sanctioned the installation of an organ.[141]

The name chosen by the Leeds secessionists in 1827 is an indication that some Methodists still regarded the Wesleyan Connexion as clinging too closely to the Church of England. Whereas, in the eighteenth century, Old Dissenters had normally held their services on Sunday mornings and afternoons, Methodists had usually preferred to conduct their main services in the evening in order to avoid clashing with those of the parish church. But in the 1820s and 1830s a combination of Methodist example and the introduction of gas-lighting led to a general movement away from afternoon to evening services.[142] The growing popularity of Sunday evening services contributed to a decline of the old Puritan and Dissenting tradition of devoting Sunday evenings to family worship, but in other respects the mid-nineteenth-century Nonconformist committed his Sundays as completely to religion as did his seventeenth- and eighteenth-century forebears. The way in which the chapel monopolized the Nonconformist's Sunday was described by John Ashton, a member of the Bunyan Meeting, Bedford, in the mid-nineteenth century:

The congregation was not made up entirely of Bedford residents. Many came from the surrounding villages in their own vehicles, or on foot, and for those who came from a distance bread, cheese, and beer were provided. There was a prayer meeting at 7 a.m. and Sunday school at 9 a.m. At 10.30 a.m. there was morning service, which

---

[139] *Minutes of the Methodist Conferences*, iv. 146.

[140] Gregory, *Side Lights on the Conflicts of Methodism*, 52.

[141] Dews, 'Methodism in Leeds', 684–5.

[142] Henderson, *History of Castle Gate Congregational Church, Nottingham*, 121; G. Hunsworth, *Memorials of the Old Meeting Congregational Church, Kidderminster* (1874), 57; K. A. C. Parsons (ed.), *St. Andrew's Street Baptist Church, Cambridge* (Cambridge, 1971), 25.

was followed by a hasty meal, and a service for the country members who then went home. At 2 p.m. there was Sunday school once more, and at 5 p.m. a young people's prayer meeting. At 7 p.m. the evening service began, and was frequently followed by another prayer meeting.[143]

When men came to look back on days so completely taken up with the round of services, Sunday school, and prayer-meetings, their reactions differed widely. For William Hale White, also a member of the Bunyan Meeting congregation, Sunday was 'a season of unmixed gloom'. 'No newspaper nor any book more secular than the *Evangelical Magazine* was tolerated', meat was cooked the day before and served up cold, and 'the only thing hot which was permitted was a boiled suet pudding, which cooked itself while we were at chapel'. The services were ruined by the long prayer, 'a horrible hypocrisy' often lasting half an hour in which the minister came 'maundering into [God's] presence [with] nothing particular to say', 'an insult upon which we should never presume if we had a petition to offer to any earthly personage'. The sermons were almost as bad, taking an hour or more to deliver and 'pretty much the same from January to December'. 'The minister invariably began with the fall of man; propounded the scheme of redemption, and ended by depicting in the morning the blessedness of the saints, and in the evening the doom of the lost.'[144] By contrast the General Baptist John Clifford recalled Sundays in the Beeston chapel in which he was brought up as the 'pearl of days'. Its members 'met in the factories and mills and fields in the week and worked long hours' and looked forward to Sunday with 'the refreshing rest of a succession of gatherings that started with seven o'clock in the morning and were not ended till after eight at night'. From this fellowship, claimed Clifford, its members 'gained their strength to face the hardships and bear the burdens of every-day existence'.[145]

Chapel gatherings were not confined to regular Sunday services. One of John Wesley's major contributions to Methodism was the borrowing from the Moravians of a whole range of interlocking activities—band-meetings, class-meetings, love-feasts, watch-night services—whereby the individual believer or potential convert was integrated into the Methodist society. The love-feast, derived from the 'agape' of the early Church, was described by the *Wesleyan Methodist Magazine* in 1836 as 'the most popular and exciting of our social meetings'.[146] It owed its popularity in part to the reluctance of early

[143] Tibbutt, *Bunyan Meeting, Bedford*, 60, citing *The Story of the Life of John Ashton* (1904).
[144] White, *Autobiography of Mark Rutherford*, 5–7. On the length of Congregational prayers and sermons see Jones, *Congregationalism in England*, 221–3.
[145] J. Clifford, *The Gospel of World Brotherhood according to Jesus* (1920), 74.
[146] F. Baker, *Methodism and the Love-Feast* (1957), 15.

Methodists to take communion at the hands of clergymen whom they regarded as unconverted, and to Wesley's opposition to the celebration of the Lord's Supper by unordained preachers.[147] The love-feast thus became a substitute for the Lord's Supper, consisting of hymns and prayers, the distribution of bread or cake and water from a two-handled mug passed round the congregation, an address by the presiding minister, and the relation of spiritual experiences.[148] Love-feasts provided the setting for much of the revivalism among the Wesleyans of Yorkshire in 1792–4, and the Cornish revival of 1814, which increased Wesleyan membership by 5,000, began in a love-feast at Camborne.[149] Love-feasts were especially popular among the Primitive Methodists who frequently held them out of doors in place of, or subsequent to, camp-meetings; on occasion they attracted crowds of several hundred and, like camp-meetings, they provided opportunities for evangelism.[150] In time regular love-feasts fell victim to the Wesleyan cult of respectability, but in some areas Primitive Methodists continued to hold them on a quarterly basis until the early twentieth century.[151] An account of a love-feast in the Hockley chapel in Nottingham in 1873 describes how, after the singing of a hymn and a prayer, the congregation sang 'Be present at our table, Lord', while stewards distributed baskets of cake and mugs of water. The minister followed with an address punctuated by exclamations from the congregation of 'Bless the Lord!' and 'Glory be to God!'. Other members then gave testimony to their spiritual experience and the love-feast was followed by a prayer-meeting: 'until a late hour the chapel walls were made to ring with the earnest appeals to get sinners to the penitent form and gain for them immediate salvation'.[152]

Class-meetings and prayer-meetings also provided opportunities for the conversion of sinners: it was said of the Primitive Methodist church at Filey in the East Riding that 'as many souls have been saved in the class-meetings as after the preaching services'.[153] Whereas in Wesleyan Methodism bands had initially consisted of four or five people who claimed to have 'remission of sins' and were subjected to searching questions on their spiritual state, classes consisted of a dozen or more people including both those who claimed to be saved and those seeking salvation. The class-meeting had originated in 1742 as an attempt to meet the debts of the Methodist society in

[147] Church, *More About Early Methodist People*, 238.

[148] Baker, *Methodism and the Love-Feast*, 15.   [149] Shaw, *Cornish Methodism*, 65.

[150] Obelkevich, *Religion and Rural Society*, 227–8; Werner, *Primitive Methodist Connexion*, 86; G. M. Morris, 'The Origin and Early Development of Primitive Methodism in Derbyshire', MA thesis (Nottingham, 1960), 146.

[151] Baker, *Methodism and the Love-Feast*, 54.   [152] Swift, *Lively People*, 137.

[153] Kendall, *Primitive Methodist Church*, ii. 106.

Bristol by dividing the society into small manageable groups under the leadership of a man or woman who undertook to collect a penny a week from each member.[154] Wesley soon realized the potential of the classes both for providing spiritual oversight of his followers and for enforcing discipline over them, and in time they came to replace the bands as the medium through which the spiritual zeal and the code of conduct of the Wesleyan societies were preserved. Methodists meeting in class once a week were expected to give accounts of their spiritual experience, and the part played by class meetings in strengthening the religious bond among Methodists led to the adoption of similar devices among the other Nonconformist denominations. Some Particular Baptist churches in London had regular 'experience meetings'; members of the Particular Baptist churches in Cambridge (in 1812), in Tiverton (in the 1820s), and at Heywood in Lancashire were divided into classes 'according to the districts of the town in which they lived'; and the Congregationalist John Campbell similarly organized the members of Whitefield's Tabernacle and the Tottenham Court Road chapel into classes in the 1830s.[155] In Wales the Calvinistic Methodists held society (*seiat*) meetings, and the Baptists and Independents fellowship (*cyfeillach*) meetings once or twice a week. 'These meetings', wrote Thomas Rees, were 'similar to the Wesleyan classes, with this difference, that the minister always presides, and that all the members . . . are expected to attend.'[156] Members, explained D. M. Evans, 'are encouraged to relate their "experience", and to give free expression to their doubts and fears: shortcomings are pointed out; encouragement and rebuke are administered; and the more aged and gifted members exhort the brotherhood'.[157] Such meetings, observed Rees, 'are considered by all the evangelical Dissenting denominations in Wales as the most important and useful of our religious services'. 'Those churches who practically neglect them are the least spiritual and efficient, and those members of our churches who seldom or never frequent them, are generally the most inactive and worthless professors we have.'[158]

[154] Church, *Early Methodist People*, 150–6.
[155] Robison, 'Particular Baptists', 217; *Church Book: St Andrew's Street Baptist Church, Cambridge*, English Baptist Records (1991), 88; H. B. Case, *History of the Baptist Church in Tiverton* (Tiverton, 1907), 56; Weston, 'Baptists of North-West England', 153; R. Ferguson and A. M. Brown, *Life and Labours of John Campbell* (1867), 141.
[156] Rees, *Miscellaneous Papers*, 76–7.   [157] Evans, *Christmas Evans*, 20–1.
[158] Rees, *Miscellaneous Papers*, 76–7.

4. 'CALLED OUT OF THE WORLD': MEMBERSHIP AND DISCIPLINE

For Wesleyans the only way of entry into the Connexion was by possession of a class ticket, renewable quarterly and introduced by Wesley to ensure that membership was confined to those that feared God and worked righteousness, and as 'a quiet and inoffensive method of removing any disorderly member'.[159] Whereas the qualification for membership of a Wesleyan class was an evident desire to seek 'the power of godliness' to enable members to help 'each other to work out their salvation',[160] qualification for entry into a Calvinistic Methodist society or a Baptist or Congregational church was evidence that the quest for salvation had already been successful. The Castle Gate Congregational church in Nottingham required applicants for membership to present 'a written account of the work of God upon their souls' and to be interviewed by two representatives of the church concerning their 'seriousness' and 'doctrinal sentiments'.[161] And Baptist churches usually, though not inevitably, expected candidates to undergo the rite of believer's baptism before being admitted to church membership.

In the first half of the nineteenth century only a minority of Baptist meeting-houses had baptistries sunk into the chapel floor, and outdoor baptismal services were common: the Nottingham, Newark, and Beeston churches all baptized converts in the River Trent; the Mansfield General Baptists used a water-mill known as the 'sheepwash'; and in Liverpool in 1839 the Particular Baptist C. M. Birrell baptized prospective members in the sea.[162] Open-air baptisms, like the Primitive Methodists' camp-meetings, could attract huge crowds and were a valuable means of advertising the Baptists' cause: it was claimed that a crowd of 10,000 people witnessed a baptismal service from Llandeilo bridge in Carmarthenshire in 1827, that another 2,000 were present at a baptism at Trosnant, Pontypool, in 1849, and that 1,500 watched seventeen being baptized in the river at Tredegar in 1852.[163] Baptisms at Christmas or in ice-covered streams were not surprisingly regarded as particularly dramatic evidence of the strength of the candidates' convictions.[164] The growing popularity of the practice of believer's baptism created a demand for a 'naming' ceremony to replace infant baptism: the covenant of the Particular

---

[159] Church, *Early Methodist People*, 170. [160] Ibid. 153–4.
[161] Castle Gate minutes, 80.
[162] Harrison, 'Baptists of Nottinghamshire', i. 101, 365; Sellers, 'Liverpool Nonconformity', 127.
[163] Bassett, *The Welsh Baptists*, 227; Jones, *Sowing Beside all Waters*, 155.
[164] Jones, *Sowing Beside all Waters*, 156.

Baptist church at Sallendine Nook, Huddersfield, which was drawn up in 1743, stated that the children of the church had been dedicated to the Lord, and a dedication service was also held for the children of what was to become the Barton New Connexion General Baptist church in Leicestershire around 1755.[165] By the beginning of the nineteenth century services of infant dedication seem to have been fairly common in Baptist churches, and in 1816 the Baptist church in Bacup even referred to such events as 'christenings'.[166]

Membership of a Baptist or Congregational church conferred on the member, if he were male, the right to attend and vote in church meetings, to participate in the election of pastors and deacons, and to share in the exercise of the church's discipline. Membership of a Quaker meeting entitled every male Friend to attend not only the relevant Monthly and Quarterly meetings but also the Yearly Meeting in London, and in the mid-nineteenth century the Yearly Meeting was attended by about a fifth of all male Quakers in Great Britain.[167] In the sixteenth and seventeenth centuries the covenants of the gathered churches, with their ideas of a voluntary agreement between free men and of a mutual contract between rulers and their subjects, had made an important contribution to the development of the theory of representative government.[168] At the turn of the eighteenth and nineteenth centuries Quaker meetings and Baptist and Congregational churches had the most democratic government of any permanent institutions in England and Wales. But the democracy of those churches was not perfect: it could be curtailed by authoritarian pastors or deacons, it could be limited by economic constraints, and it was not always extended to women.

The foundation-stone of democracy in a Baptist or Congregational church was the regular church meeting, usually held monthly, which elected and, if necessary, removed the church's deacons and ministers, controlled the church's finances, and enforced its discipline. Church meetings could, however, fall into disuse and their powers be arrogated by deacons or ministers. The Western Association of Welsh Baptists warned its member churches in 1822 not to leave church discipline to their ministers and deacons, and Arthur Jones, the pastor of the Ebenezer Independent church in Bangor (1810–15 and 1823–54), was criticized by his fellow Congregationalists for keeping not only the discipline but also the collections and pew rents of the church in his

---

[165] P. Stock, *Foundations* (Halifax, 1933), 70; *General Baptist Magazine*, 1 (1798), 359.
[166] F. Overend, *History of the Ebenezer Baptist Church* (Bacup, 1912), 187; A. N. Palmer, *History of the Older Nonconformity of Wrexham* (Wrexham, 1888), 106; *Baptist Quarterly*, 3 (1926–7), 186–7; 4 (1928–9), 75.
[167] Isichei, *Victorian Quakers*, 70–2, 78–9.
[168] Watts, *The Dissenters*, i. 3–4, 25, 29–31, 75, 117–18, 260–1.

own hands.[169] When Hugh Jones became minister of the Baptist church at Cefnbychan, Denbighshire, he found to his horror that the deacons had been in the habit of filling up vacancies in the diaconate without consulting church members, and it was only after a struggle that he was able to put a stop to the practice.[170] A similar situation existed in the Carmel Independent church at Gwaun-cae-Gurwen in Glamorgan until the 1860s when the self-perpetuating diaconate was replaced by men elected by secret ballot.[171] Such was the difficulty experienced by some churches in getting rid of deacons who had outlived their usefulness that a correspondent to the *Baptist Magazine* in 1833 suggested that all Baptist churches should follow the example of that at Christchurch in Hampshire and re-elect their deacons annually.[172] But the annual election of deacons could itself cause problems, and in 1852 the South Street Bapist church in Exeter abandoned the practice 'on account of the unpleasantness it produces'.[173]

In the case of the Carter Street Particular Baptist church in Southwark it was two deacons who reasserted against their minister the right of church members to control church business. In 1776, three years after John Rippon had begun his long pastorate at Carter Street, the principle of monthly church meetings had been established, but by the 1820s they were becoming less and less frequent. When asked by a fellow minister why his church was so peaceful, Rippon is reputed to have replied that 'we don't call a church meeting to consult about buying a new broom every time we want one, and we don't entreat every noisy member to make a speech about the price of soap the floors are scrubbed with'. But Rippon's real motive for calling church meetings infrequently may have been fear that such meetings would discuss replacing him with a younger minister: by 1828, when Rippon celebrated his seventy-seventh birthday, the number of church meetings had fallen to two a year. Two years later two deacons resigned on the ground that Rippon was claiming 'the entire management of all our church affairs', and their protest was effective: Rippon agreed to keep out of the church's temporal affairs, monthly church meetings were resumed, and the two deacons again took up office.[174]

The function of deacons was to serve at communion, to assist the minister in vetting applicants for membership, to handle the church's money, and to

[169] Bassett, *The Welsh Baptists*, 77; Lambert, *Drink and Sobriety*, 72.
[170] Bassett, *The Welsh Baptists*, 77.
[171] Evans, 'Religion in the Swansea Valley', 279–80.
[172] *Baptist Magazine*, 25 (1833), 501–2.
[173] Brockett, *Nonconformity in Exeter*, 218.   [174] Manley, 'John Rippon', 70, 87, 131.

provide for its poor.[175] It was usual for deacons to be elected from the more prosperous members of the church, but what increased the tendency of a church to be dominated by its wealthier members in the seventeenth and eighteenth centuries was the widespread practice of holding church meetings during daylight hours in the working week.[176] Some of these limitations on the democratic rights of poorer church members were discarded in the nineteenth century as churches increased their working-class membership and as more rigid work patterns restricted their leisure time. The predominantly working-class Baptist churches of Nottinghamshire held their church meetings on Sunday afternoons and their annual meetings on Christmas day or Good Friday, and in 1810 poor attendance forced the Kettering Congregational church to move its church meetings from Thursday afternoons to Wednesday evenings.[177] But among the Quakers the growing differentiation between those who were constrained by the inflexible schedules of the working week and those with the leisure and money to travel to and participate in Quarterly and Yearly meetings led to a greater concentration of power into the hands of the latter.[178] For over two hundred years the Yorkshire Quarterly Meeting was held over two days, from Wednesday morning until Thursday afternoon, and not until the 1920s was one of the meetings fixed for a Saturday.[179]

The most serious restriction on the rights of members to participate in the government of Quaker meetings and of Baptist and Congregational churches was the failure of such churches to grant equal rights to their female members. The Quakers gave women a greater share in the ministry and government of their church than did any other Nonconformist denomination, but women Friends were none the less placed in an inferior position to men. The Quakers had always asserted the right of women to preach, George Fox had established separate business meetings for women, and in some Monthly Meetings, such as that at Southwark in the mid-eighteenth century, it was the custom for women Friends to sit with the men and to be 'jointly concerned in carrying on the business thereof'.[180] But it was not until 1784 that Quaker women were allowed by male Friends to have their own Yearly Meeting, and even then it was with the restriction that it exercise no disci-

---

[175] Ibid. 92; Great Yarmouth Church Book, DWL Harmer MSS 76.2, 217–18.

[176] Watts, *The Dissenters*, i. 357.

[177] Harrison, 'Baptists of Nottinghamshire', i. 428, 430; Goodman, *The Great Meeting, Kettering*, 35.

[178] Isichei, *Victorian Quakers*, 77.

[179] W. P. Thistlethwaite, *Yorkshire Quarterly Meeting* (Harrogate, 1979), 14, 17–19.

[180] R. M. Jones, *The Later Periods of Quakerism* (1921), i. 107.

pline and make no rules without the approval of the men's Yearly Meeting.[181] 'The only real function of Women's Yearly Meeting', writes Elizabeth Isichei, 'was to issue an epistle, and the only function of its subordinate meetings was to read it.'[182]

In contrast to the Quakers, most Baptist and Congregational churches in the seventeenth century had heeded Paul's admonition that 'women keep silence in the churches',[183] and the ban on women speaking in church meetings or in church services persisted well into the nineteenth century. The Sutton-on-Trent Particular Baptist church in Nottinghamshire was unusually liberal in agreeing, on its formation in 1822, that 'every member, *male or female*, shall have full liberty to speak at church meetings'.[184] But women were sometimes permitted to vote even in the seventeenth century,[185] and in the eighteenth and nineteenth centuries a growing number of churches allowed women 'an equal vote with the men on all church matters'.[186] Two Particular Baptist churches in Suffolk, those at Wattisham (in the 1760s) and at Ipswich (in 1780) elected women to the post of deaconess, though their function was probably to care for the female members of the church rather than to share in its governance; similarly the South Parade Baptist church in Leeds elected thirteen deaconesses in 1842 to visit women members of the church and congregation; and the Baptist church at Lumb in Rossendale in Lancashire even elected a woman to its diaconate in the 1850s.[187]

Though the constitutional arrangements of Quaker meetings and of Baptist and Congregational churches may have fallen short of the democratic ideal, they were far more democratic than the polities of the newer Nonconformist denominations. The organizations both of the Unitarians, with their Presbyterian heritage, and of the Calvinistic Methodists, who were to become the Presbyterian Church of Wales, contained a popular element, but it was more circumscribed than among the Baptist and Independents. The constitutions of Unitarian congregations varied enormously from meeting to meeting. At the one extreme were the autocratic practices of Cross Street, Manchester, where a dispute between the trustees and the congregation in 1814 led to the former obtaining the legal advice that the congregation had never been consulted in the choice of trustees, in the management of the

---

[181] Ibid. 117.   [182] Isichei, *Victorian Quakers*, 108.   [183] 1 Corinthians 14: 34.
[184] Harrison, 'Baptists of Nottinghamshire', i. 353–4.   [185] Watts, *The Dissenters*, i. 320.
[186] L. A. Fereday, *The Story of Falmouth Baptists* (1950), 53; Payne, *College Street Church, Northampton*, 30; *Baptist Quarterly*, 10 (1940–1), 340; C. Binfield, 'Nonconformity in the Eastern Counties, 1840–1885', Ph.D. thesis (Cambridge, 1965), 123.
[187] Klaiber, *Suffolk Baptists*, 90; R. J. Owen, 'The Baptists in the Borough of Leeds during the Nineteenth Century', M.Phil. thesis (Leeds, 1970), 34–5; Weston, 'The Baptists of North-West England', 272.

chapel, or in the election of its minister.[188] Similarly the management of the Dob Lane chapel in Failsworth near Manchester remained in the hands of a solitary trustee until the election of a chapel committee in 1849.[189] By contrast the Birmingham New Meeting of which Joseph Priestley was minister was, from 1782, governed by a committee known as the 'vestry', elected by all male subscribers of a guinea or more annually, though it was not until 1836 that the 'vestry' began to report back to the subscribers at an annual meeting.[190] In 1811 the Hanover Square chapel in Newcastle upon Tyne was likewise governed by a committee of seven men who were elected annually by, and were responsible to, the congregation, but it was not until thirty years later that members of the congregation were allowed to vote to ratify the choice of a minister.[191]

Among the Calvinistic Methodists churches had the right to make nominations for the post of elder and deacon but the actual right of appointment to those positions lay with the Monthly Meeting for the whole county. Once appointed the Calvinistic Methodist elder held both his office and his membership of the Association for life: he could be expelled for a breach of the denomination's moral code, but he could not be removed by a vote of the church which had originally nominated him.[192] Similarly while the exercise of discipline rested in the first instance with the local church, there was a right of appeal from the church meeting to the Monthly Meeting, the Quarterly Association, and ultimately to the Associations for north and south Wales.[193]

Of all the Nonconformist denominations the Wesleyans were the least democratic. While he was alive John Wesley had personally appointed assistants—the future superintendent ministers—to govern the circuits in his absence, and had personally selected and stationed itinerant preachers. He had also either personally or through his assistants kept control over the membership of each of his societies by issuing or refusing quarterly class tickets and had maintained authority over its leadership by nominating class leaders and society stewards. After his death Wesley's powers over the Connexion had devolved on the annual Methodist Conference: it was Conference which nominated the Stationing Committee which was responsible for the appointment and settling of ministers, and it was Conference which appointed the chairmen of the District Meetings which were set up in

[188] Seed, 'Unitarianism and Liberal Culture', 272–3.
[189] A. Gordon, *Historical Account of Dob Lane Chapel, Failsworth* (Manchester 1904), 59.
[190] Bushrod, 'Unitarianism in Birmingham', 90–2.
[191] Seed, 'Unitarianism and Liberal Culture', 274, 276.
[192] J. Roberts, *The Calvinistic Methodism of Wales* (Caernarfon, 1933), 67.
[193] W. Williams, *Welsh Calvinistic Methodism* (2nd edn., 1884), 200–1.

1792 to govern the Connexion between conferences and which determined which preachers should go to Conference. In 1797, in response to the agitation for greater lay participation in church government which issued in the formation of the Methodist New Connexion, the Wesleyan Conference meeting in Leeds made important concessions to lay Methodists: leaders' meetings were given the right to oppose applications for membership, no one could be expelled for immorality 'till such immorality be proved at a leaders' meeting', and superintendents were henceforward required to submit their proposals for the appointment and dismissal of leaders and stewards to the leaders' meeting for its approval. As a further concession to lay opinion Conference stipulated that circuit Quarterly Meetings, composed of the class leaders and stewards of the circuit under the chairmanship of the superintendent minister, rather than District Meetings were the fount 'from whence all temporary regulations, during the intervals of the Conference, must now originally spring'.[194] But authority in the Wesleyan Connexion was still imposed from above, not granted from below. Leaders and stewards continued to be appointed by the superintendents, not elected by the members, and the ordinary Wesleyan had no say either in the choice of his leaders and ministers or in the exercise of his church's discipline.

The secessionist Methodist denominations gave representation to laymen at their annual conferences and gave greater powers to their Quarterly and leaders' meetings than did the Wesleyans, but although their government was more democratic than that of the Wesleyans, their democracy was indirect rather than direct, in contrast to that of the Baptists and Congregationalists. The New Connexion, unlike both the Wesleyans and the Primitive Methodists, provided for the election of class leaders by class members, for the nomination of stewards by the class leaders, and for the approval of such stewards by the society as a whole. The New Connexion also established the principle that ministers and laymen should have an equal number of representatives at Conference and the Primitive Methodists adopted the principle of two lay representatives to every ministerial representative, but in the New Connexion delegates to Conference were elected by the Quarterly Meetings, and among the Primitive Methodists they were chosen by the District Meetings, not elected by the society members. It was the influence of the District Meeting which distinguished the polity of the Primitive Methodists from that of the other Methodist denominations. The District Meetings were composed of lay and ministerial representatives of the circuit Quarterly Meetings on the same two-to-one ratio as the Conference, but because they

---

[194] *Minutes of the Methodist Conferences*, i. 375–8.

'were elected on a much broader suffrage' than the Conference, wrote Kendall, they 'grew in popularity and influence'.[195] In particular it was the District Meetings, not the Conference, which were responsible for the stationing of ministers, and Primitive Methodist ministers rarely moved from one district to another. The Quarterly Meetings, which elected the District Meetings, were composed of ministers, lay preachers, class leaders, and stewards, and the leaders' meetings consisted of stewards and class leaders. Each Primitive Methodist society was allowed to elect one representative for every hundred members to serve on the Quarterly Meeting, but the other members were nominated, not elected. Class leaders were appointed by the existing leaders' meeting, and it was the leaders' meeting which approved or refused admission to membership and exercised discipline.[196]

Though discipline was exercised among Baptists, Congregationalists, and Calvinistic Methodists in full church meetings, by Quakers in their Monthly Meetings, among the Wesleyans by the superintendent ministers in consultation with the leaders' meetings, and among the secessionist Methodist denominations by the leaders' meetings alone, the results of that discipline appear to have been very similar. We have less evidence of the day-to-day workings of Methodist discipline than we do of Baptist, Congregational, or Quaker discipline since the removal of delinquent Methodists could be achieved by the simple expedient of not renewing their class tickets and did not require decisions approved and recorded by church meetings. But we do have evidence of the discipline of Methodist local preachers and this evidence, coupled with the decisions of Methodist Conferences and the pronouncements of Methodist leaders, suggests that the standards of behaviour enforced by the Methodists were exactly the same as those insisted on by Old Dissent. Both Methodists and Old Dissenters (apart from the Unitarians) subscribed to the Reformation doctrine of justification by faith, and old and new Nonconformists alike expected evidence of that justification to be displayed in the lives of their members. Methodists believed that works were 'necessary to the continuance of faith' since 'a man may forfeit the free gift of God, either by sins by omission or commission'.[197] Calvinists denied that the elect could fall from grace, but had to insist on high moral standards from their members to avoid the charge of Antinomianism. The mainspring of Old Dissent had been the impulse of the Elizabethan Separatists to abjure the corruptions of the Church of England; the source of the Methodists' separa-

---

[195] Kendall, *Primitive Methodist Church*, ii. 366.
[196] Morris, 'Primitive Methodism in Nottinghamshire', 132–4; Currie, *Methodism Divided*, 142–3, 148–9.
[197] *Minutes of the Methodist Conferences*, i. 5.

tion from the established church was their conviction that that church was an inadequate channel to lead men to salvation. Old Dissenters and Methodists alike stressed the purity of their own denominations as against the imperfections of the Church of England, but what they emphasized even more was the gulf separating their own communities of the saved from the outside world of the damned. A Christian, announced the Glamorgan and Carmarthenshire English Baptist Association, 'is one who has been "*called out of the world*" '. 'The followers of Christ are to be to men noble examples of self-denying abstinence from all excesses ... in all things pertaining merely to this life, that they may give proof of their heavenly citizenship.'[198] If Dissent involved separation from the Church of England, far more did it imply separation from the world.

That gulf between the church and the world was particularly deep in the early decades of the nineteenth century. The industrial revolution was accompanied by the growth in popularity of brutal, cruel, and degrading sports: cock-fights, bull-baiting, duck-chasing, bullock-running, and prize-fighting, many of which were carried on on licensed premises and sponsored by publicans.[199] When a man joined a Nonconformist church he turned his back on all these activities and deliberately chose to identify himself with one set of values and one community against another. It was a more dramatic change of lifestyle for a man than for a woman, a fact which may help to explain the greater appeal of Nonconformity to women than to men. In some quarters boxing and bull-baiting were associated with manliness and Methodism was equated with effeminacy.[200] Thus when a Durham miner joined the Primitive Methodists, wrote Edward Welbourne, the Ranters took away 'his gun, his dog, and his fighting cock'. 'They gave him a frock coat for his posy jacket, hymns for his public-house ditties, prayer meetings for his pay-night frolics.'[201] During the revival which accompanied the cholera epidemic in the Black Country in 1832 it was reported from Tipton that 'most of the bull-dogs have disappeared . . . and the fighting-cocks have been consigned to the cooks'.[202] As late as the 1940s in rural Cardiganshire the fundamental division in society was not between classes but between *pobol y cwrdd* (people of the meeting) and *pobol y dafarn* (people of the tavern), while in parts of south Wales the two rival communities were known as

---

[198] Lambert, *Drink and Sobriety*, 118–19.
[199] H. Cunningham, *Leisure in the Industrial Revolution* (1980), 9–10, 22–8.   [200] Ibid. 48.
[201] E. Welbourne, *The Miners' Unions of Northumberland and Durham* (Cambridge, 1923), 57.
[202] *Wesleyan Methodist Magazine*, 55 (1832), 748.

pobol y capel (people of the chapel) and *pobol y cwn* (people of the dogs, i.e. greyhounds).[203]

In the late eighteenth and early nineteenth centuries, as in the previous period,[204] Nonconformist churches sought to secure the doctrinal orthodoxy of their members and their regular attendance at religious services; they tried to guarantee the modesty of their appearance, the propriety of their sexual behaviour, and the suitability of their marriage partners; and they attempted to regulate the ethics by which they conducted their businesses and the uses to which they put their leisure hours. The Castle Gate Congregational church in Nottingham agreed, in 1828, that censures should be 'inflicted in case of open immorality such as drunkenness, fornication, extortion, covetousness, idolatry, raillery, according to the apostolic precepts, I Corinthians 5: 11', and also in cases of heresy, insolvency, and absence from the Lord's table.[205] In the sixty-three years that John Rippon was minister of the Carter Lane Particular Baptist church in Southwark, from 1773 to 1836, 156 people were excluded from membership, of whom 38 were removed for failing to attend the church's services, 28 for sexual delinquencies, 19 for joining another church or denomination without authorization, 14 for bankruptcy, 10 for doctrinal offences, 9 for drunkenness, and 8 for stealing.[206] To a man who had long been attached to a chapel community expulsion could represent a serious loss of face. 'He felt himself disgraced in the eyes of all whose good opinion he had been accustomed to value, and became a man of the world, an outcast from the ranks of respectability.'[207] Churches were prepared to restore to communion excluded members who gave evidence of repentance, but restoration could be as humiliating as expulsion: in the Zoar Independent chapel in Merthyr Tydfil excluded members who wished 'to be received back into the church had to make public penance by standing in the aisle during the communion service'.[208]

Expulsions for doctrinal reasons seem to have been much more frequent among Baptists than in other Nonconformist churches, partly because the New Connexion of General Baptists was periodically troubled with the Unitarianism and Universalism which had led to its separation from the Old General Baptists,[209] and partly because the Particular Baptists were sensitive to what they regarded as the doctrinal heresies and spiritual declension of their Arminian cousins. As we have already seen, in 1793 nineteen members

[203] D. Jenkins, 'Aber-porth', in *Welsh Rural Communities*, 13, 61 n. 8.
[204] See Watts, *The Dissenters*, i. 321–36, 444.   [205] Castle Gate minutes, 262.
[206] Manley, 'John Rippon', 135.   [207] Jenkins in *Welsh Rural Communities*, 54.
[208] Davies, *Religion in the Industrial Revolution*, 53.
[209] Watts, *The Dissenters*, i. 455–6, and above, Ch. I, sect. 6.

of the Brighton Particular Baptist church were expelled for rejecting eternal punishment, and in 1800 Robert Aspland was excommunicated by the Devonshire Square Particular Baptist church on embracing Unitarian views.[210] In 1789 the Bacup Particular Baptist church expelled James Waugh because he rejected both 'particular redemption and eternal punishment of the finally impenitent'; in 1801 the Husbands Bosworth Particular Baptist church in Leicestershire excluded Elizabeth Bennett 'for denying the divinity of Christ'; and in 1813 four members of the Wymeswold branch of the East Leake New Connexion General Baptist church on the borders of Nottinghamshire and Leicestershire were excommunicated—and six others seceded—on the ground that they had sought 'to disseminate the tenets of Socinianism'.[211] By contrast the members of the Lutton Old General Baptist church in the Lincolnshire Fens resolved in 1791 'to mutually forbear with each other and to allow each other to think for ourselves in matters of divinity without suspecting each other's Christianity, or without attempting to irritate each other's passions on account of difference of sentiment'.[212] The price of such liberality was that by 1851 the church's congregation consisted of but twenty people.[213]

Apart from mere failure to attend a church's religious services, the largest category of offences for which members were expelled from Dissenting churches were those arising from breaches of their sexual code. Over half the forty-four members who were expelled from the Broad Street General Baptist church in Nottingham between 1818 and 1860, and at least a third of the sixty-four excommunicated by the Beeston General Baptist church between 1804 and 1837, were excluded for sexual offences.[214] There can be little doubt that the sexual taboos imposed on, and the sexual inhibitions acquired by, young men and women brought up in religious homes were a major factor in inducing feelings of guilt which rendered their subjects susceptible to Evangelical conversion,[215] and throughout the eighteenth and early nineteenth century the Nonconformists reinforced those inhibitions and taboos by means of their church discipline. Nonconformists were

---

[210] J. Rowland, 'Christ Church (Unitarian), New Road, Brighton', *TUHS* 10 (1951–4), 148; Aspland, *Memoir of Aspland*, 95, 109.

[211] K. Gray, 'Some Contributions to the Early History of Nonconformity in Rossendale', MA thesis (University of Wales, 1942), 50–1; G. Jackson, 'The Evangelical Work of the Baptists in Leicestershire, 1740–1820', MA thesis (London, 1955), 70; Harrison, 'Baptists of Nottinghamshire', ii. 640–2.

[212] Lutton General Baptist Church Book, 145. DWL MSS 38.76.

[213] Ambler, *Lincolnshire Returns*, 32.

[214] Harrison, 'Baptists of Nottinghamshire', i. 376.

[215] Watts, *The Dissenters*, i. 187, 418–21, and above Ch. I, sect. 5.

expected to be chaste before marriage, faithful to their partners after marriage, and to marry only fellow believers. However, church books of the late
eighteenth and early nineteenth centuries reveal far fewer gross sex scandals
than the church books of a century earlier.[216] In 1782 Lady Huntingdon's
chapel in Spa Fields excommunicated a man for exposing his person 'in
a shameful manner' before a chimney-sweep, baker, plumber, and cabinet-
maker; in 1806 Charles Tucker, a deacon of the Chard Baptist church in
Somerset, was excluded for behaving 'very improperly in pulling about some
boys'; and in 1843 the Stansted Congregational church in Essex accused a
woman member of living off her daughter's earnings as a prostitute.[217] But
such scandals were exceedingly rare. Most expulsions for sexual offences
were of women who got themselves pregnant before or without marriage, and
the sexual delinquencies for which men were found out and censured were
often trivial. In 1806 John Deacon, the pastor of the General Baptist church
in Friar Lane, Leicester, was excommunicated on account of his 'improper
connection' with 'our sister Elizabeth Johnson', but three years later he was
readmitted to the church's membership and in 1811 asked to resume its pastorate.[218] The Mansfield Primitive Methodists expelled Thomas Ward in 1842
for 'improperly associating with Mrs John Wild and being with her in the
fields and on the railway at a late hour at night', and in 1851 they censured W.
Clarke for having taken 'undue freedoms with Fanny Hopkinson' and having
'put his arm round Mary Ball once'.[219] But when William Wilkinson, a
Primitive Methodist class leader at Darlaston in the Black Country, was dismissed for having been 'in a house with a woman', seventy-one fellow members and two local preachers resigned in sympathy.[220]

   Most Nonconformist churches expected their members to marry other
believers. The New Connexion of General Baptists sought to persuade members 'of the impropriety and unlawfulness' of marrying unbelievers, though,
in contrast to the Old General Baptists, they declined to make a general rule
excommunicating those who were unconvinced by their arguments.[221] The
Methodist Conference of 1753 agreed that since many Methodists had

[216] Watts, *The Dissenters*, i. 327–8.

[217] C. E. Welch, *Two Calvinistic Methodist Chapels* (London Record Society publications xi,
1975), 64–5; M. Bonnington, *Chard Baptists* (Chard, 1992), 73; Binfield, 'Nonconformity in the
Eastern Counties', 361.

[218] Jackson, 'The Baptists in Leicestershire', 248–50.

[219] Minute Book of the Mansfield Primitive Methodist Circuit Committee, 20 June 1842, 17
June 1851 (Nottinghamshire Archives Office MR 6/9, 6/2).

[220] Leese, 'Impact of Methodism on Black Country Society', 265.

[221] J. H. Wood, *A Condensed History of the General Baptists of the New Connexion* (1847),
282; *TBHS* 5 (1916–17), 42.

recently 'married with unbelievers', and since few of them had won over 'the unbelieving wife or husband', Methodists who married unbelievers in the future 'should be expelled from the society'.[222] The Welsh Calvinistic Methodists, in rules drawn up in 1801, laid down that members should not be 'unequally yoked in the marriage state with unbelievers', and individual Congregational and Particular Baptist churches also attempted to prevent 'the evil consequences that arise from members of churches intermarrying with the ungodly'.[223] The extent to which such rules were enforced is difficult to gauge: cases of censure on church members for marrying unbelievers are less common in church records of the early nineteenth century than in the church books of the late seventeenth and early eighteenth centuries,[224] but that may be because the rapid expansion of Nonconformity in the period of the industrial revolution made it much easier than it had been a hundred years earlier for Dissenters to find marriage partners within their own communions. Admittedly the one denomination which tried to enforce marriage rules with the greatest consistency—the Society of Friends—was also the one which suffered a catastrophic decline in numbers. But the link between the rigid implementation of the Quakers' marriages rules and their declining numbers was probably a symptom, rather than a cause, of their decline. Had the Quakers been converting Englishmen at the same rate that the Calvinistic Methodists were converting Welshmen, it is unlikely that they would have found their marriage rules impeding their progress. As it was, the strict enforcement of the ban on Quakers marrying outside the Society of Friends gave a sharp twist to their spiralling decline. A quarter of all the losses by resignation and disownment suffered by the Bristol and Gloucester Quakers in the first half of the nineteenth century were the result of disownments for marriage; over half the disownments pronounced by the Brighouse Monthly Meeting in the same period were for breaches of the marriage rules; and two-thirds of the disownments enforced by the Marsden Monthly Meeting in Lancashire were for like cause.[225] John Stephenson Rowntree, in his winning contribution to the 1858 essay competition on the causes of Quaker decline, argued that the marriage rules were 'the most influential *proximate* cause of the numerical decline' of the Society of Friends. He

---

[222] L. Tyerman, *Life of the Rev. John Wesley* (1871), ii. 169.

[223] Jenkins in *Welsh Rural Communities*, 49–50; A. G. Matthews, *The Congregational Churches of Staffordshire* (1924), 204; Davies, *Religion in the Industrial Revolution*, 53–4; Binfield, 'Nonconformity in the Eastern Counties', 121; Urdank, 'Dissenting Community', 465; Brockett, *Nonconformity in Exeter*, 217.

[224] Watts, *The Dissenters*, i. 329–30.

[225] D. J. Hall, 'An Historical Study of the Discipline of the Society of Friends', MA thesis (Durham, 1972), 168; J. Travis Mills, *John Bright and The Quakers* (1935), i. 424–5.

calculated that a third of all marriages of Quakers were to non-Quakers, and 'that notwithstanding the entire absence of destitution, marriage in the Society of Friends is one-fifth less frequent than in the population at large'.[226] What Rowntree called the only deliberate 'act of suicide on the part of a church' in Christian history was halted in 1859 when the Yearly Meeting agreed that Friends should be permitted to marry non-Quakers who were regular attenders at meeting.[227] The decision enabled the Society to recover from the depths it reached in 1864 when there were only 13,755 Quakers in the whole of England. By 1914 membership had grown to 19,942, but this was still little more than Rowntree's estimate of the number of Quakers in 1800,[228] and the population of England in 1914 was three times as large as it had been in 1800.

The implementation of marriage rules and the enforcement of sexual morality were not the only aspects of personal relations in which churches interfered. They tried to insist that members behaved with proper concern to their husbands and wives, to their masters and apprentices, and even to their animals. Between 1774 and 1787 the Bacup Particular Baptist church was on several occasions called on to resolve disputes between Joseph Heywood and his wife: Heywood accused her of backbiting and of 'disobedience to his lawful desires', his wife claimed that on two occasions he had pulled her out of bed, and ultimately she left him.[229] In 1828 the Hilperton Particular Baptist church in Wiltshire expelled a women for 'unbecoming conduct in beating her husband'.[230] The Beeston General Baptist church excluded William Wilsley 'for inhuman conduct towards his apprentice' in 1810, and the Castle Gate Congregational church in Nottingham excommunicated a man in 1832 for having 'absconded from his master'.[231] When William Carey was pastor of the Moulton Particular Baptist church the church censured 'deacon Law and his wife, workhouse master and matron, for unkindness to the poor'.[232] And in 1830 the Particular Baptist church at Sutton-on-Trent excluded Thomas Turner for cruelty to a horse.[233]

In their business dealings as in their personalrelationships Nonconformists were expected to show concern for others. In 1848 the Mansfield Primitive Methodists ordered W. Haywood 'to regulate his frame rents according to the work done—that is, if less than a week's work be done less than a week's

---

[226] Rowntree, *Quakerism, Past and Present*, 153–7.
[227] Hall, 'Discipline of the Society of Friends', 169.
[228] Currie, Gilbert, and Horsley, *Churches and Churchgoers*, 156–9.
[229] Gray, 'Nonconformity in Rossendale', 160–2.
[230] Doel, *Twenty Golden Candlesticks*, 144.
[231] Harrison, 'Baptists of Nottinghamshire', i. 394; Castle Gate minutes, 176.
[232] Carey, *William Carey*, 48.   [233] Harrison, 'Baptists of Nottinghamshire', i. 391.

rent be charged'.[234] In 1860 Joseph and Ann Nicholls were expelled from the Congregational Dursley Tabernacle on the ground that they had been found guilty of 'using light weights and scales in their butcher's shop'.[235] It was because Nonconformists believed that Christians should conduct their businesses with a proper consideration for their creditors that they investigated the financial affairs of those of their members who fell into debt or became bankrupt. If any Methodist became bankrupt, instructed the Methodist Conference in 1770, 'let two of the principal members of the society be deputed to examine his accounts: and if he has not kept fair accounts, or has been concerned in that base practice of raising money by coining notes (commonly called the bill-trade) let him be immediately expelled from the society'.[236] The disruption of trade caused by Napoleon's attempted economic blockade of Britain and the retaliatory Orders in Council, followed by the cyclical booms and slumps of the post-war period, produced a rash of bankruptcies in the early nineteenth century. The Castle Gate Congregational church in Nottingham resolved in 1813 that since some 'professors of religion' had continued in 'business after it ought to have been given up' and had persisted in expenditure 'which must have been at the cost of the creditors', any church member who subsequently became insolvent should be 'suspended from the communion of the church, until such time as he shall either convince the church that he is not guilty of wilful negligence, delay or extravagance, or has expressed such contrition and repentance as the nature of the case renders necessary'.[237] Such appears to have been the practice of most Nonconformist churches.[238] In 1773 the Carmarthenshire and Glamorgan Monthly Meeting of the Society of Friends disowned Henry Squire, partly on account of his bankruptcy but partly on the grounds of his intemperance and his familiarity 'with loose women'.[239] By contrast a lenient attitude was taken to the insolvencies of William and Joseph Sweetman in 1819, of Alfred Hingston in 1843, and to the collapse of the Swansea bank owned by Joseph Gibbins and Robert Eaton in 1826. After investigation the problems of the Sweetmans and of Hingston were found to be due principally to 'the depressed state of business', and although Joseph Gibbins was found to be more culpable than his partner, the fact that he was prepared 'to stand the loss up to £5,000' led the

---

[234] Minute Book of the Quarterly Meeting of the Mansfield Primitive Methodist Circuit, 11 Sept. 1848 (Nottinghamshire Archives Office MR 6/2).
[235] Evans, *As Mad as a Hatter!*, 151.   [236] *Minutes of the Methodist Conferences*, i. 94.
[237] Castle Gate minutes, 124.
[238] See e.g. Manley, 'John Rippon', 96–7; Harrison, 'Baptists of Nottinghamshire', i. 386–8.
[239] M. F. Williams, 'The Society of Friends in Glamorgan, 1654–1900', MA thesis (University of Wales, 1950), 242.

Friends to conclude that 'Christian charity and forbearance should be shown to him rather than the rigorous enforcement of discipline'.[240]

In one matter Quaker discipline was much more rigorous than that of the other Dissenting denominations: they periodically sought to exclude from membership any who engaged in or benefited from war. Two General Baptist churches, those at Beeston and at Broad Street, Nottingham, expelled men for joining the army in 1808 and 1845,[241] but such disciplinary action seems to have been unusual among non-Quaker churches. The Methodists had made a special effort to evangelize British troops during the War of the Austrian Succession, and in January 1815 the Particular Baptist church in Reading agreed to admit into membership a 'private soldier in the Royal Horse Guards', though before he could be baptized he was killed at Waterloo.[242] By contrast the Friends frequently disowned those who violated their pacifist principles. Robert Foster, a Lancaster Quaker who spent three years as mate and midshipman on warships, was allowed to remain a member of the Society of Friends after he 'quitted the fighting trade at his grandfather's request' in 1779, but in 1783 'fifteen Scarborough and Whitby Friends who owned armed vessels were disowned and ten captains were debarred from acting in matters of discipline'.[243] The London Yearly Meeting agreed in 1790 that Quakers who persisted in 'fabricating or selling instruments of war' should be expelled, and as a result William Fawcett, a Liverpool merchant, was disowned in 1794 for selling weapons, and in 1795 Samuel Galton, senior, gave up his interest in his Birmingham gun-making firm and his son was disowned in the following year.[244] In 1804 the Norwich banker and future MP Richard Hanbury Gurney was expelled by the Norwich Monthly Meeting 'for contributing to a fund for military purposes'.[245]

In one area the Quakers set an example which other Nonconformists did seek to emulate, in spirit if not by the letter: matters of dress. In the first half of the nineteenth century Quaker men were still expected to wear broad-brimmed hats and coats without lapels and Quaker women were still required to wear sombre clothes and modest bonnets, and although 'gay Friends' who failed to conform to these standards of dress were not disowned,

---

[240] Ibid. 245–67, 223–8.   [241] Harrison, 'Baptists of Nottinghamshire', i. 345.

[242] Watts, *The Dissenters*, i. 416–17; Davis, *History of the Baptist Church, Kings Road, Reading*, 60–1.

[243] J. W. Steel, *A Historical Sketch of the Society of Friends in Newcastle and Gateshead* (Newcastle, 1899), 111–12; Greaves, 'Methodism in Yorkshire', 145.

[244] I. Grubb, *Quakers and Industry before 1800* (1930), 69; Sellers, 'Liverpool Nonconformity', 204.

[245] R. G. Thorne, *The History of Parliament: The House of Commons, 1790–1820* (1986), iv. 121.

their position was uncomfortable and sooner or later they opted either for plain dress or for the Church of England.[246] The Quaker 'plainness of apparel' was held up as an example to Methodists by John Wesley: he urged his women followers to avoid curling their hair and wearing gold, pearls, precious stones, rings, necklaces, laces, and ruffles, and advised male Methodists to spurn 'coloured waistcoats, shining stockings, [and] glittering or costly buckles or buttons'.[247] After his death Wesleyans continued to try to enforce modest standards of dress: in 1806 Conference exhorted Methodists 'to put an end to the unjustifiable customs of the men wearing lapelled coats, and expensive and showy stuffs, the women wearing short sleeves, and long-tailed gowns, and the children a superfluity of buttons and ribands'.[248] Some of the first Independent Methodists adopted Quaker dress, and William O'Bryan, himself descended from a family of Cornish Friends, commended the Quakers to the Bible Christians 'as patterns for plainness of dress and manner' if not for their 'worldly-mindedness'. The Bible Christians refused to have communion with any who curled their hair and wore gold, pearls, 'frills, chitterlings, lace, and bunches', and one of their preachers, Thomas Tregaskis, burned the superfluous finery of his converts 'over the flames of the chapel candles'.[249] The Primitive Methodists insisted that their preachers and stewards wore only single-breasted coats and no 'pantaloons, fashionable trousers, nor white hats', while the Calvinistic Methodists at Tredegar censured men for wearing wedding rings and women for wearing feathers.[250]

Dissenters were critical of members who wore unnecessary adornment partly because it implied personal ostentation and partly because it involved unnecessary extravagance. To strict Nonconformists money earned or inherited was not granted for selfish indulgence but was given in trust by God to be used for purposes of which he approved. 'No Christian', wrote John Wesley, 'can afford to waste any part of the substance which God has entrusted him with.'[251] The same considerations governed the Dissenters' use of leisure. The Christian, argued Wesley, had no need of what the world called 'innocent amusement', and men and women who danced or played cards could not be allowed to remain members of Methodist societies. Wesley quoted with approval the saying of 'a plain preacher in London': 'If you take away his rattles from the child, he will be angry; nay, if he can, he will scratch and bite you.

---

[246] Isichei, *Victorian Quakers*, 145–6.
[247] R. J. Wearmouth, *Methodism and the Common People of the Eighteenth Century* (1945), 244.
[248] *Minutes of the Methodist Conferences*, ii. 349.   [249] Shaw, *The Bible Christians*, 15, 110.
[250] Werner, *Primitive Methodist Connexion*, 137; Davies, *Religion in the Industrial Revolution*, 53.
[251] Tyerman, *Life of Wesley*, iii. 516.

But give him something better first, and he will throw away the rattles of himself.'[252] Moreover, the convert who continued to indulge in frivolous pursuits and to associate with worldly companions jeopardized the results of his conversion. 'If professors needlessly associate with wicked and vain persons', warned the Congregationalist George Burder, 'they will soon resemble them, learn their manners, and go back from Christ.'[253] William Bramwell gave an illustration of how the most harmless of secular hobbies could endanger a man's soul. He was introduced to a canary-fancier and was given a description of the birds' 'various beauties and excellencies'. 'Why,' Bramwell told the canary-fancier, 'these are your gods!' 'The man was offended, but, upon more serious consideration, he felt the force of the remark, disposed of the canaries . . . and his soul was set at liberty.'[254]

As a consequence of such attitudes Old General Baptists, New Connexion General Baptists, Particular Baptists, Congregationalists, and Methodists of every description all censured members who danced and played cards, attended races or cricket matches, watched cock-fighting or prize-fights.[255] The Queen Street Congregational church in Wolverhampton expelled a family of eight from church membership 'because they were unrepentant for having held a family dance'.[256] In 1790 the Midland Conference of the New Connexion of General Baptists ordered its members to refrain from fox-hunting on the grounds that it 'is a waste of precious time, is expense ill-applied, frequently exposes the person to temptation', and injures the property of others, thus substantiating Macaulay's dictum that Evangelicals objected to fox-hunting because it brought pleasure to the hunter rather than pain to the fox.[257] The theatre was anathema to most Nonconformists. In 1764 John Wesley protested against a proposal to build a new theatre in Bristol on the grounds that 'stage entertainments sap the foundation of all religion', 'efface all traces of piety and earnestness from the minds of men', and were accompanied by 'drinking and debauchery of every kind'.[258] To the Congregationalist John Angell James the theatre was the 'resort of the vicious and [a] seminary of vice', the 'broad and fiery avenue to the bottomless

---

[252] *Wesley's Letters*, viii. 12.

[253] Rosman, *Evangelicals and Culture*, 60, citing G. Burder, *Village Sermons* (1843), 395.

[254] Sigston, *Memoirs of Bramwell*, 253.

[255] Quarterly Meetings of the General Baptist churches of East Kent, 13 Apr. 1786 (DWL MSS 38.72); Harrison, 'Baptists of Nottinghamshire', i. 392–4; Jones, *Congregationalism in England*, 231; Currie, *Methodism Divided*, 132.

[256] H. A. May, *Queen Street Congregational Church, Wolverhampton: The Story of a Hundred Years* (1909), 19.

[257] *TBHS* 5 (1916–17), 123–4.   [258] *Wesley's Letters*, iv. 279.

pit'.[259] When a gunpowder explosion killed several members of the audience at a puppet show at Chester the Particular Baptist Joseph Jenkins declared it the judgement of God: 'The English theatre is the school of Satan', he proclaimed.[260]

Novels, too, were frequently condemned. Some otherwise strict Dissenters read novels. Newman Hall's mother read *Kenilworth* and *Ivanhoe* to him; John Aldis, minister of the Maze Pond Particular Baptist church, bought the latest instalment of Dickens's novels at Croydon station and took them home to read to his family; and some Congregational church book societies purchased novels by George Eliot and the Brontës.[261] By contrast when the Quakers of Newcastle upon Tyne set up a book society in 1826 it was precisely to keep out 'books of an injurious tendency', and those included the novels of Walter Scott.[262] In 1822 Adam Clarke and Robert Newton, on behalf of the Wesleyan Conference, urged parents to keep away from their children 'novels and other corrupt publications', and although John Wesley had conceded that Methodists might read 'useful history, pious and elegant poetry, or several branches of natural philosophy', other Wesleyan leaders were less tolerant of secular literature: John Pawson burned Wesley's annotated copy of Shakespeare 'as among the things which tended not to edification'.[263] The typical Dissenting attitude to the reading of novels, and to leisure in general, was summarized by Spurgeon in his usual forthright manner: 'I know that worldly people read novels; I don't blame them. I don't grudge pigs their swill. But how any converted man can waste his time over a novel I cannot imagine.'[264]

The one significant group of Nonconformists who did not subscribe to the general condemnation of novel-reading, theatre-going, and dancing were the Unitarians. According to Mrs Anna Barbauld at the Unitarians' Warrington academy 'dancing, cards, the theatre, were all held lawful in moderation'; Robert Aspland went to see John Kemble and Mrs Siddons at Covent Garden; and the Unitarian barrister Henry Crabb Robinson devoted a good deal of energy to urging Coleridge, Southey, and Wordsworth on to his reluctant Congregational friends, the Pattisons of Witham.[265] Joseph Parkes,

---

[259] Jones, *Congregationalism in England*, 231.   [260] Robison, 'Particular Baptists', 351.

[261] Newman Hall, *Autobiography*, 22; *Baptist Quarterly* NS 5 (1930–1), 6–7; Binfield, 'Nonconformity in the Eastern Counties', 370.

[262] Steel, *Society of Friends in Newcastle and Gateshead*, 96–7.

[263] *Minutes of the Methodist Conferences*, v. 347–8; Tyerman, *Life of Wesley*, iii. 518; Stevenson, *The City Road Chapel*, 135.

[264] *Baptist Quarterly*, NS 5 (1930–1), 6–7.

[265] J. Lindsay (ed.), *The Autobiography of Joseph Priestley* (Bath, 1970), 15; Aspland, *Memoir of Aspland*, 176; Binfield, *So Down to Prayers*, 45–7.

radical solicitor and member of the New Meeting, Birmingham, defended the theatre from the attacks of John Angell James and acknowledged his debt to Shakespeare and Ben Jonson.[266] And Isaac Solly, member of the Old Meeting, Walthamstow, took his seven-year-old son Henry to see *Macbeth* at Drury Lane and even acted as master-of-ceremonies at the monthly subscription 'Cinderella' dances at the Woodford Assembly rooms.[267] But then the Unitarians were not, in Spurgeon's eyes, converted men.

Some Unitarians also differed from their fellow Dissenters on the question of Sunday observance. In general Evangelical Nonconformists treated Sunday as the Jews regarded Saturday: a day on which neither work nor relaxation was permissible unless it were of a specifically religious nature. The Unitarian Thomas Belsham condemned the efforts which were made in reaction to the French Revolution to secure the implementation of laws dating back to the sixteenth century for the enforcement of 'the sabbatical observance of the Lord's day'.[268] But most orthodox Dissenters made no attempt to distinguish the Christian Sunday from the Jewish Sabbath. The Congregational church at Bradfield in Norfolk refused to admit Charles Farmery to membership in 1780 since he was 'an indentured servant and was under the necessity of standing in [his] master's shop every Lord's day morning till ten o'clock'.[269] The Beeston General Baptist church reprimanded the baker Henry Cross in 1821 'for baking on the Sabbath morning'.[270] And in 1824 the Congregational church at Handsworth near Birmingham suspended Adam Williams from membership for 'Sabbath breaking in keeping the door at Soho foundry'.[271] In rural Wales farmers made sure that 'they cut plenty of hay and brought it to the buildings before the Sabbath so that they would have nothing to do on that day apart from giving food and water to the beasts'.[272] In Yorkshire fishing villages fishermen always 'made sure to get in afore midnight of a Saturday' and would not set sail again until after midnight on Sunday, while their wives 'wouldn't even wash up of a Sunday' but put 't' dirty pots away in a cupboard'.[273] All travel on Sundays except going to chapel was frowned upon, and in 1840 the Wesleyan Conference suggested that the country's commercial distress was evidence of 'divine displeasure' at the

[266] J. K. Buckley, *Joseph Parkes of Birmingham* (1926), 19.
[267] H. Solly, *These Eighty Years* (1893), i. 34–5, 38, 184.
[268] J. Williams, *Memoirs of Thomas Belsham* (1833), 486–7.
[269] Browne, *Congregationalism in Norfolk and Suffolk*, 320.
[270] Harrison, 'Baptists of Nottinghamshire', i. 392.
[271] Matthews, *Congregational Churches of Staffordshire*, 204.
[272] Owen, 'Chapel and Community in Glan-Llyn, Merioneth,' in *Welsh Rural Communities*, 198–9.
[273] Clark, *Between Pulpit and Pew*, 56.

railway companies who prostituted the Sabbath by running their trains for 'purposes of worldly pleasure or gain'.[274] It was not until 1860 that Nottinghamshire Wesleyan local preachers overcame their Sabbatarian scruples and agreed to set up a fund to finance the hiring of a horse and trap on Sundays, and ten years later the local preachers in the Newark circuit were unanimous that they should avoid travelling by train 'in going to and from appointments on the Lord's day'.[275] When John Angell James was reprimanded for using his coach to get to chapel on Sundays, he responded by not taking his coach out on Saturdays 'so that his horse could rest on the Jewish Sabbath'.[276] To children brought up in Nonconformist homes Sunday observance could be particularly irksome. Guinness Rogers was 'punished for the sin of going with a young friend to walk in his garden and gather gooseberries', and Charles Kelly, when only six years old, was thrashed by his mother for buying apples on Sunday.[277] And William Hale White was not the only child of a Dissenting home to suffer cold dinners. In 1764 the Lancashire Particular Baptist Association agreed that, except in 'cases of necessity or mercy', 'cooking meat on the Sabbath was a breach of the Fourth Commandment'.[278]

It was, however, the morality of drinking rather than the ethics of Sabbatical cooking which the more exercised the minds of Dissenters in the nineteenth century. Most Nonconformists did not avoid alcohol before the 1830s, and indeed it was impractical to do so at a time when both water and milk were dangerous to drink and tea and coffee were dearer than beer. Dissenting churches had always expelled notorious and habitual drunkards, and Wesley had forbidden Methodists to buy, sell, or drink spirits,[279] but until well into the nineteenth century Nonconformists drank their beer like the rest of the community and regarded inns and taverns as acceptable places of meeting and refreshment. For a hundred years, from 1745 to 1844, the ministers responsible for the disbursement of the Particular Baptist Fund dined and held their annual meeting in the King's Head in the Poultry in the City of London. The same tavern was frequently used by other Dissenting organizations as a convenient meeting place, and the Sunday School Society (1785), the London Baptist Education Society (1804), and the London Baptist

---

[274] *Minutes of the Methodist Conferences*, ix. 116–17.

[275] Swift, *Lively People*, 145; Newark Wesleyan Circuit Local Preachers' Minute Book, 27 June 1870 (Nottinghamshire Archives Office, MR 5/20).

[276] Jones, *Congregationalism in England*, 233.

[277] J. Guinness Rogers, *An Autobiography* (1903), 27; C. H. Kelly, *Memories* (1910), 11.

[278] Gray, 'Nonconformity in Rossendale', 180.

[279] Watts, *The Dissenters*, i. 327; Church, *Early Methodist People*, 186, 192.

Building Fund (1824) were all founded there.[280] The committees of Congregational societies met 'chiefly at taverns' until the establishment of the Congregational Library at Finsbury Circus in 1831.[281] Although some churches would not allow publicans to remain as church members,[282] such an attitude was not general. The Wesleyan Montague Taylor kept a pub at Bilston in the Black Country and decorated the wall of his bar-room with biblical texts.[283] The Congregational lay preacher James Taylor kept the Bull Inn at Woodmancote Green in Gloucestershire, would 'never draw more than two pints at a time for any man', and condemned from the pulpit members of the Dursley Tabernacle choir when they celebrated the battle of Waterloo by getting drunk.[284] Even more strict was the Wesleyan Richard Pearce who kept the Cross Keys at Bradford-on-Avon and would not allow his customers more than one pint of beer at a time.[285]

The Cross Keys was not the only pub to allow infant Nonconformist churches to meet on its premises. The Baptists of Pontypridd met in the White Hart, the Congregationalists of Merthyr Tydfil gathered in the long room of the Crown Inn, the Calvinistic Methodists of Bangor held their first meeting in the Virgin public house in 1802, and the Wesleyans met in the same pub in the following year.[286] In Wesleyan chapels in Lincolnshire preachers were offered a glass of port after they had delivered their sermons, the Friar Lane Particular Baptist church in Nottingham gave a teaspoonful of rum to baptismal candidates after the ceremony had been carried out in the open air, and in one Welsh chapel a barrel of beer was kept under the pulpit from which the preacher could refresh himself.[287] When the Congregationalist Thomas Raffles was ordained at Hammersmith in 1809, 126 men, 'including a large number of Independent ministers', sat down to his ordination dinner and consumed between them forty-two bottles of sherry, forty-four bottles of port, and a bowl of negus.[288] When the Independent David Rees accepted an invitation to the pastorate of the Llanelli church in 1829 the church's deacons greeted him in the Mansell's Arms with a pint of beer.[289] The pioneer New Connexion General Baptist church meeting at

[280] S. J. Price, *A Popular History of the Baptist Building Fund* (1927), 16–19.
[281] J. Waddington, *Congregational History: Continuation to 1850* (1878), 352.
[282] Watts, *The Dissenters*, i. 327.
[283] Leese, 'Impact of Methodism on Black Country Society', 262.
[284] Evans, *As Mad as a Hatter!*, 115–16.
[285] Church, *More About Early Methodist People*, 10.
[286] Bassett, *The Welsh Baptists*, 133; Davies, *Religion in the Industrial Revolution*, 16–17; Lambert, *Drink and Sobriety*, 16.
[287] Obelkevich, *Religion and Rural Society*, 209; Harrison, 'The Baptists of Nottinghamshire', i. 44; Jones, *Hanes Annibynwyr Cymru*, 215.
[288] *TCHS* 20 (1966), 112.   [289] Jones, *Hanes Annibynwyr Cymru*, 216.

Barton-in-Fabis and Melbourne in Leicestershire suffered an early disaster in consequence of its willingness to provide alcoholic refreshment and dinner for members who travelled considerable distances to its services: it was accustomed to defray the cost by holding a collection and in 1759 was fined £100 for contravening the excise laws by selling alcohol.[290] Even the Primitive Methodists, who were to be pioneers in the temperance movement, discussed a proposal at their Manchester Conference in 1827 to require chapel trustees 'to provide wine for the use of preachers, either before preaching, to give them a little spirit for their work, or after preaching to revive their exhausted energies'.[291] The proposal was defeated, but it is inconceivable that such a suggestion would even have been considered a decade later.

It was in the 1820s that the tolerance with which churches regarded moderate drinking, and the friendly state of coexistence between chapel and pub, started to be questioned. An early harbinger of future conflict was a resolution of the Castle Gate Congregational church in Nottingham in 1820, 'that it is inconsistent with the duty and profession of a member of a Christian church to frequent public houses'.[292] The organized temperance movement, like the camp-meeting movement, originated in the United States in 1826, spread to Ireland and Scotland in 1829, and the influence of the Irish and Scottish movements led in turn to the foundation of the first English temperance societies in 1830. The first public temperance meeting in London was held in June 1831 to launch what was soon to be called the British and Foreign Temperance Society.[293]

From the start the temperance movement was divided into two camps. The British and Foreign Temperance Society was opposed not to the drinking of alcohol in general but to the drinking of spirits in particular, and did not contest the partaking of beer and wine in moderation. It was supported both by Evangelical Anglican clergymen and public-spirited aristocrats on the one hand and by Nonconformist ministers and Quaker businessmen on the other, but it failed to satisfy more radical temperance advocates who had knowledge of the damage that excessive beer-drinking could do to working men and their families.[294] To temperance reformers who were in close contact with working-class life the only solution for men in thrall to alcohol was total abstinence. The weakness of the case for moderation and the strength of the argument for abstinence was revealed by the members of the Treforys Temperance Society in Glamorgan. They allowed themselves 'three pots of

---

[290] *General Baptist Magazine*, 2 (1798), 504.
[291] Kendall, *Primitive Methodist Church*, i. 470.   [292] Castle Gate minutes, 145.
[293] B. Harrison, *Drink and the Victorians* (1971), 101–5.   [294] Ibid. 107, 113, 138–9.

drink per day' but then saved up their weekly allocation until Saturday night and got reeling drunk.[295]

Contrary to the widespread assumption that total abstinence was a bourgeois ploy imposed on the proletariat as part of a programme of social control, the movement did in fact originate among working-class communities in industrial Lancashire and Cheshire.[296] The first church to insist on total abstinence (and vegetarianism) as a condition of membership was the Bible Christian Christ Church in King Street, Salford, founded in 1800 by the former Swedenborgian minister William Cowherd. Cowherd emphasized the antipathy between man's material and spiritual natures and taught that the former had to be suppressed in order that the latter could realize its full potential. Since, in Cowherd's eyes, the drinking of alcohol and the eating of meat bound man to his animal nature and hindered the development of his spiritual qualities, they were forbidden to members of his church.[297] Cowherd died in 1816 and was succeeded as pastor of his church by Joseph Brotherton, a local mill-owner and future factory reformer and MP for Salford. Brotherton inherited Cowherd's convictions along with his church. His wife Martha published in 1812 *Vegetarian Cooking*, one of the earliest vegetarian recipe books, and Brotherton himself helped to found the Vegetarian Society in 1847. In 1821 Brotherton published a tract entitled *On Abstinence from Intoxicating Liquors* which was claimed to be the first pamphlet advocating total abstinence in the English-speaking world.[298]

Other Nonconformists were prominent in the early stages of the temperance movement. The future General Baptist minister Jabez Burns, father of the historian of the movement, Dawson Burns, joined a temperance society in Edinburgh in 1829 after hearing a lecture by an American minister on the subject and immediately became a temperance lecturer himself.[299] The first temperance society in England was founded in Bradford in February 1830 by a Scottish worsted manufacturer named Henry Forbes with the help of a local Wesleyan surgeon, Dr Thomas Beaumont.[300] And the second was founded in the Independent Methodist chapel at Stockton Heath, Warrington, in April 1830 by a Dublin Quaker and vegetarian George Harrison

[295] Jones, *Hanes Annibynwyr Cymru*, 216.
[296] P. Bailey, in *Leisure and Class in Victorian England* (1978), 30, sees both the temperance movement and the campaign for total abstinence as part of a 'long history' of 'concern to police the amusements of the poor'.
[297] Lineham, 'English Swedenborgians', 297–300.
[298] Axon, *Bible Christian Church*, 24; *Biographical Dictionary of Modern Radicals*, ii. 87–92.
[299] J. Burns, *A Retrospect of Forty-Five Years' Christian Ministry* (1875), 143.
[300] Harrison, *Drink and the Victorians*, 104–5.

Birkett.[301] Whereas the members of Burns's Edinburgh society were pledged to abstain only from spirits, the Warrington society from the start committed itself to the renunciation of all alcoholic drinks.

But it was Preston which was to be the Galilee of the total abstinence movement and its chief apostle the restless, tireless, radical reformer and publicist Joseph Livesey. Livesey, who in his twenties had abandoned hand-loom weaving to establish a prosperous cheesemongering business, had been baptized in the Leeming Street Particular Baptist chapel in Preston in 1811 and subsequently joined the small denomination of Scotch Baptists.[302] But by the 1830s he had come to reject 'the Christianity of the churches for that of Christ', believing that 'the best part of religion is to do good to all men'.[303] In the early 1830s he edited a monthly paper, the *Moral Reformer*, which he used to attack 'the corrupting influence of wealth' on the Church of England; in the late 1830s he led the campaign to prevent the introduction of the New Poor Law into Preston; and in 1841 he launched an illustrated paper, *The Struggle*, which became the most popular journal of the anti-Corn Law move-ment.[304] But it was to the campaign against alcohol that Livesey devoted the largest and longest share of his boundless energies. 'Convinced of the evil tendency of *moderate* drinking', from the beginning of 1831 he rejected the taking of 'ale, wine, or ardent spirits'; in March 1832 he formed the Preston Temperance Society; and in September he and six associates signed a pledge to abstain from all alcohol for a year. In February 1833 Livesey first delivered his famous *Malt Lecture* which attempted to place the case for total absti-nence on a scientific foundation, and he effectively launched the total absti-nence movement's national campaign by sending a summary of his lecture, under the title *The Great Delusion*, 'to every member of the House of Commons and the House of Lords'.[305]

Though Livesey had rejected orthodox Dissent in favour of a secularized Christianity devoted to good works, from its origin the total abstinence movement owed much to Nonconformists. The Preston reformers' first two nation-wide missionaries, James Teare and Thomas Whittaker, were both Methodist local preachers, and it was a Primitive Methodist plasterer named Richard Turner who christened the new movement in September 1833.

---

[301] Mounfield, *Short History of Independent Methodism*, 28.

[302] The Scotch Baptists had been founded in 1765 by former Presbyterians Robert Carmichael and Archibald McLean. They were extreme literalists who were influenced by the Sandemanians and rejected a paid and educated ministry (Underwood, *History of the English Baptists*, 189–90).

[303] J. Pearce, *The Life and Teachings of Joseph Livesey* (1887), pp. xii–xiii, xviii, 10–12.

[304] Ibid., pp. xiii–xiv, xxviii, lxi–lxii.   [305] Ibid., pp. lxxviii, lxxxii, lxxxviii–lxxxix.

Turner suffered from a stutter, but this did not prevent his telling a cheering meeting of the Preston Temperance Society that his renunciation of alcohol would 'be reet down out-and-out t-t-total for ever and ever'.[306]

The catalyst which transformed the fervour of a handful of temperance enthusiasts into a mass movement, and which drove an unbridgeable gulf between chapel and pub, was the Beer Act of 1830. The intention of the Act was to combat smuggling and to make beer more widely available to counter the attraction of stronger intoxicating spirits such as gin: it allowed any householder on payment of two guineas a year to obtain an excise licence to sell beer on or off his premises. The result of the Act was a huge increase in the number of beershops: by 1833 there were 35,000 in England and Wales.[307] Contemporaries believed that the Act led to a great increase in drunkenness, and while Brian Harrison has questioned the accuracy of their observations,[308] to Nonconformist churches which had always regarded drunkenness as incompatible with church membership, alcohol now appeared to be an increasingly serious problem. The Beeston General Baptist church excluded seven members for drunkenness between 1804 and 1837, but five of those seven were expelled between 1830 and 1837.[309] What is more, the Beer Act provided an opportunity for thousands of poor men (and their wives) to earn a living by selling beer. Their beershops attracted a lower class of customer than inns and taverns, and were believed to encourage behaviour which threatened both the morals of society and the security of the State. The bishop of Bath and Wells and his diocesan clergy claimed that beershops were responsible for the 'alarming increase of immorality, pauperism, and vice, among the lower orders', and beershops were blamed for instigating riots in the rural counties of south-east England in 1830–1.[310] It was not, however, only upper-class clergymen and magistrates who deplored the growth of beershops. When faced with the question of whether it is 'right for members of a Christian church to keep a beershop', the annual association of the New Connexion of General Baptists replied in 1837 that, 'while we do not wish to impugn the motives, or reflect on the character, of any respectable individuals who may keep beershops, yet the evils flowing from them are so truly fearful, so destructive of the peace and order of neighbourhoods, and so demoralizing in their tendency, that this Association can on no account approve of the keeping of these establishments by members of our churches'.[311]

---

[306] Harrison, *Drink and the Victorians*, 117–26.   [307] Ibid. 79–82.   [308] Ibid. 82–3.
[309] Harrison, 'Baptists of Nottinghamshire', i. 376.
[310] Harrison, *Drink and the Victorians*, 83–6.
[311] Wood, *History of the General Baptists*, 283.

The Beer Act brought home to Dissenters the fact that drinking places were their competitors for the leisure time and money of the working class, and ultimately for their souls. Beershops and public houses were seen as fostering a way of life which could obstruct a man's conversion and induce backsliding in those already converted. Soon inns and taverns were included in the indiscriminate denunciation of all drinking places. In 1832 the Burnley Congregational church resolved that 'if any member open a public-house he shall cease to be a member with us, not because the thing is inimical in itself in the sight of God, but because they are so many abuses connected with such a line of business', and in 1844 the Cradley Baptist church in the Black Country came to a similar decision.[312] The antagonism between chapel and pub became so intense from the 1830s onwards because they were competing for the same constituency and for much the same reasons. The same factors which induced some men to join Nonconformist churches drove others to the tavern and the beerhouse: the need for consolation and companionship after long hours of work in unhealthy and dangerous occupations, the feeling of helplessness at the hands of forces over which they had no control, the knowledge that disease or accident was likely to bring early death. It was no coincidence that Merthyr Tydfil, not only the fastest growing town in Wales but also the most unhealthy and a victim of the cholera epidemic of 1849, was distinguished both by its high level of religious observance and by its high incidence of drunkenness. The same town had 53 per cent of its population at worship on census Sunday, nearly all of them in one of 66 Nonconformist chapels, and 506 licensed drinking places, one for every 124 inhabitants.[313]

It is also significant that it was those Nonconformist denominations with the highest proportion of unskilled and semi-skilled working-class members which were the first to endorse the temperance movement and the ones to embrace teetotalism with the greatest enthusiasm. In 1831 Hugh Bourne persuaded the Primitive Methodist Conference at Leicester to instruct the editor of the connexional magazine to devote a portion of his space to articles on temperance, and in the following year Conference recommended temperance to its members.[314] The Independent Methodist leader Peter Phillips adopted total abstinence in 1833 and the Bible Christian leader James Thorne signed the pledge in 1837.[315] At the Bible Christian Conference of 1840 thirty-two of the thirty-three travelling preachers and fourteen of the

---

[312] Nightingale, *Lancashire Nonconformity*, ii. 160; Cumberland, 'Protestant Nonconformity in the Black Country', 155.
[313] Lambert, *Drink and Sobriety*, 31–3.   [314] Kendall, *Primitive Methodist Church*, i. 471.
[315] Vickers, *History of Independent Methodism*, 25; Shaw, *The Bible Christians*, 53–4.

seventeen laymen present were committed to total abstinence.[316] The South Wales Association of Calvinistic Methodists endorsed the aims of the British and Foreign Temperance Society in 1835; the North Wales Association forbade members of the denomination to engage in the drink trade in 1838, and two years later insisted that both church office-holders and Sunday school teachers be teetotal.[317] The few churches which insisted on total abstinence as a condition even of membership were very largely working class in composition. Such were the cases of the Bible Christian church in Salford and of the Particular Baptist church at Atherton in Lancashire, where the average wage of members in 1849 was said to be 7s. a week.[318] Only teetotallers were allowed to join the Calvinistic Methodist society at Coed-y-cymmer near Merthyr Tydfil, a church which included 'a great many miners and colliers'.[319] Churches with a predominantly working-class membership and leadership were all too conscious of the havoc that excessive drinking could wreak on poor families. Billy Bray's wife, before his conversion, 'had to fetch him home night after night from the beershop'. On one occasion, he later confessed, 'I went to get some coal; there was a beershop in the way . . . and coming home I went in, and stayed till I got drunk'. 'My poor wife was forced to come for me, and wheel home the coal herself.'[320]

The growth of teetotal sentiment in the Nonconformist churches did not, however, go unchallenged and it provoked opposition throughout the nineteenth century. Even among the Primitive Methodists and the Bible Christians, the denominations most ready to embrace total abstinence, there were pockets of resistance. The Darlaston circuit Primitive Methodists provided ale for members attending their quarterly meetings until the 1840s, and an attempt to restrict them to the drinking of water in 1843 was reversed in 1844 when it was decided to allow a pint of ale to any who wanted it.[321] When Bible Christians in the Michaelstow circuit in Cornwall objected to preachers and class-leaders drinking at inns, they were reminded that the Connexion's rules banned drunkenness, not drinking.[322] There was much resistance to teetotalism among the Baptists. When Jabez Burns started to use unfermented wine for communion services in the New Church Street General Baptist church in Paddington in the 1830s some forty of his members seceded; when

---

[316] W. J. Townsend, H. B. Workman, and G. Eayrs, *A New History of Methodism* (1909), i. 523.
[317] Lambert, *Drink and Sobriety*, 138.
[318] Weston, 'Baptists of North-West England', 159, 571.
[319] *Children's Employment Commission: Appendix to the First Report of Commissioners: Mines, Part II, Reports and Evidence from Sub-Commissioners*, xvii (1842), 382.
[320] Bourne, *The King's Son*, 4–5.
[321] Leese, 'Impact of Methodism on Black Country Society', 264.
[322] Shaw, *The Bible Christians*, 53–4.

Francis Beardsall, pastor of the General Baptist church in Manchester from 1834, tried to make total abstinence a condition of church membership, half the members resigned and the church subsequently died out; and the New Connexion as a whole refused to endorse total abstinence in 1847.[323] The Caersalem Baptist church in Dowlais was still buying fermented wine for communion from a church member who owned the Owain Glyndwr public house in the 1860s, and when William Morris became minister of the Baptist church in Treorchy in 1869 he claimed then, and for several years afterwards, that he was the only teetotaller in the church.[324] The most popular Baptist preacher of the century, Charles Haddon Spurgeon, resisted pressure to give up alcohol throughout most of his life, pointed out that 'the wines of the Bible were intoxicating', and referred to beer as 'the Puritan drink'.[325] And although a list of ministers of religion committed to total abstinence in 1848 showed more Congregationalists than ministers of any other denomination, again there was no unanimity.[326] The issue of teetotalism provoked bitter controversy among the Independents of Caernarfonshire in the late 1830s. William Williams ('Caledfryn'), minister of a Congregational church in Caernarfon, published a series of pamphlets in which he denied that to save a drunkard it was necessary to impose total abstinence on everyone else, and argued that the advocates of teetotalism were putting the need to abandon alcohol before the need of conversion to Christ. Williams's views led to a personal clash with his bardic rival Robert Parry ('Robyn Ddu Eryri'), a reformed drunkard and teetotal enthusiast who in 1838 sought recognition as an Independent lay preacher. Caledfryn opposed Parry's recognition on the grounds of his disreputable life, and his stand was vindicated in 1841 when Parry, who had gone to London, was reported to be drinking heavily again and associating with prostitutes.[327]

Spurgeon shared Caledfryn's suspicion that teetotallers were putting abstinence from alcohol before conversion to Christ,[328] and their misgivings could have been substantiated by the support given to teetotalism by the Quakers, who, by the nineteenth century, were characterized by the severity of their discipline and the generosity of their philanthropy rather than by their zeal to save souls.[329] The teetotal movement, with its emphasis both on

---

[323] Burns, *Retrospect of Forty-five Years*, 41; Weston, 'Baptists of North-West England', 109; *Baptist Quarterly*, 13 (1949–50), 357.

[324] Williams, *History of Caersalem, Dowlais*, 49; Lambert, *Drink and Sobriety*, 151; see also Bassett, *The Welsh Baptists*, 134.

[325] B. S. Kruppa, *Charles Haddon Spurgeon: A Preacher's Progress* (New York, 1982), 220–2.

[326] Harrison, *Drink and the Victorians*, 179.   [327] Lambert, *Drink and Sobriety*, 67–74.

[328] Kruppa, *Spurgeon*, 223–4.   [329] See Ch. I, sect. 6.

solving the problems of personal conduct and on redressing the evils of society by self-control and self-denial, had a particular appeal to Friends brought up to believe that men could work out their own salvation by following the light within. Brian Harrison, in his analysis of the leaders of the teetotal movement, found that nearly a quarter of those whose religious affiliation could be determined belonged to the Society of Friends.[330] Quaker philanthropists such as Samuel Bowly, Joseph John Gurney, Joseph Sturge, and William Wilson contributed generously to the funds of the temperance organizations and Joseph Eaton bequeathed £15,000 to the teetotal movement.[331] When the teetotal New British and Foreign Temperance Society split in 1839 over the issue of whether members should sign the short pledge to abstain from alcohol, or the long pledge both to abstain and to refrain from offering alcohol to others, the threat from the Quakers to cut off funds to the competing factions led to their reunion in 1842.[332] As usual the Quaker reliance on consensus rather than majority decisions delayed official declarations, and it was not until 1874 that the Yearly Meeting urged Friends who were engaged in the manufacture of alcohol to change their business. But moral pressure was being exercised long before that, and in 1839 the Quaker brewer William Lucas recorded that he was subjected to hints to change his trade.[333]

The most strenuous opposition to teetotalism among nineteenth-century Nonconformists came from the Wesleyans. To the Wesleyan leadership the teetotal movement, like popular revivalism, was a manifestation of working-class enthusiasm which threatened Methodist discipline and order. In 1838 the trustees of Wesleyan chapels in Cornwall, the heartland of Wesleyan revivalism, gave in to popular pressure to allow their chapels to be used for teetotal meetings, and some Cornish chapels also started using unfermented wine for their communion services, so banishing 'the destructive cup from the Lord's Table'.[334] Jabez Bunting was horrified by these developments. Wesleyans, he later wrote, were so divided over teetotalism that 'we have no right to give our chapels as the arena or battle-field to one class of the combatants against the other'.[335] To support his contention he could have cited an incident that took place in the Calverton Wesleyan chapel in Nottinghamshire in 1838 when teetotal speakers were heckled and bottles of ale distributed among their audience.[336] Bunting persuaded the Wesleyan Conference in 1841 to ban the letting of chapels for teetotal meetings and to

---

[330] Harrison, *Drink and the Victorians*, 165.
[331] Ibid. 107; Isichei, *Victorian Quakers*, 237.
[332] Harrison, *Drink and the Victorians*, 142–5.   [333] Isichei, *Victorian Quakers*, 240.
[334] Ward, *Early Victorian Methodism*, 218–19, 254.   [335] Ibid. 329.
[336] Swift, *Lively People*, 126.

insist on the use of fermented wine for the Lord's Supper.[337] The decisions were resented and widely ignored. There was a secession of 858 members from the St Ives circuit in Cornwall to form the Teetotal Methodist Connexion; a few years later Wesleyan chapels were still being used for teetotal meetings in the King's Lynn circuit; at Maldon in Essex a Baptist teetotal lecturer occupied a Wesleyan pulpit; and at Thetford in Norfolk not only was a teetotal lecturer allowed to preach in a Wesleyan chapel, but that lecturer was a woman.[338]

Bunting's critics claimed that teetotalism stimulated church expansion and that Wesleyan opposition to the movement benefited rival denominations. In 1837 a Wesleyan layman from York told Bunting that temperance societies were making rapid progress in his area, and that many of the men persuaded to renounce alcohol subsequently joined Methodist churches. But it was not the Wesleyans who benefited. 'In consequence of the zealous and almost general advocacy of teetotalism by the *ministers of the "Wesleyan Association", they* are securing the majority of these converts.'[339] The fear expressed by Caledfryn that the signing of the teetotal pledge would become a substitute for conversion was frequently countered by the argument that the abandonment of alcohol predisposed men to listen to the Gospel. 'Intemperance', claimed the Abergavenny Total Abstinence Society in 1840, 'prevents thousands from hearing the Gospel, and hinders the edification of many who attend in many of our different places of worship.'[340] The common interest which both churches and textile manufacturers had in reducing the consumption of alcohol was voiced by Joseph Evans of Carmarthen when he speculated that renouncing alcohol would enable men to 'clothe themselves with decent apparel the lack of which has kept them from frequenting the House of God'.[341] It was claimed that the revival which began in Bala and Llanuwchllyn in 1839 and which swept through much of Wales in the next four years was powerfully assisted by the temperance preaching of Benjamin Chidlaw. A native of Bala who had emigrated to Delaware in 1821, Chidlaw brought back to Merioneth a mixture of evangelical fervour and teetotalism which had already proved highly effective in the United States. In Chidlaw's revivalist campaign religious and teetotal commitments were regarded as complementary: total abstinence was seen as 'the most important outward manifestation of inner conversion'.[342]

---

[337] Gregory, *Side Lights on the Conflicts of Methodism*, 318.
[338] Shaw, *Cornish Methodism*, 80; Ward, *Early Victorian Methodism*, 268, 301–2, 313, 323–5.
[339] Ward, *Early Victorian Methodism*, 180.   [340] Lambert, *Drink and Sobriety*, 126.
[341] Turner, 'Revivals and Popular Religion in Wales', 160.
[342] Ibid. 160–1; Carwardine, *Transatlantic Revivalism*, 90–1.

It was to counter what they saw as the degrading effects of alcohol and its associated vices that all the Nonconformist denominations emulated the Primitive Methodists in deliberately staging popular religious events to draw people away from fairs, wakes, and public houses. In Peppard in Oxfordshire the annual Whit Monday celebrations brought together 'the very scum of the surrounding country to partake in, and be witnesses of, cudgelling, foot and ass racing, and all the various abominations usual on these occasions; the day always ending in intoxication, fighting, and other evils too shameful to mention'. To counter the attractions of the races and the drinking Joseph Walker, the minister of the local Congregational church, 'by the promise of a dinner . . . induced a large number of young people to spend the day at the chapel; and the following year extended the invitation to older people'.[343] Similarly the Wesleyans of Chester provided their Sunday school children with a 'currant treat and tea' during race week, and those at Camborne took their Sunday school children on a trip to the seaside in 1849 'to give the poor children pleasure and at the same time to take them away from the perils of a noisy revelling fair'.[344] Above all the tea-meeting became the characteristic Nonconformist alternative to the joviality of the pub. The members of St Mary's Particular Baptist church in Norwich decided in 1840 'to drink tea together at the Assembly Rooms at five o'clock one evening in December'. Over two hundred people attended, 'all appearing to be resolved to be happy', the church's pastor, William Brock, gave a sketch of Baptist history, and the tea-meeting became an established feature of the church's life.[345] From the 1840s the tea-urn became an essential piece of equipment for every Nonconformist chapel, the smell of tea pervading their buildings as much as the smell of polished oak.

5. BEGGING MISSIONS AND PEW-RENTS: CHAPEL FINANCES

It was one of the many Nonconformist objections to alcohol that the money spent on drink could be put to better use. The Calvinistic Methodist Thomas Levi argued that in one year alone (1869) £112,885,643 had been spent on alcohol and that 'if this money were spent to better purposes, jobs would be

---

[343] Summers, *Congregational Churches in Berks, South Oxon and South Bucks*, 153.

[344] Stigant, 'Methodism and the Working Class', 200; Rule, 'Labouring Miner in Cornwall', 311.

[345] C. B. Jewson, 'St Mary's Norwich', *Baptist Quarterly*, 10 (1940–1), 300. See also Harrison, *Drink and the Victorians*, 302.

provided for another three million workers'.[346] One of those purposes was the building and financing of Nonconformist chapels: an object which occupied a growing proportion of the time and energy of Dissenters as the nineteenth century progressed.

Kitson Clark has commented that the building of churches and chapels 'commanded more of the disinterested enthusiasm of Victorian Englishmen in all districts and classes than any other of the achievements of the reign'.[347] It was an enterprise to which Dissenters contributed almost as much as Anglicans in terms of money and far more in the way of buildings. In his report on the religious census Horace Mann calculated that between 1801 and 1851 the established church had built 2,529 new churches, of which all but 500 had been built since 1831. The total cost of this building programme Mann put at £9,087,000, of which £1,663,429 had come from government funds and £7,423,571 from private individuals.[348] He did not attempt to calculate the amount spent on Nonconformist chapels in the same period, but the census did reveal that there were 19,478 Dissenting places of worship in use in 1851. Of these 19,478 places 3,069 were not 'separate and entire buildings' and another 3,208 had been erected before 1800. If we deduct both these categories from the total number of Nonconformist places of worship we are left with a figure of 13,201 for the number of chapels built between 1801 and 1851, more than five times the number of new Anglican churches built in the same period. It is difficult to know how much these new chapels cost the Dissenters: the cost varied from the £26 which the Primitive Methodists paid for their chapel at Cloud near Congleton in Cheshire in 1815 to the £15,000 which it cost the Congregationalists to build East Parade, Leeds, in 1841.[349] The elder Edward Baines put the average cost of Dissenting chapels in 1840 at £1,000, which his son thought was too high, and the Dissenting Deputies estimated the average cost in 1853 at £400, which may have been too low.[350] The Congregationalists built twenty-five chapels in Sussex between 1818 and 1838 at an average cost of £880; the Wesleyans built eighty-two chapels in 1846–7 at an average cost of £475; and the median cost of a sample I have taken of seventy-two Primitive Methodist chapels built before 1850 was £200.[351] If one assumes that these averages were typical of those denominations

[346] Evans, 'Religion in the Swansea Valley', 214.
[347] G. Kitson Clark, *The Making of Victorian England* (1965), 172–3.
[348] *Religious Census*, p. xli.   [349] Binfield, *So Down to Prayers*, 74.
[350] Baines, *Life of Edward Baines*, 263; B. L. Manning, *The Protestant Dissenting Deputies* (Cambridge, 1952), 192.
[351] Gregory, *Side Lights on the Conflicts of Methodism*, 415; A. Peel, *These Hundred Years* (1931), 150. Samples of the cost of Congregational, Baptist, and Wesleyan chapels have yielded higher values that those cited in this paragraph and I have consequently used the lower values.

as a whole, and if one makes the conservative assumption that the Quakers, Unitarians, and Lady Huntingdon's Connexion spent no more on their meeting-houses than did the Congregationalists of Sussex, that the chapels of the Baptists, the New Connexion Methodists, and the Wesleyan Methodist Association cost on average the same as those of the Wesleyans in 1846–7, and that the Calvinistic Methodists, the Bible Christians, and the smaller denominations spent no more on their chapels than did the Ranters, one can calculate the total amount spent by Nonconformists on their chapels between 1801 and 1851 as £6,325,355. This was only £1 million less than the private benefactions given for the building of parish churches, and came from the pockets of a much poorer section of the community.

This figure helps to explain both the bitterness with which Dissenters resisted Anglican attempts to force them to pay, through church rates, for the upkeep of parish churches, and the enormous strains placed on all the Nonconformist denominations by constant demands for chapel-building. In the smaller, rural chapels, church members often did much of the construction work themselves to keep costs down. When the Primitive Methodists of Dorchester in Oxfordshire decided in 1839 that they needed a permanent place of worship they bought a piece of land for £5 and the chapel's mud walls were built by the village's inhabitants 'before and after their daily labour ... without any remuneration'.[352] When the Soar Independent chapel in Ystalyfera, Glamorgan, was built in 1847 much of the work was done by church members: William Nicholas built the walls, Lewis Rees was responsible for the woodwork, and William Thomas and his sons plastered the walls.[353] For wealthier, urban churches the first step towards building a new chapel was the opening of a subscription list. When the Benn's Garden Presbyterian (Unitarian) meeting in Liverpool contemplated moving to Renshaw Street in 1811 twenty-six members of the congregation pledged themselves to meet the total cost of £4,300.[354] Similarly the Friar Lane Particular Baptist church in Nottingham opened a subscription list in 1810 when they planned to move to George Street, and £1,000 was soon subscribed, including four subscriptions of a hundred guineas and five subscriptions of fifty guineas. However, this covered only a sixth of the ultimate cost of the new chapel and one of the church's deacons, John Barber, was sent on a collecting tour of other Particular Baptist churches in the area, and even to London, to raise another £470.[355]

---

[352] *Primitive Methodist Magazine*, NS 10 (1840), 376.
[353] Evans, 'Religion in the Swansea Valley', 155.   [354] Holt, *Walking Together*, 169.
[355] Harrison, 'Baptists of Nottinghamshire', i. 191–2.

Collecting tours, otherwise known as 'begging missions', were a much utilized and much criticized means of raising money for Nonconformist meeting-houses in the eighteenth and early nineteenth centuries. When Edward Williams was minister of the Congregational church at Oswestry (1777–91) he collected over £590 on begging missions towards the enlargement of his meeting-house, and in 1811 Richard Parsons, pastor of the Baptist church in Whitbourne, Corsley, Wiltshire, walked forty miles a day on a collecting tour which took him to Westbury, Bristol, and London, and which raised £700 for a chapel in the village.[356] Begging missions, however, aroused much opposition from Dissenters who objected to the constant demands on their pockets, disliked the opportunities they presented for dishonesty, resented the way in which they took ministers away from their churches, and calculated that the costs and efforts of collecting tours were disproportionate to the amount of money raised. Twice, in the second half of the eighteenth century, the Tacket Street Congregational church in Ipswich collected sums of £7, first for 'Breckonfield, a German who came to beg for the poor distressed Protestants in Germany', and secondly for 'Rutherford, an Anabaptist minister at Hull, to repair the meeting-house'; but on both occasions the church subsequently found that the suppliants were 'cheats'.[357] The curate of Sutton-in-Ashfield in Nottinghamshire reported to his archbishop in 1743 that there were fifty-seven Dissenting families and one meeting-house in his parish, but that for a year or more most of the Dissenters had attended the parish church since their minister spent most of his time 'collecting money for a new meeting-house'.[358] In the early nineteenth century two Merthyr Tydfil pastors, the Baptist William Price and the Independent Daniel Lewis, both went on begging tours and both returned to churches which accused them of fiddling their expenses with the result that Price was dismissed and Lewis's church divided.[359] Most unfortunate of all was the experience of Lewis Lewis, who combined the pastorate of the Baptist church at Glascoed in Monmouthshire with supplying charcoal to the local iron furnaces: he contracted a severe chill while on a begging mission and subsequently died.[360]

Particular Baptists in London tried to prevent the abuse of begging missions by insisting that persons engaged in such enterprises should first gain the approval, from 1723, of the Baptist Board (the Society of London

[356] W. T. Owen, *Edward Williams* (Cardiff, 1963), 48; M. Reeves, 'Protestant Nonconformity', *VCH, Wiltshire*, iii (1956), 138.

[357] Minute Book of Tacket Street Congregational church, Ipswich (DWL MSS 201, 11), p. 66.

[358] S. L. Ollard and P. C. Walker, *Archbishop Herring's Visitation Returns* (Yorkshire Archaeological Record Series, 1930), iv. 144.

[359] C. Wilkins, *The History of Merthyr Tydfil* (Merthyr Tydfil, 1867), 275, 282.

[360] Jones, *Sowing Beside all Waters*, 76.

Ministers of the Particular Baptist Persuasion) and, from 1784, of the Baptist Case Committee. The Baptist Case Committee provided country ministers with a guide who not only conducted them through London's unfamiliar streets and alley-ways but also supplied them with lists both of persons who were known to be generous givers and of those who would give a donation only after being subjected to considerable pleading. But even with the committee's careful supervision the begging system remained inefficient: the sums raised were often small, and even smaller after the beggar's expenses had been deducted. In one case, after expenses had been taken into consideration, '£1 only was returned to the church, and in another every farthing collected was expended'. James Hargreaves wrote in the *Baptist Magazine* in 1829 of a minister who over a period of four years had left his church on 'begging excursions' for forty-three weeks during which time he travelled 2,132 miles, much of it on foot. Yet for all his exertions, he had reduced the debt on his chapel by only £140.[361] One of the main motives behind the abortive attempt to form a Congregational Union between 1806 and 1809, and the more successful attempt in 1831–2, was to assist in the building of chapels without the 'nuisance of begging by preachers of the Gospel'. But the attempt by the Union committee in 1809 to insist that country churches should be permitted to raise funds in London only after their cases had been scrutinized by two successive meetings of that committee contributed to the collapse of the Union.[362] And the revived Congregational Union of 1832, faced with the reluctance of churches and county associations to contribute to its funds, initially had no success either in promoting chapel-building or in controlling begging missions.[363]

A writer in the *Congregational Magazine* in 1835, who regarded begging missions as 'a system of mendicity which is at once dishonourable and mischievous', pointed to the virtues of the Wesleyans' connexional system which had 'enabled them to sustain the burden of a much greater debt than the Congregational churches' and to build new chapels 'in a manner that the divided energies of our denomination will not suffer individuals to attempt'.[364] The Wesleyans had certainly built more than twice as many new chapels as the Congregationalists in the first half of the nineteenth century, but the effort had not been as painless as the contributor to the *Congregational Magazine* implied. Until 1818 begging tours were a feature of

---

[361] *Baptist Magazine*, 21 (1829), 123; Price, *Baptist Building Fund*, 30–1, 40–6, 58–9.
[362] Peel, *These Hundred Years*, 33–4, 45.
[363] K. G. Brownell, 'Voluntary Saints: English Congregationalism and the Voluntary Principle, 1825–62', Ph.D. thesis (St Andrews, 1982), 196, 201.
[364] *Congregational Magazine*, NS 11 (1835), 636.

Wesleyan as well as of Congregational fund-raising. When the trustees of the Methodist chapel in Nottingham seceded to the New Connexion in 1798, taking the chapel with them, Thomas Tatham was given permission to go on a collecting tour to raise money for a new chapel.[365] In Chester, where there was also a major secession to the New Connexion, the Wesleyans incurred the enormous debt of £5,070 in building their St John Street chapel in 1812 and their minister, Thomas Pinder, was similarly allowed by Conference to embark on a begging tour.[366] And such was the exhaustion suffered by Jabez Bunting on one begging mission that after a long journey 'he fell asleep while praying in a Leeds pulpit'.[367]

The very speed with which Methodism expanded in the late eighteenth and early nineteenth centuries and the consequent desire of local societies to build their own preaching-houses caused the Wesleyans serious financial problems. Wesley himself was constantly trying to restrain his followers from embarking on building projects which they could not afford. By 1766 the Connexion had a total debt for building of £11,383 and Methodists were told to start no new chapels until two-thirds of the cost had been subscribed; in 1770 Wesley put a ban on all new building and alterations 'unless the proposers thereof can and will defray the whole expense'; and again in 1789 Conference forbade the erection of any new chapels 'except one at Dewsbury, and those which have already been begun or set on foot'.[368] A building committee was established in 1790 with powers to veto the construction of any new chapel, and three years later its powers were delegated to the District Meetings, but all such attempts to impose central control over chapel-building were frequently ignored by local enthusiasts.[369]

In the fifteen years after Wesley's death the Connexion's debts again mounted steadily until by 1816 the post-war depression had forced them up to £5,155, and it was the opinion of Jonathan Crowther that extravagant chapel-building was a major cause of the Wesleyans' financial embarrassments.[370] In a further attempt to deal with the problem, and at the same time put an end to begging tours, in 1818 the Wesleyan Conference established a general chapel fund to raise money throughout the Connexion to help chapels to pay off their debts. Between 1818 and 1845 the fund raised

---

[365] Dunn, *Memoirs of Thomas Tatham*, 118–23.

[366] F. F. Bretherton, *Early Methodism in and around* Chester (Chester, 1903), 252–4.

[367] Bunting and Rowe, *Life of Jabez Bunting*, 474 n.

[368] *Minutes of the Methodist Conferences*, i. 55, 93, 219.

[369] Ibid. 253, 276; C. M. Elliott, 'The Social and Economic History of the Principal Protestant Denominations in Leeds', D.Phil. thesis (Oxford, 1962), 117–18.

[370] *Minutes of the Methodist Conferences*, iv. 289; *HMC*, iv. 353, citing J. Crowther, *Thoughts upon the Finances or Temporal Affairs of the Methodist Connexion* (1817).

£128,154 to assist chapels to liquidate their debts and local trustees raised another £134,555,[371] but this was insufficient to wipe out many debts or to save some trustees from disaster. The Mint Wesleyan chapel in Exeter was built in 1813 at a cost of £3,873, but by the time the debt was paid off forty-six years later interest and legal fees had pushed the total amount expended to over £7,000.[372] When the Grosvenor Street Wesleyan chapel in Manchester was built in 1820 at a cost of over £8,000, to house what was probably the wealthiest Methodist congregation in England, the society had to borrow £5,000. But thirty years later most of that debt remained and it was not extinguished until fifty years after the chapel had been built and the society had paid more than the original cost of the chapel in interest.[373] When the Wesleyans in Lincoln sold their Bank Street chapel in 1836 after worshipping in it for twenty-one years they still owed £2,500, which was £800 more than the estimated value of the property.[374] In 1820 the trustee of a Welsh Wesleyan chapel was declared bankrupt and his farm sold to meet a chapel debt, and eight years later several trustees who could not meet their liabilities were arrested.[375]

Both the Baptists and, at a distance, the Congregationalists followed the Wesleyans in thinking that greater centralization of resources would help to resolve the problem of chapel debts, but little was achieved in the first half of the nineteenth century. Particular Baptist dissatisfaction with begging missions led to the formation, in 1824, of the London Baptist Building Fund, but the sums it raised in its early years were paltry. An annual income of £1,000 in its first ten years dropped to less than £700 a year as its second decade coincided with economic depression, and debts on Baptist chapels increased from £100,000 in 1836 to an estimated £150,000 in 1847.[376] And although Welsh Independents co-operated to reduce their chapel debts by £19,000 between 1832 and 1835, in England Independent suspicion of centralization delayed the establishment of the London Congregational Building Society until 1848.[377]

Consequently the burden of raising money for the chapels of all denominations rested first and foremost on the shoulders of the individual local church. If, as was usual, the cost of building a chapel could not be covered by subscriptions raised before the chapel was opened, the difference had to be

---

[371] *HMC*, ii. 226–7.   [372] Brockett, *Nonconformity in Exeter*, 193.
[373] J. H. Huddlestone, *History of the Grosvenor Street Wesleyan Chapel, Manchester* (1920), 9, 21–2.
[374] W. Leary, *Methodism in the City of Lincoln* (Lincoln, 1969), 21–2.
[375] Bunting and Rowe, *Life of Jabez Bunting*, 541, 608.
[376] Price, *Baptist Building Fund*, 62, 75, 81, 82.
[377] *Congregational Magazine*, NS 11 (1835), 637; *Religious Census*, pp. lvii, lxii; Jones, *Hanes Annibynwyr Cymru*, 189.

made good by loans, and the preferred method of repaying the capital and interest on the loan was by means of charging rents for seats in the new chapel. Though Old Dissenters had utilized pew-rents to pay for the building and upkeep of their meeting-houses since the early eighteenth century,[378] Wesley had initially resisted the charging of rents for seats in Methodist chapels. 'We have no 5*s.* or 2*s.* 6*d.* places at the Foundry', he had written in 1744, 'nor ever had, nor ever will. . . . First come is also first served, at every time of preaching.'[379] And when Wesley's chapel in the City Road was opened in 1778, 'although large numbers paid for seats, yet none was permitted to claim a pew or sitting as his own' as long as Wesley lived.[380] But after his death the practice of raising money by charging rent for pews rapidly gained ground among Methodists, and at the City Road chapel 'the entrance to the galleries was guarded by two wicket-gates, at the foot and on the first landing of the stairs' attended by two hatch-keepers to protect 'the seatholders from the intrusion of strangers'.[381] Such was the desire of chapel trustees to wipe off their debts and secure a regular income that among prosperous urban congregations in particular few seats were left unappropriated. In Liverpool the Wesleyans sold seats in their chapels by public auction and by 1828 every seat in their huge Brunswick chapel had been let out to rent.[382] When the Wesleyan Park chapel in Sheffield was built in 1831 it was intended that all seats on the ground floor should be free, but demand for pews was such that in the event all but five pews were rented out.[383] Much the same situation existed in prosperous Congregational chapels: by 1835 demand for pews in the Albion chapel, Leeds, was so great, and the number of free sittings so small, 'as to deprive the poor, even such as were members of the church, of the privilege of attending divine worship'; by 1851 East Parade chapel, also in Leeds, had only 162 free seats out of a total of nearly 2,000; and Thomas Coleman wrote of the King Street chapel in Northampton in 1852 that the accommodation 'is not so great as it ought to be; nearly every seat being taken, so that there is no surplus room to which to invite the poor'.[384]

It is impossible to gauge the extent to which pew-rents were responsible for restricting church growth by deterring the poor from entering Nonconformist chapels. An anonymous critic of Methodism complained in 1810

---

[378] Watts, *The Dissenters*, i. 357–8. [379] *Wesley's Letters*, ii. 25.
[380] G. J. Stevenson, *City Road Chapel, London* (1872), 77.
[381] Ibid. 77. [382] Sellers, 'Liverpool Nonconformity', 41, 154.
[383] Wickham, *Church and People in an Industrial City*, 79.
[384] W. H. Stowell, *Memoir of Richard Winter Hamilton* (1850), 325; Binfield, *So Down to Prayers*, 74; T. Coleman, *Memorials of the Independent Churches in Northamptonshire* (1853), 42.

that chapels were now organized 'on the same system as those favourite haunts of Satan, the play-houses. No one is admitted who can't pay or who has not a ticket.'[385] A writer in the *Congregational Magazine* in 1836 claimed that 'in too many of our places of worship' no seating was provided for the poor, and they were 'as effectively excluded as if written over the doors "No poor persons are admitted" '.[386] And a correspondent to the *Nonconformist* in 1849 referred to a recently built chapel where the rent of a seat was from 4s. to 4s. 6d. a quarter 'which is wholly beyond the reach of a working man' and consequently 'working men are not seen there'.[387] Pew-rents, however, appear to have aroused far more opposition among Anglicans than they did among Nonconformists.[388] Wesley's chapel in the City Road was not alone in trying to combine charging for seats with maintaining free access to all parts of the chapel, and however contradictory this may have been in logic, in practice it may have modified the deterrent effect of pew-rents. The Congregational churches in Nottingham claimed in 1839 that though they had 'no sittings set apart as free', none the less they were able to 'provide for all the poor that attend'.[389] It was, in any case, much easier to justify the charging of pew-rents among Dissenters who paid for their ministers' salaries and for the building and maintenance of their chapels out of their own pockets, than among Anglicans whose church was assisted by endowments, parliamentary grants, and church rates. While pew-rents may have kept the very poor out of chapels, they were not usually set at levels which would deter the devout working man with a regular job. Thomas Rees argued that since the Nonconformist churches of Wales 'do not raise their ministers' salaries by pew-rents' they 'can afford to let the sittings at such a moderate rate, which every working man who is not a pauper can pay, and working men always had rather pay than occupy a free sitting'.[390] When the Particular Baptist chapel at Lumb in Rossendale was built in 1831 pew-rents were fixed on a scale rising from 9d. a quarter to 1s. 2d. a quarter, but in the following year they were all reduced by 2d. a quarter in view of the poverty of the members and in 1833 they were reduced by a further 1d.[391] In the Brierley Hill Wesleyan chapel in the Black Country the price for all seats in 1854 was 9d. a quarter except for seats in the front of the gallery which were 1s. a quarter and 'the four front pews in the body of the chapel which are to be free'.[392] The rents charged for

[385] Stigant, 'Methodism and the Working Class', 32, citing A Professor, *Confessions of a Methodist* (1810), 15.
[386] *Congregational Magazine*, NS 12 (1836), 24.   [387] *Nonconformist,* 10 Jan. 1849, 25–6.
[388] Davies, *Religion in the Industrial Revolution*, 112.   [389] Castle Gate minutes, 265.
[390] Rees, *Miscellaneous Papers relating to Wales,* 28–9.
[391] Weston, 'Baptists of North-West England', 262–3.
[392] Cumberland, 'Protestant Nonconformity in the Black Country', 94.

pews in the Park Wesleyan chapel in Sheffield varied from 1s. 6d. to 4s. 9d. for a half-year, while in the Broad Street General Baptist church in Nottingham they ranged from 1s. to 4s. a quarter.[393] Competition between chapels helped to keep the level of pew-rents down: in 1850 the Lady Lane Wesleyan Methodist Association church in Leeds reduced the price for seats at the back of the gallery to 7s. a year to make them competitive with the rates charged by the nearby St Peter's Wesleyan chapel.[394] Admittedly when the King's Weigh House Congregational chapel in the City of London was rebuilt in 1833 at a cost of £12,500, pew-rents were levied on a scale rising from 12s. to 24s. a year. But the membership of the King's Weigh House was exceptionally wealthy, and even so two hundred sittings were kept free.[395]

Pew-rents were levied as much among predominantly working-class congregations as by wealthy urban churches, as much by Primitive Methodists as by Congregationalists.[396] In Northumberland the Presbyterian chapel at Crookham had 740 seat-holders in 1856 and that at Branton had 526, notwithstanding the fact that seven-eighths of the Crookham congregation were labourers and the 'great majority' of the worshippers at Branton were 'poor'.[397] The Methodist Unitarians of Oldham paid pew-rents of 1s. and 1s. 6d. a quarter in 1847, although the 'supporters of the congregation' were, 'with one or two exceptions, working men of very scanty means'.[398] In some cases prosperous congregations were in fact readier to abandon pew-rents than were poor churches since they were better able to take the financial risk of relying entirely on voluntary offerings. In 1861 the large Derby Road Particular Baptist church in Nottingham abandoned pew-rents on the ground that they were 'one of the strongest prejudices entertained by the working classes against attendance at a place of worship'.[399] But the Caersalem Baptist church in Dowlais, with a large number of miners both in its membership and on its diaconate, retained pew-rents until 1928. However the Dowlais Baptists, like Wesley's chapel and the Nottingham Congregationalists, insisted that the payment of a pew-rent did not bestow 'the exclusive right to occupy a given seat'.[400]

[393] Wickham, *Church and People in an Industrial City*, 79; Harrison, 'Baptists of Nottinghamshire', ii. 566.

[394] Dews, 'Methodism in Leeds', 689.   [395] Kaye, *King's Weigh House*, 78.

[396] Harrison, 'Baptists of Nottinghamshire', ii. 567; Morris, 'Primitive Methodism in Derbyshire', 110.

[397] W. Mackie, 'Branton Congregation, Northumberland', *Journal of the Presbyterian Historical Society of England*, 13 (1964), 24–5.

[398] A. Marcroft, *Historical Account of the Unitarian Chapel, Oldham* (Oldham, 1913), 88–9, 99.

[399] Harrison, 'Baptists of Nottinghamshire', ii. 541.

[400] Williams, *History of Caersalem, Dowlais*, 140.

While we cannot know how many of the poor were kept out of chapels by pew-rents, we do know that within chapels the graduations from free seats to cheap pews to expensive pews emphasized the social divisions within the chapel community. The trustees of the Darlaston Wesleyan chapel in the Black Country resolved in 1834 that 'the largest subscriber to the enlarge-ment of the chapel shall have the first choice of new pews, and so on for the rest in proportion to their subscriptions', and in the following year a 'special high-backed pew' was constructed in the King Street Wesleyan chapel in Dudley to divide the rented pews from the free seats.[401] When the young William Booth, the future founder of the Salvation Army, persuaded a group of boys from the slums of Nottingham to attend Wesley chapel and con-ducted them to the best pews in the place he was rebuked by the chapel lead-ers and was told that 'he might bring these outcasts into the chapel only if he entered by the back door (invisible behind the pulpit)' and sat them on the benches reserved for the poor.[402] Even long after pew-rents were abolished the customary seating arrangements in Dissenting chapels reflected the social stratification of the community from which the worshippers were drawn. Emrys Jones, in his study of Tregaron in Cardiganshire in the late 1940s, found that in the Calvinistic Methodist chapel pews nearest the pulpit on the ground floor were occupied by professional, 'white-collar', and shop-keeping families, while most unskilled workers and their families sat in the gallery.[403]

The cost of building and maintaining chapels by communities of predomi-nantly poor men and women meant that many churches were heavily depen-dent on a handful of prosperous men in their congregations. The Particular Baptist church in South Parade, Leeds, had a membership of 256 in 1835, but when a subscription list was opened to clear the debt on the new chapel £2,961 of the £3,874 raised was donated by two families, the Goodmans and the Thackreys, most subscriptions consisted of 1s. or 5s., and nearly half the members gave nothing at all.[404] When the Methodist New Connexion built a new chapel at Hurst near Ashton-under-Lyne in 1857 the whole cost of £1,500 was paid by the local mill-owner, John Whittaker, on condition that the rest of the congregation raise £300 for an organ.[405] It was consequently a constant theme of the critics of Dissent that the voluntary system rendered Nonconformist ministers dependent on the whims and prejudices of wealthy paymasters. Let ministers 'offend the pride, or disclose the injustice, of a

[401] Leese, 'Impact of Methodism on Black Country Society', 130–1.
[402] Begbie, *William Booth*, i. 71.   [403] E. Jones in *Welsh Rural Communities*, 110–11.
[404] Owen, 'Baptists in the Borouth of Leeds', 28.
[405] Rose, *Methodism in Ashton-under-Lyne*, ii. 65.

powerful man', complained the former General Baptist minister Charles Lloyd, 'and occasions will not be wanting to make their situation too irksome to be retained'.[406] There were certainly cases in which men who had largely paid for the building of a chapel or for the salary of its minister sought to dictate what should be preached from its pulpit and who should preach it. In 1780 the wealthy Shrewsbury merchant William Tayleur established a trust fund of £1,000, the interest on which was to supplement the salary of the town's Unitarian minister, but only as long as he continued to use Theophilus Lindsey's liturgy.[407] In 1818 George Baring, Anglican clergyman turned Baptist and son of the banker Sir Francis Baring, provided most of the £4,000 which it cost to build the Baptist chapel in Bartholomew Street, Exeter, and as the church members 'had not contributed any thing toward the expense of the building, he would never allow them any control over it'.[408] In 1842 Henry Solly was forced to resign from the pastorate of the Unitarian congregation in Yeovil because its treasurer, a wealthy banker, objected to Solly's Chartist activities and withdrew his subscription of £20 a year, which had provided nearly a third of Solly's salary of £65.[409] Henry Wileman bought the land on which the New Church Street General Baptist chapel in Paddington was built in 1831, and was said to expect 'the same subjection and entire obedience from all in the church, including the pastor, that he enforced in his well regulated warehouse'. His attitude provoked quarrels with two successive ministers and led finally to his leaving the church.[410] And a similar position was claimed in the Queen Street Congregational church, Wolverhampton, by John Barker, a wealthy iron manufacturer who ascribed his prosperity 'to the blessing of Divine Providence'. Barker helped to bring 'two pastorates to a premature conclusion and prevented the beginning of another'. But when, for a second time, he tried to dictate the appointment of a minister 'he found himself opposed by a resolute majority, who insisted on sending an invitation to the man of their choice', and Barker resigned from the church.[411]

The fact that it was Barker who seceded from Queen Street, Wolverhampton, in 1846, just as Wileman had seceded from New Church Street, Paddington, in 1840, shows that the power of even the wealthiest supporter to dictate to Baptist or Congregational churches could be limited and in the end destroyed by the democratic constitutions of those churches. Infact in most

---

[406] C. Lloyd, *Particulars of the Life of a Dissenting Minister* (1813, repr. 1911), 175.
[407] Ditchfield, 'Unitarianism and Radicalism', 334, 371.
[408] Brockett, *Nonconformity in Exeter*, 165.   [409] Solly, *These Eighty Years*, i. 398.
[410] *General Baptist Magazine* (Apr. 1870), 102; Burns, *Retrospect of Forty-five Years*, 41.
[411] A. G. Matthews, *The Congregational Churches of Staffordshire* (1924), 217; Cumberland, 'Protestant Nonconformity in the Black Country', 120; H. A. May, *Queen Street Congregational Church, Wolverhampton: The Story of a Hundred Years* (1909), 15–16.

cases in which rich men contributed to the building of Nonconformist chapels no attempt was made to exert undue pressure on the church concerned beyond the claim to first choice in the allocation of pews. It was in a spirit of thanksgiving, not overbearance, that William Kaye paid for the building of the Toxteth Park Congregational chapel in Liverpool in 1831, in gratitude 'for his safe deliverance from an attack by highwaymen'.[412] And there is no evidence that Thomas Wilson, the most generous contributor to the building of Dissenting chapels, ever abused his position as benefactor to impose his will on the many congregations he housed. Wilson was heir to a prosperous silk manufacturer whose firm made so much money that his son was able to retire from business in 1798 at the age of thirty-four to devote the remaining forty-four years of his life to using his wealth for the building of Congregational chapels and for the support of their ministers. He assisted directly, or paid for entirely, the building of nearly a hundred chapels which cost him over £26,000 in donations and another £29,000 in largely interest-free loans.[413] In addition he was, for forty-nine years, the treasurer of the Hoxton academy, and when in 1824 it was proposed to remove the college to Highbury Wilson bought for the college, at a cost of £2,100, the four-acre site on which its new buildings were to be erected.[414] Wilson was particularly interested in buying up decayed Presbyterian meeting-houses, and he rescued seven such places for orthodox Dissent. He also used his position as treasurer of Hoxton and Highbury to provide chapels he was supporting with suitable ministers from his college. But he never attempted to dictate to such churches whom they should elect as pastor.

It was not the excessive wealth of church members, but their poverty, that was the source of most tension in Nonconformist congregations. Some poor Dissenters responded heroically to the financial needs of their churches. When, in 1849, two poor women members of the Rusholme Road Congregational church in Manchester heard that worry about the chapel debt was making their pastor ill, they made a determined effort to reduce it. One, Betty Taylor, was a seamstress and the other, a Mrs Turner, 'got a scanty living by mangling', but they and other poor members agreed to subscribe 1s. each a week so that £750 was raised and the debt eventually extinguished.[415] But the loyalty of other poor Dissenters was strained by the constant calls for money that the voluntary system necessitated with the result that some were led to desert their churches and others to organize

[412] Sellers, 'Liverpool Nonconformity', 95.
[413] J. Wilson, *Memoir of Thomas Wilson* (1849), *passim*.   [414] Ibid. 397.
[415] J. Griffin, *Memories of the Past* (1883), 141–5.

secessions. The financial demands placed on the members and regular worshippers of Nonconformist churches did not end with pew-rents and subscriptions to redeem chapel debts. Every Wesleyan, in addition to paying
for his pew, was expected to contribute 'one penny weekly (unless he is in
extreme poverty), and one shilling quarterly', primarily to pay the preachers'
allowances, and some Baptist churches reversed the Wesleyan system with
monthly or quarterly collections for church expenses and pew-rents to provide for the minister's stipend.[416] The self-sacrifice that all this could entail for
a poor Nonconformist was highlighted by an Anglican critic in 1842 who
argued that 'among Dissenters even poor servant girls, with their country
wages of £4, £5, and £6 per annum are expected to pay for a seat in the gallery,
costing them 6s. per annum; to contribute to the quarterly collections "for
defraying the expenses incidental to carrying on the worship of God"; to
subscribe to the Missionary Society one penny per week; and thus, with
ragged shoes and stockings and torn gowns, to part with twenty to twenty-
five percent of their hardly earned stipend'.[417] The Anglican writer was probably exaggerating, and in many cases servant girls would have been able to
occupy pews rented by their employers, but there is no doubt that regular
giving was one of the major contrasts between Nonconformist and Anglican
churchmanship, since Anglican clergy had no need to make regular demands
on the pockets of their congregation and often got little response when they
tried.[418] Anglican clergymen had on occasion to complain that their congregations were 'much below average' when special collections were held in
their churches,[419] but Nonconformist ministers were faced with the continual
problem of balancing the advantages of increasing the financial demands on
their churches against the risk of losing members in so doing. The Particular
Baptist church in Bacup suspended a member in 1795 for refusing to contribute to 'necessary church expenses'.[420] For seventeen years a minister at
Lowick in Northumberland tolerated in his congregation a 'person in affluent circumstances' who contributed nothing to his salary. When at length, in
1822, the minister referred the matter to the Dissenting Deputies, he was told
that no attender at Dissenting worship could be compelled to make a financial contribution 'unless he agrees to pay for a seat'.[421] The Wolverhampton

---

[416] *Minutes of the Methodist Conferences*, i. 159; Manley, 'John Rippon', 110; Harrison,
'Baptists of Nottinghamshire', ii. 563.
[417] Evans, *As Mad as a Hatter!*, 141, citing *The Church and State Gazette* (1842).
[418] Obelkevich, *Religion and Rural Society*, 207.
[419] Jones and Williams, *Religious Census, South Wales*, 323.
[420] Gray, 'Nonconformity in Rossendale', 170.
[421] Manning, *Protestant Dissenting Deputies*, 109.

circuit of the Methodist New Connexion complained in 1856 that the grant of £12 a year it received to support its minister was 'altogether inadequate' and that 'many of our subscribers have grown tired of extra-giving'. They claimed that many members 'have left both our society and congregation, chased away by the constant bore of the plate'.[422] And in Cornwall a Wesleyan woman stopped going to class-meetings after she was married because, 'with a family coming quick', she could not afford 'to pay class money and preacher's money every quarter, and to give to all the collections, as it is expected of members, however poor they may be'.[423]

The financial plight of the Wesleyan Connexion in the three decades after Wesley's death led both to increasing financial pressure on circuits and individuals and to growing resentment against the financial demands of the Wesleyan Conference that was a factor in the repeated Methodist secessions. In 1797 the Wesleyan Conference told circuits that they could not have more itinerant preachers 'than they are willing and able to provide for'.[424] In 1800 members were told to contribute 1s. each to a yearly collection in an attempt to reduce the connexional debt.[425] In 1818, when the deficit was £2,382, it was decided that the debt 'should be divided among all the circuits, in proportion to the number of members in society in each circuit'. Circuit preachers were to be responsible for collecting the quota, and if they failed to meet it they were to make up the difference with their own subscriptions.[426] This drastic action succeeded in solving the problem of the Connexion's finances, which by 1821 were showing a credit balance of £792, but it was at a cost.[427] The attempt to link the circuit quotas to circuit membership was an incentive to superintendents to prune their membership lists, and helps to explain the 5,096 drop in the membership of English Wesleyan Methodism in 1819–20. William Bramwell, in his last years, was deeply troubled by the way in which the need to wipe off the connexional debt was sapping the Wesleyans' spiritual energies. He claimed to know of a preacher who had laboured 'two years in a circuit without ever being questioned concerning the spiritual state of the people'. 'The enquiry has uniformly been "Did you make collections? . . . Have you got the money?" '[428] In June 1818, just two months before his death, Bramwell confided to a friend his concern that 'collections are become numerous, Methodists are engaged in so many new things, that it requires . . .

---

[422] Leese, 'Impact of Methodism on Black Country Society', 211.
[423] Rule, 'Labouring Miner', 225, citing W. Bottrell, *Traditions and Hearthside Stories of West Cornwall* (Penzance, 1873), 285.
[424] *Minutes of the Methodist Conferences*, i. 397.   [425] Ibid. ii. 81.
[426] Ibid. iv. 444.   [427] Ibid v. 288.
[428] Elliott, 'Protestant Denominations in Leeds', 233, citing M. Robinson, *Observations on the System of Wesleyan Methodism* (1825), 18–19.

too great exertion to accomplish our own money-matters'. 'I tremble for Zion. Can we return to our simplicity?'[429]

As always Bramwell spoke for those Methodists who longed to return to what they regarded as the primitive evangelistic fervour of early Methodism, uncomplicated by the need to worry about connexional debts and unrestrained by the decisions of the Wesleyan Conference. It was one of William O'Bryan's complaints against Wesleyanism that members were expected to contribute a penny a week and a shilling a quarter to circuit funds, and it was one of the causes of his expulsion from the Wesleyan Connexion that he proposed that preachers should be supported by voluntary contributions alone.[430] As long as O'Bryan was in control of the Bible Christians the Connexion declined to specify what subscriptions its members should pay, and hostility to the penny-a-week scheme persisted among Wesleyans in Cornwall long after O'Bryan had been excluded from their ranks. In the 1830s the Cornish Wesleyans' inability or unwillingness to pay their expected subscriptions kept their circuits short of itinerant preachers, and as late as 1871 the superintendent of the St Agnes circuit attributed the shortage of ministers in Cornwall to the fact that the 'Methodist rule of one penny per member per week' was not observed in the duchy.[431]

There were some observers who similarly ascribed Wesleyan losses to the Primitive Methodists to 'the wish for a cheaper religion'.[432] The Ranters certainly held on to their barns and cottage meeting places longer than the Wesleyans, spent far less on their chapels when they built them, and relied to a greater extent that the Wesleyans on unpaid local preachers.[433] But the Primitives did accept the principle, in July 1811, that itinerant preachers should be paid by means of voluntary contributions[434] and they were soon afflicted by the same financial problems that beset the Wesleyans. If the Ranters made fewer demands on their followers than the Wesleyans, they had more slender resources with which to meet those demands. And the means the Ranters chose to pay off their debts were all too familiar. In 1826, to clear a debt of £1,000, the Primitive Methodist Conference resolved that no circuit should be permitted to run into debt, that itinerant preachers should be paid no more than the circuits could raise, and that any deficiency should be met by preachers forgoing part of their salaries. As a result thirty preachers gave up the ministry.[435] In 1836 Conference decreed that any

---

[429] Sigston, *Memoirs of Bramwell*, 272.   [430] Shaw, *The Bible Christians*, 6–7, 24.
[431] Shaw, *Cornish Methodism*, 106, 109.   [432] Ward, *Religion and Society*, 99.
[433] Werner, *Primitive Methodist Connexion*, 13–14.
[434] Kendall, *Primitive Methodist Church*, i. 130–1.
[435] Ibid. i. 435; Wilkinson, *Hugh Bourne*, 130–1.

preacher who encouraged the building of a new chapel without 'reasonable prospect of its being supported' should 'forfeit one fourth of his salary'.[436] And in 1843 Conference tried to insist that no chapel should be built until a third of the total cost had been guaranteed.[437] The Bible Christians, too, were not long able to hold to O'Bryan's repudiation of Wesleyan money-raising methods. One of the chief complaints against O'Bryan's leadership which led to his break with the Bible Christians in 1829 concerned his handling of the Connexion's slender financial resources. His critics grumbled that he expected Conference to shoulder debts amounting to £320. 15s. while retaining control of the stationing of preachers in his own hands, and complained that his expenses were far beyond what his poverty-stricken denomination could bear.[438] In 1837 the Bible Christian rules replaced O'Bryan's objection to a fixed subscription with the recommendation 'that it would be reasonable for members to pay one penny a week'. But it was easier to make such a proposal than to get it carried out. As late as 1862 the average contribution of Bible Christian members 'was less than a halfpenny a week'.[439]

One proffered solution to the financial problems facing all the Nonconformist denominations—apart from the declining and financially sound Quakers—was 'free gospelism', the belief which a few Methodists shared with the Quakers that ministers should earn their own livings, not live off the contributions of their congregations. It was this conviction which led to the formation first of the Quaker Methodists (in 1796) and then of the Independent Methodists (in 1805–6), and it was a view that had obvious appeal to poor men who found it difficult enough to support their own families, let alone those of their preachers. John Sutton, class leader in a Wesleyan chapel in Manchester, seceded to the Independent Methodists when ordered to 'get more money' out of the members of his class. An attempt by Wesleyan officials to extract higher contributions from a congregation of cotton workers in Barnoldswick in Lancashire at a time of acute depression in 1839 led to the resignation of five class leaders and the formation of what was to become an Independent Methodist church.[440] And although the Primitive Methodists accepted in 1811 the principle that itinerant preachers should be paid, two of their early preachers, John Benton and John Wedgwood, declined either to demand class money or to accept payment and sowed the seeds of free gospelism among Ranter congregations in

[436] Biggs, 'Methodism in North Nottinghamshire', 378.
[437] Leese, 'Impact of Methodism on Black Country Society', 269.
[438] *HMC* iv. 405–6.   [439] Shaw, *The Bible Christians*, 44, 48, 60.
[440] Valenze, 'Prophetic Sons and Daughters', 255.

Nottinghamshire.[441] In 1828 some half-dozen Primitive Methodist societies in the Bingham area broke away from Primitive Methodism in protest at the payment of ministers and formed themselves into the Independent Primitive Methodist Connexion.[442] And ten years later an attempt by the superintendent minister in the Belper circuit, William Carthy, to get his salary raised from 14*s*. to 16*s*. a week, at a time of low wages and a circuit debt of nearly £50, provoked a bitter dispute that resulted in secession. Led by a congregation of coalminers at Selston on the borders of Nottinghamshire and Derbyshire another half-dozen societies left the Primitive Methodist Connexion, and to make the point that the Ranters no less than the Wesleyans had abandoned the purity of early Methodism in their quest for money, the Selston secessionists called themselves the Original Methodists.[443]

The free gospel churches may have thought they could preach the Christian message unsullied by the corrupting influence of money, but in practice they were unable to compete with the other Nonconformist denominations in England, and failed to make the sort of impact that the largely unpaid Calvinistic Methodist preachers made in Wales. By repudiating the payment of ministers the Independent Methodists denied themselves the means of sustaining a large and far-reaching itinerant ministry and they did little to advance the cause of church expansion. 'If it can be shown that a man's preaching was better because he was paid for doing it,' said the Quaker Methodists' leader Peter Phillips, 'I will admit my error.'[444] But the subsequent history of the Independent Methodists suggests that in England, at least, a paid ministry was more effective than free gospelism in expanding Christianity. In 1851 the religious census credited the Independent Methodists with only 1,500 hearers; by 1870 most of the Original Methodists had rejoined the Primitive Methodists; and in 1876 the Independent Methodists so far strayed from their early principles as to agree to pay for the maintenance, if not the salaries, of itinerant evangelists.[445] The Quaker prize essay competition of 1858 revealed that even members of the Society of Friends were questioning the wisdom of an unpaid ministry. The fact that most Quaker ministers were 'engaged in some branch of trade or commerce'

---

[441] Werner, *Primitive Methodist Connexion*, 80, 87–8.

[442] Vickers, *History of Independent Methodism*, 201–3.

[443] W. Parkes, 'The Original Methodists, Primitive Methodist Reformers', *PWHS* 35 (1965–6), 57–64; D. Grundy, 'A History of the Original Methodists', *PWHS* 35 (1965–6), 116–21, 149–53, 170–2, 189–95.

[444] Mounfield, *History of Independent Methodism*, 7.

[445] Morris, 'Primitive Methodism in Nottinghamshire', 46; Vickers, *History of Independent Methodism*, 52.

might have the advantage that they were preserved from the temptation of undertaking the ministry from worldly motives, wrote Samuel Fothergill. But equally it carried the danger that ministers might be 'tempted to neglect the oversight of the flock for the pursuit of gain'.[446] The Anglican Thomas Hancock had no doubt that the Quaker ministry was 'left untouched for the sake of business': 'were it not for the female ministry' the dearth of ministers 'would become rapidly destructive'.[447] Fothergill was even more pessimistic. The payment of ministers was 'absolutely essential to the development and conservation and diffusion of truth'. Without it, the Society of Friends would be doomed to 'irremediable decline and final extinction'.[448]

6. 'A COMPANY OF POOR GENTLEMEN': THE NONCONFORMIST MINISTRY

It was not only Quaker and Independent Methodist ministers who 'engaged in some branch of trade or commerce'. In the late eighteenth and early nineteenth centuries a vast company of Nonconformist ministers earned their living in secular occupations, not because their congregations had conscientious objections to supporting them, but because they were too poor to do so. Only the Wesleyans forbade their travelling preachers and ordained ministers from earning their living by secular means.

Initially Wesley had tried to insist, like the later Independent Methodists, that Methodist preachers should receive no payment for their services. If you are given 'food when you are hungry, or clothes when you need them', prescribed the Methodist Conference in 1744, 'it is good'. 'But not silver or gold. Let there be no pretence to say, we grow rich by the Gospel.' The rule was modified in 1752 to provide preachers with an allowance of £12 a year for clothes and £10 a year for their wives, and from the 1760s allowances were also granted for children.[449] But circuit stewards were often reluctant to find these sums and many of the early Methodist itinerants were condemned to lives of grinding poverty. Thomas Taylor, who began his fifty-five years' career as a travelling preacher in 1761, recalled that at the beginning 'what I did was gratis, not even having a penny for the turnpikes; except that the steward of Bradford circuit gave me once half-a-guinea'. In Wales he 'had no

---

[446] Fothergill, *Essay on the Society of Friends*, 101.   [447] Hancock, *The Peculium*, 189.
[448] Fothergill, *Essay on the Society of Friends*, 65.
[449] *HMC* i. 234; Elliott, 'Protestant Denominations in Leeds', 319.

quarterage, no travelling expenses, but now and then a shilling or a half-crown was put into my hands', and for most of the time he had to live off his savings of £30.[450] And in Scotland, though 'with a hungry belly', he frequently led his landlady to believe that he had dined out and asked her 'not to provide anything for dinner' to save the expense of a meal.[451]

In such circumstances it is not surprising that some enterprising Methodists sought to combine their calling as itinerant preachers with careers as travelling salesmen. Matthew Lowes, for example, sold balsam which was 'of great use to the afflicted and a source of income to the itinerant'.[452] But Wesley objected that the business interests of the preachers conflicted with their evangelistic purpose: in 1768 he ordered his preachers not to follow trades and two years later Conference resolved that preachers who traded in 'cloth, hardware, pills, drops, balsams, or medicines' would have to choose between their trade and their itinerant ministry.[453] The decision drove some men out of the itinerant ministry and meant that the burden of supporting those that remained would contribute to the Connexion's deteriorating financial position. Circuits which could not meet their financial obligations were allowed to pass on their deficiency to Conference: in 1795 the difference between what preachers and their wives and children were allowed and what the circuits raised was £1,048, and in 1801 the deficiency rose to £1,207.[454] 'The principal cause of our embarrassments', wrote the president and secretary of the Conference in 1800, was 'the sending more preachers into circuits . . . than the people could support; the carrying the Gospel into fresh places; and the great increase of families among the preachers for which we have been obliged to hire houses and buy furniture.'[455] William Myles pointed out in 1814 that since 1791 the numbers of itinerant preachers had increased from 235 to 685, and that whereas in Wesley's day only a third of preachers had been married, by 1814 three-quarters were married.[456] And, added Joseph Entwisle, those married preachers were producing thirty children a year.[457]

As long as John Wesley lived his itinerants were, in his own words, 'a company of poor gentlemen'.[458] A married preacher in Bradford in 1770 received £32. 6s. a year, including £2.5s. 6d. for his board, £2.10s. for a servant, and £1.4s. for turnpikes.[459] In the 1790s Methodist preachers in Nottingham

[450] Jackson, *Early Methodist Preachers*, v. 82–3.   [451] Ibid. v. 30.

[452] Tyerman, *Life of John Wesley*, iii. 72–3.

[453] *Minutes of the Methodist Conferences*, i. 77–8, 90.   [454] Ibid. i. 314; ii. 120.

[455] Ibid. ii. 81.   [456] Gilbert, 'Growth and Decline of Nonconformity', 380.

[457] Ward, *Religion and Society*, 97.   [458] *Wesley's Letters*, vi. 130.

[459] Ward, *Progress of Methodism in Bingley*, 31–2.

received £25. 5s. 8d. a year.[460] John Wesley himself was paid £60 a year in the 1770s, but not even he was always paid regularly and at the end of 1775 he was still owed £30.[461] From the 1790s, however, the financial situation of the Wesleyan itinerant began to improve. In 1800 Conference urged that preachers' annual salaries be increased to £16 and in 1806 their wives' allowances were increased to sixteen guineas and those for their children set at six guineas.[462] In addition allowances were paid for travel, rent, food, coal, furniture, and laundry, and Alexander Kilham calculated in 1796 that a Wesleyan preacher with a wife and four children, one of whom was being educated at the school for preachers' sons at Kingswood, could cost the Connexion £107. 10s. a year.[463] This was probably an exaggeration, but John Pawson admitted privately that there was substance to Kilham's allegations and that 'our travelling expenses have been prodigious'.[464] What is more, the sums laid down by Conference were recommended allowances, not fixed limits, and wealthy circuits could compete with each other in attracting popular preachers.[465] Jabez Bunting told the income tax commissioners in 1806 that the allowances paid to Wesleyan preachers varied 'considerably in different places': while he received £83 a year in Manchester in 1805–6, in the same year Joseph Entwisle calculated that in his predominantly working-class circuit of Rochester and Sheerness he would have to spend '£60 of my own private property'.[466] A popular preacher with a wife and two children, Jonathan Crowther noted in 1815, could expect about £100 a year, a house, and a horse.[467] While Wesleyan preachers in the comparatively poor Keighley circuit were receiving an annual income of £103 a year by 1840, the five preachers in the much more prosperous Leeds circuit were each getting an average allowance of £150 a year as early as 1807. That figure rose to £225 a year in 1824 and to £250 in 1837 at a time when prices were falling. In real terms the income of the Wesleyan preachers in Leeds doubled between 1807 and 1824:[468] in those same years they started to call themselves ministers and to appropriate to themselves the title 'Reverend'.

---

[460] J. C. Weller, 'The Revival of Religion in Nottingham', BD thesis (Nottingham, 1957), 51.
[461] Stevenson, *City Road Chapel*, 58–60.
[462] *Minutes of the Methodist Conferences*, ii. 60, 346.
[463] A. Kilham, *A Candid Examination of the London Methodistical Bull* (1796), 18.
[464] Stigant, 'Methodism and the Working Class', 272 n.
[465] Werner, *Primitive Methodist Connexion*, 10.
[466] Bunting and Rowe, *Life of Jabez Bunting*, 258, 261.
[467] Werner, *Primitive Methodist Connexion*, 10–11.
[468] P. Rycroft, 'Church, Chapel, and Community in Craven, 1764–1851', D.Phil. thesis (Oxford, 1988), 258; Elliott, 'Protestant Denominations in Leeds', 329.

The new pretensions of the Wesleyan ministry were resented by many rank-and-file Methodists who, in the years of the post-war depression, had neither the job security nor the regular income of their ministers.[469] One of the reasons for the secession of Wesleyan local preachers in Anglesey and Caernarfonshire to form Y Wesle Bach in 1831 was their complaint that chapel debts were increasing because money was 'being absorbed in maintaining ministers, nearly all of whom thought primarily of wealth, honour, and authority'.[470] Wesleyan itinerants were also regarded jealously by other Nonconformist ministers who had to combine preaching the Gospel and ministering to their congregations with earning their livings in secular employment.[471] In Wales in particular in the first half of the nineteenth century most Nonconformist ministers, apart from the Wesleyans, had to work at a second occupation in order to keep body and soul together. When the Calvinistic Methodists began to ordain their itinerant preachers in 1811 such preachers were set aside for service in the whole denomination and not for the care of a particular church (as with the Congregationalists and Baptists) or for service in a limited circuit (as with the Wesleyans).[472] Consequently nearly all Calvinistic Methodist ministers retained their secular occupations after ordination. John Jones of Blaenannerch in Cardiganshire was an agricultural worker who preached in clogs and his working clothes; Daniel Davies in nearby Aberporth was a labourer employed in lime burning;[473] and John Jones of Talysarn in Caernarfonshire worked in a quarry while his wife kept a shop. When John Jones's wife became concerned that the burden of his working in the quarry and walking twenty or thirty miles to his preaching engagements at the weekend was becoming intolerable, she expanded her business to enable her husband to devote himself entirely to the ministry.[474]

Shopkeeping was the favoured occupation of many Baptist ministers, though it could entail risks. The business of Evan Evans, pastor of the church at Garndolbenmaen in Caernarfonshire, collapsed in the post-war depression of the late 1810s, and when the drapery business of John Edwards of Nantyglo in Monmouthshire failed in the 1830s he lost both his livelihood and his pastorate.[475] Other Baptist ministers earned their living by farming, keeping schools, or by practising a whole variety of artisan crafts: as carpenters, candlemakers, clockmakers, cobblers, printers, slaters, smiths, tailors,

---

[469] Werner, *Primitive Methodist Connexion*, 11.
[470] A. H. Williams, *Welsh Wesleyan Methodism, 1800–1858* (Bangor, 1935), 320.
[471] Ibid. 320.   [472] Jones, *Great Preachers of Wales*, 369.
[473] Jenkins, 'Aber-porth', in Jenkins *et al.*, *Welsh Rural Communities*, 54.
[474] Jones, *Great Preachers of Wales*, 471.
[475] Bassett, *The Welsh Baptists*, 201; Jones, *Sowing Beside all Waters*, 50.

tanners, and weavers.[476] Most of the farmers were tenants or small freeholders, although William Williams, who was a pastor of the church which met
in the Ebenezer chapel on his estate at Tre-fach, Llanfair Nantgwyn, Pembrokeshire, inherited land which brought in £1,600 a year and enabled him
to serve both as a justice of the peace and a deputy lieutenant of Cardiganshire.[477] Some Baptist churches gave their ministers practical assistance
to enable them to combine their secular occupations with their pastorates.
The church at Rhydwilym in Carmarthenshire and that at Pentre, Llysdi-
nam, in Breconshire both paid the wages of their ministers' servants so that
they could help with the farms while the ministers devoted more time to their
pastorates, and when Jonathan Hughes became minister of the Llangian
Baptist church in Caernarfonshire in 1835 the church built a workshop for
him so that he could carry on his trade as a shoemaker.[478] Christmas Evans,
the most popular Welsh Baptist preacher of the early nineteenth century,
believed that a minister should be able to devote himself entirely to his ministry,[479] but his own career showed the privations to which a minister could
condemn himself by attempting to live off his preaching. When he moved to
Anglesey in 1792 he was responsible for preaching in two chapels and seven
or eight private houses for a salary of £17 per year 'and a bare, cold, tumble-
down cottage'. In addition he published pamphlets on current affairs and
religious books which he advertised from the pulpit and sold to his congregations after the service. When he preached to congregations other than
his own he also expected to be paid a shilling per sermon. On one occasion
when a congregation failed to produce the usual shilling a poor old woman
said to him 'Well, Christmas Evans, bach, I hope you will be paid at the resurrection; you have given us a wonderful sermon'. 'Yes,' replied Evans, 'no
doubt of that, but what shall I do till I get there? And there's the old white
mare that carries me, what will she do?—for her there will be no resurrection.'[480]

The Baptist churches in the industrial areas of south Wales were better able
to afford to pay salaries to their ministers and this led to a number of ministers
moving southwards. Robert Ellis left north Wales for Sirhowy in Monmouthshire in 1847 complaining that the Baptists of north Wales expected
'strong fare in the pulpit, roast meat and pudding, but when they come to
pay, they pay for milk and potatoes'.[481] When J. P. Davies accepted the pastorate of the Baptist church at Tredegar in 1818 it was on condition that the

[476] Bassett, *The Welsh Baptists*, 94, 201. [477] Ibid. 65; *DWB* 1078–9.
[478] Bassett, *The Welsh Baptists*, 64, 200–1. [479] Ibid. 198.
[480] Evans, *Christmas Evans*, 149. [481] Davies, *Religion in the Industrial Revolution*, 67.

church provide him with a salary of £42 a year and a house, and when Christmas Evans moved to Caerphilly in 1826 it was for a stipend of £40 per annum, a house, and a field for his horse.[482] But these salaries were exceptionally high. When Baptist ministers in Wales were paid at all in the 1820s their stipends seem to have been around £20 a year. The secretary of the Particular Baptist Fund, which assisted some of the poorest ministers, complained in 1837 that there were churches with congregations of three hundred who paid their ministers only £15 a year.[483]

The salaries of Independent ministers in Wales were similar to those of the Baptists. Enoch Salisbury, member of the Congregational church at Chester and later Liberal MP for the city, claimed in 1849 that 12s. a week was a 'fair average' for Independent ministers in north Wales.[484] When Thomas Rees began his pastoral career at Craig-y-fargod, Bedlinog, in Glamorgan in 1836 it was for a stipend of £6 a year and when he married two years later he felt obliged to open a shop. However the venture failed and he was forced to spend a week or so in the debtors' prison.[485] He moved to Aberdare in 1840 for £42 a year, but when he went to Beaufort in 1849 the church declined to offer him a fixed sum because of the fluctuations in the fortunes of the ironworks. He was told that his predecessor had been paid £77. 14s. 3d. in 1846 and £50. 11s. 1d. in 1849 and in the event Rees's salary was always higher.[486] But the minister of the Zoar Independent church in Merthyr Tydfil was paid only £5 a year in 1852 and £8 a year in 1857, and Edward Jenkins, the minister of the Bedwellty Independent church, was so poor that he confessed to the Royal Commission on the Employment of Children in 1842 that his seven-year-old son had been working as an air boy in a colliery for eighteen months, earning 8d. a day, while his fourteen-year-old son earned 9s. a week cutting coal.[487] Consequently in the middle years of the century many Welsh Independent ministers, like their Baptist and Calvinistic Methodist colleagues, continued to support themselves by secular employment. From 1840 John Davies combined the pastorate of the Mynyddbach Independent church in Glamorgan with his job as a colliery manager until, in 1854, he was killed by choke-damp in a mine shaft.[488]

The salaries of Nonconformist ministers in England varied to a far greater extent than did those of their counterparts in Wales. At the bottom end of the

---

[482] Bassett, *The Welsh Baptists*, 203.   [483] Ibid. 204.
[484] R. I. Parry, 'The Attitude of the Welsh Independents towards Working-Class Movements, 1815–70', MA thesis (University College of North Wales, 1931), 223.
[485] *DWB* 830.   [486] Davies, *Religion in the Industrial Revolution*, 66–7.
[487] Ibid. 67; *DWB* 135; Parry, 'Welsh Independents and Working-Class Movements', 101.
[488] Evans, 'Religion in the Swansea Valley', 251.

scale many Baptist, Congregational, and even Unitarian pastors either relied entirely on earnings from secular employment for their livelihood or used such earnings to supplement their ministerial salaries. Joseph Dawson, the Arian minister of the Presbyterian meeting at Idle in the West Riding from 1765 to 1790, supplemented his income of £40 a year by keeping a school, practising medicine, and opening several coalmines on a hill near his meeting-house.[489] Both Thomas Warwick, minister to the Presbyterian meeting at Rotherham between 1795 and 1816, and Thomas Southwood Smith, minister of the Unitarian meeting at Yeovil from 1816 to 1820, also combined their ministries with medical practices.[490]

The first pastors of the New Connexion General Baptist churches in Leicestershire continued to pursue secular occupations after their ordinations. Samuel Deacon, pastor of the church at Barton-in-Fabis from 1760 until his death at the age of ninety-seven in 1812, worked as a wool-comber and later kept a grocer's shop. His eldest son, also Samuel, who became his father's co-pastor in 1779, was a clockmaker and not only 'preached without remuneration' but in the course of his ministry gave away an estimated £1,000.[491] Many of the leading Particular Baptist ministers of the late eighteenth century were obliged to supplement their salaries. When the elder Robert Hall became pastor of the Arnesby church in Leicestershire in 1753 his salary was only £15 a year and to add to his income he farmed eighteen acres which had been bequeathed to the church by its first minister.[492] Andrew Fuller, pastor of the Soham church between 1775 and 1782, was paid only £13 a year by the church, received an additional £5 a year from the Particular Baptist Fund, and earned a further £3 a year from preaching four sermons a year at a neighbouring village. He tried to supplement his income 'first by opening a small shop, and afterwards by keeping a school, yet neither attempt succeeded so far as to prevent his annually sinking the little property he possessed'.[493] When William Carey became pastor of the church at Moulton in 1786 he received only £10 a year from the church—augmented by five guineas from the Particular Baptist Fund—and supplemented his salary by teaching and mending shoes. In the first decade of the following century John Warburton was paid only 4s. a week by the Strict Baptist church at Bury and continued to work as a weaver after accepting the pastorate of the

[489] Miall, *Congregationalism in Yorkshire*, 295; anon., *Fortunes Made in Business* (1894), i. 94.
[490] Lewes, *Southwood Smith*, 15; Seed, 'Unitarianism and Liberal Culture', 298.
[491] J. H. Wood, *A Condensed History of the General Baptists of the New Connexion* (1847), 215, 217–18; Jackson, 'Baptists of Leicestershire', 130, 163.
[492] Robison, 'Particular Baptists', 374; Jackson, 'Baptists of Leicestershire', 40.
[493] Ryland, *Life of Andrew Fuller*, 71.

church.[494] Isaac Double, pastor of the Baptist church at Chelmondiston in Suffolk, continued to work as a farm labourer until the chapel debt was paid off, and even then received only 12*s.* a week from his church.[495] Richard Ashworth received £13. 10*s.* 3*d.* for his services as pastor of the Particular Baptist church at Lumb in Lancashire in 1828 and although he tried to supplement his income by calico weaving this earned him only an additional 4*s.* 6*d.* a week.[496] John Jenkinson, pastor of the Ebenezer Particular Baptist church in Kettering from 1824 to 1849, worked as a nurseryman and was paid no salary by his church. When the town's rector accused him of misusing money from a charity, Jenkinson retorted that whereas the clergyman received about 'a thousand a year for leading a tolerably easy life, I have, during seventeen years, preached about four thousand sermons, and walked about ten thousand miles, without receiving a farthing for my labours'.[497] As late as 1850 when James Shaw accepted the pastorate of the Cradley Baptist church in the Black Country he was told that the church could not afford to pay him a fixed salary but that he would be allowed to open a shop which members would patronize provided that the items he sold were 'as good and as cheap' as could be bought elsewhere.[498]

As in Wales, attempts to combine the pastorate of a Dissenting church with the pursuit of a secular occupation could bring problems. Thomas Powell, minister of the Particular Baptist church in Mitchell Street, Southwark, ran a currier's business in Blue Anchor Alley. In 1784 a thief stole thirty-six calf skins and thirty-six seal skins from his shop and Powell offered a reward of five guineas for information leading to the arrest of the culprit. But when the thief was caught, tried, and hanged at Tyburn twelve members of his church withdrew in protest and formed what was to become the Upton Baptist church.[499] Similarly the Barton-in-Fabis General Baptist church was divided in 1785 by a bitter dispute occasioned by the action of a former apprentice of the younger Samuel Deacon, and a member of the church, in opening a rival clockmaking business in the village.[500] Joseph Burrows, who was a General Baptist minister for forty years from 1821, successively at Sutton-in-Ashfield in Nottinghamshire and at Alfreton in Derbyshire, endured considerable hardship in combining his pastorates with

[494] J. Warburton, *Mercies of a Convenant God* (Swengel, Penn., 1964), 79.
[495] Klaiber, *Suffolk Baptists*, 78.
[496] Weston, 'The Baptists of North-West England', 356.
[497] R. L. Greenall, 'Baptist as Radical: The Life and Opinions of the Rev. John Jenkinson', *Northamptonshire Past and Present*, 8 (1991–2), 217.
[498] Cumberland, 'Nonconformity in the Black Country', 139.
[499] S. J. Price, *Upton: The Story of One Hundred and Fifty Years* (1935), 20–1.
[500] Jackson, 'Baptists of Leicestershire', 164, 175.

his work as a lacemaker. A depression in the lace industry in the late 1830s forced him to sell a machine which had cost £600 for £120. He subsequently rented a machine until its owner found that he was a Baptist minister and deprived him of his work on the grounds that 'one trade is enough for a man to look after'.[501] Even after John Warburton had settled at Trowbridge in 1810 at a salary of £3 a week he still found it difficult to support his wife and ten children and he turned to farming to supplement his income. But his attempts to grow apples and keep pigs simply resulted in a net loss of £40 and Warburton was brought to see the force of Paul's words that 'they which preach the gospel should live of the gospel'.[502]

The experiences of Burrows and Warburton thus pointed to the conclusion that where possible Baptist and Congregational pastors should be freed from the need to engage in trade or industry to concentrate their energies on their ministries. But the salaries that many churches could afford to pay, though on the whole higher than those in Wales, were none the less very low. In 1758 Joseph Picop, minister of the Particular Baptist church in Bacup, with five children to support, was paid £17. 8s. 11d.; in the 1780s William Vidler, when minister of the Particular Baptist church at Battle in Sussex, also received a stipend of £17 a year; Benjamin Maurice, Presbyterian minister at Alcester in Warwickshire, during a ministry which lasted twenty-nine years, was never paid much more than £20 a year; and when Isaac Nortcliffe became pastor of the Congregational church at Rishworth in the West Riding in 1816 for the first three years he received no remuneration, and his payment subsequently varied between 7s. and £1. 5s. a quarter.[503] A correspondent to the *Protestant Dissenters Magazine* in 1794 complained that whereas £70 or £80 was considered 'a capital salary' for a Dissenting minister, the vast majority of churches paid their pastors less than £50 a year.[504] Half a century later many ministers were getting scarcely any more. The Chapel Street Particular Baptist church in Accrington in Lancashire paid its minister £31 a year in the 1840s; the Brettell Lane Baptist church in Brierley Hill in the Black Country gave its minister £40 a year in 1858; and although Jonathan Ingham was promised a salary of £25 a year when he became pastor of the General Baptist church in Allerton in the West Riding in 1835, in some years during the

---

[501] Harrison, 'Baptists of Nottinghamshire', i. 259–61.
[502] Warburton, *Mercies of a Covenant God*, 124, 153–4.
[503] Overend, *Ebenezer Baptist Church, Bacup*, 158; F. W. Butt-Thompson, 'William Vidler', *Baptist Quarterly*, 17 (1957–8), 4; H. McLachlan, *The Unitarian Movement in the Religious Life of England* (1934), 98–9; Miall, *Congregationalism in Yorkshire*, 340.
[504] *Protestant Dissenters Magazine*, 1 (1794), 503.

thirty years he remained the church's pastor his stipend sank as low as £16.[505] The *Congregational Magazine* estimated in 1830 that the average income of Independent ministers did not much exceed £100 and a generation later, in 1853, the Congregational Union was told that 217 of its ministers were still being paid less than £70 a year, and of those 97 got less than £50 a year.[506] Four years later, in 1857, the *Baptist Reporter* claimed that while sixty Baptist churches paid their ministers £300 or more a year, and another 120 paid £200 a year, most Baptist ministers received less than £80 a year.[507] A correspondent to the *Evangelical Magazine* in 1837 complained that the salary paid to some ministers in country districts was 'often far below that of a mechanic', and the Congregationalist John Morrison claimed in 1850 that many ministers received 'little more than the remuneration of a common artisan'.[508]

The pay of the average Baptist or Congregationalist minister in the mid-nineteenth century was thus comparable to that of Anglican curates, whose average salary in 1853 was £79 a year, but their salaries were way below those of Anglican incumbents whose median income in 1830 was £275 a year.[509] Dissenting pastors, moreover, had neither the security of tenure nor the guaranteed income of their Anglican counterparts. When John Holloway was ordained pastor of the Particular Baptist church in Reading in 1798 the minister of the town's Congregational church, Archibald Douglas, reminded the Reading Baptists of the advantage they enjoyed over members of the Church of England. Whereas, on the recent death of the Hon. William Bromley Cadogan, the Evangelical vicar of St Giles, the Evangelical Anglicans of Reading had had 'a carnal man imposed upon them', the Baptists were free to choose their own pastors.[510] But the church's liberty to elect its own ministers carried with it the freedom to depose those ministers who were deemed to have outlived their usefulness. Thirty years before John Holloway's ordination that same Reading Baptist church, when faced with a declining congregation, had asked its pastor Thomas Whitewood to assist the church's revival 'by looking out whether he could not provide for himself

[505] Weston, 'The Baptists of North-West England', 348; Cumberland, 'Nonconformity in the Black Country', 138; C. E. Shipley (ed.), *The Baptists of Yorkshire* (1912), 122.
[506] *Congregational Magazine* (1830), supplement, 689–90; Jones, *Congregationalism in England*, 230.
[507] Harrison, 'Baptists of Nottinghamshire', i. 559.
[508] Elliott, 'Protestant Denominations in Leeds', 340, citing the *Evangelical Magazine* (1837), 481.
[509] A. Haigh, *The Victorian Clergy* (1984), 223; P. Virgin, *The Church in an Age of Negligence* (Cambridge, 1989), 104 n. 50.
[510] Davis, *History of the Baptist Church, King's Road, Reading*, 53–4.

elsewhere'. The church voted that Whitewood should leave, he was unable to find another pastorate, and the poor man died soon afterwards.[511]

Whereas the income of an Anglican incumbent was usually fixed before he settled in a parish, the salary of a Dissenting minister was, to a large extent, dependent on the results of his ministry. In 1773 Job Orton had said that it was unwise for ministers to accept a pastorate at a fixed salary and cited the example of Benjamin Fawcett who agreed to serve the Kidderminster Presbyterian meeting for £80 a year and got no more when his congregation was 'larger and at least ten times richer, by the increase of their trade and manufacture'.[512] But a church's prosperity could fall as well as rise, and a minister's salary with it. When depression hit the Nottinghamshire lace industry the salary paid by the Beeston General Baptist church dropped from £80 a year in 1840 to £52 in 1846.[513] And when James Howard of the Dursley Tabernacle sold his woollen mill in 1854 the income of the church's minister dropped from £100 a year to £66. 5s. 7½d.[514] There was, however, a minority of Nonconformist ministers whose salaries enabled them to live in a fair degree of comfort and even a handful who managed to combine the Dissenting ministry with the accumulation of considerable wealth. In the late eighteenth century the best paid Dissenting pastors were those who ministered to wealthy urban Unitarian congregations. The former Anglican vicar Theophilus Lindsey may have been the highest paid Nonconformist minister in the country: his salary from his Essex Street congregation in London increased from £125 a year in 1775 to £207 a year in 1785.[515] The richest Dissenting minister was probably John Yates, the minister of the Kaye Street (from 1791 Paradise Street) Presbyterian/Unitarian meeting in Liverpool from 1777 to 1823. In 1777 the master potter Josiah Wedgwood had been impressed by Yates's social graces—'he dances admirably and sings an excellent song'—and had tried to persuade him to accept the pastorate of the Old Meeting, Newcastle-under-Lyme, at a salary of £60 a year.[516] But Yates went instead to Liverpool at £130 a year and subsequently contracted a fortunate marriage and engaged in land and commercial speculations that made him one of the wealthiest men in Liverpool. His wealth enabled him to maintain a magnificent home which on one occasion was raided by burglars armed with pistols.[517] The salary of Hugh Worthington, who was pastor of the Great

---

[511] Ibid. 34.   [512] Palmer, *Letters to Dissenting Ministers*, i. 160.
[513] Harrison, 'Baptists of Nottinghamshire', ii. 569.
[514] Evans, *As Mad as a Hatter!*, 144–6.
[515] Ditchfield, 'Unitarianism and Radicalism', 229, citing *TUHS* 3 (1926), 365.
[516] A. Finer and G. Savage, *The Selected Letters of Josiah Wedgwood* (1965), 201, 205.
[517] H. McLachlan, *The Unitarian Movement in the Religious Life of England* (1934), 100;

Meeting, Leicester, between 1741 and 1797, averaged £114. 9s. 3d. a year; Joseph Priestley had a hundred guineas a year and a house at Mill Hill, Leeds, between 1767 and 1773; and when Priestley went to the New Meeting, Birmingham, in 1780, it was at a salary of £100 per annum.[518] The salaries of Priestley's successors at Mill Hill were increased to £200 in 1808 and to £400 in 1823, but these figures reflected not only the congregation's wealth but also one of the Presbyterian/Unitarians' perennial problems, the shortage of suitable ministers. Both in 1808 and 1823 a minister was able to extract a higher salary from the Mill Hill congregation by threatening to go to another church.[519] Elsewhere the fall in Presbyterian/Unitarian numbers in the early nineteenth century made it difficult for congregations to maintain their ministers' salaries and impossible for the Presbyterian/Unitarians to retain their position as the highest paid Nonconformist ministers. In 1819 George's Meeting in Exeter was employing two ministers with salaries of £200 a year each, but twenty years later, when they agreed to pay their senior minister £300 a year and the junior minister £150 a year, they were unable to meet their commitments.[520] By 1829, according to the *Monthly Repository*, there were 'scores' of Unitarian meetings where the average number of hearers had fallen to around thirty and where the minister's salary was no more than £70 a year.[521]

The Congregationalists had by that date overtaken the Unitarians at the top of the ministerial pay-scale. George Ford, minister of the Independent church at Stepney, was rumoured to receive £1,500 a year and died leaving a fortune of £30,000, though his successor Joseph Fletcher got only £800 a year.[522] When, in 1812, Thomas Raffles accepted an invitation to the pastorate of the Congregational Newington chapel in Liverpool (which soon moved to Great George Street) he received a salary of £300 a year which was raised to £400 in 1816, to £500 in 1837, and to £700 in 1841.[523] John Leifchild also earned £700 a year as pastor of Craven chapel, Thomas Binney was paid £600 a year as pastor of the King's Weigh House, and five other London Congregational ministers in London in the late 1830s were also receiving

Sellers, 'Liverpool Nonconformity', 7; S. A. T. Yates, *Memorials of the Family of the Rev. John Yates* (1890), 74–7.

[518] A. H. Thomas, *A History of the Great Meeting, Leicester* (1908), 50; *Autobiography of Joseph Priestley*, ed. J. Lindsay (Bath, 1970), 98; Bushrod, 'Unitarianism in Birmingham', 118.
[519] Elliott, 'Protestant Denominations in Leeds', 375–6.
[520] Brockett, *Nonconformity in Exeter*, 176–7, 183.
[521] Waddington, *Congregational History to 1850*, 275.
[522] Jones, *Congregationalism in England*, 229.
[523] Raffles, *Memoirs of Thomas Raffles*, 351.

£500 a year or more.[524] The highest paid Baptist ministers appear to have received rather less. John Rippon's income at Carter Lane was dependent on fluctuating pew-rents, but was usually more than £300 a year.[525] The salaries paid to the ministers of the South Parade Baptist church in Leeds increased from £100 in 1820 to £200 in 1825, and to £300 in 1837, giving John Giles a higher income than the Wesleyan preachers in the town and the same income as that received by the vicar of Leed's Holy Trinity church.[526]

Such high ministerial salaries were, however, very exceptional. Even the £700 a year paid to Thomas Raffles or John Leifchild was no more than the lowest rates earned by senior clerks in the Civil Service,[527] and contrasted with the £19,000 a year paid to the Archbishop of Canterbury and the Bishop of Durham. Raffles's salary did, none the less, enable him to live as a member of the prosperous bourgeoisie and to travel widely through much of Europe. In 1854 he and his fellow Congregationalist Robert Halley embarked on a tour of the Mediterranean, and although the outbreak of the Crimean War and the requisition of available steamers prevented their travelling to the Holy Land, they visited Rome, Naples, Greece, Egypt, and Constantinople. In the Ottoman capital they visited the slave market and saw girls from Africa and from the shores of the Black Sea being sold for £20.[528]

There was a world of difference between the travels of Raffles and Halley and the itinerant journeys of the Primitive Methodist and Bible Christian ministers who were paid less than either Wesleyan itinerants or Baptist and Congregational pastors in England. The first paid Primitive Methodist itinerants were supported by private donations: in November 1809 Hugh Bourne agreed to pay James Crawfoot 10s. a week and from December 1810 James Nixon and Thomas Woodnorth each paid William Clowes 5s. a week. But the burden on these generous individuals could not be long sustained and in July 1811 the Primitive Methodists agreed that henceforth those itinerant preachers who could not be self-supporting should be supported by voluntary collections. From October 1811 James Crawfoot was paid 10s. 6d. a week and William Clowes, to compensate for the hospitality he was obliged to provide for his fellow Ranters, was paid 14s. a week.[529] For Crawfoot, who had hitherto been an unemployed farm labourer, this was a distinct

[524] Jones, *Congregationalism in England*, 229 n. 7; Kaye, *King's Weigh House*, 70, 78.

[525] Manley, 'John Rippon', 110.

[526] Elliott, 'Protestant Denominations in Leeds', 364–5; F. Beckwith, 'South Parade, Leeds', *Baptist Quarterly*, 21 (1965–6), 21–2.

[527] G. Best, *Mid-Victorian Britain, 1851–1875* (1971), 89.

[528] Raffles, *Memoirs of Thomas Raffles*, 154–6, 425; R. Halley, *A Short Biography of the Rev. Robert Halley* (1879), pp. lxix–lxx.

[529] Kendall, *Primitive Methodist Church*, i. 105–6, 130–2, 147–8.

improvement in his circumstances,[530] but for Clowes, who despite a depression in the pottery industry could earn '£1. 2s. 0d. in about three or four days', the decision to abandon his trade for full-time itinerant preaching involved real hardship, both for himself and for his wife. 'We endeavoured to practise self-denial to the utmost, to avoid being involved in debt: we therefore used coarser food, dining when by ourselves on a little suet and potatoes, or a piece of bread and a drink of water. But as we found our expenditure still to exceed our income, we sold the feather-bed we slept on; for it was a maxim with us never to get into debt.'[531]

The pay of Primitive Methodist itinerants did not improve for more than thirty years. The salaries of married preachers remained, with fluctuations, at £36. 8s. a year (14s. a week) until 1845 when they were increased to £49. 8s. per annum. In addition married preachers had an allowance for children which in the 1830s was 1s. 6d. a week. The salaries of unmarried preachers also varied, but in 1813 they were fixed at £15 a year and twenty years later were only £17. 5s. a year with an allowance for lodgings.[532] Even Hugh Bourne, who for years had supported himself in his ministry, was paid only £16 a year in 1824, with 10s. a week allowance for board and lodging.[533] Women preachers were even worse paid. When Sarah Kirkland embarked on her career as a travelling preacher in 1816 she was paid two guineas a quarter, and when Elizabeth Smith went on a mission to Radnorshire in 1826 she, too, was allowed two guineas a quarter, and was told she would have to raise it herself.[534] Even the small salaries recommended by the Primitive Methodist Conference were not always forthcoming, and, as we have seen, in 1826 Conference insisted that itinerant preachers should not be paid more than their circuits could raise.

Of all the English Nonconformist denominations which paid their ministers, the lowest incomes of all were provided by the Bible Christians. Initially British Christian itinerants were paid less than 10s. a week.[535] When James Way was stationed at Crewkerne in Somerset in 1826 he was forced to endure 'more privations there than I had ever done before'. 'The food generally was poor and scanty.' One morning at breakfast the woman at whose house he was lodging 'burst into tears and said she had nothing but potatoes and salt to set before me'. And his stipend for the year, 'not including board and lodging,

---

[530] E. Langton, 'James Crawfoot', *PWHS* 30 (1955), 14.
[531] J. T. Wilkinson, *William Clowes* (1951), 96.
[532] Morris, 'Primitive Methodism in Derbyshire', 109; Wilkinson, *Hugh Bourne*, 97.
[533] Herod, *Biographical Sketches*, 480–1.
[534] Ibid. 315; Kendall, *Primitive Methodist Church*, ii. 382.
[535] Shaw, *The Bible Christians*, 31.

which he had without cost, was only £8'.[536] Eleven years later, in 1837, the Bible Christians adopted a scale of salaries which provided a single man with £12. 12s. a year and board and lodging, female preachers with £7 a year, and married preachers with £30 a year, plus an allowance for their children on a scale that went down from £6 a year for the first child to £4. 10s. for a fourth and subsequent child. Married preachers were also provided with furnished houses, but only on condition that their rents should not exceed £6 a year in the towns and £4 a year in rural areas.[537]

Unmarried preachers among both the Primitive Methodists and Bible Christians were thus paid as little as the poorest agricultural labourers,[538] and the higher salaries paid to married preachers did not stop men from leaving the itinerant ministry to become local preachers once they had a wife and children to support.[539] Around 1820 a Primitive Methodist itinerant preacher with a wife and two children earned twice as much as the average Welsh Baptist pastor (though the latter could supplement his stipend with secular earnings) but only 'half the minimum salary of a Wesleyan itinerant with a comparable family'.[540] For such payment Primitive Methodist preachers sacrificed home comforts, health, and even life itself. In 1821 Joseph Reynolds, after travelling 'nearly 230 miles with a penny cake' and preaching to nearly two thousand people, 'made my supper of cold cabbage; and as I did not like to expose my poverty, I was driven to seek my lodgings in the fields, and slept under a hay stack till about four o'clock in the morning, when I was awoke by the little birds'.[541] Similarly John Petty often undertook long journeys on foot only to find that no one would offer him food and drink after his preaching, and while in Pembrokeshire in 1827 he had to sleep on straw and, on occasion, share his bed with a calf. On his thirty-fifth birthday he noted that as a result of 'many privations and sufferings' he had 'several symptoms of premature old age': greying hair, weakening eye sight, and the disorders of the stomach and liver from which he was finally to die.[542]

The privations endured by Joseph Reynolds and John Petty were not the common lot of Nonconformist ministers in the early nineteenth century and, as we have seen, by the 1820s some Unitarian and Congregational ministers were living in considerable comfort, if not luxury. But many Dissenting ministers had to combine their pastorates with secular occupations, and most of those who were able to live off the contributions of their churches had to

---

[536] Bourne, *The Bible Christians*, 175–7.   [537] Ibid. 241; *Religious Census*, p. lxxxiv.
[538] Snell, *Annals of the Labouring Poor*, 126.
[539] Werner, *Primitive Methodist Connexion*, 141.   [540] Ibid. 181.
[541] *Primitive Methodist Magazine* (1821), 184.
[542] Milburn in Dews, *From Mow Cop to Peake*, 61–3.

work hard for their salaries, and certainly far harder than their contemporary Anglican clergy.[543] The demands made of Congregational and Baptist pastors on the one hand, and of Methodist itinerants on the other, were in some ways very different but none the less burdensome. Baptist and Congregational ministers occupied settled pastorates and often in the eighteenth century, and sometimes in the nineteenth century, a man would serve the same church for the whole of his ministerial career. John Rippon was pastor of the Carter Lane Particular Baptist church, Southwark, for sixty-three years from 1773 until his death in 1836 at the age of eighty-five.[544] William Jay ministered to the Congregational church which met in the Argyle chapel, Bath, for sixty-one years from 1791 until he retired in 1852 at the age of eighty-three.[545] Andrew Reed was pastor of the Congregational church which met first in New Road and then in Wycliffe chapel, Whitechapel, for fifty years from 1811, and only resigned his pastorate when physical infirmity prevented him from preaching any longer.[546] John Clayton ministered to the King's Weigh House for forty-eight years from 1778 to 1826, and his son John was pastor to the church which met first in Camomile Street and then in the Poultry for forty-one years while his son George served the church at Walworth for fifty-one years.[547] Thomas Northcote Toller was pastor of Kettering's Congregational Great Meeting for forty-five years from 1776 to 1821, and was succeeded as minister by his son Thomas Toller who occupied the pulpit for a further thirty-four years.[548] The Independent church at Troedrhiwdalar in Breconshire had only three ministers in a period of 141 years: Thomas Morgan, who was pastor from 1725 to 1755; Isaac Price who served from 1755 to 1803; and David Williams who occupied the church's pulpit from 1803 to 1866.[549] In addition to ministering to Troedrhiwdalar David Williams was, until 1843, pastor to the church at Llanwrtyd; he also founded five branch churches which he continued to serve; and during the first forty years of his ministry he travelled twenty miles and preached three times every Sunday. When Williams celebrated the jubilee of his pastorate in 1853 the church's

---

[543] As late as 1867 just over 80% of all Anglican livings had populations of less than 2,000, and Anglican rural clergymen were considered to be underworked (Haig, *The Victorian Clergy*, 291, 293).

[544] Manley, 'John Rippon', 49.

[545] G. Redford and J. A. James, *The Autobiography of William Jay* (1851), 230–2.

[546] A. Reed and C. Reed, *Memoir of the Life and Philanthropic Labours of Andrew Reed* (1866).

[547] T. W. Aveling, *Memorials of the Clayton Family* (1867), 347, 425, 479.

[548] Goodman, *The Great Meeting, Kettering*, 47.

[549] T. G. Thomas and J. Jones, *Brecon and Radnor Congregationalism* (Merthyr Tydfil, 1912), 62–72.

senior deacon, in presenting him with a testimonial, touched on the burden
that such a long pastorate in a mountainous area carried with it. 'In fifty years
there are 2,600 Sundays, and our worthy and esteemed pastor has not been
disabled on a single Sunday in fifty years from preaching by indisposition,
or allowed flooded, bridgeless mountain streams, storms of rain, or roads
thickly covered by snow-drifts and almost impassable, to interfere with the
fulfilment of his Sabbath engagements.' Even after his retirement at the age
of eighty-seven David Williams continued to preach every Sunday. At the
age of ninety-five he travelled to London to preach five sermons, and a week
before his death three months later he rode fifteen miles and preached
twice.[550]

By the 1830s Dissenting ministers were complaining that week-night services, missionary meetings, and the need to fill the pages of denominational
periodicals were all adding to their workload.[551] The anonymous and disillusioned author of *The Autobiography of a Dissenting Minister*, first published
in 1834, claimed that it was an inevitable law of Dissenting pastorates that
congregations grew tired of listening to the same preacher year after year and
came to crave novelty.[552] The likelihood of a pastor boring his congregation
by staying in the same pulpit for too long was reduced, on the one hand, by
the ability of a Baptist or Congregational church to suggest that its pastor
look for another church, and on the other by the desire of ministers to seek
new pastorates in the hope of finding fresh challenges, larger congregations,
and higher salaries. The researches of Kenneth Brown show that 75 per cent
of Congregational and 70 per cent of Baptist pastorates begun between 1841
and 1861 lasted for less than ten years, and that half the Congregational and
43 per cent of the Baptist pastorates lasted for less than five years.[553] But in
the eighteenth century John Wesley regarded the length of Dissenting pastorates, and the number of sermons which such a ministry involved, as too
great a burden for either preacher or congregation. 'I know, were I myself
to preach one whole year in one place, I should preach both myself and most
of my congregation asleep', was his comment.[554] It was partly to avoid such

[550] Rees, *Protestant Nonconformity in Wales*, 482–4.

[551] J. Bennett, *The History of the Dissenters during the Last Thirty Years* (1839), 276–8; Evans,
'Religion in the Swansea Valley', 262.

[552] *The Autobiography of a Dissenting Minister* (6th edn., 1843), 182–3, 192. This work is usually attributed to William Pitt Scargill, who was minister to the Presbyterian meeting at Bury St
Edmunds between 1812 and 1832, but the *Autobiography* contains strong evidence to suggest
that the author was a Congregationalist. He certainly disliked Unitarianism.

[553] K. D. Brown, *A Social History of the Nonconformist Ministry in England and Wales*
(Oxford, 1988), 166.

[554] *HMC* i. 230.

outcome that Wesley insisted that his preachers should go on circuit and should change circuits at least every three years. In 1790 the Wesleyan Conference insisted that 'no preacher shall preach three times a day to the same congregation', and in the following year laid down that 'no preacher shall be stationed for any circuit above two years successively, unless God has been pleased to use him as the instrument of a remarkable revival'.[555] But if the frequency with which Methodist preachers changed pulpits made sermon preparation less of a chore than it was for Baptists or Congregationalists, the constant changes of circuit upset their home life, disrupted their children's education, and could lead to friction with the local leaders, stewards, and trustees. When, in 1845, the Wesleyan circuit stewards at Yarmouth reduced the salary of one of their preachers, H. Ransom, in order to pay off their circuit debt, Ransom complained to Jabez Bunting of the readiness of 'men living at ease in their native soil . . . to conspire against us, while we are comparatively strangers among them'.[556] What is more, the rigours of the itinerant system often made the job of a Methodist travelling preacher more physically demanding than that of settled pastors. John James left the Calvinistic Methodists for the Congregationalists and became pastor of the Castle Street Independent church, Abergavenny, 'not because of any aversion to his old friends the Methodists, but because of his inability to follow the itinerant ministry, for he had grown very corpulent'.[557] The lot of Primitive Methodist preachers was particularly arduous before the Connexion started to provide horses in the 1840s. Henry Woodcock claimed that preachers in the Driffield circuit in the East Riding were prematurely worn out by walking fifty miles a week, preaching eight sermons, and visiting forty homes.[558] And in 1839 Josiah Stamp gave the following account of his three-year ministry in the Louth Primitive Methodist circuit in Lincolnshire: 'We have built sixteen chapels, enlarged one, bought another, and fitted up a large room, and have had an increase of twenty-five local preachers and 416 members . . . I have walked more than 10,000 miles and have preached upwards of 1,500 sermons and visited near 6,000 families.' He had been paid £62. 12s. a year, while the junior minister in the circuit had received £36 a year.[559]

Such were the pressures on Methodist preachers and Dissenting pastors that they depended more than most men on the support of their wives. Some

[555] *Minutes of the Methodist Conferences*, i. 232, 246.
[556] Brown, *Nonconformist Ministry*, 138, 145–6.
[557] Price, *Penuel Calvinistic Methodist Church, Ebbw Vale*, 26.
[558] Greaves, 'Methodism in Yorkshire', 227–8.
[559] J. M. Turner in Dews, *From Mow Cop to Peake*, 5.

Methodist preachers relied on their wives' earnings to sustain them in the ministry, and Thomas Olivers 'thought it his duty to select a wife with a small competency to prevent his making the Gospel chargeable to any one'.[560] A few wives accompanied their husbands on their itinerant preaching tours. In 1820 the Bible Christian Conference recommended that 'itinerant brethren who intend to marry' should choose their partners from among the female travelling preachers, and several acted on this advice.[561] But most wives assisted their itinerant husbands by providing a haven of rest and refreshment to which they could periodically return in the course of their journeys, while the wives of settled pastors frequently acted as their husbands' unpaid curates, helping with their husbands' pastoral and charitable work, visiting the sick and the poor, receiving church members in their homes, and taking the lead in organizing women's meetings and sewing circles. It was often the wives of ministers, comments Kenneth Brown, 'who had to pay the heaviest physical and emotional price for their husbands' vocations'.[562] The Lancashire weaver and Strict Baptist John Warburton departed for a preaching engagement in Cheshire leaving his wife and six young children with 'not one penny of money or one six-penny worth of provision', and with his wife complaining that he would 'go on preaching until they were all starved to death'.[563] The wives both of the Primitive Methodist pioneer William Clowes and of the founder of the Methodist New Connexion Alexander Kilham were left for long periods during their final illnesses while their husbands went on preaching tours, and William Clowes's wife died while he was away. Kilham claimed that his wife, 'notwithstanding her extreme illness, seemed unwilling that her situation should be the cause of my neglecting my duty', but Clowes's wife 'felt her loneliness and deprivations with strong sensibility'.[564]

Although John Wesley's own evangelistic activity was probably helped by the failure of his marriage and the absence of domestic ties to keep him from his travels, lesser men who made unfortunate marriages found their lives blighted by unsympathetic partners. The biographer of John Pye Smith claimed that his first wife was a 'tribulation' to him for thirty years from the time of their marriage in 1801. Pye Smith was resident tutor, and from 1806 principal, of Homerton College, and also pastor of a Congregational church which met initially in the hall of the college and, from 1811, in the Old Gravel Pit meeting-house in which both Richard Price and Joseph Priestley had

---

[560] Elliott, 'Protestant Denominations in Leeds', 317.

[561] Shaw, *The Bible Christians*, 33.   [562] Brown, *Nonconformist Ministry*, 178.

[563] Warburton, *Mercies of a Covenant God*, 79–81. Warburton returned from Cheshire with 34s. and a bundle of cakes for his children.

[564] Brown, *Nonconformist Ministry*, 178; Kilham, *Life of Alexander Kilham*, 130–7.

once ministered. Mrs Pye Smith had a private income and did not take kindly to the role of wife of a college tutor with responsibility for the accommodation and feeding of the students. The friction which resulted between Mrs Pye Smith and the students led to two of them withdrawing from the college and to her husband resigning as resident tutor. Henceforward Mrs Smith refused to entertain either her husband's students or his friends and hampered his work by what he called the 'disabilities and hindrances [arising] from private duties and afflictions'.[565]

The Unitarian William Johnson Fox was no doubt unique among Dissenting ministers in extricating himself from an unhappy marriage by separating from his wife and living with another woman. The South Place congregation stood by their pastor, but his conduct was too outrageous even for other Unitarians and Fox's isolation emphasizes the fact that Nonconformist ministers were expected to set an example to the communities they served and to live their lives on a higher moral plane than other men. The overwhelming majority of ministers succeeded in their expected roles as exemplars to their congregations, but a handful betrayed the trust that had been placed in them. John Jenkins, who was ordained pastor of the Congregational church at Llangattock in Breconshire in 1779, absconded with the money he had collected for the building of a chapel; James Porter, minister of the Bourne General Baptist church in Lincolnshire, was accused of 'drunkenness and sodomy' and 'had to leave the town in the night for fear of the mob'; and David Llewellyn Davies, pastor of the Unitarian chapel at Dukinfield in Cheshire, was given five guineas to leave by the trustees in 1795 after he had got drunk.[566] In 1824 the Wesleyan Conference expelled four preachers of whom John Bryan was accused of 'having criminal connections with his housekeeper', Jonas Jagger was denounced 'for intemperance and imprudent conduct towards some female', and Theobald of Halifax was accused of sodomy.[567] And twenty-three years later the Conference expelled Edward Usher, superintendent of the Epworth circuit, who in five months had consumed 132 bottles of porter, '4 bottles [of] sherry, 2 bottles of port, 1½ gallons of whisky, 9 gallons of brandy, and 16½ gallons of gin'.[568] The number of Nonconformist ministers who were guilty of breaking their churches' moral code constituted only a small minority of the total, but the conduct of all of them was subjected to the constant scrutiny of their congregations. The author of *The Autobiography of a Dissenting Minister* bitterly resented the

[565] J. Medway, *Memoirs of the Life and Writings of John Pye Smith* (1853), 91–101.
[566] Thomas and Jones, *Brecon and Radnor Congregationalism*, 143; *Baptist Quarterly*, 15 (1953–4), 228; A. Gordon, *Historical Account of Dukinfield Chapel and its School* (1896), 60.
[567] Brown, *Nonconformist Ministry*, 57–8.   [568] Ward, *Early Victorian Methodism*, 347.

way in which a pastor was at the mercy of his critics, 'carping at him and objecting to him, for everything that does not exactly hit their fancy or suit their humour'. The Dissenting minister, he complained, was in a position of 'hopeless servility', subservient to his congregation 'in politics, in theology, in manners, dress, and amusements'.[569] His point was illustrated by the fate of William Lumley Evans, pastor of the Soar Baptist church in Ystalyfera, Glamorgan, in the 1840s. Evans was dismissed by his church 'not because he drank more alcoholic beverage than those brothers who belonged to the congregation under his care, nor because the alcohol he drank had a different effect on his constitution, but rather because there was more unavoidable public scrutiny of his movements, and this caused more of what is called public disgrace'.[570]

None the less, despite the heavy burden of work and the high standards expected of preachers and pastors in return for often very low pay, the Nonconformist ministry did have its compensations as a career, material as well as spiritual. Though Methodist circuits and Baptist churches did not always raise the sums they had contracted to pay their ministers, such ministers were for the most part assured of regular if uncertain incomes, which was not the case for millions of their fellow countrymen. In addition Methodist circuits were committed to providing their married preachers with houses and their unmarried preachers with lodgings, and by the turn of the eighteenth and nineteenth centuries some Congregational churches were providing their ministers with manses.[571] Moreover both the Wesleyan Connexion and the more prosperous Baptist and Congregational churches made some provision for their ministers' old age and for their widows. In 1763 John Wesley had launched his Worn-Out Preachers' and Widows' Fund to which, from 1765, every travelling preacher was expected to pay a guinea on his admission to the itinerant ministry and a subscription of half a guinea a year thereafter. In return retired itinerants were promised a pension of £10 a year, their widows a similar sum from 1767, and in 1796 the pensions were increased to £12 a year, with an additional pound for every year travelled more than twelve.[572] The sums promised to retired preachers were not always paid in full, and between 1781 and 1790 the Preachers' Fund was raided to make up the preachers' allowances.[573] But the Wesleyan scheme was far

[569] *Autobiography of a Dissenting Minister*, 144.
[570] Evans, 'Religion in the Swansea Valley', 256.
[571] Castle Gate minutes (1783), 68; Register of Chinley chapel, Derbyshire, PRO RG4.496 (1792–5); Goodman, *The Great Meeting, Kettering*, 42.
[572] Smith, *History of Wesleyan Methodism*, ii. 315–16; *Minutes of the Methodist Conferences,* i. 48, 72, 342–3.
[573] Smith, *History of Wesleyan Methodism*, ii. 315–16.

better than anything provided by the other denominations. Numerous attempts to start similar schemes for Baptist and Congregational ministers for the most part came to nothing,[574] and those that did get off the ground had only limited success. A 'Society for the Relief of the Necessitous Widows and Children of Protestant Dissenting Ministers' had been founded in 1733 and by the early nineteenth century was giving the widows of English ministers ten guineas a year and the widows of Welsh ministers eight guineas a year.[575] In 1815 the Northamptonshire Baptist Association set up the northamptonshire Provident Fund which assisted pastors and their widows in the county for more than a century,[576] and the following year the 'Society for the Relief of Aged and Infirm Baptist Ministers' was founded in Bath. The Bath Society, as it was called, had a subscription of 30s. a year or a single payment of £10, but after twenty years it had only 150 members and had paid out only £2,205 to forty-four beneficiaries.[577] The lack of proper provision for ministers' old age led, it was claimed, to 'many a good man' holding on to his pastorate long after 'he feels that his powers have become debilitated, because he has no other resources'.[578] John Brownlow, minister to the Presbyterian meeting in Ashton-in-Makerfield, agreed to retire in 1786 at the age of eighty-three only on condition that he was provided with a rent-free house and a pension of £20 a year.[579] But other Baptist, Congregational, and Unitarian churches often made generous provision for their ministers' old age without duress, though such help usually went to men who could have well afforded to save out of their own salaries. When Thomas Northcote Toller celebrated the thirtieth anniversary of his pastorate at the Congregational Great Meeting, Kettering, in 1806, the church presented him with a testimonial for £1,000.[580] Similarly when Dr Estlin retired from the ministry of Lewin's Mead Unitarian congregation in Bristol in 1816 after a pastorate lasting more than forty-five years he too was given £1,000.[581] Members of the Bowl Alley Presbyterian meeting in Hull provided John Beverley with a pension of £80 a year after his retirement in 1799; both the New Meeting and the Old Meeting of Birmingham Unitarians provided their retiring ministers with pensions of £100 a year in 1790 and 1800; and when Thomas Raffles retired from his ministry at Great George Street, Liverpool,

---

[574] Bassett, *The Welsh Baptists*, 206–8; Elliott, 'Protestant Denominations in Leeds', 351–2.
[575] Elliot, 'Protestant Denominations in Leeds', 370.
[576] E. A. Payne, *College Street Chapel, Northampton* (1947), 28.
[577] Bassett, *The Welsh Baptists*, 205; *Baptist Magazine*, 26 (1834), 208; 27 (1835), 342.
[578] Elliott, 'Protestant Denominations in Leeds', 351.
[579] G. Fox, *The History of Park Lane Chapel* (Manchester, 1897), 43–5.
[580] Goodman, *The Great Meeting, Kettering*, 42.
[581] R. L. Carpenter, *Memoirs of the Life of the Rev. Lant Carpenter* (Bristol, 1842), 208.

in 1861 he was given an annuity of £400 a year.[582] William Jay was presented with a silver salver and £650 when he completed fifty years of his pastorate at Argyle chapel, Bath, in 1841; John Alexander was given 500 guineas when he completed thirty-nine years as pastor of the Prince's Street Congregational church, Norwich, in 1856; and John Leifchild, on his retirement from his ministry at Craven chapel in 1854, was presented with a testimonial of 2,000 guineas.[583] Even some of the poorer churches tried to provide for their retired ministers and for their widows. When Stephen Edwards, the pastor of the Rhymney Baptist church in Monmouthshire, died from cholera in 1854, the church collected £210 for his widow, of which £60 was given to her to start a business and the remaining £150 invested.[584] And the Methodist Unitarian church at Padiham in Lancashire agreed in 1842 to give two elderly preachers, the former cotton weavers James Pollard and John Robinson, a gift of £5 and a promise of £10 each every year for the remainder of their lives. One of the preachers, in thanking the church for its help, said that he had not been able to see how he could raise the rent for his cottage, but now the church had fulfilled his wish, 'that my bed and cottage might be preserved for us while we live, and, freed from the poor-house, we fly to the happy reagens of life eternal hereafter'.[585]

The greatest advantage which Nonconformist ministers possessed over their contemporaries was not, however, the regularity of income, the provision of accommodation, or the far from certain hope of a pension for one's old age. The Dissenting ministry offered to its members an advantage which few could have obtained so readily in any other contemporary field of employment: the opportunity of rising with comparative ease in the social scale. Whereas Anglican clergymen were expected to be gentlemen of some social standing who had received a university education,[586] the overwhelming majority of Nonconformist ministers came from humble backgrounds. A correspondent to the *Arminian Magazine* in 1796 observed that many Methodist preachers were 'men of mean birth, without education, accustomed to earn their livelihood by manual labour'.[587] And half a century later exactly the same point was made about the Nonconformist ministers of south Wales: many were 'wholly uneducated men' who 'were, at the outset of life, daily

---

[582] W. Whitaker, *One Line of the Puritan Tradition in Hull: Bowl Alley Lane Chapel* (1910); Bushrod, 'Unitarianism in Birmingham', 120; Raffles, *Memoirs of Thomas Raffles*, 468.

[583] Redford and James, *Autobiography of William Jay*, 208; Browne, *Congregationalism in Norfolk and Suffolk*, 275; Leifchild, *John Leifchild*, 272.

[584] Bassett, *The Welsh Baptists*, 206; Jones, *Sowing Beside all Waters*, 197.

[585] MacLachlan, *Methodist Unitarian Movement*, 74–5.

[586] Haig, *The Victorian Clergy*, 142–6.

[587] Wearmouth, *Methodism and the Common People*, 228.

labourers, like the classes whom they now lead'. 'There are more miners in the Dissenting ministry than any other class of workmen', wrote a correspondent to the *Morning Chronicle*.[588] For those men who were able to secure a full-time pastorate the Nonconformist ministry offered a challenging and comparatively secure occupation which would make heavy demands on their time, yet which would provide a degree of human interest and a sense of purpose which they would have been unlikely to find in any other employment. 'Your object is the noblest and most honourable that can occupy the attention of the human mind', William Newman told students at the Stepney Baptist College. 'The physician cares for the body which will soon perish. The lawyer defends an estate which will soon pass into other hands.' But the object of the Dissenting minister was 'to save souls from death'; 'to diffuse knowledge, purity, happiness in all directions'.[589] And if the financial rewards were usually meagre, the occupation of Dissenting minister gave to its holder the respect of the church he served and prestige in the wider community outside the church which again he would have found it difficult to attain in any other walk of life. To the future Unitarian missionary Richard Wright the Dissenting ministry offered a more interesting and more challenging career than any other to which he might aspire. 'Judging from the circumstances in which I was born and spent my early years, my life seemed destined to pass away in the most humdrum obscurity.' Yet 'I panted to emerge from the lowly vale where I was placed, and to do what would give me some distinction and render me of some value in society'.[590]

For a few Dissenters entry into the ministry was literally a passport from rags to riches. Thomas Price, born in 1820 the son of 'a peasant of Maes-y-cwper, Breconshire', was employed first as a farm servant and then as a page-boy in which position he saved £21 to pay for his apprenticeship to a Brecon painter and glazier. At the age of sixteen he walked 160 miles from Brecon to London 'with 13s. 4d. in his pocket to work as a journeyman painter' and six years later entered the Baptist college at Pontypool. In 1845, at the age of twenty-five, he accepted an invitation to the pastorate of the Carmel Baptist church, Aberdare, and two years later married Mrs Anne Gilbert, the daughter and heiress of the coal proprietor William Thomas Davis. When his wife died in 1849 Price inherited her property, became a director of her son's

---

[588] P. E. Razzell and R. W. Wainwright, *The Victorian Working Class* (1973), 266, citing the *Morning Chronicle*, 15 Apr. 1850. The point is substantiated by Turner, 'Revivals and Popular Religion in Wales', 143–4.

[589] R. E. Cooper, *From Stepney to St Giles': The Story of Regent's Park College, 1810–1960* (1960), 37–8.

[590] Wright, *Missionary Life and Labors*, 18.

woollen mill in Aberdare, and subsequently became a director of the Aber-dare Gas Company.[591] Less unusual was the career of John Prichard, who was born in 1796 the son of a drunken miner. At an early age John joined his father in the mines and with the money he thus earned he was able to pay for a few months' schooling. At the age of twenty he was baptized in the sea at Llandudno and five years later entered the Baptist academy at Aber-gavenny. In 1823 he accepted a call to the pastorate of the struggling Baptist church at Llangollen, whose membership was only thirty-two, and which could offer him a salary of only £23 a year. However under Prichard's guid-ance the church flourished and when the North Wales Baptist College was established at Llangollen in 1862 Prichard was chosen president and theo-logical tutor.[592]

In England the prospect of a career as a Dissenting minister had a com-pelling attraction for the young John Clifford, who was born at Sawley in Derbyshire in 1836, the son of a warp-machine worker in a lace yard who was frequently out of work in the late 1830s and early 1840s. At the age of ten John joined his father at work in a lace factory in Beeston, working as a threader for 2s. 6d. a week. On occasion John had to leave for work 'at four o'clock on Friday morning and never reached home until six o'clock on Saturday night—working all through the night, stimulated by coffee brought in cans to keep one vital and active'.[593] Not surprisingly when, at the age of fif-teen, he paid a visit to his uncle Elam Stenson who was pastor of the General Baptist church at Nuneaton in Warwickshire, John saw a way of escape from the lace factory. He never forgot his uncle's 'severely simple attire and sober grey trousers, and black vest and coat; his necktie of fleckless white; his per-fect, unvarying neatness; his serene placidity of demeanour; his pleasant, genial face'. But what impressed John most of all was his uncle's lifestyle which presented so marked a contrast to his father's and to his own: 'a life without passionate thrills and exhausting excitements, but full of heavenly peace and real service; a life shut out from the hurrying and noisy world, but shut in with the airs of heaven and the visions of eternity'.[594] John Clifford's own life was in fact to have plenty of excitement, but that was not the prospect that inspired him to follow his uncle's example. At the age of eighteen he entered the General Baptist academy at Leicester, and at the age of twenty-two he accepted an invitation to the pastorate of the General Baptist church at Praed Street in Paddington. He thus embarked on a career that was to

---

[591] I. G. Jones, 'Dr Thomas Price and the Election of 1868 in Merthyr Tydfil', *Welsh History Review*, 2 (1964–5), 149, 155, 161–2.
[592] Rees, *Protestant Nonconformity in Wales*, 485–7.   [593] *Christian World*, 28 Nov. 1918.
[594] C. T. Bateman, *John Clifford: Free Church Leader and Preacher* (1904), 17.

bring him four university degrees (two of them firsts), two honorary doctorates, national and international fame, and ultimately the Order of the Companion of Honour 'for conspicuous service of national importance'.[595] Few Nonconformist ministers attained Clifford's eminence, but very many achieved positions of importance and prestige within their own local communities, and they did so from beginnings that were just as humble.

7. 'SURELY WE ARE TO USE ORDINARY MEANS': DISSENTING ACADEMIES AND NONCONFORMIST SCHOLARSHIP

It was no coincidence that Thomas Price, John Prichard, and John Clifford all rose from lowly origins to positions of influence by way of Baptist academies. For hundreds of future Dissenting ministers the theological college was the door by which they could abandon the life of a labourer or artisan and enter the world of scholarship and learning. And for thousands of Nonconformist pastors who had little schooling the ministry was the stimulus to continuous education. If the first concern of Evangelical Dissenters was to save their souls, for many their second concern was to improve their minds.

To some Dissenters, it is true, salvation and education were incompatible objectives. In the seventeenth century the preaching cobbler Samuel How had argued that the guidance of the Holy Spirit, unencumbered by human learning, was sufficient to interpret 'the mind of God in the holy Scriptures', and his argument had been repeated by other sectaries, by the Old General Baptists, and by the Quakers.[596] In the eighteenth century the Evangelical revival brought with it further suspicion of too much learning. John Wesley himself was obliged to defend his use of lay preachers with the argument that, apart from St Paul, all the apostles were 'common, unphilosophical, unlettered men' who were more than equal to 'that great work, the saving of souls from death'.[597] When George Whitefield's scheme to establish a training college for preachers in Georgia came to nothing, the Evangelical Anglican John Berridge rejoiced that Whitefield 'was spared from becoming the father of a race of unconverted ministers'.[598] The Wesleyan John Pawson warned in

---

[595] For Clifford's career see M. R. Watts, 'John Clifford and Radical Nonconformity, 1836–1923', D.Phil. thesis (Oxford, 1966).

[596] Watts, *The Dissenters*, i. 69–70, 192; W. T. Whitley (ed.), *Minutes of the General Assembly of the General Baptist Churches in England* (1909–10), i. 12.

[597] Elliott, 'Protestant Denominations in Leeds', 405.

[598] A. D. Belden, *George Whitefield: The Awakener* (2nd edn., 1953), 207.

1798 that 'erecting schools and endowing colleges' for the training of preachers meant 'taking the matter out of the hands of Christ and endeavouring to make ministers for him'. And two years later William Bramwell argued that too great a reliance on book-learning prevented the 'immediate influence of the Holy Spirit in the act of preaching'.[599]

As we have seen, Evangelical Nonconformity had particular appeal in largely illiterate communities and as a consequence some ministers who devoted themselves to learning aroused the suspicions of their congregations and of their colleagues. When Rees David accepted an invitation to the pastorate of the Norwich Particular Baptist church in 1770 several members seceded on the ground that he had been educated at the Bristol Baptist academy.[600] John Grimley, who was pastor of the General Baptist church at Loughborough from 1760 to 1787, kept his studies secret 'that he might not give offence to weak minds'.[601] And when in the 1790s the Calvinistic Methodist preacher John Elias asked the Caernarfonshire Monthly Meeting for permission to go to Manchester for six months to improve his education and to learn English, he was rebuked with the accusation that his request arose from 'the pride of my heart, and that it was the thirst of becoming a great preacher that made me think of going to school'.[602] Such attitudes fuelled opposition to the establishment of a Wesleyan theological institution in 1835, and led the Primitive Methodists to vote overwhelmingly against a proposal for a ministerial training college in 1843.[603]

The Evangelical view that education impeded the working of the Holy Spirit was, however, countered by a growing body of Dissenting opinion which, at the turn of the century, maintained that study could deepen one's knowledge of the Bible and understanding of the Christian message, and that an educated ministry was better placed than an ignorant one to defend Dissent from the assaults of Anglicans, papists, and secularists. Long before denominational colleges were either acceptable to uneducated congregations or within the reach of the overwhelming majority of ministerial candidates, scores of individual Nonconformists dedicated themselves to the pursuit of knowledge with an enthusiasm second only to their passion for saving souls. The Primitive Methodists were, apart from the Quakers, the last of the major denominations to acknowledge the need to provide their preachers with formal training, but their founder, Hugh Bourne, who left school at the age of twelve, taught himself Hebrew, Greek, Latin, and French, and

---

[599] Werner, *Primitive Methodist Connexion*, 17.
[600] *Baptist Quarterly*, 10 (1940–1), 285.   [601] Wood, *History of the General Baptists*, 198.
[602] Morgan, *Memoir of John Elias*, 19.
[603] Morris, 'Primitive Methodism in Nottinghamshire', 217.

wrote a substantial *Ecclesiastical History*.[604] John Elias, frustrated in his attempt to secure an education in England, had no schooling except a few months under Evan Richardson at Caernarfon, but none the less he 'attained some proficiency in the English language', 'toiled hard day and night in order to know something of Greek and Hebrew', and 'made extraordinary efforts to enrich his mind with useful knowledge, such as history [and] science'.[605] The Wesleyan local preacher Samuel Drew was taken from his St Austell school at the age of eight so that he could contribute to his family's income by working in a stamping-mill attached to a nearby tin mine. At the age of ten he was apprenticed to a shoemaker, tried to educate himself by reading at every meal, and subsequently earned fame as the author of an *Essay on the Immateriality and Immortality of the Human Soul* and of a *History of Cornwall*, and was rewarded with an MA degree from Marischal College, Aberdeen.[606] The Unitarian missionary Richard Wright 'never enjoyed the advantages of a regular education', but taught himself 'the dead languages' to enable him 'to examine any text in the Septuagint, or in the Greek New Testament'.[607] The General Baptist Thomas Goadby was, in his youth, apprenticed to a grocer in Leicester, and rose between four and five o'clock in the morning to read Virgil before the shop opened, and after closing time he would read a page of Latin, two of Greek, and thirty pages of Johnson's *Lives of the Poets*.[608] He was later president of the General Baptist College and was awarded two doctorates by American universities. The Congregationalist Thomas Binney worked for seven years in a bookshop in Newcastle upon Tyne from seven o'clock in the morning until seven o'clock in the evening, but he went on 'two evenings in the week to an old Presbyterian' minister and learned enough Latin and Greek to enable him to read Caesar and the Gospel of St John in their original tongues.[609] Rhys Pryse, the pastor of the Cwmllynfell Independent church on the border of Glamorgan and Carmarthenshire, claimed that he had attended school for only three days 'because the old cottage where the school was held was burnt before the fourth day had dawned'. None the less he taught himself to read English, Greek, Latin, and Hebrew, and studied both astronomy and botany.[610] Another Welsh Independent, Thomas Rees, had only three months' schooling, but despite his lack of scholarly training produced his

---

[604] Wilkinson, *Hugh Bourne*, 193–4.   [605] Jones, *The Great Preachers of Wales*, 279.
[606] J. H. Drew, *Life of Samuel Drew* (1834), 25–6, 30, 83–4, 140, 243, 286.
[607] Wright, *Missionary Life and Labors*, 127–8.
[608] Harrison, 'Baptists of Nottinghamshire', i. 491.
[609] E. Paxton Hood, *Thomas Binney* (1874), 3.
[610] Evans, 'Religion in the Swansea Valley', 258–60.

Hanes Eglwysi Annibynol Cwmru, one of the best histories of any Welsh denomination and, despite the fact that his knowledge of English was 'acquired after the twentieth year of his age, without the assistance of any tutor', wrote his *History of Protestant Nonconformity in Wales*, which remains, over a hundred years later, the best one-volume work on the subject.[611] Most remarkable of all was the career of John Jenkins, born in 1779 the son of a labourer of Llangynidr in Breconshire. Employed as a farm servant in his native parish, 'John Jenkins never spent a day at school in his life, and was in the fifteenth year of his age when he began to learn the alphabet'. He took advantage of evening reading classes which were held in his village, joined the Llanwenarth Baptist church, and at the age of twenty began to preach and to learn to write. In 1808 he accepted an invitation to the pastorate of the Baptist church at Hengoed in Glamorgan at a salary of £16 a year, in 1811 he published *Gwelediad y Palas Arian* (Vision of the Silver Palace), a work of theological exposition, and between 1819 and 1831 he published his *Esponiad*, a three-volume commentary on the Bible. He was rewarded, in 1852, with a doctorate of divinity from the University of Lewisburg.[612]

In the eyes of some Dissenters, however, the enthusiasm for learning displayed by individual Nonconformists did not compensate for the lack of training for the majority of their future ministers. Abraham Booth, pastor of the Prescot Street Particular Baptist church in London, in pleading the cause of the Baptist Education Society in 1804, wrote that 'we cannot but reflect with concern on that degree of illiteracy which is sometimes observable in those who preach the gospel of Christ', and he felt that his own ministry had been hampered by his lack of education.[613] From the late seventeenth century the Presbyterians and Congregationalists had had academies of their own, some of which came to earn higher repute than either Oxford or Cambridge, and the Particular Baptists had an academy at Bristol founded in accordance with the will of Edward Terrill, an elder of the Broadmead church in the reign of Charles II, which had admitted its first students in 1720.[614] But by the 1760s most of the tutors in the Presbyterian academies, and even some in those of Congregational origin, were either Arians or Socinians, and the Bristol Baptist academy was admitting only two students a year.[615] The growth of heterodox theological views in the Dissenting academies evoked a mixed

---

[611] *DWB* 830.   [612] Rees, *Protestant Nonconformity in Wales*, 445–8; *DWB* 434.
[613] Cooper, *From Stepney to St Giles'*, 26–7.
[614] Watts, *The Dissenters*, i. 366–71; N. S. Moon, *Education for the Ministry: Bristol Baptist College, 1679–1979* (Bristol, 1979), 4.
[615] Watts, *The Dissenters*, i. 465–7; Moon, *Education for the Ministry*, 11.

response among Evangelical Dissenters: the suspicion that too much learning undermined Evangelical faith was balanced by a recognition of the need for Evangelical institutions to train men for the ministry. The ambivalent Evangelical attitude towards education was typified by the Countess of Huntingdon. On the one hand she founded, in 1768, a college at Trevecca to train preachers, and on the other she discouraged her students from learning Greek and Hebrew lest they be deflected from their task of saving souls.[616] Initially Trevecca College was intended to prepare men for both the Anglican and Nonconformist ministries, but after the college moved to Cheshunt in Hertfordshire in 1792 its students increasingly found their way into Congregational pastorates.[617]

Congregationalists had always been less sceptical than the Baptists or Methodists of the value of an educated ministry, and it was they who took the lead in disputing the dominant position which heterodox tutors had achieved in the education of prospective Dissenting pastors. In 1730 the King's Head Society was formed to promote the education of future ministers in Calvinist doctrines, and from 1754 the society, together with the Congregational Fund Board, supported students at the academy run by John Conder at Mile End in east London. In 1768 the academy moved to Homerton and achieved its greatest influence under the principalship of John Pye Smith from 1806 to 1850.[618] The Congregational Fund and King's Head Society also supported students at the Western academy which was originally founded in 1751 and which for the next century followed its tutors round various West Country towns, settling in Exeter in 1828 and Plymouth in 1845.[619] And for prospective Congregational ministers in the north the Northern Education Society was founded in 1756 to dispel 'the cloud of Socinian darkness then spreading over the northern counties of England' by supporting students at James Scott's Heckmondwike academy. After Scott's death in 1783 the academy declined under his successor Samuel Walker at Northowram, but after the demise of the Northowram academy in 1794 two new Congregational colleges arose from its ashes: at Rotherham and at Idle. Congregationalists were conscious that Idle was not the happiest name for an academic institution and in 1833 the academy moved to Bradford as the Airedale Independent College.[620] Among the students educated by Scott at Heckmondwike was Robert

---

[616] G. F. Nuttall, *The Significance of Trevecca College* (1968), 7.
[617] Bennett, *History of Dissenters during the last Thirty Years*, 138–9.
[618] Jones, *Congregationalism in England*, 140, 176.
[619] Ibid. 238; Bogue and Bennett, *History of Dissenters*, iv. 273–6.
[620] Miall, *Congregationalism in Yorkshire*, 147–9, 164–8; Jones, *Congregationalism in England*, 177, 237.

Simpson, who in 1790 was appointed tutor at the academy in Mile End which had been founded in 1781 under the auspices of the Societas Evangelica.[621] The Mile End academy moved to Hoxton in 1791, and under Simpson's presidency and Thomas Wilson's treasurership it became the most successful of all the Congregational colleges. By 1814 Hoxton had forty students and these numbers were largely maintained when the college moved to Highbury in 1826.[622] In 1850 Highbury merged with Homerton and with the less successful Coward College to form New College in St John's Wood. The academy at Gosport, founded in 1789 by the Congregational minister, historian, and missionary advocate David Bogue, became after 1800 primarily a training college for missionaries and did not long survive Bogue's death in 1825.[623] But by the mid-nineteenth century three additional Congregational colleges had been founded, at Blackburn (1816, moved to Manchester 1843), Spring Hill, Birmingham (1838), and Bala (1841).

Though the Particular Baptists had more slender financial resources than the Congregationalists, and included in their membership a larger number of men opposed to an educated ministry, they, too, by the early decades of the nineteenth century had begun to make greatly improved provision for the training of their pastors. The expansion of the Bristol Baptist academy began in 1770 with the founding, by the father and son Hugh and Caleb Evans, of the Bristol Education Society. 'Are we to expect miracles, as in the Apostolic age, to qualify us for the work of the ministry', asked Hugh and Caleb Evans in appealing for funds, 'or are we to use ordinary means?' Rejecting the convictions of the Quakers, of Methodists such as William Bramwell, and of many of their fellow Baptists, they assumed that 'That we are not to expect miracles all will allow'. And if they were not to expect miracles, 'then surely we are to use ordinary means'.[624] Their appeal raised £470, including a hundred guineas from the wealthy tea-merchant Frederick Bull, a member of Abraham Booth's church in Prescot Street. Bull, a supporter of John Wilkes, was to become Lord Mayor of London in 1774 and was MP for the City from 1773 until his death in 1784 when he bequeathed 1,000 guineas to the Bristol academy.[625] The college's buildings, designed by the architect of Dartmoor

    [621] Miall, *Congregationalism in Yorkshire*, 152.
    [622] Jones, *Congregationalism in England*, 177–8; Bennett, *The History of Dissenters during the last Thirty Years*, 124.
    [623] C. Terpstra, 'David Bogue, 1750–1825: Pioneer and Missionary Educator', Ph.D. thesis (Edinburgh, 1959), *passim*.
    [624] Moon, *Education for the Ministry*, 11–12, 130.
    [625] Ibid. 12, 16; Robison, 'Particular Baptists', 183; G. Rudé, *Wilkes and Liberty* (Oxford, 1962), 5 n., 41 n., 169–70.

prison, looked to one student like the wing of a gaol,[626] but it boasted a fine library, equal 'to that of any private academy in the kingdom'. The college owed the treasures of its library to two further legacies from distinguished Baptists who died in 1783 and 1784: the classical scholar Thomas Llewellyn and Andrew Gifford, who for fifty-four years was pastor of the Eagle Street church in London and for twenty-seven years assistant librarian in the British Museum. Gifford's legacy included the only known complete copy of the first edition of William Tyndale's translation of the New Testament, printed in 1525.[627] Under the principalship of John Ryland (1792–1825) the number of students educated at the Bristol academy averaged twenty a year,[628] and the college achieved the position among Baptists that Hoxton and Highbury attained among Congregationalists.

A second Particular Baptist academy was founded at Horton, near Bradford, in 1805 under the presidency of William Steadman and two years later an academy for Welsh Baptists was established under Micah Thomas at Abergavenny. A London academy followed in 1811 as a result of the donations of William Taylor, a wealthy hosier and another member of the Prescot Street church. In 1809, at the age of eighty-one, Taylor put in trust £7,265 for 'the relief of ministers' and for 'the education of young persons for the ministry' and gave a further £3,600 for the purchase of two large houses at Stepney Green in east London.[629] The Stepney Green academy was educating nineteen students in 1830 and twenty-six in 1840, and although there was a drastic fall in numbers in the next decade, the college's fortunes revived with the appointment of Joseph Angus as president in 1840 and with its removal to Holford House, Regent's Park, in 1856.[630] The General Baptists, too, had an academy in London in the early years of the nineteenth century, founded in 1798 by Dan Taylor, the father of the New Connexion, and initially situated in the Mile End Road. However, the strength of the New Connexion in the east Midlands dictated that the academy be removed to Wisbech in Cambridgeshire in 1813, a second academy was founded at Loughborough in 1825, and in 1838 the two institutions were amalgamated and five years later moved to Leicester.[631]

The Methodists were the most reluctant of the major Nonconformist groups, apart from the Quakers, to admit the need of college education for their ministers. The fact that the absence of formal ministerial training had not prevented—and indeed may well have assisted—the rise and expansion

---

[626] F. Trestrail, *Reminiscences of College Life in Bristol* (c.1879), 9.
[627] Moon, *Education for the Ministry*, 16–17.   [628] Ibid. 30.
[629] Cooper, *From Stepney to St Giles'*, 27–8, 30.   [630] Ibid. 49, 56, 60.
[631] Wood, *History of the General Baptists of the New Connexion*, 302–8.

of the largest Nonconformist denominations in both England and Wales (the Wesleyans and the Calvinistic Methodists) was a powerful argument against setting up human learning rather than the inspiration of the Holy Spirit as the qualification for the Methodist ministry. However, those Methodist preachers who had received formal education were embarrassed by the ignorance of the majority who had not, and they were worried by the effect that illiterate preachers were having on the educated members of their congregations. Adam Clarke, the most scholarly Wesleyan of his generation, argued in 1806 that the time was coming 'when illiterate piety can do no more for the interest and permanency of the work of God than lettered irreligion did formerly'.[632] And twenty years later Joseph Sutcliffe, superintendent in the Bath circuit, pointed out to Jabez Bunting that 'all our people in trade now give a boarding school education to their children and an unlettered pastor with a provincial dialect sounds but ungracious on their ear'.[633] From 1802 the Wesleyan Conference insisted that candidates for the itinerant ministry be examined orally by their District Meeting, and from 1815 preachers on trial were required to provide a list of the books they had read since the last District Meeting.[634] The memoirs of Benjamin Gregory suggest that these examinations were more than a formality and could be nerve-racking experiences for young probationers. But the scrutiny of their book lists was designed to protect orthodoxy rather than promote academic excellence, and Gregory noted that while there was 'no *pre*scribed reading for probationers . . . there was much *pro*scribed reading'.[635]

Nothing more substantial was done for the education of Wesleyan preachers until 1833 when a committee appointed by Conference recommended the setting up of a 'theological institution' or college. The proposal was hotly contested in the Conference of 1834. James Wood, the oldest member of Conference who had been twice president and a preacher for sixty-one years, denounced the idea as 'the greatest evil ever admitted into Methodism'. Technical scholarship and linguistic proficiency, he feared, would come to be regarded as of greater importance than the 'saving doctrines which for near a hundred years had done the work of Methodism'.[636] But the theological institution was approved by Conference with only 31 dissenting votes and though

[632] J. W. Etheridge, *The Life of the Rev. Adam Clarke* (1858), 208.
[633] W. R. Ward (ed.), *The Early Correspondence of Jabez Bunting*, Camden Fourth Series, xi (1972), 192.
[634] Bowmer, *Pastor and People*, 90–1.
[635] B. Gregory, *Autobiographical Recollections* (1903), 251–2, 314.
[636] Gregory, *Side Lights*, 172–3.

the issue was the occasion of the formation of the secessionist Wesleyan Methodist Association, it was not the cause.[637]

Initially the Wesleyan theological institution occupied the premises of the old Congregational Hoxton academy, but the centenary of the founding of the first Wesleyan society in 1739 provided Conference with the opportunity of launching a major appeal for funds both for the establishment of head-quarters for the Wesleyan Missionary Society in London and for the training of ministers. The Centenary Fund raised £216,184, of which £71,600 was allo-cated to the building of a northern college at Didsbury in Manchester in 1842 and of a southern college at Richmond in Surrey in 1843.[638] The Calvinistic Methodists founded two theological colleges at the same time, at Bala in 1837 and at Trevecca in 1842; the Methodist New Connexion opened a college at Ranmoor, Sheffield, in 1864; and in the following year one of the last bastions of an untrained ministry fell when the Primitive Methodist Conference voted to make provision for the education of 'twenty students intended for the min-istry'.[639]

By 1838, when James Bennett wrote his *History of Dissenters during the last Thirty Years* and surveyed the state of the Nonconformist academies, there were eighteen such institutions in England and Wales, of which nine were Congregational, four Particular Baptist, two Presbyterian/Unitarian, one General Baptist, one Wesleyan, and one Calvinistic Methodist.[640] There were also three interdenominational colleges, at Hackney, Cheshunt, and Newport Pagnell, which were open to Anglicans as well as to Dissenters but which in practice were providing pastors largely for Congregational churches. The Congregationalists also benefited most from the Presbyterian academy at Carmarthen which was open both to Unitarians and to Calvinists: by 1850 all the students in the academy, apart from one, was an Independent, and that one exception was a Baptist.[641] The Presbyterian/Unitarians who had dominated the higher education of Dissenters in the eighteenth century had in effect only one academy left: Manchester College, which had been founded in that town in 1786, had moved to York in 1803, returned to Manchester in 1840, and in 1853 settled in University Hall, London, now the home of Dr Williams's Library.[642]

---

[637] See below, Ch. IV, sect. 2.   [638] Bunting and Rowe, *Life of Jabez Bunting*, 669–71.
[639] G. Packer (ed.), *The Centenary of the Methodist New Connexion* (1897), 139–43; Kendall, *Primitive Methodist Church*, ii. 526.
[640] Bennett, *History of Dissenters during the last Thirty Years*, 129–96.
[641] Ibid. 178–9; H. P. Roberts, 'History of the Presbyterian Academy, Carmarthen', *TUHS* 5 (1931–4), 24–35.
[642] V. D. Davis, *A History of Manchester College* (1932); Barbara Smith, *Truth, Liberty, Religion: Essays Celebrating Two Hundred Years of Manchester College* (Oxford, 1986).

The quality of the teaching and the facilities for study provided by the Dissenting academies varied as much in the nineteenth as they had in the previous century. At their best they offered their students a wide-ranging and, for their time, modern education. It was too much to expect that the Nonconformist colleges would free themselves entirely from the stranglehold with which the Classics gripped English education, and there was obviously justification for teaching New Testament Greek to future ministers of religion. But the better Dissenting academics did not confine their curricula to Greek and Latin but added Hebrew, philosophy, ancient and modern history, mathematics, physics, chemistry, and natural history.[643] Manchester College preserved the traditions of the more liberal eighteenth-century academies, and while at York its principal, Charles Wellbeloved, provided students with opposing viewpoints on controversial theological topics without attempting to impose on them his own opinions.[644] Manchester College also inherited the Warrington academy's emphasis on science, followed the Cambridge University syllabus on natural philosophy, and for seven years from 1793 enjoyed the services of the Quaker John Dalton. Dalton taught mathematics, natural philosophy, and chemistry, and was subsequently to earn fame as the author of the atomic theory.[645] But the college's outstanding tutor was John Kenrick, who was Classics tutor from 1810 to 1840, professor of history from 1840 to 1850, and also principal from 1846 to 1850. Kenrick earned the admiration of his students for breathing life into the Classics by placing his texts in their historic context, taught French, German, and modern history, and published numerous scholarly works including a two-volume history of *Ancient Egypt under the Pharaohs*.[646]

Too many of the early nineteenth-century Dissenting academies, however, continued to suffer from the limitations of their eighteenth-century predecessors: they were often dependent on one or two tutors who themselves had pastoral oversight of local churches, and as a result some academies still moved from town to town in search of tutors rather than remaining on permanent sites. Their curricula were often limited, their libraries inadequate, and they failed to stretch the minds of their more able students. Bogue and Bennett argued in 1812 that some Evangelical academies were bedevilled by a continuing suspicion of academic studies and consequently provided their

---

[643] E. A. Payne, 'Nonconformist Theological Education', in E. A. Payne, *Studies in History and Religion* (1942), 235–8.

[644] J. Kenrick, *Biographical Memoir of the late Rev. Charles Wellbeloved* (1860), 101–2.

[645] Davis, *Manchester College*, 63, 77.

[646] R. Watts, 'Manchester College and Education, 1786–1853', in Smith, *Truth, Liberty, Religion*, 90–2; Davis, *Manchester College*, 88–90.

students with only 'a half education'.[647] They were no doubt thinking of the interdenominational Hackney College which had been founded in 1803 to provide 'a slight and economical course of instruction . . . designed to prepare itinerants to publish the unsearchable riches of Christ to the poor', and so excluded 'the dead languages' except in so far as they were of use in understanding the Bible.[648] But David Bogue's own academy at Gosport was criticized by one of his former students, John Angell James, for its low academic standards. James looked back on his time at Gosport with 'much astonishment and deep regret'. To enter the academy he passed no examination 'as to piety, talents, or acquirements'; Dr Bogue's skills were restricted to theology; his students' 'literary advantages . . . were of a most slender kind'; and James strongly advised his younger brother against going to Gosport.[649] The experiences of the author of *The Autobiography of a Dissenting Minister* were similar. His college, which was reputed to be one of the more learned Dissenting institutions, did have examinations, but those exercises consisted of the tutor informing the students in advance not only of the examination questions but also of the answers to those questions! All that was required of the students to pass their examinations was that they learn the answers by heart.[650] At Cheshunt the tutors believed that the essence of a good education consisted in 'the regular drilling in . . . facts of learning', and admitted that the same lectures were delivered unchanged year after year.[651] At the Bristol Baptist College in the 1820s the principal, Thomas Crisp, read out his lectures slowly to enable the students to write them down verbatim and in the examinations 'looked rather for an exact repetition of what he had said' than for the students' own thoughts.[652] Even at Hoxton Richard Winter Hamilton, after the schooling he had received at Mill Hill, found that the lectures were 'too easy' and that mathematics were 'taught in a very limited and desultory way'.[653]

If the poorer Dissenting academies were criticized for their narrow curricula, ill-equipped tutors, and low academic standards, the better ones were frequently reproached for being over-ambitious and for placing too heavy a burden on staff and students alike. When John Pye Smith became resident tutor at Homerton College in 1801 he gave an inaugural address in which he outlined the courses he proposed to teach over the next four years: natural philosophy, which would include the history of philosophical knowledge,

---

[647] Bogue and Bennett, *History of Dissenters*, iv. 299.   [648] Ibid. iv. 268.
[649] Dale, *John Angell James*, 51–2.   [650] *Autobiography of a Dissenting Minister*, 22–3.
[651] Brown, *History of the Nonconformist Ministry*, 76–7.
[652] Trestrail, *Reminiscences of College Life*, 21.
[653] Stowell, *Memoir of Richard Winter Hamilton*, 59.

mechanics, hydrostatics, pneumatics, acoustics, optics, magnetism, and electricity; 'a general view of chemistry' and natural history, including the physiology of animal bodies, 'a more particular description of the human frame', the botanical system of Linnaeus; geology and mineralogy; astronomy, the use of globes, and geography; the art of logic, ontology, and the philosophy of the human mind; the art of composition and rhetoric; the study and use of history; mathematics, including geometry, trigonometry, 'and some properties of ionic sections'; the Greek New Testament; the Hebrew language; and the Classical languages in the works of Homer, Xenophon, Epictetus, Cicero, Virgil, Horace, and Juvenal.[654] It is perhaps not surprising that Mrs Pye Smith found marriage to a Dissenting college tutor unbearable! When Manchester College moved to York in 1803 the burden of teaching a similar syllabus fell entirely on the shoulders of the principal Charles Wellbeloved, and even after the appointment of Hugh Kerr as Classical and mathematical tutor in February 1804 Wellbeloved was forced to give four or five lectures a day for five days a week and on Saturdays to prepare his sermon for the following Sunday. Wellbeloved's health collapsed under the strain in 1807 and again in 1809 and relief did not come until 1809–10 with the appointment of two additional lecturers.[655]

By the middle of the century the situation had improved considerably, with most colleges established on secure foundations and employing several members of staff. R. W. Dale, writing in 1861, rejoiced that the days were largely gone when 'a few candidates for the ministry . . . gathered under the roof of a laborious man who [occupied] at the same time the pulpit and the professor's chair', and whose courses ranged from original sin to Jupiter's satellites, and from 'Tacitus to the principles of church polity'.[656] Academic standards, too, were rising. The Baptist college at Stepney insisted in 1828 that 'candidates entering the college must be able to read both Virgil and the New Testament in the original'.[657] Ten years later when the new Congregational college was opened at Spring Hill, Birmingham, it stipulated that no student be admitted, 'except under very special circumstances', without passing an examination in 'the elements of the Hebrew language', 'a few select authors of Greek and Roman literature', 'ancient geography and history', and 'the principles of mathematical and intellectual philosophy'.[658] A further stimulus to the increasing emphasis on academic qualifications was provided by the granting of a royal charter to the University of London in

[654] Medway, *Memoirs of John Pye Smith*, 72–7.
[655] Kenrick, *Charles Wellbeloved*, 85–93; Davis, *Manchester College*, 76–8.
[656] Dale, *John Angell James*, 44.   [657] Cooper, *From Stepney to St Giles'*, 48.
[658] Bennett, *History of the Dissenters during the last Thirty Years*, 161.

1836, authorizing it to grant degrees without a religious test. From 1840 Manchester College, and from 1841 the Bristol and Stepney Baptist colleges, obtained the right to submit candidates for London University degrees, and by 1849 the students from nine Dissenting colleges were taking the university's examinations.[659] By no means all the students at Dissenting colleges could reach the standards expected by the University of London. Although the Carmarthen College started to prepare its students for the London BA in 1841, twenty years later it reported that its students had 'not attained so high a general standard as might be reasonably expected', and that it was vain to expect 'many of our students to pass the severe examinations of London University'.[660] But, for all their faults, the Dissenting colleges gave to the future ministers they trained one clear advantage over their Anglican counterparts: a firm grounding in biblical knowledge and theological studies. While, in the first half of the nineteenth century, the majority of Anglican ordinands graduated at either Oxford or Cambridge, their education was based largely on the Classics and they left university without having received either formal education in theology or vocational training in the ministry.[661] 'England was probably the sole country in Christendom', wrote Halévy, 'where no proof of theological knowledge was exacted from candidates for ordination.'[662] Bogue and Bennett quoted the opinion of an Oxford graduate that a student educated at Cheshunt, which was hardly renowned for its scholarship, was 'ten times a better Biblical scholar than usually goes from our universities'.[663] The same could have been said of the products of any of the Dissenting colleges.

There can be little doubt that those Dissenting ministers who received a college education were better prepared for their future careers than were Anglican clergymen. The same may well have been true of many of the Dissenting laity, but not because they had access to institutions of higher education but because they were excluded from them. Until the establishment of University College, London, in 1828 and the granting of its charter in 1836 Dissenting laymen were largely debarred from higher education. Students matriculating at Oxford and graduating at Cambridge were required to conform to the Church of England, and although the sons of a few wealthy

[659] Davis, *History of Manchester College*, 98; Moon, *Education for the Ministry*, 44; Cooper, *From Stepney to St Giles'*, 51; A. C. Whitby, 'Matthew Arnold and the Nonconformists', B.Litt. thesis (Oxford, 1954), 114.

[660] H. P. Roberts, 'History of the Presbyterian Academy, Carmarthen', *TUHS* 5 (1931–4), 28–32.

[661] Haig, *The Victorian Clergy*, 27, 72–9.

[662] E. Halévy, *A History of the English People in 1815* (1924), 342.

[663] Bogue and Bennett, *History of Dissenters*, iv. 306.

Dissenters did study at Cambridge without taking their degrees, the older English universities were effectively closed to Nonconformists. Some Dissenters went to Scottish universities, but these were mainly a few select products of the Warrington and Manchester Unitarian colleges and students of the Bristol and Stepney Baptist colleges who won scholarships under the trust bequeathed by Dr John Ward, professor of rhetoric at Gresham College, London, in 1754.[664] Manchester College was unique among early nineteenth-century Dissenting academies in admitting both men destined for the ministry and men who contemplated secular careers, and indeed the fees from the latter subsidized the education of the former. From its foundation in 1786 until its move to London in 1853 over 60 per cent of the students of Manchester College were destined for secular careers, but since the fees were from eighty to a hundred guineas a session they were drawn overwhelmingly from wealthy Unitarian families.[665] Before 1828 higher education was largely out of the question for the sons of even the most prosperous orthodox Dissenters if those sons did not wish to enter the ministry. The younger Robert Hall, a Particular Baptist, complained in 1791 that the establishment's refusal to allow the sons of Dissenters to enter Oxford and Cambridge meant that the intellectual gulf between ministers and laity was greater among Nonconformists than in the established church.[666] The son and biographer of the Congregational philanthropist Thomas Wilson, commenting on his father's limited education, observed that orthodox Dissenters had 'greatly mistaken their interest . . . in making no provision for the academical training of those of their young men who were destined to the pursuits of trade, manufactures, and commerce'.[667] The exclusion of the Dissenting laity from higher education limited their intellectual horizons, thwarted much of their political activity, and provided some substance for Matthew Arnold's accusation of 'philistinism'. But it seems certain that it benefited rather than hindered their business success, and so made possible Thomas Wilson's wealth and his benefactions.[668]

Of all the Dissenters, apart from the Quakers, the Unitarians were the most successful in the field of business, and of all the Dissenters they were the most determined to use the wealth gained from commerce and industry to further the pursuit of knowledge. As the Presbyterians evolved from

---

[664] Underwood, *History of the English Baptists*, 143–4, 234–6; Cooper, *From Stepney to St Giles'*, 24; R. Brown, *The English Baptists of the Eighteenth Century* (1986), 83–4.
[665] Watts, 'Manchester College and Education', in Smith, *Truth, Liberty, Religion*, 96; Seed, 'Unitarianism and Liberal Culture', 252, 262–3.
[666] R. Hall, *Christianity consistent with a Love of Freedom* (1791), 28.
[667] Wilson, *Memoir of Thomas Wilson*, 94.   [668] See below, Ch. II, sect. 10.

Arminianism through Arianism to Socinianism so their concern for the salvation of man's immortal soul receded and the dynamic of their religion was transferred to the improvement of man's life here on earth.[669] The enthusiasm with which Unitarian ministers threw themselves into 'social, educational, literary, municipal and civic work', noted Henry Solly, arose from their 'deep convictions as to the duty of helping to cause the will of God to be "done on earth as it is in heaven", and not merely to "save men's souls" '.[670] Since the Unitarians could not proclaim that theirs was the only way to salvation, education came to fill the central place that conversion occupied in the minds of orthodox Dissenters. And just as Evangelical Dissenters formed associations to evangelize their fellow men, so Unitarians founded societies to further the pursuit of knowledge and to convert others to their intellectual enthusiasms. In the closing decades of the eighteenth century and the first half of the nineteenth century in towns throughout northern England the Unitarians constituted an energetic, questing, forward-looking intellectual aristocracy. They founded circulating and chapel libraries, Literary and Philosophical Societies, Mechanics' Institutes, and Statistical Societies. In Liverpool a group of radical intellectuals, mainly Presbyterians *en route* to Unitarianism, started the town's first circulating library in 1758, established a literary society in 1785, founded the Athenæum in 1797, the Botanic Gardens in 1802, the Literary and Philosophical Society in 1812, and in 1817 the Royal Institution 'for the promotion of literature, science, and the arts'.[671] The first chairman of Liverpool's Royal Institution was the town's most distinguished Unitarian, William Roscoe, a largely self-educated attorney whose enthusiasm for Italian art led him to write a widely acclaimed *Life of Lorenzo de Medici*, first published in 1796 and subsequently translated into French, German, and Italian. Roscoe believed that the English cities of the industrial revolution, like the Italian cities of the Renaissance, were witnessing 'the beneficial influence which commerce and literature have on each other', and that under his leadership and that of his fellow Unitarians Liverpool could become a second Florence.[672]

The same combination of civic pride and enthusiasm for learning inspired Unitarians in other towns. In Manchester the Literary and Philosophical Society (founded in 1781) originated in meetings held in the home of

[669] The secularization of the Unitarians' religious impulse is one of the themes of John Seed's University of Hull Ph.D. thesis, 'The Role of Unitarianism in the formation of Liberal Culture, 1775–1851' (1981).

[670] Solly, *These Eighty Years*, i. 391–2.

[671] Sellers, 'Liverpool Nonconformity', 251; H. Roscoe, *Life of William Roscoe* (1833), ii. 153.

[672] J. R. Hale, *England and the Italian Renaissance* (1954), 84–107.

Dr Thomas Percival, a former student of Warrington academy who had gone on to study medicine at Edinburgh and Leiden. Percival was one of the first medical men to advocate *The Use of Cod-Liver Oil* as a cure for rheumatism (1789)[673] and was largely responsible for the creation of the Manchester Board of Health in 1796. He was a trustee of the Cross Street Presbyterian meeting, then under the pastoral care of the Arian Thomas Barnes. Over a third of the Literary and Philosophical Society's members were connected with Cross Street in the 1780s, and until 1799 the society met on its premises with Percival as its first joint president and Barnes as its first vice-president and, for a time, its secretary.[674] Another member of Cross Street, Dr Edward Holme, was first president of the Manchester Natural History Society (1821) and of the Chetham (local history) Society (1844), while his fellow Cross Street member, the banker Benjamin Heywood who was briefly MP for Lancashire from 1831 to 1832, was the first president of the Manchester Mechanics' Institute (1824) and acted as host to the inaugural meeting of the Manchester Statistical Society.[675] George William Wood, who was treasurer of Manchester College, York, for thirty-five years and MP successively for South Lancashire and Kendal, was the chief instigator of the Royal Manchester Institution, founded in 1832 to foster science and the arts.[676] In York the principal of Manchester College, Charles Wellbeloved, was a leading supporter of the Philosophical Society, was from 1823 the curator of its antiquaries, in 1827 helped to found the York Mechanics' Institute, and after his retirement from his college devoted himself to the writing of *Eburacum: Or York under the Romans* (1842).[677] In Sheffield one of Wellbeloved's pupils, the Unitarian minister Joseph Hunter, was secretary of the Society for the Promotion of Useful Knowledge.[678] In Merthyr Tydfil Unitarians were the mainstay of the Cyfartha Philosophical Society, founded in 1807 with sixty members who subscribed a guinea each to buy astronomical books and instruments.[679] In Birmingham the Unitarian solicitor Joseph Parkes was the

[673] E. C. Cripps, *Plough Court: The Story of a Notable Pharmacy* (1927), 101–2.

[674] T. Baker, *Memorials of a Dissenting Chapel* (1884), 87–8; H. McLachlan, *The Unitarian Movement in the Religious Life of England* (1933), 143; Seed, 'Unitarianism and Liberal Culture', 316; A. Goodwin, *The Friends of Liberty* (1979), 143; V. A. C. Gatrell, 'Incorporation and the Pursuit of Liberal Hegemony in Manchester', in D. Fraser (ed.), *Municipal Reform and the Industrial City* (Leicester, 1982), 29.

[675] McLachlan, *Unitarian Movement*, 143; Seed, 'Unitarianism and Liberal Culture', 318.

[676] J. Raymond and J. V. Pickstone, 'The Natural Sciences and the Learning of the English Unitarians', in Smith, *Truth, Liberty, Religion*, 144–5.

[677] Kenrick, *Memoir of Charles Wellbeloved*, 162–5, 209.

[678] A. E. Musson, *Science and Technology in the Industrial Revolution* (Manchester, 1969), 148.

[679] Williams, *History of Merthyr Tydfil*, 269–70.

moving spirit behind the foundation in 1825 of the Mechanics' Institute and served as its first secretary.[680] In Hull it was another Unitarian, George Lee, the editor of the *Hull Rockingham*, who inspired the foundation of the town's Mechanics' Institute in 1833 and became its first president.[681] And in Nottingham the Unitarian George Gill gave £1,000 in 1846 towards the founding of the People's College to provide 'day schooling for boys and girls and evening classes for adults'.[682]

Two Unitarian ministers followed Priestley in making a distinctive contribution to the spread of scientific information. William Turner, another product of Warrington academy and a graduate of Glasgow University, was minister of the Hanover Square meeting, Newcastle upon Tyne, from 1782 to 1841. During his long pastorate he helped to found Newcastle's Royal Jubilee School (1810) and its Mechanics' Institute (1824), but the chief focus of his interest was the Literary and Philosophical Society which he founded in 1793. One of the chief objects of the Philosophical Society, in Turner's eyes, was the stimulation of interest in scientific research which would benefit the local coal and lead-mining industries. In 1803 he was appointed by the society to a permanent lectureship and in the next thirty years gave over six hundred lectures on science and technology, rendered George Stephenson 'valuable assistance and instruction' in the design of his first steam-engine, and also assisted Stephenson with his experiments on a new safety-lamp for miners.[683] Equally devoted to scientific research was James Yates, the son of John Yates, the wealthy minister of Paradise Street Presbyterian meeting, Liverpool. James Yates was educated at Charles Wellbeloved's Manchester College and, like William Turner, at Glasgow University, and was successively minister to Unitarian congregations in Glasgow, Birmingham New Meeting, and Little Carter Lane, Doctors' Commons, London. In 1819 he was elected Fellow of the Geological Society, in whose transactions he published several papers, and two years later he was elected Fellow of the Linnaean Society. He was a founder-member of the British Association for the Advancement of Science, the first secretary to its council (1831), and, having retired from the ministry in 1834, was elected Fellow of the Royal Society five years later.[684]

[680] J. K. Buckley, *Joseph Parkes of Birmingham* (1926), 21–2.
[681] R. W. Ram, 'The Political Activities of Dissenters in the East and West Ridings of Yorkshire, 1815–50', MA thesis (Hull, 1964), 65.
[682] R. A. Church, *Economic and Social Change in a Midland Town: Victorian Nottingham, 1815–1900* (1966), 314.
[683] Musson, *Science and Technology*, 159–60; Seed, 'Unitarianism and Liberal Culture', 311–13.
[684] S. A. T. Yates, *Memorials of the Family of the Rev John Yates* (1890), 24–36.

Yates was also an enthusiastic advocate, and subsequent benefactor, of an undenominational university in London, a scheme which in the 1820s united both Unitarian and orthodox Dissenters.[685] The Congregationalist David Bogue had in 1812 suggested the establishment of a university 'in a central part of England, upon a liberal plan, open to all denominations, Christians and Jews', and thirteen years later a committee of Dissenters was set up under the chairmanship of the Baptist Francis Cox to implement the proposal. Cox's committee was subsequently approached by the poet Thomas Campbell, who was also canvassing the idea of an unsectarian university in London, and the two groups joined forces in April 1825.[686] When the first council of University College, London, was appointed in February 1826 it included four Dissenters, and Cox acted as the university's first clerk and its first librarian.[687]

Orthodox Dissenters also played a part in founding public libraries and in supporting Mechanics' Institutes, though they were not as active as Unitarians. The establishment of the public library in Wolverhampton in 1795 was the result of a movement led by members of the Temple Street Congregational church, and forty years later John Roaf, the minister of the Queen Street Congregational church, helped to found the Wolverhampton Mechanics' Institute.[688] The launching of the Mechanics' Institute in Leeds in 1824 owed much to the advocacy of Edward Baines's *Leeds Mercury* and in subsequent years it received support from Baptist and Congregational as well as from Unitarian ministers.[689] The Mechanics' Institute in Bradford was founded in 1832 by a group of Dissenters of whom the Baptists were the most prominent.[690] In Nottingham the Mechanics' Institute, founded in 1837, was supported equally by the Unitarian Thomas Wakefield, the Quaker Samuel Fox, the Baptists William Vickers and John Rogers, and the Congregationalist Richard Morley.[691] In London in 1841 the Prescot Street Particular Baptist church established an institute which collected a library of over seven hundred volumes, provided lectures 'on philosophical and literary subjects', and organized classes in mathematics, history, geography, essay writing, and German.[692] The People's College in Sheffield was founded in

[685] H. H. Bellot, *University College, London, 1826–1926* (1929), 24.
[686] Ibid. 20, 24.   [687] Ibid. 29, 45, 66, 213.
[688] Cumberland, 'Nonconformity in the Black Country', 160; W. H. Jones, *Congregational Churches of Wolverhampton* (1894), 13, 144.
[689] J. F. C. Harrison, *Living and Learning, 1790–1960* (1961), 58–9, 176.
[690] D. G. Wright and J. A. Jowitt (eds.), *Victorian Bradford* (1982), 42; T. Koditschek, *Class Formation and Urban-industrial Society: Bradford, 1750–1850* (Cambridge, 1991), 308.
[691] Church, *Economic and Social Change in a Midland Town*, 313–14.
[692] E. F. Kevan, *London's Oldest Baptist Church* (1933), 145–6.

1842 by Robert Slater Bayley, minister of the Howard Street Congregational church, in order to raise the social and political status of working-class men.[693] And the foundation of the Liverpool public library and museum in 1852 was largely the result of the initiative of James Picton, a founder of the Wesleyan Methodist Association in Liverpool and subsequently a worshipper at Wavertree Independent chapel.[694] The Wesleyans themselves sufficiently overcame their suspicion of secular learning to found Mutual Improvement Societies. A Wesleyan Literary and Scientific Institution was formed in Truro in 1838, and six years later Wesley chapel in Nottingham established a Mutual Improvement Society.[695] And while Unitarians continued to make a distinctive contribution to the dissemination of scientific knowledge, orthodox Dissenters contributed to historical scholarship. As early as 1711 the minister of the Horsleydown Particular Baptist church in Southwark, Benjamin Stinton, had begun collecting materials for a history of the Baptists and these were used by his brother-in-law Thomas Crosby for the four volumes of his *History of the English Baptists*, published between 1738 and 1740. Crosby's work was brought up to date by Joseph Ivimey, minister of the Eagle Street Particular Baptist church in London, in his own four-volume work published between 1811 and 1830; Joshua Thomas, pastor of the Particular Baptist church at Leominster from 1745 until his death in 1797, published his history of the Welsh Baptists in 1778; and in 1818 Adam Taylor, the nephew of the founder of the General Baptist New Connexion, published his *History of the English General Baptists*.[696] Best of all was the four-volume *History of Dissenters* published by the Congregationalists David Bogue and James Bennett between 1800 and 1812 and continued in a fifth volume by James Bennett up to the year 1838. After a century and a half it remains a valuable insight into the minds of orthodox Dissenters in the great age of Nonconformist expansion.

Given the reluctance with which most Methodists conceded the need to provide their ministers with formal education, it is hardly surprising that Methodists should make a less distinguished contribution to scholarship than the Old Dissenters. But the Wesleyans did produce one outstanding scholar in this period: Adam Clarke. Born in County Londonderry around 1760, the son of an Anglican schoolmaster, Clarke was converted at the age of eighteen after listening to a Methodist preacher in a local barn, and in 1782 he sailed to

[693] S. Pollard, *A History of Labour in Sheffield* (Liverpool, 1959), 36.
[694] J. A. Picton, *Sir James Picton: A Biography* (1891), 197–9, 212–13.
[695] Shaw, *Cornish Methodism*, 119; Swift, *Lively People*, 124.
[696] Baptist historiography is surveyed by B. R. White in the introduction to *The English Baptists of the Seventeenth Century* (1983), 12–20.

England to begin his career as an itinerant minister.[697] Clarke had learned Latin, Greek, and French at his father's village school and in his early years as an itinerant preacher taught himself Hebrew. In 1786 he was appointed to the Channel Islands and while there began work on a Polyglot Bible in the public library at St Helier's, Jersey, reading and collating the Hebrew, Samaritan, Chaldee, Syrian, and Vulgate versions. After his appointment to the Bristol circuit in 1798 he taught himself Persian, Arabic, and Coptic, and it was Clarke who in 1803 identified the inscription on the third side of the Rosetta stone as being in Coptic.[698] His most substantial works of scholarship were a six-volume *Bibliographical Dictionary*, giving a chronological account of the most important printed books in Latin, Greek, Hebrew, Coptic, Syriac, Chaldee, Ethiopic, Arabic, Persian, and Armenian, and a biblical commentary which it took him thirty years to complete.[699] His learning was acknowledged in 1807 and 1808 by the University of Aberdeen which awarded him successively the degrees of MA and LLD. Clarke died from cholera in August 1832, three years before the religious communion of which he was so distinguished a member finally accepted his long-argued case for the establishment of an institution for the education of its ministers.

8. 'PEACEABLE AND USEFUL MEMBERS OF SOCIETY': SCHOOLS AND SUNDAY SCHOOLS

The division of opinion between the rational Unitarians on the one hand, and the more extreme Evangelicals on the other, over the desirability of formal education for their ministers was reflected in their conflicting attitudes towards the education of children. To the Unitarians the education of young people was essential to prepare them for adult life, to guarantee that they became upright and useful citizens, to counter ignorance and bigotry, and to further the progress of the human race. The acquisition of useful knowledge was their chief concern, and while the Unitarians did not ignore religious education, religion occupied a less central place in their curricula than it did in syllabuses drawn up by schools run by the orthodox denominations.

By contrast, in the eyes of Evangelical Nonconformists the prime function of schooling was not to inform the intellect or to train the mind, but to save the soul. Susanna Wesley had brought up her own children on the principle

---

[697] Etheridge, *Life of Adam Clarke*, 32, 45.   [698] Ibid. 262, 264–71.
[699] Ibid. 291, 324.

that, since 'self-will is the root of all sin and misery', it was the Christian mother's duty to break her children's will, lest they be damned 'soul and body for ever'. She taught her children to read at the age of five, beginning with the book of Genesis, kept them at school for six hours a day, and allowed no loud talking or playing.[700] John Wesley's recommendations for the upbringing of children followed his mother's prescription, and for the school he opened at Kingswood near Bristol in 1748, partly for the children of Methodist preachers, he instituted a similar grim regime. Children between the ages of six and twelve were to be compelled to rise at four o'clock, to spend the next hour in private reading, meditation, and prayer, and to attend a religious service at five in the morning and again at seven in the evening; they were to be kept under the constant supervision of the masters; they were to fast every Friday until three o'clock in the afternoon; they were to be allowed neither games nor holidays; they were expected to read Wesley's abridged versions of Kennett's *Antiquities of Rome*, Potter's *Greek Antiquities*, and Cave's *Primitive Christianity*; they were to be taught French, Hebrew, Latin, and Greek.[701] Fortunately for the pupils, Wesley's rigorous standards were not maintained. He complained that his rules were not observed, that masters were not keeping the children under constant surveillance, that the pupils 'ran up and down the wood, and . . . fight with the colliers' children'.[702] But if formal discipline in the Evangelical schools was not always as strict as men such as Wesley would have wished, the psychological pressure exerted on young minds was relentless and frequently effective. As we have seen, children brought up in Evangelical homes and taught in orthodox Nonconformist schools were often reared on Janeway's *Token for Children* with its warning that little children who had lied or broken the Sabbath and who died unconverted would spend eternity in hell. The same message was rammed home to children through countless numbers of tracts, sermons, and hymns. Isaac Watts had written in a hymn for children

> There is a dreadful hell,
> And everlasting pains:
> There sinners must with Devils dwell
> In darkness, fire and chains.[703]

Charles Wesley added in another children's hymn:

> Dark and bottomless the pit
> Which on them its mouth shall close;

---

[700] *Wesley's Journal*, iii. 36; *Works of John Wesley* (3rd edn., 1829–30), i. 387–93.
[701] Tyerman, *Life of John Wesley*, ii. 7–11; Church, *Early Methodist People*, 246–7.
[702] *Minutes of the Methodist Conferences*, i. 166.
[703] H. A. L. Jefferson, *Hymns in Christian Worship* (1950), 48.

> Never shall they 'scape from it;
> There they shall in endless woes
> Weep and wail and gnash their teeth,
> Die an everlasting death.[704]

And for good measure the Bible Christians added that temporal penalties also awaited the childish wrong-doer:

> Oft we see a young beginner
> Practise little pilfering ways
> Till grown up a hardened sinner
> Then the gallows ends his days.[705]

John Gregory Pike, pastor of the Brook Street General Baptist church in Derby, published *A Guide to Young Disciples* in which he told his young readers that 'the Christian belongs to a kingdom that is not of this world': 'his chief business here is to glorify God, to reach heaven, and take as many as he can with him to that kingdom of eternal peace'.[706] It was because the Evangelicals saw the chief function of education as the saving of the child's soul that they threw their energies into the founding of Sunday schools; it was because the Unitarians regarded the prime task of education to be the acquisition of useful knowledge that they excelled in the establishment of day schools.[707]

Dissenting ministers had kept schools ever since the Great Ejection of 1662 had deprived so many of them of their living in the established church,[708] and for the next two centuries thousands of Nonconformist ministers supplemented their incomes by teaching and hundreds of Dissenting churches established schools. A bequest in 1699 by William Harte led to the founding of a school by the General Baptists of Collingham in Nottinghamshire which lasted for two hundred years.[709] The Quakers established schools in Warwick and Birmingham in 1709, and at Burford in Oxfordshire in 1716.[710] The Congregational King's Weigh House church in London founded a girls' school in 1780 and a boys' school eight years later.[711] But it was the Presbyterians, and their Unitarian successors, who made by far the most

---

[704] F. J. Gillman, *The Evolution of the English Hymn* (1927), 268.

[705] Shaw, *The Bible Christians*, 97.

[706] J. G. Pike, *A Guide to Young Disciples* (1823), 261, 387.

[707] In 1851 a third of Unitarian congregations in England had no Sunday school (Seed, 'Unitarians and Liberal Culture', 300). In orthodox Wales in 1835 of 1,355 day schools only 90 were controlled by Nonconformists (Jones, *Hanes Annibynwyr Cymru*, 217).

[708] Watts, *The Dissenters*, i. 344.   [709] Harrison, 'Baptists of Nottinghamshire', ii. 729.

[710] J. Hurwich, 'Nonconformists in Warwickshire', Ph.D. thesis (Princeton, NJ, 1970), 267; R. H. M. Warner, 'Quakerism in a Country Town', *JFHS* 48 (1956–8), 169.

[711] Kaye, *King's Weigh House*, 86.

important Dissenting contribution to weekday education. The Lewin's Mead Presbyterian meeting in Bristol founded Stokes Croft school in 1722 and raised funds to accommodate, feed, and clothe thirty boys.[712] The Presbyterians at Dudley in the Black Country ran a free school from 1732 for fifty boys who were taught 'spelling, English, reading, writing, vulgar arithmetic, and the knowledge and practice of the Christian religion'.[713] The Presbyterian meeting at Gravel Lane, Southwark, and the Great Meeting at Leicester were both running schools in the 1730s; the meetings at Kidderminster and Wrexham founded schools in 1758 and 1781.[714] Since the only charity school in Nottingham, the Blue Coat school, 'was connected with the established church', in 1788 the High Pavement Presbyterian meeting founded 'a daily charity school for the children of the poor of the congregation'.[715] And in Liverpool the Presbyterian/Unitarian meetings in Benn's Garden and Paradise Street both founded charity schools in 1790 and 1792 respectively, while in 1815 John Yates, the wealthy minister of Paradise Street, founded a third school largely at his own expense.[716]

The quality of teaching in these Nonconformist schools varied enormously. The warmest tributes were paid by former pupils to the school at Palgrave in Suffolk, run from 1775 to 1785 by the Presbyterian minister Rochemont Barbauld and his wife Anna, herself the daughter and sister of Unitarian ministers (the two John Aikins), and the successful author of poetry, hymns, and children's books. At Palgrave the Norwich radical, the younger William Taylor, learnt 'as much Greek and Latin as he ever appears to have found needful', discovered 'the world of science ... opened wide before him', while 'geography and history took the lead'. Mrs Barbauld excelled at the teaching of English and drama, and among the plays performed by her pupils were *The Tempest*, *Julius Caesar*, and *Henry IV*, Part 1.[717] But the pupils of some Nonconformist schools were highly critical of the education they received. Both the future prime minister Benjamin Disraeli and the future Unitarian minister Henry Solly attended the school at Higham Hill, near Walthamstow, run by the Unitarian minister Eleazer Cogan. Disraeli praised

[712] O. M. Griffiths, 'Lewin's Mead Chapel, Bristol', *TUHS* 6 (1935–8), 117–18.

[713] Cumberland, 'Nonconformity in the Black Country', 167.

[714] A.B., 'A View of the Dissenting Interest in London' (1732), DWL MS 38.18, p. 1; A. H. Thomas, *A History of the Great Meeting, Leicester* (1908), 65–6; G. Hunsworth, *Memorials of the Old Meeting Congregational Church, Kidderminster* (Kidderminster, 1874), 51; A. N. Palmer, *A History of the Older Nonconformity of Wrexham* (Wrexham, 1888), 82.

[715] B. Carpenter, *Some Account of the Original Introduction of Presbyterianism in Nottingham* (1860), 165–6.

[716] Sellers, 'Liverpool Nonconformity', 246.

[717] B. Rodgers, *Georgian Chronicle* (1958), 74–7.

Cogan as an 'admirable instructor' in Greek and Latin,[718] and Solly was grateful 'for the formation of those intellectual habits of mental activity and power which are best provided by the severe stringency of such teaching'. But if Disraeli's account of *Vivian Grey*'s schooldays is autobiographical, he hated the years he spent at Cogan's school, and both he and Solly criticized their teacher's narrowness. While Cogan made 'feeble' attempts to teach 'a little geography and French', wrote Solly, the teaching of mathematics, history, science, and literature was either 'non-existent or despicable'.[719] Newman Hall similarly criticized the teaching at the Congregational school at Mill Hill for being 'almost entirely confined to classics and mathematics': 'history, science, poetry, logic, even the critical and grammatical study of our own language were neglected'.[720] The chemist Luke Howard made the same complaint of the education he received at the hands of Thomas Hartley's Quaker school at Burford in Oxfordshire, that he was taught 'too much Latin grammar and too little of anything else', and William Howitt was equally critical of the Friends' school at Ackworth in the West Riding where the teaching of geography, history, and natural history was either 'very defective or non-existent', and neither Latin nor French was taught.[721] James Guinness Rogers thought more highly of the school at Silcoates near Wakefield which had been founded in 1821 for the sons of Congregational ministers and missionaries. Although the principal was a capricious disciplinarian and was 'not an accurate scholar', at least he did not confine his attention 'to the literature and history of the classics, but ... was equally interested in general literature' and taught history and geography.[722] The education provided by the school for the sons of Wesleyan ministers at Woodhouse Grove near Leeds was better still, and in the late 1820s and 1830s Benjamin Gregory was taught mathematics, science, and French. But what most impressed Gregory about the school was the poor food (two out of three meals a day consisting of bread and milk), the harsh corporal punishment (one boy was beaten so severely on the shoulder that a surgeon contemplated amputation), and above all the shortage of drinking water (with nothing to drink between one dinner-time and the next). Not surprisingly there was general rejoicing in the school when in 1832 the headmaster, Samuel Ebenezer Parker, disgusted 'with the radicalism of England', emigrated to the United States.[723] The Dissenting

---

[718] W. F. Monypenny and G. E. Buckle, *The Life of Benjamin Disraeli* (1929), i. 28.
[719] Solly, *These Eighty Years*, i. 76–7, 80–1.   [720] Newman Hall, *Autobiography*, 13–15.
[721] T. A. B. Corley, *Quaker Enterprise in Biscuits: Huntley and Palmer of Reading* (1972), 12; Mills, *John Bright and the Quakers*, i. 200.
[722] J. G. Rogers, *An Autobiography* (1903), 37–41.
[723] B. Gregory, *Autobiographical Recollections* (1903), 82–96.

school to which former pupils paid greatest tribute was the Quaker school at Sidcot in Somerset. In the 1820s the school stimulated George Palmer's interest in science, which was to stand him in good stead in his career as a biscuit manufacturer, and twenty years later the continuing emphasis on science at Sidcot prepared Richard Tangye and his younger brother George for their future careers as heads of their Birmingham engineering firm.[724]

Schools such as Sidcot, Silcoates, and Woodhouse Grove catered for only a small minority of the sons of Nonconformists. Others went to one of the small private schools and a few went to grammar schools. But for the overwhelming majority of children, especially of poor parents, at the turn of the eighteenth and nineteenth centuries, educational provision in England and Wales was grossly inadequate. Yet at the same time the country's population was growing rapidly and the increasing use of child labour to supplement the earnings of poor families meant that a new generation was growing up outside the civilizing influences of both church and school. Failure to educate such children, it was believed, endangered both the safety of the children's souls on the one hand and the security of society on the other. It was in response to this challenge that the Sunday school movement emerged.

Some Nonconformist ministers had always sought to instruct the children and young people of their congregations on Sundays by means of catechetical classes. Joseph Alleine, ejected from the curacy of Taunton in 1662, moved to Bath where he taught 'about sixty or seventy children every Lord's day'. George Fowler, a Walsall Presbyterian, set up a trust in 1699 to provide the town's minister with a salary of five guineas to teach poor children on Sundays, an obligation which was still being carried out a century and a half later.[725] And when Job Orton was minister of the combined Independent and Presbyterian congregation at Shrewsbury between 1741 and 1765 adult members of his congregation used to instruct younger members on Sunday evenings.[726] But what distinguished these catechetical classes from the later Sunday schools was the latter's emphasis on the need to teach children to read. To the Evangelicals the most important weapon in the battle for conversion was the Bible, and an illiterate nation was therefore a nation which would be impervious to the call to conversion. Consequently one of the most significant aspects of the Evangelical revival was the spontaneous appearance, from the 1760s onwards, of independent and isolated Sunday schools which were designed not only to provide religious instruction, but as a prior necessity were intended to teach children to read. The transformation of

---

[724] Corley, *Quaker Enterprise*, 27; S. J. Reid, *Sir Richard Tangye* (1908), 18–20.
[725] Cliff, *Sunday School Movement*, 20–1.   [726] Palmer, *Letters from Job Orton*, 52.

these independent and localized efforts into a mass movement began in 1783 when Robert Raikes, the printer and editor of the *Gloucester Journal*, published in his paper an account of the way in which Sunday schools were being established in Gloucestershire to instruct children who could not read, and to teach those children who could read the catechism. The story was taken up by other provincial newspapers and in the next few years Sunday schools sprang up throughout the country.[727] Some Sunday schools were founded by town meetings, others were established as a result of interdenominational co-operation; but these early attempts at ecumenical enterprise broke down, usually over disputes about whether the pupils should attend the parish church or Dissenting chapel,[728] and as a result, by the second decade of the nineteenth century, there were few Sunday schools that were not affiliated to a particular church or chapel.

The contentious issue of the contribution that Sunday schools made to the growth of Nonconformity has been discussed in the first chapter; what concerns us here is the part played by the Sunday school in the life of the Dissenting community. By 1851 there were 23,135 Sunday schools in England, and of those 55 per cent were affiliated to denominations other than the Church of England. Nearly three-quarters of the 17,000 Nonconformist congregations in England must therefore have had Sunday schools attached to them. Some 2,100,000 scholars were enrolled in Sunday schools in England in 1851, and Laqueur has calculated that this represented 56.5 per cent of the population aged between five and fifteen.[729] A proportion of those scholars were, however, over the age of fifteen and in the 1830s the figure may have been as high as 10 per cent.[730] Some Sunday schools were established specifically for adults. The Grosvenor Street Congregational church in Manchester set up an adult Sunday school in 1814 and 'within two years 140 adults had attended classes and their progress was such that 75 could read easy sentences and 21 could read the New Testament'.[731] Thomas Charles founded a Sunday school for the 'aged illiterate' in 1811[732] and in Wales Sunday schools were as popular with adults as with children. In 1851 the Calvinistic Methodist chapel at Caerseddfan in Montgomeryshire reported that the ages of folk attending its Sunday school ranged from three to seventy-eight, and the Particular Baptist church at Llanidan in Anglesey claimed that the ages of its Sunday scholars varied between three and

---

[727] Cliff, *Sunday School Movement*, 27–8.
[728] Ibid. 41; Laqueur, *Religion and Respectability*, 68–9.
[729] Laqueur, *Religion and Respectability*, 44.   [730] Ibid. 90.
[731] Robinson, *William Roby*, 83.   [732] Evans, *Sunday Schools of Wales*, 175.

eighty.[733] In some Welsh Sunday schools adults outnumbered children, and as late as 1869–71 two-thirds of the scholars enrolled by the Dowlais Baptist Sunday school in Glamorgan were adults.[734]

If the quality of teaching provided by the Nonconformist day schools was variable, that provided by the Sunday schools was frequently deplorable. Many Sunday schools found it impossible to recruit satisfactory teachers and had to use teachers who were themselves in need of basic instruction. Richard Horne, reporting to the Children's Employment Commission on the Sunday schools of Wolverhampton in 1841, commented that 'the great majority of the superintendents, and all the junior teachers, were unacquainted with any methods of instruction; have had no training whatever as teachers, and are, in fact, themselves uneducated'. In neighbouring Willenhall Horne found that the superintendents were 'locksmiths, key-makers, miners, and . . . small masters or journeymen', that none of the teachers had been trained, and that some of them could not even write their own names. As a result he found boys who had 'attended Sunday schools regularly from five to seven years who could not write their names', and he believed that the religious instruction offered was equally useless. 'The great majority of children and young persons are in a state of utter confusion on all religious subjects.' One young person of sixteen thought that 'Jesus Christ was a king in London a long time ago'. Many boys had never heard of Solomon, Moses, Sampson, and St Paul. 'Only a few boys had heard of the Twelve Apostles', and if they attempted to name them they mentioned Pontius Pilate, Balaam, Job, Moses, and Jonah. Such replies, stated Horne, 'were made by children and young persons who had attended Sunday schools during five, six, and seven years'.[735] The Children's Employment Commissioners concluded that while children who had begun work were 'in almost all instances' dependent on Sunday schools for their moral and religious training, the teaching provided by such schools was 'unsystematic and feeble'. 'In all the districts great numbers of those children who had been in regular attendance on Sunday schools for a period of from five to nine years were found, on examination, to be incapable of reading an easy book, or of spelling the commonest word; and they were not only altogether ignorant of Christian principles, doctrines, and precepts, but they knew nothing whatever of any of the events of Scripture

---

[733] Jones, *Religious Census, North Wales*, 16, 335.
[734] Williams, *History of Caersalem, Dowlais*, 75.
[735] *Children's Employment Commission: Appendix to the Second Report of the Commission: Trade and Manufacturers* (1843) (432), Q 18, 51, 52.

history.'[736] Many Sunday schools, in the absence of more intelligent methods of instruction, resorted to persuading their pupils to learn either long passages of Scripture or theological catechisms by rote. In the 1860s Wesleyan Sunday schools in Cornwall were rewarding their pupils with 5*d*. for every hundred verses they could learn by heart.[737] The annual reports of Sunday schools frequently listed the number of chapters and verses which their pupils were able to repeat: that for the Penuel Calvinistic Methodist church in Ebbw Vale, for example, boasted in 1864 that its 221 scholars had learnt 1,287 chapters from the Old Testament, 798 chapters from the New Testament, and 4,861 separate verses.[738] Both the Independent Sunday school at Ganllwyd in Merioneth and the Wesleyan Sunday school at Falmouth in Cornwall claimed to have scholars who could repeat the whole of the New Testament from memory.[739] In Wales rival Sunday schools met each other at annual associations at which they vied with each other in repeating verses of Scriptures and a theological topic or *pwnc* in the form of questions and answers. In 1860 the Carmel Baptist Sunday school at Sirhowy in Monmouthshire visited the Penuel Sunday school at Rhymney to recite a *pwnc* on the ascension of Christ. The Sirhowy contingent marched *en masse* to Rhymney chapel, accompanied by the singing of the chapel choir, and between eight hundred and a thousand people 'met together to listen to the reciting'.[740]

The low level of aspiration and achievement in the Sunday schools contributed to serious problems of discipline which in turn were countered by severe and sometimes cruel punishments. The superintendent of the Stoney Street General Baptist Sunday school in Nottingham maintained order by giving recalcitrant boys 'a severe caning',[741] and the Baptist Sunday school at Wymeswold in Leicestershire punished miscreants by fastening logs to their ankles. On one occasion a Wymeswold pupil walked home with a log tied to his ankle and put the log on the fire. He was saved from the fire only by the timely arrival of his teacher and thereafter logs were dispensed with as a form of punishment.[742] The Woodgate Baptist Sunday school in Loughborough similarly forced Elizabeth Clements to 'wear the log for using saucy and indecent language', punished truants with 'holding the weights', and had twelve

---

[736] *Children's Employment Commission: Second Report of the Commissioners: Trades and Manufacturers* (1843) (430), xiii. 202.

[737] Rule, 'Labouring Miner in Cornwall', 326.

[738] Price, *Penuel Calvinistic Methodist Church, Ebbw Vale*, 64–5.

[739] Jones, *Hanes Annibynwyr Cymru*, 198; Rule, 'Labouring Miner in Cornwall', 312.

[740] Jones, *Sowing Beside all Waters*, 56–7.

[741] J. B. Goodman (ed.), *Victorian Cabinet Maker: Memoirs of James Hopkinson* (1968), 45.

[742] Harrison, 'Baptists of Nottinghamshire', ii. 742.

paper hats made 'for those children who behave ill in meeting time and for lying'.[743] The Spring Head Wesleyan Sunday school at Wednesbury in the Black Country forbade its teachers to beat their pupils, but in order to discipline truants and liars it acquired an iron cage in which delinquents were incarcerated and then 'pulled up to the ceiling of the schoolroom by means of a rope'. This form of punishment was also abandoned after one spirited lad made 'cock-a-doodle-doo' noises from inside the cage and the rest of the Sunday school dissolved into laughter.[744]

Though it was the teaching of reading that distinguished the Sunday schools of the early nineteenth century from the catechetical classes of earlier generations, the Evangelical denominations which sponsored the Sunday schools never lost sight of the fact that their prime purpose was to save the pupil's soul. The Wesleyan leadership in particular viewed with great suspicion undenominational Sunday schools which, in their opinion, placed undue emphasis on secular learning and harboured radical sentiments. Wesleyan preachers were forbidden to preach on behalf of the great undenominational Sunday school at Stockport when it opened its new buildings in 1805, and they withdrew their support from the undenominational school in Macclesfield in 1812 because it taught writing and arithmetic on Sundays.[745] But there were also many Wesleyan Sunday schools which taught their pupils to write as well as to read, and as in Nottingham, to 'cast accompts',[746] and in 1807 a Leeds surgeon named William Hey wrote a paper for the Wesleyan Conference arguing that such activities were a violation of the sanctity of the Sabbath. Unlike reading, contended Hey, the ability to write 'is a more worldly accomplishment' which 'does not in any degree promote the salvation of the hearer'.[747] Among those persuaded by Hey's argument was Jabez Bunting who now took the lead in the campaign to ban the teaching of writing in the Connexion's Sunday schools.[748] Joseph Entwisle protested that the most successful Wesleyan Sunday schools, such as that at Bolton, had 'always taught writing, and that an attempt to lay [it] aside would be ruinous', and Richard Reece, who was president of the Wesleyan Conference in 1816 and again in 1835, argued that writing could be put to religious uses: it supplied 'the defect of memory' and enabled Methodists to write notes on the sermons they heard and to record their religious experiences.[749] But on this as

---

[743] Jackson, 'Baptists in Leicestershire', 283.
[744] Leese, 'Impact of Methodism on Black Country Society', 325.
[745] Ward, *Religion and Society*, 94.   [746] Swift, *Lively People*, 101, 104.
[747] Ward, *Religion and Society*, 138.
[748] Bunting and Rowe, *Life of Jabez Bunting*, 295.
[749] Ward, *Religion and Society*, 139; Stigant, 'Methodism and the Working Class', 219.

on nearly every other matter Bunting succeeded in persuading the Wesleyan Conference to endorse his views: in 1827 Conference forbade the teaching of writing in its Sunday schools.[750]

The repeated attempts by the Wesleyan leadership to ban the teaching of writing provoked furious opposition: critics saw it as a further attempt by the clerical Conference to stifle lay initiative within the Connexion, and they deplored the move to deprive the children of poor parents of the one opportunity they had of learning basic skills. When a Wesleyan preacher named Robert Martin tried to stop the teaching of writing in the Sunday school at Bury in 1819, the radical *Manchester Observer* retorted that his opposition to writing derived not from fear of offending his Maker but from fear of the dissemination of knowledge. 'He has cunning enough to see that the Egyptian darkness which surrounds and supports his system is fast disappearing, and he dreads the approach of the age of reason, and the consequent rights and liberties of man.' To Martin's contention that the children of the poor could be taught to write on evenings in the week, the *Manchester Observer* replied 'let Robert Martin and company . . . wind bobbins from six o'clock in the morning till nine or ten at night' in a warm factory with only the same food and rest as the children of the poor, and let them see whether they still had energy left for learning at the end of the day.[751]

Attempts to enforce the ban on writing led to bitter conflicts at chapel level. When Bunting was appointed to the Sheffield circuit in 1807 he tried to suppress the teaching of writing in the circuit's Sunday schools but the defenders of writing seceded to found a rival Sunday school and two years later the leaders' meeting voted to reinstate writing.[752] Thomas Kaye tried to force the teachers at the Wesleyan Sunday school in Newchurch-in-Rossendale to abandon the teaching of writing in 1820 with the result that the teachers, the majority of the trustees, and most of the pupils left the chapel.[753] An attempt to enforce the Conference ban on writing in the Sunday school attached to the Hanover Street chapel in Bolton in 1834 led to the secession of over a thousand scholars and two hundred members who ultimately joined the Wesleyan Reformers.[754] Connexional interference with the running of Sunday schools was a powerful stimulus to the secession of the Leeds Protestant Methodists in 1827 and to the formation of the Wesleyan Methodist Association in 1835: the Association's schools in Manchester went on to teach not only 'reading and writing, but in some instances grammar,

---

[750] *Minutes of the Methodist Conferences*, vi. 288.
[751] Stigant, 'Methodism and the Working Class', 287.   [752] Ibid. 220.
[753] Laqueur, *Religion and Respectability*, 144–5.
[754] Ibid. 124; Ward, *Religion and Society*, 172.

arithmetic, and the higher branches of mathematics'.[755] In 1837 representatives of the Association welcomed the secession of yet another Sunday school, that at Burslem in the Potteries, where the Wesleyans had complained for years that while the older children were taught writing 'the public worship of Almighty God' was neglected.[756] And at Southwell in Nottinghamshire in 1844 the conflict between the pro- and anti-writing factions was so intense that at one meeting 'a scuffle ensued and books were consigned to the fire', and on the following Sunday two policemen attended both afternoon and evening services lest violence should again break out.[757] Some Wesleyan Sunday schools never accepted the conference prohibition of writing: that at Fairbottom in Ashton-under-Lyne, attended largely by the children of colliers, ignored the ban, and the Sunday school attached to Wesley chapel, Nottingham, continued to teach writing until 1860.[758]

In denominations which lacked the centralized authority of the Wesleyan Conference differences over the teaching of secular subjects in Sunday schools were resolved more amicably. When the Nottingham Sunday School Union recommended that its member schools should stop teaching arithmetic in 1809 the Friar Lane Particular Baptist school followed its advice but the Stoney Street General Baptists seceded from the Union.[759] Five years later the Friar Lane school moved the teaching of writing to week-night classes, but the General Baptist Sunday school at Basford, Nottingham, was teaching writing and 'accounts' in the 1840s, and the schools at East Kirkby and Kirkby Woodhouse in the same county were still teaching writing in the 1870s and 1880s.[760] The Carr's Lane Congregational Sunday school in Birmingham revised its rules in 1812 to include the teaching of writing, and in 1830 the Ebenezer Baptist Sunday school in Burnley appointed two teachers to teach writing on Sunday mornings.[761] While the Hope Congregational church in Oldham lost both children and adults when its Sunday school abandoned the teaching of writing in 1833, the Sunday schools in the neighbouring Congregational chapels in Delph and Dobcross continued to teach writing until at least 1860.[762] The Methodist New Connexion tried to follow its parent Connexion in banning writing, but a survey of sixty-eight of its schools

---

[755] D. A. Gowland, *Methodist Secessions: The Origins of Free Methodism in Three Lancashire Towns* (Chetham Society, Manchester, 1979), 144–6.
[756] Ward, *Early Victorian Methodism*, 43–4, 122 n. 2.
[757] Swift, *Lively People*, 110.
[758] Ibid. 100; Rose, *Methodism in Ashton-under-Lyne*, ii. 33.
[759] Harrison, 'Baptists of Nottinghamshire', ii. 737–8.   [760] Ibid. 738–9, 746.
[761] Cliff, *Sunday School Movement*, 95; Weston, 'Baptists of North-West England', 476.
[762] Smith, 'Religion in Industrial Society', 213–14.

in 1841 found that thirty-three were still teaching writing on Sundays.[763] Most Primitive Methodist Sunday schools, more responsive than the Wesleyans to working-class needs, appear to have taught writing,[764] while many Unitarian Sunday schools, repudiating the inhibitions which afflicted the Evangelical schools, taught a whole range of secular subjects. The Mill Hill Unitarian Sunday school in Leeds taught writing, arithmetic, scripture, history, and geography; that at Dukinfield in Cheshire provided advanced classes which studied Carpenter's *Scriptural Geography*, Burder's *Oriental Customs*, and Murchason's *History of England*; and even the humble Methodist Unitarian Sunday school at Oldham offered in addition to reading, writing, and arithmetic, 'geography, grammar, and the elements of natural philosophy'.[765] From its foundation in 1787 the Sunday school attached to the Unitarian Old Meeting in Birmingham taught reading, writing, and arithmetic, and by 1860 was also teaching physiology, geography, and English history. Such was the school's emphasis on secular subjects that a member of the Old Meeting complained in 1874 that 'not eight out of every ten pupils we educate ever know what our principles are, much less become Unitarians'.[766]

The teaching provided by Sunday schools was often bad and frequently useless, the range of skills taught was restricted by Sabbatarian bigotry, the discipline enforced was often uncaring and sometimes cruel. But for all their manifold faults the Sunday schools did exert a civilizing influence on the lives of many children which might otherwise have been wholly lacking, and numerous scholars later paid tribute to the benefits they had derived from the schools. If nothing else, the Sunday schools brought colour and a little excitement to otherwise drab lives. The Sunday school calendar was enlivened by processions designed to advertise the school's activities and attract new pupils, by the Sunday school anniversary originally designed to raise money for the school, and by Sunday school outings which became increasingly popular after the coming of the railways. In Dursley in Gloucestershire in 1831 the Congregational and Wesleyan Sunday schools 'joined forces to celebrate the jubilee of the Sunday school movement by processing through the streets singing hymns before attending a joint service at the Tabernacle', and then 'departed to their own chapel to be supplied with buns'.[767] Three years later at Tunstall in Staffordshire five Sunday

---

[763] Laqueur, *Religion and Respectability*, 105.

[764] Ibid. 105; Morris, 'Primitive Methodism in Nottinghamshire', 27, 208; J. T. Bradshaw in Dews, *From Mow Cop to Peake*, 41; Rose, *Methodism in Ashton-under-Lyne*, ii. 81.

[765] Seed, 'Unitarianism and Liberal Culture', 302; Laqueur, *Religion and Respectability*, 102–3; Marcroft, *Unitarian Chapel, Oldham*, 89.

[766] Bushrod, 'Unitarianism in Birmingham', 186–7, 189.

[767] Evans, *As Mad as a Hatter!*, 126–7.

schools—three Primitive Methodist, one Wesleyan, and one Methodist New Connexion, countered the attraction of the Pottery races by organizing a procession through the town's streets to celebrate 'negro emancipation in the West Indies'. The procession converged on a field where the children were addressed on the significance of the ending of slavery and afterwards they returned to their respective chapels where 'each child was presented with a cake or bun, and a pleasant drink of lemonade'.[768] The practice of holding special annual services to raise funds for Sunday schools appears to date from the first decade of the nineteenth century.[769] When the Ebenezer Baptist Sunday school at Hebden Bridge in the West Riding decided to hold its first anniversary services in 1826 it resolved that 'sermons be preached for the benefit of the Sabbath school on Easter Sunday', that special hymns be printed for the scholars and congregation, and that scholars should repeat verses from Scripture.[770] The tendency for Sunday school anniversaries to become occasions for entertainment rather than devotion was present from the start. In 1805 the Sunday school connected with the Wesleyan Octagon chapel in Chester arranged an 'elaborate musical programme' for which 'two grand pianofortes were hired' and 'the most celebrated singers of the neighbourhood engaged'. A collection at the door raised £41. 7s. 1d., but since £24. 5s. 2d. of this had to be paid out in expenses, and since some Methodists complained that the younger members of the school and congregation 'had been brought into undesirable association with worldly musicians', subsequent anniversary services were arranged without musical accompaniment.[771] But elsewhere Sunday schools continued to rely on musical performances to bolster their funds. In 1819 Thomas Jackson, minister of the Wharton Congregational church in Lancashire, protested that while he did not object 'to some instruments to aid the children in singing upon these occasions, yet I think the children's voices should be the principal music, and nothing should be sung but plain hymns, and not those pieces which render a place of worship more like a play house than a house of God'.[772] But the querulous complaints of men like Thomas Jackson failed to stem the growing popularity of Sunday school anniversaries among children and parents alike: in the Potteries, claimed Charles Shaw, even drunken fathers 'would keep themselves sober for weeks' so that they could buy their children new clothes

[768] *Primitive Methodist Magazine*, NS 4 (1834), 357–8.
[769] The Congregational Sunday school at Exeter held an anniversary service in Nov. 1801 (Brockett, *Nonconformity in Exeter*, 169).
[770] W. S. Davies, 'An Early Sunday School Minute Book', *Baptist Quarterly*, 17 (1957–8), 322.
[771] F. F. Bretherton, *Early Methodism in and around Chester* (Chester, 1903), 233–4.
[772] Nightingale, *Lancashire Nonconformity*, iv. 114.

for the great day, and the occasion rekindled cherished memories of their own childhood in 'the hearts of parents who had long been separated by poverty or folly from the sweet hopes of their youth'. By means of the anniversary services the Primitive Methodist Sunday school in Tunstall was able to raise £170 or £180 at a time when the government 'was not giving as many shillings to educate all the children in the town as these poor people were giving to educate their own poor'.[773]

Of all the Sunday school activities the most popular, among the children, was the annual outing or treat. On 28 June 1838 both the Castle Gate Congregational and the Stoney Street General Baptist Sunday schools in Nottingham celebrated the coronation of Queen Victoria by providing their pupils with special treats. The Castle Gate children, numbering 340, assembled in the market-place at ten o'clock, marched in procession to the chapel, listened to Richard Alliott, junior, preach from 2 Kings 11: 12, 'And he brought forth the king's son, and put the crown upon him', and afterwards enjoyed a meal of roast beef and plum pudding in the chapel yard.[774] The Stoney Street General Baptist scholars had a livelier celebration: tables were set up in the chapel graveyard, and the children were provided not only with 'a liberal supply of beef and plum pudding' but also with a quantity of ale which led to some of them getting drunk and discipline collapsing.[775] For the children of the Methodist New Connexion Sunday school in Tunstall the annual visit to Trentham Park by canal barge was a glimpse of paradise. The older children formed themselves into kissing-rings which often led to courtship and marriage: 'the link which widened and brightened out into many a domestic circle was first formed in a kissing-ring under the trees in Trentham Park'.[776] The parents of the Tunstall children had to pay 4*d.* for each child to travel in the canal barge, but the costs of the annual Whitsuntide outings to the botanical gardens in Sheffield or to the sea at Lytham St Anne's enjoyed by the children of the Hurst New Connexion Methodist Sunday school, Ashton-under-Lyne, were all borne by John Whittaker, the local mill-owner.[777] The children of the Dursley Tabernacle were usually taken to nearby hills or local farms for their annual outing, but the advent of the railways made possible more ambitious excursions. In July 1864 nearly three hundred scholars and teachers went by train from Dursley

[773] [Charles Shaw], *When I was a Child, by an Old Potter* (1969 edn.), 210–13.
[774] Castle Gate minutes, 180.
[775] Goodman, *Victorian Cabinet Maker*, 70–1.
[776] [Shaw], *When I was a Child*, 201–2.
[777] Rose, *Methodism in Ashton-under-Lyne*, ii. 66–7.

to Cheltenham where the children spent the time boating on the lake at Pittsville Gardens and feeding the monkeys at Jessop's Gardens.[778]

The benefits which children derived from the Sunday schools were not, however, confined to the occasional free meals and trips to the seaside or zoo. Against the deprecatory remarks of contemporary observers on the value of the education provided by Sunday schools can be set a long list of working-class leaders who claimed to have benefited from their days in Sunday school.[779] Samuel Bamford blamed the efforts of the Wesleyan leaders to ban the teaching of writing from their Sunday schools for the fact, revealed by the 1841 census, that so many 'of the working classes of Lancashire were unable to write their names'.[780] But at the same time, when looking back on the period before 1815, he concluded that 'the Sunday schools of the preceding thirty years had produced many working men of sufficient talent to become readers, writers, and speakers in the village meetings for parliamentary reform'.[781] Against the conclusion reached by the Children's Employment Commissioners that many children derived little or no advantage from Sunday schools must be set the substantial amount of evidence they collected which showed that a minority of children did obtain considerable benefit from Sunday school attendance. If Sunday school teaching was too unsystematic and too spasmodic to help the majority of children, it was often sufficiently competent to teach the intelligent minority to read. The overseer of the Cyfarthfa collieries and ironstone mines near Merthyr Tydfil estimated in 1842 that a quarter of the children in his employ 'may read or know their letters' and added that whatever reading ability they had was 'acquired by long attendance at Sunday schools'.[782] His opinion found some support from the evidence collected by Robert Franks in the collieries and ironworks of Glamorgan and Monmouthshire who discovered, despite the appalling conditions in which children worked and the horrendous burns from which some of them suffered, that a minority could read Welsh well, and that this ability was due entirely to the Sunday schools.[783]

For Charles Shaw, brought up in poverty in the Staffordshire Potteries in the 1830s, Sunday school 'leavened my life from my sixth to my tenth year and . . . determined all my future'. He was taught first by a butty collier named Ralph Lawton, 'a man whose strength of character lay in a simple and sincere

[778] Evans, *As Mad as a Hatter!*, 158–60.   [779] Laqueur, *Religion and Respectability*, 154–7.
[780] S. Bamford, *The Autobiography of Samuel Bamford*, i. *Early Days*, ed. W. H. Chaloner (1967), 106–7.
[781] Ibid. ii. *Passages in the Life of a Radical*, 7–8.
[782] *Children's Employment Commission: Appendix to the First Report of Commissioners: Miners, Part II, Reports and Evidence from Sub-Commissioners*, xvii (1842) (382), 503.
[783] Ibid. 511, 515, 518, 525, 542, 543, 561.

piety', and then at the Tunstall New Connexion Methodist Sunday school by George Kirkham, who gave 'me a dawning interest in a larger world than I had ever dreamed of'. Sixty years later Charles Shaw was still thrilled to recall the joys of his Sunday schools in contrast to the hardships of his work in a pottery, and he paid tribute to the thousands of teachers who in the week 'had to work long hours at hard labours', and on their one 'day of rest' gave 'readily, cheerfully, and with heroic self-sacrifice . . . to toil for the children under their care'.[784] Adam Rushton was taught to read by a Methodist Sunday school in Macclesfield and subsequently rejected the theological dogmas taught there and became a Unitarian minister. But he always looked back on his Methodist Sunday school with gratitude and affection. He started work in 1829 at the age of eight, working from 6 o'clock in the morning until 8 o'clock at night with only 1 hour and 40 minutes for meal-breaks, all for 1s. 6d. a week. 'But for the influence of the Sunday school', he recalled nearly eighty years later, 'I think my health would have utterly broken down.' 'The Sunday's lessons and hymns and prayers filled and uplifted my mind all through the week, and helped me to endure the long, arduous and depressing work.'[785] To the father of Ellen Wilkinson, Labour MP for Middlesbrough East in the 1920s and for Jarrow in the 1930s, 'chapel meant everything'. 'There he was taught to read, was lent books. It was his only contact with education, its pulpit his only means of self-expression.'[786] A former pupil of the Unitarian Old Meeting Sunday school in Birmingham similarly looked back with gratitude both on the work of his teachers and on the civilizing influence which the school had exerted on his life. The son of a drunken father who had emigrated to the United States, the boy had found himself at the age of twelve 'an overgrown dunce, ragged and miserable, uncared for and despised . . . with no example before me . . . but the rough and immoral conduct which is usually found in one of Birmingham's worst-conducted work shops'. But he was determined to learn to read, 'saved enough money to buy some Sunday clothes', and joined the Old Meeting Sunday school. The kind treatment he received at the hands of the teachers contrasted with the rough and vulgar usage he endured during the week, and exerted a 'moral influence' which he thought even more important than learning to read and write.[787]

The Sunday schools could not have functioned without a vast army of unpaid teachers and in so doing provided an opportunity for service and for

[784] [Shaw], *When I was a Child*, 8, 56, 135,138–9, 208.
[785] A. Rushton, *My Life as a Farmer's Boy, Factory Lad, Teacher, and Preacher* (Manchester, 1909), 32.
[786] M. Asquith (ed.), *Myself When Young, by Famous Women of To-day* (1938), 401.
[787] Bushrod, 'Unitarianism in Birmingham', 195.

study to thousands of men, and especially of women, who might not otherwise have had similar outlets for their talents. A Sunday school teacher in south Wales told a representative of the recently established Committee of the Privy Council on Education in 1840 that he and his fellow teachers periodically met together 'to expound the Scriptures, the one to the other, so far forth as we do understand them'.[788] The stimulus which Sunday schools gave to the mutual education of teachers was as important as the instruction they provided for pupils. When James Picton joined the Leeds Street Wesleyan Sunday school in Liverpool in the 1820s it opened up to him 'a new world of activity and energy'. 'Its teachers' meetings; its library; the connexions and friendships to which it led; and the constant current of healthy excitement it generated . . . were, to me, sources of the keenest enjoyment and . . . of improvement.' Picton, like many other men, met his future wife in the Sunday school.[789]

The shortcomings of the Sunday schools should also be balanced against an appreciation of the formidable obstacles with which they had to contend. The Children's Employment Commission revealed examples of children aged seven and upwards working in Nottingham lace factories for twelve to fourteen hours a day, yet still managing to attend two sessions at a Baptist Sunday school and learning to read the New Testament.[790] The Nottingham Sunday school superintendents were themselves conscious that their schools were 'most ineffective as a general system of education' and that the children's intellectual education should be carried on during each day of the week, with Sunday devoted to religious instruction.[791] But in a society in which parents could neither pay for full-time education nor indeed deprive their families of the earnings from their children's labour, Sunday schools were making heroic efforts to fill part of a yawning gap.

The ideological motive which fuelled the Sunday school movement has aroused considerable debate among historians in recent years. According to M. W. Flinn Sunday schools were one of 'the principal channels through which the middle and upper classes sought to impose their social ideas upon the working class' and were 'geared to the manning of the growing industries'.[792] E. P. Thompson similarly indicted the Sunday schools as one of the

---

[788] *Minutes of the Committee of Council on Education* (1839–40), 169.

[789] Picton, *Sir James A. Picton*, 67–9.

[790] Harrison, 'Baptists of Nottinghamshire', ii. 755–6; *Children's Employment Commission: Appendix to the Second Report of the Commissioners, Trades and Manufactures, Part I, Reports and Evidence of Sub-Commissioners*, xiv (1843) (431), fos. 70–1.

[791] Ibid. fos. 109–10.

[792] M. W. Flinn, 'Social Theory and the Industrial Revolution', in T. Burns and S. B. Saul (eds.), *Social Theory and Economic Change* (1967), 14, 17.

main agencies whereby members of the working class were indoctrinated with bourgeois values in order to induce them to accept the discipline of the factory system.[793] By contrast Thomas Laqueur, who began his study of Sunday schools with the intention of confirming 'Thompson's interpretation in one corner of nineteenth-century history', came by the end of his researches to the conclusion that Thompson was wrong. Far from being a 'bourgeois assault on working-class culture', Laqueur found that 'many of those active in founding Sunday schools in both the eighteenth and nineteenth centuries were from the working class'. 'The teachers were almost all from the same social strata as those they taught; after 1810 some sixty per cent of all teachers had once been students themselves.' The Sunday schools, concludes Laqueur, were not agents of bourgeois social control: they were 'the bastion of the respectable working class from which the leadership of popular politics was drawn'.[794]

There is evidence to support both Thompson's and Laqueur's point of view. In support of Thompson one can cite the Baptist John Fawcett who argued in 1808 that Sunday schools were 'designed to make children prudent, industrious, honest, and faithful servants and domestics'. Fawcett urged that Sunday schools should be supported as a means of guaranteeing 'the security of our persons and of our property from the violence of wicked men'.[795] Similarly the Grosvenor Street Congregational Sunday school in Manchester assured its supporters in 1828 that it had no intention of exciting 'young persons to aspire at a higher station than that which providence has placed them'. Its sole object was to qualify its pupils 'for the proper discharge of their station and thus to make them peaceable and useful members of society'. But if the social theory of the Grosvenor Street Sunday school was conservative, the practical effect of its methods could be progressive. Two of its teachers, in co-operation with the church's minister, William Roby, helped to find work for the young James Kershaw and set him on the career which led to his becoming a cotton manufacturer, town councillor, mayor of Manchester, and MP for Stockport from 1847 to 1864.[796] And James Kershaw's career, like those of Charles Shaw and Adam Rushton, illustrates why so many working-class parents and children embraced the Sunday

---

[793] E. P. Thompson, *The Making of the English Working Class* (1968), 412–16.

[794] Laqueur, *Religion and Respectability*, 186–9. Laqueur's interpretation has in turn been challenged by M. Dick, 'The Myth of the Working-class Sunday School', *History of Education*, 9 (1980), 27–41. Support for Laqueur's thesis is, however, provided by P. McCann's study of Spitalfields in *Popular Education and Socialization* (1977), 11–12.

[795] Weston, 'Baptists of North-West England', 460–3, citing J. Fawcett, *Attention and Compassion due to the Children of the Poor* (Halifax, 1808), 18, 21.

[796] Robinson, *William Roby*, 83, 87.

school movement with such enthusiasm. The Sunday schools, like the temperance movement, offered working-class children a way out of grinding poverty and provided the first rung on the ladder whereby the child might hope to rise in the social scale. The ability to read, the distinction between right and wrong, the virtues of probity, thrift, and sobriety, which were emphasized by the Sunday school and temperance movements alike, were indeed values cherished by a substantial section of the Victorian middle class, but that does not make them specifically 'bourgeois' values. They were values which were embraced with even greater enthusiasm by enormous numbers of the nineteenth-century working class. What the Sunday schools, the temperance movement, and the chapels offered to the working class above all was respectability, that most cherished of all the Victorian values. It was respectability that distinguished the decent family from the disreputable family, the responsible father from the drunken father, the cared-for children from the neglected children. And just because working-class families knew at first hand, even better than did middle-class families, the consequences of losing that respectability, they sought to have their children educated in the values taught by the Sunday schools. The assumption that such values were merely bourgeois values is destroyed by an analysis of the social structure of Nonconformity in the first half of the nineteenth century.

9. 'YE HAVE THE POOR ALWAYS WITH YOU': THE EVIDENCE OF THE DISSENTING REGISTERS

The dispute between E. P. Thompson and Thomas Laqueur on the social role of the Sunday school is part of the larger debate on the social structure of Dissent. For more than a century observers both within and without Dissent have commented on its essentially bourgeois character, and on the failure of Nonconformist churches, in company with other churches, to attract substantial support from the working and poorer classes of England. Friedrich Engels, writing in 1844, noted that 'all bourgeois writers are agreed that the workers have no religion and do not go to church'. There were exceptions: the Irish, 'a few of the older workers and those wage-earners who have one foot in the middle-class camp—overlookers, foremen, and so on'. But 'among the mass of the working-class population . . . one nearly always finds an utter indifference to religion'.[797] Four years later Algernon Wells,

---

[797] F. Engels, *The Condition of the Working Class in England* (1844, repr. Oxford, 1958), 141.

secretary of the Congregational Union, told the Union's annual meeting that all churches had failed in their mission to win over the working class: they were 'not converted by Romish zeal, or any longer gathered by Wesleyan energy, or drawn by the more intellectual discourses of Independent and Baptist preachers'. The Independents' newly built chapels gathered 'congregations of tradesmen, but never of artificers'.[798] Other ministers present challenged the accuracy of Wells's observation, but it was his view which became the accepted orthodoxy.[799] Forty years later the notion that an Englishman's religion was determined by class received classic expression from the pen of William Hale White, the erstwhile Congregationalist who recalled that the Bedford in which he was brought up in the 1830s and the 1840s was divided into three classes. 'In our town', he wrote in *Mark Rutherford's Deliverance*,

we were all formed upon recognised patterns .... The wine-merchant, for example, who went to church, eminently respectable, Tory, by no means associating with the tradesfolk who displayed their goods in the windows, knowing no 'experience', and who had never felt the outpouring of the Spirit, was a specimen of a class like him. Another class was represented by the dissenting iron-monger, deacon, presiding at prayer-meetings, strict Sabbatarian, and believer in eternal punishments; while a third was set for by 'Guffy' whose real name was unknown, who got drunk, unloaded barges, assisted in the municipal elections, and was never once seen inside a place of worship.[800]

The implication of what Mark Rutherford was saying, that Nonconformity won its support predominantly from the middle class and made little impact on the working class, has been endorsed by successive generations of writers, and especially by those whose primary concern has been with Wesleyan Methodism. Harold Faulkner, writing during the First World War, concluded that most of the Nonconformist 'sects by the second quarter of the nineteenth century represented almost entirely a middle-class constituency'.[801] Half a century later K. S. Inglis maintained that the older Nonconformist denominations were largely middle class in character and that there is little evidence that Methodism 'in any form . . . was extending its ministry far into the great body of working-class people who attended no religious worship'.[802] Tudur Jones similarly argued that 'the vast majority of Congregationalists

For other similar comments see E. Hopkins, 'Religious Dissent in Black Country Industrial Villages', *Journal of Ecclesiastical History*, 34 (1983), 411.

[798] *Congregational Year Book* (1848), 84.   [799] *Nonconformist*, 25 Oct. 1848, 809.
[800] W. H. White, *The Autobiography of Mark Rutherford and Mark Rutherford's Deliverance* (2nd edn., 1888), 178.
[801] H. U. Faulkner, *Chartism and the Churches* (1916, repr. 1970), 12.
[802] K. S. Inglis, *Churches and the Working Classes in Victorian England* (1963), 9, 13–14.

were of the middle classes', and W. R. Ward claimed that by 1830 northern Congregationalism was no longer the religion of working men but was 'the religion of an urban aristocracy'.[803] Maldwyn Edwards believed that Wesleyanism, in the early nineteenth century, was increasingly recruiting its support from the middle class; Donald Read maintained that by 1819 'Wesleyan Methodism had become middle-class in character'; and Edward Thompson concluded that by the 1830s the Methodists were tending 'increasingly to represent tradesmen and privileged groups of workers, and to be morally isolated from working-class community life'.[804] Most recently David Hempton, who writes as though Methodism and Wesleyanism were synonymous, has argued that in the half-century after 1780 British Methodism 'failed to sink deep roots into working-class culture', and that by 1820 Wesleyanism had 'lost contact with the working classes in town and country'.[805]

What all such statements have in common is the absence of any statistical evidence in their support. Those few historians who have sought to use statistical material to investigate the social structure of Nonconformity have failed to find much evidence of its supposedly bourgeois character, but they have also drawn conflicting conclusions from the available evidence. Alan Gilbert, in his *Religion and Society in Industrial England*, produces the results of researches into a sample of the Nonconformist birth and baptismal registers which were entrusted to the care of the registrar-general following the establishment, in 1836, of the Civil Registry of Births, Marriages, and Deaths. Using as his standard of comparison Patrick Colquhoun's analysis of national income in 1806, Gilbert concluded that 'whereas the proportions of tradesmen, merchants, and manufacturers in Evangelical Nonconformist communities were about the same as the proportions in the wider society, and the proportion of farmers and labourers considerably lower, the proportion of artisans was between twice and three times as high'.[806] However, Gilbert aggregated his findings in a way that obscured local and regional variations and Barry Biggs, in a detailed study of Methodism in rural north Nottinghamshire, M. A. Smith, in his work on religion in Oldham and Saddleworth, and Philip Rycroft, in his thesis on church and chapel in the Yorkshire district of Craven, have all come to quite different conclusions. Biggs compiled a card index of all persons in his area who, up to 1851, could

---

[803] Jones, *Congregationalism in England*, 228; Ward, *Religion and Society in England*, 129.

[804] M. Edwards, *After Wesley* (1935), 145; Edwards, 'John Wesley', in *HMC* i. 60; D. Read, *The English Provinces* (1964), 39; Thompson, *Making of the English Working Class*, 467.

[805] D. Hempton, *Methodism and Politics in British Society, 1750–1850* (1984), 236, 227.

[806] Gilbert, *Religion and Society*, 66.

be identified as having Methodist connections, and in the case of six villages compared the social structure of Methodism with that of the community at large, as revealed by the 1841 census. He found that whereas the proportion of shopkeepers and artisans among the Methodist churches was roughly the same as in the wider community, farmers were overrepresented among the Wesleyans and labourers among the Primitives. However, Biggs's most important conclusion was that if one takes the two branches of Methodism together, the social structure of the movement was very like that of the society from which it was drawn. Smith, in his study of Oldham and Saddleworth, and Rycroft, in his thesis on Craven, came to the same conclusion. Smith compared the evidence of the Nonconformist baptismal registers for Oldham and Saddleworth with the 1841 census and Rycroft compared the registers for his area with the Craven Muster Roll of 1803 and with the 1851 census. Both found that 'the occupational structure of the various chapels reflected the locality in which they were situated'.[807]

The whole subject is thus in need of further investigation, and to this end I have superintended the examination of all the Nonconformist birth and baptismal registers, housed in the Public Record Office, for every county in England and Wales for the period 1790–1837.[808] In addition, registers for the post-1837 period have been examined in a selection of County Record Offices.[809] A significant proportion of these registers give the occupations of the fathers of the children whose births or baptisms are recorded therein and on the basis of this evidence it has been possible to analyse the occupations of the adherents of the Independents, Quakers, and Wesleyan Methodists in most of the counties of England and, in the case of the Calvinistic Methodists, in Wales. Fewer registers have been preserved for the Baptist, Unitarian, Methodist New Connexion, or Primitive Methodist denominations but where these have been found they, too, have been analysed. The only counties for which insufficient evidence has been found for a meaningful statistical analysis to be made were the two smallest: Rutland in England and Radnorshire in Wales.

In all the calculations based on the Nonconformist registers multiple counting has been avoided by recording the name of each father entered into

---

[807] B. J. Biggs, 'Methodism in a Rural Society: North Nottinghamshire, 1740–1851', Ph.D. thesis (Nottingham, 1975), 428–32; Rycroft, 'Church, Chapel, and Community in Craven', 208, 221; Smith, 'Religion in Industrial Society', 231, 367.

[808] The list of non-parochial registers available in the PRO had been published by the List and Index Society, 42 (1969).

[809] Greater London, Chelmsford, Colchester, Maidstone, Bedford, Northampton, Leicester, Warwick, Birmingham, Nottingham, Matlock, Wakefield, Sheffield, Leeds, Bradford, Huddersfield, and Halifax.

the baptismal register and by counting his occupation once only; where a father was recorded as having two or three different occupations, each occupation was counted as a half or a third.[810] And where possible an attempt has been made to chart any changes in the occupational structure of each denomination over time by analysing the data separately in successive decades. The only cases in which this procedure has not been followed are those in which too few births were recorded in any one decade for changes over time to be charted. The results of this investigation have then been compared with the results of an analysis, on a county by county basis, of the occupational structure of the general male population derived from the printed tables of the 1841 census.[811] The consequent analyses are presented in Tables XV–LXVI at the end of this volume.

It must be admitted at the outset that objections can be raised both to using birth and baptismal registers to ascertain the occupational structure of Non-conformist congregations, and to using the printed census tables as a means of analysing the occupational structure of the population at large. Bringing one's child to a Dissenting chapel for baptism does not necessarily imply membership of its church and some of the parents who had the births of their children recorded in Nonconformist baptismal registers may have had little attachment to the chapel concerned. There is, however, a good deal of evidence to suggest that in general the baptismal registers do provide an accurate guide to the occupational structure, not necessarily of a church's membership, but certainly of the wider community which worshipped at its chapel. No parents were likely to bring their child to be baptized in a Unitarian chapel, or to have the child's name registered by a Baptist or Quaker meeting, unless they had some connection with that church. The Independents had traditionally reserved baptism for the children of members of their congregations, and the Declaration of Faith, Order, and Discipline adopted by the newly formed Congregational Union in 1833 stated that baptism should be administered only to 'converts to Christianity and their children'.[812] Similarly the Wesleyan Conference, in 1795, laid down

---

[810] Counting occupations rather than individuals can lead to serious distortions, especially in the case of small but socially significant occupational groups. For example, 25 of the 170 baptisms recorded in the Dukinfield Presbyterian register, Cheshire, were of the children of cotton masters, a proportion of 14.8%. But when multiple births are excluded, the cotton masters represented only 7.1% of the Dukinfield Presbyterian fathers.

[811] In analysing the occupational structure of the general male population men of independent means and the occupations of all employed men over the age of 20 have been counted, but men whose trade was not specified, alms people, pensioners, paupers, beggars, and 'the residue of population' have not been included.

[812] Watts, *The Dissenters*, i. 154–5; Browne, *History of Congregationalism in Norfolk and Suffolk*, 260; Peel, *These Hundred Years*, 72.

that the administration of baptism was intended 'only for the members of our own society', and in 1812 extended this provision to include the children 'of our regular hearers'.[813] The Methodist New Connexion gave more scope to its ministers in determining whom they should or should not baptize: baptism was to be administered 'to the children belonging to members of our society, of persons worshipping with us, and of others at the discretion of the preachers'.[814] But the Bible Christians were adamant that no child should 'be baptised by us, except one of its parents, at least, be a member of society, a seat-holder, or a regular attender on our ministry'.[815]

Declarations of Faith and Conference rules were, of course, one thing and the practice of individual ministers could be something else. The Primitive Methodist Hugh Bourne, the maverick New Connexion Methodist George Beaumont, and the Congregationalist Robert Halley all argued that ministers should baptize all children who were brought to them irrespective of the faith of their parents.[816] But baptism in a Nonconformist chapel was not regarded, as was Anglican baptism, as legal evidence of birth, and parents who looked upon baptism as conferring legal status, or as a social convention, were far more likely to take their children to their parish church than to a Nonconformist chapel to be baptized. Jabez Bunting admitted this in correspondence with Joshua Marsden, Wesleyan superintendent in the Worcester circuit, in 1826, and what concerned both of them was not that people who had no connection with Methodism were seeking baptism in Wesleyan chapels, but that doubts as to the legality of Methodist baptisms were driving parents to the parish churches for the baptism of their children.[817] It is in fact possible to check Nonconformist baptismal registers against other sources such as church membership lists and the 1851 religious census to gauge the extent to which parents whose names were recorded in the baptismal registers were in fact members of the relevant church or congregation. In the case of Congregational churches such evidence suggests that in most if not all churches virtually every father whose child's baptism was recorded in a church register was either a church member, was married to a church member, or was a member of the congregation. What is more, such comparisons show that while in some chapels those fathers who were church members were of higher social standing than those who were merely attenders, in other

---

[813] N. W. Mumford, 'The Administration of the Sacrament of Baptism in the Methodist Church', *London and Holborn Quarterly Review*, 172 (1947), 115.

[814] B. G. Holland, *The Doctrine of Infant Baptism in Non-Wesleyan Methodism* (1970).

[815] *HMC* iv. 464.

[816] Holland, *Doctrine of Infant Baptism, passim*; Jones, *Congregationalism in England*, 226–7.

[817] Ward, *Early Correspondence of Bunting*, 169–71.

chapels there was actually a higher proportion of poor men among church members than among fathers who had the baptism of their children recorded in the church registers, and that in yet other chapels the occupational profile of those fathers who were church members was very similar to that of fathers who were simply members of the congregation.[818] And in the case of Methodist congregations, comparison of the evidence of the baptismal registers with that of the 1851 religious census suggests that the baptismal registers underrepresent rather than overrepresent the size of the chapel community.[819] This evidence substantiates the fears of Bunting and Marsden that many parents who were attending Nonconformist chapels in the 1820s and 1830s were continuing to have their children baptized in Anglican churches,[820] and as late as the 1890s clergymen in rural areas were reporting that chapel-goers often went to the parish church for the baptism of their children.[821] All the evidence thus points to the conclusion that to have one's child baptized in a Nonconformist chapel in the first half of the nineteenth century involved a degree of commitment on the part of at least one of the parents and signified membership of the Dissenting or Methodist communities if not of their churches.

A more substantial objection to the drawing of conclusions about social structure from either the baptismal registers or the census tables is based on the knowledge that the mere description of a man's occupation often gives no real clue either to his economic worth or to his social standing.[822] Thus a man described as 'tailor' might be a prosperous master tailor employing others, a man whose business was in retailing rather than manufacture, or an employee earning a low wage in a sweat shop. Similarly the 1841 census tables tried to subsume all men engaged in cotton manufacture under the same heading, whether they were big manufacturers or poverty-stricken handloom weavers. However, one can be confident that the overwhelming majority of men described as tailors, shoemakers, or engaged in cotton manufacture were poorly paid wage-earners rather than employers,[823] and in other trades

---

[818] See Appendix II.   [819] See Appendix II.

[820] This is also supported by the comments of Anglican clergymen in 1831 (E. A. Wrigley and R. S. Schofield, *The Population History of England, 1541–1871* (1981), 96 n. 11).

[821] H. Pelling, *Popular Politics and Society in late Victorian Britain* (2nd edn., 1979), 23–4.

[822] Geoffrey Crossick, for example, argues that 'social structure cannot be reconstructed from the printed census tables' (*An Artisan Elite in Victorian Society* (1978), 37–40).

[823] E. P. Thompson and E. Yeo (eds.), *The Unknown Mayhew* (1971), 181; R. S. Neale, *Bath, 1680–1850: A Social History* (1981), 269–70. It is sometimes possible for the local historian to distinguish manufacturers from workers by reference to local trade directories and M. A. Smith does this in his analysis of baptismal registers in 'Religion in Industrial Society', 222, 235, 366. The result of Smith's detailed researches supports my own contention that the vast majority of men who described themselves, for example, as cotton spinners were workers rather than

the differences between masters and men were often differences of age rather than differences of class. R. J. Morris has concluded from a study of the manuscript returns to the 1851 census 'that the status of employer and wage-earner in many craft occupations was a life-cycle stage rather than a class division'. He found that 75 per cent of men who described themselves as masters or employers were over the age of thirty-five, while 66 per cent of journeymen, 97 per cent of apprentices, and 59 per cent of manual workers were under the age of thirty-five.[824] While the occupational terms used in the Dissenting registers and the census tables cannot be regarded as an infallible guide to the social status of individuals, they can be used as rough indicators of the social structure of the communities in which they lived and worshipped.

It is customary to use the registrar-general's fivefold classification of 1951 when interpreting occupational data, but the resulting categories are too broad for useful comparative purposes and lead to absurd results.[825] I have therefore devised the following elevenfold classification:

    I.   Gentlemen and men of independent means
    II.   Businessmen
    III.   Professional men
    IV.   Farmers and yeomen
    V.   Retail traders, dealers, and food manufacturers
    VI.   White-collar workers
    VII.   Labour aristocracy
    VIII.   Higher-skilled workers
    IX.   Lower-skilled workers
    X.   Depressed workers
    XI.   Unskilled workers

employers. A comparison between Smith's analysis and my own calculations for Oldham and Saddleworth suggests that I have underestimated the proportion of businessmen among the Congregationalists by a mere 1.1%, among the Wesleyans by 3.1%, and among the New Connexion Methodists by 2.9%.

[824] R. J. Morris, *Class, Power, and Social Structure in British Nineteenth-Century Towns* (Leicester, 1986), 13.

[825] e.g. W. A. Armstrong's use of the registrar-general's classification produced, as he admits, 'a swollen Class III' when applied both to all males in England and Wales in 1951 and to heads of households in York in 1851 (W. A. Armstrong, 'The Use of Information about Occupation', in E. A. Wrigley, *Nineteenth-Century Society* (Cambridge, 1972), 212). K. D. Brown, following Armstrong, places civil servants, grocers, miners, and weavers in the same Class III, *A Social History of the Nonconformist Ministry in England and Wales* (Oxford, 1988), 21–2.

This classification calls for explanation. Class II includes bankers, brokers, coal proprietors, corn dealers, coach owners, factors, land agents, manufacturers, merchants, railway contractors, ship owners, and wine merchants. The class is underrepresented in the census returns which, in industrial occupations, failed to distinguish employers from employees. Class III comprises architects, attorneys, auctioneers, barristers, physicians, surgeons, surveyors, and clergymen, but not Dissenting ministers[826] whom I have placed in Class VI alongside accountants, actors, artists, bailiffs, civil servants, clerks, commercial travellers, warehousemen, and schoolteachers. The term 'farmer' in Class IV covers a whole spectrum of wealth and social standing but does not generally include men described as husbandmen since that term is frequently used in the baptismal registers as an alternative for labourer. An exception has been made for the Quakers of the north of England in whose registers the term husbandman is used consistently as a synonym for farmer rather than labourer. Class V comprises both retail traders and men engaged in the manufacture of foodstuffs such as bakers, brewers, maltsters, and millers. The category will include some men of lower social status because the Dissenting registers rarely, and the published census returns never, distinguish between master butchers and master brewers and their assistants, but where the registers do indicate that a father was a butcher's assistant or a common brewer he has been placed in Class IX. A particular problem is posed by the terms 'clothier' and 'hosier'. Throughout most of the country these terms appear to have been used to denote the sellers of cloth, clothes, or hosiery goods and they have been placed in Class V, but in the West Riding of Yorkshire the term clothier was applied to a small capitalist who owned several spinning jennies and looms and employed his own family and a few spinners and weavers, while in Nottinghamshire and Leicestershire the term hosier was used both of merchants and of employers of framework knitters.[827] Consequently I have placed the Nottinghamshire and Leicestershire hosiers with the businessmen in Class II, but since most of the West Riding clothiers went into a steady decline from the early years of the nineteenth century,[828]

[826] The frequency with which Methodist ministers changed circuits and some Dissenting ministers changed chapels means that to have recorded every minister whose wife gave birth to a child would have inflated the number of Nonconformist white-collar workers, especially in smaller congregations. I have therefore divided the number of Nonconformist ministers by half in registers where there was more than one per decade.

[827] W. B. Crump and G. Ghorbal, *History of the Huddersfield Woollen Industry* (Huddersfield, 1935), 91; P. Hudson, *The Genesis of Industrial Capital: A Study of the West Riding Wool Textile Industry* (Cambridge, 1986), 35; Church, *Economic and Social Change in a Midland Town*, 32–3.

[828] Hudson, *Genesis of Industrial Capital*, 35; Thompson, *Making of the English Working Class*, 301, 598.

and since by the 1830s clothiers were sometimes being described alternatively as weavers in the Dissenting registers, I have found it impossible to classify them and have placed them in a category of their own.

Skilled workers have been divided into four categories determined not by any subjective judgement on the degree of skill involved in performing their differing crafts but according to the level of their earnings in the 1830s and 1840s. Information on workers' earnings in the period is sparse and widely scattered, and earnings varied from year to year and from region to region, but enough information is available to enable workers to be arranged in a hierarchical scale according to income.[829] Thus Class VII, the labour aristocracy, comprises workers who were accustomed to earning 30s. a week or more: block cutters, bookbinders, brass founders, calico printers, clockmakers, coach-builders, carvers and gilders, coppersmiths, engravers, engine makers, furnacemen, glassmakers, grinders, hatters, iron founders and moulders, millwrights, pattern makers, printers, shipwrights and ships' carpenters. Class VIII, the higher-skilled workers, includes men who usually received between 21s. and 30s. a week: blacksmiths, boat-builders, boilermakers, brickmakers and bricklayers, cabinet-makers and carpenters, cotton dressers, curriers, cutlers, file cutters, flatmen, flax dressers, locksmiths, masons, mechanics, overlookers, painters, plasterers, plumbers, saddlers, sawyers, slaters, spinners, tinplate workers, turners, upholsterers, wheelwrights, and woolsorters. Class IX, the lower-skilled workers, comprises men who usually earned between 15s. and 20s. a week: bleachers, carders, carriers, coachmen, colliers, dyers, hairdressers, lacemakers, police constables, tailors, tanners, shoemakers, and woolcombers. Class X, the depressed workers, is reserved for those domestic workers who may have been reason-

---

[829] The principal sources used to ascertain workers' earnings were: E. Baines, *History of the Cotton Manufacture in Great Britain* (1935); E. Baines, 'On the Woollen Manufacture of England', *Journal of the Statistical Society of London*, 22 (1859), 24–5; G. J. Barnsby, 'The Standard of Living in the Black Country during the Nineteenth Century', *Economic History Review*, 2nd ser. 14: 2 (1971); R. D. Baxter, *National Income* (1868); A. L. Bowley, *Wages in the United Kingdom in the Nineteenth Century* (Cambridge, 1900); D. Chadwick, 'On the Rate of Wages in Manchester and Salford and the Manufacturing Districts of Lancashire, 1839–59', *Journal of the Statistical Society*, 23 (1860), 1–36; W. Felkin, 'The Lace and Hosiery Trades of Nottingham', ibid. 24 (1866), 536–41; L. Levi, *Wages and Earnings of the Working Classes* (1885); W. Neill, 'Comparative Statement of the Income and Expenditure of Certain Families of the Working Classes in Manchester and Dukinfield in the Years 1836 and 1841', *Journal of the Statistical Society*, 4 (1841), 320–34; G. R. Porter, *The Progress of the Nation (1847); Returns of Wages, published between 1830 and 1886* (Parliamentary Papers, 1887, vol. 89); Thompson and Yeo (eds.), *The Unknown Mayhew*; W. H. Warburton, *History of Trade Union Organisation in the North Staffordshire Potteries* (1931), 242–5; G. H. Wood, *Rates of Wages and Hours of Labour in Various Industries in the United Kingdom 1851–1906* (1908); and G. H. Wood, *The History of Wages in the Cotton Trade during the Past Hundred Years* (1910).

ably well paid at the turn of the eighteenth and nineteenth centuries but whose wages by the 1830s had been depressed to a good deal less than 15*s*. a week, and in some cases to less than those earned by agricultural labourers: chain-makers, framework knitters, nailers, silk workers, and weavers.[830] Finally Class XI comprises unskilled workers, again men whose earnings were usually less than 15*s*. a week: domestic servants, fishermen, gamekeepers, gardeners, labourers, porters, sailors, and soldiers. Since the 1841 census placed all military and naval men in the categories of 'army' and 'navy' a number of generals, colonels, and admirals will have been placed in this bottom category, but since I have found no such person in any Nonconformist congregation the distorting effect of these and similar errors on the totals in the comparative tables will be minimal. In counties with a significant proportion of workers in a single occupation, for example weavers in the West Riding and miners and potters in Staffordshire, these have been listed separately in the tables and enclosed in square brackets to indicate that they have also been included in the class to which they have been assigned. In every county labourers have been both listed separately and also included in the totals for unskilled workers.

It was argued in the first volume of this work, partly on the basis of evidence from Congregational, Presbyterian, and Quaker registers from the late seventeenth and early eighteenth centuries, that Dissent appealed chiefly to the economically independent, to men who were beholden neither to king and courtiers on the one hand nor to parsons or squires on the other either for their social standing or for their economic well-being.[831] As those members of the aristocracy and gentry who had given shelter to ministers ejected from their parishes in 1662 died the links between the landed classes and Dissenting meeting-houses were one by one severed, and by the turn of the eighteenth and nineteenth centuries only exceptional and eccentric members of the aristocracy and gentry frequented Nonconformist chapels. Those wayward sons of George III, the brutal Duke of Kent and the liberal Duke of Sussex, were reputed to have attended on occasion the Congregational chapel at Peckham ministered by Dr William Bengo Collyer,

---

[830] The printed census returns for Lancashire in 1841 pose a special problem because while 21,190 adult males are listed as weavers, another 45,619 are listed under the blanket term 'cotton manufacture'. In my analysis of the 1841 census I have assumed that half those workers included in 'cotton manufacture' were weavers, 30% spinners, and 20% carders. E. Baines, *History of the Cotton Manufacture in Great Britain*, calculated that of 18,049 people employed in 225 cotton mills, 36.1% were weavers, 41.5% were spinners, and 18.3% carders, but these figures do not of course include the still very substantial proportion of cotton workers who scraped a living as hand-loom weavers in the 1830s.

[831] Watts, *The Dissenters*, i. 346–54.

and the Duchess of Sutherland worshipped in Hornton Street chapel in Kensington when Robert Vaughan was pastor.[832] Robert Carr Brackenbury, the squire of Raithby in Lincolnshire in the later eighteenth century, was a Methodist lay preacher who gave John Wesley hospitality when he was in his native county, accompanied him on a preaching tour of Scotland, and from 1784 to 1790 served as Methodist preacher in the Channel Islands.[833] The Particular Baptist church at Rugby in Warwickshire was founded in the 1790s by a baronet, Sir Egerton Leigh, who held services in his drawing-room, provided the church with its first two chapels, and served as its first pastor.[834] And even the Primitive Methodists claimed a solitary member of the gentry, Robert Shafto of Bavington Hall near Hexham in Northumberland, though they also recorded that despite a Cambridge education it was evident that 'nature had not gifted him with the higher qualities of mind'.[835] But such cases are notable for their singularity. At least one member of the gentry who secretly sympathized with Nonconformity dared not show that sympathy openly. Weston Cracroft, the squire of Hackthorn in Lincolnshire, 'confided to his diary that he was really a Dissenter but that he wanted to live with his own social class and among gentlemen'.[836]

Professional men, and especially members of professions for which a university degree, and hence conformity to the established church, were prerequisites, were similarly rarely to be found in Nonconformist congregations. The Royal College of Surgeons, unlike the Royal College of Physicians, did not insist that its entrants had an Oxford or Cambridge degree,[837] and consequently a few Dissenting congregations numbered surgeons among their members. There were three surgeons among the fathers who had their children baptized in the Independent Trevor chapel in Brompton Road in London's West End in the 1820s, and another four in the 1830s. Two surgeons were recorded in the registers of the Staindrop Independent church in County Durham in the 1820s and another two at Barnard Castle. The Baptist church at Abingdon in Berkshire had in its congregation two surgeons, a physician, and an attorney. The Quakers attracted a disproportionate number of professional men in general and of surgeons in particular. Of the 112 fathers who had the births of their children registered by the Quakers of

---

[832] Jones, *Congregationalism in England*, 228; Guinness Rogers, *Autobiography*, 158.

[833] T. R. Leach, 'The Methodist Squire of Raithby: Robert Carr Brackenbury, 1752–1818', *The Epworth Witness and Journal of the Lincolnshire Methodist History Society*, 1, parts xiii and xiv (1969–70).

[834] Jackson, 'Baptists in Leicestershire', 75.

[835] Kendall, *Primitive Methodist Church*, ii. 159–61.

[836] F. Hill, *Victorian Lincoln* (Cambridge 1974), 180.

[837] W. J. Reader, *Professional Men* (1966), 16, 34.

Devon between 1790 and 1837, four were surgeons, three surveyors, two physicians, and one an attorney. Among the Quakers in London (both north and south) in the 1810s there were four surgeons, four architects and surveyors, two barristers, a doctor of medicine, an apothecary, a solicitor, and a notary. A few Unitarian congregations also attracted a handful of professionals: the Cross Street meeting in Manchester in the 1820s numbered among its congregation a surgeon, a physician, an architect, an attorney and three solicitors, and the Renshaw Street meeting in Liverpool in the 1830s included two surgeons and a solicitor. But such congregations were very exceptional. In so far as their baptismal registers are an accurate guide to their occupational structure, the overwhelming majority of Nonconformist congregations appear to have contained not a single professional man.

The observations of contemporaries and the assumptions of historians that early nineteenth-century Nonconformity was predominantly bourgeois in character receives support from some birth and baptismal registers. In every county in which they had a following the Quakers were by far the most prosperous of the Dissenting communities and in most of those counties they were overwhelmingly middle class. If one assumes that all the men in Classes II–VI were middle class, then in only four counties (Cheshire, Derbyshire, Dorset, and Lancashire) were fewer than half the Quaker fathers members of the bourgeoisie by the early years of the nineteenth century. In every county for which evidence is available the Quakers attracted a disproportionate number of businessmen and retailers, and in most a disproportionate number of farmers. In the period 1810–37 28.5 per cent of Quaker fathers in Warwickshire were businessmen; in north London in the 1820s the proportion was 19.0 per cent; in Norfolk in the years 1810–37 the figure was 18.1 per cent. Over half the Quaker fathers of Berkshire, Buckinghamshire, Hertfordshire, Kent, and Sussex were engaged in retail trade or the manufacture of foodstuffs. Over a third of the Quakers of Cumberland, Lincolnshire, Westmorland, and the North Riding of Yorkshire were farmers. The evidence from several counties shows that Quaker prosperity was growing from decade to decade. In Durham, Gloucestershire and Bristol, and the West Riding the proportion of Quakers in the five middle-class categories went up from around 50 per cent in the 1790s to around 70 per cent in the 1830s; in Lancashire the increase was from 44.5 per cent to 62.4 per cent, and in Westmorland from 59.1 per cent to 75.0 per cent. By the end of the period three-quarters of the Quaker fathers in Devon, Essex, Gloucestershire and Bristol, Hertfordshire, Lincolnshire, Westmorland, and the North Riding belonged to one of the middle-class categories. The only blips on the rising graph of the Quaker prosperity were the decline in the proportion of businessmen in Suffolk from 8.2 per cent in 1790–1809 to 3.5 per cent in 1810–37, and in the West Riding from 17.8 per cent in the 1810s to 10.2 per cent in the 1830s, suggesting that the Quakers were losing some of their wealthier members to the Church of England.

The Unitarians also boasted a number of prosperous congregations, though as a denomination they were far less wealthy than the Quakers. Nearly half the sixty-three fathers who had their children baptized in the Lewin's Mead chapel in Bristol in the 1780s fall into categories I–VI, eight of them merchants. Thirty of the seventy fathers attached to the Bowl Alley Lane chapel in Hull between 1790 and 1837 were middle class; they included eight merchants, four bankers, and four doctors. Three-quarters of the thirty-six fathers who had their children baptized in the Renshaw Street chapel in Liverpool in the 1830s were middle class, seventeen of them merchants. And two-thirds of the eighty-one fathers whose names were recorded by the Cross Street chapel in Manchester in the 1830s were middle class, twenty of them merchants. It was the prosperity of the members of Cross Street that led an American visitor to Manchester to remark in 1777 that the Dissenters in the town were 'some of the most wealthy merchants and manufacturers here'.[838] On the other hand the Unitarians, unlike the Quakers, also attracted a considerable proportion of poor people. While 36.7 per cent of the Presbyterian Unitarians of Lancashire were employed in middle-class occupations in the 1830s, and 13.4 per cent were businessmen, nearly a quarter were poverty-stricken weavers. Thirty per cent of Glamorgan Unitarians in the 1830s were unskilled, and another 22.2 per cent were lower-skilled workers, earning less than £1 a week. The Methodist Unitarians of Lancashire were, after the Primitive Methodists, the poorest of all the Nonconformists of the county, with more than half their fathers scraping a living as weavers in the 1820s and 1830s.

A number of Independent churches, while not as wealthy as the most prosperous Unitarian congregations, were also strongly bourgeois in character. Ten of the small band of forty-eight fathers whose children were baptized by Thomas Binney in the King's Weigh House in the 1830s were businessmen, three of them merchants and two bankers, and three-quarters of those King's Weigh House fathers earned their living in one of the middle-class occupations. Of the forty-three fathers whose occupations were recorded by the Independent Nether chapel in Sheffield in the 1830s ten were merchants, four manufacturers, and two were described as gentlemen. Two-thirds of the

---

[838] G. A. Ward (ed.), *Journal and Letters of the Late Samuel Curwen* (New York, 1942), cited by Seed, 'Unitarianism and Liberal Culture', 66.

fathers attached to the Independent church at Cirencester in Gloucestershire and half those associated with the Castle Gate Congregational church in Nottingham in the 1830s fall into the five middle-class categories, while 47 per cent of the fathers associated with the George Street Independent church in Liverpool in the 1820s and with the Congregational churches in Manchester in the 1830s were middle class. At county level the Congregational churches of Lancashire, Norfolk, Nottinghamshire, Staffordshire, Worcestershire, and the West Riding all contained a much higher proportion of businessmen than was present in the population at large, and in nearly every county in England (but not in Wales) the Congregationalists attracted a disproportionately high number of retailers and white-collar workers. The tables for Middlesex and north London and for Surrey and south London explain why metropolitan-based Independent leaders such as Algernon Wells were so worried by the bourgeois bias of Congregationalism. A quarter of the Independents of north London and nearly 20 per cent of those of Surrey and south London were retailers in the 1830s. The proportion of Middlesex and north London Congregationalists who were in categories II–VI was 42.9 per cent in the 1830s, while the figure for south London was 37.5 per cent, whereas less than a quarter of the general population of those counties was middle class.[839] The Congregationalists of south London would have appeared even more bourgeois had it not been for the presence of a large and predominantly working-class congregation of Welsh Independents in Guildford Street, Southwark: 48.7 per cent of the English Independents of south London were middle class.

My analysis of the Dissenting registers also provides some support for Alan Gilbert's thesis that artisans were overrepresented in Nonconformist congregations. The Congregationalists attracted a disproportionate number of members of the labour aristocracy and higher-skilled workers in fourteen counties in England: Berkshire, Buckinghamshire, Cheshire, Cornwall, Derbyshire, Devon, Dorset, Hampshire, Leicestershire, Oxfordshire, Suffolk, Wiltshire, and the East and North Ridings of Yorkshire. Similarly Wesleyan Methodist congregations contained a disproportionate number of

---

[839] In my computation of the occupations of London Dissenters I have treated the large Upper Street church, Islington, as Calvinistic Methodist although it is described in the registrar-general's list as Congregational. The cause was a proprietary chapel which from 1800 to 1827 was owned and preached in by Evan-John Jones who in 1805 joined the London Association of Calvinistic Methodists. It was not until 1828, the year after Jones's death, that the church established church meetings, and not until 1830 that it stopped using the liturgy of the Church of England. Even then Jones's successor, Charles Gilbert, tried to follow Jones's one-man method of government (anon., *Brief History of Islington Chapel* (1865)); L. D. Dixon, *Seven Score Years and Ten: The Story of Islington Chapel* (1938), 13, 18–19; *TCHS* 8 (1920–3), 320.

labour aristocrats and higher-skilled workers in fourteen English counties: Buckinghamshire, Cheshire, Devon, Hampshire, Herefordshire, Hertford-shire, Middlesex and north London, Staffordshire, Surrey and south Lon-don, Sussex, Warwickshire, Westmorland, Worcestershire, and the East Riding. The Wesleyans also attracted a disproportionate number of labour aristocrats and higher-skilled workers in Anglesey and Caernarfonshire, and in the south Welsh counties of Breconshire and Glamorgan where workers in the iron industry made up a significant proportion of their con-gregations. The available evidence suggests that the Baptists also attracted a disproportionate number of better-paid workers in Buckinghamshire, Northumberland, Warwickshire, Carmarthenshire, and Glamorgan, though the small number of Baptist registers which have survived from the early nineteenth century makes one wary of drawing firm conclusions from the data.

However, the two denominations which had the most notable success among the higher-paid manual workers were the Unitarians (in Cheshire, Dorset, and the West Riding) and the Methodist New Connexion (in Cheshire, Lancashire, Staffordshire, and the East Riding). The success of both denom-inations among the higher-skilled workers of Cheshire, and of the Kilhamites among those same workers in Lancashire, was due to their ability to attract considerable numbers of cotton spinners, who in the 1830s could earn between 20s. and 45s. a week, between twice and five times the earnings of weavers.[840] Most spectacular of all was the support won by the Methodist New Connexion in the Potteries of Staffordshire where they were the largest Nonconformist denomination in 1851. Potters, who were earning between 17s. and 28s. a week in the 1830s,[841] made up 40 per cent of the fathers who had their children baptized in the three Kilhamite chapels for which evidence is available in the 1820s and 1830s. It is significant that among the largest employers in the Potteries were John and William Ridgway of Hanley who, like many of their workers, were members of the Methodist New Connexion and who had reputations as considerate employers, philanthropists, and advocates of political reform.[842]

The accompanying analysis of Nonconformist occupations also contains no surprises by confirming that Quakers and Unitarians were usually more prosperous than Congregationalists, that Independent congregations were

---

[840] Chadwick, 'Wages in Manchester, Salford, and Lancashire', 24; *Returns of Wages* (1887), 6–8; Wood, *History of Wages in the Cotton Trade*, 23, 44, 58.

[841] Warburton, *Trade Union Organisation in North Staffordshire*, 242.

[842] J. H. Y. Briggs, 'The Radical Saints of Shelton', in D. J. Jeremy (ed.), *Business and Religion in Britain* (Aldershot, 1988), 47–71.

often more prosperous than those of the Wesleyan Methodists, and that Wesleyan societies were of higher social standing than those of the Primitive Methodists or Bible Christians. In Lancashire in the 1830s Quakers and Presbyterian Unitarians had proportionately three times as many business-men as had the Independents who had twice as many as the Wesleyans. In the West Riding the Quakers had, in percentage terms, twice as many busi-nessmen and five times as many retailers as the Independents, who in their turn had four times as many businessmen and twice as many retailers as the Wesleyans. In Suffolk the Quakers had three times as many retailers as the Independents who had twice as many as the Wesleyans. Conversely the Wesleyans of Suffolk, like the Wesleyans of Dorset and Lincolnshire, attracted twice the proportion of unskilled workers as did the Independents. In Leicestershire and Oxfordshire the percentage of Wesleyan fathers who were unskilled was three times that of Independent fathers who were unskilled. In Berkshire, Herefordshire, and Wiltshire the proportion of unskilled workers among the Primitive Methodists was double the propor-tion among the Wesleyans. Similarly in Cornwall, Hampshire, and Somerset the Bible Christians attracted, in percentage terms, twice as many unskilled workers as did the Wesleyans.

However, the most important conclusion to emerge from my analysis of the Dissenting registers is not that Bible Christian congregations were poorer than those of the Wesleyans, or that Wesleyan congregations were usually less prosperous than those of the Independents: it is the fact that in the vast majority of counties the adherents of *all* the Evangelical Noncon-formist denominations, with the partial exception of the Independents, were predominantly poor. Alan Gilbert was led to conclude that labourers were underrepresented in the Dissenting registers because fathers' occupations were more frequently listed in the baptismal registers for the counties of northern England than for those in the south. As a result any national sample is going to be biased in favour of industrial occupations against those con-cerned with agricultural. But a county by county analysis enables one to see that in many rural counties Nonconformity did in fact enjoy the support of a substantial number of agricultural labourers. In Buckinghamshire in the 1830s 44.5 per cent of Independent fathers were labourers. In Essex the percentage of Congregationalists who were labourers was 43.8; in Mont-gomeryshire 42.4; in Cardiganshire 43.2; and in six other Welsh counties it was over 30 per cent. In Bedfordshire 59.9 per cent of Wesleyans were labourers in the 1830s; in Huntingdonshire 54.0 per cent; in Suffolk 49.8 per cent; in Cambridgeshire 43.2 per cent; in Northamptonshire 42.6 per cent; and in Anglesey 41.6 per cent. In Norfolk 47.4 per cent of Primitive

Methodists were labourers, in Essex 44.1 per cent, and in Herefordshire 40.0 per cent. The proportion of Calvinistic Methodists who were labourers was 35.6 per cent in Denbighshire and around 30 per cent in Cardiganshire, Carmarthenshire, Merioneth, and Pembrokeshire. In all these cases the proportion of labourers among Nonconformist fathers was roughly the same as the percentage of labourers in the population at large. But in some cases the proportion of labourers among the Dissenters was very much larger than the proportion in the general population. This was true of the Independents of Merioneth (46.2 per cent), the Baptists of Suffolk (66.7 per cent), the Primitive Methodists of Huntingdonshire (85.1 per cent in the 1850s), Northamptonshire (77.2 per cent in the 1840s), Bedfordshire (68.5 per cent), Wiltshire (61.7 per cent), and Berkshire (61.2 per cent), and of the Bible Christians in every county in which they were represented. In many rural counties the occupational structure of Nonconformist denominations was very similar to that of the population at large, apart from the fact that rural Dissenters could claim the support of very few gentlemen and of virtually no professional men. But in a significant number of cases the baptismal registers reveal that the adherents of rural Nonconformity were in fact considerably poorer than the inhabitants of the wider community from which they were drawn.

If one turns to industrial England one finds that here, too, Nonconformity attracted a surprising number of the urban poor. The argument that skilled artisans were overrepresented in Dissenting congregations is valid for some denominations in some counties, but the extent of that overrepresentation has been grossly exaggerated by the assumption that highly-paid iron founders and printers, reasonably well-paid blacksmiths and carpenters, and desperately poor hand-loom weavers and framework knitters belonged to the same social category. They did not. Neither in terms of their position in the social hierarchy nor often in terms of their earnings were the depressed workers I have allocated to class X far removed from agricultural labourers. The occupations of hand-loom weaver, framework knitter, nailer, chainmaker, and even some occupations such as that of shoemaker, which had once been better paid, were often merely the jobs undertaken by rural labourers when they moved to towns.[843] Throughout industrial England the repeal of the apprenticeship clauses of the Elizabethan Statute of Artificers in 1814 opened hitherto skilled crafts to a flood of unskilled workers with the result that wages in those crafts were depressed to a level as low or sometimes

---

[843] D. Bythell, *The Handloom Weavers* (Cambridge, 1969), 45; J. Foster, *Class Struggle and the Industrial Revolution* (1974), 86–7, 102–3.

lower than those of agricultural labourers.[844] The reason why Alan Gilbert found a comparatively low proportion of labourers in his nation-wide sample of Nonconformist baptismal registers was because men who described their occupation as that of labourer, in the early nineteenth century as a hundred years earlier, were confined very largely to rural areas and to ports such as Liverpool and were in a small minority in manufacturing towns.[845] In Lancashire, according to the 1841 census, 18.5 per cent of the total adult male population were labourers, and 20.9 per cent of the male population of Liverpool were labourers, but the proportion of labourers in Manchester was only 10.3 per cent, in Bolton 7.9 per cent, and in Oldham only 6.0 per cent. The term 'labourer' thus covers most of the rural poor (apart from Wales, where the standard of living of farmers was often not much better than that of labourers[846]), but only a small proportion of the urban poor. The urban and industrial poor comprised not only unskilled labourers but also semi-skilled workers such as hand-loom weavers and framework knitters whose earnings had been depressed by competition from rural and Irish immigrants and, in the case of weavers, by competition from power-driven machinery. And also among the urban poor were numerous workers such as lacemakers and woolcombers, shoemakers and tailors, who even in good years usually earned less than £1 a week and whose livelihood was frequently threatened by unemployment. The standard of living of a working-class family was determined only in part by the wage rates paid to the father of the household. It was even more dependent on the regularity of his income, on the size of his family, and on whether his wife and children could themselves contribute to the family budget. An analysis of the incomes of working-class families in Manchester and Dukinfield in the late 1830s found that the incomes of families in which the father was a labourer were often higher than those in which the father was a weaver, dyer, warehouseman, or even spinner, and that the families of dressers and overlookers were only marginally better off. The only families which were significantly more prosperous than those of the labourers were those headed by a machine printer and a millwright—men I have classified as belonging to the labour aristocracy.[847]

It is therefore legitimate, when looking at the accompanying analysis of the occupations of Dissenting fathers, to regard the men in Classes IX and X as

---

[844] Thompson, *Making of the English Working Class*, 279–86.

[845] Cf. Watts, *The Dissenters*, i. 348–52. Liverpool had a higher 'proportion of its labour force engaged in casual work' than any town in England (D. Fraser, *Power and Authority in the Victorian City* (Oxford, 1979), 39–40).

[846] D. Williams, *The Rebecca Riots* (Cardiff, 1955), 101–3, 109.

[847] W. Neil, 'Income and Expenditure of the Working Classes in Manchester and Dukinfield', *Journal of the Statistical Society*, 4 (1841), 320–34.

belonging to the mainly urban and industrial poor. If one adds to their number the predominantly rural poor in Class XI one comes to the conclusion that in most of the counties in England and Wales in which they were represented at least a third of Congregationalist fathers, nearly half of New Connexion Methodist fathers, a majority of Baptist, Calvinistic Methodist, and Wesleyan fathers, and at least two-thirds of Bible Christian and Primitive Methodist fathers were poor men earning less than £1 a week. In all 36 English counties for which we have evidence, apart from Middlesex and north London, over a third of Congregationalists were in Classes IX–XI in the 1830s, in two-thirds of those counties over 40 per cent of Congregationalists were in the bottom three categories, and in nine counties over half the Congregationalists were in Classes IX–XI. In Wales over half the Independents were in the bottom three categories in every county apart from Breconshire and in six Welsh counties over 60 per cent of Independents were in Classes IX–XI. The proportion of male Congregationalists who were lower-skilled, depressed, or unskilled workers was 70.8 per cent in Flintshire, 67.2 per cent in Monmouthshire, 66.9 per cent in Caernarfonshire, 65.4 per cent in Cumberland, and 63.1 per cent in Essex. And if one can assume that all workers from the labour aristocracy downwards belonged to the working class, then one can conclude that in every county in England and Wales, again apart from Middlesex, more than half the Congregationalist fathers were working class, that in 41 counties out of 48 two-thirds of Congregationalists were working class, and that in 18 over 75 per cent of Independent fathers were working class. The social structure of provincial Congregationalism was thus very different from that of metropolitan Congregationalism, and the contrast was pointed to by an anonymous contributor to the *Congregational Magazine* in 1836. 'A tolerably extensive acquaintance with county congregations' had led the writer to conclude that between 'two-thirds or three-fourths of each congregation consists of the poor', that is of mechanics or of agricultural labourers. But after living in London for two years he had come to the conclusion that in the metropolis the poor constituted only a quarter of some congregations and in others 'scarcely any such individuals are to be found'.[848] His observations are confirmed exactly by my analysis of Congregational baptismal registers.

Provincial Wesleyans were even poorer than provincial Congregationalists. In 33 of 40 English counties and in 9 out of 11 Welsh counties for which we have evidence at least 50 per cent of Wesleyan fathers were in Classes IX–XI, and in 16 English counties and 7 Welsh counties over 60 per cent of Wesleyan

---

[848] *Congregational Magazine*, NS 12 (1836), 24.

fathers were in one of those bottom three categories. That figure rose to 75.6 per cent in Northamptonshire, 74.4 per cent in Bedfordshire, 72.0 per cent in Shropshire, 70.8 per cent in Huntingdonshire, and 70.3 per cent in Nottinghamshire. At least 50 per cent of Baptists were in Classes IX–XI in 9 out of 14 counties for which we have evidence, and in Leicestershire, Monmouthshire, and Suffolk the figure was over 80 per cent. Over 60 per cent of Primitive Methodists fell into the bottom three categories in 19 of the 22 counties for which data are available, and the proportion was over 80 per cent in Bedfordshire, Cumberland, Derbyshire, Huntingdonshire, Leicestershire, Northamptonshire, and Nottinghamshire. At least 60 per cent of Bible Christian fathers in all the counties in which they were represented were in Classes IX–XI, as were half the Calvinistic Methodist fathers in every Welsh county, except Breconshire and Montgomeryshire, and also in Middlesex and north London. And again on the assumption that all workers from the labour aristocracy downwards can be described as working class, then working-class men constituted over 60 per cent of the Baptist fathers in every county for which we have evidence apart from Bedfordshire, where the data are limited to the period 1790–1819. At least 70 per cent of both Wesleyan and New Connexion Methodist fathers belonged to the working class in every county for which we have evidence, and for the Wesleyans in 31 out of 51 counties the figure was over 80 per cent. As for the Primitive Methodists, over 80 per cent of their fathers were working class in every county for which data are available, and in 17 out of 22 counties over 90 per cent of Ranter fathers were working class.

It is evident from the accompanying tables that Nonconformity had a special appeal not only to skilled artisans but also to those depressed workers whose standard of living was being so cruelly eroded in the first four decades of the nineteenth century. Framework knitters were heavily overrepresented among the Baptists and Primitive Methodists of Leicestershire and among the Primitive Methodists and New Connexion Methodists of Nottinghamshire. Few framework knitters appear among the Congregationalists of Leicestershire, but that is because the registers which have survived from the Congregational churches in Leicestershire in the 1820s and 1830s rarely give fathers' occupations. A London Missionary Society deputation to Hinckley in 1840 found that the congregation at the town's Independent chapel consisted largely of stockingers 'with their aprons wrapped round them . . . most of them distressingly poor with families and earning 8 or 10s a week'.[849] All

---

[849] B. Stanley, 'Home Support for Overseas Missions in Early Victorian England, 1838–73', Ph.D. thesis (Cambridge, 1979), 189.

the Dissenting denominations in Lancashire apart from the Quakers and the New Connexion Methodists contained a much higher proportion of weavers than was present in the population at large. Some of the Independent weavers had either deserted the denomination or found alternative employment by the 1830s, and the proportion of weavers among the Baptists, which was over 50 per cent in the 1810s, fell over the next two decades. But even in the 1830s weavers constituted a huge 31.4 per cent of Baptist fathers in Lancashire. In 1842 the pastor of the Stockport Particular Baptist church in Cheshire reported that nearly all his members were 'factory operatives whose wages have been reduced nearly fifty per cent in five years', and seven years later the members of the Atherton Baptist church in Lancashire were said to be earning on average only 7s. a week.[850] The proportion of weavers among the Wesleyans of Lancashire appears actually to have risen from 24.9 per cent in the 1810s to 32.1 per cent in the 1830s. And the plight of the Primitive Methodists and Methodist Unitarians in the county was even worse, with 45.7 per cent and 52.4 per cent still trying to scrape a living as weavers in the 1830s. In the West Riding of Yorkshire 45.9 per cent of Baptists, 42.0 per cent of Moravians, 33.6 per cent of Primitive Methodists, and 22.3 per cent of Wesleyans were weavers in the 1830s. The baptismal registers fail to distinguish hand-loom weavers from power-loom weavers, but both groups were badly paid and by the 1830s were often earning less than agricultural labourers.[851] The same was true of the shoemakers of Northamptonshire[852] who constituted 20.1 per cent of the Baptists in the county in the 1820s, and of the silk weavers of Warwickshire who made up 26.2 per cent of the Independents in the county in the 1830s.

But the occupational group above all others to whom all the major Evangelical Nonconformist denominations had a special appeal were the miners.[853] Miners constituted 41.2 per cent of Wesleyan fathers in Cornwall in the 1830s and 42.5 per cent of those in Shropshire. In Cumberland 30.9 per cent of Independents, 33.5 per cent of Wesleyans, and 72.9 per cent of Primitive Methodists were miners. In Durham a quarter of Wesleyans and a third of Ranters were miners. So, too, were 29.0 per cent of New Connexion Methodists, 32.6 per cent of Wesleyans, and 38.6 per cent of Primitive

---

[850] *Baptist Magazine*, 34 (1842), 591; Weston, 'Baptists of North-West England', 159.

[851] Chadwick, 'Rates of Wages in Manchester, Salford, and Lancashire', 24, 29; Bythell, *Handloom Weavers*, 134–6.

[852] Foster, *Class Struggle and the Industrial Revolution* (1974), 86–7, 102–3.

[853] Miners' wages varied enormously from coalfield to coalfield and fluctuated with demand, but they rarely exceeded 20s. a week and on occasion could be as low as 5s. a week (R. Challinor and B. Ripley, *The Miners' Association* (1968), 54–5, 57, 111, 131; *Returns of Wages* (1887), 24).

Methodists in Northumberland.[854] The proportion of Baptists who were miners was 34.1 per cent in Staffordshire and 70.4 per cent in Monmouthshire. In Flintshire and Monmouthshire over 40 per cent of Independents were miners, as were 35.1 per cent in Glamorgan. In Monmouthshire 38.2 per cent of Calvinistic Methodists were miners and nearly 30 per cent of Welsh Methodists in both Flintshire and Glamorgan were similarly employed. The Dissenting baptismal registers prove conclusively the appeal of Evangelical Nonconformity to tightly knit communities whose menfolk worked in continual fear of sudden death.

Not only do the Dissenting registers reveal that, outside London, the majority of men in the overwhelming majority of Evangelical Nonconformist congregations were poor, they also suggest that as Evangelical Nonconformity expanded in the first four decades of the nineteenth century, so it went down the social scale. The evidence presented in the county tables of changes in the occupational structure of denominations from decade to decade must be treated with caution, for such variations may be due to changes in the availability of data rather than to real changes in the occupations of Dissenting fathers. The apparent decline in the number of miners among the Independents of the North Riding from the early 1820s is due entirely to the fact that the Swaledale Congregational church stopped recording fathers' occupations in 1822. However, the evidence from numerous counties suggests that in the first forty years of the nineteenth century the proportion of unskilled and lower-skilled workers among the fathers having their children baptized in Nonconformist chapels was rising from decade to decade. Far from Dissent becoming more bourgeois, outside the major towns the reverse was happening: at least until the 1830s Nonconformity was increasingly successful in recruiting the poor. Thus the percentage of unskilled workers among the Wesleyans of Bedfordshire rose from 26.9 per cent in the 1810s to 63.6 per cent in the 1830s. In Cornwall the proportion of Wesleyans in categories IX–XI increased from 40.4 per cent in the 1810s to 59.7 per cent in the 1820s and to 64.3 per cent in the 1830s. In Buckinghamshire the proportion of unskilled workers among the Independents went up from 32.9 per cent in the 1810s to 46.7 per cent in the 1830s. Among Northamptonshire Independents the proportion of unskilled workers rose from 27 per cent in the 1800s and 1810s to around 40 per cent in the 1820s and 1830s. Among the

---

[854] The humble status of Northumberland Methodists is also confirmed by J. P. Horner's analysis of chapel trustees in south Northumberland for the period 1821–1914. He found that 27% of both Wesleyan and Primitive Methodist trustees were 'unskilled labourers', which term he took to include miners (Horner, 'The Influence of Methodism on the Social Structure and Culture of Rural Northumberland, 1820–1914', MA thesis (Newcastle upon Tyne, 1971), 137).

Congregationalists of Leicestershire the proportion of unskilled workers rose from 20.7 per cent in the period 1822–39 to 38.5 per cent in the period 1840–9. Similar evidence of Nonconformist denominations going down the social scale is revealed by the Wesleyans of Northumberland, Oxfordshire, Staffordshire, Suffolk, and Flintshire, by the Independents of Hertfordshire and Shropshire, by the Bible Christians of Kent, and by the Calvinistic Methodists of Anglesey. Most impressive of all is the evidence of the Wesleyans of Denbighshire, for the information on fathers' occupations for the 1810s, the 1820s, and the 1830s all comes from the same six chapels and circuits. This evidence shows that the proportion of unskilled workers among the Denbighshire Wesleyan fathers increased from 26.7 per cent in the 1810s to 33.4 per cent in the 1820s and to 38.3 per cent in the 1830s, while the proportion of fathers in the bottom three categories IX–XI rose from 56.2 per cent in the 1810s to 68.6 per cent in the 1830s. There is thus considerable evidence to suggest that the rapid expansion of Evangelical Nonconformity in the first half of the nineteenth century was achieved very largely by the success of Methodists and Dissenters in appealing not so much to the middle classes but to the industrial and rural poor.

Finally it must be emphasized that the picture of Nonconformist congregations which emerges from a study of their baptismal registers may well appear more prosperous than it was in reality, for the registers reveal the occupations only of fathers and heads of families and exclude those of wives (unless they were recently widowed), and of men and women who could not afford to marry. Yet women made up the majority of the membership in virtually every Nonconformist church, they were barred from the best-paid occupations, and in the worst-paid occupations they were forced to accept much lower wages than men. All this is not to deny, of course, that a majority of working-class men and women in mid-nineteenth century England attended neither church nor chapel. Horace Mann believed that the most important fact revealed by the religious census of 1851 was the 'alarming number of non-attendants', and he concluded that the majority of those absentees from public worship were labourers and artisans.[855] But the fact that the absentees from religious worship were largely members of the working class does not invalidate the evidence of the Dissenting registers that the majority of chapel worshippers were also drawn from the working class. The evidence of those registers does in fact reinforce the conclusions from the study of the geographic distribution of Dissent and of its psychological motivation: that the massive expansion of Nonconformity in the first half of the

---

[855] *Religious Census*, p. clviii.

nineteenth century took place predominantly among people who were poor, ill-educated, unsophisticated, and superstitious.

10. 'HE THAT HASTETH TO BE RICH HATH AN EVIL EYE': THE WEBER THESIS

The Dissenting baptismal registers emphasize, more dramatically than any other evidence, the gulf separating the often wealthy, sophisticated, and educated congregations of the Unitarians, the Quakers, and occasionally the Congregationalists, from the humble and barely literate congregations of much of Evangelical Nonconformity. But while the poverty and ignorance of the great mass of Evangelical Dissenters has rarely been noted, the success of a tiny minority of Dissenting entrepreneurs has frequently been commented on. Indeed, such was the prominence and wealth won by numerous Dissenters during the industrial revolution that many historians and sociologists have concluded that there was a special relationship between religious Nonconformity and successful business entrepreneurship.

The roll-call of firms founded and run by Dissenters which were to become household names is certainly impressive. At the turn of the eighteenth and nineteenth centuries Quaker firms such as Backhouses, Barclays, Lloyds, and Overend and Gurney were already pre-eminent in banking.[856] In the late eighteenth century the Quaker Abraham Darby III presided over the largest iron-making business in Britain at Coalbrookdale in Shropshire, and between 1777 and 1779 his firm built the country's most famous monument of the industrial revolution, the Iron Bridge across the River Severn.[857] Much of the industrial development of north-east England was sponsored by the Quaker Pease family. Edward Pease was the chief promoter of the Stockton–Darlington railway and he also provided the bulk of the capital for the firm of Robert Stephenson and Company which manufactured George Stephenson's *Rocket*. Edward's son, Joseph Pease, played a leading part in the subsequent railway development of the north-east, in founding the town of Middlesbrough, and in developing the coal and iron industries of the region.[858] In East Anglia Ransomes, the firm of agricultural implement makers, was founded by a Quaker in the late eighteenth century and was run by

---

[856] A. Raistrick, *Quakers in Science and Industry* (1950), 319–33.
[857] Ibid. 141; D. B. Windsor, *The Quaker Enterprise* (1980), 54.
[858] M. W. Kirby, *Men of Business and Politics: The Rise and Fall of the Quaker Pease Dynasty of North-East England, 1700–1943* (1984), 10–17, 22–43.

Quakers throughout the nineteenth century.[859] Similarly at Street in Somerset the shoemaking firm of Clarks was founded and run by Quakers. And Quaker firms dominated sections of the new food manufacturing industries: the biscuit firms of Huntley and Palmers of Reading and of Carrs of Carlisle, the chocolate and cocoa manufacturing firms of Cadbury, Rowntree, and Fry were all founded and run by Friends.

Unitarians were, like the Quakers, prominent in banking: two of Manchester's major banks, the firms of Heywood Brothers and John Jones, were founded by members of Cross Street chapel, and the marriage of John Jones's daughter to a former Unitarian minister, Lewis Loyd, led to the establishment of the firm of Jones, Loyd, and Company which subsequently merged with the Westminster Bank.[860] England's most celebrated pottery manufacturer, Josiah Wedgwood, was also a Unitarian. But it was in the textile industry that the Unitarians made their greatest impact. The list of leading Unitarian textile manufacturers includes Jedediah Strutt, who in partnership with Richard Arkwright built the first water-driven cotton mill at Cromford in Derbyshire in 1771; John Fielden, whose Quaker father Joshua started the cotton-spinning business at Todmorden in 1782 which, under his son, was to become the largest textile firm in the country; Samuel Greg, who in 1783 founded the mill at Quarry Bank at Styal in Cheshire which was to become the basis of one of the largest cotton manufacturing firms; John Marshall, who in 1788 started the Leeds flax-spinning business which was to make him one of Britain's wealthiest manufacturers; and Samuel Courtauld, who in 1816 established at Bocking in Essex what was to become the largest manufactory of crape in the world.[861] Independents were also prominent in textiles: Samuel Morley, who was a member of Thomas Binney's prosperous King's Weigh House church, and who owned the largest hosiery business in Great Britain, Francis Crossley, who at Halifax headed the largest carpet manufacturing business in the world, and Titus Salt, who in Bradford controlled the largest worsted factory in the world, were all Congregationalists.[862] So, too, was Henry Overton Wills, the founder of what was to become the largest tobacco producing firm in Britain. And Particular Baptist

[859] Raistrick, *Quakers in Science and Industry*, 210–13.
[860] R. V. Holt, *Unitarian Contribution to Social Progress in England* (1938), 60; Seed, 'Unitarianism and Liberal Culture', 210.
[861] R. S. Fitton and A. P. Wadsworth, *The Strutts and the Arkwrights, 1758–1830* (Manchester, 1958), 65; S. A. Weaver, *John Fielden and the Politics of Popular Radicalism* (Oxford, 1987), 19–20; M. B. Rose, *The Gregs of Quarry Bank Mill* (Cambridge, 1986), 18; W. G. Rimmer, *Marshall of Leeds: Flax-Spinners, 1788–1886* (Cambridge, 1960), 23; D. C. Coleman, *Courtaulds: An Economic and Social History* (Oxford, 1969), 48.
[862] S. D. Chapman, 'Samuel Morley', *Dictionary of Business Biography* (1985), iv. 319–23.

entrepreneurs included Jeremiah Colman, the founder of the Norwich mustard firm, and Sir Samuel Morton Peto, the building and railway contractor whose firms were responsible for the building of Nelson's Column, the Reform Club, and the Houses of Parliament, and for railway construction throughout much of southern and eastern England, and in Argentina, Algeria, Australia, and Canada.[863]

The supposed connection between Nonconformity and successful business activity formed one of the central themes of the famous thesis put forward by Max Weber in 1905.[864] Weber argued that both Calvinism and Methodism produced what he called 'worldly asceticism': that the notion that a Christian was 'called' to serve God in a secular trade combined with the need to restrict consumption in accordance with the demands of a strict moral code to issue in the accumulation of capital and in business success. Weber's thesis led to one of the great historiographical debates of the twentieth century, and both historians and sociologists have found it as difficult to agree with Weber as they have found it impossible to ignore him.[865] T. S. Ashton argued that the significant part played by Nonconformist entrepreneurs in the industrial revolution was the result not so much of their religious teaching as of the appeal of the individualism and spontaneity of Dissent to men of 'self-reliance, assertiveness, and adventurous enterprise' and of their superior education. The schools and universities of Scotland and the Dissenting academies in England, contended Ashton, provided Scottish Presbyterians and English Nonconformists with an education, and in particular with a scientific education, which was far in advance of that which was available to Anglicans.[866] Everett Hagen took the argument a stage further by investigating the religion of ninety-two entrepreneurs mentioned in Ashton's history of the *Industrial Revolution* and discovering that '41 per cent of the English and Welsh entrepreneurs whose religion is known' were Nonconformists. But again, like Ashton, Hagen argued that the fact that Dissenters provided 'a disproportionate number of the innovators was due not to religious dogma but to the independence of mind fostered by Dissent'.[867] Hagen's conclusions have, however, been challenged by W. D. Rubinstein who has made a study of the very wealthy in Britain based on the

[863] Underwood, *History of the English Baptists*, 239–40; C. Binfield, 'Sir Samuel Morton Peto', *Biographical Dictionary of Modern British Radicals* (1984), ii. 407–11.

[864] M. Weber, *The Protestant Ethic and the Spirit of Capitalism*, trans. T. Parsons (1930).

[865] In a vast literature the most trenchant criticism of Weber is K. Samuelsson, *Religion and Economic Action*, trans. E. G. French (Stockholm, 1961).

[866] T. S. Ashton, *Iron and Steel in the Industrial Revolution* (Manchester, 1968), 211–12; T. S. Ashton, *The Industrial Revolution* (1947), 17–21.

[867] E. Hagen, *On the Theory of Social Change* (1962), 294–8.

wills of 1,300 men who died leaving £500,000 or more between 1809 and 1939, those who left more than £160,000 between 1809 and 1829, and those who left more than £250,000 between 1850 and 1869.[868] Rubinstein criticizes Hagen for omitting bankers, financiers, merchants, and shipowners when extracting names from Ashton's book, and for confusing innovators with entrepreneurs. 'Many key inventors', argues Rubinstein, 'were incompetent or luckless as businessmen.' In contrast to Ashton and Hagen, Rubinstein found that the proportion of Nonconformists among the very wealthy was similar to the proportion of Nonconformists in the population at large, although he admits that Quakers were 'quite dramatically over-represented' among the very wealthy, that Baptists were 'slightly under-represented', and that Methodists 'were grossly under-represented'. Entrepreneurial success, he concludes, had 'little or nothing to do with religion'.[869] Anthony Howe, in his study of 351 cotton masters, similarly found only an 'extremely marginal predominance of Nonconformists' and concluded that religion 'was not a major factor contributing to economic success'.[870]

The conclusions of Rubinstein and Howe are, however, themselves open to qualification. Rubinstein was measuring wealth at death, not entrepreneurial success, and there is a good deal of evidence to suggest that many Nonconformist businessmen regarded the hoarding of wealth as an evil to be avoided. Wesley had told his followers that the Lord forbade them to lay up 'treasures upon earth' as surely as he proscribed adultery: if they received £500 a year, spent only £200, and failed to give £300 back to God then they robbed God of that £300.[871] Wealthy Methodists, said Wesley, 'having gained all they can and saved all they can, they should give all they can',[872] and up to a point his prescription was followed both by his own followers and by other Nonconformists. It was said of the wealthy Liverpool Baptist, Richard Haughton, that 'his only wish was to give away all that he possessed'.[873] The Congregational worsted manufacturer Titus Salt reputedly gave away £250,000 in the course of his life; his fellow Independent Thomas Wilson donated nearly £30,000 towards the building of Congregational chapels and Highbury College, besides many other benefactions; another Congregationalist, the hosiery manufacturer Samuel Morley, gave away between £20,000 to £30,000; the woolcombing firm headed by the Wesleyan Isaac Holden donated at least £20,000 in ten years to Bradford charities; Richard Reynolds, the Quaker partner of Abraham Darby II and manager of

---

[868] W. D. Rubinstein, *Men of Property* (1981), 10–11.   [869] Ibid. 148–63.
[870] A. Howe, *The Cotton Masters, 1830–1860* (Oxford, 1984), 61–71.
[871] *Wesley's Works*, v. 373; vii. 36.   [872] Ibid. vii. 9.
[873] Sellers, 'Liverpool Nonconformity', 132.

the ironworks at Coalbrookdale, reputedly gave away around £8,000 a year in the late eighteenth century; the Quaker stuff merchant William Wilson gave away nearly £40,000 while spending less than £150 a year on his personal and domestic needs; and the Quaker biscuit manufacturer William Issac Palmer was said to have given away £10,000 a year, donated £25,000 to Reading municipal library, and left only £123,000 when he died in 1893.[874] At least three prominent Dissenters would have died millionaires had they not given away much of their wealth. Sir Francis Crossley, the Halifax carpet manufacturer and Liberal MP, left £800,000 when he died in 1872, but in 1857 he had presented the people of Halifax with a park which, with money invested for its maintenance, cost him £41,300; in 1870 he gave £20,000 to the London Missionary Society; he gave two sums of £10,000 to funds for retired Congregational pastors and their widows; and he similarly endowed funds for almshouses, orphanages, and schools in Halifax.[875] The Wesleyan Thomas Ferens, chairman of the Quaker firm of Reckitts, would also have died a millionaire had he not given away the bulk of his fortune to good causes in general and £250,000 to University College, Hull, in particular. And, most spectacularly of all, in the late nineteenth and first half of the twentieth centuries, the Wesleyan flour miller Joseph Rank gave away some £4 million to Methodism so that on his death in 1943 he left a mere £70,954.[876] There were thus quite a number of successful Dissenting entrepreneurs whose very generosity excluded them from Rubinstein's analysis of the very wealthy.

There is, however, a more substantial objection to Rubinstein's conclusion that entrepreneurial success had 'little or nothing to do with religion': it is not in fact supported by his own statistics. Rubinstein admits that some denominations were overrepresented among the very wealthy and that others were underrepresented, but he fails to see the significance of such denominational differences. The point can be reinforced by comparing Rubinstein's analysis of the religion of his millionaires and half-millionaires with my analysis of the 1851 religious census. Exact comparison is difficult because Rubinstein's figures cover the whole of Great Britain, not just England and Wales, and he omits from his analysis those wealthy men whose religion cannot be discovered, and such men are unlikely to have been Dissenters. I have therefore reworked Rubinstein's figures by deducting members of the Church of

---

[874] R. Balgarnie, *Sir Titus Salt* (1877), 201; anon., *Fortunes made in Business* (1884), i. 38; I. C. Bradley, *Enlightened Entrepreneurs* (1987), 43; Raistrick, *Quakers in Science and Industry*, 144–5; H. R. Hodgson, *Society of Friends in Bradford* (Bradford, 1926), 48–9; Corley, *Quaker Enterprise*, 120–2.

[875] *DNB*.

[876] G. E. Milburn, 'Piety, Profit, and Paternalism: Methodists in Business in the North-East of England', *PWHS* 44 (1983), 59, 65, 74, 83.

Scotland (but some Scottish Episcopalians may remain among the Anglicans), and by adding those men whose religion he was unable to discover, to
give a total of 675.[877] A comparison with my analysis of the religious census for
England and Wales is given in Table VII, and the results of that comparison
are exactly in line with my analysis of the Nonconformist birth and baptismal
registers. Dissent as a whole produced fewer wealthy men than their strength
in the total population would have predicted. As Rubinstein himself pointed
out the Methodists in particular were signifi-cantly underrepresented among
the millionaires and half-millionaires, a fact which is entirely consistent
with the predominantly working-class profile of Methodism revealed by
their baptismal registers. The Congregationalists produced significantly
more very wealthy men than the Methodists, again a fact consistent with the
existence of a minority of wealthy Independent congregations in the early
nineteenth century. But again the proportion of the very rich who were
Congregationalists was smaller than the proportion of Congregationalists in
the population at large. By contrast not only the Quakers, but also the
Unitarians, were heavily overrepresented among the very rich. There were
nearly ten times the proportion of Unitarians among the millionaires and
half-millionaires as in the general population; the proportion of Quakers
among the very wealthy was fifty times their proportion in the population at
large.

TABLE VII. *Comparison of the proportion of Nonconformist millionaires and
half-millionaires with the proportion of Nonconformists in the population at large*

	Nonconformist millionaires and half-millionaires		Nonconformists in England and Wales, 1851
	Number	%	%
Independents	23	3.4	4.4
Baptists	8	1.2	3.3
Quakers	29	4.3	0.09
Unitarians	12	1.8	0.2
Arminian Methodists	3	0.4	8.7
Presbyterians	2	0.3	0.3
Others	18	2.7	1.7
TOTALS	95	14.1	18.6

Similar objection can be made against the conclusions which Howe draws
from his analysis of the religion of the cotton masters. Howe grossly exagger-

[877] Rubinstein, *Men of Property*, 150–3.

ated the proportion of Dissenters in the total population and failed to appreciate the peculiar weakness of Nonconformity in the cotton-manufacturing areas. The Wesleyans constituted 7.7 per cent of Howe's 351 cotton masters, but only 3.8 per cent of the total population of Lancashire; the Congregationalists also made up 7.7 per cent of the cotton masters, but only 2.8 per cent of Lancashire's general population; the Quakers accounted for 4.3 per cent of the cotton masters, whereas they comprised only 0.1 per cent of Lancastrians; and most notable of all, 15.1 per cent of the cotton masters were Unitarians, compared with only 0.4 per cent in the general population of the county.[878] In total, Nonconformists accounted for 142 of Howe's 351 cotton masters, a proportion of 40.5 per cent, whereas they constituted only 12.0 per cent of the total population of Lancashire in 1851. Something, therefore, remains to be explained.

There is no doubt that one of the points made by Weber is valid: that conversion and subsequent membership of a Nonconformist church both produced a conscientious attitude towards work and curtailed opportunities to waste one's time and substance on frivolous pursuits, and so created a situation in which hard work and savings could result in modest prosperity. Wesley noted this consequence of adhering to Methodist discipline as early as 1763, and regarded it with grave misgivings. He had given his followers in Bristol, he wrote, 'a solemn caution not to "love the world, neither the things of the world" '. 'This', he added, 'will be their grand danger: as they are industrious and frugal, they must needs increase in goods.' Already Methodists in trading towns 'who are in business have increased in substance seven-fold; some of them twenty, yea, an hundred-fold'.[879] Forty years later the president and secretary of the Wesleyan Conference made a similar point, but they did so not to warn against the spiritual dangers of growing prosperity but to touch the consciences and the pockets of their wealthier members in appealing for funds to pay off the connexional debt. Methodists, they claimed, 'save much more by religion than is desired of them for its support', for 'superfluities are cut off by the reception of the Gospel' and 'the grace of God excites to diligence and frugality'.[880] Whereas Wesley was troubled by the evidence that conversion could be followed by an increase in wealth, his nineteenth-century followers all too often regarded such prosperity as a token of God's favour. The son of William Stockdale, a Wesleyan farmer from Burnsall in the West Riding, claimed that his father, 'prior to his conversion . . . was in poor and humble circumstances,

---

[878] Howe, *The Cotton Masters*, 62. In order to compare like with like, I have taken the proportion of Nonconformists to the total number of cotton masters, not just of those whose religious affiliation is known.

[879] *Wesley's Journal*, v. 31–2.   [880] *Minutes of the Methodist Conferences*, ii. 81.

but no sooner had he taken the Lord for his portion . . . than Providence began to smile on him . . . God blessed him in his field and cattle and family, and made him successful in his undertakings'.[881]

Membership of a Nonconformist church could on occasion set a Dissenter on the road to prosperity, not only by removing temptations to fritter away time and money on ephemeral pleasures but also by providing business contacts. Chapels and meeting-houses furnished opportunities for people who would not normally enjoy social contact to come together, and in such a situation it was only natural that Nonconformist employers would find work for fellow Dissenters who were looking for a job, and that Nonconformist tradesmen would strike bargains with, and give credit to, fellow Dissenters whose membership of the same church inspired confidence that the agreement would be honoured and the debt repaid. When the Bentnall family of Maldon in Essex joined the town's Independent church they found that their drapery business acquired 'a new class of trade' from the farmers and timber merchants in the congregation.[882] And the first step on the road to success that was to make Josiah Mason the largest maker of steel pens in the world was taken when a fellow Wesleyan introduced him to a small Birmingham pen manufacturer.[883] Whereas in the eighteenth century membership of a Dissenting church or Methodist society had frequently resulted in the convert's finding difficulty in obtaining work,[884] by the early nineteenth century attendance at a Nonconformist chapel was often seen as an economic advantage. A Bolton employer told the Wesleyan preacher Robert Miller in 1793 that 'numbers of Methodists worked for him' and that 'he liked them better than he did others, because he could depend on them'.[885] Sir Robert Peel, the master cotton-spinner and father of the future prime minister, stated that he 'left most of my works in Lancashire under the management of Methodists, and they serve me excellently well'.[886] A critic of Halifax Methodism in 1797 noted the change that was coming over the economic fortunes of the Wesleyans:

The state of Methodism is now the reverse almost of what it was at first; originally the Methodists were poor, despised, persecuted people, and suffered many things on account of their religion. Now, when a man becomes serious and enters the society, it is often a means of his advancement in the world. He forms new connexions, and these introduce him into business. And so far are they from being persecuted in general at

    [881] *Wesleyan Methodist Magazine*, 64 (1841), 177–8.
    [882] L. Davidoff and C. Hall, *Family Fortunes* (1987), 102.
    [883] *Fortunes Made in Business*, i. 142–3.
    [884] See e.g. Taylor, *History of the General Baptists*, ii. 12–13; Jackson, *Early Methodist Preachers*, ii. 271; D. D. Wilson, *Many Waters cannot Quench* (1969), 40–1.
    [885] *Methodist Magazine*, 24 (1801), 237.   [886] Tyerman, *Life of Wesley*, iii. 499.

present, that many amongst them are held in esteem, and looked upon as respectable characters, even by men of the world.[887]

There was, though, a vast difference between gaining modest prosperity and respectability and achieving the entrepreneurial success that would make one's name and one's products familiar household names: it was a gulf crossed by very few Dissenters, and then only after several generations. This is one reason why the successful entrepreneurs of the early nineteenth century were more often Quaker and Unitarian than Methodist, and why successful Methodist entrepreneurs became more prominent in the late nineteenth and twentieth centuries. But it is only one reason, and does not explain why successful entrepreneurs of the early nineteenth century were more likely to be Quakers or Unitarians than members of the even older denominations of Congregationalists and Particular Baptists. Indeed, it must be a major qualification of Weber's insistence on the Calvinist concept of predestination as an 'extraordinarily powerful' driving force for asceticism, and by implication for capitalist development,[888] that the tiny denominations of Quakers and Unitarians who rejected Calvinism produced far more entrepreneurs, both in proportionate and even in absolute terms, than did the far larger denominations of Congregationalists and Particular Baptists who clung to Calvinist theology. To what, then, are we to attribute the business success of so many Quakers and Unitarians?

To begin with, on the eve of the industrial revolution Quakers and Unitarians often found themselves in the right place at the right time. Entrepreneurial success was seldom achieved by one generation but was usually the culmination of a gradual accumulation of capital and expertise over several generations,[889] and the prominence achieved by some Quaker and Unitarian firms in the nineteenth century is in part explained by the geographic distribution and social structure of their ancestors a hundred or so years earlier. In the early eighteenth century Dissenters were more urbanized than was the population at large and they were heavily involved in the manufacture of textiles and in retail trade.[890] Although the Unitarians constituted only a tiny proportion of the population in industrial areas in 1851, a century and a half earlier their Presbyterian forebears had constituted a significant proportion of the population in the mercantile and manufacturing towns of Liverpool, Manchester, Bolton, Newcastle upon Tyne, Sheffield,

---

[887] Anon., *A Candid Address to the Methodist Societies in Halifax and Neighbouring Circuits* (1797), cited by Stigant, 'Methodism and the Working Class', 328.

[888] Weber, *The Protestant Ethic and the Spirit of Capitalism*, 128.

[889] Rubinstein, *Men of Property*, 178.   [890] Watts, *The Dissenters*, i. 285–9, 346–56.

and Nottingham, and in the future textile counties of Lancashire and Cheshire.[891] In the seventeenth and early eighteenth centuries Dissent had much greater appeal to economically independent clothiers, grocers, and ironmongers than to either landowners or landless labourers, and it was these Presbyterian clothiers and Quaker grocers who so often laid the basis of their descendants' fortunes two, three, or four generations later. Country banking in the eighteenth century grew out of wholesale trading in wool, cloth, iron, and tea, and David Pratt has calculated that by 1785 nineteen of the 119 country banks in England were either run or had been founded by Quakers.[892] The founders of two leading Quaker banking houses, Henry Gurney and James Backhouse, were both descended from two generations of wool dealers, and the railway promoter Edward Pease was descended from a grandfather who had a woolcombing business and a father who combined woolcombing with banking.[893] The Unitarian Samuel Greg's lucrative cotton-spinning business was founded on the successful firm built up by his uncles; the Quaker Joseph Crosfield's soap-making enterprise in Warrington was made possible by capital borrowed from his father's wholesale grocery business; the basis of John Marshall's fortune was laid by his father's achievement as a linen draper.[894] Josiah Wedgwood was descended from three generations of Burslem potters, and the success of Cadburys and Rowntrees as chocolate manufacturers grew logically out of long-established family grocery businesses.[895]

The geographic distribution and urban concentration of Dissenters a century before the industrial revolution does not, however, fully explain why it was Quakers and Presbyterians rather than Congregationalists and Baptists who produced the highest proportion of successful entrepreneurs. Admittedly the Congregationalists around 1700 were concentrated, as far as England was concerned, in Essex, Suffolk, and the south Midlands, the Particular Baptists were similarly at their strongest in the south Midlands and also in Wiltshire, and the General Baptists were most numerous in Kent, Buckinghamshire, Lincolnshire, and Sussex.[896] These were all areas largely untouched by the industrial revolution. But the Congregationalists and

---

[891] Ibid. 272, 277–8.

[892] D. H. Pratt, *English Quakers and the First Industrial Revolution* (New York, 1985), 73, 76.

[893] Raistrick, *Quakers in Science and Industry*, 76–80; Kirby, *Men of Business*, 1–3.

[894] Rose, *The Gregs of Quarry Bank Mill*, 15; A. E. Musson, *Enterprise in Soap and Chemicals: Joseph Crosfield and Sons* (Manchester, 1965), 7, 11, 16; Rimmer, *Marshalls of Leeds*, 13–14, 22–3.

[895] B. Trueman, 'Josiah Wedgwood: An Eighteenth-century Entrepreneur', Ph.D. thesis, (Nottingham, 1960), 48; Windsor, *Quaker Enterprise*, 79–80, 131–2.

[896] Watts, *The Dissenters*, i. 273–4, 508.

Baptists had their strongest following of all in south Wales, and especially in Monmouthshire and Glamorgan, and yet they did not make the contribution to the development of the south Wales iron and coal industries that was made by the numerically insignificant Quakers.[897] Moreover, by 1851 the Congregationalists and Baptists were far more numerous than were either the Quakers or the Unitarians in the industrial regions of Lancashire, Cheshire, the West Riding, and the north Midlands, and this had probably been the case since at least the 1790s.[898] Indeed, by the middle of the nineteenth century there was almost an inverse correlation between a denomination's popular support and its economic prosperity. Whereas the proportion of Congregationalists and Baptists in the total population of England trebled between 1718 and 1851, and in absolute terms the combined number of their adherents increased nearly tenfold, the proportion of Quakers and Presbyterian/Unitarians decreased sixfold, and in absolute terms their numbers halved. But just as the Congregationalists and Baptists grew by going down the social scale, so the Quakers and Presbyterian/Unitarians in shedding much of their popular support ascended the ladder of economic success. While Evangelical Nonconformity was becoming a mass movement with an increasingly working-class membership, the Quakers and Unitarians were becoming dwindling bands increasingly distinguished by the high proportion of bankers, merchants, and manufacturers among their members. And as their numbers declined so their social isolation, in the case of the Quakers, and their theological isolation, in the case of the Unitarians, endowed them with a strong instinct of self-preservation and mutual support. It was one of the Quakers' principles, wrote Augustine Birrell, 'to give employment to one another, to entertain one another, and to fall in love with one another'.[899] And much the same was true of the Unitarians.

There is a mass of evidence to illustrate the way in which the chapel community launched young men on their careers, facilitated the making of business contacts, and fostered the birth of business partnerships.[900] The obtaining of credit within the chapel community was of especial importance in an age before the enactment of the principle of limited liability: the Quaker reputation for honesty, and the knowledge that Quakers investigated

---

[897] M. F. Williams, 'The Society of Friends in Glamorgan', MA thesis (Aberystwyth, 1950), 204–10.

[898] See Watts, *The Dissenters*, i. 467–9, 477, for the growth of Congregationalism in northern England in the late 18th cent.

[899] A. Birrell, 'Sketch of the Earlier William Rathbones', in E. A. Rathbone, *Records of the Rathbone Family* (Edinburgh, 1913), 90.

[900] See e.g. Sellers, 'Liverpool Nonconformity', 81–2, for advancement in shipping through membership of orthodox Presbyterian congregations.

the affairs of, and often disowned, those who became bankrupt was an important factor in the minds of Friends and non-Friends alike, and goes far to explain Quaker success in banking and the ease with which Quaker entrepreneurs were able to raise loans.[901] Joshua Fielden, the Quaker yeoman farmer and woollen weaver, started what was to become the largest textile manufacturing business in the United Kingdom in three cottages in Todmorden in 1782, bought with money borrowed from a friend, probably a fellow Quaker.[902] Though the strict enforcement of the Society of Friends' marriage regulations contributed to the decline in Quaker numbers, it may also have helped to keep and augment wealth within the Quaker community in the way that arranged marriages are designed to preserve wealth in other societies. The chief backing for Edward Pease's promotion of the Stockton–Darlington railway was provided by the Backhouses and the Gurneys who were Pease's fellow Quakers and who were, or were to become, his relations. The Gurneys and Backhouses between them put up a third of the capital for the railway; Edward Pease's aunt Ann had married Jonathan Backhouse in 1774, his son Joseph was to marry Emma Gurney in 1826, and Emma's elder sister was in turn married to the son of Ann Pease, the second Jonathan Backhouse.[903] The Gurneys also provided financial backing for Robert Ransome's first iron foundry in Norwich, and Robert Ransome was the brother-in-law of another east England Quaker entrepreneur, Isaac Reckitt, who started his starch milling business with capital borrowed from his Quaker mother-in-law and whose 'Reckitt's Blue' was yet another Quaker product to become a household name.[904]

The nexus of business acquaintances and profitable marriages provided by the chapel community was also important for Unitarian and Congregational entrepreneurs. Jedediah Strutt's business success owed a good deal to his partnership with Samuel Need, a wealthy Nottingham hosier who was once a member of the High Pavement Presbyterian congregation and subsequently joined the Independents.[905] Samuel Greg's business ventures clearly benefited from his marriage to Hannah Lightbody, the daughter of a Liverpool Unitarian merchant, who brought him both a dowry of £10,000 and contacts through her sisters' husbands with other textile manufacturers and bankers.[906] In Leeds John Marshall found a succession of partners among his fellow Unitarians, and both he and the Congregationalist newspaper proprietor

[901] Watts, *The Dissenters*, i. 363, 365.   [902] Weaver, *John Fielden*, 19.
[903] Kirby, *Men of Business and Politics*, 3, 11, 21.
[904] Raistrick, *Quakers in Science and Industry*, 210; Davidoff and Hall, *Family Fortunes*, 221.
[905] Fitton and Wadsworth, *The Strutts and the Arkwrights*, 38.
[906] Rose, *Gregs of Quarry Bank Mill*, 16–17.

Edward Baines at critical points in their careers raised loans among the worshippers at the Mill Hill Unitarian chapel.[907] And an important ingredient in the early success of Henry Overton Wills's tobacco firm was the credit allowed him by his fellow Bristol Congregationalist and West India merchant, Stephen Prust.[908]

The Quakers did, however, have one further commercial advantage which was denied to other adherents of the Old Dissent: a nation-wide, and indeed international,[909] network of organized itinerant journeyings and hierarchical meetings which meant that leaders in their community were constantly on the move, addressing their fellow Quakers, conducting the business of the Society of Friends, and at the same time contacting potential financial backers, business partners, suppliers of materials, and outlets for their sales. This can be seen most clearly in the career of Joseph Huntley, the founder of the biscuit firm of Huntley and Palmers. While his son Thomas made the biscuits Joseph 'acted as his son's commercial traveller . . . turning his visits to Monthly Meetings, Quarterly Meetings and other gatherings of the body to good account . . . and as Friends welcomed Joseph to their homes, so they gave orders for fresh supplies of biscuits'.[910] A Quaker grocer supplied the firm's ingredients, Thomas's Quaker brother Joseph made its tins, a Quaker firm printed its labels, the Quaker owner of the Banbury cake shop provided it with its largest retail outlet, and after George Palmer became effective manager of the business in 1841 he employed Quaker commission agents to sell his biscuits.[911] When, in 1768, John Wesley forbade his itinerant preachers to engage in trade he closed one avenue by which his followers might have become as rich as the Quakers.

The refusal of John Wesley to allow Methodist preachers to combine their itinerant ministry with travelling in trade supplies a clue to the major reason for the greater entrepreneurial success of the Quakers and Unitarians in comparison with that of other Nonconformists: Quakers and Unitarians were readier than other Dissenters to subvert their religious concerns to the aim of making money.

The critics of Max Weber have frequently, and rightly, pointed out that there was much in Puritan and Evangelical teaching that was inimical rather than conducive to capitalist enterprise.[912] After the Wesleyan Adam Clarke

---

[907] Rimmer, *Marshall of Leeds*, 26, 40, 44, 58; R. G. Wilson, *Gentlemen Merchants: The Merchant Community in Leeds 1700–1830* (Manchester, 1970), 189.

[908] B. W. E. Alford, *W. D. and H. O. Wills* (1973), 50.

[909] On this see Pratt, *English Quakers and the First Industrial Revolution*, 41.

[910] Corley, *Quaker Enterprise*, 9.   [911] Ibid. 9, 21, 38–9.

[912] e.g. Samuelsson, *Religion and Economic Action*, 47.

preached a sermon in which he 'inculcated the most inflexible principles on the subject of commercial integrity', he was confronted by a businessman who complained that on Clarke's premises 'few commercial men will be saved'. 'I cannot help that sir,' retorted Clarke, 'I may not bring down the requirements of infinite justice to suit the selfish chicanery of any set of men whatever.'[913] The silk merchant Thomas Wilson wrote in the front of one of his ledgers words from the Book of Proverbs, 'He that maketh haste to be rich shall not be innocent . . . he that hasteth to be rich hath an evil eye'.[914] And he was moved to give up business and devote his life to the extension of Congregationalism by listening to a series of sermons delivered by Andrew Fuller in 1794 in which he was warned that 'if your main object is to amass a fortune, you live to yourself, and not to God'.[915] When the Calvinistic Methodist Ebenezer Morris bought a cow and subsequently found he had paid less than the market price he gave the vendor of the cow an extra guinea; when the Wesleyan corn dealer Samuel Hitchen saw that during the war with revolutionary France the high price of corn was causing distress to the poor, he 'sold his corn at a rate far below market prices'; when the General Baptist John Calrow Means found that his late father had been trading in adulterated wine, he recompensed his father's customers, closed down the business, and entered the General Baptist ministry.[916]

Such scruples against dishonest practices and misgivings about the hoarding of wealth were, it is true, shared by many Quakers and Unitarians. Indeed Quakers were sometimes confronted by obstacles to economic activity not faced by other Dissenters. Quaker manufacturers were forbidden to make armaments, Quaker merchants were barred from trafficking in the sinews of war, Quaker craftsmen worried about the propriety of making luxury items such as silk stockings and painted china.[917] The Quaker banker Joseph John Gurney continually worried whether his wealth was compatible with his religious profession, the Quaker railway promoter Edward Pease regretted that in accumulating wealth Friends were carried away 'from the purity of our principles', and the Unitarian merchant William Rathbone VI confided to his wife that when a man was worth more than £200,000 'he is too rich for the

---

[913] Etheridge, *Life of Adam Clarke*, 167.

[914] Wilson, *Memoir of Thomas Wilson*, 70–1; Proverbs 28: 20, 22.

[915] Wilson, *Memoir of Thomas Wilson*, 121–4.

[916] Williams, *Welsh Calvinistic Methodism*, 229–30; Bretherton, *Early Methodism in Chester*, 19; Solly, *These Eighty Years*, i. 129.

[917] Ashton, *Iron and Steel in the Industrial Revolution*, 218; I. Grubb, *Quakers in Industry before 1800* (1930), 106.

kingdom of heaven'.[918] But these periodic qualms of conscience did not stop the Gurneys, Peases, or Rathbones from amassing fortunes, and Quakers and Unitarians were far less inhibited about making money, both by the practice and by the teaching of their churches, than were Baptists, Congregationalists, or Methodists. Jedediah Strutt was a loyal Unitarian and built Unitarian chapels for his workers at Cromford, Belper, and Milford, but a visit to London in 1765 prompted the thought that 'whatever some divines would teach to the contrary' the getting of money 'is the main business of the life of man'.[919] Edward Pease worried about the effect that the pursuit of profit was having upon Quaker principles, but this did not prevent his son Joseph from ruthlessly seeking to destroy his commercial rivals.[920] Thomas Clarkson, in his sympathetic *Portraiture of Quakerism* of 1807, observed that 'a money-getting spirit . . . is considered as belonging so generally to the individuals of this Society that it is held by the world to be almost inseparable from Quakerism'.[921] Half a century later Thomas Hancock commented acidly that the fact that the Quakers had 'gathered gold rather than men must be looked upon as the declaration of the Word of God . . . that their procedure was grounded upon a delusion'.[922]

Many of the factors which are usually brought forward to explain Quaker and Unitarian business success are equally applicable to the other Dissenters. They were all members of tightly knit communities which provided opportunities for fortunate marriages and business contacts; they all fostered the virtues of honesty, hard work, sobriety, and thrift which were likely to issue in modest prosperity; apart from the Unitarians they all disciplined bankrupts and censured those few of their number who were ever suspected of dishonest business practice; and in the eighteenth century they were all excluded from the English universities, from the political establishment, and to a large extent from the professions, and so gravitated naturally towards trade and industry. But what distinguished the Quakers and the Unitarians on the one hand from the Baptists, Congregationalists, and Methodists on the other was their lack of Evangelical purpose. The same factors which explain the failure of the Quakers and the Unitarians to expand their numbers explain their success in making money.[923] For Evangelical Nonconformists, even for those engaged in business, the chief end of their endeavours was not worldly prosperity, it was the saving of souls. They

---

[918] D. E. Swift, *Joseph John Gurney* (Middletown, Conn., 1961), 74–6, 85, 87; Kirby, *Men of Business and Politics*, 7; Sellers, 'Liverpool Nonconformity', 241.

[919] Fitton and Wadsworth, *The Strutts and the Arkwrights*, 102, 109–10.

[920] Kirby, *Men of Business and Politics*, 25–6.   [921] Isichei, *Victorian Quakers*, 183–4.

[922] Hancock, *The Peculium*, 177.   [923] See above, Ch. I, sect. 6.

looked upon their fellow men first and foremost not as potential customers but as potential converts, not primarily as men whose desires required satisfaction in this life, but as men whose souls needed saving after death. Conversely the Quakers and the Unitarians were more successful in business than the Baptists or Congregationalists not because they adhered more rigidly to the values of the Reformation, but for the quite opposite reason that they were readier than Calvinists and Evangelicals to escape the straitjacket of Puritan restraint. While Weber was right to stress that Puritan frugality and abstinence would lead to modest prosperity but wrong to imply that Calvinists and Methodists were in some peculiar way called to achieve worldly success, so Kurt Samuelsson was right to suggest that it was the secularization of the Protestant ethic, not its inner logic, which stimulated the spirit of capitalism.[924]

It will be obvious from much that has already been written that by the turn of the eighteenth and nineteenth centuries the Quakers and Unitarians were far more this-worldly than were the other denominations of Dissenters. The Quaker opposition to a salaried ministry, which grew out of the Protestant belief in the priesthood of all believers, led in practice to the secularization of all ministers. As has been seen, by the middle of the nineteenth century there were Quakers who believed that only a professional ministry could save the Society of Friends from extinction. But while the absence of a paid ministry led to the dilution of Quaker theology and to the attenuation of Quaker missionary effort, it also freed Quakers from the constant demands made on the pockets of other Dissenters and this, coupled with the absence of the need for constant rebuilding which afflicted the rapidly expanding denominations, assisted the private accumulation of Quaker capital. The Unitarians did retain a salaried ministry, but that ministry did not have the same career status among Unitarians that it had among the Evangelical denominations. Joseph Dawson, Arian minister to the Presbyterian meeting at Idle in the West Riding from 1765 to 1790, and friend of Joseph Priestley, was 'too much occupied in scientific speculation and in the promotion of his material prosperity' to be a successful minister, and he saw his congregation dwindle to half a dozen. After opening a number of coalmines he became a partner in the Low Moor Iron Company, resigned his pastorate in 1790, the year before the company started up its first blast furnace, and acquired an 'immense fortune'.[925] Two other prominent entrepreneurs, the cotton manufacturer Samuel Greg and the banker Lewis Loyd, similarly turned their backs on the

---

[924] Samuelsson, *Religion and Economic Action*, 55–6.
[925] Miall, *Congregationalism in Yorkshire*, 295; *Fortunes Made in Business*, 94–101.

Unitarian ministry in order to pursue lucrative business careers, and they were representative of others of their co-religionists.[926]

There is no question that many Unitarians, through their enthusiasm for philosophical and statistical societies, fostered an interest in science and technology in the early nineteenth century, but T. S. Ashton's argument, that the education provided by the Dissenting academies prepared potential entrepreneurs for their future careers, is difficult to substantiate, and a recent study of Manchester College suggests that there is little evidence to support the theory of the college's 'early significance as a training ground for industry and trade'.[927] It is true that a quarter of the students educated at the Warrington academy between 1757 and 1786 subsequently embarked on careers in commerce and industry, the majority as merchants or bankers.[928] But such an education was more often a consequence rather than a cause of business success. Both the Warrington academy and Manchester College, with their high fees for students who were not studying for the ministry, attracted the sons of men who had already achieved entrepreneurial success rather than the innovators of the future.[929] Five members of the Heywood banking dynasty of Liverpool and Manchester were educated at Warrington, but not the founder of the family fortunes, Arthur Heywood. John Wedgwood went to Warrington, but not his more famous father Josiah. The elder John Milnes of Wakefield, one of the leading West Riding merchants, sent his son to Warrington, but the younger John Milnes was not thereby conditioned to pursue a successful business career, and 'by a strange series of eccentricities' managed to divest himself of his father's fortune.[930] As for the Quakers, the education provided by their schools was rudimentary and, apart from Sidcot, they provided little systematic teaching of science until the second half of the nineteenth century.[931]

What was of crucial importance to the success of Nonconformist entrepreneurs was not so much that their education was better than that of other men, but that after only basic schooling they ended their education around the ages of fourteen or fifteen to go straight into a business or counting-house, or

---

[926] Rose, *Gregs of Quarry Bank*, 15; Holt, *Unitarian Contribution to Social Progress*, 60. David Wykes has found that 'a significant proportion of the divinity students' at the Unitarian Manchester College 'failed to enter the ministry and followed secular careers' (Wykes, 'Sons and Subscribers, 1788–1840', in Smith, *Truth, Liberty, Religion*, 66). When Lewis Loyd died in 1858 he left £1,878,730 (R. G. Thorne, *History of Parliament: The House of Commons 1790–1820* (1986), iv. 466).

[927] Wykes, 'Sons and Subscribers', 53.

[928] *Monthly Repository*, 9 (1814), 202–5, 262–7, 386–90, 526–9.

[929] Wykes, 'Sons and Subscribers', 62–3.   [930] *Monthly Repository*, 9 (1814), 264.

[931] W. A. Campbell Stewart, *Quakers and Education* (1953), 29, 148–50.

to be apprenticed to a co-religionist in a trade which offered opportunities for advancement. Such was the experience of the Congregationalist worsted manufacturer Titus Salt whose career, like that of many Quaker and Unitarian entrepreneurs, represented a partial secularization of the Protestant ethic. Salt does not appear to have had an Evangelical experience and did not become a communicant of his church until he reached the age of fifty-eight, but he displayed a degree of thrift which would have endeared him to Max Weber by denying himself the luxury of a gold watch until his savings amounted to £1,000.[932] His father was an unsuccessful farmer who turned to woolstapling at the point at which the wool trade was on the verge of huge expansion, but the seeds of Titus's own success were sown by 'a plain, commercial education' provided by the school attached to the Salem chapel, Wakefield, which he attended until the age of fourteen, and by two years' experience as a woolsorter in a Bradford factory.[933]

The Quakers in particular took care to apprentice their sons to masters who were themselves Friends. George Palmer's career was launched when, at the age of fourteen, he was apprenticed to an uncle who was a confectioner and a miller; the foundation of the fortunes of Joseph Crosfield, the Quaker soap manufacturer of Warrington, was laid when he was apprenticed to a Quaker chemist and druggist in Newcastle upon Tyne; and the first step on the road which led Richard Tangye to the head of one of Birmingham's largest engineering firms was taken when, at the age of nineteen, he gave up his teaching post at the Quaker school at Sidcot to accept a position as clerk in a Birmingham engineering firm run by a fellow Quaker.[934] Such apprenticeships were of far greater value to potential entrepreneurs than were years spent studying Greek and Roman authors at either the Dissenting academies or the English universities. Indeed, there is much evidence to suggest that the technological innovations of the industrial revolution were achieved by 'practical men' with only elementary schooling, and that higher education was inimical to business success.[935] Josiah Wedgwood's friend and partner, the Liverpool merchant Thomas Bentley, was educated at Ebenezer Latham's academy at Findern near Derby, but what he acquired there was 'a very fair amount of classical learning', and the basis of his commercial success was laid not by his Dissenting academy but by his apprenticeship in a

---

[932] Balgarnie, *Titus Salt*, 48–9, 197.   [933] Ibid. 23–5, 36–7.

[934] Corley, *Quaker Enterprise*, 28; Musson, *Enterprise in Soap and Chemicals*, 10; Reid, *Richard Tangye*, 37–40.

[935] S. Pollard, *The Genesis of Modern Management* (1965), 106; Wykes, 'Sons and Subscribers', 34–5.

Manchester warehouse at the age of sixteen.[936] Wedgwood himself argued that the time spent by young men in studying the Classics from the ages of fourteen to twenty were precisely the years 'which should be devoted to learning a business', and while he conceded that a knowledge of Latin was useful for discerning the origins of words, that involved 'learning a *thousand* things to make use of *one*'.[937] The Quaker cotton manufacturer Henry Ashworth was educated at the Quaker boarding-school at Ackworth, where the syllabus was limited to reading, writing, arithmetic, history, and geography, sent most of his own children to Quaker schools, and terminated their education when they reached their middle teens.[938] Ashworth was scathing in his criticism of the universities for neglecting science and making little contribution to technological advance, and Quaker business success was undoubtedly assisted by Quaker inability to enter Oxford and Cambridge before the second half of the nineteenth century. Whereas in the Church of England many of the best brains went to the universities and thence into the Church or into the secular professions, and whereas among Evangelical Dissenters some of the best brains went into the ministry, among the Quakers and Unitarians most of the best brains went into banking, trade, and manufacture.

The Unitarian enthusiasm for secular knowledge, the rational discourses elegantly enunciated in Unitarian pulpits, the undemanding requirements for communion in Unitarian meetings, the Unitarian toleration of social activities such as dances and theatre-going, all appealed to both potential and successful entrepreneurs far more than did the narrow religious preoccupations, the emotional insistence on self-revelation and personal conversion, and the narrow ethical codes and inquisitorial disciplinary procedures of the Evangelical Dissenters. When Presbyterian congregations divided in the eighteenth century, it was usually the wealthy minority who followed the heterodox path to Arianism and Socinianism and the poorer majority who remained loyal to orthodox Calvinism.[939] On the eve of the foundation of their families' fortunes John Marshall's father Jeremiah left the Baptists, and Samuel Courtauld's father George left the Huguenots, both for the Unitarians.[940] Whether their sons would have achieved fame and fortune had their fathers remained in their ancestral denominations cannot of course be known, but in joining the Unitarians they guaranteed that their sons would

---

[936] E. Meteyard, *Life of Josiah Wedgwood* (1865), i. 303–4.
[937] Pollard, *Genesis of Modern Management*, 109.
[938] R. Boyson, *The Ashworth Cotton Enterprise* (Oxford, 1970), 246.
[939] Watts, *The Dissenters*, i. 380.
[940] Rimmer, *Marshalls of Leeds,* 14; Coleman, *Courtaulds,* i. 33.

be brought up in communities whose ethos, teachings, and values were conducive to business success. The qualities which transformed the prosperous linen draper and the unsuccessful silk manufacturer of one generation into the wealthy entrepreneur of the next were intelligence, drive, initiative, energy, imagination, and a single-mindedness of purpose. These were not qualities which were peculiar to Quakers or to Unitarians. They were shared by William Carey, contending for forty years with the death of his son, the illness of his wife, the hostility of the East India Company, the carping criticism of his backers, and with the complexities of at least six different Indian languages, to establish the Baptist mission to Bengal; they were shared by Thomas Coke, labouring almost single-handed for thirty years to raise money to send Wesleyan missionaries to the West Indies and to India; they were shared by Hugh Bourne, teaching himself to read Hebrew, Greek, Latin, and French, editing the *Primitive Methodist Magazine*, writing his *Ecclesiastical History*, and walking forty or fifty miles a day to preach the Gospel. What distinguished Carey and Coke and Bourne from Courtauld and Marshall were not their abilities but their motives. The former were moved by their passion to save the souls of their fellow men from eternal death; the latter were motivated by their desire to achieve for their families a comfortable life. The hearts and minds of the Quakers and Unitarians were concentrated on this world; the eyes of the Evangelicals were fixed on heaven.

III

'The Stormy Element of Political Debate'
The Politics of Dissent, 1791–1833

1. 'A REPUBLICAN SPIRIT IS INJURIOUS TO RELIGION':
THE IMPACT OF THE FRENCH REVOLUTION

The contrast between the this-worldly orientation of the Unitarians with their prosperous congregations, their enthusiasm for secular knowledge, and their flair for business success, and the other-worldliness of the Evangelical Nonconformists, with their unsophisticated following, their humble status, and their passion for saving souls, was reflected in their differing attitudes towards politics. For the Unitarians political activity was the corollary of their belief that human problems could be solved by the rational application of knowledge. John Edwards, who succeeded Priestley as minister of the Unitarian New Meeting in Birmingham after the riots of 1791, argued that politics and religion were inextricably linked: it was as logical to protest against politics being introduced into the pulpit as it was to 'exclaim against a volume of sermons being introduced into a manufactory'.[1] The Unitarians' conviction that politics were a legitimate field of Christian endeavour was often shared by Calvinists among the Old Dissenters, no matter how much they might detest the Unitarians' theology. The central Calvinist tenet of the sovereignty of God provided Old Dissenters with a standard with which to judge, and if necessary challenge, the authority of the State: it provided Calvinistic Nonconformists with the grounds from which to criticize the governments of George III just as it had given their forefathers justification for

---

[1] Seed, 'Unitarianism and Liberal Culture', 145, citing J. Edwards, *A Discourse on Friday, April 19, 1793*, pp. iv–v.

contesting the rule of Charles I.[2] The Independents of the mid-seventeenth century, believing that salvation was either ordained or denied by God's sovereign decrees, had not shared the later Evangelicals' preoccupation with proselytizing: their concern was with preparation for the second coming of Christ and the establishment of his thousand-year rule on earth.[3] And although widespread hopes of the return of Christ were destroyed by the restoration of Charles II and were not revived until the 1790s, Dissenters who treasured memories of the Interregnum could hardly regard politics as outside their concern.

However, the passage of wealthy Presbyterians into the Church of England, the debarring of conscientious Congregationalists, Baptists, and Quakers from local government by the Corporation Act, and the numerical decline of Dissent in the first half of the eighteenth century, all took their toll of Nonconformist political influence. The number of Nonconformist MPs fell from an estimated maximum of sixty in 1661 to only three or four in 1685, and although the number rose to a possible thirty in 1689, in the hundred years after the accession of George I there were never more than five Dissenters in the House of Commons at any one time.[4] Dissenters who either had no scruples about taking the Anglican sacrament to qualify for membership of a borough corporation, or who avoided the sacramental test because their right to sit on a corporation went unchallenged, had greater political influence. Nonconformists sat on some thirty borough corporations at some point in the eighteenth century, and for most of the century the corporations at Bridport and Nottingham, and in the early part of the century that at Bridgwater, were controlled by Dissenters.[5] And there is considerable evidence to suggest that while distinctions between Whig and Tory were obliterated at Westminster, they survived in many constituencies as Dissenters in alliance with Low Church Anglicans continued to struggle with High Anglicans for influence over MPs and borough corporations.[6] The dissociation between parliamentary and local politics came to an end with the outbreak of the War of American Independence in 1775 when Dissenters took the lead in organizing petitions pleading for the conciliation rather than the

---

[2] J. Bradley, *Religion, Revolution, and English Radicalism* (Cambridge, 1990), 136–8.

[3] Watts, *The Dissenters*, i. 129–51.

[4] Ibid. 218, 256, 259; D. R. Lacey, *Dissent and Parliamentary Politics in England, 1661–1689* (New Brunswick, NJ, 1969), 165, 224, 476–9; J. E. Bradley, 'Whigs and Nonconformists: Presbyterians, Congregationalists, and Baptists in English Politics, 1715–1790', Ph.D. thesis (University of Southern California, 1978), 525.

[5] Watts, *The Dissenters*, i. 482–3; Bradley, 'Whigs and Nonconformists', 115, 171; E. B. Short, *A Respectable Society, Bridport 1593–1835* (Bradford-on-Avon, 1976), 30–1.

[6] Bradley, 'Whigs and Nonconformists', 517–19, 531–2.

coercion of the American colonists, and in some constituencies the terms 'Tory' and 'Whig' were revived to describe the supporters and opponents respectively of the government's policy.[7] Whereas most Dissenters, when they had the opportunity to vote, voted before 1760 for candidates loyal to the House of Hanover, after 1760 they increasingly gave their support to candidates who were critical of the government's handling of the American problem, and in particular to the Rockingham Whigs.[8] And although Dissenting unity was fractured by the formation of the Fox–North coalition in 1784, Pitt's opposition, in 1787 and again in 1789, to motions for the repeal of the Test and Corporations Acts, the outbreak of the French Revolution, and Pitt's consequent sharp turn to the right, all helped to revive the alliance between Unitarians, old-time Calvinists, and the Whigs under Charles James Fox.[9] The wealthy Unitarian MP William Smith, who had been elected to Parliament in 1784 as a supporter of Pitt and opponent of the Fox–North coalition, broke with Pitt in April 1792 when the prime minister opposed Charles Grey's motion in favour of parliamentary reform.[10] The continuity of the radical Dissenting political tradition was epitomized by John Bowring of Exeter, grandfather of the future Unitarian MP. 'A fine mezzotint of Oliver Cromwell' hung in Bowring's parlour; 'he took a strong part with the Americans in their war of independence'; and in 1791 his sympathies with revolutionary France led to his being burnt in effigy in Exeter's cathedral yard.[11]

The outbreak of war between Britain and France in February 1793 further alienated much Nonconformist opinion from Pitt's government. There were some Dissenters who supported the prime minister's policy towards France, and Sir Henry Hoghton, the orthodox Presbyterian MP for Preston, praised Pitt in the House of Commons 'for his high spirit and wise conduct'.[12] But in the eyes of many Dissenters Pitt had provoked the French declaration of war by restricting Anglo-French trade and by expelling the French ambassador. Unitarians objected to the war because it violated the rational, God-given order of the universe;[13] orthodox Dissenters opposed it

[7] Bradley, *Religion, Revolution, and Radicalism*, 233, 317, 331, 348–51, 356–7, 389–90, 415.

[8] Bradley, 'Whigs and Nonconformists', 371–3, 386–7, 397, 427, 434–6, 550–1; J. A. Phillips, *Electoral Behaviour in Unreformed England* (Princeton, NJ, 1982), 291–2, 295.

[9] Bradley, 'Whigs and Nonconformists', 532–51; Phillips, *Electoral Behaviour*, 165–6; J. E. Cookson, *The Friends of Peace* (Cambridge, 1982), 15–17; A. Goodwin, *The Friends of Liberty* (1979), 83–4.

[10] R. W. Davis, *Dissent in Politics: The Political Life of William Smith, MP* (1971), 67.

[11] J. Bowring, *Autobiographical Recollections* (1877), 31–2.

[12] R. G. Thorne, *History of Parliament: The House of Commons, 1790–1820* (1986), iv. 212–13.

[13] Cookson, *Friends of Peace*, 46–7.

because it was the means of sending unconverted souls to hell. The Quaker Meeting for Sufferings urged the king on the eve of war 'to prevent a measure which may consign to death and danger thousands of our fellow countrymen'.[14] The Congregational philanthropist Thomas Wilson heard a Dissenting preacher in 1793 denounce the war for compelling 'nameless numbers of unconverted sinners to fall, murdering and murdered, amongst flashes of fire into a fire infinitely worse'.[15] The Particular Baptist churches in Tiverton, Cullompton, and Bampton lamented in 1794 'a war by which thousands in different countries are reduced to penury and starving; and thousands on thousands have been unnecessarily hurried into the eternal state'.[16]

The anti-war movement of the 1790s was predominantly a Dissenting affair, and its provincial basis often the local Unitarian chapel.[17] The Dissenters who controlled the Nottingham corporation opposed the war with France as two decades earlier they had opposed the war with the American colonies: in February 1793 they were the first people in the whole of England to present a petition for peace to Parliament.[18] Robert Aspland's Baptist father 'held in the strongest dislike the measures of Mr Pitt, and both in private and public expressed hostility to that unscrupulous statesman'; the Liverpool Quaker William Rathbone tried to organize a meeting to petition for the prime minister's dismissal; and Fox's opposition to the war made him Thomas Wilson's favourite politician.[19] For the younger Robert Hall, pastor of the Cambridge Particular Baptist church, Pitt was 'a veteran in fraud while in the bloom of youth' who had first betrayed and then persecuted 'his earliest friends and connexions', while Fox was the honoured leader of a 'band of illustrious patriots'.[20] The author of *The Autobiography of a Dissenting Minister* recalled that the students at the academy he attended in the 1790s 'hated the name of William Pitt, and all but worshipped that of Charles James Fox'.[21] And John Parkes, worsted manufacturer and trustee of the

[14] M. E. Hirst, *The Quakers in Peace and War* (1923), 208–9.

[15] Wilson, *Memoir of Thomas Wilson*, 102.

[16] J. Rippon, *Baptist Annual Register*, ii (1794–7), 184.

[17] Cookson, *Friends of Peace*, 9, 22.

[18] Ibid. 276 n. 16; L. Namier and J. Brooke, *History of Parliament: The House of Commons, 1754–1790* (1964), i. 355; M. I. Thomis, *Politics and Society in Nottingham, 1785–1835* (Oxford, 1969), 173–4.

[19] Aspland, *Memoirs of Aspland*, 5; I. Sellers, 'William Roscoe, the Roscoe Circle, and Radical Politics in Liverpool, 1787–1807', *Transactions of the Historic Society of Lancashire and Cheshire*, 120 (1968), 52; Wilson, *Memoir of Thomas Wilson*, 101.

[20] *Works of Robert Hall*, ed. O. Gregory (1832), iii. 82, 117.

[21] *Autobiography of a Dissenting Minister*, 33.

Unitarian chapel in Warwick, had one of his sons christened 'Charles James'.[22]

Such displays of political radicalism were anathema to the Wesleyan leadership. Government in Wesley's view was a trust, 'not from the people' but from God, and in England was delegated to the king as 'the fountain of all power'.[23] Wesley could find 'no single instance in above seven hundred years of the people of England's conveying the supreme power' to their rulers, and he saw no reason why matters should be changed in his day.[24] London citizens and Newcastle colliers were alike incompetent to pass judgement on government measures, for political understanding required 'more time than common tradesmen can spare, and better information than they can possibly procure'.[25] Wesley had detested the rational Dissenters' support both for the American Revolution and for parliamentary reform, and four months after the outbreak of the French Revolution the *Arminian Magazine* reprinted a letter sent to Wesley ten years earlier in which the writer argued that 'a republican spirit is injurious to religion among Methodists: as I find most fallen Methodists . . . are Republicans'.[26] A few Methodists—including Jabez Bunting's father William and the preacher Samuel Bradburn[27]—initially welcomed the French Revolution, but as events in France became increasingly violent and as France and Britain drifted into war so the Wesleyan leadership became increasingly voluble in its protestations of loyalty to Pitt's government. In 1792 the Wesleyan ministers gathered in the Methodist Conference agreed that 'none of us shall, either in writing or conversation, speak lightly or irreverently of the Government under which he lives'; in 1793 Joseph Benson, finding 'a spirit of disloyalty and rebellion manifesting itself' in Manchester, preached on Titus 3: 1, 'inculcating subjection to higher powers'; again in 1793 William Thompson, Wesley's successor as president of the Conference, wrote to Pitt to pledge 'Methodist support for him as prime minister'; and in 1798 the Conference expressed its determination 'to suppress whatever tends to molest the quiet of the best of kings or derange . . . the happiest of all civil constitutions'.[28]

[22] G. B. M. Finlayson, 'Joseph Parkes of Birmingham', *Bulletin of the Institute of Historical Research*, 46 (1973), 187.

[23] *Works of John Wesley* (3rd edn., 1829–30), xi. 47, 105.   [24] Ibid. 52.

[25] Ibid. 19.   [26] *Arminian Magazine*, 12 (1789), 614.

[27] J. W. Etheridge, *Life of the Rev Adam Clarke* (1858), 137; Bunting and Rowe, *Life of Jabez Bunting*, 11; B. Semmel, *The Methodist Revolution* (1974), 120.

[28] *Minutes of the Methodist Conferences*, i. 260, 414; Stigant, 'Methodism and the Working Class', 248; J. Macdonald, *Memoirs of the Rev Joseph Benson* (1822), 243.

At the root of the political quietism of so many Methodists lay the Evangelical conviction that political activity was an irrelevance which could distract them from their chief purpose of saving souls. The point was made by the self-taught Cornish Wesleyan metaphysician Samuel Drew. When he opened his shoemaker's shop in 1787 he was, he recalled, 'a great politician' who 'entered as deeply into newspaper argument as if my livelihood depended on it', and his shop 'was often filled with loungers who came to canvass public measures'. As a consequence he often had to work until midnight to make up for the hours he had lost until, one night, 'some little urchin' shouted through the key-hole of his door, 'Shoemaker! shoemaker! work by night and run about by the day!'. Stung by the rebuke, Drew henceforward 'ceased to venture on the restless sea of politics, or trouble myself about matters which did not concern me'.[29] Similarly the biographer of William Bramwell recorded that at a tea-party held in London in 1804 the Wesleyan preacher 'ruled the conversation, so that not a sentence concerning politics . . . was permitted to transpire', and 'the attention of the company was directed exclusively to the great concerns of their present and eternal salvation'.[30] And in 1836 the *Wesleyan Methodist Magazine* published a memoir of Joseph Gee, a hosier of Hull, whom it praised for having 'seldom intermeddled in worldly politics'.

Being absorbed in the prosecution of his high calling; feeling habitually impressed with a sense of the shortness of time, and the paramount importance of eternal things; and having long observed that those professors who devote their time and talents to the correction and settlement of civic and state abuses, become . . . unsteady in their walk, censorious in their discourse, fiery in their tempers, dogmatic in their dispositions, tyrannical in their families, and troublous in the church of God, he dreaded and instinctively shunned the arena of political strife.[31]

The contrast between the political radicalism of Old Dissent and the otherworldliness of the New was drawn by George Eliot in *Felix Holt*. Comparing the attitudes of Dissenters in the manufacturing towns of the Midlands with those of their co-religionists in the fictional market-town of Treby Magna, Eliot wrote that in the former 'were multitudinous men and women aware that their religion was not exactly the religion of their rulers, who might therefore be better than their rulers, and, if better, might alter many things which now made the world more painful than it need be'. By contrast in Treby Magna there were Nonconformists 'of the melancholy sort' who 'said it would be well if people would think less of reforming parliament and more

---

[29] Drew, *Life of Samuel Drew*, 102.   [30] Sigston, *Memoir of William Bramwell*, 57.
[31] *Wesleyan Methodist Magazine*, 59 (1836), 569.

of pleasing God'. They were typified by Mrs Muscat 'whose youth had been passed in a short-waisted bodice and tight skirt, had never been animated by the struggle for liberty, and had a timid suspicion that religion was desecrated by being applied to the things of this world'.[32]

That suspicion came to be shared, in the course of the 1790s, by many of the Old Dissenters as well as by the New. The threats of violence from 'Church and King' mobs, the execution of Louis XVI and the Jacobin Terror in France, the treason trials, suspension of Habeas Corpus, and restrictions on public meetings in Britain, all combined to encourage Baptists, Congregationalists, and even Unitarians to adopt the apolitical and conservative stance of the Methodists. The destruction of the Unitarian meeting-houses and of Priestley's home and laboratory in Birmingham in July 1791 was followed in April 1792 with attacks on homes and mills of Unitarians in Nottingham.[33] In June attempts were made to batter down the doors of the Unitarian meeting-houses in Manchester and on Christmas day the Baptist chapel at Guilsborough in Northamptonshire was gutted by fire.[34] When, in November 1792, the Unitarian cotton manufacturer William Strutt tried to distribute copies of Tom Paine's *Rights of Man* to his workers in Belper, rioters flooded his mills and burned his books.[35] The fury of loyalist mobs was similarly directed against the signatories of Nottingham corporation's anti-war petition of 1793: in July the home of the mayor, the Particular Baptist grocer Joseph Oldknow, was attacked, a blunderbuss was fired at the rioters, and a young man was killed; in June 1794 'Republicans' in the town were forcibly 'baptized' in the River Leen; and another signatory of the anti-war petition, the Unitarian cotton manufacturer Robert Denison, had the workshops attached to his mill set on fire.[36] In Derby an attempt by John Thelwall of the London Corresponding Society to give a lecture in the Baptist chapel led to an attack by the mob in which the lecturer and his audience were expelled and the windows of the chapel were smashed.[37] At Taunton in Somerset an effigy of Tom Paine was burned outside the door of the Unitarian minister Joshua Toulmin, and his wife was forced to give up the 'trade of a bookseller in which [she] had been long engaged'.[38] In Oxford

---

[32] George Eliot, *Felix Holt, the Radical* (Oxford, 1980), 8, 169–70.

[33] S. D. Chapman, *The Early Factory Masters* (Newton Abbot, 1967), 189.

[34] A. Prentice, *Historical Sketches and Personal Recollections of Manchester* (1851), 6–7; *A Sketch of the History of the Deputies . . . of the Protestant Dissenters* (1813), 57.

[35] Goodwin, *Friends of Liberty*, 231.

[36] J. F. Sutton, *The Date-Book of Remarkable and Memorable Events connected with Nottingham* (1852), 199–200, 207–13; Thomis, *Politics and Society in Nottingham*, 175–6.

[37] J. C. Marshman, *The Life and Times of Carey, Marshman, and Ward* (1859), i. 94.

[38] Murch, *Presbyterian and General Baptist Churches in the West of England*, 196.

early in 1793 Dr Edward Tatham, the Rector of Lincoln College, preached a university sermon against Methodists and Dissenters, charging them with disaffection 'to the king and government', which led to rioting against Nonconformists in the city. And in nearby Woodstock in May of the following year the Baptist minister at Oxford, James Hinton, and other Dissenters were beaten up by a mob consisting in part of Irish soldiers, who accused them of being 'Jacobin rascals'.[39]

In the wake of the destruction wrought by mobs, there followed legal prosecution brought by the government. On 5 November 1792 William Winterbotham, assistant pastor at How's Lane Particular Baptist church, Plymouth, preached a sermon in commemoration of the landing of William of Orange at Torbay in 1688. In the following July he was put on trial at Exeter for sedition. Winterbotham was charged with having asserted that the British 'have as much right to stand up as they did in France for our liberty', and that if the king did not observe the laws of the land he had 'no more right to the throne than the Stuarts had'. Such a sermon, argued the prosecution, 'was most improper in an assembly of two and three hundred of low, ignorant people', and Winterbotham was sentenced to a fine of £200 and to four years in prison.[40]

Unitarians who criticized Church or State were particularly exposed to charges of seditious libel. Thomas Fyshe Palmer, minister to a Unitarian meeting in Dundee, was sentenced in 1793 to seven years' transportation to Botany Bay for his part in publishing a pamphlet in favour of parliamentary reform. After serving his sentence he was shipwrecked on one of the Ladrone Islands on his homeward voyage and died from dysentery in a Spanish gaol.[41] James Belcher, a Unitarian bookseller in Birmingham, was also imprisoned in 1793 for selling the works of Thomas Paine.[42] Jeremiah Joyce, tutor to the sons of the Earl of Stanhope and future secretary of the Unitarian Society, was arrested in 1794 and held for twenty-three weeks on suspicion of treason.[43] Gilbert Wakefield, tutor successively at Jesus College, Cambridge, and at the Warrington and Hackney academies, was sentenced to two years' imprisonment for seditious libel in 1799; he had characterized Pitt's government as 'the most pestilential ministry ever commissioned by the wrath of Heaven to sink a great but guilty nation in the gulf of disgrace and misery'.[44]

[39] *Protestant Dissenter's Magazine*, 2 (1795), 252–6.
[40] *The Trial of William Winterbotham* (1794), 1–4, 67.
[41] Belsham, *Memoirs of Theophilus Lindsey*, 268–9, 272–3.
[42] Bushrod, 'Unitarianism in Birmingham', 231.
[43] Goodwin, *Friends of Liberty*, 215–16, 333; Ditchfield, 'Unitarianism and Radicalism', 18.
[44] G. Wakefield, *A Reply to Some Parts of the Bishop of Llandaff's Address* (1798 2nd edn.), 46–7.

Benjamin Flower, editor of the *Cambridge Intelligencer*, was sent to Newgate for six months in 1799 for referring to the government apologist Bishop Watson of Llandaff as a 'time-server and apostate'.[45] Thomas Evans, hymn-writer and minister to the Unitarian meeting at Cwm Cothi in Carmarthen-shire, was sentenced in 1801 to stand in the pillory and to two years in prison for reputedly singing a seditious song.[46] And a more celebrated hymn-writer, the Moravian James Montgomery, author of 'Angels in the Realms of Glory' and editor of the *Sheffield Iris*, was sentenced in 1795 and again in 1796 to two terms of imprisonment, of three and six months, on the ground of having published seditious libels.[47]

This combination of persecution and prosecution led some Dissenters to flee abroad, others to retreat into apolitical quietism. Priestley was but one of a number of Unitarian ministers who sailed to the United States in 1793 and 1794.[48] Other radical Dissenters who found refuge in America included Joseph Gales, Unitarian editor of the *Sheffield Register* and founder-member of the Sheffield Constitutional Society; Benjamin Vaughan, Unitarian MP for Calne, who was accused of treasonable correspondence with the French; and Morgan John Rhys, former minister of the Penygarn Baptist church, Pontypool, whose proud boast was that he had stood on the ruins of the Bastille.[49] The Baptist Robert Hall compared the lot of Dissenters in the early 1790s 'to that of the primitive Christians, against whom, though in themselves the most inoffensive of mankind, the malice of the populace was directed', and the Unitarian Theophilus Lindsey likened the exodus of radical Dissenters to America to that of the Puritans and Separatists in the days of Archbishop Laud.[50]

Robert Hall himself, however, typified the change that came over the political outlook of many Dissenters in the 1790s. The man who in 1791 had proclaimed *Christianity consistent with a Love of Freedom* and who in 1793 penned *An Apology for the Freedom of the Press* subsequently came to the conclusion that the Christian ministry lost 'something of its energy and sanctity by embarking on the stormy element of political debate'.[51] Hall had once regarded the French Revolution as 'the most splendid event recorded in the annals of history',[52] but by 1800 he was equating it with *Modern Infidelity*.

---

[45] Cookson, *Friends of Peace*, 101.
[46] D. E. Davies, *They Thought for Themselves* (Llandysul, 1982), 106–8.
[47] Goodwin, *Friends of Liberty*, 380–3.
[48] Seed, 'Unitarianism and Liberal Culture', 167.
[49] Goodwin, *Friends of Liberty*, 333, 487; Thorne, *History of Parliament: The House of Commons, 1790–1820*, v. 442–3; Bassett, *The Welsh Baptists*, 109–11.
[50] *Works of Robert Hall*, iii. 149; Seed, 'Unitarianism and Liberal Culture', 168.
[51] *Works of Robert Hall*, vi. 34.   [52] Ibid. iii. 172.

'The diffusion of scepticism and of revolutionary principles went hand in hand', he lamented. The barbarities which had stained the revolution in France were 'chargeable on the prevalence of atheism'.[53] Hall's sermon on *Modern Infidelity* earned him the praise both of Bishop Porteous of London and of William Windham, Pitt's Secretary of War, but the Baptist preacher who had once denounced Pitt for his apostasy was now similarly denounced by Benjamin Flower in the *Cambridge Intelligencer*.[54]

Hall was not alone. Until William Carey sailed to India in 1793 he held republican views, but he subsequently repudiated them 'for things of greater consequences' and in 1797 wrote that 'the Bible teaches me to act as a peaceful subject under the government which is established'.[55] The Congregationalist David Bogue, who in 1792 had seen the French Revolution as a step towards the expansion of Christ's kingdom, subsequently wrote that he considered himself 'as restrained by my office from an active interference' in politics, that he had never attended a political meeting, and that although entitled to vote for MPs for Hampshire 'I have forborne to avail myself of that privilege'.[56] As anti-revolutionary sentiment intensified, so the official representatives and leaders of Dissent vied with those of the Methodists in their declarations of loyalty to king and country. In December 1792 the London Dissenting Deputies responded to the accusation that Dissenters had fomented the American rebellion by praising the British constitution as 'excellent in its principles, and wisely framed for the extension of solid happiness and real liberty'; the same year the Yorkshire Quarterly Meeting of the Society of Friends warned its members against 'imbibing or promoting a spirit of disaffection to the king and to the government'; and in March 1794 the newly launched *Protestant Dissenter's Magazine* claimed that 'the majority of Dissenters are abhorrent' of French principles. The Baptist Thomas Tayler and the Arian Presbyterian Abraham Rees both celebrated Britain's naval victories in 1798 as evidence of God's sanction of her war effort, and in 1800 the Staffordshire Congregational Association announced that 'in worldly politics we have no concern, for our desire is to advance that kingdom which is not of this world and therefore not dependent upon it'.[57]

[53] R. Hall, *Modern Infidelity with Respect to its Influence on Society* (1800), 42.

[54] *Works of Robert Hall*, vi. 63–5. Flower had once been a member of Hall's congregation in the latter's more radical, and heretical, days.

[55] Carey, *William Carey*, 64; Potts, *Baptist Missionaries in India*, 171.

[56] Bogue, *Sermon Preached at Salters Hall*, 46–8; Morison, *Fathers and Founders of the London Missionary Society*, 184.

[57] *Sketch of the History of the Deputies*, 55; R. M. Jones, *The Later Periods of Quakerism* (1921), 315; *Protestant Dissenter's Magazine*, 1 (1794), 102; T. W. Davis, 'Conflict and Concord

Some Dissenters remained loyal to their radical traditions. In April 1795 the Norwich Baptist Mark Wilks preached two sermons to raise money to pay for the defence of Thomas Hardy, Horne Tooke, and John Thelwall, who had been acquitted of treason in the previous autumn, and four months later at York two Congregational ministers gave evidence in defence of Henry Yorke against a charge of conspiracy.[58] The Congregationalist Thomas Wilson denounced the renewal of war with France in 1803 and was saddened by the 'wholesale massacre at Trafalgar'; the Unitarian Robert Aspland refused to pray for the success of British armies since 'we worship not the God of Britain merely, but the God of the whole earth'; and his fellow Unitarian William Roscoe published a pamphlet criticizing the British government for violating 'the laws of morality and justice' by attacking neutral Denmark in 1807.[59] But such was the hostility of a section of the congregation of George's Meeting, Exeter, to the radical views of their Unitarian minister, Timothy Kenrick, that in 1793 he offered to resign.[60] And so devoted to the policy of William Pitt was the retired Baptist minister Josiah Thompson that he gave £100 out of his private fortune to assist the prosecution of the war against France.[61] It was thus not without cause that Thomas Walker, the Anglican founder of the Manchester Constitutional Society, complained that the Dissenters had 'constantly fallen short of their own principles', or that the Congregationalist Walter Wilson bemoaned the 'unaccountable notion' of the Evangelicals that 'the affairs of governments should be left to the wicked'.[62] But the authentic voice of Evangelical Dissent at the turn of the century was not that of Walter Wilson, it was that of Andrew Fuller. In a pamphlet entitled *The Backslider* the minister of the Kettering Particular Baptist church argued that a major cause of departing from God was 'taking an eager and deep interest in political disputes'. 'There is scarcely any thing in all the New Testament inculcated with more solemnity', he added, than that 'Christians should be obedient, peaceable, and loyal subjects'.[63]

---

among Protestant Dissenters in London, 1787 to 1813', Ph.D. thesis (University of North Carolina, 1972), 235–6; Matthews, *Congregational Churches of Staffordshire*, 197–8.

[58] M. Wilks, *Athaliah, or the Tocsin sounded by Modern Alarmists* (1795); Goodwin, *Friends of Liberty*, 375; Wickham, *Church and People in an Industrial City*, 65.
[59] Wilson, *Memoir of Thomas Wilson*, 271; Aspland, *Memoir of Robert Aspland*, 357–8; Roscoe, *Life of William Roscoe*, i. 414.
[60] The offer was declined (Brockett, *Nonconformity in Exeter*, 142–5).
[61] Aspland, *Memoir of Robert Aspland*, 20.
[62] Prentice, *Historical Sketches of Manchester*, 20; I. Sellers, *Nineteenth-century Nonconformity* (1977), 3.
[63] A. Fuller, *The Backslider* (1801), 25, 28.

2. 'THE VOICE OF THE PEOPLE IS THE VOICE OF GOD': THE REVOLT OF ALEXANDER KILHAM

Just as many Old Dissenters, either from conviction or through circumspection, came in the 1790s to adopt the apolitical stance of the Methodists, so conversely some Methodists refused to accept the conservative and quietist position of their own leaders. It was a characteristic of the Wesleyan Connexion that whereas it was the most centralized, most clerically dominated, and most conservative of all the Nonconformist denominations, in its chapels it fostered lay participation, free debate, and frequently radicalism.[64] The resulting tension between Conference and chapel was at the root of the series of schisms which disrupted Wesleyanism for sixty years after the death of its founder, and the coincidence of the removal of their founder's authority and the divisions produced by the French Revolution meant that for Wesleyans the 1790s were a decade of particular bitterness. There is a good deal of evidence to suggest that the pro-government stance taken by the Wesleyan Conference in the aftermath of the French Revolution was resented by a minority of Methodists. Adam Clarke attended a District Meeting in London in 1795 at which a preacher was rebuked—no more—for 'having given utterance to republican sentiments by praying that our fleets might be defeated'.[65] Seven Methodists served on the committee of the Sheffield Society for Constitutional Information and others apparently joined the London Corresponding Society, for they seceded in 1795 in protest at the society's refusal to ban atheists and Deists from membership.[66] The radical Samuel Bamford claimed that both his father Daniel and his uncle Thomas, though they left the Methodists, none the less adhered to the doctrines of John Wesley as long as they lived, read Paine's *Rights of Man*, and held political discussions with other men whom their neighbours at Middleton, near Manchester, branded as 'Jacobins'.[67] By February 1796 John Pawson was alarmed by evidence, some of which had reached the government, that the Methodists were a 'disaffected people', and he proposed to counter it by drawing up a loyal address to the king. But the proposal aroused so much opposition, especially from preachers in London, that it was dropped.[68]

---

[64] This is the theme of ch. 2 of Robert Currie's *Methodism Divided*.

[65] J. Everett, *Adam Clarke Portrayed* (1844), ii. 29–30.

[66] J. Baxter, 'The Great Yorkshire Revival', in M. Hill (ed.), *A Sociological Yearbook of Religion in Britain*, vii (1974), 66; Thompson, *Making of the English Working Class*, 164.

[67] Chaloner (ed.), *The Autobiography of Samuel Bamford*, i. 43.

[68] Stigant, 'Methodism and the Working Class', 249–50, 259–60; N. Murray, 'The Influence of the French Revolution on the Church of England and its Rivals', D.Phil. thesis (Oxford, 1975), 256.

Antipathy to the abortive loyal address was particularly bitter in the Stockport circuit in Cheshire where the Wesleyan superintendent, Jeremiah Brettell, preached a sermon on *Fear God: Honour the King*. People whom Brettell described as having been 'degenerated by Jacobinical politics' accused him of preaching 'violent political party sermons' and petitioned Conference for his removal. Conference ignored the petition, but one of the towns in Brettell's circuit, Ashton-under-Lyne, was to become a stronghold of the Methodist New Connexion.[69]

The willingness of the Ashton radicals to support Alexander Kilham's protest movement illustrated how easily the sympathy of a minority of Methodists for parliamentary reform and the French Revolution could lead to criticism of the Wesleyan Connexion and to demands for democratic control of its government. Kilham was born of Methodist parents in the Wesleys' home town of Epworth in 1762, was converted at the age of eighteen, and was accepted by Wesley as a travelling preacher in 1785. Described by a contemporary as being of low stature with a 'countenance common almost to coarseness', a 'clumsy hobbling sort of walk', and a weak, faltering, and unharmonious preaching voice, Kilham's unattractive appearance may well have contributed to his querulousness.[70] As long as John Wesley lived, Kilham explained, he thought it his duty 'to comply with his will in many things not essential to salvation . . . out of affection to him as our father in the Gospel',[71] but as soon as Wesley was dead Kilham felt free to challenge the leadership of the Connexion.

Kilham's initial conflict with the Wesleyan hierarchy was over the reluctance of the Methodist Conference to allow Methodists to receive the Lord's Supper in their own chapels and at the hands of their own preachers. Kilham had regarded himself as a Dissenter from the moment he had been obliged to declare himself as such in 1784 in order to obtain a preacher's licence under the terms of the Toleration Act,[72] and henceforward he saw no reason why he and his fellow Methodists should be forced to rely on the Church of England for the administration of the sacrament. On 4 May 1791, only two months after Wesley's death, eighteen Methodist trustees in Hull issued a circular letter urging Methodists to remain within the established church and Kilham wrote a letter in reply pointing out that, since many Methodists 'never

---

[69] A. Kilham, *An Address to the Members and Friends of the Methodist Society in Newcastle* (1792), p. v.

[70] E. A. Rose, 'The Methodist New Connexion', *PWHS* 47 (1990), 243, citing *Methodist New Connexion Magazine* (1846), 13.

[71] Rose, *Methodism in Ashton-under-Lyne*, i. 31–2, 41.

[72] J. Blackwell, *Life of the Rev Alexander Kilham* (1838), 76–7.

communicate anywhere because their consciences will not suffer them to go among sinners to receive [the sacrament] from the hand of an ungodly minister', they were already 'Dissenters in fact, though not in profession'.[73] Kilham sent his reply to like-minded Methodists in Newcastle upon Tyne who first published it under their own name and then, later in 1791, persuaded Conference to appoint Kilham to their circuit as one of their preachers. And when a handful of Newcastle Methodists seceded in protest at their preachers' action in administering the sacrament Kilham penned another letter in which he argued that the only reasons for maintaining connections with the Church of England were 'political, or, in other words, carnal, and sold under sin'.[74]

Historians have characterized Kilham both as a custodian of 'England's libertarian past' and as the harbinger of nineteenth-century Liberal Nonconformity.[75] But in his eagerness for disputation, in the tactlessness which infuriated friends as well as enemies, above all in his faith in the inspired common sense and hence political rights of the ordinary Christian believer, Kilham was both in temperament and in doctrine the reincarnation of the eponymous Elizabethan Separatist Robert Browne.[76] In his *Address to . . . the Methodist Society in Newcastle* Kilham both censured the Church of England and set forth his own conception of the true church in words which recalled those used by Browne more than two hundred years before. The discipline of the established church was 'like a city broken down, and without walls', so that 'a man may be drunk on a Saturday evening' yet be admitted to the sacrament the next day; most of its clergy had 'never renounced their sins and turned sincerely to God'; and while they did not preach the Gospel, they denounced those who knew their sins were forgiven, and those who witnessed to their Christian experience, 'calling these doctrines enthusiasm'. For Kilham, as for the first Separatists, the church 'is a number of faithful people assembled together, where the pure word is preached and the sacrament duly administered', no matter whether they meet in the open air, in a barn, or in a Methodist chapel.[77]

One unfortunate fact spoilt the logic of Kilham's argument: as the 'Church Methodists' of Hull emphasized, John Wesley had always insisted that he had no design to separate from the Church of England, and to counter the argument Kilham was reduced to denying that 'Mr Wesley was infallible'.[78]

---

[73] Ibid. 131–2.   [74] Kilham, *Address to . . . the Methodist Society in Newcastle*, 20.
[75] Hempton, *Methodism and Politics*, 67–8; E. R. Taylor, *Methodism and Politics* (Cambridge, 1935), 72.
[76] Watts, *The Dissenters*, i. 27–34.
[77] Kilham, *Address to . . . the Methodist Society in Newcastle*, 8–11.   [78] Ibid., p. iv.

Such an admission was regarded by Thomas Coke and William Thompson as sufficient provocation to warrant Kilham's expulsion from the Connexion, and at the Methodist Conference in July 1792 Coke declared that Kilham's 'reproach upon Mr Wesley . . . was like dragging his ashes from the tomb and exposing them in a most infamous manner'. But Kilham had powerful supporters, above all Samuel Bradburn, and he escaped with a censure and was sent off to Aberdeen where Methodist preachers were already administering the sacrament.[79]

As long as Kilham confined his polemics to urging the right of Methodist societies to have the sacrament at the hands of their own preachers he was protected by many of his fellow preachers who similarly saw themselves as spiritually superior to Anglican clergymen. But once he began to advocate the rights of lay Methodists to participate in the government of their Connexion, and so diminish rather than augment the power of the preachers, he found his support in the Methodist Conference dwindling away.[80] Kilham ministered in the Aberdeen circuit for three years, time enough for him to observe and admire the lay participation of the Church of Scotland's Presbyterian system, and long enough for him to reveal his antagonism towards the government's war policy. Later biographers of Kilham thought it prudent to omit all reference to his antipathy to Pitt's government from their works, but in his private correspondence Kilham confessed to his 'republican principles'.[81] In the autobiography printed just after his death his publisher revealed how Kilham had listened with embarrassment to a fellow preacher who was 'fond of shewing his strong attachment to the war and present measures of administration'. Kilham prayed that the preacher's 'mouth might be stopped', and 'had the happiness to find [that] he could not get on at all as he intended'.[82]

Kilham's experience of Presbyterianism led him to the conclusion that every Methodist circuit or district should 'be represented in Conference by a delegate of its own choosing'.[83] Consequently the Plan of Pacification, which in 1795 resolved the controversy over the sacrament by allowing it to be administered in chapels where a majority of trustees, stewards, and leaders were in favour, did not touch what Kilham now regarded as the fundamental issue of church government. The Conference of 1795 appointed Kilham to the Alnwick circuit in Northumberland and it was from there, in the closing stages of the year, that he issued his most controversial pamphlet, *The Progress of Liberty*. The Wesleyan leadership, Kilham argued, was guilty of

---

[79] Blackwell, *Life of Kilham*, 157–8, 173. [80] Ibid. 215. [81] *HMC*, iv. 270.
[82] Kilham, *Life of Alexander Kilham*, 66. [83] Blackwell, *Life of Kilham*, 176.

spiritual tyranny: 'We detest the conduct of persecuting Neros, and all the bloody actions of the great whore of Babylon, and yet in our measure we tread in their steps.'[84] To remedy the situation he advocated a major shift of power from the preachers to the people: members should be received into and excluded from Methodist societies 'by the consent of our people'; class leaders should be chosen by the people; local preachers should be appointed and dismissed by leaders' meetings; itinerant ministers should be chosen from the ranks of local preachers by Quarterly Meetings; and one or two lay delegates should be nominated from every District Meeting to attend Conference. To justify his argument Kilham repeated the radical dictum of the Separatist Robert Browne: the 'voice of the people is the voice of God'.[85]

The radical nature of Kilham's proposals, and the intemperate language which he used to support them, undermined his position in the Wesleyan Connexion. Joseph Benson claimed that Kilham's *Progress of Liberty* opened the eyes of his erstwhile supporters to the fact that his principles would issue in the 'entire subjection of the preachers to the people, and in the utter loss of all discipline'.[86] Samuel Bradburn, whose support for Kilham had been so crucial in 1792, was prepared by April 1795 'to give up a good deal rather than divide' the Connexion.[87] As late as February 1796 Jonathan Crowther was assuring Kilham of his support, but within a matter of months he, too, had changed sides.[88] In May Kilham added insult to injury by claiming that 'no government under heaven, except absolute monarchies, or the papal hierarchy', was as despotic and oppressive as that of the Methodists,[89] and when Conference met in London in July the outcome was a foregone conclusion. Kilham's expulsion was confirmed by every preacher being 'required to sign a paper signifying the justness and uprightness of the transaction'. 'The paper was taken to the communion table', and Kilham recorded with tears in his eyes that Samuel Bradburn, the secretary of the Conference, 'who had formerly professed himself a friend to liberty', stood 'like the governor of the inquisition' by the rails of the communion table 'to see that none omitted' to sign.[90]

Kilham responded to his expulsion by touring Yorkshire, Lancashire, Cheshire, Staffordshire, and Nottinghamshire, putting his case in Methodist

---

[84] Ibid. 235.   [85] Taylor, *Methodism and Politics*, 79.

[86] J. Macdonald, *Memoirs of Joseph Benson* (1822), 301.

[87] Blackwell, *Life of Kilham*, 210.

[88] Kilham, *Life of Alexander Kilham*, 106, 113, 206.

[89] A. Kilham, *An Appeal to the Methodist Societies of the Alnwick Circuit* (1796), 2.

[90] Kilham, *Life of Alexander Kilham*, 120–1; T. W. Blanshard, *Life of Samuel Bradburn* (1870), 175.

chapels in places where the trustees were sympathetic to his movement, and in Independent, Baptist, or Presbyterian meeting-houses in places where they were not. In August 1797 he met with three other former Methodist preachers and a number of lay supporters in the former Baptist Ebenezer chapel in Leeds to found the Methodist New Connexion; by the time of their second conference at Sheffield in May 1798 they had a membership of 5,037; and there they drew up a constitution based on the proposals Kilham had put forward in his *Progress of Liberty*.[91]

The progress of the New Connexion was in fact slow. Even preachers who were sympathetic to Kilham were reluctant to forfeit their regular incomes by joining him at a time of high unemployment, and a high proportion of those that did join did not stay the course. The salaries of New Connexion preachers failed to keep pace with those of the Wesleyans,[92] and nearly half the eighty-four preachers admitted to the Kilhamite ministry between 1797 and 1814 resigned after serving an average of six years.[93] It was a major blow to Kilham's hopes when William Bramwell, having convinced Kilham that he was determined either to secure reform or leave the Wesleyans, decided to remain with the parent body.[94] Similarly the Nottingham grocer Thomas Tatham, after writing to Kilham that God intended, by the formation of the New Connexion, 'to separate the precious from the vile', elected to remain with the vile and played a leading part, in alliance with Bramwell, in restoring Wesleyan fortunes in the town.[95] It was not until 1821 that the New Connexion recorded over 10,000 members and at the time of the religious census it had only 16,932 members.

It is possible that the initial success of the New Connexion in areas of recent Methodist revivals, such as the West Riding and Nottingham, meant that a proportion of its early supporters were recent converts without deep Methodist roots. Jonathan Saville claimed that the damage done to the Wesleyan society at Greetland near Halifax, the scene of a major revival in 1793–4, was the result of 'some of the inexperienced converts having been made leaders'.[96] But a more likely explanation of the New Connexion's comparative lack of success is the failure of the radical views which inspired Kilham's protest to find an echo among more than a small minority of

[91] W. J. Townsend, *Alexander Kilham: The First Methodist Reformer* (1889), 89–92; Rose, 'First Methodist New Connexion Chapels', *PWHS* 36 (1967–8), 7–15.

[92] William Driver, in one of the largest and most prosperous New Connexion circuits, received only £55. 4s. in 1804 (Rose, *Methodism in Ashton-under-Lyne*, ii. 10).

[93] Townsend, Workman, and Eayrs, *New History of Methodism*, i. 501.

[94] Kilham, *Life of Alexander Kilham*, 149, 191–2.

[95] Ibid. 216; Swift, *Lively People*, 43–4.

[96] F. A. West, *Memoirs of Jonathan Saville of Halifax* (1863), 24.

reasonably intelligent, comparatively prosperous, and politically conscious Methodists. The constitution of the New Connexion, giving a select band of lay 'ruling elders' equality with its ministers, meant that it was particularly attractive to wealthy and ambitious men who had the leisure to take part in the government of the Connexion.[97] In Ashton-under-Lyne, one of the few places where the New Connexion outnumbered the Wesleyans, the Kilhamites included in their membership the Heginbottom family, prosperous cotton-spinners, and claimed in Samuel Heginbottom the wealthiest manufacturer in the town.[98] Similarly in nearby Hurst both the New Connexion chapel and the community as a whole were dominated by the mill-owner John Whittaker who gave employment to nearly everyone in the area.[99] In Hanley in Staffordshire the Kilhamites were led by Job Ridgway, a pottery manufacturer whose son John was to become one of the largest employers in the district. John Ridgway's biographer noted that the New Connexion in the Potteries was given 'firmness and strength' by having at its head men who were 'growing into respectable commercial positions'.[100] In Halifax the New Connexion was supported by the worsted manufacturers James Akroyd and his son Jonathan. The latter was the largest textile manufacturer in the town and when he died in 1847 he left nearly £1,750,000.[101] In Sheffield two members of the committee of the radical Society for Constitutional Information, Richard Beale and Edward Oakes, left the Wesleyans for the Kilhamites in 1797, but since Beale was a shopkeeper and Oakes a silver plater they are unlikely to have been very poor men.[102] Forty years later the Methodist New Connexion in Cheshire, Lancashire, Staffordshire, and the West Riding was still attracting a much higher proportion of well-paid skilled workers than were the Wesleyans.[103] In Nottingham 'nearly the whole of the influential and wealthy' section of the Methodist society joined the New Connexion.[104] Among their leaders were the textile manufacturer Robert Hall of Basford Hall and the publisher Charles Sutton, later founder of the radical *Nottingham Review*. Hall's radical views did not prevent him from carrying a musket and enrolling, in May 1798, in a company of 'persons of property . . . for the defence of their houses and property', and Sutton was significantly the son of Unitarian parents.[105] By contrast the

[97] J. Stacey, *A Prince in Israel* (1862), 97.
[98] Rose, *Methodism in Ashton-under-Lyne*, ii. 18–19.   [99] Ibid. 24–6.
[100] Stacey, *A Prince in Israel*, 87.
[101] J. A. Hargreaves, 'Political Attitudes and Activities of Methodists in the Parish of Halifax, 1830–48', MA thesis (Huddersfield Polytechnic, 1985), 32.
[102] Baxter, 'Great Yorkshire Revival', 66–7.   [103] Tables XIX, XXXIII, XLIV, LIV.
[104] Sutton, *Nottingham Date-Book*, 233.   [105] Swift, *Lively People*, 33–7, 41–2.

280 Nottingham Methodists who initially stayed with the Wesleyans were described as the 'poorer brethren', and in 1798 they received as one of their itinerant preachers William Bramwell, who had greater appeal to working-class people than any other contemporary Methodist preacher. After some hesitation Bramwell spurned both Kilhamite reforms and political involvement and for the next two years devoted himself to inspiring a revival which doubled the Wesleyans' membership in Nottingham and enabled them rapidly to outdistance the New Connexion.[106] The example of Nottingham emphasizes the fact that among Nonconformists radicalism in the 1790s was the concern primarily of middle-class Unitarians and a small minority of like-minded men in the other denominations. For the vast majority of working-class Methodist men and women the apolitical revivalist message of William Bramwell had far greater appeal than the democratic arguments of Alexander Kilham.

For Alexander Kilham the founding of the New Connexion represented the failure of his hopes of injecting a democratic element into the Wesleyan Connexion and was attended by personal tragedy. His expulsion was followed by the serious illness of his wife, and his preaching tours were conducted against the background of her growing weakness and ultimate death. He married again fourteen months later, but by the end of 1798 the punishing schedule he had set himself was taking its toll. In November, while travelling through south Wales, he was twice wet through by rain, journeyed to Merthyr 'on one of the coldest days I ever travelled, and thence rode to Brecon through deep snow'. He returned home to Nottingham, where he had been stationed since May, developed a violent cold, began coughing up blood, and died on 20 December.[107] His death was compared by the Wesleyan Robert Melson to that of Korah, the leader of a rebellion against Moses, whose followers were swallowed up by an earthquake and taken 'alive into the pit'.[108]

There can be no doubt that the disputes which issued in the formation of the New Connexion were at bottom political. The leaders of the Kilhamites denied that they had separated from the parent Connexion on account of politics, but the attitudes of the two sides towards the government of their church were but a reflection of their attitudes towards the government of the State. Kilham and his supporters were demanding for ordinary Methodists the right to choose their leaders just as parliamentary reformers were

---

[106] Ibid. 35, 44–5.   [107] Kilham, *Life of Alexander Kilham*, 130–8, 165–77.
[108] R. Melson, *Defensive Armour against the Devouring Sword of Calumny* (Ashton-under-Lyne, 1815), 15; Numbers 16: 31–3.

demanding for Englishmen the right to elect their MPs; the Wesleyan leadership maintained that democracy would be as damaging to the discipline of the church as Tories claimed it would undermine the stability and authority of the State. Kilham's fundamental complaint against the government of the Wesleyan Connexion was that 'our people are . . . ruled without being consulted'. Methodists had no voice in the choice of their officers, in the formation of their laws, or in the disbursement of their financial contributions.[109] Joseph Benson argued conversely that there was no foundation in the Scriptures for 'the idea of a people choosing or appointing their own preachers'.[110] The founders of the New Connexion complained that leading Wesleyans had been all too ready 'to offer their services, and influence in the societies' to Pitt's government.[111] The Wesleyans retorted that Kilham 'was the same to the Methodists as Tom Paine was to the nation'.[112] Radical Methodists at Barnsley and Illingworth in the West Riding, the Wesleyans claimed, had graduated from the works of Tom Paine to the writings of Alexander Kilham.[113] Eighty years later the Wesleyan Conference conceded one of Kilham's basic points—the principle of lay representation[114]—but for the moment his expulsion, and the comparatively small number of Methodists who left with him, confirmed the victory of conservative forces within the Wesleyan Connexion. Benson's biographer, James Macdonald, writing in 1822, claimed that the consequences of Kilham's agitation reinforced the lessons to be learnt from 'the atrocities which accompanied the French Revolution': they brought into 'deserved contempt the absurd doctrine of annual parliaments and universal suffrage'. 'It holds equally good in church as in civil government that several theories which, on a superficial view, seem founded in truth, are demonstrated to be false by an attempt to reduce them to practice.'[115]

[109] Kilham, *Appeal to the Methodist Societies of Alnwick*, 2.
[110] Macdonald, *Memoirs of Joseph Benson*, 295.
[111] Kilham, *Life of Alexander Kilham*, p. xxii.   [112] Ibid. 144.
[113] Entwisle, *Memoir of Joseph Entwisle*, 147; J. U. Walker, *A History of Wesleyan Methodism in Halifax* (Halifax, 1836), 216–17.
[114] Townsend, Workman, and Eayrs, *New History of Methodism*, i. 442.
[115] Macdonald, *Memoirs of Joseph Benson*, 301.

3. 'WE MEAN TO CLEAR OURSELVES': LORD SIDMOUTH'S BILL AND THE HALÉVY THESIS

A major reason for the oft-expressed conservatism of the Wesleyan leadership, and for their detestation of Alexander Kilham, was the fear that the government would use any evidence of Methodist radicalism as a pretext for curbing Methodist evangelism. 'We know, in general, we are not enemies to the king, nor have we a wish to alter the government of our country,' wrote Samuel Bradburn as he was abandoning Kilham, but 'we are charged as if we were otherwise'.[116] 'We mean to clear ourselves', he added, and he and his fellow Methodists went on to do so with such success that they initiated one of the great debates of modern British historiography.

Just as the Wesleyans accused the Kilhamites of Jacobinism so Anglicans claimed that Methodists of all varieties were guilty of sedition. In August 1799 a correspondent from Denbigh wrote to the *Gentleman's Magazine* that 'the sect of Methodists called Jumpers', presumably the Calvinistic Methodists, were spreading throughout the whole of north Wales. Their preachers, he alleged, were 'the instruments of Jacobinism, sent into this country to disseminate their doctrines' and to distribute the works of Tom Paine.[117] Two years later Thomas Ellis Owen, rector of Llandyfrydog in Anglesey, claimed that the Methodists were 'either blind instruments, or wilful tools, in the hands of anarchists or atheists, for the purpose of bringing about in this once happy country, a revolution similar to those which have deluged the continent with blood'. And he cited the evidence of a sermon by John Pawson on false prophets to show that the Methodists would be satisfied with 'no less than the absolute murder of all the clergy; the total extermination of the priesthood, root and branch'.[118] Such accusations served simply to make their authors look ridiculous, but one did not need to see in every Methodist a Jacobin in sheep's clothing to realize, at the turn of the century, that the Methodists and other itinerants were transforming the religious landscape of England and Wales. Some Anglican clergymen responded to the challenge posed by the growth of Nonconformity by urging that the Church make efforts to improve the quality of its ministry.[119] But other clergymen appealed directly to the government for help in curbing the activities of the itinerant preachers: they urged the amendment of the Toleration Act of 1689.

[116] Hempton, *Methodism and Politics*, 69.   [117] *Gentleman's Magazine*, 69 (1799), 741.
[118] T. E. Owen, *Hints to Heads of Families* (3rd edn., 1802), 8, 13.
[119] Watts, *Religion in Victorian Nottinghamshire*, i, p. xvii.

By the end of the eighteenth century there was a swelling chorus of Anglican clerics demanding restrictions on Dissenters' freedom to preach. In the spring of 1799 the Anglican Evangelical William Wilberforce was alarmed by rumours that the government was contemplating legislation to curb the granting of licences to itinerant preachers and warned Pitt 'against any infringement of perfect toleration'.[120] In August the Bishop of Lincoln, Pitt's former tutor Dr Pretyman-Tomline, invited the clergy of his diocese to meet and report on the state of their parishes. They responded with the information that fewer than one person in three attended their services and advised that part of the solution lay in the amendment of the Toleration Act.[121] In November Bishop William Cleaver of Chester wrote to Lord Grenville, the Foreign Secretary, that anyone who rode 'from Manchester through Yorkshire to Richmond, the extremity of my diocese' would be convinced that 'without some aid from the legislature . . . the established religion cannot exist much longer in the country'. He suggested that Dissenting ministers who sought to benefit from the Toleration Act should be required to produce both 'a certificate of their moral lives' and a statement of the 'doctrines they profess to teach', and should be 'confined in their function to certain districts, and in buildings distinct, and appropriated to divine worship only'.[122] And in 1800 Bishop Horsley of Rochester, in a charge to the clergy of his diocese, warned that 'in many parts of the kingdom new conventicles have been opened in great number', led by pastors who were illiterate peasants or mechanics and 'visited occasionally by preachers from a distance'. 'These new congregations of non-descripts', added the bishop, 'have been mostly formed since the Jacobins have been laid under the restraint of those two most salutary statutes commonly known by the names of the Sedition and the Treason Bill.' The Seditious Meetings and Treasonable Practices Acts of 1795 had prohibited all public meetings of more than fifty people without a magistrate's consent, and had prescribed seven years' transportation for inciting hatred or contempt of the king or government. By these Acts, implied Bishop Horsley, opponents of the State had been driven underground only to re-emerge as opponents of the Church. It was a circumstance which gave 'much ground for suspicion that sedition and atheism', not religion, were the real object of these Methodist conventicles.[123]

---

[120]   R. I. Wilberforce and S. Wilberforce, *The Life of William Wilberforce* (1838), ii. 335–6.

[121]   Jenkins, *Life of Thomas Charles*, ii. 370.

[122]   *Report on the Manuscripts of J. B. Fortescue preserved at Dropmore*, Historical Manuscripts Commission (1908), vi. 20–1.

[123]   S. Horsley, *The Charge of Samuel Horsley, Lord Bishop of Rochester, to the Clergy of his Diocese* (1800), 19–20.

An attempt was made in February 1800 to carry out the bishops' wishes. Michael Angelo Taylor, MP for Durham, proposed to amend the Toleration Act by restricting the granting of preachers' licences to the settled pastors of separate congregations. Taylor was a Foxite Whig whose antipathy to Evangelical itinerants derived from his rational Anglicanism.[124] The story is told of an encounter between Taylor and the Wesleyan blacksmith-preacher, Samuel Hick. Taylor, as a magistrate, broke up a Methodist service at Ledstone in the West Riding at which Hick was present and the following day Hick went to see Taylor to remonstrate that the Member of Parliament had broken the law. Taylor retorted that when his bill came law Hick would have to go to his parish church: Hick replied that his parish church was more than three miles from his home.[125]

Taylor was persuaded to drop his bill as a result of pressure from his own Nonconformist constituents and Wilberforce's influence on Pitt.[126] But eleven years later a more determined effort was made to limit the application of the Toleration Act, this time by Henry Addington, Viscount Sidmouth, the former prime minister. Sidmouth was an amiable muddle-headed politician who thought he could legislate for the defence of the Anglican establishment while at the same time retaining the goodwill of respectable Dissenters.[127] In June 1809 he had expressed concern that men were licensed as Dissenting preachers solely for the purpose of 'obtaining an exemption from parish officers and the militia' and requested information of the number of licences granted under the Toleration Act. The returns revealed that whereas 179 licences for preachers had been granted in the seven years from 1774 to 1780, in the years 1795–1801 the number granted had increased to 1,318. Over the same twenty years the number of registrations for Dissenting places of worship had risen from 898 in 1774–80 to 3,578 in 1795–1801.[128] At the same time Sidmouth collected information from clerical correspondents throughout the country to support the contention that many of the newly licensed preachers were unfit to fill the office of Dissenting preacher. He was told of assemblies of sectaries who gathered in barns 'to hear the wild effusions of a mechanic or a ploughboy, perhaps not more than fifteen years of age'; of eighteen licensed preachers in Middlesex who could not properly spell 'preacher of the Gospel' in their applications; and of a licensed preacher

---

[124] Murray, 'Influence of the French Revolution', 207.

[125] J. Everett, *The Village Blacksmith* (15th edn.), 83–6.

[126] Murray, 'Influence of the French Revolution', 8; Ward, *Religion and Society*, 52.

[127] Davis, *Dissent in Politics*, 165–6. Davis gives the best account of the controversy provoked by Sidmouth's proposals.

[128] *Sketch of the History of the Deputies*, 83–6.

in Staffordshire who admitted he could neither read nor write. The rector of Sedstone in Herefordshire particularly disliked the claim of uneducated preachers to the direct inspiration of God: he knew of one who told his congregation that 'all the knowledge of the clergy was bought learning, whereas *his* knowledge was inspired'.[129]

Armed with such information Sidmouth gave notice, in June 1810, of his intention of bringing in a bill to prevent anyone from taking out a licence 'unless he had attained the age of twenty-one, was appointed to a congregation, and could produce testimonials of his fitness for office from some persons of the same religious persuasion'.[130] The Dissenting Deputies, representing the congregations of Old Dissent in the London area and thus containing a number of Unitarians, had already sent a deputation to Sidmouth in which they argued that 'though their own regular ministers were in general stationary', they were 'strenuously opposed, upon principle', to his attempt to curtail Methodist itinerants.[131] Sidmouth took the point and he dropped the proposal to confine the granting of licences to the pastors of separate congregations. But the bill he introduced into the House of Lords on 9 May 1811 still contained provisions which would have severely curtailed the issue of licences to Dissenting preachers. Whereas magistrates were hitherto required, or so Dissenters claimed, to administer the oaths prescribed by the Toleration Act to all preachers, whether ordained or lay, who sought licences, justices were henceforward to be given discretionary powers to issue or deny licences. Sidmouth proposed that the granting of licences should be confined to pastors of separate congregations who could produce testimonials signed by six 'substantial and reputable householders' belonging to their congregations, or to ordained ministers and probationers who, although not attached to specific churches, could produce certificates similarly signed by six householders testifying to their 'sober life and conversation'.[132] Magistrates were thus to be left free to refuse licences to ministers who could not convince them that their sponsors were 'substantial and reputable' and, what was worse, there was no provision for the granting of licences to lay preachers at all.[133]

Sidmouth argued that he was motivated only by a concern to improve the quality of the Dissenting ministry and to stop men from obtaining licences in order to avoid public service. He alleged that men were seeking licences as Dissenting preachers who were 'cobblers, tailors, pig-drovers, and chimney-

---

[129] G. Pellew, *The Life and Correspondence of the Rt. Hon. Henry Addington, First Viscount Sidmouth* (1847), iii. 41–3, 45.
[130] *Sketch of the History of the Deputies*, 91.   [131] Ibid. 88–9.
[132] *Monthly Repository*, 6 (1811), 336.   [133] *Methodist Magazine*, 34 (1811), 558–9, 628–9.

sweepers', and claimed that his measure had the support of 'respectable' Dissenting ministers.[134] Sidmouth's proposals did in fact meet with favourable reactions from the Unitarian Thomas Belsham, who believed it 'an insult upon common sense' 'for an ignorant booby, who can neither read nor write . . . to assume the office of a Christian teacher'; from Thomas Coke, always ready to appease the establishment; and from the scholarly Adam Clarke, increasingly embarrassed by the ignorance of his fellow Methodist preachers.[135] But Sidmouth did not strengthen his case by linking his proposed amendment of the Toleration Act with the need to use public money to 'prevent us from having a nominal established church, and a sectarian people'.[136] And the overwhelming majority both of Old Dissenters and of Methodists regarded Sidmouth's bill as an assault on religious liberty in general and on lay preaching in particular. The Dissenting Deputies, already worried by a narrow interpretation of the Toleration Act which was leading some magistrates to reject applications for preachers' licences, believed that more could be achieved by discreet diplomacy than by public agitation.[137] The lead in opposing Sidmouth's bill was taken, as a result, by the Wesleyan Committee of Privileges, set up in 1803 to defend their religious freedom, and by the newly formed Protestant Society for the Protection of Religious Liberty. The Protestant Society, eschewing the cautious policy of the Unitarian-led Dissenting Deputies, was dominated by Congregationalists and Calvinistic Methodists and elected as its secretary John Wilks, a City lawyer who was the son of Matthew Wilks, the pastor of the Calvinistic Methodist Moorfields Tabernacle. At the foundation meeting of the Protestant Society in the London Tavern in Bishopsgate on 15 May three Wesleyans, the connexional solicitor, Thomas Allan, Joseph Butterworth, soon to be MP for Coventry, and Joseph Benson agreed to join with the Protestant Society in forming a committee to co-ordinate opposition to Sidmouth's bill.[138] This, the first occasion on which Methodists and Old Dissenters had come together in defence of religious liberty, was a portent for the future.

Only twelve days elapsed between the introduction and second reading of Sidmouth's bill, but in that time the Dissenters and Methodists were able to

---

[134] *Parliamentary Debates*, xix (1812), cols. 1129–30.
[135] Pellew, *Life of Sidmouth*, iii. 49–53. Belsham did, however, urge Sidmouth to modify his bill (Davis, 'Dissenters in London', 304).
[136] *Parliamentary Debates*, xix (1812), col. 1131.
[137] Davis, *Dissent in Politics*, 159–64.
[138] M. B. Whittaker, 'The Revival of Dissent, 1800–1835', M.Litt. thesis (Cambridge, 1958), 122–3; Hempton, *Methodism and Politics*, 100.

collect nearly 700 petitions against the measure. 'The peers', recalled Lord Holland, 'could hardly get to the doors, the avenues were so crowded with men of grave deportment and puritanical aspect; when there, they had almost equal difficulty in gaining their seats, for loads of parchment encumbered and obstructed their way to them'.[139] The government, alarmed by the hornets' nest that Sidmouth had stirred, gave him no backing and the bill was defeated without a division.

It was in response to successive Anglican and Tory attacks on their ecclesiastical polity and religious principles that Methodists developed the argument that, far from undermining the country's constitution and the people's loyalty to the throne, they had contributed substantially to the stability of England in the decades following the French Revolution. John Whitehead took the opportunity of John Wesley's funeral in 1791 to argue that since Methodists were 'friends to the king and government', 'the more numerous this body of people is, the better it will be for this country'.[140] A writer in the *Evangelical Magazine* in 1801 countered Bishop Horsley's charges that Jacobins, driven underground, had reappeared in Methodist conventicles, with the argument that the tranquillity of the country was in large measure due to the Methodists' success in 'diverting the attention of the people from political debates to subjects of higher importance and of everlasting interest'.[141] John Sutcliffe in 1805 asked how it was that 'vast groups of loose and disorderly men, subjected as they have been to sudden stoppages in trade [and] to exorbitant advances in provisions, have been governed without mobbing and confusion?'. And he gave as his answer that it was due to the influence of Methodist preachers whose sermons and writings 'abound with effusions of loyalty and patriotic affection'.[142] Five days after Lord Sidmouth introduced his bill to amend the Toleration Act the Wesleyan Committee of Privileges pointed to 'the manifest effect which the diffusion of religion has had for the last fifty years, in raising the standard of public morals, and in promoting loyalty in the middle ranks, as well as subordination and industry in the lower orders of society'.[143] And in Manchester Wesleyan ministers maintained that it was England's religious liberty which had preserved 'this happy country from the horrors of that revolutionary frenzy which has so awfully

---

[139] Davis, *Dissent in Politics*, 155.
[140] J. Whitehead, *A Discourse delivered at the Funeral of the late Rev. Mr John Wesley* (1791), 53.
[141] *Evangelical Magazine*, 9 (1801), 164.
[142] Stigant, 'Methodism and the Working Class', citing J. Sutcliffe, *A Review of Methodism* (1805), 37–8.
[143] *Methodist Magazine*, 34 (1811), 559.

desolated the nations of the continent'.[144] This argument, that it was Evangelical religion in general and Methodism in particular which saved England from the series of revolutions which racked so much of Europe in the sixty years after 1789, was endorsed by the Irish historian William Lecky and by the president of the United States Woodrow Wilson.[145] But it is with the name of the Frenchman Elie Halévy, the greatest historian of nineteenth-century England, that the thesis is most closely associated.

What fascinated Halévy was the contrast between his own country's recent history and that of England. Halévy was puzzled by the fact that the world's pioneer industrial country did not experience the violent class conflict issuing in revolution which, on the Marxist interpretation of history, it should have suffered. 'If the materialistic interpretation of history is to be trusted', wrote Halévy in the first volume of his monumental *History of the English People*, 'the England of the nineteenth century was surely, above all countries, destined to revolution, both political and religious.' But in fact 'in no other country of Europe have social changes been accomplished with such a marked and gradual continuity'. The key to the problem Halévy found in the Methodist and Evangelical revival. England escaped revolution because both 'the élite of the working class' and 'the hard-working and capable bourgeois had been imbued by the Evangelical movement with a spirit from which the established order had nothing to fear'. The role of Nonconformity was crucial. 'For all their freedom of theological difference the sects agreed among themselves and with the national authorities to impose on the nation a rigorous ethical conformity and at least an outward respect for the Christian social order.'[146]

In recent years Halévy's thesis has been the subject of much debate among historians. In an article first published in 1957 the Marxist historian Eric Hobsbawn denied that Methodism 'could have prevented a revolution had other conditions favoured one', partly because the Methodists in 1811 had only 150,000 members out of a population in England and Wales of ten million, partly because much of the 'revolutionary unrest of the period' took place in areas where Methodism was weak, and partly because 'Methodism advanced when Radicalism advanced and not when it grew weaker'.[147] Seven years later another Marxist historian, Edward Thompson, in his classic *Making of the English Working Class*, repeated Hobsbawm's point that even

[144] B. Semmel, *The Methodist Revolution* (1974), 132.
[145] W. H. H. Lecky, *A History of England in the Eighteenth Century* (1878), ii. 636; R. F. Wearmouth, *Methodism and the Common People of the Eighteenth Century* (1945), 14.
[146] Halévy, *History of the English People in 1815*, 334–5, 339, 371.
[147] E. Hobsbawm, *Labouring Men* (1964), 28, 32.

if every Methodist 'shared the Tory principles of their founder' there were not enough of them 'to have stemmed a revolutionary tide'. But he did agree with Halévy that Methodism acted as a stabilizing force among working people, though he regarded this as something for which they should be damned rather than praised. The growth of Methodism during the wars with France 'was a component of the psychic process of counter-revolution' and in contrast to Hobsbawm's view that Methodism advanced when radicalism advanced, Thompson postulated the theory 'that religious revivalism took over just as the point where "political" or temporal aspirations met with defeat'. Instead of Methodism and radical protest advancing together Thompson suggested that the social process oscillated between the opposing poles of religious revivalism and radical politics.[148]

Ten years later, in 1974, the Halévy thesis was reformulated by Bernard Semmel who argued that what he called *The Methodist Revolution* was the English equivalent of the American and French revolutions. Writing under the influence of R. R. Palmer's *Age of the Democratic Revolution*, Semmel wrote that in the last quarter of the eighteenth and the first quarter of the nineteenth centuries all of western society was prepared 'for a revolution whose message was to be *liberté*, *egalité*, and *fraternité*'. But in England alone was 'this explosion of the energies of the masses ... accompanied by a minimum of physical violence and bloodshed', and a major reason for England's peaceful transition to the modern world was the Methodist revival.[149] As Halévy had argued for Dissent as a whole, so Semmel argued for Methodism in particular, that its major contribution was to reconcile liberty with order. The genius of Methodism was to balance its liberating, Arminian, theology, emphasizing free will and spiritual equality, with obedience to connexional discipline and to the authority of the State.[150] A similar point was made by Alan Gilbert in an article published in 1979. Like Semmel, Gilbert emphasized not the conservatism of Methodism but its potential liberalism. He pointed to the evidence that Methodist laymen often rejected the political views of the Wesleyan hierarchy and argued that many Methodists shared with Old Dissenters an attitude of 'moderate radicalism' which was critical of the establishment but which was not revolutionary. The 'moderate radicalism' of the Nonconformists, argued Gilbert, provided a non-violent channel for social and political deviance and so acted as a ' "safety valve" in early industrial politics'.[151]

[148] Thompson, *Making of the English Working Class*, 49, 50, 419, 428–9.
[149] Semmel, *The Methodist Revolution*, 192.   [150] Ibid. 171.
[151] A. D. Gilbert, 'Methodism, Dissent, and Political Stability in Early Industrial England', *Journal of Religious History*, 10 (1978–9), 381–99.

The reasons for the differing interpretations of Hobsbawm and Thompson on the one hand and of Semmel and Gilbert on the other are in part ideological. As a Marxist Hobsbawm is reluctant to admit that a substantial proportion of the working class could ever have been caught up in anything as other-worldly, irrational, and disciplined as Evangelicalism and so he underestimates its numerical strength. And while Thompson is readier than Hobsbawm to acknowledge that a significant proportion of the working class was for a time attracted to Methodism, his explanation of the appeal of Methodism is one that can fit only the small minority of politically conscious workers with whom a twentieth-century Marxist can have some sympathy. Thompson's explanation of the growth of Methodism—that it represented 'the chiliasm of despair' of people whose political and economic aims were frustrated—can be applied to the handful of radicals whom John Baxter found caught up in the Yorkshire revival of the mid-1790s, and to a number of Chartists, of whom Thomas Cooper and Joseph Barker were the most prominent, who rejected radical politics in favour of Evangelical religion, but even in these cases it appears that it was their political radicalism, not their religious enthusiasm, which was the deviation from the norm.[152] And Thompson's thesis is scarcely adequate to explain a mass movement of people who were unsophisticated, ill-educated, and predominantly female.

Hobsbawm's contention that there were only some 150,000 members of Methodist societies in 1811 is true, but is beside the point.[153] The evidence of the 1851 census suggests that for every Methodist member there were three Methodist worshippers, and that throughout England and Wales the number of Evangelical Nonconformists who were not followers of John Wesley—the Baptists, Congregationalists, and Calvinistic Methodists—exceeded the number of Arminian Methodists. If the proportion of Arminian Methodists to other Evangelical Nonconformists was the same in 1811 as it was in 1851, then this means that the size of the Nonconformist worshipping community at the earlier date was around 900,000. Not perhaps enough to prevent revolution, but a considerable force for peace none the less. And by the 1840s, when political frustration was more intense and the threat of violence greater than at any time since the accession of George III, the proportion of Nonconformists in England and Wales had risen to over 18 per cent. Halévy's explanation of the stability of English society in the nineteenth century was founded not on Methodism alone, but on the wider Evangelical movement

---

[152] Thompson, *Making of the English Working Class*, 429; Baxter, 'The Great Yorkshire Revival', 66–7.

[153] The combined membership of the Wesleyan and New Connexion Methodists in England and Wales in 1811 was 151,328; Currie, Gilbert, and Horsley, *Churches and Churchgoers*, 140.

which brought 'under its influence first the dissenting sects, then the establishment [and] finally secular opinion'.[154]

If Hobsbawm and Thompson underestimate the contribution of Methodism to England's political stability, Semmel and Gilbert exaggerate its liberalizing role. This is not because one cannot point to individual Methodists who rejected the conservatism of the Wesleyan leadership and embraced radical politics, but because such people were an unrepresentative minority. The essential appeal of Evangelical religion was to people for whom the prospect of altering the country's government was as remote as was the hope of changing the country's weather. It has been argued above that the mass following of Evangelical Nonconformity was drawn from people who were poor, uneducated, prone to superstition, young, and disproportionately female. Some Nonconformists educated themselves to understand affairs of state; others were driven by economic hardship and by revulsion against injustice to challenge the political system under which they lived; but for the majority the brevity of life, the certainty of death, and the sense of helplessness in a frightening world, all which had predisposed them to accept the Evangelical message in the first place, militated against either political involvement or revolutionary action. Obedience to the will of God offered more certain rewards than disobedience to the authority of the State.

The reason for the coincidence of Methodist revivalism and radical agitation to which Hobsbawm rightly drew attention for the years 1793–4, and for the oscillation between the growth of Methodism and political disturbances which Thompson again rightly noted for the 1810s, was not that in every working-class Methodist there was a radical agitator fighting to get out, but because economic distress, which inevitably stimulated popular political protest, could have contradictory effects on church growth. As explained in Chapter I, the economic hardship which would impel some men to riot would induce others, and more so their wives, to seek the consolation of Methodist meetings, and this appears to have happened during the Yorkshire revival of 1793–4. Alternatively unemployment could also force Methodists to avoid class membership in order to save their subscriptions, just as that same unemployment would drive their fellow men to smash machinery, burn ricks, and riot for the vote. This appears to be the explanation for the slump in Methodist growth rates at the turn of the century. The year 1800–1 marked the lowest point in the index of real wages in the century after 1767 and also, apart from the years of disruption following the Fly Sheets controversy, the years in which Methodist membership figures suffered their greatest set-

[154] Halévy, *History of the English People in 1815*, 339.

back. 'The year 1800', wrote James Sigston, Bramwell's biographer, 'was rendered memorable by a great dearth of provisions.' The price of corn shot up, unemployment increased, and 'in several manufacturing towns the population became outrageous and vented their anger on those who had brought provisions for sale'. But in Nottingham, where Bramwell for two years presided over a major revival, 'and in every town where religion had its legitimate influence over the hearts and conduct of professors, not one person connected with Methodism was concerned in any riotous act'. 'The power of religion', concluded Sigston, 'is manifested in such instances as these, when it teaches the poor and needy to exercise resignation and patience.'[155]

In his Ford lectures Ian Christie explored the reasons for the stability of British society in the late eighteenth century.[156] He emphasized the degree of social mobility, the country's buoyant economy, the affluence of a sizeable and growing minority of the population, the safety-net provided by the poor law, and the freedom with which the British criticized their rulers: all factors which distinguished late eighteenth-century Britain from contemporary France. Professor Christie did not place great emphasis on religion, but he did argue 'that the pluralistic character of British society gave it an enormous capacity to absorb pressures of internal conflict generated by the ideals and aspirations of dissident groups, without this seriously menacing the nation's political stability'.[157] That pluralist society had been established by the victory of the parliamentary army and the proliferation of Dissenting congregations during the Civil Wars; it was secured by the defeat of Anglican and Roman Catholic intolerance between 1686 and 1689; and was underwritten by the successful opposition to Tory attempts to contain the expansion of Evangelical Nonconformity in 1800 and 1811. The growth of Evangelical Nonconformity in the first half of the nineteenth century did not prevent political upheaval, radical protest, or growing class conflict; but it did guarantee that most of that protest and conflict would be contained within constitutional limits, accompanied by a minimum of violence, and expressed for much of the time in the language of the Bible.

---

[155] Sigston, *Memoir of Bramwell*, 117–18.
[156] I. R. Christie, *Stress and Stability in late Eighteenth-century Britain* (Oxford, 1984), *passim*.
[157] Ibid. 188.

4. 'LIBERAL SENTIMENTS' AND MIDDLE-CLASS VIRTUES:
THE RISE OF THE DISSENTING PRESS

On the defeat of Lord Sidmouth's bill the Dissenting Deputies passed a resolution expressing their satisfaction with 'those declarations against every
species and degree of persecution' which had emanated from the House of
Lords, and looked forward to the day 'when the legislature shall expunge
from the statute book ... all penalties, restrictions, and disabilities on account
of religion'. Their victory in 1811, and their optimism for the future, they
explained, arose 'not from any accidental circumstance, but from the gradual
and silent increase of just and liberal sentiments'.[158]

By 1811 it was too late for Lord Sidmouth to turn the clock back to the seventeenth century. The coincidence of the French and industrial revolutions
and of the expansion of Evangelical Dissent meant that while the super-
structure of British politics was dominated by the younger Pitt and his Tory
successors for nearly half a century after 1784, the economic, social, and religious changes of those fifty years were shifting the substructure of the country
in a fundamentally liberal direction. The rapid growth of Britain's economy,
the increasing wealth of the commercial and manufacturing classes—many of
whom were Dissenters—and the rapid growth of Nonconformity all contributed to the 'increase of just and liberal sentiments'. The use of the term
liberal to describe a distinctive political viewpoint was employed with increasing frequency in the last quarter of the eighteenth century. To a 'liberal mind,
what is life without liberty?' asked Caleb Evans, principal of the Bristol Baptist College, in a sermon preached in 1775 against the government's policy
towards the American colonies.[159] To 'the liberal-minded Members of Parliament who voted for the repeal of the Test and Corporations Acts' was the
toast proposed by Sir Thomas Beevor at a meeting of the Independent Club
at the Angel Inn in Norwich in 1789.[160] That Charles James Fox was a man
whose 'general views in politics are as liberal, as his conduct open and manly'
was the accolade bestowed on him by the Unitarian John Aikin in 1790.[161] And
when, in February 1796, Aikin and Richard Phillips launched the *Monthly
Magazine* they pledged themselves 'to the propagation of those liberal principles ... which have been either deserted or virulently opposed by the other
periodical miscellanies'.[162]

---

[158] B. L. Manning, *The Protestant Dissenting Deputies* (Cambridge, 1952), 140.
[159] Bradley, *Religion, Revolution, and Radicalism*, 128 n. 19.
[160] C. B. Jewson, *The Jacobin City: A Portrait of Norwich, 1788–1802* (1975), 14.
[161] J. Aikin, *An Address to the Dissidents of England on their late Defeat* (1790), 19.
[162] *Monthly Magazine*, 1 (1796), p. iii.

John Aikin was the son of Dr John Aikin who was for a time assistant minister to Philip Doddridge at Northampton and later Classical and divinity tutor at the Warrington academy where he espoused Arian views. The younger John, although only eleven when his father went to Warrington, was for three years allowed to attend the academy's lectures and subsequently studied medicine at Edinburgh and surgery in London. He gained a doctorate in medicine from the University of Leiden and set up in medical practice, first in Warrington and from 1784 in Great Yarmouth.[163] But the campaign for the repeal of the Test and Corporation Acts in 1789–90 prompted Aikin to publish two pamphlets which so angered the clergy of Great Yarmouth that they schemed to invite a rival physician to the town to ruin his practice, and in 1792 Aikin moved to London intending to divide his time between medicine and his literary interests.[164] For the next thirty years Aikin was at the centre of a circle of liberal and Dissenting intellectuals whom Henry Brougham described as 'the best of the professional writers',[165] and although he lacked the originality of Joseph Priestley he shared his friend's encyclopaedic range of interests. Aikin wrote biographies of Samuel Johnson, John Selden, Archbishop Ussher, and John Howard; he edited the writings of the younger Pliny and the poems of Edmund Spenser, Milton, Samuel Butler, Oliver Goldsmith, and Alexander Pope; he translated from French A. Baumé's *Manual of Chemistry* and from Latin Johann Forster's *Essay on India*; he wrote a much-reprinted *England Delineated, or a Geographical Description of Every County in England and Wales*, and *Geographical Delineations, or a Compendious View of the Natural and Political State of all Parts of the Globe*; he compiled a two-volume *Annals of the Reign of George III* and the *Biographical Memoirs of Medicine in Great Britain*; but the work which occupied the greater part of his time over a period of nineteen years was his ten-volume *General Biography . . . of the Most Eminent Persons of all Ages, Countries, Conditions, and Professions*, the last volume of which was published in 1815.[166]

Three years after Aikin was obliged to leave Great Yarmouth for London, in 1795, he met Richard Phillips, a former Leicester bookseller and proprietor and editor of the *Leicester Herald* who had also suffered for his radical political views. Phillips had been sentenced to eighteen months in prison in 1793 for selling Paine's *Right of Man*, and in 1795 the unpopularity of his views and falling sales had forced him to close his newspaper. However a fortuitous fire at his shop in November enabled him to move to London; with

---

[163] Lucy Aikin, *Memoir of John Aikin, M.D.* (1823), i. 3–15, 64–5, 99.
[164] Ibid. 130–2, 151.   [165] Cookson, *Friends of Peace*, 91.
[166] Aikin, *Memoir of John Aikin*, i. 190, 261.

the insurance money he founded the *Monthly Magazine* with John Aikin as editor; and Phillips was thus launched on the path to wealth and social acceptance which was to lead to his election as sheriff of London and to the award of a knighthood.[167]

It was not the intention of Phillips and Aikin that the *Monthly Magazine* should be primarily a political journal. Its aim was rather the publication of 'full information of every new thing that is going forward in science and the arts', and with a circulation of 5,000 copies it achieved a readership far larger than that of any other contemporary periodical.[168] The *Monthly* did not eschew political controversy: it called for a national system of education and inveighed against the government of the younger Pitt.[169] But what was most significant about the *Monthly Magazine*'s political stance was the fact that it was the first periodical to voice the awakening consciousness of the liberal, and largely Nonconformist, middle class. In the same way that Linnaeus was categorizing the world of plants so writers in the later eighteenth century were beginning to divide society into 'higher', 'middling', and 'lower' classes,[170] and it is not surprising that Aikin, an enthusiastic botanist,[171] should adopt the new classification. Aikin was insistent that the middle class was both more deserving than other classes in society yet more burdened by the taxation policies of Pitt's government. In 1790, in the same pamphlet in which he praised Fox for his liberal views, Aikin addressed his fellow Dissenters as belonging to 'the most virtuous, the most enlightened, the most independent part of the community, the *middle class*'.[172] Yet it was this very class which, in Aikin's eyes, was being unjustly penalized by government policy. The trebling of assessed taxes, the *Monthly Magazine* complained in November 1797, would rob 'the middle industrious classes of society . . . of all their little savings'.[173] The *Monthly*'s very success, it claimed in the following year, was evidence that 'the great mass of information, and of public and private virtues' were to be found in the middle class.[174] And Aikin contrasted the virtues of the middle class with 'the ignorant apathy of the lowest classes' on

---

[167] A. T. Patterson, *Radical Leicester* (Leicester, 1954), 67–77; F. S. Herne, 'An Old Leicester Bookseller', *Transactions of the Leicester Literary and Philosophical Society*, NS 3 (1892–5), 65–73. Herne claims that Phillips was still editing the *Leicester Herald* at the time of the fire.

[168] Aikin, *Memoir of John Aikin*, i. 155; I. Sellers, 'Some Political Ideas of Representative English Unitarians, 1795–1850', B.Litt. thesis (Oxford, 1956), 16–17. Sellers's thesis provides the fullest account of the *Monthly Magazine*.

[169] *Monthly Magazine*, 4 (1797), 146; 5 (1798), 26.

[170] P. J. Corfield, 'Class by Name and Number in Eighteenth-century Britain', *History*, 72 (1987), 55.

[171] Rodgers, *Georgian Chronicle*, 57.

[172] Aikin, *Address to the Dissidents of England*, 18.

[173] *Monthly Magazine*, 4 (1797), 397.   [174] Ibid. 5 (1798), p. i.

the one hand and with the greed of the upper classes on the other. Among the latter he numbered the clergy, the landowners, 'and a large portion of the mercantile and manufacturing interest' in the pursuit of whose 'ambitions and rapacious projects has been accumulated the enormous burden under which we now groan'.[175]

John Aikin, in common with other Dissenters, subsequently became disillusioned with events in France and the antipathy he had once shown towards Pitt was henceforward directed against Napoleon.[176] He finally quarrelled with Richard Phillips in 1806 and broke with the *Monthly Magazine*. However, his son Arthur, who returned to Unitarianism after a brief flirtation with Deism, became editor of the *Annual Review* in 1802 when it was founded by Thomas Longman III in partnership with the Unitarian Owen Rees.[177] By entrusting the historical and political section of the *Annual Review* to the Norwich radical William Taylor, Arthur Aikin ensured that it would continue the *Monthly*'s policy of defending the interests of the Dissenting middle class. The *Annual Review* complained that Pitt's financial policy had benefited 'the great monopoly companies to the prejudice of unprivileged trade', and that the majority of his taxes were inequitable since they levied 'on the poor and on the rich an equal sum'.[178] The privileges of the East India Company, of the Bank of England, and of colonial agriculture had been upheld at the expense of domestic manufactures with the result that 'the middle class has sunken step by step, until at length it is reduced to recruit the numbers of the poor'.[179] And so the *Review* demanded an end to the monopolies of the Bank of England and of the East India Company, the resumption of cash payments, the replacement of income tax with a tax on capital, and a policy of *laissez-faire*.[180] Above all the 'Parliament of landlords' should be swept away by the granting of universal male suffrage.[181]

The activities of John Aikin and Richard Phillips in the *Monthly Magazine*, and of Arthur Aikin and William Taylor in the *Annual Review*, were but early manifestations of what was to become one of the major developments of the late eighteenth and early nineteenth centuries: the concerted effort by middle-class Nonconformists and other liberals to establish periodicals through whose columns they could campaign against the injustice of monopolies, the privileges of landlords, and the disabilities of Dissenters. Such papers were often started to counter the influence of existing Tory

[175] Ibid. 178.   [176] Sellers, 'English Unitarians', 18, 25–7.
[177] Rodgers, *Georgian Chronicle*, 163; Cookson, *Friends of Peace*, 105.
[178] *Annual Review*, 2 (1803), 238.   [179] Ibid. 4 (1805), 302.
[180] Ibid. 2 (1803), 383–5; 3 (1804), 265, 292; 5 (1806), 194.   [181] Ibid. 4 (1805), 242.

journals, but they frequently came to exceed them in influence and circulation,[182] and the most successful were based on the manufacturing towns of the north and the Midlands where the expansion of industry and the growth of Dissent provided them with a receptive readership and essential advertising revenue.[183] In Newcastle upon Tyne both the Whig *Newcastle Chronicle* (from 1784) and the more radical *Tyne Mercury* (founded in 1802) were owned and edited by two families, the Hodgsons and the Mitchells, who were both members of the Hanover Square Unitarian chapel.[184] Another Unitarian, Joseph Gales, founded the *Sheffield Register* in 1787, and after he fled to the United States in 1794 his mantle fell on his former assistant, the Moravian James Montgomery, though the two spells he spent in prison in 1795 and 1796 cooled Montgomery's radical ardour.[185] Under the editorship of the Unitarian Benjamin Flower the *Cambridge Intelligencer* from 1793 to 1803 was the most outspoken voice of those liberal Dissenters who were opposed to the war with France and he, too, spent six months in prison in 1799.[186]

The most successful of all the Dissenting newspaper editors and proprietors was Edward Baines, who bought the *Leeds Mercury* in 1801. Baines was the son of a Preston grocer who had been forced to close his business by the town's Tory corporation, an event which lay at the root of Baines's lifelong antipathy to closed corporations and trade monopolies.[187] After he walked from Preston to Leeds in 1795 to begin work on the paper he was subsequently to own, Baines divided his Sunday worship between Salem Congregational chapel and the Mill Hill Unitarian meeting. His motive, his son implied, was primarily political: 'belonging to the party of reformers . . . Mr Baines found his only congenial associations among the Dissenters'.[188] But like other enterprising young men Edward Baines found that attendance at Dissenting chapels brought economic benefits: in 1801, when the circulation of the *Leeds Mercury* had fallen to 700 or 800, Baines bought the paper with the help of a loan of £1,000 from eleven wealthy backers who wanted Leeds to have a paper which would support liberal causes. The majority of Baines's backers were Unitarians, including Richard Slater Milnes, who was Whig MP for York from 1784 to 1802, and John Marshall, the wealthy flax-

---

[182] D. Fraser, 'The Press in Leicester, c.1780–1850', *Leicestershire Archaeological and Historical Society*, 42 (1966–7), 60.
[183] Cookson, *Friends of Peace*, 113–14.
[184] Seed, 'Unitarianism and Liberal Culture', 242, 347.
[185] D. Read, *Press and People, 1790–1850* (1961), 69–73.
[186] Cookson, *Friends of Peace*, 97–8.   [187] Baines, *Life of Edward Baines*, 13–15.
[188] Ibid. 29, 57.

spinner and future MP for Yorkshire.[189] Baines's vacillation between Salem and Mill Hill was ultimately resolved, under the influence of his wife, in favour of the Congregationalists, although he did not join the church until 1840, when he was sixty-five years old. By that date he had increased the weekly sales of the *Leeds Mercury* to 10,000, giving it the largest circulation of any provincial newspaper apart from Feargus O'Connor's *Northern Star*.[190]

Unitarians ran the liberal papers in Wakefield and Hull. Rowland Hurst printed, and Thomas Lums helped to edit, the *Wakefield Star* which was founded in 1804 and continued from 1811 as the *Wakefield and Halifax Journal*. William Spence (1808–11) and George Lee (1811–42) edited the *Hull Rockingham* in succession after its foundation in 1808.[191] It was also in 1808 that the *Nottingham Review* was founded and edited by Charles Sutton, the friend of Alexander Kilham and pillar of the Methodist New Connexion. Such was the depth of Sutton's antagonism to the government and to the war with the United States that in October 1814, after British troops had sacked Washington and burned down the Congressional buildings, he printed a satirical letter, allegedly from the machine-breaker 'General Ludd', in which the latter claimed that his son Ned was now serving with the British army in the United States. What he and his son had done in Nottinghamshire, claimed 'General Ludd', was 'not half so bad as what my son has done in America'. For publishing the letter Sutton was prosecuted and found guilty of libel and spent eighteen months in prison.[192]

The *Leicester Chronicle* was founded in 1810 by a group of Whigs and Liberals. Its first editor was the Baptist John Ryley and from 1813 it was edited by the Congregationalist Thomas Thompson who became sole proprietor of the paper in the following year and whose family was to retain control for more than sixty years.[193] The *Sheffield Independent*, founded in 1819, was edited from 1823 to 1829 by the Unitarian Thomas Asline Ward and in 1829 was bought by the Congregationalist Robert Leader, whose wife was cousin to the wife of the elder Edward Baines. Like the *Leeds Mercury* the *Independent* was the spokesman for middle-class reformers and under the editorship of Robert Leader II (1833–74) it became the most influential newspaper in Sheffield.[194] Similarly journalism in Manchester was dominated by the *Manchester Guardian*, founded in 1821 by a group of middle-class

---

[189] Read, *Press and People*, 76.   [190] Ibid. 78, 210, 212.

[191] Seed, 'Unitarianism and Liberal Culture', 349.

[192] Sutton, *Nottingham Date-Book*, 316–18.

[193] Cookson, *Friends of Peace*, 111; Fraser, 'The Press in Leicester', 60.

[194] Read, *Press and People*, 91–3, 201.

radicals who were mainly Unitarians. It was edited by the Unitarian John Edward Taylor, and printed by the Unitarian Jeremiah Garnett. However, Taylor's politics proved to be too moderate for some of his backers, and two of them, Thomas and Richard Potter, Unitarian cotton merchants, withdrew their support and bestowed it on the much more radical Archibald Prentice, a Scottish Presbyterian who shared the political aims of the English Dissenters.[195] Prentice bought the *Manchester Gazette* in 1824 and from 1828 edited the *Manchester Times*, but the majority of Manchester's middle class preferred the more cautious politics of the *Manchester Guardian* and Prentice's papers were never able to challenge its supremacy.[196]

What provoked much of this middle-class Dissenting interest in journalism in the early nineteenth century was the conviction that Britain was being governed in the interests of monopolists and the landed classes at the expense of the manufacturing classes, and the belief that newspapers could play a crucial role in arousing public opinion against what was regarded as inequitable class legislation. The radical middle class complained bitterly of the increase in import duties and of the introduction, in 1799, of income tax to pay for the war with France; they resented the East India Company's monopoly of trade with the Indian subcontinent; above all they objected to the Orders in Council which from 1807 sought to compel neutral countries to trade with France and her allies via British ports and which produced a retaliatory embargo from the United States. It was the disruption of Norwich's overseas trade by the war which led that city's popular electorate to choose the Unitarian and future chairman of the Dissenting Deputies, William Smith, as its MP in 1802.[197] And it was the worse disruption of the nation's trade by the Orders in Council which provoked a mass agitation against measures which were seen to benefit British shipowners and West Indian merchants at the expense of northern manufacturers and their workers and of merchants who traded with the United States. The public campaign against the Orders in Council began in February 1808 with a petition of Liverpool merchants, led by the Unitarians William Roscoe and William Rathbone. The Liverpool merchants initially received little support from the rest of the country, apart from Manchester, but they renewed the agitation in 1812 after two years of depression and they received enthusiastic support from the

---

[195] For the Potters see G. Meinertzhagen, *From Ploughshare to Parliament, a short memoir of the Potters of Tadcaster* (1908).

[196] Read, *Press and People*, 80–2, 87–8.

[197] Davis, *Dissent in Politics*, 120–7. Smith had hitherto sat in Parliament for the corrupt borough of Sudbury (1784–90, 1796, 1802) and for the pocket borough of Camelford (1791–6). He was to represent Norwich from 1802 to 1806, and from 1807 to 1830.

Potteries, where the protest was led by the Unitarian Josiah Wedgwood II and the New Connexion Methodist John Ridgway, from Sheffield, where the campaign was led by some of the Dissenters who seven years later were to found the *Sheffield Independent*, and from Leeds and Birmingham. The political crisis following the assassination of the prime minister, Spencer Perceval, on 11 May 1812, destroyed the government's will to withstand the public agitation and on 23 June the Foreign Secretary, Viscount Castlereagh, announced the revocation of the Orders in Council.[198] It was, wrote Edward Baines in the *Leeds Mercury*, 'the most beneficial victory which has been achieved during the present war'.[199]

On the very day that Castlereagh announced the withdrawal of the Orders in Council the new prime minister, Lord Liverpool, met a delegation from the Dissenting Deputies and assured them that the government had no objection to the repeal of the Five Mile Act or to the suspension of the operation of the Conventicle Act.[200] The Toleration Act of 1689 had allowed Dissenting ministers to avoid the penalties prescribed by the Five Mile Act of 1665 by subscribing to thirty-six of the Thirty-nine Articles, and permitted Dissenting congregations to escape the consequences of the Conventicle Act of 1670 by enabling them to take out licences for their meeting-houses on condition of one of their number taking the oaths of allegiance and supremacy.[201] But neither the Five Mile Act nor the Conventicle Act had been repealed, and their continued presence on the statute-book was used from time to time by unsympathetic magistrates as a pretext for refusing licences to Dissenting meeting-houses and ministers. In 1766 magistrates in Derbyshire refused a request from the General Baptists at Kegworth to license either their houses for preaching or one of their preachers and it cost the Kegworth Baptists £50 to get a mandamus from the King's Bench to overturn the magistrates' decision.[202] And with the growing Anglican concern at the expansion of Nonconformity at the turn of the eighteenth and nineteenth centuries came an increasing readiness by clergymen to prosecute Dissenters who did not comply with the letter of the law. In 1791 magistrates at Brecon somewhat reluctantly fined Thomas Bowen £20 for preaching at an unlicensed farmhouse at Llansantffraid on the evidence of the local vicar, a man named Frew. It was with grim satisfaction that six weeks later Brecon Dissenters were able to record that Frew had fallen from his horse, fractured

---

[198] Cookson, *Friends of Peace*, 214–37; A. Briggs, *The Age of Improvement* (1959), 164–6; J. H. Y. Briggs, 'The Radical Saints of Shelton', in D. J. Jeremy (ed.), *Business and Religion in Britain* (Aldershot, 1988), 62.

[199] Read, *Press and People*, 108.   [200] Davis, *Dissent in Politics*, 180–1.

[201] Watts, *The Dissenters*, i. 259–60.   [202] Taylor, *History of the General Baptists*, ii. 51–3.

his skull, and died.[203] Nine years later, in 1800, Charles Farmery, pastor of the Particular Baptist church at Diss in Norfolk, preached at the home of one of his members for which a licence had been applied for but not yet granted. As a result a magistrate who was also an Anglican clergyman fined both Farmery and the cottager £20 each, and the eight other people present 5s. each.[204]

The culmination of magisterial hostility towards Dissenters coincided with the Anglican panic which led to Sidmouth's abortive bill of 1811. An attempt by Congregationalists to hold services in a house in Wickham Market, Suffolk, in 1810 provoked a series of riots. Vast crowds of noisy protesters used squibs, fireworks, 'an Indian gong, cow's horns, [and] old kettles' to disturb the worshippers, threw 'stones, dirt, muck, [and] human dung' at them, and subjected the women of the congregation 'to the most brutal insults'. The local magistrates refused to take action against the rioters, and it was not until the matter was referred to the King's Bench, with help of the Protestant Society and at a cost of £800, that the troublemakers were indicted. At the subsequent Suffolk assizes the ringleaders of the rioters apologized and paid 200 guineas by way of compensation, a sum which was donated to the British and Foreign Bible Society.[205]

The hands of unsympathetic magistrates had been strengthened by an amendment of the Toleration Act in 1779 which could be interpreted as restricting the granting of licences to ministers in charge of particular congregations to the exclusion of itinerants and probationers.[206] In 1806 Suffolk magistrates refused an application for a licence from Samuel Squirrel unless he could prove that he ministered to a specific congregation; in 1809 Buckinghamshire magistrates refused a licence for William Carr on the grounds that he was not the pastor of a settled church; in 1811 Denbighshire magistrates declined to tender the oaths prescribed by the Toleration Act to a preacher who ministered to several different congregations.[207] Gloucestershire magistrates refused a licence to John Packer of Dursley because he 'itinerated to various congregations' and to Thomas Brittain of Bristol, a student who preached to different congregations as part of his preparation for the ministry.[208] It was fear that public agitation against

---

[203] Rees, *Protestant Nonconformity in Wales*, 380–1.

[204] C. B. Jewson, *The Baptists of Norfolk* (1957), 65; Browne, *Congregationalism in Norfolk and Suffolk*, 202.

[205] Browne, *Congregationalism in Norfolk and Suffolk*, 540; Lovegrove, *Established Church, Sectarian People*, 119.

[206] Davis, *Dissent in Politics*, 39–40, 160.

[207] Lovegrove, *Established Church, Sectarian People*, 138; Davis, *Dissent in Politics*, 151.

[208] Evans, *As Mad as a Hatter!*, 111.

Sidmouth's bill would further provoke magistrates to a strict interpretation of the Toleration Act that dictated the cautious policy of the Dissenting Deputies in 1811,[209] and subsequent events gave some substance to their fears: by January 1812 magistrates in thirty counties were refusing to grant licences to preachers not in charge of settled congregations.[210]

The withdrawal of Sidmouth's bill in May 1811 was thus followed by the determination, on the part of both Methodists and Dissenters, to campaign for the repeal of the Five Mile and Conventicle Acts.[211] The government, for its part, was anxious not to inflame Nonconformist opinion further lest the Dissenters made common cause with the Catholics in opposition to all religious tests.[212] At three o'clock on the afternoon of 11 May 1812 Robert Aspland and John Wilks of the Protestant Society had what they described as a 'satisfactory interview' with the prime minister, Spencer Perceval, on the question of the Five Mile and Conventicle Acts. That same day William Smith, the Unitarian MP and chairman of the Dissenting Deputies, wrote to his fellow Whig MP Samuel Whitbread that Perceval would support their repeal. Smith arranged to meet Whitbread in the lobby of the House of Commons at five o'clock in the afternoon, but as soon as he arrived he heard a shot fired and Perceval collapsed at his feet.[213] The assassination of the prime minister did not, however, impede the campaign for repeal. Perceval's successor, Lord Liverpool, repeated his predecessor's assurance of support and in July Parliament approved the Little Toleration Act abolishing both the Five Mile and Conventicle Acts and requiring all magistrates to administer the oaths prescribed by the Toleration Act. Two main pillars of the Clarendon Code were thus removed: only the Test and Corporation Acts remained.

The defeat of Sidmouth's bill, the withdrawal of the Orders in Council, and the repeal of the Five Mile and Conventicle Acts were followed by other liberal victories. In 1813 Parliament revised the charter of the East India Company, securing for commercial interests the revocation of the company's trading monopoly with the subcontinent and for Evangelicals the right to send missionaries to those parts of India under the company's control. In the same year William Smith secured the approval first of the Archbishop of Canterbury and then of Parliament for an Act absolving Unitarians of the

---

[209] Davis, *Dissent in Politics*, 161–2.
[210] Lovegrove, *Established Church, Sectarian People*, 140.
[211] Hempton, *Methodism and Politics*, 101–2; Davis, *Dissent in Politics*, 174.
[212] Pellew, *Life of Sidmouth*, iii. 62.
[213] Aspland, *Memoir of Robert Aspland*, 272; Davis, *Dissent in Politics*, 178–9.

crime of blasphemy.[214] Annoying 'penalties, restrictions, and disabilities on account of religion' still remained: while magistrates could no longer refuse to grant licences to Nonconformist preachers, they could and did prosecute itin-erants for obstructing the highway and for gathering riotous assemblies;[215] in 1817 a Congregational deacon, to his discredit, initiated proceedings against John Wright, brother of the Unitarian missionary, for holding blasphemous services on unlicensed premises in Liverpool; and as late as 1838 two inhabi-tants of Llanelli were sent to prison for not attending their parish church.[216] It was nevertheless true that in the three years from 1811 to 1813 the Noncon-formist middle class had made significant political gains and the Dissenting Deputies' faith in the 'increase in just and liberal sentiments' had been vin-dicated.

5. 'BE YE THEREFORE PATIENT': METHODISM, WORKING-CLASS CONSCIOUSNESS, AND LUDDISM

While Unitarian editors and the Congregationalist newspaper proprietors Edward Baines and Robert Leader were seeking to foster the class conscious-ness and defend the class interests of their middle-class readers, exactly the reverse process was at work among the Wesleyan Methodists: in the first quar-ter of the nineteenth century the Wesleyan leadership did all in its power to thwart the development of class consciousness among its own working-class membership.

Working-class consciousness developed later, or at least was articulated later, than middle-class consciousness. The term 'working class' seems to have been used first by the Scottish writer John Gay in 1789, was taken up by John Aikin in 1795, and passed into common usage in the early nineteenth century, or forty years after the term 'middle class'.[217] The origins of working-class consciousness have been the subject of much controversy among histo-rians. Edward Thompson's attempt to trace its genesis back to Thomas Hardy's London Corresponding Society of the 1790s is open to the objection that a third of its members whose occupations are known were in fact middle class, and that it contained far more attorneys, merchants, and tradesmen, and far fewer labourers, than most contemporary Nonconformist congrega-

---

[214] Davis, *Dissent in Politics*, 190–3.   [215] See Ch. I, sect. 9.
[216] Sellers, 'Liverpool Nonconformity', 291; Aspland, *Memoir of Robert Aspland*, 375–8; Manning, *Dissenting Deputies*, 180; D. Paterson, 'John Wright', *TUHS* 6 (1935–8), 29–43.
[217] Corfield, 'Class by Name and Number', *History*, 77 (1987), 56–7.

tions.[218] Joseph Birch, Whig candidate in Nottingham in 1803, was perhaps the first parliamentary candidate to make a specific bid for 'working-class' support, but the Nottingham voters refused to divide on class lines.[219] Harold Perkin dates the origin of working-class consciousness to the years between 1815 and 1820 when post-war distress turned the agitation of a minority of radicals for parliamentary reform into a mass movement of popular protest.[220] Thompson agrees that the end of the wars against France brought a new dimension to working-class radicalism, transforming 'a movement of an organized minority' into 'the response of the whole community'.[221] And while Robert Glen, in his detailed study of Stockport, doubts whether 'a class-conscious working class existed during the industrial revolution', he concedes that in the years 1818–20 'radicalism reached a peak', in part the result 'of the adherence of increasing numbers of hand-loom weavers'.[222] The Manchester radical Archibald Prentice also placed the emergence of working-class radicalism in the years after Waterloo. Whereas it was the homes and meeting-houses of Dissenters that had been assaulted by mobs in the names of Church and King in 1791, it was the establishment which felt threatened by working-class violence after the end of the war. The working class of Manchester, wrote Prentice with a degree of bitterness, had found 'a new and more truthful teacher' than the Anglican pulpit and the Tory press: that teacher was 'WANT'. 'The working classes were the first to experience the consequences of that general folly in which they had so largely participated.'[223]

Prentice's comment serves to remind us that conservative loyalism rather than radicalism was often the distinguishing characteristic of working-class attitudes, and that working-class Toryism was to be an important feature of the political landscape throughout the nineteenth and twentieth centuries. Conversely, in the late eighteenth and early nineteenth centuries, radicalism was often a middle-class, and frequently a Dissenting middle-class, rather than a working-class phenomenon. Richard Davis argues that in Norwich 'from 1802 to 1818 it was middle-class Dissenting radicalism' which led the movement for parliamentary reform 'and "the people did not respond" '. Norman McCord similarly concludes that on Tyneside it was 'the liberal

[218] M. Thale (ed.), *Selections from the Papers of the London Corresponding Society* (Cambridge, 1983), p. xix; H. Perkins, *The Origins of Modern English Society* (1969), 30.
[219] Thomis, *Politics and Society in Nottingham*, 56–7.
[220] Perkins, *Modern English Society*, 209.
[221] Thompson, *Making of the English Working Class*, 663.
[222] R. Glen, *Urban Workers in the Early Industrial Revolution* (1984), 278, 284.
[223] Prentice, *Historical Sketches of Manchester*, 25, 30.

middle-classes, for whom the Unitarian-owned *Tyne Mercury* and *Newcastle Chronicle* primarily catered', rather than local coalminers, seamen, or keelmen, who were most aroused by the massacre at Peterloo.[224] And, as we have seen, among Nonconformists the radical Unitarians and liberal New Connexion Methodists attracted a more bourgeois following than the conservative Wesleyans.

Yet against the evidence which suggests that radicalism was a predominantly middle-class rather than a working-class phenomenon must be set the fact that middle-class radicals were often worried that the reform movement would split along class lines. From the 1790s onwards it was the constant theme of radical Dissenters that the working and middle classes had a common interest in curtailing the privileges and monopolies of the landed and mercantile interests. And it was the continual fear of some Dissenters that the working class, far from making common cause with the bourgeoisie, would come to see the middle class and the upper class as a common enemy. In 1792 the London Society for Constitutional Information was divided between the radical followers of Tom Paine and the more moderate supporters of Christopher Wyvill who criticized the former for holding out to 'the lower classes of the people . . . the prospect of plundering the rich'.[225] When, in April, the Norwich Revolution Society, with the elder William Taylor as secretary, wrote to the Society for Constitutional Information to ask for a form of association, it made plain that it did not subscribe to the view that the interests of the rich and poor were opposed. The Revolution Society claimed that 'the interests of all the industrious in the community are the same: to lessen the number of unproductive and to do away with such impositions and imposts as do away with the means of maintenance'.[226]

While middle-class radicals thus stressed the common ground between the middle and working classes in the interests of the movement for reform, the leaders of the Wesleyan Methodism sought to unite them in defence of the status quo. For Wesleyans the growth of working-class militancy jeopardized Methodism's essential task of winning souls, put into the hands of their opponents pretexts on which to restrict their freedom to preach, posed a threat to the Connexion's undemocratic structure, and threatened to disrupt Methodist communities along class lines. The leaders of both the Wesleyans and of the New Connexion Methodists were alarmed, and with good reason, by the campaign of machine-breaking which swept through the industrial

---

[224] Davis, *Dissent in Politics*, 134–5; N. McCord, 'Tyneside Discontents and Peterloo', *Northern History*, 2 (1967), 110–11.

[225] Thompson, *Making of the English Working Class*, 120.   [226] Jewson, *Jacobin City*, 29.

regions of northern England in the second decade of the nineteenth century, the movement which claimed to take its inspiration from the mythical General Ludd.

The Luddite outbreak began in the industrial village of Arnold, near Nottingham, on 11 March 1811 when a decision by hosiery manufacturers to cut the wages of stockingers sparked off riots in which more than sixty stocking-frames were smashed. From Nottinghamshire Luddism spread to Leicestershire and Derbyshire and in January 1812 entered the West Riding of Yorkshire. It was provoked by the same trade depression which prompted Midland and northern manufacturers to campaign against the Orders in Council, and their repeal in June 1812 brought a rapid improvement of trade and the decline of Luddism. However the post-war depression led to a brief revival of machine-breaking in the Midlands which lasted from the summer of 1816 until the beginning of 1817.[227] Although short-lived, the Luddite outbreak produced bitter divisions in Methodist communities. The New Connexion in particular was sensitive to the charge that it had encouraged Luddite violence and responded with the same apolitical gestures with which the Wesleyans had greeted the French Revolution. In 1813 George Beaumont, a New Connexion minister in Sheffield, was accused of inspiring the Luddite disturbances in the Huddersfield area. Beaumont, originally from Stockport, had been one of the leaders of the revolt against Jeremiah Brettell in 1796, and after he entered the New Connexion ministry he continued to advocate radical views.[228] He had published pamphlets in 1808 and 1809 denouncing war and pleading the cause of the poor without incurring the censure of his Connexion.[229] But the allegation that his pamphlets had incited Luddite machine-breaking led the New Connexion Conference to take note of his activities in 1813. Conference dissociated itself from all 'political books which may have been published by any of our preachers' and registered its disapprobation 'of our ministers writing or disseminating works of a political nature'. Beaumont responded with a third pamphlet attacking monopolies, place-men, and press-gangs and was expelled from the ministry.[230]

---

[227] Thompson, *Making of the English Working Class*, 605–9, 627, 657; M. Thomis, *The Luddites* (Newton Abbot, 1970), 43–8.

[228] Rose, *Methodism in Ashton-under-Lyne*, i. 32.

[229] G. Beaumont, *The Warrior's Looking Glass* (Sheffield, 1808), *passim*; Werner, *Primitive Methodist Connexion*, 195 n. 75.

[230] Werner, *Primitive Methodist Connexion*, 24, 195 n. 75; Thompson, *Making of the English Working Class*, 512–13.

Beaumont was not the only Kilhamite to voice dangerously radical political views. In January 1813 the Quarterly Meeting of the Ashton-under-Lyne New Connexion circuit felt obliged to dissociate itself from sentiments 'inconsistent with the duty we owe as subjects to the government of this country . . . expressed by one of our preachers' at Stalybridge.[231] And two years later Charles Sutton, the Kilhamite editor of the radical *Nottingham Review*, was accused of sympathy with the Luddites and the charge played a part in his conviction for libel.[232] But in the same year of 1815 the New Connexion Methodists in Ashton were able to turn the tables on Wesleyan critics such as Robert Melson who accused them of rebellion.[233] Not only did the Kilhamites claim that the local Wesleyans had in their societies 'men who have been among the Luddites', but they asserted that a preacher who had been reproved for uttering Jacobin opinions in New Connexion pulpits had 'left us, joined the Wesleyans and [become] their best local preacher'.[234]

The accusation that Wesleyan societies were harbouring Luddites, and the knowledge that some of the men accused of violence had been brought up in Methodist homes, were acutely embarrassing to the Wesleyan leadership. Wesleyan preachers were faced with the difficult task of denouncing the Luddites without alienating the working-class communities from which they were drawn, and they were fortunate that Lord Sidmouth's bill for regulating Methodist preachers had been defeated before the worst of the Luddite outbreaks occurred. After two Luddites had been mortally wounded in an attack on William Cartwright's mill at Rawfolds in the Spen Valley on 11 April 1812, friends of one of the men, Samuel Hartley, demanded a Methodist funeral for him. Jabez Bunting, who at the time was superintendent in the Halifax circuit, refused to conduct the service and threats were made against his life.[235] On the following Sunday the Wesleyan chapel in Halifax attracted the largest congregation it had ever seen as 'people came from far and wide to show their sympathy for the deceased'. Hundreds stood outside, unable to get in, and 'constables walked before the doors to keep the peace'. The crippled preacher Jonathan Saville chose the occasion to contrast the death of a Christian believer with that of an infidel, with the implication that Hartley belonged to the latter category. His sermon appeared 'to have a great effect', but a few days later some of the local inhabitants showed

[231] Rose, *Methodism in Ashton-under-Lyne*, ii. 21.
[232] Thomis, *Politics and Society in Nottingham*, 136, 194.
[233] Melson, *Defensive Armour against the Devouring Sword of Calumny, passim*.
[234] Rose, *Methodism in Ashton-under-Lyne*, ii. 21.
[235] Walker, *Wesleyan Methodism in Halifax*, 254–5.

their resentment by throwing stones at him.[236] A similar problem confronted the Wesleyans at nearby Greetland. Six of the seventeen men executed at York in January 1813 for their part in the Luddite disturbances were the sons of Methodists, and when mourners attempted to bring some of their bodies to the Greetland chapel for a funeral service they found the doors of the chapel and the gates of the graveyard locked against them.[237] Greetland had been one of the scenes of the Yorkshire revival of twenty years before, and Bunting commented that the executions at York confirmed him in his 'fixed opinion that the progress of Methodism in the West Riding . . . has been more swift than solid'.[238] The same Wesleyan Conference which rejoiced at the defeat of Sidmouth's bill looked upon the principles which had given birth to Luddism with 'the utmost horror [as] alike destructive to the happiness of the poor and of the rich'. The Wesleyan preachers sympathized with the poor in 'their want of employment, and the dearness of provisions' and urged the 'richer brethren' to assist them. But the only advice they could give to the poor was 'Be ye therefore patient'. 'Let all hope and trust in Him who hath said, "I will never leave thee, nor forsake thee", and in due time you shall reap your reward if you faint not.'[239]

6. 'DESIGNS AGAINST THE PEACE AND GOVERNMENT OF OUR BELOVED COUNTRY': PARLIAMENTARY REFORM, PENTRICH, AND PETERLOO

The Wesleyan leadership not only recoiled with horror from the violence of the Luddite movement, it was deeply distrustful of the peaceful campaign for parliamentary reform. And the Wesleyan hierarchy's opposition to electoral reform placed it at loggerheads both with some working-class members of its own Connexion and with radical, middle-class leaders among Old Dissent. Opinion on the extent of the Dissenting commitment to electoral reform is divided. John Cannon noted the connection between Nonconformity and reform running 'from Overton and Lilburne in the 1640s, through Priestley and Price in the 1780s, to the enactment of Catholic Emancipation'.[240] By

---

[236] West, *Memoirs of Saville*, 26–7.

[237] R. F. Wearmouth, *Methodism and the Working-class Movements of England, 1800–1850* (1937), 63; T. Jackson, *Recollection of My Own Life and Times* (1873), 136–7; J. A. Hargreaves, 'Methodism and Luddism in Yorkshire', *Northern History*, 26 (1990), 179.

[238] Ward, *Religion and Society*, 86.   [239] *Minutes of the Methodist Conferences*, iii. 306.

[240] J. Cannon, *Parliamentary Reform, 1640–1832* (Cambridge, 1973), 22.

contrast James Bradley has argued that the Dissenters' involvement in the unreformed political system, even to the extent of accepting government patronage and of receiving and giving bribes, militated against any reforming impulse. And he further notes the Dissenters' 'near absence from the pages of books on parliamentary reform'.[241] Bradley's first point can, however, be countered with the argument that only a tiny minority of Dissenters were actively engaged in the political process, either as members of borough corporations or as MPs, and is undermined by evidence that even those Dissenters who did benefit from the unreformed system were not thereby inhibited from criticizing it. The Dissenters' parliamentary spokesman, the wealthy Unitarian wholesale grocer and art collector William Smith, first entered the House of Commons for the corrupt borough of Sudbury in 1784. When he lost Sudbury in 1790 he purchased the seat for Camelford in the following year for £2,000 and was again returned for Sudbury in 1796. But all this did not prevent Smith from advocating household suffrage and triennial parliaments.[242]

The 'near absence' of Dissenters from 'the pages of books on parliamentary reform' can in part be explained by the fact that the historians who have written such books have not usually troubled themselves with the religion of their heroes. In fact a significant minority of the most consistent and vociferous advocates of electoral reform were either Dissenters or men who managed to combine Unitarian theological views with continued adherence to the established church. What has been called 'the definitive statement of the reforming case' was put by James Burgh, whose father was a Scottish Presbyterian minister and who came to England in the 1740s and for twenty-five years kept a school at Stoke Newington. Burgh was a close friend of Richard Price and an acquaintance of Joseph Priestley and under Price's influence became an Arian. In the three volumes of his *Political Disquisitions*, published in 1774–5, Burgh argued that 'all lawful authority, legislative and executive, originates from the people'.[243] It was Burgh's book which furnished the material for the speech which John Wilkes made in the Commons in March 1776 when he introduced a motion calling for a more

[241] Bradley, 'Whigs and Nonconformists', 37, 211, 513–14; J. Bradley, 'Whigs and Nonconformists: "Slumbering Radicalism" in English Politics, 1739–1789', *Eighteenth-Century Studies*, 9 (1975–6), 4, 14–15; J. Bradley, 'Nonconformity and the Electorate', *Parliamentary History* (1986–7), 251.

[242] Davis, *Dissent in Politics*, 16–19, 57–8, 93–4, 100.

[243] J. C. D. Clark, *English Society, 1688–1832* (Cambridge, 1985), 322–3; J. T. Rutt (ed.), *The Theological and Miscellaneous Works of Joseph Priestley*, i (1831), part i, 258 n.; part ii, 109 n.; J. O. Baylen and N. J. Gossman, *Biographical Dictionary of Modern British Radicals* (1979), i. 72–6.

equal representation of the people.[244] Among Wilkes's most loyal supporters was Alderman Frederick Bull, a member of Abraham Booth's Particular Baptist church in Prescot Street and, as we have seen, a benefactor of the Bristol Baptist College. When Bull contested a by-election for the City of London in November 1773 he pledged himself 'to endeavour to obtain a more fair and equal representation of the people', and he was the first man to be elected to Parliament after giving such pledges to his electorate.[245]

It was also Burgh who popularized the notion of an extra-parliamentary National Association to agitate for reform, and the man who first put the idea into practice, Christopher Wyvill, although an Anglican clergyman, sympathized with Unitarian theological views.[246] Burgh's ideas also influenced Dr John Jebb, a tutor at Peterhouse, Cambridge, whose evolving Unitarian views led him to leave the university for a career in medicine. It was Jebb who developed the idea of an alternative parliament, consisting of delegates chosen in proportion to the population of the counties and boroughs, to challenge the authority of the unrepresentative Parliament.[247] Major John Cartwright, who campaigned for electoral reform for more than fifty years, also embraced Unitarian views but, like Wyvill, did not sever his links with the established church.[248]

Jebb and Cartwright both played a prominent part in the founding in 1780 of the Society for Constitutional Information. The society, which complained 'that under the present imperfect constitution of Parliament it is impossible we can be free, safe, and happy at home, or respected abroad' endorsed Jebb's concept of an alternative parliament or convention.[249] It was supported by numerous Dissenters,[250] and in many parts of England Dissenters were the most outspoken advocates of parliamentary reform. In Nottingham George Walker, the minister of the High Pavement Presbyterian meeting, spoke in support of Wyvill's Association movement in 1780 and in 1793 drew up a petition signed by 2,500 Nottingham citizens in favour of manhood suffrage.[251] In Yorkshire Presbyterian Unitarians, led by the Wakefield merchant Pemberton Milnes, were prominent in the leadership

---

[244] Cannon, *Parliamentary Reform*, 66–7.
[245] Rudé, *Wilkes and Liberty*, 195; I. Christie, *Wilkes, Wyvill, and Reform* (1962), 48, 58–9.
[246] Christie, *Wilkes, Wyvill, and Reform*, 53, 70–1.   [247] Ibid. 77–9.
[248] R. V. Holt, *The Unitarian Contribution to Social Progress* (1938), 89–90.
[249] E. C. Black, *The Association: British Extraparliamentary Political Organisation, 1769–1793* (Harvard, Mass., 1963), 176–7, 192–4.
[250] Davis, *Dissent in Politics*, 22–3, 26–7.
[251] Bradley, *Religion, Revolution, and Radicalism*, 132; Thomis, *Politics and Society in Nottingham*, 217–18.

of the Association.[252] Wyvill claimed that one in five of the men who signed his petition in Yorkshire were Dissenters, and that in a county where fewer than one person in twenty was a Dissenter.[253] In London Richard Price, in his famous sermon celebrating the Glorious Revolution of 1688, drew attention to 'the imperfect state in which the Revolution left our constitution' and singled out 'the inequality of our representation' as its most gross and palpable defect.[254] In Manchester the Unitarian merchant and future MP, George Philips, urged the *Necessity of a Speedy Reform of Parliament*, including votes for women, in 1792. And at Stockport in Cheshire in January 1793 the ministers and trustees of seven Dissenting congregations countered a loyal address to the king from local Wesleyans with a declaration calling for 'an impartial representation of the people'.[255]

James Bradley's own researches have shown that in Cambridge Dissenters who were divided over the issue of the American Revolution united in 1780 in support of Wyvill's Association. William Cole, the Anglican rector of Milton, claimed that the Cambridge Association was initiated by Robert Robinson's Particular Baptist church and reported that a meeting called to petition for economic reform and addressed by John Wilkes attracted 'Dissenters of all hues, colours, and denominations in every part of the country, called together . . . by the Anabaptist Alderman Purchase'.[256] In 1783 Robinson formed the Cambridge Constitutional Society to advocate parliamentary reform and the two chairmen of the society were both members of his church.[257] Robinson's policy was continued by his successor Robert Hall. In his *Apology for the Freedom of the Press and for General Liberty*, published in 1793, Hall argued that 'the disproportion between those who vote for representatives and the population at large is so great, that the majority of our House of Commons is chosen by less than eight thousand, in a kingdom consisting of as many millions'. Nothing rendered parliamentary reform more urgent than the ascendancy of the aristocracy. 'This colossus bestrides both houses of parliament; legislates in one and exerts a domineering influence over the other. It is humiliating at the approach of an election, to see a

---

[252] Seeds, 'Unitarianism and Liberal Culture', 121–5.

[253] Christie, *Wilks, Wyvill, and Reform*, 229. Dissenters constituted 3.7% of the population of Yorkshire in 1715 and even in 1851 Old Dissenters comprised only 5.7% of Yorkshiremen and women.

[254] R. Price, *A Discourse on the Love of our Country* (1789), 39.

[255] V. A. C. Gattrell, 'The Commercial Middle Class in Manchester', Ph.D. thesis (Cambridge, 1971), 191; Glen, *Urban Workers in the Industrial Revolution*, 124–5.

[256] J. E. Bradley, 'Religion and Reform at the Polls: Nonconformity in Cambridge Politics, 1774–1784', *Journal of British Studies*, 23 (1984), 67–70.

[257] Ibid. 75–6.

whole county send a deputation to an Earl or Duke, and beg a representative as you would beg an alms.'[258]

Robert Hall's radical ardour was subsequently moderated, though never extinguished, by the course of the revolution in France, and organizations pledged to the reform of parliament such as the Society for Constitutional Information and the London Corresponding Society were silenced by the government in the 1790s. But the resurgence of liberal sentiment which occurred in the following decade was accompanied by a revival of interest in electoral reform. The election of William Smith for the large, popular, constituency of Norwich in 1802 was greeted by Thomas Grenville as a 'Jacobin triumph'.[259] The spending of over £12,000 to secure the election of Smith's fellow Unitarian, William Roscoe, the biographer of Lorenzo de Medici, for Liverpool in 1806 did not inhibit Roscoe, as corruption similarly did not prevent Smith, from advocating 'gradual and temperate' parliamentary reform.[260] And the victory of the Whig Lord Milton by 187 votes in Yorkshire in 1807, in one of the most hotly contested and expensive elections in British history, may well have been swayed by the active support he received from Dissenting ministers.[261]

Milton, the heir of Earl Fitzwilliam, was initially opposed to electoral reform, and it was not until 1821 he was convinced he should support reform because 'the great mass of the middle classes are in favour'.[262] But, according to Thomas Belsham, the enthusiasm with which the Dissenting ministers of Yorkshire supported Milton in the election of 1807, coupled with the zeal with which Dissenters throughout the country supported the Ministry of All the Talents in 1806–7, the government which abolished the slave trade, gave the leaders of the Whig party 'a more favourable opinion of Dissenters, and induced some of them to desire an interview with a few of the Dissenting ministers in London'. Early in July 1807 the Arian ministers Abraham Rees, James Lindsay, and Thomas Jervis and the Socinians Thomas Belsham and Robert Aspland accepted an invitation to a dinner held at the home of the Unitarian serjeant-at-law Samuel Heywood. Also present were the Whig peers Holland, Lauderdale, Stanley, and Howick and the Whig MPs Samuel Whitbread and William Smith. In March 1807 George III had provoked the resignation of Whig ministers and the collapse of the Ministry of All the

[258] *Works of Robert Hall*, iii. 105–6, 113.   [259] Cannon, *Parliamentary Reform*, 147–8.

[260] Sellers, 'Liverpool Nonconformity', 278–80; F. E. Sanderson, 'The Liverpool Abolitionists', in R. Anstey and P. E. H. Hair, *Liverpool, the African Slave Trade, and Abolition* (1976), 221–3.

[261] E. A. Smith, 'The Yorkshire Elections of 1806 and 1807', *Northern History*, 2 (1967), 85.

[262] Cannon, *Parliamentary Reform*, 162, 171, 174, 183.

Talents by demanding a written promise never to raise the issue of Roman Catholic emancipation, and James Lindsay, the minister of the Monkwell Street Presbyterian meeting, seized the opportunity to argue that only electoral reform could give a future Whig ministry a chance of survival. 'You will do no good, my Lord,' he told Howick, 'until you do something for the people. If you were to come in again tomorrow, you would be turned out the next day, if you brought forward any measure that was offensive to the Court. If you would bring forward your own plan of parliamentary reform, you might do some good, but till then you can do nothing.' Howick replied that were he to bring forward a proposal for parliamentary reform at the present time, he would find himself 'in a very small and a very unpopular minority'. Twenty-five years later Howick, as Earl Grey, was to head the ministry that would act on Lindsay's advice. But for the moment, added Lord Holland, 'the people stood in great need of being enlightened, for . . . if we had, at this time, a House of Commons which spoke the sense of the great mass of the people, we should be in a much worse situation than we are at present.'[263]

Lord Holland's challenge that 'the people stood in need of being enlightened' was taken up by the veteran reformer Major Cartwright. In May 1812 he resolved to turn the discontent revealed by the Luddite outbreaks 'into a legal channel favourable to parliamentary reform'[264] and, at the age of seventy-two, embarked on a series of tours to rouse public opinion. Cartwright's initiative proved to be premature, for the improvement in trade which followed the repeal of the Orders in Council in June 1812 removed much of the discontent which had provoked the Luddite movement. But the depression which followed the ending of the war with France in July 1815, as a fall in government spending and the return of troops coincided with renewed competition from the Continent and a run of poor harvests, gave Cartwright his opportunity. In June 1815 the Hampden Club in London endorsed an appeal by Cartwright and the radical MP Sir Francis Burdett for petitions in favour of electoral reform, and by March 1817 Burdett was claiming they had attracted the support of nearly a million people.[265] The petitioning movement of 1816–17 divided Nonconformity, as it divided the nation as a whole, into three schools of thought: radical reformers, moderate reformers, and conservatives. Radicals were represented by a group of Nottingham Dissenters led by the Congregationalist mayor William Wilson, the Baptist alderman John Ashwell, and the Unitarian Robert Denison. At 'an immense public meeting'

[263] Williams, *Memoirs of Thomas Belsham*, 575–6.
[264] Thompson, *Making of the English Working Class*, 666.
[265] Cannon, *Parliamentary Reform*, 166–8.

addressed by these men at Weekday Cross in January 1817 a petition calling for universal suffrage and annual parliaments 'was unanimously adopted, and subsequently received the signatures of six thousand male inhabitants'.[266] Similar views were held by the Oldham Methodist Unitarian preacher and journeyman machine-maker William Browe. In September 1816 Browe chaired a meeting of the Oldham Union Society which pledged itself to work in conjunction with the London Hampden Club, but when Habeas Corpus was suspended in the following March he fled to the United States to avoid arrest.[267]

At the other end of the Nonconformist spectrum in Oldham was the Wesleyan preacher William France. In November 1816 France wrote to Thomas Jackson that the Wesleyans' 'fair blossoms' in the circuit were in danger of being 'blasted this winter by the nipping frost of politics'. The labouring classes were starving; radicals were using the opportunity 'to fill them with discontent against the government'; and it was 'with many an almost unpardonable crime to pray for kings and for all that are in authority'. One of France's congregation had asked him to preach from the fifth chapter of Nehemiah in which the Jews complained that they had mortgaged their 'lands, vineyards, and houses' that they might buy corn. He would have preferred to have preached from Romans 13: 1, 'the powers that be are ordained of God', but refrained from doing so because he feared he was 'in danger of having my head broken'.[268] His views were shared by Christmas Evans and the Baptist ministers of Anglesey. In March 1817 they drew up a declaration which they sent to a local magistrate in which they dissociated themselves from the agitation for parliamentary reform and promised to excommunicate any of their members who spoke disparagingly of the king and government. 'It is not the province of Christians to debate and discuss politics', they assured their JP; it was their duty 'to behave humbly towards their superiors'.[269]

In between the Nonconformist radicals represented by William Browe and conservatives such as William France lay a group of moderate reformers such as the MP William Smith, the Sheffield Unitarian Thomas Asline Ward, and Edward Baines of the *Leeds Mercury*. While this group favoured parliamentary reform, they would commit themselves to no more than triennial parliaments and a suffrage linked to the payment of rates or direct taxes, and

---

[266] Sutton, *Nottingham Date-Book*, 326; Harrison, 'Baptists of Nottinghamshire', ii. 840.
[267] McLachlan, *Methodist Unitarian Movement*, 117.
[268] Stigant, 'Methodism and the Working Class', 283; P. Stigant, 'Wesleyan Methodism and Working-class Radicalism', *Northern History*, 6 (1971), 105.
[269] Bassett, *Welsh Baptists*, 131–2.

they were as worried as the conservatives that the popular agitation for reform would lead to a breakdown of public order. Thomas Ward, a master cutler, had been in the forefront of the campaign for parliamentary reform in 1810 and had drawn up a petition for reform which was sent to the House of Commons. But food riots in Sheffield in August 1812 dampened the enthusiasm of Sheffield's middle class for reform and when Major Cartwright visited the town a month later Ward refused to attend a dinner at which Cartwright was to be the chief speaker. Ward did have breakfast with Cartwright, and found him to be a 'good humoured, mild man', but was glad he had not attended the dinner since he had heard that it was a disreputable gathering. The 'tickets were priced so low that the company were of the lowest rank', and the proceedings were dominated by 'the annual parliament and universal suffrage men'.[270]

Similar views were entertained by Edward Baines. In January 1817 he was the principal speaker in support of the petitioning movement held in falling snow in the Cloth Hall Yard in Leeds and received three rounds of applause. But Baines warned his audience that 'they should employ no other force than the force of argument' to obtain their objectives,[271] and the wisdom of his caution seemed justified when two months later the government used the pretext of the riots which attended the reform meetings in Spa Fields to suspend Habeas Corpus. When, in June 1819, Baines attended a radical meeting on Hunslet Moor near Leeds he again warned against the holding of weekly meetings lest they give the government an excuse to increase military force. Though in a minority of one, and to the 'considerable disapprobation' of the crowd, Baines argued in favour of triennial rather than annual parliaments and a taxpayers' franchise rather than universal suffrage.[272] 'Universal suffrage', he warned in the *Leeds Mercury* in 1819, 'would create an overwhelming democracy; it would bring soldiers in battalions, paupers by crowds, menial servants, and even vagrants, in hosts to the polls.'[273]

Despite his opposition to universal suffrage, Baines's concern that excessive militancy on the part of the radicals would be used by the government as a pretext to curb civil liberties was genuine enough. His greatest and most famous service to the cause of reform was his exposure, in the *Leeds Mercury* in June 1817, of the doings of William Oliver. Oliver was a former carpenter and unsuccessful surveyor who, after being released from a debtors' prison, made contact in March 1817 with both the leaders of the radical underground

[270] A. B. Bell, *Peeps into the Past* (1909), 163, 189.
[271] Baines, *Life of Edward Baines*, 88–9.   [272] Ibid. 105–6.
[273] R. W. Ram, 'Dissent in Urban Yorkshire', *Baptist Quarterly*, 22 (1967–8), 10.

in London and with the Home Secretary Lord Sidmouth. On 23 April Oliver began a tour of the Midlands and the north of England, laying plans for an insurrection and claiming at each town he visited 'that the other towns were . . . ready for action, eager to begin the great fight for liberty'.[274] The message was taken seriously by groups of radicals in the West Riding and on the borders of Derbyshire and Nottinghamshire, and although ten Yorkshire men were arrested prematurely by troops under the command of General Byng at Thornhill Lees near Dewsbury on 6 June, plans for the Yorkshire and east Midlands risings went ahead. On 8 June several hundred clothing workers began to march on Huddersfield and on the following evening between two and three hundred men gathered under the leadership of Jeremiah Brandreth, a framework knitter, in the villages of Pentrich and Ripley on the Nottinghamshire–Derbyshire border with intent to march on Nottingham. Both bands of would-be rebels fled at the sight of troops, but on the way to Nottingham Brandreth accidentally killed a man and he and two of his fellow conspirators were found guilty of treason and condemned to death.

Once again the incident emphasizes the dilemma which working-class protest could pose for Nonconformist churches. Brandreth claimed to be a Baptist and one of his fellow sufferers, Isaac Ludlam, was a Methodist who was said to have been 'the ablest local preacher in the Belper circuit'. The Wesleyans tried to dissociate themselves from Ludlam and claimed that he had been expelled eighteen months before the rising.[275] But on this occasion, at least, moderate Nonconformist reformers and working-class radicals found common cause. Four days after the Pentrich rising Edward Baines received a letter claiming that Oliver was a government spy who had tried to persuade a Quaker printer named James Willan to attend the meeting at Thornhill Lees. Baines and his son Edward immediately took a chaise to Dewsbury and met both James Willan, who asserted that for two months Oliver had been endeavouring 'to seduce him into acts of violence and situations of danger', and a linen-draper named John Dickinson whose evidence was even more damning. Dickinson claimed that Oliver had been taken, along with the ten men arrested at Thornhill Lees, to Wakefield. But Oliver was then allowed to go free and was seen by Dickinson in conversation with a servant of General Byng who told Dickinson that Oliver had been at the general's house a few days earlier. The following day, 14 June, Baines published the whole story in the *Leeds Mercury*. Why, asked Baines, was the

---

[274] J. L. and B. Hammond, *The Skilled Labourer* (1979), 288.
[275] Thompson, *Making of the English Working Class*, 433, 731–2; Gregory, *Autobiographical Recollections*, 129; Werner, *Primitive Methodist Connexion*, 121 n. 20.

wretched Oliver, 'the mainspring and master-piece of the conspiracy by which the country had been thrown into its present state of alarm and agitation . . . suffered to escape, while the poor unfortunate victims of his machinations are held in confinement?' And, most pertinent of all, 'who were his employers?.'[276]

The government refused the inquiry into the episode which Baines and the Whigs in Parliament demanded. But Baines's revelations discredited the government's use of *agents provocateurs* (for the testimony of the Quaker James Willan clearly reveals that that is what Oliver was) and secured both the release of the men arrested at Thornhill Lees and the acquittal of those who had marched on Huddersfield. Baines's exposé also united moderate and radical reformers in defence of civil liberties, as did the Peterloo incident two years later. The action of the Manchester magistrates in ordering the Manchester yeomanry to break up a peaceful reform meeting in St Peter's Field on 16 August 1819, causing eleven deaths and another four hundred injuries, infuriated liberal Dissenters. It was the Unitarian John Edward Taylor and the Presbyterian Archibald Prentice, soon to be rivals as the editors of the *Manchester Guardian* and the *Manchester Gazette*, who immediately sent off accounts of the outrage to *The Times*, and Taylor who followed this up with a weekly publication which ran for fourteen weeks called the *Peterloo Massacre*.[277] The younger Edward Baines, sent to report the meeting for the *Leeds Mercury*, described the military's assault on the unarmed crowd as 'a mad, savage, and wicked act'; the Congregational philanthropist Thomas Wilson, who also witnessed the attack, characterized it as 'a wanton, cruel act of despotism'; and the Welsh Baptist Joseph Harris, the editor of *Seren Gomer*, denounced the behaviour of the yeomanry as the 'inexcusable shedding of his neighbours' blood'.[278]

Less moderate men were driven to even more forthright expressions of outrage. Joseph Harrison combined radical politics with the pastorate of an Independent church in Stockport, though the church appears to have been independent by virtue of its lack of denominational ties rather than because of its Congregational polity. Certainly Harrison was much more radical than any contemporary Congregational minister. He was the inspiration behind, and secretary of, the Stockport Union for the Promotion of Human Happiness which was founded in October 1818 to campaign for universal suf-

---

[276] Baines, *Life of Edward Baines*, 92–4.
[277] D. Read, *Peterloo* (Manchester, 1958), 143, 164.
[278] Baines, *Life of Edward Baines*, 107; Wilson, *Memoirs of Thomas Wilson*, 340; O. Parry, 'The Parliamentary Representation of Wales and Monmouthshire during the Nineteenth Century', MA thesis (Bangor, 1922), 126.

frage, annual parliaments, and voting by ballot. He presided over a day school, evening classes, and a Sunday school where two thousand scholars were taught 'the basis of true Christian morality and the spirit of genuine liberty'. And he rode in Orator Hunt's coach on the way to Peterloo. In a sermon preached in December 1819 Harrison denounced kings, princes, lords, commons, bishops, and constables as alike corrupt and urged the people 'to rise *en masse*' to overthrow their tyrannical government. A week later Harrison was arrested and sentenced to three and a half years in prison.[279]

Harrison's sermon was just the sort of inflammatory talk, aimed at working-class congregations, which terrified the leaders of Wesleyan Methodism. In their address to Wesleyan societies on 7 August 1819 Jonathan Crowther and Jabez Bunting, as president and secretary of Conference, warned Methodists against 'unreasonable and wicked men' who sought to use 'the privations of the poor' as 'instruments of their own designs against the peace and the government of our beloved country'.[280] The events in St Peter's Field nine days later illustrated dramatically the gulf between the Wesleyan leadership and the radical working class. In Manchester members of the Wesleyan Sunday school were expelled for wearing white hats or radical badges; the Wesleyan preacher Thomas Jackson was obliged by the magistrates to tour the streets of the town at night 'for the purpose of reporting any suspicious movements that might appear'; and his superintendent minister John Stephens preached on *The Mutual Relations, Claims, and Duties of the Rich and the Poor*, asserting that he had no difficulty in deciding where his loyalty lay 'when the contest is between a vile demagogue and his venerable king'.[281] In Newcastle upon Tyne the Wesleyan preacher John Rigg pleaded with his fellow Methodists to boycott a radical meeting on the Town Moor on 11 October and in the following year the Duke of Northumberland showed his appreciation by contributing £50 towards the cost of the new Wesleyan Brunswick chapel.[282] However, a young Wesleyan local preacher named William Stephenson, who taught at the Burton colliery school, ignored Rigg's admonition and proceeded to speak at the Town Moor meeting and to denounce the magistrates at Peterloo. As a result Stephenson was sacked by his employers, and his speech gave 'very great offence to most of the travelling preachers', but his fellow local preachers refused to take him off the

---

[279] Glen, *Urban Workers in the Industrial Revolution*, 224–30, 248, 251. Harrison subsequently became pastor of the General Baptist church in Stockport in 1840 (Wood, *History of the General Baptists*, 230).
[280] *Minutes of Methodist Conferences*, v. 63.
[281] Jackson, *Recollections*, 173; Stigant, 'Methodism and the Working Class', 142.
[282] Horner, 'Influence of Methodism on Northumberland', 152.

preaching plan.[283] Stephenson's case was taken up in London by the Wesleyan Committee of Privileges which, on 12 November, passed resolutions expressing 'strong and decided disapprobation of certain tumultuous assemblies which have lately been witnessed in several parts of the country'; exhorted Methodists to abstain from such meetings; and advised preachers to expel all members who persisted 'in identifying themselves with the factious and disloyal'.[284]

The Wesleyan Methodists were not the only Evangelical Nonconformists to urge submission to the government in the aftermath of Peterloo. The Congregationalist John Angell James claimed that the neglect of piety, immorality, and drunkenness, not low wages or lack of representation, lay at the root of the crisis.[285] A number of Independent ministers in Manchester were said to have signed a declaration thanking the magistrates for their action at Peterloo.[286] And a Congregational minister at Leigh exhorted his people 'to patience and to peace' with the result that 'almost all the weavers . . . were offended', they donned white hats 'as flags of defiance', a deacon resigned, and some of the congregation left the chapel.[287] But it was the Wesleyans who chiefly earned the antipathy of working-class radicals for their protestations of loyalty to Lord Liverpool's government. The Committee of Privileges' resolutions of 12 November were widely circulated and as widely resented. The radical *Manchester Observer* attacked the double standards of the Wesleyan leaders who were free to 'think and act against reform' while other Methodists were prohibited 'from giving it encouragement'.[288] The paper expressed astonishment that Wesleyan preachers such as John Stephens should 'appear more eager to support harsh and coercive measures than almost the clergy of the establishment', and denied Stephens's contention that 'the discontent of the lower orders' was based on 'hatred and contempt for God's Word'. The workers' anger arose rather 'from their being obliged to labour six days in the week, and sixteen hours in the day' and from being forced 'for that time to live on less food' than Stephens would consume in one day.[289] In Rochdale a Wesleyan class leader who admitted to subscribing to the *Manchester Observer* was forced to resign.[290] And from Haslingden the Wesleyan superintendent James Holroyd reported that the

---

[283] Wearmouth, *Methodism and the Working Class*, 182–3; W. R. Ward (ed.), *The Early Correspondence of Jabez Bunting, 1820–1829* (1972), 21–4.
[284] Wearmouth, *Methodism and the Working Class*, 179–80.
[285] L. Davidoff and C. Hall, *Family Fortunes* (1987), 93–4.
[286] Read, *Peterloo*, 204; Jones, *Congregationalism in England*, 191.
[287] Waddington, *Congregational History to 1850*, 285.
[288] Stigant, 'Methodism and the Working Class', 293.   [289] Ibid. 293–5.
[290] Read, *Peterloo*, 203.

Committee of Privileges' address was very unpopular, that the sentiments of the *Manchester Observer* were widely endorsed, and that both he and the Anglican incumbent were marked for assassination when the revolution came. 'There is no part of the kingdom where the distresses of the poor are more general than in this neighbourhood', Holroyd wrote to Jabez Bunting just before Christmas 1819. The workers 'are principally cotton weavers, who by working hard six days, cannot earn above 7*s*. or 8*s*. per week'. Radical views had rapidly gained ground in the town and had led some Methodists to refuse to renew their class tickets: 'they do not think it right to give anything towards the support of those who encourage and pray for . . . tyrants'. On the previous Sunday Holroyd claimed that after the service he had been confronted by three class leaders, two local preachers, one steward, and several ordinary members seeking to protest against the address of the Committee of Privileges: 'they told me in plain terms that Methodist preachers were as bad as the Church ministers in supporting government'.[291]

The policy of refusing to pay class money was urged on working-class Wesleyans by the *Manchester Observer*: it was better to give class money 'to the wife towards providing for a needy family; rather than to the indulgence of those who wish to support bribery, peculation, and oppression'.[292] In Bolton the adoption of such a policy led to a secession from the Wesleyan society. Despite the poverty of the members of his congregation the superintendent Thomas Hill 'lectured them on the support of the ministry', reproached them 'for non-payment of class money', and struck their names 'from the class-book with little ceremony'. Radicals replied by attending a week-night meeting in their white hats and placing them on the table in front of the superintendent who, with a 'contemptuous sweep of his arm', knocked them on to the floor. Rumour went round the town that John Stephens had received from Sidmouth a cheque for £10,000 for his services to the government, and the radicals seceded to form, in February 1820, an Independent Methodist church.[293]

Such was the antipathy between the Wesleyan ministry and working-class radicals in Lancashire in the aftermath of Peterloo that some historians have argued that the mutual antagonism did permanent damage to Wesleyan Methodism. 'The years 1819–20 were the moment of truth for the Wesleyans', writes W. R. Ward; 'Wesleyanism was never going to be a popular urban religion.'[294] Paul Stigant agrees that 'after 1821 Wesleyan

---

[291] Ward, *Early Correspondence of Bunting*, 25–6.
[292] Stigant, 'Methodism and Radicalism', *Northern History*, 6 (1971), 111.
[293] Vickers, *History of Independent Methodism*, 147–8; Ward, *Religion and Society*, 89.
[294] Ward, *Religion and Society*, 94.

Methodism was no longer a predominantly working-class religion', and David Hempton similarly argues that the era which ended with Peterloo 'also saw the end of Wesleyan Methodism as a force in working-class culture and politics'.[295] In the years 1819–20 Wesleyan membership in England fell by 5,096—only the second time in the history of the Connexion thus far that a decrease in membership had been recorded—and Adam Clarke placed the blame squarely on 'what is called Radicalism'.[296] Jonathan Crowther, president of the Wesleyan Conference in 1819, advised the superintendent of the North Shields circuit in favour of political neutrality and against the expulsion of William Stephenson and other radicals on the ground that 'the Kilhamites and Ranters will greedily gather them up'.[297] And although the membership of the New Connexion also fell slightly in 1819–20, that of the Primitive Methodists doubled in 1821–2.[298]

Yet, despite the pessimism of contemporary Wesleyans and the verdict of later historians, the year 1819–20 proved to be only a temporary blip on the rising graph of Wesleyan membership. Between 1820 and 1829 Wesleyan membership in England rose by 51,793, an increase of nearly 29 per cent. If Methodists left the Wesleyans for the Ranters it can hardly have been because the leadership of the latter was more sympathetic towards political radicalism. The founders of Primitive Methodism regarded radicalism with as much suspicion as any Wesleyan: William Clowes complained of the people of Dewsbury in 1820 that their minds were 'so much exercised with the politics of the day, that the story of the cross had but little charm for them', and in the following year Hugh Bourne demanded, and secured, the expulsion of a 'speeching Radical' from the Ranters' Conference at Tunstall.[299] George Herod claimed that the Primitive Methodists had saved the east Midlands from rebellion in 1817 just as a generation earlier the Wesleyans had claimed to have saved England as a whole from revolution. Herod recalled that in the village of Countesthorpe, five miles south of Leicester, working men had been 'drilling for fighting' and a barn had been converted 'into a storehouse for ammunition' in readiness for the uprising which Oliver was planning. After the failure of the Pentrich rising a Primitive Methodist preacher visited Countesthorpe, 'all the leading men belonging to the

---

[295] Stigant, 'Methodism and Radicalism', 111; Hempton, *Methodism and Politics*, 110.
[296] Currie, Gilbert, and Horsley, *Churches and Churchgoers*, 140; Ward, *Religion and Society*, 93.
[297] Ward, *Early Correspondence of Bunting*, 22.
[298] Currie, Gilbert, and Horsley, *Churches and Churchgoers*, 140.
[299] Werner, *Primitive Methodist Connexion*, 121; Kendall, *History of the Primitive Methodist Church*, i. 339.

Levellers in that village were convinced of sin, of righteousness, and of a judgement to come', two of the ringleaders became local preachers, and the barn in which the ammunition was stored became the Ranters' place of worship.[300]

In so far as Wesleyan numbers did decline in 1819–20, and in so far as they did suffer losses to the Primitive Methodists, the causes were economic rather than political. As we have seen, the decision of the Wesleyan Conference in 1818 that circuits should help to pay off the connexional debt in proportion to their numbers encouraged superintendents to prune their membership lists, and it was claimed that the Ranters in comparison with the Wesleyans offered Methodists a cheaper religion. But once the economic situation began to improve in 1821 the working class began to turn their backs on radicalism and Wesleyan numbers resumed their upward spiral. Thomas Cheetham, a Wesleyan local preacher of Ripponden near Halifax, was caught up in the radical ferment of 1819 and 1820 and his conversation and his leisure hours were devoted to politics. But when the agitation died down he resolved to 'fear God and honour the king' and to meddle no more with 'the affairs of the State'.[301] The overwhelming majority of the working class lacked the ideological commitment to reform of radical Unitarians or even of liberal Congregationalists such as Edward Baines, and when work became more plentiful their interest in politics dwindled. Far from the chapels acting as a temporary refuge for men and women suffering the 'chiliasm of despair', it was radical politics which were suddenly taken up, and as suddenly dropped, with the downturns and upsurges of the trade cycle. Sixty per cent of the men who had their children baptized in the Wesleyan chapels of Lancashire in the 1820s earned less than £1 a week, and over a third of the total were weavers. But Thomas Jackson was able to write from Manchester in March 1821 that radical feeling had 'subsided very much among the lower classes' and that the *Manchester Observer* had ceased publication.[302] And in the following month John Stephens, also in Manchester, reported that 'the poor people are getting better wages'; 'provisions are cheap'; £200 had been collected for the Wesleyan Missionary Society; and that 'such a religious feeling has been excited, as, I trust, will produce everlasting good'.[303] Thirty-nine per cent of male Manchester Wesleyans in the 1820s were either lower-skilled workers, weavers, or unskilled workers. The Grosvenor Street circuit was the wealthiest in England, dominated by a group of merchants and

---

[300] Herod, *Biographical Sketches*, 12–15.
[301] A. E. Teale, 'Methodism in Halifax and District', M.Sc. thesis (Bradford, 1976), 175.
[302] Ward, *Early Correspondence of Bunting*, 63.
[303] Stigant, 'Methodism and Radicalism', 114.

manufacturers of whom the most important was James Wood, the first president of the Manchester Chamber of Commerce and Wesleyanism's most influential layman.[304] But in the 1820s 'working men and poor women thronged the places reserved for their use' in the Grosvenor Street chapel,[305] and of the fathers who had their children baptized there in that decade 38 per cent were lower-skilled or unskilled workers and another 29 per cent higher-skilled manual workers.[306] In the three years 1824–7 membership of the Grosvenor Street circuit doubled. And the circuit's superintendent minister in those years was James Wood's lifelong friend Jabez Bunting.[307]

7. 'THE MOST FORMIDABLE ENEMY TO THE METHODIST LIBERALS': JABEZ BUNTING AND THE LEEDS ORGAN CASE

The success of the conservative, autocratic, and Tory Jabez Bunting in maintaining control over a predominantly poor and working-class Connexion is one of the most remarkable features of Nonconformist history. His rule was never undisputed, and it contributed to secessions in 1827 and 1835, but that it lasted so long, and that it coincided with the most successful period in the history of English Methodism, is both a tribute to the respect with which Bunting was regarded by his fellow ministers, and evidence of the fact that Wesleyanism's spiritual appeal to working-class people was sufficiently powerful for much of the period to counter any hostility which may have been provoked by its political conservatism. To many poor Wesleyans the hope of eternal life which their Connexion offered was a more substantial prospect than the hope of temporal betterment which the radicals held out. The improvement in the country's economy, which began in 1820, continued, with brief interruptions in 1825–6 and 1829–30, until the late 1830s, and to a large extent cushioned Bunting from the effects of radical criticism. The secessions of 1827 and 1835 had little adverse effect on the upward swing of Wesleyan membership and left Bunting in a stronger position than ever before. Only in 1849, when the Wesleyan leadership appeared to be frustrating the spiritual zeal as well as the political aspirations of its working-class following, did Bunting find that the strategy he had been pursuing successfully for thirty years was no longer adequate to hold the Connexion together.

[304] J. H. Huddleston, *The History of Grosvenor Street Wesleyan Chapel, Manchester* (Manchester, 1920), 13–14.
[305] Ibid. 15.   [306] PRO. RG 4/1465.
[307] Bunting and Rowe, *Life of Jabez Bunting*, 571.

Jabez Bunting was a second-generation Methodist, a man who inherited his faith from his parents rather than having it forged in the fires of his own experience. His mother was converted in 1769 by a preacher named Richard Boardman who stopped at her village of Monyash in Derbyshire *en route* for Bristol and America. Ten years later, when she gave birth to her son, Mary Bunting remembered the text of Richard Boardman's sermon: 'Jabez was more honourable than his brethren: and his mother called his name Jabez, saying, because I bare him with sorrow'.[308] Jabez's father was a Methodist tailor in Manchester who sympathized with the French Revolution, sent Jabez to Unitarian ministers for his education, and apprenticed him to the Unitarian doctor Thomas Percival, founder of the Manchester Literary and Philosophical Society and public health pioneer.[309] As so often happened in this period, maternal religion proved to be a more decisive influence than paternal politics, and Jabez gave up thought of a medical career for the Methodist ministry.[310] But he was an unemotional man and his conversion was prompted not by a sense of sin and the need for forgiveness, but by the discovery that he could not attend a love-feast without first joining the Methodist society.[311] It was in the same calculating manner that, when contemplating marriage a few years later, he drew up a list of his proposed wife's pros and cons and asked her to marry him only when he found that her advantages outweighed her disadvantages by ten points to six.[312]

The same cold, ruthless efficiency characterized Bunting's career as a Wesleyan minister and enabled him to dominate his Connexion for thirty years. While he rejected the Manchester radicalism in which he had been nurtured he retained its distrust of enthusiasm. When he was stationed in the Macclesfield circuit in 1803 he came into conflict with the enthusiasm of the self-styled Christian Revivalists and, as we have seen, was of the opinion that Wesleyanism would be well rid of revivalists such as William Bramwell and James Sigston. His suspicion of revivalism remained throughout his career. John Kent claims that Bunting was the 'last Wesleyan' who was only seeking to follow in the founder's footsteps,[313] but Bunting specifically denied that Methodist ministers of the nineteenth century should continue Wesley's apostolic mission. Methodist ministers, Bunting is reported as having told Conference in 1829, cannot be 'proved to be evangelists'. 'Our proper office

---

[308] G. Smith, *History of Wesleyan Methodism* (1863), ii. 516; 1 Chronicles 4: 9.
[309] Ward, *Early Correspondence of Bunting*, 10.
[310] Smith, *History of Wesleyan Methodism*, ii. 518.
[311] Bunting and Rowe, *Life of Jabez Bunting*, 34–6.   [312] Ibid. 131–4.
[313] J. Kent, *Jabez Bunting, the Last Wesleyan* (1955).

is pastors and teachers.'[314] And Bunting commented tartly on a revival at Yeadon in the West Riding in 1834, which claimed to have produced nearly six hundred converts, that he wished that 'there was less parade about revivals'. Wesleyans, he complained, were prepared to 'spend money to *win* souls, but not to *keep* them'.[315]

From his days in Macclesfield Bunting was convinced that the function of the Wesleyan minister was not evangelism but the 'proper ministerial *pastorship* and *oversight* of the flock'.[316] Over the next thirty years the Wesleyan leaders developed the doctrine of the pastoral office in order to assert the validity of their ministry against, on the one hand, Anglican critics who pointed to their lack of episcopal ordination and, on the other, Methodist laymen who questioned the distinction between itinerant and local preachers. Wesleyan ministers could not claim, as could Anglican clergymen, that their ministry was validated by apostolic succession, nor could they claim, as could Dissenters, that their commission derived from the choice of their church. So they took the higher ground that the validity of the Methodist ministry derived directly from God.[317] The eloquence with which Bunting proclaimed the supremacy of the pastoral office, coupled with the efficiency with which he applied himself to successive connexional offices, endeared him to two generations of Wesleyan ministers. They guaranteed his supremacy both within the Methodist Conference and within the committees to which Conference was increasingly delegating much of its powers.[318]

Jabez Bunting was elected secretary to the Wesleyan Conference in 1814, served in that office for the next five years, and from 1818 to 1824 served as senior secretary of the newly formed Wesleyan Methodist Missionary Society. He was partly responsible for the financial changes of 1818 which made the circuits responsible for the connexional debt in proportion to their membership and which resolved the Connexion's financial problems at the cost of a fall in numbers.[319] In 1820 he was elected president of the Conference for the first time and impressed members by the authority with which he presided over their deliberations and kept them 'in their places, and to their business'.[320] He was appointed editor of the *Wesleyan Methodist Magazine* in 1821; gave up the post in 1824 to become secretary of the Conference; and remained as secretary until 1828 when he was elected to the presidency for the second time. He returned to the Wesleyan Missionary Society as its

---

[314] Gregory, *Side Lights on the Conflicts of Methodism*, 83.
[315] Ibid. 168; Smith, *History of Wesleyan Methodism*, iii. 296.
[316] Ward, *Early Correspondence of Bunting*, 12.   [317] Kent, *Jabez Bunting*, 18, 23–4.
[318] Smith, *History of Wesleyan Methodism*, iii. 43.   [319] Ibid. 41–2.
[320] *HMC* iv. 365, 373.

senior secretary in 1834, a post which gave him a permanent power base in London,[321] and he was re-elected as president of the Conference for third and fourth terms in 1836 and 1841.

From the Conference of 1820 Bunting dominated its proceedings and for the next thirty years 'framed the great majority of [its] Acts'.[322] He was respected even by those Methodists who did not like him, and the man who was to become his most bitter critic, James Everett, said that Bunting was unequalled as a preacher, and that when he prayed there was 'a stronger resemblance of God and man holding converse with each other as face to face' than in any other person, apart from William Bramwell, he had ever known.[323] That the members of the Wesleyan Conference submitted to Bunting's growing authority was due partly to his undoubted ability and partly to the fact that they knew that he in return would support their rising status.[324] His only defeat in Conference occurred in 1818 when he failed to secure its approval for the ordination of Methodist preachers by the laying on of hands.[325] But that same year, when drawing up the list of preachers on the committee of the missionary society, Bunting prefixed their names with the title of 'Reverend' and the decision was never rescinded.[326] For the next two decades the income of Wesleyan ministers rose while prices were falling and Bunting's efforts to increase the status of Wesleyan ministers culminated in the Conference decision to approve ordination by the imposition of hands in 1836. By 1837 Bunting had made himself so indispensable that when he was absent from a single session of Conference, business was brought to a standstill and the session was adjourned until he could return. Whoever was president of the Wesleyan Conference, commented Benjamin Gregory, 'Bunting was the prime minister who never went out of office'.[327]

The corollary to Bunting's emphasis on the supremacy of the pastoral office was his belief in the subjection of the Wesleyan laity. 'The minister of God is your judge as God's minister', the laity were told by Conference in 1847, 'and you are not to judge him.'[328] Bunting admittedly did extend the policy, begun with the Committee of Privileges, of co-opting wealthy and influential laymen on to connexional committees, but such men were in no sense

---

[321] Gregory, *Side Lights on the Conflicts of Methodism*, 140.
[322] Smith, *History of Wesleyan Methodism*, iii. 455.
[323] [J. Everett], *Wesleyan Takings* (1840), 13, 31.
[324] Smith, *History of Wesleyan Methodism*, iii. 33–5.
[325] Bunting and Rowe, *Life of Jabez Bunting*, 517.
[326] Smith, *History of Wesleyan Methodism*, iii. 35.
[327] Gregory, *Side Lights on the Conflicts of Methodism*, 251, 176.
[328] *Minutes of the Methodist Conferences*, x. 569.

representative of the Wesleyan laity as a whole.[329] Bunting may not have said, as his opponents alleged, that Wesleyanism was as much opposed to democracy as it was to sin, but at times he came near to uttering such sentiments. 'Taking the sense of the people in classes,' he wrote in 1821, 'is unmethodistical, absurd, and mischievous.' 'Our system is not democracy', for 'nothing could be more fatal to real liberty, whether in church or state' than universal suffrage.[330] 'A government carried on by endless debates and majorities would ruin the real work of God among us.'[331] Bunting was, wrote John Scott with warm approval in 1830, 'the most formidable enemy to the Methodist liberals'.[332]

While the overwhelming majority of Wesleyans—and the overwhelming majority of working-class Wesleyans—accepted the rule of Bunting and his ministerial colleagues without question throughout the 1820s and 1830s, the growing authority of Bunting within the Conference, and the rising status of Wesleyan ministers *vis-à-vis* the laity, provoked resentment among a minority of ministers and laymen. Bunting impressed many of his fellow Wesleyans with his modesty and his humility,[333] but he could be petty-minded, had a sharp tongue which turned critics into enemies, and was suspected of using his dominance of the stationing committee to reward his friends with comfortable circuits and to punish his opponents with impoverished ones.[334] But the irritation of a small minority of Wesleyan ministers with Bunting's ascendancy would have been of no significance had he and his colleagues not alienated a much larger body of Wesleyan laymen. Wesleyan local preachers in particular resented the tendency of the itinerant preachers to set themselves up as a clerical caste distinct from the laity, and liberal Wesleyans in general were induced by their demands for fairer representation in the affairs of state to seek greater lay participation in the government of their church. In the year of Peterloo local preachers in Manchester were said to be comparing the Wesleyan constitution 'unfavourably with the unreformed constitution of the land', and in the following year the shoemaker and philosopher Samuel Drew told a visiting American Methodist that the local preachers 'are looked down on by the travelling [preachers] and held in too much degradation, which is sorely felt and will in time cause an explosion'.[335] Local preachers complained that the largest services in the urban chapels were always taken

[329] Gregory, *Side Lights on the Conflicts of Methodism*, 497.
[330] Ward, *Early Correspondence of Bunting*, 74.   [331] Ibid. 191.
[332] Ward, *Early Victorian Methodism*, 1.
[333] J. H. Rigg, *Wesleyan Methodism Reminiscences ... Sixty years Ago* (1904), 26–8.
[334] Gregory, *Side Lights on the Conflicts of Methodism*, 128, 134, 137, 144–5, 525, 528.
[335] Ward, *Religion and Society*, 88; *HMC* iv. 367, 373.

by the itinerant preachers; itinerants complained that local preachers were 'urging the people to build chapels in country places where we cannot visit them on the Lord's day'.[336] Drew told his American visitor that local preachers outnumbered itinerant preachers by ten to one, and the point underlines the difficulty faced by the Wesleyan leadership in trying to control what was going on at chapel level.

Far from the Wesleyans losing contact with the working classes in the 1820s and 1830s, as some historians have claimed, the very success of the Connexion in expanding its numbers and in pushing down the social scale contributed to the tensions of those two decades. The Sunday schools constituted a major focus of discontent. These institutions were for the most part run by lay men and women for the benefit of the children of the poorer sections of society and often with little control by the ministers who preached in the chapels on whose premises the Sunday schools met. Wesleyan preachers complained that Sunday schools violated the Lord's day by teaching writing and that scholars did not always attend religious worship; ministers of all denominations grumbled that only a small proportion of Sunday scholars ever became members of their churches; and in Manchester after Peterloo scholars offended Wesleyan preachers by openly displaying evidence of their radical sympathies. A particular source of Wesleyan complaint were those Sunday schools in the north of England which had begun as undenominational enterprises but which were now in effect funded by Wesleyans and conducted on Wesleyan premises though still claiming to be schools for the 'children of all denominations'.[337] Consequently in the late 1810s and 1820s the Wesleyan hierarchy under Bunting's leadership made a determined attempt to tie such schools more closely to the Connexion and to insist that their functions should be primarily spiritual. In 1817 the Wesleyan Conference insisted that Sunday school sessions should be held at times which did not prevent the attendance of teachers and pupils at chapel; in 1826 Bunting began a four-year campaign to bring the Sunday schools of Manchester firmly under connexional control; and his experiences in Manchester led him to persuade Conference in 1827 to insist that Wesleyan Sunday schools 'should be strictly and entirely religious institutions' from which writing should be banned.[338] The policy of tighter connexional control met with resistance in a number of northern towns. In Marple in Cheshire in 1820 there took place a six-week battle for the control of the Sunday school

---

[336] Currie, *Methodism Divided*, 52–3; Ward, *Early Correspondence of Bunting*, 47.
[337] Ward, *Early Correspondence of Bunting*, 148–9, 228.
[338] *Minutes of the Methodist Conferences*, iv. 337; vi. 284, 288.

which issued in a victory for the Wesleyans and their policy of enforcing chapel attendance on the scholars.[339] In Newchurch-in-Rossendale an attempt to ban the teaching of writing led to the secession from the chapel of all the teachers and most of the pupils.[340] And, most serious of all, the clash between radicals and conservatives for control of the Wesleyan Sunday schools in Leeds prepared the ground for the dispute over the Brunswick chapel's organ.[341]

The proposal of the trustees of the Brunswick chapel to install an organ in defiance of the wishes of a majority of the society leaders and of many of its members highlighted the tensions developing between the Wesleyan hierarchy's pursuit of ministerial status and respectability and the concerns of the Connexion's radical and working-class members. In October 1826 sixty local preachers in the Leeds circuit protested against the organ not only on the grounds that it was designed 'to please the ear and captivate the passions' rather than to promote spiritual worship, but also because the expenditure of £1,000 on the organ could not be justified at a time 'when many members of our society are wanting the common necessaries of life'.[342] The dispute was interpreted by Jabez Bunting in terms of class conflict: while 'the great majority of the society' at Leeds 'and nearly all of our respectable friends' were in favour of the organ, 'the great mass of disaffection' was among persons who worshipped at the downtown Old chapel, guided by 'the poor leaders, and younger leaders and local preachers'.[343] The Wesleyan Conference came down on the side of the respectable against the poor and in 1827, in defiance of a resolution of the Leeds District Meeting, sanctioned the erection of the organ. When a local preacher, Matthew Johnson, called a meeting of his fellow preachers to protest against the Conference decision, he was expelled from the Connexion, and nine hundred members, fifty-six class leaders, and twenty-eight local preachers resigned in protest at the high-handed and unconstitutional proceedings of Conference.[344] The seceders formed themselves into the denomination of Protestant Methodists which in 1836 joined up with the Wesleyan Methodist Association. Foremost among them was the Leeds schoolmaster and friend and biographer of William Bramwell, James Sigston, who in 1803 had led a previous secession of the 'Kirkgate Screamers' out of Wesleyanism.[345] The seceders of 1827, claimed Edmund Grindrod, the

[339] Stigant, 'Methodism and the Working Class', 289.
[340] Laqueur, *Religion and Respectability*, 144–5.
[341] Smith, *History of Wesleyan Methodism*, iii. 112–13.   [342] *HMC* iv. 396–7.
[343] Ward, *Early Correspondence of Bunting*, 164.
[344] Gregory, *Side Lights on the Conflicts of Methodism*, 52–4; Smith, *History of Wesleyan Methodism*, iii. 123.
[345] Gregory, *Side Lights on the Conflicts of Methodism*, 66–7.

Wesleyan superintendent in Leeds, were 'generally of the very poorest' of the town's Methodists: he and his fellow ministers calculated that they had contributed on average only a shilling per quarter to connexional funds, considerably less than other members of the Brunswick and Old chapels.[346]

The protest of the Leeds secessionists spread to other towns: the Sheffield Quarterly Meeting complained that the decisions of Conference deprived Wesleyan members of their rights 'as Englishmen, as Methodists, and as Christians', and the Liverpool Quarterly Meeting asserted that 'the local government of every circuit is vested in the Leaders, Local Preachers, and Quarterly Meetings'.[347] The Southwark Quarterly Meeting, whose proceedings one preacher claimed 'would have disgraced a tavern', passed resolutions advocating 'the supreme authority of the local courts in Methodist circuits', and when Conference responded by dividing the circuit in an attempt to quell the agitation, ten local preachers and seven class leaders resigned.[348] Once again the conflict was in part a clash between working-class radicals and authoritarian preachers. David McNicoll, superintendent of the newly created Lambeth circuit, told Bunting that many of the Wesleyans in south London were 'as little able to discuss' the issues dividing the Connexion 'as a number of stragglers in a barber's shop would be to settle the question of the justice or policy of a nation going to war'. 'We Methodists are peculiarly in danger here from the multitudes of poor connected with us . . . for the people of a circuit are taught to believe that they do almost everything in the management of a circuit, and that the preachers are and ought to be their mere servants.'[349]

Yet once again it must be emphasized that the overwhelming mass of working-class Wesleyans remained loyal to their Connexion. The Protestant Methodists never had more than 4,000 members and of these over 40 per cent were in Leeds. For the first three years of their existence the Leeds Protestant Methodists were racked by disputes over whether they should or should not have a paid itinerant ministry and whether a local preacher should or should not be expelled for marrying his deceased wife's sister. By the early 1830s the Leeds Protestant Methodists were losing members while the Leeds Wesleyans more than recouped their losses of 1827 and were continuing to attract a predominantly working-class constituency.[350] Elsewhere the losses

[346] Ward, *Early Correspondence of Bunting*, 176; Elliott, 'Protestant Denominations in Leeds', 228–9.

[347] Ward, *Early Correspondence of Bunting*, 187, 197.

[348] Ibid. 210–11, 213–14; Smith, *History of Wesleyan Methodism*, iii. 132.

[349] Ward, *Early Correspondence of Bunting*, 214–15.

[350] Dews, 'Methodism in Leeds', 584–5, 589, 653; see below, Table VIII.

suffered by the Wesleyans in 1827–8 were for the most part insignificant. The largest secession outside Leeds, that at York, involved some 230 persons.[351] In Southwark only thirty members followed their local preachers out of the Connexion and after their withdrawal the Wesleyans' 'evening congregation was more than usual'.[352] In Sheffield a secession was avoided when the Quarterly Meeting agreed unanimously to a compromise resolution asking Conference to allow leaders' meetings to have a veto over organs as they did over the Lord's Supper. The circuit superintendent, William Henshaw, wrote that there was such 'a general dread on men's minds as to the consequences of separation' that the adoption of the peace-keeping resolution was greeted with 'floods of tears from most eyes, sobs, praises, singing "Praise God", Hallelujah, confessions of sin, mighty prayers [and] loud shouts'.[353] Seven months later Henshaw reported from Sheffield that in six years 'the society has increased in number about 500 members [who] almost wholly consist of poor persons'.[354]

The success of the Wesleyan leadership in minimizing the damage done by the Leeds organ case can be explained in part by reference to an address which John Stephens gave in the town at the height of the dispute. Stephens, president of the Conference in 1827, told his audience how he had been present at the deathbed of an old friend who had once led a secession from the Wesleyan Connexion. His friend subsequently returned to the fold, but he was tormented to the end by the knowledge that he had been 'instrumental in taking away two or three hundred souls' and, claimed Stephens, he got to heaven only 'by the skin of his teeth'.[355] Stephens's point would have struck a chord in the hearts of his hearers: to the vast majority of Wesleyans of all classes their spiritual message of salvation was of far greater consequence than disputes over connexional government. It was only in the 1840s, when the Wesleyan leadership seemed to be impeding the preaching of that message of salvation, that a permanently damaging secession from Wesleyanism occurred.

There was thus no major working-class revolt from Wesleyanism in 1827. Even the radical secessionists of Leeds identified themselves not with working-class leaders, nor even with popular agitators such as William Cobbett or Orator Hunt, but with Whig and radical parliamentarians. Several of the leaders of the Leeds Sunday school, the fount of much of the dissatisfaction with the Brunswick chapel organ, 'were known among their companions by the names of the principal members of the opposition' in the House of

---

[351] Dews, 'Methodism in Leeds', 575.
[352] Ward, *Early Correspondence of Bunting*, 224.   [353] Ibid. 188–9.   [354] Ibid. 208.
[355] Smith, *History of Wesleyan Methodism*, iii. 122.

Commons. 'One was called Lord John Russell; another was known as Mr Hume; a third, as Mr Grey Bennett.'[356]

8. 'RELIEF TO ALL HIS MAJESTY'S SUBJECTS':
THE REPEAL OF THE TEST AND CORPORATION ACTS
AND CATHOLIC EMANCIPATION

The political sympathies of those radical Leeds Methodists who identified themselves with leaders of the parliamentary opposition in 1827 were not entirely misplaced. While Grey Bennett has left little mark on history, Joseph Hume was to campaign in the 1830s for the opening of the English universities to Nonconformists, and in 1828 Lord John Russell earned the gratitude of Dissenters for introducing into the House of Commons the bill which was to issue in the repeal of the Test and Corporation Acts.

The Test and Corporation Acts dated from the restoration of Charles II and the attempts by Parliament to purge the State of the men who had rebelled against his father. The Corporation Act of 1661 required that all mayors, aldermen, councillors, and borough officials should take the oaths of supremacy and allegiance and should have taken the 'sacrament of the Lord's Supper according to the rites of the Church of England' in the twelve months before their election. The Test Act of 1673 laid down similar requirements for the holders of civil and military officers under the crown, except that it allowed the Anglican sacrament to be taken within three months of entry into office.[357] The extent to which the two Acts were effective in keeping Dissenters out of corporation and public offices has been much debated. The Indemnity Acts which were passed by Parliament in most years from 1727 to 1867 were designed not so much to relieve Dissenters from the operation of the Corporation Act as to allow 'careless churchmen' who had neglected to take the sacrament before election to a borough office to qualify for that office *after* their election.[358] Stanhope's Act of 1719 for Quieting and Establishing Corporations was a more substantial concession to Dissenters: it provided that men elected to corporations without taking the sacramental test could not be removed or prosecuted unless their right to

---

[356] Ibid. 113.
[357] K. R. M. Short, 'The English Indemnity Acts, 1726–1867', *Church History*, 42 (1973), 366.
[358] J. Bennett, *History of the Dissenters during the last Thirty Years* (1839), 59; Short, 'The Indemnity Acts', 373–5; N. C. Hunt, *Two Early Political Associations* (Oxford, 1961), 122–4.

office was challenged within six months of their election.[359] However, orthodox Presbyterians, like many Methodists, had no theological objection to
taking the Anglican sacrament.[360] Dissenting baptismal registers frequently
reveal that the fathers of the children baptized were employed as excise officers, and Dissenters in dockyard towns such as Plymouth and Chatham
earned their living in government employment.[361] Dissenters sat on some
thirty borough corporations in the course of the eighteenth century, and by
the early nineteenth century both the Test and Corporation Acts had in some
places simply fallen into disuse. By 1827 only ninety of the 260 members of
the corporation of the City of London had taken the sacramental test and in
1828 John Smith, MP for Midhurst, told the House of Commons that he knew
of a director of the Bank of England and of army officers who had no idea
that they were supposed to take the sacramental test to qualify for office.[362]

But despite the apparent ease with which Dissenters could frustrate the
intention of the Corporation Act—either by practising occasional conformity or by avoiding challenge to their office for six months after their election—the Act none the less rankled as a badge of their second-class
citizenship. Baptists who practised occasional conformity were sometimes
deprived of their church membership as a result. As Presbyterians adopted
Unitarian views they found it increasingly distasteful to have to take the
sacrament at Trinitarian services:[363] in 1807 the Liverpool Unitarian William
Roscoe, having just lost his seat in Parliament, declined the deputy lieu-
tenancy of Lancashire because acceptance would involve taking the Anglican sacrament.[364] And Dissenters of all shades of opinion objected to
the 'profanation of the Lord's Supper by making it a mere civil or political
test'.[365] The conservative reaction which followed the outbreak of the
French Revolution brought with it attempts to enforce the Corporation Act
against Nonconformist councillors and mayors who had neglected to take the
Anglican sacrament. Though Dissenters had held the mayoralty of Nottingham for sixty-six years in the eighteenth century without provoking
legal action, the election of William Smith to that office late in 1789 was
challenged on the ground that he had failed to take the Anglican sacrament
and the dispute was not settled until a successor was elected in April 1791.
Similarly in 1819–20 an attempt was made to deprive the Baptist William

---

[359] Bradley, *Religion, Revolution, and Radicalism*, 69–70; Hunt, *Early Political Associations*, 125.
[360] Watts, *The Dissenters*, i. 265.
[361] Bradley, *Religion, Revolution, and Radicalism*, 81–2.
[362] *The Test-Act Reporter* (1829), 46–7, 111–12.   [363] Watts, *The Dissenters*, i. 483–5.
[364] Thorne, *History of Parliament, 1792–1820*, v. 43–5.   [365] *The Test-Act Reporter*, 13.

Soars of the mayoralty of Nottingham, and although the challenge was unsuccessful the legal proceedings cost the corporation, which paid for Soars's defence, £89. 7s. 9d.[366] During council elections in Norwich in 1801 Tories warned that they would challenge the right of Dissenters to sit on the corporation, though legal confrontation was avoided since all the Dissenting candidates elected had in fact taken the sacrament.[367]

The Dissenting campaign against the Test and Corporation Acts had foundered in the wake of the French Revolution. Fox's bill for repeal had been rejected by the Commons in 1790 by 294 votes to 105 and, as Timothy Kenrick noted two years later, 'for the Protestant Dissenters to renew their claims at this time would only furnish their adversaries with a pretence for setting the mob upon them'.[368] However, the growth of 'liberal sentiments' in the second decade of the nineteenth century, and with it the defeat of Lord Sidmouth's bill, the withdrawal of the Orders in Council, and the repeal of the Five Mile and Conventicle Acts, all encouraged hope that pressure for the removal of the Test and Corporation Acts might now succeed. Following the repeal of the Five Mile and Conventicle Acts the Dissenting Deputies called for the abolition of every remaining 'shackle on the entire freedom of religious profession'; in 1820 William Smith presented to the House of Commons a petition seeking the abolition of 'every remnant of that system of coercion and restraint on religious profession which had its origins in times of darkness and intolerance'; and in 1823 the general meeting of the Dissenting Deputies voiced the opinion that repeal of the Test and Corporation Acts would be 'most effectually and honourably accomplished by active and unremitted efforts to enlighten the public mind . . . and by earnest application to the legislature at every possible opportunity'.[369]

At this juncture, however, the committee of the Dissenting Deputies, under Smith's chairmanship, was very doubtful as to whether the sort of public agitation their members were demanding would in fact serve the cause of repeal. Smith was conscious that following the union of Great Britain and Ireland in 1800 many MPs, and especially the more liberal Tory MPs, regarded the removal of Roman Catholic grievances as a more pressing issue than the satisfaction of Dissenting claims: whereas no bill to relieve Dissenters of

---

[366] F. M. W. Harrison, 'Nonconformity and the Corporation of Nottingham', *Baptist Quarterly*, 21 (1965–6), 366; Harrison, 'Baptists of Nottinghamshire', ii. 944–5.

[367] Davis, *Dissent in Politics*, 124–5 n. 4.   [368] *TUHS* 4 (1927), 74.

[369] Manning, *Dissenting Deputies*, 143, 219–21; Davis, *Dissent in Politics*, 217; R. G. Cowherd, in his *Politics of English Dissent* (1959), 29, is incorrect in stating that Smith's petition of 1820 carried 100,000 signatures. In fact it bore only a hundred signatures, but Smith claimed that, since nearly every signatory represented a separate congregation, 'it was the petition of a great number of congregations' (*Parliamentary Debates*, NS, ii (13 July 1820) 424).

the sacramental test had been introduced in the House of Commons since the failure of Fox's bill in 1790, a motion to consider the claims of Roman Catholics passed the House of Commons by a majority of six in February 1821.[370] What was worse, some liberal Tories such as William Huskisson feared that if Dissenting grievances were remedied before those of the Catholics, a majority of Dissenters would turn round and oppose the emancipation of Catholics.[371] Dissent had, after all, as one of its chief original motives the conviction that the Elizabethan Church of England was insufficiently purged of the taint of Catholicism, and in some Dissenting chapels in the eighteenth century copies of Foxe's *Book of Martyrs* 'were laid on the sacrament table by the side of the Bible'.[372] When Lord George Gordon presented petitions to Parliament against the relief of Roman Catholics in 1780 his resolutions were seconded by the Baptist Alderman Frederick Bull, and in some quarters the subsequent riots were blamed on Dissenters.[373] Forty years later the Baptist historian Joseph Ivimey strenuously opposed the Dissenting Deputies' support for Catholic emancipation on the ground that English Papists, 'from the nature of their subjection to the pope', were 'incompetent to give the required pledge of allegiance . . . to the supreme authority in the State'.[374] Robert Hall also opposed concessions to the Catholics on the ground that Romanism was a 'vast politico-religious system aiming at supremacy over all law, education, science, and morals' which, 'whilst loudly demanding freedom for itself . . . would not give it to others'.[375] And the Congregationalist John Clayton of the King's Weigh House, together with his ministerial sons, were even reluctant to support a campaign for the repeal of the Test and Corporation Acts lest it lead to Catholic emancipation.[376]

The most substantial Nonconformist opposition to the Catholic claims came, however, from the Methodists, both Wesleyan and Calvinistic. John Wesley disliked Catholic doctrine, loathed what he regarded as its low moral standards, and deplored its effects on the people of Ireland.[377] But his prime

---

[370] Davis, *Dissent in Politics*, 217–20; G. I. T. Machin, *The Catholic Question in English Politics, 1820 to 1830* (Oxford, 1964), 26.

[371] *Test-Act Reporter*, 133–4.   [372] J. Hunter, *Life of Oliver Heywood* (1842), 250.

[373] J. Steven Watson, *The Reign of George III* (Oxford, 1960), 236; Black, *The Association*, 180; Thompson, *Making of the English Working Class*, 77; A. Lincoln, *Some Political and Social Ideas of English Dissent* (Cambridge, 1938), 48.

[374] J. Ivimey, *An Address to Protestant Dissenters on the Present State of the Roman Catholics* (1819), p. xxiii.

[375] F. Trestrail, *Reminiscences of College Life in Bristol* (1879), 98.

[376] Jones, *Congregationalism in England*, 196.

[377] M. Edwards, *John Wesley and the Eighteenth Century* (1955), 99–101; Hempton, *Methodism and Politics*, 36–43.

objection to concessions to Catholics lay in their untrustworthiness: for the Council of Constance in 1414 had avowed that 'no faith is to be kept with heretics', and the maxim had never been openly disclaimed.[378] Consequently Wesley supported Lord George Gordon's Protestant petition, though he deplored the violence it incited, and his antipathy to Roman Catholicism was to make a lasting impression on the Wesleyan Connexion. From 1799 the Methodist Conference dispatched Gaelic-speaking missionaries throughout rural Ireland and the reports they sent back intensified Wesleyan antagonism to Catholicism.[379] In 1812 Joseph Butterworth, the Methodist MP for Coventry, terrified the Committee of Privileges with a 'mass of information' collected from Ireland and he persuaded at least one member that if the Papists 'had the power they would not leave [one] Protestant alive in the kingdom'; in the following year Butterworth and the connexional solicitor, Thomas Allan, took the initiative in launching the Protestant Union for the Defence and Support of the Protestant Religion and British Constitution; and in 1813 the *Methodist Magazine* quoted at length a pamphlet whose author argued that a people 'whose conduct has been deeply and repeatedly stained by the crimes of murder, rebellion, and high treason, should not be admitted to any participation in political power'.[380] When an anti-Catholic petition was sent to the Nonconformist churches of Manchester in 1825 it was rejected by the Congregationalists and Baptists but accepted by the Wesleyans.[381] Similarly among the Welsh Calvinistic Methodists their most powerful preacher, John Elias, was forthright in his opposition to the Papists, the 'chief agents' of Satan.[382] By the 1820s Elias had come to occupy the dominant position among Welsh Methodists that Bunting enjoyed among the Wesleyans: critics called his home town of Llangefni the 'Ottoman Porte' of the Calvinistic Methodists and likened his home at Y Fron to the 'seraglio of the sultan'.[383] When, in 1828, members of the Jewin Crescent Calvinistic Methodist church in London signed a petition in favour of Catholic emancipation Elias was furious and the signatories were excommunicated on the orders of the North Wales Association. Conversely a petition against

---

[378] *Letters of John Wesley*, vi. 371.

[379] Hempton, *Methodism and Politics*, 120–1.

[380] Ward, *Religion and Society*, 119; Hempton, *Methodism and Politics*, 127–8; *Methodist Magazine*, 36 (1813), 188.

[381] Prentice, *Historical Sketches of Manchester*, 255.

[382] E. Morgan, *John Elias: Life, Letters, and Essays* (1973), 210.

[383] R. I. Parry, 'The Attitude of the Welsh Independents towards Working-class Movements, 1815–70', MA thesis (Bangor, 1931), 4.

emancipation from the Calvinistic Methodists of Caernarfonshire attracted, so it was claimed, 11,000 signatures.[384]

All this had grave implications for the Dissenting campaign against the Test and Corporation Acts. While the more prosperous and better-educated metropolitan congregations, represented by the Dissenting Deputies, favoured the repeal of legislation which discriminated against Dissenters and Catholics alike, Dissenters outside London were not always prepared to pay the price of Catholic emancipation in order to secure the repeal of the Test and Corporation Acts.[385] Antipathy towards the Roman Catholic claims led John Wilks's Protestant Society for the Protection of Religious Liberty to decline to support the Dissenting Deputies' proposed campaign against the Test and Corporation Acts in 1824, and in the following year William Smith was acutely embarrassed by the presentation to Parliament of twenty-six petitions from Nonconformist congregations protesting against the emancipation of Catholics.[386] Consequently William Smith advised the Dissenting Deputies against agitation to secure the repeal of the Test and Corporation Acts in 1825 and action was once again postponed.[387]

The prospects for repeal were, however, improved as a result of the general election of 1826. The election campaign revealed something of the strength of anti-Catholic feeling in the country; candidates opposed to Catholic emancipation made a net gain of thirteen seats; and when Sir Francis Burdett introduced a motion for Catholic emancipation into the Commons on 7 March 1827 it was defeated by 4 votes—the first time a pro-Catholic resolution had been defeated in the lower house since 1819.[388] This rebuff to the Catholics redounded to the advantage of the Dissenters. Since the Catholic claims had been temporarily shelved anti-Catholics were prepared to consider the Dissenters' case on its own merits, while pro-Catholics were ready to remedy the Dissenters' grievances as a precedent for Catholic emancipation.[389] Two days after the defeat of Burdett's motion the committee of the Dissenting Deputies decided that the time was now opportune to press for the repeal of the Test and Corporation Acts; representatives of the Protestant Society, the General Body of London Dissenting ministers, the Board of Congregational ministers, and the Unitarian Association were invited to send representatives to a conference to establish a United

---

[384] R. T. Jones, 'The Origins of the Nonconformist Disestablishment Campaign', *Journal of the Historical Society of the Church in Wales*, 20 (1970), 49.

[385] R. W. Davis, 'The Strategy of Dissent in the Repeal Campaign of 1820–28', *Journal of Modern History*, 38 (1960), 385–6; Davis, *Dissent in Politics*, 229–35.

[386] Davis, 'Strategy of Dissent', 380–2.   [387] Ibid. 386.

[388] Machin, *The Catholic Question*, 70–1, 86, 91.

[389] Davis, 'Strategy of Dissent', 387; Machin, *The Catholic Question*, 114.

Committee to campaign for repeal; and Lord John Russell was requested to move resolutions to that end in the House of Commons.[390] A temporary setback to Dissenting hopes was provided by the appointment of George Canning as prime minister in April and by his declaration in May that 'under no circumstances would he consider repeal before emancipation'.[391] However, prospects brightened with the death of Canning in August and when the Duke of Wellington became prime minister in January 1828 the Whig leader Earl Grey was convinced that all 'chance of carrying the Catholic question' was destroyed.[392] Once again as hopes of relieving the Catholics receded so Lord John Russell's chances of relieving the Dissenters improved.

Lord John Russell, son of the sixth Duke of Bedford, was descendant and biographer of the Whig William, Lord Russell, who had been executed for seeking to exclude the Catholic James, Duke of York, from succession to the throne in 1683. Lord John appealed to the memory of his martyred ancestor as evidence that it was the special mission of the liberal aristocracy to advocate liberty combined with order,[393] and it was he who rose in the Commons on 26 February 1828 to move that the House go into committee on the question of the sacramental qualification in the Test and Corporation Acts. Russell claimed that since Fox's similar resolution of 1790 'a great improvement . . . in the public mind' had taken place on the issue, 'especially among the middle classes of society',[394] and his motion was approved by 237 votes to 193. Crucially important to Russell's majority of 44 were twenty MPs who a year later would oppose Catholic emancipation.[395] Two days later, on 28 February, a resolution calling for the repeal of the sacramental test passed without a division. Robert Peel, the Home Secretary, pronounced government support for the measure if some means could be found of protecting the Church, and in April the bill passed the Lords with the provision that candidates for office should make a declaration 'on the true faith of a Christian' not to weaken the established church.[396] The declaration excluded Jews from the benefit of the Act and would prove difficult for the advocates of disestablishment, but for the first time since Cromwell's Protectorate conscientious Dissenters who had scruples against taking the Anglican sacrament were free to sit on borough corporations and to accept public office without fear of prosecution. And for the first time in a century the Dissenters who

[390] *Test-Act Reporter*, 2–4.   [391] Davis, 'Strategy of Dissent', 389.
[392] Clark, *English Society*, 393.   [393] J. Prest, *Lord John Russell* (1972), 20.
[394] *Test-Act Reporter*, 98.   [395] Machin, *The Catholic Question*, 113 n.
[396] Davis, *Dissent in Politics*, 245–7.

controlled the Bridport corporation did not attend the parish church to receive the sacrament.[397]

Neither the Quakers nor the Wesleyan Methodists contributed to the campaign for the repeal of the Test and Corporation Acts, and they would hardly have approved of the manner in which the victory was celebrated by the aristocracy of metropolitan Dissent. More than four hundred men, including forty-three MPs (with seventy ladies looking down from the gallery) attended a banquet at the Freemasons' Tavern on 18 June. Tickets were priced at two guineas (refreshments were provided for the ladies at a cost of 2s. a head); a vast quantity of turtles, salmon, beef, veal, chickens, turkeys, ducks, geese, and tarts were consumed; twenty-four toasts were drunk; and the festivities lasted for seven-and-a-half hours, from 6 p.m. until 1.30 in the morning.[398] The banquet was presided over by the younger brother of George IV, the Duke of Sussex, who proposed toasts to the king, Lord John Russell, Lord Holland, William Smith, 'the immortal memory of Charles James Fox', and to 'the Protestant Dissenting ministers, the worthy successors of the ever memorable two thousand who sacrificed interest to conscience' on St Bartholomew's day, 1662. The Unitarian minister Robert Aspland, in responding to the duke, expressed the hope that repeal was 'but the harbinger of good things to come': among them the opening of the universities to Dissenters and the reform of Parliament, so that 'the future government of this country' shall be 'the government of the people and *for* the people'. Aspland's speech was greeted with repeated cheers, but one of the loudest cheers of the evening was in response to the Duke of Sussex's welcome to three Roman Catholic peers, and to his toast to the relief of all who still laboured 'under any legal disabilities on account of their religion'.[399]

A fortnight after the banquet the victory of the Roman Catholic Daniel O'Connell in the by-election for County Clare persuaded the Duke of Wellington that the settlement of the Catholic claims could no longer be delayed, and in February 1829 the government announced its intention of repealing the laws against the Catholics. The decision was welcomed by all Unitarians and by many Congregationalists and Baptists: in 1829 petitions from Dissenting congregations in favour of Catholic emancipation outnumbered those against by nearly two to one.[400] The United Committee which had campaigned for the repeal of the Test and Corporation Acts at its final

---

[397] Short, *Respectable Society*, 60.   [398] Manning, *Dissenting Deputies*, 245–9.
[399] *Report of the Speeches and Proceedings at a Dinner to Commemorate the Abolition of the Sacrament Test* (1828), 37–8, 10.
[400] There were 116 for, 62 against (G. I. T. Machin, 'Resistance to Repeal of the Test and Corporation Acts', *Historical Journal*, 22 (1979), 120).

meeting in December 1828 called 'for the entire abolition' of all religious tests; the General Body of London Dissenting ministers resolved to support emancipation by a large majority; the Dissenters who controlled the corporation of Nottingham voted unanimously in favour of Catholic relief. Even John Wilks's Protestant Society gave an enthusiastic reception to an uninvited visit from Daniel O'Connell, and Henry Solly's Dissenting schoolmaster, Dr Morrell, would not let the pupils in his Hove school display their hostility towards the Catholics by having a bonfire on Guy Fawkes's day.[401] Many Methodists, by contrast, continued to oppose the Catholic claims. Adam Clarke believed that Wellington's government was 'betraying the king, the country, and the Church by delivering them into the hands of the Papists', and Wesleyan ministers in Cornwall, Leeds, Sheffield, and Hull played a prominent part in the anti-Catholic campaign.[402] But Jabez Bunting favoured 'a wise and reasonable concession' to the Catholics and, although 'in a minority of one', he prevented the Wesleyan Committee of Privileges from openly expressing its opposition to emancipation.[403] Even among the humble Bible Christians there was sympathy for the Catholics: James Thorne 'supported Catholic emancipation even when it was most unpopular to do so'.[404] With the government now supporting emancipation the Catholic Relief Bill passed both Houses of Parliament with surprisingly large majorities: 180 on its second reading in the Commons and 105 on its second reading in the Lords.[405] But opponents of emancipation were concerned that both government and Parliament had ridden roughshod over public opinion and some drew the conclusion that a House of Commons more representative of the people would never have allowed Catholic relief to pass. On 2 June 1829 the ultra-Tory Marquess of Blandford introduced into the Commons a motion for parliamentary reform. The Catholic Relief Bill, commented William Smith, 'appeared to have transformed a number of the highest Tories in the land to something very nearly resembling radical reformers'.[406]

Smith himself retired from Parliament in 1830 when the death of George IV in June necessitated a dissolution: for more than forty years Smith had represented the Dissenting interest in the House of Commons and the repeal of

---

[401] Aspland, *Memoir of Robert Aspland*, 492–3; Machin, *The Catholic Question*, 146; *Congregational Magazine*, NS 5 (1829), 336; Solly, *These Eighty Years*, 105.

[402] Smith, *History of Wesleyan Methodism*, iii. 133; P. Hayden, 'Culture, Creed, and Politics: Methodism and Politics in Cornwall, 1832–1979', Ph.D. thesis (Liverpool, 1982), 80; R. W. Ram, 'The Political Activities of Dissenters in the East and West Ridings of Yorkshire, 1815–1850', MA thesis (Hull, 1964), 103–5.

[403] Ward, *Early Correspondence of Bunting*, 201 n. 2, 202.

[404] Bourne, *Life of James Thorne*, 140.   [405] Machin, *The Catholic Question*, 174, 177.

[406] Ibid. 185–6.

the Test and Corporation Acts was a fitting climax to his career. In the subsequent general election, according to Brougham's calculations, the government won only 79 seats in open constituencies against the opposition's 141.[407] And when the new Parliament met in November thirty-three ultra-Tories, still seething at what they regarded as Wellington's betrayal over Catholic emancipation, voted with the Whigs to bring down the government.[408] In so doing they provided the first opportunity, since the Commonwealth 180 years earlier, of effecting the reform of Parliament.

9. 'THE REVOLUTION IS MADE': THE GREAT REFORM ACT

On 17 November 1830 Earl Grey took office at the head of a Whig government and within a couple of weeks appointed a committee to draft proposals for parliamentary reform. The issue divided Nonconformists in 1830 as it had divided them in the years leading up to Peterloo. Radical Dissenters supported the union of the middle and the working classes to force the establishment to make substantial concessions to democracy. At the other extreme conservative Nonconformists opposed any tampering with the constitution. Between them moderate Dissenters followed the Whig government in advocating a limited measure of reform which would enfranchise the middle class and thus unite them with the landed class in the defence of property. It was this third viewpoint which was to triumph in 1832.

Renewed popular agitation for electoral reform had begun ten months before the formation of Grey's government with the setting up of Thomas Attwood's Birmingham Political Union in January 1830. Attwood wanted his organization to be 'a general union between the lower and middle classes of the people', but he was a Tory who saw parliamentary reform chiefly as a means of introducing a paper currency and Birmingham Dissenters were suspicious both of his Toryism and of his inflationary currency policy.[409] It was for these reasons that Joseph Parkes, the Birmingham solicitor and member of the Unitarian New Meeting who was to become one of the most effective advocates of parliamentary reform, initially opposed the formation of the Birmingham Political Union, though he was subsequently to be a frequent speaker on Union platforms.[410] However, similar political unions were

---

[407] Cannon, *Parliamentary Reform*, 198–9.   [408] Ibid. 202.
[409] J. A. Langford, *A Century of Birmingham Life* (1868), ii. 534; C. Flick, *The Birmingham Political Union and the Movement for Reform in Britain, 1830–39* (Hamden, Conn., 1978), 24, 56.
[410] J. K. Buckley, *Joseph Parkes of Birmingham* (1926), 61, 73. Parkes was married to Joseph Priestley's granddaughter.

formed over the next two years in Nottingham (March 1830), Leeds and Huddersfield (May 1830), Manchester (November 1830), Sheffield and Todmorden (January 1831), London (October 1831), and Leicester (November 1831), and in each of these towns radical Dissenters were prominent in the campaign for parliamentary reform. In Nottingham the New Connexion Methodist Richard Sutton, who had become owner of the *Nottingham Review* on the death of his father in 1829, was a member of the committee of the Political Union and used the columns of his paper to advocate universal male suffrage, annual parliaments, and voting by secret ballot.[411] The Political Unions at Huddersfield and nearby Almondbury also received a good deal of support from New Connexion Methodists, including the former Kilhamite preacher George Beaumont.[412] Beaumont addressed a mass meeting held on Hunslet Moor to inaugurate the Leeds Political Union and another New Connexion Methodist, Joshua Bower, was elected president.[413] In Manchester the council of the Political Union included the radical Presbyterian Archibald Prentice and the Methodist Unitarian cotton manufacturer John Fielden.[414] It was Fielden who took the chair at the inaugural meeting of the Todmorden Political Union and of the twenty members of its council at least seven were Methodist Unitarians.[415] In London W. J. Fox 'addressed the people daily in Leicester Square' on behalf of the Political Union; in Sheffield the committee of the Political Union included numerous Dissenters under the chairmanship of Thomas Asline Ward; and in Leicester the Political Union was dominated by Unitarian manufacturers such as William Biggs, Robert Brewin, and Joseph Whetstone, by the Unitarian and Baptist ministers Charles Berry and James Phillippo Mursell, and by the General Baptist publisher Joseph Foulkes Winks.[416] From Stockport, in June 1831, the Political Union sent the radical preacher and future General Baptist minister Joseph Harrison to London with a petition calling for universal male suffrage, annual parliaments, and voting by ballot.[417]

---

[411] Thomis, *Politics and Society in Nottingham*, 224.

[412] Ram, 'Dissenters in the East and West Ridings', 113–14. Although Beaumont had been expelled from the New Connexion ministry in 1814, he continued to contribute to its funds (Werner, *Primitive Methodist Connexion*, 195 n. 75).

[413] A. S. Turberville and F. Beckwith, 'Leeds and Parliamentary Reform, 1820–32', *Publications of the Thoresby Society*, 41 (1954), 29–30; Ram, 'Dissenters in the East and West Ridings', 111.

[414] Prentice, *Historical Sketches of Manchester*, 368–9.

[415] McLachlan, *Methodist Unitarian Movement*, 117–19.

[416] Mineka, *Dissidence of Dissent*, 187; Ram, 'Dissenters in the East and West Ridings', 112–13; A. Temple Patterson, *Radical Leicester, 1780–1850* (Leicester, 1954), 187–8.

[417] Weston, 'Baptists of North-West Lancashire', 609.

In other towns, too, Dissenters were in the forefront of the agitation for parliamentary reform: in Islington the Congregationalist Thomas Wilson chaired a reform meeting in the Canonbury Tavern; in Bradford the Baptist minister Benjamin Godwin addressed a similar meeting; and at Machynlleth in Montgomeryshire an Independent minister, David Morgan, spoke on a reform platform.[418] In Merthyr Tydfil both Independent and Unitarian ministers addressed a reform meeting in the parish church, and notwithstanding the venue the Unitarian David John (who was also a blacksmith) launched into 'a fiery denunciation of bishops who starved their clergy, proclaimed that the poor were living on carrion, and indulged in revolutionary exhortation to loud cheers and the stamping of feet'.[419]

At the other end of Wales, geographically, religiously, and politically, John Elias denounced parliamentary reform as he had denounced Catholic emancipation.[420] And the leaders of Wesleyan Methodism, as always, were suspicious of political radicalism: in August 1831 the president and secretary of Conference warned Methodists not to let 'worldly politics engross too much of your time and attention' since the political excitement of the year had been 'unfriendly to the work of God'.[421] But the Methodists' gravest disservice to the cause of reform was to oppose Lord John Russell's re-election to Parliament for his Bedford constituency in 1830. In the previous year Russell had published his *Memoirs of the Affairs of Europe* in which he had criticized eighteenth-century Methodism for 'the intolerance it is too apt to engender', for its doctrines which bordered on those 'destructive of all morality', and for the 'encouragement it affords to fraud and every species of cant'.[422] Not surprisingly Russell's opponent circulated extracts from his book throughout his strongly Methodist constituency; Jabez Bunting published a letter urging Wesleyans in Bedford to oppose Russell; and the young Whig leader lost his seat by one vote.[423] Russell had the embarrassment of having to seek the shelter of his family pocket borough of Tavistock, and it was as MP for Tavistock that on 1 March 1831 he introduced the government's Reform Bill into the House of Commons. The bill proposed to disfranchise 60 boroughs and to halve the representation of 48 others; to transfer 106 of the 168 seats thus released to the counties and the larger towns; and to give the vote to house-

---

[418] Wilson, *Memoirs of Thomas Wilson*, 434; Parry, 'Welsh Independents', 50; Wearmouth, *Methodism and Working-class Movements*, 188. Wearmouth is in error in describing Godwin as a Wesleyan.

[419] G. Williams, 'The Making of Radical Merthyr', *Welsh History Review*, 1 (1960–3), 175–6.

[420] *DWB* 204.   [421] *Minutes of the Methodist Conferences*, vii. 74.

[422] Lord John Russell, *Memoirs of the Affairs of Europe* (1829), ii. 579–81.

[423] Prest, *Lord John Russell*, 37; Gregory, *Side Lights on the Conflicts of Methodism*, 202.

holders in the towns whose homes were rated at £10 a year. The bill passed its second reading by 302 votes to 301 and the *Baptist Magazine* rejoiced that the majority of one—like the majority for the Act of Succession in 1702—was evidence that 'this is the finger of God'.[424] But in April an amendment opposing a reduction in the number of MPs for England and Wales was carried against the government by 8 votes and a new election was called to give the government a majority of around 140. This time Russell was returned to Parliament for the county of Devonshire, and the Dissenting Deputies atoned for the Wesleyans' opposition in the previous year by opening a subscription list to cover his election expenses with a donation of £500. It was, so Russell claimed, the Dissenters' 'prompt liberality' that secured for him an unopposed election.[425]

The government's motive in persevering with its Reform Bill was not, however, that of the political unions. 'If any persons suppose that this Reform will lead to ulterior measures', Grey told the House of Lords in November 1831, 'they are mistaken; for there is no one more decided against annual parliaments, universal suffrage, and the ballot than I am. My object is not to favour, but to put an end to such hopes and projects.'[426] The Whigs sought not to aid democracy, but to prevent it by uniting the landed and middle classes in defence of the established order. Without concessions to the middle class, Grey wrote privately, the changes which had taken place in Europe since 1815 would 'lead rapidly to republicanism and to the destruction of established institutions'.[427] The moderate Dissenters who followed the lead of Edward Baines were similarly concerned to contain the threat to property. Throughout the crisis of 1830–2 the *Leeds Mercury* continued to oppose universal suffrage, a stance which contributed to the rapidly worsening relations between Baines and the Leeds radicals.[428] In Sheffield the Congregationalist editor of the *Sheffield Independent*, Edward Leader, told the workers in the town to leave the direction of the reform movement to their 'natural leaders', the middle-class reformers.[429] In Nottingham Richard Sutton was 'one of the few middle-class people to be associated with' the Political Union.[430] And in Manchester Archibald Prentice noted that the council of the Political Union, apart from the Fielden family, 'consisted

[424] *Baptist Magazine*, 3rd ser. 6 (1831), 155.
[425] *Congregational Magazine*, NS 8 (1832), 326; Manning, *Dissenting Deputies*, 474.
[426] Thompson, *Making of the English Working Class*, 892.
[427] Cannon, *Parliamentary Reform*, 250–1.
[428] Turberville and Beckwith, 'Leeds and Parliamentary Reform', 27–9.
[429] Ram, 'Dissent in Urban Yorkshire', 11–12.
[430] Thomis, *Politics and Society in Nottingham*, 224.

principally of shopkeepers, with a few men of the working class'.[431] That the threat to property was real enough was confirmed in October 1831 when the rejection of the second Reform Bill by the House of Lords led to rioting in many parts of the country. In London the Duke of Newcastle's home was attacked and the Duke of Wellington's windows were broken; in Derby the gaol was forced open and in Nottingham the castle, also owned by the Duke of Newcastle, was burned to the ground; in Bristol for three days the gaols, the custom house, and the bishop's palace were fired and looted. In Manchester a meeting called on Camp Field by moderate reformers to protest against the action of the Lords attracted over 80,000 people and a 'furious mob' forced the chairman, the Unitarian cotton manufacturer Thomas Potter, to accept a resolution in favour of universal suffrage, annual parliaments, and voting by ballot.[432]

From their different standpoints Joseph Parkes, Edward Baines, and John Fielden were all alarmed that the government would seek to appease the House of Lords by raising the qualification for the vote in boroughs above the occupancy of houses rated at £10 a year proposed in the original bill. In November Lord Althorp, the Whig leader in the House of Commons, and Lord John Russell sought the views of Joseph Parkes and Edward Baines respectively for their reaction to a raising of the £10 household qualification and they both received similar replies. Parkes told Althorp that he regarded the £10 qualification as already too high and that any further limitation on the number of men entitled to vote 'would probably wreck the bill with the public'.[433] Russell asked Baines for his opinion on the effects of either a £10 or a £15 household franchise in Leeds. Baines replied that even with a £10 franchise 'not one householder in fifty would have a vote' in working-class districts, and that in the opinion of Liberal canvassers in the town the £10 qualification would exclude 'a great number of persons whom they thought might be entrusted with the franchise with safety and advantage to the public'. Baines added his 'strong conviction . . . that the raising of the qualification for voting in the boroughs above £10 house-rent, would make the Reform Bill nearly as unpopular as it has been popular, and that it would greatly diminish the blessing which that measure confers upon the people'.[434] Similarly John Fielden and his fellow radicals in the Todmorden Political Union, in a district where 'thousands of families are absolutely in a state of starvation', warned the government in April 1832 against raising the £10

---

[431] Prentice, *Historical Sketches of Manchester*, 369.
[432] Watkin, *Extracts from his Journal*, 153–4.   [433] Buckley, *Joseph Parkes*, 79.
[434] Baines, *Life of Edward Baines*, 157–8.

householder qualification: such a move would 'produce great dissatisfaction in the manufacturing districts and consequences might follow which it is awful to contemplate'.[435]

In the end the government stood firm. A slightly modified third Reform Bill passed the Commons by 355 votes to 239 in March 1832 only to be defeated on amendment in the Lords in May and Grey's government resigned. William IV's attempts to find a Tory who could form a government was met with mass protests throughout the country: Attwood was said to have addressed an audience of 200,000 in Birmingham, Edward Baines 30,000 in Leeds, John Fielden 20,000 on St Peter's Fields, Manchester. It was Fielden who suggested to Attwood and Francis Place that the Tories could be thwarted by a run on the banks, and Birmingham, Manchester, and London were placarded with the slogan, 'To Stop the Duke, Go for Gold'.[436] But Wellington found it impossible to construct a government and the king was forced to agree to Grey's request to create, if necessary, sufficient Whig peers to secure the passage of the bill through the upper house. The threat alone was enough to break the peers' resistance: on 4 June the Reform Bill passed the Lords by 106 votes to 22 and three days later it received the royal assent. The Act disfranchised 56 English and Welsh boroughs, halved the representation of another 31, and transferred 65 of the seats thus made available to the counties and another 63 to large towns hitherto unrepresented in Parliament. The Act retained the 40s. freeholder franchise in the counties, added leaseholders and tenants-at-will paying rents of £50 a year, and in the boroughs the government followed Baines's advice in not abandoning the £10 rating qualification. Under the new electoral system some 808,000 men throughout the United Kingdom now had the vote: perhaps nearly twice the number entitled to the franchise before 1832.[437]

The passage of the Great Reform Bill was greeted by Dissenters with much rejoicing. John Fielden presided over a huge open-air dinner in the grounds of his Todmorden mill at which all his 3,000 employees sat down to eat.[438] Thomas Asline Ward chaired another at Sheffield, attended by 1,500 people.[439] William Biggs, in presiding over a third at Leicester, told his audience that their next objective must be municipal reform.[440] At Belper the Strutt family of Unitarian manufacturers gave every householder a pound of

[435] McLachlan, *Methodist Unitarian Movement*, 120.
[436] Weaver, *John Fielden*, 50–1; Brock, *The Great Reform Act*, 295–8; Turberville and Beckwith, 'Leeds and Parliamentary Reform', 52.
[437] Cannon, *Parliamentary Reform*, 259; Brock, *The Great Reform Act*, 312–13.
[438] Weaver, *John Fielden*, 52.   [439] Ram, 'Dissenters in the East and West Ridings', 128.
[440] Patterson, *Radical Leicester*, 198.

meat for every person of meat-eating age and a pound of plum pudding. And Benjamin Gregory, the twelve-year-old son of a Wesleyan minister who took no part in politics, joined in Belper's triumphal procession.[441] In February a group of Congregationalists and Baptists, buoyed up with optimism at the prospect of the imminent passage of the Reform Bill, had launched a new 7*d*. weekly, the *Patriot*, to remind Evangelical Dissenters that they were 'descendants of the Puritans' and that Nonconformity was 'one of the bulwarks of freedom'.[442] Once the Reform Bill had passed the *Patriot* claimed that it would free Dissenting voters from having to choose between Tories 'whose political sentiments were dramatically opposed to their own' and Whigs of 'whose religious opinions they could not approve'. Henceforward 'in a great number of small towns, and in more than one of the new metropolitan districts', Dissenters could send to Parliament 'whom they please'.[443] In similar vein the *Congregational Magazine* rejoiced that 'the happy extension of the elective franchise has at length convinced the nation of the numerical strength and moral influence of the Protestant Dissenters'.[444] By the same token the Duke of Wellington was plunged into gloom. 'The revolution is made', he wrote in March 1833; 'power is transferred from one class of society, the gentlemen of England, professing the faith of the Church of England, to another class of society, the shopkeepers, being Dissenters from the Church.'[445]

In fact there was no transfer of power in 1832, nor would there be until the Great Reform Act was itself reformed. Few Dissenters had sat in Parliament before 1832 and few were to sit in Parliament after it. William Smith was unique among Dissenting MPs in making much impact on the unreformed House of Commons, and when he first entered Parliament in 1784 there were only two other members who can be definitely identified as Dissenters: Sir Henry Hoghton, the Lancashire baronet and orthodox Presbyterian who represented Preston from 1768 until his death in 1795, and Richard Slater Milnes, son of a wealthy Wakefield cloth merchant who sat for York from 1784 until 1802.[446] In addition there was a small group of MPs who were attracted to Unitarian theology and who attended Theophilus Lindsey's meeting-house in Essex Street. They included the barrister John Lee, who

---

[441] Gregory, *Autobiographical Recollections*, 129–30.   [442] *Patriot*, 22 Feb. 1832, 4.
[443] Ibid. 13 June 1832, 168.   [444] *Congregational Magazine*, NS 8 (1832), 703.
[445] L. J. Jennings (ed.), *The Correspondence and Diaries of John Wilson Croker* (1884), ii. 205–6.
[446] Namier and Brooke, *History of Parliament, 1754–1790*, ii. 628–9; iii. 142; Thorne, *History of Parliament, 1790–1820*, iv. 212–13, 598.

was MP successively for Earl Fitzwilliam's pocket boroughs of Clitheroe (1782–90) and Higham Ferrers (1790–3); the banker James Martin who represented Tewkesbury from 1776 to 1807; Joshua Grigby, who was MP for Suffolk from 1784 to 1790; the banker Robert Smith who sat for Nottingham from 1779 to 1797; and the wine merchant Thomas Whitmore who represented Bridgnorth from 1771 to 1795. But Lee and Whitmore certainly, and Martin possibly, continued to retain connections with the Church of England, and Smith deserted the Dissenters in 1791 to oppose the repeal of the Test and Corporation Acts.[447] Two more Dissenters entered Parliament in the 1790s: James Adair who had sat for Cockermouth from 1775 to 1780, and who succeeded Lee as MP for Higham Ferrers in 1793, and Benjamin Vaughan who sat for Calne from 1792 to 1796.[448] And there were two other MPs who may have been Unitarians: Benjamin Hobhouse, who bought the seat for Bletchingley for £4,000 in 1797 and subsequently represented Grampound (1802–6) and Hindon (1806–18), and Robert Wigram, a merchant who married into a family of Unitarians, became a half-millionaire, and sat for Fowey from 1802 to 1806 and for Wexford from 1806 to 1807. Yet in both cases there is evidence to suggest that their attachment to Unitarianism was but temporary: Hobhouse was for a time a member of Lewin's Mead chapel in Bristol, but by 1800 was being described by Lady Holland as a 'Humanitarian' rather than a 'Unitarian', and Wigram's attachment to Unitarianism may not have long survived the death of his first wife.[449]

Even though the group of Dissenters in the House of Commons was tiny they failed to act in unison. While William Smith, James Martin, and Benjamin Hobhouse all opposed the war with France in 1793, and Benjamin Vaughan's fear of prosecution at the hands of Pitt's government prompted him to flee to France and thence to America, Sir Henry Hoghton and James Adair both supported the war and Robert Wigram fitted out four of his merchant ships as troop transports for the government in 1795. The election of two more Unitarian MPs in 1806 brought little significant additional strength to the Dissenters in Parliament. William Roscoe was returned for Liverpool and Robert Pemberton Milnes for Pontefract, but both men had unhappy parliamentary careers. Roscoe disliked being separated from his family, suffered from a nervous disorder, and felt ill at ease in the House of Commons.

---

[447] Namier and Brooke, *History of Parliament, 1754–1790*, i. 115; Ditchfield, 'Unitarianism and Radicalism', 103, 176; Seed, 'Unitarianism and Liberal Culture', 118; Thorne, *History of Parliament, 1790–1820*, v. 199–201.

[448] Namier and Brooke, *History of Parliament, 1754–1790*, ii. 6–7; Thorne, *History of Parliament, 1790–1820*, iii. 21–4; v. 442–3.

[449] Thorne, *History of Parliament, 1790–1820*, iv. 202–12; v. 554–6; Seed, 'Unitarianism and Liberal Culture', 118.

After he voted in favour of the abolition of the slave trade he was met on his return to Liverpool by a hostile demonstration of seamen 'chiefly consisting of the crews of vessels lately engaged in the African trade, armed with bludgeons', and he decided not to defend his seat in 1807.[450] And although Pemberton Milnes continued to represent Pontefract until 1818, he failed to fulfil the promise of a brilliant maiden speech and gained an unenviable reputation for inconsistency.[451]

The first Methodist MP, the banker Thomas Thompson, entered Parliament for Lord Carrington's pocket borough of Midhurst in 1807 and held the seat until 1818, and in 1812 a second Wesleyan, the law publisher Joseph Butterworth, entered Parliament for Coventry.[452] However, the first two Wesleyan MPs were no more able than the Unitarians to agree on the major issues of the day. While Thompson consistently voted for Catholic emancipation, Butterworth as consistently voted against, and in 1818 the electors of Coventry accused Butterworth of voting too often with the government and he lost his seat. He returned to the House of Commons in 1820 as MP for Dover and served until his death in 1826. A solitary Baptist, Benjamin Shaw, merchant and later treasurer of the Baptist Missionary Society, represented Westbury from 1812 to 1818 and he, too, was regarded as a government supporter though he did vote for Roman Catholic emancipation.[453]

Three more Unitarians were elected to Parliament in the 1810s and 1820s, all representatives of northern industrial and mercantile interests. Benjamin Gaskell of Wakefield was MP for Maldon from 1812 to 1826; George Philips, partner in a Lancashire cotton-spinning firm, who sat in Parliament from 1812 to 1830 successively for the Ilchester, Steyning, and Wootton Bassett, was regarded as the 'unofficial member for Manchester'; and the wealthy Leeds flax-spinner John Marshall, supported by Baines and the *Leeds Mercury*, was returned unopposed for Yorkshire in 1826.[454] But Marshall, who had bought estates in the Lake District worth £66,500, had sought a seat in Parliament partly in order to secure 'an introduction to good society', and

---

[450] Roscoe, *Life of William Roscoe*, i. 362–4, 392.

[451] Thorne, *History of Parliament, 1790–1820*, iv. 598–601.

[452] Ibid. v. 368–9; iii. 348–9.

[453] Ibid. v. 132; B. Stanley, *History of the Baptist Missionary Society* (Edinburgh, 1992), 209.

[454] Holt, *Unitarian Contribution to Social Progress*, 46; Rimmer, *Marshalls of Leeds*, 111–13. Cowherd, *Politics of English Dissent*, 76, states that two MPs for the City of London, Matthew Wood (MP 1817–43) and Robert Waithman (MP 1818–20, 1826–33) were also Dissenters, but there appears to be no hard evidence to identify them as such. *The History of Parliament, 1790–1820* states that though Wood was the 'son of a Dissenting serge maker at Tiverton', it is doubtful whether he was himself a Dissenter (v. 645–7). His obituary in the *Christian Reformer*

he made little impression on the House of Commons.[455] Marshall, along with William Smith, relinquished his seat in 1830, and the House of Commons before which Russell introduced his first Reform Bill contained but one MP who was unquestionably a Dissenter: John Wilks, the Calvinistic Methodist secretary of the Protestant Society, who was elected for Boston in 1830. Wilks was joined by a second Dissenter in 1831: Benjamin Heywood of the Unitarian banking family and a trustee of Cross Street chapel, Manchester, was elected for Lancashire, but he did not seek re-election the following year.[456]

The general election of December 1832, the first held under the reformed franchise, brought some modest increase in Dissenting strength in Parliament with the election of twelve Nonconformist MPs. John Wilks was re-elected for Boston and George Philips, created a baronet in 1828, returned to represent South Warwickshire after an absence from the House of two years. A total of nine Unitarian MPs were elected in 1832: in addition to George Philips, another member of the same family, Mark Philips, was returned for Manchester, the younger John Marshall for Leeds, Daniel Gaskell for Wakefield, Rawdon Briggs for Halifax, George Wood for South Lancashire, Richard Potter for Wigan, Matthew Hill for Hull, and the Methodist Unitarian John Fielden for Oldham.[457] In addition Joseph Pease, the first Quaker to sit in Parliament, was elected for South Durham and the Bible Christian (Swedenborgian) Joseph Brotherton was returned for Salford.[458]

The fact that nine of the twelve Dissenting MPs elected in December 1832 were Unitarians, and that five of the Dissenting MPs were returned for Lancashire constituencies, is clear evidence that what Dissenting representation there was in Parliament in the 1830s was based on the economic influence of rational Dissent in northern manufacturing towns, not on the mass support of Evangelical Dissent throughout the rest of the country. Against the handful of Unitarian MPs elected in 1832 must be set the fact that there was no representative of the four largest Nonconformist denominations—

(10 (1843), 730) stated that 'on his coming to London he attached himself to the late Dr Abraham Rees's congregation', but that he was 'never sectarian in his feelings', and he had his eldest son educated at Winchester and Trinity College, Cambridge. Manning, in his *Dissenting Deputies*, i. 486, is in error in stating that Waithman was a deputy.

[455] Rimmer, *Marshalls of Leeds*, 102, 111–13.
[456] T. Baker, *Memorials of a Dissenting Chapel* (1884), 115.
[457] Seed, 'Unitarianism and Liberal Culture', 352.
[458] Kirby, *Men of Business*, 55, 57. The Quaker John Archdale had been elected to Parliament for High Wycombe in 1698 but declined to take the oaths to enable him to take his seat (D. Wykes, 'Religious Dissent and the Penal Laws', *History*, 75 (1990), 58).

the Wesleyan Methodists, Congregationalists, Baptists, and Primitive Methodists—although Edward Baines was elected for Leeds at a by-election in February 1834. And against the return of Nonconformist industrialists for places like South Lancashire, Manchester, Salford, Oldham, and Wigan, in all of which places Dissent was numerically weak, must be set the fact that no Nonconformist was returned for predominantly Dissenting towns such as Bristol or Nottingham, or for overwhelmingly Nonconformist counties such as Bedfordshire and Cornwall. Most telling of all, the parliamentary representation of Wales was to remain almost exclusively Anglican for the next thirty years.

The Unitarian MPs elected in 1832, apart from John Fielden, were all cautious, Whiggish men who made little impact on Parliament. Mark Philips, entrusted with presenting petitions for the redress of Dissenting grievances in 1834, was so overcome by 'nervous anxiety' that he confessed he was 'a very poor advocate for the cause', and five years later George Wood so angered members of the Manchester Chamber of Commerce, of which he was president, with the maladroitness with which he put the case against the Corn Laws that they removed him from the presidency.[459] The Whig tactic of detaching 'from the working classes a large portion of the middle ranks', to quote Bronterre O'Brien, and of engaging those middle ranks in the service of the aristocracy, appeared to have been very largely successful.[460] In some constituencies such as Colchester and Lancaster the Reform Act deprived existing working-class voters of the franchise, and in Parliament the overwhelming majority of MPs continued to be connected with the nobility, baronetage, or gentry.[461]

Yet if the Duke of Wellington was entirely wrong when he spoke of power being transferred to Dissenters in 1832, there was a sense in which under the reformed electoral system the growing numerical strength of Dissent could now more easily be brought to bear on the political scene. If there was no great influx of Dissenting MPs into the House of Commons in the 1830s, there was evidence of growing Dissenting influence over MPs who were not Dissenters. In 1832 the Dowlais ironmaster and colliery proprietor Josiah John Guest was returned unopposed to Parliament for the newly created borough of Merthyr Tydfil. Guest was a Wesleyan-turned-Anglican and had sat in Parliament for Honiton from 1825 to 1831 as a moderate Tory. He was

---

[459] McKerrow, *Memoir of William McKerrow*, 47; A. Prentice, *History of the Anti-Corn-Law League* (1853), i. 108–11.

[460] Thompson, *Making of the English Working Class*, 903.

[461] Cannon, *Parliamentary Reform*, 257; W. D. Aydelotte, 'The House of Commons in the 1840s', *History*, 39 (1954), 254–5.

The Politics of Dissent, 1791–1833

to keep his seat for Merthyr for twenty years, until his death in 1852, but he retained the loyalty of this, one of the most strongly Nonconformist of all parliamentary boroughs, only by transforming himself into 'a spokesman for militant Dissent'.[462] And militant Dissent, over the next twenty years, would become the political expression not so much of the diminishing number of radical Unitarians but of a growing number of Evangelical Nonconformists. More significant for the future than the election of a small band of Unitarian MPs was a meeting held in October 1832 in a field behind Ebenezer chapel, Carmarthen, said to have been attended by a hundred Nonconformist ministers and thousands of their members. These Evangelical Welsh Dissenters agreed to support, in the forthcoming general election, only those candidates who would pledge themselves to vote for the abolition of slavery and of compulsory church rates.[463] The Bible Christian Conference, in the summer of 1832, likewise urged those of its members who now had the vote to cast it in favour of candidates who 'will use their influence to abolish that deep national disgrace, the existence of slavery in the British colonies, and who will also further such measures as will remove all abuses in Church and State'.[464] Early in June 1832 the Baptist missionary William Knibb returned to England from riot-torn Jamaica. When a pilot came on board his ship in the English Channel Knibb asked him 'Well, pilot, what news?' 'The Reform Bill has passed', replied the pilot. 'Thank God', retorted Knibb. 'Now I'll have slavery down.'[465]

10. 'THE EXECRABLE SUM OF ALL VILLAINIES': THE ANTI-SLAVERY CAMPAIGN

The campaign for the abolition of the slave-trade and for the emancipation of slaves throughout the British Empire began as a Quaker initiative, developed into a mainly Evangelical and Dissenting enterprise, and culminated in a largely Nonconformist protest.

The attempt by Dr Eric Williams, the first prime minister of independent Trinidad, to offer a Marxist interpretation of abolition and emancipation has been rejected by all recent students of the subject. Williams argued that the

---

[462] G. A. Williams, 'The Making of Radical Merthyr, 1800–1836', *Welsh History Review*, 1 (1960–3), 179–80, 184–7; *DWB*.

[463] Jones, *Hanes Annibynwyr Cymru*, 207; *Patriot*, 31 Oct. 1832, 330.

[464] Bourne, *The Bible Christians*, 213.

[465] J. N. Hinton, *Memoir of William Knibb* (1849), 140.

independence of Britain's continental American colonies disrupted trade between the West Indies and what became the United States and left the sugar planters of the British West Indies in a disadvantageous position to face growing competition from the French colony of Saint Domingue, the present Haiti. The plight of the sugar planters was made worse by the war between Britain and Napoleonic France and by Bonaparte's continental blockade. The result was that by 1807 the British West Indian islands were suffering from a crisis of overproduction which could be resolved only by restricting sugar production, and that restriction could be achieved only by abolishing the slave-trade.[466] Williams's case has been demolished by Roger Anstey and Seymour Drescher. Anstey pointed out that Williams made no attempt to study the political processes in Britain whereby abolition and emancipation were achieved, and noted that 'in all the long debates on the 1807 Abolition Bill, in both Lords and Commons', only two speakers 'commended abolition as a remedy for overproduction'.[467] Drescher argues that 'in terms of both capital value and of overseas trade, the slave system was expanding, not declining, at the turn of the nineteenth century': the property values of the slave colonies doubled between 1789 and 1814 and 'as late as 1821 the West Indies accounted for more of British overseas trade in both imports and exports than they had fifty years before'. The decline of the West Indian slave colonies, concludes Drescher, followed and not preceded abolition.[468]

The springs of abolition and emancipation thus have to be sought in the changing moral and political climate of Great Britain, not in the economies of the West Indies, and in that changing climate the expansion of Dissent was of critical importance. Dissenters had not always regarded slavery and Christianity as incompatible. George Fox accepted slavery, William Penn bought and owned slaves, Quaker merchants in Philadelphia and Rhode Island traded in negroes, and Quaker farmers in Maryland, Virginia, and North Carolina owned slaves.[469] In England eighty-four Quakers were listed, in 1756, as members of the Company of Merchants Trading to Africa and therefore likely to have been implicated in slavery; in Liverpool sixteen members of Benn's Garden Presbyterian meeting owned ships which traded in slaves; and the Heywood banking family of Liverpool and Manchester was

---

[466] E. Williams, *Capitalism and Slavery* (1964), 121–3, 149.

[467] R. Anstey, 'The Historical Debate on the Abolition of the British Slave Trade', in Anstey and Hair, *Liverpool, the African Slave Trade, and Abolition*, 161; R. Anstey, 'Capitalism and Slavery: A Critique', *Economic History Review*, 2nd ser. 21 (1968), 314.

[468] S. Drescher, *Econocide: British Slavery in the Era of Abolition* (Pittsburgh, 1977), 19–24, 132.

[469] D. B. Davis, *The Problem of Slavery in Western Culture* (Ithaca, NY, 1966), 304–5.

involved in the slave-trade.[470] But Richard Baxter had characterized the slave-trade as a 'heinous sin' perpetuated by 'incarnate devils' as early as 1665; eleven years later the Quaker missionary William Edmundson issued from Newport, Rhode Island, a letter to Friends which also equated slave-holding with sin; and in 1688 Dutch-speaking Quakers in Germantown, Pennsylvania, sent the first Quaker anti-slavery resolution to their Monthly Meeting.[471] Eight years later, in 1696, the Philadelphia Yearly Meeting urged Friends to avoid trading in slaves; in 1719 they disciplined Friends who ignored this advice; and in 1727 the London Yearly Meeting resolved that Quakers who engaged in the slave-trade were deserving of censure.[472]

Why were Quakers in the forefront of the fight against slavery? It was in part a consequence of the high moral standards and concern for others enforced and encouraged by the discipline of a gathered church; it was in part the result of the fact that the Quakers, until the advent of Methodism, were the best organized of all the Nonconformist denominations with adherents on both sides of the Atlantic; it was in part a logical development from the fundamental bases of Quaker theology. The capturing and enslaving of negroes against their will was akin to the warfare against which Quakers had born witness since the 1660s; the denial of liberty to negroes hindered, for slaves and slave-holders alike, that search for sinless perfection which George Fox had set as his own and his followers' goal; the treatment of negroes as inferior beings violated the principle of the spiritual equality of all men implicit in the Quaker doctrine of the inner light; and the discrimination which had prompted so many Quakers to leave Europe for the New World gave Friends a bond of sympathy with the negroes and at the same time brought them face to face with the realities of slavery and the slave-trade.[473] As Roger Anstey has pointed out, many of the early Quaker witnesses against slavery—William Edmundson, the authors of the Germantown resolution, George Keith, John Farmer, Ralph Sandiford, Benjamin Lay—were men born in Europe for whom contact with slavery in the New World was a traumatic experience.[474] But what transformed the revulsion with which individual Quakers viewed slavery into a mass movement to rid the Anglo-Saxon world of the traffic in human beings was the crisis of conscience which afflicted

---

[470] R. Anstey, *The Atlantic Slave Trade and British Abolition* (1975), 218; A. D. Holt, *Walking Together: A Study of Liverpool Nonconformity* (1938), 155–7; Williams, *Capitalism and Slavery*, 47.

[471] Davis, *Slavery in Western Culture*, 338, 307–9.

[472] Anstey, *Atlantic Slave Trade*, 204; Jones, *Later Periods of Quakerism*, i. 320.

[473] Davis, *Slavery in Western Culture*, 291–308.

[474] Anstey, *Atlantic Slave Trade*, 202–3.

Pennsylvania Quakers in 1755 following raids by Indians, backed by the French, into their colony. The Quakers were divided over whether they should or should not vote taxes for the defence of Pennsylvania, and as pacifist Quakers withdrew from the Pennsylvania Assembly so they looked for a new role in which to assert their influence without either compromising their consciences or endangering their colony. In 1758 the Philadelphia Yearly Meeting excluded from business meetings Friends who bought or sold slaves; in 1775 Quakers founded what was to become the Pennsylvania Society for the Abolition of Slavery; and in 1776 the Philadelphia Yearly Meeting resolved that any Friends who still owned slaves should be disowned.[475]

The Pennsylvania Quakers were, however, convinced that 'this crying evil' of slavery 'principally originates from the trade carried on by Great Britain',[476] and for more than twenty years, under the leadership of the Philadelphia schoolmaster Anthony Benezet, they constantly prodded English Friends to initiate a public campaign against the slave-trade. In 1761 the London Yearly Meeting, probably under American pressure, resolved that Friends who engaged in the slave-trade should be disowned; in 1767 the London Meeting for Sufferings ordered the printing of 1,500 copies of Benezet's *Observations on the Enslaving, Import, and Purchasing of Negroes* and sent copies to every member of both Houses of Parliament; and in 1783 Quakers presented to Parliament the first petition for the total abolition of the slave-trade.[477] By the 1780s Quakers had succeeded in mobilizing a significant section of Christian opinion in England in opposition to the slave-trade. Benezet's *Historical Account of Guinea* inspired John Wesley to publish his own *Thoughts on Slavery* in 1774; it provided the Evangelical Anglican Thomas Clarkson with material for his 1785 Cambridge prize essay on the evils of slavery; and it was one of Benezet's pupils, another Philadelphia Quaker, William Dillwyn, who became what Clarkson described as 'the chief organiser of the British anti-slavery movement'.[478] That movement was provided with a focus, in 1787, with the formation of the London Committee for the Abolition of the Slave Trade, comprising nine Quakers and three non-Quakers including Clarkson and Granville Sharp. Sharp was the man who in 1772 had secured judgment in Somerset's case that a slave could not be removed from England against his will, and who tried unsuccessfully in 1783 to prosecute the captain of the slave ship *Zong* which had thrown 132 negroes

[475] Ibid. 209–11; D. B. Davis, *The Problem of Slavery in the Age of Revolution, 1770–1823* (Ithaca, NY, 1975), 216; Jones, *Later Periods of Quakerism*, i. 319.
[476] Anstey, *Atlantic Slave Trade*, 224.   [477] Ibid. 220–2, 229.
[478] Ibid. 232–3; Davis, *Slavery in the Age of Revolution*, 234.

overboard to their deaths when the ship was running short of water.[479] It was Sharp who now became chairman of the London Abolition Committee.

The speed with which the Abolition Committee won both mass support in the country and influence in Parliament indicated that years of patient Quaker propaganda had done their work. Dissenters of all shades of theological opinion responded to the abolition campaign. In Liverpool, the most important slave-trading port in the Old World, the Unitarian William Roscoe published, in 1787, a poem entitled *The Wrongs of Africa* and a pamphlet giving *A General View of the African Slave Trade*, and in the following year joined with two other Unitarians and four Quakers to form a Liverpool abolition committee.[480] In Bristol, also a slave-trade port, the younger Robert Hall, then tutor at the Bristol Baptist College, wrote anonymous articles in the local press attacking the trade in the face of 'much opposition by the merchants and their dependants'.[481] In Cambridge the Baptist Robert Robinson, and in Birmingham the Unitarian Joseph Priestley, along with other ministers both Anglican and Dissenting, preached sermons against the slave-trade in the early months of 1788.[482] The Baptist Morgan John Rhys tried to persuade his fellow Welshmen, and the Wesleyan Samuel Bradburn tried to persuade his fellow Methodists, to abstain from sugar and treacle until abolition had been achieved.[483] The Norfolk and Suffolk Congregational Association resolved in 1783 that the slave-trade should be regulated or 'even abolished'; the Northamptonshire Particular Baptist Association voted to support the movement for the abolition of the slave-trade in 1787; the Western Particular Baptist Association voted to give five guineas to the Abolition Committee in 1787; and the Old Connexion General Baptist Assembly resolved in 1788 that the trade was 'inconsistent with every rational and humane principle'.[484]

The growth of support for abolition in the country was paralleled by the growth of support among MPs. James Martin, the Unitarian MP for Tewkesbury, and William Morton Pitt, cousin of the prime minister and MP for Poole, joined the Abolition Committee in 1788. Seven more MPs were added in 1791, including Charles James Fox, William Smith, and William

---

[479] Anstey, *Atlantic Slave Trade*, 32, 246–7.

[480] Roscoe, *Life of William Roscoe*, 77, 83; Sellers, 'Liverpool Nonconformity', 272.

[481] *Works of Robert Hall*, vi. 23.

[482] G. W. Hughes, *With Freedom Fired: The Story of Robert Robinson* (1955), 48; *Works of Joseph Priestley*, i, part ii, 7.

[483] G. A. Catherall, 'British Baptist Involvement in Jamaica, 1783–1865', Ph.D. thesis (Keele, 1970), 11; W. Warner, *The Wesleyan Movement in the Industrial Revolution* (1930), 244.

[484] Browne, *Congregationalism in Norfolk and Suffolk*, 201; E. A. Payne, *The Prayer Call of 1784* (1941), 6; J. Ivimey, *History of the English Baptists* (1830), iv. 63; *Minutes of the General Baptist Assembly*, ii. 188.

Wilberforce.[485] Wilberforce, the young MP for Yorkshire who, after his Evangelical conversion, was looking for a cause whereby to justify the continuance of his political career, became the leader of the abolitionist cause in the House of Commons. His motion for abolition was defeated by 163 votes to 88 in April 1791, and although in the following year a motion that the slave-trade be abolished by 1796 passed the Commons, the reaction which followed the Terror in France and the outbreak of war guaranteed that nothing would be done.[486] Motions in favour of abolition were defeated in the Commons by narrow majorities in 1797, 1798, and 1799, but the union of Great Britain and Ireland in 1800 led to the influx of Irish MPs into Westminster who were for the most part in favour of abolition, and the death of Pitt in 1806 and the formation of the Ministry of All the Talents brought into office a group of men, including Charles James Fox, who were also supporters of abolition.[487] The abolitionists began by securing the consent of both Houses of Parliament, in May 1806, to the prohibition of the supply of slaves to the colonies Britain had conquered in the course of the war, and in June Fox followed this up with a resolution, which again passed both Houses, that the British slave-trade be abolished completely. He had sat in Parliament for thirty-four years, Fox told the Commons, and 'if I had done nothing else, but had only been instrumental in carrying through this measure, I should think my life well spent'.[488] Sadly Fox did not live to see the final completion of his work, for he died in September 1806, but in the general election which followed his death, and in which, as we have seen, Dissenters in some parts of the country gave enthusiastic support to Whig candidates, the government made an estimated gain of forty-six seats.[489] The prime minister, Lord Grenville, took charge of the Abolition Bill in the Lords which was passed by the upper house, in February 1807, by 100 votes to 34 and by the lower house by 283 votes to 16.[490] As far as the British Empire was concerned what John Wesley had described as the 'execrable sum of all villainies' was at an end.[491] It was not entirely a coincidence that it was ended in a Britain in which the Evangelical revival was both influencing an important section of the Anglican church and stimulating the rapid growth of Nonconformity, and in which Dissenters were beginning to recover their political nerve after the reaction, disillusionment, and persecution of the 1790s.

The abolition of the slave-trade throughout the British Empire brought no relief to those negroes already in captivity, and the emancipation of the

---

[485] Anstey, *Atlantic Slave Trade*, 261.   [486] Ibid. 273–8.   [487] Ibid. 322, 342, 357.
[488] Ibid. 366–81.   [489] Ibid. 391.   [490] Ibid. 396–8.
[491] *Wesley's Journal*, v. 445–6.

slaves was to prove a much more difficult task than the abolition of the slave-trade. Abolition was regarded as part of the government's admitted right to regulate trade, emancipation was seen as an illegitimate assault on the rights of property.[492] Two of the most dedicated opponents of the slave-trade, William Wilberforce and William Smith, both denied in 1807 that they were in favour of the emancipation of the slaves.[493] Wilberforce hoped that abolition of the slave-trade would lead planters to take greater care of those slaves already in their custody and that the slaves in time would become free peasants, and it was only slowly that he and his fellow abolitionists realized that such optimism was groundless.[494] Consequently it was not until the early 1820s that the earlier concern with the plight of negroes caught up in the slave-trade developed into a campaign for the emancipation of negroes already enslaved. As in the 1780s, so in the 1820s the initiative lay with the Quakers. But in the 1830s, unlike the early 1800s, Evangelical Nonconformity acted not merely in a supporting role to the anti-slavery cause: the mass support which Evangelical Dissent could now mobilize was a factor of increasing significance in a political system in which, in the wake of the Great Reform Act, public opinion counted for more than at any previous time in British history.

The campaign for emancipation opened with a series of letters which the Quaker merchant James Cropper wrote to Wilberforce in 1821 and which he published in the *Liverpool Mercury*.[495] Cropper's initiative led to the London Yearly Meeting of 1822 authorizing the Meeting for Sufferings 'to take any measures for the gradual abolition of slavery' and to the formation, in Liverpool in December 1822, of a Society for the Amelioration and Gradual Abolition of Slavery.[496] Cropper also urged the formation of a similar society in London which was founded in January 1823 with William Smith as chairman and with a committee largely composed of Evangelical Anglicans such as Wilberforce and Zachary Macaulay, and of Quakers such as Luke Howard and Samuel Gurney.[497] By the autumn of 1822, however, Wilberforce's health was failing and he handed over the leadership of the anti-slavery group in the House of Commons to Thomas Fowell Buxton, the tall, broad-shouldered

---

[492] Anstey, *Atlantic Slave Trade*, 256.

[493] W. L. Mathieson, *British Slavery and its Abolition, 1823–1838* (1926), 20; Davis, *Dissent in Politics*, 106.

[494] R. Furneaux, *William Wilberforce* (1974), 401.

[495] K. Charlton, 'James Cropper and Liverpool's Contribution to the Anti-Slavery Movement', *Transactions of the Historic Society of Lancashire and Cheshire*, 123 (1971), 57–9.

[496] R. Anstey, 'The Pattern of British Abolitionism', in C. Bolt and S. Drescher, *Anti-Slavery, Religion, and Reform: Essays in Memory of Roger Anstey* (Folkestone, 1980), 23–4.

[497] Charlton, 'James Cropper', 61.

and eloquent Whig MP for Weymouth. Although himself an Evangelical Anglican, Buxton's mother, Anna, was a member of the Quaker banking and brewing family of Hanbury; he was on close terms with the Quaker Gurneys of Earlham Hall and married Hannah Gurney; and he often attended Quaker meetings. On Buxton's election to Parliament his brother-in-law, Joseph John Gurney, tried to persuade him to make his chief objective the reform of the criminal code, but other Quakers urged on him the cause of the slaves. Most poignant of all were the pleadings of his sister-in-law, Priscilla Gurney, a Quaker minister, as she lay dying in March 1821. Two or three days before she died she sent for him, and though 'seized with a convulsion of coughing, which continued for a long time, racking her feeble frame, she still seemed determined to persevere, but, at length, finding all strength exhausted, she pressed my hand and said, "The poor, dear slaves!" '. Wilberforce himself came to the conclusion that Buxton was the man to succeed him, after hearing him deliver a devastating attack against the use of capital punishment for forgery in the House of Commons in May 1821, and he wrote to him the day after to ask him to take up the cause of slave emancipation.[498] Buxton pondered the issue for eighteen months, held back by fear that raising the issue of emancipation would precipitate slave rebellions, but finally, in October 1822, he acceded to Wilberforce's request.[499]

On 18 March 1823, on presenting a Quaker petition against slavery to the House of Commons, Wilberforce announced that Buxton, not he, intended to give notice of a motion on the state of slavery.[500] Two months later, when Buxton moved his first resolution for the abolition of slavery, the Foreign Secretary George Canning responded for the government with resolutions promising 'decisive measures' to ameliorate the conditions of the slaves. Canning's resolutions were carried and the government sent out circular letters to the colonies urging them to end Sunday labour for slaves, to legalize their marriages, to abolish the flogging of women, to admit the testimony of slaves in court, and to prohibit the use of the driving whip in the fields. Colonial legislatures and governors ignored the circulars but news that the British Parliament had taken up their cause filtered down to the slaves. Rumours circulated that the colonial authorities were ignoring government orders to free the negroes and, as Buxton had feared, precipitated a slave rebellion. On the night of 18 August some 13,000 slaves in Demerara rose in revolt, and although they showed great restraint in imprisoning rather than killing their masters, and only a couple of whites died in the rebellion, savage

---

[498] C. Buxton, *Memoirs of Sir Thomas Fowell Buxton* (2nd edn., 1849), 83, 125–9.
[499] Ibid. 130–1.   [500] *Parliamentary Debates*, NS vii (1823), 630.

reprisals were exacted: over a hundred slaves were shot and forty-seven were hanged.[501] It was claimed that the rising had originated among negroes attached to the chapel presided over by John Smith, a Congregational missionary with the London Missionary Society. Smith, already suffering from tuberculosis, was arrested on 21 August; kept in close confinement for seven weeks; tried by court-martial and sentenced to death; and died in prison on 6 February 1824. The only Anglican clergyman in Demerara, a man named Austin who was chaplain to the British garrison in Georgetown, wrote during the trial that it was only those 'principles of the gospel of peace' which Smith had been preaching which had 'prevented a dreadful effusion of blood here and saved the lives of those very persons who are now, I shudder to write it, seeking his life'. To the sin of slave-holding the West Indian planters had, in the eyes of English Dissenters, added the crime of effectively murdering one of their own number.[502]

The growth of Evangelical Nonconformity, and its close ties through its missionaries with the West Indies, was a major factor in mobilizing British public opinion against slavery. By the early 1830s there were fifty-eight Methodist missionaries in the British West Indies, seventeen Baptists, and twelve other Dissenters, and it is estimated that 11 per cent of the slave population were members of, or attenders at, Nonconformist chapels.[503] All the missionaries had left Europe with instructions not to meddle with politics. When John Smith left England for Demerara in 1816 he had been warned by the London Missionary Society that 'not a word must escape you in public or private which might render the slaves displeased with their masters or dissatisfied with their station'. 'You are not sent to relieve them from their servile condition, but to afford them the consolations of religion.'[504] The Wesleyan Missionary Society told its agents in the West Indies that they should impress on the slaves Paul's advice to the Ephesians: 'Servants, be obedient to them that are your masters'.[505] And the Baptist Missionary Society made the same point to William Knibb when he sailed for Jamaica in 1825: 'The gospel of Christ . . . so far from producing or countenancing a spirit of rebellion or insubordination, has a directly opposite tendency'.[506]

The missionary societies knew full well that any hint that their agents were inciting the slaves to rebellion would lead to the shutting down of their missions and to the frustration of their chief objective, the saving of the negroes' souls. The Wesleyan Conference of 1824 censured two of its missionaries in

---

[501] Mathieson, *British Slavery and its Abolition*, 130–1.   [502] Ibid. 146.
[503] M. Craton, 'Slave Culture, Resistance and the Achievement of Emancipation in the British West Indies', in J. Walvin, *Slavery and British Society* (1982), 110.
[504] Ibid. 109.   [505] *HMC* vi. 384.   [506] Hinton, *Memoir of William Knibb*, 151.

Jamaica and took them off the island because they had criticized the institution of slavery. Four of the missionaries that remained, meeting in Kingston in September, thanked the magistrates on the island for the goodwill they had shown 'towards the spread of morality and religion among the slaves' and voiced their opinion that the abolition of slavery would be 'injurious to the slaves, unjust to the proprietors, and ruinous to the colonies'.[507] But in the course of the 1820s, notwithstanding the missionaries' constant admonitions to the slaves to remain patient, their missions were closed down and their preachers were thrown into prison, and the missionary societies came to realize that slavery not only deprived the negroes of their rights as men, it jeopardized their hopes of eternal life as Christians. The slave rebellion in Demerara prompted a white mob in Barbados to attack and destroy both the Wesleyan chapel in Bridgetown and the home and library of the Wesleyan missionary, William Shrewsbury, and he and his wife were forced to flee to St Vincent.[508] Five years later in 1829, a mob in St Ann's, Jamaica, destroyed the Wesleyan chapel and a missionary, Joseph Grimsdall, was arrested and imprisoned in a 'fetid dungeon' in which he died.[509]

The growing persecution in the West Indies provoked Wesleyans in England into taking a decisive stand against slavery. The committee of the Wesleyan Missionary Society in London disavowed the pro-slavery resolutions of the missionaries in Kingston and the Wesleyan Conference of 1825 went on to resolve that while it was 'the Christian duty of the slaves in our colonies to yield obedience to their masters', it was 'the equally Christian duty of the religious public at home' to work for the ultimate extinction of slavery.[510] The Conference of 1829 urged Wesleyans to unite with other Christians in petitioning Parliament for 'the mitigation and ultimate abolition of the state of negro colonial slavery'.[511] And when, in July 1830, the Anti-Slavery Society called on its supporters to demand from parliamentary candidates in the forthcoming general election a pledge to vote for the abolition of slavery, its move was endorsed by the Wesleyan Conference, the Dissenting Deputies, and the London Board of Congregational ministers.[512] Two thousand six hundred petitions against slavery were presented to

---

[507] *Wesleyan Methodist Magazine*, 48 (1825), 115–17.
[508] Smith, *History of Wesleyan Methodism*, iii. 69–70; *Wesleyan Methodist Magazine*, 47 (1824), 49–52.
[509] Smith, *History of Wesleyan Methodism*, iii. 138–9.
[510] *Wesleyan Methodist Magazine*, 48 (1825), 117; *Minutes of the Methodist Conferences*, vi. 52.
[511] *Minutes of the Methodist Conferences*, vi. 515.
[512] Ibid. 615; Cowherd, *Politics of English Dissent*, 57; Jones, *Congregationalism in England*, 201.

Parliament in the autumn of 1830: of these 2,200 were sponsored by Non-conformists.[513]

By 1830 it was clear that the government policy of amelioration, announced by Canning in 1823, was a total failure. The colonial legislatures refused to sanction the government recommendations and the government made no attempt to enforce them. In April 1831 Buxton produced in the House of Commons the devastating statistic that whereas in fourteen years the free black population of Demerara had registered a natural increase of 50 per cent, in ten years the slave population of Britain's West Indian colonies, no longer replenished by the slave-trade and excluding manumissions, had fallen by over 45,000.[514] But the Whig government would do no more than offer fiscal advantages to those colonies which implemented the amelioration proposals of 1823,[515] and despair at the failure of the Anti-Slavery Society to make progress led to its more radical members demanding a propaganda campaign to raise public opinion. A subcommittee, known as the Agency Committee, was established in June to raise money to send paid agents round the country to lecture on the evils of slavery. James Cropper subscribed £500 and his fellow Quaker Joseph Sturge of Birmingham gave £250.[516] Six months later the slaves in Jamaica rose in rebellion: the barbarity with which the rising was suppressed, and in particular the persecution of Nonconformist missionaries and their congregations, not only provided the Anti-Slavery Society with its most dramatic evidence of the viciousness of slavery, it also gave to the Agency Committee its most effective propagandist.

William Knibb was born in Kettering in 1803, the son of a struggling tailor who later became bankrupt and of a mother who was a member of the town's Congregational church. William's mother sent him to her chapel Sunday school and when he was thirteen his teacher, a Mr Gill, obtained for William and his elder brother Thomas apprenticeships with a local printer, J. G. Fuller, who was the son of Andrew Fuller, pastor of the Kettering Baptist church and secretary of the Baptist Missionary Society. When J. G. Fuller moved his business to Bristol he took the Knibb brothers with him and they subsequently joined the Broadmead Baptist church. In 1822 Thomas offered his services to the Baptist Missionary Society and was accepted as a teacher for a school in Kingston, Jamaica. However, Thomas died only three months

---

[513] Brock, *The Great Reform Act*, 81.   [514] Buxton, *Life of Buxton*, 270–1.

[515] Mathieson, *British Slavery*, 199.

[516] Charlton, 'James Cropper', 69. Between 1826 and 1832 Quakers contributed a total of £7,300 to the Anti-slavery Society (R. Anstey, 'Religion and British Emancipation', in D. Eltis and J. Walvin, *The Abolition of the Atlantic Slave Trade* (Madison, Wis., 1981), 58 n. 46).

after his arrival and on hearing the news William, always more impulsive and high-spirited than his more studious brother, immediately offered to fill Thomas's place. William arrived in Jamaica in February 1825 to become first teacher in his brother's school in Kingston and, in 1830, pastor of the Baptist church in Falmouth.

William Knibb was already a convinced opponent of slavery before he set foot in Jamaica, but he claimed that he had initially abided by the Baptist Missionary Society's instruction to avoid political controversy. He had, he maintained, kept his thoughts on slavery to himself until the planters deprived him 'of the privilege of telling the poor, ill-used, and oppressed slave that he would, if a believer in the gospel, spend an eternity of happiness in heaven'.[517] What transformed Knibb from a passive to an active opponent of slavery was the reaction of the planters to the rebellion which broke out in Jamaica on 27 December 1831. The immediate cause of the rebellion, as in Demerara eight years earlier, was a rumour that the king had freed the slaves and that the planters were refusing to carry out the emancipation edict. The rising was quickly suppressed and although only fourteen whites died in the rebellion the vengeance wreaked on the slaves was even more savage than that which had followed the Demerara insurrection: according to the official figures at least two hundred negroes were killed and another 312 were executed after trials by court-martial, often for the most trivial offences.[518] The leader of the slaves, a negro named Samuel Sharpe, who had advocated nothing more than a refusal to return to work after the Christmas holiday, was among those executed, and he was a deacon of the Baptist church at Montego Bay. And although William Knibb had told the slaves to defend their masters' property, and although he claimed that 'not one estate where we have members connected with Falmouth had been burned',[519] the missionaries were blamed for inciting the rebellion. Knibb and five other missionaries were arrested and then released on bail, and on 8 February riots broke out which forced Knibb and his family to take refuge on a royal navy ship anchored in Montego Bay. White mobs looted and burned the missionaries' homes and went on to destroy fourteen Baptist and six Wesleyan chapels. A month later Knibb's fellow missionaries asked him to return to England to plead their cause and seek redress for the damage done to their missions. He sailed from Jamaica on 26 April 1832.

Knibb arrived in England just as the Reform Act had received the royal assent. The Reform Act, by abolishing many of the rotten boroughs which

---

[517] Hinton, *Memoir of Knibb*, 147.
[518] M. Reckford, 'The Jamaica Slave Rebellion of 1831', *Past and Present*, 40 (1968), 121–2.
[519] Hinton, *Memoir of Knibb*, 120.

had secured the representation of the West Indian interest in the unreformed Parliament, and by increasing the voting strength of middle-class Dissenters, sealed the fate of slavery. A fortnight before William IV assented to the Reform Act, on 24 May, Buxton had moved in the House of Commons for the appointment of a select committee to consider measures 'for the purpose of effecting the extinction of slavery throughout the British dominions at the earliest period compatible with the safety of all classes in the colonies'. Both Lord Althorp, Whig leader in the Commons, and Lord Howick, the colonial under-secretary, pleaded with Buxton to drop the motion lest it embarrass the government while the Reform Bill had yet to pass the House of Lords.[520] Buxton refused to yield and Althorp carried against him an amendment that the committee's recommendations should be in conformity with the amelioration proposals of 1823.[521] But ninety of Buxton's supporters voted against the government amendment and Althorp later told the Member for Weymouth that the division had settled the issue. If Buxton could get 'ninety to vote with him when he is wrong . . . he can command a majority when he is right'.[522]

The committee of the House of Commons set up in accordance with Buxton's resolution was appointed on 6 June, and one of its most important witnesses was William Knibb. Some supporters of the Baptist Missionary Society, including its secretary, John Dyer, still wished to maintain a ban on political activity by its missionaries, but Knibb told the committee of the BMS on 19 June that though he and his family were entirely dependent on the mission, had landed in England without a shilling, and 'may at once be reduced to penury', he would if necessary 'take them by the hand, and walk bare-foot through the kingdom [to] make known to the Christians of England what their brethren in Jamaica are suffering'. Two days later he told the annual meeting of the BMS that the Jamaican negro would never again 'enjoy the blessings of religious instruction' until slavery was overthrown, and in an emotional peroration pleaded with children for 'the infant slave whom I saw flogged on Macclesfield estate', with parents 'by the blood-streaming back of Catherine Williams who . . . preferred a dungeon to the surrender of her honour', and with all Christians 'by the lacerated back of William Black [which], a month after flogging, was not healed'. Knibb's speech was greeted with prolonged applause, and the missionary committee authorized him to tour the United Kingdom to awaken the conscience of the nation to what was happening in the West Indies.[523] By early September he

---

[520] Buxton, *Memoirs of Buxton*, 298.
[522] Buxton, *Memoirs of Buxton*, 307.

[521] Mathieson, *British Slavery*, 223.
[523] Hinton, *Memoir of Knibb*, 143–4, 148–53.

had already visited the major towns of England and had travelled over 1,300 miles, speaking nearly every night. From October to January 1833 he toured Scotland, and he then proceeded to the north of England and in the summer to the West Country.[524] Among Knibb's triumphs was to persuade Lord Howick, under-secretary at the colonial office, that only emancipation would prevent another and much bloodier slave rebellion.[525] The Jamaican planters, commented Knibb's biographer, John Hinton, 'had flung the firebrand from their hearths, and it had fallen on the powder magazine'.[526]

Slavery was a major issue in the general election of December 1832. The Anti-Slavery Society urged supporters to vote only for candidates who would pledge themselves to vote for 'the total and immediate abolition' of slavery, and between 140 and 200 candidates so pledged were elected, the overwhelming majority of them Liberals.[527] A total of 5,020 petitions calling for the abolition of slavery were presented to the new Parliament in the early months of 1833, with a total of 1,309,931 signatures. Over half of those petitions, containing 27 per cent of the signatures, originated with Nonconformist congregations.[528] The campaign for the emancipation of the slaves was the most successful of all the petitioning movements of the nineteenth century, and attracted far more Dissenting signatures than the petitions for the repeal of the Test and Corporation Acts.[529] 'The religious persecutions in Jamaica', Zachary Macaulay wrote to Brougham in May 1833, have aroused the Nonconformists 'to a feeling of intense interest in the matter and they have not only caught fire themselves but have succeeded in igniting the whole country'.[530]

When the new Parliament met in February 1833 there was, to Buxton's disgust, no mention of slavery in the king's speech and he immediately gave notice that on 19 March he would introduce a motion of his own for the abolition of slavery. Buxton, now with the knowledge that the Dissenters had mobilized mass public support against slavery, thus forced the government itself to take up the issue. On 14 May the Colonial Secretary, Edward Stanley, the future Earl of Derby and Conservative prime minister, announced the government proposals in the House of Commons. From 1 August 1834 slave children under the age of six were to be freed; slavery for their elders was to be replaced by a twelve-year apprenticeship during which time the

---

[524] Ibid. 153, 178.   [525] P. Wright, Knibb, 'the Notorious' (1973), 120.
[526] Hinton, Memoir of Knibb, 196.
[527] Anstey, 'The Pattern of British Abolitionism', in Bolt and Drescher, Anti-Slavery, 28.
[528] Wesleyan Methodist Magazine, 57 (1834), 229.
[529] Walvin, Slavery and British Society, 8; Hurwitz, Politics and the Public Conscience, 83.
[530] Anstey, 'The Pattern of British Abolitionism', 28.

negro would earn sufficient to purchase his freedom; and £15,000,000 was to be paid to the slave-holders as compensation. The abolitionists disliked the apprenticeship system and Buxton moved an amendment which obliged the government to reduce the length of apprenticeship for field workers to six years and for other slaves to four years. At the same time supporters of the planters increased the amount of government compensation to £20,000,000. With these alterations the Act for the Abolition of Slavery became law on 29 August 1833. When it passed its second reading in the Commons on 26 July Wilberforce, now very frail and in his seventy-fourth year, commented 'Thank God that I should have lived to witness a day in which England is willing to give twenty millions sterling for the abolition of slavery'.[531] Three days later he died.

The victory of the anti-slavery forces was not, however, complete. They bitterly resented the apprenticeship system, and especially the provision in the 1833 Act whereby apprentices could still be flogged for idleness and disobedience. In 1835 William Knibb wrote from Jamaica that nearly forty women passed his door in chains every morning; that negroes were still flogged while working treadmills; that a pregnant woman who was beaten gave birth to a child as she left the wheel and then died.[532] The £20,000,000 paid in compensation to the slave-owners was in marked contrast both to the sums extracted from the slaves to enable them to purchase their freedom, and to the £5,510 offered by the government to the BMS for the damage done to their chapels, the costs of which the Baptists put at £17,900.[533] The abolitionists in England led by the Birmingham Quaker corn merchant Joseph Sturge waged a continuing campaign against the apprenticeship system. To collect evidence to support his claim that the apprenticeship system was 'slavery under another name' Sturge sailed to the West Indies in November 1836 and brought back to England in the following May a young apprentice whose freedom he had purchased. The apprentice's story, published as *The Narrative of John Williams*, revealed evidence of the brutal conditions in which negroes in Jamaica continued to work.[534] In August 1837 the anti-slavery campaigners took advantage of the accession to the throne of the young Queen Victoria to draw up an address to the throne by the women of Britain calling for the ending of the apprenticeship system, and by the time

---

[531] Furneaux, *William Wilberforce*, 454.   [532] Hinton, *Memoir of Knibb*, 232, 233, 237.

[533] Wright, *Knibb 'the Notorious'*, 134, 136. The government subsequently agreed to add £6,195 to the £5,510 if the Baptists could raise a similar sum (K. R. M. Short, 'A Study in Political Nonconformity: The Baptists, 1827–1845', D.Phil. thesis (Oxford, 1972), 184).

[534] A. Tyrell, *Joseph Sturge and the Moral Radical Party in Early Victorian Britain* (1987), 64, 76–9.

the petition was presented in February 1838 it had attracted 449,000 signatures. It was a pioneering exercise in women's political activity even though the petition was presented to the queen by four men, including Buxton, the Quaker William Allen, and the Baptist Henry Waymouth.[535] The campaign against the apprenticeship system reached its climax with a Commons resolution of 22 May 1838 to end the system by 1 August. Although the resolution did not have the force of law, fear that further delay would provoke another negro rebellion led the Jamaican legislature to abolish the apprenticeship system on its own initiative and the other colonies followed suit.[536]

The emancipation of slaves throughout the British Empire was thus an untidy and an unjust business, but it was none the less a very significant triumph for England's Evangelical, and increasingly Nonconformist, conscience. In England Dissenters celebrated the victory as their own. On the day that the Abolition Act came into operation, 1 August 1834, many of the shops in Nottingham were closed, there were celebratory teas in all the Dissenting chapels, and Sunday school children were 'regaled with cake and wine'.[537] William Knibb returned to Jamaica in October 1834 to a hero's welcome. Vast crowds greeted his landfall, and people who assumed he was dead believed he had risen from the grave. To the former slaves he was 'King Knibb': 'Him fight de battle, him win de crown.' And two negro women, whose babies had been born since 1 August, came after the Sunday service to thank him for their children's freedom. Knibb, completely overcome, 'left them, and retired to weep'.[538]

---

[535] Short, 'Political Nonconformity', 278–9, 288.   [536] Tyrell, *Joseph Sturge*, 81–2.
[537] Sutton, *Nottingham Date-Book*, 444; Castle Gate minutes, 177.
[538] Hinton, *Memoir of Knibb*, 196–8.

IV

'On Equal Footing with the Church'
The Dissidence of Dissent, 1833–1869

1. 'A GREAT NATIONAL EVIL': THE CAMPAIGN FOR THE SEPARATION OF CHURCH AND STATE

The King's Weigh House was one of the wealthiest Congregational churches in London. It took its name from a building in Little Eastcheap near London Bridge in which merchants were required to have their goods weighed for customs purposes and above which the church was able to build a room for worship in 1697. The origins of the church are obscure, but it probably began as a Presbyterian meeting in the reign of Charles II, transferred its allegiance to the Congregational Fund in 1728, reverted to the Presbyterian Fund in 1743, and finally moved back to the Congregational Fund in 1784 at the behest of its pastor, John Clayton.[1] Clayton ministered to the King's Weigh House from 1778 until 1826, and although a Congregationalist he was a very conservative Congregationalist and it was he who, when confronted by the French Revolution, wrote of *The Duty of Christians to Magistrates*. Clayton retired from his pastorate in 1826 at the age of seventy-one, and after an unhappy two years under the ministry of Edward Parsons, who was sacked for excessive drinking, the church in 1829 chose as its minister a man of very different stamp from John Clayton: the thirty-one-year-old Northumbrian Thomas Binney.[2]

Binney was a tall, thin man, rather quietly spoken for a Dissenting minister, and when the King's Weigh House chose him as its pastor it can hardly have known that it was electing a man who was soon to be the centre of furious

---

[1] Kaye, *King's Weigh House*, 11–19, 24, 38, 42, 53.   [2] Ibid. 64–5.

controversy. In 1832 the church received notice that the Weigh House was to be demolished as part of a road-widening scheme and a site for a new chapel was found nearby on Fish Street Hill. Binney used the opportunity presented by the laying of the foundation-stone of the new chapel on 16 October 1833 to draw a contrast between the strengths of Dissent and the weaknesses of the establishment: whereas among Dissenters Unitarian churches were decaying as Evangelical churches were multiplying, in the Church of England anti-Evangelical clergymen were in a majority and immovable, and so 'a sort of immortality was conferred on ignorance, imbecility, and error'. After the ceremony Binney was asked to publish his address and he did so with an appendix in which he stated his objections to the established church in even more forthright terms. 'It is with me, I confess, a matter of deep, serious, religious conviction, that the Established Church is a great national evil; that it is an obstacle to the progress of truth and godliness in the land; that it destroys more souls than it saves; and that, therefore, its end is most devoutly to be wished by every lover of God and man.'[3]

Binney's remarks provoked a storm of protest. His address was attacked for its 'poisonous doctrine', for its 'monstrous falsehoods', for the 'bitterness and the blasphemy of the Weigh-house orator'.[4] Its publication signified an end of the era in which Dissenters had struggled to free themselves from the restrictions of the Clarendon Code and to establish their right to full participation in the affairs of state. It marked the arrival of a new militancy on the part of Dissenters in which they would move on to the offensive and challenge the position of the Church of England. One of Binney's critics, the Evangelical Anglican clergyman Josiah Pratt, noted the change. 'It is no longer Dissent for conscience sake, with the thankfulness for the quiet enjoyment of the privilege of worshipping and preaching according to their own judgement; but it is a claim to be placed on equal footing with the Church and to have the Church separated from the State.'[5]

The evidence that Dissenters were seeking an 'equal footing with the Church' was provided in May 1830 by John Wilks, secretary of the Protestant Society for the Protection of Religious Liberty and soon to be MP for Boston. Wilks told the annual meeting of his society that notwithstanding the repeal of the Test and Corporation Acts, Dissenters still did not have equality with members of the established church. There were five outstanding grievances

    [3] T. Binney, *An Address delivered on laying the first stone of the New King's Weigh House* (5th edn., 1834), 16–17, 34.
    [4] Ibid., p. iii.
    [5] R. H. Martin, *Evangelicals United* (Metuchen, NJ, 1973), 197–8, citing J. Pratt, *Memoir of the Rev. Josiah Pratt* (1849), 292.

which his committee proposed to bring to the notice of Parliament: the frequent refusal of clergymen to allow the bodies of Dissenters to be buried in parish graveyards; the liability of Dissenting chapels to demands for the poor rate when parish churches were exempt; the refusal of the courts to accept the validity of Dissenting baptismal and birth registers in the absence of a civil registry of births and deaths; the forcing of Dissenters, apart from Quakers, to submit to the rites of the Church of England for marriage; and the levying on Dissenters of church rates for the support of the established church.[6] Wilks's proposed application to Parliament was soon submerged by the Reform Bill crisis, but the successful resolution of that crisis encouraged Dissenters to hope that the way was now open 'to other remedial measures of every kind'.[7] The *Congregational Magazine* of November 1832 suggested that Dissenters should exact from candidates seeking election to Parliament pledges to redress the five grievances outlined by John Wilks and to his list it added a sixth, that Dissenters should be free to enter Oxford and to take degrees at Cambridge.[8] And to co-ordinate a new Dissenting campaign on these issues a United Committee of representatives of the Protestant Society, the Dissenting Deputies, and the General Body of Dissenting Ministers in London was set up in March 1833.[9]

Four months later, on 14 July, John Keble, Fellow of Oriel College, Oxford, stung by the Whig government's proposal to abolish ten Irish bishoprics, preached the sermon on 'national apostasy' which came to symbolize the birth of the Oxford movement and the attempt to return the Church of England to its Catholic roots. These two events, the formation of the United Committee and the launching of the Oxford movement, signalled a deepening division between an increasingly militant Nonconformity on the one hand and an increasingly aggressive Catholic party within the Church of England on the other. The result was to polarize Christian England to a greater extent than at any time since the Civil War. And that religious divide was to be reflected in England's political divide to a greater degree than at any time since the 1660s.

Ever since the Civil War the dichotomy of Laudian and Puritan, of High Anglican on the one side and of Nonconformist and Low Anglican on the other, had been the most persistent division in England's political life. Ever since the 1670s, when the terms Tory and Whig were applied to those who supported, and those who opposed, the succession of the Roman Catholic

---

[6] *Congregational Magazine*, NS 6 (1830), 437–43.
[7] *The Claims of Protestant Dissenters* (1833), 1.
[8] *Congregational Magazine*, NS 8 (1832), 703.
[9] G. I. T. Machin, *Politics and the Churches in Great Britain, 1832–1868* (Oxford, 1977), 42.

Duke of York to the throne, Dissenters had looked to the Whigs to protect their interests and High Anglicans had looked to the Tories to uphold the principle of the identity of Church and State. The researches of James Bradley have shown how the distinctions between Whig and Tory, based on differences of religion, often continued to be an important factor in local politics long after they ceased to have much meaning at Westminster.[10] As we have seen, the alliance between the Dissenters and the Whigs was revived by the War of American Independence and Pitt's opposition to the repeal of the Test and Corporation Acts, assisted by Dissenting support for the Ministry of All the Talents in 1806–7, cemented by Lord John Russell's initiative in securing the repeal of the Test and Corporation Acts, and crowned by Dissenting support for the Great Reform Act. With the widening of the franchise in 1832 the identity of religious and political affiliation became even closer. The term Liberal, used by radical Dissenters to describe their political views since the 1770s, was in common usage to denote the party of reform by 1834.[11] In every constituency, claimed Halévy, Dissenters 'were probably the majority of the Liberal party, and in certain localities perhaps the majority of the electorate'.[12] His contention is borne out by the evidence of the pollbooks which have preserved a record of the way men voted in the days before the secret ballot. From 1820 Dissenters in Buckinghamshire voted *en bloc* for candidates who described themselves initially as 'Reformers' and after 1832 as Liberals, and the identification of Dissenters with Liberals became closer after the passing of the Reform Act as some pre-1832 Anglican Reformers went over to the Conservatives.[13] In Leicester in 1832, in Devizes in 1835, in Christchurch in 1837, around 90 per cent of those Dissenters who voted gave their support to Liberal candidates.[14] Those 'Tory Dissenters' who wrote to *The Times* affirming their loyalty to Sir Robert Peel represented a tiny minority,[15] and conversely a majority of Anglicans voted Conservative. However, a substantial minority of Anglicans voted Liberal and consequently the Whig leaders never felt they could alienate those Churchmen who supported them by acceding to all the Dissenters' demands. Of the list of grievances drawn up by John Wilks in 1830 only one was settled in 1833–4: in

[10] Bradley, 'Whigs and Nonconformists', 517–19, 531–2.
[11] N. Gash, *Reaction and Reconstruction in English Politics, 1832–1852* (Oxford, 1965), 165 n. 3.
[12] Halévy, *History of the English People*, iii. 63.
[13] R. W. Davis, *Political Change and Continuity, 1760–1885; A Buckinghamshire Study* (Newton Abbot, 1972), 65, 102–3, 137.
[14] Machin, *Politics and the Churches*, 40, citing D. H. Close, 'The General Elections of 1835 and 1837', D.Phil. thesis (Oxford, 1966), 141; *The Times*, 11 Dec. 1835.
[15] *The Times*, 10, 16 Jan. 1835.

July 1833 Parliament approved Wilks's bill to exempt Nonconformist chapels from payment of the poor rate.[16] But a bill introduced by Lord Althorp in April 1834 to replace church rates by taking £250,000 from the proceeds of the land tax was opposed by Dissenters on the ground that it would mean taking 'the money out of one pocket instead of out of the other' and was dropped.[17] And a bill sponsored by George Wood, the Unitarian MP for South Lancashire, to admit Dissenters to study at Oxford and to degrees at Cambridge passed the Commons in June but was thrown out by the Lords.

The failure of the Whigs to remedy the more serious Dissenting grievances in 1833 had led, by the end of the year, to increasing criticism of the government and a growing demand for the disestablishment of the Church of England. In November George Hadfield, a Congregationalist solicitor from Sheffield and future Liberal MP, wrote to the *Patriot* to complain that Dissenters had been 'asking for trifles' when they should have been 'contending for great principles', the 'total disconnection between Church and State'.[18] As the campaign launched by the United Committee gathered momentum in December 1833 and January 1834, with scores of meetings throughout England, the Dissenters' demand for the redress of specific grievances was often widened to a general call for disestablishment. In Leeds Congregationalists and Baptists pointed out that in ten years £30,000 had been spent from public funds in the creation of Anglican churches in the town; that Dissenters in Leeds had spent a similar sum out of their own pockets on the erection and enlargement of places of worship; that the number of people who worshipped in Dissenting chapels in the area greatly exceeded those who attended the services of the established church; and that 'equal justice cannot be done to all classes' until the alliance between Church and State was severed. In Bradford Dissenters declared the connection between Church and State to be unscriptural; in Nottingham they called upon the government 'to abolish all State religion'; in Leicester they proclaimed 'the alliance between the Church and State . . . to be inconsistent with the law of Christ'.[19] When, in February 1834, the Whigs lost a by-election at Dudley it was claimed that the government defeat was the result of Dissenters withholding their support. It was subsequently denied that the Dissenters of Dudley had deserted the Whig cause, but one disgruntled Dissenter wrote to *The Times* that his co-religionists were so angry at the 'abandonment of them

---

[16] Machin, *Politics and the Churches*, 43.   [17] Ibid. 44.

[18] *Patriot*, 13 Nov. 1833, 387.

[19] *Memorials Addressed to His Majesty's Government by Various Bodies of Dissenters* (1834), pp. v–vi, ix, xi, xix.

by the government, that unless a different policy be pursued, the scene of Dudley will be reacted in not a few other places'.[20]

All this the Whig leadership found intensely irritating. In January 1834 the prime minister, Earl Grey, told a deputation of Nottingham Dissenters that their demands for the separation of Church and State 'would embarrass ministers, would alarm both Houses of Parliament, and would startle the country'. 'He considered it the sacred duty of every government to maintain an establishment of religion.'[21] In February Lord Holland warned Robert Aspland that Grey and the cabinet were 'not a little displeased at the conduct of the violent party' among the Dissenters.[22] Moderate Dissenters for their part were alarmed that the campaign for disestablishment would impede rather than help the redress of specific grievances. Josiah Conder, the Congregationalist who had taken over the editorship of the *Patriot*, argued that to demand disestablishment was to 'ask for nothing tangible' and Edward Baines's *Leeds Mercury* claimed that a breach between the Whigs and the Dissenters could only help the Tories and delay reform.[23] But when Baines, recently elected MP for Leeds, presided over a conference of four hundred delegates from Dissenting congregations throughout England in London in May 1834, those delegates ignored his advice that to campaign for the separation of Church and State would be to delay the settlement of their practical complaints.[24] The conference resolved that the 'complete separation of Church and State' was the only basis on which equal rights could be secured to all subjects, and recommended the setting up of Voluntary Church Societies to secure that end.[25]

2. 'NO POLITICS': JOSEPH RAYNER STEPHENS AND THE WARRENITE SECESSION

The politicization of Dissent in the 1820s and 1830s did not go unchallenged. Not only Wesleyan Methodists but Evangelical Baptists, conservative Congregationalists, quietest Quakers, and Primitive Methodists continued to argue that a preoccupation with politics was contrary to the Christian's calling. The General Baptist minister John Gregory Pike, in his *Guide to*

---

[20] *The Times*, 1, 6, 10 Mar. 1834.
[21] *Patriot*, 29 Jan. 1834, 39; *Annual Register*, 1834, Chronicle, 7.
[22] Aspland, *Memoir of Robert Aspland*, 534.   [23] *Patriot*, 29 Jan. 1834, 37.
[24] Baines, *Life of Edward Baines*, 197.
[25] *Patriot*, 14 May 1834, 167; *Evangelical Magazine*, NS 12 (1834), 232.

Young Disciples, warned that 'to take a warm interest in the political discussions of the day, is in many respects unsuitable to a follower of the Lamb'. 'Religion languishes or dies in the heart that is continually agitated by political subjects.'[26] The Particular Baptist James Lister claimed that he had never seen 'one example in which devotedness to politics did not injure the spirituality and piety of the individual'.[27] The younger John Clayton argued that 'excepting on rare occasions, it is well for the ministers of the gospel of peace to abstain from political intermeddlings', and on his retirement from the ministry in 1845 claimed that for more than forty years he had avoided 'the political, which is only one form of a worldly spirit'.[28] The Methodist New Connexion forbade its ministers to take part in political discussions in 1831.[29] The North Wales Calvinistic Methodist Association, meeting at Bala in 1834, resolved on the motion of John Elias to deplore the agitation for the disestablishment of the Church of England, and urged its members to 'meddle not with them that are given to change'.[30] The Primitive Methodist Conference resolved in 1835 that no itinerant preachers should make speeches at political meetings or at parliamentary elections and that none of its chapels should be let out for 'political or religious controversy'. In the previous year the *Primitive Methodist Magazine* had published the confession of a local preacher who had admitted that he had been 'full of zeal for the separation of the Church from the State' until persuaded by a travelling preacher that 'the work of converting sinners to God' was the more important task. As a result he 'gave up politics at once'.[31]

Among Quakers there was a good deal of opposition to Friends participating in politics. The London Yearly Meeting warned Quakers against involving themselves in politics in 1818 and Thomas Shillitoe, a Quaker minister from Hitchin in Hertfordshire, urged Friends to avoid the reading of 'political publications and newspapers as much as possible'.[32] The banker and Quaker minister Joseph John Gurney was reprimanded by Norwich Monthly Meeting for speaking on behalf of his cousin, the disowned Quaker Richard Hanbury Gurney, when the latter won one of Norwich's two seats alongside William Smith in the election of 1818. For the next fourteen years Joseph Gurney remained aloof from 'the proceedings of either party and

[26] J. G. Pike, *A Guide to Young Disciples* (1823), 387–8.

[27] *Baptist Magazine*, 41 (1849), 5.

[28] *The Times*, 20 Feb. 1835; T. W. Aveling, *Memorials of the Clayton Family* (1867), 429.

[29] Leese, 'Impact of Methodism on Black Country Society', 282.

[30] Parry, 'Parliamentary Representation of Wales', 170.

[31] Wearmouth, *Methodism and Working-Class Movements* 192; *Primitive Methodist Magazine*, NS 4 (1834), 436.

[32] Isichei, *Victorian Quakers*, 188; Jones, *Later Periods of Quakerism*, i. 73.

from subscribing a single shilling to any of our elections' on account of the corruptions of Norwich politics. And when, in January 1833, Gurney was tempted to stand for Parliament, he went through 'intense conflict' before concluding that such a step would be incompatible with 'the duties of the ministry' and against the will of God.[33] When Joseph Pease was invited to stand for Parliament in 1833 his acceptance was strongly opposed by both his family and his Monthly Meeting, and when the radical wine merchant Joseph Metford wrote letters on political issues to the *Bath Journal* he was silenced as a Quaker minister in 1834.[34] In the London Yearly Meeting of 1838 there was 'a strong disposition to declare' that Quakers should not become magistrates or sit on borough corporations, and five years later it reprimanded Joseph Sturge for his activities with the Complete Suffrage Union.[35]

However, as so often happened in the nineteenth century, the issue of whether Christians should or should not take part in politics was debated with the most ferocity, and with the most serious consequences, in the Wesleyan Connexion. The Wesleyan Conference repeatedly reminded Methodists in the early 1830s that they sought a kingdom which 'is not of this world' and warned them against political partisanship.[36] But the 'no politics rule' was seen by radical Wesleyans as a means of silencing those who wished to advocate Liberal causes while allowing Methodists who supported the Tories free rein to uphold the status quo. The 'no politics rule' had not stopped Jabez Bunting from publicly opposing the election of Lord John Russell for Bedford in 1830. It did not prevent him from supporting the Tory factory reformer Michael Sadler against the Whigs Thomas Babbington Macaulay and John Marshall, junior, in Leeds in the general election of 1832.[37] Nor did it inhibit him from openly supporting the Tory Lord Sandon against the Whig Thomas Thornley in Liverpool in the same election. Bunting justified his partisanship by reference to the fact that both Thornley and Marshall were Unitarians, but what was particularly scandalous to liberal Methodists was the knowledge that Macaulay and Thornley were outspoken opponents of slavery whereas neither Sadler nor Sandon had taken a stand on the issue.[38]

Criticism of Bunting's pro-Tory stance was voiced by two newspapers launched in 1830, the *Circular to Wesleyan Methodists* and the *Christian*

---

[33] D. E. Swift, *Joseph John Gurney* (Middletown, Conn., 1961), 93; J. B. Braithwaite, *Memoirs of Joseph John Gurney* (1854), i. 478–83.

[34] *Journal of the Friends Historical Society*, 24 (1927), 45.

[35] R. F. Jones, *Later Periods of Quakerism,* ii. (1921) 945; Isichei, *Victorian Quakers*, 189; Tyrell, *Joseph Sturge*, 192–3.   [36] *Minutes of the Methodist Conferences*, vii. 74, 183.

[37] Ward, *Early Victorian Methodism*, 17.

[38] Ibid. 17 n. 3; Semmel, *Methodist Revolution*, 179–80.

Advocate. The *Circular* was published anonymously in Liverpool by David
Rowland and James Picton in the belief that the principles of the movement
for parliamentary reform 'were applicable to ecclesiastical as well as to political institutions'.[39] The more successful *Christian Advocate*, with which the
Circular merged in 1833, was founded by a group of sons of Methodist
preachers and edited by John Stephens, the son of the minister of the same
name and former Conference president who had rallied to the support of the
government in the aftermath of Peterloo. It was initially assumed that John
Stephens's parentage would be a guarantee of his paper's respectability and
the *Christian Advocate* was regarded 'in some sense as an unofficial organ of
the Connexion'.[40] But its criticisms of Bunting's leadership led to its being
condemned by Conference in 1833, and a vote of confidence was given to
Bunting's 'fidelity and integrity'. The elder John Stephens stated that he
would rather follow 'his son to the grave than that he should promulgate such
principles', and the paper soon folded.[41] Within twelve months, however,
John Stephens was to be given even more pain by the political radicalism of
another son.

Joseph Rayner Stephens, the elder brother of John, was born in 1805,
entered the Wesleyan ministry in 1825, spent four years as a missionary
in Stockholm, and returned to England in 1829 to be stationed first in
Cheltenham and, in 1832, at Ashton-under-Lyne.[42] Ashton, a town of some
14,000 people with forty large cotton firms, had a long tradition of radical
Methodism. It had been a centre of the revolt against Jeremiah Brettell and
the abortive loyal address in 1796, and as a result the New Connexion had
become the dominant form of Methodism in town.[43] Nearby Stockport had
produced both the radical Kilhamite George Beaumont in the 1790s and
the radical Independent Joseph Harrison twenty years later. Beaumont,
expelled from the New Connexion ministry for refusing to keep silent on
political issues in 1814, had five years later published a pamphlet in which he
ridiculed those preachers who 'tell us that religious people have not any thing
to do with politics'. 'For what is this but to say that kings must be infidels, and
unbelievers ministers of state; that all public questions must be discussed, all

[39] Currie, *Methodism Divided*, 62; D. A. Gowland, *Methodist Secessions: The Origins of Free
Methodism in Three Lancashire Towns*, Chetham Society (Manchester, 1979), 31.

[40] Smith, *History of Wesleyan Methodism*, iii. 188.

[41] Gregory, *Side Lights on the Conflicts of Methodism*, 131–2; Smith, *History of Wesleyan
Methodism*, iii. 189.

[42] G. J. Holyoake, *Life of Joseph Rayner Stephens* (1881), 26–41; J. T. Ward, 'Revolutionary
Tory: The Life of Joseph Rayner Stephens of Ashton-under-Lyne', *Transactions of the
Lancashire and Cheshire Antiquarian Society*, 68 (1958), 93–4.

[43] Rose, *Methodism in Ashton-under-Lyne*, i. 31–2.

public offices filled, and all public affairs managed by wicked men?'[44] These were views which Joseph Rayner Stephens, two decades later, was to endorse wholeheartedly.

If, in appointing Joseph Stephens to Ashton-under-Lyne in 1832, the Wesleyan stationing committee was hoping that he would curb radicalism in the circuit, just as his father had sought to contain radicalism in Manchester in 1819, it was to be grievously disappointed. Though in subsequent years Joseph Stephens returned part way back towards his father's Toryism, soon after his arrival in Ashton he came under the influence of Charles Hindley, a Moravian cotton manufacturer and future Liberal MP. Stephens supported Hindley's unsuccessful attempt to secure election to Parliament for Ashton in December 1832 and for a time allied himself to the radical Dissenting movement which Hindley represented. Relations between Nonconformists and Anglicans were particularly bad in Ashton, for most of the land in the town was owned by the Earl of Stamford who did his utmost to prevent Nonconformists from obtaining sites on which to build places of worship. The earl was also patron of the living of St Michael's which he had bestowed on his nephew, George Chetwode, who collected between £1,500 and £2,000 a year, lived in a vicarage in Buckinghamshire, and visited Ashton at intervals of three or four years.[45] The local tension between church and chapel combined with Hindley's influence to prompt Stephens to join the campaign for the redress of Dissenting grievances in January 1834.[46]

Stephens was not the only Wesleyan to back the United Committee's campaign. Wesleyans attended meetings calling for the redress of Dissenters' grievances at Newport in the Isle of Wight and at Launceston in Cornwall; at Petersfield in Hampshire a Wesleyan minister, Thomas Jewell, sat on a Dissenting platform; and in Birmingham a dozen Wesleyan local preachers made public their common cause with political Dissent.[47] The change that was to come over Wesleyan political attitudes in the second half of the century was presaged in the city of Durham where a meeting in support of the United Committee's campaign was held in the Wesleyan chapel in Old Elvet and a principal speaker was John Bramwell, solicitor son of William

---

[44] Stigant, 'Methodism and the Working Class', 297, citing G. Beaumont, *To the Professors of Religion* (1819).

[45] E. A. Rose, 'Ashton Churches and Chapels', in S. A. Harrop and E. A. Rose, *Victorian Ashton* (Ashton-under-Lyne, 1974), 65–6.

[46] Rose, *Methodism in Ashton-under-Lyne*, ii. 33–4.

[47] *Memorials Addressed to His Majesty's Government by Various Bodies of Dissenters* (1834), pp. xxi, xxxvi, xli; Shaw, *Cornish Methodism*, 122; *Patriot*, 16 Apr. 1834, 130.

Bramwell, and subsequently five times Liberal mayor of the city.[48] But Stephens was a minister, not a layman; his opposition to the established church was more extreme than that of his fellow Wesleyans; and it was made public in the politically sensitive area of Manchester. Stephens not only obtained a hundred signatures for a Dissenting petition from 'almost all the local preachers and leaders with other male members of the Methodist society in Ashton' but agreed to become 'corresponding secretary' of the Ashton Church Separation Society.[49] Jabez Bunting was scandalized by the 'violent and wholly unmethodistical character' of Stephens's behaviour[50] and in April the Manchester District Meeting condemned Stephens for expressing views 'at variance with the general sentiments of Mr Wesley and the Conference' and called upon him to resign his office as secretary of the Church Separation Society. When Stephens refused he was suspended from the exercise of his ministry and the matter was referred to the next Conference.[51]

Stephens's case occasioned a two-day debate on the relationship between the Wesleyan Connexion and the Church of England. Bunting maintained that Wesley 'was nearer to the Church than to Dissent' and that 'this is our proper position'. Samuel Warren argued that Wesleyans 'should be as neutral as possible, and maintain our middle position between Church and Dissent'. William Atherton commented that to say that the Methodists were indebted to the Church of England for Wesley was like saying that they were indebted to the Church of Rome for Luther. Joseph Beaumont claimed that 'Wesley's bearings towards the Church was like that of a rower in a boat; his face was always steadily fixed on the Church, but every stroke of his oars took him farther away from it'. He added that it was 'very difficult to answer for the conduct of brethren who, whilst gagging others, allow themselves to speak and do what they please'—a reference to the fact that Bunting, while condemning Stephens for his political activities, had recently written in support of the Tory candidate in a by-election at Finsbury.[52] The extent to which passions were aroused was indicated by rounds of applause which greeted the opposing sentiments of both Bunting and Atherton, an innovation at Wesleyan Conferences. But when it came to the vote only three preachers supported an amendment critical of Stephens's suspension and the action

[48] *Patriot*, 22 Jan. 1834, 30; G. E. Milburn, 'Piety, Profit, and Paternalism', *PWHS* 44 (1983–4), 72.

[49] Rose, *Methodism in Ashton-under-Lyne*, ii. 35.

[50] Ward, *Early Victorian Methodism*, 51.

[51] Rose, *Methodism in Ashton-under-Lyne*, ii. 35; Smith, *History of Wesleyan Methodism*, iii. 208–11.

[52] Gregory, *Side Lights on the Conflicts of Methodism*, 156–66; Smith, *History of Wesleyan Methodism*, iii. 219; Ward, *Early Victorian Methodism*, 76.

of the Manchester District Meeting was endorsed almost unanimously.[53] The business of Methodists, said George Marsden, was 'to save souls, not to unsettle institutions'.[54] Stephens disagreed and resigned from the Connexion.

Stephens's suspension produced yet another haemorrhage from Wesleyan Methodism. Six hundred and fifty members in the Ashton circuit refused to renew their class tickets and the Wesleyan society at Stalybridge was reduced to seven members.[55] The Oldham circuit lost 195 members and the Bolton circuit another 170.[56] From Stroud in Gloucestershire John Gordon told the president of the Wesleyan Conference that he could not 'remain a member of a body of ministers who, in their corporate and official capacity, maintain, as a "great principle", the establishment of a Church by the State'. Gordon returned to his native Black Country and organized a secession which reduced Wesleyan membership in the Dudley circuit by 1,564 and in the Stourbridge circuit by 653.[57] Old Dissenters were delighted at the evidence that even Wesleyans were coming to see the injustice of the union of Church and State. In Hexham in Northumberland Joseph Parker's Congregationalist father, a stonemason, bought a portrait of Joseph Stephens, 'framed it in maple . . . and hung it above a chest of drawers in the principal spare bedroom'.[58]

Stephens and Gordon were, however, both too extreme to act as the catalysts of a major protest movement against the Wesleyan hierarchy. Stephens tried to organize his followers into a new denomination but he became increasingly devoted to politics and increasingly violent in his language. In 1836 he took up the cause of factory reform, told his followers that he would 'preach nothing but factory sermons . . . until the question be settled', and as a result lost five of his seven meeting-houses. Stephens's espousal of the cause of factory workers brought working-class gains to compensate for middle-class losses, and a preaching plan of 1839 reveals that he had thirty lay preachers serving ten societies. But decline continued and his last two chapels, at Ashton and Stalybridge, were closed in 1856 and 1875.[59] As for John Gordon, the majority of his followers eventually united with the

---

[53] Smith, *History of Wesleyan Methodism*, iii. 219–20.
[54] Gregory, *Side Lights on the Conflicts of Methodism*, 159.
[55] Rose, *Methodism in Ashton-under-Lyne*, ii. 37.
[56] Gowland, *Methodist Secessions*, 34.
[57] Leese, 'Impact of Methodism on Black Country Society', 152.
[58] J. Parker, *A Preacher's Life* (1899), 48.
[59] Rose, *Methodism in Ashton-under-Lyne*, ii. 48–52.

Methodist New Connexion, but Gordon himself came to reject Methodism altogether and in 1837 joined the Unitarians.[60]

A more moderate focus of discontent with the leadership of Wesleyan Methodism emerged at the 1834 Conference: Dr Samuel Warren. In his early fifties and the co-author, with the elder John Stephens, of a standard work on Methodist law,[61] Warren was an unlikely rebel. In 1827 he had praised the 'maturity and perfection' of Wesleyan government and it is difficult to escape the conclusion that his emergence seven years later as the spokesman of disaffected Wesleyans was in part motivated by personal jealousy of Jabez Bunting.[62] Warren had voiced no criticism of the Wesleyan hierarchy before 1834, but he was superintendent of the Manchester, Oldham Street, circuit at the time of Joseph Rayner Stephens's suspension and had shown some sympathy with the accused at the District Meeting. During the subsequent Conference debate Warren complained of the double standards whereby Conference censured Stephens's political activities but condoned those of Bunting. 'If one brother lets off a squib, and you extinguish *him* for doing so, you ought to extinguish a brother who lets off a rocket on the other side of the street'.[63] But the issue which provoked Warren's own protest was not overtly political: it was the proposal to establish a training college for Methodist preachers.

Warren was a member of the committee which had been set up by Conference in 1833 to consider the question of the education of itinerant preachers and he had originally concurred with the committee's unanimous recommendation that Conference should establish a 'theological institution' with Bunting as its president. However, when it came to recommending tutors for the new college Warren put forward the names of two preachers— John Burdsall and Jonathan Crowther—whose nominations were opposed by the rest of the committee. It seems likely that Warren, a Classical scholar who had both an MA and a doctorate from the University of Glasgow, had nominated Burdsall and Crowther as a ploy to stake his own claim to one of the posts, and when the other members of the committee passed over his qualifications for the college he was bitterly disappointed.[64] Instead the committee proposed that Bunting, who was already secretary of the Missionary Society and president designate of the college, should be one of the college's theological tutors as well. Warren told Bunting to his face that he would never consent to 'such an extraordinary assumption of power' by one

[60] Leese, 'Impact of Methodism on Black Country Society', 195–6.
[61] Ward, *Early Victorian Methodism*, 60 n. 3.   [62] Gowland, *Methodist Secessions*, 37–8.
[63] Gregory, *Side Lights on the Conflicts of Methodism*, 167.
[64] Gowland, *Methodist Secessions*, 37.

person.[65] Was there such a 'dearth of intellect and learning amongst us', he asked of the Wesleyan Conference in 1834, 'that throughout the whole length and breadth of the Connexion, not one preacher . . . can be found to rescue this individual from being overwhelmed and smothered under this accumulation of offices?'[66]

Unwisely, however, Warren tried to subsume his objection to the concentration of power into the hands of Jabez Bunting under a general onslaught on the principle of a theological institution. It was a tactic which exposed him to charges of inconsistency and self-seeking. At the 1834 Conference Warren's amendment to postpone action on the theological institution attracted only 31 votes and a motion to implement the committee's recommendations was carried by a large majority. Warren followed up his defeat in Conference by publishing a pamphlet containing the substance of his speech and as a result was suspended from his ministerial duties by the Manchester District Meeting. Warren's supporters organized themselves into a Grand Central Association whose inaugural meeting was held in Manchester in November 1834.[67] The Association agreed, at a further meeting in Manchester in April 1835, 'that the basis of a plan for a reformation of the existing abuses of Methodism shall be the principle of the right of interference, on the part of the members of the Church, in the regulation of all its affairs'. No rule was to 'be considered binding upon the Connexion until it has the approbation of a majority of the societies, through the medium of their respective Quarterly Meetings'; circuit Quarterly Meetings were to be the final court of appeal from the leaders and local preachers' meetings 'without the interference of either District Meeting or Conference'; and lay delegates were to sit in Conference alongside the preachers.[68] There was no likelihood whatever that such proposals would be accepted by the Wesleyan Conference and Warren undermined his own position by challenging, unsuccessfully, the legality of his exclusion from the pulpits of the Oldham Street and Oldham Road chapels. The Conference of 1835 expelled Warren and two of his supporters from its membership and the Wesleyan Methodist Association became yet another secessionist Methodist denomination.

Within two years the Wesleyan Methodist Association had 21,262 members, making it the third largest Methodist denomination in England after the Wesleyans and the Primitives.[69] Support for the Association was particu-

[65] Smith, *History of Wesleyan Methodism*, iii. 233–4.   [66] *HMC* iv. 421.

[67] Smith, *History of Wesleyan Methodism*, iii. 244, 255, 262.

[68] Ibid. 279, 555; M. Baxter, *Methodism: Memorials of the United Methodist Free Churches* (1865), 254–6.

[69] Currie, Gilbert, and Horsley, *Churches and Churchgoers*, 141.

larly strong in Cornwall and south Lancashire. In Manchester Wesleyan membership fell from 7,488 in 1834 to 4,820 in 1835, and that of Warren's old Oldham Street circuit from 2,145 to 650. When Warren's successor, Robert Newton, tried to take over his pulpits he had to be ushered into Oldham Street by a police escort through a hostile crowd, and at Oldham Road the service was disrupted and Newton was chased down the road by a chanting mob.[70] In Rochdale Wesleyan membership fell from 1,911 in 1835 to 745 in 1836, and two-thirds of the class leaders and local preachers and a majority of Sunday school teachers joined the Association.[71] In Camelford in Cornwall a wealthy Boscastle merchant named Thomas Roseveare, a devotee of the *Christian Advocate*, took 634 of the Wesleyan circuit's 702 members into the Association.[72] And the Association was also joined by some of the smaller secessionist groups: the Leeds Protestant Methodists, Y Wesle Bach of Anglesey and Caernarfonshire, the Arminian Methodists of Derby, the Independent Primitive Methodists of Scarborough, and the supporters of Joseph Rayner Stephens in Oldham.[73]

Such was the ground swell of support for the Association that it was evident that Warren's protest against the founding of the theological institution was but the occasion and not the cause of a wider revolt against the rule of Bunting and the Wesleyan Conference.[74] The demand for popular participation in the affairs of state which issued in the Great Reform Act led to lay demands for a share in the government of the church in the same way that radical political views in the 1790s had helped to provoke the secession of Alexander Kilham. John Bicknell, a Wesleyan preacher in the Hull circuit, who considered that the constitution of the Connexion was 'already *too liberal*', wrote to Bunting in March 1835 that the unnecessary and injurious Reform Act had produced 'such a lust of power in a considerable number of our people, that it is becoming very difficult . . . to exercise that pastoral authority . . . which is indispensable to order and good government'.[75] And to prove his point in October the Liverpool coffee dealer Richard Farrer contrasted the representation offered to the people in Parliament by the Reform Act, and soon to be offered to them in town councils through the Municipal Corporations Act, with the 'irresponsible and irresistible power' of the Wesleyan Conference.[76] The divisions revealed within Methodism by the

[70] Gowland, *Methodist Secessions*, 43–4.   [71] Ibid. 72–5.

[72] Shaw, *History of Cornish Methodism*, 82–3.

[73] Marcroft, *Unitarian Chapel, Oldham*, 59–63.

[74] Gowland, *Methodist Secessions*, 104; Bowmer, *Pastor and People*, 120–1.

[75] Ward, *Early Victorian Methodism*, 125.

[76] Baxter, *Memorials of the United Methodist Free Churches*, 451; Gowland, *Methodist Secessions*, 127.

formation of the Association in 1835 reflected differences of political opinion. In Manchester, Liverpool, and Rochdale those Methodists who were later to go over to the Association 'gave solid support to the Whig candidates' in the general election of 1832, while those chapel trustees who remained loyal to Wesleyanism were to give overwhelming support to Tory candidates in Liverpool in 1835 and 1837 and in Manchester in 1839.[77] Robert Newton, Warren's successor in the Oxford Street circuit, travelled to Tavistock in 1835 to campaign against Lord John Russell's re-election to parliament.[78] In Rochdale, said one of the Association's leaders, 'most of those who go to the Association chapel are Radicals; there are hardly any Tories amongst us'.[79]

However, the subsequent history of the Association, as that of the New Connexion and Joseph Rayner Stephens's chapels, showed that a Methodist secession motivated by political protest rather than by evangelistic zeal would never have the dynamic impetus for growth of the parent Connexion. Whereas the formation of the Association made scarcely a dent in the rising graph of Wesleyan membership, which in England increased by over 60,000 in the fifteen years after Warren's expulsion, membership of the Association peaked at 23,493 in 1839 and then went into a steady decline.[80] The Association leaders in Liverpool quarrelled amongst themselves, sacked their first preacher soon after his appointment, and then went off to join other denominations. Some attached themselves to a revivalist group known as the Christian Society which Robert Aitkin collected at Hope Hall, others went back to the Wesleyans, and in fifteen years Association membership in Liverpool fell by nearly a thousand.[81] The Association in Manchester also lost members to Aitkin's Christian Society and others went off to the Quakers and the Mormons.[82] Samuel Warren himself soon tired of the Association of which he was elected president in 1836. From the start he had disliked the Association's rule that circuits should be self-governing without reference to the annual assembly. And he was further annoyed in 1836 when the Association's assembly resolved that it should be composed of representatives elected by the circuits in proportion to their membership. Circuits were to be free to choose either ministers or laymen, and ministers were thus denied guaranteed representation. Warren decided that this was making too many concessions to democracy, resigned from the Association, and went on

---

[77] Gowland, *Methodist Secessions*, 123, 128, 171–2.
[78] Ibid. 124–5; Gregory, *Side Lights on the Conflicts of Methodism*, 202.
[79] Ward, *Religion and Society*, 169.
[80] Currie, Gilbert, and Horsley, *Churches and Churchgoers*, 141.
[81] Gowland, *Methodist Secessions*, 105–8.   [82] Ibid. 57–8.

to join the Church of England as vicar of the downtown parish of Ancoats in Manchester.[83] The leadership of the Association thus devolved on Robert Eckett, a small, rotund, but wealthy Yorkshire builder who in 1839 gave up his business to enter the Association ministry. Eckett steadfastly maintained free representation and circuit independence as the twin pillars of Association Methodism, principles which prevented union with the Methodist New Connexion in talks in 1836–7 and which delayed union of the two liberal Methodist denominations until 1907.[84]

The importance of the Wesleyan Methodist Association was essentially political, not religious: even more than the New Connexion it gave institutional form to a Methodism that was Dissenting and Liberal, not quasi-Anglican and Tory. The Association's new chapel in Baillie Street, Rochdale, attracted some of the most important manufacturers in the town: George Ashworth, woollen manufacturer, Thomas Booth and Abraham Tweedale, cotton manufacturers, James and John Hoyle, corn merchants, John Howard and Stephen Broad, woolstaplers, and, above all, John Petrie, whose engineering works manufactured the first steam engines in the region.[85] Their devotion to commerce was illustrated by their decision to finance the building of Baillie Street, which cost £6,200, by issuing shares of £1 which, it was hoped, would yield a dividend of up to 7½ per cent from the chapel's pew-rents.[86] The scheme failed to raise much more than a third of the total cost of the chapel and was abandoned in 1841, but the very fact of its conception was an illustration of the enterprise, wealth, and self-confidence of the Baillie Street leadership. And it was these same families who provided much of the leadership of Rochdale Liberalism; who in the 1840s sat on the board of the town's improvement commissioners; and who, in the thirty-seven years after the town's incorporation in 1856, gave it sixteen of its mayors.[87] What was true of Rochdale was true of many other English towns in the mid-nineteenth century. The Great Reform Act of 1832 had given the Dissenters influence but not power. The Municipal Corporations Act of 1835 was to give them power.

---

[83] Ibid. 59.   [84] Currie, *Methodism Divided*, 77–8.

[85] Gowland, *Methodist Secessions*, 73–5.

[86] Ibid. 80–1. Similar schemes were launched to pay for the WMA chapels in Liskeard and Redruth in Cornwall and in Armley and Holbeck in Leeds (Shaw, *History of Cornish Methodism*, 39; Dews, 'Methodism in Leeds', 688).

[87] D. A. Gowland, 'Methodist Secessions and Social Conflict in South Lancashire, 1830–1857', Ph.D. thesis (Manchester, 1966), 325–7.

3. 'THE STEAM-ENGINE FOR THE MILL BUILT BY
PARLIAMENTARY REFORM':
THE MUNICIPAL CORPORATIONS ACT

The most important political advance achieved by Dissenters in the 1830s, indeed in the whole of the nineteenth century, had not figured in either John Wilks's or the United Committee's list of Dissenting grievances: it was the reform of England's municipal corporations.

Although Dissenters had controlled the corporations of Nottingham and Bridport for most of the previous hundred years, and had sat on nearly thirty other corporations in the course of the eighteenth century, by the time of the passing of the Great Reform Act the overwhelming majority of corporations were under Anglican control. Since most corporations were self-elected, the repeal of the Test and Corporation Acts in 1828, though a great symbolic victory for Dissent, made no practical difference to their composition. When the Unitarian Ralph Eddowes had challenged the right of the corporation of Chester to fill its own vacancies in the early 1790s, he had lost the case in the House of Lords, was faced with heavy legal costs, and in 1794 emigrated to the United States.[88] And since, in numerous towns, politics in the late eighteenth and early nineteenth centuries had revolved round a struggle between Anglican-dominated corporations facing an opposition consisting of Low Church Anglicans and Dissenters, Anglican control of corporations meant Tory control.[89] Until 1832 municipal corporations controlled the representation of numerous parliamentary boroughs, directly in the case of twenty-nine boroughs and indirectly through the power to create freemen in many more,[90] and their influence was wielded in a blatantly partisan fashion. In 1817 the Whig–Dissenting corporation of Nottingham began to create honorary burgesses from among its supporters who did not live in the town in order to swell the Whig vote in parliamentary elections, and it was claimed that by 1826 over 1,200 extra votes had thus been manufactured.[91] The Tory–Anglican corporation of Leicester responded by creating 800 new Tory freemen in readiness for the 1826 general election, and by agreeing to pay £7,000 towards the expenses of one of the Tory candidates. According to the Dissenting *Leicester Chronicle* the corporation spent £19,550 from its

---

[88] W. B. Kenrick, *Chronicles of a Nonconformist Family* (Birmingham, 1932), 73–4, 78.

[89] Namier and Brooke, *History of Parliament, 1754–1790*, i. 12, 28, 67, 114, 253, 260, 317, 322, 342, 425; Patterson, *Radical Leicester*, 63, 110–11; Bradley, *Religion, Revolution and Radicalism*, 413.

[90] Brock, *Great Reform Act*, 22–3.   [91] Thomis, *Politics and Society in Nottingham*, 146.

funds to secure the election of two Tory MPs, and as a result had to mortgage part of its property for a loan of £10,000.[92]

Consequently one of the first tasks of Grey's Whig government after the passing of the Great Reform Act was to appoint first a select committee of the House of Commons and then, in July 1833, a Royal Commission, to inquire into municipal corporations. The Royal Commission was itself a partisan body: eighteen of its twenty members were either Whigs or Radicals and its secretary was Joseph Parkes, the Unitarian lawyer who, during the Reform Bill crisis, had acted as intermediary between the government and the Birmingham Political Union. Parkes applied himself to the work of the commission with efficiency and enthusiasm, determined that 'the most important and popular results will follow this enquiry—most beneficial to the ministry, and useful in accelerating good government'.[93] But despite the commission's one-sided political complexion, the essential justice of its aims and its work is revealed by the fact that Sir Robert Peel, the Tory leader, in his Tamworth Manifesto of 1834 pledged himself not to interrupt its work, and fulfilled that pledge during his short-lived ministry of December 1834–April 1835.[94]

The commission's report was published in April 1835, the month in which the Whigs under Viscount Melbourne returned to office. The commission damned the existing corporations as 'self-elected municipal councils whose powers are subject to no popular control', and which used those powers to divert local revenues 'away from their legitimate use'.[95] The government accepted the commission's recommendation that 178 corporations should be swept away and be replaced by elected town councils, and Joseph Parkes was jubilant that he was successful in persuading first the commission and then the cabinet to accept the principle of household suffrage. Parkes was sorry that the government proposed that one-third of the councillors should seek re-election annually instead of the whole council retiring every three years, and that household suffrage was conditional on a three-year rate-paying qualification.[96] The House of Lords further diluted the democratic intentions of the commission by passing an amendment to ensure that a quarter of the new councils should consist of aldermen elected by the rest of the council for

[92] Brock, *Great Reform Act*, 26–7; Patterson, *Radical Leicester*, 146, 150, 155; D. Fraser, 'The Press in Leicester, c.1790–1850', *Transactions of the Leicester Archaeological Society*, 42 (1966–7), 62.

[93] G. B. M. Finlayson, 'The Municipal Corporation Commission and Report, 1833–5', *Bulletin of the Institute of Historical Research*, 36 (1963), 41.

[94] Ibid. 48   [95] Ibid. 43.   [96] Buckley, *Joseph Parkes*, 121–2.

a period of six years. But, by the Municipal Corporations Act, wrote Parkes to Lord Durham, 'We have again incalculably increased the democratical action of the people and at the same time weakened the coercive power of the government'. The Act was 'the steam-engine for the mill built by Parliamentary reform'.[97]

For Dissenters Parkes's analogy proved to be exact. Though in practice the Municipal Corporations Act proved to be less democratic than Parkes had hoped, and in scores of towns the three-year rate-paying qualification limited the municipal franchise to fewer people than possessed the vote for parliamentary elections,[98] the Act did for Dissenters what neither the repeal of the Test and Corporation Acts nor the Great Reform Act had achieved: it gave them political power. In at least fifty towns throughout England and Wales the first elections for the new councils in December 1835 issued in dramatic changes of control: Tory corporations were replaced by Liberal councils, and in many of the new councils Dissenters now exercised a preponderant influence.[99] In Leicester, which had been singled out for special opprobrium by the commissioners, the old corporation had been entirely Anglican and Tory. Of Leicester's 56 new councillors and aldermen, 40 were Nonconformists and only 4 were Tories.[100] In Liverpool the Liberals won 43 council seats against the Tories' 5 and a majority of the Liberals were Nonconformists.[101] In Leeds the Liberals won 42 out of 48 council seats and over half the new councillors were Dissenters.[102] In Coventry Liberals won 44 out of 48 council and aldermanic seats and of those 28 were held by Dissenters.[103] In Stockport 41 of the 42 new councillors were Liberals and most of those were Nonconformists.[104] In Hull of the 39 victorious Liberal candidates 16 were Dissenters and only 3 Tories were elected to the new council.[105] In Preston 11 of the 20 Liberals who now controlled the council

---

[97] Ibid. 129–30.

[98] B. Keith-Lucas, *The English Local Government Franchise* (Oxford, 1952), 60–1.

[99] The most complete list of Liberal victories is printed in the *Patriot*, 30 Dec. 1835, 434, 437; 6 Jan. 1836, 3. The *Patriot*'s list is supplemented by Keith-Lucas, *Local Government Franchise*, 57.

[100] Patterson, *Radical Leicester*, 214–15. Leicester's new council consisted of 16 Anglicans, 12 Unitarians, 12 Baptists, 10 Independents, 3 Quakers, 2 Wesleyans, and 1 member of Lady Huntingdon's Connexion.

[101] Sellers, 'Liverpool Nonconformity', 302.   [102] Binfield, *So Down to Prayers*, 61.

[103] P. Searby, *Coventry Politics in the Age of the Chartists* (Coventry, 1964), 5.

[104] P. T. Phillips, *The Sectarian Spirit: Sectarianism, Society, and Politics in Victorian Cotton Towns* (Toronto, 1982), 92.

[105] R. A. Smith, 'The Passing of the Municipal Corporations Act', MA thesis (University of East Anglia, 1974), 165.

were Dissenters.[106] In Banbury the Liberals won every council seat and the new council was dominated by Unitarians.[107] In Lyme Regis the Liberals again won all 12 council seats and 9 of the new councillors were Nonconformists.[108] In Saffron Walden 9 of the 16 new councillors were either Quakers or Independents.[109] For Joseph Parkes the municipal election results were 'the greatest political revolution ever accomplished'.[110]

Not every council changed hands in December 1835. The Tories retained control in boroughs such as Guildford, Hertford, Salisbury, Southampton, Grantham, and Stamford where Anglicans outnumbered Dissenters and they gained control of the strongly Anglican city of Gloucester from the Liberals.[111] In Bristol the drawing of ward boundaries on the basis of rateable value rather than population gave the Conservatives control of the city for the rest of the century.[112] In Exeter the Liberals and Conservatives won an equal number of council seats, but the Liberal contingent was reduced by one when a Quaker declined to take the qualifying oath to enable him to take his council seat, and the Conservatives went on to fill 11 of the 12 aldermanic seats with their supporters. But even in Exeter the Conservatives felt it prudent to elect as first mayor of the reformed corporation a Tory Unitarian ironmonger named Sam Kingdon.[113] Two other councils did not change hands in 1835: the two corporations which had been controlled by Dissenters before 1835, Nottingham and Bridport, continued to be dominated by them afterwards. In Nottingham 27 Nonconformists were elected to the new council against 18 Anglicans,[114] and in Bridport 15 Liberals and Dissenters were returned against 3 Tories and Churchmen.[115]

The denominational balance within Dissent varied from town to town. The majority of Nonconformist councillors in Liverpool were Unitarians and after Manchester became a corporate town in 1838 its council was also dominated by Unitarians who provided ten of the town's first twenty-eight mayors.[116] The apolitical attitude of the Wesleyans was reflected in the fact that

---

[106] Ibid. 165.   [107] P. Horn, *The Rural World, 1780–1850* (1980), 197.

[108] *The Times,* 4 Jan. 1836.   [109] Davidoff and Hall, *Family Fortunes,* 49.

[110] D. Fraser, *Municipal Reform and the Industrial City* (Leicester, 1982), 5, citing W. E. S. Thomas, *The Philosophical Radicals* (1979), 289–90.

[111] *The Times,* 20, 30, 31 Dec. 1835, 1, 2, Jan. 1836; A. T. Patterson, *A History of Southampton* (Southampton, 1971), ii. 23–4.

[112] D. Fraser, *Power and Authority in the Victorian City* (Oxford, 1979), 114–15.

[113] R. Newton, *Victorian Exeter, 1837–1914* (Leicester, 1968), 6–7, 30–1.

[114] The Nonconformists consisted of 8 Baptists, 8 Independents, 7 Unitarians, and 4 Methodists (J. C. Weller, 'The Revival of Religion in Nottingham, 1780–1850', BD thesis (Nottingham, 1957), 176).

[115] *Patriot,* 30 Dec. 1835, 434.

[116] H. McLachlan, *Essays and Addresses* (Manchester, 1950), 103.

Methodists were underrepresented in all the new councils, and many Quakers shared the attitude of the Friends of Newcastle upon Tyne who resolved in 1835 that 'no member of this society can consistently accept the office of alderman, town clerk or councillor in any borough'.[117] But the composition of many of the new councils suggests that those Baptists and Congregationalists who had been urging their co-religionists to eschew political activity were losing the argument. Seven of the first nine mayors of the reformed Bridport council were Independents; the Baptists had as many seats as the Unitarians on the Leicester council in 1836; the largest Dissenting contingent on the Hull council came from the Fish Street Independent church; and after Bradford received its charter of incorporation in 1847 five of the town's first eight mayors worshipped at Horton Lane Congregational chapel.[118] From the beginning of the century the Unitarians of the High Pavement chapel in Nottingham had had to share power with the Congregationalists of Castle Gate and the Particular Baptists of George Street,[119] and in the council elections of 1835 both the Baptists and Congregationalists won more seats than the Unitarians. The days when political Dissent could be equated with rational Dissent were over.

The change in the composition of councils wrought by the Municipal Corporations Act did not, however, bring any immediate improvement in the government of the towns for whose benefit the Act had been passed. The Act permitted, but did not compel, the new corporations to take over responsibility for the paving, cleaning, and lighting of streets from the improvement commissioners who had hitherto been in charge of such functions, and it imposed only one new obligation on the corporations, the establishment of a police force.[120] The revenues as well as the powers of the new corporations were severely limited. The unreformed Whig corporation in Nottingham and the Tory corporation in Leicester both bequeathed to their successors debts of over £20,000, while the Tory corporation in Leeds paid its entire balance of £7,000 into a trust fund for Anglican churches and charities and left not a penny to its Dissenting-controlled successor.[121] Some of the largest of the

---

[117] J. W. Steel, *A Historical Sketch of the Society of Friends in Newcastle and Gateshead* (Newcastle, 1899), i. 80.

[118] Short, *Respectable Society*, 62; Ram, 'Dissenters in the East and West Ridings', 183; A. Elliott, 'Municipal Government in Bradford', in D. Fraser, *Municipal Reform and the Industrial City* (Leicester, 1982), 142.

[119] Thomis, *Politics and Society in Nottingham*, 135, 138; Church, *Economic and Social Change in a Midland Town*, 167–8.

[120] E. P. Hennock, *Fit and Proper Persons* (1973), 186–7; Fraser, *Power and Authority*, 70–1.

[121] Church, *Economic and Social Change in a Midland Town*, 180; Patterson, *Radical Leicester*, 210; Fraser, *Power and Authority*, 55.

manufacturing towns such as Birmingham, Bolton, Bradford, and Manchester did not even have corporations in 1835 and in each of these towns Dissenters were in the forefront of the campaigns to secure charters of incorporation.[122]

Birmingham, Bolton, and Manchester all received their charters in 1838, and Bradford in 1847, and by degrees both the new and the reformed corporations began to expand their activities. The initiative in attempts to improve the urban environment was often take by Dissenters. The Leeds council took over the functions of the town's improvement commissioners in 1842, and although it took the cholera epidemic of 1849 to persuade the council to accept responsibility for the town's sewerage, the council fought a long campaign to acquire control of the Leeds water supply.[123] A council committee under the chairmanship of George Goodman, a Baptist woolstapler, recommended in 1836 that the town's water supply should be placed under municipal control; opposition by Tory shareholders in the Leeds Waterworks Company led to a compromise in 1837 whereby the council was allowed to appoint half the members on the board; and the Waterworks Company was finally bought up by the council in 1852.[124]

Dissenters could not always be relied on to give first priority to the health of their towns. The Nonconformists who controlled the Leicester town council were divided into 'Economists' and 'Improvers', but the latter, led by the Unitarian hosier brothers John and William Biggs were more concerned to 'improve' Leicester with a new town hall, post office, and cattle market than by providing it with adequate water and sewerage systems. It was, however, the Biggses' fellow Unitarian, the worsted manufacturer Joseph Whetstone, who led the opposition to their schemes of urban aggrandizement and who took the initiative in persuading the council to constitute itself as the local board of health in 1849. This action in its turn led to the passing of the Leicester Sewerage Act of 1851 and to the completion of the town's first sewerage scheme by 1855.[125] Similarly the Dissenters who controlled the Nottingham corporation were responsible both for frustrating the town's development before 1845, by opposing the enclosure of the common land on the town's periphery, and for the urban improvements which followed. One of the chief proponents of the moves which led to the Nottingham Enclosure

---

[122] Bushrod, 'Unitarianism in Birmingham', 224; Phillips, *The Sectarian Spirit*, 28; D. James, 'William Byles and the *Bradford Observer*', in D. G. Wright and J. A. Jowitt, *Victorian Bradford* (Bradford, 1982), 125–6; Baker, *Memorials of a Dissenting Chapel*, 117.

[123] Fraser, *Power and Authority*, 61–6.

[124] D. Fraser, *Urban Politics in Victorian England* (Leicester, 1976), 155–9.

[125] Patterson, *Radical Leicester*, 330–41, 348–9, 370; Fraser, *Urban Politics*, 166–9.

Act of 1845 was the Baptist lace manufacturer William Felkin and it was another Baptist, Alderman John Heard, who took the initiative in the setting up of a committee to investigate the town's health in 1847.[126] As a result of the committee's findings a sanitary committee was appointed under Felkin's chairmanship, and it was so successful in draining and paving courts and alleys, and in demolishing houses built above privies, that it was able to claim credit for the fact that Nottingham largely escaped the cholera epidemic of 1849.[127] In smaller towns, too, Dissenters were prominent in endeavours to improve public health. In Aberdare in Glamorgan the initiative in persuading the town to apply for the setting up of a board of health, an application which was finally successful in 1854, was taken by Dr Thomas Price, minister of the Carmel Baptist church.[128] And in Wisbech in Cambridgeshire another Baptist, George Dawbarn, who was mayor in 1864, was primarily responsible for improving the town's drainage, lighting, and water supplies.[129]

Urban improvement was, however, far from the thoughts of most political Dissenters in the 1830s. Though in retrospect the Municipal Corporations Act stands out as the most substantial political gain of Dissenters in the first two-thirds of the nineteenth century, and though it subsequently provided some aspiring Dissenting politicians with their first political experience before embarking on careers at Westminster, the prime focus of Dissenters' political interest in the 1830s was not their borough corporation. It was their parish vestry.

4. 'FOR THE SUPPORT OF A CORRUPT CHURCH': CHURCH RATES

All ratepayers in England and Wales had the right to attend meetings of the parish vestry and their consent was necessary for expenditure on poor relief or on the fabric and running costs of the parish church.[130] Money for the latter was raised by means of a church rate levied on all ratepayers and until the second decade of the nineteenth century it was rarely a source of conflict. Quakers sometimes refused to pay church rates as they refused to pay tithes,

---

[126] Harrison, 'Baptists of Nottinghamshire', ii. 948–52.
[127] Church, *Economic and Social Change in a Midland Town*, 194–6.
[128] I. G. Jones, 'Dr. Thomas Price and the Election of 1868 in Merthyr Tydfil', *Welsh History Review*, 2 (1964–5), 160.
[129] Binfield, 'Nonconformity in the Eastern Counties', 458.
[130] Fraser, *Urban Politics*, 25.

and in theory they could be disowned for agreeing to pay for the maintenance of the established church.[131] However, by the second half of the eighteenth century the Meeting for Sufferings was making frequent complaints of Friends' laxity 'as to the payment of tithes and steeple-house rates' and there were well-tried ways of avoiding conflict over tithes, such as having them paid by a neighbouring farmer.[132] The Tithe Commutation Act of 1836, which replaced the tithe by a rent charge, led to a further dilution of the Quaker testimony against tithes for, outside Wales, the new charge was paid by landowners rather than by farmers, and in 1873 the London Yearly Meeting finally abrogated the ban on payment of tithes.[133]

By contrast the second quarter of the nineteenth century witnessed a growing protest against church rates, and it was a protest in which Quakers were ultimately joined by a majority of Old Dissenters and by many Methodists as well. Outside rural Wales the question of tithes was a problem only for the consciences of a dwindling band of Quaker farmers, but the issue of church rates was an affront to the principles and pockets of a rapidly growing number of urban Dissenters. What turned the scruples of a handful of Quakers into a mass protest movement was the government's decision, in 1818 and 1824, to grant £1.5 million for the building of new Anglican churches, and its abortive attempt, in 1828, to force ratepayers in existing parishes to pay for the upkeep of the new parish churches as well as for the old.[134] By the 1830s church rates were raising £560,000 a year for the established church,[135] and of all the Dissenting grievances of the second quarter of the nineteenth century the issue of church rates was by far the most deeply resented. Fifty years later Joseph Lawson of Pudsey recalled the disputes of the 1830s with enduring bitterness. Though the established church 'had so many favours and advantages in the shape of national wealth and royal patronage and privileges' it 'compelled all those who had either chapels of their own to support, or those who attended neither church nor chapel, to help pay for the washing of the clergyman's surplice, the ringing of bells, for church repairs, and for the wine church people drank at sacrament'. 'Such barefaced robbery made a deep impression' on the minds of the youth of Pudsey, and they concluded 'that the people who went to Pudsey church

---

[131] Rowntree, *Quakerism, Past and Present*, 24.

[132] Jones, *Later Periods of Quakerism*, i. 153–5; E. J. Evans, *The Contentious Tithe* (1976), 59–61.

[133] Isichei, *Victorian Quakers*, 149–50.

[134] Elliott, 'Protestant Denominations in Leeds', 197–8; Ram, 'Dissenters in the East and West Ridings', 199–201.

[135] Machin, *Politics and the Churches*, 44.

were not religious folk at all'. 'They appeared to us usurpers of power, hard and cruel dictators, gathering where they had not sown.'[136]

There were three avenues of redress open to Dissenters in their struggle against church rates: they could seek to obtain their abolition by Act of Parliament; failing that they could end their imposition at parish level by taking control of their local vestry; and failing that they could publicize the injustice of church rates by refusing to pay and by allowing their goods to be seized and sold in public to cover the charge. Viscount Melbourne, who succeeded Earl Grey as Whig prime minister in July 1834, was more inclined than his predecessor to satisfy what he regarded as reasonable Dissenting demands. In August Melbourne asked four of his ministers to prepare legislation for the redress of Dissenting grievances, and although the plans were interrupted by William IV's dismissal of Melbourne's government in November, the return of the Whigs to office in April 1835 was followed by Melbourne's appointment of a committee in September to try to settle the Dissenters' claims.[137] In 1836 the government satisfied two of the six grievances against which the United Committee had been campaigning since 1833, and went some way to meeting the Dissenting case on a third. The passing of the Marriage Act legalized marriages in Dissenting chapels; the establishment of the Civil Registry of Births, Marriages, and Deaths removed the legal disabilities which had hitherto attended Nonconformist baptisms; and the granting of a charter to the University of London gave to Dissenters for the first time the opportunity of obtaining a degree at an English university.

Satisfaction of the Dissenting complaint against church rates proved, however, to be much more difficult. Dissenters had opposed Althorp's abortive attempt in 1834 to replace church rates with a charge on the land tax on the ground that parish churches would still be supported by public money. Three years later another Whig Chancellor of the Exchequer, Thomas Spring Rice, proposed to abolish church rates and to pay for the maintenance of parish churches by revising the terms on which church lands were leased. Since Spring Rice's bill involved raising additional revenue from the Church's own resources rather than from taxation it was supported by Dissenters and, for the same reason, was opposed by a minority of Anglican Whigs. The government had a majority of only twenty-three on the bill's first reading and it fell to five on the second. The death of William IV in June 1837 prevented the bill's further progress and Whig losses in the subsequent general election killed any prospect that the government would reintroduce it in the new

---

[136] Lawson, *Progress in Pudsey*, 87–8.

[137] R. Brent, 'The Whigs and Protestant Dissent in the Decade of Reform: The Case of Church Rates, 1833–41', *English Historical Review*, 102 (1987), 900–1.

Parliament. It was Melbourne's belief that the issue had cost the Whigs seats in rural areas where 'the church rate is no burden . . . and where the Dissenters are not strong nor collected together'.[138]

One of the reasons for Dissenting opposition to Althorp's abortive bill of 1834 was the knowledge that the substitution of a national tax for a local rate in support of parish churches would remove from Dissenters the opportunity of frustrating that support at local level. Dissenters may not have been able to persuade Parliament to abolish church rates, but if they could secure control of their parish vestry they could prevent the imposition of a church rate on their own locality. In 1819 a meeting of the ratepayers in Sheffield parish church refused to allow the levy of a 2*d*. rate on the grounds 'that the expenses of providing necessaries of the performance of divine service ought to be defrayed by the pew owners, who have excluded the rest of the parishioners from the use of the church'.[139] In Manchester in 1820 the parish vestry refused by 720 votes to 418 to sanction a church rate for new parish churches.[140] In Leeds in 1827 the parish vestry adjourned without approving a rate; in 1833 Dissenters were elected as churchwardens, with Edward Baines as chairman of the vestry; and henceforward no church rate was levied in the town.[141] But most significant of all were two meetings held in St Martin's parish church in Birmingham in the second half of 1832. In August a meeting of parishioners which filled St Martin's to overflowing voted to petition Parliament to relieve ratepayers from compulsory church rates.[142] In October an equally crowded meeting refused to approve a 3*d*. rate.[143] And when the decision of the parish vestry was challenged by Anglicans in a poll of ratepayers, the rate was rejected by 6,699 votes to 1,723.[144]

The decision of the Birmingham parish vestry in October 1832 prompted *The Times* to warn that the 'existing establishment of the Church of England is now in serious peril',[145] and it encouraged Dissenters in hundreds of other towns to take control of their vestries. Church rates were refused in June 1833 at Chatham; in July at Chard; in August at Gateshead, Tavistock, and St Mildred's, Canterbury; in September at Tiverton, St Michael's, Coventry, and in the West Riding towns of Attercliffe, Hunslet, Morley, and Selby.[146]

[138] Brent, 'Whigs and Protestant Dissent', 903–6.
[139] Wickham, *Church and People in an Industrial City*, 71.   [140] Fraser, *Urban Politics*, 37.
[141] Ram, 'Dissenters in East and West Ridings', 199–203; D. Fraser (ed.), *A History of Modern Leeds* (Manchester, 1980), 252.
[142] *Patriot*, 15 Aug. 1832, 239.   [143] *The Times*, 8 Oct. 1832.   [144] Ibid. 17 Dec. 1834.
[145] Ibid. 9 Oct. 1832.
[146] *Patriot*, 12 June 1833, 210; 31 July, 263; 7 Aug., 275; 28 Aug., 298; 18 Sept., 319, 322; *The Times*, 27 Aug.; 23 Sept.; 24 Sept. 1833.

Thereafter the trickle of vestries refusing to approve church rates became a flood. In some towns, as in four parishes in the Tory stronghold of Southampton in 1841, attempts to refuse church rates were defeated in the parish vestry.[147] In others Anglicans were able to counter an adverse vote in the vestry with a poll of ratepayers in which, thanks to Sturge Bourne's Act of 1818, wealthy ratepayers had an additional vote for every £25 they were rated up to a maximum of six votes.[148] Plural voting thus saved the church rate in Brighton in 1836. A rate was refused by the Brighton parish vestry in 1835 and the decision confirmed in a poll, but in a poll in the following year Sturge Bourne's Act had the effect of reversing the popular verdict of the ratepayers. Whereas 994 people voted against the rate and only 704 for it, the plural voting provision of the 1818 Act gave 1,702 votes for the church rate and 1,389 against.[149] However, in the overwhelming majority of cases attempts by Dissenters to prevent the levying of church rates by parish vestries were successful: in the twenty years from 1831 there were 632 challenges to the church rate, and in 484 of these cases the church rate was refused.[150]

The church rate contest was particularly bitter in Manchester. Having persuaded the vestry to refuse a church rate for new parish churches in 1820 the Dissenters were defeated five years later when a rate for new silver plate was approved. In 1833 the church rate was defeated both in the vestry and in a subsequent poll by five votes, but the decision was reversed on a scrutiny called by the wealthy Wesleyan businessman and lifelong friend of Jabez Bunting, James Wood.[151] A second poll was held in 1834 which George Hadfield claimed caused a stir greater than that 'at any election for Members of Parliament'. 'Mills were stopped that men might vote, bands of music preceded long lines of voters, and waggons and carts full of voters poured in from the out townships, amidst loud cheers from the people.'[152] The rate was again defeated in the poll, by 7,119 votes to 5,897, and again reversed on scrutiny. However, in 1835 the Anglicans in Manchester tired of the struggle and gave up the attempt to levy a compulsory rate.[153]

Similar passions were aroused in Rochdale. When a vestry meeting was called to consider levying a rate in June 1839 the church was soon filled and 'hundreds of parishioners were not able to enter the church in consequence of every available space of standing room being occupied'. The rate was

---

[147] Patterson, *History of Southampton*, ii. 77.
[148] Keith-Lucas, *Local Government Franchise*, 23–4.
[149] *The Times*, 21 Dec. 1835; 30 Nov. 1836.   [150] Chadwick, *Victorian Church*, i. 152.
[151] *Patriot*, 5 June 1833, 199; 14 Aug. 1833, 281.
[152] Machin, *Politics and the Churches*, 45.
[153] Read, *Peterloo*, 28–9; Ward, *Religion and Society*, 178–82; Fraser, *Urban Politics*, 37–40.

opposed on a show of hands by two to one but the vicar called another meeting a fortnight later in an attempt to reverse the decision and 'about a thousand persons waited in the churchyard for about an hour, in the midst of incessant rain, until the doors were opened'. An amendment opposing a rate was again carried by an overwhelming majority, but in a subsequent poll of ratepayers plural-voting enabled the rate to be approved by 2,897 votes to 2,886.[154] In the following year the rate was defeated in a poll by 4,047 votes to 3,981 but the vicar chose to ignore the result and called for a second poll. This time the anti-rate party brought into Rochdale 'almost seven hundred of the operatives of Messrs. Fielden of Todmorden, who were regularly dragooned, and walked through the streets with a band of music at their head', while the Anglicans countered by opening the public houses 'in all parts of the parish where free drink and refreshments . . . were liberally distributed to all who would promise to vote for the rates'. The church rate was approved by 6,594 votes to 6,481, but it was a Pyrrhic victory. Such was the level of disturbance that the local Tories called out the troops to calm the situation and after 1841 no further attempt was made to levy a compulsory rate on the citizens of Rochdale.[155] Of all the political issues of the 1830s and 1840s that of church rates was the most important in crystallizing the division between Conservatives and Liberals at grass-roots level. And it guaranteed that that division was in large measure a reflection of the dichotomy between church and chapel.

In those parishes where church rates were still being levied in the late 1830s and 1840s Dissenters had one further recourse open to them: they could register their protest against an unfair tax by refusing to pay. It was this tactic which helped the Dissenters of Rochdale to defeat the compulsory rate in 1841 when an attempt made to prosecute nine men for non-payment failed on a technicality.[156] Similarly after over eight hundred ratepayers in Newport in Monmouthshire refused to pay the rate in 1833 churchwardens gave up the attempt to collect it.[157] More often, however, churchwardens tried to recover the unpaid rate by issuing summonses against defaulters: 1,200 summonses were issued in St Mary Abbott's parish in Kensington for non-payment of the rate in March 1837, and more than a thousand were issued in St John's parish in Hackney in the spring of 1841.[158] If this failed to produce payment then the churchwardens could seize the goods of objectors and sell them in public, but

---

[154] W. Robertson, *Social and Political History of Rochdale* (Rochdale, 1889), 28–30.
[155] Ward, *Religion and Society*, 185–8; Gowland, 'Methodism Secessions', 287.
[156] Gowland, 'Methodist Secessions', 287–8.
[157] Davies, *Religion in the Industrial Revolution*, 42.
[158] *The Times*, 20 Mar. 1837; *Nonconformist*, 9 June 1841, 163.

such displays inevitably produced sympathy for the victims and adverse publicity for the established church. When, in June 1833, an auctioneer in Sevenoaks tried to sell the goods of a Mr Chatfield who had refused to pay the church rate, the sale was announced by a placard stating that 'the property of a poor man with a large family of small children [had] been seized for the support of a corrupt church', and the auctioneer was followed round the town by a hostile crowd yelling abuse.[159] After the bailiffs in Rochdale in 1834 seized the family Bible of James Brierley, a poor weaver who lay dying, the supporters of church rates were henceforth branded as the men 'who robbed the dying man of his Bible'.[160] When John Childs, a printer of Bungay in Suffolk, refused to pay a rate of 17s. 6d. in 1835 he was sent to prison.[161] An attempt to auction the goods of an ironmonger in Colchester in 1836 provoked a riot in which four or five hundred people 'made a sudden rush towards the auctioneer, knocked him down and, uttering loud cries against the Church and its exactions trampled upon and completely destroyed the goods that had been seized and sold'.[162] When an auctioneer in Truro in 1838 tried to sell the distrained goods of Dissenters he was hooted by the crowd, the window of his shop was shattered, and his shelves were broken.[163] In 1849 Robert Best, the minister of the Kirkham Congregational church in Lancashire, refused to pay a rate of 9½d., and the bailiffs responded by seizing eight mahogany chairs valued at £4.[164] Such incidents made a permanent contribution to the mythology of Dissent. Jacob Bright, the Rochdale Quaker cotton manufacturer, suffered more than twenty distraints for his refusal to pay church rates and his son John, the future Liberal MP, was long remembered in the town for having climbed on to a tombstone in Rochdale churchyard to harangue a church rates demonstration in 1840.[165] Alfred Illingworth, the future Liberal MP for Bradford, claimed that the seizure of his father's goods for non-payment of the church rate was the most important determinant of his political future.[166] Joseph Tangye, a Quaker shopkeeper of Illogan near Redruth in Cornwall, lost his cow because he refused to pay the church rate and as a result his son Richard, the future head of the Birmingham engineering firm, 'could never forgive the established church

---

[159] *The Times*, 13 June 1833.   [160] Ward, *Religion and Society*, 184–5.
[161] Machin, *Politics and the Churches*, 55.
[162] A. F. J. Brown, *Chartism in Essex and Suffolk* (Chelmsford and Ipswich, 1982), 36.
[163] Chadwick, *Victorian Church*, i. 147–8.
[164] B. Nightingale, *Lancashire Nonconformity* (1890), i. 98–9.
[165] G. M. Trevelyan, *Life of John Bright* (1913), 36, 39.
[166] T. Jowitt, 'The Pattern of Religion in Victorian Bradford', in Wright and Jowitt, *Victorian Bradford*, 42.

for putting [such] people under the harrow'.[167] And sixty years after the young John Clifford was taken by his father to Nottingham market-place to watch the sale of goods taken from the Quaker Samuel Fox for refusing to pay the church rate, Clifford used the incident to inspire resistance to the Balfour Education Act.[168]

In some cases disputes over church rates issued in bitter legal wrangles. In the Carmarthenshire parishes of Llanelli and Llanon the action of Dissenters in blocking church rates in 1837 by electing some of their number as church-wardens backfired when the pugnacious vicar of Llanelli, Ebenezer Morris, had both the Congregationalist John James and the Unitarian David Jones clapped in gaol for failing to fulfil their duties. John James was a prosperous farmer and was released from prison after a few days on payment of £20 in costs, but David Jones was a poor weaver who spent nearly seven months in gaol before being released in June 1839 after appeal had been made to the Queen's Bench. Morris did not, however, give up his prosecution of David Jones who sought to escape a new writ by taking refuge with his son at Cadle, near Swansea, and died on the journey in February 1840. Morris commented that Jones 'died to all appearance under a most awful judgement of God', but three years later Morris was himself declared bankrupt and he was deprived of his livings to pay his creditors.[169]

Two of the most notorious church-rates cases came from the county of Essex, where both the Church of England and Old Dissent were strongly entrenched. When a Chelmsford cobbler named John Thorogood refused to pay a church rate of 5s. 6d. and ignored a summons to attend the Consistory Court of the diocese of London he was declared to be in contempt of court and in January 1839 was imprisoned in Chelmsford gaol. He could not, how-ever, be released from prison unless he purged his contempt and this he refused to do. He remained in prison for eighteen months until a special Act of Parliament allowed a judge to release a prisoner charged with contempt once he had served six months in gaol.[170] The longest-running of all church-rates disputes was the Braintree case. The campaign against church rates in Braintree and in the neighbouring towns of Halstead and Bocking, one of the oldest Dissenting centres in England, was led by the Unitarian crape manu-facturer Samuel Courtauld. In 1834 the vestries of all three parishes refused to levy a rate but three years later a Braintree solicitor and churchwarden named Augustus Veley began legal proceedings against one of the objectors.

---

[167] S. J. Reid, *Sir Richard Tangye* (1908), 8.   [168] *Daily News*, 25 July 1903.
[169] W. T. Morgan, 'Disciplinary Cases against Churchwardens in the Consistory Courts of St Davids', *Journal of the Historical Society of the Church in Wales*, 10 (1960), 27–41.
[170] Chadwick, *Victorian Church*, i. 149–50.

Veley based his case on a forgotten decision of 1799 that a single church-warden could legally levy a rate against the wishes of a majority of the rate-payers, and in 1841 the Braintree churchwardens levied a rate despite the opposition of the parish vestry. It was not until 1853, after Veley's case had been heard by twenty-six judges in front of eight courts, that the House of Lords finally decided that the Braintree rate was illegal.[171]

The most widely publicized church-rates case of all was that of William Baines of Leicester. While church rates had been refused by the vestries in St Nicholas's parish in 1833 and in St Margaret's parish in 1837, a rate con-tinued to be approved by the small parish of St Martin's until 1848. Twenty-seven of St Martin's Dissenters countered by refusing to pay the rate and in November 1840 Baines, a Congregationalist draper, was imprisoned in Leicester county gaol for refusing to pay either the rate of £2. 5s. or the £125. 3s. costs which the churchwardens were claiming, or to appear before the Court of Arches. The conditions of Baines's imprisonment were relaxed—he was allowed to play cricket in the prison yard—and in May 1841 his costs were paid by an anonymous donor and, thanks to Thorogood's Act, he was set free.[172] But the consequences of the church-rates contest in Leicester were far-reaching: Baines was a member of the Bond Street Congregational church and his pastor since 1834 had been Edward Miall.

Miall, the son of a Portsmouth general dealer who subsequently became a schoolmaster, was only twenty-five years old when he went to Leicester and although unassuming, diffident, and an indifferent speaker he soon gained a reputation as a militant radical who had no qualms about mixing politics with religion. He refused to pay the church rate in St Margaret's parish in 1836; he joined with John Phillippo Mursell, Robert Hall's successor as pastor of the Harvey Lane Baptist church, in forming the Leicester Voluntary Church Society; and so much time did he devote to politics that the resulting criticism from a section of his congregation was a factor in his decision to resign the pastorate of his church in the autumn of 1839.[173] Miall's letter of resignation shows that his hostility to what he called the 'adulterous' connection between Church and State was already the obsession that it was to remain for the rest of his life. The Church's 'forced union with the powers of this world defaces her beauty, cripples her energy, misrepresents her character, and does dis-honour unto her Lord'. Christianity was 'converted into a mere political engine' and the Church of England served 'chiefly as a stepping stone to power and place'. The clergy of the established church were 'reviving the

---

[171] Ibid. 155–8; Coleman, *Courtaulds*, i. 218–20.
[172] Patterson, *Radical Leicester*, 247–55; Fraser, *Urban Politics*, 49–53.
[173] A. Miall, *Life of Edward Miall* (1884), 29–32; Patterson, *Radical Leicester*, 249.

arrogant pretensions of the papal priesthood, and . . . setting forth the doctrines of Popery under the garb of Protestantism'. By 1839 the failure of the Dissenters to secure the abolition of church rates was leading to a search for new weapons in the battle against the impost. John Wilks, the secretary of the Protestant Society and former MP for Boston, had died in 1836 and the society held its last annual meeting in 1839.[174] In February 1839 Josiah Conder founded the Religious Freedom Society which was intended to unite Dissenters and liberal Anglicans on a common platform, but as a corollary the society refused to commit itself to disestablishment and Conder's moderation alienated the more militant Dissenters. The *Leicestershire Mercury* complained in May that the leaders of the London Dissenters had 'betrayed the cause . . . for the sake of bolstering up the Whigs',[175] and John Childs, the church-rates martyr from Bungay, criticized the continuing support which Conder's *Patriot* gave to Melbourne's government and urged the setting up of a radical Dissenting newspaper.[176] Miall and Mursell took up Childs's suggestion and travelled to London to try to persuade an experienced writer to take on the editorship of such a journal. They failed. But on their return journey, on the platform of Rugby station, Mursell turned to Miall and urged him to undertake the task himself. Miall thus embarked on the career that was to dominate the rest of his working life. From August 1840 until March 1841 he toured England to raise money in support of the venture and on 14 April 1841 he published the first number of the *Nonconformist*.[177] From the very start the new paper proclaimed from its masthead its loyalty to 'The Dissidence of Dissent and the Protestantism of the Protestant Religion'. Its chief task was to show 'that a national establishment of religion is essentially vicious in its constitution'.[178]

5. 'JUDAS ISCARIOT, THE FIRST DISSENTER': TRADE UNIONS, FACTORY REFORM, AND THE NEW POOR LAW

Edward Miall launched the *Nonconformist* at a critical juncture in the history of Dissent. The issues which we have so far considered in this chapter, the

[174] Jones, *Explorations and Explanations*, 240–1.
[175] A. C. Whitby, 'Matthew Arnold and the Nonconformists', B.Litt. thesis (Oxford, 1966), citing *Leicestershire Mercury*, 25 May 1839.
[176] H. R. Martin, 'The Politics of the Congregationalists, 1830–1856', Ph.D. thesis (Durham, 1971), 170–1, 183.
[177] Miall, *Life of Miall*, 38–40.   [178] *Nonconformist*, 14 Apr. 1841.

redress of Dissenting grievances, the reform of municipal corporations, the campaign against church rates, divided Englishmen on vertical lines, according to whether they thought that the Church of England should retain its privileged position or whether they believed that the Dissenting denominations should be given equality of status in a pluralist society. But the 1830s not only witnessed an intensification of the conflict between church and chapel, they also saw a worsening of class divisions along horizontal lines. While members of the middle class who had received the vote in 1832 were temporarily satisfied with the settlement, the Great Reform Act had left six out of seven men disfranchised and those working-class men who had agitated for the vote and had then been denied it felt a deep sense of grievance. Once the Reform Act was on the statute-book workers hoped to obtain higher wages through the trade union movement and to secure shorter working hours by legislation; middle-class manufacturers for the most part opposed them. Middle-class ratepayers sought to limit expenditure on the poor law by the Poor Law Amendment Act of 1834; but working men and women had always regarded the poor law as a safety net in the event of poverty or old age and to them the New Poor Law was a denial of their birthright. From 1837 overproduction led to falling prices and rising unemployment which further intensified class antagonism: middle-class radicals argued that the way out of the recession lay in the repeal of the corn laws; to the working class the solution to their problems was the People's Charter and one man, one vote. By 1841 class conflict was pushing religious conflict into the background, dividing Dissenting employer against Dissenting workman and thus threatening to emasculate Dissent's new-found political strength.

As we have seen, ever since the 1790s radical Dissenters had been willing to inflame middle-class resentment against the aristocracy while at the same time insisting that the industrious classes—the middle and working classes alike—had a common interest in curtailing the power of the upper class.[179] These attitudes persisted into the 1830s and 1840s. The middle-class Dissenters who supported the Anti-Corn Law League saw their campaign as part of a wider mission to free Britain from the stranglehold of aristocratic rule. Yet at the same time they denied that there was any conflict of interest between the middle and working classes. Edward Miall in particular worked to unite middle- and working-class radicals against the aristocracy. From October 1841 he regularly allocated space in the *Nonconformist* to the bringing about of 'a better understanding between the middle and labouring classes'. 'We are certain their interests are bound up together,' he wrote.[180] But the

---

[179] Ch. III, sects. 4 and 5.   [180] *Nonconformist*, 13 Oct. 1841, 456.

hopes entertained by men like Miall for the co-operation of the middle and working classes in the 1830s and 1840s had one enormous obstacle to overcome: the commitment of so many middle-class Dissenters to the philosophy of *laissez-faire*. While many working men were prepared to acknowledge that freer trade would benefit the country's economy, and thus themselves, they were bitterly resentful of the application of *laissez-faire* to social issues such as industrial relations, poor relief, and factory reform. Miall himself illustrated the confusion at the heart of radical Dissent: while on the one hand he devoted much time and energy in 1842 in working for the union of working-class men and middle-class radicals, in the same year he published in the *Nonconformist* a series of letters from Herbert Spencer, the extreme advocate of *laissez-faire*. In May 1842 Miall denounced the cold-blooded atrocities committed by coal-owners on children in mines and described factories as 'hecatombs of youthful victims'.[181] But he confessed that he did not know how to remedy such evils and a month later published the first of Herbert Spencer's letters arguing that it was not the function of government to regulate commerce, educate the people, or to administer charity, or to do anything but 'protect person and property'.[182] In June 1842 Miall criticized the 'awful deterioration of character' produced by the 'severity' of the New Poor Law, but three weeks later gave space to one of Spencer's letters urging that the poor law be abolished completely.[183] And in 1844, while arguing that an eight-hour day was the most that was consistent with the 'physical, intellectual, or moral well-being' of the worker, at the same time he opposed legislation to limit hours of work and believed that such matters should be left 'in the hands of providence'.[184] The failure of the majority of Nonconformist leaders to support the working class on issues such as factory reform and the poor law constitutes the most glaring failure of compassion in the whole history of Dissent.

Not all Dissenters were thus guilty. The Unitarian William Taylor, in articles in the *Annual Review* in 1802 and 1805, had suggested that the poor law should be administered by overseers elected by the poor themselves; that workhouses should be converted into hospitals for the poor; and that the Combination Laws should be repealed in order to raise wages. Higher wages would benefit, not damage, British industry, since manufacturers would thus be provided with 'an additional nation of customers'.[185] Another Unitarian, Joseph Hanson, a Manchester check manufacturer and member of Stand

---

[181] Ibid. 18 May 1842, 335.   [182] Ibid. 15 June 1842, 411.
[183] Ibid. 13 July 1842, 474–5.   [184] Ibid. 15 May 1844, 356.
[185] *Annual Review*, 1 (1802), 424–5; 4 (1805), 302–3.

chapel, supported the weavers' petition for a minimum wage in 1807. When the House of Commons rejected the petition a mass demonstration was held in St George's Fields, Manchester, in May 1808. The magistrates ordered a regiment of cavalry to disperse the crowd but Hanson, who was a colonel in the Volunteers, rode among them telling them 'to stick to your cause and you will certainly succeed'. As a result Hanson was prosecuted for incitement to sedition, found guilty, and sentenced to a fine of £100 and six months in prison.[186]

The Particular Baptist Robert Hall also tried to keep up the wages of poor workers. While minister of the Harvey Lane church in Leicester in 1819 he gave his support to a Framework Knitters' Friendly and Relief Society which was designed to protect wage rates. The society set up a fund, subscribed to by working stockingers and well-wishers outside the industry, to provide unemployed framework knitters with 8s. a week to stop them from undercutting the wages of their fellow workers. Hall defended the scheme on the grounds that of all species of property labour was the most defenceless and the most in need of protection, and like Taylor argued that higher wages would increase the market for the products of both industry and agriculture. Two years later Hall claimed that the Framework Knitters' Society had raised wages by 'at least one-third' and, although the scheme had collapsed by 1824, for three years the average wage of stockingers was kept steady at 10s. or 11s. a week.[187] Hall's successor, James Phillippo Mursell, tried to initiate a similar scheme in the depths of the 1838 depression, but was rebuffed by the employers.[188] The Methodist Unitarian cotton manufacturer John Fielden also tried in 1826 to promote a scheme to maintain the wages of hand-loom weavers by guaranteeing a steady income to unemployed weavers.[189] Both William Smith, when he was Unitarian MP for Norwich in 1828, and Fielden, when he was MP for Oldham in 1835, introduced abortive bills to secure a minimum wage for weavers. And in 1830, shortly before his retirement from Parliament, William Smith introduced a bill to abolish the truck system.[190]

However, a second and increasingly dominant strand in Unitarianism embraced the *laissez-faire* views of the classical economists. *Laissez-faire* views were advocated by Unitarian periodicals such as the *Monthly Magazine* and the *Monthly Repository*,[191] and two of Jeremy Bentham's closest

---

[186] R. T. Herford, 'Joseph Hanson, the Weavers' Friend', *TUHS* 8 (1943–6), 17–26; Thompson, *Making of the English Working Class*, 307–8.

[187] *Works of Robert Hall*, iii. 237–9, 263, 268; Patterson, *Radical Leicester*, 126–7, 135.

[188] Patterson, *Radical Leicester*, 298–9.　　[189] Weaver, *John Fielden*, 48.

[190] Ibid. 118–36; Davis, *Dissent in Politics*, 251–2.

[191] Sellers, 'Social and Political Ideas of English Unitarians', 25–6, 57–8.

associates, John Bowring and Southwood Smith, were Unitarians. Southwood Smith was the man to whom Bentham bequeathed his body for medical
research; Bowring edited Bentham's works and wrote his biography. Elected
MP for Kilmarnock in 1835, Bowring was one of the most vociferous opponents of Fielden's Minimum Wages Bill.[192] At the same time many Evangelical Dissenters subscribed to the notion that poverty was a consequence of sin.
Wesleyans such as Samuel Bradburn and Thomas Olivers argued that in
most cases the distress of the poor was their own fault, the consequences of
idleness and drunkenness, and the Congregationalist William Jay denied
that anything could be done to improve their lot.[193] In 1841 the Sick Visiting
Society attached to the Philip Street Congregational church in Dalston was
horrified by the 'poverty and misery of the most appalling and distressing
description' in the neighbourhood of the chapel, but concluded that in the
vast majority of cases that poverty was caused by intemperance.[194] The
Evangelical belief that social improvement was a question of personal morality and the *laissez-faire* conviction that individuals pursuing their own selfish
ends would do most to advance the common good united in the philosophy of
the younger Edward Baines. The editor of the *Leeds Mercury* acknowledged
that in all large towns and cities there were 'sinks of iniquity, into which all
the sores and all the filth of society . . . empty themselves', but denied that
there was any governmental power that could reform them. What hope there
was for the inhabitants of such places lay not in state action but in ministers
of religion, town missionaries, tract distributors, and Sunday school teachers.
The function of government was to restrain violence and crime, to protect
person and property, to administer laws, to sanction public works, and to
guard against external attack. It was not the duty of government 'to feed the
people, to clothe them, to build houses for them, to direct their industry or
their commerce, to superintend their families, to cultivate their minds, to
shape their opinions, or to supply them with religious teachers, physicians,
schoolmasters, books, or newspapers'.[195]

The Evangelical conviction that social conditions could be improved only
by individual conversion clashed head-on with the belief of the pioneer
Socialist Robert Owen that it was social conditions that determined personal
morality. As the *Baptist Magazine* argued in 1821, Owen failed to realize
'that man in his native state is universally and totally corrupt', and that only

---

[192] Weaver, *John Fielden*, 129–31, 136.
[193] Semmel, *Methodist Revolution*, 119; Elliott, 'Protestant Denominations in Leeds', 466;
Jones, *Congregationalism in England*, 189.
[194] F. R. Salter, 'Congregationalism in the Hungry Forties', *TCHS* 17 (1952–5), 113.
[195] E. Baines, jr., *Letters to the Rt Hon Lord John Russell on State Education* (1846), 13, 22–3.

the 'renewing grace of God' could change the 'rebellious creature'.[196] Unitarians, however, did not share the Calvinist conviction that man is totally corrupt and some gave Owen their support. His advocacy of co-operation received sympathy from writers in the *Monthly Repository*; John Collier Farn, a Unitarian ribbon-weaver from Coventry, served as an Owenite lecturer in the Midlands in the late 1830s; and John Finch, a Liverpool corn merchant and member of the Renshaw Street Unitarian church, was also an enthusiastic Owenite and governor of the Owenite colony at Harmony Hall, Tytherley, Hampshire, from 1842 to 1846, though he ultimately left the Unitarians and urged Owen to found a Millennial Christian church.[197] Owen's attempts to improve industrial relations were also sup-ported by a group of Quakers. When a bitter quarrel between Owen and his business partners jeopardized his management of the cotton mills at New Lanark in 1813, Owen's control was secured by a new partnership which included a number of wealthy Friends, among them the pharmaceutical manufacturer and philanthropist William Allen. Owen's new partners enabled him to turn New Lanark into a model industrial village. But Allen gave his backing to Owen in apparent ignorance of the latter's antipathy towards religion and Allen was soon complaining that he had been 'made a dupe to designs which my heart could never approve'. In 1828, after years of disagreement on whether religion should or should not be taught in the schools of New Lanark, the partnership between Allen and Owen was finally dissolved.[198]

As Owenism became identified with infidelity so Nonconformists of all shades of opinion felt impelled to repudiate Socialism. John Giles, minister of the South Parade Baptist church in Leeds, gave a series of lectures in 1838 in which he described a Socialist as an infidel, a libertine, and a scoffer whose object was 'the sweeping away of all existing laws, religions, and institutions'.[199] Owenite lecturers and Methodist preachers clashed frequently in Bilston, Dudley, and Stourbridge in 1838–9.[200] When the anti-Socialist lecturer James Brindley formed a society in Halifax in 1840 'for the refutation of infidelity and the suppression of blasphemy' he received strong Wesleyan support. And even the radical minister of the Methodist New Connexion, Joseph Barker, who later became a Chartist, toured the north of England in

---

[196] *Baptist Magazine*, 13 (1821), 358.
[197] Mineka, *Dissidence of Dissent*, 163–5, 186; Searby, *Coventry Politics*, 4–5; G. J. Barnsby, *The Working-Class Movement in the Black Country* (Wolverhampton, 1977), 37, 44–5; J. F. C. Harrison, *Robert Owen and the Owenites* (1969), 122–6.
[198] G. D. H. Cole, *Robert Owen* (1925), 83–5, 159–62; *Life of William Allen* (1846), i. 180–2, 209, 244–5; ii. 236–7; iii. 8.
[199] J. E. Giles, *Socialism as a Religious Theory, Irrational and Absurd* (1838), 2.
[200] Barnsby, *Working Class Movements in the Black Country*, 37, 42–3, 46.

1840 lecturing against Socialism and holding public debates with Socialist missionaries. Barker claimed that 'in every place I was voted triumphant', and certainly in Halifax a meeting of two thousand people resolved 'that the religion of Christ is calculated . . . to eradicate the evils of society' and that 'the system of Robert Owen, if brought into general practice' would 'make mankind vicious and miserable'.[201]

The high incidence of Unitarians and Quakers among manufacturers, especially in the textile industries, and the rapid growth of both Wesleyan and Primitive Methodism among the poorer sections of the working class in the 1830s, guaranteed that Nonconformists would be on both sides of the industrial divide. Some Nonconformist employers, such as Joseph Hanson, 'the weavers' friend', made strenuous efforts to retain the goodwill of their workers and to give substance to the claim that the industrious classes—both employer and employee—had a common interest against the ruling class. John Ridgway, the Hanley pottery manufacturer and pillar of the Methodist New Connexion, in 1820 gave his workmen time off, with pay, to attend a public meeting and oppose a resolution in support of the government, and he later earned praise from the trade union pioneer John Richards for his radical views.[202] John Fielden encouraged trade unions and in 1833 co-operated with Robert Owen in the National Regeneration Society which aimed to use strikes to force employers to grant an eight-hour day for 'the present full day's wages'. Though the society lasted barely five months it paralysed every mill in Oldham for a fortnight in a dispute in which one striker was killed and a factory owner's home and mill were wrecked.[203] And another Unitarian, James Hawkes, minister at Nantwich in the early 1830s, supported the shoe-makers in the town in their attempts to form a trade union.[204]

But the majority of Nonconformist employers were opposed to the formation of trade unions and their attitude was very largely supported by the denominational leaders and by the Dissenting press. The Quaker cotton manufacturer Henry Ashworth was a firm believer in the identity of interest of worker and employer: he provided substantially built stone cottages for his workers at New Eagley and Egerton near Bolton and even critics of the factory system praised the clean and healthy conditions in which his employees worked. But when a reduction in wage rates led to a strike at his mills in

---

[201] Teale, 'Methodism in Halifax', 178–85; J. T. Barker, *Life of Joseph Barker* (1880), 248–9.

[202] Wearmouth, *Methodism and Working-class Movements*, 211; R. Fyson, 'Aspects of the National Union of Operative Potters', in J. Rule (ed.), *British Trade Unionism, 1750–1850* (1988), 209.

[203] Weaver, *John Fielden*, 80–105; J. T. Ward, *The Factory Movement* (1962), 114.

[204] Chaloner, *Autobiography of Samuel Bamford*, i. 18.

1830 Ashworth warned his workers that anyone who joined the strike would never again be employed by him; from that date all his workers had to sign a paper agreeing not to join a union; and workers who subsequently broke the rule were sacked. The Quaker Ashworths, comments Rhodes Boyson, thus denied in industrial relations the value of arbitration which they advocated in international affairs.[205] The same accusation could be levelled against John Tregelles Price, Quaker owner of the Neath Abbey ironworks in Glamorgan and founder of the Peace Society. Price was an enlightened employer who would not employ anyone under fourteen years of age, but he, too, threatened all his workers who joined a union with dismissal in 1831.[206] And the same combination of a paternalist approach to their workforce and resolute opposition to trade unions was shared by the Unitarian cotton manufacturers, the Gregs of Quarry Bank, at Styal in Cheshire.[207]

One reason for Henry Ashworth's intense opposition to the trade union movement was the intimidation and violence which often accompanied strike action culminating, in 1831, in the murder of Thomas Ashton, the son of a Hyde cotton manufacturer. Such violence, associated as it was with the swearing of secret oaths and the frequent malversation of union funds by dishonest officials, helped to alienate uncommitted observers from the trade union cause. The Welsh Independent periodical *Y Dysgedydd* condemned trade unionists for intimidating non-members in 1825 and deplored the violence with which the miners of Merthyr Tydfil protested against a cut in wages in 1831.[208] Josiah Conder's *Patriot* in 1834 attacked trade union leaders for administering illegal oaths and for fraudulently misusing money entrusted to their care.[209] The Congregationalist Thomas Rees regarded the promoters of strikes as 'dissatisfied idlers who seldom settle for any length of time under the same employer', and in July 1834 and again early in 1835 his shop at Craig-y-fargod was wrecked by bands of colliers known as 'Scotch Cattle' because of his criticisms of the trade union movement.[210] In 1859 the Independent *Y Chronicl* condemned a strike of London joiners on the ground that it had deprived the workers and their families of £60,000.[211] And the Baptist Thomas Price, minister of the church at Aberdare, although a

[205] Boyson, *The Ashworth Cotton Enterprise*, 87, 91–4, 118–19, 140–8, 152–3.
[206] M. F. Williams, 'The Society of Friends in Glamorgan, 1654–1900', MA thesis (Aberystwyth, 1950), 238–9.
[207] Rose, *The Gregs of Quarry Bank*, 136.
[208] Parry, 'Welsh Independents and Working-class Movements', 109–10.
[209] *Patriot*, 21 May 1834, 183.
[210] Rees, *Miscellaneous Papers relating to Wales*, 19–20; Davies, *Religion in the Industrial Revolution*, 77 n. 2; I. Wilks, *South Wales and the Rising of 1839* (1984), 86.
[211] Parry, 'Welsh Independents and Working-class Movements', 111.

staunch defender of workers' Friendly Societies, also argued that trade unions were against workers' real interests.[212]

The Wesleyan leadership, with its anxiety to convince the country's rulers of its loyalty to the established constitution and its concern to counter the spread of radicalism among its predominantly working-class constituency, was particularly censorious of members who took part in trade union activities. When coalminers in the Newcastle district organized themselves into a 'Brotherhood' in 1810 and swore secret oaths the Wesleyan preachers Daniel Isaac and H. Taft 'visited all the collieries where we had societies, instructed our members and hearers respecting the evil of the Brotherhood . . . and exhorted those who had taken the oath to abjure it'. As a result Daniel Isaac was attacked by men armed with bludgeons as he 'was returning home after preaching at a colliery . . . but being provided with a good stick' he fought his way through.[213] Two years later Wesleyan preachers in the Dudley circuit forbade members to join Friendly Societies such as the Druids, Loyal Britons, or Odd Fellows.[214] In 1818 John Hickling, superintendent minister in Barnsley, ordered nine striking linen-weavers who were members of the Wesleyan society to go back to work, and when they refused had them expelled.[215] And in 1833 the Wesleyan Conference warned Methodists to avoid 'associations which are subversive to the principles of true and proper liberty, employing unlawful oaths, and threats, and force to acquire new members, and to accomplish purposes which would tend to destroy the very framework of civil society'.[216] Industrial unrest in the Flintshire coalfield and in the collieries and ironworks of Monmouthshire similarly prompted the Calvinistic Methodist Associations of both north and south Wales to resolve in 1831 that 'no member of the Union of Colliers, Miners, and Firemen' could be tolerated as a church member.[217] As a result some Calvinistic Methodists were excommunicated for joining unions, and the Dowlais ironmaster and future MP for Merthyr Tydfil, Josiah John Guest, claimed that the opposition of the Calvinistic Methodists to the strikes in 1831 was a major factor in their collapse. Guest subsequently made generous donations to the Nonconformist

[212] I. G. Jones, 'Dr Thomas Price and the Election of 1868 in Merthyr Tydfil', *Welsh History Review*, 2 (1964–5), 162–3.

[213] J. Everett, *The Polemic Divine: Memoirs of Daniel Isaac* (1839), 73–4; Wearmouth, *Methodism and Working-class Movements*, 62–3.

[214] Leese, 'Impact of Methodism on Black Country Society', 291.

[215] F. J. Keijage, 'Labour Barnsley', Ph.D. thesis (Warwick, 1975), 64–5.

[216] Wearmouth, *Methodism and Working-class Movements*, 188.

[217] J. Roberts, *The Calvinistic Methodism of Wales* (Caernarfon, 1933), 9; Turner, 'Revivals and Popular Religion in Wales', 153–5.

chapels in Merthyr, thus creating the suspicion that he was rewarding them for their part in combating trade unionism.[218]

But, as always, the resolutions of denominational conferences and editorials in the religious press did not necessarily reflect or influence the opinions of the man or woman in the Nonconformist pew. It was inevitable, given the large working-class membership of most Nonconformist churches, that at least some of those workers would be caught up in the trade union movement. And it was equally inevitable, given the training in self-expression, organization, and leadership provided for laymen by the chapels, that many of the leaders of the trade union movement should come from the ranks of Nonconformity. To some extent the incidence of Nonconformist involvement in the trade union movement was a reflection of the geographic and occupational distribution of Dissent. Nonconformists were evident in the trade union movement among agricultural workers, West Country textile workers, and Staffordshire pottery workers; Methodists in particular were often dominant in the mining unions of the Midlands and the north-east. But the present state of historical knowledge suggests that Nonconformists were absent from artisan unions in London, and in the cotton districts of Lancashire it was as employers, not as trade unionists, that Dissenters made their mark.

The oft-repeated fear of Nonconformist leaders that society was dividing along class lines was given substance by the experience of some individual churches. A violent strike of weavers in the textile district of Gloucestershire in 1825, during which employers were assaulted, special constables ducked in a pond, and the Tenth Hussars called out, led to bitter divisions in the Baptist church at Shortwood near Nailsworth, with some members taking a leading part in the strike and others as vociferous in its denunciation.[219] In the same year a strike of worsted workers in Bradford threatened to divide Dissenters on class lines. Benjamin Godwin, pastor of the town's Sion Baptist church, confided in his autobiography that 'ministers were obliged in their preaching to be fastidiously careful of any language which might be construed as an attack on the [trade] union. The members who were working men had scarce any charity towards their fellow members who were masters.'[220] Of all the Nonconformist denominations the Primitive Methodists were most sympathetic towards working-class interests, but in 1838 a Ranter preacher in the Stalybridge circuit was reprimanded 'for naming cotton masters in his

---

[218] Turner, 'Revivals and Popular Religion in Wales', 155–7.

[219] Urdank, 'Dissenting Community', 364–70, 397.

[220] T. Koditschek, *Class Formation and Urban-industrial Society: Bradford, 1750–1850* (Cambridge, 1990), 280–1.

preaching'.[221] And in south Wales Independents were to be found on both sides in industrial disputes. While Thomas Rees and the denominational press attacked trade unions, it was claimed during a coal strike in Aberdare in 1850 that the deacons of the Siloah Independent church had resolved that no members should work in the colliery during the strike and that a miner who insisted on continuing to work was excommunicated.[222]

The accusations against the Siloah church were subsequently denied, but the incident does illustrate the fact that it was in coalmining districts that the connection between trade unionism and Nonconformity—usually Primitive Methodism—was strongest. The harsh working conditions, the ever-present danger of sudden death, the closely knit and isolated communities in which they lived, all meant that miners and their families were peculiarly susceptible to the Evangelical appeal of the Methodists. Even so, the Ranters in the Durham coalfield in particular exercised an influence on the trade union movement out of all proportion to their numbers. At the 1851 religious census fewer than 5 per cent of the population of Durham attended a Primitive Methodist chapel and only in the districts of Weardale and Easington did that figure approach 10 per cent. But for nearly a century the Ranters played a leading role in the mining unions of Durham. Methodists were put forward as spokesmen for the miners, a colliery manager told a Royal Commission in 1842, and were 'most decidedly the hardest to deal with', because they were better educated than their fellow colliers.[223]

The repeal of the Combination Laws in 1824 and the agitation for parliamentary reform was followed closely by the rapid growth of trade union activity, and in 1830 the miners of Durham and Northumberland united in a union under the leadership of Tommy Hepburn, a Primitive Methodist from Hetton in County Durham whom Sidney Webb described as 'the first recorded effective leader of the miners'.[224] Until 1872 a Durham miner contracted to work for a year in the same colliery under an annual 'bond' which detailed his conditions of service but which gave him no guarantee of full employment or regular wages in return. Encouraged by the mounting campaign for parliamentary reform Hepburn's union organized mass meetings in March 1831 which demanded improved working conditions: in particular shorter working hours for boys and an end to the system whereby a colliery owner could close his pits for three days a week and so reduce his workers' earnings by

[221] Rose, *Methodism in Ashton-under-Lyne*, ii. 43.
[222] Parry, 'Welsh Independents and Working-class Movements', 122–4.
[223] *Children's Employment Commission: Appendix to the First Report of the Commissioners (Mines)* (1842), xvi. 381.
[224] S. Webb, *The Story of the Durham Miners* (1921), 28.

half. The miners agreed that every pit should send a delegate to a union committee to give effect to their resolutions and refused to sign new bonds until their demands were met.[225] The union delegates, commented a hostile observer, 'are chiefly Ranter preachers, who have acquired a considerable fluency and even in some cases considerable proficiency in public speaking'.[226]

The colliery owners conceded a twelve-hour maximum working day for boys and the men went back to work. But in March 1832 the owners of half the collieries refused to re-engage workers unless they abandoned their union membership and another strike ensued. The 1832 strike was marked by increasing bitterness on both sides: miners vandalized pits and assaulted blacklegs, colliery owners evicted workers and their families from their homes. Hepburn made a desperate attempt to stem the violence but a blackleg, named Errington, was murdered and a local magistrate, Nicholas Fairless, was attacked and beaten to death. The cholera epidemic drained union funds, the importation of blacklegs undermined the miners' bargaining power, and the strike collapsed in September 1832. Hepburn was forced to try to earn a living hawking tea, and when this failed to yield a livelihood he was given work at Felling colliery on condition that he promised never again to become involved in union activities. Not surprisingly the events of 1832 embittered his spirit and temporarily shattered his faith: for a time he abandoned the Primitive Methodists but in later life returned to the fold.[227]

Other union leaders lost their faith in 1832, and the miners' defeat took away from some Ranter chapels many of the gains they made during the cholera epidemic,[228] but in subsequent disputes Primitive Methodist influence grew rather than diminished. In 1844 the Durham and Northumberland miners put forward a series of demands which included half-yearly contracts instead of the annual bond and a guaranteed minimum of five days' work a week at 3s. a day.[229] When the colliery owners refused these demands the miners went on strike. Mark Dent, who chaired most of the Durham miners' meetings in 1844, was a Primitive Methodist, and nine of the 'Twelve Apostles' who went to London in a vain attempt to rally public support for

---

[225] The fullest accounts of Hepburn's union are in R. Fynes, *The Miners of Northumberland and Durham* (publ. 1873, repr. 1963), 17–36, and in E. Welbourne, *The Miners' Unions of Northumberland and Durham* (Cambridge, 1923), 25–44. There are, however, numerous discrepancies between the two accounts.

[226] R. Colls, *The Pitmen of the Northern Coalfield* (Manchester, 1987), 189.

[227] G. E. Milburn in Dews, *From Mow Cop to Peake*, 65.

[228] Ibid. 65; Colls, *Pitmen of the Northern Coalfield*, 152, 199.

[229] Welbourne, *Miners' Unions*, 72–3.

the strikers were Primitive Methodist local preachers.[230] Seymour Tremen-heere, who two years later toured the mining districts as a government commissioner, claimed that in Primitive Methodist chapels 'prayers were publicly offered up for the successful result of the strike', and the commis-sioners were told that while the Wesleyans were among the first miners to return to work, 'the Ranters were the worst agitators'.[231] The colliery owners responded to the strike, as in 1832, by importing blacklegs from Wales and Ireland, and to make room for the blacklegs thousands of miners' families were evicted from their homes. The evictions had a devastating effect on Primitive Methodist circuits. The membership of the Durham circuit fell from 1,500 in 1843 to 520 in 1844[232] and after five months, in August 1844, the strike itself collapsed. The coal strike of 1844 again revealed Dissenters to be on both sides of the industrial divide: against Primitive Methodist support for the strike must be placed the attitude of the Quaker railway proprietor and colliery owner Joseph Pease, MP for South Durham, who was denounced for his lack of sympathy with the miners and for his suggestion that waggoners, masons, and joiners should go down the pits to break the strike.[233]

Similar divisions among Nonconformists were revealed by the case of the Tolpuddle martyrs. Four of the six members of the Friendly Society of Agricultural Labourers who were arrested at Tolpuddle in Dorset in February 1834 were Wesleyan Methodists, and two of them, George and James Loveless, were local preachers. The six men were charged with the administration and taking of illegal oaths, found guilty, and sentenced to seven years' transportation to New South Wales and Van Dieman's Land. The sentences provoked public outcry and two Dissenting MPs, Mark Philips and Joseph Brotherton, presented petitions to Parliament for the men's release. When, in June 1835, Thomas Wakley introduced a motion to pardon the labourers seven of the ten Nonconformist MPs then in Parliament voted for the motion, though it was defeated by 308 votes to 82.[234] But outside Parliament no Dissenting denomination, least of all the Wesleyans, con-tributed to the campaign for the men's pardon which resulted, in 1837 and 1838, in five of the six returning home. None the less the case of the Tolpuddle martyrs provides yet another example of the way in which Methodism, by virtue of its spiritual appeal, was able to retain the adher-ence of its working-class members despite the hostility of the Wesleyan

---

[230] Wearmouth, *Methodism and Working-class Movements*, 231.   [231] Ibid. 232–3.
[232] Ibid. 231.   [233] Fynes, *Miners of Northumberland and Durham*, 61.
[234] *Parliamentary Debates*, 3rd ser., xxviii (26 June 1835), cols. 1261–2, 1272–3. E. Baines, J. Bowring, J. Brotherton, C. Hindley, J. Fielden, M. Philips, and J. Wilks voted for the motion. The Nonconformist MPs who did not vote for a pardon were D. Gaskell, J. Pease, and R. Potter.

Conference to their political and economic aspirations. The Methodist Tolpuddle martyrs emigrated to Canada in the 1840s where they remained loyal to their faith: James Loveless had a son christened 'Wesley' and George Loveless helped to build a Methodist chapel near London, Ontario.[235]

The failure of official Nonconformity to give succour to the trade union movement was, to a very large extent, paralleled by its reluctance to support the movement to restrict by law the hours worked by children and adults in the country's textile mills. Indeed, J. T. Ward, in the most comprehensive twentieth-century history of the *Factory Movement*, sees it very largely in terms of a struggle of compassionate, protectionist, Tory Evangelical Anglicans against heartless, free-trade, Dissenting Liberal manufacturers.[236] And certainly many of the leading protagonists in the struggle to control working conditions in factories by legislation fall into these categories. Richard Oastler, the steward of the Fixby estate near Huddersfield, who launched his campaign for factory reform with the first of a series of letters on 'Yorkshire Slavery' in the *Leeds Mercury* in September 1830, was the son of a Methodist local preacher who later joined the New Connexion. When only eight months old Richard had been taken by John Wesley in his arms and blessed by him; he too became a Methodist local preacher; and he married Mary Tatham, the daughter of Thomas Tatham, the bastion of Nottingham Wesleyanism. But Oastler subsequently moved to the Church of England[237] and expounded a protectionist philosophy which was the very antithesis of the *laissez-faire* views of Dissenting anti-state church manufacturers. He demanded protection for industrial workers, the landed interest, the established church, and the monarchy. 'The Altar, the Throne, and the Cottage', he declared, 'should share alike the protection of the law.'[238] Michael Sadler, the MP for Aldborough, who in 1832 introduced a bill to limit the hours of work of children and young people in factories to ten hours a day, and who chaired a select committee on child labour, was also an Evangelical Anglican Tory. And when Sadler failed to secure re-election in December 1832 his place as leader of the factory reformers in Parliament was taken by another Evangelical Tory, Lord Ashley, MP for Dorset. Outside Parliament numerous Anglican clergymen supported factory reform, led by George Bull, the curate of Bierley near Bradford.[239]

Ranged against the factory reformers were many of the Unitarian and Quaker manufacturers whose prominence in the textile industry was empha-

[235] J. Marlow, *The Tolpuddle Martyrs* (1971), *passim*.
[236] J. T. Ward, *The Factory Movement* (1962), 40–1, 417, 423, 425.
[237] C. Driver, *Tory Radical: The Life of Richard Oastler* (New York, 1946), 5, 13, 21, 23, 29.
[238] Ward, *Factory Movement*, 77, 79.   [239] Ibid. 48, 87.

sized in Chapter II. The Ashworths of Bolton, the Gregs of Quarry Bank, the Marshalls of Leeds were all vocal in their opposition to parliamentary interference with the way they ran their factories, and they used their money and influence to try to thwart the factory reformers.[240] Dissenting newspapers which spoke for, and to an extent were financed by, the textile manufacturers, papers such as the *Leeds Mercury*, *Manchester Guardian*, and *Bradford Observer*, were all critical of the short-time movement. So, too, were the Unitarian *Inquirer* and *Christian Reformer* and the Independent *Diwygiwr*. It was the younger John Marshall, allied with Macaulay, who defeated Michael Sadler's attempt to gain election as MP for Leeds in December 1832. In the course of the election campaign Marshall argued that Sadler's Ten Hours Bill would not benefit the working class because it would result in lower wages. Oastler responded by contrasting the elder Marshall's fortune of £2 million with the average weekly wage of 6s. 11d. earned by his workers.[241]

Ashley's attempt to rescue the ten hours proposal in 1833 was defeated by 238 votes to 93, and five of the dozen Dissenting MPs, representing northern manufacturing interests, spoke against Ashley's bill. Richard Potter warned that the cotton industry faced mounting competition from the Continent, the United States, and India; Sir George Philips argued that if the Ten Hours Bill passed manufacturers would have to cut wages by 25 per cent; George Wood claimed that if hours of work were further reduced many masters would be ruined.[242] Lord Althorp, for the government, did, however, carry his own measure which prohibited the employment of children under nine in textile mills, restricted the hours of children between the ages of nine and thirteen to eight hours a day, and of young people under the age of eighteen to twelve hours a day. But the Act did not extend to the lace industry: the Baptist lace manufacturer William Felkin argued successfully that extension of the provisions of the Act to cover his own industry would retard the application of steam power.[243] And three years later, in 1836, when Poulett Thomson made a vain attempt to restrict the eight hours' limitation to children under twelve instead of thirteen, he was supported by half the Dissenting MPs: Edward Baines, John Bowring, Joseph Pease, Mark Philips, and Richard Potter.[244]

---

[240] Boyson, *Ashworth Cotton Enterprise*, 158–64; Ward, *Factory Reform*, 169, 171, 202; Rose, *Gregs of Quarry Bank*, 135–6.

[241] Driver, *Tory Radical*, 201–2; Ward, *Factory Movement*, 116.

[242] Joseph Pease and Mark Philips also spoke against Ashley's bill (*Parliamentary Debates*, 3rd ser., xix (18 July 1833), cols. 894, 897, 903).

[243] Thomis, *Politics and Society in Nottingham*, 245; Church, *Economic and Social Change in a Midland Town*, 331.

[244] *Parliamentary Debates*, 3rd ser., xxxiii (10 May 1836), cols. 788–90.

Oastler's most bitter invective was reserved for his Dissenting opponents. Oastler's first letters on 'Yorkshire Slavery' had been published in the Baineses' *Leeds Mercury*; the younger Baines declared that the evidence of Sadler's committee called 'imperatively for legislative interference'; and the elder Baines claimed that he had always favoured an eleven-hour day for children.[245] But when, in March 1831, the *Mercury* published the views of Halifax worsted manufacturers that restrictions on the hours of work of children would ruin British industry, and when the younger Baines cut Oastler's very long reply by half, the stage was set for acrimonious conflict between the Dissenting newspaperman and the Anglican factory reformer.[246] When the first reports of the inspectors appointed under Althorp's Act suggested to the *Mercury* that the factory reformers had exaggerated the abuses of the factory system, Oastler published a pamphlet characterizing Edward Baines, with a phrase he borrowed from William Cobbett, as 'the Great Liar of the North'.[247] When Joseph Schofield, a mill owner and deacon of Ramsden Street Congregational church, Huddersfield, was fined £5 for violating Althorp's Act by keeping a girl at work for thirteen hours without a break, Oastler described such Dissenters as 'just as holy . . . as the filthiest strumpet who walks the streets of Leeds'.[248] Oastler claimed to know of 'liberal, dissenting deaconised blood-hounds' who showed their respect for the Lord's day by keeping children at work until twenty minutes before midnight on Saturday and starting them back at work as the clock struck midnight on Sunday. Judas Iscariot, said Oastler, was 'the first Dissenter from the Church of Christ'.[249]

But for all Oastler's invective, and for all Professor Ward's scholarship, there were Dissenters who campaigned for factory reform and there was one Dissenter who secured the movement's greatest legislative victory. One of the first men to draw attention to the damaging effect that employment in cotton factories had on children's health was the Unitarian Manchester doctor Thomas Percival to whom the young Jabez Bunting was for a time apprenticed. Percival set up the Manchester Board of Health in 1796 to find ways 'of freeing the town from the contagion of an infectious fever . . . amongst the manufacturing poor' and blamed the factories for the speed with which such diseases were propagated. He called for legislation to regulate working conditions in factories and his Board of Health included both Robert Owen and the elder Sir Robert Peel, who, with Percival's assistance,

---

[245] Driver, *Tory Radical*, 208; Baines, *Life of Edward Baines*, 254.
[246] Driver, *Tory Radical*, 65–75.   [247] Ibid. 299.
[248] Ibid. 299–300; Ward, *Factory Movement*, 136–7.
[249] Ward, *Factory Movement*, 163, 127.

introduced and carried through Parliament the first, though ineffective, Acts to control child labour in factories in 1802 and 1819.[250] The Unitarian MP William Smith consistently supported early efforts to legislate for better conditions in factories and in 1825 told the House of Commons that negro slaves worked shorter hours than Manchester children.[251] In the early 1830s the factory reform movement received a good deal of support from Nonconformist ministers and laymen and from sections of the Dissenting press. The Baptist pastor James Acworth in Leeds and the Wesleyan minister William Dawson in Halifax both supported the Ten Hours campaign early in 1832.[252] In April of the same year the Quaker William Allen and the former Quaker Samuel Hoare founded the Society for the Improvement of the Condition of Factory Children, and in February 1833 the society organized a London meeting in support of Ashley's Ten Hours Bill at which Oastler, Sadler, and Bull shared a platform with the Dissenting MP John Wilks and veteran Dissenting politician William Smith.[253] Oastler's Wesleyan father-in-law, Thomas Tatham, collected subscriptions for the factory reform movement in Nottingham and presumably helped to organize a meeting held in the town in March 1833 in support of the Ten Hours Bill. Oastler was the main speaker but the chair was taken by Richard Alliott, minister of the Castle Gate Congregational church, and Tatham and the Quaker Samuel Fox also spoke.[254] And although many Nonconformist newspapers were critical of the short-time movement, it did gain early support from Dissenting periodicals such as the *Baptist Magazine*, the *Patriot*, and Joseph Livesey's *Moral Reformer*.[255] But from 1834 Nonconformist support for the Ten Hours movement became noticeably less vocal. The Society for the Improvement of the Condition of Factory Children was short-lived and Bradford factory reformers contrasted the £1,000 Quakers had given towards the emancipation of slaves with £3 they gave to the Ten Hours movement.[256] The inactivity of William Allen's society was blamed by Oastler on the Quaker MP Joseph Pease,[257] but the indiscriminate virulence with which Oastler branded all Dissenters as hypocrites, and his attempt to turn the reform movement into an ultra-Tory crusade, cannot have endeared him to the leaders of Nonconformist opinion.

---

[250] S. E. Maltby, *Manchester and the Movement for National Elementary Education, 1800–1870* (Manchester, 1918), 15–19, 121–2.

[251] Ward, *Factory Movement*, 21, 25, 29.

[252] Ibid. 50; Owen, 'Baptists in Leeds', 142; Everett, *Memoir of William Dawson*, 380.

[253] *Life of William Allen*, iii. 35; Ward, *Factory Movement*, 63; *Patriot*, 27 Feb. 1833, 69.

[254] *Nottingham Review*, 21 Sept. 1832, 8 Mar. 1833.

[255] *Baptist Magazine*, 25 (1833), 131; *Patriot*, 22 Mar. 1832, 38; 9 Jan. 1833, 12; 10 Apr. 1833, 210; Pearce, *Joseph Livesey*, p. lii.

[256] Ward, *Factory Movement*, 109.   [257] Ibid. 63.

None the less there were many Nonconformists who shrugged off Oastler's abuse and continued to give his campaign their support. As always it is a mistake to assume that the mass of forgotten working-class men and women who filled up the pews in Dissenting chapels shared the political views of either the Unitarian and Quaker manufacturers or of their own denominational leaders. Most of the men in the deputation which urged Oastler to accept the leadership of the short-time movement in June 1831 were described as Nonconformists; meetings of the factory reformers were often held in Primitive Methodist and sometimes in Methodist New Connexion chapels; some Baptist ministers in the north of England supported the short-time campaign; and if some Nonconformist editors cooled towards the Ten Hours issue, a new one, the Wesleyan Tory James Walker, who became proprietor of the *Halifax Guardian* in 1838, gave it enthusiastic support.[258] Nonconformist MPs gave the Ten Hours movement more help than one would imagine from Oastler's blanket condemnations. Four of the twelve Nonconformist MPs voted for Ashley's bill in July 1833,[259] and one, Joseph Brotherton, spoke in its support. Brotherton, who represented Salford in Parliament from 1832 until his death in 1857, was the son of a master cotton-spinner and had worked in his father's mill until the age of fifteen. Brotherton subsequently became a partner in the firm but retired from the business in 1819 in order to devote himself to the pastorate of the Bible Christian church in Salford. He had joined the church in 1805 when it was a branch of the Swedenborgian New Jerusalem church, but the church had seceded from the Swedenborgians four years later and Brotherton was ordained pastor in 1817. He was, as we have seen, a pioneer advocate of teetotalism and vegetarianism, and even after his election to Parliament continued to minister to his church during parliamentary recesses. As MP for Salford Brotherton was a consistent advocate of factory reform and always argued that limitations on hours of work should apply to adults as well as to children. In supporting Ashley's bill in 1833 he told the Commons that he knew at first hand of the hardships suffered by factory children, for until his sixteenth year 'he had worked twelve and fourteen hours a day and had undergone all the privations which factory children endured'.[260]

---

[258] Driver, *Tory Radical*, 87–8, 101; Ward, *Factory Movement*, 84, 133, 138, 165, 272, 275, 296, 329, 330; Teale, 'Methodism in Halifax', 155.

[259] Brotherton, Fielden, Gaskell, Wilks. *Parliamentary Debates*, 3rd ser., xix (18 July 1833), cols. 913–14.

[260] *DNB*; *Biographical Dictionary of Modern British Radicals*, ii. 87–92; *Parliamentary Debates*, 3rd ser., xix (5 July 1833), cols. 233–4.

A second Dissenting MP who was prominent in the factory reform movement was Charles Hindley, who represented Ashton-under-Lyne from 1835 until his death in 1857. Hindley was a Moravian cotton manufacturer who, simply because he was a mill-owner, was asked, in preference to Ashley, to sponsor a new Ten Hours Bill in 1836. However, Hindley received an unsympathetic response both from the government and from the House of Commons and withdrew his bill.[261] Henceforward what was regarded as Hindley's excessive caution earned him the distrust of Oastler and the bitter enmity of his erstwhile political ally, Joseph Rayner Stephens, who took up the cause of factory reform in 1836 and tried, unsuccessfully, to capture Hindley's seat in the general election of 1837.[262] It did not help Hindley's reputation as a factory reformer that his own firm, managed in his absence, was prosecuted for violating Althorp's Act, but he voted consistently for reductions of hours of work and was, according to the trade union leader John Doherty, one of the chief financial backers of the Ten Hours movement.[263]

However, the chief financial supporter of the factory reform movement, and its most important advocate among the mill-owners, was John Fielden, MP for Oldham from 1832 to 1847. John Fielden was the son of the Quaker Joshua Fielden who had founded his cotton-spinning business at Todmorden in 1782, two years before John was born, and by the time John entered Parliament Fielden Brothers had grown to become the largest textile firm in the United Kingdom, employing three thousand workers. John Fielden, like Joseph Brotherton, was sent to work in his father's mill at an early age, and from the age of ten until nineteen worked ten hours a day, an experience which convinced him that such a working day was too long either for children or for adults and that a ten hours' day should be but the stepping-stone towards an eight hours' day. At the age of seventeen Fielden was converted to Methodism but in 1806 he followed Joseph Cooke out of the Wesleyan Connexion and twelve years later joined Cooke's Methodist Unitarian disciples.[264] The membership of the Methodist Unitarian denomination was overwhelmingly working class, with more than half their fathers attempting to earn their living by weaving in the 1820s and 1830s, and Fielden's accession not only strengthened the ties between the employer and his employees but also gave him moral as well as economic leadership of his community. Fielden was superintendent of the Methodist Unitarian Sunday school at Todmorden, helped to start a chapel library, and when the church found itself unable to pay off the chapel debt bought the property for £480 on

---

[261] Driver, *Tory Radical*, 324.   [262] Ward, *Factory Movement*, 165, 181.
[263] Weaver, *John Fielden*, 161, 236 n. 78.   [264] Ibid. 32–4.

condition that he discharged its liabilities.[265] And as an employer who had worked on the factory floor, and as a leader of a religious community of predominantly poor people, Fielden took up the cause of the social as well as the spiritual well-being of the workers of Lancashire. In 1816 the Fielden brothers and their employees petitioned Parliament to restrict the hours of labour of adults as well as of children; in 1826 John Fielden organized a campaign to secure a minimum wage for hand-loom weavers; and in 1831 and 1832 he played a leading role in the Manchester and the Todmorden Political Unions' campaign for electoral reform. It was his contribution to the popular agitation which culminated in the passing of the Great Reform Act that led to his being urged to contest Oldham in the general election of December 1832.[266] Three Methodist Unitarians stood for Parliament in that election: Edmund Grundy failed to win Bury and James Taylor, a future pastor of the Todmorden church, was defeated at Rochdale.[267] But Fielden, contesting Oldham alongside the radical journalist William Cobbett and facing weak Whig and Tory opponents who were both tainted by connections with the slave-trade, was returned with an overwhelming majority.[268]

As MP for Oldham Fielden was a poor and often inaudible speaker whose habit of drumming his hat to emphasize his points produced laughter from his fellow parliamentarians.[269] But of all MPs in the 1830s and 1840s he was the most consistent champion of the interests of the working class, supporting not only measures to restrict hours of work but, unlike so many of the Tory Evangelicals, advocating universal male suffrage, annual parliaments, voting by ballot, and abolition of the Corn Laws.[270] In 1833 he joined with Robert Owen in founding the National Regeneration Society in an attempt to secure an eight-hour day; in 1834 he was a determined opponent of the Poor Law Amendment Act; in 1835 he brought before Parliament a bill to guarantee a minimum wage to hand-loom weavers; and in 1836 he responded to Poulett Thompson's attempt to amend the 1833 Factory Act with his most famous pamphlet, *The Curse of the Factory System*. But by far the most significant of all Fielden's many contributions to the cause of the poor was the Act of 1847 limiting the hours of work of women and of young people between the ages of thirteen and eighteen to ten hours a day. In January 1846 Ashley, feeling that his support for the repeal of the Corn Laws violated his

[265]   Ibid. 36; McLachlan, *Methodist Unitarian Movement*, 67.
[266]   Weaver, *John Fielden*, 43–63.
[267]   H. McLachlan, *Essays and Addresses* (Manchester, 1950), 214.
[268]   R. A. Sykes, 'Some Aspects of Working-class Consciousness in Oldham', *Historical Journal*, 23 (1980), 173–6.
[269]   McLachlan, *Methodist Unitarian Movement*, 131.   [270]   Ibid. 121.

pledge to his Dorset constituents, resigned from the House of Commons and Fielden was chosen parliamentary leader of the factory reformers in his place. In the eyes of some commentators the wealthy cotton manufacturer was a more appropriate sponsor of a Ten Hours Bill than the southern aristocrat, and in moving the second reading of such a bill in April 1846 Fielden declared that if it were as destructive of the textile interest as some of its opponents asserted 'it is a bill to abolish the business of myself and my family'. Fielden's bill was defeated by only 10 votes and, with Peel's government tottering to its fall, it augured well for the future that Fielden was supported by leading members of the Whig opposition.[271] Fielden reintroduced his bill in January 1847 and, notwithstanding the strenuous opposition of the Quaker John Bright and the attempt by the prime minister Lord John Russell to effect an eleven-hours compromise, on 17 March the crucial ten-hour clause was approved by 144 votes to 66. The third reading was carried by a majority of 63 on 3 May and Fielden's Ten Hours Act received the royal assent on 8 June.[272]

Fielden's triumph was not quite complete. He had always admitted that one of his motives for seeking to reduce the hours of work of young people was thereby to reduce the hours of work of adults, since the textile mills were so dependent on juvenile labour.[273] But factory owners soon found that they could bend the spirit if not the letter of Fielden's Act by employing children and young people in relays and thus keeping adult males at work for up to fifteen hours a day. The government resolved the problem by an Act of 1850 which outlawed the relay system, but only at the price of extending the maximum working day to ten-and-a-half hours. Fielden did not live to see the 1850 compromise. He lost his seat in the general election of 1847—ironically to another Unitarian, William Johnson Fox—and he died in May 1849. Twenty years later his sons built a massive Gothic Unitarian chapel, with a spire rising to 196 feet, as his memorial at Todmorden.

After Fielden's rejection by the voters of Oldham in 1847 the working men of the town complained bitterly that the 'Religious, Dissenting, and Non-conforming part of the electors' had voted for his opponents,[274] and their complaint illustrates the point that although there were important sympathizers with the working class among prominent Nonconformists, those sympathizers often came from minority and heretical groups within Dissent. Fielden was a Methodist Unitarian, Joseph Brotherton a Bible Christian (Swedenborgian), Charles Hindley a Moravian. Much the same was true of

---

[271] Weaver, *John Fielden*, 259–61.   [272] Ibid. 265–6.   [273] Ibid. 260.
[274] J. Vincent, *Pollbooks: How Victorians Voted* (Cambridge, 1967), 156.

the Nonconformist opposition to the Poor Law Amendment Act of 1834: a minority of vocal Dissenters tried to frustrate its passage through Parliament and its implementation in the country, but to a large extent the leadership of mainstream Dissent gave the New Poor Law its support.

The mounting campaign against the Elizabethan Poor Law, based on its soaring cost, the supposed subsidies it gave to the idle, and the stimulus it was alleged to give to population growth, met with a favourable response from many Nonconformists from the late eighteenth century onwards. The Unitarian Joseph Priestley, the *Monthly Magazine*, and the *Monthly Repository* all demanded the abolition or the drastic alteration of the old Poor Law.[275] In Manchester in 1821 the Unitarian John Taylor, editor of the *Guardian*, was accused by his future rival, the Presbyterian Archibald Prentice, of imbibing 'the leading principles of Malthus' and of wishing to deny poor relief to all persons who got married after a certain date.[276] In Nottingham Absalom Barnett, a deacon of the George Street Particular Baptist church and assistant overseer of the poor from 1819, tried to reform the administration of the Poor Law by setting the unemployed to work and paying them less in poor relief than was earned by men in regular employment.[277] The principle of 'less eligibility' which Absalom Barnett tried to enforce in Nottingham was enshrined in the Poor Law Commissioners' *Report* of February 1834 which was itself the basis of the Poor Law Amendment Act of August of the same year. The Act created a centralized Poor Law Commission with powers to amalgamate existing parishes into poor law unions administered by guardians elected by the ratepayers. The Poor Law Commissioners had powers to order the building of workhouses and to insist that poor relief should be given to the able-bodied and their families only within the walls of those workhouses. In order to ensure that only people in genuine need of relief applied for assistance the condition of the paupers within the workhouse was to be 'less eligible', that is more uncomfortable, than that of the poorest workers outside. The Poor Law Commissioners were given powers to transport the unemployed from rural areas to districts where their labour was needed. 'The New Poor Law', commented Oastler, 'was only one branch of the factory system, intended to drive the agricultural poor into the factories.'[278]

---

[275] Sellers, 'Social and Political Ideas of English Unitarians', 26, 57; Mineka, *Dissidence of Dissent*, 267.

[276] Prentice, *Historical Sketches*, 212–14, 235.

[277] Church, *Economic and Social Changes in a Midland Town*, 112–13; Harrison, 'Baptists of Nottinghamshire', ii. 860–3.

[278] Ward, *Factory Movement*, 123–4.

The Poor Law Amendment Act was warmly supported by Dissenting manufacturers such as the Ashworths: Edmund Ashworth confirmed the truth of
Oastler's accusation by telling Edwin Chadwick, secretary to the Poor Law
Commissioners, 'that every facility [should] be given to the removal of
labourers from one county to another' in order to reduce wages and prevent
strikes in industrial districts.[279] The Act was, on the whole, well received by
the Nonconformist press. The *Patriot* asserted that 'a more well-considered
and beneficial measure never emanated from any administration'.[280] The
Unitarian *Christian Reformer* claimed that it would be 'a far greater boon to
the poor than to the rich', restoring to the British peasantry their independence.[281] The *Baptist Magazine* published a short criticism of the Act and a
long defence of it.[282] And the Independent *Dysgedydd*, while it disliked the
provision that husbands and wives should be kept apart in workhouses,
regarded it as a largely satisfactory measure.[283] The Baptist *Seren Gomer* was
a rare exception to this chorus of approval, its editor, Hugh William Jones,
denouncing the workhouses as 'the Bastilles of the poor'.[284]

There were a number of other orthodox Dissenters who shared Hugh
Jones's antipathy to the Poor Law Amendment Act. John Hart, minister of
the Ebenezer chapel, Middleton, led an anti-Poor Law procession into Oldham in 1837 and publicly burnt a copy of the Act.[285] John Hanson, minister of
the Loxley Congregational church in Sheffield, claimed that it was because
of his opposition to the New Poor Law that he was deprived of his share of
the Regium Donum by John Pye Smith.[286] John Jenkinson, pastor of the
Ebenezer Particular Baptist church in Kettering, was treasurer of the
Kettering Radical Association which in 1837 drew up a petition against
the Poor Law Act.[287] John Markham, who became secretary of the Leicester
Anti-Poor Law Society in 1838, was a former Primitive Methodist local
preacher.[288] The Liberal Wesleyan George Browne, who topped the poll in
the elections for the Halifax poor law guardians in 1837, resigned a year later

---

[279] Boyson, *Ashworth Cotton Enterprise*, 185–90.   [280] *Patriot*, 21 May 1834, 184.

[281] Sellers, 'Social and Political Ideas of Unitarians', 96.

[282] *Baptist Magazine*, 28 (June 1836), 225–9.

[283] Parry, 'Welsh Independents and Working-class Movements', 141–2.

[284] Bassett, *Welsh Baptists*, 140.

[285] J. Knott, *Popular Opposition to the 1834 Poor Law* (1986), 148.

[286] *Northern Star*, 23 Feb. 1839, 7; C. M. Elliott, 'The Political Economy of English Dissent', in
R. M. Hartwell (ed.), *The Industrial Revolution* (Oxford, 1970), 158. The Regium Donum was a
Treasury grant to poor Dissenting ministers and their widows, amounting to £1,000 a year, which
dated from the reign of George I and which was a constant source of embarrassment to the advocates of disestablishment until its abolition in 1851 (Manning, *Dissenting Deputies*, 22, 387–8).

[287] Greenall, 'Baptist as Radical', *Northamptonshire Past and Present*, 8 (1991–2), 215.

[288] Patterson, *Radical Leicester*, 295–6.

when the Poor Law Commissioners 'cruelly' refused to let him continue to provide outdoor relief.[289] The Quaker Joseph Sturge appeared on an anti-Poor Law platform alongside Oastler in Birmingham in 1844.[290] And, somewhat surprisingly, the elder Edward Baines objected to parts of the Act and moved an unsuccessful amendment to keep the Poor Law Commissioners out of districts where there had been no abuses in poor law administration.[291] When the third reading of the Poor Law Amendment Bill was carried by 187 votes to 50 in July 1834, Baines was one of five Dissenting MPs to vote with the minority.[292]

The most energetic opponents of the New Poor Law were, however, members of small and heretical sects on the fringes of Nonconformity. Joseph Rayner Stephens denounced the New Poor Law as the work of 'Beelzebub, the Prince of the Devil' and urged workers at Rochdale in 1838 to resist its implementation by force. 'If it were right to confiscate the property of the people' by denying them outdoor relief, 'it was right for the poor to take a dagger in one hand and a torch in the other, and do their best for themselves.' The violence of Stephens's language led to his arrest on a charge of sedition in December 1838, and in the following year meetings in his defence were held in Baptist, Unitarian, New Connexion and Association Methodist, and above all in Primitive Methodist chapels and schoolrooms in the north of England. But such displays of radicalism often incurred the censure of denominational authorities and Stephens's extremism alienated many of the men who had left the Wesleyan Connexion with him in 1834.[293] Two other unorthodox ministers who gave active support to the campaign against the New Poor Law were James Taylor, the Methodist Unitarian, and William Hill, pastor of the Swedenborgian Bethel chapel in Hull.[294] The opposition to the implementation of the Poor Law Amendment Act in Preston was led by Joseph Livesey, the former Scotch Baptist and temperance pioneer who topped the poll in the elections for the town's poor law guardians in 1837.[295] By the 1830s, though, Livesey had rejected orthodox Christianity in favour of a religion of good works.

---

[289] Hargreaves, 'Methodists in the Parish of Halifax', 49–50, 82.

[290] Ward, *Factory Movement*, 300.   [291] Baines, *Life of Edward Baines*, 199–200.

[292] The others were Brotherton, Fielden, Potter, and Wilks (*Parliamentary Debates*, 3rd ser. xxiv (1 July 1834), col. 1061).

[293] Knott, *Opposition to the Poor Law*, 249; Rose, *Methodism in Ashton-under-Lyne*, ii. 48–4; J. T. Ward, 'Revolutionary Tory: The Life of Joseph Rayner Stephens', *Transactions of the Lancashire and Cheshire Antiquarian Society*, 68 (1958), 102; *Northern Star*, 23 Feb. 1839, 4; 9 Mar., 3, 6; 16 Mar., 4; 23 Mar., 8; 30 Mar., 4, 7; 6 Apr., 4; 13 Apr., 6; 20 Apr., 4, 5, 6; 4 May, 6.

[294] N. Edsall, *The Anti-Poor Law Movement* (Manchester, 1971), 63; Knott, *Opposition to the Poor Law*, 104.

[295] Phillips, *Sectarian Spirit*, 59.

The most effective opponent of the New Poor Law was John Fielden. He opposed the bill when it was first presented to Parliament; he moved for its repeal in 1838, receiving only 17 votes; and he led a determined campaign to prevent the introduction of the New Poor Law into either his constituency of Oldham or his home town of Todmorden. In Oldham ratepayers boycotted the elections of guardians and no board of guardians met from 1837 to 1847.[296] Some guardians had been elected in the Todmorden union in 1837, but when the Poor Law Commissioners ordered them to take over the administration of poor relief in July 1838 Fielden tried to compel the resignation of the guardians by closing his mills and forcing his three thousand workers on to poor relief. Fielden's attempt to remove the guardians failed and eleven days later he reopened his mills, but at Fielden's behest the Todmorden overseers refused to collect the poor rate, distress warrants were issued against them, and when an attempt was made to seize the possessions of one of the over-seers two constables were prevented from carrying out the distraint by a hostile crowd, which assaulted them, stripped them naked, and covered them with mud. The mob went on to ransack and burn the homes of the guardians and both the *Manchester Guardian* and the *Leeds Mercury* urged that Fielden be prosecuted for complicity in the riot.[297] But the violence achieved its objective. The New Poor Law was not enforced in Todmorden; in 1844 the commissioners authorized the guardians to sell all the workhouses in the Todmorden union; and until 1877 Todmorden 'found itself in the unique position of being a Poor Law union without workhouses'.[298]

In Nottingham the attempt by Absalom Barnett, now relieving officer and clerk to the board of guardians, to enforce the full rigour of the New Poor Law provoked bitter criticism. Barnett's reluctance to grant poor relief, claimed William Roworth, 'has produced the greatest distress among the industrious poor, and brought on disease, which would have caused death had not others provided that which the relieving officers ought to have given'.[299] Barnett, said Roworth, was the 'best hated man in Nottingham'. But depression in the hosiery and lace trades forced the Nottingham guardians, in 1837 and again in 1839, to suspend the workhouse test and grant outdoor relief to the able-bodied.[300] The suspension of the workhouse test in Nottingham, and the failure of the commissioners to impose the New Poor

---

[296] Edsall, *Anti-Poor Law Movement*, 79–80; Knott, *Opposition to the Poor Law*, 147–8.
[297] Knott, *Opposition to the Poor Law*, 206–15; Weaver, *John Fielden*, 192–4, 200–5.
[298] Edsall, *Anti-Poor Law Movement*, 224.
[299] W. Roworth, *Observations on the Administration of the New Poor Law in Nottingham* (1840), 69.
[300] Church, *Economic and Social Change in a Midland Town*, 114–18.

Law in Todmorden, were symptomatic of the concessions which the commissioners were forced to make throughout the north of England in the late 1830s and 1840s. They culminated in the Outdoor Relief Regulation Order of 1852, which acknowledged the necessity of granting, on occasion, outdoor assistance to the able-bodied in violation of the Poor Law Report of 1834.[301]

The conflicting policies of Absalom Barnett and John Fielden, of the Particular Baptist and the Methodist Unitarian, epitomized the contrasting attitudes of orthodox and heterodox Dissenters to working-class problems. To Barnett the object of legislation was to provide moral restraint and stimulus to virtue; Fielden by contrast derided men who thought that 'the morals, and virtues, and well-being of the people would be best promoted by pinching their bellies'.[302] Critics of orthodox Dissenters frequently contrasted their coolness towards factory reform with their enthusiasm to free colonial slaves. As William Cobbett, Fielden's fellow MP for Oldham, complained in 1824, while Methodists railed 'against the West India slave-holders . . . not a word do you ever hear from them against the slave-holders in Lancashire and Ireland'.[303] Whereas in 1833 Parliament limited the hours of work of negroes in the West Indies to forty-five hours a week, in 1836 it nearly increased the hours of work of twelve-year-olds in English factories from forty-eight to sixty-nine hours a week. 'What a pity,' exclaimed Fielden, 'that these 35,000 factory children happen to be white instead of black!'[304]

But the great crime of the slave owners, in the eyes of Evangelical Dissenters, was not that they tortured the negroes' bodies by overworking them, but that they imperilled their souls by denying missionaries access to them. No such accusation could be levelled against the factory owners of northern England who, if they took any interest in such matters at all, encouraged rather than discouraged their factory children to attend Sunday school. But heterodox Dissenters such as Joseph Rayner Stephens, Joseph Livesey, James Taylor, and John Fielden were more concerned with their fellow countrymen's bellies than with their souls. Their political radicalism, like the entrepreneurial success of the Ashworths and the Gregs and the Marshalls who opposed them, came from a religious impulse that was well on the way to being secularized. John Fielden's compassion for the pauper and the factory child was the conscience of a Quaker and Unitarian family whose devotion to making money rather than saving souls had brought immense wealth. By contrast the great strength of Evangelical Nonconformity was that it

[301] Knott, *Opposition to the Poor Law*, 216–18.
[302] Church, *Economic and Social Change in a Midland Town*, 119; Weaver, *John Fielden*, 173.
[303] *Cobbett's Weekly Register*, 49, 3 Jan. 1824, col. 36.
[304] J. Fielden, *The Curse of the Factory System* (2nd edn., 1969), 14, 41.

offered consolation, companionship, and ultimately eternal salvation to a working class threatened by disease, natural disaster, and early death. Yet for this very reason the great weakness of orthodox Dissent was its inability to offer convincing solutions when working people began to see the cause of their problems not in natural disasters or immutable laws, but in the policies of government, the demands of factory owners, and the tight-fistedness of poor law guardians. The dilemma facing working-class Dissenters was expressed by the New Connexion Methodists of Ambler Thorn near Halifax when they were reprimanded by their Quarterly Meeting for allowing a sermon to be preached on behalf of Joseph Rayner Stephens in 1839. 'Whether our poverty derives from the just and merciful decrees of the Supreme Governor of the universe,' they complained, 'or from the free agency of wicked men, very few attempt to instruct us.'[305] But if the Methodists were reluctant to instruct them in such matters, by 1839 a new body of men had arisen which was only too willing to provide an answer to the question they posed: they were the Chartists.

6. 'WHAT SAYS CHRISTIANITY TO THE PRESENT DISTRESS?': CHARTISM, THE ANTI-CORN LAW LEAGUE, COMPLETE SUFFRAGE

The Chartist movement, with its demand for universal male suffrage, annual parliaments, and voting by ballot, imposed greater political strains on Dissent than any of the other political issues of the first half of the nineteenth century. Simply because it had far more popular support than the trade union movement, the factory reformers, or the anti-Poor Law agitation, simply because it subsumed all these movements under the single banner of the People's Charter, Chartism threatened to disrupt Nonconformity to a greater extent than any of the earlier agitations. Chartism was what some Dissenting leaders had been dreading for twenty years or more: a mass movement which would divide society, and hence the chapels, on class rather than on religious lines.

After the disappointment of the 1832 Reform Act, frustration at the early failures of the trade union and Ten Hours movements, anger against the New Poor Law, and rapidly declining living standards which accompanied the depression of 1837–42, working-class radicals were no longer prepared to

[305] *Northern Star*, 20 Apr. 1839, 5.

accept what middle-class radicals told them about the common interest of the working and middle classes. Even more than in the case of the trade union movement, the high proportion of working-class people in Nonconformist chapels guaranteed that Dissenters would be much in evidence in the Chartist movement. What little statistical evidence there is suggests that Nonconformists were more heavily represented among active Chartists than they were in the population at large. Many of the five thousand colliers and ironworkers who marched in pouring rain down the Monmouthshire valleys to Newport on the night of 3–4 November 1839 must have been Dissenters. No doubt some were forced to join the march against their will, and during the Sunday evening services at Rhyd chapel, Rassa, and Carmel Independent chapel, Beaufort, bands of Chartists entered the chapels and compelled male worshippers to accompany them.[306] The marchers were armed with guns, pikes, and mandrils, and in the clash with the 45th Regiment in front of the Westgate Hotel on the morning of Monday, 4 November, at least twenty Chartists were killed and perhaps another fifty injured. Anglicans blamed the rising on Dissent and a recent Marxist historian has ascribed it to the workers' 'linguistic and cultural exclusivity', which comes largely to the same thing.[307] Thomas Thomas, principal of the Baptist college at Pontypool, claimed that not more than fifty of the marchers were members of Nonconformist churches, but the chaplain of Monmouth gaol interviewed forty-nine Chartist prisoners incarcerated therein in 1840 and revealed that forty-one of them were Dissenters.[308] The leader of the rising, the draper and former mayor of Newport John Frost, attended the Hope Congregational chapel and its minister, Benjamin Byron, supported the Chartists and after Frost's imprisonment prayed for his release 'and the destruction of his enemies'.[309] One of the columns that advanced on Newport on that disastrous night was led by John Reynolds who was known as a Nonconformist preacher.[310] Interviews with seventy-three of the longest-serving Chartist prisoners held in thirteen different gaols in England and Wales in the winter of 1840–1 also revealed a disproportionately high number of Nonconformists: twenty-four, a proportion of 32.9 per cent.[311] Of the fifteen men still being held in con-

---

[306] I. Wilks, *South Wales and the Rising of 1839* (1984), 194.

[307] D. Williams, *John Frost* (Cardiff, 1939), 323–5; Wilks, *The Rising of 1839*, 231–2.

[308] J. V. Morgan, *Welsh Religious Leaders in the Victorian Era* (1905), 149; Williams, *John Frost*, 324.

[309] Williams, *John Frost*, 16, 136, 186, 242.

[310] D. J. V. Jones, *The Last Rising* (Oxford, 1985), 122, 124; Wilks, *The Rising of 1839*, 176, 189.

[311] PRO HO 20/10. The 24 included 7 Independents, 7 Baptists, 3 Calvinistic Methodists, 2 Wesleyans, 1 Primitive Methodist, 3 followers of J. R. Stephens, and W. Jackson, a former Wesleyan minister who had formed his own breakaway congregation. C. Godfrey, in his article

nection with the Newport rising, ten were Nonconformists. Similarly of fifteen men arrested in Oldham for speaking at Chartist meetings in 1842, ten were Nonconformists and of these seven were local preachers.[312] After the Plug Plot riots in the Manchester area in August 1842 James Gwyther defended Dissenters from the charge of inciting the violence by claiming that of 425 prisoners serving sentences for their part in the disturbances only 92 were Nonconformists, a proportion of 21.6 per cent.[313] But this was in an area where Dissenters were hard pressed to win the allegiance of 10 per cent of the population in 1851, and again suggests that active Nonconformist participation in Chartist disturbances was much greater than the proportion of Nonconformists in the general population would lead one to expect.

While neither the free-thinking Feargus O'Connor, the infidel Zephaniah Williams, nor the former Bryanite William Lovett could claim that their devotion to Chartism was motivated by religion, many of the second tier of Chartist leaders were active Nonconformists. Unitarians were prominent in the Chartist as in other radical movements. John Fielden took the chair at a mass Chartist demonstration on Kersal Moor, Manchester, in September 1838, and at that meeting his friend and pastor James Taylor, now minister of the Todmorden Methodist Unitarian church, was chosen to represent Rochdale at the first Chartist Convention in February 1839.[314] Fielden, along with Thomas Attwood, was chosen to present the first Chartist petition to Parliament in June 1839. When the petition was rejected by 235 votes to 46 those Nonconformist MPs present divided on the issue: against the Charter were Edward Baines and George Philips but in its favour were Brotherton, Fielden, and Charles Hindley who had been a member of the original committee appointed to draw up the Charter.[315] As Chartism became increasingly violent from the summer of 1839 Fielden, along with other middle-class supporters, distanced himself from the movement, but he did not abandon his commitment to universal male suffrage.[316]

The leading Chartist in Gloucester was the Unitarian Thomas Sidaway, a master chain-maker who had also been prosecuted for his refusal to pay

on 'The Chartist Prisoners, 1839–1841', found 32 Dissenters, but he appears to have included a number whose connections with Dissent were very tenuous by the time of their imprisonment (*International Review of Social History*, 24 (1979), 235–6).

[312] Smith, 'Religion in Industrial Society', 478.
[313] Wearmouth, *Methodism and Working-Class Movements*, 72–3.
[314] McLachlan, *Methodist Unitarian Movement*, 123–4, 132–3.
[315] *Parliamentary Debates*, 3rd ser. xlix (12 July 1839), cols. 274–8; J. T. Ward, *Chartism* (1973), 83.
[316] Weaver, *John Fielden*, 215–17.

church rates and had organized a meeting in favour of the Tolpuddle martyrs.[317] In Merthyr Tydfil the Unitarian minister, the blacksmith David John, supported Chartism as he had earlier supported parliamentary reform, and his son, also David John, printed and published the Chartist *Udgorn Cymru* (Trumpet of Wales) from March 1840 until October 1842.[318] Other Welsh Unitarian ministers who supported Chartism were John Jones of Trecynon and Owen Evans of Cefn Coed, Merthyr.[319] Two Unitarian ministers in England lost their pastorates as a result of their adherence to the Chartist cause. Henry Solly of Yeovil was converted to Chartism by working-class members of his congregation and published his support for Chartism in a pamphlet, *What Says Christianity to the Present Distress?* But his radical views angered other members of his church and when its main financial backer withdrew his subscription Solly was forced to look for another congregation.[320] Similarly John Cameron, minister of Wakefield's Unitarian Westgate church, supported the Chartists and criticized the 'pride of wealth' from his pulpit. But he provoked such opposition from the chapel trustees that they closed the building to him in 1844, and when he broke down the door to gain access to the pulpit he was removed by legal action.[321]

The connection between religious heterodoxy and political radicalism can also be seen in the cases of two other ministers who supported the Chartist movement. James Scholefield, apothecary and minister to the Bible Christian (Cowherdite) church at Ancoats, Manchester, provided hospitality for Feargus O'Connor when he visited the town and allowed his chapel to be used for a meeting of the Chartist executive in 1842.[322] Even more devoted to the Chartist cause was the Swedenborgian minister William Hill, a former hand-loom weaver from Barnsley who was pastor of the Bethel chapel in Hull from 1837 until 1848. For the first six years of his pastorate Hill preached on Sundays and in the week worked in Leeds editing Feargus O'Connor's *Northern Star.* Under Hill's editorship the paper reached a circulation of 42,000 a week in the spring of 1839, four times that of its rival, the *Leeds Mercury.*[323]

---

[317] D. Thompson, *The Chartists* (1984), 162–3.
[318] A. Briggs (ed.), *Chartist Studies* (1967), 221, 242.
[319] Davies, *They Thought for Themselves*, 84.
[320] Solly, *These Eighty Years*, i. 343–51, 398.
[321] J. Seed, 'Theologies of Power: Unitarianism and the Social Relations of Religious Discourse', in R. J. Morris (ed.), *Class, Power, and Social Structure in British Nineteenth-Century Towns* (Leicester, 1986), 144–5.
[322] Lineham, 'English Swedenborgians', 314–17; Read, *Press and People*, 216; Thompson, *The Chartists*, 168–9.
[323] Lineham, 'English Swedenborgians', 437–8; Thompson, *The Chartists*, 51–2.

While unorthodox Dissenters were prominent in the Chartist movement, they were not alone. Some Nonconformist ministers and numerous lay preachers from the orthodox denominations put their oratorical skills at the service of the Chartists. A Chartist meeting held on Northampton racecourse in August 1838 was addressed by John Jenkinson, pastor of the Ebenezer Baptist church in Kettering, on the theme 'Justice for all'.[324] At the huge Chartist demonstration held on Peep Green (Hartshead Moor) in the West Riding on Whit Monday, 1839, the Primitive Methodist local preacher William Thornton opened the proceedings with prayer. When he had finished Feargus O'Connor promised that 'when we get the People's Charter I will see that you are made the Archbishop of York'.[325] Chartism was supported consistently by Richard Sutton, the Methodist New Connexion editor of the *Nottingham Review*, and a leading figure among Nottinghamshire Chartists was George Harrison, a Calverton farmer who claimed to have been a Primitive Methodist local preacher for twelve years.[326] Harrison took the chair at a Chartist demonstration on the Forest in May 1839, attended by several thousand people despite a severe hailstorm and the presence of 'three pieces of artillery'; he represented Nottingham at the second Chartist Convention in May 1842; and in July he organized a great Chartist fête on one of his fields in Calverton in honour of Feargus O'Connor.[327] Another local preacher who threw himself into the Chartist cause was the Tunstall blacksmith Joseph Capper, who was said to have been 'one of the first converts at the great Primitive Methodist camp meeting held on Mow Cop in 1807'.[328] In Leicester a prominent Chartist was a framework knitter named Finn who was also a General Baptist pastor, and in Coventry John Watts, assistant minister at the Cow Lane Particular Baptist church, declared his sympathy for Chartism in 1842.[329] The ministers of two Particular Baptist churches in Lancashire, Archibald McPhail of Huncoat and T. S. Baker of Millwood, gave lectures on behalf of the Chartists in the 1840s, and in 1842 Chartists thanked three Baptist ministers at West Bromwich and Coseley in the Black Country for supporting the Chartist cause from their pulpits.[330]

[324] Greenall, 'Baptist as Radical', *Northamptonshire Past and Present*, 8, 215.

[325] B. Wilson, *The Struggles of an Old Chartist* (1887), 3.

[326] *Nottingham Review*, 20 July 1838, 4; 21 Sept. 1838, 2; 29 Mar. 1839, 7; 10 May 1839, 4; Morris, 'Primitive Methodism in Nottinghamshire', 247.

[327] *Nottingham Review*, 24 May 1839, 3; 29 July 1842, 6; J. Epstein and D. Thompson (eds.), *The Chartist Experience* (1982), 228, 248.

[328] Shaw, *When I was a Child*, 144.

[329] Patterson, *Radical Leicester*, 300, 302–3; Searby, *Coventry Politics*, 18; Cunningham, *Everywhere Spoken Against*, 186.

[330] Weston, 'Baptists of North-West England', 660–2; Barnsby, *Working Class Movement in the Black Country*, 92–3.

In two areas where Old Dissent attracted a good deal of working-class support—south Wales and the eastern counties—there was considerable orthodox Dissenting sympathy for Chartism. Hugh Jones, the editor of the Baptist *Seren Gomer*, supported the six points of the People's Charter when they were first published in 1837.[331] In the following year David Rees, minister of the Independent church at Llanelli and editor of *Y Diwygiwr* (The Reformer) urged Welshmen to support Chartism, though his own preference was for household rather than universal suffrage on the ground that universal education should precede one man, one vote.[332] The Chartists at Dinas were led by William David, a shopkeeper and trustee of the Baptist chapel who fled to America after the Newport rising.[333] And in April 1839 the Baptist church at Rhayader in Radnorshire altered the time of its evening service so that members could attend a Chartist meeting to be addressed by Henry Hetherington.[334]

Similarly in Essex and Suffolk the considerable working-class following which both the Congregationalists and Baptists attracted was reflected in the large number of Dissenters among the Chartists of those counties.[335] Among the leading Chartists of Ipswich was Robert Booley, a spring-maker at a coachworks and a lay preacher. The Chartists at Witham were led by Charles Fish, a Baptist shoemaker. In Colchester the Chartists were supported in 1840 by T. W. Davis, minister of the Lion Walk Congregational church. And in Chelmsford John Thorogood, the cobbler and future church-rates martyr, spoke at a Chartist rally in 1838.[336] The Chartists argued that church rates would never be repealed until parliament was reformed, and that middle-class Dissenters who were opposed to universal suffrage were helping to perpetuate 'the unhallowed union of Church and State'.[337]

In Coventry, in Gloucester, in Truro, as well as in Chelmsford the local Chartist leaders were Dissenters who had earlier been prominent in the campaign against church rates.[338] Although historians of Nonconformity have always emphasized that those Dissenters who supported Chartism repudiated the use of physical force, for a minority the breaking of the law to resist the imposition of church rates was but the prelude to threatening violence to secure the People's Charter. William Taunton, a Coventry

---

[331] Bassett, *Welsh Baptists*, 140.
[332] Williams, *John Frost*, 98; Parry, 'Welsh Independents and Working-class Movements', 52, 58.
[333] Briggs, *Chartist Studies*, 233, 239; Jones, *The Last Rising*, 170–1.
[334] Williams, *John Frost*, 144.
[335] A. F. J. Brown, *Chartism in Essex and Suffolk* (Chelmsford and Ipswich, 1982), 39–41, 86.
[336] Ibid. 39–40, 49, 80–2, 94, 101.   [337] Ibid. 87.
[338] Searby, *Coventry Politics*, 6, 13; Thompson, *The Chartists*, 162–3, 203.

Congregationalist and Sunday school teacher, Owenite, and manager of the city's first co-operative store, was also a physical force Chartist. In the summer of 1839 he urged the Chartists of Coventry to arm themselves, and even in the aftermath of the Newport rising warned that the 'government never will concede anything till they are obliged through fear'.[339] Similarly in the West Riding one of the leaders of an abortive rising in January 1840 was Samuel Holberry, a General Baptist distillery worker from Sheffield, who was arrested before the planned insurrection could materialize.[340] Holberry died in York Castle in June 1842 and his death was blamed by Chartists on the harsh conditions of his imprisonment.[341]

Yet against the mass of evidence which indicates a substantial degree of Nonconformist support for Chartism, must be set the equally striking evidence of Dissenting hostility to the movement. Much of Evangelical Nonconformity, and especially official Nonconformity, regarded Chartism as anathema. Henry Solly's experiences at Yeovil and John Cameron's ejection from Wakefield remind us that by no means all Unitarians supported Chartism: with the usual exception of John Fielden prominent Unitarian manufacturers were as opposed to universal suffrage as they were to factory reform. From their widely differing theological standpoints Wesleyan and Primitive Methodist preachers, prosperous Congregationalists, and wealthy Unitarians could all be found denouncing the People's Charter. The Dissenting establishment, no less than the Anglican, felt threatened by Chartism.

Given the traditional Wesleyan hostility to radicalism, it is hardly surprising that the Connexion should denounce those who supported the six points of the Charter. In May 1839 Wesleyan preachers in the Bath circuit resolved that any Methodist who joined the Chartists should be expelled and both the Halifax and Huddersfield Wesleyan circuits expelled local preachers who had attended the meeting on Peep Green.[342] When the Chartist Convention in March 1839 sent Robert Lowery as a missionary to Cornwall he found the hold which Methodism and teetotalism had on the people of the duchy was an effective barrier to the growth of Chartism. Are there any radicals or Chartists in the town? he asked of an inhabitant of St Ives. 'No', replied the

---

[339] Searby, *Coventry Politics*, 5, 14.

[340] PRO HO 20/10; J. L. Baxter, 'Early Chartism and Labour Class Struggle: South Yorkshire, 1837–40', in S. Pollard and C. Holmes, *Essays in the Economic and Social History of South Yorkshire* (Sheffield, 1976), 144–50.

[341] *Nottingham Review*, 10 July 1842, 2.

[342] *Northern Star*, 25 May 1839, 4; 6 July 1839, 4; E. V. Chapman, *John Wesley and Co.* (Halifax, 1952), 44, 61.

bewildered man; 'they catch nothing here but pilchards and mackerel.'[343] The Wesleyan Conference, in 1842, condemned 'infidels and irreligious men' who charged 'all the sufferings of the community upon the selfish policy of rulers'.[344] Official Primitive Methodism was no more sympathetic to Chartism than was official Wesleyanism. The Ranters of Nottinghamshire regarded Chartism as an evil influence on their members. When one of their local preachers, Henry Dorman, was advertised to preach at Stapleford on 'Chartism in accordance with the Scriptures' he was ordered to preach no more political sermons. And when a Nottingham Primitive Methodist was expelled in 1841 he was described as 'a bad man, fond of ale, a desperate tobacco smoker, and a great Chartist'.[345]

There was a good deal of opposition to Chartism among the Baptists. The support which Archibald McPhail of the Huncoat Baptist church gave to the Chartists prompted the chapel trustees and four local Baptist ministers to take legal action in an attempt to remove him from his pulpit in 1843. Their action led to the closure of the chapel for two years and a five-year-long dispute which cost the church £538 in legal fees.[346] The South Parade Baptist church in Leeds excommunicated one of its members, P. B. Templeton, a reporter on the *Northern Star*, for publishing a paragraph critical of the church's minister, John Giles, the opponent of Socialism.[347] The General Baptist church at Basford near Nottingham expelled Robert Arms for 'uniting with a body of Chartist religionists' in 1839, though he was received back into church membership five months later.[348] John Gent Brooks, an unemployed Baptist framework knitter from Hinckley in Leicestershire, supported the Chartists for two years until repelled by the advocates of physical force. When a Leicester Chartist arrived in Hinckley to organize a demonstration Brooks was let out of the workhouse to address the crowd and to urge them not to follow the Chartists.[349] Among Congregationalists Josiah Conder's *Patriot* regarded Chartism as an 'enormous evil'; John Blackburn bracketed it with rationalism and atheism; and Jonathan Glyde castigated its supporters as 'radical subverters of our constitution'.[350] William Byles's *Bradford Observer* accused the Chartists of 'attempting to exercise the worst

[343] Rule, 'Labouring Miner in Cornwall', 362, 365, 370.
[344] Wearmouth, *Methodism and Working-class Movements*, 190.
[345] Morris, 'Primitive Methodism in Nottinghamshire', 246–8.
[346] Weston, 'Baptists of North-west England', 371–2, 660–2.
[347] F. Beckwith, 'South Parade, Leeds', *Baptist Quarterly*, 21 (1965–6), 112.
[348] Harrison, 'Baptists of Nottinghamshire', ii. 858–9.
[349] J. Ryan, 'Religion and Radical Politics in Birmingham, 1830–50', M.Litt. thesis (Birmingham, 1979), 61–2.
[350] Martin, 'Politics of the Congregationalists', 247, 266.

species of tyranny, threatening not only loss of custom but even loss of life itself to those who dare to differ from them in opinion'.[351] The younger Edward Baines countered the six points of the People's Charter with six points of his own: Education, Religion, Virtue, Industry, Sobriety, Frugality.[352] The Unitarian mill-owner Robert Hyde Greg opposed any further extension of the franchise after 1832: the lower one descended down the social scale, he claimed, the greater was the degree of ignorance, since the poor man's time 'must be spent in providing for existence, not acquiring knowledge'.[353] John Taylor, the Unitarian editor of the *Manchester Guardian*, agreed: to grant universal suffrage would be to give the vote 'to every drunkard and blackguard in the kingdom'.[354]

In Wales the Newport rising of November 1839 prompted many Nonconformists to distance themselves from Chartism, just as the violence and intimidation which had accompanied early trade unionism had provoked their criticism of workers' combinations. Both the Independent David Rees, who sympathized with Chartism, and the Calvinistic Methodist John Elias, who did not, agreed that the rising was a disgrace to Wales.[355] In December 1839 the South Wales Calvinistic Methodist Association, meeting at Blackwood in Monmouthshire, excommunicated two of its members who had joined the Chartists, and in the following January its monthly paper, *Y Drysorfa*, argued that Chartism and Christianity were incompatible.[356] So delighted was Sir Josiah Guest, now MP for Merthyr, with the Calvinistic Methodists' opposition to Chartism that he gave £2,000 towards the erection of their new chapel at Dowlais.[357]

The attempt by Chartists to force Dissenters to accompany them on the march to Newport on the night of Sunday, 3 November, did not endear them to Nonconformist pastors. When Chartists interrupted the service at Carmel Independent chapel, Beaufort, the minister, John Ridge, took refuge under the pulpit stairs.[358] Richard Jones, Independent minister at Sirhowy, spent the same night up to his neck in the reeds of a local river while Chartists armed with swords and crowbars crossed the bridge above his head to find him. Not surprisingly Jones retaliated by excommunicating church members who

[351] Koditschek, *Class Formation and Urban-industrial Society*, 336.
[352] Read, *Press and People*, 132.   [353] Rose, *Gregs of Quarry Bank*, 126.
[354] Briggs, *Chartist Studies*, 38.
[355] R. Wallace, *Organise! Organise! Organise!* (Cardiff, 1991), 37; E. Morgan, *John Elias: Life, Letters, and Essays* (1973), 331.
[356] Williams, *John Frost*, 325.
[357] Turner, 'Revivals and Popular Religion in Wales', 157, 173.
[358] Williams, *John Frost*, 217.

were known to be Chartists.[359] Four members of the Salem Baptist church at Blaina were also excommunicated for taking part in the march on Newport, though they were later restored, and Thomas Morris, minister of a Baptist church at Newport, argued that the torrential rain which soaked the marchers on the evening of 3 November was the judgement of God on men who dared to break the Sabbath.[360] *Seren Gomer*, hitherto sympathetic towards Chartism, argued that the march on Newport had delayed rather than assisted the cause of electoral reform, and to prove the point it published, in 1841, an article on 'The Evil Effects of Chartism in Wales'.[361]

Inevitably the chorus of criticism levelled against the Chartist movement from Nonconformist pulpits and the Dissenting press brought its own retribution: working-class Dissenters voted with their feet. The Chartists who gathered on Peep Green in May 1839 resolved to boycott places of worship where the services were 'inimical to civil liberty' and the ministers refused 'to declare the whole truth unto the people'.[362] When Evan Williams, minister of the Ebenezer Independent church at Cefn-coed-y-cwmmer near Merthyr Tydfil, refused to administer communion unless the church members repudiated Chartism, the members retaliated by forcing him to resign his pastorate.[363] The extent of working-class disillusionment with official Nonconformity can be seen in the formation and growth of separate Chartist churches whose members were overwhelmingly ex-Dissenters. The Primitive Methodist chapels in Keighley and Northowram in the West Riding transformed themselves into Chartist churches in 1839; the Chartists in Nottingham, again in 1839, obtained a former Methodist chapel which they henceforward called the Democratic Chapel; and in Birmingham in the following year Arthur O'Neill founded a Christian Chartist church which was composed largely of former Baptists and Methodists.[364] Numerous Independent churches were founded in Wales between 1839 and 1842 by secession from existing churches, and the cause of those secessions was often disputes about the People's Charter.[365]

---

[359] Parry, 'Welsh Independents and Working-class Movements', 75; Williams, *John Frost*, 326.
[360] Jones, *Sowing Beside all Waters*, 310; Bassett, *Welsh Baptists*, 141; Williams, *John Frost*, 326.
[361] Bassett, *The Welsh Baptists*, 142; Williams, *John Frost*, 326.
[362] *Northern Star*, 25 May 1839, 1.
[363] Parry, 'Welsh Independents and Working-class Movements', 78.
[364] E. Yeo, 'Christianity in the Chartist Struggle', *Past and Present*, 91 (1981), 117; Epstein and Thompson, *Chartist Experience*, 233–4; H. U. Faulkner, *Chartism and the Churches* (1916), 44–5. The fullest account of the Birmingham Christian Chartist church is in J. Ryan's Birmingham M.Litt. thesis, 'Religion and Radical Politics in Birmingham' (1979).
[365] Lambert, *Drink and Sobriety in Victorian Wales*, 50 n. 16.

None the less, the congregational polity of the Independents and the Baptists was more successful than the connexional polity of the Wesleyans and Primitive Methodists in containing the divisions brought about by Chartism. Whereas the Baptists and Congregationalists who supported Chartism in Wales and eastern England tended to remain with their denominations, even if they were temporarily excommunicated or if they seceded to form new churches, the Chartist movement in the north of England and the east Midlands contained numerous activists who had once been Wesleyan, New Connexion or Primitive Methodists, but who had been expelled by, or had resigned from, their denominations on account of their radical political activities. Joseph Rayner Stephens for a time gave limited support to Chartism, though of the six points of the People's Charter he approved only of universal male suffrage. As a man who repudiated the name of radical and cared nothing for political rights, Stephens supported one man one vote only because it might be the means of providing every working man with 'a good coat to his back, a comfortable abode in which to shelter himself and his family [and] a good dinner upon his table'. His primary concern remained opposition to the Poor Law Amendment Act, and it was the inflammatory language he used to incite men to resist the Act that led to his arrest at the end of 1838 and to his being sentenced in August to eighteen months in prison.[366] At his trial Stephens denied that he had ever supported the Chartist 'rigmarole', but Chartists persisted in regarding him as their first martyr. Another former Wesleyan minister, William Vickers Jackson of Leigh, had, like Stephens, formed his own congregation of radical sympathizers and denounced 'all sects of Methodists' for having 'deviated from the truth of God' and having 'condemned Mr Stephens for preaching it'.[367] In 1840 Jackson was himself sentenced to two years imprisonment at the Liverpool assizes for unlawful assembly and seditious conspiracy.[368] Another ex-Wesleyan who was prominent in the Chartist movement in the north-west was Isaac Johnson, a Stockport blacksmith who had been expelled from the Wesleyans for wearing a radical hat at the time of Peterloo.[369] In 1840 he told a prison inspector that he now 'forms his own ideas as to religion', a sentiment echoed by another ex-Methodist prisoner, Isaac Armitage, who cited their treatment of J. R. Stephens as evidence that the Wesleyans were 'the most avaricious men under the sun'.[370]

---

[366] Ward, 'Revolutionary Tory', 103–9.
[367] *Northern Star*, 16 Mar. 1839, 1; Thompson, *The Chartists*, 171.
[368] R. G. Gammage, *History of the Chartist Movement* (1969), 178–9.
[369] Yeo, 'Christianity in the Chartist Struggle', 125.   [370] PRO HO 20/10.

In Yorkshire a popular Chartist leader was Ben Rushton, a hand-loom weaver from Ovenden near Halifax who had once been a Methodist New Connexion local preacher but who had been dismissed for introducing politics into his sermons. It was Rushton who seconded the resolution at the Peep Green rally in May 1839 calling on Chartists to boycott churches and chapels whose ministers were unsympathetic to Chartism, and in accordance with the spirit of that resolution Rushton became a regular preacher at Chartist chapels. In the Chartist chapel at Littletown near Heckmondwike he preached from Matthew 26: 11, 'Ye have the poor always with you'. Rushton 'depicted in glowing language the miseries of the poor man's lot and the sin of those who lorded it so unjustly over him', and was greeted by cries from the congregation of 'damn 'em, damn 'em'.[371] Another Methodist speaker at the Peep Green meeting was the Wesleyan local preacher Abram Hanson, a shoemaker from Elland, who told his audience to boycott those churches and chapels where ministers preached passive obedience and non-resistance. For his speech he was expelled by the Halifax circuit.[372] Throughout the north of England the Chartists emulated the organization of the Methodists, dividing their members into classes, electing class leaders, and holding camp-meetings. This was scarcely surprising, commented the *Sheffield Mercury*, since 'there are some renegade Methodists among the Chartists in this town'.[373]

In the east Midlands much of the Chartist leadership was provided by former Primitive Methodists. George Black was a Nottingham framework knitter and ex-Ranter preacher who preached at the Nottingham Democratic Chapel and lost his frames because of his Chartist activities.[374] After Henry Dorman was reprimanded by the Nottingham Primitive Methodists for preaching political sermons he left the Connexion of his own volition, having 'caused great trouble . . . by taking an active part with the Chartists', and opened a temperance hotel which served as a meeting place for Chartists.[375] The Loughborough Chartists were led by James Skevington, a straw bonnet maker and newsagent who had been a Primitive Methodist itinerant preacher for six years before lameness compelled him to settle down in Loughborough as a circuit steward, class leader, and local preacher.

---

[371] F. Peel, *Spen Valley: Past and Present* (Heckmondwike, 1893), 317–19; Thompson, *Making of the English Working Class*, 438; Hargreaves, 'Methodists in Halifax', 90.

[372] Thompson, *Making of the English Working Class*, 437–8; Chapman, *John Wesley and Co.*, 44, 61.

[373] Wearmouth, *Methodism and Working-class Movements*, 217–18; Morris, 'Primitive Methodism in Nottinghamshire', 248.

[374] Epstein and Thompson, *Chartist Experience*, 245, 252.

[375] Morris, 'Primitive Methodism in Nottinghamshire', 246; Epstein and Thompson, *Chartist Experience*, 231.

However, he was accused of embezzling circuit funds in 1836, was expelled from membership, and thenceforward devoted himself to radical politics, representing his town at the first Chartist Convention in 1839.[376] The first leader of the Leicester Chartists, the shoemaker John Markham, was also a Primitive Methodist local preacher until expelled in 1841.[377] The middle-class Dissenting Liberals who now controlled Leicester's corporation, he complained, no longer had any use for the people now that 'they had got municipal honours and privileges'.[378]

James Skevington, despite his expulsion from the ranks of the Ranters, appears to have retained his religious faith, and towards the end of his life (he died in 1851) wrote that 'though a man may be a Chartist and not a Christian, a man cannot be a Christian and not a Chartist unless through ignorance'.[379] But some of the Chartists who journeyed from religious Dissent to radical politics jettisoned their religious belief along the way. Such was the experience of two of the most colourful Chartist personalities: Joseph Barker and Thomas Cooper. Both men came from humble Methodist backgrounds; both men were influenced, at one remove, by the great Wesleyan preacher William Bramwell and by his biographer James Sigston; both men were largely self-educated, sharing the Nonconformist passion for learning and having an equal passion to pass on their learning to their fellow men; and both men came to reject orthodox Christianity in the 1840s in favour of secularized humanitarianism which led to involvement in the Chartist cause.

Barker was born in Bramley in the West Riding in 1806, the son of an unsuccessful clothier who was forced by the failure of his business to become a labourer. His parents were typical working-class Yorkshire Methodists, combining a belief in witchcraft, boggards, and fairies with a devotion to William Bramwell, and Joseph attended James Sigston's school at Leeds. Although for a time a Wesleyan local preacher, Barker was alienated by the Wesleyans' 'everlasting begging' and became a minister in the Methodist New Connexion. Despite his rough and slovenly appearance Barker was a popular preacher, but he angered his new denomination's hierarchy by contending that baptism was not divinely ordained, and that Christians were under no permanent obligation to observe the Lord's Supper, and he was expelled from the Connexion in 1841.[380] However, Barker's contention that the New Connexion Conference had 'conformed itself to the likeness of the

---

[376] Dews, *From Mow Cop to Peake*, 49–51.   [377] Briggs, *Chartist Studies*, 130.
[378] Patterson, *Radical Leicester*, 303.
[379] Harrison, 'Chartism in Leicester', in Briggs, *Chartist Studies*, 131.
[380] *Life of Joseph Barker*, 16–19, 78, 104, 181, 246, 260; S. Hume, *Memoir of Rev Thomas Allin* (1881), 147–8; Rose, *Methodism in Ashton-under-Lyne*, ii. 27.

Old' struck a chord with many of its members: twenty-nine churches left the New Connexion with Barker and its membership dropped by 4,348, a fifth of its total. The seceders tended to be the poorer members of the Connexion and some at least were Chartist sympathizers.[381] Barker himself became pastor to a church of New Connexion seceders at Newcastle upon Tyne. He tried to organize his church on liberal principles without requiring members to subscribe to a creed and promising complete freedom of discussion and speech. The result was that several members 'entered on a career of scepticism', 'many joined the Unitarians', and 'some few went to the Quakers'. By 1845 Barker had himself become a Unitarian and as a result of contacts with John Bowring, then MP for Bolton, was given a printing press, bought with £600 raised for him by Unitarians, on which he proceeded to print cheap literary and religious works. In 1846 Barker took up radical politics, advocated repeal of the Act of Union for Ireland and republicanism for England, and in 1848 attended the Chartist Convention. He emigrated to the United States in 1851 where he was befriended by Garrisonian abolitionists under whose influence he came to reject Christianity altogether and stood on the brink of 'the dreadful abyss' of atheism.[382]

The passionate enthusiasm with which Joseph Barker embraced an ever-changing kaleidoscope of new ideas was paralleled in the career of Thomas Cooper. Born in Leicester in 1805 but brought up in Gainsborough by his widowed mother, Cooper was converted by the Primitive Methodists at the age of thirteen and at the age of twenty-four claimed to have received 'entire sanctification' after reading Sigston's *Memoirs of William Bramwell*. He joined the Wesleyans, became a local preacher, quarrelled with his circuit superintendent, went to Lincoln to become a schoolmaster, left the Wesleyans, and began a new career as a newspaper reporter. In 1840 he became a correspondent on the *Leicestershire Mercury* and his first-hand experience of the sufferings of the Leicester framework knitters transformed him into a Chartist activist.[383] 'A large, pock-marked man' with a swinging walk, long hair that fell on ample shoulders, and 'a voice that proclaimed a man', Cooper soon came to dominate Leicester Chartism.[384] He was sacked by the *Leicestershire Mercury*, took over the editorship of the Chartist *Midland Counties Illuminator*, opened a coffee-shop which became a venue for the town's Chartists, started an adult Sunday school, and gave lectures on Milton, English history, and geology in the Shakespearean Room.[385] But all

---

[381] Yeo, 'Christianity in the Chartist Struggle', 117.
[382] *Life of Joseph Barker*, 269–71, 280–9, 305, 313–15.
[383] *The Life of Thomas Cooper* (Leicester, 1971), 37, 84, 97–102, 138–9.
[384] J. Parker, *A Preacher's Life* (1899), 55–6.   [385] *Life of Cooper*, 146–8, 162.

this destroyed his Christian faith. The comradeship of the Chartist movement militated against a theological system which divided men into sheep and goats. Class unity triumphed over religious division. Cooper found that in Leicester he 'could not preach eternal punishment to poor starving stockingers'.[386]

Nonconformist divisions over Chartism contrasted with the enthusiasm with which Old Dissent at least united behind the Anti-Corn Law League. Middle-class Dissenters had resented the attempt by Parliament to protect British corn growers from foreign competition from the inception of that policy in 1815, but it was the economic depression of 1837 which provoked the organized anti-Corn Law campaign, its supporters convinced that the fundamental cause of the depression was artificial restrictions on the freedom of trade. The citadel of the free trade movement was Manchester: the Manchester Anti-Corn Law Association was founded in September 1838 as a result of a meeting called by Archibald Prentice, the Presbyterian editor of the *Manchester Times* and first historian of the movement, to hear John Bowring, the former Unitarian MP for Kilmarnock. Bowring had recently returned from a trade mission to the Continent and told his audience that Frenchmen, Prussians, and Hungarians had all told him that the Corn Laws prevented them from buying British manufactures.[387] Prentice moved that an organization be set up to work for the repeal of the Corn Laws, and at the inaugural meeting of the Manchester Anti-Corn Law Association held a fortnight later six of the seven men present were worshippers at the Lloyd Street chapel of the United Secession Church (from 1847 the United Presbyterian Church) ministered to by a radical Scotsman from Kilmarnock, William McKerrow.[388] A provisional committee of the Manchester Association was formed in October which included, in addition to Prentice, the Quaker cotton manufacturer John Bright, the Congregationalists Elkanah Armitage, George Hadfield, and James Kershaw, and the Unitarians Thomas Potter and John Benjamin Smith. A week after the formation of the provisional committee the names of the Unitarian editor of the *Manchester Guardian*, John Taylor, and of Richard Cobden were added to it, and the Unitarian lawyer Joseph Parkes acted as their London agent.[389] Though Cobden was an Anglican, his closest political allies for the next twenty-five years were to be radical Dissenters: 'the principle of religious equality', he wrote to John

---

[386] Ibid. 260.   [387] Prentice, *Anti-Corn-Law League*, i. 65–71.
[388] *Memoir of McKerrow*, 90–1.
[389] Prentice, *Anti-Corn-Law League*, i. 73–4; N. McCord, *The Anti-Corn Law League* (1958), 36, 39.

Bright in 1851, 'stands in my judgement before that of commercial free-dom'.[390] The Manchester Association formed the basis of the national Anti-Corn Law League which was founded in March 1839. J. B. Smith was elected president and was the League's standard-bearer in the Walsall by-election in January 1841 in which the League, though it failed to win the seat by 27 votes, for the first time demonstrated the electoral appeal of its arguments.[391]

Dissenters committed themselves to the campaign for cheap corn with an enthusiasm second only to their devotion to the abolition of slavery. The *Eclectic Review*, in January 1839, urged the 'religious world' to protest against 'the evils inflicted by the remnant of feudal barbarism contained in the restrictions on commerce'; the General Body of Dissenting Ministers similarly denounced commercial restrictions in June 1841; innumerable sermons were preached on Proverbs 11: 26: 'He that withholdeth corn, the people shall curse him'.[392] John Childs, the church-rates martyr from Bungay in Suffolk, published a *Corn Law Catechism* and was rewarded by having Prentice's *History of the Anti-Corn-Law League* dedicated to him.[393] In Wales the Congregationalist Walter Griffith toured the principality on behalf of the League; Dissenting ministers presided at Anti-Corn Law meet-ings; and in May 1841 at Denbigh more than two thousand people heard Griffith and a local Independent minister, William Rees, denounce the Corn Laws from a cart.[394] Dissent provided the Anti-Corn Law League with two of its most effective orators: W. J. Fox, the maverick Unitarian and minister of South Place chapel, who became a paid propagandist for the League, and John Bright, the Rochdale Quaker, who in the autumn of 1841 took up Richard Cobden's suggestion that he should try to deaden the pain of the loss of his wife by throwing himself into the free trade movement.[395]

The climax of the Dissenting campaign against the Corn Laws came with a conference of ministers held under the auspices of the League in Manchester in August 1841. Out of 636 ministers present 276 were Congregationalists, 182 Baptists, 30 Scottish Seceders, 23 Unitarians, 21 Methodist New Con-nexion, 21 Wesleyan Methodist Association, 12 Scottish Relief, 9 Primi-tive Methodists, 8 Presbyterians, and only 2 Wesleyans.[396] A subsequent

[390] J. Morley, *Life of Richard Cobden* (1906), 560.

[391] McCord, *Anti-Corn Law League*, 53, 84–90.

[392] Cowherd, *Politics of English Dissent*, 135; Martin, 'Politics of the Congregationalists', 215–18.

[393] Prentice, *Anti-Corn-Law League*, i. 112.

[394] Parry, 'Welsh Independents and Working-class Movements', 162–74.

[395] R. Garnett, *Life of W. J. Fox* (1910), 258–63; Mineka, *Dissidence of Dissent*, 200–1; Trevelyan, *Life of John Bright*, 43–4.

[396] *Patriot*, 23 Aug. 1841, 571.

conference of Welsh ministers held in Caernarfon in December 1841 revealed a similar composition: Congregationalists and Baptists predominated, a number of Calvinistic Methodists were present, but only three Wesleyans attended.[397] The free trade controversy does, however, reveal some evidence of rank-and-file Wesleyan dissatisfaction with their leaders' hostility towards liberal political movements. When the Wesleyan *Watch-man* sneered at the anti-Corn Law agitation with the comment that 'the cry for "cheap bread" was the prelude to the horrors of the French Revolution', Wesleyans in Huddersfield responded by forming their own Anti-Corn Law society and six thousand Wesleyans in Leicester signed a petition against the Corn Laws.[398] And when the Calvinistic Methodists in Anglesey ordered their ministers to boycott the Caernarfon conference Thomas Charles, the grandson and namesake of the denomination's most famous pastor, protested that the Connexion 'had no power to interfere with my right of judgement in political matters'.[399]

If the Anti-Corn Law League attracted enthusiastic support from Congregationalists, Baptists, and Unitarians, it provoked bitter hostility from many Chartists. The free trade agitation was regarded by Chartists as a middle-class strategy to defuse working-class anger against their employers by redirecting their hostility towards the landlords. They suspected that the urge of cotton manufacturers to reduce the price of bread was motivated by a desire to reduce the rates of wages. The Lancashire entrepreneurs who provided the financial backing for the Anti-Corn Law League, men such as the Unitarian Gregs and the Quaker Ashworths, were the very same men who opposed trade unions and factory reform and supported the New Poor Law.[400] John Bright, who was elected MP for Durham in 1843, regarded Fielden's Ten Hours Act as 'one of the worst measures ever passed', and his opposition to factory reform earned him the title of 'the heartless Quaker'.[401]

Yet the issue of the Corn Laws did not divide men neatly into middle-class free traders and working-class Chartists and factory reformers. A significant minority of free traders supported radical working-class causes and a substantial proportion of working-class radicals supported the anti-Corn Law campaign. What usually distinguished such protagonists of class co-operation in the name of reform was their common religious Dissent. The factory reformers Joseph Brotherton and Charles Hindley were both

[397] Parry, 'Welsh Independents and Working-class Movements', 185.
[398] *Patriot*, 20 May 1841, 348; 10 June 1841, 405.
[399] Parry, 'Welsh Independents and Working-class Movements', 161.
[400] Rose, *Gregs of Quarry Bank*, 131; Boyson, *Ashworth Cotton Enterprise*, 200–2.
[401] Isichei, *Victorian Quakers*, 246; Ward, *Factory Movement*, 342.

members of the Anti-Corn Law League, while John Fielden spoke and voted for the repeal of the Corn Laws in Parliament and his brother Thomas attended the inaugural dinner of the Manchester Anti-Corn Law Association.[402] John Jenkinson, the radical Baptist pastor from Kettering, published in 1839 a pamphlet on *The Just Claims of the Working Classes* in which he combined advocacy of the People's Charter and a demand for the repeal of the New Poor Law with calls for free trade and the separation of Church and State.[403] Archibald Prentice, the founder and first historian of the Anti-Corn Law League, was a vigorous defender of the old Poor Law, recommended Fielden as parliamentary candidate for Rochdale in 1831, and in 1842 declared himself to be a Chartist 'to the whole extent'.[404] Joseph Livesey, the temperance pioneer, was another opponent of the New Poor Law and advocate of factory reform who was also an active campaigner on behalf of the Anti-Corn Law League. In December 1841 he launched a weekly illustrated paper called the *Struggle* which survived for four and a half years and which addressed itself primarily to the 'struggle for cheap bread'. With its simple woodcuts and homely arguments supported by biblical quotations, the *Struggle* was designed to bring the arguments for free trade to a popular audience. It attained an average circulation of 12,000 weekly copies, making it the most popular of all the anti-Corn Law papers.[405] There is much evidence to show that the free trade campaign met with a notable measure of success among the working class. Both the framework knitters of Nottinghamshire (in 1833) and the hand-loom weavers of Manchester (in 1837) petitioned for the repeal of the Corn Laws.[406] While Feargus O'Connor was bitterly opposed to the Anti-Corn Law League, John Markham, the former Primitive Methodist who led the Leicester Chartists, said that three-quarters of the local Chartists disagreed with O'Connor on this issue.[407] In Derby, Sheffield, and Wolverhampton the Anti-Corn Law League attracted considerable working-class support, and Operative Anti-Corn Law Associations were set up in numerous towns.[408] Even Henry Ashworth managed to persuade the Operative Cotton Spinners' Association of Bolton to support the repeal of the Corn Laws and in return his brother Edmund supported the People's Charter.[409]

---

[402] Weaver, *John Fielden*, 212, 237.   [403] Greenall, 'Baptist as Radical', 216.

[404] Weaver, *John Fielden*, 47; Prentice, *Anti-Corn-Law League*, i. 330.

[405] Pearse, *Life of Joseph Livesey*, pp. lxi–lxxi.

[406] *Nottingham Review*, 8 Mar. 1833; Prentice, *Anti-Corn-Law League*, i. 70–1.

[407] Patterson, *Radical Leicester*, 306.

[408] L. Brown, 'Chartists and the Anti-Corn Law League', in Briggs, *Chartist Studies*, 343, 356–9.

[409] Boyson, *Ashworth Cotton Enterprise*, 205–6, 211.

The need for co-operation between free traders and Chartists was emphasized by the result of the general election of 1841. The failure of Melbourne's government either to abolish church rates or to overcome the House of Lords' refusal to accept the abolition of university tests had led to widespread Dissenting disillusionment with the Whigs.[410] While the Whigs' partial conversion to the cause of Corn Law reform prompted Josiah Conder's *Patriot* to urge support for the government, Miall's *Nonconformist* had no faith in the Whigs' change of heart.[411] The Dissenters were 'the bond and muscle of the Liberal party,' said the *Nonconformist*, but the government had ignored their grievances.[412] In the West Riding the Leeds Baptist minister John Giles, writing on behalf of his co-religionists, publicly criticized the views on church rates of the sitting Whig member Lord Morpeth and threatened the withdrawal of Baptist support.[413] But, as the *Patriot* warned would happen, the subsequent victory of Peel's Conservatives in the general election hardly increased the political prospects of the Dissenters for the better.[414] Only six Nonconformist MPs were returned in 1841: John Bowring for Bolton, Joseph Brotherton for Salford, John Fielden for Oldham, Charles Hindley for Ashton-under-Lyne, Mark Philips for Manchester, and George Wood for Kendal. Four of the six were Unitarians and even this tiny band was not united: on issues such as factory reform, the Poor Law, and Chartism, Fielden (and Brotherton) would vote the opposite way to Bowring, Philips, and Wood. Political Nonconformity was weaker than at any time since the passing of the Great Reform Act.

The defeat of the Whigs also increased the frustrations of the free traders and led some to conclude that only with a further extension of the franchise could the Corn Laws be repealed. In like manner the failure of the first Chartist Convention in 1839 and the defeat of the Newport rising was leading some Chartists to the opinion that only with middle-class support could universal male suffrage be attained.[415] To an assortment of Dissenters, Chartists, and free traders, the alliance between middle- and working-class radicals which had helped to bring about the 1832 Reform Act, and which had been fractured by the subsequent workings of that Act, was in urgent need of resurrection.

The Dissenting insistence that the working and middle classes had a common interest in combating the privileges of the landed interest and of the established church, which dated back to the 1790s, was voiced with

---

[410] *Nonconformist*, 19 May 1841, 97; *Patriot*, 3 May 1841, 284; 31 May 1841, 380.
[411] *Patriot*, 24 June 1841, 436; *Nonconformist*, 5 May 1841, 57; 16 June, 186.
[412] *Nonconformist*, 26 May 1841, 121.   [413] *Patriot*, 21 June 1841, 427.
[414] Ibid. 28 June 1841, 444.   [415] J. Epstein, *The Lion of Freedom* (1982), 263, 285.

increasing urgency in the late 1830s and early 1840s. Richard Sutton's *Nottingham Review* argued in March 1839 that there was 'a close affinity between the middle and poorer classes of society' and urged the Chartists and the opponents of the Corn Law to unite on a platform of household suffrage and the ballot.[416] Archibald Prentice published two articles in the *Manchester Times* in October advocating a union of the working and middle classes on the basis of free trade, triennial parliaments, the ballot, and an educational qualification for the right to vote.[417] In August 1840 Arthur O'Neill, the founder of the Birmingham Christian Chartist church, urged Chartists to make 'a junction with the middle classes'.[418] And in the same month the Leeds Parliamentary Reform Association was founded on the initiative of Hamer Stansfeld, a Unitarian cloth merchant, and James Marshall, the Unitarian flax-spinner, to advocate household suffrage, triennial parliaments, and the ballot.[419] But by far the most important manifestation of the movement to unite working- and middle-class radicals was the Complete Suffrage Union led by the Quaker anti-slavery campaigner Joseph Sturge and powerfully supported by Edward Miall's *Nonconformist*.

In the autumn of 1841 Miall published a series of articles on the need for 'reconciliation between the middle and labouring classes'.[420] Such reconciliation, argued Miall, was in the best interests of both classes. For the working class he advocated 'complete suffrage': a vote for every adult male apart from paupers and criminals. Complete suffrage he justified on the grounds that 'the people are the only legitimate source of power', for 'government is made for man and not man for government'.[421] Yet the Reform Act of 1832 had left the right of electing MPs almost exclusively in the hands of the middle class, with the result that the working class was 'almost wholly unprotected'. It was the aristocracy, not the industrialists, who were the chief enemy of the working class. Working people were 'taxed more heavily than any other class'. 'The fruits of their toil are wrested from them, and industry and skill, their only property, taken from them to augment the boundless wealth of the landlords.'[422] Miall was scornful of the argument that a House of Commons elected by complete suffrage could be any more ignorant or any more corrupt than the one chosen under the 1832 system.[423] And he was equally scornful of the argument that the working class, if they had the vote, would use it to plunder the rich. 'Encroachment upon the property of the poor by the

---

[416] *Nottingham Review*, 15 Mar. 1839, 4.   [417] Read, *Press and People*, 166.
[418] Epstein, *Lion of Freedom*, 271.   [419] Fraser, *Urban Politics in Victorian England*, 260.
[420] *Nonconformist*, 13 Oct. 1841, 456–7.   [421] Ibid. 20 Oct. 1841, 472–3.
[422] Ibid. 27 Oct. 1841, 489.   [423] Ibid. 17 Nov. 1841, 536.

rich'—the current situation—was as much to be deprecated as the 'encroach-ment upon the property of the rich by the poor'.[424]

To the middle class Miall argued that the franchise reform of 1832 had given them the vote, but not political power. Parliament continued to be dominated by the aristocracy who imposed on middle and working classes alike class legislation such as the Corn Laws, Poor Laws, and Game Laws. Only with a further extension of the franchise would the Corn Laws be repealed.[425] Alone the middle class could not defeat the aristocracy, but the working class could provide 'the additional force to compel the surrender of the common foe'.[426] The middle class thus had to decide between the aristoc-racy and the people. Sooner or later 'the oligarchy must fall' and the only issue was whether 'it shall fall by peaceful or by violent means'. If the middle and working classes united the former could guide the latter and guarantee that change would be peaceful. But if the middle class stood aloof from the working class they took the risk of leaving them 'under the control of any demagogue who may inspire to place himself at their head'.[427]

Miall's most important co-operators in the Complete Suffrage movement were the Quaker brothers Joseph and Charles Sturge. Joseph Sturge was the sixth of that name in a long line of Quakers who traced their ancestry back to the earliest Friends. His father was a farmer at Elberton in Gloucestershire but the foundations of Joseph's own fortune were laid when, at the age of twenty, he entered into partnership with a corn factor of Bewdley in Worcestershire. He moved to Birmingham in 1822, taking part in the politics of his adopted town and earning the censure of his fellow Quakers for his public support of the Birmingham Political Union. But it was his opposition to the apprenticeship system established in the West Indies following the Emancipation Act of 1833 that earned Sturge national fame and best illus-trated his chief characteristics: his high moral purpose, his tenacity, and his total refusal to compromise with what he regarded as evil.

For Sturge his advocacy of complete suffrage was a logical extension of his opposition to slavery. While engaged in his campaign against the apprentice-ship system, he explained in 1841, it had been pressed upon him 'that the suf-ferings of my fellow-countrymen had a prior claim on my attention'. 'Our unenfranchised countrymen', he wrote to the American abolitionist Lewis Tappan, 'are *politically* much in the same position as your slaves, and in many of the electors there is nearly as strong a feeling against giving them the franchise as there is against giving it to the slave with you.'[428] Sturge was a

---

[424] Ibid. 1 Dec. 1841, 569.   [425] Ibid. 568.   [426] Ibid. 27 Oct. 1841, 489.
[427] Ibid. 19 Jan. 1842, 41.   [428] H. Richard, *Memoirs of Joseph Sturge* (1864), 296, 298.

generous supporter of the Anti-Corn Law League, doubling his subscription to £200 a year in 1841, and his first move in favour of complete suffrage was to propose a conference on the subject to delegates at an Anti-Corn Law gathering in Manchester in November 1841. Sturge's proposed conference met in Birmingham in April 1842 to establish the National Complete Suffrage Union. The conference attracted both Chartists such as William Lovett, Henry Vincent, and James Bronterre O'Brien, and radical Dissenters such as John Bright, John Childs, Samuel Fox, Edward Miall, John Phillippo Mursell, Thomas Potter, Archibald Prentice, and Henry Solly. Although the *Nonconformist* claimed that 'the most conciliatory temper' was shown throughout the debates there was none the less tension between the two groups. The conference approved all six points of the People's Charter despite the misgivings of Bright, Miall, and Mursell about the wisdom of annual parliaments. More ominously, William Lovett went on to persuade the meeting to call another conference to discuss the Charter itself, notwithstanding Miall's warning that he would vote against any move to commit the Complete Suffrage movement to the Charter.[429] At the conclusion of the conference the *Nonconformist* rejoiced that 'the middle and labouring classes, through the medium of delegates fairly representing their wishes, have shaken hands', but it went on to warn that 'the aristocratic among the middle classes' and 'the factious among the working classes' would stand aloof. It was soon proved right.[430]

Feargus O'Connor denounced Sturge's movement as 'complete humbug' and the *Northern Star* argued that the Complete Suffragists' reluctance to accept the name of the Charter proved that they desired 'to effect not union but disunion among the people'.[431] Among the Dissenting newspapers the *Patriot*, the *Leeds Mercury*, and the *Manchester Guardian* were all critical of the Complete Suffrage movement, and the *Nonconformist*'s commitment to the cause led to an immediate fall in its circulation.[432] The movement was cheered in April when a motion in favour of its programme secured 67 votes in the House of Commons, but disappointed in August when Sturge, with O'Connor's support, contested a by-election at Nottingham and was defeated by 84 votes. The *Patriot* expressed little regret at Sturge's defeat in view of the company he was keeping,[433] and the fears which working-class refusal to abandon the Charter aroused among middle-class Dissenters were

[429] *Nonconformist*, 13 Apr. 1842, 234–44.   [430] Ibid. 13 Apr. 1842, 232; 20 Apr., 257.
[431] Epstein, *Lion of Freedom*, 288–9.
[432] J. S. Newton, 'The Political Career of Edward Miall', Ph.D. thesis (Durham, 1975), 182, 190.
[433] *Patriot*, 8 Aug. 1842, 532.

powerfully articulated by William Byles's *Bradford Observer*. 'If the working classes stick with such tenacity to favourite dogmas,' commented Byles, 'what guarantee do they give us that, should we help them to obtain the franchise . . . they would not adhere to their dogmatism and thus reduce us, by the mere force of numbers, to utter insignificance?'[434]

The fear that the middle class would be swamped by working-class numbers was heightened by the strike movement of August 1842 which became known as the Plug Plot. A threatened 25 per cent reduction in wages at cotton mills in Stalybridge and Ashton-under-Lyne led to employees coming out on strike on 5 August and workers throughout the cotton-manufacturing areas and the West Riding woollen districts proceeded to put mills out of action by removing the plugs from boilers.[435] A meeting of strikers on Mottram Moor near Stalybridge on 7 August resolved 'that all labour should cease until the People's Charter became the law of the land'; the resolution was seconded in towns throughout Lancashire in the following week; and on 15 August Thomas Cooper, who was passing through Staffordshire on his way to a Chartist conference in Manchester, chaired a mass meeting at Hanley in the Potteries at which the same resolution was carried.[436] The Hanley gathering sparked off twenty-four hours of rioting in which police offices and the homes of manufacturers and magistrates were looted and burned, and the home of Benjamin Vale, the rector of Longton, was fired and the contents of his cellar drunk. The rioting extended to Burslem on 16 August and ended with a troop of dragoons firing into the crowd, killing one man and seriously injuring others.[437] Among the men prosecuted for their part in the Hanley riots were Joseph Whiston, a potter and Primitive Methodist who was sentenced to twenty-one years' transportation for his part in leading the attack on Vale's house; Joseph Capper, the Tunstall blacksmith and Primitive Methodist local preacher, who was sentenced to two years' imprisonment on a charge of inciting riot; and Thomas Cooper who in May 1843 was sentenced to two years in Stafford gaol for sedition and conspiracy.[438]

The strike movement collapsed in late August and September 1842 in an atmosphere of worsening class tension. Even at the height of the strike Edward Miall continued to urge the middle class to 'unite with the people'

---

[434] Ram, 'Dissenters in the East and West Ridings', 297.   [435] Ward, *Chartism*, 162–4.
[436] *Life of Thomas Cooper*, 185, 191.
[437] Shaw, *When I was a Child*, 158–66; R. Fyson, 'The Crisis of 1842: Chartism, the Colliers' Strike, and the Outbreak in the Potteries', in Epstein and Thompson, *The Chartist Experience*, 207–8.
[438] Fyson, 'Crisis of 1842', 211; Wearmouth, *Methodism and Working-class Movements*, 72–3.

rather than 'side with the aristocracy',[439] and the Fieldens persisted in acting on such principles. John Fielden voluntarily closed his works and one of his brothers gave money to the strikers.[440] But such displays of continuing class harmony were very exceptional. The Chartists blamed John Bright and the League for precipitating the crisis by urging employers to close their mills in order to force the government to repeal the Corn Laws. The middle class saw the violence as evidence that the working class were unfit to have the vote. All this did not augur well for the crucial conference of the Complete Suffrage Union which was scheduled for December 1842. In preparation for the conference the Union's council proposed that equal numbers of electors and non-electors should be chosen as delegates by joint meetings, but, beginning with Sturge's Birmingham, Chartists took control of such meetings in over thirty towns and, often with threats of violence, secured the election of their own nominees as delegates.[441] Miall tried to rebuff the argument that the Chartists' behaviour invalidated the case for manhood suffrage, but at the same time he advised that if the Chartists gained control of the conference his supporters should withdraw.[442] When the conference met in Birmingham on 27 December 1842 the council of the Complete Suffrage Union wanted it to discuss a detailed parliamentary bill which embodied the six points of the People's Charter without mentioning its name. The Chartists, led by William Lovett, countered with an amendment stating that the Charter, the document for which 'vast numbers have suffered imprisonment, transportation, and death' had 'a prior claim over all other documents'. The middle-class radicals retorted that adopting the Charter would 'prevent that union of all classes which was so essential to their ultimate success'. The meeting adopted Lovett's amendment by 193 votes to 94 and Miall, Sturge, and their supporters walked out.[443]

The failure of the Complete Suffrage initiative left political Nonconformity in a divided and parlous state. Moderate Dissenting papers such as the *Patriot* and the *Leeds Mercury* gloated over the failure of Sturge's conference.[444] The Complete Suffragists' hope of uniting middle- and working-class radicals seemed doomed. At the end of 1842 British society was more bitterly divided along class lines than at any other time in the nineteenth century and religious issues had been forced into second place. Yet within

---

[439] *Nonconformist*, 24 Aug. 1842, 576–7.   [440] Weaver, *John Fielden*, 241.
[441] Martin, 'Politics of the Congregationalists', 255; A. Wilson, 'The Suffrage Movement', in P. Hollis (ed.), *Pressure from Without in Early Victorian England* (1974), 88 n. 28.
[442] *Nonconformist*, 20 Nov. 1842, 800–1; 7 Dec. 1842, 816–17.
[443] Ibid. 31 Dec. 1842, 875–80.
[444] *Patriot*, 5 Jan. 1843, 12; Martin, 'Politics of the Congregationalists', 257–8.

seven months of the collapse of Sturge's conference Peel's government was to unite not only Baptists and Congregationalists but even Wesleyans on a common platform. The cause was Sir James Graham's Factory Education Bill of 1843.

7. 'THE VOLUNTARY EFFORTS OF THE VARIOUS DENOMINATIONS': THE EDUCATION CONFLICT

Religion, politics, and education were inextricably mixed in the nineteenth century. The massive increase in population and the shift of much of that population towards industrial areas threw into sharp relief the inadequacy of the country's educational system, just as it highlighted the shortcomings of the rest of England's social, political, and religious institutions. At the same time the experience of the French Revolution abroad and the threats of Radicalism, Luddism, and Chartism at home led many respectable citizens to conclude that educating the mass of the people in Christian principles was the only way to underpin the stability of society. It was partly to address this problem that the Sunday school movement had been started in the 1780s and went on to enjoy mounting support, but the reports of the Children's Employment Commissioners in the 1840s revealed that the Sunday schools were scratching only the surface of the problem.

In retrospect it seems incredible that the wealthiest country in the world should have found it impossible to establish a national system of education before 1870, and that the politicians of nineteenth-century England should have so neglected the country's education that they paved the way for her decline in the twentieth century. But much of the reason for that failure lies in the basic theme of this book: the enormous expansion of Evangelical Nonconformity prevented the establishment of any system of education in which the Church of England would play a predominant part, while the continued, if diminished, strength of the established church delayed the creation of an educational system which was not dominated by the Anglican church. In this way the religious divisions of nineteenth-century England contributed to Britain's economic decline in the twentieth century.

The religious issue thus lay at the heart of England's educational problem, and in the early nineteenth century there were broadly three contrasting responses to the question: the secular, the undenominational, and the Anglican. The Utilitarian followers of Jeremy Bentham wanted a national system of education financed by the State and teaching secular subjects only. This would have been a logical solution to the religious problem but had no chance of success in the nineteenth century when the overwhelming majority of MPs, voters, and leaders of opinion, whatever else they might disagree about, were united in the view that religion and education were inseparable. What did divide them was the question of what sort of religion should be taught. Most Nonconformists were of the opinion that children should receive simple Bible teaching uncomplicated by the tenets of any particular religious denomination. This was the objective of the British and Foreign School Society which owed its origin to the quixotic educational pioneer Joseph Lancaster. Lancaster, born in 1778, the son of a Southwark sieve-maker, was, like Joseph Barker and Thomas Cooper, a largely self-taught Dissenter whose own lack of formal education prompted a missionary-like enthusiasm for the education of others. At the age of fourteen he ran away from home with the intention of travelling to Jamaica to teach negroes. He started his own free school in his father's house in 1796, moved to permanent premises in the Borough Road, Southwark, two years later, began to worship with the Quakers, and was admitted into membership in 1801. Lancaster organized his school on the monitorial system advocated by Andrew Bell and claimed that a thousand or more children could be educated economically by other children acting as monitors, or assistants, under the supervision of a single master. Lancaster's scheme attracted the support of George III, who agreed to subscribe £100 a year, but royal patronage did not prevent Lancaster from falling deeply into debt and by 1808 he owed over £5,000. His school was rescued by a committee of supporters which included William Corston, a Moravian hatter who had founded a 'school of industry' at Fincham in Norfolk; Joseph Fox, a Baptist dentist who worked at Guy's Hospital; Thomas Sturge, Joseph Sturge's elder brother; and William Allen, the Quaker pharmaceutical manufacturer who five years later was similarly to rescue Robert Owen's experiment in humane factory production in New Lanark. The new society was known initially as the Royal Lancasterian Institution and between 1807 and 1810 Lancaster travelled seven thousand miles throughout England to establish nearly a hundred new schools. However, control of the society in effect passed into the hands of Fox as secretary and Allen as treasurer, a development Lancaster bitterly resented. In 1814 the society changed its name to the British and Foreign School Society; in April Lancaster severed all connection with it; and two months later he was disowned by the Quaker Horsleydown Monthly Meeting for bankruptcy. He responded to his misfortunes by publishing abusive pamphlets against Fox and Allen and not surprisingly they replied by contributing to a fund to enable him to emigrate to the United States in 1818. Fox died in 1816 but

Allen continued to serve the society as treasurer until his own death in 1843. Under Allen's guidance the society extended its operations to the Continent, Russia, the West Indies, South America, and India, but most of its efforts were devoted to the founding of undenominational schools for the children of the poor in Britain.[445]

The foundation of the Lancasterian Institution, coming as it did when many Anglicans were thrown into a state of panic by the expansion of Dissent, prompted a group of High Churchmen to set up, in 1811, the rival National Society for the Education of the Children of the Poor in the Principles of the Established Church. The conflicting programmes of the British and Foreign and the National Society were to remain the rival standards around which were to gather opposing armies for another hundred years: Dissenting and moderate Anglicans content that children should receive undenominational Bible teaching, the majority of Anglicans insisting that the nation's children should be instructed in the catechism and liturgy of the established church.

For the next sixty years the mutual antagonism of Church and Dissent frustrated all attempts to establish a national system of education in England. In 1807 the Whig Samuel Whitbread introduced a bill to provide poor children in every parish with two years' education paid for by the poor rate. Although the bill received a third reading in the Commons it was thrown out by the Lords because the proposed schools would not be under the control of the established church.[446] In 1820 it was the hostility of Dissenters which led to the withdrawal of a bill introduced by Henry Brougham. Brougham, like Whitbread, proposed a system of parish schools but to meet Anglican objections he suggested that the schoolmaster should be a communicant of the established church, and that while the Bible alone should be used for reading lessons, all children, apart from those of Dissenting parents, should be obliged to receive instruction in the catechism on Sundays.[447] William Allen described Brougham's bill as the worst attack on religious liberty, apart from Lord Sidmouth's bill, since the days of Queen Anne,[448] and in the face of Dissenting opposition the bill was withdrawn.

Thirteen years later Brougham had more success. In July 1833 the radical MP John Roebuck introduced into the Commons a resolution for a national system of compulsory education, for children between the ages of seven and fourteen, to be financed by the State. Lord Althorp, for the government,

---

[445] H. B. Binns, *A Century of Education* (1908), 7–110; *Life of William Allen*, i. 96, 100, 246–7.
[446] D. G. Paz, *The Politics of Working-class Education in Britain, 1830–50* (Manchester, 1980), 5–6.
[447] Cowherd, *Politics of English Dissent*, 43–4.   [448] *Life of William Allen*, ii. 193.

opposed Roebuck's motion on the ground that massive state intervention would lead to the drying up of voluntary contributions and Roebuck withdrew his resolution. But the government, acting on a proposal of Brougham's, did make a modest grant of £20,000 towards the building of schoolrooms.[449] The grant was available only to schools whose applications were approved either by the National or by the British and Foreign School Societies, and only to schools which could raise half the cost of building from voluntary contributions. As a result the bulk of the government grant went to the wealthier National rather than to the British schools, and to rural rather than to urban schools. By 1839 70 per cent of government money had gone to Anglican schools, a fact which led some Dissenters to ponder whether state aid to education, like state aid to religion, was wrong in principle.[450]

A solution to the religious problem which was much canvassed in the 1830s was the system adopted by the government for Ireland in 1831. A Board of Commissioners of National Education was set up and charged with the task of providing Ireland with a national system of education. In schools assisted by the Board all children, irrespective of their parents' religion, were to receive the same secular education, but they were to be allowed to receive separate religious teaching according to their parents' wishes at times specifically set apart. To meet the objection that religious education should not be separated from secular education certain specially translated sections of the Bible were to be read by children of all religious persuasions during the normal school day.[451]

The Irish system was subjected to bitter criticism from the advocates of denominational education, but it survived for more than forty years[452] and in 1836 an attempt was made to introduce it into the English town whose religious divisions most closely mirrored the gulf between Catholic and Protestant in Ireland: Liverpool. When the Liberals gained control of the Liverpool town council in 1835 they also gained control of two schools which had been founded by the corporation in 1827 to educate the children of poor parents in the doctrines of the established church. The new Liberal education committee, under the chairmanship of the Unitarian William Rathbone IV, was concerned with the lack of provision in Liverpool for the children of Roman Catholic parents and it was on the proposal of a Congregationalist surgeon, Thomas Blackburn, that the council voted to introduce the Irish system into the corporation schools. The Liberals' action produced a furious

---

    [449] Paz, *Politics of Working-class Education*, 12–13.

    [450] J. Murphy, *Church, State and Schools in Britain, 1800–1970* (1971), 16–17, 41; Paz, *Politics of Working-class Education*, 17, 35.

    [451] Murphy, *Church, State and Schools*, 15–16.   [452] Ibid. 64.

Protestant backlash, led by the fiery Hugh M'Neile, an Ulsterman who was vicar of St Jude's who contended, with scant regard for the truth, that the Liberals were keeping the Authorized Version out of corporation schools and that the council's policy would issue in atheism. Initially M'Neile's campaign made little impact on Liverpool's voters, but nation-wide dissatisfaction with the Whigs led to Conservatives winning most wards in the town in the municipal elections of 1840 and when, in 1841, the Conservatives won thirteen of Liverpool's sixteen wards both the Liberals' brief control of Liverpool and the attempt to introduce the Irish educational system into England were at an end.[453]

The declining electoral fortunes of the Whigs in 1837–8 inspired militant Anglicans with the prospect of tightening their grip on the nation's schools and it was to counter the National Society's hopes of gaining monopolistic control over primary education that Lord John Russell, Home Secretary in Melbourne's government, put forward new proposals in February 1839.[454] Russell proposed to set up a committee of the Privy Council to administer the education grant for England and Wales, to increase that grant to £30,000 a year, to allow schools other than National or British schools to receive aid, and to establish an undenominational teachers' training college with a model school for children attached. Most Old Dissenters welcomed Russell's proposals, but the Wesleyan leadership protested against the prospect of government money going to Roman Catholic schools and against 'the training and employment by the State of Romish . . . teachers'.[455] As in the case of Whitbread's bill in 1807 and of the Liverpool Liberals' scheme of 1836, an educational proposal which would have denied the Church of England monopolistic control provoked Anglican anger. *The Times* claimed that Russell's undenominational scheme would issue in the herding of the children of Protestants 'with the leprous brood of Papists, Socinians, Free-thinkers, and fanatics'. Lord Ashley contended that 'the State adopted the Church of England as the true church, and if it did not enforce her tenets in education, it had no right to countenance others'. And a large meeting of the National Society on 28 May resolved that religious instruction in schools 'should be under the superintendence of the clergy and in conformity with the doctrines of the church of this realm'. The Bishop of London claimed that three thousand petitions had been collected against the government's

---

[453] J. Murphy, *The Religious Problem in English Education* (Liverpool, 1959), *passim*.

[454] I. D. C. Newbould, 'The Whigs, the Church, and Education, 1839', *Journal of British Studies*, 26 (1987), 339–41.

[455] Hempton, *Methodism and Politics*, 161; Bunting and Rowe, *Life of Jabez Bunting*, 672.

proposals, and in June Russell abandoned his plan for an undenominational college.[456]

The argument which the Tories had used to defeat Russell's proposed training college in 1839—that only Anglican-sponsored education should be assisted from public funds—produced from many Dissenters the reaction that no education should be paid for out of public money. The *Patriot* was one of the few Dissenting papers to oppose the Whig proposals of 1839 on the ground that 'the teaching of religion ought not to be undertaken, or to be provided, or to be controlled by the State'.[457] But that opinion was to become increasingly widespread in the 1840s. From its early issues Edward Miall's *Nonconformist* adopted the position that the provision of schools, like the provision of chapels, should be a matter for voluntary effort alone. In August 1841 it claimed that there was 'not a single argument [which] can be adduced for state education which is not equally powerful for state religion'.[458] A state system of education would have to be funded out of either taxes or rates, and such imposts would be open to the same objection as church rates: people would be compelled to finance religious teaching of which they disapproved. Even worse, state-controlled education would be a threat to liberty. 'An educational establishment in the hands of government would constitute about the most fearful weapon with which a nation could entrust its rulers . . . to surrender to the "powers that be" the task of moulding the habits, shaping the character, and fixing the elemental principles . . . of succeeding generations is just to let down the drawbridge, and raise the portcullis, which at present guard the citadel of national freedom.' The experiences of Austria and Prussia were evidence of the way in which governments could maintain despotic rule by controlling their countries' education systems.[459]

Miall's voluntaryist position was powerfully strengthened by Sir James Graham's abortive Factory Education Bill of 1843. Graham, Home Secretary in Peel's Conservative government, proposed to amend the 1833 Factory Act by lowering the age at which children could start work from nine to eight while at the same time cutting the hours of work of children under the age of thirteen from eight to six and a half. The reduction in hours of work was intended to enable children to attend school for three hours a day and to this end special factory schools were to be built with government loans and their running costs to be met out of the rates. The most controversial part of

---

[456] Murphy, *Church, State, and Schools*, 20, 22; Murphy, *Religious Problem in English Education*, 179.

[457] *Patriot*, 6 June 1839, 381; Newton, 'Edward Miall', 14.

[458] *Nonconformist*, 4 Aug. 1841, 297.

[459] Ibid. 20 July 1842, 497; Newton, 'Edward Miall', 24.

Graham's scheme was his proposal that the factory schools should be in effect under Anglican control: the chairman of the governing body was to be the incumbent of the parish; the appointment of all schoolmasters was to be approved by the local bishop; teachers would have to be competent to give religious instruction to members of the Church of England; and such teaching was to be given daily, though Dissenting parents would have the right to withdraw their children from such lessons.[460]

Dissenting fury at Graham's proposals was even fiercer than Anglican reaction to Russell's scheme four years earlier. The *Patriot* denounced it as 'the greatest encroachment upon religious liberty that has been attempted since the days of Lord Sidmouth'.[461] The *Nonconformist* went further and described Graham's bill as 'the boldest inroad attempted upon our liberties since the revolution of 1688'.[462] To the *Eclectic Review* the measure was in reality 'a church extension scheme' designed to buttress a 'tottering church'.[463] The Leeds Baptist minister John Giles saw the bill in similar light. 'It was a mere artifice to add to the £7m or £8m a year possessed by the Church of England at the present moment.'[464] Edward Baines was doubly alarmed that the Church of England which was to receive this back-door subsidy was a church which was falling under the spell of the Oxford movement. 'The mighty and fatal corruption which has been growing up within the last few years in the Church, and which is rapidly bringing back the clergy of the establishment to the doctrines, the rites, and the spirit of Popery, would make the attempt to place clergymen over the schools incomparably more hateful and revolting than it would have been before that great corruption took its rise.'[465] The Congregational minister Andrew Reed similarly warned that Dissenters could not trust the Church of England 'when so many of her sons are blotting the name of Protestant from their brow'.[466]

The growth of Anglo-Catholic sentiment within the Church of England had a particularly profound effect on the Wesleyans. The divisions on political issues that had disturbed the harmony of the Wesleyan Connexion ever since the 1790s became especially critical in the later 1830s. The official connexional line remained that of Jabez Bunting: loyalty to the 'Christian and Protestant constitution of England', which in practice meant support for the Conservative party and the established church.[467] Bunting's continuing

---

[460] J. T. Ward and J. H. Treble, 'Religion and Education in 1843: Reaction to the Factory Education Bill', *Journal of Ecclesiastical History*, 20 (1969), 79–82; Machin, *Politics and the Churches, 1832–1868*, 152–3.

[461] *Patriot*, 13 Mar. 1843, 164.   [462] *Nonconformist*, 22 Mar. 1843, 185.

[463] Machin, *Politics and the Churches*, 156.

[464] Ward and Treble, 'Religion and Education', 86.   [465] Ibid. 90.   [466] Ibid. 87.

[467] *Wesleyan Methodist Magazine*, 60 (1837), 310–11.

dominance over his fellow ministers was signalled by his election as president of Conference for the third time in 1836, and it was entirely in keeping with Bunting's conception of the role of the Wesleyan Connexion that his successor as president of Conference, Edmund Grindrod, should attend a meeting in support of church rates in Exeter Hall.[468] The attempt by Bunting's old friend James Wood to unseat Charles Hindley as MP for Ashton-under-Lyne in 1837, the Wesleyan leaders' support for church rates in Liverpool, Manchester, and Rochdale, and Wesleyan opposition both to Liverpool's adoption of the Irish education system and to Russell's proposed undenominational training college, all followed from the desire to preserve the country's 'Protestant constitution'.[469] But the antagonism of many Wesleyans towards what they regarded as their leaders' political partisanship did not end with the secessions of the Leeds Protestant Methodists in 1827, of the followers of Joseph Rayner Stephens in 1834, and of the supporters of the Wesleyan Methodist Association in 1835. As we have seen, Stephens was not the only Wesleyan to brave the wrath of Conference by supporting the campaign for the redress of Dissenting grievances in 1834, and in Leeds, Leicester, Northampton, Todmorden, and Rotherham, Wesleyans joined the agitation for the abolition of church rates.[470] John M'Owan, superintendent in the Northampton circuit, told Bunting that the action of Wesleyans in the town in supporting a petition against church rates was 'contrary to the feelings and judgement of both their preachers' and against the wishes 'of our best and most intelligent members', but he added that the latter were in a minority.[471]

The launch, in 1835, of a weekly paper called the *Watchman* by a group of Tory Wesleyans, including Bunting and James Wood, further intensified political divisions and led John Davis, superintendent in the Penzance circuit, to protest that the editor was 'greatly mistaken as to what is the opinion of our people on the church rate question'.[472] The pro-Tory bias of the *Watchman* was also the subject of an anonymous letter which appeared in the *Leeds Mercury* in March 1837, apparently from the pen of Thomas Galland, a minister in the Leeds circuit, which led to a clash between Galland and Bunting at the subsequent Conference.[473] Galland denied that those

[468] Gregory, *Side Lights on the Conflicts of Methodism*, 252.
[469] Gowland, *Methodist Secessions*, 150–2.
[470] Gregory, *Side Lights on the Conflicts of Methodism*, 237; Patterson, *Radical Leicester*, 249; Ward, *Early Victorian Methodism*, 181; *Patriot*, 24 July 1833, 251; 18 Apr. 1834, 128.
[471] Ward, *Early Victorian Methodism*, 181–2.
[472] Hempton, *Methodism and Politics*, 183; Ward, *Early Victorian Methodism*, 182.
[473] Ward, *Early Victorian Methodism* 184–5 n., 198–9 n.; Gregory, *Side Lights on the Conflicts of Methodism*, 237–40.

Wesleyans who had petitioned for the abolition of church rates had departed 'from the public and recognised principles of the Wesleyan body', and two years later he again clashed with Bunting when he complained of being ordered to circulate a petition against the Whig government's education proposals. The Wesleyan Conference, said Galland, was 'wrong to charge the government with "teaching Popery and promoting infidelity" '.[474]

Bunting, in defending the official Wesleyan line on education in 1839, argued that the leadership had the support of the Wesleyan laity,[475] but there is a good deal of evidence to suggest that by that date it was Galland, not Bunting, whose views best reflected those of the politically conscious rank-and-file Wesleyans. Increasingly those Wesleyans who had the vote were using it to support the Liberals, not the Conservatives. In Horncastle in Lincolnshire in 1836 nineteen Wesleyans voted against church rates and only five in favour,[476] and a similar move to the Liberals was beginning among the Calvinistic Methodists of Wales. In 1837 in a by-election for Anglesey two Calvinistic Methodist ministers and a deacon rebelled against the authority of the denomination's patriarch, John Elias, by supporting the Liberal candidate, William Owen Stanley, and when Stanley was elected he was presented with a memorial signed by thirty-nine Calvinistic Methodist elders.[477] While Wesleyan trustees, who were by definition more prosperous than rank-and-file members, voted for the Tories in Liverpool in 1835 and 1837 and in Manchester in 1839,[478] the *Wesleyan Chronicle*, founded in 1843 to give voice to the opinions of Liberal Wesleyans, claimed that in nearly thirty constituencies in the general election of 1841 two-thirds of Wesleyan voters had supported Liberal candidates.[479] In Northampton the Wesleyans supported the Liberals by 87 votes to 19; in Exeter by 85 votes to 3; in Yarmouth by 84 votes to 10; and in Norwich by 65 votes to 12.[480] Only in Aylesbury did Wesleyans support the Tories rather than the Liberals, by 17 votes to 11.[481]

---

[474] Gregory, *Side Lights on the Conflicts of Methodism*, 268–70, 276.   [475] Ibid. 277.

[476] R. J. Olney, *Lincolnshire Politics, 1832–1885* (Oxford, 1973), 60–1.

[477] D. Pretty, 'Richard Davies and Nonconformist Radicalism in Anglesey, 1837–68', *Welsh History Review*, 9 (1978–9), 435; R. T. Jones, 'The Origins of the Nonconformist Disestablishment Campaign', *Journal of the Historical Society of the Church in Wales*, 20 (1970), 62–3.

[478] Gowland, *Methodist Secessions*, 128, 171–2.

[479] *Wesleyan Chronicle*, 1 Dec. 1843–20 Sept. 1844. The statistics cited in *Victorian Pollbooks* by John Vincent from the *Wesleyan Chronicle* for 19 July 1844, 458, showing that 74.3% of Wesleyans voted Liberal in 1841, are inaccurate since they refer not only to the general election but also to subsequent by-elections and include, at least in the case of Rochdale, members of the Wesleyan Methodist Association.

[480] *Wesleyan Chronicle*, 16 Feb. 1844, 105; 8 Dec. 1843, 507; 29 Mar. 1844, 202; 12 Jan. 1844, 24.

[481] Ibid. 29 Dec. 1843, 554.

All this gave substance to the argument advanced by Dr William Small of Boston in 1841, that while Wesleyan preachers were 'to a great extent under the direction of a powerful party, wholly devoted to Toryism', 'fifteen out of every twenty Methodists are favourable to a Liberal government'.[482] The tensions that such differences of opinion could produce in a local Wesleyan society were revealed by John Stevens, superintendent of the Lewes circuit, in 1837. Because he had voted for two Conservative candidates, he wrote to Jabez Bunting, some Methodists 'will leave the society, one of the leaders has resigned—and things look very discouraging'.[483]

By the early 1840s, however, not only rank-and-file Wesleyans but even the Wesleyan leadership was beginning to question the traditional relationship between their Connexion and the Church of England, and hence the Tory party. No matter how much Jabez Bunting emphasized the Wesleyans' 'most friendly feelings towards the Church'[484] the spread of Anglo-Catholic ideals in the Church of England deepened the gulf between the established church and the Wesleyan Connexion. Wesleyan hostility towards the Whig educational proposals of 1839 was motivated by anti-Popery sentiments, but Popery appeared to be rising up within the body of the Church of England itself. In 1840 the vicar of Gedney in Lincolnshire caused a scandal by not only refusing to bury a child who had been baptized by a Wesleyan minister but also by characterizing such preachers as 'ministers of hell'.[485] In 1841 the Tractarian leader Edward Pusey published a tract accusing the Methodists of heresy and Antinomanism and was replied to by the former Wesleyan president Thomas Jackson. Pusey, said Jackson, was advocating 'a union between the Church of England and the Church of Rome'. But before members of the established church followed such advice, they should remember that 'the church with which he recommends them to identify themselves stands convicted of some millions of atrocious murders, of which the burnings of Smithfield are only a slight specimen'.[486] Even Bunting was moved to tell the Methodist Conference in 1841 that 'unless the Church of England will protest against Puseyism . . . it will be the duty of Methodists to protest against the Church of England'.[487] And finally Sir James Graham's Factory Education Bill caused leading Wesleyans as much as leading Congregationalists to express alarm that the church which would thus be supported out of public funds was a church in which Catholic principles were making rapid headway. The wealthy Wesleyan layman Thomas Farmer told the

[482] Currie, *Methodism Divided*, 49.   [483] Ward, *Early Victorian Methodism*, 195.

[484] Ibid. 59.   [485] Townsend, Workman, and Eayrs, *New History of Methodism*, i. 403.

[486] T. Jackson, *Recollections of my own Life and Times* (1873), 317–20.

[487] Gregory, *Side Lights on the Conflicts of Methodism*, 317.

Connexion's Committee of Privileges that because the Church of England was moving away from the scriptural foundations of the Reformation Wesleyans were now Dissenters from it, and Bunting himself agreed that Wesleyans were in a sense Dissenters.[488] When, in April 1843, Graham received a Wesleyan protest against his measure he wrote to Peel that is 'goes the whole length of the bitterest dissent'. 'It is quite clear that the Pusey tendencies of the Established Church have operated powerfully on the Wesleyans and are converting them rapidly into enemies.' Lord Ashley agreed. 'The Wesleyan Methodists, hitherto friendly to the Church, as they showed in 1839, are actuated by a deep and conscientious fear of Popery in the Church of England.'[489] The Wesleyan leaders were not yet prepared to accompany the bulk of their followers into the Liberal camp, but the rift between the Wesleyan hierarchy and the Conservative party which opened up in 1843 was never entirely healed. By the end of April over two million signatures had been collected on 13,369 petitions against the bill, and on 15 June Graham announced the withdrawal of its education provisions.[490]

The fear aroused among Dissenters that the government would use the inadequacies of the country's educational system as a pretext for strengthening the position of the established church prompted both Congregationalists and Wesleyans to make strenuous efforts to make good the failings of the voluntary system. In October 1843 the Congregational Union resolved that 'both the general and the religious education of the people ... must be chiefly provided and conducted by the voluntary efforts of the various denominations of Christians', and to that end launched an education fund which raised £100,000 in three years. In the next ten years, so the younger Edward Baines claimed, the Congregationalists founded 453 schools with 50,000 scholars.[491] The Wesleyans did not commit themselves so firmly to the voluntary principle but they, too, responded to the threat posed by Graham's Factory Education Bill with a gallant effort to plug the gaps in the country's educational system. The Wesleyan Conference had approved the setting up of day schools in 1833 and ten years later had 290 schools with 20,804 scholars. In the aftermath of the storm provoked by Sir James Graham the Conference established a committee under the chairmanship of its president, John Scott, which set itself a target of establishing 700 schools in seven years. The target was never reached but by 1857 the Wesleyans had 434 day schools with 52,630 pupils.[492]

---

[488] Ibid. 511–12.   [489] Ward and Treble, 'Religion and Education in 1843', 84–5.
[490] Machin, *Politics and the Churches*, 158.   [491] Peel, *These Hundred Years*, 177–82.
[492] *HMC* ii. 242–3; Gregory, *Side Lights on the Conflicts of Methodism*, 352; Hempton,

Graham's ill-fated bill not only encouraged the growth of voluntaryist principles and the accompanying school-building programmes among Dissenters, it also gave a powerful stimulus to the campaign for disestablishment. In October 1843 a group of Dissenting ministers in the Midlands, led by Miall's old friend John Phillippo Mursell, published a letter in both the *Nonconformist* and the *Patriot* calling for a conference to promote 'the dissolution of the union between the Church and the State'.[493] Miall took up the suggestion and in December travelled to Leicester, along with the Baptists Francis Cox and Thomas Price, editor of the *Eclectic Review*, to discuss the idea. The result was a conference which met in the Crown and Anchor in the Strand from 30 April to 2 May 1844 to found the British Anti-State Church Association.[494]

The inaugural conference of the Anti-State Church Association was attended by 728 delegates, of whom the majority were Baptists and Congregationalists. Miall and his supporters did not, however, carry all the representatives of even Old Dissent with them. The Baptist Union was the only denominational organization to send official representatives,[495] and many Congregationalists were hostile. John Blackburn, editor of the *Congregational Magazine*, complained that the new association was open to 'Christians, Socinians, and men of no religion' and argued that 'Christian churches and congregations, as such' should not concern themselves with the redress of civil grievances.[496] John Campbell, John Angell James, and Thomas Raffles all opposed the Anti-State Church Association. The committee of Homerton College tried, in vain, to persuade its principal, John Pye Smith, to resign his membership. And Robert Vaughan, president of the Lancashire Independent College which had just moved to Manchester, was so angered by the *Eclectic Review*'s support for disestablishment that he set in motion plans for a rival periodical, the *British Quarterly Review*.[497]

A handful of Quakers, including Joseph Sturge, attended the inaugural conference of the Anti-State Church Association, as did Robert Eckett, the leader of the Wesleyan Methodist Association.[498] Unsurprisingly few

---

Methodism and Politics, 171; M. Edwards, *John Wesley and the Eighteenth Century* (1985), 143–4.

[493] *Patriot*, 2 Oct. 1843, 685; *Nonconformist*, 4 Oct. 1843, 674.
[494] Patterson, *Radical Leicester*, 257; D. Thompson, 'The Liberation Society', in Hollis, *Pressure from Without*, 214–16.
[495] E. A. Payne, *The Baptist Union* (1959), 84.
[496] Waddington, *Congregational History to 1850*, 573.
[497] Ibid. 569–70, 574–8; Jones, *English Congregationalism*, 213.
[498] Machin, *Politics and the Churches*, 161.

Calvinistic Methodists and few Wesleyans supported the new movement, though the Liberal *Wesleyan Chronicle*, proclaiming 'eternal war with the Establishment', urged its readers to join forces with their 'Dissenting brethren to obtain equal rights'.[499] More surprisingly few Unitarians attended the new association's foundation meeting. Until the 1830s there was much Unitarian support for disestablishment: Priestley had argued that the dissolution of the bond between Church and State would strengthen Christianity; Henry Turner claimed that the alliance between Church and State was 'a conspiracy against the rights and liberties of mankind'; John Beard maintained that the church establishment was among the greatest of public nuisances.[500] But the growing militancy of Evangelical Dissent in the 1830s alarmed Unitarians and led them to distance themselves from their orthodox brethren. As the United Committee's campaign of 1833–4 for the redress of Dissenting grievances developed into an agitation for disestablishment so those Unitarian leaders who were in close contact with Whig politicians recoiled in horror. Robert Aspland refused to attend a meeting of the United Committee in March 1834 and consoled himself with the thought that he and his co-religionists were demonstrating to 'the sane portion of the old Church of England that the Unitarians, the descendants from . . . the old English Presbyterians, are not . . . the rancorous enemies of the establishment'.[501] The bitter disputes over the Unitarians' legal title to meeting-houses and funds which had once been Presbyterian and Calvinist, culminating in the Wolverhampton chapel and Lady Hewley's charity cases, further increased tension. Unitarians seceded both from the lay Protestant Dissenting Deputies and from the ministerial Committee of the Three Denominations in 1836, and in the same year the gulf between orthodox and heterodox Dissenters was further emphasized when Trinitarian Presbyterian congregations in Lancashire and north-west England organized themselves into a synod which three years later called itself the Presbyterian Church in England.[502]

Peel sought to resolve the issue of the disputed meeting-houses in favour of the Unitarians with the Dissenters' Chapels Act of 1844. The Act gave congregations a legal title to buildings in which they had worshipped for twenty-five years provided that the beliefs they held were not in conflict with the chapels' trust deeds. While the Dissenting Deputies launched an

---

[499] *Wesleyan Chronicle*, 22 Mar. 1844, 185.
[500] C. Robbins, *The Eighteenth-Century Commonwealthman* (New York, 1968), 227–8; Mineka, *Dissidence of Dissent*, 140, 222.
[501] Aspland, *Memoir of Robert Aspland*, 535.
[502] Chadwick, *The Victorian Church*, i. 399.

agitation against the bill, a minority of orthodox Dissenters, including the younger Edward Baines, Thomas Price, and Edward Miall, supported the measure.[503] But Miall's backing of the Dissenters' Chapels Bill did not spare the Anti-State Church Association from the censure of many Unitarians. The *Christian Reformer*, under the editorship first of Robert Aspland and then of his son R. B. Aspland, condemned both the campaign against church rates and the disestablishment agitation. Far worse than the ascendancy of the Church of England, argued the *Christian Reformer*, was 'the fanaticism, intolerance, hollowness, and spiritual pride of those leagued' for its destruction.[504] John James Tayler, minister of the Unitarian chapel in Upper Brook Street, Manchester, made the same point in 1845: 'the temper and views, often exhibited by those who are most eager for the separation of the Church from the State, have created some apprehension . . . that the tyranny of a fanatical public opinion might prove more intolerable than the ascendancy of a favoured Church'.[505]

When the results of the religious census were published in 1854 Edward Miall rejoiced that those who worshipped in Nonconformist chapels were almost as numerous as those who attended parish churches. But the reactions of most Wesleyans, many Unitarians, and a significant minority of Congregationalists to the foundation of the Anti-State Church Association suggested that a substantial body of Nonconformist opinion did not share Miall's vision of the ultimate separation of Church and State. If one makes the generous assumption that half of all regular Nonconformist worshippers in England were in favour of disestablishment, that means that nearly four-fifths of all worshippers were not, and most of those people who attended neither church nor chapel were unlikely to have been moved by the issue. In other words, the campaign for the separation of Church and State probably had the support of fewer than 10 per cent of the total population of England, and it is therefore difficult to escape H. R. Martin's conclusion that the cause of the disestablishment of the Church of England was doomed from the beginning.[506] The *Nonconformist* newspaper never reached more than a tiny fraction of its intended constituency. Its circulation by the end of its first year was only 2,000, and for the first five years of its life it was dependent for its continued existence on the generous financial support of Joseph Sturge and his brother Charles.[507] By the 1850s the circulation of the *Nonconformist* had

---

[503] Manning, *Dissenting Deputies*, 87–91; Martin, 'Politics of the Congregationalists', 310.
[504] Sellers, 'English Unitarians', 128, 142.
[505] J. J. Tayler, *A Retrospect of the Religious Life of England* (1845), 466–7.
[506] Martin, 'Politics of the Congregationalists', 536.
[507] Miall, *Life of Miall*, 54; Newton, 'Edward Miall', 346.

reached 3,200, but this was less than a tenth of the circulation of the *Northern Star* at the height of its influence.[508] In 1845 the executive committee of the Anti-State Church Association resolved to select half a dozen candidates for parliamentary elections, but its first intervention in an electoral contest was disastrous. In September Miall stood as a radical candidate in a parliamentary by-election for Southwark against the official Liberal Sir William Molesworth. The *Patriot* condemned Miall for standing on a platform which tried to unite Dissenting and Chartist principles and the *Leeds Mercury* denounced him as 'one of the most impracticable men in the three kingdoms'.[509] Miall came a bad third, polling only 10 per cent of the total vote.[510]

But if the disestablishment of the Church of England was a forlorn hope, the disestablishment of the Anglican Church of Ireland, in a country in which 80 per cent of the population were Roman Catholics, was a more likely prospect. Miall convinced himself that the disestablishment of the Church of Ireland would lead inevitably to the disestablishment of the Church of England,[511] and it was partly for this reason that he tried desperately to avoid alienating Roman Catholics when Peel, in 1845, raised a storm of protest by increasing the government's grant to the Roman Catholic college at Maynooth in County Kildare. Half the Tory party in Parliament, the Evangelical wing of the Church of England, the Wesleyan Methodists, and many Congregationalists opposed the grant on anti-Catholic grounds. Miall also opposed the grant, but he took pains to point out that he did so not because he disliked the Roman Catholic church, but because he disliked all state endowments of religion.[512] When the Anti-Maynooth committee organized a meeting in Exeter Hall in April 1845 Miall and his supporters walked out, claiming that they had not been allowed to put the case against all church establishments.[513] The split in the Conservative party over the Maynooth grant presaged the more serious split in the following year when Peel announced the government's intention to repeal the Corn Laws. Nearly all the Conservative MPs who opposed Peel over Maynooth also voted against him on the Corn Laws,[514] and many voted with the opposition in June 1846 to defeat the government and bring the Whigs back into office.

Most political Dissenters regarded the return of the Whigs with little enthusiasm. Peel had carried the Maynooth grant through Parliament only because he had the support of the Whig opposition and the new prime minister, Lord John Russell, was known to favour not the disestablishment of

[508] Newton, 'Edward Miall', 4.   [509] Ibid. 198–200.
[510] Miall, *Life of Miall*, 108–10.   [511] Newton, 'Edward Miall', 266.
[512] Ibid. 247, 253.   [513] Ibid. 260.
[514] R. Stewart, *Party and Politics, 1830–1852* (1989), 75.

endowed churches but the concurrent endowment of all churches, Roman Catholic as well as Protestant.[515] Both the *Eclectic Review* and the *Patriot* suggested that Whig support for Maynooth warranted the ending of the Whig–Dissenting alliance,[516] and Nonconformist hostility to the Whigs further increased with the publication, in December 1846, of the minutes of the Education Committee of the Privy Council. Hitherto government grants for education had been made only to assist the building of schools, but now the Education Committee proposed that grants be given to aid training colleges and pupil teachers, to supplement the salaries of trained teachers, and to provide such teachers with pensions after fifteen years' service. The grants were to be conditional on both the colleges in which teachers trained, and the schools in which they taught, being inspected by government inspectors, and on teachers in receipt of government grants being examined.[517]

This potentially vast increase in government intervention aroused the fury of those Dissenters who believed that state subvention for education could be no more justified than state support for religion. When the British and Foreign School Society voted to accept government aid, prominent Congregationalists including Samuel Morley and the younger Edward Baines withdrew their subscriptions.[518] For Edward Baines and his father the controversy provided one of their last opportunities to co-operate on a political issue. The younger Baines argued that state aid was unwanted and unnecessary. Given the supreme importance of giving religious instruction 'in our schools to the children of the poor, we are shut up by our principles from receiving money doled out by the civil power, and raised by taxes, for that purpose'.[519] The deficiencies in school accommodation could be remedied by the people themselves, for in thirteen years voluntary effort had contributed nearly four times as much as government grants to the building of schools.[520] In March 1847, in the Cloth Hall Yard, Leeds, the elder Baines, now aged seventy-three, addressed a huge meeting of 15,000 people for an hour in one of his last public appearances. The meeting resolved by a proportion of two to one to condemn the government scheme and over half a million signatures were collected in 4,203 petitions against the proposals.[521] It was all to no avail. In April the House of Commons agreed by 372 votes to 47 to increase the education grant to £100,000 a year.[522] The Nonconformists who were opposed to the Whigs' education policy in 1847 were unable to

---

[515] Newton, 'Edward Miall', 266–7.   [516] Martin, 'Politics of the Congregationalists', 342.

[517] Murphy, *Church, State and Schools*, 34–5.   [518] Binns, *A Century of Education*, 145–6.

[519] Martin, 'Politics of the Congregationalists', 409.

[520] Baines, *Letters to Russell on State Education*, 37–9.

[521] Baines, *Life of Edward Baines*, 332–5.   [522] Machin, *Politics and the Churches*, 184.

repeat their success of 1843 because Russell's government, unlike Peel's, had the support of the opposition. But in any case, in contrast to their campaign against Graham's Factory Education Bill, Dissenters in 1847 were far from united. In Leeds prominent Unitarians such as Charles Wicksteed and Hamer Stansfeld opposed the Baineses' voluntaryist agitation.[523] The Unitarian *Christian Reformer* argued that if opposition to state aid succeeded it would be not a victory for voluntaryism but a defeat for a decent education for the children of the poor.[524] In Manchester in July the United Presbyterian minister William McKerrow laid the foundations of the Lancashire Public School Association for 'the establishment of a general system of secular education for the county of Lancaster', by which he meant the Irish and now defunct Liverpool systems.[525] Among Congregationalists Jonathan Glyde thought that Dissenters should accept the government grants and Thomas Binney maintained that secular and religious education could be kept separate: 'it was legitimate for the State to assist the former if the latter were left to the churches'.[526] But the most important Nonconformist group to accept state aid were the Wesleyans. At a crucial meeting of the Connexional Education Committee early in 1847 Samuel Jackson and William Bunting urged their fellow Wesleyans to adopt the voluntaryist position, but a dramatic and unexpected visit from Lord Ashley strengthened the hands of those committee members who were opposed to voluntaryism and the committee's chairman, John Scott, persuaded the committee and the subsequent Wesleyan Conference to accept government aid.[527] Opposition to the government's proposals, as Vaughan's *British Quarterly Review* pointed out, had 'been left almost exclusively to the Congregational and Baptist denominations, and to a portion only even of those bodies'.[528] In the case of education, as in the case of disestablishment, Edward Miall voiced the opinions of fewer than half the politically aware Nonconformists for whom his newspaper by its very title claimed to speak.

None the less, such was the disillusionment of Miall's supporters with the government's education policy, and such was their fear that the Whig support for the Maynooth grant foreshadowed a policy of concurrent endowment, that they resolved to bring pressure to bear on the Whigs in the forthcoming general election. The result was the most determined effort that the Dissenters had yet made to influence the composition of Parliament. In March 1847 the executive committee of the Anti-State Church Association

---

[523] Ram, 'Dissenters in the East and West Ridings', 260–2.
[524] Newton, 'Edward Miall', 20.   [525] *Memoir of McKerrow*, 153–5.
[526] *Nonconformist*, 24 Feb. 1847, 188; 6 Apr. 1847, 246.
[527] Rigg, *Wesleyan Methodist Reminiscences*, 107–14.   [528] Newton, 'Edward Miall', 51.

urged all Dissenters 'to withhold their votes at the ensuing general election from all candidates who are not prepared to resist every attempt to extend the power, patronage, and possessions of the established church'.[529] In April a conference on education, attended by nearly five hundred Dissenters, told electors to vote only for candidates who held 'sacred the claims of religious liberty', and a Dissenters' Parliamentary Committee was set up to organize the Nonconformist campaign. The chairman was the wealthy Congregationalist hosiery manufacturer and member of the King's Weigh House, Samuel Morley. After a decade and a half in which militant Dissenters had become increasingly alienated from the Whigs, they now concluded that so little separated the Whigs from the Tories that no harm could be done by opposing both.[530]

Miall claimed that in 1847 twenty-six supporters of his Anti-State Church Association were returned to Parliament and that more than sixty MPs were now opposed to a further extension of state endowments for religion.[531] However, only thirteen English Nonconformist MPs were returned, plus one Scottish United Presbyterian, and of those English Nonconformists only five were members of the Anti-State Church Association: John Bowring, John Bright, Joseph Brotherton, Charles Hindley, and John B. Smith. Four of the six Unitarian MPs remained aloof from Miall's movement (William J. Fox, James Heywood, J. Thornley, and James Marshall). And four of the orthodox Dissenters returned for the first time in 1847 were similarly not supporters of the Anti-State Church Association: James Pilkington, the Congregationalist MP for Blackburn, Samuel Morton Peto, the Baptist railway contractor who was MP for Norwich, and two Wesleyan merchants from Manchester who sat on opposite sides of the House—Joshua Westhead, Liberal MP for Knaresborough, and James Heald, Conservative MP for Stockport.[532]

Indeed the election of 1847 highlighted the divisions as much as the achievements of political Dissent. In Oldham John Fielden's attempt to secure the election of his son-in-law John Cobbett resulted in the defeats of both Fielden and Cobbett. Fielden was replaced by his fellow Unitarian,

---

[529] *Nonconformist*, 10 Mar. 1847, 156.

[530] Gash, *Reaction and Reconstruction in English Politics*, 102.

[531] Miall, *Life of Miall*, 128.

[532] *Nonconformist*, 1 Sept. 1847, 634–5. The Congregationalist J. Kershaw was subsequently returned for Stockport at a by-election in 1847 and two more Dissenters, the Baptist hosiery manufacturer Richard Harris and the Quaker John Ellis, were returned for Leicester at a by-election in 1848. They were elected to 'keep the seats warm' for Sir Joshua Walmsley and Richard Gardner who had been elected in 1847 and had subsequently been unseated on petition on grounds of corruption (Patterson, *Radical Leicester*, 348).

W. J. Fox, whom Fielden's supporters claimed was backed by the local mill-owners in revenge for the Ten Hours Act.[533] In Norwich Samuel Morton Peto's refusal to commit himself to disestablishment led to his own pastor, William Brock, supporting a rival candidate.[534] In Halifax Edward Miall stood on a voluntaryist platform in alliance with the Chartist Ernest Jones with the result that both were defeated by a Whig–Tory combination. Even in Baines's Leeds the voluntaryists went down to defeat. Joseph Sturge stood as a voluntaryist candidate against the Unitarian James Marshall who had the support of Hamer Stansfeld. Stansfeld told Baines that he intended 'to rescue the town of Leeds from being disgraced in the eyes of the country by the adoption of so narrow and sectarian a policy [on education] as that which you advocate'.[535] He succeeded: Marshall and a Tory were elected and Sturge came bottom of the poll.

If the general election of 1847 illustrated the limited political appeal of voluntaryism, the next twenty years revealed its glaring educational inadequacies. Most Dissenting communities were already overstretched financially, with constant demands being made on their resources to fund ministers' salaries, the building and maintenance of chapels, missionary societies, and numerous philanthropic organizations, and it is hardly surprising that they found difficulty in shouldering the additional burden of finding money for denominational schools. In 1843 John Scott had set the Wesleyans the target of building 700 schools in seven years, but it took them twenty-five years to build 670 schools, and the Wesleyans were in receipt of state aid.[536] The schools which the Wesleyans and Congregationalists had set up since 1843, William McKerrow argued five years later, had been founded on no rational plan and were often 'a lamentable waste of money and effort'. Such schools 'abounded where they were least needed, and were rarely to be met with where schools were most required'.[537] Antipathy to voluntaryism was reflected in the growing support for McKerrow's Lancashire Public School Association, both from Dissenters and from other radicals. It numbered among its vice-presidents the MPs Joseph Brotherton, Richard Cobden, William Sharman Crawford, and Thomas Milner Gibson, and was supported by the Unitarian MPs John Bowring and W. J. Fox, the Quaker Jacob Bright, the Congregationalists Elkanah Armitage, Samuel Davidson, and Robert Vaughan, and in Liverpool by the former pillar of the Wesleyan Methodist Association, James Picton.[538] In 1850 the Lancashire Association was

---

[533] Weaver, *John Fielden*, 269–73.   [534] C. M. Birrell, *Life of William Brock* (1878), 156.
[535] Ram, 'Dissenters in the East and West Ridings', 168–9.   [536] *HMC* ii. 243.
[537] *Memoir of McKerrow*, 157.
[538] Ibid. 156; Martin, 'Politics of the Congregationalists', 415; Picton, *Sir James Picton*, 188–90.

transformed into the National Public School Association. It advocated a system of free schools, providing secular instruction only, 'supported by local rates, and managed by local authorities specifically elected for that purpose by the ratepayers'.[539] It was supported in Leicester by the Unitarian hosier William Biggs, in Nottingham by two Baptist ministers and by the Baptist lace manufacturer William Felkin, and in Bradford by the Quaker woollen manufacturer William E. Forster.[540] It was Forster who, twenty years later, was to carry through Parliament the Act establishing rate-supported schools.

The inadequacies of the voluntary system were particularly evident in Wales. The depression of the early 1840s, which in urban England fuelled the Plug Plot riots of August 1842, led in rural south-west Wales to the Rebecca riots. For twelve months from November 1842 gangs of men, some of whom disguised themselves in women's clothes, roamed the Welsh countryside attacking toll-gates, taking their inspiration from Genesis 24: 60, 'And . . . they said unto [Rebecca] . . . let thy seed possess the gate of those which hate them'. As in the case of the Newport rising, Anglicans blamed Dissenters for fomenting the violence and, as in 1839, there was some evidence to support their accusation. The outbreak was centred on Carmarthenshire where nearly half the population was to attend a Nonconformist chapel on census Sunday and where Dissenting ministers sympathized with the complaints against the toll-gates even if they disapproved of Rebecca's methods.[541] When the rioters went on from wrecking toll-gates to chastising bad neighbours, violent husbands, and the fathers of illegitimate children, they were enforcing the moral code of the Dissenting churches, and Rebecca's reprimands were sometimes conveyed to her victims by chapel officers.[542] The Independents of Cardiganshire condemned the violence in the summer of 1843 and in October the South Wales Calvinistic Methodist Association, meeting at Newport in Pembrokeshire, urged their societies to expel members who either joined or justified the riots.[543] But, as in the case of the Newport rising, the laity did not always obey ministerial injunctions. On 18 June 1843 John Thomas, minister of the Independent church at Bwlch-newydd in Carmarthenshire, preached from Jeremiah 29: 7, 'Seek ye the peace of the city', but this did not prevent many of his congregation from joining the march on Carmarthen the following morning.[544] Two of the most

---

[539] *Memoir of McKerrow*, 174.
[540] Patterson, *Radical Leicester*, 258; Harrison, 'Baptists of Nottinghamshire', ii. 794.
[541] Parry, 'Welsh Independents and Working-class Movements', 138–9.
[542] D. J. V. Jones, *Rebecca's Children* (Oxford, 1989), 267–73.
[543] Ibid. 333; D. Williams, *The Rebecca Riots* (Cardiff, 1955), 155.
[544] Williams, *Rebecca Riots*, 154.

violent of Rebecca's leaders, both of whom were sentenced to transportation, had Nonconformist affiliations. John Jones, alias Shoni Sgubor Fawr, a prize-fighter with a reputation for hard drinking, was said to have been a Baptist and David Davies, alias Dai'r Cantwr, was once a Wesleyan local preacher.[545]

If Dissent was one of the perceived causes of the Rebecca riots, another was ignorance of the English language. In March 1846 William Williams, a native of Carmarthenshire who was radical MP for Coventry, moved in the House of Commons for an inquiry into the state of education in Wales, and 'especially into the means afforded to the labouring classes of acquiring a knowledge of the English language'. Sir James Graham agreed on behalf of the government to institute such an inquiry and his Whig successor, Sir George Grey, appointed three commissioners who began work in October 1846.[546] When the commissioners' report was published in 1847 it provoked a storm of protest. The three commissioners were English barristers who knew nothing of the Welsh language, and of the eight Welsh assistants who served them throughout the inquiry seven were Anglicans. The commissioners and their assistants thus had no sympathy either for the culture or for the religion of the majority of the Welsh people. They reported that while the poor in Wales were 'far superior to the same class of Englishmen in being able to read the Bible in their own language' and were skilled in discussing 'abstruse points of polemic theology', they were inferior 'in every branch of practical knowledge and skill'. While serious crimes were rare in Wales, there were few countries in Europe 'where the standard of minor morals is lower'. 'Petty thefts, lying, cozening, every species of chicanery, drunkenness . . . and idleness' prevailed 'among the least educated part of the community'. Above all the Welsh were guilty of pre-marital sex, with chapel prayer-meetings and evening classes providing opportunities for 'immoralities between the young persons of both sexes, who frequently spend the night afterwards in haylofts together'. The solution to the ignorance and immorality of the Welsh was to educate them in the English language. The Welsh language was a 'manifold barrier to the moral progress and commercial prosperity of the people'. 'It is not easy to over-estimate its evil effects.'[547]

The report of the Welsh Education Commission was deeply and bitterly resented in Wales: it became known as 'Brad y Llyfrau Gleision', the 'Treachery of the Blue Books'. Evan Jones, alias Ieuan Gwynedd, former

---

[545] Ibid. 247–8.
[546] D. Salmon, 'The Story of a Welsh Education Commission', *Y Cymmrodor*, 24 (1913), 191–5.
[547] Ibid. 207–15.

minister of Saron Independent church in Tredegar, argued that 'a vast number of the published depositions' were worthless as 'the productions of interested, incompetent and immoral witnesses', among them 'broken-down Dissenting ministers expelled from their respective denominations', 'Englishmen and Irishmen entirely unacquainted with the language of the country', and clergy who 'could hardly be expected to give a fair description of a nation of Dissenters'.[548] The Caernarfon Independent minister William Williams (Caledfryn) complained that he had spent four hours with one of the commissioners, Henry Johnson, detailing how a 'great work of reformation had been promoted among us' since the beginning of the Evangelical revival a hundred years earlier, and that Johnson had totally ignored Williams's evidence in his report.[549] In Aberdare 2,500 people attended a public meeting to censure the evidence of the vicar, that there was 'no religion whatever' in a parish which housed sixteen Dissenting chapels.[550] But there were some Nonconformists who admitted that much of the report was true and that its indictment of Welsh education was valid.[551] 'Why is the Scotchman a manager in the office, and the Welshman but a labourer in the ditch?' asked the Calvinistic Methodist Henry Rees in 1845. It was 'because the Welshman never received the Scotchman's advantages in education'.[552] And while the initial reaction of most Welsh Dissenters to the commission's report was to confirm them in their attachment to voluntaryism, since any other response would be seen as acceptance of the slander on their nation,[553] in subsequent years the voluntaryist position foundered on the rocks of Welsh poverty. The Congregationalist Enoch Salisbury, later Liberal MP for Chester, wrote in 1849 that he had 'no faith in the voluntary principle': many of the Independent churches in Wales were deeply in debt, their chapels were unfit for the worship of God, and they were hard pressed to pay their ministers more than 12s. a week. Salisbury had no confidence in their ability to finance an adequate system of schools as well.[554] His point was proved by the fate of the Nonconformist teachers' training college which was established at Brecon in 1846. When a meeting of subscribers resolved in 1847 that the college should be run on voluntary principles the Wesleyans withdrew their support and in the following year the college moved to new buildings at

[548] E. Jones, *Facts, Figures, and Statements in Illustration of the Dissent and Morality of Wales* (1849), 19–20.
[549] Parry, 'Welsh Independents and Working-class Movements', 207–8.
[550] I. J. Jones, *Mid-Victorian Wales* (Cardiff, 1992), 162.
[551] Parry, 'Welsh Independents and Working-class Movements', 192, 206.
[552] A. M. Davies, *Life and Letters of Henry Rees*, 140.
[553] Salmon, 'Welsh Education Commission', 235.
[554] Parry, 'Welsh Independents and Working-class Movements', 223.

Swansea which it could not afford. With subscriptions failing to meet expenditure the college closed in 1850.[555] Over the next few years Nonconformist opposition to government aid for education was progressively weakened. The Calvinistic Methodists followed the Wesleyans in repudiating voluntaryism and co-operated with the state-aided British and Foreign School Society. From 1843 the society's agent in north Wales was John Phillips, a Calvinistic Methodist minister, and it was largely as a result of Phillips's initiative that a state-assisted teachers' training college was founded in Bangor in 1863. Phillips was the college's first principal and the Calvinistic Methodists its chief supporters, providing £10,786 of its first £13,520.[556] In south Wales David Rees's *Y Diwygwr*, the leading Independent periodical, abandoned voluntaryism in the early 1850s, and in 1853 William Roberts, minister of the Salem Baptist church, Blaina, was appointed agent for the British and Foreign School Society notwithstanding the society's acceptance of state aid.[557] The Independents of Denbighshire and Flintshire also voted to support the British and Foreign School Society in 1863.[558]

In England the advocates of voluntaryism abandoned their opposition to state-aided education with greater reluctance, but in the end they bowed to the inevitable. Edward Miall opposed bills introduced by W. J. Fox in 1850 and 1851 to provide for rate-supported secular schools on the ground that the State was no more responsible for the people's education than it was for 'their food, their employment, and their health'.[559] And he similarly opposed Lord John Russell's Borough Education Bill of 1853 which proposed to use rate aid to support voluntary schools.[560] But by the end of the 1850s it was clear that the voluntaryist refusal to accept state grants for education was benefiting only the Church of England. In 1859 the established church received two-thirds of the government grant and three years later Welsh Nonconformists were complaining that the money was being used not only for church schools but also for buildings accommodating church services.[561] Miall was appointed to the Royal Commission set up under the chairmanship of the Duke of Newcastle in 1858 to inquire 'into the present state of popular

---

[555] Ibid. 236–42; A. H. Williams, *Welsh Wesleyan Methodism*, 173–6.

[556] Parry, 'Welsh Independents and Working-class Movements', 229–31, citing J. V. Morgan, *Welsh Political and Educational Leaders in the Victorian Era* (1908), 293–302; *DWB* 756–70.

[557] Parry, 'Welsh Independents and Working-class Movements', 228; Bassett, *Welsh Baptists*, 298; Evans, 'Religion in the Swansea Valley', 307.

[558] Parry, 'Welsh Independents and Working-class Movements', 227.

[559] *Nonconformist*, 6 Mar. 1850, 191; 28 May 1851, 417.

[560] Newton, 'Edward Miall', 58–9.

[561] Chadwick, *The Victorian Church*, i. 345; Parry, 'Welsh Independents and Working-class Movements', 212.

education in England', and when its report was published three years later he and Goldwin Smith submitted a minority report expressing the voluntaryist point of view. But Miall undermined the consistency of his own position by also signing, as 'the second resort', the majority report proposing that elected boards be set up in counties and boroughs with powers to levy rates and make grants to schools.[562] Edward Baines's voluntaryism was similarly undermined by his membership of the Taunton Commission, set up in 1864 to inquire into the condition of endowed secondary schools, an experience which persuaded him of the value of government inspection and control.[563] In October 1867 both Miall and Baines publicly announced their abandonment of the cause of voluntary education: 'as a practical politician', Baines told the Congregational Union, 'he must bow to forces which he cannot withstand'.[564] One might ask how a 'practical politician' could have fought for so futile a cause for so long.

8. 'A BETTER UNDERSTANDING BETWEEN THE MIDDLE AND LABOURING CLASSES': CLASS RECONCILIATION

The educational conflicts of the 1840s were evidence that issues that were fundamentally religious could still divide men as bitterly as could issues of class. That point was reinforced over the next two decades as both Chartists and middle-class radicals were increasingly inclined to put behind them the class hostility of the late 1830s and early 1840s and to unite against privilege in both Church and State. If the 1832 Reform Act, the defeat of the Ten Hours movement in 1833, the Poor Law Amendment of 1834, and the economic crisis of 1837 set the scene for class conflict, the repeal of the Corn Laws, the Ten Hours Factory Act, the decline of Chartism, and the economic recovery which accompanied the railway boom laid the basis for class reconciliation. The 'better understanding between the middle and labouring classes' which Edward Miall had been urging ever since 1841 and in support of which Joseph Sturge had launched the Complete Suffrage Union, though it foundered on the rocks of the Plug Plot in 1842, was refloated later in the decade and twenty years later sailed triumphantly into harbour.

---

[562] Newton, 'Edward Miall', 70–3; Miall, *Life of Miall*, 235; Murphy, *Church, State and Schools*, 45.
[563] Binfield, *So Down to Prayers*, 89.
[564] Newton, 'Edward Miall', 79; D. Fraser, 'Edward Baines', in Hollis, *Pressure from Without*, 202.

From the point of view of the Chartist leadership, the growing emphasis on the need to work with the radical middle class was simply an acceptance of the obvious: Parliament's rejection of the three Chartist petitions underlined the fact that without support from within the established political parties one man one vote would never be achieved. Feargus O'Connor, one-time advocate of class war, called in October 1849 for 'union between the veritable middle classes and the working classes'.[565] But the movement for class reconciliation in the 1850s and 1860s was not merely a tactical ploy on the part of the frustrated Chartist leadership, it was a recognition of the part of a substantial section of the working class that what they had in common with the radical middle class was more important than what separated them. They shared a common belief in the virtues of hard work, self-help, and self-discipline, a common regard for the value of education, sobriety, and thrift, a common disdain for unmerited wealth, rank, and aristocratic privilege. These were also the values of the Nonconformist churches, and in the class reconciliation of the third quarter of the century Dissent played a crucial role.

The significance of the contribution of Nonconformity to class reconciliation in mid-Victorian England can in part be gauged by the fact that even in the 1840s Dissenting chapels were attracting a far larger active working-class following than was the Chartist movement. Chartism undoubtedly provoked expulsions from some chapels and caused secessions from others, and it prompted individual Nonconformists to question, and in some cases to reject, their faith. None the less the damage that Chartism did to Nonconformity was limited in extent and not always permanent in duration. The year of the Newport rising also saw the beginnings of a religious revival in Wales, sparked off by the preaching of the Welsh-born evangelist Benjamin Chidlaw, recently returned from America, and stimulated by the publication, in 1839, of a Welsh translation of Charles Grandison Finney's *Lectures on Revivals of Religion*.[566] The revival is said to have added some 20,000 members to the Welsh Nonconformist churches, especially to the Independents and the Calvinistic Methodists. And Wesleyan membership in Wales rose by 3,234 between 1838 and 1841, an increase of 20 per cent, though by 1847 it had dropped back to its 1839 level.[567]

One might have expected the Wesleyan Connexion, with its large working-class membership and its unflinching antagonism to radical politics, to

[565] A. Wilson, 'The Suffrage Movement', in Hollis, *Pressure from Without*, 95.

[566] Jones, *Hanes Annibynwyr Cymru*, 200–1.

[567] R. Carwardine, 'The Welsh Evangelical Community and "Finney's Revival" ', *Journal of Ecclesiastical History*, 29 (1978), 465; Currie, Gilbert, and Horsley, *Churches and Churchgoers*, 140.

have been harmed by the Chartist movement, and indeed Wesleyan membership in England did drop by 1,865 in 1841–2 and by 2,248 in the two years 1846–8.[568] In 1840–1 there were more Wesleyans per head of the adult population than at any previous time in British history, but thereafter the proportion of Wesleyans to the adult population went into decline.[569] At the Wesleyan Conference of 1843 Jabez Bunting acknowledged that there had been a fall in the 'attendance of poor people at our services' and blamed it on 'radicalism, infidelity, and Socialism'.[570] But one must not exaggerate the extent of Wesleyan decline in the 1840s nor oversimplify its causes. In absolute terms Wesleyan membership in England rose by 48,451 during the Chartist years (1838–49), an increase of 17.5 per cent, and by 1850 the Welsh Wesleyans had similarly more than recouped the losses of the middle years of the decade. What losses Wesleyans suffered in the 1840s were probably much more the result of economic depression than of political disaffection. The Wesleyans of Leeds, the Primitive Methodists of Mansfield, and the Wesleyan Methodist Association all attributed membership losses in the late 1830s and early 1840s to commercial distress rather than to political discontent.[571] In 1847 the president and secretary of the Methodist Conference claimed that over a thousand Wesleyans had emigrated from Cornwall alone.[572]

The leadership of the Primitive Methodist Connexion was no more sympathetic to Chartism than was that of the Wesleyans, but Ranter membership grew even more dramatically than did Wesleyan in the Chartist years, rising by 25,678 between 1838 and 1849, an increase of 37.9 per cent. The membership of the National Charter Association at its peak in the autumn of 1842 was around 70,000, and this is a generous figure since it is the aggregate of the number of membership cards issued over a period of two years and includes people who had dropped out over that time.[573] But even so that figure of 70,000 is smaller than the membership of the Primitive Methodists in 1842, is less than a quarter of the membership of the Wesleyans, and only one-seventh of the total Methodist membership (both Arminian and Calvinist) in England and Wales. And if one makes the assumption, justified by the 1851 religious census, that Methodists of all persuasions constituted just over half the total Nonconformist population, then this means that in 1842 the membership of the Nonconformist churches in England and Wales outnumbered that of the National Charter Association in the proportion of fourteen to one.

---

[568] Currie, Gilbert, and Horsley, *Churches and Churchgoers*, 140.
[569] Ibid. 65.   [570] Gregory, *Side Lights on the Conflicts of Methodism*, 346.
[571] See above, Ch. I, sect. 5.   [572] *Minutes of the Methodist Conferences*, x. 564.
[573] Epstein, *Lion of Freedom*, 229, 232.

And, as we have seen, the adherents of most of those Nonconformist churches were overwhelmingly working class.

Not only did Nonconformist membership dwarf support for the National Charter Association, even at the height of the Chartist agitation, once that agitation had subsided numerous once-active Chartists became Dissenters or, if they were lapsed Nonconformists, returned to the fold. Arthur O'Neill, founder of the Birmingham Christian Chartist church, was baptized in the Cannon Street Baptist chapel in May 1846, baptized twenty of his own Chartist supporters a month later, and united his following with the Baptist church in Newhall Street in 1847 with himself as pastor.[574] Isaac Jefferson, the blacksmith who was known as the 'Wat Tyler' of the Bradford Chartists and who forged pikes in anticipation of a rising in 1848, devoted his last years to his Primitive Methodist chapel.[575] At Lowton near Leigh in Lancashire both the radical democrat John Birchall and the Owenite John Roughly were converted in the 1850s and joined the Independent Methodists, and at Bingley in the West Riding an Independent Methodist church evolved out of Chartist meetings held in 1848.[576] But the most remarkable cases of free-thinking Chartists returning to the religion of their youth were those of Thomas Cooper and Joseph Barker.

Cooper's rejection of orthodox Christianity had followed his conversion to Chartism in 1840. He was powerfully influenced by Charles Hennell's and George Eliot's translation of D. F. Strauss's demythologizing *Life of Jesus*, gave lectures on Strauss which he published in one of his many short-lived periodicals, *Cooper's Journal*, and would have called himself an agnostic had Huxley then invented the term. But in the middle of the 1850s Cooper began to have doubts about his scepticism and a narrow escape from death in a train crash led him to vow to dedicate the rest of his life to God. In 1858 he embarked on a new career as a lecturer on the evidences of Christianity, and on Whit Sunday 1859 he was baptized in the Friar Lane Baptist chapel in Leicester by his old friend Joseph Foulkes Winks.[577]

Barker's experience was very similar. While in the United States in the 1850s he earned a living as a free-thought lecturer and after his return to England in 1860 edited the secularist *National Reformer* alongside Charles Bradlaugh. Barker was so astounded by the news of Cooper's re-conversion that he challenged him to a public debate, to be held either in England or America, on the claims of Christianity. Cooper took up the challenge and an

---

[574] A. S. Langley, *Birmingham Baptists: Past and Present* (1939), 151–2.
[575] J. Reynolds, *The Great Paternalist* (1983), 136, 154.
[576] Valenze, 'Prophetic Sons and Daughters', 227, 236, 238.
[577] Cooper, *Life of Thomas Cooper*, 262–3, 320, 361–2, 370, 377–8, 380–2.

ill-tempered debate, continuing over six nights, took place in Bradford in September 1860. Barker boasted that 'so completely does the old belief appear to be without foundation' that it was impossible that he could ever be re-converted,[578] but re-converted he was. Barker's scepticism, like Cooper's, was undermined by reminders of the brevity of life. The death of his mother and the illness of his sons were followed by a request, in 1863, from an old friend that he pray with him as he lay dying. That friend was a saddler named Medley from Millbridge near Heckmondwike who had been a Chartist and a follower of Barker in the early 1840s but who had retained his orthodox religious faith. When the dying Medley asked Barker to pray for him, the secularist propagandist found himself 'praying not only for his comrade but also for himself' and agreed to his friend's request that he conduct his funeral service. Vast numbers of people flocked to the funeral and were astounded to hear the renegade Methodist preach from Numbers 23: 10, 'Let me die the death of the righteous, and let my last end be like his'. Barker joined the Primitive Methodists, became a local preacher, and returned to America in 1868 where he preached for both the Methodists and Presbyterians and died in 1875.[579]

The re-conversions of Cooper and Barker are evidence of the continuing appeal of Nonconformity to intelligent men from working-class backgrounds and was a factor in softening working-class attitudes in the 1850s and 1860s. The most convincing analysis of working-class moderation in those decades, that by Neville Kirk, emphasizes not so much the improved living standards of the majority of workers, which were at best marginal, but the success of working-class leaders in rising in the social scale.[580] And a significant number of Kirk's sample of upwardly mobile working-class leaders were Nonconformists.[581] They included William Marcroft, an Oldham Unitarian mechanic, the illegitimate son of a Middleton weaver who began work at the age of six collecting horse manure, and who rose to become a director of the Sun Mill Company and left property worth £14,753 on his death in 1894. Similarly James Lowndes, a Primitive Methodist from Ashton-under-Lyne, progressed from being a shoemaker's apprentice to insurance agent; William Barnett, a Macclesfield Congregationalist, advanced from being a bookbinder's apprentice to become chairman of the Macclesfield Silk

[578] J. Barker, *Confessions of Joseph Barker* (1858), 15–16; *Belief in a Personal God and a Future Life: Six Nights' Discussion between Joseph Barker and Thomas Cooper* (1860).
[579] Barker, *Life of Joseph Barker*, 326–7, 333, 338–9, 345–84; Peel, *Spen Valley*, 321.
[580] N. Kirk, *The Growth of Working Class Reformism in Mid-Victorian England* (1985), 79–82, 98–106, 132–4.
[581] Ibid. 161–2.

Manufacturing Company; and William Bates, a Pendleton Methodist who started work in a calico printing works and was involved in Chartism in the 1840s, left £2,000 when he died in 1908.[582]

What united these men was not only their Nonconformity but also their commitment to the co-operative movement. From the start there was a close connection between the co-operative movement and Dissent. Several founder-members of the Rochdale Equitable Pioneers' Society, the most influential of the early co-operative societies, were associated with the Clover Street Methodist Unitarian chapel.[583] The ethos of the co-operative movement, with its emphasis on working-class self-help rather than class confrontation, was perfectly attuned to the improving, thrifty, communal values of working-class Nonconformity. The first secretary of the Birmingham Co-operative Society when it was established in 1846 was the Baptist John Langford, chair-maker and future historian of the town.[584] William Marcroft, once the secretary of the Oldham branch of the Machine Grinders' Society, abandoned trade unionism for co-operation in the 1850s, took the initiative in forming the Oldham Industrial Co-operative Society in 1850, helped to found the North of England Co-operative Wholesale Society, and played a leading role in the adoption of a profit-sharing scheme for skilled workers at the Hibbert and Platt's machine-building plant where he worked.[585] John Thomas Mitchell, who was secretary to the Rochdale Pioneers from 1857 and president of the Co-operative Wholesale Society from 1874 until his death in 1895, was also teacher and superintendent at the Providence and Milton Congregational Sunday schools.[586] The Manchester and Salford Co-operative Society was founded in 1859 by a group of men associated with the Congregational Roby chapel Sunday school.[587] The co-operative society at Cwmbach near Aberdare also dates from 1859, begun in Bethania Baptist chapel by a group of colliers who were in the main Dissenters.[588] The Colchester Co-operative Society was started by the Congregationalist John Castle in the 1860s.[589] The foundation-stone of the Ipswich Co-operative Society's first building commemorated the names of

---

[582] Ibid. 137–40.
[583] McLachlan, *Methodist Unitarian Movement*, 136–7; G. D. H. Cole, *A Century of Co-operation* (Manchester, 1944), 49.
[584] Ryan, 'Religion and Politics in Birmingham', 85; *DNB*.
[585] Kirk, *Working Class Reformism*, 136–8; J. Foster, *Class Struggle and the Industrial Revolution* (1974), 227–8; R. E. Tyson, 'William Marcroft and the Limited Liability Movement in Oldham', *Transactions of the Lancashire and Cheshire Antiquarian Society*, 80 (1979), 64.
[586] A. S. Mayor, *The Churches and the Labour Movement* (1967), 153–4.
[587] Ibid. 154; W. E. A. Axon, *The Annals of Manchester* (Manchester, 1886), 279.
[588] Turner, 'Revivals and Popular Religion in Wales', 276.
[589] Binfield, 'Nonconformity in the Eastern Counties', 406.

two members of the congregation of Stoke Green Baptist church.[590] Samuel Steinthal, minister to the Unitarian Domestic Mission in Liverpool from 1857 to 1863, was president of the town's co-operative society.[591] A founder and first treasurer of the co-operative society in Ashton-in-Makerfield in Lancashire was the village's Unitarian Minister George Fox, and the society's secretary was also a member of Fox's congregation.[592] James Lowndes was chairman of the Ashton-under-Lyne Co-operative Society in the 1870s, William Barnett was secretary and manager of the Macclesfield Co-operative Society, and William Bates was president of the Eccles Co-operative Society.[593]

The evidence that working-class leaders such as William Bates were shifting the focus of their activities away from Chartism and towards the co-operative movement strengthened the arguments of those middle-class radicals who wanted to extend the franchise to include at least the 'respectable' working class. The failure of the Complete Suffrage conference in December 1842 to unite Chartists and middle-class reformers on a common platform frustrated, but did not end, hopes that the two classes would be able to join forces. In the next two years Sturge devoted much energy to attempts to revive the Complete Suffrage Union, but Sharman Crawford's amendment to the queen's speech on behalf of the movement in February 1844 was supported by only twenty-two MPs and when, in July, Sturge contested a by-election for his home town of Birmingham he came a poor third.[594] However, the downturn in the economy in 1847–8, which provoked the third and final Chartist petition, and the establishment, in February 1848, of the second French republic on the basis of universal manhood suffrage revived middle-class demands for an extension of the franchise.[595] Early in April 'a meeting of gentlemen of the middle classes' in Leicester resolved that it was 'absolutely essential for the peace of society that a union be effected between the working and middle classes'. And in Bradford fifty-two prominent electors, including the Congregationalists William Byles, Titus Salt, and J. G. Miall, and the Quaker W. E. Forster, signed an address to non-electors deprecating 'the policy which dissociates the middle classes from the operatives' and urging the extension of the franchise to every taxpayer.[596] The anti-climax of the

[590] Klaiber, *Suffolk Baptists*, 179.
[591] A. Holt, *A Ministry to the Poor* (Liverpool, 1936), 69.
[592] Fox, *History of Park Lane Chapel*, 215.   [593] Kirk, *Working Class Reformism*, 139–40.
[594] Tyrrell, *Joseph Sturge*, 146–8; Wilson, 'The Suffrage Movement', in Hollis, *Pressure from Without*, 92.
[595] For the impact of the French Revolution on the reform movement see R. Quinault, '1848 and Parliamentary Reform', *Historical Journal*, 31 (1988), 832–6.
[596] *Nonconformist*, 12 Apr. 1848, 256.

Chartist demonstration on Kennington Common on 10 April, at which O'Connor requested his followers to disperse at the behest of the metropolitan police, both convinced many Chartists of the need for middle-class support and assured middle-class radicals that the Chartists posed no threat to public order.[597] Members of the bourgeoisie not only enrolled as special constables to counter a possible outbreak of violence, many of them also voiced their support for at least some of the working-class demands. It was the special constables of Nottingham who called a 'meeting of the middle classes' for 17 April at which resolutions were passed expressing sympathy with the working class in their distress and calling for an extension of the franchise. Both James Edwards, pastor of the George Street Particular Baptist church, and William Linwood, minister of the Unitarian Old Meeting in Mansfield, were loudly cheered when they declared themselves in favour of universal male suffrage.[598] In Leicester on the same day a joint meeting of Chartists and middle-class radicals was held at which the Baptist Joseph Winks argued that they should concentrate on securing manhood suffrage and the Chartist and former Primitive Methodist John Markham looked forward to a union of the working and middle classes.[599] And in Manchester a meeting of former members of the Anti-Corn Law League council, including prominent Dissenters such as John Bright, James Kershaw, Archibald Prentice, and J. B. Smith, sought to 'promote a cordial union of all classes of reformers' by advocating household suffrage, triennial parliaments, voting by ballot, and equal electoral districts.[600] These proposals, which became known as the 'Little Charter', formed the basis of a motion which the radical MP Joseph Hume put before the House of Commons in June. Hume's motion was defeated by 351 votes to 84,[601] but ten of the Dissenting MPs present voted for the motion, with only the Wesleyans James Heald and Joshua Westhead voting against. And the debate elicited from the prime minister, Lord John Russell, the hint that he might, in the not too distant future, bring forward measures 'for the improvement of the representation'.[602]

The 'Little Charter' was adopted as the platform of the Parliamentary and Financial Reform Association which was founded early in 1849 to unite the causes of electoral reform and economy in public expenditure. Initially it seemed possible that the Parliamentary and Financial Reform Association might achieve the class collaboration that had eluded the Complete Suffrage

---

[597] Ibid. 254.   [598] *Nottingham Review*, 21 Apr. 1848, 2–3.
[599] Patterson, *Radical Leicester*, 358.   [600] *Nonconformist*, 3 May 1848, 317.
[601] *Parliamentary Debates*, 3rd ser., xcix, 879 (20 June 1848); c, 226–9 (7 July 1848).
[602] Ibid., xcix, 929 (20 June 1848).

Union. Its leader, Sir Joshua Walmsley, once MP for Leicester and now MP for Bolton, echoed the hopes of his former Dissenting constituents for the 'cordial' union of the middle and working classes, and Walmsley's association won the support not only of the usual radicals and Nonconformists but also that of Feargus O'Connor. In July O'Connor told a meeting of the association that he had decided to give it his support to 'assist the coalition out of doors . . . to meet the coalition of Whig and Tory within', and in August added 'that there were now no differences between the middle and working classes'.[603] Such optimism was, however, premature. A group of Chartists, led by Ernest Jones, were irreconcilable and denounced the association's programme as a bourgeois conspiracy; O'Connor himself changed course again in 1851 and began attacking the association; and both Cobden and Bright disliked what the latter described as Walmsley's 'hardly disguised Chartism'.[604] The radicals in Parliament did achieve a solitary success in 1851 when they carried against the government a motion to bring the voting qualification in the counties in line with that in the towns and extracted from Russell a promise to introduce a government bill in the following year. But Russell's bill of February 1852, designed to reduce the borough qualification to £5 and that in the counties to £20, without providing for a significant redistribution of seats, failed to satisfy even the most moderate of reformers. In London eighty-two Dissenting ministers signed a letter dismissing Russell's bill as inadequate and urging that, 'through advanced and wide-spread intelligence the working classes of this country are . . . as fit to be trusted with the franchise as the men who now hold it'.[605] With the government's defeat, on its Local Militia Bill, imminent, Russell's Franchise Bill was withdrawn.

The subsequent general election, held in July 1852, in which Lord Derby's minority Conservative government made an abortive attempt to gain a majority, saw the number of Nonconformists in the House of Commons double. A total of twenty-seven Nonconformists were returned for English and Welsh constituencies, plus two United Presbyterians elected for Scottish constituencies and four members of the Free Church of Scotland who were *de facto* Dissenters. The Nonconformist MPs returned for English constituencies included the veterans Joseph Brotherton and Charles Hindley, eight Unitarians,[606] two Baptists (Samuel Peto and Sir George Goodman),

---

[603] *Nonconformist*, 25 July 1849, 583; 15 Aug. 1849.

[604] F. E. Gillespie, *Labor and Politics in England, 1850–67* (1966), 86–94; N. C. Edsall, 'A Failed National Movement: The Parliamentary and Financial Reform Association, 1848–54', *Bulletin of the Institute of Historical Research*, 49 (1976), 122, 125.

[605] *Nonconformist*, 14 Apr. 1852, 280.

[606] W. Biggs, S. Carter, J. Crook, J. Heywood, W. P. Price, J. B. Smith, E. Strutt, J. Thornley.

two Quakers (James Bell and John Bright), and the Wesleyan Joshua West-head. An English Unitarian, the coal-owner Walter Coffin, was also elected for Cardiff, the first Nonconformist to represent a Welsh con- stituency since the Interregnum. But Coffin gave no support to Dissenting political campaigns and far more portentous for the future of Welsh politics was the attempt by the wealthy Calvinistic Methodist shipowner, the younger Richard Davies, to win Caernarfon boroughs for the Liberals. Davies contested the election in response to an appeal from the Dissenting electors, and *Yr Amserau* welcomed Davies as the first Welsh Nonconformist to come forward 'in the principality to fight the battle of our political and religious principles'.[607] Davies was defeated by 93 votes, but the very fact that he stood at all was an indication of the way in which Anglican exclusiveness was driving what had hitherto been the most apolitical of all the Nonconformist denominations into the arms of political Dissent. Both in Anglesey and in Denbighshire the Calvinistic Methodists were resentful at Anglican attempts to frustrate the setting up of British and Foreign Schools, and their periodical *Y Drysorfa* warned in the course of the election campaign that no Welsh Methodist could vote for men who forbade their servants to attend Nonconformist chapels, who refused their custom to Dissenting tradesmen, and who declined to let Dissenters have sites for their chapels.[608]

What was most significant about the 1852 election from a Nonconformist point of view, however, was the increase in the number of Congregationalist MPs from two to eleven, thus outnumbering the Unitarian MPs for the first time. Admittedly the new Independent MPs included one oddity—a Conservative Congregationalist in the person of Edward Ball who was returned for Cambridgeshire—but they also comprised radicals such as Francis Crossley, the carpet manufacturer who was elected for Halifax, George Hadfield, the Manchester solicitor who was returned for Sheffield, James Kershaw, the Manchester cotton manufacturer who was re-elected for Stockport, and Apsley Pellatt, the glass manufacturer returned for Southwark. Most significant of all, the new band of Congregationalist MPs included Edward Miall, the leading advocate of class reconciliation, who was elected for Rochdale.[609]

---

[607] Parry, 'The Parliamentary Representation of Wales', 221–2, 225; D. A. Pretty, 'Richard Davies and Nonconformist Radicalism in Anglesey, 1837–68', *Welsh History Review*, 9 (1978–9), 440–5.

[608] Pretty, 'Richard Davies', 438; Parry, 'Representation in Wales', 211, 216.

[609] The other Congregationalist MPs elected in 1852 were T. Barnes, T. Challis, T. Chambers, J. Cheetham, and J. Pilkington (*Nonconformist*, 4 Aug. 1852, 597–8; 11 Aug., 617–18).

Edward Miall was on the crest of a wave. The Nonconformist MPs, he pointed out, sat in the main for populous urban constituencies and so represented a fifth both of the electorate and of the population of Great Britain. Fifteen months after the election Miall was overjoyed by the publication, in January 1854, of the results of the religious census of 1851. 'For the first time,' he wrote in the *Nonconformist*, Dissenters were 'dealt with in a State paper in accordance with their actual professions and deeds' and were shown to command the active support of as nearly as many people as the Anglicans. It was 'as if the son of a peer, treated from birth as a menial by his own relatives ... should find himself all at once in the saloon of his ancestral residence ... receiving the attention due to his birth'.[610] By 1853 the circulation of the *Nonconformist* had increased to 3,200 copies a week and in the following year its circulation exceeded that of all other Dissenting newspapers.[611] His favourite pressure group, the Anti-State Church Association, was increasing its support and its influence. Its organization was improved with the appointment, in 1847, of a full-time secretary, the Congregationalist John Carvell Williams, and in 1853 it made a successful attempt to widen its appeal by changing its name, at the suggestion of Edward Baines, to the Society for the Liberation of Religion from State Patronage and Control. It was rewarded by an increase in its annual income from £1,789 in 1854 to £3,208 in 1856, and in 1855 was able to start publication of its own monthly, the *Liberator*, sent free to subscribers of more than half a guinea a year.[612] In 1854 the Liberation Society set up two subcommittees to further its political aims: a parliamentary subcommittee which developed a whipping system whereby the attention of sympathetic MPs was drawn to issues of concern to the society, and an electoral subcommittee, under the chairmanship of Samuel Morley, to employ election agents with the object of increasing the number of Dissenting voters on the electoral register and securing the election of Nonconformist MPs.[613]

Miall's first Parliament provided Dissenters with their most significant political advances since the Municipal Corporations Act of 1835. In June 1854 James Heywood, Unitarian MP for North Lancashire, carried amendments against the government to allow Dissenters to enter and to take first degrees at Oxford, and the government incorporated the amendments into the bill which became law in August. Two years later Dissenters were also

[610] *Nonconformist*, 4 Jan. 1854, 1.

[611] Martin, 'Politics of the Congregationalists', 15; *Nonconformist*, 7 Mar. 1855, 186.

[612] Martin, 'Politics of the Congregationalists', 288; A. H. Welsh, 'John Carvell Williams: The Nonconformist Watchdog', D.Phil. thesis (Kansas, 1968), 36.

[613] Thompson, 'The Liberation Society', in Hollis, *Pressure from Without*, 219–21.

admitted to all non-theological degrees at Cambridge, though individual colleges at both universities were able to frustrate the intentions of the university Acts by imposing their own religious tests.[614] Parliamentary support for the abolition of compulsory church rates was also growing, though again ultimate victory eluded the Dissenters. An abolition bill, introduced by Sir William Clay, the liberal Anglican MP for Tower Hamlets, was rejected by the House of Commons in 1854, but Clay's bill passed its second reading with a majority of 28 in 1855 and with a majority of 43 in 1856. Both the 1855 and 1856 bills had to be abandoned for lack of parliamentary time, but no church-rates abolition bill had ever got this far before.[615]

Most dramatic of all was the evidence elicited in 1856 of the extent of support in the House of Commons for the disestablishment of the Anglican Church of Ireland. Miall hoped that the disestablishment of the Church of Ireland would lead inevitably to the disestablishment of the Church of England and for this reason he had always tried to avoid antagonizing Roman Catholic opinion.[616] He had explained that his opposition to the Maynooth grant derived from his hostility to all state endowments of religion, not from antipathy to the Roman Catholic church, and he refused to join the outcry against 'papal aggression' when Pius IX established an episcopal hierarchy in England in 1850.[617] Miall's care in avoiding offence to Roman Catholics brought fruit in 1856. His motion that the House of Commons consider state support for religion in Ireland received the surprisingly high figure of 93 votes, and though 163 votes were cast against the motion Miall's initiative resulted in a group of Irish Catholics, under the leadership of William O'Neill Daunt, offering to co-operate with the English Liberationists.[618]

The encouraging progress made by political Dissent in the Parliament elected in 1852 was, however, impeded by questions of foreign policy. British politics in the 1850s were dominated by Lord Palmerston whose truculent foreign policy both endeared him to a majority of Englishmen and alienated a minority of Dissenters who were increasingly committed to the peace movement. Pacifism had of course been an article of faith for Quakers ever since they had sought to demonstrate that they posed no threat to the restored Charles II because they forswore all bearing of arms. What became known as the London Peace Society owed its origin to a Glamorgan Quaker, Joseph Tregelles Price, who owned the Neath Abbey ironworks. A meeting

---

[614] Machin, *Politics and the Churches*, x. 267–9, 275; Newton, 'Edward Miall', 132, 136.

[615] *Parliamentary Debates*, 3rd ser., cxxxviii (24 May 1855), 692; cxl (5 Mar. 1856), 1924; Machin, Politics and the Churches, 265–6, 274–5.

[616] Newton, 'Edward Miall', 273.   [617] Miall, *Life of Miall*, 163–7.   [618] Ibid. 202.

to discuss the formation of such a society was held at the London home of William Allen in 1814 and the society founded two years later.[619] From the start the London Peace Society was pacifist, opposing 'all war, upon any pretence', though it did allow supporters of defensive war to join its local auxiliaries, and it directed its appeal specifically at Christians.[620] The absence of British involvement in any major war for the next quarter of a century was accompanied by a lack of interest in the peace movement, but concern revived in the 1840s with the outbreak of war between Britain and China following the latter country's attempts to curb the import of opium. In March 1840 Joseph Sturge published an address to 'The Christian Public of Great Britain' claiming that the action of the British government 'in slaughtering the peaceable inhabitants of China' would 'cast a deep stain upon the Christian profession which time will never efface', and he went on to organize a public meeting at the Freemasons' Hall in London to protest against the war.[621] The disastrous results of British intervention in Afghanistan between 1839 and 1842 gave an additional boost to the peace movement: the Peace Society was revitalized, 270 public meetings were held throughout Britain in 1844–5, and the movement won the support of radical Dissenting ministers such as William McKerrow and Arthur O'Neill.[622] The Peace Society also gained the adherence of two Nonconformist MPs: Joseph Brotherton, who presented a petition to Parliament in 1842 which condemned not only the wars in China and Afghanistan in particular but all war in general, and Charles Hindley, who accepted the presidency of the Peace Society in 1842 and in the following year presided over the first international Peace Convention in London.[623]

A further stimulus to the peace movement was provided by the threat of war between Britain and the United States over the boundary between Oregon and British Columbia in 1845–6. The dispute led Joseph Sturge to invite to Britain Elihu Burritt, the visionary 'learned blacksmith' from Connecticut who came hoping to encourage co-operation between British and American pacifists. While in England Burritt founded the League of Universal Brotherhood whose distinctive feature was a personal pledge taken by all members never to join the armed forces or to assist in prepara-

---

[619] Hirst, *Quakers in Peace and War*, 243–4; A. C. F. Beales, *The History of Peace* (1931), 46; Williams, 'The Society of Friends in Glamorgan', 186–91.

[620] P. Brock, *Pacifism in Europe to 1914* (Princeton, NJ, 1972), 378–9, 382–3.

[621] *The Times*, 20 Mar. 1840, 5; 25 Apr., 5; H. Richard, *Memoirs of Joseph Sturge* (1864), 288–9.

[622] Tyrrell, *Joseph Sturge*, 144; *Memoir of William McKerrow*, 141; *Nonconformist,* 25 May 1842, 362–4.

[623] Richard, *Memoirs of Joseph Sturge*, 353; Beales, *History of Peace*, 59, 66.

tions for war. It was supported by Sturge's collaborators in the Complete Suffrage movement—Edward Miall, Arthur O'Neill, and Henry Vincent—and by the end of 1846 Burritt was claiming ten thousand members on both sides of the Atlantic. Burritt also revived the idea of an international peace convention and organized a series of congresses in European cities between 1848 and 1851. The first congress, that in Brussels in 1848, agreed on proposals for international arbitration, disarmament, and a Congress of Nations which were incorporated into the Covenant of the League of Nations seventy years later. But for the moment the great weakness of the peace movement was its overwhelmingly Anglo-Saxon complexion. At the Paris congress in 1849 670 of the 840 delegates were British and at the London congress in 1851 over 1,000 of the 1,200 delegates were also British.[624] Burritt and Sturge co-operated closely with the London Peace Society which from May 1848 was under the control of its dynamic secretary, the Welsh Congregational minister and future Liberal MP Henry Richard. When Richard visited Germany for the Frankfurt Peace Congress in 1850 he found few Germans present and discovered that in all parts of the country Germans believed that their national unity could be achieved only by war.[625]

The British pacifists were convinced that Britain could secure peace by setting Europe an example, just as Britain had set Europe an example by abolishing the slave trade and by liberalizing commerce. At the Brussels Peace Congress in 1848 a resolution was passed urging Britain and the United States to take the initiative in disarmament,[626] thus beginning the unilateralist delusion that was to lead Britain and the world to disaster ninety years later. In September 1848 Sturge and Cobden launched a campaign to prepare public opinion for a motion in favour of international arbitration that Cobden was to introduce into the House of Commons on 12 June 1849. The campaign was supported by over a thousand petitions but Cobden's motion was defeated by 176 votes to 79.[627] A second major peace campaign was launched in 1852, following Louis Napoleon's *coup d'état* against the second French Republic and the British government's Militia Bill in response to fear of a French invasion. In January 1853 Sturge and Henry Richard organized a peace conference in Manchester which was attended by nine MPs, seven of them Nonconformists.[628] In the next nine months over £8,000 was raised for a campaign which sponsored a team of lecturers, organized 160 public meetings, and distributed half a million pamphlets.[629]

---

[624] Beales, *History of Peace*, 71–82; Tyrrell, *Joseph Sturge*, 162–5.
[625] C. S. Miall, *Henry Richard, MP* (1889), 74, 78.   [626] Beale, *History of Peace*, 76.
[627] Ibid. 77–8; Tyrrell, *Joseph Sturge*, 167–8.   [628] *Nonconformist*, 2 Feb. 1853, 93.
[629] Tyrrell, *Joseph Sturge*, 204–7.

Europe, however, refused to be impressed by the British example. In September 1850 Sturge and Burritt earned a good deal of ridicule by travelling to Berlin, Rendsburg, and Copenhagen in a vain attempt to prevent the renewal of war between Prussia and Denmark over Schleswig-Holstein.[630] And in January 1854 Sturge provoked even greater scorn when, in the company of two fellow Quakers, Robert Charlton and Henry Pease, he travelled to St Petersburg to appeal to Tsar Nicholas I to avert what became the Crimean War. The tsar received the Quakers courteously but insisted that it was his duty to protect the Orthodox Christians of the Turkish Empire.[631] In the previous June Russian troops had occupied the Turkish province of Moldavia and four days after the three Quakers returned to England the British and French governments issued an ultimatum demanding that the Russians withdraw from Turkish territory. The tsar did not reply and on 31 March Britain and France declared war on Turkey.

The Crimean War demoralized the peace movement and divided Dissent. The Quaker mission to the tsar was blamed for giving the Russians the impression that Britain would not fight and for thus precipitating the war. Joseph Sturge threw himself into a 'Stop the War' campaign with his usual energy, but the effort led to a heart attack in December 1855 which nearly killed him.[632] John Bright denounced the government for fighting on behalf of the Ottoman Empire—'the most immoral and filthy of all despotisms'—and as a result found himself attacked by the *Manchester Guardian*, deserted by many of his Manchester constituents, and burned in effigy in the town's streets.[633] The moderate Dissenter Edward Baines supported the war on the ground that Russia was the aggressor.[634] The radical Dissenter W. J. Fox supported it because 'of the part which Russia took in putting down the Hungarians, and upholding the despotism of Austria'.[635] And Edward Miall deserted his old friends in the peace movement by asserting that 'no one can impugn' 'the moral right of Europe to punish Russia, as a reckless disturber of its peace'.[636]

But if Dissenters disagreed over the justice of the war, they could agree that its prosecution was less than vigorous. The evidence of military and administrative incompetence, against which Florence Nightingale struggled in the hospital at Uskudar and which was reported from the Crimea in W. H. Russell's dispatches to *The Times*, powerfully strengthened the radical Dissenting argument that Britain was ill-served by the aristocrats who gov-

---

[630] Ibid. 171–2.   [631] Ibid. 210–12.   [632] Ibid. 213–14.
[633] H. Ausubel, *John Bright* (New York, 1966), 70–1.
[634] D. Fraser, 'Edward Baines', in Hollis, *Pressure from Without*, 200.
[635] Garnett, *Life of W. J. Fox*, 326.   [636] *Nonconformist*, 29 Mar. 1854, 267.

erned it. The disasters of the war caused the resignation of Lord Aberdeen's coalition government and his replacement as prime minister by Lord Palmerston in February 1855, and prompted the founding in May of the Administrative Reform Association. The chairman of the new association was Samuel Morley, who two months earlier had also become chairman of the Liberation Society's electoral committee. The objectives of the Administrative Reform Association, Morley told a mass meeting in the Drury Lane theatre in June, were the exposure of abuses, the opening to public gaze of every government department, and the throwing open of entry into the civil service to public competition by examination.[637] Though Palmerston responded by setting up the Civil Service Commission, he rejected the Administrative Reform Association's proposals for open competition and so provided further evidence that the aristocracy was the major obstacle to the political reforms desired by radicals and Dissenters alike.

The challenge which radicals and Dissenters had thus flung down in the face of Palmerston's aristocratic rule was taken up in the general election of 1857. In the previous October the Chinese authorities in Canton had boarded a British-registered ship named the *Arrow* in search of a pirate and when the Chinese refused to apologize for the incident the British governor of Hong Kong ordered a British squadron to bombard Chinese forts in the Canton River. Ironically the governor of Hong Kong was the Unitarian Sir John Bowring, formerly Liberal MP for Kilmarnock and Bolton and one-time member of the Peace Society and its foreign secretary from 1820 to 1823.[638] Miall in the *Nonconformist* denounced the bombardment of Canton as 'cruel and barbarous in the extreme',[639] and when Palmerston defended Bowring's action in Parliament Cobden carried a censure motion against the government by 263 votes to 247. Forty-eight Liberals voted in the majority.[640]

In response to his defeat Palmerston called a general election which in effect became a referendum for and against his foreign policy. The election of March 1857 brought mixed fortunes for Dissenters. Samuel Morley's electoral committee targeted eleven county constituencies with a view to increasing the number of supporters of the Liberation Society on the electoral

---

[637] E. Hodder, *Life of Samuel Morley* (1887), 122–6.

[638] S. Conway, 'John Bowring and the Nineteenth-century Peace Movement', *Historical Research*, 64 (1991), 346.

[639] *Nonconformist*, 7 Jan. 1857, 11.

[640] A. H. Welch can find no evidence, in Carvell Williams's detailed minutes, to support J. Vincent's contention that supporters of the Liberation Society voted to bring down the government in revenge for its failure to provide parliamentary time for Sir William Clay's Church Rates Abolition Bill in the previous year (Welch, 'Carvell Williams', 78; J. Vincent, *Formation of the Liberal Party, 1857–1868* (1972), 111).

register and claimed that twenty seats were gained for religious liberty while another nine were lost.[641] The *Nonconformist* reported more optimistically that the 'religious liberty party' had made a net gain of thirty-six seats, but some of the losses were serious. The Quaker James Bell was defeated in Guildford, the Congregationalists T. Barnes and Apsley Pellatt lost their seats for Bolton and Southwark, the Unitarian W. J. Fox was defeated in Oldham, and the Congregationalist Sir Elkanah Armitage failed to win the Salford seat held until January 1857 by the now deceased Joseph Brotherton. Sir William Clay, the liberal Anglican who had introduced the Church Rates Abolition bills of 1854, 1855, and 1856, lost his seat for Tower Hamlets. Charles Hindley held on to his seat at Ashton but only, he claimed, because he had abstained on Cobden's censure motion and had refrained from denouncing the bombardment of the Chinese forts, despite his being president of the Peace Society.[642] The most serious losses of all were those of John Bright and Edward Miall. Bright's attacks on Palmerston's aggressive foreign policy angered Manchester merchants who saw gun-boat diplomacy as a means of opening up foreign markets to Lancashire's exports, and Bright and his colleague, Thomas Milner Gibson, were rejected by the Manchester electorate in favour of two Unitarian businessmen, Sir John Potter and J. Aspinall Turner, who stood as Palmerstonian Liberals.[643] In Rochdale Miall was opposed by a Conservative, Sir Alex Ramsay, who defended Palmerston's record and denounced ' "the peace-at-any-price party" who had encouraged the tsar of Russia and governor of Canton to believe that Britain would not fight'. When Miall lost his seat by 42 votes the *Nonconformist* blamed his defeat on the drink interest since many of Ramsay's voters had been taken 'to the polls in cabs in a state of beastly intoxication', a claim that has been vindicated by modern scholarship.[644] While Bright returned to the House of Commons in August, following the death of one of Birmingham's MPs, it was to be another twelve years before Miall returned to Parliament.

The defeat of Edward Miall threw into sharp relief the problem of the leadership of the Dissenting members in the House of Commons. In some ways John Bright would have been an ideal leader of political Dissent. He was proud of his descent from John Gratton, a Quaker who had suffered imprisonment under Charles II; one of his earliest forays into politics had been in

    [641] Thompson, 'Liberation Society', in Hollis, *Pressure from Without*, 223.
    [642] *Nonconformist*, 8 Apr. 1857, 262, 273; 15 Apr., 281.
    [643] V. A. C. Gattrell, 'The Commercial Middle Class in Manchester, *c*.1820–57', Ph.D. thesis (Cambridge, 1971), 432; D. Fraser, *Urban Politics in Victorian England* (Leicester, 1976), 208–9.
    [644] *Nonconformist*, 1 Apr. 1857, 253; Vincent, *Pollbooks*, 166.

the church-rates contest in Rochdale; he had supported the Complete Suffrage Union; he advocated a 'firm confederacy' of the middle and working
classes; he was opposed to state aid for education; he supported the peace
movement without being a pacifist. What is more, he was one of the greatest
orators of his age who had earned a national reputation as a consequence of
his advocacy of free trade. And Bright's great weakness, his inability to deal
with details of legislation or with the burdens of public office, was not a major
disadvantage at a time when Dissenters still saw themselves as a permanent
opposition rather than as an alternative government. Yet Bright turned
down an offer to lead the Liberation Society's supporters in the Commons in
1854 and thereafter distanced himself from other political Dissenters.[645]
Bright was never an Evangelical, never talked about religion at home, and
said on one occasion that he felt no more sympathy with Wesleyans, Congregationalists, or Baptists than he did with Anglicans.[646] And although he
occupied the same seat in the Quaker meeting-house in Rochdale for more
than forty years it is an astonishing fact that Bright, for all his oratorical skills,
never once spoke in a meeting for worship. When the American evangelist
Dwight L. Moody invited Bright to speak at one of his meetings in 1875, the
Quaker's comment was, 'How little I feel qualified to attempt the conversion
of others, and how much I need help for myself'.[647] Bright was frequently at
loggerheads with his fellow Quakers. While they distrusted his particular
brand of political activism, he resented their restrictive morality. He was particularly contemptuous of the marriage rule which led to the disownment of
his sister Priscilla when she married Duncan McLaren, the future Liberal
MP, in 1848. The Society of Friends, he feared, was doomed to extinction.
'There seems nothing but decay in our monthly meetings,' he wrote in 1852,
'we are too few to afford any warmth, nobody comes in and the children
born in do not remain in.'[648] Holding such pessimistic views of the future of
his own denomination, it is perhaps not surprising that Bright regarded
Dissent as too insubstantial a basis for his future political campaigns. Instead
he returned to the vision that had inspired the Complete Suffrage movement: a union of the working and middle classes in the cause of a wider franchise.

The ground was prepared for Bright's new crusade by the London Reform
Association, formed at the end of 1858 to further a 'thorough union between

[645] Machin, *Politics and the Churches*, 258.
[646] R. A. J. Walling (ed.), *The Diaries of John Bright* (1930), p. xi; D. Read, *Cobden and Bright* (1967), 168.
[647] J. T. Mills, *John Bright and the Quakers* (1935), i. 374, 376.
[648] K. Robbins, *John Bright* (1979), 118.

the middle and working classes'.[649] The possibility that this new union might succeed where the Complete Suffrage movement had failed was raised by the defeat of Palmerston's government in Parliament in February 1858 for 'truckling to France', in Bright's words, following Orsini's attempt to murder Napoleon III. Derby and Disraeli came into office to form the second Conservative minority government of the decade and Disraeli, and more reluctantly Derby, came to the conclusion that the only way to remedy their party's permanent position of inferiority was to change the electoral system which had given them only one general election victory since 1832.[650] Radicals believed that a popular agitation might force Derby and Disraeli to accept a more radical measure than they had intended, just as popular agitations had forced earlier Tory governments to accept repeal of the Test and Corporations Acts, Roman Catholic emancipation, and abolition of the Corn Laws.[651] Bright's campaign began in his new constituency of Birmingham on 27 October 1858 when he spoke to an audience of five thousand in the town hall. He proposed that the vote should be given to every householder in the boroughs who paid rates; to £10 occupiers in the counties; and that seats be transferred from the smaller boroughs to the industrial towns. Bright's proposals disappointed the advocates of manhood suffrage: Joseph Sturge, now nearing the end of his life, still clung to the basis of his Complete Suffrage movement, 'the right of every man to a vote', but Bright told him that he was 'not working for failure, but for success', and that to advocate manhood suffrage would be to doom his cause.[652] The government accepted Bright's proposal of a £10 householder qualification for the counties, since '£10 occupiers in villages are tradesmen all under the thumb of agriculturalists ... who are mostly Conservatives', but proposed no extension of the right to vote in the boroughs apart from 'fancy franchises' for university graduates or men who had £60 in a savings bank. The government thus alienated both 'radicals who wanted more reform and Palmerstonians who did not want any' and was defeated on 31 March 1859 by 39 votes.[653]

In the subsequent general election the Conservatives gained some thirty seats but remained in a minority. The election brought little comfort to Dissenters. Some prominent Dissenters were elected to Parliament for the first time: Edward Baines won the Leeds seat from which his father had retired eighteen years earlier and Titus Salt, the Congregationalist worsted

---

[649] Wilson, 'The Suffrage Movement', in Hollis, *Pressure from Without*, 98–9.
[650] F. B. Smith, *The Making of the Second Reform Bill* (Cambridge, 1966), 38–9.
[651] Gillespie, *Labor and Politics in England, 1850–67*, 149.
[652] Tyrrell, *Joseph Sturge*, 230; Trevelyan, *Life of John Bright*, 270–1.
[653] Smith, *Second Reform Bill*, 40, 44.

manufacturer, was returned for Bradford. But there appears to have been no overall increase in the number of Nonconformist MPs and the new Parliament witnessed a reaction against the politics of militant Dissent. In June Russell and Palmerston set aside the personal differences of a decade and agreed to unite to defeat Derby's government on a vote of confidence. Palmerston returned to Downing Street as prime minister and for the next six years his lack of enthusiasm for reform frustrated Dissenting desires both to change the electoral system and to abolish church rates. A bill to widen the franchise by extending the vote to men who occupied houses whose rent was £6 in the boroughs and £10 in the counties was introduced by Russell in March 1860 but was greeted by apathy both within and without the House of Commons and was withdrawn in June.[654] No further measure of electoral reform was sponsored by Palmerston's government and the cause of church-rates abolition fared no better. With the defeat of Sir William Clay, the sponsor of the church rates bills of 1854–6, in the general election of 1857 the Liberation Society had asked another liberal Anglican, Sir John Trelawny, MP for Tavistock, to take charge of the issue. In May 1857 Trelawny obtained from Palmerston an assurance that the government would itself bring forward a church-rates abolition bill in the current session.[655] However, the pledge was broken and in January 1858 Palmerston told a deputation from the Liberation Society that the government could give no guarantee that it would introduce a church-rates bill in that session either.[656] None the less on 17 February Trelawny's bill for the Abolition of Church Rates secured a majority of 54 on its second reading, the first such bill to pass all its stages in the Commons before being rejected in the House of Lords. And a year later, in March 1859, the second reading of Trelawny's bill secured a majority of 74 before being aborted by the general election.[657]

Thereafter reaction set in. The Conservative gains in the election made it likely that the new Parliament would be less amenable than the old to the redress of Dissenting grievances and there was evidence that in some areas the clash between church and chapel was becoming increasingly bitter. Following the election eleven tenants-at-will in Merioneth who had either abstained or had voted for a Liberal candidate pledged to the abolition of church rates were evicted by their landlords, one of whom was Sir Watkin

---

[654] Ibid. 46–7.   [655] *Parliamentary Debates*, 3rd ser., cxlv (11 May 1857), 109.
[656] T. A. Jenkins (ed.), *The Parliamentary Diaries of Sir John Trelawny, 1858–65*, Camden Fourth Series, cl (1990), 10–11.
[657] *Parliamentary Debates*, 3rd ser., cxlviii (17 Feb. 1858), col. 1583; cliii (15 Mar. 1859), col. 194.

Williams Wynn.[658] And in the following year the tenants of Mary Morice of Llanddeiniol in north Cardiganshire were similarly told that they would have to choose between attending the Anglican church and supporting its princi- ples or losing their farms.[659] In July 1859 Samuel Morley and Dr C. J. Foster, chairmen of the Liberation Society's parliamentary committee, found diffi- culty in denying before a select committee of the House of Lords that the campaign for the abolition of church rates was but a step on the road to the disestablishment of the Church of England, and their evasive replies provided welcome ammunition for the defenders of church rates.[660] Church Defence Associations sprang up throughout the country; in February 1860 the majority for Trelawny's abolition bill fell to 29; in December Disraeli in a speech in his Buckinghamshire constituency urged Churchmen to redouble their efforts to save church rates.[661] On the third reading of Trelawny's abo- lition bill in 1861 opponents and supporters of church rates tied, with 274 votes for and against the measure, and the Speaker gave his casting vote with the 'Noes'. This was the first time a Church Rates Abolition Bill had been defeated in the Commons since 1854. Worse was to follow. In 1862 Trelawny's bill was defeated by 1 vote on its second reading; in 1863 it was defeated by 10 votes; and the MP for Tavistock gave up the fight.[662]

The salvation of radical Dissent was to come from an unlikely source. William Ewart Gladstone was the son of a wealthy Liverpool merchant and future Tory MP, a slave-owner whose Demerara plantations had been the scene of the negro insurrection of 1823 which had issued in the death of the LMS missionary John Smith. Gladstone had been brought up as an Evan- gelical but at Oxford he befriended James Milnes Gaskell, descendant of the family of Unitarian Wakefield merchants, and while on a visit to Gaskell's home Gladstone's Evangelical orthodoxy was disturbed by a comment of Gaskell's mother that anyone who believed in Christ was saved, no matter what his theological opinions.[663] However, Gladstone's deviation from Evan- gelicalism ultimately took a High Church, not a Unitarian, route: he became convinced of the validity of the doctrine of baptismal regeneration and a visit to Italy in 1832 brought home to him both the scandal of the Church's disunity and the Catholic tradition of the Church of England. He returned to

---

[658]   Jones, *Explorations and Explanations*, 128, 138–40.

[659]   Turner, 'Revivals and Popular Religion in Wales', 257.

[660]   Whitby, 'Matthew Arnold and the Nonconformists', 212–13; Jenkins, *Trelawny Diaries*, 12.

[661]   Thompson, 'Liberation Society', in Hollis, *Pressure from Without*, 232; Machin, *Politics and the Chuches*, 313; *The Times*, 8 Dec. 1860, 10.

[662]   *Parliamentary Debates*, 3rd ser., clxvi (14 May 1862), col. 1727; clxx (29 Apr. 1863), col. 974; Machin, *Politics and the Churches*, 308.

[663]   P. Butler, *Gladstone: Church, State, and Tractarianism* (Oxford, 1982), 19.

England to secure election to the first reformed Parliament as MP for Newark, seeing his political role 'chiefly as a means of being useful in church affairs'. He defended the West Indian slave-owners from their critics; he opposed the admission of Dissenters to universities; he argued for the retention of church rates. When he published his first book in 1838, *The State in its Relation with the Church*, maintaining that it was the function of the State to promote the truth, that is the religion of the Church of England, Macaulay retorted that the logical tendency of Gladstone's argument was to justify the roasting of Dissenters at slow fires.

Yet the man who advocated such outrageously reactionary views in the 1830s was to become, by the end of his career, the idol of the Nonconformists. In the thirty years following the writing of *The State in its Relation with the Church* Gladstone's views became progressively more liberal. Within a few years of its publication he was forced to accept that its thesis was anachronistic. He acknowledged that the United Kingdom was a pluralist society by voting for the Dissenters' Chapels Bill in 1844, for the Maynooth grant in 1845, and for the admission of Jews to Parliament in 1847.[664] He supported Peel over the repeal of the Corn Laws and the savagery with which Peel was attacked by Disraeli prompted Gladstone to refuse to serve in the Conservative government of 1852. As for Palmerston, Gladstone disliked his foreign policy as much as did Cobden and Bright, but the one issue which united them was sympathy for the Italians in their struggle for independence from Austrian domination. It was this issue which persuaded Gladstone to accept Palmerston's offer to join his government as Chancellor of the Exchequer in 1859. By the 1860s Gladstone was becoming increasingly sympathetic to two of the fundamental positions of radical Dissent: he came to see the need for 'respectable' working men to be accepted as part of the political nation, and he came to share, at least in part, the Dissenting dislike of too close a connection between Church and State.

The independence, industry, sobriety, and thrift of those working men, many of them Nonconformists, who enrolled in the Mechanics' Institutes and ran the co-operative societies, and which have so impressed historians, also impressed the new Chancellor of the Exchequer. Gladstone was pleased with the use working men made of the Post Office Savings Bank which he set up in 1861; he was flattered by the warm reception accorded him by the radicals of Tyneside in 1862; he was conscious of the restraint shown by the workers of Lancashire during the cotton famine occasioned by the American Civil War. The younger Edward Baines was similarly impressed. Through the

[664] Ibid. 93–123, 134–5.

medium of his *Leeds Mercury* Baines had denounced Chartism, scoffed at the Complete Suffrage movement, and dismissed Joseph Sturge as a man lacking in sound judgement and mental capacity. But he supported Joseph Hume's 'Little Charter' in 1848, from 1852 took part in meetings designed to unite the middle and working classes, and along with John Bright attended the inaugural meeting of the Leeds Working Men's Parliamentary Reform Association in 1860.[665] Baines remained adamantly opposed to manhood suffrage, but he wanted the support of such working men as were 'members of Mechanics Institutions, teachers in Sunday schools, and enrolled in clubs of mutual insurance or as depositors in Savings Banks', and to this end he moved in the Commons in 1861 that the borough franchise qualification be reduced to £6. Such a proposal, he told the House on repeating his motion in 1864, would not threaten property because 'the upper and middle classes would still constitute two-thirds of the voters in the boroughs'.[666] To the astonishment of the House of Commons Gladstone spoke in favour of Baines's motion: 'every man who is not presumably incapacitated by some consideration of personal unfitness or of political danger is morally entitled to come within the pale of the constitution'.

Gladstone had said more than he had intended and was taken aback by the reception accorded his speech. 'I have unwarily ... set the Thames on fire', he wrote to the Congregational minister Newman Hall, and added that he hoped that the Thames would realize that 'he had no business ... to catch the flame, and will revert to its ordinary temperature'.[667] But the beacon Gladstone had lit was not so easily extinguished: working men who had hitherto been denied access to political power and influence now began to convince themselves that they had in Gladstone a national political leader and cabinet minister who would voice their political desires and support their political objectives. 'You have spoken words that have sunk deep into the hearts of every working man in every corner of the land', so the workers of York addressed Gladstone after his speech on Baines's motion. 'We look upon you as a powerful and consistent advocate of our cause, and may God preserve your life.'[668]

Gladstone had thus emerged, in the words of F. B. Smith, as 'the prophet of ordered social unity'.[669] Even more surprisingly he came to be regarded, by the mid-1860s, as the standard-bearer of religious equality.[670] Gladstone had

[665] D. Fraser, 'Edward Baines', in Hollis, *Pressure from Without*, 199 n. 80, 204 n. 105; Gillespie, *Labor and Politics*, 238.

[666] Fraser, 'Edward Baines', 205–6.   [667] N. Hall, *An Autobiography* (1901), 265.

[668] Vincent, *Formation of the Liberal Party*, 266.   [669] Smith, *Second Reform Bill*, 48.

[670] This was the view of the *Daily News*; *Nonconformist*, 26 July 1865, 593.

defended the close connection between Church and State in 1838 because he believed that it was the function of the State to promote truth. But in 1850 he had to face the fact that the State could no longer be relied on to promote truth as he saw it. In that year the judicial committee of the Privy Council upheld the right of an Evangelical clergyman, George Gorham, to a living in the diocese of Exeter despite the fact that he repudiated the doctrine of baptismal regeneration. High Churchmen were scandalized and Gladstone's friend Henry Manning was provoked to secede to the Church of Rome. Gladstone's reaction was quite different: he concluded that what the Church needed of the State was not greater support, it was greater freedom.

Gladstone thus came to sympathize with the Dissenters' antipathy to the state control of religion. In March 1863 he wrote to Bishop Samuel Wilberforce of Oxford that it was in the Church of England's own interests to 'avoid all points of sore contact with Dissenters', and his growing liberalism in religion, coupled with the likelihood that he would succeed to the leadership of the Liberal party when Russell and Palmerston passed from the scene, made him receptive to overtures he received from Newman Hall, who followed up his earlier correspondence with Gladstone by inviting him, in November 1864, to meet himself and thirteen other Nonconformists ministers at his home in Hampstead. The ministers tried to persuade the Chancellor of the Exchequer that church rates were 'unjust to Dissenters, unnecessary for Episcopalians [and] religiously injurious to the ungodly' and that the established Church of Ireland retarded Protestantism and was detrimental 'to the peace and prosperity of that country'.[671] On both issues they were largely successful.

While Gladstone had long favoured some scheme to exempt Dissenters from the payment of church rates, provided that the impost continued to be levied on the rest of the community,[672] the meeting at Newman Hall's home seems to have convinced him that a more radical remedy was necessary. In April of the following year he wrote to his son that 'it would be a wise concession for the Church of England to have the laws of church rate abolished in all cases where it places her in fretting conflict with the Dissenting bodies'.[673] In the case of the Irish church Gladstone's meeting with the Dissenting ministers also appears to have had some influence on his thinking. Three months after the gathering, in February 1865, he wrote to Robert Phillimore that the continued establishment of the Church of Ireland was 'no

[671] G. I. T. Machin, 'Gladstone and Nonconformity in the 1860s: The Formation of an Alliance', *Historical Journal*, 17 (1974), 352.

[672] *Parliamentary Debates*, 3rd ser., cxxvii (26 May 1853), col. 645; cl (13 May 1858), col. 1724.

[673] J. Morley, *Life of Gladstone* (1903), ii. 159.

more favourable to religion . . . than it is to civil justice and to the contentment and loyalty of Ireland'.[674] And when, in March, Lewis Dillwyn, the Liberal MP for Swansea, brought before the Commons a motion for the disestablishment of the Church of Ireland Gladstone, while declaring the motion premature, endorsed Dillwyn's criticism of that church. 'The eleventh hour of the bondage of the Church has come', rejoiced the General Baptist Thomas Goadby; 'God has sent us a man to be the prophet of the new era.'[675]

Dissenters thus approached the general election of July 1865 in confident mood. In the years preceding the election, with parliamentary support for the abolition of church rates slipping, the Liberation Society had adopted an increasingly aggressive electoral strategy and by 1865 this appeared to be producing results. In 1862 the society had made a determined attempt to arouse the political consciousness of Welsh Dissenters. The principality's Nonconformists, wrote the Congregationalist Thomas Rees in 1858, had 'culpably neglected their political rights'. In a country in which the majority of the population, and 'three-quarters of the electors', were Dissenters, all the Welsh MPs were Anglicans, 'most of them Conservatives of the old school'.[676] To remedy the situation the Liberation Society called a conference in Swansea in September 1862 and urged Dissenters to take practical steps to bring Welsh representation 'into harmony with the views and feelings of the population'.[677] Thirteen months later, in October 1863, Miall presented to the society's executive committee a paper in which he urged that it was useless to try to change the minds of members of the existing House of Commons: what was needed was a strategy to determine the composition of the next. He suggested that the Liberation Society's future co-operation with the Liberal party should depend on the latter's willingness to advance the society's interests, in proportion to the society's strength in each constituency, and that if the Liberal party refused to recognize the Liberation Society's claims, then the society's supporters should withhold co-operation 'whatever may be the consequences of our abstention to the Liberal party'. Miall's strategy was endorsed by a conference in London in November and he followed this up with a series of conferences in Manchester, Bristol, and Norwich. There was some opposition from Dissenters such as the Ashton-under-Lyne cotton manufacturer Hugh Mason, who argued that half a Liberal loaf was better than no bread at all, but most Liberationists supported Miall's strategy.[678]

[674] Ibid. 142.
[675] Binfield, 'Nonconformity in the Eastern Counties', 225, citing *General Baptist Year Book* (1865), 10–11.
[676] Rees, *Miscellaneous Papers*, 81.   [677] Miall, *Henry Richard*, 121.
[678] D. A. Hamer, *The Politics of Electoral Pressure* (1977), 102–8.

That strategy was vindicated in the next two years: a warning shot was fired across Liberal bows in a by-election at Exeter in 1864 when Nonconformist abstentions led to the defeat of the Liberal candidate J. D. Coleridge, a High Churchman who refused to commit himself to the total abolition of church rates, and in January 1865 Dissenters in Aylesbury forced the retirement of a prospective Liberal candidate who declined to support the removal of the impost. When the general election came in July 1865 the Liberation Society's journal, the *Liberator*, claimed that nearly every Liberal candidate was sound on the church-rates issue and that most of those that were not were defeated.[679] There was no significant increase in the number of Dissenting MPs: thirty-three were elected,[680] and there were some disappointments. Edward Miall failed to secure adoption as candidate for Manchester, Henry Richard failed to secure the candidature for Cardiganshire, and although Samuel Morley was elected for Nottingham after a violent contest in which the Riot Act was read, he was subsequently unseated on an accusation of bribery. But the Liberal party secured a majority of seventy seats and the Liberation Society's activities, coupled with the election of radical MPs such as John Stuart Mill, Thomas Hughes, Joseph Cowen, and G. O. Trevelyan, meant that the new Parliament would be much more amenable to Dissenting pressure than had the old.[681] Ironically one of the Liberal candidates who failed to give a satisfactory pledge on church rates and who lost his seat was Gladstone. But the severance of the link between Gladstone and his constituents of Oxford University, and his return 'unmuzzled' for South Lancashire, removed the last factor inhibiting his emergence as the advocate of electoral reform, of the abolition of compulsory church rates, and of the disestablishment of the Church of Ireland. When Palmerston died in October 1865 and Russell succeeded him as prime minister, it was Gladstone to whom Russell entrusted the task of introducing the government's Reform Bill in the Commons in March 1866.

Gladstone's views on franchise reform were not as radical as his speech in favour of Baines's motion in 1864 had suggested. He wanted to enfranchise the more prosperous members of the working class without endangering the position of the upper and middle classes and so proposed a £7 rental qualification for the boroughs and a £14 qualification for the counties. Such a move, he calculated, would increase the electorate by some 400,000 voters, of whom half would be working class. It was, said Frances Gillespie, 'a more restricted measure than had been presented by any Liberal government since 1848',[682]

[679] Ibid. 111–15.　　　[680] *Nonconformist*, 26 July 1865, 593.
[681] Machin, *Politics and the Churches*, 332; Gillespie, *Labor and Politics*, 247–9.
[682] Gillespie, *Labor and Politics*, 259.

and it was a measure of the frustration and limited expectations of reformers that it was accepted by the two pressure groups which had been agitating outside Parliament for electoral reform. Both the Manchester-based National Reform Union, founded in 1864 to campaign for household suffrage, and the London-based Reform League, founded in 1865 to campaign for universal male suffrage, backed the government bill, and Bright urged that it be used as a 'lever' to secure more radical demands.[683] But the likelihood that Gladstone's modest proposals would be but the thin end of a much larger wedge alarmed both many Tories and the more conservative Liberals led by Robert Lowe, who denied that the majority of working men deserved the vote. 'If you want venality, if you want ignorance, if you want drunkenness ... [if] you want impulsive, unreflecting and violent people', asked Lowe, 'do you go to the top or to the bottom?' The government's opponents, retorted Gladstone, spoke as though 'they were engaged in ascertaining the numbers of an invading army; but the persons to whom their remarks apply are our fellow-subjects, our fellow-Christians, our own flesh and blood'.[684] Once again Gladstone's rhetoric was much more radical than his proposals warranted but once again he had placed himself on the side of working men against their detractors. On 19 June Lowe and his supporters voted with the Conservatives to defeat the government on an amendment to replace the £7 rental qualification with a rating qualification, a change which would have nearly halved the number of new voters in the boroughs. Russell resigned and Derby formed his third minority Conservative administration.

Previous government reform bills had been dropped or defeated in 1852, 1854, 1859, and 1860 and the country had shown little interest. But by the summer of 1866 Britain was in the midst of an economic recession: in May both the Quaker financial house of Overend and Gurney and Samuel Morton Peto's firm had collapsed with the result that share prices plummeted and the number of people seeking poor relief rose. Moreover, Gladstone's bill appeared to have had a much greater chance of success than any similar measure since 1832, and the pent-up frustrations of both middle- and working-class radicals now exploded into anger. The Reform League launched a series of mass demonstrations, beginning in Trafalgar Square on 27 June and continuing in Hyde Park on 23 July. When the police commissioner forbade the Hyde Park rally a huge crowd of some 20,000 surged against the park railings and they collapsed. Some demonstrators fought with the police, one policeman subsequently died, and over a hundred people were seriously injured. But, in contrast to what happened after the Plug Plot riots of 1842,

---

[683] Ibid. 260–2.   [684] Smith, *Second Reform Bill*, 80, 86–7.

there was no middle-class backlash. The Reform League, although predominantly working class, had, unlike the Chartist movement, significant middle-class, and largely Nonconformist middle-class, backing. Samuel Morley was the League's most important source of finance and donated nearly £1,000, besides the contribution he was to make to the election fund in 1868; two Unitarian MPs, Thomas Bayler Potter, MP for Rochdale and son of Sir John Potter, and Peter Taylor, partner in the firm of Courtaulds and MP for Leicester, both contributed to its funds; and over £400 was given by a group of Bradford textile manufacturers including the Quakers Robert and Samuel Kell, the Baptist Alfred Illingworth, and the Congregationalist Titus Salt.[685] In Kettering in August 1866 Dissenting ministers supported a working-class meeting calling for universal male suffrage.[686] From Wales in November the Reform League's lecturer George Mantle reported that in Brecon and Merthyr Tydfil eleven Nonconformist ministers had given him 'most hearty, unqualified, and valuable support'. And in Denbigh, Newtown, and Brecon the same men served on the local committees of both the Liberation Society and the Reform League. As John Jones, Baptist minister of Brymbo near Wrexham, told a meeting of his Liberation Society branch, the success of the movement for 'the liberation of the church from state control' depended in great measure on the success of the reform movement.[687]

Some tension between the middle-class advocates of household suffrage and the working-class supporters of one man one vote remained, and Edward Baines refused to attend a West Riding demonstration in Leeds because the organizers declined to limit their demands to household suffrage. But what was impressive about the mass demonstrations in the summer and autumn of 1866 was the number of occasions on which the Reform League and the Reform Union co-operated. In June Randal Cremer and Edmond Beales, speaking for the League, indicated that they were prepared to co-operate with the Union on the basis of household suffrage.[688] In August John Bright addressed an estimated crowd of 150,000 at a joint League–Union meeting in Birmingham. In October, notwithstanding Baines's opposition, a joint League–Union demonstration went ahead on Woodhouse Moor, near Leeds, and Titus Salt closed his factory at Saltaire to enable his workers to attend.[689] And in December the League and the Union again co-operated in organizing a march of 25,000 people through London's

---

[685] F. M. Leventhal, *Respectable Radical: George Howell and Victorian Working-class Politics* (1971), 63–6, 87, 106, 235 n. 57; Coleman, *Courtaulds*, i. 226–8.

[686] Greenall, 'Baptist as Radical', *Northamptonshire Past and Present*, 8 (1991–2), 223.

[687] Wallace, *Organise!*, 115–16.   [688] Gillespie, *Labor and Politics*, 264.

[689] Reynolds, *Great Paternalist*, 217, 308.

West End.[690] The reason for this class co-operation was explained by Bright in a speech he gave at a banquet organized by the Reform Union in Manchester in November. It was not true, he argued, that since 1832 political power had been in the hands of the middle class. 'The middle class have votes, but those votes are rendered harmless and nugatory by the unfair distribution of them.' Under the existing political system, while 'workingmen are almost universally excluded, roughly and insolently, from political power, . . . the middle class, whilst they have the semblance of it, are defrauded of the reality'.[691] By the end of 1866 Bright had helped to achieve the goal that had eluded Joseph Sturge and Edward Miall a generation earlier: the co-operation of middle- and working-class radicals in the cause of electoral reform.

It was not the Hyde Park riots and the subsequent mass demonstrations that converted the government to the need for reform: ever since 1857–8 Disraeli and Derby had been convinced that a suitably manipulated measure of electoral reform could be the means of restoring the Conservative party's fortunes. But the mass protest movement made easier their task of convincing their followers of the need to widen the franchise. In December Derby proposed that there should be household suffrage in the boroughs, coupled with the safeguard of plural voting in the form of 'fancy franchises'; other Conservative MPs urged the additional safeguard that only householders who paid their rates personally, and not through their landlords, should have the vote; and these proposals formed the basis of the bill which Disraeli introduced into the Commons on 18 March.[692] The government proposed to extend the franchise in the boroughs to householders who paid their rates in person and had lived at the same address for two years and to give additional votes to university graduates, men who had £50 in a savings bank, and men who paid 20s. a year in direct taxation. But it was one thing for the government to introduce such proposals before Parliament: it was another to get them through a House of Commons in which the Liberals had a large majority. Disraeli was repeatedly faced with Liberal amendments which were designed to widen the scope of his bill, and repeatedly faced with the choice of either accepting such amendments or facing defeat. Every time he was confronted by such a dilemma Disraeli gave way and as a result the borough franchise was widened to a far greater extent than Gladstone or Russell or Derby or Disraeli had ever intended. The fancy franchises were swept away; the residential qualification was reduced from two years to twelve months;

---

[690] Smith, *Second Reform Bill*, 139–43.
[691] *Speeches by John Bright*, ed. J. E. T. Rogers (1868), ii. 215–17.
[692] Smith, *Second Reform Bill*, 139, 147, 151–4, 167–8.

the vote was given to lodgers of rooms worth £10 a year; most important of all, the franchise was extended to ratepayers who paid their rates through their landlords.[693] As a result something like real household suffrage was established in the boroughs and the size of the electorate was increased from 1,357,519 to 2,476,745.[694] And although only fifty-three seats were redistributed, and the continued inequitable distribution of seats favoured the Conservatives at the expense of the Liberals, the Reform Act of 1867 was the most significant advance towards democracy in nineteenth-century Britain. 'We can scarcely realise the magnitude of this result', commented Miall in the *Nonconformist*. 'It fairly takes one's breath away.'[695] Twenty-five years on, the tactics of his once-despised Complete Suffrage movement had been vindicated.

In the eyes both of Edward Miall and of his opponents one of the consequences of an extension of the franchise would be the further curtailment of the privileges of the established church. In 1864 Richard Masheder, Fellow of Magdalene College, Cambridge, had warned of the mutual relations between *Dissent and Democracy*. Dissenters wanted to extend the franchise, introduce the ballot, and achieve annual parliaments, equal electoral districts, and the payment of MPs as the means to their ultimate goal—the separation of Church and State.[696] Masheder's forebodings were in part born out, for the years immediately following the passage of the 1867 Reform Act saw significant political gains for militant Dissent.

By the 1860s the success of Dissenters in gaining control of parish vestries and preventing the levying of church rates had removed the issue as a practical grievance in most of the large towns of England and Wales. The total amount raised by church rates had fallen from £519,000 in 1829 to £232,905 in 1862, and by 1864 the rate was not being levied in 4,912 parishes out of 12,085.[697] But in those small towns and rural parishes where the hated impost was still being levied church rates remained a burning issue. There was a bitter dispute at Ystradgynlais in Glamorgan in 1864 when a shoemaker's leather was seized and sold by auction for non-payment of the rate and the rector of the parish subsequently ignored a vote in the vestry against the further levying of the rate.[698] In 1865 a Mr Jones of Shrewsbury was forced into bankruptcy when he was forced to pay legal expenses of well over £1,000 in a church-rates case which went against him.[699] In 1867 a Mr Hatton of

---

[693] Ibid. 184–207.   [694] Ibid. 236.   [695] *Nonconformist*, 22 May 1867, 422.
[696] R. Masheder, *Dissent and Democracy* (1864), 3–4.
[697] *Nonconformist*, 23 Mar. 1864, 223; 10 Apr. 1867, 285.
[698] Evans, 'Religion in the Swansea Valley', 267–8.
[699] *Nonconformist*, 2 Aug. 1865, 617.

Mattishall in Norfolk was similarly 'faced with entire ruin' as a result of losing a court action over non-payment of a church rate.[700] And worst of all was
the case of a maltster of Kettleburgh in Suffolk named Grant who was not
only ruined by a legal case arising out of his refusal to pay £1. 13s. 5¾d. in
church rates, but was also 'committed to Whitecross Street prison'.[701] But
the increased Liberal majority in the general election of 1865, the rise in
the number of radical Liberal MPs, the death of Palmerston, and the links
being forged between Gladstone and the leaders of Dissent, all helped
to strengthen the hands of the opponents of church rates. When J. A.
Hardcastle, liberal Anglican MP for Bury St Edmunds, introduced yet
another Church Rates Abolition Bill in March 1866 Gladstone, from the
government benches, announced his support on condition that the measure
would be amended in committee, and on that understanding he voted for
the bill which passed the Commons by 285 votes to 252. What Gladstone
suggested was not merely the exemption of Dissenters, as he had in previous
years, but the abolition of 'the compulsory power of collecting church rates'
while retaining the levy for those still willing to pay it.[702] And to this end he
introduced, on 8 May, a bill to prevent the legal enforcement of the payment
of any church rate in any place in England or Wales.[703] The *Nonconformist*
and the Liberation Society would have preferred Hardcastle's bill for total
abolition, but they supported Gladstone's bill on the ground that it met their
fundamental objection to the church-rates system.[704] The government's
defeat, on an amendment to its Reform Bill in June, ended any hope of a
government measure to resolve the church-rates issue, but in the following
month the new minority Conservative administration undertook not to
oppose the second reading of Gladstone's bill provided that it went no
further.[705]

   In February 1867 Hardcastle's bill passed its second reading in the
Commons by 263 votes to 187—the largest majority ever achieved for a
Church Rates Abolition Bill—only to be rejected by the Lords by 82 votes
to 24. But by the following year the growing support for abolition in the
Commons coupled with the passage of the Second Reform Act suggested
that the defenders of church rates would be wise to compromise if they
were to salvage anything from the wreck which now appeared to be

---

[700] Brown, *Congregationalism in Norfolk and Suffolk*, 353–4.
[701] *Nonconformist*, 10 Apr. 1867, 285.
[702] *Parliamentary Debates*, 3rd ser., clxxxi (7 Mar. 1866), col. 1668.
[703] Ibid., clxxxiii (8 May 1866), col. 621.   [704] *Nonconformist*, 23 May 1866, 409.
[705] O. Anderson, 'Gladstone's Abolition of Compulsory Church Rates', *Journal of Ecclesiastical History*, 25 (1974), 186–8.

inevitable. In 1867 Lord Morley warned his fellow peers that 'there could hardly be any doubt that when the new Reform Bill came into operation a large number of Dissenters would get into Parliament', and that their lordships would be well advised to settle the church-rates dispute 'before that occurred'.[706] And Sir Michael Hicks-Beach urged from the Conservative benches in the Commons that the question had 'better not be left to the tender mercies of the Reformed Parliament'.[707] Such warnings made Conservatives now willing to accept Gladstone's compromise measure which he reintroduced into the Commons in February 1868. Gladstone's bill proposed not to abolish church rates but to remove the mechanism by which their payment could be enforced on unwilling ratepayers. The bill for the Abolition of Compulsory Church Rates thus passed its second readings in both Commons and Lords without a division and received the royal assent on 31 July 1868. Church rates survived and long continued to be levied in some rural areas. But except in parishes such as Marylebone and Southwark, where it was claimed that local Acts of Parliament permitted the continued imposition of a compulsory rate,[708] churchwardens abandoned the attempt to force Dissenters to contribute to the upkeep of the parish church. The cause for which William Baines and John Thorogood had been imprisoned, for which Bright had harangued the crowds in Rochdale churchyard, and to which Edward Miall had devoted much of his life, had finally been won.[709]

Five weeks after Gladstone introduced his bill for the Abolition of Compulsory Church Rates he moved and carried against the government resolutions calling for the disestablishment of the Anglican Church of Ireland. The timing of Gladstone's move had less to do with the growing political influence of Dissent or with pressure from the Liberation Society than with an Irish terrorist attack on Clerkenwell gaol in the previous December in which twelve people had been killed and another 120 injured.[710] But Edward Miall had long argued that Irish disestablishment would be the first and easiest step on the road to English disestablishment and Gladstone

---

[706] *Parliamentary Debates*, 3rd ser., clxxxix (8 Aug. 1867), col. 1081.

[707] Ibid., cxc (19 Feb. 1868), col. 979.

[708] Manning, *Dissenting Deputies*, 195–7; Chadwick, *Victorian Church*, ii. 195; J. Cox, *English Churches in a Secular Society: Lambeth, 1870–1930* (Oxford, 1982), 184.

[709] The attempt by Olive Anderson to minimize the Dissenting contribution to the abolition of church rates is wrong-headed. As David Thompson asks rhetorically: 'Who deserves the credit: the person who takes the decision or those who make it necessary for a decision to be taken?' (Anderson, 'Abolition of Compulsory Church Rates', 196–7; Thompson, 'The Liberation Society', in Hollis, *Pressure from Without*, 236).

[710] P. M. H. Bell, *Disestablishment in Ireland and Wales* (1969), 81.

had hit on an issue which would unite English and Welsh Nonconformists, Scottish Free Churchmen, and Irish Roman Catholics in opposition to the Conservative government now headed by Disraeli. Following his defeat in the Commons on the Irish church issue Disraeli announced that an election would be held in November on the new electoral register, and in that election the Liberation Society found itself in the unusual position, not of pressuring reluctant Liberal MPs, but of campaigning on behalf of the Liberal leadership. The Liberation Society spent £3,145 in publishing over a million tracts, employing twenty-seven special lecturers, and organizing 515 meetings.[711] The alliance between middle- and working-class radicals held. George Howell, the secretary of the Reform League, offered his services to the Liberation Society; the Liberation Society for its part voted £50 to the Reform League and £40 to the London Working Men's Association to assist their campaigns for Irish disestablishment; and Samuel Morley was the chief contributor to a fund of £1,900 raised by the Reform League to help the Liberals 'win a number of seats from the Tories'.[712] In Wales Calvinistic Methodist ministers appeared on Liberation Society platforms and Calvinistic Methodist chapels were used for Liberal election meetings.[713] In Liverpool the Wesleyan Conference, alienated by the 'rationalistic and ritualistic movements in the Church of England', refused to support the established Church of Ireland.[714]

Not all movement was in the Liberals' direction. The Irish church issue prompted the Wesleyan Benjamin Gregory to desert the Liberals and vote Conservative because 'he dreaded any weakening of Protestantism, any triumph, even apparent, of Popery'.[715] There was a Protestant backlash against the Liberals in Lancashire where the Conservatives won twice as many seats as their opponents[716] and Gladstone himself was defeated in South-West Lancashire, though he had already taken the precaution of securing election for Greenwich. But elsewhere the Liberals were triumphant, winning 65 of 105 seats in Ireland, 53 of 60 seats in Scotland, while in Wales and Monmouthshire the Liberation Society at last succeeded in mobilizing Welsh Nonconformity and the Liberals captured 23 of the principality's 33 seats.[717] The Liberals had a majority of 110 in the new Parliament and the

[711] Machin, *Politics and the Churches*, 373; Bell, *Disestablishment*, 107.

[712] Newton, 'Edward Miall', 311–13; Machin, *Politics and the Churches*, 365; Hodder, *Samuel Morley*, 268–9; Leventhal, *Respectable Radical*, 106, 235 n. 57.

[713] Pretty, 'Richard Davies', *Welsh History Review*, 9 (1978–9), 459; J. Morgan, 'Denbighshire's *Annus Mirabilis*: The Borough and County Elections of 1868', ibid. 7 (1974–5), 83.

[714] *The Times*, 3 Aug. 1868.   [715] Gregory, *Autobiographical Recollections*, 452.

[716] Vincent, *Formation of the Liberal Party*, 27.   [717] Bell, *Disestablishment*, 107.

number of Nonconformist MPs rose from 33 to 62. They comprised 19 Unitarians, 14 Independents, 11 nonconforming Presbyterians, 9 Quakers, 6 Baptists, 2 Wesleyans, and 1 Calvinistic Methodist.[718] There were some notable individual triumphs: in Liverpool the Unitarian merchant and pioneer of district nursing, William Rathbone VI, was elected as the third member for the town's three-member constituency and so became the first Dissenter to represent Liverpool in Parliament since William Roscoe's defeat sixty-one years earlier. Three Nonconformists were returned for Welsh constituencies: the Calvinistic Methodist Richard Davies was elected for Anglesey, the Baptist Evan Richards won Cardiganshire, and the Congregationalist Henry Richard came top of the poll in Merthyr Tydfil, with 4,054 more votes than the second Liberal elected.[719] In December 1868 Gladstone formed his first administration and offered John Bright the Presidency of the Board of Trade. The Rochdale Quaker thus became the first Dissenter ever to sit in a British cabinet.

One of the few disappointments suffered by Dissenters in the general election of 1868 was the defeat of Edward Miall in his attempt to secure election for Bradford. But his Conservative opponent was subsequently unseated for bribery and Miall was elected MP for Bradford at a by-election in the following March.[720] Twelve days after Miall returned to Parliament Gladstone's bill to disestablish the Irish church passed its second reading in the Commons with a majority of 118. In the previous spring the Lords had rejected by 95 votes a bill by which Gladstone had sought to suspend further appointments to livings in the Irish church. But now Lord Stratford de Redcliffe warned his fellow peers of 'the consequences of throwing out a bill which is backed by a very large majority in the Commons, who are understood to express the deliberate conviction of their respective constituencies'.[721] On 19 June the Lords approved the second reading of the bill by 179 votes to 146 and after they tried, and failed, to graft on to it the principle of concurrent endowment the bill received the royal assent on 26 July. Within the space of two years Miall had seen the seeds of the alliance between middle- and working-class radicals which he had sown a generation earlier brought triumphantly to fruition. The vote had been given to householders in the boroughs; compulsory church rates had been abolished; the number of Nonconformist MPs

---

[718] *Nonconformist*, 16 Dec. 1868, 1220; I have not included Jacob Bright among the Quaker MPs since he had been disowned in 1852 (Mills, *John Bright and the Quakers*, i. 432).
[719] Miall, *Henry Richard*, 150.   [720] Miall, *Life of Miall*, 291.
[721] *Parliamentary Debates*, 3rd ser., cxcvi (14 June 1869), col. 1700.

had doubled; the Anglican Church of Ireland had been disestablished. The future did not turn out quite as Miall would have hoped or could have expected. But the newly elected MP for Bradford, along with other politically active Dissenters, had reason to feel that their long years of campaigning had been well rewarded.

V

'Intellectuality and Surface Culture'
The Respectability of Dissent, 1840–1859

1. 'PERSONS OF INTELLIGENCE AND RESPECTABILITY':
UPWARD SOCIAL MOBILITY

By the late 1840s it seemed possible that the period of virtually uninter-
rupted expansion which the Nonconformist denominations had enjoyed for
eighty years might be coming to an end. Wesleyan membership fell by 1,641
in 1846–7 and by another 607 in 1847–8. The Primitive Methodists, the Bible
Christians, the Methodist New Connexion, the Wesleyan Methodist Association, and the New Connexion General Baptists all lost members in 1846–7,
and General Baptist membership fell again in 1848–9.[1] Statistics for the Particular Baptists are less complete than those for the Methodist denominations, but those churches which did make a return to the Baptist Union
showed a slackening in their growth rate in the years 1845–7.[2] And although
the Congregationalists did not collect national membership figures in the
1840s, the paper which Algernon Wells read to the annual meeting of the
Congregational Union in October 1848, on the failure of the churches to
evangelize the working class, indicated that leading Independents were also
worried by their denomination's lack of progress.[3]

Following that annual meeting of the Congregational Union Edward Miall
invited working men to write to the *Nonconformist* to give their opinions on
the reasons for working-class alienation from the churches. Scores responded
to the invitation and the letters published from them over the next three

---

[1] Currie, Gilbert, and Horsley, *Churches and Churchgoers*, 141, 148.
[2] Gilbert, *Religion and Society*, 190.   [3] See above, Ch. II, sect. 9.

months shed a flood of light on working-class attitudes to the churches in the mid-nineteenth century. As one would expect of correspondents to the *Nonconformist*, many writers blamed the established church for workers' antipathy to religion. 'The poor of our country', wrote a shoemaker from Cambridge, 'have been accustomed to look upon religion through the medium of a State Church.' 'They behold men arrayed in purple and fine linen, and faring sumptuously every day . . . whilst thousands around them are sunk in the lowest depths of degradation, crime, and suffering.'[4] Other writers blamed Dissenting ministers for the absence of working men from places of worship: ministers were accused of lack of sympathy for the poor and of failing to support the Chartist movement.[5] One correspondent ascribed workers' alienation from Wesleyan chapels to the latter's failure to provide adequate support for their sick members; another complained that churches did not provide sick and benefit clubs; a third was convinced that the pew-rents charged by chapels were 'wholly beyond the reach of a working man'.[6] Several writers claimed that workers were reluctant to attend chapels because ministers refused to take up the cause of total abstinence. A 'Tyneside teetotaller' who asked the editor to 'put the stops and mend the spelling' of his letters since he was 'put to work when only nine years old', wrote that some of his associates who were reclaimed drunkards expressed 'astonishment at the silence of preachers and professors' on the temperance movement.[7] One correspondent claimed that ministers were too grounded in the Classics to be able to preach to working men; another complained that ministers knew nothing of modern science; a third argued that they spent too much time dwelling on 'those gloomy doctrines of man's depravity . . . and his sure condemnation to eternal punishment'.[8] Four writers drew attention to the gulf separating Christian employers from their workers. 'A Norwich operative' pointed out that when workers 'find a Christian employer, whose liberality in matters pertaining to the diffusion of religious knowledge is undoubted, driving a bargain with his labourers upon such terms as closely border upon starvation', it was hardly surprising that his workers should be prejudiced against the employer's religion.[9]

But what these working-class correspondents complained of most was not the uncaring attitude of Nonconformist employers or Dissenting ministers' antipathy to Chartism: by far and away their most frequently voiced complaint was that both ministers and churches had grown too respectable.

---

[4] *Nonconformist*, 27 Dec. 1848, 991.   [5] Ibid. 15 Nov. 869; 29 Nov. 909; 6 Dec. 931.
[6] Ibid. 6 Dec. 931; 13 Dec. 950; 10 Jan. 1849, 25–6.
[7] Ibid. 20 Dec. 1848, 967–8; 27 Dec., 991.   [8] Ibid. 20 Dec., 968; 15 Nov., 869, 870.
[9] Ibid. 6 Dec., 930; 20 Dec., 967; 27 Dec., 991; 31 Jan. 1849, 33.

'From false notions of respectability', wrote one working man, 'the poor are despised, their poverty is reckoned a disgrace, they are not even spoken to in the street, and the rich, however base, are bowed to.'[10] Another working man, a church member for more than twelve years, complained that ministers' 'visits and prayers . . . are confined principally to the affluent and respectable, who are in the least need of them'.[11] A sailmaker argued that some Congregational churches repelled the artisan classes because they 'pander to the pride of a conventional respectability'.[12] A Leicester correspondent pointed out that if a worker entered a chapel on a Sunday morning he would be shown to 'a free bench in some remote corner of the building'; he would find wealthy members of the congregation 'lolling idly on their velvet cushions, enclosed with brass rails and damask hangings'; he would hear prayers 'for the choicest blessings of heaven to be showered on the royal family', though not a word would be said 'on behalf of the starving poor, hundreds of whom were living in the same neighbourhood'; and he would listen to a sermon which was 'a scholastic effusion, put together to please the respectable of the congregation'.[13] The same point was made by a speaker at the Wesleyan Conference in 1848 when the Connexion's fall in membership was discussed. 'We have looked too much to respectability and intellectuality and surface culture', said F. A. West.[14] To the Cambridge shoemaker, writing in the *Nonconformist*, the identity between religion and respectability was at the root of the alienation of working-class people from the churches: 'to be a professor is . . . to be respectable, and in fact to be respectable you must make some profession'.[15]

Respectability had become, by the mid-nineteenth century, the great idol of the middle and upper working classes. The obsession with respectability was the product of a hierarchical yet mobile society in which substantial sections of every class sought to emulate the lifestyle and manners of those above them and to distance themselves from those they imagined to be beneath them. The working-class correspondents to the *Nonconformist* in 1848 despised the cult of respectability, but to many skilled workers respectability was as much the goal of their endeavours as it was of the bourgeoisie.[16] The conventions of respectability were flouted at one end of the

---

[10] Ibid. 22 Nov. 1848, 889.   [11] Ibid. 29 Nov., 909.   [12] Ibid. 29 Nov., 910.
[13] Ibid. 13 Dec., 950.   [14] Gregory, *Side Lights on the Conflicts of Methodism*, 427.
[15] *Nonconformist*, 27 Dec. 1848, 991. There was no hint in this correspondence that the term 'respectability' could denote moral as opposed to social standing. Cf. the discussion in B. Harrison, *Peaceable Kingdom* (Oxford, 1982), 157 *et seq*.
[16] A. L. Calman, *Life and Letters of John Ashworth* (Manchester, n.d.), 38; G. Crossick, *An Artisan Elite in Victorian Society: Kentish London, 1840–1880* (1978), 135–6; D. Vincent, *Bread, Knowledge, and Freedom* (1981), 55.

social scale by members of the upper class whose wealth, social position, and self-confidence obviated the need to imitate anyone else, and at the other by those people whose economic conditions were so depressed that they despaired of ever being able to improve their lot. But sections of all other classes were caught up in the quest for respectability: wealthy members of the bourgeoisie who spent much of the fortunes they made in industry in buying country houses and estates, lower middle-class families who sought to escape from the working-class inner cities by moving to substantial villas in the newer suburbs, working-class men and women who by hard work, self-improvement, thrift, and sobriety tried to emphasize the gulf that separated them from the drunkards, paupers, prostitutes, and criminals at the bottom of society, were all seeking the approbation of those whose social status they envied.

Since Dissent was so powerful a stimulus to upward social mobility, it was inevitable that it, too, should become entangled in the pursuit of respectability. As a Wesleyan minister, John Dyson, put it in 1856, while Methodism had 'not reached the outcast and the dregs of society', it 'had taken hold of the comparatively poor' and had 'lifted them up and bettered their condition'. It had saved many a man 'from rags—put him on his feet—[given] him a character, and placed him in the path of industry in which he has found both affluence and position', and Dyson's claim can be made equally for all the other Nonconformist denominations.[17] One must not exaggerate the effect that this upward social mobility was having on Dissenting congregations by the mid-nineteenth century. The complaints voiced by Algernon Wells and some of the correspondents to the *Nonconformist* in 1848 about the alienation of the working class from chapel worship were countered by equally confident assertions that Dissenters were appealing to the working class as much as they had ever done. John Angell James, minister of the Carr's Lane Congregational church in Birmingham, argued that Wesleyan societies 'were chiefly gathered from the working classes' and that the proportion of working-class people attending Congregational chapels was greater than when he began his ministry more than forty years earlier. A Mr Parsons who had spent twenty-two years ministering to a manufacturing population at Ebley in Gloucestershire maintained that Congregational churches 'were almost wholly composed of the working classes'.[18] And Joseph Drew, a Newbury Baptist, claimed that while Congregationalists were more bourgeois than

---

[17] J. B. Dyson, *The History of Wesleyan Methodism in the Congleton Circuit* (1856), 178. J. Lea has a long list of Lancashire Baptists who 'began life in poverty but rose to affluence', 'Baptists in Lancashire 1837–87', Ph.D. thesis (Liverpool, 1970), 87–8.

[18] *Nonconformist*, 25 Oct. 1848, 809.

other Evangelical Dissenters, among Wesleyans, Baptists, and Primitive Methodists the proportion of working-class to middle-class people was three to one.[19] A religious census published in the *Liverpool Mercury* in 1853 calculated that half the people attending Wesleyan chapels in the town, and 70 per cent of those attending Wesleyan Methodist Association chapels, were working class.[20]

A clear guide to what was happening to the social composition of Nonconformity is provided by those baptismal and marriage registers that have survived from the middle decades of the nineteenth century. The Public Record Office's holding of Nonconformist baptismal registers, apart from a handful of exceptions, ends with the year 1837, and although baptismal registers for the subsequent decades are housed in most County Record Offices they are far less numerous than those for the pre-1837 period. What is worse is the fact that the Wesleyan Methodists, who provided the greater proportion of baptismal registers for the pre-1837 period, after 1837 issued a new-style baptismal register which omitted the column in which fathers' occupations had hitherto been recorded. However, many Congregational churches and Primitive Methodist circuits, some New Connexion Methodist and Free Methodist societies, and a few Wesleyan chapels continued to record fathers' occupations after 1837, and the information that can be gleaned from such registers can sometimes be supplemented by information from marriage registers, taking the occupations of the bridegrooms as the equivalent of those of the fathers in the baptismal registers. I have supervised the examination of baptismal and marriage registers for the period 1837–69 in seventeen County Record Offices,[21] and where the material is sufficiently plentiful to enable a county-wide analysis to be made it has been incorporated in Tables XV–LIV.

The first conclusion to be drawn from these tables is that throughout most of England the appeal of Nonconformity in the 1840s, 1850s, and 1860s continued to be primarily to the working class. The proportion of retailers among the Congregationalists of Essex rose from 8.7 per cent in the 1820s to 18.3 per cent in the 1860s, but even in that latter decade the Independents of Essex remained predominantly poor: 46 per cent were unskilled workers and over half were in the bottom three categories. The proportion of weavers among the Congregationalists of the West Riding fell from 14 per cent in the 1820s to 8 per cent in the 1860s, and the clothiers almost completely

[19] Ibid. 17 Jan. 1849, 44.   [20] Gowland, 'Methodist Secessions', Ph.D. thesis, 487–8.
[21] Bedford, Birmingham, Bradford, Chelmsford, Colchester, Greater London, Halifax, Huddersfield, Leeds, Leicester, Northampton, Nottingham, Maidstone, Matlock, Sheffield, Wakefield, and Warwick.

disappeared, but the decline of the weavers and clothiers was balanced not by any corresponding increase in the proportion of middle-class fathers but by a rise in the proportion of higher-skilled workers who by the 1860s constituted nearly a third of West Riding Congregationalists. In the 1860s over 80 per cent of Independent fathers in the West Riding still belonged to the working class. Similarly the Leicestershire Congregationalists were still overwhelmingly working class in the 1860s, with nearly half of them unskilled workers and over 60 per cent falling into categories IX–XI. The evidence for the occupations of Wesleyan fathers after 1837 is too fragmentary to permit county-wide analyses, but the records of individual chapels show that many remained predominantly working class. The proportion of miners having their children baptized in the Midsomer Norton circuit in Somerset fell from 56.2 per cent in the 1830s to 41.1 per cent in the 1850s, but this was accompanied not by any significant increase in the proportion of fathers with middle-class occupations but by a doubling of the percentage of unskilled workers from 9.1 to 19.8.[22] Of the men married in the Wesleyan chapel in Newark in the 1850s and 1860s over a third were unskilled workers and, together with the lower-skilled workers, they constituted more than half the total number of bridegrooms.[23] A third of the men married in the Broad Street Wesleyan chapel in Halifax in the 1860s belonged to one of the bottom three categories—lower-skilled, depressed, or unskilled—and together with the higher-skilled manual workers made up 69 per cent of the men married in the chapel.[24] As for the Primitive Methodists, in Bedfordshire, Essex, and Northamptonshire, more than half their fathers were unskilled workers in the 1860s, and in Leicestershire although the proportion of unskilled Ranters was only 39.6 per cent in the 1850s another 35.6 per cent were equally poor framework knitters.

The only county table which reveals much in the way of upward social mobility between 1840 and 1869 is that for Middlesex and north London which shows that metropolitan Congregationalism, already more bourgeois than anywhere else in the country, had a growing attraction for white-collar workers, who increased from 12.0 per cent of the total number of fathers in the 1830s to 24.4 per cent in the 1850s and to 33.7 per cent in the 1860s. At the same time the proportion of London Congregationalists who were in the bottom three categories fell from 28.7 per cent in the 1830s to 13.9 per cent in the 1850s and to 11.1 per cent in the 1860s. The evidence from other urban churches suggests that what was happening to London Congregationalism in

---

[22] PRO RG 4/1732, 3267.   [23] Nottinghamshire Archives Office, MR 5/34/8; 5/34/9.
[24] WYAS, Halifax, MR 253–6.

the middle decades of the nineteenth century was not exceptional. While the Congregationalists of Essex as a whole remained predominantly poor and working class in the 1850s and 1860s, those attached to the Lion Walk church in Colchester were moving up the social scale. The proportion of Lion Walk fathers who were in the top six categories rose from 35.3 per cent in the 1840s to 49.5 per cent in the 1860s, while the proportion in the bottom four categories fell from 59.6 per cent in the 1840s to 42.5 per cent in the 1860s.[25] Similarly in Leicestershire while the limited evidence available suggests that the proportion of unskilled workers among the county's Congregationalists was increasing from the 1840s to the 1860s, in the market town of Melton Mowbray the reverse was happening: the proportion of retailers among the town's Congregationalists rose from 12.7 per cent in the period 1822–39 to 22.0 per cent in the 1840s and 33.3 per cent in the 1860s. Whereas 26 per cent of Melton's Congregationalist fathers fell into the five middle-class categories in the years 1822–39, by the 1840s the figure was 37 per cent and by the 1860s it was 43 per cent.[26] In Birmingham the proportion of retailers among the Constitution Hill Wesleyans doubled from 17.6 per cent in the 1840s to 35.1 per cent in the 1860s.[27] In Nottingham the proportion of middle-class men associated with the Castle Gate Congregational church rose from 47.8 per cent in the period 1831–43 to 60.9 per cent in the years 1850–62.[28] In the same town the proportion of middle-class adherents of the Methodist New Connexion chapel in Parliament Street rose from 10 per cent in the 1820s to 20 per cent in the 1830s and to 38.5 per cent in the 1860s, while the proportion of men in the bottom three categories fell from 81.9 per cent in the 1810s to 69 per cent in the 1830s and to 30.8 per cent in the 1860s.[29]

Most instructive of all is the evidence of what was happening to the Wesleyans of Leeds. Because Brunswick chapel, Leeds, was one of the few Wesleyan chapels to record fathers' occupations in its baptismal registers from the late 1830s onwards, and because four other Wesleyan chapels in Leeds (Hunslet, Oxford Place, St Peter's, and Wesley[30]) began to marry couples earlier than in most towns, it is possible to build up a picture of the changing occupational structure of Leeds Wesleyanism over six successive decades. Leeds is the only town for which I have found such evidence, and the accompanying analysis of Leeds Wesleyanism in Table VIII is thus all the more valuable. The table shows that in the second decade of the nineteenth

[25] Colchester RO, D/NC 52/1/3.   [26] Leicestershire CRO, N/C/219/1–2.
[27] Birmingham Reference Library, M25/1–3.
[28] Castle Gate records, Nottingham University Library, CU/R 4/1.
[29] Nottinghamshire Archives Office, MR 12/304.
[30] WYAS, Leeds, OP 3/1; LS 22/2; OP 3/17; OP 3/37.

century 68 per cent of male Leeds Wesleyans earned their living in manual occupations, and that notwithstanding the bitter dispute and schism occasioned by the Leeds organ case Leeds Wesleyanism remained overwhelmingly working class throughout the 1820s and 1830s. As late as the 1830s three-quarters of the fathers who had their children baptized in the Wesleyan chapels in Leeds belonged to the working class. It was in the 1840s, not in the 1820s, that the middle-class element in Leeds Wesleyanism began to grow and that the working-class element began to shrink. Between the 1830s and

TABLE VIII. *Occupations of male Wesleyans in Leeds,*
1810–1869, in percentages

		1810–19	1820–9	1830–9	1840–9	1850–9	1860–9
I	Gentlemen	—	—	—	0.7	0.7	0.4
II	Business	3.4	2.1	1.9	4.9	4.9	4.9
III	Professions	—	0.3	—	1.0	1.1	0.8
IV	Farmers	2.1	0.3	1.0	1.4	1.1	2.9
V	Food and retail	5.5	8.8	8.3	20.8	22.1	17.7
Va	Clothiers	14.7	9.3	7.0	0.7	—	—
VI	White collar	5.8	2.4	6.8	17.0	15.6	20.2
VII	Labour aristocracy	4.2	5.6	5.8	5.2	3.2	10.3
VIII	Higher skilled	20.5	30.0	22.6	24.0	24.6	24.7
IX	Lower skilled	27.9	21.4	27.2	18.1	20.9	14.0
X	Depressed	11.6	11.7	6.0	—	—	—
	[Weavers]	[10.5]	[11.1]	[5.6]	[—]	[—]	[—]
XI	Unskilled	4.2	8.2	13.3	6.2	6.0	4.1
	[Labourers]	[2.4]	[6.1]	[7.5]	[2.1]	[3.2]	[1.2]
	Number of churches/circuits	3	3	5	5	5	4
	Number of fathers/grooms	190	337	301	288	285	243

the 1840s the proportion of businessmen, retailers, and white-collar workers among the Leeds Wesleyans doubled while the proportion of unskilled workers halved and the weavers disappeared. While the proportion of higher-skilled workers among Leeds Wesleyans remained fairly steady from the 1830s to the 1860s, the proportion of middle-class men rose from 25.0 per cent in the 1830s to 46.5 per cent in the 1860s, the proportion of labour aristocrats also nearly doubled, and the proportion of men in the bottom three categories fell from 46.5 per cent in the 1830s to 18.1 per cent in the 1860s.

The evidence provided by the baptismal and marriage registers from the middle decades of the nineteenth century thus suggests that throughout rural England and its smaller industrial towns the occupational structure of Dissent remained predominantly working class. But in market towns such as Colchester and Melton Mowbray and in the larger urban centres such as London, Birmingham, Nottingham, and Leeds, Nonconformity was becoming increasingly respectable and bourgeois. There is consequently evidence both to justify the pessimism of urban-based ministers like Algernon Wells about the failure of the churches to recruit working-class members, and to support the claims of his critics that throughout most of England and Wales Nonconformity was retaining the loyalty of its working-class adherents. While a minority of Dissenting congregations were becoming increasingly prosperous, upwardly mobile, and eminently respectable, the vast majority continued to be made up of poor, unsophisticated, semi-skilled and unskilled men and women whose plight, in the 1840s, was rendered all the more desperate by economic depression. Among Congregationalists, in 1848–9, the gulf that was opening up between prosperous middle-class churches and the denomination's working-class adherents produced lengthy debate; among the Wesleyans, with their centralized connexional system, it contributed to disaster.

2. 'THE RIGHT OF A DISSENTING CHAPEL TO LOOK LIKE A PARISH CHURCH': EMULATING THE ESTABLISHMENT

The readiness of Dissenting churches to embrace the cult of respectability was not only the consequence of the growing prosperity of some of their members; it was also an attempt on their part to emulate the Church of England. Though Dissenters were disdainful of Anglican subservience to the State they were at the same time anxious to show that their ministers were as well educated, that their members were of equal social standing, that their chapels were as decorous, and that their services were as dignified, as those of the established church. But just as the quest for respectability could cut the cotton manufacturer off from the industrial community which produced his profits and could entice the working man into the ranks of the *petite bourgeoisie*, so could it encourage prosperous Dissenters to leave their chapels for their parish churches and at the same time cut off Nonconformist churches from the unevangelized working class. 'It would be difficult to find an instance of families who, for three generations, have kept their carriage and continued Dissenters', wrote a contributor to the *Monthly Magazine* in 1798,[31] and there was plenty of evidence to support his contention. The Quaker woolstapler John Hustler played a large part in establishing the wool and worsted industry in Bradford in the eighteenth century, but he also bought a country estate of ninety acres at Undercliffe and built a large country house. His son, also John Hustler, remained true to the Society of Friends and helped to found the Friends' Provident Institution in 1832, but his grandson, John Mildred Hustler, threw himself into the social whirl of upper-class society and brought the family to the verge of financial ruin.[32] When the Snow Hill Congregational chapel, Wolverhampton, was built in 1849 £1,200 of the cost was donated by the banker Sidney Cartwright. But when at a subsequent church meeting a poor member suggested that every church member should give personal service as well as money to the work of the church Cartwright resigned in protest and henceforward worshipped in an Anglican church.[33] Jonathan Akroyd, a wealthy Halifax manufacturer, gave £2,330 towards the building of Salem Methodist New Connexion chapel in 1845, and when he died in 1847 he was buried in the new chapel. But his son joined the Church of England and in 1854 obtained Home Office permission to have his father's body exhumed and reinterred in the parish cemetery.[34] Those few Dissenters who sent their sons to Cambridge often by the same act sent them into the established church. This was the fate of Joseph Clarke, son of the Wesleyan scholar Adam Clarke, who became an Anglican clergyman, and of Matthew Talbot Baines, eldest son of the elder Edward Baines, who was MP for Hull from 1847 to 1852 and for Leeds from 1852 to 1859, and who in 1855 entered Palmerston's cabinet as Chancellor of the Duchy of Lancaster.[35] The most spectacular illustration of the truth of the *Monthly Magazine*'s dictum was the case of Samuel Jones Loyd, grandson of the Manchester Unitarian banker John Jones and son of the former Unitarian minister Lewis Loyd who left the ministry for banking and founded the London branch of Jones, Loyd and Company.[36] When Lewis Loyd died in 1858 he left a fortune of nearly £2 million. His son was brought up as an Anglican; was Tory MP for Hythe from 1819 to 1826; and in 1850 entered the House of Lords as Baron Overstone.[37]

[31] *Monthly Magazine*, 5 (1798), 170.
[32] H. R. Hodgson, *The Society of Friends in Bradford* (Bradford, 1926), 46.
[33] Jones, *Congregational Churches of Wolverhampton*, 93–4.
[34] E. V. Chapman, *John Wesley and Co.* (Halifax, 1952), 47–8.
[35] J. W. Etheridge, *Life of the Rev Adam Clarke* (1858), 399; Binfield, *So Down to Prayers*, 55.
[36] Holt, *Unitarian Contribution to Social Progress*, 60.
[37] Thorne, *History of Parliament*, iv. 466.

On a more modest level the threat posed to Dissent by the quest for respectability was epitomized by the character of Mrs Furze in William Hale White's novel *Catherine Furze*. Until 1840 the tradesmen of Eastthorpe had all lived behind their shops but in the late 1830s a new row of villas was built at 'The Terrace' at the north end of the town, three of which were taken by a doctor, a brewer, and a wealthy grocer. Mrs Furze persuaded her ironmonger husband to follow the town's upper bourgeoisie to 'The Terrace' and at the same time urged that they should leave their Nonconformist chapel for the parish church. 'There is no denying that the people who go to church are vastly more genteel', explained Mrs Furze, 'and so are the service and everything about it—the vespers—the bells—somehow there is a respectability in it.'[38]

The huge expansion of Evangelical Nonconformity in the first four decades of the nineteenth century had been made possible in part by the failure of the Church of England to adapt its organization to the changes brought about in English society by the demographic and industrial revolutions, but by the 1840s the church-building programme, substantially assisted by parliamentary grants, the work of the Ecclesiastical Commission, and the legislation passed by the Whigs in the 1830s had all helped to revitalize the established church. As far as its ability to minister to the people of England was concerned, the reformation of the Church of England occurred not in the 1530s but three hundred years later. Between 1831 and 1851 2,029 new Anglican churches were built and between 1813 and 1858 the number of non-resident clergymen fell from over 6,000 to 2,000. By 1839 John Angell James was conscious that the reawakening of the Church of England posed a threat to Dissent. 'It seems to be the present policy of the Church of England', he warned his fellow Congregationalists, 'to build us *down* and to build us *out*'. The Anglicans were 'multiplying chapels and churches, many of which are erected in the immediate vicinity of ours, for the purpose of drawing into them the people *we* have gathered'. To meet this challenge Congregationalists 'must catch the building spirit of the age'. 'We must *build, build, build*.' 'We must not wait for congregations to be gathered before we build: we must build to gather.'[39]

Denominational rivalry was thus a great spur to chapel-building. According to Herbert Skeats the number of chapels belonging to the major Nonconformist denominations rose by 4,350 between 1851 and 1876, an

---

[38] W. H. White ('Mark Rutherford'), *Catherine Furze* (1894), 23.

[39] A. Peel, *These Hundred Years: A History of the Congregational Union of England and Wales* (1931), 149.

increase of 24.8 per cent.[40] If a denomination was slow to build a chapel in any particular town, it incurred the risk of being overtaken by rivals. The Bible Christians bemoaned the fact that at Nailsea near Bristol and at Ventnor in the Isle of Wight they had pioneered Evangelical preaching and had formed strong societies, only to have 'the fruits of their toil' snatched from them by other denominations which had been the first to build chapels.[41] Even the Primitive Methodists were abandoning their cottages and converted barns for purpose-built chapels. Whereas in 1847 the Ranters used twice as many rented rooms as permanent chapels for worship, by 1868 the number of their permanent chapels had increased from 1,421 to 3,235, and these now out-numbered the rented rooms.[42] But competition between voluntary chapels did not necessarily produce an adequate number of pews in places where they were most needed, any more than competition between voluntary schools created educational provision in areas of greatest deprivation. The use of pew-rents to pay for new buildings limited the number of free seats available to the poor and among Wesleyans the proportion of free seats in their chapels fell from 43 per cent in 1851 to 26 per cent in 1873.[43] Yet in rural areas, especially in Wales, denominational rivalry was by the 1850s produc-ing more chapels and more accommodation than was necessary for the reli-gious needs of the people. In 1851 Botwnnog in Caernarfonshire had two Dissenting chapels and a parish church to serve a population of 163, and the Calvinistic Methodist chapel alone had room for nearly three times the total population of the village.[44]

Denominational rivalry produced more elaborate as well as more numer-ous chapels. Until the 1830s virtually all Nonconformist chapels had been built either in the style of contemporary domestic architecture or on the model of the Greek temple. But many of the Anglican churches erected with the proceeds of the £1 million grant made by Parliament in 1818 were built in the Gothic style, partly because the Romantic movement had revived inter-est in medieval architecture and partly because Gothic churches made of brick were far cheaper than classical churches constructed of stone.[45] The apostle of the Gothic revival was Augustus Pugin, whose *Contrasts*, empha-sizing the gulf between the 'noble edifices of the middle ages' and the 'decay

---

[40] H. S. Skeats, 'Statistics Relating to the Support of Religious Institutions in England and Wales', *Journal of the Statistical Society*, 39 (1876), 333.

[41] Bourne, *Life of James Thorne*, 87; Bourne, *The Bible Christians*, 243.

[42] Kendall, *Primitive Methodist Church*, ii. 456.

[43] R. B. Walker, 'Wesleyan Methodism in Victorian England and Wales', *Journal of Eccle-siastical History*, 24 (1973), 283.

[44] Jones, *Explorations and Explanations*, 24–5.

[45] H. Davies, *Worship and Theology in England*, iv (1962), 42–4.

of taste' in the nineteenth century, was published in 1836. But even before the publication of Pugin's book Nonconformist chapels were displaying Gothic features, and it was no doubt the financial advantage which Gothic brick had over Greek stone which explains the surprising fact that some of the earliest manifestations of the Gothic revival among Nonconformists were found not in the meeting-houses of wealthy urban congregations but in the humble chapels of Primitive Methodists and rural Congregationalists. Both the Primitive Methodist chapel built at Lynn in Norfolk in 1826 at a cost of £205 and that built at Morton Common in Shropshire in 1838 at a cost of £97 were fitted with Gothic windows.[46] One of the first Congregational chapels to be built in the Gothic style was that at March in the Cambridgeshire Fens in 1836.[47] And comparative cheapness was certainly a factor in the decision of the Mosley Street Unitarian congregation in Manchester to build their Upper Brook Street chapel in the Gothic style in 1837. Charles Barry's Gothic design was priced at £6,000, exactly half the estimated cost of Barry's classical plan for the same congregation.[48]

But, notwithstanding the fact that Gothic brick was far cheaper than Greek stone, Nonconformists embraced Gothic architecture as evidence that Dissent was of equal social standing with the established church. When J. G. Robberds spoke at the opening of the Gee Cross Unitarian chapel at Hyde in Cheshire in 1848 he claimed that its Gothic spire asserted 'the right of a Dissenting chapel to look like a parish church, and to be used as a parish church'.[49] Not all Dissenters were convinced that Gothic was an appropriate style for a Nonconformist meeting-house. Spurgeon's Metropolitan Tabernacle, built in 1860–1 in south London near the Elephant and Castle with seating for 4,600 at a cost of £21,500, was built in classical style. At the laying of the foundation-stone Spurgeon said that 'every Baptist place should be Grecian, never Gothic'.[50] In 1863 J. A. Tabor published *A Nonconformist Protest* against Dissenting chapels being built in imitation of Roman Catholic churches.[51] But these were isolated islands of resistance in the rising tide of Nonconformist Gothic. In 1850 the Wesleyan F. J. Jobson, in his influential *Chapel and School Architecture*, urged his co-religionists to abandon imitation pagan temples where 'the blood of bulls and goats is not to be shed' and which were indistinguishable from town halls or concert rooms, in favour of Gothic edifices whose 'ecclesiastical form' was unmistakable.[52] In 1847 the

[46] *Primitive Methodist Magazine* 8 (1827), 142; 2nd ser. 11 (1841), 363.
[47] Wilson, *Memoir of Thomas Wilson*, 457.
[48] L. Smith, 'Unitarians and the Gothic Revival', *TUHS* 17 (1980), 83–4.   [49] Ibid. 85.
[50] W. Y. Fullerton, *C. H. Spurgeon* (1920), 137, 139.
[51] Davies, *Worship and Theology*, iv. 49.   [52] *HMC* iv. 492.

Congregational Year Book announced the opening of three new chapels, at Dalston in London, at Lymington in Hampshire, and at Pendleton in Manchester, all costing over £3,000, all in Gothic style, and, in the case of the Dalston edifice, described significantly as a 'Congregational church'. Such buildings were praised in the same issue of the *Year Book* by John Blackburn for their beauty, flexibility, and above all their 'moderate cost'. 'Most fervently' Blackburn expressed the hope that ' "the religion of barns" is passing away from amongst us.' 'When money is to be spent for the service of God, we are bound to use it with taste and judgement, so as to attract, rather than repel, persons of intelligence and respectability.'[53]

'Persons of intelligence and respectability' could also be attracted by the relocation of chapels. In the late eighteenth and early nineteenth centuries Nonconformist chapels were usually sited in the most populous parts of towns, but as those areas became either increasingly industrialized or increasingly overcrowded so churches sought to move to more congenial neighbourhoods. The first Wesleyan chapel in Windsor was built in 1816 'in a very obscure . . . part of the town called Beer Lane', but in 1837, with the aid of donations from the Duke of Cambridge and the Duchess of Kent, the society moved to a new chapel 'in the best part of one of the principal streets'.[54] In the eighteenth century both Congregational meeting-houses in Leeds, White chapel and Salem chapel, were built south of the River Aire in Hunslet and Holbeck, but as those areas became industrialized and predominantly working class so 'the great proportion of the respectable population' moved out and the churches followed. The White chapel congregation moved north of the river to Queen Street in 1825 and the Salem congregation followed to East Parade in 1840.[55] Even the Primitive Methodists deserted their chapel at Silver Street, Newcastle upon Tyne, in 1838, though it was 'greatly needed in that wicked part of the town', and built 'a costly edifice' in Nelson Street for £2,950.[56] The way in which the interests of the poor could be sacrificed to those of the rich by the relocation of chapels was illustrated by the decision of the Unitarian New Meeting in Birmingham to move from Moor Street to Broad Street in 1858. The move was favoured by wealthy Unitarians who lived in the suburbs of Edgbaston and Harborne and opposed by Sunday school teachers concerned for the education of their poorer charges. But the issue was decided in favour of the move at a meeting held at 12 noon on a Tuesday in October at which only the economically independent could be present, and in consequence many of the Sunday school teachers seceded to

---

[53] *Congregational Year Book* (1847), 161–8.   [54] *Wesleyan Magazine*, 9 (1837), 692–4.
[55] Elliott, 'Protestant Denominations in Leeds', 165–6.
[56] Kendall, *Primitive Methodist Church*, ii. 192.

form the Free Christian Society.[57] It was an ominous portent for the future progress of Dissent that when the Baptists abandoned chapels in working-class districts of Sheffield in 1857 and Preston in 1858 for more attractive neighbourhoods, those buildings were taken over by the Church of England.[58]

The building of Gothic chapels in fashionable thoroughfares was accompanied by a move towards formality in worship. The change that was coming over worship in some London chapels was noted by a correspondent to the *Baptist Magazine* in 1835. Having recently settled in the capital, he wrote to complain that he had been 'greeted in one or two Baptist meeting-houses in the city with the sound of an organ', an instrument whose use he had always assumed 'to be at variance with that primitive simplicity at which we profess to aim'.[59] The Congregationalist Thomas Binney was opposed to the use of organs in Nonconformist chapels, but he nevertheless introduced the chanting of psalms and the recitation of the Apostle's Creed into services in the King's Weigh House and the practice spread slowly to other Congregational churches.[60] When the new Gothic Congregational chapel was opened at Snow Hill, Wolverhampton, in 1849 worshippers were presented with an order of service which included the chanting of psalms and which was headed 'Snow Hill Congregational Church'.[61] Similarly when the Derby Road Particular Baptist chapel in Nottingham, built in the 'thirteenth-century early English style', was opened in 1850 at a cost of £6,525, an organ was installed and the singing of chants was introduced.[62] Henry Allon gave music an important place in the life of the Congregational Union chapel in Islington. In 1847 a psalmody class was begun which subsequently gave performances of oratorios; chanting was introduced into the church's services around 1856; and three years later a chapel choir was formed.[63] Among Wesleyans the Conference's prohibitions of anthems, musical festivals, and selections of sacred music went the way of its banning of organs. A performance of Handel's *Messiah* was given in the Wesleyan Square chapel in Halifax in 1821 in order to raise funds for an organ. Since the concert was held at 2.30 on a Wednesday afternoon and the price of tickets ranged from 1s. 6d. to 4s. 0d. members of the working class were obviously not expected to attend

[57] Bushrod, 'Unitarianism in Birmingham', 12–13.
[58] D. Smith, *Conflict and Compromise* (1982), 244; P. T. Phillips, *Sectarian Spirit* (1982), 50.
[59] *Baptist Magazine*, 27 (1835), 58.
[60] Davies, *Worship and Theology*, iv. 226; Kaye, *King's Weigh House*, 73–4.
[61] Jones, *Congregational Churches of Wolverhampton*, 73–4.
[62] Harrison, 'Baptists of Nottinghamshire', i. 208–9.
[63] W. H. Harwood, *Henry Allon* (1894), 34–5.

in large numbers.[64] Similarly among New Connexion Methodists when 740 teachers and friends of the Stamford Street Sunday school in Ashton-under-Lyne took over the town hall on Christmas day 1849 for their annual meeting, they were entertained by the chapel choir and orchestra's rendering of Handel's 'And the glory of the Lord' and to music by Mozart and Mendelssohn.[65] Choirs began to appear in the Dissenting chapels in Wales in the 1840s and so inaugurated the choral tradition which was to become one of the outstanding characteristics of Welsh Nonconformity. The Tredegar Baptists staged a concert on Christmas day in 1850; twelve months later the choir of the Jerusalem Baptist chapel, Rhymney, sang selections from Handel and Mozart; excerpts from Haydn's *Creation* and the *Messiah* were performed at the Hebron Independent chapel at Clydach in Glamorgan in 1858; and the Independent church at Morriston even overcame its antipathy to Roman Catholicism to permit a performance of Mozart's *Twelfth Mass* in 1860.[66] The development of choral singing was powerfully assisted by the use of the tonic sol-fa system which helped people with no musical training to sing at sight, a system which was popularized in the 1840s by a Congregational minister, John Curwen, who was minister successively to churches at Stowmarket and Plaistow.[67] And the popularity of chapel music was further enhanced by the eisteddfod movement in which chapel choirs vied with each other in friendly competition. A correspondent in the Anglican *Yr Haul* in 1858 claimed that eisteddfodau were turning chapels into theatres, 'where every kind of trash is acted, and the ministers perform the role of stage managers'.[68]

If people of taste were to be attracted to Dissent by Gothic chapels, choral singing, and organs, persons of intelligence were to be lured by an educated ministry. The connection between education and respectability was recognized by the *General Baptist Magazine* as early as 1798 when it argued that a denominational academy was necessary 'to remove the prejudices of mankind, to conciliate their esteem, [and] to render our preachers and our cause respectable'.[69] After the colleges at Homerton and Highbury amalgamated to form the New College in 1850 the Congregationalists had nine training colleges for ministers, the Particular Baptists four, the Unitarians, Wesleyans, and Calvinistic Methodists two each, and the General Baptists

---

[64] Teale, 'Methodism in Halifax', 130.

[65] Rose, *Methodism in Ashton-under-Lyne*, ii. 16, 60.

[66] Jones, *Sowing Beside all Waters*, 292; Bassett, *Welsh Baptists*, 268; Evans, 'Religion in the Swansea Valley', 409.

[67] *DNB*.   [68] Evans, 'Religion in the Swansea Valley', 414, 426.

[69] *General Baptist Magazine*, i (1798), 62.

one. By the mid-nineteenth century over 70 per cent of men entering the Congregational ministry and nearly half those entering the Wesleyan and Baptist ministries had been college trained.[70] In 1856 the Calvinistic Methodist Associations for both north and south Wales resolved that henceforward candidates for the ministry must pass examinations testing their 'abilities, knowledge, and ministerial experience before being presented for ordination', and the first examinations were held in 1859.[71] But if an educated ministry was needed to attract and retain intelligent congregations, it could also inhibit evangelism and alienate the ignorant and unsophisticated who had hitherto been the backbone of Evangelical Dissent. In 1852 the Congregationalist Dr Robert Ferguson warned the young William Booth against going to college since such institutions were doing 'nothing in reference to the salvation of souls'.[72] And some of the working-class correspondents to the *Nonconformist* in 1848 were of the opinion that too much education was opening up a gulf between ministers and the poorer members of their congregations. That gap was made worse by ministers' social pretensions. Ministers were increasingly designating themselves as 'Reverend', wearing gowns in the pulpit, and expecting higher salaries. The *Methodist Magazine* complained in 1815 that a preacher 'fills a respectable station in society; and he and his family are . . . expected to appear becoming in that station; but for this, his income, in general, will not afford him the means'.[73] A generation later the General Baptist minister John Gregory Pike was even blunter: poorer church members did not understand the 'extra calls and expenses' made on ministers occupying 'the middle sphere of life', and did not appreciate that people who moved in that sphere found £100 a year 'altogether inadequate'.[74] And that was in 1840, at the depths of the economic recession.

Well-educated ministers dressed in clerical black, wearing white cravats, calling themselves 'Reverend', preaching in large Gothic buildings at services dignified by organ voluntaries and choral anthems, simply did not have the same appeal to working-class audiences as did carpenters and shoemakers preaching in local dialects on village greens or in converted barns to the accompaniment of the singing of hymns set to popular tunes. As the energies of church members were increasingly devoted to building chapels and raising money for ministers' salaries so their enthusiasm for evangelism declined, and

[70] Brown, *Nonconformist Ministry*, 60.
[71] D. E. Jenkins, *Calvinistic Methodist Holy Orders* (Caernarfon, 1911), 233–6.
[72] Booth-Tucker, *Catherine Booth*, i. 75.   [73] *Methodist Magazine*, 38 (1815), 779.
[74] J. G. Pike, 'Christian Exertion: Letter to the Churches', in *General Baptist Minutes* (1840), 39. I owe this reference to Frank Rinaldi.

as ministers became increasingly dependent on well-filled chapels for their stipends so they became reluctant to engage in the itinerant evangelism which had been one of the most fruitful means of Nonconformist expansion.[75] This was as true of Wesleyan preachers whose very *raison d'être* was itinerancy as it was of Baptist or Congregational ministers. As early as 1819 William Myles was arguing that the tendency of Wesleyan preachers to 'live in great towns such as Hull, York, Sheffield, and Leeds' was the reason why Primitive Methodists were increasing in the countryside, and in the 1820s local preachers were complaining that Wesleyan ministers monopolized the pulpits of large urban chapels, leaving small rural chapels to laymen.[76] The justice of that complaint has been fully substantiated by John Vickers's analysis of Wesleyan preaching plans, and indeed Vickers concludes that by the 1820s it was the local preachers in Wesleyan Methodism who had become the true itinerant preachers, preaching in the open air and starting new rural causes, while the supposed full-time itinerants were confining their ministries to established urban congregations.[77] It was significant that Robert Twinem, a steward of the Pitt Street circuit in Liverpool, should complain to Jabez Bunting in 1846 that members of the society had taken to preaching in the open air; it was even more significant that he added that he had never known 'of volunteers required in this way before' in his membership of more than twenty years.[78] The same ignorance of the way in which Nonconformity had spread in the first place was shown by the Congregational minister Richard Knill who in 1849 advocated village preaching to the Cheshire Congregational Union as though it was something of which he had just thought.[79] Even Jabez Bunting, who in 1829 had said that the proper function of Wesleyan ministers was to be pastors and teachers, not evangelists, had by 1841 come to the opinion that 'fewer chapels and more horses would save more souls'. 'We should preach in barns, the cottages of the poor, and out of doors.'[80]

In Wales the itinerant system was brought into disrepute by the ease with which supposedly dubious characters could become preachers for the sake of the 6*d.* they were paid for each sermon. The Baptist Christmas Evans complained that 'almost any man with strong lungs and a feeble intellect' could become an itinerant preacher, and that the growth in their numbers 'threat-

[75] Lovegrove, *Established Church, Sectarian People*, 155–7.
[76] Ward, *Religion and Society*, 99; Currie, *Methodism Divided*, 52–3.
[77] J. Vickers, 'Methodism and Society in Central Southern England, 1740–1851', Ph.D. thesis (Southampton, 1987), 159–60, 173.
[78] Gowland, 'Methodist Secessions', Ph.D. thesis, 482.
[79] Gilbert, *Religion and Society*, 160.
[80] Gregory, *Side Lights on the Conflicts of Methodism*, 83, 315.

ened to become a worse calamity than any of the plagues of Egypt'.[81] The Baptist Associations of south-west Wales (in 1817), Glamorgan, and Monmouthshire (1832) all tried to control the activities of itinerants by insisting that they had the approval either of their own churches or of the Association or of both.[82] The itinerant system survived longest among the Calvinistic Methodists and in the first half of the nineteenth century their preachers retained their secular occupations and were ordained to serve the whole denomination, not a particular society. But an exception was made for Henry Rees, who in 1836 accepted the pastoral charge of three congregations of exiled Welshmen in Liverpool and a salary to go with it, and the Liverpool example was followed by Calvinistic Methodist societies in Wales in the 1850s.[83]

The rise of respectability and the decline of itinerancy were accompanied by the neglect of many of the other means by which Nonconformity had attracted working-class people in the earlier, less inhibited, years of the century. By the mid-nineteenth century love-feasts in many Wesleyan chapels were being held on an annual rather than on a half-yearly or quarterly basis.[84] Similarly among Primitive Methodists there were 'loud complaints from the societies' in 1835 that camp-meetings were deteriorating and by the 1850s village societies were holding only one a year.[85] For Baptists open-air baptisms in rivers and ponds were just as much a means of witnessing to the outside world as were camp-meetings among the Ranters, but, as William Steadman had said of the Bradford Baptists early in the century, the custom of baptizing converts in muddy streams kept away persons of 'more genteel or delicate feelings'.[86] Consequently from the 1840s it was increasingly usual for new Baptist chapels to be built with indoor baptistries and for existing buildings to be altered to contain them.[87] Other victims of the cult of respectability were those female preachers who had held such an attraction for male audiences. Women preachers provoked controversy among the Primitive Methodists as they had among the Wesleyans whose Conference had banned them in 1803. When Ann Carr, Martha Williams, and Sarah Healand (the first two former Wesleyans) were appointed preachers in the Leeds Primitive Methodist circuit in 1821 they refused to accept the constraints of the circuit

---

[81] Evans, *Christmas Evans*, 137, 139–40.   [82] Bassett, *Welsh Baptists*, 194.

[83] A. M. Davies, *Life and Letters of Henry Rees* (Bangor, 1904), 75; Price, *Penuel Calvinistic Methodist Church, Ebbw Vale*, 54.

[84] Baker, *Methodism and the Love-Feast*, 41–2.

[85] Kendall, *Primitive Methodist Church*, i. 197; Obelkevich, *Religion and Rural Society*, 227.

[86] Jowitt, 'The Pattern of Religion in Victorian Bradford', in Wright and Jowitt, *Victorian Bradford*, 38.

[87] Harrison, 'Baptists of Nottinghamshire', i. 368.

plan, insisted on preaching in places to which male preachers had been appointed, and seceded in 1822 to form the sect of Female Revivalists.[88] Thereafter the number of women preachers declined, and the last female Primitive Methodist preacher, Elizabeth Bultitude, retired in 1862.[89] Similarly among the Bible Christians women preachers, who constituted a quarter of all travelling preachers in 1829, had by 1872 dwindled to one.[90]

The Nonconformist preoccupation with respectability was responsible for a steady trickle of secessions out of the established Dissenting denominations and into the newest denomination of all, the Brethren. The movement initially took its name from a church established in Plymouth in 1831 by a group of evangelical Anglicans disillusioned with the established church. Many of the criticisms levelled by the Brethren against the Church of England were a repetition of the arguments of the founding fathers of Dissent: 'a church consists not in rites and ceremonials, but "where two or three are gathered together in His Name, there He is in the midst of them" '.[91] But the Brethren also rejected the existing Dissenting denominations on account of their worldliness, their lack of spirituality, and their political activism. In 1848 the movement was torn apart by a bitter dispute between two of its leaders, the former Anglican clergymen Benjamin Newton and John Nelson Darby. The quarrel was provoked by Newton's teaching that Christ's sufferings were a necessary consequence of his identification with the human condition, a theory which his opponents claimed could undermine the doctrine of the atonement.[92] The vitriol exchanged in the dispute exceeded anything that disgraced the controversies of mainstream Dissenters: Newton's teaching, said Darby, was received 'by direct inspiration from Satan'.[93] And the rift led to the permanent division of the movement between the exclusive and the independent Brethren. But initially the Brethren appeared to offer a more spiritual haven to Nonconformists disillusioned with the respectability of Dissent. The movement attracted a number of former Quakers, including the distinguished chemist Luke Howard, the Congregationalist William Henry Dorman, and the Wesleyan Philip Gosse.

In 1835 Dorman had become minister of Islington chapel which was in the process of moving from Calvinistic Methodism to Congregationalism and which had used the Anglican liturgy until 1830.[94] However, the process of transformation was not happening fast enough for Dorman, who objected to the fact that the chapel's trust deed placed all 'power and responsibility in the

---

[88] Dews, *From Mow Cop to Peake*. 21–4.
[89] Kendall, *Primitive Methodist Church*, ii. 216.   [90] Shaw, *The Bible Christians*, 30, 42.
[91] F. R. Coad, *A History of the Brethren Movement* (1968), 65.   [92] Ibid. 147.
[93] Ibid. 160.   [94] L. D. Dixon, *Seven Score Years and Ten* (1938), 19–20.

hands of three managers' instead of deacons. In other ways, too, Dorman believed that the practice of Islington chapel departed from 'gospel simplicity'.

The organ, the graduated desks,—from the clerk's upward to the pulpit—the brass trellis-work, to separate the poor from the rich; the gates at the end of the aisles, effectively to shut out those who could not pay for a seat, and, above all, the fact that the floor of the chapel is made six inches lower in the compartment appropriated to the poor (which has the effect . . . of marking more effectually the distinction), and that at the greatest distance from the pulpit.

Dorman objected to the system of pew-rents, 'for which I see no more countenance in the New Testament than for tithes'; he complained of the influence wielded by wealthy members in chapels, so that on one occasion a minister was warned that if one of their number were subjected to discipline thirty subscriptions would be withdrawn; and he criticized 'the political spirit into which the Dissenters . . . have so grievously fallen, and which is so entirely opposed to the spirit of discipleship of Christ'. Dorman left the Independents for the Brethren in 1838, complaining that 'a Dissenting minister is honoured by his brethren much more in proportion to the strength of his intellect . . . and the respectability of his congregation, and the amount of subscriptions raised by his flock for the religious and benevolent institutions of the day, than for his devotion to the cause of the Lord'.[95] The respectability of Wesleyanism similarly helped to drive the naturalist Philip Gosse into the arms of the Brethren. When, after eleven years in North America, he returned to England in 1849 with the intention of becoming a Wesleyan minister he was distressed to discover the contrast between the Methodism of Alabama and the Methodism of Liverpool. 'The large and fine Wesleyan chapels of Liverpool, the fashionable attire of the audiences, and the studied refinement of the discourses' were 'thoroughly out of keeping with my own fresh and ardent feelings'.[96]

The developments against which Gosse protested were the culmination of changes that had been taking place in Wesleyanism since the first decade of the century. For forty years the onward march of respectability among the Wesleyans had met with vigorous though mainly localized resistance. The uninhibited revivalism of the Ranters and Bible Christians, Zachariah Taft's spirited defence of women preachers, the Leeds protest against the Brunswick chapel's organ, the rebellion against Bunting's theological institution, were all part of the opposition to the process whereby the exuberance

---

[95] W. H. Dorman, *Reasons for Retiring from the Independent or Congregational Body and from Islington Chapel* (1862), 73, 81, 85, 88, 99.
[96] E. Gosse, *Life of Philip Henry Gosse* (1890), 153.

and excitement of the great age of expansion were giving place to 'showy chapels, pealing organs, and other formal appendages'.[97] For forty years repeated but limited secessions had drained off the enthusiasts and the malcontents from the Wesleyan Connexion without impairing either the continuing expansion of its numbers or the rising social aspirations of its ministers. But the very success of the Wesleyan hierarchy in containing the effects of the successive protest movements meant that there built up beneath the Connexion's surface calm a deep reservoir of men embittered by the leadership's political conservatism, ecclesiastical authoritarianism, and social snobbery. In 1849 the dam burst.

3. 'SPARKS ON A MAGAZINE OF GUNPOWDER': THE *FLY SHEETS*

The conflicts between the opposing tendencies in Wesleyanism, the respectable and the revivalist, the educated and the enthusiastic, the liturgical and the spontaneous, the conservative and the liberal, reached their deepest intensity in the 1840s. The extremes of wealth and poverty in the Connexion were emphasized by the decision of Conference to set up a fund in 1839, at the depths of the economic recession, to celebrate the centenary of the founding of the first Wesleyan society. The fund was to be used for the building of a permanent home for the Connexion's theological institution, Bunting's threatened dominance of which had provoked the Warrenite secession in 1835, and for a new headquarters for the Wesleyan Missionary Society, and thus for its senior secretary, Jabez Bunting. At a meeting held to launch the fund in Manchester in November 1838 a wealthy widow named Mrs Bealey promised a thousand guineas and 'others instantly caught her spirit and resolved to follow her example': ten more people offered £1,000 each, another fifteen promised £500 each, and within a fortnight £45,000 had been raised.[98] The fund eventually totalled £216,184, of which £8,438 came from Wesleyanism's wealthiest circuit, Grosvenor Street, Manchester.[99] But the majority of the members of Grosvenor Street remained people in humble circumstance—when the circuit was divided in 1846 the average contribution to circuit funds was only 2s. 9¼d.[100]—and there is evidence that poor

[97] Currie, *Methodism Divided*, 78.
[98] Jackson, *Recollection of My Life and Times*, 294; Smith, *History of Wesleyan Methodism*, iii. 369–70.
[99] Huddlestone, *History of Grosvenor Street*, 33.   [100] Ibid. 30.

Wesleyans resented their leaders' lavish expenditure on connexional headquarters and colleges. Local preachers criticized the fact that no money was
set aside for 'distressed or destitute local preachers' and to emphasize the
point the Wesleyan Methodist Association in Halifax started a fund for
needy local preachers.[101] To one anonymous Methodist the missionary society's Centenary Hall was further evidence that the Connexion's respectability was an affront to the Gospel. 'Is not this Hall a temple erected to
Mammon?' he asked in 1846. 'The mahogany, the mirrors, the carpets, the
curtains, with other costly decorations, are they not offerings made to the god
of this world?'[102] The Wesleyan hierarchy's extravagance was made the more
scandalous, in the eyes of its critics, by the discovery that the cellars of the
Centenary Hall were hired out to two wine merchants to store their wares.[103]
Methodist teetotallers were further affronted by the decision of Conference,
in 1841, to insist, on Bunting's initiative, on the use of fermented wine in the
Lord's Supper and on the banning of teetotal meetings from Wesleyan
chapels.[104] The ban was widely resented, often ignored, and led to the secession of 858 members from the St Ives circuit in Cornwall. They formed themselves into the Teetotal Methodist Connexion and subsequently joined the
Wesleyan Methodist Association.[105]

What did most damage to Wesleyan Methodism in the 1840s, though, was
not its leaders' extravagance nor their opposition to teetotalism, it was their
hostility to the revivalist missions of the Irish-born American evangelist
James Caughey. After a successful campaign in Dublin in 1841 Caughey
obtained permission from the American Methodist Episcopal Church to
conduct an itinerant mission in England and between 1842 and 1847 he led a
series of revivalist meetings in some of the major industrial towns of northern
England and the Midlands. Caughey was a tall, imposing man with dark eyes
and a melodious voice, but the secret of his success lay in the uninhibited
manner in which he warned those that did not respond to his message that
they would spend eternity in the fiery furnace of hell. 'This year thou shalt
die' was one of his favourite texts. Throughout his meetings Caughey built up
the psychological pressure on those who feared they were damned until they
were invited to find release from tension, and salvation from their sins, by
coming forward to the communion rail while the rest of the congregation was
singing hymns. As in the case of Bramwell half a century earlier, one can
trace the impact of Caughey by the way in which Wesleyan membership

---

[101] Chapman, *John Wesley and Co.*, 70–1.   [102] Currie, *Methodism Divided*, 79.
[103] *Wesleyan*, 29 Oct. 1845, 704.
[104] Gregory, *Side Lights on the Conflicts of Methodism*, 318.
[105] Shaw, *Cornish Methodism*, 80.

increased in the towns through which he passed. Wesleyan membership rose by 529 in Leeds in 1843–4; by 935 in Hull in 1843–5; by 864 in Sheffield in 1844–5; by 546 in Huddersfield in 1844–6; and by 523 in Birmingham in 1845–7. After six years in the British Isles it was claimed that Caughey had effected the conversions of 21,625 people, while another 9,222 had experienced 'entire sanctification'. His converts shared the same characteristics as the sample of Nonconformist converts analysed in Chapter I: nearly all had had a religious upbringing and most of them were between the ages of sixteen and thirty.[106]

Not all Wesleyans, however, were grateful for the boost which Caughey gave to their membership figures in the mid-1840s. There was much discussion at the Conferences of 1843 and 1844 as to the propriety of inviting Caughey to preach in Methodist chapels, and on the latter occasion Bunting gave his opinion that the 'brethren who have given up their pulpits to Mr Caughey have been guilty of a great violation of godly discipline'.[107] Benjamin Gregory accused Caughey of employing 'the unworthy trickery of decoy penitents' whereby people who were already converted rose from their seats and moved towards the communion rail in order to encourage others to do likewise.[108] At the Conference of 1846 Caughey's methods were subjected to a good deal of criticism. Robert Newton, chairman of the Manchester District, regarded him as a charlatan. Caughey claimed to have been praying on his knees for hours between services when people knew that for most of the time he had been engaged in conversation. He acquired information about people in his congregation before the service and then revealed that information from the pulpit as if 'learnt by supernatural intuition'. Bunting proposed that a letter be sent to the Methodist bishops in America requesting Caughey's recall and the resolution was carried 'amidst much clamour' with 'many objecting'.[109] Despite a subsequent resolution that no Wesleyan superintendent should henceforward employ Caughey, he continued to preach both in Wesleyan circuits in Huddersfield, Nottingham, and York, and in Primitive Methodist, New Connexion, and Wesleyan Methodist Association pulpits, and returned to America in the summer of 1847.[110] But the Conference's hostility to Caughey was deeply resented by a substantial number of Wesleyans. Robert Newton stated that 'even in the Warrenite dissensions he had not experienced such unpopularity, such odium, and such vituperation as he had to face from Mr Caughey's partisans'.[111] John Haswell,

---

[106] Carwardine, *Transatlantic Revivalism*, 109–24; *HMC* ii. 235.
[107] Gregory, *Side Lights on the Conflicts of Methodism*, 344, 368–9.   [108] Ibid. 345.
[109] Ibid. 400–1.   [110] Ibid. 412; Carwardine, *Transatlantic Revivalism*, 130–1.
[111] Gregory, *Side Lights on the Conflicts of Methodism*, 402.

superintendent in the Exeter circuit, pointed out that had it not been for Caughey and the rise in membership of 2,199 in the four districts in which he had campaigned, the Connexion's modest increase in membership in 1846–7 would have been a decrease.[112] And one of Caughey's supporters castigated the Wesleyan leadership's attitude to the American evangelist as, 'in effect, one of distinct opposition to revivals of religion and the salvation of souls'.[113]

To those Wesleyans for whom Caughey was 'a messenger from God'[114] the Wesleyan Conference's decision to ban him from its pulpits was yet another example of the overweening influence which Bunting exercised over the Connexion. In the short run the controversy over the theological institution in 1834 and the formation of the Wesleyan Methodist Association in 1835 had strengthened Bunting's hold over his denomination. He was elected president of Conference for a third time in 1836, and at the Conference of 1837 his 'absence for a single session brought business to a standstill' and it had to adjourn until his return.[115] But not all of Bunting's critics had seceded with the Protestant Methodists in 1827 and the Warrenites in 1835. A vocal minority of ministers within the Wesleyan Conference continued to challenge Bunting's authoritarianism throughout the 1840s. They were led by Joseph Beaumont who came to be regarded by friends and enemies alike as 'the leader of the opposition in the Conference'.[116]

Beaumont's antipathy to Bunting derived both from the latter's opposition to teetotalism and revivalism and from his one-sided interpretation of the 'no politics' rule. As a doctor of medicine and brother of the temperance pioneer Dr Thomas Beaumont, Joseph Beaumont used his knowledge of the effects of alcohol to support the cause of total abstinence, and he opposed Conference's attempt in 1841 to ban the use of Wesleyan chapels for teetotal meetings.[117] As a man who did not believe that Methodism should be 'tacked on to the established church', Beaumont protested against Bunting's action in trying to silence Wesleyan Liberals while retaining his own freedom to support Tory candidates: in 1847 he objected to the suspension of Conference business to allow the admission to Conference of the recently elected Conservative MP for Stockport, the wealthy Wesleyan merchant James Heald.[118] And as minister in the two Liverpool circuits (south 1839–42, north 1842–5), Beaumont resisted the rising tide of Wesleyan respectability by

---

[112] Ward, *Early Victorian Methodism*, 342.

[113] Carwardine, *Transatlantic Revivalism*, 131.

[114] Ward, *Early Victorian Methodism*, 342.

[115] Gregory, *Side Lights on the Conflicts of Methodism*, 214–15, 251.   [116] Ibid. 448.

[117] Gowland, 'Methodist Secessions', Ph.D. thesis, 503; Gregory, *Side Lights on the Conflicts of Methodism*, 318.

[118] Gregory, *Side Lights on the Conflicts of Methodism*, 161, 166, 265, 415.

opposing hired singers, chanting, and liturgies, and by supporting James Caughey who was invited to conduct campaigns in the town in 1843 and 1845.[119] The personal animosity between Beaumont and Bunting was evident at the 1842 Conference when Bunting, after suggesting that Beaumont should become the new bishop of New Zealand, revealed that he had once offered himself as a missionary for service in India. Beaumont retorted sarcastically that those who had turned Bunting down 'incurred a very grave responsibility'.[120]

Beaumont's hostility to the Wesleyan leadership was open and avowed. Far more serious for Bunting, because they were anonymous, were the papers launched against him in five successive editions between 1844 and 1849 and circulated to all Wesleyan ministers: the *Fly Sheets*. The burden of Bunting's unknown assailant was that his 'whole system of government has been opposed to the advice and practice of Mr Wesley'. Bunting was criticized for neglecting his work as a Methodist minister by basing himself in London; he was accused of 'flagrant injustice' to itinerant preachers by living a life of 'fleshy ease and sloth' in the capital while they were 'compelled to be out in all weathers'; he was criticized for encouraging Conference to exclude evangelists such as Caughey from its pulpits, men who 'in a couple of years have formed more new classes' than Bunting had throughout his whole career; and he was accused of stifling free discussion in Conference and of packing the connexional committees with his cronies, in particular the stationing committee, 'the slaughter house of ministerial character'. Finally, claimed the author of the *Fly Sheets*, Bunting was guilty both of financial extravagance and of political prejudice. He had allowed '£40,000 to be abstracted from the Centenary Fund for a couple of spirit cellars, a large room, and two rooms each for himself and his colleagues', and he had used another £800 from the fund 'to preserve the *Watchman* from sinking', a Tory paper 'raised to support the interests of a Church and State party'.[121]

No one ever claimed responsibility for the authorship of the *Fly Sheets* but they were widely assumed to be the work of James Everett, who at the time of the publication of the first number had been a Wesleyan preacher for thirty-seven of his sixty years. In some ways James Everett, like Samuel Warren, was an unlikely rebel. A bibliophile, poet, biographer of Adam Clarke and Samuel Hick, and collector of antiquities, Everett was devoted to the memory of John Wesley and had built up a considerable collection of Wesleyana. For

[119] Ibid. 368; Sellers, 'Liverpool Nonconformity', 169.

[120] Gregory, *Side Lights on the Conflicts of Methodism*, 322.

[121] *All the numbers of the 'Fly Sheets' now first reprinted in one pamphlet* (Birmingham, 1849), 1–2, 6–7, 28, 53.

much of his life Everett suffered from bronchitis and he gave his illness as a reason for retiring from the itineracy in 1821 and again in 1842. But after both breaks in his itinerant ministry he continued to preach as a supernumerary and indeed claimed to have travelled a total of 320,000 miles in the course of his ministerial career.[122] This was by far the largest claim of any nineteenth-century preacher whose ministry was confined to the British Isles, a claim larger even than that of John Wesley, and opened Everett to the charge that although supposedly too ill to carry the burden of an ordinary itinerant preacher, he endured 'as a popular orator far more exposure and exertion than would be required by circuit work'.[123] For much of his career Everett was thus freed from the responsibilities of a full-time minister and had more opportunities than most Wesleyan ministers to spend time in his study and greater freedom than others to preach where and when he wished: more opportunity, indeed, to listen to the grievances of Wesleyans up and down the country, and more time to commit their complaints to paper. It was significant that as a tobacconist's assistant in Alnwick in the 1790s the young John Everett had sympathized with the French Revolution, and that as a prospective Wesleyan preacher in Sunderland in 1806 he had worked under William Bramwell and was deeply influenced by the latter's 'kindness, example, industry, influence, ministerial success, and unparalleled zeal'.[124] Bunting's Toryism and his antipathy to revivalism antagonized both Everett's liberalism and his faithfulness to the tradition of Bramwell.

Everett's first clash with Bunting had come around 1820 when he had written an article for the *Methodist Magazine* defending himself against an attack by an Anglican and Bunting had refused to publish it as being too critical of the establishment.[125] When Everett became a supernumerary for the first time in 1821 he opened a bookshop in Sheffield and wrote a *History of Methodism in Sheffield* with a view to preserving 'the simplicity' of Methodism's 'primitive times'.[126] He subsequently moved his bookselling business to Manchester and was obviously annoyed when, attending the 1834 Conference in London, he was pressurized by Bunting into returning to circuit work. He was given three weeks to move house and to entrust his business to a nephew in whose hands it failed four years later.[127] If Everett was the author of the *Fly Sheets*, the contrast he drew between the trials of itinerant preachers and the comforts enjoyed by Bunting and his colleagues comfortably settled in London was obviously rooted in the resentment he felt at being forced back into the circuit system despite his indifferent health and at the

---

[122] Chew, *James Everett*, 489.
[123] Gregory, *Side Lights on the Conflicts of Methodism*, 434.
[124] Chew, *Everett*, 27–8, 60–1.   [125] Ibid. 156.   [126] Ibid. 162.   [127] Ibid. 266–8.

cost of his carefully nurtured business. The resentment was felt all the more keenly because it was at that same Conference that it was proposed to establish a theological institution with Bunting as president and tutor, thus giving him, in Everett's words, 'a pretext for quietly settling down in London ... for the remainder of his life'.[128] Everett did not follow Samuel Warren and the Associationists in 1835, but he did write two anonymous works which were critical of Bunting, *The Disputants* in 1834 on the theological institution, and *Wesleyan Takings* in 1840 which questioned the wisdom of allowing any Methodist, apart from Wesley, 'to have such force of influence concentrated in himself'.[129] Both publications were followed by attempts by the Wesleyan leadership to discover their authorship, and on both occasions Everett was asked, and refused, to sign a declaration disowning the offending work. The fact that no disciplinary action other than a mild rebuke followed no doubt encouraged Everett to believe that he could attack Bunting with greater vehemence in the *Fly Sheets* and get away with it.[130] In this he was mistaken.

The Conference of 1847 resolved, on the motion of George Osborn, to deal with the *Fly Sheets* as Bunting's supporters had reacted to Everett's earlier anonymous attacks, by drawing up and circulating among Wesleyan ministers a declaration for their signature repudiating the alleged slanders and disowning knowledge of their publication.[131] But, in contrast to what had happened in 1834 and 1841, the pressure on ministers was unremitting and Everett was not allowed, as on the two previous occasions, to escape with evasive replies. When the first circulation of Osborn's declaration repudiating the *Fly Sheets* did not produce sufficient signatures in August 1847, the document was circulated again in October 1847 and for a third time in October 1848. By the summer of 1849 only thirty-six ministers had refused to sign the declaration and the Wesleyan leadership was determined to suppress the recalcitrant minority.[132] The high moral position assumed by the Wesleyan hierarchy in the face of the *Fly Sheets* was not, however, strengthened by the publication, in January 1849, of the first of the equally anonymous and equally scurrilous *Papers on Wesleyan Matters*, which tried to do to liberal Methodists what the *Fly Sheets* had done to Bunting and his supporters. Nor was the Bunting party's non-too-glowing reputation for impartiality strengthened by the decision of the Wesleyan Book Committee that the *Papers on Wesleyan Matters* should be offered for sale in the Methodist Book

[128] Ibid. 293.   [129] *Wesleyan Takings* (1840), 7.   [130] Chew, *Everett*, 290, 325–7.
[131] Gregory, *Side Lights on the Conflicts of Methodism*, 407.
[132] Chew, *Everett*, 366–8, 385.

Room.[133] The reformers were compared to Judas Iscariot who, 'whilst maturing his sad character as a traitor, yet remained with the disciples as long as he could', and they were accused of thinking that they could enjoy assurance of salvation while being 'full of envy, murder, debate, deceit, [and] malignity', 'which was Antinomianism in one of its vilest forms'.[134] The beleaguered liberal minority responded, also in January 1849, with two new publications, the weekly *Wesleyan Times*, to which Everett himself contributed, and the monthly *Wesley Banner*, edited by the Nottingham minister Samuel Dunn. Dunn protested against Osborn's declaration against the *Fly Sheets* being turned 'into a compulsory test', but it was to no avail.[135] Everett was summoned to appear before the Conference which met in Manchester in July 1849; he was asked whether he was the author of the *Fly Sheets*; and when he declined to answer he was expelled.

Had the Wesleyan Conference contented itself with the expulsion of Everett catastrophe might have been avoided, for there was scant sympathy for a man who had continually attacked his brethren under a cloak of anonymity. But the dominant party did not rest with punishing Everett, it seized the opportunity to root out all opposition from the Conference. George Osborn caused an uproar in the Conference by attributing the *Fly Sheets* to 'Dr Beaumont's party and friends' and went on to argue, 'amidst volleys of applause', that Methodism could no longer exist 'if the Conference be divided into two parties—a Government and an Opposition'.[136] And so Conference went on to condemn Samuel Dunn for editing the *Wesley Banner* and William Griffith, superintendent in the Ripley circuit, for reporting the proceedings of Conference for the *Wesleyan Times*. When Griffith pointed out that other ministers present were reporting for the *Watchman*, Bunting retorted that 'the *Watchman* is altogether conservative of Methodism, the *Wesleyan Times* is thoroughly hostile to it'. Dunn refused to give an undertaking to suspend the *Wesley Banner*, Griffiths refused to give a pledge to stop contributing to the *Wesleyan Times*, and both men were expelled alongside Everett.[137]

The expulsions of Everett, Dunn, and Griffith were followed by the most catastrophic of all the secessions suffered by the Wesleyans in the sixty years after the death of their founder. Between 1850 and 1852 the Wesleyan Methodist Connexion in England lost 75,529 members, 22.6 per cent of its total membership. In previous secessions the Wesleyans had either alienated

---

[133] Gregory, *Side Lights on the Conflicts of Methodism*, 437–42.
[134] *Papers on Wesleyan Matters* (1849), 1 Mar. 1849, 37; 1 May 1849, 71.
[135] Gregory, *Side Lights on the Conflicts of Methodism*, 450.   [136] Ibid. 448, 453.
[137] Ibid. 456, 458.

revivalists by attempting to restrain their activities by connexional discipline (the Independent Methodists, the Primitive Methodists, the Bible Christians), or had antagonized liberals by their authoritarian and clerically dominated government and by their pro-Tory political bias (the Methodist New Connexion, the Protestant Methodists, the Wesleyan Methodist Association). But in the 1840s the Wesleyan hierarchy managed to alienate both groups at one and the same time—the revivalists by their antipathy to James Caughey and the liberals by their attempts to silence criticism. As in the case of Samuel Warren in 1835, so in the case of James Everett in 1849, the expulsion of a prominent rebel was the occasion and not the cause of the disaster. The *Fly Sheets*, commented Everett's biographer, Richard Chew, 'fell like sparks on a magazine of gunpowder'.[138]

There was, as in 1827 and 1835, a political dimension to the dispute. In Derby the superintendent minister, William Clarkson, the man who had first urged disciplinary action against Samuel Dunn, referred to the Reformers as 'the radical party'; George Birley, superintendent in the Market Rasen circuit, condemned the Reformers as 'ecclesiastical Chartists'; William Griffith was a committed Liberal who was sympathetic towards Chartism and who had been election agent for the brewer Michael Bass when he was elected MP for Derby in a by-election in 1848; and Alderman Schofield, expelled by the Wesleyans in Sheffield for attending reform meetings, was an advocate of a wider suffrage.[139] But politics was only one of the issues at stake in 1849–50. Samuel Dunn denied that he had ever meddled in party politics or had even voted for a member of parliament, and his *Wesley Banner* was intended not only as a platform for criticizing the Wesleyan leadership, it was also a *Revival Record*.[140] The *Fly Sheets* controversy did far more damage to the Wesleyan Connexion than did the disputes over the Leeds organ or the theological institution just because the grievances it tapped went far deeper than complaints about the leadership's political bias or authoritarian rule. First and foremost, argued the *Wesleyan Times*, the reform agitation was a crusade to free Methodism 'from the hands of those parties who are seeking to make it respectable at the cost of its primitive character'.[141]

Everett, Dunn, and Griffith responded to their expulsions by touring the country to rally support, beginning with a packed meeting in Exeter Hall at the end of August, and in the next twelve months addressed an estimated

---

[138] Chew, *Everett*, 407.
[139] Ward, *Early Victorian Methodism*, 376–82, 413; Taylor, *Methodism and Politics*, 206; Greaves, 'Methodism in Yorkshire', 68.
[140] Wearmouth, *Methodism and Working-class Movements*, 191.
[141] Gowland, 'Methodist Secessions', Ph.D. thesis, 152.

167,430 people in 139 public meetings.[142] The three men claimed, like the Associationists in 1835, that they wanted the reform, not the disruption, of the Wesleyan Connexion. They were reluctant to found yet another Methodist denomination, and for seven years meetings of the Reformers' delegates were held at the same time and place as those of the Wesleyan Conference in the hope that the latter would heed the petitions of the former.[143] But the wounds inflicted by the *Fly Sheets* on the one hand and by the expulsions on the other went far too deep to be easily healed. When Thomas Jackson, president of the Wesleyan Conference in 1849, attempted to preach in the Langton Street chapel in Bristol to a congregation restricted to ticket-holders, supporters of the reform movement forced open the chapel doors, occupied the 'principal pews both in the gallery and on the ground floor', and for an hour prevented Jackson from conducting the service by shouting him down.[144] When Thomas Thomas of Pen-y-cae in Denbighshire tried to attend a class-meeting despite his having been expelled, his minister, William Rowlands, removed him by force and Thomas brought a charge of assault against him.[145] When at Carlton, near Nottingham, the Reformers tried to seize Sunday-school equipment and furniture the Wesleyans resisted them by force, and when five of the Reformers were put on trial for causing a riot their acquittal was greeted in court with the 'most extraordinary uproar of applause ... stamping, clapping, and shouting'. And when, in nearby Arnold, the bass viol player Thomas Parkinson left the Wesleyans for the Reformers and took the instrument with him, he was waylaid by three Wesleyans on his way home from chapel, was knocked down, and had the bass viol wrested from him.[146]

With their hopes of reforming the Wesleyan Connexion dashed, the Reformers turned to the dissenting Methodist denominations for support. An approach was made to the New Connexion, but the Reformers laid down as a condition of co-operation the independence of local church courts and the Kilhamites would contemplate union only on the basis of their own laws.[147] The Reformers' emphasis on local independence meant that in constitutional matters little divided them from the Wesleyan Methodist Association, but the Association's dominant personality, Robert Eckett, stood in the way. By the 1850s Eckett had achieved a position within the Association analogous to that of Bunting among the Wesleyans: Eckett supported the Wesleyan Conference's action in expelling Everett, Dunn, and

[142] Chew, *Everett*, 423, 431–3.   [143] *HMC* ii. 321–2; Currie, *Methodism Divided*, 223.
[144] Jackson, *Recollections of My Life and Times*, 339–40.
[145] Williams, *Welsh Wesleyan Methodism*, 268–9.   [146] Swift, *Lively People*, 93–4.
[147] Currie, *Methodism Divided*, 229.

Griffith; argued that the Association would have responded similarly to anonymous attacks on its ministers; and secured the secession or expulsion of those who disagreed with him.[148] Everett for his part thought no more highly of Eckett than he did of Bunting: the Association leader had 'an evil eye, a sinister look, [and] a brazen meretricious leer' he confided in his diary.[149] However, by 1854 the Wesleyan Reformers found that some of their supporters were slipping back to the old Connexion, they were in financial difficulties, and Eckett tried to soothe their fears by pointing out that the Association's central principle of circuit independence was close to the Reformers' demand for the independence of all local church courts.[150] Negotiations between the Reformers and the Association were opened and in 1857 the two bodies united to form the United Methodist Free Churches with Everett as president and Eckett as secretary.

The *Fly Sheets* controversy and the subsequent secessions were a disaster for Methodism in general and for Wesleyanism in particular. Resentment against the Wesleyan leadership which had festered for a generation erupted after 1849 and many of those who now seized the opportunity to harass the representatives of Conference were lost to Methodism for ever. In Norwich a circuit superintendent was denounced as 'the agent of the devil'; in Bramley a preacher was told he was 'too bad even for hanging'; in Ilkeston another was faced with men 'who squared their fists in my face in regular pugilistic style'.[151] Between 1850 and 1855 Wesleyan membership in England fell by 95,322, a loss of 28.5 per cent. But only half those lost joined the Wesleyan Reformers, who claimed a membership of only 46,609 in 1856. And less than half the Wesleyan Reformers—19,113—joined the United Methodist Free Churches in 1857, though more joined in subsequent years.[152] A substantial minority of Reformers initially refused to unite with the Association and constituted themselves into the Wesleyan Reform Union. The Wesleyan Reform Union was based in Sheffield where its congregations were almost entirely working class, but it subsequently suffered a loss of churches to the United Methodist Free Churches and its membership fell from just over 17,000 in 1859 to just over 12,000 in 1861.[153] A few thousand disillusioned Wesleyans no doubt joined the New Connexion, Primitive Methodists, and Bible Christians, but their modest gains in the 1850s in no way compensated for the huge Wesleyan losses or for the failure of the Wesleyan Reformers

---

[148] Ibid. 220–1, 226.   [149] Gowland, *Methodist Secessions*, 112.
[150] Currie, *Methodism Divided*, 223–4, 227–8.   [151] Ward, *Religion and Society*, 267–9.
[152] Ibid. 230.
[153] E. R. Wickham, *Church and People in an Industrial City* (1957), 130–1; W. H. Jones, *History of the Wesleyan Reform Union* (1952), 50–1.

and the United Methodist Free Churches to retain the loyalty of the majority of those who seceded from the parent Connexion. Total Methodist membership in England in 1857 was 46,000 down on that in 1850, a loss of 9.4 per cent.[154]

The *Fly Sheets* controversy was a personal tragedy for Jabez Bunting. The policies which he had advocated for half a century and of which he had been the personal embodiment for thirty of those fifty years had brought the Wesleyan Connexion to its most bitter controversy and to its most disastrous secession. At the time of the crucial Manchester Conference in 1849 Bunting was seventy years old, suffering like his opponent Everett from bronchitis, and like other former itinerants racked by rheumatism.[155] Deeply hurt by Everett's attacks, he offered to retire from the secretaryship of the missionary society in 1847 and again in 1848, but his offers to stand down were declined and he finally retired in 1851.[156] When he died in 1858, at the age of seventy-nine, the Wesleyans had fewer members per head of the adult population than when he had first been elected secretary of the Conference over forty years before.[157]

4. PATERNALISM AND PHILANTHROPY: SOCIAL CONTROL OR SOCIAL HARMONY?

The arrogance of the overweening Bunting, the cowardice of the anonymous Everett, the fickleness of the poacher-turned-gamekeeper Robert Eckett, all raise the question of whether the behaviour of these Methodist politicians was any better than that of the secular politicians of their age, of whether Palmerston was ever as domineering, Disraeli ever as caustic, or Peel ever as changeable as these three, of whether in fact the public conduct of leading Methodists provided any evidence that they were regenerate men, born again, and set apart from others. And did the violence which followed the expulsions of 1849, the conflicts for control of chapels, Sunday schools, and bass viols, suggest that the contenders were any different from men who

---

[154] Currie, Gilbert, and Horsley, *Churches and Churchgoers*, 141. I have added the Wesleyan Reform Union membership figure for 1859 to those of the other Methodist denominations for 1857.

[155] Bunting and Rowe, *Life of Jabez Bunting*, 705.

[156] Gregory, *Side Lights on the Conflicts of Methodism*, 410, 423; Bunting and Rowe, *Life of Jabez Bunting*, 718.

[157] Currie, Gilbert, and Horsley, *Churches and Churchgoers*, 65.

protested against workhouses, clamoured for the Charter, and engaged in picketing?

Certainly one of the reasons advanced by correspondents to the *Nonconformist* in the winter of 1848–9 for the alienation of working men from places of worship was the fact that Dissenting employers were no better, and often worse, than employers who had no deep religious convictions. A Cambridge shoemaker wrote that working men complained that religious bosses were 'grasping, selfish, and niggardly', and that 'men of the world' were 'often the best employers'.[158] A Bristol man observed that if an 'unemployed mechanic' asked the official of a local chapel for a job he was met 'with a cold repulsive reply' from a man who sometimes preached from the pulpit and eloquently prayed that 'men may be converted'.[159] And a correspondent from London, who stated that he had been a working man until very recently but now employed 'one or two hands', attributed the absence of working men from chapels to the antagonism between masters and men. He described how he had once visited a chapel only to find his master in the congregation, 'a man of wealth', a deacon of the church, and 'a large donor to most religious societies'. Yet this was the same man who 'injured me and my fellow workmen every day of the week', and his employer's presence in the chapel 'spoiled the service' for him. The former workman had no wish to frequent the same chapel as his master, and he 'certainly would never join the same church'.[160]

Such complaints lend credence to the argument of Edward Thompson and his followers that religion in the first half of the nineteenth century was a weapon used by industrialists to discipline their workforce. Thompson, himself the son of a Methodist minister and a product of Kingswood school, elaborates Weber's emphasis on the 'interpenetration of the capitalist mode of production and the Puritan ethic'. Not only does Thompson argue that Methodism's 'elevation of the values of discipline and of order' were 'exceptionally well-adapted' to the needs of manufacturers, foremen, and overlookers, but he maintains that the Methodist emphasis on discipline was even more important in providing factory workers with the 'inner compulsion' to accept the constraints of the factory system, the rhythms of its machinery, and the tyranny of the factory clock.[161] The result was to cut off a substantial section of the working class from their freer, more alcoholic, more rumbustious, more spontaneous heritage and to subject them to the rule of the Methodist class-meeting and the factory foreman. In so doing, claims

---

[158] *Nonconformist*, 27 Dec. 1848, 991.   [159] Ibid. 20 Dec. 1848, 967.
[160] Ibid. 31 Jan. 1849, 83.   [161] Thompson, *Making of the English Working Class*, 390–8.

Thompson, 'Methodism condemned working people to a kind of moral civil war'.[162]

Thompson's accusations have been repeated and developed by others. Paul Stigant cites John Wesley as evidence that Methodists saw a connection between industrialization and an increase in 'swearing, drunkenness, Sabbath-breaking, and all manner of wickedness', and he argues that in consequence Wesleyan preachers supported industrial work discipline as helping 'to impose "habits of order" upon the poor'.[163] A. P. Donajgrodzki, in an influential book, claims that 'the church was a crucial agency of social control' and asserts that Nonconformist ministers and Roman Catholic priests, as well as Anglican clergy, 'explained and often justified the existence of poverty and inequality in society, preached the merits of due subordination, discerned a divine basis for wealth and authority in society, and asserted its harmonious nature'.[164] And Philip McCann maintains that even the charitable work undertaken by the 'Evangelical and Dissenting upper and middle class' had as its objective the control of 'the populace in the interests of social and economic stability'.[165]

There is no doubt that Methodists in particular tried to inculcate in their followers respect for the country's rulers and that Methodists and Dissenters alike sought to instil into servants obedience to their masters. The Particular Baptist Samuel Pearce argued in 1797 that in the Bible 'the servant is taught diligence, submission, cheerful obedience, an inviolable fidelity to his master; and should he ever become a master himself, to deal kindly and justly by those who serve him'.[166] A Wesleyan Sunday school catechism of 1810 taught that servants should be 'subject to [their] masters with all fear'.[167] And the *Scripture Lessons for Schools* which the Quaker William Allen drew up for the British and Foreign School Society in 1820 contained biblical passages emphasizing 'the duties of subjects to government' and 'the duties of servants to masters'.[168] But such injunctions were impressed on children because they were in the Bible, not because Evangelical Nonconformists had a special mission to discipline the industrial workforce. The very terms 'master' and 'servant' were taken from the King James's version of the Bible and were more appropriate to the personal relationships of the household and the workshop

---

[162] Ibid. 50.
[163] *Wesley's Journal*, v. 454; Stigant, 'Methodism and the Working Class', 180.
[164] A. P. Donajgrodzki (ed.), *Social Control in Ninteenth Century Britain* (1977), 16–17.
[165] P. McCann (ed.), *Popular Education and Socialization in the Nineteenth Century* (1977), 2.
[166] Robison, 'Particular Baptists', 195.
[167] Stigant, 'Methodism and the Working Class', 187.
[168] J. M. Goldstrom, 'The Content of Education and Socialization of the Working Class Child', in McCann, *Education and Socialization*, 96.

than to the conditions of the industrial factory. When Edward Thompson criticizes Evangelicals for teaching their followers the importance of 'redeeming the time' he similarly fails to appreciate that their purpose was entirely spiritual and had nothing to do with obedience to the foreman's watch.[169] The exhortation 'to improve each shining hour' was far more likely to lead working men on the path of self-education rather than that of self-abasement. Employers had at their disposal weapons such as fines, stoppages from pay, and ultimately dismissal which were far more effective in disciplining their workforce than were Sunday school catechisms. And contemporaries often observed that factory workers led more disciplined lives than independent artisans simply because their working hours were regulated for them.[170]

There is in fact much more evidence of mill-owners using their position as employers to make their workers religious than there is of churches using their religious teaching to make workers subservient to their bosses. Many Dissenting employers and managers tried to compel their workers to attend a place of worship. In the 1830s Morgan Thomas, agent to the Llanarth family and deacon of the Babell Calvinistic Methodist chapel at Ynysddu, Monmouthshire, was reluctant to give work to men who would not give an undertaking to attend his chapel.[171] It was said of James Howard, principal partner in the family firm which owned three cloth mills in Dursley, Gloucestershire, and member of the town's Congregational Tabernacle, that he insisted that his workmen attend a place of worship and that children in his employ went to Sunday school regularly.[172] The Quaker Henry Ashworth similarly insisted that his employees attended 'on Sabbath days, either at a place of worship or Sunday school'.[173] The Wesleyan Jonas Sugden, owner of a worsted mill at Bingley in the West Riding, had a notice at the entrance to his mill informing workers that they were expected to attend 'some place of divine worship every Lord's day'.[174] And both at Chipping Norton in Oxfordshire and at Mere in Wiltshire Anglican incumbents accused Dissenting manufacturers of using their positions as employers to influence the religious allegiance of their workpeople.[175]

[169] E. Thompson, 'Time, Work-discipline, and Industrial Capitalism', *Past and Present*, 38 (1967), 87–8, 95.

[170] R. D. Storch, 'The Problem of Working-class Leisure', in Donajgrodzki, *Social Control*, 140, 146–7.

[171] Turner, 'Revivals and Popular Religion', 313.   [172] Evans, *As Mad as a Hatter!*, 130.

[173] Boyson, *Ashworth Cotton Enterprise*, 95.

[174] R. Spence Hardy, *Commerce and Christianity: Memorials of Jonas Sugden* (1858), 94.

[175] P. Horn, *The Rural World, 1780–1850* (1980) 157; P. T. Phillips, 'Religion and Society in the Cloth Region of Wiltshire', *Journal of Religious History* (1980), 100–1.

How much of this pressure on employees to attend a place of worship was due to a desire to secure a docile workforce, how much of it was due to a wish to strengthen the employer's chapel or political party, and how much of it was due to a sincere concern for the salvation of the workers' souls, it is impossible to say. The attitude of some employers was comparable to that of those landlords who expected obedience from their subordinates in matters of both politics and religion. In Oldham in 1852 a trade union leader accused Nonconformist employers of using the same tactics that Anglican landlords in Merioneth were to use seven years later: of sacking nearly fifty workers who 'would not vote for their candidate in the municipal elections'.[176] Many, but by no means all, employers in the early nineteenth century believed that it was in their interests to have a thrifty, sober, and religious workforce,[177] and numerous businessmen contributed to the building of places of worship. The Unitarian mill-owner Jedediah Strutt helped the Primitive Methodists to build a chapel at Belper in 1817 because, in the words of William Clowes, he had noticed the 'decided change wrought by our instrumentality in many of his work-people'.[178] Josiah John Guest was reputed to have contributed to the building of every Nonconformist chapel in Merthyr Tydfil, though he himself had deserted Wesleyanism for the Church of England. And both the Bethania Independent chapel in Aberdare and the Blaenycwm Baptist chapel in the Rhondda received generous donations from local colliery owners.[179]

There is some evidence that employer confidence in the moderating influence of religion was not entirely misplaced for Nonconformists among early trade unionists could on occasion be less militant than other men. In the autumn of 1833 an attempt by Robert Owen to influence the National Union of Operative Potters provoked the hostility of Methodist trade unionists and threatened to split the union. 'The warehousemen as a body refused to pay any more subscriptions until they were assured that no union money was to be used for the furtherance of Owenite schemes', and a short-lived attempt to set up a co-operative for the manufacture of pottery went ahead only after it was made clear that it would be kept entirely separate from the potters' union.[180] A strike of colliers in the Black Country in 1842 came to an end when

[176] J. Foster, *Class Struggle and the Industrial Revolution* (1974), 180–1.

[177] W. E. Lambert gives examples of employers who made no effort to restrict their workers' drinking habits ('Drink and Work-discipline in Industrial South Wales', *Welsh History Review*, 7 (1974–5), 297, 304–5).

[178] Werner, *Primitive Methodist Connexion*, 80.

[179] Turner, 'Revivals and Popular Religion', 157, 203–4.

[180] W. H. Warburton, *The History of Trade Union Organisation in the North Staffordshire Potteries* (1931), 71–6.

a mass meeting of colliers on Swan Field, West Bromwich, repudiated Chartist influence and elected twenty deputies, led by a Methodist local preacher named Shelton, to negotiate with the employers. Shelton told Lord Dartmouth, the chief colliery-owner, that the men's main grievances were ill-treatment at the hands of the butties, having to work three-quarters of a day for only half-a-day's pay, and the continuance of the truck system. The employers listened sympathetically to the men's complaints, the colliers went back to work, and they subsequently passed resolutions denouncing Chartism.[181]

If Nonconformity had a moderating influence on trade unionism, did it similarly have a liberalizing influence on management? What evidence there is suggests that the majority of Dissenting employers were firm but fair, strict disciplinarians but careful of their workers' welfare. However, the historical record is inevitably biased in favour of the more celebrated and successful businesses whose owners could afford to be generous and whose good works have been recorded for posterity. There is less evidence of struggling employers who may have had a greater temptation to get every ounce of work out of their workforce. While the supposedly bad Dissenting employers remained anonymous when their misdeeds were catalogued in the columns of the *Nonconformist* in 1848–9, many of the good employers had their virtues trumpeted in numerous contemporary hagiographies. None the less, surprisingly few Nonconformist employers appear to have been criticized by name for lack of consideration to their workpeople. The Wesleyan James Fernley, a Manchester cotton manufacturer, was criticized by the *Poor Man's Guardian* for forcing his employees to work at night and his mill was singled out for attack during the Plug Plot of 1842.[182] The Salford factory of the Congregationalist Elkanah Armitage was hit by a bitter seven months' strike in 1850–1, and mass demonstrations were held against Armitage's refusal to recognize trade unions.[183] And the Methodist New Connexion local preacher Joseph Love was a notorious Durham colliery-owner who was generous to his Connexion—donating £12,000 in 1871 and another £10,000 in 1874[184]— yet who earned the hatred of his workers. Love, himself a former collier, paid his men according to the number of full tubs of coal sent to the surface, but if coal had fallen from the tubs or had been shaken down below the rim of the tub during its journey to the top the miners were fined and received no pay for the incomplete tubs. When Love's miners went on strike in October 1863

[181] Leese, 'Black Country Society', 301–5.
[182] Gowland, 'Methodist Secessions', Ph.D. thesis, 122.
[183] Kirk, *Growth of Working Class Reformism*, 245.
[184] R. Moore, *Pit-men, Preachers, and Politics* (Cambridge, 1974), 81–2.

he evicted workers and their families from tied cottages and imported black-leg labour so that the strike collapsed in January 1864.[185]

However, Fernley, Armitage, and Love appear to have been in a minority among Nonconformist employers. If contemporary opinion can be trusted, and we have little else to go on, those workmen who were employed by Non-conformist bosses were fortunate. Josiah Wedgwood insisted that his workers obey a strict time-keeping regime and introduced a clocking-in system, but he laid down clear regulations to protect his workers' health, he provided them with much-improved housing, and the wages of some of his workers more than doubled while they were in his employ.[186] John Marshall is said to have dismissed any overseer found talking to workers in his mill during working hours, but he forbade the use of corporal punishment in his factories, and in the 1830s Marshalls provided their workers with changing-rooms and baths, installed fans to keep the temperature even, and engaged a surgeon to visit their mills twice a week.[187] Henry Ashworth worked his employees for a sixty-nine-hour week, would not allow them to join a trade union, and in 1830 warned would-be strikers that if they went on strike they would lose their jobs. But the Ashworths' employees worked in exceptionally clean and well-ventilated conditions; they were provided with stone-built houses which were 'furnished much in the same fashion as those of the middling Manchester class'; both Ashworth industrial villages had their own doctor; and their workers were provided with a library and news-room and a school for their children. The machines in Ashworth's New Eagley mill did not require constant attention and workers were encouraged to read books and newspapers while tending them.[188] John Bright earned the hatred of factory reformers for his opposition to the Ten Hours movement, but he built a row of four-roomed cottages with gardens for his workers, built a school for their children, founded a factory library, and during the cotton famine of 1862–4 continued to give workers whom he was forced to lay off two-thirds of their usual wages.[189] The Congregationalist cotton manufacturer James Kershaw, who was Liberal MP for Stockport from 1847 to 1864, incurred considerable financial loss by keeping his mills running throughout the American Civil War and his firm was the first to provide relief for its workers.

    [185] R. Fynes, *The Miners of Northumberland and Durham* (1873), 225–30; E. Welbourne, *The Miners' Unions of Northumberland and Durham* (Cambridge, 1923), 115–21.

    [186] N. McKendrick, 'Josiah Wedgwood and Factory Discipline', *Historical Journal*, 4 (1961), 39–45, 53.

    [187] Rimmer, *Marshalls of Leeds*, 119–29, 215–16.

    [188] Boyson, *Ashworth Cotton Enterprise*, 91–4, 116–19, 124–5, 128, 134; Kirk, *Working Class Reformism*, 110.

    [189] J. T. Mills, *John Bright and the Quakers* (1935), ii. 188–91.

Even the Conservative *Stockport Advertiser* regarded Kershaw as 'the greatest and best employer' in the area.[190] Another Liberal MP, the Baptist hosiery
manufacturer Richard Harris who represented Leicester from 1848 to 1852,
similarly suffered financial loss by keeping elderly men, 'who had long been
in the service of the firm', at work on obsolete knitting-frames because 'they
were too old to take charge of new machinery'.[191] The New Connexion
Methodist John Ridgway, head of one of the largest pottery firms in
Staffordshire, provided some of his workers with 'clean and comfortable
housing' and started for all of them an insurance scheme to enable them to
enter hospital should the need arise.[192] His fellow Kilhamite John Whittaker,
who employed virtually every working person in the village of Hurst near
Ashton-under-Lyne in his cotton mill, was criticized by a group of anonymous workers in 1848 for compelling workers to begin early and finish late,
but during the cotton famine he gave £5,000 to relieve unemployed workers
and their families and in 1867 trade unionists exempted Whittaker's mills
'from strike action on the grounds that the family paid higher wages, and
treated their workers better, than other employers in the area'.[193] The
Congregationalist Hugh Mason, also of Ashton-under-Lyne, like Ashworth
refused to employ trade unionists, but he built recreation rooms for his workers which cost £4,500, followed this up by providing a swimming bath and
gymnasium, paid his workers higher wages than any other employer in the
district, and angered his fellow manufacturers in 1871 by reducing his workers' hours to fifty-eight per week with a half-holiday on Saturdays.[194] And
during the Franco-Prussian war the Bradford woolcombing firm headed by
the Wesleyan Isaac Holden provided the workers at its two factories in
France with two free meals a day.[195]

   The Nonconformist employer at his best was epitomized by the Bradford
Congregationalist Titus Salt. Salt was a shy, nervous man, whose domination
of worsted manufacture rested on his discovery that the wool of the Peruvian
alpaca could be woven with cotton or silk to produce an attractive cloth.[196]
Like other employers Salt distrusted trade unions, and in 1868 refused to

[190] M. Ellison, *Support for Secession: Lancashire and the American Civil War* (Chicago, 1972),
26; Kirk, *Working Class Reformism*, 51.
[191] T. Lomas, *Character and its Conquests: A Memoir of Richard Harris* (1855), 79.
[192] J. H. Y. Briggs, 'The Radical Saints of Shelton', in D. Jeremy, *Business and Religion in
Britain* (Aldershot, 1988), 55, 67.
[193] Rose, *Methodism in Ashton-under-Lyne*, ii. 67; Kirk, *Working Class Reformism*, 298–9.
[194] J. Holland, 'Hugh Mason', in S. A. Harrop and E. A. Rose, *Victorian Ashton* (Ashton-
under-Lyne, 1974), 79.
[195] Anon., *Fortunes Made in Business* (1884), i. 38.
[196] Reynolds, *The Great Paternalist* (1983), 51–3.

negotiate with strikers until they returned to work. And like most manufacturers Salt believed that factory legislation would render British industry
vulnerable to foreign competition, though in 1846 he recommended an
eleven-hour day as a compromise with the Ten Hour movement.[197] But so
considerate an employer was Salt in other respects that he even gained the
praise of that scourge of textile manufacturers, Joseph Rayner Stephens.[198]
During the slump of 1845–8 Salt kept all his workers in employment until the
revolution in France in February 1848 disrupted trade with the Continent; he
took on a hundred unemployed woolcombers and stockpiled the fruits of
their labour; and in 1850 he organized the first of what were to become
annual outings for his employees by enabling two thousand of them to
travel by train to Malham in Craven.[199] But Salt's most important contribution to the well-being of his workers was the inauguration, in 1853, of the
model industrial village of Saltaire on the banks of the River Aire between
Bradford and Bingley. Salt's decision to move his factory out of Bradford was
prompted partly by the knowledge that further expansion would be difficult
in the town itself, partly by the advantages of concentrating his manufacturing processes on one instead of five different sites, and partly by the desire to
enable his workers to escape the overcrowding, dirt, and smoke of Bradford
where Salt had fought a fruitless campaign to reduce the levels of atmos-
pheric pollution.[200] The new mill, the largest in Europe, was built in an Italian
style with a factory chimney resembling a campanile, and particular attention
was paid in its construction to ventilation and the health of workers. A total of
895 houses were built, 850 for workers and their families and 45 almshouses
for the elderly, at a cost of £106,562. The houses were subsequently criticized
for their austere design and for being too closely crowded together, but they
were far better than houses available elsewhere for industrial workers in the
1850s and the rents charged were lower than those in Bradford. Saltaire was
also provided with baths and wash-houses, with a classically designed
Congregational chapel which has been described as the finest Nonconformist building in the north of England, with a club and institute which
were intended to 'supply the advantages of a public house without its evils',
and with three factory schools opened in 1868. Two years later the local
school inspector said that the boys' school at Saltaire was 'rapidly becoming
one of the best, as it is already the handsomest in my district'.[201] Such was

[197] R. Balgarnie, *Sir Titus Salt* (1877), 44;Reynolds, *The Great Paternalist*, 63, 71, 130–1.
[198] Reynolds, *The Great Paternalist*, 283.
[199] Balgarnie, *Salt,* 97, 102; Reynolds, *The Great Paternalist*, 70.
[200] Reynolds, *The Great Paternalist*, 73, 263–4.
[201] Balgarnie, *Salt*, 131–42; Reynolds, *The Great Paternalist*, 270–85.

Salt's workers' appreciation of his model village that three years after its opening, in 1856, three thousand of them travelled by train to his country home at Crow Nest, Lightcliffe, to present him with a marble bust as a 'token of their affection and regard' and as a tribute to 'the high and noble spirit of philanthropy which you have always manifested . . . in securing the happiness and prosperity of your workpeople'. The workers in return were regaled in a large marquee with a feast of beef, ham, tongue, pies, and plum bread.[202]

Philanthropy revealed Nonconformity at its best. Cynics could dismiss philanthropy as balm for guilty consciences, as bestowing distinction on the donor rather than benefit on the recipient, as the product of an inequitable society.[203] The Quaker William Allen, in urging the readers of his *Philanthropist* to greater generosity, used both the argument that charity was a blessing to the giver as well as to the receiver and the suggestion that philanthropy was a means of social control. Allen contended that people 'who make all their actions and exertions centre in self' forfeited 'much solid and substantial happiness', and certainly Allen himself found in his philanthropic activities consolation from a tragic personal life in which three wives and a beloved only daughter predeceased him. Allen further supported his argument for beneficence by reference to the interdependence of 'the different orders of society'. The rich needed 'the services of the poor' just as the poor needed 'the aid of the rich', but if the moral and material standards of the poor fell to a point where they ceased to recognize that society provided them with any benefit, the result might well be revolution. As the security of the rich, 'in the enjoyment of their possessions, may be materially affected by the degree of virtue which exists in the great mass of the people, it becomes the interest as well as the duty of those in elevated stations . . . to improve the moral conditions and increase the comforts of the poor'. But the argument that philanthropy would contribute to social stability was a way of getting money out of wealthy donors, it was not a reflection of Allen's own motives. For Allen philanthropy was first and foremost obedience to God's will. 'A human being, in fulfilling the purpose of his creation, and promoting his own happiness, must of necessity promote that of his fellow creatures, for he then acts harmoniously with the Divine intention, and it will be found that as we approach more nearly to the standard of perfection, we shall be more fully imbued with love to our species.'[204]

Allen's twin passions were science and philanthropy. Born in 1770, the son of a Spitalfields silk manufacturer, Allen joined the pharmaceutical firm

---

[202] Balgarnie, *Salt*, 160–4.

[203] For a discussion of the motives of philanthropists see Isichei, *Victorian Quakers*, 213–19.

[204] *Philanthropist*, 1 (1811), 1–2, 7.

owned by his fellow Quaker John Gurney Bevan, a distant cousin of the Gurneys of Norwich, at Plough Court, Lombard Street, in the City of London in 1792. Bevan retired from the business in 1794 and Allen became a partner in the following year. From 1797 to 1806 Allen was in partnership with another Quaker, Luke Howard, and from 1818 with John Thomas Barry, to whom he relinquished effective control of the business.[205] In his early years at Plough Court Allen carried out original chemical research, gave lectures on chemistry and physics at Guy's Hospital and the Royal Institution, became a Fellow of the Linnaean Society in 1801, was elected Fellow of the Royal Society in 1807, was a founder-member of the Geological Society in the same year, and in 1843 he was elected first president of the Pharmaceutical Society of Great Britain. Allen's career as a philanthropist began in 1798 when he and other Quakers, faced with the worsening conditions of the poor of Spitalfields, launched a society to provide them with soup. For the remainder of his life, until his death in 1843, philanthropy was Allen's major preoccupation. In 1808 he was one of a number of Dissenters who came to the rescue of Joseph Lancaster's schools and served what was to become the British and Foreign School Society as treasurer for the rest of his life. In 1811 he launched a journal, the *Philanthropist*, which for seven years sought to stimulate its readers 'to virtue and active benevolence'.[206] In 1813 Allen, in company with other Quakers, bailed out Robert Owen's New Lanark enterprise just as he had bailed out Lancaster's schools five years earlier. The example of Robert Owen and the inspiration of the seventeenth-century Quaker John Bellers prompted Allen to set up his own farm colony and School of Industry at Lindfield in Sussex in 1826. He was a founder-member of a society which was set up to oppose capital punishment in 1808, when a new Society for the Abolition of Capital Punishment was formed in 1828 Allen was its chairman, and the meeting that was to result in the formation of the Peace Society met at his home in 1814.

Allen's work for the British and Foreign School Society brought him into contact with the Dukes of Kent, Sussex, and Bedford, while in his capacity as a Quaker minister and apostle of the British and Foreign School Society he travelled widely on the Continent and was granted audiences by King Charles XIV of Sweden in 1818 and by Tsar Alexander I of Russia in 1819. Such was Allen's success in resolving the financial problems of Lancaster's schools that in 1813 the Duke of Kent asked the Quaker to sort out his own embarrassed financial situation and invited him to become a trustee of his

---

[205] E. C. Cripps, *Plough Court: The Story of a Notable Pharmacy* (1927), 21–6, 53–4.
[206] *Life of William Allen*, i. 123.

property.[207] A quarter of a century later Allen presented the women's petition calling for the abolition of the apprenticeship system in the West Indies
to the Duke of Kent's daughter, the newly enthroned Queen Victoria.[208] It
was Allen's conviction that it was important 'to be known in the higher ranks
of society' if he was to be 'more extensively useful',[209] and he tried to put his
contacts with high society to good use when he visited Vienna and Verona for
the Congress of European leaders in 1822. He saw both the Duke of Wellington and Alexander I and was assured that both men would use their influence
to have the slave-trade treated as piracy, though French opposition prevented acceptance of the proposal. While in Vienna and Verona Allen also
took up the cause of the Greeks of Chios, who were fleeing from massacres
at the hands of the Turks, and urged the tsar to press the king of Sardinia to
halt the persecution of the Waldensians. Allen undoubtedly enjoyed hob-
nobbing with royalty, but he never forgot that he was first and foremost
a Quaker minister. When, in May 1819, he and his fellow Quaker Stephen
Grellet tried to obtain an interview with the deputy governor of Tula in central Russia they were reprimanded for refusing to take off their hats in front
of the tsar's picture. Grellet informed the Russians that the tsar himself had
allowed the Quakers to keep their hats on in his presence and so they were
permitted to see the deputy governor.[210] Notwithstanding Allen's predilec-
tion for dukes and emperors, Thomas Clarkson believed that he was 'the
greatest man in Europe'. 'He does more good than any man living', he wrote
in 1822.[211]

William Allen was fortunate in having a business partner, John Barry,
to whom he could entrust the running of his business and unusual in the
range of his philanthropic activities, but he was by no means alone. All Nonconformist denominations taught that their members had a duty to the poor,
the sick, the widowed, and the orphaned. Wesley warned Methodists that
they had to help the poor if they hoped to 'escape everlasting fire and
to inherit eternal life'.[212] Most Nonconformist churches accepted a responsibility for their own poor and many acknowledged an obligation to help
the needy outside their own congregations. Congregational and Baptist
churches took up regular collections for the poor, often after the monthly
communion service; Wesleyans formed Strangers' Friend Societies to 'relieve
strangers who had no habitation—no clothes—no food—no friends';[213]

[207] Ibid. i. 171.   [208] Ibid. iii. 278.   [209] Ibid. i. 303.   [210] Ibid. ii. 51–2.
[211] L. H. Doncaster, *Friends of Humanity* (1965), 8.
[212] F. Prochaska, *Women and Philanthropy in Nineteenth-century England* (Oxford, 1980), 9.
[213] R. F. Wearmouth, *Methodism and the Common People of the Eighteenth Century* (1945),
212.

Unitarians organized Domestic Missions to cater for the spiritual and material needs of people who did not attend their services. In twenty years from 1770 the London Methodists gave £15,000 to the poor and in twelve years from 1790 the Manchester Wesleyans' Strangers' Friend Society raised £6,403 to assist over 60,000 people.[214] In twenty-five years from 1843 the Congregational church in Allen Street, Kensington, collected £5,480 for its poor.[215] The Hammersmith Baptist church in London had a Society for the Distribution of Bread which, between 1813 and 1832, gave away 7,000 loaves.[216] In 1842 the pastor of the poverty-stricken Baptist church in Stockport appealed to readers of the *Baptist Magazine* for help in relieving his poor members and as a result was able to provide forty families with coal, potatoes, and 'weekly doles of oatmeal or flour'.[217] The Wesleyans of Nottingham had a long tradition of helping the needy. During the depression of 1800, when many Wesleyans in Nottingham 'were in deep distress', William Bramwell spoke of their plight at a quarterly dinner with the result that those who were 'in affluent circumstances' vied with each other in generosity, with one offering to 'administer medicines gratis' and others offering coal, money, and clothing.[218] During the subsequent slump of 1837 the Nottingham Wesleyans collected £60 and 312½ sacks of potatoes for their poorer members, and in 1861 when unemployment again rose the Halifax Place Wesleyan chapel provided a hundredweight of coal and half a stone of bread for every needy person.[219]

The generosity of individual Dissenters such as Titus Salt, Thomas Wilson, William Isaac Palmer, and Thomas Ferens was, as we have seen, spectacular. One can cite scores of examples of individuals who were helped by acts of Nonconformist charity. William Bramwell was known to have given 'his only top-coat, in severe weather, to one without', and on one occasion, when 'visiting a sick man, who was very poor and lay in bed without a shirt', Bramwell 'retired into another room, took off his shirt, and gave it to the poor man'.[220] When John Jones of Wolverhampton travelled to London in search of work his fellow members of the Temple Street Congregational church provided for his family until his return; when 'poor old Joe Sudborough' lost his cow the Kettering Congregational church gave him 15*s*.; when Brother Swain's

---

[214] E. D. Bebb, *Nonconformity and Economic and Social Life* (1935), 143; Wearmouth, *Methodism and the Common People*, 214.

[215] J. Stoughton, *Congregationalism in the Court Suburb* (1883), 90.

[216] Manley, 'John Rippon', 103. [217] Weston, 'Baptists of North-West England', 161.

[218] Dunn, *Memoirs of Thomas Tatham*, 155–6.

[219] G. H. Harwood, *History of Wesleyan Methodism in Nottingham* (1859), 99; Swift, *Lively People*, 121.

[220] Sigston, *Memoir of Bramwell*, 50.

mill was blown down in a gale the members of the Loughborough General Baptist church took up a collection on his behalf; when the Baptist William Swain lost his job at Billingsgate fish market the deacons of his church gave him 10s.; and when Ann Watkins's husband was thrown out of work by the fraudulent actions of his employer the Quakers of Birmingham contributed £40 to the support of his family.[221] During his wanderings through north Wales George Borrow came across a Calvinistic Methodist in Llangollen who earned only 5s. a week, but he was able to support his family, so he told Borrow, because 'the people of our congregation are very kind to each other'.[222] Dissenting churches were especially ready to help at times of public emergency. In 1805 the Falmouth Baptists collected £17 for the widows and orphans of men killed at Trafalgar, and ten years later the Particular Baptist church at Church Street in Southwark collected £16. 16s. 10d. for the families of the men who had fallen at Waterloo.[223] During the trade depression of 1825 the Norwich Quaker Joseph John Gurney helped to raise £3,300 in five days to provide bread and soup for the unemployed, and twenty years later Gurney gave £1,000 to a Norwich committee to set up a fund to find work for those without it.[224] At the time of the Irish famine of 1846–7 George Armstrong, minister of the Lewin's Mead Unitarian church in Bristol, collected £190 for its victims; the Congregational Union sent £13,000 to Ireland to help to relieve the suffering; and in urging the congregation of the Renshaw Street Unitarian chapel in Liverpool to assist the Irish its minister, John Hamilton Thom, 'could not be silent in dealing with the miseries inflicted on the Irish Catholics by an English aristocracy and a Protestant domination'.[225] During the Lancashire cotton famine the Lancashire and Cheshire Baptist Association raised £6,785 to assist those thrown out of work as a consequence of the American Civil War.[226]

The elderly, the sick, the orphaned, the imprisoned, were all beneficiaries of Dissenting philanthropy, and churches of all denominations held regular

[221] W. H. Jones, *History of the Congregational Churches of Wolverhampton* (1894), 30–1; Goodman, *The Great Meeting, Kettering*, 34; Jackson, 'Baptists in Leicestershire', 212; G. Swan, *The Journals of Two Poor Dissenters* (1970), 10–11; Davidoff and Hall, *Family Fortunes*, 101.

[222] G. Borrow, *Wild Wales* (n.d.), 57–8.

[223] L. A. Fereday, *The Story of Falmouth Baptists* (1950), 68; S. J. Price, *Upton: The Story of One Hundred and Fifty Years* (1935), 56–7.

[224] J. B. Braithwaite, *Memoirs of Joseph John Gurney* (Norwich, 1854), i. 384; ii. 452.

[225] O. M. Griffiths, 'Records of Lewin's Mead Chapel, Bristol', *TUHS* 6 (1935–8), 128; F. R. Salter, 'Congregationalism in the Hungry Forties', *TCHS* 17 (1952–3), 113; A. Holt, *Walking Together* (1938), 200.

[226] Lea, 'Baptists in Lancashire', 296.

collections for dispensaries and hospitals.[227] Wesley's London headquarters at the Foundry, Matthew Wilks's Whitefield's Tabernacle, John Rippon's Baptist church in Carter Lane, Southwark, and the Particular Baptist church in Church Street, Southwark, all supported their own almshouses for the elderly.[228] Thomas Guy, who endowed the hospital that bears his name with £220,134 made out of selling shares in the South Sea Company before the bubble burst in 1720, was a Baptist.[229] John Wesley opened what 'was probably the first free dispensary in the City of London' in 1746, the Quakers of York helped to start a dispensary in their city in 1788, and the Quaker Richard Phillips founded a dispensary for the poor in Swansea around 1808 out of which grew the Swansea General Hospital.[230] In Liverpool the Unitarian physician James Currie promoted the town's lunatic asylum in 1790 and its fever hospital in 1806; in Manchester the Unitarian Thomas Percival was responsible for the establishment of the town's first Board of Health in 1796; and in London the Unitarian Southwood Smith, physician to the London Fever Hospital, was one of the first men to draw attention to the connection between epidemics and insanitary conditions in articles he wrote for the *Westminster Review* in 1825.[231] The opening of hospitals to women visitors was initiated by another Unitarian, Catherine Cappe, who persuaded the York County Hospital to admit such visitors in 1813.[232] And district nursing was pioneered by yet another Unitarian, William Rathbone VI, who was moved by the devoted nursing received by his first wife during her terminal illness to found, in 1862, the Liverpool Training School and Home for Nurses.[233]

Orphans were the particular concern of Andrew Reed, who for fifty years from 1811 was minister to the New Road Congregational church and later to the Wycliffe chapel in Whitechapel. His motive he described as simple Christian charity: his own mother had been an orphan and had been given a home, she in turn had provided a home for an orphan, and when he visited 'a dying man whose great sorrow in death was leaving his motherless children',

[227] Fereday, *Falmouth Baptists*, 68; Castle Gate minutes, 176; Sellers, 'Liverpool Nonconformity', 244; Jewson, *Jacobin City*, 137.

[228] G. J. Stevenson, *City Road Chapel* (1873), 41; W. Salmon, *TCHS* 18 (1956–9), 96; Manley, 'John Rippon', 107–8; Price, *Upton*, 61.

[229] H. C. Cameron, *Mr Guy's Hospital* (1954), 28–9, 61.

[230] Stevenson, *City Road Chapel*, 40; S. Wright, 'Friends in York: the Dynamics of Quaker Revival, 1780–1860', M.Phil. thesis (York, 1991), 201; M. F. Williams, 'The Society of Friends in Glamorgan', MA thesis (University of Wales, 1930), 173.

[231] Sellers, 'Liverpool Nonconformity', 241; C. L. Lewes, *Dr Southwood Smith* (1893), 21.

[232] Prochaska, *Women and Philanthropy*, 141–2.

[233] E. Rathbone, *William Rathbone: A Memoir* (1905), 155–81.

Reed gave 'a promise to befriend them'.[234] Reed founded the London Orphans' Asylum in 1813 and the East London Infant Orphans' Asylum in 1827, but he resigned from the boards of both institutions in 1843–4 when their governing bodies resolved that the children in their care be instructed in the Anglican catechism. Undeterred, Reed founded a third, undenominational, Asylum for Fatherless Children in 1844, and went on to found an Asylum for Idiots in 1847 from which sprang the Eastern Counties Idiot Asylum at Colchester in 1859. Finally, in 1854, Reed founded the Royal Hospital for Incurables. By the time of his death in 1862 a total of £1,043,566 had been raised for these six institutions and they had provided homes for 6,423 people, of whom 1,760 were in residence when he died.[235] Not only had the chief burden of fund-raising fallen on Reed's shoulders, but he had also supervised the planning and construction of four of the six buildings and had contributed £4,540 to their cost out of his salary as a Dissenting minister.[236] Since Reed's salary was never more than £500 a year, and often a good deal less, this meant that he gave at least a fifth of his income to the orphanages.[237] Nor were Reed's philanthropic activities confined to orphans, lunatics, and incurables. In 1837 he started a Savings Bank for the people of the East End of London, which by 1862 had annual receipts of over £600,000, and in the depression of 1842 he raised over £150 which he used to provide relief for over 700 distressed people in Lancashire.

Dissenters were prominent in efforts to mitigate the severity of the penal code at a time when the death penalty was exacted for trifling offences. In 1817 two soldiers took part in a wrestling match with a man named Read in Wolverhampton churchyard. During the contest Read dropped 1s. 1d. from his pocket which one of the soldiers picked up and when Read complained to the town constable, a man named Roberts, the constable suggested that Read should allege that he had been robbed and that if the soldiers were convicted Read and Roberts should divide between them the £40 'blood money' paid to witnesses for the prosecution. The two soldiers were condemned to death at the Stafford assizes but Charles Mander, a Wolverhampton varnishmaker and member of the Queen Street Congregational church, rode to London to see the Home Secretary, Lord Sidmouth, with the result that the execution was stayed and in the following year the payment of blood money to prosecution witnesses was stopped.[238] William Allen's partner, John

---

[234] A. and C. Reed, *Memoirs of the Life and Philanthropic Labours of Andrew Reed* (1863), 94.
[235] Ibid. 582–3.   [236] Ibid. 359–61, 371.
[237] R. J. Helmstadter, 'Rev. Andrew Reed', in R. W. Davis and R. J. Helmstadter, *Religion and Irreligion in Victorian Society* (1992), 17.
[238] Jones, *Congregational Churches of Wolverhampton* (1894), 44–8.

Thomas Barry, was also active in the movement against capital punishment and claimed to have 'spent over £500 in cab fares to the House of Commons in his endeavours to obtain reprieves for criminals who had been condemned on what he found to be inadequate evidence'. In 1830 Barry organized a petition which was signed by over a thousand bankers urging the abolition of the death penalty for crimes of forgery, a request to which Parliament acceded three years later.[239]

A succession of Dissenters showed concern for the plight of men and women in prisons. The pioneer prison reformer John Howard was a Congregationalist who seceded from the Bunyan Meeting, Bedford, in 1773 when its minister was converted to Baptist views, and he gave £400 towards the building of a new Congregational chapel which subsequently bore his name.[240] Howard's father was a prosperous upholsterer whose death in 1742 and bequest of £7,000 enabled his son to live as a country gentleman at Cardington and to be appointed High Sheriff of Bedfordshire in 1773. Howard's sympathy with prisoners was first stirred in 1756 when a ship on which he was travelling to Portugal was seized by a French privateer and he spent six uncomfortable nights in a prison in Brest before being released on parole. He subsequently devoted two months in France to investigating the conditions of English prisoners who were 'treated with such barbarity that many hundreds perished'.[241] But the main impulse to Howard's work as a prison reformer came as a result of his experiences as High Sheriff of Bedfordshire. He was horrified to find that people who had either not been tried, or had been tried and found not guilty, were none the less kept in prison until they could pay the fees demanded of them by gaolers who relied on fees, in the absence of salaries, for their livelihoods.[242] The experience led him to embark on a tour of prisons throughout Great Britain and Ireland, and then of virtually every European country, recording the state of the prisons, making recommendations for the improvement of the lot of prisoners, and publishing his detailed findings in *The State of Prisons* in 1777. Howard died at Kherson in Russian Tartary in January 1790 at the age of sixty-three, having caught a fever from a sixteen-year-old girl whom he had tried in vain to cure.[243]

Howard's role as the benefactor of prisoners was taken over by three more Dissenters, Sarah Martin, Elizabeth Fry, and Thomas Wright. Sarah Martin, a dressmaker from Caister near Great Yarmouth, was converted at the age of

[239] Cripps, *Plough Court*, 58–61.
[240] H. G. Tibbutt, *A History of the Howard Congregational Church, Bedford* (Bedford, 1961), 17.
[241] J. Stoughton, *Howard the Philanthropist* (1884), 26.   [242] Ibid. 98.   [243] Ibid. 324.

nineteen, in 1810, and in the following year joined the Congregational church
at Great Yarmouth. She began visiting the prisoners in Yarmouth gaol in
1819 and continued until her death twenty-four years later, reading the Bible
and preaching sermons to the inmates, providing them with work such as
bookbinding and needlework, and obtaining accommodation for them when
they left prison.[244] Whereas Sarah Martin was a humble dressmaker, Elizabeth Fry came from a wealthy family, daughter of the Norwich Quaker wool-
stapler John Gurney and sister of the banker and leading Evangelical
Quaker Joseph John Gurney.[245] Raised in a 'gay Quaker' household in which
music and dancing were permitted, she experienced an Evangelical conversion at the age of eighteen in 1798. Soon afterwards she felt called to become
a Quaker minister, but a decision was postponed by her marriage, in 1800, to
the wealthy London merchant Joseph Fry and by the subsequent birth of ten
children. However, in 1811 she was accepted as a Quaker minister and was
encouraged by her brother-in-law Thomas Fowell Buxton, himself concerned with the state of British prisons, to visit Newgate. Elizabeth's regular
visitation of Newgate began in December 1816, and in the following
February she founded an Association for the Improvement of the Female
Prisoners in Newgate. Its aims were 'to provide for the clothing, instruction,
employment of the women; to introduce them to a knowledge of the Holy
Scriptures', and to form in them 'habits of order, sobriety and industry'. To
achieve these aims Elizabeth obtained the consent both of the prison authorities and of the prisoners themselves to the division of the women prisoners
into classes of not more than twelve led by monitors, copied from Lancaster's
school system, 'chosen from among the most orderly of the prisoners'.
Elizabeth Fry's 'primary intention', writes John Kent, 'was to give the Newgate women the chance of leaving prison better equipped to live a normal
life'.[246] This, too, was the aim of Thomas Wright, who was born in Manchester in 1789, converted under the ministry of William Roby, and served
as deacon of the Grosvenor Street Congregational church for half a century.
Wright began work at the age of fifteen as an apprentice iron founder, was
promoted to foreman at the age of twenty-three, and until a public subscription enabled him to retire at the age of sixty-two worked from 5 o'clock
in the morning until 6 o'clock in the evening. But after work on weekdays
and on Sunday afternoons he visited the prisoners in Salford gaol and,
following a request from the prison chaplain in 1838, devoted himself to

---

[244] Prochaska, *Women and Philanthropy*, 164–8; Browne, *Congregationalism in Norfolk and Suffolk*, 249.

[245] The most recent biography is John Kent, *Elizabeth Fry* (1962).

[246] Kent, *Elizabeth Fry*, 66, 93.

finding work for discharged convicts. Over the next sixteen years Wright found employment for nearly three hundred prisoners on their release, often providing financial guarantees for their future good behaviour out of his own pocket, and helped over nine hundred to emigrate.[247] Thomas Wright's efforts to assist prisoners were better appreciated by the authorities than were those of Elizabeth Fry. The first prison inspectors, appointed in 1835, objected to Elizabeth's interference in the affairs of Newgate and complained that the presence of visitors at her weekly Bible readings tended 'to diminish the necessary gloom of the prison, and to mitigate the punishment which the law has sentenced the prisoner to undergo'. The prison inspectors circumscribed, though they did not end, Elizabeth's influence at Newgate. It was not until 1948, commented Sir Lionel Fox, that Parliament tried to implement her ideas.[248]

Sir Lionel Fox's verdict serves to invalidate one of the most frequent criticisms levelled against nineteenth-century philanthropists, that in their attempts to relieve suffering they were dealing with its symptoms and not with its underlying causes. When John Joseph Gurney was raising money for the unemployed of Norwich, when Andrew Reed was founding his orphanages, when Elizabeth Fry was visiting prisoners, the publication of Keynes's *General Theory*, the implementation of the Beveridge Report, and the foundation of the National Health Service were more than a century away. Had the philanthropists devoted their energies to drawing up blueprints for the reform of society rather than to dealing with immediate needs, by the time those reforms could be implemented the people whom they sought to help would have been long dead. 'Unlike social theorists who had rarely held the hand of a dying child in a hovel', writes Frank Prochaska, 'philanthropists had to clean up the mess: . . . they had to deal with conditions as they were, not as they might be.'[249]

A second criticism levelled against the philanthropists is that the means resorted to by many charities to distinguish the deserving from the undeserving—the visitation of the poor in their own homes—were designed to subordinate the poor to the rich. Visiting, writes Philip McCann, 'was the essence . . . of social control; it enabled the middle class not only to detect imposture but also to deliver a homily to those whose conduct failed to come up to their standards, an activity at which Evangelicals and Quakers excelled'.[250]

---

[247] T. W. McDermid, *The Life of Thomas Wright of Manchester, the Prison Philanthropist* (1876), *passim*.

[248] Kent, *Elizabeth Fry*, 124; Prochaska, *Women and Philanthropy*, 169.

[249] F. Prochaska, *The Voluntary Impulse* (1988), 51.

[250] McCann, *Popular Education and Socialization*, 17.

Charities employed the visitation method in obedience to the Epistle of James, 'to visit the fatherless and widows in their affliction',[251] and in the knowledge that this was the most efficient way of directing their limited resources to those most in need. The pattern was set by the Methodists' Strangers' Friend Societies, of which the first was founded in London in 1785 by a former soldier, John Gardner, after he had visited 'a poor man dying of fistula' and lying on a floor 'covered only with a sack, without shirt, cap, or sheet'.[252] As the *Methodist Magazine* pointed out in 1798, people living in cellars and garrets who were too proud or too ill to beg were often in greater distress than street-beggars whose very visibility attracted a modicum of charity. And the Strangers' Friend Societies, as their name implies, were particularly concerned to discover and help those who, because they had moved from the parish of their birth or marriage, could claim no relief from the poor law. The Methodist visitors, claimed Adam Clarke, took upon themselves the dangerous task 'of visiting the wretches in cellars and garrets, where poverty and distress had taken up their abode, and where the most virulent contagion had dwelt for many years with increasing, because undisturbed, malignity'.[253]

The Methodists' system of home visitation was adopted both by William Allen's Spitalfields Association for the Relief of the Poor, which between 1812 and 1816 raised £43,369 for destitute silk weavers and their families,[254] and by the Unitarians' Domestic Mission in Liverpool. The latter was founded in 1836, primarily for religious purposes. 'If the people will not come to the gospel', said John Hamilton Thom of the Renshaw Street chapel, 'the gospel must be brought to the poor.'[255] But under its first missioner, the Unitarian minister John Johns, the mission 'assumed the magnitude . . . of a considerable charity'.[256] Johns provided clothes, sheets, and blankets for the needy, acted as banker to working men, started a Friendly Loan Society, obtained sixteen acres which he divided up into 143 allotments on which workers could grow their own food, and founded three schools and a library.[257] Unlike some Dissenters, Johns recognized that environment could influence character: 'if condition is to be improved by the improvement of character, character is also to be improved by the improvement of condition'.[258] But he was sickened by the clamour from the poor for hand-outs and came to the conclusion that

---

[251] James 1: 27.   [252] L. Tyerman, *Life of John Wesley* (1882), iii. 253.
[253] Wearmouth, *Methodism and the Common People*, 212–14.
[254] Doncaster, *Friends of Humanity*, 20–1.
[255] A. Holt, *A Ministry to the Poor* (Liverpool, 1936), 13.
[256] B. A. Packer, 'The Founding of the Liverpool Domestic Mission', *TUHS* 18 (1984), 112.
[257] Holt, *Ministry to the Poor*, 30–1, 38–42, 48.
[258] Packer, 'Liverpool Domestic Mission', 115.

his most important task was 'to induce my poor people to help themselves'.[259] Johns died from typhoid in June 1847 after visiting the home of one of its victims.

John Johns's emphasis on the need to help the poor to help themselves was one that was shared by all Dissenting churches. In the late eighteenth and early nineteenth centuries very many churches had their own Friendly Societies to which members could contribute their savings in order to protect themselves against the financial burdens of sickness, old age, and widowhood. One of the earliest was that founded by the General Baptist church at Fleet in Lincolnshire in 1773 to which members contributed 1*s.* a month. Between 1800 and 1817 it distributed over £2,200 and by the latter date had more than 250 members.[260] Some Baptist churches in Nottinghamshire objected to their members joining secular Friendly Societies such as the Oddfellows in the 1840s, probably because they often met in public houses, but in south Wales Nonconformist ministers supported and on occasion served on the committees of such societies.[261] Churches also helped their poorer members by acting as labour exchanges. As early as 1693 the Congregational church at Rothwell in Northamptonshire resolved that its deacons ought 'to take care if any be out of employ to labour to get them into employ', and in 1769 the Kent General Baptist Association adopted a plan, which lasted until at least 1786, to find apprentices for masters seeking them.[262] From the late seventeenth century onwards the Quakers also arranged apprenticeships for the sons of their members,[263] and the custom of apprenticing Quaker boys to Quaker masters was an important factor in Quaker economic advancement. In other churches informal contacts between prosperous potential employers and unemployed members worked to the benefit of the latter. William Pearce, a wealthy industrialist in London's East End, 'found work for a disabled docker who was a class leader at his Methodist chapel', and John Bezer obtained one of his first jobs in the ham and beef shop owned by his Sunday school superintendent.[264]

[259] Holt, *Ministry to the Poor*, 27, 30–1.

[260] Taylor, *History of the General Baptists*, iii. 466–7.

[261] Harrison, 'Nottinghamshire Baptists', i. 392–3; Evans, 'Religion in the Swansea Valley', 227, 234.

[262] Rothwell Congregational Church Book, 1655–1708, DWL MSS 201.42, 47; Kent General Baptist Association Minute Book, DWL MSS 38.79b, 63–4; Journal of the Quarterly Meetings of the General Baptist Churches of East Kent, DWL MSS 38.72, 1782–1786.

[263] K. Gray, 'Some Contributions to the Early History of Nonconformity in Rossendale', MA thesis (University of Wales, 1942), 88.

[264] C. Caine, *William Pearce of Poplar: A Chapter in the History of Methodism in London* (1894), 44; Vincent, *Testaments of Radicalism*, 165.

Dissenting philanthropy is open to criticism, but not on the grounds that its motives were ignoble or that its practitioners spent their time helping the poor rather than reordering society. Two working-class correspondents of the *Nonconformist* in 1848 complained not that the churches were using their benevolent institutions to exert control over their lives, but that the churches with which they were associated had no such institutions.[265] Dissenters, so often generous, could like other men sometimes be mean. The enormous sums they spent on building and adorning their chapels on occasion contrasted unfavourably with the money they gave to the poor. The Particular Baptists of Reading set up a Friendly Society in 1834 to assist the poor, but insisted that financial help should not exceed '1*s*. at each visit, except in urgent cases'; three months later the same church opened a new chapel at King's Road at a cost of £2,837.[266] The Unitarians of George's Meeting, Exeter, gave £30 to the poor in 1831 but paid £112 for a silver vase.[267] A Nonconformist church could sometimes fail its poorer members. John Ward, Wesleyan minister at Bingley in the 1860s, recorded with distaste the fact that a hundred years earlier Benjamin Wilkinson, 'a simple-hearted, zealous, and good old pilgrim . . . was suffered to end his days in the workhouse'.[268] Similarly John Mackfarland, the founder of Methodism in Retford, had to enter the workhouse after his hardware business went bankrupt, and he refused a place at Trinity Hospital because that would necessitate attendance at the parish church.[269] But instances of churches being unwilling or unable to help their poorer members are rare and, as was suggested above, the readiness of Methodist societies to help destitute people who were refused assistance from the poor law may well have contributed to Methodist growth in the late eighteenth and early nineteenth centuries. The overwhelming mass of evidence suggests that Nonconformist charity, both to the poor of its own congregations and to the suffering of the wider world, was one of its most attractive features.

Did, then, Nonconformist religion add or subtract to the sum of human happiness? To some, as to a writer in the *Cornish Magazine* in 1898, Evangelical religion was a scourge with which they were tormented in childhood and which could haunt them for the rest of their lives. The doctrine of eternal punishment, he wrote, 'dealt with by a preacher of an active imagina-

---

[265] *Nonconformist*, 6 Dec. 1848, 931; 13 Dec. 1848, 950.
[266] C. A. Davis, *History of the Baptist Church, King's Road, Reading* (1891), 64, 66.
[267] Brockett, *Nonconformity in Exeter*, 182.
[268] J. Ward, *Historical Sketches of the Rise and Progress of Methodism in Bingley* (Bingley, 1863), 23.
[269] Biggs, 'Methodism in a Rural Society', 461.

tion, and capable of clothing his ideas in vivid language, created the utmost terror in the minds of the poor, struggling, uneducated, unread people, adding intense mental misery to their many physical woes'.[270] But to the many thousands of men and women who were converted under such preaching the change wrought brought a sense of freedom, joy, and often material improvement. John Wesley himself told his doubting elder brother Samuel in 1739 that not only had he seen 'very many persons changed in a moment from the spirit of horror, fear, and despair to the spirit of hope, joy, peace', but that by the act of conversion 'the whole tenor of their life' was changed. Men who had been wicked were from the time of their new birth 'holy, just, and good'.[271] 'Not a few whose sins were of the most flagrant kind', he wrote in his *Journal*, 'drunkards, swearers, thieves, whoremongers, adulterers, have been brought "from darkness into light, and from the power of Satan unto God".'[272]

It must, however, be admitted that the effects of supposed conversion experiences were often superficial and short-lived. Many of the conversions occasioned by the cholera epidemic of 1831–2 proved to be transient, and Thomas Tatham, on hearing of the apostacy of some cholera-induced converts, commented on how often 'the terrors of the thunderstorm excite the fears of many, who afterwards return as the dog to his vomit'.[273] Conversion was often an emotional crisis which failed to transform a convert's behaviour, and the frequency with which the disciplinary procedures of the Dissenting churches had to be resorted to is sufficient evidence that the habits of a lifetime were not always discarded overnight. Church rolls were in a constant state of flux and in some chapels existing members were removed as fast as new ones were added. In seventeen years from 1832 the Hexham Primitive Methodist society gained 263 members but in the same period lost 281 and of these losses only six were through death.[274] In the Fakenham Primitive Methodist circuit in Norfolk in the 1820s 'very large numbers of preachers were taken off the plan for various reasons, including debt, intemperance, harvest frolicking, improper conduct, quarrelling, bad language, gambling, non-attendance at the means of grace and often neglect of appointments'.[275] The 'backsliding' of converts was a common phenomenon. The accounts of

[270] Rule, 'Labouring Miner in Cornwall', 277, citing the *Cornish Magazine*, 2 (1898), 224 *et seq*.

[271] *Letters of John Wesley*, i. 290–1.   [272] *Wesley's Journal*, ii. 67–8.

[273] Dunn, *Memoirs of Thomas Tatham*, 226.

[274] J. Horner, 'The Influence of Methodism on the Social Structure and Culture of Rural Northumberland', MA thesis (Newcastle upon Tyne, 1971), 93.

[275] D. Yarham, 'The Influence of Primitive Methodism in East Anglia', in E. S. Leedham-Green, *Religious Dissent in East Anglia* (Cambridge, 1991), 98–9, citing E. A. Harvey, *The Tale of the Years* (Watton, Norfolk, 1908), 19.

religious experience published in the *Primitive Methodist Magazine* frequently refer to their subjects as having been converted, usually by the Wesleyans, as having subsequently lost their faith and returned to their evil ways, and as having had to be re-converted by the Ranters.[276] John Tewson, a drunken, quarrelsome blacksmith of Caythorpe in Lincolnshire, was converted at a Primitive Methodist camp-meeting in 1827 and for eight months was a member of a Ranter society. But he soon returned to drink and 'for nine years he remained in his backsliding' until he was re-converted in 1837.[277]

It was significant, however, that the account of Tewson's conversion revealed that he was 'not religiously educated'. There is a mass of evidence to suggest that the conversion experience was more likely to be permanent when the subject had been brought up in a religious home and had received a religious education. My analyses of the conversion experiences of the Independents and the Quakers in the mid-seventeenth century, of the *Early Methodist Preachers* in the eighteenth century, and of Nonconformists who were converted between 1780 and 1850 all suggest that the overwhelming majority of converts came from religious homes and had strict religious upbringings.[278] John Wesley himself noted in 1780 that young converts who had 'pious parents' were much more likely to remain true to their religious profession than children of parents who 'did not fear God'.[279] But this does not alter the fact that even the products of religious homes were often caught up in the conflict between two cultures, and that for the children of Christian parents, just as for some children from irreligious homes, conversion was a conscious decision to opt for the values of the chapel, the Sunday school, and the temperance society, rather than those of the pub, the brothel, and the music-hall. In 1743 the Methodist Thomas Butts made a claim for the beneficial effects of Evangelical conversion that was to be repeated time and again over the next 150 years. Whereas, before their conversion, many families 'used to be sotting and quarrelling at alehouses in the evenings, so as often to make themselves unfit for work in the mornings', now after work they 'hear the preaching, and hereby their hearts are made so glad that they can rise at five to hear the Word, and go cheerfully to work at six, and are better husbands on all accounts'.[280] One can cite many examples from the early nineteenth century which substantiate Butts's point. The *Primitive Methodist Magazine* for 1829 recorded the biography of James Cocker of Huddersfield

---

[276] *Primitive Methodist Magazine*, 7 (1826), 129–30, 166–7, 373–4; 8 (1827), 200.
[277] Ibid. 3rd ser. 1 (1843), 204–5.
[278] Watts, *The Dissenters*, i. 174, 200, 422; above, Ch. I, sect. 5.
[279] *Wesley's Journal*, vi. 273.   [280] L. F. Church, *The Early Methodist People* (1949), 3.

whose life 'previous to his conversion was grossly wicked'; he lied, swore, and rolled about the streets drunk, but after entering a Ranter chapel in a state of intoxication he was converted and his life transformed.[281] Similarly Charles Wilkins, in his *History of Merthyr Tydfil*, told the story of a workman who was 'a bad man, a bad husband, and a bad father' and whose favourite entertainment was to get drunk and then challenge the men who lived in the same row of houses to fight him one by one. But the drunkard went to a revival meeting, 'came from it a stricken, humbled being', and was subsequently a changed man.[282] Mrs Hopper of Chatham in Kent recalled how both she and her husband had once lived 'shocking' lives. On Saturday nights, after her husband had received his wages, he used to tour the local public houses and between ten and eleven o'clock his wife followed him to search him out and to reprimand him. When she found him they quarrelled and cursed each other 'for the devil was in him as well as in me', and their children copied their example until 'our house was like a little hell'. But one Sunday she persuaded her husband to hear a Bible Christian woman preacher, both were converted, and now her 'husband brings home the money on Saturday nights, I tidy up the house, then we go and get our marketing', and on Sundays they attend the services 'throughout the day, and close with singing and prayer in our home, and the children sing with us, and we are all happy together'.[283]

Even more impressive than the testimony of Methodists and Dissenters of the way in which the conversion experience changed individual lives is the evidence of men who were not themselves Dissenters of the way in which the influence of Evangelical Nonconformity changed whole communities. Observers of nineteenth-century Cornwall, of the Durham and Northumberland coalfields, and of the manufacturing towns of the Black Country all commented on the change that Methodism and Dissent had wrought in working-class communities. In 1808 Richard Warner, an Anglican clergyman, praised the Methodists for the fact that in Cornwall 'desperate wrestling matches . . . and inhuman cockfights . . . and riotous revellings' were becoming less frequent.[284] In 1857 a writer in the *Quarterly Review* contrasted the sober, peaceable, orderly, and law-abiding people of predominantly Methodist Cornwall with the drunkenness, turbulence, pugnacity, and shipwrecking for which the Cornish had been notorious a

[281] *Primitive Methodist Magazine*, 10 (1829), 332–3.
[282] Wilkins, *History of Merthyr Tydfil*, 225.
[283] Bourne, *Life of James Thorne*, 66–7; Valenze, 'Prophetic Sons and Daughters', 165.
[284] J. Rule, 'Methodism, Popular Beliefs, and Village Culture in Cornwall', in R. D. Storch (ed.), *Popular Culture and Custom in Nineteenth-century England* (1982), 54.

century earlier.[285] The commissioners investigating children's employment in 1842 and the state of the mining districts in 1846 were told time and again that the Methodists were largely responsible for the marked improvement in the conduct of the people in the north-east coalfield. George Elliot, though not a Methodist himself, admitted that the 'Methodists have done more to ameliorate the pitmen than the whole Church put together', and commissioner Seymour Tremenheere concluded that the improvements in the coalfield were 'greatly attributable' to the Methodists' exertions.[286] Similarly in the Black Country the glass manufacturer William Chance of Smethwick told the Midland Mining Commission in 1843 that thanks to the Methodists 'the moral condition of the people . . . is a great deal better than it was about twenty years ago'.[287] Prayer-meetings organized by Methodists at dinner times in the pits were said to have had a sobering and calming effect on miners in the aftermath of the strike of 1842.[288] And William Brown, a leader of the Derbyshire miners, speaking in Ilkeston in 1873, admitted that while 'about fifteen per cent of the mining population of the present day drank too freely, gambled too much, and neglected their work, causing their families to suffer', there were among the miners 'more Sunday school teachers, more local preachers, more tract distributors [and] more Good Templars . . . than in any other operative class they could name'.[289]

Not only did Dissenters assert that they had improved the morals of the working class in general, they claimed to have reduced the crime rate in particular. They pointed out that of 887 prisoners incarcerated in the Middlesex county gaol in 1838, only one was a Congregationalist, only two were Baptists, and only eleven Methodists, a proportion of 1.6 per cent.[290] Welsh Nonconformists were especially prone to argue that fewer people were committed for indictable offences in the principality than in England, and that the difference could be explained by the dominant position occupied by Dissent in the life of the Welsh nation. Richard Davies, the wealthy Calvinistic Methodist shipowner who was later to become Liberal MP for Anglesey, argued in 1851 that 'religious instruction under the supervision of Dissenters accounted for the paucity of crime in Wales'.[291] Thomas Rees pointed out that

---

[285] *Quarterly Review*, 102 (1857), 328–9.
[286] R. Colls, *The Pitmen of the Northern Coalfield* (Manchester, 1987), 119.
[287] *Midland Mining Commission: First Report, Staffordshire* (1843) [508], xiii., 186.
[288] Leese, 'Impact of Methodism on Black Country Society', 306.
[289] J. E. Williams, *The Derbyshire Miners* (1962), 134.
[290] Peel, *These Hundred Years*, 148. There were also 11 Presbyterians, but they were probably Scotsmen.
[291] D. A. Pretty, 'Richard Davies and Nonconformist Radicalism in Anglesey', *Welsh History Review*, 9 (1968–9), 439.

whereas 0.60 per cent of the population of England was committed for trial in 1860, only 0.34 per cent of the population of Wales was so committed, and that at least 42.5 per cent of the crimes committed in Wales were perpetrated by people born outside the principality.[292] And even Jelinger Symons, the member of the Welsh Education Commission who was most condemnatory of the morals of the Welsh people, admitted that the principality's 'jails are empty'.[293] Recent research on crime in nineteenth-century Wales emphasizes the reluctance of the Welsh to prosecute offenders and their willingness to accept compensation rather than legal punishment for wrongs done to them, but even with such qualifications David Jones concludes that the claims by Welsh Dissenters of the comparative paucity of crime in the principality are substantially correct.[294]

There can be little doubt that the expansion of Evangelical Nonconformity, for good or ill, had a pacifying and civilizing influence on the working class. A Welsh magistrate told the Calvinistic Methodist preacher Ebenezer Morris that the justices were 'under great obligation to you, Mr Morris, for keeping the country in order, and preserving peace among the people'. 'You are worth more than any dozen of us.'[295] When the Primitive Methodist preacher Samuel Waller was arrested in 1821 on charges of holding a 'tumultuous' meeting in a street in Ashton-under-Lyne and of obstructing the public highway, he told the magistrates in his defence how the overseers of one parish had given the Ranters £5 towards the building of a chapel because their preaching had led to the poor 'becoming sober, orderly, industrious, [and] virtuous', and so less of a charge on the poor rate.[296] During the Swing riots of 1830–1, so a farmer of Bluntisham in Huntingdonshire told the Primitive Methodist preacher Robert Key, 'a gang of vermin' destroyed seventeen houses and it cost him 'two shillings a night, during the whole winter', to pay a man to watch his premises, and even then his family went to bed full of fear lest they 'should be burnt out before morning'. But when the Ranters 'came here and sang and prayed about the streets (you could not get these vermin into a church or chapel), the word was brought to bear upon them in the open air . . . and they are now good men in your church'.[297]

In a sentence, Nonconformity made a section of the working class respectable. Harold Perkin has argued that between 1780 and 1850 there

---

[292] T. Rees, *Miscellaneous Papers on Subjects Relating to Wales* (1867), 17.
[293] I. G. Jones, *Mid-Victorian Wales* (Cardiff, 1992), 143.
[294] D. J. V. Jones, *Crime in Nineteenth-Century Wales* (Cardiff, 1992), 5, 7, 239–40.
[295] W. Williams, *Welsh Calvinistic Methodism* (1872), 236.
[296] *Primitive Methodist Magazine*, 3 (1822), 261–3.
[297] R. Key, *The Gospel among the Masses* (1872), 126–7.

took place a 'moral revolution' in which the 'traditional puritanism of the English middle ranks' was imposed on the whole of society. In those seventy years 'the English ceased to be one of the most aggressive, brutal, rowdy, out-spoken, riotous, cruel, and bloodthirsty nations in the world, and became one of the most inhibited, polite, orderly, tender-minded, prudish, and hypocritical'.[298] Yet it would be wrong to see this moral revolution simply as a bourgeois revolution. Working-class Methodists and Baptists were more certain than middle-class Unitarians and Quakers that those who rejected the Evangelical message would spend eternity in hell. It was working-class communities, not middle-class society, which were most at risk from occupational hazards and cholera epidemics and so most susceptible to appeals to escape the wrath to come. It was working-class men and women who knew best the havoc that alcohol could wreak on individual lives and on family budgets and who were most insistent that total abstinence was the only answer. It was working-class families who were most conscious of the need to work hard and to practise thrift if they were to avoid the ultimate shame and degradation of the workhouse, and it was working-class people who best appreciated that education offered an escape route out of poverty and towards modest prosperity.

By making the working class respectable Dissent also helped to promote social harmony. England and Wales in the nineteenth century were divided by two conflicts which set citizen against citizen: the conflict between church and chapel, and the conflict between capital and labour. The conflict between capital and labour for a time became a dominant theme in the 1840s, but it was not until the second decade of the twentieth century, when the Labour party was replacing the Liberal party as one of the two main political parties, that class conflict again became the main theme of British domestic history. For many people for most of the time in nineteenth-century England and Wales the clash between church and chapel was far more significant than the conflict between capital and labour. Thomas Jones, the future confidant and biographer of Lloyd George, recalled of Rhymney in the south Wales coalfield in which he was brought up in the 1870s and 1880s that religious divisions were far more important than class divisions. His family was never invited to tea at the large houses standing at either end of the terrace in which he lived, the one owned by the manager of the company shop and the other by the colliery manager, because 'they were Church and we were Chapel'. 'We did not then speak of the bourgeoisie and the proletariat.'[299] Though the

---

[298] H. Perkin, *The Origins of Modern English Society* (1969), 280.
[299] T. Jones, *Rhymney Memories* (Newtown, 1938), 79–80.

expansion of Evangelical Nonconformity deepened the religious divisions which split England and Wales, it helped to prevent class division from threatening the stability of society. As we have seen, although Nonconformity itself suffered from the intensification of class antagonism in the 1840s, it made a significant contribution to the social harmony of the 1850s and 1860s. Nonconformist employers united with working-class radicals in an assault on privilege and in defence of workers' rights. Francis Crossley, the Congregationalist carpet manufacturer, spoke in support of the Chartist Ernest Jones in Halifax in the general election of 1847.[300] Twenty years later his fellow Congregationalist Samuel Morley chaired a lecture by Ernest Jones on 'Capital and Labour'. When Morley was criticized by the press he retorted that his great fear was not that 'communism will proceed to universal confiscation', but that wealthy and educated Englishmen would fail to reduce and eradicate 'the poverty, disease, and vice of so many of our own flesh and blood'.[301] Morley and Titus Salt both subsidized the trade union newspaper the *Beehive* to enable it to reduce its price in 1870.[302] Four years later Morley contributed £500 to a relief fund for locked-out agricultural workers.[303] The Nonconformist disdain for class conflict—apart from criticism of the idle and privileged classes—comes out time and again. In 1843 the Leeds Baptist minister John Giles was loudly applauded when he told a meeting, composed largely of Chartists, that he 'repudiated the idea of a different class in British society'. 'Were they not brothers? (Applause). Were they not all Englishmen? (applause) . . . Then away with the absurd idea of upper and middle and lower classes! (Tremendous applause).'[304] The Bratton Particular Baptist church in Wiltshire was proud of the fact that 'servants and employees sat alongside masters on the church's diaconate', and 'it was entirely accepted that the children of "the master" were taught in Sunday school by their father's employees'.[305] The Nonconformist faith in class co-operation was epitomized in Mrs Gaskell's novel *Mary Barton*. Elizabeth Gaskell, the daughter of a one-time Unitarian minister and wife of William Gaskell, who from 1828 until his death in 1884 was minister to the Cross Street Unitarian church in Manchester, leapt to fame with the publication of her first novel, *Mary Barton*, in that year of revolutions, 1848. The central

[300] K. Tiller, 'Late Chartism: Halifax 1847–58', in J. Epstein and D. Thompson, *The Chartist Experience* (1982), 315.

[301] Hodder, *Life of Samuel Morley*, 250–1.

[302] J. Vincent, *Formation of the British Liberal Party* (Penguin edn., 1972), 75.

[303] Owen, *English Philanthropy*, 405.

[304] C. M. Elliott, 'The Political Economy of English Dissent', in R. M. Hartwell, *The Industrial Revolution* (Oxford, 1970), 162.

[305] M. Reeves, *Sheep Bell and Ploughshare* (Bradford-on-Avon, 1978), 136–7.

theme of *Mary Barton* is the clash between a hard-hearted employer, a Mr Carson, and impoverished weavers led by the trade unionist John Barton. The weavers were so driven to despair that they drew lots to commit an act of violence against their employer, a lottery which issued in the murder of their employer's son, Harry Carson, at the hands of John Barton, an incident based on the murder of the mill-owner Thomas Ashton in 1831. But the novel ends with the elder Carson visiting the dying John Barton, with Barton pleading for the forgiveness of his victim's father, with Carson granting his request, and with John Barton dying in the arms of the man whose son he had murdered. In his last moments John Barton recognized that 'rich and poor, masters and men, were . . . brothers in the deep suffering of the heart', and saw in Carson not 'a being of another race' but 'a very poor and desolate old man', mourning the loss of his son. And after his shattering experience Carson was determined 'that a perfect understanding, and complete confidence and love, might exist between masters and men; that the truth might be recognised that the interests of one were the interests of all'.[306]

The way in which Nonconformity helped to inhibit the development of working-class consciousness was illustrated by Beatrice Webb's observations on the Lancashire cotton town of Bacup which she visited in the 1880s. Beatrice Webb, née Potter, was the granddaughter of two successful entrepreneurs and former MPs, of Richard Potter, the Unitarian cotton merchant who represented Wigan in the first reformed Parliament in 1832, and of Lawrence Heyworth, a Liverpool merchant whose family came from east Lancashire and who was elected MP for Derby in 1847. It was to visit her mother's working-class relatives, whom she had never met, that Beatrice, as the daughter of a wealthy upper middle-class family, travelled incognito to Bacup in 1883, and she was enchanted by the community of working-class Dissenters she found there. She stayed in an 'old-fashioned house at the back of the chapel', the home of the chapel-keeper John Ashworth, a 'regular old Puritan'. Beatrice and her companion were greeted by Ashworth and his daughter, a mill-hand, 'in the most hearty fashion'. Prayers were 'offered up for our safety and spiritual well-being while under their roof', and the travellers were refreshed with 'some delicious tea and home-made bread and butter'. The agnostic and future Fabian Socialist found herself at the centre of 'the only society I have ever lived in, in which religious faith really guides thought and action, and forms the basis of the whole life of the community'. The Dissenters' religious faith 'seemed to absorb the entire nature, to claim as its own all the energy unused in the actual struggle for existence'. Each

---

[306] E. Gaskell, *Mary Barton* (1848; 1906), 425–32, 451.

chapel was 'a self-governing community, regulating not only chapel matters but overlooking the private life of its members'. 'What an excellent thing', exclaimed Beatrice, 'these dissenting organisations have been for educating this class for self-government.' 'Public opinion—which means religiously guided opinion—presses heavily on the misdoer or the non-worker,—the outcasting process, the reverse of the attracting force of East End life, is seen clearly in this small community, ridding it of the ne'er-do-well and the habitual out-o-work.' The 'co-op' flourished and provided 'amusement and interest, free of expense to all members, and through the system of deposit account, a mutual insurance company'. But trade unionism was not strong in Bacup. Those mills which were not controlled by companies were 'owned by quite small men of working-class origin and connected with working people'. 'Class spirit hardly exists.'[307]

Bacup was not typical of Lancashire. It was situated in the Haslingden registration district which in 1851 had by far the highest Nonconformist attendance in the county, with 34.4 per cent of the people worshipping in chapel on census Sunday, 13.2 per cent at Wesleyan chapels, and 9.9 per cent at Baptist chapels. But Bacup was representative of hundreds of working-class communities in the mining districts of Cornwall, in the smallware manufacturing towns of the west Midlands, in the hosiery villages of Nottinghamshire and Leicestershire, in the agricultural regions of Wales, Lincolnshire, East Anglia, and the south Midlands, in the fishing villages of Yorkshire, and in the coal-mining areas of Durham, Northumberland, and south Wales. If one wants to brand the Nonconformist influence on such communities as 'social control' it must be with the recognition that it was social control imposed by the working class on the working class. And against those historians who deplore the role of Nonconformity in fostering social harmony one must argue that the muted class antagonism of nineteenth-century England and Wales was preferable to the turmoil unleashed on Paris in 1871, on Russia in 1917, and on Spain in 1936–9, and preferable to the order which the threat of such turmoil helped to provoke in Italy in 1922 and in Germany in 1933.

This is not to ignore the fact that Dissenters marched on Newport in 1839, were involved in the Rebecca riots in 1842–3, and from time to time participated in strike action. When the ending of the Crimean War produced a trade depression in 1857 and the colliery-owners at Aberdare sought to impose a wage cut of 15 per cent, the miners replied by calling a strike which lasted seven weeks and at the end of which they were forced to accept a 20 per cent reduction in wages. The failure of the strike caused great bitterness and led

---

[307] B. Webb, *My Apprenticeship* (2nd edn., n.d.), 131–43.

the Dissenting leaders in the area to argue that strikes damaged relations between the classes without producing any benefit for the workers. In an attempt to heal the wounds David Price, the minister of Siloa Independent church, urged the holding of prayer-meetings to bring the colliery-owners and miners together. Early in 1858 David Davis, the Wesleyan owner of the Blaengwawr and Aberaman pits, organized such prayer-meetings both in chapels and in the pits he controlled, meetings which were attended both by himself and by his workers.[308] Out of the desire to reduce class hostility was thus sown one of the seeds of the religious revival of 1857–9.

5. 'HELL-FIRE FLASHED BEFORE THEIR FACES': THE REVIVAL OF 1857–1859

In July 1859 Richard Cope Morgan, the thirty-two-year-old son of a Congregationalist printer from Abergavenny, launched a weekly newspaper, the *Revival*, designed to be a 'record of events connected with the present revival of religion'. In his first issue Morgan explained how the revival had begun in New York in September 1857, when financial panic had prompted business men and their clerks to gather for lunch-time prayer-meetings in the Dutch Reformed church in Fulton Street. It had then spread to Ireland, beginning with prayer-meetings in Kells in the parish of Connor near Ballymena in County Antrim, and in September 1858 revival had broken out in Scotland, beginning with the holding of 'special and united prayer meetings for the outpouring of the Holy Spirit' in Aberdeen.[309] In August 1859 the *Revival* announced the holding of a daily prayer-meeting in the Crosby Hall in London's Bishopgate Street and by January 1860 the paper was reporting twenty-seven daily and fifty-two weekly prayer-meetings in London and scores of others in towns throughout England.[310] Ninety years later Morgan's thesis of a revival originating in the United States in 1857, spreading across the Atlantic to Ulster, Scotland, and Wales, and ultimately reaching England in 1859, was elaborated in detail by an American evangelist, Edwin Orr, in what he called *The Second Evangelical Awakening in Britain*.

Edwin Orr's thesis has been challenged by other scholars, and John Kent has argued that 'it would be wrong to suggest that in 1859–60 either the pro-

---

[308] Turner, 'Revivals and Popular Religion in Wales', 266–70.
[309] *Revival*, 30 July 1859, 2–3.   [310] Ibid. 10 Sept. 1859, 53; 14 Jan. 1860, 15.

fessional or the amateur revivalists succeeded in England'.[311] Orr claimed that as a result of the revival the Nonconformist churches of England 'gained at least 400,000 accessions',[312] but his conclusion is based on a good deal of optimistic guesswork as far as the Baptists and the Congregationalists are concerned. The New Connexion of General Baptists, the one non-Methodist denomination to keep accurate statistics, recorded even in the best of their revival years, 1861–2, an increase of only 648, a mere 3.3 per cent.[313] However, the figures for the Arminian Methodist churches do show an upsurge in the late 1850s and early 1860s. The Arminian Methodist churches in England increased their membership by 16,806 in 1857–8, an increase of 3.9 per cent, by 28,986 in 1858–9, a rise of 6.5 per cent, and by 21,256 in 1859–60, an increase of 4.3 per cent.[314] The increase in 1858–9 was the highest annual increase since the cholera revival of 1832–3, and in the decade 1857–67 the Arminian Methodists in England and Wales increased their membership by 136,534, an increase of 30.7 per cent. However two points need to be made about these figures. Although by 1860 total Methodist membership figures had made good the losses occasioned by the disaster of the *Fly Sheets* controversy, in percentage terms total Methodist membership in England and Wales, per head of population over the age of 15, was never again to attain the level of 4.42 per cent it had reached in 1850.[315] Secondly, although there was an impressive growth in Methodist membership figures in the late 1850s and 1860s, the most significant gains were made in the year 1858–9, in the twelve months *before* the period in which Morgan and Orr claimed that the Evangelical revival had begun to affect England.

In so far as there was a religious revival in England in the late 1850s and early 1860s it was the result not of the prayer-meetings which were held in New York in September 1857, but of an older revivalist tradition which went back to James Caughey, William Bramwell, and John Wesley himself. Many of the Methodists who were expelled, or seceded, from the Wesleyan Connexion in the aftermath of the *Fly Sheets* controversy did so not so much

---

[311] J. Kent, *Holding the Fort* (1978), 71.

[312] J. E. Orr, *The Second Evangelical Awakening in Britain* (1949), 207.

[313] Currie, Gilbert, and Horsley, *Churches and Churchgoers*, 148–9.

[314] These calculations are based on figures in *Churches and Churchgoers*, 141, but include in the comparative figures for 1859 and 1860 statistics for the Wesleyan Reform Union which had approximately 17,000 members in 1859 but only 12,516 in 1860, the result, presumably, of churches leaving the Wesleyan Reform Union for the United Methodist Free Churches (Jones, *History of the Wesleyan Reform Union*, 50; W. J. Townshend, *et al.*, *A New History of Methodism* (1909), ii. 539).

[315] Gilbert, 'Growth and Decline of Nonconformity', 39.

because they sympathized with James Everett but because they were disgusted with Conference's decision to bar Caughey from its pulpits in 1846. Such men were determined to maintain in Free Methodism the revivalist tradition which they believed was being stifled by the Old Connexion. Their numbers included Richard Poole of Sheffield, 'a plain, simple preacher [whose] word was attended by a power that was very remarkable', and Poole's young protégé, the pale-skinned, long-haired William Booth, who, frustrated at the Wesleyan Reformers' reluctance to establish a permanent organization, threw in his lot with the Methodist New Connexion in 1854.[316] The activities of these Free Methodist revivalists were publicized in a monthly paper called the *Revivalist*, edited by Edwin Squire, a Louth bookseller, and financed, at least in part, by Page Woodcock, a Lincoln manufacturer of 'wind pills' which were claimed to be 'the most effective remedy' for most human disorders. The Free Methodists promised a cure for spiritual as well as for physical ill-health. Their object was not only the conversion of sinners but also, in the tradition of Wesley, Bramwell, and Caughey, the 'entire sanctification' of those already justified.[317] '*Preach holiness*', urged William Braimbridge to the editor of the *Revivalist* in 1856. 'Methodism has betrayed its trust in this point; Mr Wesley esteemed it as a talent entrusted by the Lord to the societies, but now it has been lost sight of.'[318]

From April 1854 the *Revivalist* carried news of the dramatic results of Free Methodist revivalism. In December 1853 Methodist revivalists at Caistor in north Lincolnshire seceded from the Wesleyans, started their own services in a hired room, and attracted so many people that they had to move to a former Congregational chapel. 'Evening after evening did its walls echo the sighs and mournings of numerous penitents.'[319] In February 1854 the holding of special services in the Leather Lane chapel in Holborn and the distribution of 1,200 handbills produced large congregations, and 'every evening was the vestry filled with penitents, many of whom experienced the power of God to save'.[320] The *Wesleyan Methodist Association Magazine* reported a revival in its Lever Street chapel in Manchester in November 1854 during which 'upwards of a hundred testified to their conversion'.[321] At the end of 1854 the Methodist New Connexion released William Booth from circuit duties to enable him to devote himself to special evangelistic services and in the next two years he claimed to have won 460 converts at Longton and Hanley in the Potteries, 290 at Newcastle-under-Lyme, 270 in Hull, 663 in Sheffield, 440 in

[316] Begbie, *William Booth*, i. 211, 224–5; Booth-Tucker, *Catherine Booth*, i. 101.
[317] Watts, *The Dissenters*, i. 432–4.   [318] *Revivalist*, Mar. 1856, 73.
[319] Ibid. Apr. 1854, 167.   [320] Ibid. 169.
[321] *Wesleyan Methodist Association Magazine*, 17 (Dec. 1854), 591.

Dewsbury, 800 in Leeds, 641 in Halifax, another 646 in Sheffield, and 740 in his native Nottingham.[322] In November 1855 Richard Poole conducted the first of a series of revival services at Mount Tabor chapel, Sheffield, towards the end of which a man cried out from the gallery 'Lord save me! Lord have mercy upon me!' and the preacher's voice was drowned in the subsequent shouting and sobbing. After four weeks of such services Poole claimed that 650 people were either justified or sanctified.[323] A revival in the Wesleyan Methodist Association Camelford circuit in Cornwall was said to have resulted in 770 conversions in the winter of 1855–6.[324] In March 1857 Poole conducted evangelistic services in London, attracting crowds of over 1,300 people to St George's chapel in Cannon Street and claiming 360 converts in one week.[325] He went on to lead campaigns in Newcastle-under-Lyme, in Kingswood, and in Louth where, in December 1857, nearly 300 'professed to get spiritual profit'.[326] Free Methodist revivals produced 700 conversions in the Camborne circuit in the summer of 1858, over 200 in Wigan, more than 400 at Rotherham in the autumn, and 400 at Doncaster in the spring of 1859.[327]

The climax of Free Methodist revivalism came with Caughey's return to England, at their request, in the summer of 1857. He began his mission on 10 August in the Free Methodists' stronghold of Sheffield and for the next twelve months conducted revival services in chapels belonging to the United Methodist Free Churches, the Wesleyan Reform Union, the Methodist New Connexion, and the Primitive Methodist Connexion. When the Wesleyan Reform Union Chapel in Watery Street proved too small for the crowds who wanted to hear him Caughey moved to the Surrey Music Hall where he attracted capacity audiences of 4,000, but particularly poignant were the services he conducted in the Reformers' Garden Street chapel, a pulpit 'once occupied by the Rev William Bramwell, a name endeared to thousands'.[328] By the time a thousand representatives of the Free Methodists, Wesleyan Reformers, New Connexion, and Primitive Methodists gathered in the music-hall to honour Caughey on 31 August 1858 he was claiming to have effected the conversions of 5,264 men and women and to have been instrumental in obtaining the entire sanctification of another 2,393.[329] Caughey followed up his success at Sheffield by conducting evangelistic missions in Hanley where over 950 people were said to have been either justified or

---

[322] Booth-Tucker, *Catherine Booth*, i. 131–86.   [323] *Revivalist*, Mar. 1856, 46–7.
[324] *Wesleyan Methodist Association Magazine*, 19 (Jan. 1856), 46; (Apr. 1856), 199; (June 1856), 294.
[325] *Revivalist*, May 1857, 72.   [326] Ibid. Feb. 1858, 25.
[327] Ibid. July 1858, 111; Nov. 1858, 174; Feb. 1859, 22; Mar. 1859, 43; June 1859, 93.
[328] Ibid. May 1858, 76–7; June 1858, 89.   [329] Ibid. Oct. 1858, 145, 158.

sanctified; in Manchester, where 2,202 professed conversion and 467 entire sanctification; in Hull, with 544 converted and 182 sanctified; and Louth where 166 were converted and 121 sanctified.[330] Caughey could not expect dramatic results at Louth since the town had already been the scene of numerous revivals, but his presence was significant since he attended a circuit meeting in August 1859 at which the Wesleyan Reformers decided unanimously to join the United Methodist Free Churches.

In time all the branches of Methodism benefited from the revival of 1857–9, though not as dramatically as did the Free Methodists. A revival prompted by the preaching of the Free Methodist, William Tomlins, at Tremar Coombe near Liskeard in Cornwall in May 1857 spread to the neighbouring Bible Christians and in total over 200 people were converted.[331] A revival in the Free Methodists' St Austell circuit in March 1858 similarly led to revivals in the Wesleyan and Bible Christian chapels.[332] During a revival which began in the Downham Market Primitive Methodist circuit in Norfolk in December 1858 600 people 'professed to find peace with God'.[333] A revival broke out among the Wesleyans of Brackley and Turweston on the borders of Northamptonshire and Buckinghamshire in April 1859 and 174 were placed on trial for membership.[334] Much of this revival activity took place among people who were totally unaware of the contemporary revivals in the United States and in Ulster. The *Revivalist* did not mention the 'great awakening' in America until April 1858, and the Irish revival was not referred to until July 1859.[335] It was not until the end of 1858 that there was a conscious attempt to export the American revival to England when the veteran American preacher Charles Grandison Finney, now aged sixty-six, decided to see whether 'the same influence would not pervade' Britain and he set sail for Liverpool. At the invitation of a wealthy Congregationalist miller from Huntingdon, Potto Brown, Finney conducted revival services in Houghton, St Ives, and Huntingdon itself, and went on to London, Edinburgh, and Aberdeen.[336] But Finney's main success came in Bolton where Congregationalists and Methodists united to canvass every house in the town and where he claimed to have converted up to 1,200 people in three months.[337] Two more American revivalists, Walter and Phoebe Palmer, also came to England in 1859 and in September began a series of evangelistic ser-

---

[330] Ibid. Feb. 1859, 32; June 1859, 92; Aug. 1859, 125; Sept. 1859, 140.
[331] Ibid. June 1857, 91–2; July 1857, 109.   [332] Ibid. Apr. 1858, 63.
[333] *Primitive Methodist Magazine*, 17 (Aug. 1859), 491.
[334] *Wesleyan Methodist Magazine*, 82 (June 1859), 550.
[335] *Revivalist*, Apr. 1858, 64; July 1859, 106.
[336] C. G. Finney, *Memoirs of the Rev C. G. Finney* (1876), 447–57.
[337] Carwardine, *Transatlantic Revivalism*, 176–9.

vices in the Brunswick Place Wesleyan chapel in Newcastle upon Tyne. In five weeks 1,400 people claimed 'to have received religious good' and by July 1860 the Wesleyan circuits in the area were reporting an increase of 1,593 members with another 1,851 on trial.[338]

The enthusiasm with which the Wesleyans of the north-east rallied to the Palmers was, however, exceptional and many respectable Wesleyans continued to harbour the misgivings about revivalism which had led to the banning of Caughey from Wesleyan pulpits in 1846. In the course of a sermon preached to the Wesleyan Conference in 1860 its president, Samuel Waddy, referred to 'the damage which may be done to the position and usefulness of your ministers in having recourse to . . . revival schemes' and warned that revivals often produced a reaction which took years to overcome.[339] Two years later Conference, though it claimed it did not wish 'to discourage efforts to promote revivals of religion', ordered Wesleyan superintendents 'not to sanction the occupation of any of our chapels for continuous services by persons who are not amenable to our regular discipline'.[340] Wesleyan ministers were not alone in resenting the intrusion of freelance evangelists into their pulpits. The success of William Booth's revival methods incurred the jealousy of some of his fellow ministers in the Methodist New Connexion. In 1857 the New Connexion Conference voted by 44 votes to 40 to deprive Booth of his commission as a roving evangelist and to insist that he become a circuit minister and when, four years later, Conference refused to let him return to full-time evangelistic work Booth left the Connexion.[341] Booth's opponents argued, as had Samuel Waddy, that revivalists often left circuits in a worse state than that in which they found them, and that it was an insult to circuit ministers to bring outsiders into their pulpits.[342] Even the Primitive Methodists had become so respectable that they resented revivalists who might poach on the reserves of regular ministers. In the summer of 1859 James Milbourn held a series of evangelistic services in the Old End Lyng Primitive Methodist chapel in West Bromwich in the Black Country. In eight weeks Milbourn claimed that 550 people had been justified and another 294 sanctified, but he was obliged to interrupt his mission by the deaths of his wife and his infant son, and when he tried to resume his campaign he was ordered by the circuit authorities to stop.[343] In 1862 the Primitive Methodist Conference, meeting in Sheffield of all places, urged its 'station authorities to

---

[338] *Wesleyan Methodist Magazine*, 83 (Aug. 1860), 738.
[339] *Messenger of Life*, Sept. 1860, 451.
[340] R. Sandall, *History of the Salvation Army* (1947), i. 16.
[341] Booth-Tucker, *Life of Catherine Booth*, i. 202, 289, 303.   [342] Ibid. i. 289.
[343] *Revivalist*, July 1859, 111; Aug. 1859, 128; Jan. 1860, 9–10.

avoid the employing of revivalists, so called'.[344] All the Methodist denominations in England enjoyed rising membership figures in the ten years after
1857: Wesleyan membership increased by 24 per cent, that of the New Connexion by 25 per cent, that of the Bible Christians by 34 per cent, and that of
the Primitive Methodists by 36 per cent. But it was the growth of the United
Methodist Free Churches which was most spectacular in percentage terms:
between 1857 and 1867 their membership grew by 23,771, an increase of
61 per cent.[345]

Religious revival began in Wales, as in England, independently of the
revival in the United States. A revival in the Wesleyan society at Llanfair-
fechan in Caernarfonshire early in 1858 led to an increase in membership of
134 and its influence spread to the Calvinistic Methodists in the town, who
increased their membership by sixty, and to other towns on the coast of north
Wales. A similar revival broke out in the Congregational chapel at Llangybi,
Cardiganshire, in April.[346] But the American revival appears to have been a
much more direct stimulus to revival in Wales than it was in England. The
Calvinistic Methodists of south Wales, meeting in Aberystwyth in April, and
those of north Wales, meeting at Holywell in June, discussed the need to
encourage the revivalist spirit which had broken out in parts of Wales and
in America, and William Jenkins, pastor of the Rehoboth Congregational
church in Bryn-mawr, Monmouthshire, was prompted by the American
revival to launch a series of prayer-meetings which led to eighty-five new
members being added to his church.[347] But the main impact of the American
revival on Wales came with the return to his native country of a young Welshman named Humphrey Jones in June 1858.

Humphrey Jones had been born at Tre'r-ddol in north Cardiganshire in
1832. Converted at the age of sixteen, he had applied for admission to the
Wesleyan ministry six years later and, on being rejected, emigrated to
the United States. He briefly served the Methodist Episcopal Church in
Wisconsin before becoming a freelance preacher and earning a reputation as
a revivalist. He returned to his native village in June 1858 to visit relatives and
to convert his fellow countrymen. After a fortnight's preaching he won fifty-
one converts in Tre'r-ddol, which was regarded 'as a major revival in such a
small congregation', and another seventy-six in the lead-mining village of
Ystumtuen. In October Jones persuaded David Morgan, a Calvinistic
Methodist minister from Ysbyty Ystwyth, to join him in his evangelistic cru-

---

[344] *Minutes of the Annual Conferences of the Primitive Methodist Connexion* (1862), 28.
[345] Some of this increase was due to societies of Wesleyan Reformers joining the Methodist
Free Churches subsequent to the union with the Wesleyan Methodist Association in 1857.
[346] E. Evans, *When He is Come* (Bala, 1959), 30–1.   [347] Ibid. 31, 33.

sade, and by the end of January 1859, so David Morgan's son claimed, three hundred of the three thousand inhabitants of the Ysbyty Ystwyth district had been converted. By the end of 1858 the revival had spread to other parts of Cardiganshire and during the first six months of 1859 the membership of the Calvinistic Methodist churches of Cardiganshire increased by 4,726, with another 1,474 on trial.[348]

The climax of the Cardiganshire revival came on 4 August 1859 with the South Wales Calvinistic Methodist Quarterly Association at Llangeitho, the village hallowed by the memory of the Connexion's pioneer evangelist David Rowland. At six o'clock in the morning thousands gathered in a field to hear Daniel Rowlands of Llanidloes preach and a young man in the audience 'began to tremble like a leaf', fell to the ground in a swoon, and 'poured forth a succession of sublime sentences'. Two hours later twenty thousand people attended a prayer-meeting at which the prayers offered from the platform 'were submerged by billows of praise sweeping up from the sea of worshippers'. In the evening Dr Owen Thomas preached in the chapel from Hebrews 9: 14, 'How much shall the blood of Christ . . . purge your conscience from dead works'. In the course of the sermon a farmer in the congregation cried out 'God be thanked for the blood!' 'A mighty chorus of "Hallelujahs" and "Praise God" broke out all over the building', and 'the rejoicing lasted for hours'.[349]

From Cardiganshire the revival spread, early in 1859, to Merioneth, Carmarthenshire, and Glamorgan and then to the rest of Wales. All the Evangelical Nonconformist denominations, and some Anglican churches, benefited. The Independent churches of Aberdare claim to have increased their membership by 1,400; by June 1860 the Calvinistic Methodist churches of Merioneth had added 4,000.[350] In Aberystwyth eight publicans took down their signs and became teetotallers, in Bethesda in Caernarfonshire a mixture of changed convictions and falling sales led to twelve public houses being closed.[351] In the early days of the revival David Morgan and Humphrey Jones toured the pubs of Ysbyty Ystwyth holding prayer-meetings which emptied the bar rooms of customers, and at Morlais Castle near Dowlais beer-drinking sessions which young men began early on Sunday mornings in the summer months were transformed into prayer-meetings.[352] During the time of the revival virtually no cases of drunkenness came before the courts in Denbigh, and in Cardiff criminal cases dwindled.[353] It may not have been

[348] J. J. Morgan, *The '59 Revival in Wales* (Mold, 1909), 2–18, 76–7.   [349] Ibid. 76–81.
[350] Ibid. 99, 117.   [351] T. Phillips, *The Welsh Revival* (1860), 19, 96.
[352] Morthan, *The '59 Revival*, 14; E. Davies, *Revivals in Wales* (1859), 40.
[353] Phillips, *Welsh Revival*, 97; Orr, *Second Evangelical Awakening*, 91–2.

entirely a coincidence that the religious revival coincided with the beginning of a decline in the number of indictable offences in Wales which continued until the end of the century.[354]

The results of the revival were far more dramatic in Wales than they were in England. Membership of the Calvinistic Methodists rose from 58,678 in 1850 to 90,650 in 1861, an increase of 54.3 per cent.[355] We do not have precise membership figures for the Welsh Baptists and the Welsh Independents in the mid-nineteenth century, but we can estimate attendance at their chapels on census Sunday, 1851, and by assuming a ratio of members to attenders of 1 : 3 we can estimate their membership.[356] Such figures can then be compared with the membership statistics for 1861 which Thomas Rees produced in his *History of Protestant Nonconformity in Wales*.[357] These comparisons suggest that the growth of Old Dissent in Wales was as impressive, if not more impressive, as that of the Calvinistic Methodists. The membership of the Welsh Baptists rose from an estimated 38,376 in 1851 to 50,903 ten years later, an increase of 32.6 per cent. As for the Welsh Independents, their estimated membership rose from 48,409 in 1851 to 97,647 in 1861: if Thomas Rees's figure for the latter year can be believed, this represents an increase of an astounding 101.7 per cent. The statistics may not be wholly reliable, but there can be little doubt that Wales, by 1861, was even more overwhelmingly Nonconformist than it had been at the time of the religious census ten years earlier.

The revival of the late 1850s replicated the features of the earlier revivals of the eighteenth century and of the 1830s. There was the same appeal to unsophisticated and ill-educated working-class audiences; the same notable successes among adolescents and in isolated communities of miners; the same hysterical convulsions, swooning, jumping, and dancing; the same urgent entreaties to escape the fires of eternal damnation. William Booth knew that 'nothing moves people' like terror. 'They must have hell-fire flashed before their faces, or they will not move.'[358] In one of his most memorable sermons David Morgan compared the unconverted person to 'a man collecting sea-birds' eggs on a rock-bound coast'.

While his friends above hold the rope which was tied around him, he descends on his perilous quest. It is a stormy day; the wind swings him . . . and the rope rubs against the

---

[354] Jones, *Crime in Nineteenth-century Wales*, 31–3, 51.

[355] Williams, *Welsh Calvinistic Methodism*, 216; Rees, *Protestant Nonconformity in Wales*, 451.

[356] In these calculations I have included the estimates for Monmouthshire in the totals for Wales.

[357] Rees, *Protestant Nonconformity in Wales*, 450–1.

[358] Booth-Tucker, *Catherine Booth*, i. 116.

teeth of the rocks. To his consternation he observes that the sharp precipice above has already severed one strand of the rope. He shouts to his mates above, but his cry is lost in the whistling of the wind. 'Haul me up! haul me up!' he shrieks as he swings, horror-struck to see another and yet another strand severed by the jagged crag. You hang by a frail and fraying rope over the abyss of eternity. What means that shooting pain in your head? A strand of the rope is gone. What is that crick in your back? Another strand has parted. Your lost sleep the other night! Another fibre severed! The last strand will snap one of these next days. You may be raised to safety tonight and your feet set upon a rock.[359]

A contemporary critic of the revival, John Chapman, the editor of the *Westminster Review*, believed that overwork and an inadequate diet made people particularly receptive to the evangelists' message. 'Ignorant men and women, and the youth of both sexes, many of them ill fed, most of them phys-ically exhausted already by their daily toil, are crowded in a building where . . . the imagination is goaded and stimulated until it conjures up conceptions of hell and the devil with a vividness approaching reality.'[360] Certainly Cardiganshire, the focus of the Welsh revival, was one of the poorest coun-ties in Britain and its people suffered from a poor diet and consequent dis-ease.[361] The revivalists frequently commented on their successes in poor, working-class communities. A majority of the converts won by William Tomlins at Tremar Coombe in Cornwall in May 1857 were 'young men who work in the copper mines'.[362] Tomlins won another eighty converts at Batley in the West Riding later in the same year where the church was 'composed entirely, with one exception, of working men', and a few months later Richard Poole was suprised at his success in winning over a hundred more converts at Batley 'notwithstanding the badness of trade and the extreme want of the people'.[363] The revival presided over by James Milbourn in the Park Gate chapel, Rotherham, in the autumn of 1858, was aided by a coalminers' strike which led to a stoppage in the ironworks with the result that the forge men, who constituted 'the principal part of the members . . . consecrated a whole day to God, by praying and preaching in and out of doors'.[364] Finney's congregations in Bolton 'generally consisted of working people, the majority of whom were female'.[365] The Wesleyan revival in Brackley and Turweston in 1859 was 'among the poor'; that at Brede, Beckley, Northiam, and Peasmarsh in east Sussex in 1860 affected 'to a large

---

[359] Morgan, *The '59 Revival*, 60.
[360] J. Chapman, *Christian Revivals: Their History and National History* (1860), 28.
[361] Turner, 'Revivals and Popular Religion', 215.   [362] *Revivalist*, June 1857, 91–2.
[363] Ibid. Jan. 1858, 12; Mar. 1858, 40.   [364] Ibid. Feb. 1859, 22.
[365] Carwardine, *Transatlantic Revivalism*, 193.

extent young men of the labouring class'.[366] In Cardiganshire 'the lead-miners cried out of the depths of the earth unto God', and it was reported of the Frongoch lead mines near Aberystwyth in 1860 that there was not a company of miners 'small or large, without its prayer-meeting, held under-ground previous to the commencement of work'.[367] In Wales and in Cornwall a significant proportion of the converts were under the age of twenty, in Newcastle upon Tyne the converts included 'a vast number of young persons belonging to the senior classes of Sunday schools', and in Sheffield more than half the 982 converted by Caughey's preaching in the Surrey Music Hall were under the age of twenty-one.[368]

Their conversions were often accompanied by the signs, groans, sobbing, and clapping which John Chapman, a member of the Royal College of Physicians, diagnosed as hysteria.[369] Richard Poole said of the revival over which he presided at Louth in December 1857 that while there might have been confusion, 'it was the confusion of battle when the enemy is routed'.[370] Revival services in the villages surrounding Louth in 1857 were marked by similar manifestations. At Legbourne 'one after another began to weep and mourn and [made] their way with throbs and sighs to the penitent form'.[371] At Carlton a woman in her twenties was afraid to go home after listening to William Braimbridge, had a fit which lasted for two hours while 'she appeared bound or torn by the devil', and after Braimbridge was summoned to her home at three o'clock in the morning she cried for mercy, exclaiming 'I do believe' and 'instantly she was free from the manacles of the devil'.[372] And when Braimbridge preached at Grimoldby, 'one female fairly danced for joy, and a young man fell as he was speaking of the grace of God'.[373] The Cardiganshire revival was similarly marked by spontaneous outbreaks of hysteria and emotion. At Tregaron in November 1858 a seventy-two-year-old deacon vaulted over the top of the high-backed 'big seat' reserved for the deacons and proceeded to dance in front of the congregation with an eighty-year-old woman who was said to be crippled with rheumatism. Four months later, also at Tregaron, when the lay preacher David Morgan of Pontrhydfendigaid was conducting the service, during the singing of the hymn 'the congregation burst into thunders of praise, not ceasing for two hours'.[374] A sermon preached by Richard Poole at Breage in Cornwall in

[366] *Wesleyan Methodist Magazine*, 82 (June 1859), 550; *Revivalist*, 3 Mar. 1860, 68.

[367] Morgan, *The '59 Revival*, 15. Phillips, *Welsh Revival*, 107.

[368] Phillips, *Welsh Revival*, 89; Orr, *Second Evangelical Awakening*, 114, 148; *Revivalist*, May 1858, 78.

[369] Chapman, *Christian Revivals*, 34–5.   [370] *Revivalist*, Feb. 1858, 25.

[371] Ibid., Apr. 1857, 49.   [372] Ibid., May 1857, 80.   [373] Ibid., July 1857, 107.

[374] Morgan, *The '59 Revival*, 25–7.

April 1859 was accompanied by weeping and crying by members of the congregation and by cries of 'Lord save me!', 'God have mercy on my soul', and 'What must I do to be saved'. On the following day 'one soul believed and burst forth into such shouts of "Glory" as to stop the sermon for a time'. 'Revivals without excitement', commented Poole, 'are revivals without spiritual life and power.'[375] The revival's most extravagant manifestation came in June 1859 in the Wesleyan chapel in Queen Street, Aberystwyth, where Humphrey Jones had been preaching since the previous November. Jones announced that 'at eleven o'clock on a certain morning the Holy Ghost would descend in visible form in Queen Street chapel', at the expected hour the chapel was crowded, and Jones lifted up his arms crying 'He is coming! He is coming'. When nothing happened Jones fled back to his rooms and subsequently returned to Wisconsin.[376]

The extravagances of Humphrey Jones were an extreme example of the way in which the revivalists rejected the cult of respectability and attempted to return to the more emotional, more vibrant, more aggressive Evangelicalism of the earlier years of the century. Jones was just one of several freelance evangelists who devoted themselves to revivalist preaching. Another celebrated evangelist was Richard Weaver, a former collier and prizefighter who began his missionary work in 1856 by trying to dissuade people from attending Chester races and who claimed numerous converts in the Black Country in 1859: 500 in Willenhall, 600 in Bilston, and 700 in Darlaston.[377] Among lay preachers employed to attract working-class audiences at Wednesbury in the Black Country in 1863 were a former pickpocket, a convicted train-robber, and a bear wrestler. In Nottingham an expugilist, a former housebreaker, and a converted actor achieved a great 'in-gathering of souls' in 1864.[378] Women preachers reappeared in Free Methodist and New Connexion pulpits: Sarah White in the Lincolnshire Wolds, Elizabeth Bennett in Shropshire, Flintshire, Cheshire, and Lancashire, and William Booth's redoubtable wife Catherine in Gateshead.[379] When a Congregational minister, Arthur Rees, attacked the American evangelist Phoebe Palmer for preaching in Newcastle Catherine Booth replied with a pamphlet defending the right of women to preach. 'When the true light shines and God's words take the place of man's traditions', forecast Catherine, 'the Doctor of Divinity who shall teach that Paul commands women to be silent when God's Spirit urges her to speak, will be

---

[375] *Messenger of Life*, May 1859, 115.   [376] Morgan, *The '59 Revival*, 16–17.
[377] R. C. Morgan, *Life of Richard Weaver* (1906), 83–7.
[378] Orr, *Second Evangelical Awakening*, 139, 143.
[379] *Revivalist*, Apr. 1857, 49; May 1858, 78; Booth-Tucker, *Catherine Booth*, i. 255.

regarded much as the same as we should regard an astronomer who should teach that the sun is the earth's satellite.'[380] But whatever the unusual means employed, the revivalists would always claim that they were justified by souls saved, lives sanctified, and criminals reformed. A pickpocket converted by Caughey one night in Sheffield returned to a publican a handkerchief he had stolen from him earlier in the day; it was also in Sheffield that a thief affected by Caughey restored to a jeweller a diamond he had stolen; and in Staffordshire a poacher converted by the Free Methodist Thomas Whitehouse 'sold his ferrets, went to a bookseller's shop, and bought a Bible with the money'.[381]

The converted poacher illustrated the dilemma of the Dissenting revivalists. The means used to convert him were hardly respectable, but in selling his ferrets and buying a Bible he took the first step on the road to respectability. For the moment, though, the awakening of 1857–9 appeared to mark the triumph of revivalism over respectability. Notwithstanding the misgivings of the Wesleyan, New Connexion, and even the Primitive Methodist leadership, Nonconformity seemed to have regained the Evangelical fervour which had led to its massive expansion in the first half of the nineteenth century. The revival produced a huge increase in the already overwhelming strength of Nonconformity in Wales and enabled the Methodist denominations in England to recover almost all the losses they had suffered as a result of the *Fly Sheets* controversy ten years earlier. We can be far less certain of the effects of the revival on the English Baptists and Congregationalists, but it was during the years of revival, from October 1856 until December 1859, that the Baptists' most popular preacher, Charles Haddon Spurgeon, was preaching to audiences of up to 10,000 people in London's Surrey Gardens Music Hall. The revival enhanced the important position which the 1851 religious census had shown Dissent to occupy in English and Welsh society. In arguably the most Christian period in English and Welsh history half the churchgoers were Dissenters and their numbers were increasing. Dissenters dominated much of British industry and, if not yet adequately represented in Parliament, occupied positions of local and potentially national importance in the municipal corporations. Nonconformity had the loyalty of a minority, but a substantial minority, of the English working class and its adherents occupied increasingly influential positions in working-class institutions such as co-operative societies and trade unions. By the late 1850s the class conflict which had threatened to tear Nonconformity apart in the previous decade

---

[380] Booth-Tucker, *Catherine Booth*, i. 242–5.
[381] *Revivalist*, Dec. 1857, 187; Apr. 1858, 57; Apr. 1859, 61.

had very largely subsided and Dissent was playing a significant role in healing class divisions and bringing a degree of harmony to industrial and social relations. The growing confidence of English and Welsh Dissent was revealed with the enthusiasm, and indeed sometimes aggression, with which Dissenters celebrated, in 1862, the two hundredth anniversary of the ejection of two thousand Nonconformist ministers on St Bartholomew's day, 1662.

And yet there was an ominous cloud on the horizon. In the same year that David Morgan was dangling the peasantry of Cardiganshire over the precipice of eternity, five months after Humphrey Jones waited for the Holy Ghost to appear in the Wesleyan chapel in Aberystwyth, a grandson of the Unitarian pottery manufacturer Josiah Wedgwood, a man who in his childhood had attended the Unitarian meeting in Shrewsbury, published his most famous work. The author was Charles Darwin; the book, *On the Origin of Species*.

Interpreting the Religious Census of 1851

The basic problem which confronts any historian who seeks to make use of the religious census of 1851 is that of converting the statistics for attendance into an estimate of the size of the worshipping community. Horace Mann's formula, of counting all the morning attendances, half the afternoon attendances, and a third of the evening attendances, was arbitrary in conception and unfair to Nonconformists in operation. Attempts have been made by K. S. Inglis and W. S. F. Pickering to use Mann's figures for comparative purposes while avoiding the problems arising from the use of his formula for converting attendances into worshippers. Inglis added morning, afternoon, and evening attendances together and expressed the resultant sum as a percentage of the total population, to give what he calls 'the index of attendance', while Pickering, to avoid double counting, considered only the best-attended services for each denomination, to give what he calls the 'maximum–minimum' number.[1] But while useful for comparative purposes, neither method can be used for arriving at an estimate of the approximate strength of the various denominations in 1851, for Inglis's method, by including a large element of double and treble counting, produces a figure which is impossibly high, and Pickering's method, by excluding persons not present at the best-attended service, gives a figure which is too low. Inglis's index of attendance for the whole of England and Wales is 61; Pickering's figure for the number of persons present at the best-attended services, expressed as a percentage of the total population, is 35. The actual size of the worshipping community on 30 March 1851 must lie somewhere in between.

It is, however, possible to devise a method which is as valid as those of Inglis and Pickering for comparative purposes, and yet brings us closer to the actual strength of the denominations in 1851. Such a result can be achieved by taking the figures for the best-attended services as the basis, and adding a proportion of the worshippers at the less well-attended services. The major problem is, what proportion? The only attempt, so far as I know, which has been made to calculate the proportion of worshippers who attended services more than once on a Sunday was made by Richard Mudie-Smith and his enumerators when they conducted a religious census in London for the *Daily News* in 1902–3.[2] Mudie-Smith's statistics were based on a small sample

---

[1] K. S. Inglis, 'Patterns of Religious Worship: 1851', *Journal of Ecclesiastical History*, 11 (1960), 79; W. S. F. Pickering, 'The 1851 Religious Census—a Useless Experiment?', *British Journal of Sociology*, 18 (1967), 393.

[2] R. Mudie-Smith, *Religious Life of London* (1904), 449–50.

of seventeen Anglican and fifty-two Nonconformist places of worship, and they show that an average of 62.8 per cent of people (71.8 of Anglicans and 58.8 per cent of Nonconformists) who attended the least well-attended service did not attend any other. Given the increased facilities for Sunday leisure at the beginning of the twentieth century, it seems likely that the proportion of people who attended only one service would have been much higher in 1902–3 than in 1851. Consequently in my own calculations I have made the conservative assumption that a third of the people who attended one of the less well-attended services on census Sunday did not attend any other. Such a formula can be justified by the frequent comments of ministers of religion who completed the census returns. The minister of the General Baptist church in Fleet in Lincolnshire estimated his morning congregation at 320, with 33 Sunday scholars, and his evening congregation at 170, but added that the congregations were 'not composed of the same persons' since 'in the evening those who attended are principally servants etc. who have not an opportunity of attending in the morning'.[3] Similar points were made by the vicar of All Saints church, Stamford, in the same county, by the vicar of East Retford in Nottinghamshire, by the minister of the Calvinistic Methodist church at Llanelli in Carmarthenshire, and by the minister of the Baptist church at Brynmawr in Monmouthshire.[4] My formula is entirely consistent with the observations of the minister of the Ebenezer Independent church at Pontypool that 'about one third of the evening congregation do not attend morning service', and with the comment of the Baptist pastor at Poole that his congregation at any one service consisted of no more than 'two-thirds of the persons who are in the habit of attending this place of worship'.[5]

The statistics presented in Tables II and XIV are thus based on the totals for the best-attended services for each denomination in each registration district, with the addition of a third of the total for attendances at the less well-attended services. The chief criticism which can be levelled against this formula is that it may exaggerate the strength of Nonconformity as compared with that of the Church of England and the Church of Rome, since the proportion of Anglicans and Catholics who went to church once only on census Sunday was almost certainly higher than the proportion of Dissenters. But while the extent of the exaggeration cannot be gauged, it is probably only marginal and will not be as great as using Inglis's index of attendance.

Two further problems arise from any attempt to interpret the published results of the religious census. In the first place the census report stated that out of returns for 34,467 places of worship, 1,394 were 'defective as to attendance'.[6] In some, but not all, of those returns which failed to produce a figure for attendance, a figure was given for the seating accommodation in the place of worship concerned. Unfortunately the published returns failed to distinguish between those churches and chapels for which no attendance figure was given because they were redundant by 1851, those which were open at fortnightly or monthly intervals, but not on 30 March, and those which were 'defective as to attendance' because the clergyman or minister entrusted with filling in

[3] Ambler, *Lincolnshire Returns*, 35.

[4] Ibid. 3; PRO HO.129/435.2.12.18; Jones and Williams, *Religious Census, South Wales*, 283, 615.

[5] Jones and Williams, *Religious Census, South Wales*, 79; J. Vickers, 'Methodism and Society in Central Southern England', Ph.D. thesis (Southampton, 1987), 324.

[6] *Religious Census*, p. clxxxii.

the form flatly refused to do so. As the incumbent of St Paul's, Preston, wrote on his census form, he was unwilling to answer the question concerning the number of his hearers 'because the congregations are no reflection of the labours of the clergy and such returns must be fallacious'.[7] However the number of returns which were defective because the clergyman concerned declined to reveal the size of his congregation was probably larger than the number which were defective because the places of worship concerned were closed on census Sunday. I have therefore made estimates for those churches and chapels for which accommodation figures, but not attendance figures, are provided in the published returns. The estimates have been calculated on the basis of the ratio between sittings and attendants for other places of worship of the same denomination in the same registration district, or, in the case of small denominations, the same county. No estimates have been provided for places of worship for which the census returns provided neither accommodation nor attendance figures.

The second problem confronting the historian who seeks to make use of the published returns concerns their accuracy. The most serious defects in Horace Mann's figures arose not from the incompetence or dishonesty of the ministers who made the returns and of the enumerators who checked them, but from the carelessness of the clerks who added them up and transferred their results to the published totals. A spot check has suggested that in general the calculations were done accurately, but numerous errors undoubtedly crept in.[8] In cases where the totals for the registration districts appeared to be either suspiciously high or incredibly low, I have checked the original returns in the Public Record Office. The two worst errors which came to light concerned the Dursley district of Gloucestershire and the Preston district of Lancashire. The return for the Slimbridge Independent chapel in the Dursley district was filled in by the ill-educated chapel manager, a Mrs Mary Lees. The chapel contained 150 sittings, and the good woman initially calculated the attendance for both morning and evening service at 100. She then evidently had second thoughts and tried to alter her estimate to 140. But she changed only the last digit of her original entry and added another, so that the clerk who added up the totals for the Dursley district credited the Slimbridge Independents with 1,040 attendants at both morning and evening services.[9] At Preston in Lancashire the reverse happened. The total number of sittings in Anglican churches in Preston which did not produce an estimate for attendance was 8,350, but the figure given in the published returns was 83.[10]

The statistics produced in Tables II and XIV are thus only rough guides to the strengths of the various religious denominations in England and Wales in 1851, but their general reliability can be substantiated by comparison with contemporary membership figures for those denominations which were producing them by 1851. Table IX shows that the ratios of known membership to the estimated number of worshippers derived from the census returns was, for all denominations apart from the Friends, between 1 : 2.93 and 1 : 3.71. In view of the mass of evidence which suggests that church and chapel attendance in 1851 was greatly in excess of church membership,

[7] PRO HO.129/482.2.2.9. [8] Watts, *Religion in Victorian Nottinghamshire*, i, p. xi.

[9] PRO HO.129/133. An even more grotesque error was made by the steward of the Primitive Methodist chapel at Willoughton in Lincolnshire. He gave the attendance at the evening service in his chapel as 10,010 when presumably he intended to write 110, but on this occasion the error was not transmitted to the published returns (Ambler, *Lincolnshire Returns*, 261).

[10] PRO HO.129/482.

and in the light of the fact that the census figures include both children in the main congregations and scholars who attended Sunday schools which met at the same time as adult services, ratios of one to three or one to three and a half seem not unreasonable.[11]

TABLE IX. *Ratio of church members to worshippers in 1851*

England and Wales	Number of members[a]	Estimated number of worshippers	Ratios
Wesleyan Methodists	298,406	982,278	3.29
Methodist New Connexion	16,962	62,891	3.71
Primitive Methodists	105,656	335,658	3.18
Bible Christians	13,324	48,135	3.61
Wesleyan Methodist Association	20,557	62,579	3.04
Calvinistic Methodists	58,678	179,941	3.07
Quakers	15,345	16,898	1.10
Swedenborgians	2,559	7,503	2.93

[a] Membership figures are derived from Currie, Gilbert, and Horsley, *Churches and Churchgoers*, from Williams, *Welsh Calvinistic Methodism*, 216, and from Lineham, 'The English Swedenborgians', 379.

The final totals arrived at by using my formula of counting attendances at the best-attended services plus a third of attendances at other services are not very different from those which Mann arrived at by taking the morning service as the basis for his calculations, as can be seen in Table X. The chief difference in the results achieved by the two methods of calculation is that my formula, by removing the in-built bias in

TABLE X. *Estimates of church and chapel attendance, 30 March 1851: totals for England and Wales*

	Mann's formula		Watts's formula	
	No.	%	No.	%
Church of England	3,773,474	21.05	3,528,535	19.68
Nonconformists	3,151,695	17.58	3,338,885	18.62
Roman Catholics	305,393	1.70	292,030	1.63
Others	30,470	0.17	39,197	0.22
TOTAL	7,261,032	40.50	7,198,647	40.15

[11] Richard Alliot, the pastor of the Castle Gate Congregational church, Nottingham, observed in 1817 that of a congregation of between 900 and 1,000 people fewer than 200 were church members, and added that 'such a disproportion was the case generally with most [churches] of the Independent denomination' (Minutes, 134). Deryck Lovegrove produces evidence to suggest that the ratio of members to congregation could vary from 1 : 3 to 1 : 7 (*Established Church, Sectarian People*, 149).

favour of the Church of England in Mann's formula, reduces the gap between the established church and Nonconformists from 3.47 to 1.07 per cent. It must be remembered, though, that my calculations have been based on the published returns for the 624 registration districts. I have applied a similar formula to the original returns for Nottinghamshire[12] and the results have produced a consistently higher, though marginal, result (Table XI). The discrepancies are due partly to the fact that using the published returns as a basis for calculation leads to a reduction by two-thirds of the

TABLE XI. *The 1851 religious census: calculations for Nottinghamshire based on the original and on the published returns, in percentages*

	Original returns	Published returns
Church of England	18.6	16.7
Nonconformists	24.3	21.3
Roman Catholics	0.8	0.8
Mormons	0.4	0.4
TOTAL	44.0	39.2

figures for the best-attended services in a minority of places of worship where the best-attended services for the rest of the denomination in the same registration district were held at a different time of day, and partly to the fact that a study of the original returns leads to a reinstatement of some of the Sunday school statistics arbitrarily discarded by Horace Mann. The comparison between the figures arrived at for Nottinghamshire on the basis of the original returns and of the published returns shows that reliance on the published returns leads to a marginal underestimate of Nonconformist strength, thus helping to counter any in-built bias in favour of Dissent in my formula. If any qualification needs to be made of the statistics presented in Tables II and XIV, it is that they may slightly underestimate the size of the worshipping community as a whole.

[12] Watts, *Religion in Victorian Nottinghamshire*, i, pp. xxiv–xxx.

The Reliability of Baptismal Registers as a Guide to the Occupational Structure of Nonconformist Congregations

A major question raised by the use of Nonconformist baptismal registers to ascertain the occupational structure of Dissenting congregations is the extent to which parents who took their children to Nonconformist chapels to be baptized were in fact committed to those chapels. Many parents who took their children to Anglican parish churches to be baptized rarely if ever attended the services of those churches and one needs to know whether the relationship between the parents of baptized children and Nonconformist chapels was any different.

To resolve the question one can compare the evidence of the baptismal registers with other evidence provided by the records of individual churches and with the 1851 religious census. Unfortunately very few church membership lists have survived for the earlier period covered by this volume, but from the 1850s a number of Congregational registers began to record not only the occupations of the fathers whose children were baptized in their chapels but also the parents' 'church relation': whether in fact the parents were or were not members of the church. The evidence from these registers suggests that the overwhelming majority of parents who had their children baptized in Congregational chapels were members either of the churches or of the congregations which met in those chapels. Of the 137 sets of parents who had children baptized in the Southgate Road Congregational chapel in Hoxton between 1850 and 1869, in 64 cases both parents were church members, in 3 cases either the father (2) or the mother (1) alone was a member, 4 sets of parents were members of other (presumably Congregational) churches, 2 sets of parents are described as Anglicans, and in the remaining 64 cases both parents are described as members of the congregation.[1] Similarly, of the 135 sets of parents who had children baptized in the Zion Congregational chapel in Wakefield between 1860 and 1879, in 41 cases both parents were church members, in 18 cases one parent was a church member (16 mothers and 2 fathers), in 70 cases parents were described as 'hearers', and in only 6 cases does it appear that the parents had no connection with the church: 4 sets of parents are described as 'strangers' and in 2 cases no 'church relation' is given.[2]

---

[1] Greater London Record Office, N/C/20/1.   [2] WYAS, Wakefield, C28/4.

The only Congregational baptismal register I have found in which the columns headed 'church relation' have been completed and in which a substantial proportion of parents are not described as members either of the church or of the congregation is that for Charlesworth in Derbyshire (1852–69) in which 57 out of 113 sets of parents are given no 'church relation'.[3] However, one wonders whether the pastor of the Charlesworth church understood what information he was supposed to supply in the column headed 'church relation'. The terms 'hearer' or 'member of the congregation' do not appear before 1864, but we are frequently told that the grandfather or the grandmother of the child baptized was a member of the church! It is possible to compare the occupations of those parents who were described as having a 'church relation' with those who were not, and the results presented in Table XII show that the inclusion in the Charlesworth register of parents with no apparent 'church relation' in the statistics for the congregation as a whole leads to an underestimate of 6.4 per cent in the proportion of retailers and to an overestimate of 4.3 per cent in the proportion of labour aristocrats, but that is all.

In the remaining Congregational baptismal registers, in which most parents are described either as church members, as members of the congregation, or as 'hearers', it is possible to compare the occupations of those fathers where one or both parents were church members with the occupations of those fathers where neither parent was a church member. The results of these comparisons are also given in Table XII. The table provides some evidence, which is hardly surprising, that those people who were prepared to commit themselves to the responsibilities of church membership were of higher social standing than those who were not. Of the Gravesend fathers where either one or both parents were church members 67.8 per cent fell into one of the middle-class categories; the figure for non-church members was only 38.9 per cent.[4] Of the Heckmondwike fathers where neither parent was a church member 49.9 per cent fell into the bottom three categories, compared with only 27.3 per cent of fathers of families where one or both parents were church members. However, the records of the Burley-in-Wharfdale and Warley churches reveal that a significant proportion of male church members were in fact lower down the social scale than were the fathers who had their children baptized in those chapels. Of the men admitted to membership of the Burley-in-Wharfdale church between 1839 and 1869, 27.8 per cent were either depressed or unskilled workers, compared with only 16.1 per cent of fathers who had their children baptized in the chapel.[5] Similarly 35 per cent of the male members of the Warley Congregational church fell into the bottom three categories, compared with only 23 per cent of the fathers of the children baptized.[6] And in three of the larger Congregational churches whose records I have analysed, those at Southgate Road, Hoxton, City Road, Finsbury, and Wakefield, the occupational profiles of the fathers in cases where one or both parents were church members, of the total number of fathers listed in the baptismal registers, and of the men admitted to church membership,

[3] Derbyshire County Record Office, Matlock, D 2343.
[4] Maidstone Record Office, N/C 159/1.1A.
[5] WYAS, Bradford, 51 D89. Only 13 of the 70 Burley-in-Wharfdale fathers, or their wives, were church members, but again they were lower down the social scale than fathers who were not church members.
[6] WYAS, Halifax, WHW/B 3.

TABLE XII. Comparison of the occupations of male members and non-members in Independent congregations, in percentages

		Charlesworth, Derbyshire			Gravesend, Kent			Southgate Road, Hoxton, London			City Road, Finsbury, London			
		Church relation	No church relation	All fathers	Parents members	Parents non-members	All fathers	Parents members	Parents non-members	All fathers	Parents members	Parents non-members	All fathers	New male members
		1852–69			1856–69			1850–69			1850–9			1853–63
I	Gentlemen	—	—	—	1.5	—	0.7	—	—	—	1.4	—	0.7	2.8
II	Business	—	—	—	2.3	2.1	2.2	5.6	1.5	3.6	4.1	1.3	2.6	3.9
III	Professionals	—	—	—	6.8	0.7	3.6	2.1	—	1.1	—	1.3	0.7	3.9
IV	Farmers	8.9	7.0	8.0	—	—	—	—	—	—	—	—	—	—
V	Food and retail	17.9	5.3	11.5	36.4	25.7	30.8	7.0	15.2	10.9	28.8	26.6	27.6	23.9
VI	White collar	3.6	5.3	4.4	22.3	10.4	16.1	44.3	49.2	46.7	24.7	19.0	21.7	30.6
VII	Labour aristocracy	5.4	14.0	9.7	9.1	11.1	10.1	12.7	15.2	13.9	21.9	22.8	22.4	15.8
VIII	Higher skilled	26.8	33.3	30.1	12.6	6.9	9.6	16.9	9.8	13.5	11.0	13.9	12.5	8.8
IX	Lower skilled	7.1	7.0	7.1	4.5	29.2	17.4	9.9	7.6	8.8	8.2	10.1	9.2	6.0
X	Depressed	10.7	12.3	11.5	—	—	—	—	—	—	—	—	—	0.7
XI	Unskilled	19.6	15.8	17.7	4.5	13.9	9.4	1.4	1.5	1.5	—	5.1	2.6	3.5
	Numbers	56	57	113	66	72	138	71	66	137	73	79	152	284

TABLE XII (cont.). *Comparison of the occupations of male members and non-members in Independent congregations, in percentages*

	Burley-in-Wharfdale, West Riding		Heckmondwike, West Riding			Wakefield, West Riding				Warley, West Riding	
	All fathers	New male members	Parents members	Parents non-members	All fathers	Parents members	Parents non-members	All fathers	New male members	All fathers	Male members
	1856–69	1839–69	1857–69			1860–79			1854–70	1863–9	1861–9
I Gentlemen	—	1.9	—	—	—	—	—	—	3.8	—	—
II Business	—	1.9	13.6	3.2	5.2	1.7	4.6	3.3	—	3.8	—
III Professionals	2.9	3.7	—	1.1	0.9	3.4	1.3	2.2	1.2	—	—
IV Farmers	—	7.4	—	—	—	—	1.3	0.7	—	1.9	10.0
V Food and retail	2.9	3.7	—	11.8	9.6	23.7	27.0	25.6	17.5	11.5	7.5
VI White collar	5.7	5.6	9.1	1.1	2.6	16.9	21.1	19.3	28.8	11.5	—
VII Labour aristocracy	4.3	2.7	2.3	3.2	3.0	6.8	5.9	6.3	10.0	7.5	—
VIII Higher skilled	41.4	20.4	47.7	29.6	33.0	22.0	4.6	12.2	22.5	40.4	47.5
IX Lower skilled	26.6	24.1	15.9	22.0	20.9	23.7	22.4	23.0	15.0	11.5	5.0
X Depressed	4.7	3.7	11.4	24.7	22.2	—	—	—	—	—	15.0
XI Unskilled	11.4	24.1	—	3.2	2.6	1.7	11.8	7.4	1.2	11.5	15.0
Numbers	70	54	22	93	115	59	76	135	80	26	20

were very similar.[7] There were a handful of 'gentlemen' among the new members admitted to the City Road and Wakefield churches who, because they were probably retired, would not have appeared in the baptismal registers. Similarly there was a higher proportion of clerks among the new members of the City Road and Wakefield churches than among the fathers of baptized children, presumably because some of those clerks were as yet unmarried. There were a few more businessmen among the fathers who were church members in the Southgate Road and City Road registers than among the fathers who were not church members, but the reverse was true in Wakefield. And again in Wakefield there were 17 per cent more higher-skilled workers among fathers who were church members, and 10 per cent fewer unskilled workers, than among non-member fathers. But these were the only significant differences. Of the fathers who had their children baptized in the Southgate Road chapel, 44.3 per cent of church members and 49.2 per cent of non-church members were white-collar workers. Of the fathers associated with the City Road chapel 28.8 per cent of church members and 26.6 per cent of non-church members were retailers.[8] And of the fathers who had their children baptized in the Zion chapel in Wakefield, 23.7 per cent of those who were church members were retailers compared with 27.0 per cent of those who were not church members. In all three congregations the proportion of middle-class to working-class fathers among members and non-members alike was roughly the same.

This study of Congregational baptismal registers from the 1850s and 1860s thus enables one to state with confidence that those registers present an accurate picture of the occupational profile of the men of those congregations, apart from the fact that they do not include the unmarried and do not include men whose wives were past child-bearing age. And, apart from the unsurprising fact that in some, but by no means all, congregations unskilled and lower-skilled workers were more reluctant than other workers to incur the responsibilities of church membership, the social standing of those fathers and/or their wives who were church members was very similar to that of fathers who were merely 'hearers' or 'attenders'.

I have not found any comparable membership lists for Methodist societies which can be compared with their baptismal records, but it is possible to compare the evidence of Methodist baptismal registers with membership statistics and with the 1851 religious census. If one counts the number of baptisms recorded in a register over one or two decades and assumes an annual birth rate of 39.4 per thousand in the 1820s and of 35.7 per thousand in the 1830s,[9] one can thus calculate the size of the community whose childrens' baptisms are so recorded. For example, we know that fifty baptisms were recorded by the Chester Wesleyans from 1830 to 1837, and also that the Chester Wesleyan society in 1833 had 361 members.[10] Fifty baptisms in eight years means an average of 6.25 births a year (making no allowance for children who died before they could be baptized), and if one assumes a birth rate of 35.7 per thousand this means that those fifty births represented a community of 175. This suggests that only half the

[7] The list of new male members joining the Zion Congregational church in Wakefield includes 12 schoolboys who have not been included in the statistics in Table XII.

[8] Greater London Record Office, N/C/4/1.

[9] The birth-rate figures for the two decades are based on E. A. Wrigley and R. S. Schofield, *Population History of England*, 534.

[10] PRO RG 4/162; Bretherton, *Early Methodism in and around Chester*, 260.

members of the Chester Wesleyan society were having their children baptized by Wesleyan ministers, and that the rest were still taking their children to the parish church to be baptized. If one compares the evidence of the baptismal registers with that of the religious census one comes to a similar conclusion. The original returns to the 1851 religious census can be used as a basis from which to estimate the size of the worshipping community attached to any chapel by taking the figure for the best-attended service for the general congregation, by making an allowance for other services by adding a third of the total attendances at the least well-attended services, and by including those present at the best-attended Sunday school session but ignoring other Sunday school attendances.[11] Table XIII gives the results of such calculations for

TABLE XIII. *Comparison of the size of Nonconformist communities estimated from baptismal registers and from the 1851 religious census*

Congregation or circuit	Size of community estimated from	
	baptismal registers	1851 religious census
Beeston, Wesleyan Methodist, 1831–6	364	349
Beggarlee, Primitive Methodist, 1830–6 (inc. Kimberley)	484	253
Mansfield, Wesleyan Methodist, 1820–9	444	440 +
[Wesleyan Reformers]		[240]
Mansfield, Primitive Methodist, 1830–6		
(inc. Sutton-in-Ashfield and Bagthorpe)	412	731
Newark, Wesleyan Methodist, 1820–9	287	1086
1830–6	324	
Nottingham, Castle Gate Independent, 1831–9	405	1214
Nottingham, New Connexion Methodist, 1820–9	642	898
1830–7	522	

seven congregations and circuits in Nottinghamshire where one can compare estimates of the size of the worshipping community derived from the baptismal registers with estimates based on the religious census. In five of the cases in Table XIII the estimates of the size of the worshipping community derived from the baptismal registers are considerably less than the estimates based on the religious census and in one case, that of the Beeston Wesleyan Methodists, the resulting estimates are very similar. In only one case, that of the Beggarlee Primitive Methodists, does the evidence suggest that the church may have been baptizing numerous children whose parents rarely attended its services. A comparison between the baptismal registers, church membership lists, and the 1851 religious census thus suggests that the registers underestimate rather than overestimate the size of the Nonconformist congregations. While it cannot be claimed that every single parent who had his or her child baptized in a Nonconformist chapel was a regular attender at that chapel, all the evidence points to the conclusion that in the overwhelming majority of cases at least one such parent must have been a member of the chapel community. We can therefore be confident that the occupations listed in the Nonconformist baptismal registers are a reasonably accurate guide to the social structure of those congregations.

[11] The justification for this method is explained in Watts, *Religion in Victorian Nottinghamshire*, i, pp. xi–xiii.

TABLE XIV. *Estimates of church and chapel attendance, 30 March 1851,*

Registration District	Population	Church of England	Indepen- dents	Baptists	Quakers	Unitar- ians	Presby- terians	Wesleyan Methodists
LONDON	2,362,236	15.6	4.0	2.0	0.05	0.08	0.4	1.4
Kensington	120,004	17.1	2.0	1.4	—	—	0.2	1.1
Chelsea	56,538	18.5	0.6	0.8	—	—	1.2	3.5
St George, Hanover Square	73,230	25.9	1.7	0.7	—	—	—	0.1
Westminster	65,609	23.6	5.7	—	—	—	—	1.5
St Martin- in-the-Fields	24,640	16.4	6.4	—	0.5	—	2.1	—
St James, Westminster	36,406	12.9	4.7	—	—	—	—	0.4
Marylebone	157,696	15.9	2.4	2.1	—	0.2	0.7	1.7
Hampstead	11,986	40.8	—	2.1	—	1.1	0.8	0.6
St Pancras	166,956	21.6	5.1	1.4	—	—	0.8	1.1
Islington	95,329	18.2	5.8	0.5	—	—	0.8	1.3
Hackney	58,429	19.2	11.2	4.3	0.5	1.1	—	2.3
St Giles	54,214	13.4	—	4.9	—	—	—	1.9
Strand	44,460	13.9	2.8	1.8	—	—	—	—
Holborn	46,621	14.1	1.9	4.4	—	—	—	0.1
Clerkenwell	64,778	8.4	3.0	2.2	0.2	—	0.5	—
St Luke	54,055	6.8	11.3	2.2	—	—	—	2.9
East London	44,406	12.4	5.0	1.6	—	0.2	0.6	3.1
West London	28,790	20.3	—	—	—	—	—	0.2
City of London	55,932	27.4	6.7	1.6	0.4	0.4	3.4	—
Shoreditch	109,257	6.7	3.3	2.1	—	—	—	1.1
Bethnal Green	90,193	9.5	6.1	1.0	—	0.1	—	0.9
Whitechapel	79,759	10.9	1.6	3.0	—	—	—	0.9
St George -in-the-East	48,376	7.6	0.5	1.2	—	—	—	2.3
Stepney	110,775	10.1	6.1	1.1	0.1	—	0.4	1.4
Poplar	47,162	6.0	4.4	1.5	—	—	—	2.7
St Saviour's, Southwark	35,731	9.9	9.3	2.7	0.2	—	—	0.4
St Olave, Southwark	19,375	18.2	4.7	4.9	—	—	—	0.7
Bermondsey	48,128	9.1	2.4	3.9	—	—	—	3.5
St George, Southwark	51,824	10.0	3.0	5.2	—	—	0.7	0.3
Newington	64,816	10.6	3.4	4.3	—	—	—	2.0
Lambeth	139,325	15.4	2.7	1.9	—	0.2	—	2.3
Wandsworth	50,764	33.7	5.3	3.0	0.1	—	—	1.7
Camberwell	54,667	20.6	7.2	0.6	0.4	—	—	0.7
Rotherhithe	17,805	16.5	0.6	—	—	—	—	2.6
Greenwich	99,365	16.0	3.2	3.8	—	—	1.4	1.6
Lewisham	34,835	27.4	2.9	0.6	—	—	—	2.3

according to registration districts, in percentages of total population

Methodist New Connexion	Primitive Methodists	Bible Christians	Wesleyan Methodist Association	Wesleyan Reformers	Other Nonconformists	Total Nonconformists	Roman Catholics	Others	Total attenders	Level of Illiteracy
0.02	0.1	0.03	0.1	0.1	0.6	8.9	2.0	0.5	27.0	18.1
—	0.1	—	—	0.1	0.1	4.9	1.8	0.3	24.2	19.8
—	—	—	0.4	—	—	6.6	1.4	0.6	27.0	14.8
—	—	—	—	0.4	—	2.8	1.4	0.3	30.3	4.8
—	0.1	—	—	—	0.2	7.5	1.0	—	32.2	17.5
—	—	—	—	—	—	9.0	4.5	9.8	39.7	10.1
—	—	—	—	—	—	5.1	2.8	1.3	22.3	7.3
—	0.1	—	0.3	—	0.1	7.6	3.9	0.5	27.9	11.1
—	—	—	—	—	—	4.5	3.5	—	48.9	3.9
—	—	—	—	—	0.6	9.0	10.2	0.1	31.9	12.5
—	—	—	0.4	—	0.6	9.5	2.1	0.1	30.6	9.6
—	0.2	—	—	—	0.3	19.8	0.6	—	39.7	17.8
—	—	—	—	—	1.7	8.5	6.0	—	28.0	21.6
—	—	—	—	—	0.7	5.3	7.9	0.6	27.7	9.7
—	0.5	—	—	—	0.8	7.7	0.9	0.9	23.6	11.6
—	—	—	—	—	3.8	9.7	2.2	—	20.3	16.1
—	0.2	—	0.4	0.3	—	17.4	—	0.4	24.6	18.6
—	—	—	—	—	2.4	12.9	—	—	25.3	18.6
—	—	—	—	—	0.7	0.9	—	—	21.2	10.5
—	—	—	—	—	1.0	13.4	2.4	1.9	45.2	15.1
0.1	0.2	0.3	0.3	—	0.9	8.4	—	0.2	15.3	20.6
—	0.5	—	—	—	0.6	9.1	—	—	18.7	38.8
—	—	—	—	0.3	0.1	6.0	2.9	1.6	21.5	33.8
0.1	0.8	—	—	0.8	0.2	5.9	2.4	0.2	16.1	23.3
—	—	—	—	0.6	1.6	11.4	3.3	0.8	25.5	26.7
—	—	—	—	—	1.4	10.7	3.3	0.1	19.5	21.6
—	—	—	—	—	—	13.2	—	—	23.1	7.1
—	—	—	—	—	0.6	10.9	7.6	—	36.7	22.8
—	—	—	0.4	—	—	10.3	5.6	—	25.1	21.2
—	0.2	—	0.2	—	0.1	9.6	9.3	—	28.9	24.8
0.4	—	—	—	—	0.8	11.0	—	0.9	22.5	14.8
—	0.1	0.2	0.1	0.1	0.1	7.5	—	0.1	23.3	18.5
—	—	—	—	—	0.1	10.2	1.1	0.1	45.2	17.8
—	0.1	—	—	—	0.1	9.0	—	0.6	30.2	9.8
—	—	—	—	1.1	—	4.3	—	—	20.9	13.1
—	0.2	0.2	0.7	0.1	0.7	12.0	1.6	0.4	30.0	22.9
0.1	0.3	—	—	—	0.1	6.4	—	—	33.8	19.4

TABLE XIV. *(cont.) Estimates of church and chapel attendance, 30 March 1851,*

Registration District	Population	Church of England	Independents	Baptists	Quakers	Unitarians	Presbyterians	Wesleyan Methodists
SURREY	202,521	29.9	3.4	1.8	0.2	—	—	1.5
Epsom	19,040	32.8	3.7	0.4	—	—	—	2.4
Chertsey	16,148	29.6	1.2	4.0	—	—	—	3.4
Guildford	25,072	30.4	4.9	1.6	0.1	—	—	1.3
Farnham	11,743	27.3	3.6	2.7	—	—	—	0.5
Farnborough	7,839	40.6	0.4	1.2	—	—	—	1.0
Hambledon	13,552	33.7	3.6	0.6	—	—	—	1.0
Dorking	11,353	20.3	3.8	—	0.4	—	—	2.2
Reigate	14,329	22.3	5.3	3.1	0.2	—	—	—
Godstone	8,868	32.7	0.9	4.0	—	—	—	2.8
Croydon	31,888	31.0	4.3	2.3	0.9	—	—	1.1
Kingston	26,783	30.2	3.2	1.6	0.1	—	—	1.1
Richmond	15,906	28.2	2.5	0.5	—	—	—	1.4
KENT	485,021	25.6	3.6	3.7	0.05	0.07	—	5.0
Bromley	17,637	21.5	6.2	3.1	—	—	—	3.4
Dartford	27,330	19.6	4.8	5.2	—	—	—	2.4
Gravesend	16,633	16.6	5.1	4.2	—	—	—	3.9
North Ayleford	16,569	21.7	4.4	4.3	—	—	—	2.5
Hoo	2,845	23.7	—	0.9	—	—	—	3.9
Medway	42,796	18.1	2.9	2.9	0.1	—	—	6.1
Malling	19,579	27.0	0.5	4.6	—	—	—	2.6
Sevenoaks	22,095	26.7	3.1	4.7	—	—	—	3.6
Tunbridge	28,545	28.3	3.3	6.6	—	—	—	4.4
Maidstone	36,097	29.2	3.7	4.5	0.1	0.4	—	2.4
Hollingbourn	13,751	21.1	4.9	0.8	—	—	—	4.3
Cranbrook	13,069	27.3	7.2	3.7	—	—	—	4.6
Tenterden	11,279	36.0	—	3.9	—	1.6	—	6.4
West Ashford	13,314	31.4	—	6.1	0.1	—	—	6.0
East Ashford	11,960	23.7	—	1.0	—	—	—	6.4
Bridge	11,164	32.7	0.9	—	—	—	—	5.5
Canterbury	14,100	19.4	5.8	4.1	0.1	—	—	7.3
Blean	14,661	29.9	3.6	—	—	—	—	3.9
Faversham	16,684	26.7	4.7	0.5	—	—	—	9.6
Milton	12,026	32.0	5.4	—	0.1	—	—	7.5
Sheppey	13,385	13.8	6.4	1.7	—	—	—	8.1
Thanet	31,798	28.2	4.3	6.3	0.1	—	—	7.1
Eastrey	25,162	28.6	5.8	3.6	—	—	—	3.6
Dover	28,325	28.3	2.2	4.5	0.1	—	—	5.2
Elham	18,780	31.1	2.6	2.5	0.1	—	—	7.5
Romney Marsh	5,437	36.5	—	2.3	—	—	—	12.1
SUSSEX	339,604	27.4	3.9	3.1	0.1	0.3	—	2.6
Rye	12,349	21.2	2.6	2.4	—	—	—	10.9

according to registration districts, in percentages of total population

Methodist New Connexion	Primitive Methodists	Bible Christians	Wesleyan Methodist Association	Wesleyan Reformers	Other Noncon-formists	Total Noncon-formists	Roman Catholics	Others	Total attenders	Level of Illiteracy
—	0.02	0.4	—	—	0.3	7.7	0.7	—	38.3	31.8
—	—	—	—	—	0.3	6.8	—	—	39.6	30.4
—	—	0.6	—	—	—	9.2	0.3	—	39.1	38.5
—	—	—	—	—	0.6	8.6	0.3	0.1	39.5	37.7
—	—	2.6	—	—	—	9.4	—	—	36.7	45.0
—	—	4.8	—	—	—	7.5	—	—	48.1	47.6
—	—	—	—	—	0.4	5.6	—	—	39.3	42.0
—	—	—	—	—	2.2	8.5	—	—	28.8	26.4
—	—	—	—	—	0.6	9.1	—	—	31.4	36.6
—	—	—	—	—	—	7.7	—	—	40.5	34.0
—	0.1	—	—	—	0.3	9.1	1.9	—	41.9	26.0
—	—	0.1	—	—	—	6.2	0.4	—	36.8	19.2
—	—	—	—	—	—	4.4	2.6	—	35.2	14.1
—	0.4	0.4	0.06	0.03	0.9	14.2	0.4	0.1	40.3	31.4
—	—	—	0.2	—	—	12.9	—	—	34.4	32.7
—	—	—	0.4	—	0.6	13.4	0.5	—	33.5	38.1
—	1.2	—	—	—	—	14.5	0.8	—	32.0	18.0
—	0.8	—	0.1	—	—	12.2	—	—	33.9	35.8
—	—	5.4	—	—	1.2	11.5	—	—	35.1	60.7
—	—	1.0	0.3	—	0.1	13.6	0.8	0.2	32.7	32.7
—	0.6	—	—	—	—	8.3	—	—	35.3	39.4
—	—	—	—	0.7	—	12.1	—	—	38.8	33.5
—	0.3	—	—	—	1.3	15.8	0.5	—	44.6	32.0
—	0.5	—	—	—	2.1	13.8	—	—	43.0	33.8
—	0.3	0.4	—	—	—	10.8	—	—	31.9	52.2
—	0.5	0.2	—	—	3.2	19.3	—	—	46.7	33.7
—	—	2.9	—	—	—	14.8	—	—	50.8	32.9
—	—	0.5	—	—	3.2	15.9	0.3	—	47.7	31.1
—	—	1.0	—	—	—	8.4	—	—	32.1	36.1
—	1.0	—	—	—	—	7.4	—	—	40.1	31.9
—	1.1	—	—	—	2.5	20.9	—	—	40.3	22.7
—	0.4	—	—	—	—	7.9	—	—	37.9	36.5
—	0.2	1.5	—	—	—	16.5	—	0.7	43.9	31.9
—	—	2.1	—	—	—	15.1	—	—	47.2	44.0
—	0.9	0.9	—	—	—	17.9	2.0	1.7	35.4	34.3
—	0.7	—	—	—	4.1	22.7	0.8	—	51.7	22.1
—	0.4	—	—	—	1.4	15.0	0.8	—	44.4	24.0
—	0.2	—	—	—	—	12.2	1.0	0.6	42.2	21.7
—	0.4	0.9	—	—	—	14.0	—	—	45.1	19.8
—	—	—	—	—	—	14.4	—	—	50.9	25.8
—	0.2	0.3	—	—	1.6	12.2	0.3	0.1	40.0	29.2
—	—	—	—	—	—	16.0	—	—	37.1	40.6

TABLE XIV. *(cont.) Estimates of church and chapel attendance, 30 March 1851,*

Registration District	Population	Church of England	Indepen- dents	Baptists	Quakers	Unitar- ians	Presby- terians	Wesleyan Methodists
Hastings	21,215	29.4	1.8	2.3	—	—	—	5.5
Battle	14,232	16.0	—	2.7	—	1.2	—	7.4
Eastbourne	8,347	44.5	5.1	0.6	—	—	—	2.1
Hailsham	13,289	28.9	9.2	11.2	—	—	—	3.1
Ticehurst	15,507	22.4	2.5	9.5	—	—	—	7.4
Uckfield	17,631	20.6	2.2	2.7	—	—	—	3.6
East Grinstead	13,216	29.6	1.7	8.4	—	—	—	1.6
Cuckfield	15,607	23.1	8.5	3.6	—	—	—	0.7
Lewes	25,719	26.1	10.8	2.7	0.3	0.6	—	1.7
Brighton	65,569	22.4	3.4	3.9	0.2	1.1	—	1.3
Steyning	16,867	39.0	1.4	3.1	—	—	—	1.8
Horsham	14,018	29.0	4.2	3.2	0.2	—	—	0.4
Petworth	9,629	29.2	3.8	0.7	—	—	—	—
Thakeham	7,434	33.0	0.4	—	—	—	—	—
Worthing	18,746	31.9	3.9	—	—	—	—	3.1
Westhampnett	14,649	36.2	1.0	—	—	—	—	0.4
Chichester	15,037	29.7	3.4	0.7	0.1	—	—	1.4
Midhurst	13,599	27.5	4.3	1.0	—	—	—	—
Westbourne	6,944	43.5	3.6	1.1	—	—	—	—
HAMPSHIRE	402,016	27.3	6.6	3.1	0.05	0.3	—	3.4
Havant	7,212	36.8	6.9	3.4	—	—	—	0.9
Portsea Island	72,126	14.2	6.2	5.1	—	0.5	—	4.2
Alverstoke	16,908	25.0	6.0	2.1	—	—	—	2.5
Fareham	13,924	30.5	8.8	0.4	—	—	—	0.5
Isle of Wight	50,324	23.8	7.7	2.5	0.03	0.3	—	8.5
Lymington	12,153	33.9	8.7	11.3	—	—	—	—
Christchurch	8,482	27.9	23.9	2.9	—	—	—	3.1
Ringwood	5,675	27.9	13.1	2.6	—	2.5	—	4.2
Fording- bridge	6,834	38.3	11.6	2.6	0.3	—	—	7.2
New Forest	13,540	32.3	4.2	4.3	—	—	—	2.9
Southampton	34,098	22.8	7.6	1.8	0.2	1.2	—	2.5
South Stoneham	15,974	30.7	3.8	1.9	—	—	—	4.1
Romsey	10,810	23.6	7.3	3.7	—	0.2	—	2.6
Stockbridge	7,480	20.8	2.2	6.3	0.1	—	—	7.2
Winchester	25,661	30.6	2.0	1.6	—	—	—	1.1
Droxford	10,697	42.5	0.6	—	—	—	—	—
Catherington	2,493	47.2	22.4	—	—	—	—	—
Petersfield	7,814	37.5	8.5	—	—	—	—	1.6
Alresford	7,418	40.0	2.0	0.5	—	—	—	—
Alton	11,910	36.6	5.8	0.2	0.4	—	—	1.5
Hartley Wintney	11,223	37.4	7.3	6.3	—	—	—	—
Basingstoke	17,466	32.1	5.6	0.5	0.2	—	—	—

according to registration districts, in percentages of total population

Methodist New Connexion	Primitive Methodists	Bible Christians	Wesleyan Methodist Association	Wesleyan Reformers	Other Nonconformists	Total Nonconformists	Roman Catholics	Others	Total attenders	Level of Illiteracy
—	—	0.6	—	—	0.8	11.0	—	—	40.4	22.4
—	—	—	—	—	—	11.5	—	—	27.5	34.0
—	—	—	—	—	0.2	8.0	—	—	52.5	23.5
—	—	—	—	—	6.1	29.7	—	—	58.6	28.9
—	—	—	—	—	2.2	19.7	—	—	42.1	41.5
—	—	—	—	—	3.1	11.6	—	—	32.3	47.4
—	—	—	—	—	4.0	15.8	—	—	45.4	42.5
—	—	—	—	—	—	12.9	—	—	36.0	41.6
—	0.9	—	—	—	1.6	18.5	—	—	44.6	23.6
—	0.6	0.3	—	—	2.6	13.7	1.0	0.6	37.7	18.7
—	0.5	—	—	—	2.7	9.4	—	0.1	48.5	24.0
—	—	—	—	—	—	8.1	0.7	—	37.7	32.1
—	—	—	—	—	0.8	5.3	—	—	34.5	47.4
—	—	—	—	—	1.5	1.9	—	—	35.0	53.2
—	—	—	—	—	1.4	8.5	0.2	—	40.6	27.0
—	—	2.8	—	—	—	4.3	—	—	40.5	32.6
—	—	0.3	—	—	0.9	6.8	1.1	—	37.5	23.2
—	—	1.0	—	—	0.1	6.4	0.2	—	34.2	42.3
—	—	1.5	—	—	—	6.2	—	—	49.6	26.7
—	1.8	1.1	0.2	—	0.5	17.1	0.8	0.1	45.3	30.4
—	—	—	—	—	—	11.5	1.4	—	49.6	31.4
—	0.3	1.2	—	—	0.1	17.6	1.3	0.2	33.2	26.7
—	—	—	0.6	—	0.3	11.4	1.2	0.3	38.0	36.9
—	—	—	0.5	—	1.0	11.2	—	—	41.7	21.0
—	1.4	5.5	—	—	0.9	26.8	1.6	—	52.3	25.1
—	2.3	—	—	—	2.3	24.6	0.3	0.5	59.3	32.1
—	—	—	—	—	—	29.9	0.3	—	58.1	14.7
—	—	—	—	—	—	22.4	—	—	50.4	27.4
—	8.8	—	—	—	—	30.5	—	—	68.8	53.3
—	1.9	—	—	—	—	13.3	—	—	45.6	20.7
—	1.1	0.6	—	—	1.5	16.5	1.8	0.6	41.7	20.2
—	—	0.8	—	—	—	10.6	—	0.1	41.4	24.5
—	3.0	—	—	—	—	16.8	—	0.2	40.6	39.8
—	5.3	—	5.1	—	0.7	26.9	—	—	47.6	35.9
—	0.7	0.4	1.0	—	—	6.8	2.3	—	39.8	31.5
—	1.6	—	—	—	—	2.3	0.4	—	45.2	42.4
—	—	—	—	—	—	22.4	—	—	69.7	45.2
—	0.9	—	—	—	1.1	12.1	—	—	49.6	47.9
—	1.3	—	—	—	—	3.8	1.1	—	44.9	34.1
—	—	1.4	—	—	—	10.6	—	—	47.2	45.9
—	—	1.3	—	—	—	14.9	—	—	52.3	47.7
—	5.0	—	—	—	2.2	13.5	—	—	45.6	43.3

TABLE XIV. *(cont.) Estimates of church and chapel attendance, 30 March 1851,*

Registration District	Population	Church of England	Independents	Baptists	Quakers	Unitarians	Presbyterians	Wesleyan Methodists
Whitchurch	5,619	29.6	8.0	7.6	—	—	—	9.3
Andover	17,266	35.5	5.2	3.3	—	—	—	4.7
Kingsclere	8,909	32.9	6.7	1.2	—	—	—	3.6
BERKSHIRE	199,224	31.3	4.3	3.1	0.07	0.05	—	4.2
Newbury	20,815	22.9	6.3	2.6	—	0.4	—	4.9
Hungerford	20,404	30.9	2.4	0.6	—	—	—	13.7
Faringdon	15,732	32.8	5.2	3.9	—	—	—	1.3
Abingdon	20,946	40.5	3.4	6.2	—	—	—	3.5
Wantage	17,433	34.7	—	3.3	—	—	—	8.4
Wallingford	14,163	27.7	3.2	5.7	0.2	—	—	1.5
Bradfield	16,380	35.1	3.0	0.9	—	—	—	1.1
Reading	22,175	27.6	9.1	4.9	0.4	—	—	2.2
Wokingham	13,668	32.7	2.1	4.5	—	—	—	0.9
Cookham	11,767	32.9	6.0	—	—	—	—	6.9
Easthampstead	6,352	36.5	2.6	—	—	—	—	—
Windsor	19,389	26.8	6.2	1.5	—	—	—	2.1
MIDDLESEX	150,606	24.7	5.7	2.2	0.2	—	—	1.6
Staines	13,973	24.9	4.9	5.2	0.4	—	—	1.3
Uxbridge	19,475	22.0	5.4	3.1	0.2	—	—	2.4
Brentford	41,325	20.5	4.4	1.3	0.1	—	—	1.7
Hendon	15,916	43.0	2.0	1.3	—	—	—	2.4
Barnet	14,619	34.2	8.5	0.7	—	—	—	1.5
Edmonton	45,298	20.1	7.6	2.4	0.5	—	—	1.1
HERTFORDSHIRE	173,962	28.7	8.9	6.4	0.2	0.1	—	5.2
Ware	16,482	26.9	0.7	—	0.2	—	—	6.6
Bishop Stortford	20,356	34.5	14.6	1.6	0.2	—	—	1.9
Royston	26,355	33.9	29.1	2.1	—	0.4	—	5.9
Hitchin	24,729	25.5	4.0	7.1	0.6	—	—	7.8
Hertford	15,090	33.6	5.6	1.7	0.3	—	—	1.9
Hatfield	8,499	32.8	5.2	—	—	—	—	1.1
St Albans	18,004	25.5	6.0	5.6	—	0.8	—	8.4
Watford	18,800	25.2	2.8	11.7	—	—	—	3.7
Hemel Hempstead	13,120	19.3	4.1	13.3	0.2	—	—	9.1
Berkhampstead	12,527	28.4	3.2	26.6	0.2	—	—	2.2
BUCKINGHAMSHIRE	143,655	29.4	5.8	8.7	0.04	—	—	6.5
Amersham	18,637	27.0	4.5	23.6	—	—	—	2.4
Eton	21,490	32.3	4.3	2.2	—	—	—	1.8
Wycombe	33,562	24.3	7.0	8.6	0.04	—	—	6.6

according to registration districts, in percentages of total population

Methodist New Connexion	Primitive Methodists	Bible Christians	Wesleyan Methodist Association	Wesleyan Reformers	Other Noncon-formists	Total Noncon-formists	Roman Catholics	Others	Total attenders	Level of Illiteracy
—	11.3	—	—	—	—	36.1	—	—	65.9	53.7
—	7.2	—	—	—	0.3	20.8	—	—	56.2	42.6
—	7.3	—	—	—	—	18.7	—	—	51.7	49.3
—	4.1	—	—	—	0.7	16.5	0.5	0.1	48.5	36.0
—	8.9	—	—	—	0.7	23.8	1.4	1.0	49.1	31.4
—	8.2	—	—	—	—	25.0	—	0.2	56.1	47.1
—	3.1	—	—	—	1.8	15.2	0.9	—	48.9	40.4
—	0.5	—	—	—	1.0	14.7	—	—	55.2	46.1
—	6.8	—	—	—	0.3	18.8	0.9	—	54.5	46.3
—	3.4	—	—	—	0.9	15.0	0.6	—	43.2	41.6
—	4.9	—	—	—	1.7	11.6	—	—	46.8	48.9
—	3.1	—	—	—	0.2	20.0	1.2	0.2	49.0	24.2
—	2.8	—	—	—	—	10.3	—	—	43.1	40.2
—	2.3	—	—	—	1.4	16.6	—	—	49.5	29.7
—	2.6	—	—	—	—	5.2	—	—	41.7	25.8
—	0.1	—	—	—	—	9.9	—	—	36.6	23.8
—	0.1	—	0.04	0.03	0.5	10.4	0.4	—	35.6	28.5
—	0.4	—	—	—	—	12.3	—	—	37.1	33.8
—	—	—	—	—	1.1	12.2	—	0.3	34.5	38.1
—	0.2	—	—	—	0.1	7.8	0.7	—	29.1	30.3
—	—	—	—	—	0.1	5.9	0.3	—	49.2	26.5
—	—	—	—	—	—	10.8	0.3	—	45.3	22.4
—	—	—	0.1	0.1	1.0	12.9	0.5	—	33.6	20.2
—	0.7	—	—	—	0.6	22.1	0.2	0.2	51.3	50.6
—	0.3	—	—	—	0.7	8.6	2.0	0.3	38.0	41.7
—	0.7	—	—	—	0.2	19.0	—	—	53.5	61.5
—	0.5	—	—	—	—	38.0	—	—	71.8	46.6
—	1.1	—	—	—	0.9	21.6	—	—	47.1	57.6
—	1.5	—	—	—	—	11.0	0.4	—	45.1	45.9
—	1.3	—	—	—	3.1	10.7	—	—	43.5	43.1
—	0.5	—	—	—	1.5	22.8	0.2	0.2	48.7	52.8
—	—	—	—	—	0.3	18.4	—	0.5	44.2	41.8
—	1.0	—	—	—	—	27.7	—	1.5	48.5	57.1
—	—	—	—	—	—	32.3	—	—	60.7	50.0
—	3.6	—	—	0.5	0.6	25.8	0.2	—	55.5	46.5
—	3.9	—	—	1.7	—	36.2	—	—	63.1	46.3
—	2.0	—	—	—	—	10.3	0.3	—	43.0	30.2
—	4.8	—	—	1.1	0.2	28.3	0.3	—	53.0	55.7

TABLE XIV. *(cont.) Estimates of church and chapel attendance, 30 March 1851,*

Registration District	Population	Church of England	Indepen- dents	Baptists	Quakers	Unitar- ians	Presby- terians	Wesleyan Methodists
Aylesbury	23,071	27.6	2.6	10.5	0.05	—	—	10.2
Winslow	9,376	33.7	7.4	5.3	—	—	—	10.1
Newport Pagnell	23,109	33.9	8.6	7.6	0.1	—	—	7.6
Buckingham	14,410	33.2	6.3	0.7	—	—	—	8.6
OXFORD- SHIRE	170,247	30.6	3.0	3.5	0.2	0.2	—	6.7
Henley	17,895	30.5	6.4	0.1	0.05	—	—	3.0
Thame	15,640	28.9	5.8	8.2	—	—	—	4.5
Headington	15,771	31.2	3.1	0.6	—	—	—	0.5
Oxford	20,172	31.8	2.2	7.0	0.5	—	—	3.9
Bicester	15,562	35.6	5.3	0.7	—	—	—	9.0
Woodstock	14,453	34.5	1.4	1.3	—	—	—	10.6
Witney	23,558	26.5	2.0	3.2	0.2	—	—	8.2
Chipping Norton	17,427	33.2	0.8	6.8	0.4	—	—	6.5
Banbury	29,769	29.0	1.7	3.1	0.7	0.9	—	11.2
NORTHAMPTON- SHIRE	213,844	29.9	6.1	7.8	0.3	0.1	—	7.8
Brackley	13,747	45.6	2.5	5.2	0.1	—	—	—
Towcester	12,806	31.1	3.3	12.7	—	—	—	14.2
Potterspury	10,663	23.0	8.5	6.3	—	—	—	5.8
Hardingstone	9,157	34.8	8.2	15.0	—	—	—	5.8
Northampton	33,857	19.1	5.2	9.3	1.4	0.8	—	6.1
Daventry	21,926	30.5	8.5	5.1	—	—	—	5.5
Brixworth	14,771	34.6	4.9	10.2	—	—	—	10.3
Welling- borough	21,367	27.6	8.6	9.4	0.2	—	—	15.3
Kettering	18,097	31.0	11.3	8.7	0.2	—	—	8.0
Thrapston	12,841	35.0	3.4	14.9	—	—	—	9.6
Oundle	15,655	35.7	5.0	2.7	—	—	—	6.9
Peterborough	28,957	26.2	4.1	1.8	—	—	—	6.6
HUNTINGDON- SHIRE	60,319	29.1	3.3	14.9	0.06	0.2	—	10.5
Huntingdon	20,900	27.5	0.6	7.8	—	—	—	11.1
St Ives	20,594	28.5	4.7	22.8	0.2	0.6	—	8.3
St Neots	18,825	31.5	4.9	14.2	—	—	—	12.2
BEDFORD- SHIRE	129,805	26.0	4.4	12.6	0.1	—	—	15.9
Bedford	35,523	31.2	10.7	10.1	—	—	—	10.2
Biggleswade	23,436	31.5	3.3	15.7	—	—	—	13.4
Ampthill	16,542	32.2	2.6	5.2	0.2	—	—	14.6
Woburn	12,075	25.3	4.3	7.4	—	—	—	14.9

according to registration districts, in percentages of total population

Methodist New Connexion	Primitive Methodists	Bible Christians	Wesleyan Methodist Association	Wesleyan Reformers	Other Nonconformists	Total Nonconformists	Roman Catholics	Others	Total attenders	Level of Illiteracy
—	4.2	—	—	—	2.2	29.8	—	—	57.4	50.3
—	8.9	—	—	—	1.5	33.4	—	—	67.1	45.0
—	1.8	—	—	—	0.4	26.2	0.8	—	60.9	40.9
—	1.4	—	—	—	0.5	17.6	—	—	50.8	45.5
—	2.3	—	—	0.06	0.1	16.2	0.7	—	47.4	37.7
—	0.4	—	—	—	—	10.0	0.9	—	41.4	42.1
—	1.9	—	—	—	—	20.4	—	0.2	49.5	54.9
—	1.3	—	—	—	0.2	5.8	0.3	—	37.3	27.5
—	0.7	—	—	0.5	—	14.9	—	—	46.7	21.5
—	0.7	—	—	—	—	15.7	1.0	—	52.2	36.8
—	2.3	—	—	—	—	15.7	—	—	50.2	37.4
—	3.5	—	—	—	0.2	17.3	—	—	43.8	53.3
—	1.9	—	—	—	—	16.4	1.7	—	51.4	47.3
—	5.4	—	—	—	0.3	23.4	1.7	—	54.2	31.8
—	1.1	0.1	0.1	0.5	0.8	24.7	0.2	0.1	54.9	40.6
—	6.8	—	—	0.7	1.4	16.7	—	—	62.3	45.7
—	1.2	—	—	0.5	0.4	32.4	—	—	63.4	46.9
—	1.7	—	—	—	—	22.4	—	—	45.4	37.5
—	—	—	—	1.4	3.1	33.5	—	—	68.4	37.9
—	0.7	—	0.5	—	0.4	24.4	0.9	0.3	44.7	30.5
—	0.5	—	—	—	0.8	20.5	0.6	—	51.6	42.2
—	—	—	—	—	1.2	26.6	—	—	61.2	46.3
—	0.6	—	—	—	0.5	34.6	—	0.4	62.6	51.7
—	0.6	—	—	2.1	2.9	33.8	—	—	64.8	34.7
—	—	—	—	—	0.1	28.6	—	0.8	64.3	50.5
—	—	—	—	—	0.4	15.1	0.1	—	51.0	42.7
—	1.3	0.6	—	1.5	0.2	16.2	0.3	—	42.7	39.2
—	1.8	—	—	—	4.0	34.8	—	0.1	64.0	44.2
—	0.7	—	—	—	4.7	24.9	—	—	52.4	46.3
—	3.2	—	—	—	2.5	42.3	—	0.2	70.9	40.6
—	1.6	—	—	—	4.8	37.7	—	0.2	69.4	46.3
—	2.8	—	—	0.1	3.2	39.1	0.04	0.3	65.6	53.5
—	2.7	—	—	—	5.3	39.0	—	0.3	70.5	43.6
—	0.6	—	—	—	0.6	33.6	0.2	0.4	65.6	61.6
—	2.1	—	—	—	3.3	27.9	—	—	60.1	63.5
—	4.4	—	—	—	—	31.0	—	—	56.4	55.5

TABLE XIV. *(cont.) Estimates of church and chapel attendance, 30 March 1851,*

Registration District	Population	Church of England	Independents	Baptists	Quakers	Unitarians	Presbyterians	Wesleyan Methodists
Leighton Buzzard	17,142	16.7	0.8	17.9	0.2	—	—	23.0
Luton	25,087	16.2	—	16.8	0.3	—	—	22.9
CAMBRIDGE-SHIRE	191,894	24.6	3.2	10.0	0.03	0.03	—	6.8
Caxton	11,065	29.6	4.1	19.6	—	—	—	4.8
Chesterton	5,170	31.9	2.1	21.3	—	—	—	4.3
Cambridge	27,815	27.0	1.5	9.0	—	—	—	3.3
Linton	14,148	40.9	11.1	3.6	—	—	—	—
Newmarket	30,655	26.6	6.3	5.8	—	0.2	—	5.6
Ely	22,896	16.8	0.4	10.3	—	—	—	14.1
North Witchford	16,243	12.4	1.5	13.2	0.2	—	—	15.7
Whittlesey	7,687	24.8	3.9	8.0	—	—	—	7.4
Wisbech	36,215	18.2	1.7	5.0	0.06	—	—	6.5
ESSEX	344,130	30.5	11.0	4.1	0.2	—	—	3.1
West Ham	34,395	22.1	5.4	0.6	0.3	—	—	1.2
Epping	15,631	30.1	5.4	7.6	0.3	—	—	—
Ongar	11,855	36.4	3.5	1.4	—	—	—	—
Romford	24,607	21.6	3.9	3.3	—	—	—	2.8
Orsett	10,642	24.0	5.2	1.4	—	—	—	1.7
Billericay	13,787	22.8	10.8	—	—	—	—	6.5
Chelmsford	32,272	30.9	12.6	2.0	0.5	—	—	0.8
Rochford	15,838	40.6	7.6	5.3	—	—	—	3.6
Maldon	22,137	32.0	11.6	3.7	0.2	—	—	2.1
Tendring	27,710	26.5	2.1	1.8	—	—	—	16.1
Colchester	19,443	30.9	13.2	6.7	0.4	—	—	3.3
Lexden	21,666	34.4	13.4	2.4	0.1	—	—	4.6
Witham	16,099	44.6	14.3	3.3	0.4	—	—	1.5
Halstead	19,273	30.7	20.3	12.8	0.5	—	—	—
Braintree	17,561	28.1	31.9	6.5	0.2	—	—	2.2
Dunmow	20,498	35.4	21.1	2.5	0.2	—	—	0.7
Saffron Walden	20,716	37.6	8.7	10.3	0.3	—	—	0.9
SUFFOLK	336,136	33.0	8.6	8.0	0.1	0.3	—	2.9
Risbridge	18,125	40.9	22.3	4.6	0.06	—	—	—
Sudbury	30,814	38.2	8.3	4.9	0.2	0.2	—	0.3
Cosford	18,107	39.6	15.0	6.1	—	—	—	1.2
Thingoe	19,014	44.1	0.7	3.9	—	—	—	1.1
Bury St Edmunds	13,900	25.7	6.3	7.2	0.2	1.0	—	1.3
Mildenhall	10,354	24.4	2.4	10.0	—	—	—	16.5
Stow	21,110	33.7	14.8	14.8	—	—	—	2.4
Hartismere	19,028	28.1	2.0	12.8	—	—	—	5.0
Hoxne	15,900	27.5	3.1	17.2	—	—	—	0.4

according to registration districts, in percentages of total population

Methodist New Connexion	Primitive Methodists	Bible Christians	Wesleyan Methodist Association	Wesleyan Reformers	Other Nonconformists	Total Nonconformists	Roman Catholics	Others	Total attenders	Level of Illiteracy
—	3.6	—	—	0.7	—	46.2	—	0.8	63.7	61.0
—	4.3	—	—	—	6.6	50.9	—	0.8	67.9	49.8
—	3.6	—	—	0.7	1.7	26.1	0.3	0.1	51.0	44.1
—	0.5	—	—	—	—	29.0	—	—	58.6	54.8
—	0.5	—	—	—	0.6	28.8	—	—	60.6	43.7
—	1.0	—	—	—	—	14.8	1.4	0.4	43.7	19.8
—	7.2	—	—	—	2.6	24.5	0.3	—	65.7	60.5
—	4.5	—	—	—	0.2	22.6	—	—	49.3	51.1
—	2.8	—	—	—	7.5	35.1	—	—	51.9	54.6
—	5.5	—	—	2.4	4.5	43.1	—	0.4	55.9	39.8
—	0.8	—	—	2.5	—	22.5	—	—	47.3	39.2
—	6.8	—	—	2.3	0.6	23.0	0.2	—	41.4	45.1
—	0.8	—	0.04	0.08	0.8	20.1	0.5	—	51.2	44.7
—	0.2	—	0.4	—	—	8.2	2.2	—	32.4	16.1
—	—	—	—	—	0.5	13.7	—	—	43.8	37.2
—	—	—	—	—	—	4.8	—	—	41.2	54.5
—	—	—	—	—	1.1	11.1	—	0.1	32.8	46.3
—	0.4	—	—	1.3	0.2	10.2	—	—	34.2	50.8
—	—	—	—	—	—	17.3	3.0	—	43.2	46.6
—	—	—	—	—	2.5	18.5	1.6	0.2	51.2	32.8
—	—	—	—	—	2.2	18.7	—	—	59.3	49.5
—	0.3	—	—	—	0.6	18.4	—	0.3	50.7	49.7
—	1.9	—	—	0.5	0.9	23.3	—	—	49.9	44.9
—	2.1	—	—	—	1.9	27.6	0.5	0.7	59.7	37.3
—	3.1	—	—	—	1.2	24.7	—	—	59.1	49.1
—	0.3	—	—	—	—	19.8	0.2	—	64.6	47.7
—	—	—	—	—	0.5	34.1	—	—	64.8	58.9
—	—	—	—	—	—	40.8	—	—	68.9	43.4
—	—	—	—	—	—	24.6	—	—	60.0	58.8
—	5.2	—	—	—	—	25.5	—	—	63.2	49.2
—	2.2	—	0.06	0.1	0.2	22.5	0.1	—	55.8	44.7
—	4.5	—	—	—	0.7	32.2	—	—	73.1	68.7
—	0.4	—	—	—	—	14.4	0.4	—	53.0	64.1
—	3.0	—	—	—	—	25.3	—	0.2	65.1	57.4
—	1.5	—	—	0.9	0.6	8.7	—	—	52.9	45.9
—	—	—	—	—	—	16.0	—	—	41.7	24.3
—	4.5	—	—	—	0.3	33.7	—	—	58.1	47.7
—	3.8	—	—	—	1.8	37.7	—	—	71.4	50.4
—	3.0	—	—	1.1	—	24.0	—	—	52.1	59.3
—	1.4	—	—	—	—	22.1	—	—	49.6	50.6

TABLE XIV. *(cont.) Estimates of church and chapel attendance, 30 March 1851,*

Registration District	Population	Church of England	Independents	Baptists	Quakers	Unitarians	Presbyterians	Wesleyan Methodists
Bosmere	17,219	32.5	14.6	6.7	0.1	—	—	0.6
Samford	12,493	40.2	11.9	4.1	—	—	—	4.4
Ipswich	32,759	24.7	4.9	8.3	0.4	1.7	—	1.3
Woodbridge	23,776	30.9	8.2	16.1	0.2	—	—	1.7
Plomesgate	21,477	38.2	9.1	8.3	—	—	—	3.3
Blything	27,883	30.6	8.6	0.8	0.1	—	—	6.5
Wangford	14,014	29.8	12.4	13.2	—	—	—	5.4
Mutford	20,163	31.4	3.6	2.1	0.05	—	—	5.9
NORFOLK	433,716	24.8	2.2	3.6	0.04	0.2	—	4.9
Yarmouth	26,880	18.5	1.9	2.8	0.1	0.9	—	3.2
Flegg	8,497	31.4	—	2.3	—	0.2	—	—
Tunstead	15,614	30.1	0.8	10.7	—	—	—	4.5
Erpingham	21,722	27.3	1.8	1.0	—	—	—	4.7
Aylsham	20,007	29.7	1.7	4.7	—	—	—	5.2
St Faiths	11,890	44.2	—	4.6	—	—	—	6.6
Norwich	68,195	14.7	3.1	4.1	0.1	0.8	—	1.5
Forehoe	13,565	26.3	6.3	2.0	0.1	—	—	3.2
Henstead	11,545	30.4	0.7	4.9	—	—	—	2.2
Blofield	11,574	26.6	2.0	0.7	—	—	—	2.4
Loddon	15,095	28.9	1.2	4.4	—	0.2	—	6.0
Depwade	26,395	18.4	3.8	6.1	0.1	0.3	—	4.5
Guiltcross	12,744	28.4	—	6.1	0.1	—	—	6.3
Wayland	12,141	29.3	1.3	6.4	—	—	—	4.4
Mitford	29,389	29.1	3.2	1.6	—	—	—	3.3
Walsingham	21,883	24.9	4.0	2.5	—	—	—	6.2
Docking	18,148	28.3	2.2	—	—	—	—	7.6
Freebridge Lynn	13,557	27.8	—	2.9	—	—	—	9.1
King's Lynn	20,530	15.6	3.2	4.9	—	0.6	—	5.4
Downham	20,985	23.5	—	2.7	—	—	—	10.3
Swaffham	14,320	32.6	0.1	3.9	—	—	—	6.7
Thetford	19,040	30.1	2.5	—	—	—	—	11.1
WILTSHIRE	240,966	30.4	6.9	8.2	0.02	0.1	—	5.8
Highworth	17,620	24.1	6.6	3.5	—	—	—	7.2
Cricklade	11,402	28.1	3.5	2.3	—	—	—	0.5
Malmsbury	14,899	26.4	9.3	4.6	—	—	—	0.4
Chippenham	21,407	25.4	8.1	6.8	—	—	—	3.0
Calne	9,173	21.0	1.5	7.7	0.2	—	—	6.9
Marlborough	10,263	42.8	4.8	2.6	—	—	—	4.2
Devizes	22,236	30.1	5.8	7.9	—	—	—	4.8
Melksham	18,815	20.6	7.1	26.5	0.2	0.8	—	10.5
Bradford	11,607	27.8	10.7	13.2	—	—	—	6.3
Westbury	12,530	20.6	8.9	24.0	—	—	—	8.5
Warminster	17,067	41.3	12.6	6.9	—	0.6	—	3.9
Pewsey	12,503	35.3	—	6.6	—	—	—	9.9
Amesbury	8,250	42.1	2.1	8.2	—	—	—	8.5

according to registration districts, in percentages of total population

Methodist New Connexion	Primitive Methodists	Bible Christians	Wesleyan Methodist Association	Wesleyan Reformers	Other Nonconformists	Total Nonconformists	Roman Catholics	Others	Total attenders	Level of Illiteracy
—	0.8	—	—	—	—	22.8	—	—	55.3	52.0
—	0.8	—	—	—	—	21.2	—	—	61.4	47.3
—	0.9	—	0.4	—	0.2	18.1	0.8	—	43.7	25.0
—	0.2	—	0.2	—	—	26.7	—	—	57.6	33.7
—	1.6	—	—	—	0.2	22.5	—	—	60.7	37.0
—	7.5	—	—	—	—	23.5	—	—	54.2	42.9
—	2.9	—	—	—	—	33.9	0.5	0.2	64.5	41.4
—	0.7	—	—	—	—	12.4	—	0.5	44.4	35.4
0.1	6.3	0.1	0.04	1.4	0.2	19.5	0.4	0.1	44.8	43.0
2.1	4.7	—	—	2.2	1.6	19.5	—	—	38.0	36.6
—	9.8	—	—	0.2	—	14.7	—	—	46.1	52.7
—	7.4	—	—	0.7	—	24.2	—	—	54.3	53.8
—	9.1	—	—	3.4	0.5	20.5	—	0.2	48.0	48.6
—	6.9	—	—	6.7	—	25.2	—	—	55.0	52.8
—	2.5	—	—	0.8	—	14.5	—	—	58.7	41.9
—	1.7	—	—	0.7	2.9	14.9	0.4	0.3	30.3	30.3
—	5.7	—	—	—	0.8	18.2	6.9	1.1	52.5	53.3
—	0.9	—	—	—	0.2	8.8	—	—	39.2	45.1
—	8.9	—	—	—	—	14.2	—	—	40.7	55.3
—	6.6	—	—	—	—	18.4	—	—	47.3	51.7
—	4.5	—	—	—	—	19.4	0.1	—	37.9	47.2
—	7.6	—	—	—	2.0	22.2	—	0.1	50.7	50.6
—	11.0	—	—	—	—	23.1	—	—	52.4	49.3
—	8.2	—	—	2.5	—	18.9	—	0.4	48.4	48.8
—	12.4	—	—	2.0	—	27.0	—	—	51.9	41.1
—	9.9	—	—	1.9	—	21.6	—	—	49.8	42.1
—	9.2	1.2	—	1.4	—	23.7	—	—	51.5	50.0
—	2.8	—	0.8	2.2	—	20.0	1.0	0.1	36.7	32.6
—	10.5	—	—	1.3	—	24.8	—	—	48.4	54.4
—	7.4	1.3	—	0.8	0.1	20.3	1.0	—	53.9	45.5
—	4.6	—	—	—	—	18.2	0.3	0.4	49.1	44.4
—	3.9	—	—	0.04	1.0	25.9	0.5	0.2	57.0	44.4
—	7.7	—	—	—	0.1	25.2	—	—	49.3	47.7
—	11.6	—	—	—	—	18.0	—	—	46.1	40.3
—	3.5	—	—	—	2.0	19.8	—	—	46.2	43.2
—	4.6	—	—	0.4	0.7	23.7	—	—	49.1	43.0
—	3.8	—	—	—	1.9	22.1	—	—	43.1	47.3
—	5.8	—	—	—	1.4	18.8	—	—	61.5	47.8
—	1.3	—	—	—	3.5	23.4	—	—	53.5	47.7
—	2.3	—	—	—	—	47.5	—	1.9	70.1	54.8
—	2.7	—	—	—	2.0	35.0	—	—	62.8	39.6
—	1.1	—	—	—	0.7	43.2	—	0.5	64.4	47.0
—	1.2	—	—	—	1.8	27.0	—	—	68.3	45.8
—	4.0	—	—	—	—	20.5	—	—	55.8	61.8
—	1.9	—	—	—	—	20.8	—	—	62.9	43.7

TABLE XIV. *(cont.) Estimates of church and chapel attendance, 30 March 1851,*

Registration District	Population	Church of England	Indepen-dents	Baptists	Quakers	Unitar-ians	Presby-terians	Wesleyan Methodists
Alderbury	14,908	30.1	0.2	4.0	—	—	—	10.0
Salisbury	8,930	37.5	12.3	6.1	—	—	—	6.7
Wilton	10,742	46.7	11.0	0.6	—	—	—	2.4
Tisbury	10,181	37.4	7.6	4.7	—	—	—	6.8
Mere	8,433	26.3	9.8	1.9	—	—	—	4.1
DORSET	177,095	33.9	7.6	0.9	0.03	0.3	—	7.0
Shaftesbury	13,029	26.5	3.4	2.8	0.1	—	—	5.8
Sturminster	10,382	42.7	4.1	—	0.1	—	—	8.8
Blandford	14,837	41.0	12.5	—	—	—	—	6.2
Wimborne	17,284	25.9	8.9	0.3	—	—	—	9.4
Poole	12,890	27.3	12.8	1.9	0.1	0.5	—	7.1
Wareham	17,417	32.5	11.4	0.3	—	0.7	—	11.0
Weymouth	22,037	27.7	5.7	1.9	—	—	—	8.4
Dorchester	25,002	39.5	4.0	0.8	—	0.2	—	3.6
Sherborne	13,081	37.8	6.3	—	—	—	—	7.9
Beaminster	14,270	40.6	5.5	1.2	—	—	—	3.2
Bridport	16,866	33.5	9.9	1.0	0.1	2.0	—	6.4
DEVON	572,330	27.7	4.8	3.2	0.04	0.3	—	5.7
Axminster	20,303	38.2	10.1	2.6	—	1.2	—	3.9
Honiton	23,824	33.0	8.3	2.2	—	0.4	—	5.0
St Thomas	48,806	33.9	3.0	0.9	—	0.3	—	2.9
Exeter	32,823	35.2	2.3	4.5	0.2	1.4	—	4.1
Newton Abbot	52,306	34.2	6.6	3.9	—	—	—	6.0
Totnes	34,022	32.6	7.4	3.1	—	—	—	7.4
Kingsbridge	21,377	38.8	4.7	6.2	0.2	—	—	9.3
Plympton St Mary	19,723	21.8	2.0	0.8	—	—	—	7.2
Plymouth	52,221	15.9	3.9	2.0	0.1	0.5	—	3.8
East Stone-house	11,979	14.8	2.8	3.9	—	—	—	6.6
Stoke Damerel	38,180	14.7	6.1	4.0	—	0.2	—	7.8
Tavistock	27,850	17.9	2.9	1.7	0.1	0.7	—	9.1
Okehampton	20,401	24.3	3.5	2.4	—	—	—	3.8
Crediton	21,728	32.1	6.3	0.8	—	0.6	—	2.1
Tiverton	39,563	27.1	4.9	6.4	—	0.5	—	3.8
South Molton	20,566	38.4	4.2	1.9	—	—	—	5.2
Barnstaple	38,178	27.8	5.1	5.4	—	—	—	4.9
Torrington	17,491	24.9	3.7	4.8	—	—	—	5.3
Bideford	19,607	22.7	5.5	3.5	—	—	—	13.7
Holsworthy	11,382	22.6	—	1.3	—	—	—	9.3
CORNWALL	356,641	13.7	1.8	0.9	0.1	—	—	19.7
Stratton	8,580	22.2	—	—	—	—	—	9.8
Camelford	8,448	15.2	—	—	—	—	—	7.2

according to registration districts, in percentages of total population

Methodist New Connexion	Primitive Methodists	Bible Christians	Wesleyan Methodist Association	Wesleyan Reformers	Other Nonconformists	Total Nonconformists	Roman Catholics	Others	Total attenders	Level of Illiteracy
—	4.5	—	—	—	—	18.8	—	—	49.9	30.6
—	—	—	—	—	0.7	25.8	2.3	—	65.5	19.0
—	4.8	—	—	—	—	18.7	—	—	65.5	44.7
—	2.4	—	—	—	—	21.5	8.5	0.5	67.9	37.2
—	8.1	—	—	—	0.9	24.8	1.1	0.3	52.6	51.5
0.1	1.7	—	—	0.2	0.5	18.4	0.5	0.2	53.1	36.9
—	5.3	—	—	—	—	17.4	—	—	43.9	50.0
—	8.2	—	—	—	—	21.2	0.9	0.8	65.7	58.5
—	1.9	—	—	—	—	20.7	1.1	—	62.9	26.1
—	3.0	—	—	—	—	21.6	1.1	—	48.6	38.7
—	2.1	—	—	—	1.6	26.2	1.2	0.5	55.1	27.1
—	0.4	—	—	—	0.2	24.0	1.8	—	58.3	39.8
0.9	0.7	—	—	1.3	2.3	21.3	0.3	—	49.4	24.3
—	0.3	—	—	0.6	—	9.5	—	—	49.1	36.4
—	0.5	—	—	—	0.7	15.4	—	0.3	53.5	38.2
—	0.3	—	—	—	—	10.2	—	—	50.8	37.4
—	—	—	—	—	—	19.3	—	1.3	54.1	52.0
—	—	2.4	0.1	0.2	2.3	19.0	0.3	0.1	47.0	31.3
—	—	1.0	—	—	—	18.7	0.6	—	57.5	30.0
—	—	—	—	—	0.2	16.1	—	—	49.2	31.4
—	—	0.1	—	0.1	2.3	9.7	—	—	43.6	24.3
—	—	1.0	—	1.4	3.9	18.8	0.8	—	54.7	19.5
—	—	0.3	—	—	2.0	18.8	0.6	—	53.6	28.6
—	—	—	—	0.7	2.3	20.9	0.1	—	53.7	29.2
—	—	4.4	—	—	3.1	27.9	—	—	66.8	33.5
—	—	0.4	0.2	—	1.2	11.8	—	—	33.6	28.9
—	—	1.1	0.2	—	8.6	20.1	—	0.2	36.2	35.6
—	—	1.3	—	—	1.8	16.4	5.6	—	36.7	43.0
—	—	1.0	0.5	0.2	2.9	22.7	—	0.7	38.0	34.1
—	—	7.0	0.7	—	0.4	22.6	—	—	40.4	40.8
—	—	4.5	—	—	0.9	15.1	—	—	39.4	35.1
—	—	2.0	—	0.2	2.5	14.5	—	—	46.6	46.3
—	—	1.7	—	0.7	0.1	18.3	0.2	—	45.6	35.3
—	—	5.0	—	—	1.2	17.4	—	0.3	56.2	39.5
—	—	2.5	—	—	1.9	19.9	—	—	47.7	26.6
—	—	8.6	—	—	0.3	22.7	—	—	47.6	48.8
—	—	5.8	—	—	0.3	28.8	—	—	51.5	31.2
—	—	17.9	0.5	—	—	29.0	—	—	51.6	42.2
0.2	1.7	5.8	3.0	0.2	0.3	33.8	0.2	—	47.7	44.4
—	—	10.6	8.4	—	—	28.8	—	—	51.0	36.4
—	—	16.3	14.5	—	—	38.1	—	—	53.3	42.1

TABLE XIV. *(cont.) Estimates of church and chapel attendance, 30 March 1851,*

Registration District	Population	Church of England	Independents	Baptists	Quakers	Unitarians	Presbyterians	Wesleyan Methodists
Launceston	16,773	20.0	6.7	0.7	—	—	—	17.7
St Germans	16,545	30.4	4.0	2.9	0.1	—	—	15.0
Liskeard	33,831	13.2	1.5	0.7	0.2	—	—	15.6
Bodmin	20,493	17.6	—	—	—	—	—	12.1
St Columb	17,402	17.2	2.6	0.2	—	—	—	23.4
St Austell	32,073	8.2	3.7	0.9	0.1	—	—	19.6
Truro	42,270	14.7	2.6	0.5	0.1	—	—	29.5
Falmouth	22,052	13.9	3.5	3.2	0.3	—	—	20.9
Helston	28,402	9.1	0.1	1.0	—	—	—	14.4
Redruth	53,628	5.8	—	0.7	0.4	—	—	21.3
Penzance	53,517	14.1	1.2	1.0	—	—	—	22.8
Scilly Islands	2,627	36.7	—	—	—	—	—	16.5
SOMERSET	456,259	28.8	4.9	3.5	0.1	0.3	—	5.8
Williton	19,895	40.2	0.8	2.9	—	—	—	4.4
Wellington	22,121	35.5	7.3	5.1	0.2	—	—	5.2
Taunton	35,114	36.9	6.6	2.9	0.1	0.8	—	3.1
Bridgwater	33,188	31.3	5.4	1.5	0.1	0.8	—	4.7
Langport	18,567	33.6	6.5	2.2	0.1	—	—	3.3
Chard	26,085	28.2	6.1	4.9	—	0.9	—	4.0
Yeovil	28,463	29.4	6.1	3.6	—	0.2	—	6.1
Wincanton	21,311	31.9	7.8	1.8	—	—	—	5.8
Frome	25,325	26.4	5.9	11.2	—	—	—	6.0
Shepton Mallet	16,957	24.7	2.6	0.4	—	0.6	—	13.0
Wells	21,342	24.1	3.6	2.0	0.3	—	—	4.7
Axbridge	33,059	25.1	1.8	5.0	0.4	—	—	7.9
Clutton	25,227	21.1	2.2	1.9	—	—	—	15.7
Bath	69,847	31.0	2.7	4.1	0.1	0.3	—	2.5
Keynsham	21,615	22.3	10.9	3.5	—	—	—	9.9
Bedminster	38,143	19.1	5.3	1.1	0.2	—	—	4.8
GLOUCESTERSHIRE	419,514	27.2	5.9	4.8	0.2	0.3	—	3.4
Bristol	65,716	21.2	8.4	5.6	0.8	1.2	—	1.2
Clifton	77,950	19.8	3.6	1.6	0.1	0.1	—	2.5
Chipping Sodbury	18,526	28.8	11.2	4.0	—	0.1	—	3.5
Thornbury	16,454	24.2	8.9	2.9	0.1	—	—	11.4
Dursley	14,803	34.0	24.9	5.4	—	—	—	5.1
Westbury-upon-Severn	18,124	20.3	6.0	5.1	—	—	—	2.8
Newent	12,575	18.3	1.5	2.3	—	—	—	6.7
Gloucester	32,045	29.1	1.8	2.8	0.1	0.4	—	3.6
Wheatenhurst	7,987	41.7	5.0	2.4	—	—	—	6.1
Stroud	37,386	34.3	10.1	11.1	—	—	—	5.5
Tetbury	6,254	38.7	3.6	8.6	—	—	—	0.6
Cirencester	21,327	33.3	2.1	3.5	0.3	0.2	—	1.1

according to registration districts, in percentages of total population

Methodist New Connexion	Primitive Methodists	Bible Christians	Wesleyan Methodist Association	Wesleyan Reformers	Other Nonconformists	Total Nonconformists	Roman Catholics	Others	Total attenders	Level of Illiteracy
—	—	9.6	5.3	—	1.1	41.1	—	—	61.1	41.6
—	—	0.7	0.2	0.5	—	23.3	—	—	53.7	35.5
—	—	3.5	4.2	—	0.3	26.0	0.3	—	39.5	51.3
—	0.2	9.9	12.4	—	1.3	35.9	0.5	—	54.0	35.0
—	—	11.3	—	—	—	37.5	0.7	—	55.3	28.3
—	3.4	11.3	1.6	—	1.1	41.7	—	—	49.9	44.6
1.6	2.8	7.4	0.1	—	0.1	44.7	—	—	59.5	40.3
—	2.2	1.5	—	—	0.9	32.5	0.6	0.5	47.5	30.6
—	—	2.8	4.4	—	—	22.8	0.1	—	32.0	46.4
—	2.2	3.3	3.5	1.1	—	32.5	—	—	38.3	58.1
—	4.0	2.9	—	—	0.1	32.1	0.5	—	46.6	45.1
—	—	16.6	—	—	—	33.1	—	—	69.8	13.6
—	1.0	0.6	0.1	1.2	1.1	18.6	0.4	0.2	47.9	39.4
—	0.3	1.5	—	—	—	9.9	—	—	50.1	34.3
—	—	1.1	—	—	0.4	19.5	—	—	55.0	41.7
—	—	0.9	—	—	0.1	14.5	1.1	—	52.6	37.6
—	0.4	0.3	—	—	0.2	13.6	1.1	0.1	46.2	41.8
—	—	2.0	—	—	0.5	14.6	—	—	48.2	46.0
—	—	0.7	—	—	0.6	17.2	—	0.4	45.8	47.0
—	0.1	1.0	—	—	2.8	19.9	—	—	49.3	50.8
—	2.1	0.3	—	0.3	—	18.1	—	0.2	50.2	46.0
—	6.3	—	—	2.1	—	31.5	—	—	57.9	42.8
—	1.8	0.5	—	0.2	—	19.2	0.4	—	44.3	45.2
—	0.4	2.2	—	—	0.4	13.7	—	0.3	38.1	35.9
—	—	1.3	1.3	—	0.1	18.0	—	—	43.1	45.3
—	1.9	0.2	—	3.6	—	25.6	0.1	—	46.8	44.2
—	1.6	—	0.2	2.4	4.6	18.5	1.3	0.6	51.4	24.3
—	1.5	—	—	5.8	0.6	32.2	—	—	54.5	50.5
—	—	0.4	0.3	2.4	0.6	14.9	—	—	34.0	43.4
—	0.6	0.1	—	1.5	1.9	18.8	1.3	0.3	47.6	33.0
—	—	—	—	5.2	5.3	27.6	3.1	—	52.0	26.7
—	1.3	—	0.1	2.7	0.3	12.2	2.0	0.5	34.6	29.5
—	1.3	—	—	—	0.1	20.3	0.2	—	49.4	52.6
—	—	—	—	0.5	1.1	24.9	—	—	49.1	48.3
—	—	—	—	—	—	35.5	—	—	69.5	39.7
—	1.3	—	—	4.1	—	19.3	—	—	39.6	42.4
—	—	0.4	—	—	—	10.8	1.1	—	30.3	54.3
—	—	—	—	—	3.9	12.6	0.6	—	42.3	34.4
—	—	—	—	—	0.6	14.1	—	—	55.8	44.7
—	2.0	—	—	—	3.4	32.2	0.7	0.3	67.5	38.5
—	—	—	—	—	4.6	17.3	—	1.2	57.2	36.0
—	2.9	—	—	—	0.2	10.4	0.9	—	44.6	33.2

TABLE XIV. *(cont.) Estimates of church and chapel attendance, 30 March 1851,*

Registration District	Population	Church of England	Independents	Baptists	Quakers	Unitarians	Presbyterians	Wesleyan Methodists
North Leach	10,984	40.2	3.1	5.0	—	—	—	2.7
Stow-on-the-Wold	9,932	33.4	2.1	13.4	—	—	—	5.1
Winchcomb	10,136	33.5	—	5.6	—	—	—	3.1
Cheltenham	44,184	34.1	3.0	4.9	—	0.2	—	2.6
Tewkesbury	15,131	23.2	5.3	5.5	—	—	—	4.5
HEREFORDSHIRE	99,115	24.9	1.6	2.1	0.1	—	—	2.3
Ledbury	13,139	30.7	1.4	1.1	—	—	—	4.0
Ross	15,502	25.6	3.5	3.1	0.1	—	—	4.3
Hereford	35,154	26.1	1.3	3.1	0.1	—	—	1.5
Weobly	8,718	26.1	0.3	—	—	—	—	1.7
Bromyard	11,692	21.3	3.0	—	—	—	—	1.2
Leominster	14,910	17.3	—	2.2	0.2	—	—	2.0
SHROPSHIRE	244,898	25.9	3.0	1.2	0.02	0.04	—	4.2
Ludlow	17,051	20.8	2.1	—	—	—	—	7.6
Clun	10,119	19.3	1.4	0.3	—	—	—	1.6
Church Stretton	6,167	32.4	—	—	—	—	—	1.9
Cleobury Mortimer	8,633	30.3	—	0.1	—	—	—	2.3
Bridgnorth	15,608	32.8	1.4	1.4	—	—	—	2.4
Shiffnall	11,483	22.5	2.5	1.4	—	—	—	4.4
Madeley	27,627	15.3	0.7	2.0	0.1	—	—	8.9
Atcham	19,174	29.1	3.9	1.6	—	—	—	0.9
Shrewsbury	23,104	38.5	4.0	1.5	—	0.5	—	2.2
Oswestry	22,795	22.2	7.8	2.3	—	—	—	2.6
Ellesmere	15,680	30.5	2.8	0.2	—	—	—	3.2
Wem	16,948	27.5	7.2	1.3	—	—	—	5.0
Market Drayton	14,160	36.2	3.3	0.8	—	—	—	2.8
Wellington	20,729	16.2	1.1	1.0	0.1	—	—	9.7
Newport	15,620	25.1	2.6	1.7	—	—	—	0.4
STAFFORDSHIRE	639,545	15.5	2.2	1.4	0.02	0.1	0.2	6.5
Stafford	22,787	21.2	1.5	—	—	—	0.8	1.7
Stone	19,344	29.8	2.4	—	—	—	—	0.8
Newcastle-under-Lyme	20,814	19.4	1.4	0.4	—	—	—	8.7
Wolstanton	41,916	7.3	0.6	0.2	—	—	—	11.6
Stoke-on-Trent	57,942	11.1	2.1	0.8	0.1	—	0.4	3.5
Leek	23,031	11.6	1.6	—	—	—	—	12.1
Cheadle	18,142	17.4	3.6	—	—	—	—	3.3
Uttoxeter	15,140	20.2	2.8	0.4	0.1	—	—	5.5

according to registration districts, in percentages of total population

Methodist New Connexion	Primitive Methodists	Bible Christians	Wesleyan Methodist Association	Wesleyan Reformers	Other Nonconformists	Total Nonconformists	Roman Catholics	Others	Total attenders	Level of Illiteracy
—	1.4	—	—	—	0.8	13.0	—	0.4	53.6	44.2
—	—	—	—	—	—	20.6	—	—	54.0	32.4
—	—	—	—	—	2.3	11.0	—	—	44.5	55.6
—	—	—	0.2	—	1.8	12.7	1.4	1.5	49.7	22.0
—	—	0.2	—	—	0.5	16.0	1.1	—	40.3	47.3
—	2.2	0.1	—	—	1.6	9.9	0.4	0.1	35.4	40.4
—	0.8	—	—	—	0.8	8.1	—	—	38.8	45.7
—	0.7	0.8	—	—	1.8	14.3	—	0.2	40.2	41.8
—	2.5	—	—	—	2.3	10.8	1.2	—	38.1	37.4
—	4.2	—	—	—	0.9	7.0	—	—	33.2	39.4
—	1.8	—	—	—	0.5	6.5	—	0.6	28.4	50.9
—	3.4	—	—	—	1.7	9.4	—	—	26.8	36.5
0.6	4.7	—	0.2	0.1	0.9	15.0	0.7	0.1	41.7	44.1
—	6.5	—	—	—	0.7	16.8	—	—	37.6	38.5
—	9.2	—	—	—	—	12.4	0.6	—	32.4	41.8
—	4.2	—	—	—	—	6.1	—	—	38.4	48.1
—	3.6	—	—	—	—	6.0	1.7	—	37.9	47.7
—	0.1	—	—	—	—	5.4	1.5	1.1	40.8	36.8
1.9	0.2	—	—	—	—	10.4	—	—	32.9	50.5
1.5	2.5	—	—	—	—	15.8	1.5	—	32.5	52.3
0.2	4.0	—	—	—	0.6	11.3	1.1	0.2	41.8	37.4
1.8	1.3	—	—	0.5	2.1	13.9	—	0.3	52.7	29.1
—	8.4	—	1.3	0.4	5.5	28.4	—	—	50.5	42.1
—	9.2	—	1.1	—	—	16.6	—	—	47.1	38.4
0.3	5.3	—	—	—	0.2	19.4	—	—	46.9	38.3
—	6.7	—	—	—	1.5	15.0	0.4	—	51.6	43.8
1.2	7.2	—	—	—	—	20.3	1.4	—	38.0	62.2
—	2.9	—	—	—	—	7.6	2.2	—	34.9	53.3
2.4	3.4	—	0.1	0.03	0.1	16.6	1.9	0.1	34.1	52.6
2.0	1.0	—	—	—	0.5	7.6	2.3	—	31.1	39.9
1.7	0.2	—	—	—	—	5.2	3.4	—	38.4	51.4
4.1	5.5	—	—	—	0.1	20.2	2.4	—	42.0	48.7
2.7	5.0	—	2.2	—	—	22.4	1.7	—	31.5	55.7
5.4	1.0	—	0.1	—	0.2	13.6	1.2	—	25.8	51.2
0.9	2.2	—	—	—	—	16.8	1.2	—	29.6	37.5
1.7	6.0	—	—	—	—	14.5	8.5	—	40.5	39.4
—	5.0	—	—	—	—	13.7	0.7	0.1	34.7	24.7

TABLE XIV. *(cont.) Estimates of church and chapel attendance, 30 March 1851,*

Registration District	Population	Church of England	Independents	Baptists	Quakers	Unitarians	Presbyterians	Wesleyan Methodists
Burton								
-upon-Trent	31,843	22.2	2.1	1.7	—	—	—	7.8
Tamworth	13,996	28.5	1.8	1.9	—	0.2	—	3.5
Lichfield	25,279	28.5	2.3	—	—	—	—	2.2
Penkridge	16,850	21.2	2.8	—	—	—	—	3.6
Wolver-								
hampton	104,158	17.2	2.1	1.6	—	0.1	—	5.7
Walsall	43,044	12.2	1.6	1.7	—	—	—	6.3
West								
Bromwich	69,729	13.1	3.7	1.4	—	0.2	—	7.4
Dudley	106,530	11.1	2.4	3.9	—	0.6	0.5	9.7
WORCESTER-								
SHIRE	258,733	22.9	1.8	1.7	0.1	0.4	—	3.8
Stourbridge	57,350	14.9	2.7	1.1	0.1	0.7	—	4.5
Kidderminster	32,917	22.8	1.9	1.4	—	1.1	—	8.3
Tenbury	7,047	29.7	—	1.5	—	—	—	1.7
Martley	13,811	28.7	0.9	—	—	—	—	0.8
Worcester	27,677	26.9	2.0	2.0	0.4	—	—	2.9
Upton-								
on-Severn	18,070	32.5	0.1	1.4	—	—	—	1.8
Evesham	14,463	29.9	3.0	5.9	0.2	0.6	—	4.5
Pershore	13,553	30.6	—	5.9	—	—	—	2.5
Droitwich	18,152	25.9	0.7	0.4	—	—	—	1.8
Bromsgrove	24,822	26.6	3.2	1.6	—	—	—	4.8
King's Norton	30,871	13.1	1.1	1.4	—	0.5	0.1	2.3
WARWICK-								
SHIRE	480,120	18.9	3.5	3.0	0.1	0.6	0.1	3.0
Birmingham	173,951	12.6	2.7	2.5	0.4	1.2	0.3	2.4
Aston	66,852	11.8	1.4	2.9	—	—	—	2.6
Meriden	11,267	21.2	2.7	—	—	—	—	2.2
Atherstone	11,448	32.4	13.3	0.7	—	—	—	5.0
Nuneaton	13,532	29.5	8.2	3.3	—	—	—	4.3
Foleshill	19,490	19.7	8.5	12.9	—	—	—	4.5
Coventry	36,812	12.2	5.0	3.1	0.1	1.0	—	0.8
Rugby	23,477	20.6	4.4	3.4	—	—	—	4.4
Solihull	11,931	32.0	1.8	0.3	—	—	—	0.5
Warwick	41,934	33.2	5.0	1.4	—	0.5	—	2.4
Stratford-								
on-Avon	20,789	35.6	3.2	1.7	—	—	—	4.9
Alcester	17,482	20.3	1.0	8.7	—	1.3	—	4.6
Shipston-								
on-Stour	20,651	26.0	1.7	4.1	0.2	—	—	6.0
Southam	10,504	32.3	2.2	—	—	—	—	7.9
LEICESTER-								
SHIRE	234,957	24.8	4.0	8.1	0.04	0.2	—	6.2

according to registration districts, in percentages of total population

Methodist New Connexion	Primitive Methodists	Bible Christians	Wesleyan Methodist Association	Wesleyan Reformers	Other Nonconformists	Total Nonconformists	Roman Catholics	Others	Total attenders	Level of Illiteracy
—	4.2	—	—	0.7	—	16.5	0.7	0.2	39.6	33.6
—	0.2	—	—	—	—	7.6	1.6	—	37.7	38.7
0.4	1.6	—	—	—	—	6.4	2.1	—	37.0	35.3
2.2	1.5	—	—	—	0.5	10.5	3.1	—	34.8	40.1
0.8	1.9	—	—	—	0.2	12.6	2.1	0.1	32.0	56.0
—	4.3	—	—	—	—	14.0	3.0	—	29.2	58.5
1.8	4.3	—	—	—	0.2	19.0	1.0	0.2	33.4	48.0
6.0	6.0	—	—	—	0.2	29.5	1.4	0.1	42.0	65.7
1.0	2.1	—	0.1	—	0.9	12.0	1.0	0.1	36.0	41.6
4.3	5.6	—	—	—	0.1	19.2	0.9	0.2	35.0	60.5
—	1.4	—	—	—	1.2	15.3	1.3	—	39.4	48.8
—	2.1	—	—	—	—	5.3	—	—	35.0	47.4
—	—	—	0.1	—	1.7	3.6	—	—	32.3	40.8
—	0.5	—	—	—	3.3	11.0	2.0	0.7	40.7	34.2
—	—	—	—	—	0.7	4.0	3.6	—	40.1	43.8
—	—	—	—	—	—	14.2	0.8	—	44.9	48.6
—	1.0	—	—	—	—	9.4	1.5	—	41.5	46.8
—	0.4	—	—	—	1.5	4.8	1.0	—	31.7	40.2
—	4.4	—	1.0	—	—	15.0	—	—	41.5	47.4
0.3	0.9	—	0.1	—	0.9	7.7	—	—	20.8	22.0
0.2	0.8	—	0.2	0.04	0.7	12.3	2.0	0.4	33.6	37.0
0.4	0.3	—	0.4	—	1.5	12.1	1.5	0.9	27.1	38.3
—	0.1	—	—	0.2	—	7.3	3.3	0.2	22.7	30.7
—	—	—	—	—	—	4.8	—	0.2	26.2	31.9
—	0.7	—	—	—	1.9	21.6	0.6	—	54.6	43.0
—	1.7	—	—	—	1.9	19.4	3.1	—	52.0	51.0
—	5.7	—	—	—	—	31.7	—	—	51.4	54.8
—	0.6	—	—	—	—	10.7	3.8	0.2	26.9	38.1
—	1.4	—	—	—	0.4	13.9	2.1	—	36.5	32.3
—	—	—	—	—	—	2.6	1.0	—	35.6	41.6
—	0.2	—	—	—	0.3	10.0	1.8	0.1	45.1	24.3
—	0.7	—	—	—	0.3	10.9	2.2	0.1	48.6	39.2
—	0.2	—	—	—	—	15.7	5.6	—	41.6	36.8
—	2.9	—	—	—	—	15.0	1.3	—	42.3	44.4
—	3.0	—	—	—	0.5	13.6	—	—	45.8	36.0
—	3.1	—	0.5	0.5	0.6	23.2	1.1	0.3	49.4	36.7

TABLE XIV. *(cont.) Estimates of church and chapel attendance, 30 March 1851,*

Registration District	Population	Church of England	Independents	Baptists	Quakers	Unitarians	Presbyterians	Wesleyan Methodists
Lutterworth	16,194	33.4	9.3	5.4	—	—	—	0.5
Market Harborough	15,839	36.0	9.9	6.8	—	—	—	3.9
Billesdon	7,009	29.4	1.7	2.2	—	—	—	8.9
Blaby	14,190	31.5	12.0	8.7	—	—	—	3.4
Hinckley	15,595	21.3	8.1	5.4	—	0.3	—	10.0
Market Bosworth	13,633	31.2	0.9	10.1	—	—	—	6.9
Ashby-de -la-Zouch	25,895	22.8	0.7	7.8	—	—	—	8.7
Loughborough	25,368	19.0	1.7	12.4	—	0.3	—	8.9
Barrow- upon-Soar	20,059	20.6	—	8.8	—	—	—	7.7
Leicester	60,642	19.8	3.5	10.1	0.1	0.7	—	1.8
Melton Mowbray	20,533	29.9	2.5	1.5	—	—	—	15.1
RUTLAND	24,272	31.7	3.3	6.1	—	—	—	6.7
Oakham	11,513	31.5	2.0	6.3	—	—	—	8.4
Uppingham	12,759	32.0	4.5	5.9	—	—	—	5.2
LINCOLN- SHIRE	400,236	20.0	1.7	2.1	0.06	0.07	—	13.0
Stamford	19,755	30.9	2.9	2.0	—	—	—	4.3
Bourne	22,362	22.8	2.4	3.2	—	—	—	5.7
Spalding	21,290	19.6	2.5	5.9	0.1	—	—	8.0
Holbeach	19,134	17.7	1.3	7.2	0.2	0.1	—	10.5
Boston	38,444	16.1	2.1	3.5	—	0.3	—	10.9
Sleaford	24,551	21.8	2.8	1.7	—	—	—	11.8
Grantham	29,850	29.1	2.0	0.6	—	—	—	5.1
Lincoln	42,062	20.1	1.8	1.0	0.3	0.1	—	15.7
Horncastle	25,089	18.4	1.0	1.2	—	0.1	—	22.2
Spilsby	28,937	21.4	0.8	1.1	—	—	—	16.8
Louth	33,427	17.2	0.8	2.9	—	—	—	15.1
Caistor	34,291	16.4	0.7	1.4	—	—	—	17.3
Glanford- Brigg	33,786	16.7	2.3	1.1	0.1	—	—	15.1
Gainsborough	27,258	17.1	1.4	0.2	0.1	0.4	—	16.3
NOTTINGHAM- SHIRE	294,380	16.7	2.1	3.6	0.06	0.2	—	8.1
East Retford	22,758	19.0	1.3	1.6	—	—	—	13.4
Worksop	19,153	22.5	1.2	—	—	—	—	7.1
Mansfield	30,146	17.4	3.2	3.6	0.1	0.3	—	5.9
Basford	64,943	12.9	1.3	6.7	—	—	—	5.7
Radford	26,776	7.2	1.0	0.7	—	—	—	2.3
Nottingham	58,419	12.3	4.4	6.0	0.2	1.0	—	4.9
Southwell	25,616	27.0	0.3	1.5	—	—	—	11.3

according to registration districts, in percentages of total population

Methodist New Connexion	Primitive Methodists	Bible Christians	Wesleyan Methodist Association	Wesleyan Reformers	Other Nonconformists	Total Nonconformists	Roman Catholics	Others	Total attenders	Level of Illiteracy
—	0.9	—	—	—	—	16.1	—	0.4	50.0	34.8
—	—	—	—	—	1.7	22.3	0.3	—	58.6	30.0
—	0.4	—	—	—	2.3	15.6	—	—	44.9	28.3
—	2.9	—	0.7	0.5	1.5	29.8	—	—	61.3	47.4
—	2.7	—	—	—	—	26.3	1.6	—	49.1	52.7
—	5.3	—	—	—	—	23.3	—	—	54.5	36.7
—	4.1	—	—	0.6	—	21.9	1.3	—	46.1	45.0
—	3.2	—	—	—	0.2	26.8	3.5	0.7	50.0	35.9
—	9.3	—	1.5	—	—	27.3	0.4	0.3	48.6	35.8
—	2.0	—	1.1	1.5	1.0	21.9	1.4	0.5	43.7	35.4
—	2.9	—	—	0.2	0.1	22.4	1.0	—	53.3	21.1
—	0.7	—	—	0.7	0.9	18.5	—	0.2	50.3	32.9
—	1.4	—	—	—	—	18.1	—	—	49.5	35.6
—	—	—	—	1.4	1.7	18.8	—	0.3	51.5	30.1
0.2	5.3	—	—	0.7	0.1	23.3	0.5	0.1	43.9	34.2
—	0.3	—	—	—	—	9.5	1.1	0.1	41.6	22.7
—	0.4	—	—	0.8	—	12.5	1.2	0.2	36.7	34.2
—	4.0	—	—	—	0.4	20.8	—	0.7	41.2	30.1
—	5.1	—	—	2.4	—	26.7	—	—	44.4	35.1
1.2	2.3	—	—	0.1	—	20.5	0.8	0.3	37.7	33.4
—	3.4	—	—	—	0.4	20.2	—	—	42.0	45.0
—	2.5	—	—	4.1	0.3	14.6	0.4	—	44.1	31.8
—	3.4	—	—	2.3	0.2	24.8	0.8	—	45.7	32.3
—	5.5	—	—	—	—	30.0	—	—	48.4	34.3
—	2.7	—	—	—	—	21.5	—	—	42.9	34.3
—	7.9	—	—	—	—	26.7	0.2	—	44.2	38.5
—	8.2	—	—	—	—	27.6	1.1	—	45.1	36.8
—	11.4	—	—	—	—	30.0	0.5	—	47.3	34.7
1.9	13.9	—	—	—	—	34.2	0.3	—	51.6	32.7
1.4	3.7	—	0.6	0.8	0.6	21.3	0.8	0.4	39.2	39.4
—	1.9	—	0.2	—	—	18.4	—	—	37.5	35.6
—	0.6	—	3.0	—	0.3	12.2	1.6	0.1	36.4	24.6
1.2	4.1	—	—	1.4	2.4	22.2	—	0.9	40.5	43.3
2.8	4.1	—	1.1	1.4	0.2	23.4	—	0.7	37.0	49.3
2.5	1.7	—	0.3	—	—	8.7	—	0.7	16.6	41.8
1.5	3.9	—	0.5	1.5	0.6	24.6	2.9	0.5	40.4	38.8
—	6.2	—	—	—	—	19.4	—	—	46.4	31.0

TABLE XIV. *(cont.) Estimates of church and chapel attendance, 30 March 1851,*

Registration District	Population	Church of England	Indepen-dents	Baptists	Quakers	Unitar-ians	Presby-terians	Wesleyan Methodists
Newark	30,348	21.8	2.1	2.9	0.1	—	—	15.4
Bingham	16,241	26.7	1.4	0.1	—	—	—	17.2
DERBYSHIRE	260,693	16.0	2.8	2.9	0.06	0.3	—	8.3
Shardlow	32,322	19.0	1.5	5.5	0.1	—	—	11.2
Derby	43,684	18.5	3.0	4.8	0.1	0.6	—	3.3
Belper	46,872	14.5	2.9	6.1	—	0.6	—	10.5
Ashbourne	20,932	25.3	1.3	0.3	—	—	—	6.3
Chesterfield	45,795	12.9	2.0	0.7	0.1	0.4	—	6.0
Bakewell	29,880	15.5	3.1	0.4	0.1	0.3	—	9.2
Chapel-en -le-Frith	11,496	15.1	0.8	0.4	—	—	—	13.5
Hayfield	29,712	10.8	6.8	0.8	0.1	—	—	11.1
CHESHIRE	423,526	16.8	3.0	0.8	0.1	0.4	0.3	6.2
Stockport	90,208	11.1	5.6	1.0	—	0.6	—	5.8
Macclesfield	63,327	14.9	1.2	0.6	0.1	0.5	—	5.5
Altrincham	34,043	17.9	6.4	1.4	0.1	1.5	—	8.9
Runcorn	25,797	17.7	3.6	1.8	—	—	—	10.7
Northwich	31,202	17.6	2.2	0.7	—	0.1	—	5.9
Congleton	30,512	17.7	2.1	0.2	—	0.2	—	10.9
Nantwich	37,986	18.0	1.1	1.0	0.1	0.3	0.3	6.8
Great Boughton (Chester)	53,294	21.4	2.3	0.2	0.1	0.2	0.1	4.3
Wirrall	57,157	20.8	1.6	0.4	0.2	—	2.1	3.0
LANCASHIRE	2,067,301	14.4	2.8	1.2	0.1	0.4	0.5	3.8
Liverpool	258,236	11.3	1.0	0.6	0.1	0.4	1.6	1.1
West Derby	153,279	18.9	1.7	1.1	—	0.1	—	3.8
Prescot	56,074	17.4	1.8	—	—	0.2	—	3.0
Ormskirk	38,307	23.9	2.9	—	0.1	—	—	2.8
Wigan	77,539	14.4	3.7	1.0	—	0.2	0.1	2.6
Warrington	36,164	20.8	2.6	0.9	0.4	0.7	—	5.6
Leigh	32,734	13.0	2.3	1.0	—	1.2	0.2	4.7
Bolton	114,712	12.7	4.2	0.3	0.1	0.6	0.2	5.0
Bury	88,815	13.6	4.3	1.0	—	0.8	0.8	5.5
Barton- upon-Irwell	31,585	17.6	4.1	—	—	0.3	—	8.0
Chorlton	123,841	11.2	3.5	0.7	—	0.3	1.4	4.0
Salford	87,523	12.1	3.5	0.7	—	—	—	3.6
Manchester	228,433	10.1	1.8	0.8	0.2	0.5	1.0	2.6
Ashton- under-Lyne	119,199	13.8	4.1	1.1	—	0.6	—	1.8
Oldham	86,788	8.5	3.6	0.9	—	0.2	—	3.2
Rochdale	72,515	11.4	2.6	4.9	0.1	0.6	—	4.4
Haslingden	50,424	16.6	1.3	9.9	—	1.3	—	13.2
Burnley	63,868	12.8	3.9	3.2	—	0.5	—	8.7

according to registration districts, in percentages of total population

Methodist New Connexion	Primitive Methodists	Bible Christians	Wesleyan Methodist Association	Wesleyan Reformers	Other Nonconformists	Total Nonconformists	Roman Catholics	Others	Total attenders	Level of Illiteracy
1.4	2.4	—	—	0.4	0.1	24.7	0.8	—	47.4	31.1
—	8.8	—	—	—	3.1	30.7	0.5	—	57.9	37.6
0.7	5.6	—	0.3	1.8	0.4	23.1	1.2	0.1	40.5	34.2
3.3	4.1	—	—	1.4	1.0	28.0	—	—	47.1	33.6
1.1	3.5	—	—	2.1	0.4	18.9	3.6	—	41.1	26.0
0.1	6.5	—	—	3.5	0.1	30.4	—	0.1	45.0	35.1
—	10.1	—	—	1.3	1.9	21.2	—	0.1	46.6	26.4
0.6	4.9	—	0.3	1.7	—	16.5	0.8	0.3	30.5	45.9
—	8.3	—	—	1.8	0.2	23.5	1.0	—	40.0	32.8
—	4.3	—	—	—	—	19.0	—	—	34.1	27.8
—	4.1	—	2.0	—	—	24.9	3.4	—	39.2	43.5
0.9	2.6	—	1.1	—	0.5	16.0	2.2	0.2	35.2	43.9
1.5	1.8	—	0.7	—	0.2	17.3	2.8	0.4	31.5	53.7
1.7	1.8	—	1.0	—	0.2	12.7	2.6	0.4	30.5	42.2
0.4	1.6	—	0.1	—	—	20.3	1.1	0.1	39.4	34.5
—	1.5	—	1.7	—	2.0	21.3	1.9	—	40.9	46.5
0.3	3.8	—	5.0	—	0.5	18.4	1.0	0.1	37.2	50.8
1.2	4.2	—	1.8	—	—	20.6	0.9	—	39.2	53.0
—	8.0	—	2.2	—	—	19.9	0.6	—	38.6	40.1
1.6	2.3	—	0.1	—	1.7	13.0	0.8	0.5	35.7	36.8
—	1.1	—	0.1	—	0.6	9.3	5.2	—	35.3	19.5
0.4	1.0	—	0.9	0.05	0.9	12.0	5.8	0.2	32.4	49.3
0.2	0.3	—	0.3	—	1.6	7.3	12.3	0.4	31.3	40.1
0.3	—	—	0.1	—	1.2	8.3	9.4	—	36.6	23.5
—	0.3	—	0.6	—	0.4	6.3	8.5	0.6	32.8	56.7
—	2.0	—	—	—	0.4	8.2	7.4	—	39.5	56.5
—	0.7	—	—	—	0.2	8.6	7.8	0.3	31.0	70.6
—	1.0	—	—	—	1.4	12.4	6.3	—	39.6	63.8
—	3.3	—	0.4	—	1.7	14.8	2.3	0.2	30.3	63.7
0.2	1.2	—	0.3	—	0.6	12.9	1.9	0.1	27.6	60.3
0.8	0.9	—	1.1	—	0.8	15.9	1.3	0.6	31.4	54.0
0.7	0.8	—	1.4	—	1.3	16.7	1.2	—	35.5	50.1
0.2	0.9	—	0.6	—	0.7	12.3	2.3	0.1	25.8	27.0
0.3	0.7	—	0.7	—	0.6	10.3	3.3	0.4	26.0	34.3
0.5	0.2	—	1.2	—	0.4	9.4	8.3	0.1	28.0	44.5
2.7	1.5	—	0.7	—	1.3	13.8	1.6	0.4	29.5	53.3
0.3	1.5	—	0.8	—	1.6	12.2	0.7	0.2	21.7	63.3
0.7	1.8	—	5.3	0.3	1.9	22.6	0.7	—	34.7	70.7
—	4.4	—	3.1	—	1.1	34.4	0.8	—	51.9	52.5
—	4.1	—	2.3	—	1.8	24.6	1.5	—	38.9	62.8

TABLE XIV. *(cont.) Estimates of church and chapel attendance, 30 March 1851,*

Registration District	Population	Church of England	Independents	Baptists	Quakers	Unitarians	Presbyterians	Wesleyan Methodists
Clitheroe	22,368	23.9	5.7	1.9	—	—	—	8.0
Blackburn	90,738	16.2	5.3	1.0	0.1	—	0.8	3.3
Chorley	37,701	17.0	2.0	0.1	—	0.3	—	5.5
Preston	96,545	15.4	1.7	0.5	0.2	0.1	—	2.7
Fylde	22,002	29.9	5.4	0.2	0.1	—	—	4.0
Garstang	12,695	25.5	3.6	1.7	0.4	—	—	5.4
Lancaster	34,660	26.3	4.6	0.2	0.5	0.3	—	4.0
Ulverstone	30,556	32.8	1.1	1.2	0.1	—	—	2.1
YORKSHIRE:								
WEST RIDING	1,340,051	12.8	3.6	2.2	0.2	0.2	0.05	8.9
Sedbergh	4,574	28.0	6.0	—	1.3	—	—	7.7
Settle	13,762	23.0	1.3	1.3	0.2	—	—	8.4
Skipton	28,766	18.3	2.2	4.1	1.1	—	—	13.4
Pateley Bridge	7,579	9.3	2.7	—	—	—	—	21.0
Ripon	18,648	23.8	1.1	2.1	—	—	—	11.8
Knaresborough	27,783	26.7	2.0	0.4	—	—	—	11.8
Otley	28,644	10.3	2.1	1.5	0.7	—	—	15.1
Keighley	45,903	7.9	3.5	8.3	—	—	—	15.3
Todmorden	29,727	10.6	3.2	13.8	—	0.7	—	9.3
Saddleworth	17,799	7.1	7.2	0.1	—	—	—	4.7
Huddersfield	123,860	14.4	3.7	3.3	0.1	0.1	0.1	7.4
Halifax	120,958	11.3	6.4	1.8	0.1	0.3	—	7.2
Bradford	181,964	7.7	4.9	3.6	0.1	0.1	0.3	7.1
Hunslet	88,679	11.8	1.0	1.8	—	0.3	—	7.8
Leeds	101,343	11.6	3.5	1.5	0.4	0.4	—	9.1
Dewsbury	71,768	14.4	8.9	1.2	0.1	—	—	9.9
Wakefield	48,956	19.5	3.7	0.8	0.1	0.5	—	5.8
Pontefract	29,937	14.7	2.3	—	0.1	—	—	14.2
Hemsworth	8,158	25.3	—	—	6.1	—	—	14.9
Barnsley	34,980	12.6	1.1	0.8	0.1	—	—	4.4
Wortley	32,012	11.2	3.3	0.7	0.2	—	—	7.6
Ecclesall-Bierlow	37,914	6.1	0.1	—	—	—	—	6.0
Sheffield	103,626	11.1	3.0	1.5	0.2	0.7	—	5.0
Rotherham	33,082	14.4	3.6	0.5	—	0.2	—	10.4
Doncaster	34,675	24.3	1.4	0.5	0.1	0.2	—	13.4
Thorne	15,886	10.6	1.2	0.5	—	0.9	—	14.3
Goole	13,686	8.6	3.5	—	—	—	—	19.2
Selby	15,429	10.8	1.9	—	0.2	0.8	—	16.0
Tadcaster	19,953	25.0	0.6	—	—	—	—	12.9
YORKSHIRE:								
EAST RIDING	254,352	16.6	3.4	0.7	0.2	0.1	0.06	11.2
York	57,116	21.7	3.0	—	0.6	0.2	—	8.4
Pocklington	16,098	13.8	2.2	—	0.1	—	—	13.6
Howden	14,436	14.2	3.2	—	0.1	—	—	19.0

according to registration districts, in percentages of total population

Methodist New Connexion	Primitive Methodists	Bible Christians	Wesleyan Methodist Association	Wesleyan Reformers	Other Nonconformists	Total Nonconformists	Roman Catholics	Others	Total attenders	Level of Illiteracy
—	0.7	—	3.1	—	0.1	19.6	10.7	0.3	54.5	43.3
—	1.9	—	1.4	0.6	0.3	14.7	2.5	0.1	33.6	64.0
—	0.5	—	0.7	—	—	9.2	11.6	—	37.9	59.4
—	0.7	—	0.7	—	0.4	7.2	10.5	—	33.2	56.6
—	0.7	—	—	0.6	—	11.0	6.5	—	47.4	43.0
—	—	—	—	—	—	11.1	14.3	—	50.9	46.8
—	0.5	—	—	0.3	0.1	10.5	3.9	—	40.7	29.3
—	—	—	—	—	0.1	4.6	—	—	37.4	30.1
1.1	2.6	—	0.6	1.0	0.6	21.1	1.2	0.1	35.3	45.9
—	6.7	—	—	—	—	21.8	—	—	49.8	28.8
—	2.4	—	—	—	—	13.6	0.2	—	36.7	28.1
—	3.6	—	5.0	—	1.9	31.3	1.0	—	50.6	41.5
—	7.9	—	—	—	—	31.8	—	—	41.2	42.9
2.4	2.9	—	—	—	—	20.3	1.3	—	45.3	28.9
—	3.2	—	—	1.5	—	18.9	1.4	0.1	47.2	30.6
0.7	3.3	—	1.9	0.9	2.3	28.6	0.5	—	39.4	46.9
—	4.7	—	0.7	—	0.9	33.4	0.7	—	42.0	55.6
—	2.6	—	5.3	—	1.3	36.4	—	—	47.0	66.5
0.4	—	—	—	—	2.7	15.2	0.4	—	22.7	52.3
2.2	2.1	—	—	0.7	0.5	20.3	0.4	0.1	35.2	46.7
2.3	1.5	—	—	1.4	0.2	21.2	0.5	—	33.0	57.7
0.5	2.1	—	0.5	1.6	0.4	21.8	1.9	0.3	31.7	52.4
1.6	2.5	—	1.4	0.8	0.3	17.5	—	—	29.4	36.4
0.9	1.0	—	1.4	1.2	0.7	20.1	4.0	0.3	36.1	39.6
1.7	2.6	—	—	2.2	2.0	28.6	0.6	—	43.6	56.0
0.7	4.6	—	—	3.4	—	19.8	0.7	—	40.0	46.0
—	3.9	—	—	—	—	20.6	0.8	—	36.1	38.9
—	2.6	—	—	—	0.5	24.2	0.8	—	50.3	19.7
2.4	2.9	—	1.7	1.2	—	14.7	1.1	—	28.3	52.8
2.0	2.2	—	—	1.1	1.2	19.1	—	—	30.3	38.6
1.7	4.9	—	—	0.3	—	13.1	—	—	19.2	15.4
0.8	—	—	0.3	—	0.1	11.8	2.2	0.4	25.5	57.4
—	2.6	—	—	1.6	0.2	19.1	0.6	—	34.2	39.0
0.3	4.6	—	—	0.1	—	20.6	0.4	0.1	45.4	32.7
3.2	9.6	—	—	—	0.1	29.8	—	—	40.5	40.5
—	10.3	—	—	—	—	33.1	—	—	41.7	38.9
—	3.5	—	—	—	—	22.4	—	—	38.9	38.9
—	2.9	—	—	—	0.3	16.7	3.1	—	44.9	35.3
0.3	5.2	—	0.1	1.2	0.6	23.1	1.7	0.1	41.5	30.2
—	1.3	—	0.5	3.2	0.4	17.7	3.0	—	42.4	28.3
—	7.2	—	—	—	—	23.1	3.4	—	40.3	36.6
—	6.7	—	—	—	—	29.0	1.9	0.2	45.3	40.1

TABLE XIV. *(cont.) Estimates of church and chapel attendance, 30 March 1851,*

Registration District	Population	Church of England	Indepen-dents	Baptists	Quakers	Unitar-ians	Presby-terians	Wesleyan Methodists
Beverley	20,040	25.0	1.6	3.0	—	—	—	14.8
Sculcoates	44,719	13.9	6.0	0.8	—	—	—	7.3
Hull	50,670	11.5	3.9	0.7	0.3	0.5	0.3	7.0
Patrington	9,407	17.2	0.6	—	—	—	—	9.9
Skirlaugh	9,279	17.6	2.4	—	—	—	—	13.6
Driffield	18,265	13.1	3.0	1.2	—	—	—	14.8
Bridlington	14,322	19.2	3.0	1.4	—	—	—	27.5
YORKSHIRE: NORTH RIDING	194,644	19.1	2.6	0.7	0.2	0.1	0.2	14.4
Scarborough	24,615	17.8	3.2	2.0	0.3	—	—	15.2
Malton	23,128	17.3	1.4	0.6	0.2	0.4	—	12.5
Easingwold	11,450	26.7	0.8	—	—	—	—	19.0
Thirsk	12,760	27.1	2.6	—	0.3	—	—	14.9
Helmsley	12,455	14.4	2.5	—	0.1	—	—	18.5
Pickering	9,978	16.2	2.9	—	0.1	—	—	13.4
Whitby	21,592	14.1	4.8	—	0.1	0.4	1.5	13.8
Guisborough	12,202	15.8	2.3	3.1	0.4	—	—	14.5
Stokesley	8,666	14.1	1.3	—	1.6	—	—	8.1
Northallerton	12,460	22.0	3.1	0.8	0.1	—	—	7.4
Bedale	8,980	26.8	—	3.2	—	—	—	19.0
Leyburn	10,057	19.0	2.4	—	—	—	—	16.9
Askrigg	5,635	13.6	8.8	0.1	0.5	—	—	14.2
Reeth	6,820	9.7	4.1	—	—	—	—	31.2
Richmond	13,846	30.4	0.6	—	—	—	—	7.3
DURHAM	411,679	11.3	1.5	1.0	0.1	0.1	1.1	6.4
Darlington	21,618	23.0	1.8	0.4	—	—	—	11.6
Stockton	52,934	16.1	2.3	0.9	0.3	0.1	0.8	5.4
Auckland	30,083	11.6	0.3	1.3	0.1	—	—	5.4
Teesdale	19,813	11.5	2.6	3.3	0.2	0.3	—	8.3
Weardale	14,567	7.4	0.8	—	—	—	—	16.0
Durham	55,951	9.0	0.5	0.2	0.1	—	—	5.8
Easington	21,795	8.7	—	—	—	—	—	7.3
Houghton-le-Spring	19,564	13.4	0.4	0.1	—	—	0.9	9.1
Chester-le-Street	20,907	9.8	0.8	—	—	—	—	6.4
Sunderland	70,576	9.6	2.9	2.5	0.2	0.3	3.2	3.8
South Shields	35,790	8.6	1.6	1.2	—	—	2.8	5.8
Gateshead	48,081	9.9	1.3	—	—	—	0.9	5.4
NORTHUMBER-LAND	303,568	11.7	1.2	0.8	0.1	0.2	6.4	3.5
Newcastle upon Tyne	89,156	12.0	1.1	1.5	0.3	0.6	2.5	2.0
Tynemouth	64,248	7.5	1.6	0.5	0.2	—	3.8	6.1

according to registration districts, in percentages of total population

Methodist New Connexion	Primitive Methodists	Bible Christ-ians	Wesleyan Methodist Associa-tion	Wesleyan Reformers	Other Noncon-formists	Total Noncon-formists	Roman Catholics	Others	Total attenders	Level of Illiteracy
—	6.6	—	—	—	—	26.0	0.6	—	51.7	28.3
1.5	5.4	—	—	2.7	—	23.8	3.5	—	41.2	29.1
—	4.0	—	—	—	2.6	19.3	—	0.4	31.2	26.3
—	11.0	—	—	—	—	21.5	—	—	38.7	42.8
—	6.5	—	—	—	0.3	22.9	1.6	—	42.2	29.7
—	11.2	—	—	—	—	30.1	—	—	43.3	38.7
—	6.5	—	—	—	—	38.4	—	—	57.6	32.8
—	5.1	—	0.3	0.1	0.3	24.0	1.6	—	44.7	28.3
—	6.8	—	0.7	—	0.2	28.5	1.3	—	47.6	25.1
—	5.2	—	—	—	0.5	20.9	1.0	—	39.2	33.8
—	2.9	—	—	—	—	22.8	1.5	—	51.1	33.3
—	2.8	—	—	1.4	—	22.0	0.7	—	49.9	26.6
—	4.5	—	—	—	—	25.6	1.3	—	41.3	36.9
—	12.6	—	—	—	—	29.0	—	—	45.2	28.8
—	6.9	—	1.4	—	0.2	29.1	5.2	—	48.3	25.0
—	4.0	—	—	—	—	24.2	—	—	40.1	23.2
—	5.9	—	—	—	—	16.9	0.4	—	31.4	31.5
—	6.6	—	—	—	—	18.1	0.2	—	40.3	32.5
—	3.7	—	—	1.2	—	27.1	0.5	—	54.4	19.2
—	3.1	—	—	—	—	22.5	1.4	—	42.9	21.9
—	3.6	—	—	—	6.2	33.4	—	—	47.0	40.2
—	1.9	—	—	—	0.5	37.7	—	—	47.5	42.5
—	1.1	—	0.4	—	—	9.4	5.7	—	45.4	17.1
0.9	4.7	—	0.8	0.6	0.2	17.3	2.5	—	31.1	27.6
—	1.4	—	0.5	—	—	15.7	2.3	—	41.0	21.4
—	3.4	—	1.0	0.9	0.4	15.5	2.8	0.1	34.5	29.2
—	7.6	—	0.5	—	—	15.3	0.8	—	27.7	50.8
—	7.2	—	—	—	—	21.9	2.4	—	35.8	20.8
—	10.6	—	—	—	—	27.3	1.1	—	35.9	30.8
0.7	4.7	—	—	—	—	12.0	6.2	—	27.3	42.1
—	9.0	—	0.5	—	—	16.8	1.8	—	27.4	46.6
0.3	7.1	—	2.7	—	—	20.6	2.3	—	36.3	55.1
1.1	0.8	—	0.5	—	—	10.0	—	—	19.8	59.3
0.8	3.7	—	1.5	2.3	0.4	21.6	1.3	—	32.6	38.3
1.5	6.0	—	2.3	0.2	0.6	22.1	1.3	0.1	32.1	32.6
3.8	2.7	—	0.4	—	—	14.5	3.2	—	27.6	37.8
0.7	1.9	—	—	1.1	1.1	15.9	2.3	1.0	31.0	29.4
0.6	1.3	—	—	1.2	0.2	11.2	4.4	1.1	28.7	32.0
2.2	3.3	—	—	2.9	0.1	20.7	1.4	0.1	29.7	35.5

TABLE XIV. *(cont.) Estimates of church and chapel attendance, 30 March 1851,*

Registration District	Population	Church of England	Indepen-dents	Baptists	Quakers	Unitar-ians	Presby-terians/ Calvinistic Methodists	Wesleyan Methodists
Castle Ward	13,897	12.4	—	—	—	—	0.6	5.6
Hexham	30,436	11.7	1.2	0.4	—	—	1.2	7.5
Haltwhistle	7,286	4.9	—	—	0.2	—	0.9	7.7
Bellingham	6,553	10.9	—	—	—	—	20.1	0.5
Morpeth	18,127	15.4	1.6	0.8	—	—	7.3	2.9
Alnwick	21,122	15.2	2.0	—	—	0.3	10.3	2.5
Belford	6,871	22.8	—	—	—	—	18.0	—
Berwick-on-Tweed	24,093	13.2	1.3	1.5	—	—	19.0	0.6
Glendale	14,348	11.2	—	0.7	—	—	21.7	—
Rothbury	7,431	17.7	1.5	—	—	—	7.4	—
CUMBER-LAND	195,492	15.2	1.8	0.3	0.2	—	1.4	3.7
Alston	6,816	6.6	2.8	—	0.1	—	—	13.8
Penrith	22,307	16.8	1.8	—	0.1	—	0.6	7.0
Brampton	11,323	11.0	1.2	—	—	—	1.9	3.0
Longtown	9,696	5.6	—	—	0.2	—	3.0	2.6
Carlisle	41,557	11.2	1.4	0.2	0.3	—	1.1	1.8
Wigton	23,661	11.6	3.9	—	0.3	—	0.3	1.3
Cockermouth	38,510	16.8	2.6	0.7	0.5	—	3.0	4.3
Whitehaven	35,614	23.5	1.0	0.2	0.1	0.1	1.2	3.4
Bootle	6,008	24.5	0.2	1.5	—	—	—	5.1
WESTMOR-LAND	58,387	24.0	1.3	0.4	0.2	0.3	0.3	4.3
East Ward	13,660	22.1	2.2	1.7	0.1	—	—	8.9
West Ward	8,155	26.3	—	—	0.1	—	—	2.5
Kendal	36,572	24.1	1.3	—	0.3	0.4	0.5	3.1
MONMOUTH-SHIRE	177,130	12.7	7.1	12.9	—	—	3.3	7.3
Chepstow	19,057	20.4	0.8	3.4	—	—	0.4	3.6
Monmouth	27,379	23.1	2.2	7.4	—	—	—	3.5
Abergavenny	59,229	9.8	9.7	17.7	—	—	7.1	8.1
Pontypool	27,993	13.6	7.0	16.5	—	—	1.9	14.0
Newport	43,472	5.9	9.5	11.5	—	—	2.3	6.0
GLAMORGAN	240,095	6.8	15.8	13.0	0.03	0.3	9.5	3.5
Cardiff	46,491	8.8	7.7	12.5	—	—	11.5	5.6
Merthyr Tydfil	76,804	3.3	16.3	20.4	—	0.4	7.3	3.0
Bridgend	23,422	9.4	15.5	12.1	—	—	14.7	4.6
Neath	46,471	6.6	21.7	7.3	0.1	0.4	12.0	1.4
Swansea	46,907	9.3	17.3	7.5	—	0.6	6.0	3.8
CARMARTHEN-SHIRE	94,672	13.9	20.5	12.0	—	0.3	11.9	2.6

according to registration districts, in percentages of total population

Methodist New Connexion	Primitive Methodists	Bible Christians	Wesleyan Methodist Association	Wesleyan Reformers	Other Nonconformists	Total Nonconformists	Roman Catholics	Others	Total attenders	Level of Illiteracy
—	1.5	—	—	2.2	—	9.8	1.3	—	23.6	15.8
—	4.1	—	—	—	—	14.5	2.1	—	28.3	25.3
—	2.8	—	—	—	0.7	12.3	—	—	17.2	11.9
—	0.6	—	—	—	—	21.1	1.0	—	33.0	1.9
—	0.1	—	—	—	—	12.8	2.0	—	30.2	19.1
1.2	—	—	—	—	—	16.3	1.2	—	32.7	16.4
—	—	—	—	—	—	18.0	0.8	5.1	46.8	3.3
—	1.5	—	—	—	0.2	24.1	1.5	5.3	44.1	14.3
—	2.0	—	—	—	—	24.5	0.5	2.9	39.2	12.9
—	—	—	—	—	—	8.8	3.3	—	29.8	4.2
—	1.4	—	1.1	—	0.3	10.3	1.6	0.2	27.4	23.4
—	16.2	—	—	—	—	32.8	—	—	39.5	10.0
—	1.1	—	—	—	0.4	11.1	0.6	—	28.5	8.3
—	—	—	—	—	—	6.1	—	—	17.2	20.8
—	—	—	0.4	—	—	6.2	—	0.9	12.7	8.6
—	0.8	—	3.5	—	0.1	9.1	3.2	0.7	24.3	22.7
—	0.1	—	—	—	—	6.0	1.7	—	19.3	16.7
—	1.4	—	—	—	0.5	13.0	1.3	0.1	31.2	22.5
—	1.6	—	1.7	—	0.5	10.0	2.3	0.2	35.9	38.6
—	—	—	—	—	—	6.8	—	—	31.3	20.0
—	1.6	—	1.4	0.3	1.7	12.0	1.0	—	36.9	22.8
—	4.1	—	5.4	—	—	23.4	—	—	45.5	20.6
—	—	—	0.8	—	—	3.4	—	—	29.7	23.8
—	1.0	—	—	0.6	2.4	9.7	1.6	—	35.4	23.4
—	2.3	0.4	—	0.5	0.3	34.1	1.6	0.6	49.0	55.0
—	1.0	2.4	—	—	1.0	12.7	0.7	0.3	34.0	46.1
—	3.9	0.4	—	0.7	—	18.1	1.1	—	42.3	41.6
—	2.7	—	—	—	0.5	45.8	0.7	0.5	56.8	69.5
—	3.2	0.2	—	—	0.3	43.1	1.7	—	58.4	61.9
—	0.5	0.3	—	1.4	0.1	31.6	3.7	1.6	42.9	44.6
—	0.5	—	—	0.05	0.7	43.5	1.0	1.0	52.3	61.4
—	—	—	—	—	0.2	37.6	2.8	0.7	49.9	56.8
—	0.7	—	—	0.2	0.7	49.0	0.8	2.2	55.4	74.1
—	—	—	—	—	—	46.9	—	—	56.3	50.5
—	0.2	0.3	—	—	—	43.4	—	0.2	50.2	62.4
—	1.3	—	—	—	2.3	38.9	0.8	0.5	49.5	47.8
—	—	—	—	—	—	47.3	0.1	0.4	61.7	57.0

TABLE XIV. *(cont.) Estimates of church and chapel attendance, 30 March 1851,*

Registration District	Population	Church of England	Independents	Baptists	Quakers	Unitarians	Calvinistic Methodists	Wesleyan Methodists
Llanelly	23,507	14.9	17.9	19.6	—	—	9.5	3.8
Llandovery	15,055	12.8	26.9	6.6	—	—	14.4	1.1
Llandilofawr	17,968	14.5	17.9	10.8	—	0.3	12.3	3.5
Carmarthen	38,142	13.3	20.9	10.0	—	0.6	12.2	2.0
PEMBROKE-SHIRE	84,472	14.7	13.3	12.5	—	0.1	4.8	5.8
Narberth	22,130	14.6	19.3	11.5	—	0.3	3.1	2.2
Pembroke	22,960	21.6	7.4	9.9	—	—	5.0	8.8
Haverford-west	39,382	10.7	13.3	14.6	0.1	—	5.7	6.2
CARDIGAN-SHIRE	97,614	13.6	15.1	11.1	—	1.5	23.8	3.0
Cardigan	20,186	14.7	14.4	26.8	—	—	14.9	0.6
Newcastle Emlyn	20,173	12.0	23.5	10.3	—	2.9	14.3	2.3
Lampeter	9,874	10.6	24.1	7.1	—	4.9	6.0	1.8
Aberayron	13,224	16.0	23.1	2.8	—	3.0	26.1	1.3
Aberystwyth	23,753	14.2	6.9	6.8	—	—	41.1	8.3
Tregaron	10,404	12.9	—	5.9	—	—	34.1	0.6
BRECONSHIRE	59,178	13.8	17.5	10.9	—	—	8.3	4.9
Builth	8,345	10.1	15.2	6.9	—	—	9.6	—
Brecknock	18,174	22.4	14.1	8.8	—	—	11.2	3.3
Crickhowell	21,697	6.8	27.0	15.4	—	—	6.5	8.9
Hay	10,962	16.3	5.9	8.6	—	—	6.1	3.4
RADNOR-SHIRE	31,425	16.3	4.6	5.2	0.1	—	2.3	2.9
Presteigne	15,149	18.9	1.8	4.2	0.2	—	2.2	2.9
Knighton	9,480	14.8	0.4	2.2	—	—	—	3.2
Rhayader	6,796	12.8	16.6	11.8	—	—	5.7	2.6
MONTGOMERY-SHIRE	77,142	13.5	8.3	4.3	—	—	13.0	11.9
Machynlleth	12,116	10.6	18.1	1.7	—	—	24.8	16.0
Newtown	25,107	8.8	3.6	9.3	—	—	12.8	8.8
Montgomery	20,381	23.3	4.0	1.6	—	—	5.6	4.4
Llanfyllin	19,538	11.1	12.7	2.2	—	—	13.8	21.3
FLINT: Holywell	41,047	15.9	8.0	4.0	—	—	15.2	13.5
DENBIGH-SHIRE	96,915	12.3	6.7	5.9	—	0.3	18.7	7.4
Wrexham	42,295	14.1	5.5	9.0	—	0.8	8.6	6.0
Ruthin	16,853	9.8	7.1	3.0	—	—	25.4	6.5
St Asaph	25,288	12.6	6.7	4.6	—	—	22.9	10.1
Llanrwst	12,479	8.8	10.1	2.3	—	—	35.6	7.7

according to registration districts, in percentages of total population

Methodist New Connexion	Primitive Methodists	Bible Christians	Wesleyan Methodist Association	Wesleyan Reformers	Other Nonconformists	Total Nonconformists	Roman Catholics	Others	Total attenders	Level of Illiteracy
—	—	—	—	—	—	50.8	—	1.2	66.9	59.2
—	—	—	—	—	—	48.9	—	—	61.7	67.1
—	—	—	—	—	—	44.7	—	0.2	59.5	53.6
—	—	—	—	—	—	45.7	0.3	0.3	59.5	53.6
—	0.7	—	—	—	0.5	37.9	0.2	0.1	52.8	39.4
—	1.3	—	—	—	—	37.7	—	—	52.4	45.2
—	1.2	—	—	—	0.4	32.8	0.5	—	54.9	33.1
—	0.2	—	—	—	0.8	40.8	0.1	0.2	51.8	40.6
—	0.1	—	0.1	—	—	54.8	—	0.1	68.5	51.7
—	—	—	—	—	—	56.6	—	—	71.4	45.7
—	—	—	—	—	—	53.3	—	0.3	65.7	54.1
—	—	—	—	—	—	43.9	—	0.3	54.8	53.3
—	—	—	—	—	—	56.2	—	—	72.3	50.7
—	0.6	—	0.6	—	—	64.3	—	—	78.6	53.5
—	—	—	—	—	—	40.6	—	—	53.5	52.1
—	1.8	—	—	—	0.5	44.0	0.3	—	58.1	53.4
—	0.2	—	—	—	—	31.9	—	—	42.1	45.5
—	—	—	—	—	—	37.4	1.1	—	60.9	38.1
—	3.6	—	—	—	1.5	62.9	—	—	69.7	65.7
—	2.5	—	—	—	—	26.6	—	—	42.9	50.7
—	3.7	—	—	—	—	18.8	—	—	35.1	42.7
—	4.3	—	—	—	—	15.6	—	—	34.5	46.8
—	5.2	—	—	—	—	11.1	—	—	25.9	36.1
—	—	—	—	—	—	36.7	—	—	49.5	39.1
—	1.1	—	0.1	—	0.7	39.5	—	0.1	53.0	49.2
—	—	—	0.6	—	3.2	64.5	—	0.4	75.4	45.0
—	0.3	—	—	—	—	34.9	—	—	43.7	43.6
—	3.5	—	—	—	—	19.2	—	—	42.4	48.9
—	0.3	—	—	—	0.7	51.0	—	—	62.1	52.6
0.9	0.5	—	—	—	1.5	44.2	1.1	—	61.2	62.5
0.6	0.5	—	0.8	—	0.2	41.2	0.4	0.2	54.0	55.6
1.4	1.2	—	1.8	—	0.2	34.5	0.7	0.2	49.5	55.5
—	—	—	—	—	—	42.0	—	—	51.8	49.1
—	—	—	—	—	0.3	44.6	0.3	0.3	57.8	59.6
—	—	—	—	—	—	55.7	—	—	64.6	57.5

TABLE XIV. *(cont.) Estimates of church and chapel attendance, 30 March 1851,*

Registration District	Population	Church of England	Indepen-dents	Baptists	Quakers	Unitar-ians	Calvinistic Methodists	Wesleyan Methodists
MERIONETH	51,307	6.2	12.2	6.6	—	—	29.2	6.9
Corwen	15,418	6.6	6.7	12.4	—	—	24.3	9.2
Bala	6,736	5.6	15.5	0.8	—	—	38.7	0.6
Dolgelly	12,971	5.6	17.1	3.2	—	—	26.0	11.5
Festiniog	16,182	6.4	12.0	6.1	—	—	32.5	3.6
CAERNARFON-SHIRE	94,674	9.6	12.2	3.9	—	—	33.4	8.0
Pwllheli	21,788	5.9	10.1	5.7	—	—	38.0	6.2
Caernarfon	30,446	5.5	13.0	2.7	—	—	36.0	4.4
Bangor	30,810	14.6	13.4	3.0	—	—	31.5	10.1
Conway	11,630	13.9	10.8	6.4	—	—	22.9	15.4
ANGLESEY	43,243	7.2	8.3	5.6	—	—	29.0	5.6

according to registration districts, in percentages of total population

Methodist New Connexion	Primitive Methodists	Bible Christians	Wesleyan Methodist Association	Wesleyan Reformers	Other Noncon- formists	Total Noncon- formists	Roman Catholics	Others	Total attenders	Level of Illiteracy
—	—	—	0.2	—	0.8	55.8	—	—	62.0	56.7
—	—	—	—	—	—	52.7	—	—	59.3	62.5
—	—	—	—	—	—	55.7	—	—	61.2	52.7
—	—	—	0.6	—	2.0	60.5	—	—	66.1	48.8
—	—	—	—	—	0.9	55.1	—	—	61.5	59.3
—	—	—	—	—	0.6	58.2	0.1	0.2	68.1	54.3
—	—	—	—	—	1.2	61.2	—	—	67.1	56.6
—	—	—	—	—	—	56.1	—	0.2	61.9	56.8
—	—	—	—	—	—	58.0	0.4	0.3	73.3	53.3
—	—	—	—	—	2.7	58.2	—	—	72.2	43.0
—	—	—	—	—	1.0	49.7	—	—	56.9	57.9

TABLE XV. *Bedfordshire: occupations of male Dissenters in percentages*

	General male population 1841	Baptists 1790–1819	Wesleyan Methodists			Primitive Methodists		
			1810–19	1820–9	1830–9	1840–9	1850–9	1860–9
I Gentlemen	1.9	1.2	—	0.8	—	—	—	—
II Business	0.3	—	—	0.4	0.7	0.6	0.9	0.5
III Professions	1.1	—	—	—	0.1	—	—	—
IV Farmers	5.6	32.4	8.8	6.0	4.1	7.6	1.9	6.1
V Food and retail	9.1	13.5	15.4	11.6	8.1	1.3	7.5	0.5
VI White collar	2.0	2.4	8.2	2.2	1.7	—	0.4	1.6
VII Labour aristocracy	1.0	—	3.3	1.6	1.6	7.6	0.4	—
VIII Higher skilled	11.5	4.1	11.0	8.2	9.4	12.7	9.2	16.3
IX Lower skilled	8.0	6.5	26.4	13.9	10.5	—	13.2	19.4
X Depressed	0.5	1.2	—	0.8	0.3	—	—	0.2
XI Unskilled	59.2	38.8	26.9	54.4	63.6	70.1	66.5	55.4
[Labourers]	[52.5]	[36.5]	[19.8]	[48.8]	[59.9]	[68.5]	[64.3]	[52.7]
Number of churches/circuits		2	3	4	5	2	2	2
Number of adults/fathers	23,634	85	91	249	1,039	157	234	410

TABLE XVI. *Berkshire: occupations of male Dissenters in percentages*

		General male population 1841	Independents 1818–37	Quakers 1790–1837	Wesleyan Methodists 1813–37	Primitive Methodists 1831–7
I	Gentlemen	3.8	1.4	2.1	—	—
II	Business	0.5	—	6.2	0.3	—
III	Professions	1.2	1.4	4.2	0.3	—
IV	Farmers	4.5	1.4	—	3.4	4.7
V	Food and retail	8.7	21.8	58.3	12.7	3.5
VI	White collar	2.4	3.5	3.1	6.4	1.2
VII	Labour aristocracy	1.6	8.5	5.2	2.9	—
VIII	Higher skilled	13.4	23.9	8.3	19.8	14.1
IX	Lower skilled	8.7	8.5	10.4	17.6	9.4
X	Depressed	0.8	—	—	1.5	2.4
XI	Unskilled	54.4	29.6	2.1	35.1	64.7
	[Labourers]	[42.8]	[19.7]	[2.1]	[30.4]	[61.2]
	Number of churches/circuits		1		6	4
	Number of adults/fathers	38,582	71	48	296	85

TABLE XVII. *Buckinghamshire: occupations of male Dissenters in percentages*

		General male population	Independents			Baptists	Quakers	Wesleyan Methodists
		1841	1810–19	1820–9	1830–7	1796–1837	1790–1837	1804–37
I	Gentlemen	2.6	—	—	—	1.3	—	0.5
II	Business	0.3	—	0.5	0.9	—	4.8	2.7
III	Professions	1.0	1.4	0.5	—	—	6.0	—
IV	Farmers	6.3	7.9	2.9	3.7	9.0	9.6	3.2
V	Food and retail	9.4	15.7	12.2	9.4	20.5	55.4	10.9
VI	White collar	2.1	4.3	2.7	2.2	5.1	1.2	2.7
VII	Labour aristocracy	1.4	1.4	2.3	1.7	5.1	3.6	2.7
VIII	Higher skilled	12.5	21.4	34.9	25.8	26.9	9.6	26.7
IX	Lower skilled	7.3	13.6	11.7	9.6	20.5	2.4	12.0
X	Depressed	0.3	1.4	—	—	—	—	0.5
XI	Unskilled	56.8	32.9	32.4	46.7	11.5	7.2	38.2
	[Labourers]	[49.2]	[32.9]	[31.1]	[44.5]	[9.0]	[4.8]	[34.8]
	Number of churches/circuits		2	5	6	2		4
	Number of adults/fathers	35,634	70	222	229	78	83	221

TABLE XVIII. *Cambridgeshire: occupations of male Dissenters in percentages*

	General male population 1841	Independents 1819–37	Wesleyan Methodists		
			1810–19	1820–9	1830–7
I Gentlemen	2.8	0.8	—	—	—
II Business	0.4	1.9	0.4	0.7	1.9
III Professions	1.1	0.8	—	—	0.3
IV Farmers	8.3	9.3	10.0	10.3	5.8
V Food and retail	8.6	14.3	5.2	7.1	6.8
VI White collar	2.4	5.4	1.6	2.4	1.4
VII Labour aristocracy	1.5	3.9	0.8	0.8	5.2
VIII Higher skilled	11.1	16.3	12.4	14.5	18.8
IX Lower skilled	9.5	13.2	14.0	12.9	12.6
X Depressed	0.1	—	0.8	0.3	—
XI Unskilled	54.2	34.1	54.8	51.0	47.2
[Labourers]	[47.2]	[31.8]	[53.2]	[46.3]	[43.2]
Number of churches/circuits		3	3	3	4
Number of adults/fathers	37,839	129	125	372	317

TABLE XIX. Cheshire: occupations of male Dissenters in percentages

| | | General male population 1841 | Independents | | | Quakers | Unitarians | |
			1810–19	1820–9	1830–7	1790–1837	1817–29	1830–9
I	Gentlemen	2.6	—	—	0.1	—	—	—
II	Business	0.9	0.5	1.2	1.2	10.8	2.5	6.5
III	Professions	0.9	0.7	0.2	0.1	1.0	0.6	1.3
IV	Farmers	7.0	4.9	2.0	2.7	15.7	6.3	1.6
V	Food and retail	6.2	5.4	5.9	5.8	13.2	4.6	7.8
VI	White collar	2.7	4.0	4.1	3.3	6.9	2.6	11.8
VII	Labour aristocracy	4.2	8.1	6.8	10.5	4.4	14.7	9.1
VIII	Higher skilled	15.4	23.4	30.7	25.0	15.2	24.8	30.5
IX	Lower skilled	15.4	19.9	16.8	17.4	10.8	28.5	13.8
X	Depressed	12.6	21.4	17.7	19.4	14.7	10.4	6.7
	[Weavers]	[7.1]	[21.0]	[17.2]	[18.8]	[11.8]	[10.4]	[6.7]
XI	Unskilled	32.0	11.8	14.7	14.4	7.3	4.9	10.8
	[Labourers]	[25.1]	[8.1]	[11.1]	[9.9]	[1.5]	[3.7]	[8.5]
	Number of churches/circuits		4	9	12		2	2
	Number of adults/fathers	92,286	297	588	913	102	163	153

TABLE XIX. (cont.) *Cheshire: occupations of male Dissenters in percentages*

	Wesleyan Methodists			Methodist New Connexion	Primitive Methodists	
	1808–19	1820–9	1830–9	1830–7	1820–9	1830–7
I Gentlemen	—	0.2	0.2	—	—	—
II Business	1.1	0.9	0.6	2.8	—	—
III Professions	—	0.3	0.2	—	—	—
IV Farmers	8.1	5.2	6.5	1.9	6.5	3.9
V Food and retail	4.2	4.3	6.9	3.3	1.9	2.0
VI White collar	4.2	4.0	3.8	2.6	3.2	3.2
VII Labour aristocracy	3.7	6.1	5.4	4.3	5.6	3.1
VIII Higher skilled	24.5	23.7	21.4	35.5	11.1	21.7
IX Lower skilled	24.7	22.8	22.3	17.3	27.3	18.3
X Depressed	11.2	13.6	13.6	23.0	7.4	20.0
[Weavers]	[10.1]	[12.2]	[12.8]	[21.3]	[6.5]	[19.3]
XI Unskilled	18.1	18.7	19.0	9.2	37.0	27.8
[Labourers]	[14.5]	[15.5]	[14.8]	[8.3]	[35.2]	[23.4]
Number of churches/circuits	9	16	16	4	3	4
Number of adults/fathers	356	1,231	1,220	211	108	451

TABLE XX. *Cornwall: occupations of male Dissenters in percentages*

	General male population 1841	Independents 1812–37	Quakers		Wesleyan Methodists			Bible Christians	
			1790–1809	1810–37	1810–19	1820–9	1830–7	1820–9	1830–7
I Gentlemen	2.8	—	—	—	0.3	0.3	0.1	—	0.1
II Business	0.4	0.5	20.2	14.5	1.8	0.5	0.8	0.6	0.1
III Professions	1.0	1.9	2.4	4.7	0.6	0.6	0.2	—	—
IV Farmers	10.4	4.4	14.3	10.3	18.7	11.7	8.5	10.8	10.4
V Food and retail	4.8	13.3	21.4	22.9	8.7	6.0	5.8	3.2	3.3
VI White collar	2.3	5.6	7.1	12.0	5.9	3.9	3.3	0.6	0.7
VII Labour aristocracy	2.5	6.5	2.4	5.3	3.6	2.4	2.6	0.3	0.4
VIII Higher skilled	12.8	23.8	13.1	16.6	20.1	15.1	14.4	9.6	9.1
IX Lower skilled [Miners]	30.2 [23.4]	22.4 [2.6]	16.7 [2.4]	11.6 [9.5]	16.7 [5.1]	28.5 [15.5]	41.2 [31.5]	34.7 [23.2]	31.7 [22.2]
X Depressed	0.4	—	—	—	—	0.1	—	0.3	0.3
XI Unskilled [Labourers]	32.4 [22.8]	21.5 [13.3]	2.4 [—]	2.1 [—]	23.7 [17.5]	31.1 [22.4]	23.1 [17.5]	39.8 [37.9]	44.0 [42.1]
Number of churches/ circuits		6			10	20	22	11	10
Number of adults/ fathers	73,683	214	42	95	335	1,592	2,135	680	1,036

TABLE XXI. *Cumberland: occupations of male Dissenters in percentages*

		General male population	Independents	Quakers				
		1841	1818–37	1790–9	1800–9	1810–19	1820–9	1830–7
I	Gentlemen	4.6	—	—	0.9	—	—	—
II	Business	0.4	—	1.4	5.3	6.8	3.0	4.3
III	Professions	1.1	—	1.9	0.9	0.4	—	—
IV	Farmers	11.8	2.8	42.5	38.1	33.6	44.6	39.8
V	Food and Retail	6.6	7.7	5.2	10.2	13.0	15.4	19.4
VI	White collar	2.8	8.9	3.8	2.2	4.1	5.1	1.1
VII	Labour aristocracy	3.2	3.3	3.8	5.3	4.9	3.0	5.4
VIII	Higher skilled	15.3	11.8	11.3	19.0	15.0	13.7	13.4
IX	Lower skilled	16.2	35.8	15.1	8.0	6.0	6.8	6.5
	[Miners]	[6.9]	[30.9]	[—]	[0.9]	[—]	[—]	[—]
X	Depressed	6.4	9.3	7.5	4.9	6.0	3.4	3.2
XI	Unskilled	31.5	20.3	7.5	5.3	10.0	5.0	7.0
	[Labourers]	[22.0]	[15.4]	[—]	[1.8]	[2.6]	[3.0]	[5.9]
	Number of churches/circuits		4					
	Number of adults/fathers	40,743	123	106	113	133	117	93

TABLE XXI. (cont.) Cumberland: occupations of male Dissenters in percentages

		Wesleyan Methodists			Primitive Methodists	
		1810–19	1820–9	1830–7	1820–9	1830–7
I	Gentlemen	—	—	—	—	0.5
II	Business	0.5	1.7	2.2	1.3	1.9
III	Professions	0.5	0.1	0.3	—	—
IV	Farmers	4.3	4.2	5.1	1.3	3.2
V	Food and retail	2.9	2.3	1.8	1.3	1.9
VI	White collar	3.3	2.5	4.0	—	0.5
VII	Labour aristocracy	4.5	3.1	4.0	—	5.4
VIII	Higher skilled	17.7	18.3	22.4	5.8	6.6
IX	Lower skilled	43.1	45.3	45.6	87.7	77.3
	[Miners]	[36.8]	[34.1]	[33.5]	[86.4]	[72.9]
X	Depressed	9.3	7.8	4.4	—	1.1
XI	Unskilled	13.9	14.8	10.3	2.6	1.6
	[Labourers]	[5.3]	[7.5]	[6.8]	[2.6]	[1.6]
	Number of churches/circuits	4	5	5	2	2
	Number of adults/fathers	209	501	340	77	189

TABLE XXII. *Derbyshire: occupations of male Dissenters in percentages*

		General male population	Independents		Quakers	Wesleyan Methodists			Primitive Methodists	
		1841	1820–9	1830–7	1790–1837	1810–19	1820–9	1830–7	1820–9	1830–7
I	Gentlemen	2.2	0.3	0.2	—	—	0.1	0.4	—	—
II	Business	0.6	1.4	1.4	6.3	0.7	1.1	1.6	—	0.3
III	Professions	0.9	0.3	—	1.6	—	0.1	0.3	—	—
IV	Farmers	9.4	5.5	4.5	15.9	4.1	3.2	2.8	1.9	2.5
V	Food and retail	6.3	5.5	6.3	15.9	4.4	4.6	6.7	0.8	0.9
VI	White collar	2.2	2.3	3.7	0.8	2.1	2.6	2.6	2.0	1.2
VII	Labour aristocracy	3.7	3.6	8.5	15.9	3.4	5.2	4.9	3.1	3.0
VIII	Higher skilled	14.5	20.6	24.1	16.7	14.6	17.4	17.4	12.0	10.9
IX	Lower skilled	17.8	24.2	27.7	10.3	21.6	24.9	28.9	27.9	35.4
	[Miners]	[7.8]	[13.5]	[12.9]	[—]	[14.8]	[14.5]	[14.5]	[21.4]	[26.5]
X	Depressed	12.1	16.5	11.2	16.7	34.2	20.4	15.0	27.8	21.4
	[Framework knitters]	[5.6]	[11.5]	[6.6]	[15.1]	[20.4]	[12.9]	[9.8]	[14.7]	[13.7]
XI	Unskilled	30.5	19.7	12.3	—	14.8	20.5	19.4	24.4	24.4
	[Labourers]	[24.5]	[19.0]	[12.0]	[—]	[13.2]	[18.9]	[17.6]	[23.3]	[23.3]
	Number of churches/circuits		7	8		7	9	11	5	6
	Number of adults/fathers	66,011	697	487	63	497	1,372	1,126	367	651

TABLE XXIII. *Devon: occupations of male Dissenters in percentages*

	General male population 1841	Independents						Quakers 1790–1837
		1780–9	1790–9	1800–9	1810–19	1820–9	1830–7	
I Gentlemen	4.2	3.9	0.7	0.9	0.2	0.5	1.0	—
II Business	0.7	—	3.7	3.5	1.2	1.2	1.5	16.3
III Professions	1.6	—	1.5	1.8	0.2	1.8	2.7	8.9
IV Farmers	9.4	3.9	6.7	4.4	3.5	2.9	3.9	10.5
V Food and retail	6.8	8.7	8.5	9.2	6.7	8.8	10.8	32.1
VI White collar	2.3	2.9	3.7	6.6	2.7	3.7	4.9	7.1
VII Labour aristocracy	1.6	5.8	5.9	7.9	4.7	7.7	6.6	0.9
VIII Higher skilled	17.3	15.5	18.1	28.1	26.4	26.3	24.2	8.5
IX Lower skilled	11.2	22.3	25.9	19.3	23.4	17.9	19.2	—
X Depressed	1.2	8.7	5.2	—	1.7	0.4	0.4	—
XI Unskilled	43.8	28.2	20.0	18.4	29.2	28.8	24.9	0.9
[Labourers]	[30.8]	[10.7]	[7.4]	[5.3]	[17.7]	[17.2]	[15.2]	[0.9]
Number of churches/circuits		4	5	7	14	26	29	
Number of adults/fathers	119,621	103	135	114	404	1,009	1,020	112

TABLE XXIII. (cont.) *Devon: occupations of male Dissenters in percentages*

		Wesleyan Methodists			Bible Christians	
		1810–19	1820–9	1830–7	1820–9	1830–7
I	Gentlemen	0.2	0.1	0.1	—	—
II	Business	—	0.7	1.2	0.4	0.2
III	Professions	0.8	0.4	0.4	—	—
IV	Farmers	2.0	2.2	4.7	14.8	18.4
V	Food and retail	4.1	5.5	7.8	4.3	3.8
VI	White collar	1.9	1.9	2.0	1.5	0.6
VII	Labour aristocracy	9.0	9.7	5.7	1.1	1.3
VIII	Higher skilled	26.9	23.4	22.8	14.8	15.3
IX	Lower skilled	18.4	19.3	22.7	11.8	11.0
X	Depressed	1.7	1.0	0.6	0.4	0.3
XI	Unskilled	34.9	35.8	32.0	50.9	49.0
	[Labourers]	[16.5]	[16.2]	[18.0]	[46.6]	[47.3]
	Number of churches/circuits	8	14	15	5	5
	Number of adults/fathers	515	3,539	2,616	267	463

TABLE XXIV. *Dorset: occupations of male Dissenters in percentages*

		General male population 1841	Independents			Quakers	Unitarians	Wesleyan Methodists	
			1810–19	1820–9	1830–7	1790–1837	1820–37	1820–9	1830–7
I	Gentlemen	3.6	0.7	1.0	1.1	—	1.1	—	—
II	Business	0.6	3.3	3.3	1.3	8.0	4.6	0.5	0.3
III	Professional	1.3	1.3	1.5	0.4	4.5	1.1	0.2	0.2
IV	Farmers	7.1	4.6	1.9	2.9	6.2	1.1	2.9	3.6
V	Food and retail	6.8	9.9	13.5	15.4	25.0	6.3	6.9	9.3
VI	White collar	2.6	1.3	3.9	3.5	3.6	8.6	5.2	3.0
VII	Labour aristocracy	1.5	—	2.9	4.8	0.9	5.7	2.0	2.0
VIII	Higher skilled	15.0	37.8	23.4	23.4	26.8	31.6	16.6	19.6
IX	Lower skilled	10.5	25.0	26.1	26.1	12.5	25.3	21.1	22.2
X	Depressed	0.9	4.3	3.6	3.2	1.8	4.6	1.4	1.3
XI	Unskilled	50.1	11.8	18.8	18.0	10.7	9.8	43.1	38.4
	[Labourers]	[40.2]	[9.9]	[11.7]	[10.6]	[—]	[6.9]	[33.1]	[32.3]
	Number of churches/circuits		5	9	13		1	5	6
	Number of adults/fathers	38,211	152	344	475	56	87	400	471

TABLE XXV. *Durham: occupations of male Dissenters in percentages*

		General male population	Independents		Quakers				
		1841	1820–9	1830–7	1790–9	1800–9	1810–19	1820–9	1830–9
I	Gentlemen	2.1	0.6	—	—	—	—	—	1.0
II	Business	0.9	3.2	1.2	2.9	10.0	11.8	14.0	11.8
III	Professions	1.4	3.2	2.8	0.7	1.0	—	4.5	8.3
IV	Farmers	4.2	1.6	3.5	12.3	6.7	9.5	12.6	3.9
V	Food and retail	6.2	12.2	12.7	31.2	32.2	40.6	34.8	38.6
VI	White collar	2.7	5.1	5.3	2.9	1.9	4.5	7.3	9.7
VII	Labour aristocracy	7.5	8.9	14.8	6.5	5.8	2.3	3.4	1.0
VIII	Higher skilled	18.4	22.0	17.1	21.7	24.1	18.9	15.5	13.6
IX	Lower skilled	27.8	15.8	12.0	14.5	13.0	8.6	5.6	9.2
	[Miners]	[17.4]	[1.3]	[0.5]	—	—	—	[1.1]	[1.5]
X	Depressed	1.5	1.9	1.4	4.3	3.4	0.9	1.1	1.0
XI	Unskilled	27.2	25.6	29.2	2.9	1.9	2.7	1.1	1.9
	[Labourers]	[18.6]	[5.1]	[12.3]	[1.4]	[1.0]	[1.8]	—	[1.0]
	[Mariners]	[3.3]	[13.6]	[11.1]	—	—	[0.9]	—	[1.0]
Number of churches/circuits			6	7					
Number of adults/fathers		77,386	158	216	69	104	110	89	103

TABLE XXV. (cont.) *Durham: occupations of male Dissenters in percentages*

	Wesleyan Methodists			Methodist New Connexion	Primitive Methodists	
	1810–19	1820–9	1830–7	1807–40	1820–9	1830–7
I Gentlemen	0.6	0.2	0.1	—	—	—
II Business	1.3	1.2	0.7	—	—	—
III Professions	1.3	0.8	0.9	—	—	—
IV Farmers	3.2	2.3	2.4	—	0.9	—
V Food and retail	7.0	6.4	9.1	6.3	4.1	2.6
VI White collar	3.8	3.1	3.4	3.1	3.7	4.2
VII Labour aristocracy	10.2	7.1	5.8	6.3	0.9	4.5
VIII Higher skilled	22.6	24.1	22.9	24.5	17.4	20.6
IX Lower skilled	38.2	38.7	39.6	34.4	56.9	46.5
[Miners]	[21.7]	[21.3]	[25.4]	[5.2]	[49.5]	[33.5]
X Depressed	2.5	2.0	1.3	—	0.9	0.6
XI Unskilled	9.2	14.1	13.7	25.5	15.1	21.0
[Labourers]	[4.1]	[6.3]	[5.3]	[10.9]	[4.6]	[9.4]
[Mariners]	[0.6]	[4.8]	[5.0]	[13.0]	[6.4]	[10.3]
Number of churches/circuits	6	8	8	3	2	3
Number of adults/fathers	157	498	674	96	109	155

TABLE XXVI. *Essex: occupations of male Dissenters in percentages*

| | | General male population | Independents | | | | Quakers | |
		1841	1820–9	1830–9	1850–9	1860–9	1790–1809	1810–37
I	Gentlemen	2.3	—	0.4	0.2	0.4	—	—
II	Business	0.6	1.5	1.0	1.0	1.6	2.5	6.1
III	Professions	1.3	0.2	1.3	0.9	0.5	0.8	1.4
IV	Farmers	5.5	5.6	6.4	2.8	4.7	26.5	22.2
V	Food and retail	7.4	8.7	11.7	13.5	18.3	37.7	45.1
VI	White collar	2.3	3.7	4.7	5.5	3.7	0.4	2.0
VII	Labour aristocracy	1.5	0.6	0.8	2.1	4.3	2.5	5.4
VIII	Higher skilled	11.8	10.6	10.7	14.7	11.9	12.9	8.8
IX	Lower skilled	7.5	13.4	11.3	9.6	7.3	9.2	4.4
X	Depressed	0.8	1.8	1.6	2.4	1.1	0.8	1.4
XI	Unskilled	59.0	53.9	50.2	47.4	46.2	6.7	3.4
	[Labourers]	[49.5]	[45.5]	[43.8]	[31.8]	[29.7]	[5.4]	[3.4]
	Number of churches/circuits		12	14	8	9		
	Number of adults/fathers	83,212	481	850	457	585	120	148

TABLE XXVI. (*cont.*) *Essex: occupations of male Dissenters in percentages*

	Wesleyan Methodists		Primitive Methodists		
	1820–9	1830–7	1840–9	1850–9	1860–9
I Gentlemen	—	0.3	—	—	—
II Business	0.7	0.2	—	—	0.5
III Professions	—	—	—	—	—
IV Farmers	3.2	3.6	1.2	—	0.7
V Food and retail	6.3	8.3	5.3	4.6	5.0
VI White collar	2.1	2.3	2.4	1.5	1.7
VII Labour aristocracy	2.2	3.7	3.5	3.6	1.9
VIII Higher skilled	14.3	12.2	12.9	14.9	16.3
IX Lower skilled	12.8	12.1	11.8	9.8	6.4
X Depressed	0.6	0.8	2.4	—	—
XI Unskilled	57.7	56.5	60.6	65.5	67.6
[Labourers]	[44.3]	[39.8]	[44.1]	[51.5]	[59.1]
Number of churches/circuits	6	6	1	1	1
Number of adults/fathers	481	661	85	194	423

TABLE XXVII. *Gloucestershire and Bristol: occupations of male Dissenters in percentages*

	General male population 1841	Independents			Quakers					Wesleyan Methodists		
		1810–19	1820–9	1830–7	1790–9	1800–9	1810–19	1820–9	1830–7	1810–19	1820–9	1830–7
I Gentlemen	3.8	0.7	0.8	0.2	1.9	0.9	—	0.9	1.0	—	1.0	0.3
II Business	0.6	6.5	3.5	2.4	6.7	11.5	10.9	9.4	10.8	3.7	2.1	1.9
III Professions	1.4	2.5	2.2	1.3	3.8	1.7	3.6	5.4	4.9	1.5	1.4	0.3
IV Farmers	4.5	2.2	4.1	2.6	2.9	4.3	5.5	3.1	4.4	1.5	4.1	4.0
V Food and retail	9.0	11.5	12.9	17.2	33.8	42.3	36.4	45.5	39.7	6.0	9.1	11.8
VI White collar	3.4	9.4	5.4	7.8	4.3	3.4	7.3	10.7	17.7	9.0	6.0	5.3
VII Labour aristocracy	4.0	7.2	5.3	4.9	7.6	5.1	3.6	3.1	6.4	3.7	5.8	4.9
VIII Higher skilled	17.5	13.7	21.4	17.4	25.2	19.7	18.6	8.9	6.9	26.1	22.0	19.3
IX Lower skilled	13.3	19.8	18.0	18.0	6.2	9.0	13.2	11.6	7.4	20.1	20.2	27.1
X Depressed	3.6	14.4	15.9	15.3	1.9	1.3	0.9	—	—	14.2	13.0	11.9
XI Unskilled	38.7	12.2	10.5	12.9	5.7	0.9	—	1.3	1.0	14.2	15.6	13.2
[Labourers]	[30.2]	[7.9]	[8.6]	[8.5]	[1.0]	[0.9]	[—]	[1.3]	[1.0]	[10.4]	[9.3]	[10.1]
Number of churches/circuits		6	13	16						8	12	14
Number of adults/fathers	100,640	139	362	430	105	117	110	112	102	154	538	721

TABLE XXVIII. *Hampshire: occupations of male Dissenters in percentages*

	General male population 1841	Independents		Wesleyan Methodists			Bible Christians
		1820–9	1830–7	1810–19	1820–9	1830–7	1830–7
I	Gentlemen	3.5	1.1	—	0.6	0.4	0.3	—
II	Business	0.6	1.4	1.7	—	—	0.4	—
III	Professions	1.4	2.2	1.2	—	—	0.8	—
IV	Farmers	4.1	3.3	3.7	0.6	0.7	1.6	6.4
V	Food and retail	8.0	23.5	19.5	10.8	12.5	12.0	2.1
VI	White collar	2.9	4.9	3.9	4.5	3.2	5.2	1.1
VII	Labour aristocracy	3.1	4.4	4.2	5.1	5.1	8.6	1.1
VIII	Higher skilled	14.2	20.8	25.2	24.7	22.7	24.5	8.8
IX	Lower skilled	9.1	18.6	22.3	17.9	17.9	17.7	8.6
X	Depressed	0.2	1.1	—	1.7	1.4	0.3	—
XI	Unskilled	53.0	18.9	18.2	34.1	36.1	28.8	71.9
	[Labourers]	[38.7]	[15.3]	[13.7]	[21.6]	[26.2]	[18.5]	[63.1]
Number of churches/circuits			7	9	4	4	5	2
Number of adults/fathers		84,246	183	321	176	277	384	187

TABLE XXIX. *Herefordshire: occupations of male Dissenters in percentages*

		General male population 1841	Baptists 1810–37	Wesleyan Methodists 1820–37	Primitive Methodists 1828–37
I	Gentlemen	3.4	—	—	—
II	Business	0.2	—	—	—
III	Professions	1.3	—	1.0	—
IV	Farmers	10.9	3.3	9.9	6.7
V	Food and retail	5.7	17.2	12.9	4.2
VI	White collar	2.1	5.0	4.0	4.5
VII	Labour aristocracy	0.9	1.1	—	—
VIII	Higher skilled	14.9	19.4	26.7	20.1
IX	Lower skilled	8.2	30.6	21.3	24.3
X	Depressed	0.5	1.1	2.0	—
XI	Unskilled	52.0	22.2	22.3	40.0
	[Labourers]	[42.6]	[20.0]	[20.3]	[40.0]
	Number of churches/circuits		3	2	2
	Number of adults/fathers	29,189	90	101	67

TABLE XXX. *Hertfordshire: occupations of male Dissenters in percentages*

		General male population 1841	Independents		Baptists		Quakers	Wesleyan Methodists
			1820–9	1830–9	1780–99	1800–19	1790–1837	1830–7
I	Gentlemen	3.1	2.5	1.0	1.1	—	—	—
II	Business	0.3	2.5	1.3	—	—	2.3	0.8
III	Professions	1.4	0.3	0.2	—	—	6.8	1.2
IV	Farmers	4.4	6.2	4.3	29.3	20.3	14.7	7.3
V	Food and retail	9.1	15.7	13.2	12.2	10.1	60.2	9.8
VI	White collar	2.3	7.1	7.1	2.1	4.4	2.3	5.3
VII	Labour aristocracy	1.5	1.2	2.1	3.2	1.3	4.5	1.2
VIII	Higher skilled	13.3	18.2	17.5	15.6	19.0	2.3	24.8
IX	Lower skilled	8.1	8.3	12.2	10.1	17.7	2.3	15.4
X	Depressed	0.6	0.6	—	1.1	—	—	0.8
XI	Unskilled	55.7	37.3	40.9	25.5	27.2	4.5	33.3
	[Labourers]	[46.6]	[32.1]	[37.2]	[24.5]	[22.2]	[4.5]	[32.5]
	Number of churches/circuits		9	11	1	1		3
	Number of adults/fathers	36,614	162	312	94	79	44	123

TABLE XXXI. *Huntingdonshire: occupations of male Dissenters in percentages*

	General male population	Wesleyan Methodists		Primitive Methodists	
	1841	1819–29	1830–7	1850–9	1860–9
I Gentlemen	2.2	—	0.5	—	—
II Business	0.3	0.7	0.3	—	—
III Professions	1.0	—	—	—	—
IV Farmers	7.6	5.9	2.7	—	1.6
V Food and retail	8.7	6.2	8.8	1.4	7.9
VI White collar	2.2	2.9	2.1	2.7	3.2
VII Labour aristocracy	1.3	1.5	2.1	—	1.1
VIII Higher skilled	12.1	15.8	12.6	5.4	10.5
IX Lower skilled	8.9	13.6	14.4	1.4	6.8
X Depressed	0.2	—	0.5	—	—
XI Unskilled	55.4	53.3	55.9	89.2	68.9
[Labourers]	[48.8]	[50.4]	[54.0]	[85.1]	[61.6]
Number of churches/circuits		2	2	1	1
Number of adults/fathers	13,532	136	187	74	95

TABLE XXXII. *Kent: occupations of male Dissenters in percentages*

	General male population 1841	Independents			Quakers	Wesleyan Methodists			Bible Christians	
		1810–19	1820–9	1830–7	1790–1837	1810–19	1820–9	1830–9	1820–9	1830–7
I Gentlemen	4.0	1.3	—	1.1	—	—	0.3	0.3	—	—
II Business	0.7	—	—	0.4	3.8	0.3	0.2	0.3	0.6	—
III Professions	1.4	—	0.6	1.3	2.5	—	0.3	0.2	—	—
IV Farmers	3.9	7.6	5.6	7.2	3.8	7.4	4.0	5.0	0.6	1.2
V Food and retail	8.6	16.4	9.9	14.4	53.8	4.7	7.6	10.6	1.1	4.8
VI White collar	3.3	6.3	8.6	7.2	—	3.3	1.5	3.5	1.1	1.2
VII Labour aristocracy	3.5	3.8	4.3	1.4	8.9	7.6	5.1	3.1	15.7	9.0
VIII Higher skilled	13.2	27.8	19.1	18.6	15.2	22.2	20.3	15.7	26.8	15.8
IX Lower skilled	9.3	8.9	6.8	14.1	5.1	10.8	13.4	14.8	13.8	11.2
X Depressed	0.1	1.3	—	—	—	0.5	0.8	0.3	—	—
XI Unskilled	51.8	26.6	45.1	34.3	7.0	43.3	46.4	46.2	40.3	56.8
[Labourers]	[34.6]	[20.3]	[37.7]	[28.0]	[1.3]	[34.8]	[36.5]	[39.4]	[30.9]	[47.8]
Number of churches/circuits		7	12	13		19	26	27	3	4
Number of adults/fathers	129,907	79	162	277	79	397	1,576	1,318	181	250

TABLE XXXIII. *Lancashire: occupations of male Dissenters in percentages*

	General male population	Independents					Baptists			Quakers				
	1841	1790–9	1800–9	1810–19	1820–9	1830–7	1810–19	1820–9	1830–7	1790–9	1800–9	1810–19	1820–9	1830–7
I Gentlemen	2.1	—	—	0.1	0.2	0.1	—	—	—	—	—	—	—	—
II Business	0.8	4.2	9.0	5.7	4.6	4.3	1.0	1.6	0.7	20.1	16.1	11.5	14.0	14.9
III Professions	0.9	—	0.2	0.3	0.8	1.1	—	—	0.1	2.6	2.6	1.2	1.9	1.9
IV Farmers	3.8	0.5	1.1	2.6	4.0	3.0	5.2	2.5	2.7	9.7	7.3	8.0	8.2	7.6
V Food and retail	6.8	9.5	10.2	5.7	9.1	8.9	3.0	4.5	5.7	10.8	17.8	19.2	21.3	29.8
VI White collar	4.6	4.8	9.2	7.0	8.2	8.4	2.6	2.3	1.9	1.3	5.7	5.4	6.8	8.2
VII Labour aristocracy	7.2	11.4	7.1	5.2	6.7	8.4	9.3	9.0	9.6	12.2	9.4	7.9	6.7	4.2
VIII Higher skilled	20.0	23.0	21.3	18.7	20.1	25.3	9.8	14.0	18.5	14.7	12.2	14.5	14.0	10.3
IX Lower skilled	18.0	12.2	14.1	12.1	13.3	15.2	4.6	8.2	10.3	22.2	16.7	15.3	16.1	15.1
X Depressed	13.4	30.2	22.5	19.3	21.0	14.6	53.7	44.9	31.7	6.3	11.7	15.2	9.7	5.3
[Weavers]	[11.2]	[29.1]	[22.5]	[19.0]	[20.8]	[14.1]	[53.3]	[44.9]	[31.4]	[5.6]	[11.3]	[14.6]	[9.7]	[5.3]
XI Unskilled	22.4	4.2	5.3	23.3	12.1	10.6	10.9	12.8	18.7	—	0.4	1.7	1.3	2.7
[Labourers]	[16.3]	[1.1]	[3.1]	[15.4]	[6.2]	[7.1]	[8.1]	[9.3]	[12.5]	—	[0.4]	[0.9]	[0.6]	[1.5]
Number of churches/circuits		4	9	18	38	43	4	5	6					
Number of adults/fathers	391,440	189	481	1,054	2,384	2,935	252	495	693	152	233	322	361	310

TABLE XXXIII. (cont.) Lancashire: occupations of male Dissenters in percentages

		Presbyterian Unitarians				Methodist Unitarians		Wesleyan Methodists					Methodist New Connexion			Primitive Methodists
		1800–9	1810–19	1820–9	1830–7	1820–9	1830–7	1790–9	1800–9	1810–19	1820–9	1830–7	1810–19	1820–9	1830–7	1830–7
I	Gentlemen	1.2	—	0.7	0.2	—	—	—	—	0.1	—	0.1	—	—	0.4	—
II	Business	7.3	15.2	13.1	13.4	0.6	1.7	0.8	1.9	1.8	1.2	0.7	1.3	0.9	1.4	0.4
III	Professions	0.6	1.8	2.0	2.9	—	—	1.1	0.6	0.3	0.1	0.2	0.4	—	—	—
IV	Farmers	6.7	9.9	4.4	4.7	—	0.4	0.7	0.8	3.1	2.8	2.0	—	—	0.8	3.0
V	Food and retail	8.8	10.6	9.8	8.3	3.0	2.7	3.1	5.2	4.7	3.8	4.5	1.1	3.9	2.7	1.9
VI	White collar	6.0	8.5	10.4	7.4	0.6	0.4	1.6	3.7	4.4	3.2	2.9	3.3	4.6	4.5	1.9
VII	Labour aristocracy	3.5	5.1	7.4	7.4	3.8	10.5	5.1	6.3	9.0	8.4	9.2	19.7	17.4	10.0	7.8
VIII	Higher skilled	17.0	12.9	15.9	13.2	10.4	10.7	16.5	22.0	22.8	19.5	20.2	29.4	32.6	35.7	17.7
IX	Lower skilled	14.0	8.5	7.7	11.9	18.0	16.7	13.2	17.2	18.7	16.0	16.7	17.3	19.8	22.5	10.8
X	Depressed	22.2	18.0	23.5	23.5	58.9	52.4	54.9	33.6	25.2	35.4	32.5	21.9	12.6	9.6	45.8
	[Weavers]	[22.2]	[18.0]	[22.9]	[23.4]	[58.9]	[52.4]	[54.9]	[33.6]	[24.9]	[34.9]	[32.1]	[21.9]	[12.4]	[9.0]	[45.7]
XI	Unskilled	12.7	9.4	4.9	7.1	4.7	4.6	3.2	8.6	9.9	9.7	11.2	5.5	8.2	9.3	10.7
	[Labourers]	[4.6]	[6.0]	[3.8]	[5.4]	[2.4]	[4.2]	[2.1]	[4.8]	[6.0]	[9.1]	[8.2]	[2.0]	[5.2]	[5.0]	[6.2]
	Number of churches/circuits	4	4	10	11	2	2	4	13	37	57	66	4	6	7	7
	Number of adults/fathers	171	217	400	517	169	239	376	1,267	2,463	4,700	4,829	228	427	512	765

TABLE XXXIV. *Leicestershire: occupations of male Dissenters in percentages*

		General male population	Independents				Baptists
		1841	1822–39	1840–9	1850–9	1860–9	1820–37
I	Gentlemen	2.5	—	—	1.0	—	—
II	Business	1.0	2.9	2.3	—	1.6	—
III	Professions	1.0	—	—	—	—	—
IV	Farmers	6.6	7.0	4.2	6.1	5.2	0.3
V	Food and retail	8.2	15.3	18.5	11.5	18.8	3.3
VI	White collar	2.3	5.0	3.8	6.1	3.1	—
VII	Labour aristocracy	2.2	3.3	3.1	—	1.0	3.0
VIII	Higher skilled	10.6	21.5	11.5	19.2	9.4	8.3
IX	Lower skilled	11.6	19.4	18.1	10.1	8.1	17.3
X	Depressed	21.7	5.0	—	—	4.2	60.3
	[Framework knitters]	[19.6]	[2.9]	—	—	[4.2]	[60.0]
XI	Unskilled	32.2	20.7	38.5	46.0	48.4	7.3
	[Labourers]	[25.1]	[16.5]	[25.8]	[39.4]	[39.0]	[5.0]
	Number of churches/circuits		4	3	3	4	2
	Number of adults/fathers	51,002	121	130	99	191	150

TABLE XXXIV. (cont.) *Leicestershire: occupations of male Dissenters in percentages*

		Wesleyan Methodists			Primitive Methodists	
		1810–19	1820–9	1830–7	1825–39	1850–9
I	Gentlemen	0.3	0.2	0.1	—	—
II	Business	3.0	1.8	1.5	0.4	0.4
III	Professions	—	0.3	0.4	—	—
IV	Farmers	4.4	4.8	4.2	0.8	0.8
V	Food and retail	7.7	7.6	7.7	2.8	1.4
VI	White collar	2.7	1.7	2.5	0.6	2.0
VII	Labour aristocracy	2.7	2.9	2.7	1.8	—
VIII	Higher skilled	11.2	13.9	13.8	9.7	8.5
IX	Lower skilled	20.0	20.1	19.4	26.3	10.0
X	Depressed	29.5	24.3	19.3	42.4	37.2
	[Framework knitters]	[27.2]	[22.3]	[17.8]	[42.0]	[35.6]
XI	Unskilled	18.5	22.4	28.4	15.1	39.6
	[Labourers]	[15.1]	[20.5]	[24.6]	[11.9]	[37.0]
	Number of churches/circuits	7	12	13	4	4
	Number of adults/fathers	298	931	1,100	474	246

TABLE XXXV. *Lincolnshire: occupations of male Dissenters in percentages*

	General male population 1841	Independents		Quakers	Wesleyan Methodists			Primitive Methodists
		1820–9	1830–7	1790–1837	1810–19	1820–9	1830–9	1830–7
I Gentlemen	2.7	1.6	0.2	—	—	0.1	—	—
II Business	0.3	2.3	0.9	4.1	0.3	0.6	0.3	—
III Professions	1.0	0.9	2.4	0.7	0.3	0.2	0.4	—
IV Farmers	12.0	8.0	8.6	47.1	13.9	11.5	11.1	11.9
V Food and retail	7.4	15.1	18.3	28.0	9.7	10.5	11.9	3.7
VI White collar	2.2	8.0	10.8	—	5.8	4.2	3.1	1.1
VII Labour aristocracy	1.3	2.8	4.0	0.7	0.9	1.6	2.1	1.1
VIII Higher skilled	12.3	27.5	18.9	13.8	16.8	15.4	15.2	13.0
IX Lower skilled	8.4	14.2	14.3	1.4	13.0	13.5	15.5	10.1
X Depressed	0.3	1.4	1.3	—	1.2	0.7	0.4	—
XI Unskilled	52.0	18.1	20.3	4.3	38.0	41.8	39.9	59.3
[Labourers]	[45.8]	[13.5]	[15.9]	[4.3]	[34.5]	[38.3]	[35.8]	[54.0]
Number of churches/circuits		13	12		13	16	17	5
Number of adults/fathers	88,174	218	227	69	330	983	1,306	189

TABLE XXXVI. *Middlesex and north London: occupations of male Dissenters in percentages*

		General male population 1841	Independents					Quakers				
			1810–19	1820–9	1830–9	1850–9	1860–9	1790–9	1800–9	1810–19	1820–9	1830–7
I	Gentlemen	5.6	3.4	2.6	1.2	1.0	0.7	—	0.4	—	—	0.6
II	Business	1.7	5.0	2.2	2.7	3.0	2.0	11.6	10.1	12.1	19.0	15.2
III	Professions	3.0	3.1	2.6	2.7	0.9	2.0	3.5	2.9	5.7	5.2	5.4
IV	Farmers	0.3	—	0.3	0.3	—	—	0.5	1.8	3.2	0.7	0.6
V	Food and retail	13.3	20.9	23.2	25.2	21.1	19.3	37.6	37.5	39.7	38.0	34.5
VI	White collar	6.2	13.5	11.0	12.0	24.4	33.7	5.7	7.2	6.9	6.7	8.9
VII	Labour aristocracy	7.5	8.4	8.0	8.4	17.8	14.4	10.4	10.7	12.9	8.1	8.9
VIII	Higher skilled	17.6	17.5	20.4	18.7	17.8	17.0	16.3	13.7	10.4	16.0	17.9
IX	Lower skilled	17.7	11.1	15.0	13.8	7.7	8.5	8.7	13.2	7.7	4.9	6.2
X	Depressed	1.0	3.4	1.0	1.4	0.8	—	1.0	0.4	0.5	0.5	0.6
XI	Unskilled	26.1	13.5	13.6	13.5	5.4	2.6	4.7	2.2	0.7	1.0	1.2
	[Labourers]	[11.3]	[3.1]	[5.3]	[6.8]	[2.0]	[0.7]	[—]	[0.4]	[—]	[—]	[—]
	Number of churches/circuits		8	19	22	5	3					
	Number of adults/fathers	399,468	208	572	931	383	153	202	228	201	203	168

TABLE XXXVI. *(cont.) Middlesex and north London: occupations of male Dissenters in percentages*

		Wesleyan Methodists		Calvinistic Methodists		
		1820–9	1830–9	1810–19	1820–9	1830–9
I	Gentlemen	0.7	—	—	—	2.7
II	Business	2.9	1.2	—	0.9	—
III	Professions	2.9	0.6	0.5	0.7	0.9
IV	Farmers	—	0.6	—	—	1.2
V	Food and retail	15.8	8.6	6.5	7.6	11.1
VI	White collar	4.4	2.5	2.8	3.0	3.6
VII	Labour aristocracy	3.7	11.0	8.3	9.0	7.6
VIII	Higher skilled	29.4	24.5	28.0	26.2	21.1
IX	Lower skilled	18.4	27.9	21.2	20.0	20.0
X	Depressed	11.4	2.8	0.5	0.8	0.3
XI	Unskilled	10.3	20.2	32.1	31.8	31.5
	[Labourers]	[5.1]	[10.4]	[19.9]	[18.0]	[21.4]
	Number of churches/circuits	4	5	2	2	3
	Number of adults/fathers	136	163	375	555	330

TABLE XXXVII. *Norfolk: occupations of male Dissenters in percentages*

		General male population	Independents		Baptists		Quakers	
		1841	1820–9	1830–7	1820–9	1830–7	1790–1809	1810–37
I	Gentlemen	2.7	0.5	1.0	1.7	—	—	1.2
II	Business	0.5	3.2	4.6	1.3	1.2	15.8	18.1
III	Professions	1.0	1.3	1.9	—	—	3.5	1.2
IV	Farmers	7.3	8.2	9.2	5.2	4.9	7.0	10.6
V	Food and retail	8.2	20.0	15.3	9.5	10.2	36.8	34.7
VI	White collar	2.7	8.9	8.3	1.7	4.1	3.5	6.0
VII	Labour aristocracy	1.8	2.1	2.9	3.4	3.3	4.4	6.2
VIII	Higher skilled	13.3	18.9	11.5	22.0	18.0	10.5	8.1
IX	Lower skilled	10.0	14.2	11.8	11.6	11.1	14.0	9.1
X	Depressed	3.1	7.4	9.0	7.8	7.8	4.4	3.1
XI	Unskilled	49.3	15.3	24.5	35.8	39.3	—	1.2
	[Labourers]	[40.9]	[11.8]	[21.1]	[30.6]	[31.6]	[—]	[1.2]
Number of churches/circuits			7	8	5	4		
Number of adults/fathers		95,377	190	206	116	122	57	80

TABLE XXXVII. *(cont.) Norfolk: occupations of male Dissenters in percentages*

		Wesleyan Methodists			Primitive Methodists
		1810–19	1820–9	1830–7	1830–7
I	Gentlemen	—	0.2	0.4	—
II	Business	0.4	0.9	0.2	0.2
III	Professions	—	0.2	—	—
IV	Farmers	8.9	5.1	4.5	3.5
V	Food and retail	8.5	9.2	11.9	4.0
VI	White collar	3.0	3.1	3.9	1.8
VII	Labour aristocracy	1.3	2.3	2.0	1.4
VIII	Higher skilled	10.4	14.2	15.5	15.2
IX	Lower skilled	15.9	16.4	15.0	12.4
X	Depressed	10.2	9.3	4.5	8.0
XI	Unskilled	41.5	39.1	42.1	53.3
	[Labourers]	[37.5]	[34.8]	[38.0]	[47.4]
Number of churches/circuits		7	17	17	8
Number of adults/fathers		236	695	852	523

TABLE XXXVIII. *Northamptonshire: occupations of male Dissenters in percentages*

	General male population 1841	Independents				Baptists		
		1800–9	1810–19	1820–9	1830–7	1810–19	1820–9	1830–7
I Gentlemen	2.3	—	—	—	—	—	—	—
II Business	0.3	—	0.7	0.5	1.0	3.1	2.1	0.8
III Professions	1.0	—	0.7	1.9	0.4	1.0	0.7	—
IV Farmers	6.4	20.9	14.6	13.6	8.3	4.1	5.4	5.5
V Food and retail	8.7	10.0	15.9	9.1	13.0	10.2	7.5	6.4
VI White collar	2.1	1.8	2.0	1.9	1.2	2.0	0.7	1.7
VII Labour aristocracy	1.3	—	4.0	1.4	2.0	2.0	0.7	0.8
VIII Higher skilled	12.1	10.9	8.6	10.3	15.2	9.2	13.9	16.1
IX Lower skilled	15.6	26.4	23.5	16.0	18.8	27.6	30.3	26.3
[Shoemakers]	[11.0]	[17.3]	[16.6]	[11.0]	[13.0]	[12.2]	[20.1]	[18.2]
X Depressed	1.3	2.7	2.6	2.4	1.2	5.1	9.2	11.9
XI Unskilled	49.0	27.3	27.5	42.8	38.9	35.7	29.6	30.5
[Labourers]	[42.0]	[20.1]	[25.5]	[36.8]	[35.6]	[33.2]	[25.2]	[26.3]
Number of churches/circuits		3	4	6	7	4	4	4
Number of adults/fathers	47,825	110	151	209	253	98	147	118

TABLE XXXVIII. (cont.) Northamptonshire: occupations of male Dissenters in percentages

		Wesleyan Methodists		Primitive Methodists		
		1820–9	1830–7	1840–9	1850–9	1860–9
I	Gentlemen	—	—	—	—	—
II	Business	1.0	0.7	—	—	—
III	Professions	—	—	—	0.5	0.3
IV	Farmers	3.9	3.8	3.1	—	0.3
V	Food and retail	5.4	6.3	4.9	2.9	5.9
VI	White collar	1.7	1.5	1.2	1.4	1.1
VII	Labour aristocracy	—	1.1	—	0.5	3.2
VIII	Higher skilled	14.0	11.1	4.9	9.6	9.0
IX	Lower skilled	29.8	20.8	6.2	7.7	5.9
	[Shoemakers]	[20.2]	[14.1]	[4.9]	[2.9]	[2.2]
X	Depressed	5.6	8.0	—	—	—
XI	Unskilled	38.7	46.8	79.6	77.5	74.3
	[Labourers]	[36.1]	[42.6]	[77.2]	[73.7]	[72.6]
	Number of churches/circuits	7	8	1	1	1
	Number of adults/fathers	411	608	81	209	372

TABLE XXXIX. *Northumberland: occupation of male Dissenters in percentages*

	General male population	Independents	Baptists		Wesleyan Methodists				
	1841	1830–7	1820–9	1830–7	1790–9	1800–9	1810–19	1820–9	1830–7
I Gentlemen	2.2	—	1.4	—	—	—	—	—	0.1
II Business	1.6	—	6.8	12.8	0.9	1.1	1.2	0.5	1.7
III Professions	1.1	0.8	1.4	—	—	0.6	—	—	0.5
IV Farmers	4.7	0.8	—	—	1.3	1.4	1.2	0.3	1.1
V Food and retail	7.6	10.8	14.9	12.8	3.4	7.1	4.9	5.3	7.9
VI White collar	3.0	4.6	6.8	5.7	6.0	1.4	3.0	6.6	4.5
VII Labour aristocracy	5.8	3.3	10.8	17.1	12.1	12.4	8.0	6.1	5.1
VIII Higher skilled	17.1	20.4	21.6	22.9	18.5	16.1	18.0	16.3	13.2
IX Lower skilled	22.5	24.6	21.6	15.7	40.5	44.1	45.9	51.6	46.0
[Miners]	[10.1]	[7.5]	[8.1]	[4.3]	[22.4]	[30.5]	[32.0]	[37.4]	[32.6]
X Depressed	0.9	—	1.4	—	3.4	0.6	1.6	1.1	0.5
XI Unskilled	33.6	34.6	13.5	12.8	13.8	15.3	16.2	12.2	19.3
[Labourers]	[25.4]	[7.9]	[1.4]	[1.3]	[8.6]	[3.4]	[7.6]	[4.9]	[7.2]
Number of churches/ circuits		4	3	3	2	3	4	4	5
Number of adults/ fathers	60,498	120	74	70	116	177	417	374	374

TABLE XXXIX. *(cont.) Northumberland: occupation of male Dissenters in percentages*

		Methodist New Connexion		Primitive Methodists	
		1800–9	1810–29	1820–9	1830–7
I	Gentlemen	—	—	—	—
II	Business	0.9	0.5	—	0.3
III	Professions	—	1.1	—	0.2
IV	Farmers	2.6	2.2	1.5	1.4
V	Food and retail	4.8	4.3	5.1	2.1
VI	White collar	3.1	1.6	2.2	2.0
VII	Labour aristocracy	6.6	5.4	—	4.2
VIII	Higher skilled	26.8	20.4	11.0	16.0
IX	Lower skilled	36.4	45.2	34.6	52.5
	[Miners]	[16.2]	[29.0]	[20.6]	[38.6]
X	Depressed	4.4	3.2	1.5	0.2
XI	Unskilled	14.5	16.1	44.1	21.0
	[Labourers]	[4.4]	[7.5]	[21.3]	[13.6]
Number of churches/circuits		2	2	4	4
Number of adults/fathers		114	93	136	511

TABLE XL. *Nottinghamshire: occupations of male Dissenters in percentages*

		General male population 1841	Independents 1820–39	Quakers 1790–1837	Wesleyan Methodists 1820–9	1830–7
I	Gentlemen	2.2	—	—	0.2	—
II	Business	0.7	8.1	14.9	2.0	0.7
III	Professions	0.9	3.1	4.8	0.2	0.2
IV	Farmers	5.8	5.0	3.6	1.8	3.0
V	Food and retail	8.1	19.1	28.0	7.2	7.2
VI	White collar	2.4	11.2	3.0	2.4	2.5
VII	Labour aristocracy	2.7	1.2	2.4	5.2	3.1
VIII	Higher skilled	11.4	16.9	22.6	15.8	13.0
IX	Lower skilled	17.9	18.1	10.7	27.5	38.7
	[Laceworkers]	[5.9]	[4.4]	[—]	[14.2]	[22.9]
X	Depressed	17.0	11.2	8.9	27.9	18.1
	[Framework knitters]	[15.8]	[11.2]	[8.9]	[24.9]	[16.1]
XI	Unskilled	30.9	6.0	1.2	9.7	13.5
	[Labourers]	[25.8]	[2.8]	[—]	[8.6]	[12.2]
	Number of churches/circuits		5		4	12
	Number of adults/fathers	59,435	160	84	452	544

TABLE XL. (cont.) Nottinghamshire: occupations of male Dissenters in percentages

		Methodist New Connexion			Primitive Methodists
		1810–19	1820–9	1830–7	1826–37
I	Gentlemen	—	—	—	—
II	Business	0.6	1.3	2.9	—
III	Professions	0.6	0.7	—	—
IV	Farmers	2.3	0.7	1.0	0.5
V	Food and retail	4.7	2.6	6.3	1.9
VI	White collar	1.8	3.3	4.9	0.9
VII	Labour aristocracy	1.8	4.0	4.9	2.4
VIII	Higher skilled	6.4	12.6	11.2	7.6
IX	Lower skilled	20.5	25.8	33.5	39.1
	[Laceworkers]	[0.6]	[2.6]	[12.6]	[—]
X	Depressed	56.1	38.7	24.3	30.3
	[Framework knitters]	[56.1]	[38.1]	[23.3]	[30.3]
XI	Unskilled	5.3	10.3	11.2	17.3
	[Labourers]	[4.1]	[7.9]	[7.8]	[16.6]
	Number of churches/circuits	1	1	1	2
	Number of adults/fathers	171	151	103	211

TABLE XLI. *Oxfordshire: occupations of male Dissenters in percentages*

		General male population 1841	Independents 1804-37	Quakers 1790-1809	Quakers 1810-37	Wesleyan Methodists 1810-19	Wesleyan Methodists 1820-9	Wesleyan Methodists 1830-7
I	Gentlemen	3.6	—	—	—	0.9	—	—
II	Business	0.4	—	—	3.4	—	1.0	1.3
III	Professions	1.7	—	1.5	2.8	—	0.3	—
IV	Farmers	5.8	14.5	14.6	11.8	7.1	5.3	3.7
V	Food and retail	9.1	14.5	26.9	39.6	15.2	9.4	13.5
VI	White collar	2.4	10.8	2.3	4.9	3.6	5.0	4.4
VII	Labour aristocracy	1.9	1.2	1.5	6.9	3.6	5.5	2.1
VIII	Higher skilled	13.7	22.9	12.3	6.9	22.8	23.8	19.6
IX	Lower skilled	9.1	15.7	14.6	10.4	15.6	15.1	15.0
X	Depressed	1.4	8.4	15.4	6.9	7.1	8.0	6.0
XI	Unskilled	50.9	12.0	10.8	6.2	24.1	26.6	34.4
	[Labourers]	[44.2]	[10.8]	[6.9]	[6.2]	[24.1]	[22.0]	[30.7]
	Number of churches/circuits		4			4	4	4
	Number of adults/fathers	37,447	83	65	72	112	302	423

TABLE XLII. *Shropshire: occupations of male Dissenters in percentages*

	General male population	Independents				Wesleyan Methodists		Primitive Methodists	
	1841	1800–9	1810–19	1820–9	1830–7	1820–9	1830–37	1820–9	1830–7
I Gentlemen	2.5	0.9	1.6	1.6	1.0	—	—	—	—
II Business	0.4	—	—	1.4	1.0	—	0.5	—	—
III Professions	1.2	1.8	2.3	2.2	1.9	0.4	0.3	1.1	—
IV Farmers	7.6	16.5	13.2	4.7	3.6	2.2	2.5	1.1	3.7
V Food and retail	7.1	11.5	13.2	12.4	11.4	4.6	3.5	2.4	2.5
VI White collar	2.4	3.9	8.9	4.9	4.9	1.6	1.3	2.4	1.3
VII Labour aristocracy	3.0	9.9	4.7	1.6	1.9	8.0	9.3	3.2	6.5
VIII Higher skilled	14.2	14.4	12.4	17.6	16.2	16.3	10.6	17.1	14.7
IX Lower skilled	16.8	18.5	20.2	15.4	21.4	53.2	56.0	46.0	41.0
[Miners]	[7.6]	[5.4]	[7.0]	[4.4]	[7.3]	[38.6]	[42.5]	[27.6]	[28.1]
X Depressed	2.2	2.7	2.7	2.7	3.1	1.2	1.1	2.6	0.8
XI Unskilled	42.7	19.8	20.9	35.4	33.6	12.5	14.9	24.2	29.6
[Labourers]	[36.7]	[18.0]	[20.2]	[31.0]	[28.6]	[12.5]	[14.9]	[22.1]	[27.4]
Number of churches/circuits		9	12	15	18	5	5	4	5
Number of adults/fathers	58,868	111	129	182	308	251	398	190	382

TABLE XLIII. *Somerset: occupations of male Dissenters in percentages*

		General male population	Independents			Quakers	
		1840	1810–19	1820–9	1830–9	1800–19	1820–37
I	Gentlemen	4.0	0.8	0.9	2.0	—	—
II	Business	0.4	—	—	0.4	2.6	15.0
III	Professions	1.6	0.4	0.9	1.4	—	2.4
IV	Farmers	8.2	5.8	4.8	5.4	28.9	25.6
V	Food and retail	7.5	12.5	17.6	17.9	30.3	26.8
VI	White collar	2.5	5.8	4.8	4.2	5.3	4.3
VII	Labour aristocracy	1.7	6.0	4.3	2.1	1.3	1.2
VIII	Higher skilled	15.8	20.5	24.4	22.1	10.5	4.9
IX	Lower skilled	12.6	17.1	17.3	24.6	17.1	14.4
	[Miners]	[2.5]	[4.4]	[3.9]	[0.8]	[—]	[—]
X	Depressed	2.1	4.2	3.0	4.5	—	—
XI	Unskilled	43.5	26.7	22.0	15.4	3.9	5.2
	[Labourers]	[36.8]	[23.8]	[18.1]	[13.4]	[—]	[2.8]
Number of churches/circuits			7	11	13		
Number of adults/fathers		99,709	240	346	355	76	82

TABLE XLIII. (*cont.*) *Somerset: occupations of male Dissenters in percentages*

		Wesleyan Methodists			Bible Christians
		1810–19	1820–9	1830–9	1830–7
I	Gentlemen	—	0.4	0.2	—
II	Business	—	0.6	0.8	—
III	Professions	0.5	0.8	0.6	—
IV	Farmers	5.3	6.2	6.4	4.7
V	Food and retail	12.1	13.9	12.1	2.3
VI	White collar	5.3	3.5	4.5	1.2
VII	Labour aristocracy	3.9	4.1	3.1	—
VIII	Higher skilled	25.0	18.7	19.2	19.8
IX	Lower skilled	24.5	29.3	33.3	19.8
	[Miners]	[4.4]	[6.9]	[17.1]	[—]
X	Depressed	4.4	1.7	2.9	3.5
XI	Unskilled	18.9	20.8	17.0	48.8
	[Labourers]	[16.5]	[16.0]	[13.3]	[47.7]
Number of churches/circuits		9	12	14	2
Number of adults/fathers		206	522	841	86

TABLE XLIV. *Staffordshire: occupations of male Dissenters in percentages*

		General male population	Independents			Baptists	
		1841	1800–19	1820–9	1830–7	1820–9	1830–7
I	Gentlemen	1.8	—	0.3	—	—	—
II	Business	0.6	1.2	0.8	4.5	—	2.3
III	Professions	0.8	—	1.0	0.2	—	—
IV	Farmers	4.7	2.4	3.0	2.8	—	—
V	Food and retail	6.1	5.9	8.7	8.9	0.8	3.9
VI	White collar	2.5	3.6	3.3	5.9	4.1	—
VII	Labour aristocracy	9.2	8.9	5.7	6.4	26.8	20.2
VIII	Higher skilled	23.8	27.2	24.6	27.4	24.4	16.3
	[Potters]	[5.7]	[12.1]	[10.5]	[10.1]	[—]	[0.8]
IX	Lower skilled	20.3	26.6	23.3	20.9	32.1	45.0
	[Miners]	[11.3]	[8.9]	[11.6]	[9.1]	[21.5]	[34.1]
X	Depressed	3.0	16.6	9.4	5.1	0.8	—
XI	Unskilled	27.3	7.7	19.9	17.9	11.0	12.4
	[Labourers]	[23.5]	[5.9]	[19.5]	[13.9]	[11.0]	[12.4]
Number of churches/circuits			8	12	12	3	4
Number of adults/fathers		124,077	169	362	287	123	129

TABLE XLIV. *(cont.) Staffordshire: occupations of male Dissenters in percentages*

		Wesleyan Methodists			Methodist New Connexion		Primitive Methodists	
		1810–19	1820–9	1830–7	1820–9	1830–7	1820–9	1830–7
I	Gentlemen	—	0.1	0.1	—	—	—	—
II	Business	0.6	0.7	1.0	0.1	0.4	—	—
III	Professions	—	0.3	0.3	0.1	0.2	—	—
IV	Farmers	1.6	2.7	2.6	1.3	0.5	0.8	1.3
V	Food and retail	4.6	3.9	4.8	2.7	2.5	3.0	3.6
VI	White collar	2.4	2.6	2.5	1.4	2.0	1.5	1.2
VII	Labour aristocracy	10.8	10.0	10.8	10.9	13.0	5.3	7.3
VIII	Higher skilled	50.5	37.3	33.3	57.6	57.7	47.7	42.1
	[Potters]	[33.4]	[21.7]	[16.1]	[39.8]	[42.8]	[25.0]	[24.1]
IX	Lower skilled	17.9	27.2	27.9	15.4	14.0	12.9	19.0
	[Miners]	[9.8]	[15.7]	[16.7]	[7.2]	[5.9]	[6.1]	[10.3]
X	Depressed	2.0	2.6	2.7	1.0	1.3	1.5	1.6
XI	Unskilled	9.6	12.6	14.1	9.5	8.3	27.3	23.8
	[Labourers]	[8.9]	[11.6]	[12.9]	[8.4]	[7.2]	[25.4]	[23.2]
Number of churches/circuits		15	15	16	3	3	5	7
Number of adults/fathers		864	1741	1908	941	1150	132	583

TABLE XLV. *Suffolk: occupations of male Dissenters in percentages*

	General male population 1841	Independents						Baptists
		1790–9	1800–9	1810–19	1820–9	1830–7		1810–37
I Gentlemen	2.8	0.9	1.1	—	0.3	—		—
II Business	0.6	2.8	2.6	2.1	0.8	1.9		—
III Professions	1.1	—	0.8	0.2	0.3	1.1		—
IV Farmers	6.8	3.8	4.7	5.1	2.2	3.2		1.1
V Food and retail	7.7	10.4	11.6	15.8	17.4	16.2		4.4
VI White collar	2.4	4.7	3.2	1.3	1.9	2.5		1.1
VII Labour aristocracy	1.7	0.9	2.6	3.4	6.0	9.8		0.6
VIII Higher skilled	13.0	17.9	21.3	23.3	27.6	21.7		12.2
IX Lower skilled	9.1	17.9	8.9	10.0	7.7	12.6		7.8
X Depressed	0.8	5.7	7.4	2.8	4.9	6.7		—
XI Unskilled	54.0	34.9	35.8	35.9	30.9	24.3		72.8
[Labourers]	[46.6]	[15.6]	[16.6]	[26.3]	[24.6]	[17.5]		[66.7]
Number of churches/circuits		3	3	4	6	6		3
Number of adults/fathers	72,831	106	190	234	317	265		90

TABLE XLV. *(cont.) Suffolk: occupations of male Dissenters in percentages*

		Quakers		Wesleyan Methodists			
		1790–1809	1810–37	1810–19	1820–9	1830–7
I	Gentlemen	—	—	—	—	—
II	Business	8.2	3.5	0.8	0.2	0.3
III	Professions	2.0	1.8	0.2	0.3	0.4
IV	Farmers	15.3	11.4	4.2	4.2	4.3
V	Food and retail	32.7	47.5	8.5	7.8	8.5
VI	White collar	6.1	7.5	4.4	4.2	2.1
VII	Labour aristocracy	7.1	12.3	1.2	0.7	1.1
VIII	Higher skilled	9.2	7.0	17.6	13.9	14.0
IX	Lower skilled	16.3	5.3	13.9	11.9	13.6
X	Depressed	—	—	1.2	1.1	0.6
XI	Unskilled	3.1	3.5	48.1	55.6	55.0
	[Labourers]	[2.0]	[0.9]	[42.1]	[50.9]	[49.8]
Number of churches/ circuits				8	8	8
Number of adults/fathers		49	57	259	603	835

TABLE XLVI. *Surrey and south London: occupations of male Dissenters in percentages*

		General male population	Independents			Quakers					Wesleyan Methodists
		1841	1810–19	1820–9	1830–9	1790–9	1800–9	1810–19	1820–9	1830–7	1812–37
I	Gentlemen	5.1	1.6	2.6	3.0	—	0.5	—	—	—	0.6
II	Business	1.8	—	2.9	2.7	14.2	20.6	19.3	16.8	18.0	3.1
III	Professions	1.9	2.1	2.3	1.2	2.6	0.9	3.4	3.7	2.2	0.6
IV	Farmers	1.3	1.6	0.1	0.3	4.2	0.9	4.2	2.8	1.1	0.6
V	Food and retail	11.3	16.0	17.8	19.6	31.0	30.4	34.0	36.0	32.6	11.4
VI	White collar	6.6	5.2	11.8	13.7	6.8	8.4	13.4	9.8	12.9	7.4
VII	Labour aristocracy	6.4	5.8	3.4	5.6	5.3	5.6	4.6	7.9	12.4	7.4
VIII	Higher skilled	18.2	21.5	18.4	16.8	20.0	20.6	10.9	12.6	15.7	28.4
IX	Lower skilled	13.7	25.4	20.0	16.2	14.7	10.7	6.7	9.3	4.5	17.3
X	Depressed	0.4	1.0	1.1	0.3	—	—	—	0.9	—	—
XI	Unskilled	33.1	19.9	19.5	20.5	1.1	1.4	3.4	—	0.6	23.1
	[Labourers]	[22.9]	[13.6]	[10.6]	[8.9]	[—]	[0.9]	[1.7]	[—]	[—]	[12.7]
	Number of churches/circuits		8	14	16						4
	Number of adults/ fathers	142,441	191	348	331	95	107	119	107	89	162

TABLE XLVII. *Sussex: occupations of male Dissenters in percentages*

		General male population	Independents		Quakers	Wesleyan Methodists		Countess of Huntingdon's Connexion
		1841	1820–9	1830–7	1790–1837	1820–9	1830–7	1821–37
I	Gentlemen	3.7	2.9	0.7	—	0.3	0.6	1.3
II	Business	0.5	0.5	1.0	2.4	0.4	0.3	2.5
III	Professions	1.4	1.9	1.6	1.8	0.3	0.3	—
IV	Farmers	5.4	4.9	3.3	7.8	3.3	1.5	—
V	Food and retail	8.0	14.6	15.0	57.6	9.9	10.7	24.7
VI	White collar	3.1	6.8	7.1	0.1	5.0	7.2	6.3
VII	Labour aristocracy	1.6	3.4	1.9	3.6	2.0	3.9	7.6
VIII	Higher skilled	14.0	25.2	20.3	16.9	27.8	23.6	41.8
IX	Lower skilled	8.8	12.6	14.1	4.8	15.1	15.4	12.0
X	Depressed	0.1	—	—	—	—	0.3	—
XI	Unskilled	53.3	27.2	35.0	4.0	35.9	36.4	3.8
	[Labourers]	[43.3]	[23.3]	[27.1]	[2.8]	[28.1]	[26.9]	[1.3]
	Number of churches/circuits		11	11		3	5	2
	Number of adults/fathers	70,139	206	290	83	352	363	79

TABLE XLVIII. *Warwickshire: occupations of male Dissenters in percentages*

	General male population	Independents		Baptists		Quakers		Wesleyan Methodists		Primitive Methodists
	1841	1820–9	1830–9	1820–9	1830–7	1790–1809	1810–37	1820–9	1830–9	1830–7
I Gentlemen	2.3	0.5	0.2	—	0.6	—	—	—	—	—
II Business	0.6	2.3	2.0	3.0	4.9	11.5	28.5	—	0.7	—
III Professions	1.3	0.2	0.3	3.0	1.7	0.5	0.9	—	—	—
IV Farmers	3.6	1.6	2.0	1.0	0.8	3.6	3.3	—	—	—
V Food and retail	9.8	10.2	9.0	14.0	16.3	32.1	28.1	3.0	5.0	2.4
VI White collar	3.6	7.6	4.1	6.0	4.9	4.5	15.9	1.5	4.4	1.2
VII Labour aristocracy	11.1	10.3	11.6	29.0	31.4	8.3	3.7	4.1	8.5	8.5
VIII Higher skilled	20.3	16.2	15.0	30.0	26.9	18.0	12.0	16.8	31.4	33.5
IX Lower skilled	12.6	14.1	15.7	8.0	10.2	17.7	7.5	12.7	16.8	7.3
X Depressed	6.0	26.4	26.7	1.0	0.4	2.6	—	47.0	18.1	37.2
[Weavers]	[1.9]	[26.0]	[26.2]	[1.0]	[—]	[2.6]	[—]	[45.5]	[17.4]	[14.6]
XI Unskilled	28.7	10.5	13.3	5.0	1.9	1.0	[—]	14.9	15.1	9.8
[Labourers]	[22.7]	[9.8]	[11.6]	[—]	[0.8]	[1.0]	[—]	[12.7]	[13.8]	[9.8]
Number of churches/circuits		10	10	1	1			4	9	1
Number of adults/fathers	97,422	554	808	100	236	96	107	134	282	82

TABLE XLIX. *Westmorland: occupations of male Dissenters in percentages*

	General male population 1841	Quakers						Wesleyan Methodists	
		1790–9	1800–9	1810–19	1820–9	1830–7		1820–9	1830–7
I	Gentlemen	5.6	—	—	—	—	—		—	—
II	Business	0.5	3.9	6.4	4.3	6.1	11.0		0.7	1.7
III	Professions	1.4	—	—	1.3	1.9	—		—	1.0
IV	Farmers	17.2	48.1	36.1	34.1	37.7	49.3		14.5	18.0
V	Food and retail	6.2	7.1	15.8	16.0	15.1	13.2		5.4	6.2
VI	White collar	2.8	—	—	1.7	2.8	1.5		4.3	1.5
VII	Labour aristocracy	1.3	3.9	2.0	3.4	3.8	—		4.3	1.2
VIII	Higher skilled	13.3	11.7	13.4	9.1	13.2	9.6		7.2	22.7
IX	Lower skilled	12.8	17.5	20.3	13.8	10.4	9.6		23.6	18.5
X	Depressed	6.8	3.9	2.0	1.7	0.9	—		17.0	9.5
XI	Unskilled	32.4	3.9	4.0	5.2	8.0	5.9		22.8	19.5
	[Labourers]	[25.0]	[3.9]	[4.0]	[5.2]	[8.0]	[5.1]		[20.0]	[15.0]
	Number of churches/circuits								3	3
	Number of adults/fathers	13,344	77	101	116	106	68		138	200

TABLE L. *Wiltshire: occupations of male Dissenters in percentages*

| | | General male population | Independents | | | | | Wesleyan Methodists | | Primitive Methodists |
		1841	1790–9	1800–9	1810–19	1820–9	1830–7	1820–9	1830–7	1830–7
I	Gentlemen	2.8	—	0.9	0.4	0.9	0.5	0.5	0.7	—
II	Business	0.3	—	0.9	0.7	0.4	0.5	—	—	—
III	Professions	1.0	—	—	0.4	0.2	0.5	—	—	—
IV	Farmers	7.0	5.3	3.7	2.2	2.0	1.9	1.5	4.9	7.0
V	Food and retail	6.4	9.6	8.4	9.5	12.8	15.0	14.2	16.0	3.1
VI	White collar	2.0	3.2	1.9	2.5	5.2	2.4	3.5	2.0	0.8
VII	Labour aristocracy	1.2	1.1	0.9	1.8	3.3	2.6	2.0	2.5	0.8
VIII	Higher skilled	12.0	7.4	15.9	23.1	22.7	22.4	15.9	18.3	12.5
IX	Lower skilled	8.0	20.7	15.4	30.4	21.4	20.5	18.9	20.4	9.4
X	Depressed	5.0	45.7	35.5	15.5	10.0	8.2	5.7	7.9	3.1
XI	Unskilled	54.2	6.9	13.6	13.6	21.1	25.5	37.8	27.2	63.3
	[Labourers]	[48.7]	[5.9]	[13.1]	[10.4]	[17.2]	[22.2]	[32.8]	[24.3]	[61.7]
	Number of churches/circuits		3	4	8	13	12	4	5	2
	Number of adults/fathers	59,229	94	107	275	541	421	201	406	128

TABLE LI. *Worcestershire: occupations of male Dissenters in percentages*

| | | General male population | Independents | | Quakers | Wesleyan Methodists | | |
		1841	1820–9	1830–7	1790–1837	1810–19	1820–9	1830–7
I	Gentlemen	2.6	1.7	0.5	—	—	0.4	—
II	Business	0.6	4.8	4.7	5.3	0.2	1.0	1.7
III	Professions	1.1	0.6	1.1	3.2	—	0.1	0.3
IV	Farmers	5.3	1.1	0.5	6.3	1.2	0.6	0.6
V	Food and retail	7.2	14.4	16.2	32.9	6.1	3.3	3.6
VI	White collar	2.5	9.0	9.1	7.7	2.7	3.1	3.3
VII	Labour aristocracy	4.1	5.9	5.5	4.2	3.5	8.2	11.7
VIII	Higher skilled	14.1	13.6	15.7	11.1	19.2	17.4	20.0
IX	Lower skilled	15.1	20.9	25.0	27.7	40.4	36.7	38.0
X	Depressed	9.7	22.6	18.4	—	17.5	19.6	11.2
XI	Unskilled	37.6	5.4	3.3	1.6	9.1	9.5	9.8
	[Labourers]	[31.6]	[3.7]	[1.0]	[1.1]	[6.9]	[8.2]	[8.6]
	Number of churches/circuits		5	4		4	7	7
	Number of adults/fathers	56,084	177	182	95	328	782	720

TABLE LII. *Yorkshire, East Riding: occupations of male Dissenters in percentages*

	General male population	Independents						Quakers
	1841	1780–9	1790–9	1800–9	1810–19	1820–9	1830–7	1790–1837
I Gentlemen	3.8	—	1.0	1.0	—	—	—	—
II Business	1.2	—	—	—	2.8	3.0	1.8	6.7
III Professions	1.0	—	—	—	0.8	2.1	1.8	1.0
IV Farmers	8.6	16.3	9.1	10.6	13.7	12.0	4.5	25.5
V Food and retail	8.8	8.3	15.7	8.7	7.7	10.6	12.4	35.6
VI White collar	3.4	3.2	2.0	4.1	3.2	2.1	5.8	1.0
VII Labour aristocracy	3.0	—	—	1.2	4.8	7.0	3.6	3.4
VIII Higher skilled	14.3	15.1	17.2	15.7	22.6	26.4	28.5	15.4
IX Lower skilled	10.9	17.1	21.2	21.2	14.5	14.8	14.2	6.7
X Depressed	0.7	3.2	1.0	1.9	1.6	0.7	1.2	1.0
XI Unskilled	44.3	36.9	32.8	35.6	28.2	21.1	26.1	3.8
[Labourers]	[35.3]	[34.9]	[27.3]	[22.1]	[18.1]	[15.5]	[17.6]	[3.8]
Number of churches/circuits		2	1	2	5	7	7	
Number of adults/fathers	48,189	126	99	104	124	142	165	104

TABLE LII. *(cont.) Yorkshire, East Riding: occupations of male Dissenters in percentages*

	Unitarians	Wesleyan Methodists		Methodist New Connexion		Primitive Methodists
	1790–1837	1820–9	1830–7	1800–19	1820–37	1830–7
I Gentlemen	—	1.6	—	—	—	0.5
II Business	15.7	1.6	2.3	3.9	1.1	1.1
III Professions	5.7	—	—	—	—	—
IV Farmers	—	5.1	5.7	5.9	1.1	1.6
V Food and retail	8.6	1.6	11.2	10.3	7.8	6.0
VI White collar	12.9	3.1	5.7	2.0	3.3	3.9
VII Labour aristocracy	7.1	2.4	5.5	8.8	11.1	3.7
VIII Higher skilled	12.9	28.7	26.1	28.0	27.2	24.5
IX Lower skilled	15.7	13.8	15.2	10.3	10.0	16.7
X Depressed	—	0.8	—	2.9	1.1	2.1
XI Unskilled	21.4	41.3	28.2	28.0	37.2	39.8
[Labourers]	[4.3]	[33.5]	[27.0]	[10.3]	[18.3]	[19.8]
Number of churches/circuits	1	5	8	1	1	2
Number of adults/fathers	70	127	174	102	90	374

TABLE LIII. *Yorkshire, North Riding: occupations of male Dissenters in percentages*

	General male population 1841	Independents					
		1780–9	1790–9	1800–9	1810–19	1820–9	1830–7
I	Gentlemen	4.0	—	0.8	—	—	1.3	1.7
II	Business	0.5	0.9	0.8	—	1.3	1.3	1.7
III	Professions	1.1	0.9	—	—	—	—	1.7
IV	Farmers	14.9	5.0	3.1	2.8	7.6	6.1	7.7
V	Food and retail	6.9	6.4	3.9	1.6	8.9	9.4	10.3
VI	White collar	2.5	1.8	1.2	4.8	5.4	4.5	9.4
VII	Labour aristocracy	1.9	1.8	1.6	—	1.3	3.9	8.1
VIII	Higher skilled	15.4	7.7	10.9	13.7	15.6	21.6	22.6
IX	Lower skilled	12.2	70.0	70.9	66.5	44.4	25.2	13.7
	[Miners]	[2.5]	[64.5]	[62.8]	[56.0]	[36.2]	[13.5]	[—]
X	Depressed	1.4	—	0.8	3.2	1.3	3.2	1.7
XI	Unskilled	39.1	5.5	6.2	7.3	14.1	23.5	21.4
	[Labourers]	[31.9]	[2.7]	[4.7]	[7.3]	[6.5]	[9.0]	[5.1]
	Number of churches/circuits		3	4	6	8	11	13
	Number of adults/fathers	48,904	110	129	124	224	155	117

TABLE LIII. (cont.) *Yorkshire, North Riding: occupations of male Dissenters in percentages*

	Quakers				Wesleyan Methodists		
	1790–9	1800–9	1810–19	1820–37	1810–19	1820–9	1830–7
I Gentlemen	—	—	—	—	—	—	—
II Business	4.8	3.8	2.9	1.5	—	—	0.7
III Professions	—	1.1	1.9	1.5	—	—	0.8
IV Farmers	42.9	47.3	48.6	40.9	7.3	5.0	9.6
V Food and retail	18.6	22.6	21.1	28.8	6.6	3.8	9.7
VI White collar	1.9	—	2.8	4.5	4.4	5.0	3.8
VII Labour aristocracy	8.1	5.4	2.8	0.8	1.5	2.6	2.2
VIII Higher skilled	7.6	6.5	7.8	12.9	4.4	7.6	10.4
IX Lower skilled	11.4	6.5	9.0	7.6	73.0	71.9	56.9
[Miners]	[1.0]	[—]	[—]	[—]	[69.3]	[66.0]	[45.2]
X Depressed	0.5	1.6	1.9	1.5	—	—	1.2
XI Unskilled	4.3	5.4	—	—	2.9	4.3	4.6
[Labourers]	[2.4]	[3.2]	[—]	[1.5]	[2.2]	[3.3]	[3.0]
Number of churches/circuits					4	8	9
Number of adults/fathers	105	93	105	66	137	210	250

TABLE LIV. *Yorkshire, West Riding: occupations of male Dissenters in percentages*

	General male population 1841	Independents						
		1800–9	1810–19	1820–9	1830–9	1840–9	1850–9	1860–9
I Gentlemen	2.0	—	0.4	0.2	0.3	—	—	—
II Business	1.0	2.0	2.4	3.9	5.3	2.2	3.8	3.9
III Professions	0.8	0.4	0.4	0.6	0.6	0.3	0.7	0.2
IV Farmers	5.7	3.2	6.2	5.4	4.9	4.4	3.0	2.8
V Food and retail	6.3	7.3	5.4	6.8	7.0	8.0	5.8	7.0
Va Clothiers	3.2	14.7	14.9	9.3	13.4	9.7	1.5	0.2
VI White collar	2.8	1.3	2.5	3.3	4.0	1.9	3.8	5.9
VII Labour aristocracy	4.1	4.5	4.9	3.5	3.8	6.1	12.2	8.7
VIII Higher skilled	17.8	31.6	23.1	22.0	23.3	20.2	27.5	32.4
IX Lower skilled		18.0	16.8	19.1	17.6	20.5	18.7	21.4
X Depressed	36.7	9.5	12.2	14.3	11.8	14.7	9.0	8.2
[Weavers]	[—]	[8.6]	[12.2]	[14.0]	[11.4]	[14.1]	[9.0]	[8.0]
XI Unskilled	19.8	7.3	10.8	11.5	8.0	11.9	14.0	9.4
[Labourers]	[15.0]	[4.1]	[8.5]	[7.2]	[5.5]	[9.7]	[10.9]	[4.2]
Number of churches/circuits		11	27	36	55	9	13	15
Number of adults/fathers	268,405	451	823	1,438	2,066	361	726	1,020

TABLE LIV. (cont.) Yorkshire, West Riding: occupations of male Dissenters in percentages

	Baptists					Quakers					Unitarians			
	1790-9	1800-9	1810-19	1820-9	1830-7	1790-9	1800-9	1810-19	1820-9	1830-7	1800-9	1810-19	1820-9	1830-7
I Gentlemen	—	—	0.2	0.1	0.1	—	11.9	18.2	15.1	10.2	—	—	—	0.9
II Business	5.3	4.1	2.6	2.2	2.3	8.0	1.0	2.4	3.0	3.1	1.2	2.6	2.1	1.9
III Professions	—	0.6	0.2	—	—	1.9	7.9	12.9	7.6	5.7	1.2	2.6	2.1	0.9
IV Farmers	1.9	5.2	4.1	2.9	2.6	9.8	17.7	15.0	26.2	36.2	3.3	6.2	4.2	1.9
V Food and retail	5.3	3.5	2.2	1.9	3.0	13.9	15.1	11.9	10.1	8.6	1.8	1.7	2.1	2.8
Va Clothiers	27.6	19.0	11.6	9.5	5.0	14.6	4.7	4.9	4.3	4.2	4.8	—	—	—
VI White collar	2.9	2.6	0.7	1.0	1.9	2.2	2.7	3.8	3.3	4.0	3.6	3.8	1.0	6.5
VII Labour aristocracy	0.4	1.2	0.9	0.6	1.0	4.3	18.1	17.7	12.3	9.8	24.8	26.9	30.7	29.4
VIII Higher skilled	8.0	9.3	10.8	12.2	13.7	19.7	11.0	4.5	7.8	10.0	29.5	26.0	24.8	31.3
IX Lower skilled	16.9	9.7	12.6	14.8	20.0	13.8	7.4	6.0	6.6	4.2	16.7	19.9	14.4	14.0
X Depressed	27.9	42.7	50.2	51.4	46.7	9.3	5.7	4.9	6.0	4.2	3.6	5.1	2.1	1.9
[Weavers]	[27.9]	[42.7]	[50.2]	[51.2]	[45.9]	[6.0]	[5.7]	[4.9]	[6.0]	[4.2]	[2.4]	[5.1]	[2.1]	[0.9]
XI Unskilled	3.8	2.0	3.8	3.5	3.8	2.4	2.7	2.6	3.8	4.0	9.5	5.1	16.5	8.4
[Labourers]	[3.4]	[1.5]	[2.3]	[2.0]	[3.1]	[1.1]	[0.7]	[0.9]	[2.6]	[2.9]	[6.0]	[4.5]	[11.2]	[7.5]
Number of churches/circuits	6	8	10	11	9						3	6	4	4
Number of adults/fathers	263	344	542	831	733	312	299	293	302	261	84	78	96	107

TABLE LIV. *(cont.)* Yorkshire, West Riding: occupations of male Dissenters in percentages

		Moravians		Wesleyan Methodists				Methodist New Connexion				Primitive Methodists	
		1820–9	1830–7	1800–9	1810–19	1820–9	1830–8	1800–9	1810–19	1820–9	1830–7	1820–9	1830–7
I	Gentlemen	—	—	—	—	0.1	0.1	—	—	—	—	—	—
II	Business	2.2	1.5	2.2	2.7	1.9	1.4	1.2	1.2	1.6	1.5	—	0.5
III	Professions	0.7	—	—	—	0.2	0.2	0.4	0.2	0.2	0.2	—	0.1
IV	Farmers	0.7	1.0	2.9	3.6	3.4	4.8	3.3	2.0	1.0	0.9	2.3	1.2
V	Food and retail	8.2	8.0	3.3	2.8	4.2	4.4	2.3	3.2	3.5	3.6	2.9	2.2
Va	Clothiers	10.4	7.0	16.9	16.0	19.5	15.0	9.6	10.1	15.9	20.2	1.6	1.3
VI	White collar	6.0	7.0	1.8	2.6	2.3	3.1	1.6	1.8	3.2	2.9	2.7	1.6
VII	Labour aristocracy	2.2	1.0	2.2	2.5	2.6	2.1	3.3	2.6	2.5	2.3	0.4	0.4
VIII	Higher skilled	16.8	12.0	14.2	19.7	18.9	15.3	22.1	20.0	20.6	22.3	12.6	13.2
IX	Lower skilled	25.7	15.5	19.2	23.2	24.7	21.3	30.9	24.1	22.8	27.3	39.0	35.2
X	Depressed	23.1	42.0	26.3	20.0	13.3	22.6	20.5	28.2	22.6	13.2	30.0	33.7
	[Weavers]	[23.1]	[42.0]	[26.0]	[19.9]	[13.0]	[22.1]	[19.3]	[26.9]	[22.4]	[12.8]	[29.7]	[33.6]
XI	Unskilled	3.7	5.0	10.9	6.7	8.8	9.7	4.7	6.5	6.2	5.7	8.5	10.5
	[Labourers]	[2.2]	[3.0]	[5.2]	[4.3]	[6.3]	[6.6]	[4.7]	[4.1]	[5.6]	[4.4]	[6.6]	[9.2]
Number of churches/circuits		4	4	21	46	65	78	7	8	9	11	9	14
Number of adults/fathers		134	100	670	1,386	3,009	3,436	244	454	516	516	258	768

TABLE LV. *Anglesey: occupations of male Dissenters in percentages*

		General male population	Independents			Wesleyan Methodists		Calvinistic Methodists			
		1841	1810–19	1820–9	1830–7	1820–9	1830–7	1800–9	1810–19	1820–9	1830–7
I	Gentlemen	1.5	—	—	—	—	—		0.2	—	0.1
II	Business	0.4	1.1	0.4	—	—	—	0.7	0.3	0.4	0.3
III	Professions	0.7	—	0.4	—	—	—	—	0.2	0.2	0.1
IV	Farmers	19.1	10.6	9.0	13.5	6.3	6.5	25.5	21.8	18.1	17.4
V	Food and retail	3.7	2.1	4.5	4.9	5.5	3.8	5.1	4.2	3.3	3.5
VI	White collar	1.8	0.5	0.4	1.6	0.8	1.9	3.6	1.2	0.8	0.6
VII	Labour aristocracy	1.5	2.1	6.0	10.0	—	0.9	0.7	0.9	1.4	0.8
VIII	Higher skilled	11.0	12.2	14.2	10.2	13.4	19.6	13.1	9.9	8.5	10.2
IX	Lower skilled	14.6	16.1	18.3	12.3	14.2	16.4	8.8	12.1	14.8	13.2
X	Depressed	1.7	2.6	1.1	1.2	1.6	1.9	5.1	3.7	3.0	2.6
XI	Unskilled	44.1	52.6	45.9	46.1	58.3	49.1	37.2	45.5	49.6	51.1
	[Labourers]	[38.1]	[50.5]	[38.1]	[36.2]	[51.2]	[41.6]	[36.5]	[43.2]	[47.6]	[47.9]
Number of churches/circuits			4	8	8	1	1	25	36	40	44
Number of adults/fathers		10,822	189	268	244	127	107	137	865	1,065	861

TABLE LVI. *Breconshire: occupations of male Dissenters in percentages*

		General male population	Independents			Wesleyan Methodists			Calvinistic Methodists		
		1841	1810–19	1820–9	1830–7	1810–19	1820–9	1830–7	1810–19	1820–9	1830–7
I	Gentlemen	3.7	—	—	0.4	1.1	1.9	—	—	—	—
II	Business	0.3	—	—	—	—	—	0.5	—	—	0.3
III	Professions	0.8	—	—	0.4	—	—	—	0.7	—	—
IV	Farmers	13.7	25.5	28.5	33.6	15.1	11.3	5.4	32.8	29.0	29.1
V	Food and retail	5.1	1.1	1.9	2.4	4.3	4.2	4.2	5.2	6.4	4.3
VI	White collar	2.2	5.3	1.9	1.2	3.2	1.9	3.4	4.5	2.6	2.2
VII	Labour aristocracy	3.9	1.1	0.5	—	7.5	6.6	19.2	0.7	1.2	1.7
VIII	Higher skilled	12.0	18.1	13.5	12.8	12.4	20.8	20.0	18.7	14.7	13.1
IX	Lower skilled	24.6	11.7	9.7	8.0	28.0	27.4	31.3	15.7	21.9	27.1
	[Miners]	[17.0]	[—]	[—]	[—]	[15.1]	[5.7]	[16.5]	[5.2]	[11.0]	[12.8]
X	Depressed	1.3	3.2	1.0	0.8	2.2	0.9	1.0	2.2	1.7	1.0
XI	Unskilled	33.4	34.0	43.0	39.6	26.3	25.0	15.0	19.4	22.6	21.0
	[Labourers]	[27.8]	[32.4]	[38.6]	[33.4]	[26.3]	[23.1]	[15.0]	[17.9]	[21.9]	[19.5]
	Number of churches/circuits		5	5	6	1	1	2	16	20	18
	Number of adults/fathers	14,126	94	207	250	93	106	203	134	290	290

TABLE LVII. *Caernarfonshire: occupations of male Dissenters in percentages*

	General male population	Independents			Wesleyan Methodists		Calvinistic Methodists		
	1841	1810–19	1820–9	1830–7	1820–9	1830–7	1810–19	1820–9	1830–7
I Gentlemen	2.0	–	–	–	–	0.5	0.1	0.1	0.2
II Business	0.5	0.8	0.2	0.6	–	–	0.7	0.2	0.2
III Professions	0.8	–	0.2	0.6	–	–	0.2	0.3	–
IV Farmers	16.2	13.0	11.3	8.4	4.2	4.1	26.4	24.0	19.1
V Food and retail	4.3	4.2	4.8	5.2	4.9	4.1	3.6	3.5	3.4
VI White collar	1.7	0.4	0.7	1.5	1.4	1.5	0.3	0.9	0.8
VII Labour aristocracy	1.7	5.0	2.7	3.2	6.3	3.0	0.8	0.8	0.7
VIII Higher skilled	11.1	11.1	10.7	13.6	17.5	25.4	12.4	9.4	9.9
IX Lower skilled	9.7	10.9	14.6	10.3	14.0	12.2	7.8	10.3	11.0
X Depressed	1.4	3.3	1.8	0.8	2.1	1.5	3.8	2.0	1.3
XI Unskilled	50.7	51.3	53.1	55.8	49.7	47.7	44.0	48.6	53.5
[Labourers]	[29.1]	[22.6]	[29.7]	[31.4]	[27.6]	[23.9]	[28.0]	[30.1]	[31.0]
[Quarrymen]	[16.3]	[16.1]	[11.9]	[17.2]	[7.7]	[14.2]	[12.6]	[14.8]	[19.9]
Number of churches/circuits		6	11	12	1	1	49	59	66
Number of adults/fathers	18,908	239	586	912	143	197	769	1,150	1,332

Appendix

TABLE LVIII. *Cardiganshire: occupations of male Dissenters in percentages*

		General male population	Independents			Wesleyan Methodists			Calvinistic Methodists		
		1841	1810–19	1820–9	1830–7	1810–19	1820–9	1830–7	1810–19	1820–9	1830–7
I	Gentlemen	2.8	0.6	0.2	0.3	—	0.4	0.5	0.3	0.1	0.1
II	Business	0.4	—	0.3	0.3	—	—	0.5	0.5	0.2	0.2
III	Professions	1.0	—	—	0.3	—	0.4	—	—	—	0.1
IV	Farmers	22.0	26.9	23.3	23.1	13.0	11.5	15.1	25.0	24.0	27.0
V	Food and retail	4.2	5.6	2.5	2.9	1.2	3.4	3.5	1.8	4.1	4.2
VI	White collar	2.0	1.8	0.9	1.0	3.1	1.3	2.0	0.9	1.0	0.8
VII	Labour aristocracy	2.0	0.6	0.9	1.1	3.7	5.1	5.5	5.0	3.8	2.4
VIII	Higher skilled	13.1	14.8	13.8	13.2	14.3	15.8	16.6	15.9	12.4	13.3
IX	Lower skilled	13.3	8.0	11.4	9.2	16.8	20.9	20.6	8.8	13.9	13.7
X	Depressed	2.2	1.8	2.9	2.1	3.1	3.4	2.5	2.9	2.8	2.2
XI	Unskilled	37.0	39.9	43.9	46.5	44.7	37.9	33.2	38.8	37.6	36.1
	[Labourers]	[30.0]	[38.2]	[40.6]	[42.3]	[34.8]	[31.1]	[28.1]	[30.1]	[31.2]	[31.8]
	Number of churches/circuits		4	11	11	2	2	2	30	44	45
	Number of adults/fathers	13,977	169	1,061	1,193	161	235	199	380	968	1,238

TABLE LIX. *Carmarthenshire: occupations of male Dissenters in percentages*

		General male population	Independents		Baptists		Wesleyan Methodists	Calvinistic Methodists		
		1841	1820–9	1830–7	1820–9	1830–7	1810–37	1810–19	1820–9	1830–7
I	Gentlemen	2.6	1.8	1.0	—	0.6	—	—	—	0.2
II	Business	0.4	0.1	0.4	0.6	0.6	—	0.5	0.2	0.3
III	Professions	0.9	—	0.1	—	0.6	—	—	0.1	0.3
IV	Farmers	21.6	26.2	22.2	2.9	1.8	19.2	27.8	26.3	25.4
V	Food and retail	4.9	4.3	4.5	3.4	12.2	3.1	4.0	3.9	4.3
VI	White collar	2.4	0.8	1.1	2.3	2.4	3.1	2.5	2.8	1.8
VII	Labour aristocracy	2.8	1.2	4.9	9.2	5.4	—	1.5	1.7	1.7
VIII	Higher skilled	13.7	13.2	14.2	32.2	27.1	21.9	14.4	14.0	15.7
IX	Lower skilled	13.3	8.0	11.7	18.7	22.0	18.8	13.4	16.4	17.5
X	Depressed	1.7	1.0	1.6	2.3	2.4	—	3.5	2.4	1.8
XI	Unskilled	35.5	43.5	38.2	28.4	25.0	33.8	32.3	32.4	31.0
	[Labourers]	[31.1]	[41.3]	[36.1]	[21.6]	[14.6]	[30.8]	[30.8]	[30.8]	[29.1]
	Number of churches/circuits		12	12	2	2	1	34	36	36
	Number of adults/fathers	22,289	1,384	1,358	174	168	130	198	544	609

TABLE LX. *Denbighshire: occupations of male Dissenters in percentages*

		General male population	Independents			Baptists	Wesleyan Methodists			Calvinistic Methodists		
		1841	1810–19	1820–9	1830–7	1810–37	1810–19	1820–9	1830–7	1810–19	1820–9	1830–7
I	Gentlemen	2.3	0.2	–	0.1	–	0.7	0.2	0.3	0.4	0.1	0.2
II	Business	0.4	–	0.1	0.1	–	–	0.2	–	0.4	0.4	0.2
III	Professions	0.9	–	–	–	–	–	0.2	0.1	–	0.1	–
IV	Farmers	14.5	7.1	11.3	16.1	8.0	11.8	8.4	7.9	24.7	24.4	20.3
V	Food and retail	5.8	4.3	4.4	4.3	8.0	8.3	3.6	5.0	4.8	5.7	7.3
VI	White collar	2.0	1.0	0.7	0.6	3.1	6.2	2.2	1.4	1.4	1.5	0.9
VII	Labour aristocracy	2.1	1.9	2.2	1.5	1.8	0.7	2.6	1.6	0.4	0.7	1.5
VIII	Higher skilled	11.2	11.4	10.2	11.6	24.8	16.0	15.6	15.1	14.3	10.8	11.2
IX	Lower skilled	18.1	40.6	32.1	23.7	14.2	22.2	29.8	28.2	15.4	15.7	17.3
	[Miners]	[9.0]	[31.1]	[22.6]	[12.9]	[0.9]	[12.3]	[17.4]	[11.3]	[3.7]	[6.1]	[7.9]
X	Depressed	1.8	1.9	1.0	1.7	6.2	8.3	3.8	2.1	3.6	2.7	2.2
XI	Unskilled	40.9	31.6	38.1	40.2	34.1	25.7	33.4	38.3	34.6	37.9	38.9
	[Labourers]	[35.3]	[30.3]	[34.5]	[35.4]	[32.3]	[25.0]	[31.1]	[32.6]	[31.8]	[34.6]	[35.6]
	Number of churches/ circuits		8	12	17	1	6	6	6	36	48	56
	Number of adults/ fathers	20,795	576	1,113	1,186	113	144	544	700	492	731	863

TABLE LXI. *Flintshire: occupations of male Dissenters in percentages*

	General male population 1841	Independents			Wesleyan Methodists			Calvinistic Methodists		
		1810–19	1820–9	1830–7	1810–19	1820–9	1830–7	1810–19	1820–9	1830–7
I Gentlemen	1.7	0.6	0.2	0.4	—	—	0.2	—	0.4	0.3
II Business	0.6	—	0.4	0.1	—	0.2	—	—	0.2	1.0
III Professions	0.9	—	0.2	—	—	0.2	0.2	—	0.4	—
IV Farmers	9.7	1.8	3.2	3.2	8.2	3.6	4.3	14.5	12.2	12.2
V Food and retail	5.7	4.8	4.4	4.2	2.4	2.7	4.8	5.9	10.7	8.2
VI White collar	2.3	1.2	1.2	1.2	1.2	1.7	1.3	3.2	—	1.3
VII Labour aristocracy	2.6	3.0	3.8	5.4	1.2	6.1	7.2	2.3	1.9	1.6
VIII Higher skilled	13.1	21.0	19.0	14.7	24.7	18.9	14.1	18.8	12.2	15.0
IX Lower skilled	29.7	44.3	42.7	48.7	47.1	43.9	44.4	38.3	43.4	38.2
[Miners]	[21.3]	[35.3]	[34.3]	[42.1]	[37.6]	[36.1]	[36.7]	[28.9]	[32.5]	[29.3]
X Depressed	1.2	4.2	2.2	0.4	3.5	2.5	1.5	6.3	2.6	1.6
XI Unskilled	32.6	19.2	22.6	21.7	11.8	20.2	22.1	10.9	16.0	20.6
[Labourers]	[26.4]	[16.8]	[20.3]	[20.5]	[10.6]	[19.1]	[19.6]	[10.9]	[16.0]	[19.0]
Number of churches/circuits		5	7	7	1	1	1	15	26	26
Number of adults/fathers	15,469	167	499	498	85	524	653	128	266	312

TABLE LXII. *Glamorgan: occupations of male Dissenters in percentages*

	General male population 1841	Independents		Baptists		Unitarians	Wesleyan Methodists			Calvinistic Methodists		
		1820–9	1830–7	1820–9	1830–7	1830–7	1810–19	1820–9	1830–7	1810–19	1820–9	1830–7
I Gentlemen	1.8	—	—	—	—	—	—	—	—	—	—	—
II Business	0.6	—	—	—	—	—	—	—	0.4	—	0.1	0.4
III Professions	0.8	0.1	0.1	—	—	—	—	0.2	0.2	0.7	—	—
IV Farmers	6.6	9.8	11.4	6.1	3.6	18.6	1.6	1.3	2.0	8.5	7.9	5.2
V Food and retail	5.0	3.2	3.0	5.5	10.4	8.2	1.2	3.0	3.6	2.0	2.1	3.8
VI White collar	2.3	0.9	1.4	2.6	2.1	5.2	4.1	2.0	2.2	3.4	1.7	1.2
VII Labour aristocracy	7.8	10.7	12.9	12.2	16.7	4.1	21.1	21.3	27.0	11.2	14.2	15.1
VIII Higher skilled	16.5	12.3	10.4	24.0	24.5	9.3	9.8	14.5	16.4	16.7	11.8	16.3
IX Lower skilled	27.6	43.0	43.3	17.8	15.6	22.2	49.4	40.2	35.9	39.8	45.3	40.6
[Miners]	[19.7]	[33.5]	[35.1]	[6.5]	[8.3]	[14.4]	[42.1]	[33.6]	[25.2]	[29.6]	[34.3]	[29.4]
X Depressed	1.1	0.9	0.8	0.9	3.1	2.1	0.8	0.9	1.4	4.1	2.7	2.1
XI Unskilled	29.9	19.1	16.7	30.9	24.0	30.4	12.0	16.6	10.9	13.6	14.2	15.3
[Labourers]	[25.0]	[17.3]	[14.7]	[30.0]	[21.9]	[29.9]	[10.0]	[12.7]	[7.9]	[12.9]	[14.2]	[13.7]
Number of churches/circuits		8	10	4	3	2	3	4	5	8	12	12
Number of adults/fathers	44,599	686	1,177	115	96	97	246	574	813	147	353	485

TABLE LXIII. *Merioneth: occupations of male Dissenters in percentages*

		General male population	Independents			Wesleyan Methodists		Calvinistic Methodists		
		1841	1810–19	1820–9	1830–7	1820–9	1830–7	1810–19	1820–9	1830–7
I	Gentlemen	2.9	—	0.4	—	—	—	—	—	—
II	Business	0.5	1.1	—	—	—	1.0	0.7	0.2	0.2
III	Professions	0.9	—	—	—	—	0.5	—	0.1	—
IV	Farmers	23.0	25.3	23.0	27.5	15.3	15.0	33.1	33.0	28.7
V	Food and retail	4.2	2.3	3.4	5.2	4.1	2.9	3.8	3.3	3.6
VI	White collar	1.8	2.3	0.7	—	0.6	1.5	1.1	1.0	1.4
VII	Labour aristocracy	0.9	—	0.4	—	0.6	—	1.1	0.7	0.9
VIII	Higher skilled	10.5	8.0	8.5	7.5	13.2	16.5	10.7	7.0	8.7
IX	Lower skilled	9.4	4.6	5.7	8.6	13.8	16.5	10.9	11.0	11.5
X	Depressed	2.3	3.4	2.7	2.2	4.1	2.4	3.5	2.1	1.8
XI	Unskilled	43.6	52.9	55.3	49.0	48.2	43.7	35.1	41.5	43.2
	[Labourers]	[31.4]	[51.7]	[53.9]	[46.2]	[44.1]	[39.8]	[32.9]	[35.0]	[32.7]
	Number of churches/circuits		6	8	11	2	2	33	38	39
	Number of adults/fathers	9,162	87	281	440	170	206	275	541	544

TABLE LXIV. Monmouthshire: occupations of male Dissenters in percentages

	General male population	Independents		Baptists		Wesleyan Methodists			Calvinistic Methodists		
	1841	1820–9	1830–7	1820–9	1830–7	1810–19	1820–9	1830–7	1810–19	1820–9	1830–7
I Gentlemen	1.8	—	0.3	—	—	—	—	—	1.4	0.4	—
II Business	0.4	0.5	0.1	—	—	—	—	0.6	—	1.1	—
III Professions	0.8	—	—	1.1	—	0.7	—	0.3	—	—	—
IV Farmers	6.1	4.7	3.4	2.1	1.0	5.1	2.8	1.6	4.9	9.0	8.5
V Food and retail	5.0	3.1	3.6	5.3	3.1	1.5	3.6	5.3	—	2.5	2.4
VI White collar	2.3	0.5	1.7	2.1	2.0	5.9	3.0	2.5	4.2	0.4	1.7
VII Labour aristocracy	8.6	10.0	10.7	4.3	6.1	17.6	11.7	12.4	4.2	5.4	12.3
VIII Higher skilled	13.2	9.8	13.1	12.8	4.1	18.4	18.1	14.4	13.9	11.7	14.6
IX Lower skilled	26.6	58.4	53.0	58.5	75.5	30.5	38.8	39.3	45.8	53.2	45.3
[Miners]	[19.6]	[47.8]	[41.7]	[47.3]	[70.4]	[19.1]	[26.0]	[26.5]	[44.4]	[44.1]	[38.2]
X Depressed	0.6	0.2	0.4	—	—	0.7	0.6	1.1	2.8	—	0.8
XI Unskilled	34.5	12.9	13.8	13.8	8.2	19.5	21.3	22.5	22.9	16.4	14.3
[Labourers]	[28.1]	[10.4]	[10.2]	[13.8]	[8.2]	[15.1]	[18.9]	[18.5]	[21.5]	[15.6]	[11.6]
Number of churches/circuits		9	9	5	4	3	7	7	15	20	19
Number of adults/fathers	37,195	425	769	94	98	136	497	731	72	278	318

TABLE LXV. *Montgomeryshire: occupations of male Dissenters in percentages*

		General male population 1841	Independents			Wesleyan Methodists			Calvinistic Methodists		
			1810–19	1820–9	1830–7	1810–19	1820–9	1830–7	1810–19	1820–9	1830–7
I	Gentlemen	2.5	0.4	0.3	—	—	0.3	0.2	—	—	—
II	Business	0.2	0.4	0.6	0.6	0.5	1.4	1.4	0.3	0.5	0.6
III	Professions	0.9	—	—	0.1	—	—	0.2	—	—	—
IV	Farmers	20.3	9.1	18.6	21.5	13.8	17.4	15.0	32.5	27.4	32.1
V	Food and retail	5.2	6.6	6.3	5.0	3.6	3.5	4.2	5.5	8.0	9.0
VI	White collar	1.9	0.8	1.6	1.5	3.1	1.3	1.0	1.9	1.8	1.5
VII	Labour aristocracy	1.0	1.2	0.3	0.7	2.1	2.1	1.8	1.0	0.5	0.5
VIII	Higher skilled	12.3	16.9	11.4	12.2	16.9	19.4	18.8	11.6	12.7	11.4
IX	Lower skilled	8.9	13.2	11.9	8.9	14.1	13.0	12.1	7.1	9.3	9.4
X	Depressed	7.5	10.7	8.8	6.1	13.0	11.1	12.5	24.1	17.8	10.3
XI	Unskilled	39.3	40.7	40.2	43.3	32.8	30.6	32.7	16.0	21.9	25.3
	[Labourers]	[35.0]	[37.7]	[39.2]	[42.4]	[31.8]	[29.3]	[31.4]	[16.0]	[21.2]	[23.8]
	Number of churches/circuits		6	11	12	4	4	4	28	36	36
	Number of adults/fathers	15,482	243	687	816	192	797	845	297	603	487

TABLE LXVI. *Pembrokeshire: occupations of male Dissenters in percentages*

		General male population	Independents			Calvinistic Methodists		
		1841	1810–19	1820–9	1830–7	1810–19	1820–9	1830–7
I	Gentlemen	3.2	0.5	0.5	0.3	—	—	—
II	Business	0.4	0.5	0.2	0.4	1.3	—	—
III	Professions	1.0	—	0.2	0.5	—	—	—
IV	Farmers	14.5	17.2	11.6	12.9	13.3	18.7	18.0
V	Food and retail	4.5	5.0	2.9	3.4	4.0	4.9	4.4
VI	White collar	2.3	3.2	1.5	2.3	3.3	4.9	2.5
VII	Labour aristocracy	3.2	1.8	2.2	3.5	4.0	2.7	1.1
VIII	Higher skilled	15.8	11.5	15.7	14.7	20.7	21.2	20.5
IX	Lower skilled	10.9	9.0	9.9	10.3	14.7	8.2	10.4
X	Depressed	0.8	2.7	1.5	1.2	1.3	2.2	1.6
XI	Unskilled	43.3	48.6	53.7	50.5	37.3	37.2	41.5
	[Labourers]	[34.5]	[44.1]	[42.8]	[39.5]	[20.0]	[20.1]	[30.6]
	Number of churches/circuits		9	19	19	9	12	12
	Number of adults/fathers	18,095	221	581	863	75	184	183

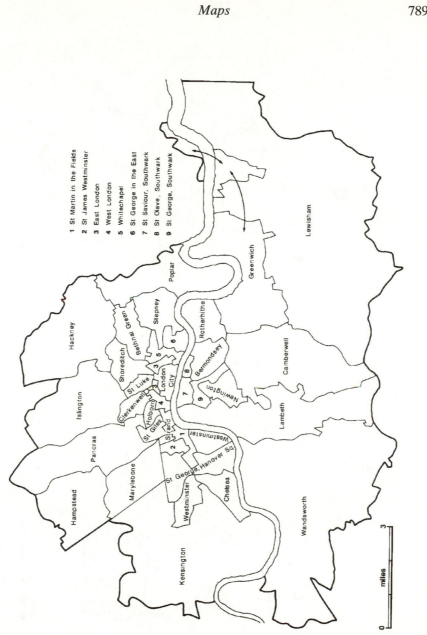

1 St Martin in the Fields
2 St James Westminster
3 East London
4 West London
5 Whitechapel
6 St George in the East
7 St Saviour, Southwark
8 St Olave, Southwark
9 St George, Southwark

MAP 1. London: registration districts, 1851

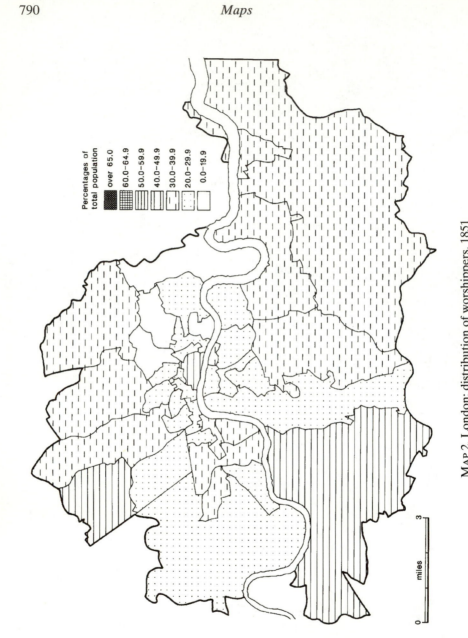

MAP 2. London: distribution of worshippers, 1851

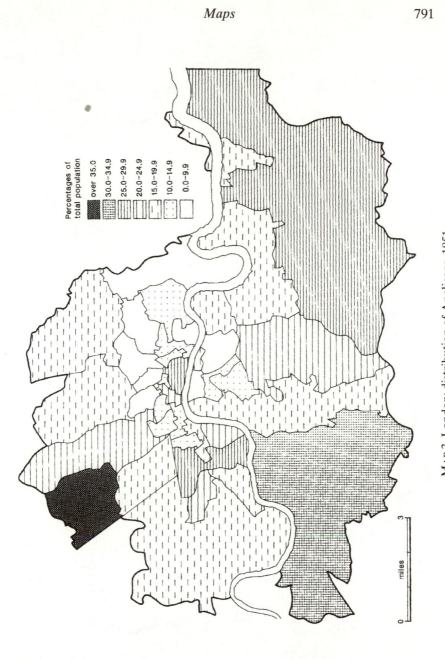

Percentages of
total population

- over 35.0
- 30.0–34.9
- 25.0–29.9
- 20.0–24.9
- 15.0–19.9
- 10.0–14.9
- 0.0–9.9

MAP 3. London: distribution of Anglicans, 1851

miles

0   3

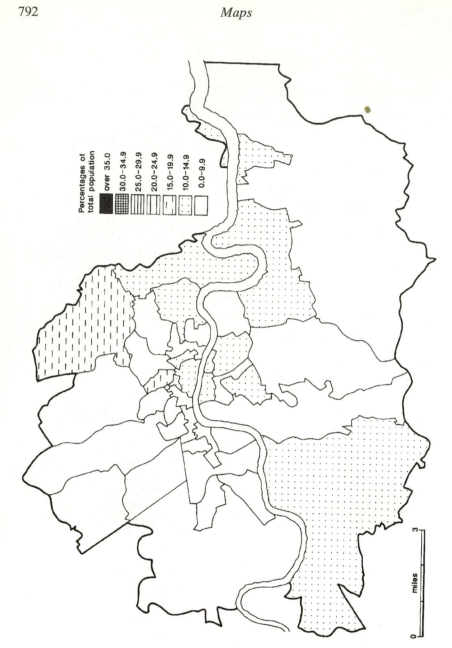

MAP 4. London: distribution of Nonconformists, 1851

Percentages of
total population

over 35.0
30.0–34.9
25.0–29.9
20.0–24.9
15.0–19.9
10.0–14.9
0.0–9.9

0   miles   3

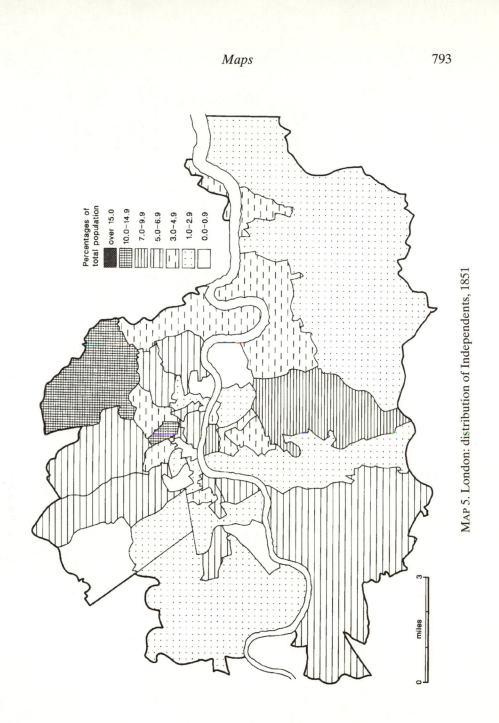

MAP 5. London: distribution of Independents, 1851

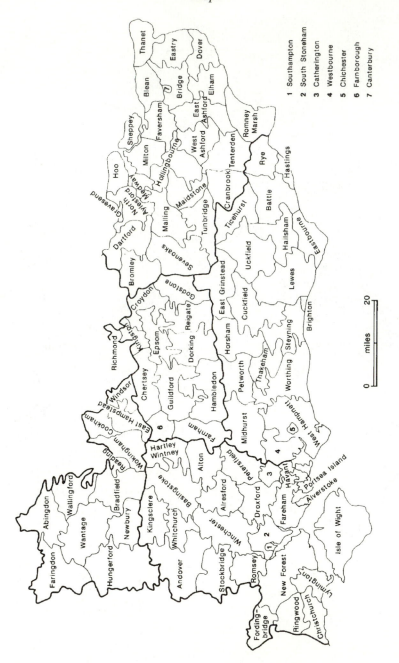

MAP 6. South-east England registration districts, 1851

1 Southampton
2 South Stoneham
3 Catherington
4 Westbourne
5 Chichester
6 Farnborough
7 Canterbury

0 miles 20

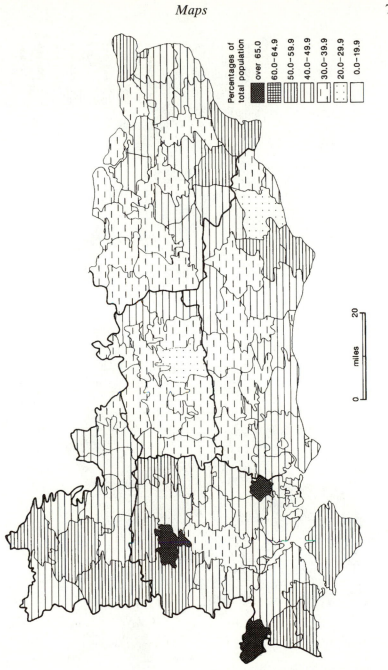

MAP 7. South-east England: distribution of worshippers, 1851

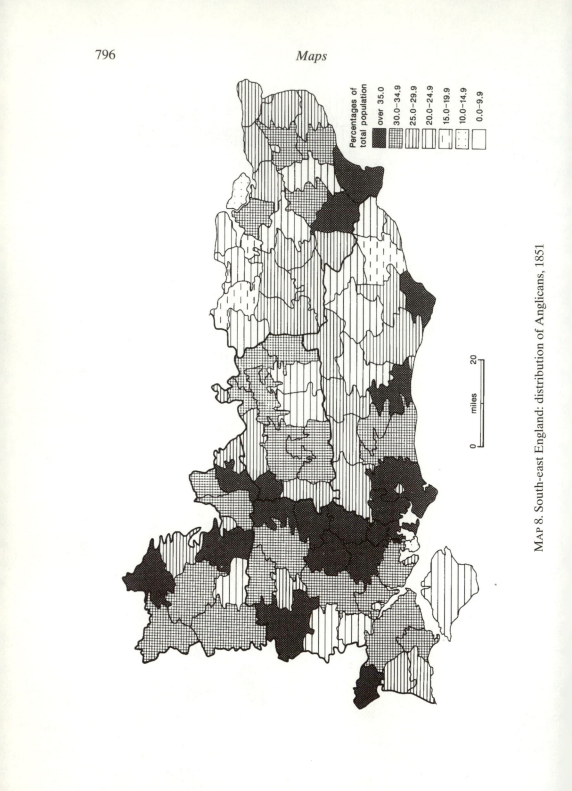

MAP 8. South-east England: distribution of Anglicans, 1851

Percentages of
total population

over 35.0
30.0–34.9
25.0–29.9
20.0–24.9
15.0–19.9
10.0–14.9
0.0–9.9

0   20
    miles

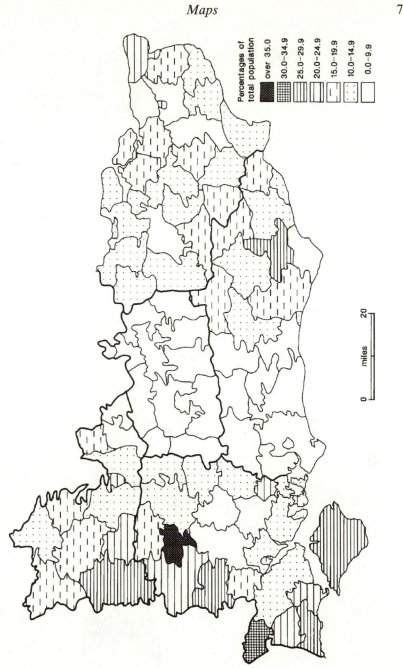

MAP 9. South-east England: distribution of Nonconformists, 1851

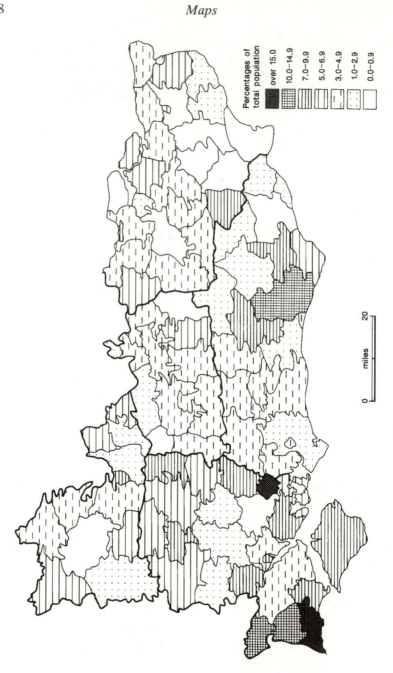

MAP 10. South-east England: distribution of Independents, 1851

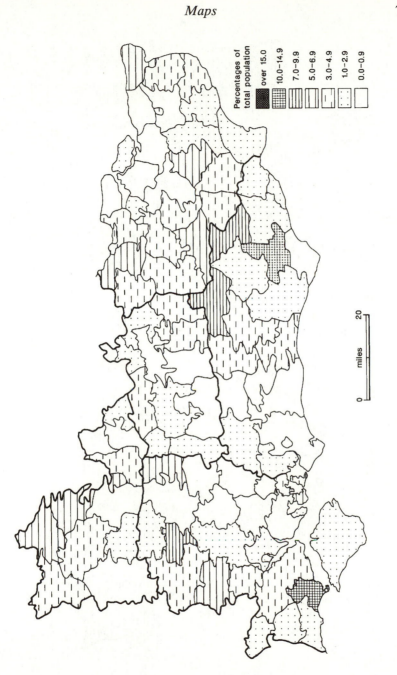

MAP 11. South-east England: distribution of Baptists, 1851

Percentages of
total population

over 15.0
10.0–14.9
7.0–9.9
5.0–6.9
3.0–4.9
1.0–2.9
0.0–0.9

0   miles   20

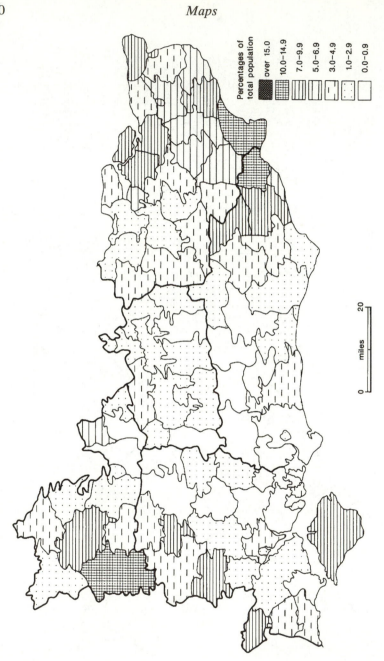

MAP 12. South-east England: distribution of Wesleyan Methodists, 1851

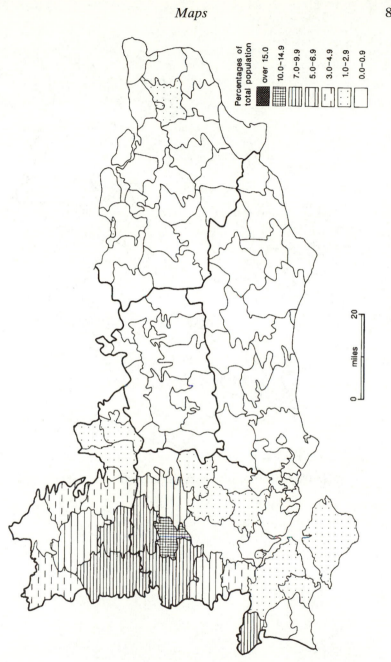

MAP 13. South-east England: distribution of Primitive Methodists, 1851

Percentages of
total population

over 15.0
10.0–14.9
7.0–9.9
5.0–6.9
3.0–4.9
1.0–2.9
0.0–0.9

0   miles   20

MAP 14. South Midlands: registration districts, 1851

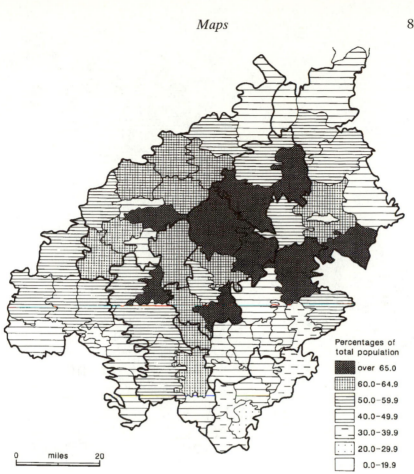

Percentages of
total population

over 65.0

60.0–64.9

50.0–59.9

40.0–49.9

30.0–39.9

20.0–29.9

0.0–19.9

0   miles   20

MAP 15. South Midlands: distribution of worshippers, 1851

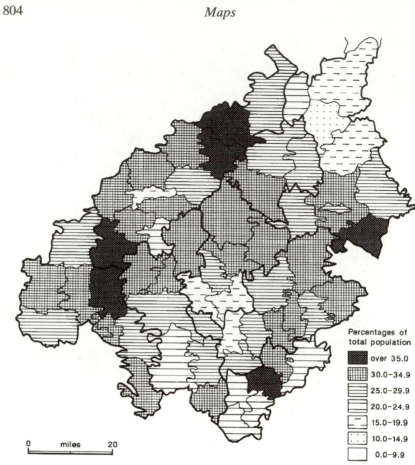

Percentages of
total population

over 35.0

30.0–34.9

25.0–29.9

20.0–24.9

15.0–19.9

10.0–14.9

0.0–9.9

0   miles   20

MAP 16. South Midlands: distribution of Anglicans, 1851

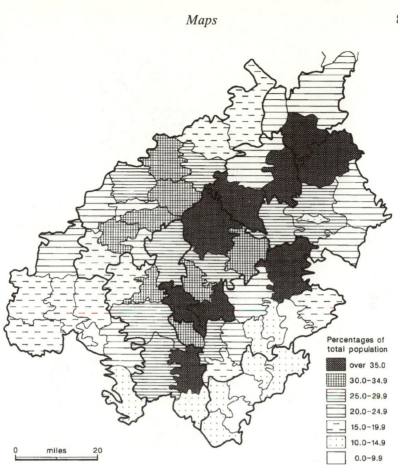

MAP 17. South Midlands: distribution of Nonconformists, 1851

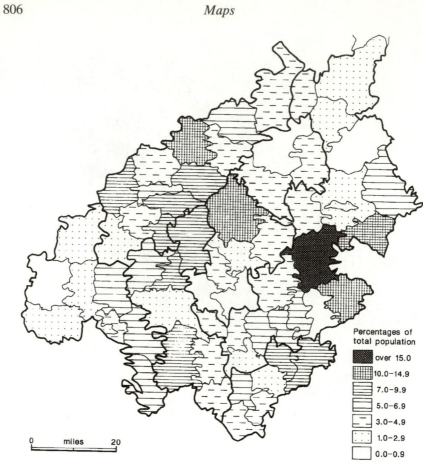

MAP 18. South Midlands: distribution of Independents, 1851

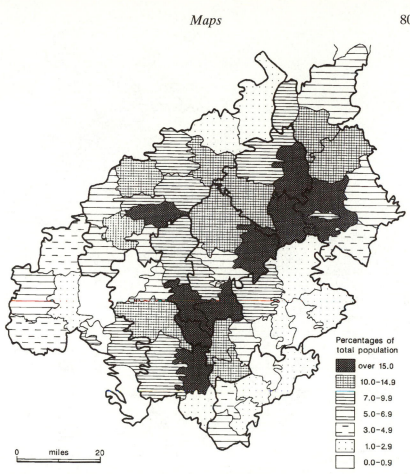

MAP 19. South Midlands: distribution of Baptists, 1851

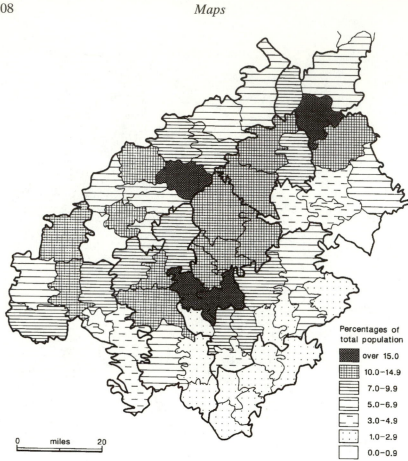

MAP 20. South Midlands: distribution of Wesleyan Methodists, 1851

MAP 21. Eastern England: registration Districts, 1851

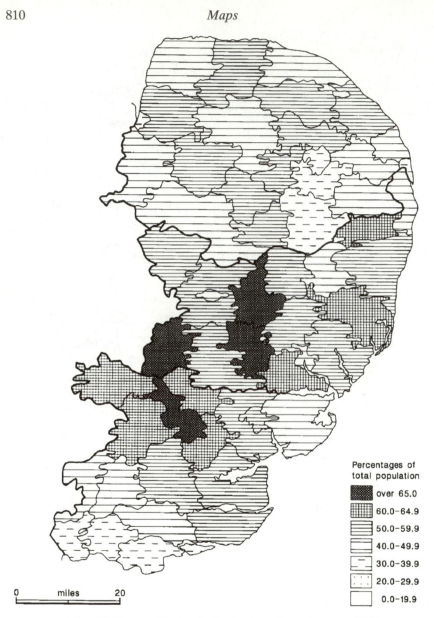

Percentages of
total population

over 65.0

60.0–64.9

50.0–59.9

40.0–49.9

30.0–39.9

20.0–29.9

0.0–19.9

0   miles   20

MAP 22. Eastern England: distribution of worshippers, 1851

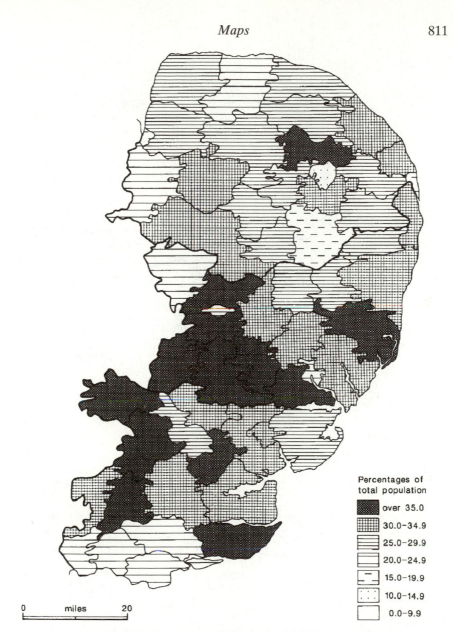

Percentages of
total population

■ over 35.0

▦ 30.0–34.9

▤ 25.0–29.9

▭ 20.0–24.9

15.0–19.9

10.0–14.9

0.0–9.9

0 ___ miles ___ 20

MAP 23. Eastern England: distribution of Anglicans, 1851

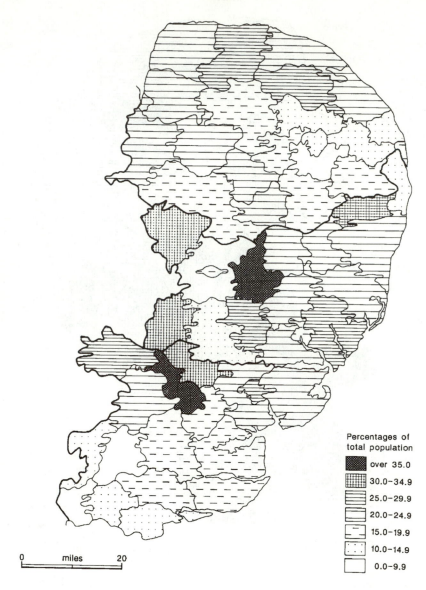

MAP 24. Eastern England: distribution of Nonconformists, 1851

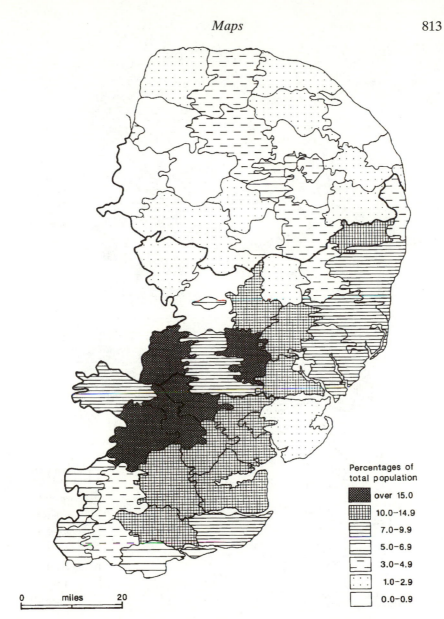

Percentages of
total population

over 15.0

10.0–14.9

7.0–9.9

5.0–6.9

3.0–4.9

1.0–2.9

0.0–0.9

0   miles   20

MAP 25. Eastern England: distribution of Independents, 1851

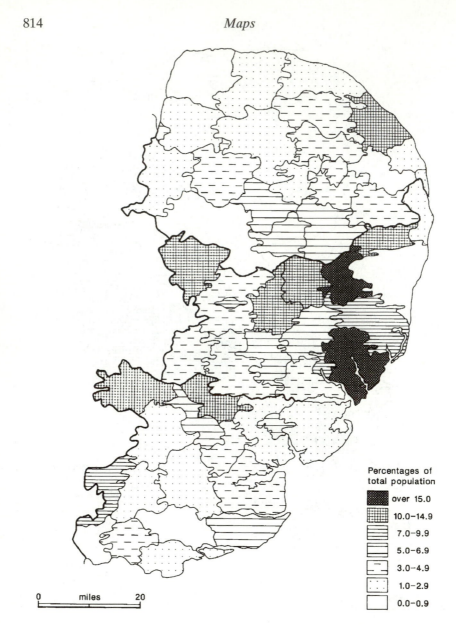

Percentages of
total population

over 15.0

10.0–14.9

7.0–9.9

5.0–6.9

3.0–4.9

1.0–2.9

0.0–0.9

0   miles   20

MAP 26. Eastern England: distribution of Baptists, 1851

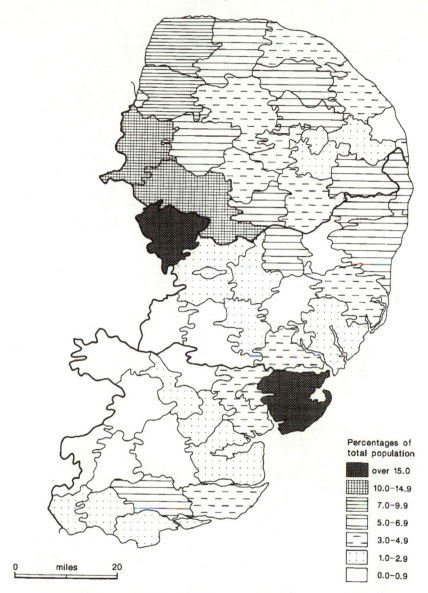

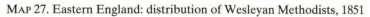

MAP 27. Eastern England: distribution of Wesleyan Methodists, 1851

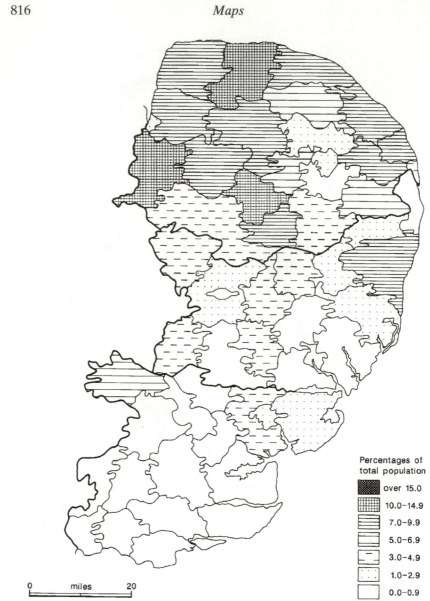

Percentages of
total population

▓ over 15.0
▦ 10.0–14.9
▤ 7.0–9.9
▥ 5.0–6.9
⊟ 3.0–4.9
⋯ 1.0–2.9
☐ 0.0–0.9

0   miles   20

MAP 28. Eastern England: distribution of Primitive Methodists, 1851

MAP 29. South-west England: registration districts, 1851

1 Bradford
2 Melksham
3 Sherborne
4 Sturminster
5 Shaftesbury
6 Salisbury

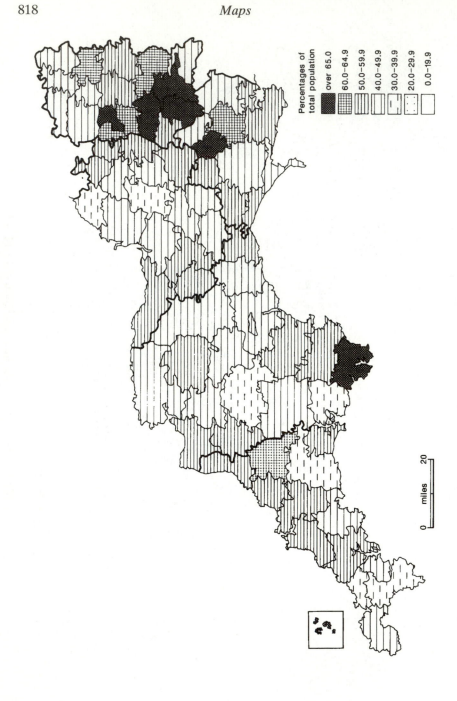

MAP 30. South-west England: distribution of worshippers, 1851

Percentages of
total population

over 65.0
60.0–64.9
50.0–59.9
40.0–49.9
30.0–39.9
20.0–29.9
0.0–19.9

0   miles   20

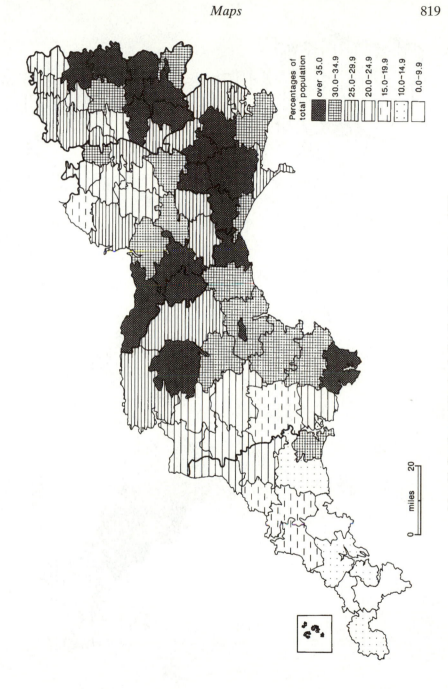

MAP 31. South-west England: distribution of Anglicans, 1851

Percentages of
total population

over 35.0
30.0–34.9
25.0–29.9
20.0–24.9
15.0–19.9
10.0–14.9
0.0–9.9

0   miles   20

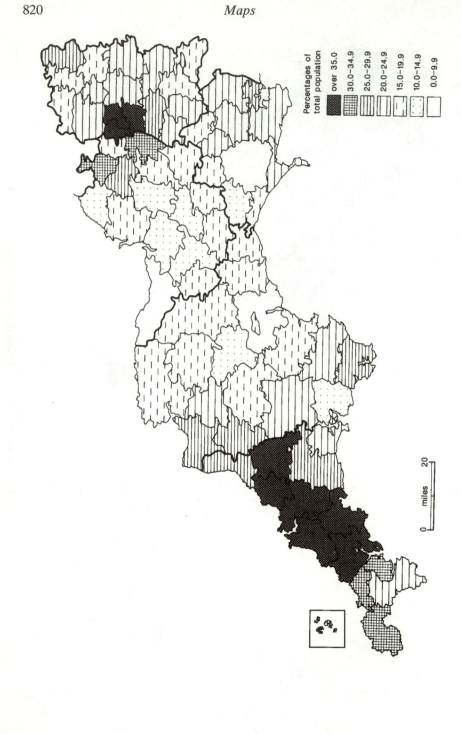

MAP 32. South-west England: distribution of Nonconformists, 1851

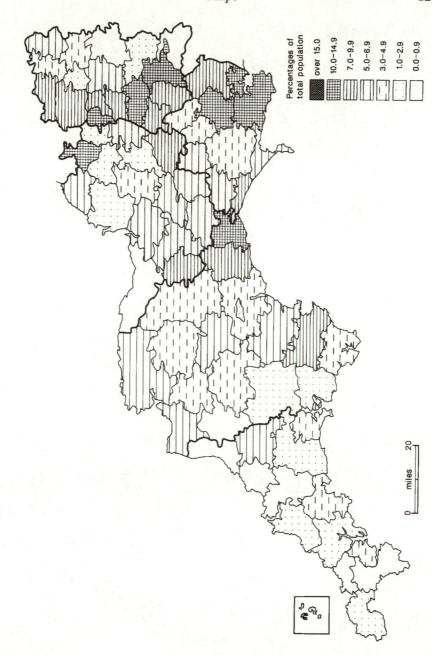

MAP 33. South-west England: distribution of Independents, 1851

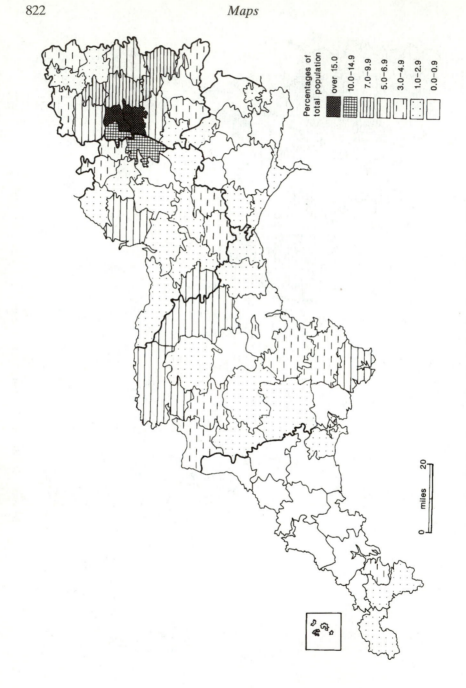

MAP 34. South-west England: distribution of Baptists, 1851

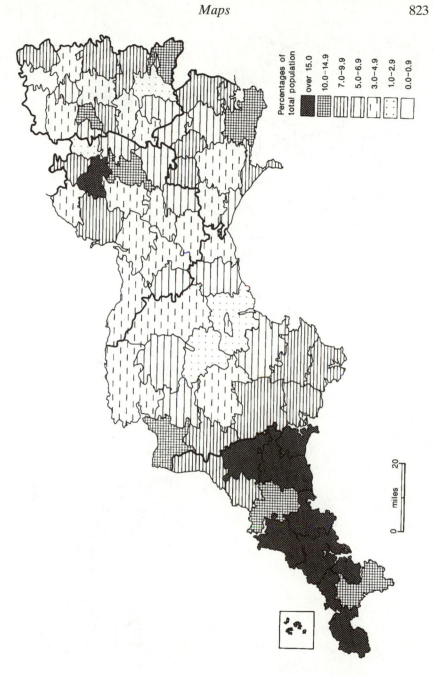

MAP 35. South-west England: distribution of Wesleyan Methodists, 1851

MAP 36. South-west England: distribution of Primitive Methodists, 1851

Percentages of
total population

over 15.0
10.0–14.9
7.0–9.9
5.0–6.9
3.0–4.9
1.0–2.9
0.0–0.9

0   miles   20

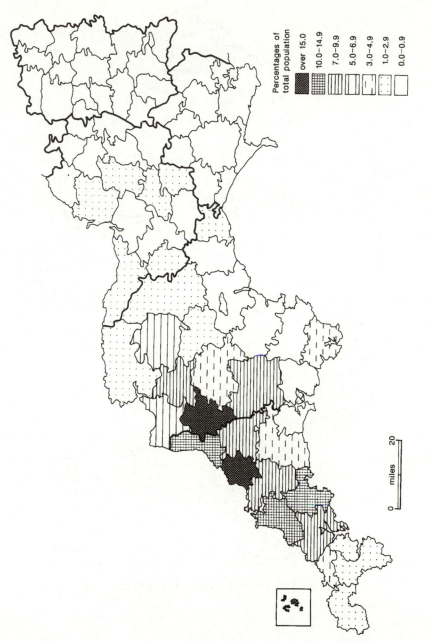

MAP 37. South-west England: distribution of Bible Christians, 1851

Percentages of
total population

over 15.0
10.0–14.9
7.0–9.9
5.0–6.9
3.0–4.9
1.0–2.9
0.0–0.9

1 Wolstanton
2 Stoke on Trent
3 West Bromwich
4 Birmingham
5 Coventry
6 Stourbridge
7 Worcester
8 Wheatenhurst

MAP 38. West Midlands: registration districts, 1851

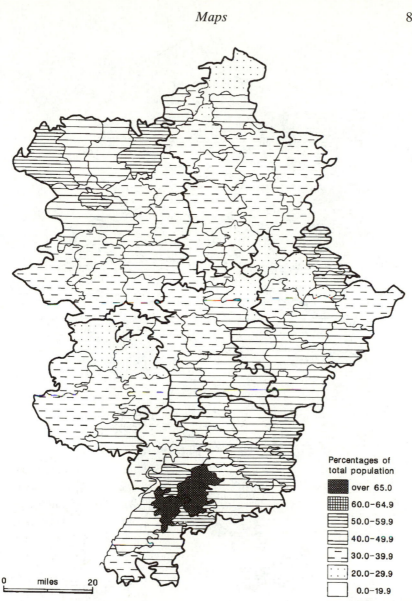

MAP 39. West Midlands: distribution of worshippers, 1851

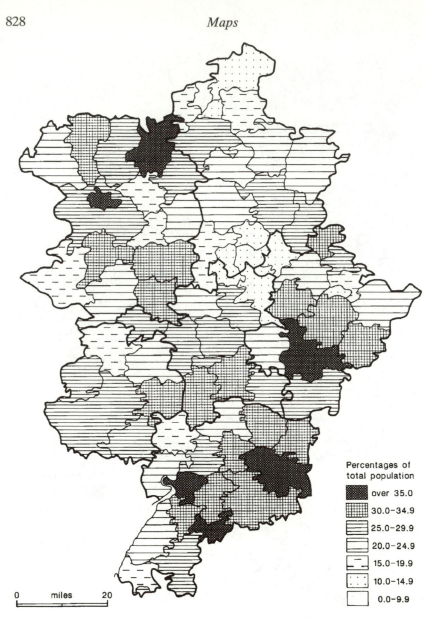

MAP 40. West Midlands: distribution of Anglicans, 1851

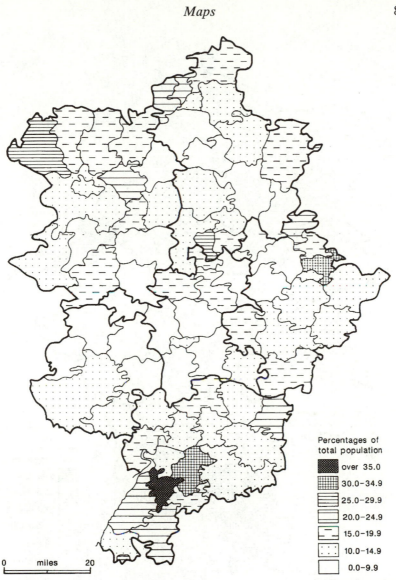

Percentages of
total population

over 35.0

30.0–34.9

25.0–29.9

20.0–24.9

15.0–19.9

10.0–14.9

0.0–9.9

0   miles   20

MAP 41. West Midlands: distribution of Nonconformists, 1851

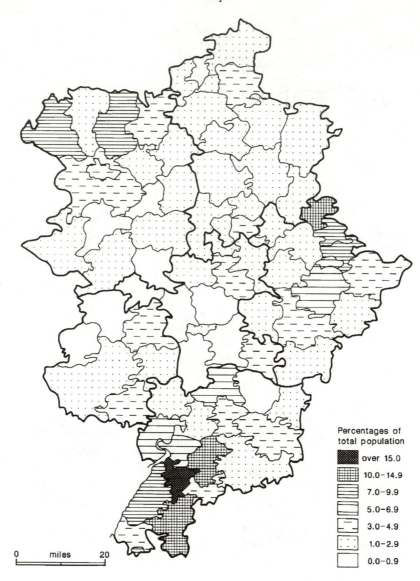

MAP 42. West Midlands: distribution of Independents, 1851

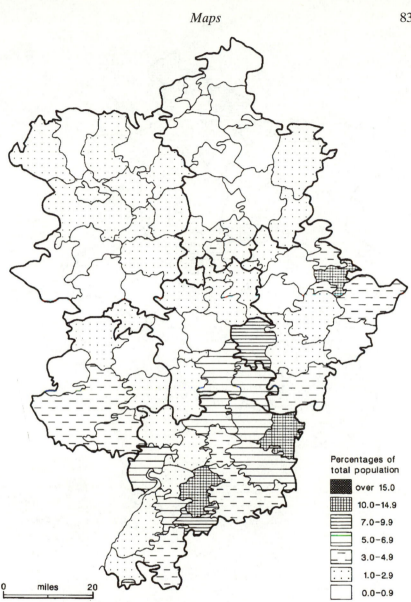

MAP 43. West Midlands: distribution of Baptists, 1851

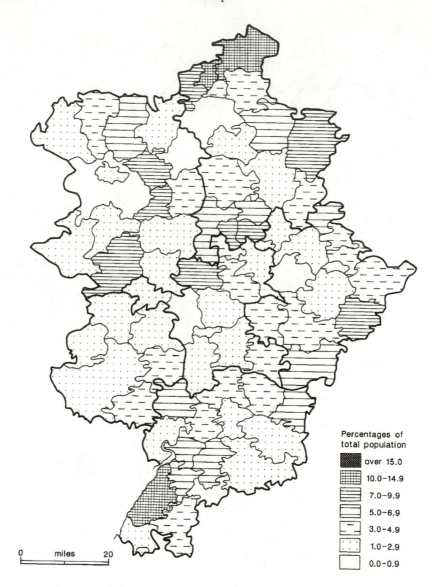

MAP 44. West Midlands: distribution of Wesleyan Methodists, 1851

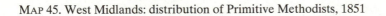

MAP 45. West Midlands: distribution of Primitive Methodists, 1851

MAP 46. North Midlands: registration districts, 1851

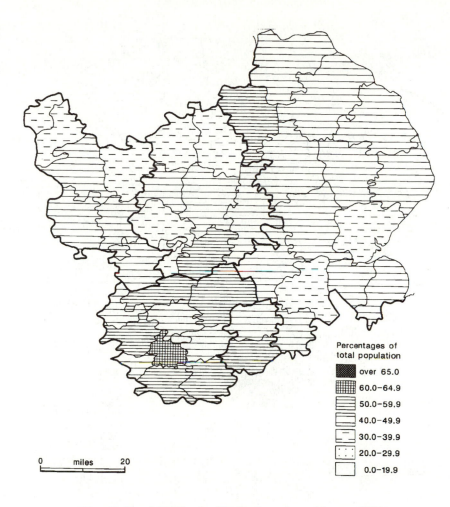

Percentages of
total population

over 65.0

60.0–64.9

50.0–59.9

40.0–49.9

30.0–39.9

20.0–29.9

0.0–19.9

0   miles   20

MAP 47. North Midlands: distribution of worshippers, 1851

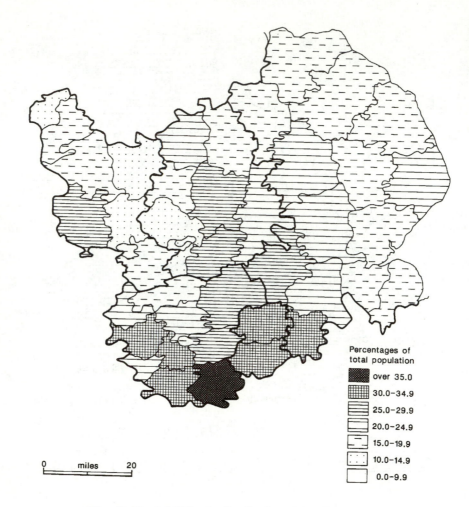

MAP 48. North Midlands: distribution of Anglicans, 1851

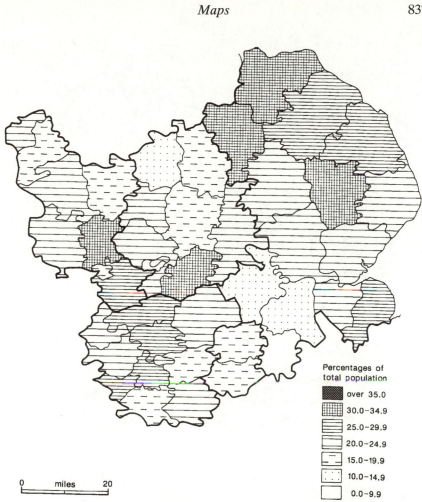

Percentages of
total population

▓	over 35.0
▦	30.0–34.9
▤	25.0–29.9
▢	20.0–24.9
⊡	15.0–19.9
⋯	10.0–14.9
□	0.0–9.9

0   miles   20

MAP 49. North Midlands: distribution of Nonconformists, 1851

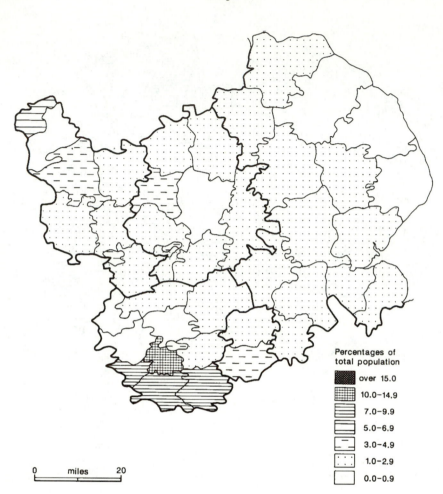

MAP 50. North Midlands: distribution of Independents, 1851

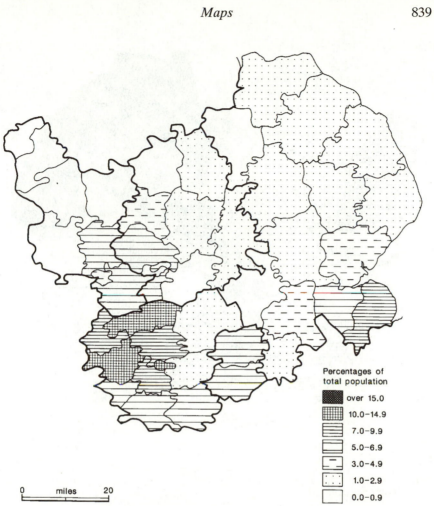

Percentages of
total population

▨	over 15.0
▦	10.0–14.9
▤	7.0–9.9
▢	5.0–6.9
▭	3.0–4.9
⋯	1.0–2.9
▢	0.0–0.9

0   miles   20

MAP 51. North Midlands: distribution of Baptists, 1851

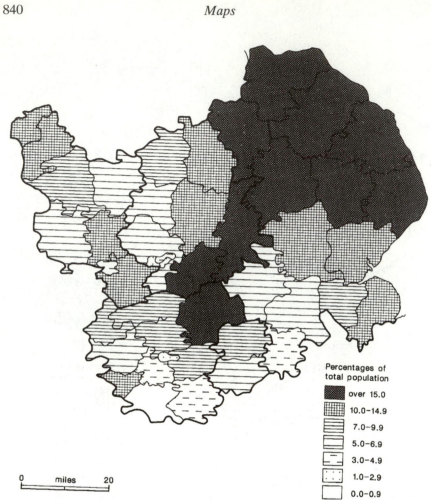

Percentages of
total population

	over 15.0
	10.0–14.9
	7.0–9.9
	5.0–6.9
	3.0–4.9
	1.0–2.9
	0.0–0.9

0   miles   20

MAP 52. North Midlands: distribution of Wesleyan Methodists, 1851

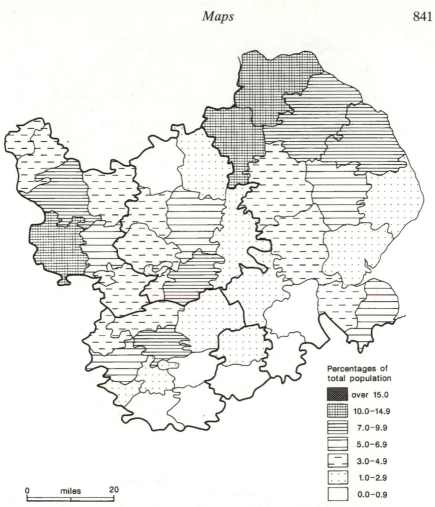

MAP 53. North Midlands: distribution of Primitive Methodists, 1851

Ulverstone

1   Barton upon Irwell
2   Liverpool
3   Salford

Lancaster

Garstang

Clitheroe

Fylde

Preston

Burnley

Blackburn

Haslingden

Choriey

Rochdale

Ormskirk

Bolton

Bury

Wigan

Oldham

Manchester

West Derby

Leigh

3

Ashton under
Lyne

1

Prescot

Chorlton

2

Warrington

Stockport

Wirrall

Altrincham

Runcorn

Macclesfield

Great Boughton

Northwich

Congleton

Nantwich

0   miles   20

MAP 54. North-west England: registration districts, 1851

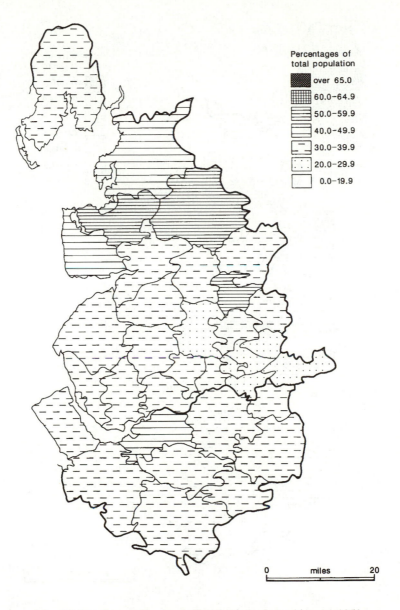

MAP 55. North-west England: distribution of worshippers, 1851

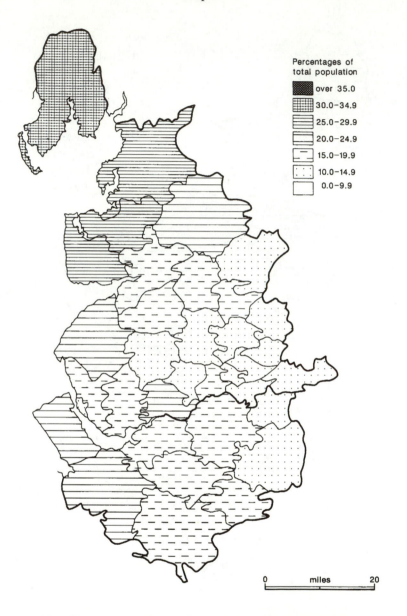

Percentages of
total population

over 35.0

30.0–34.9

25.0–29.9

20.0–24.9

15.0–19.9

10.0–14.9

0.0–9.9

0   miles   20

MAP 56. North-west England: distribution of Anglicans, 1851

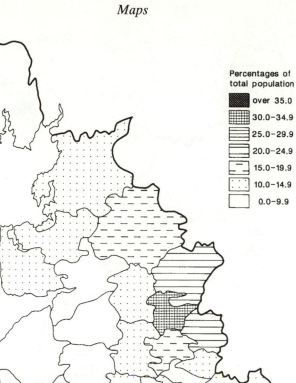

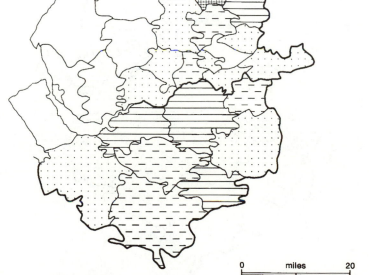

Map 57. North-west England: distribution of Nonconformists, 1851

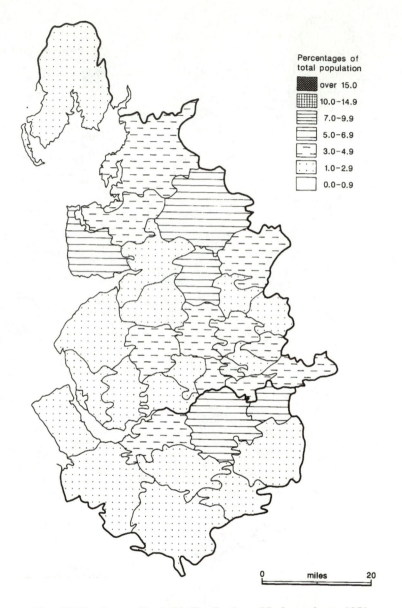

MAP 58. North-west England: distribution of Independents, 1851

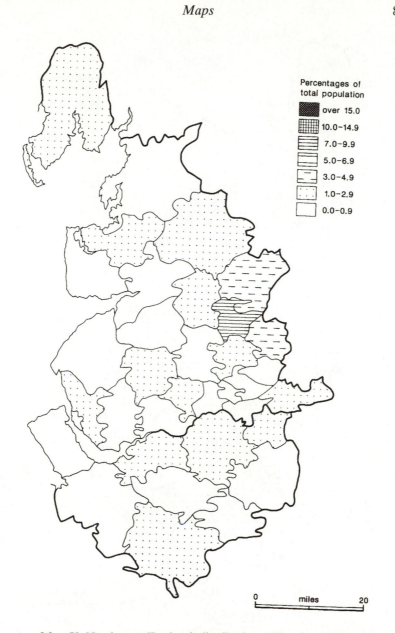

MAP 59. North-west England: distribution of Baptists, 1851

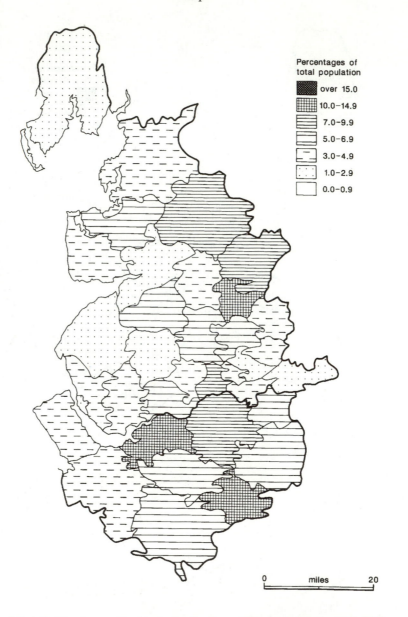

Percentages of
total population

over 15.0

10.0–14.9

7.0–9.9

5.0–6.9

3.0–4.9

1.0–2.9

0.0–0.9

0   miles   20

MAP 60. North-west England: distribution of Wesleyan Methodists, 1851

Map 61. Yorkshire: registration districts, 1851

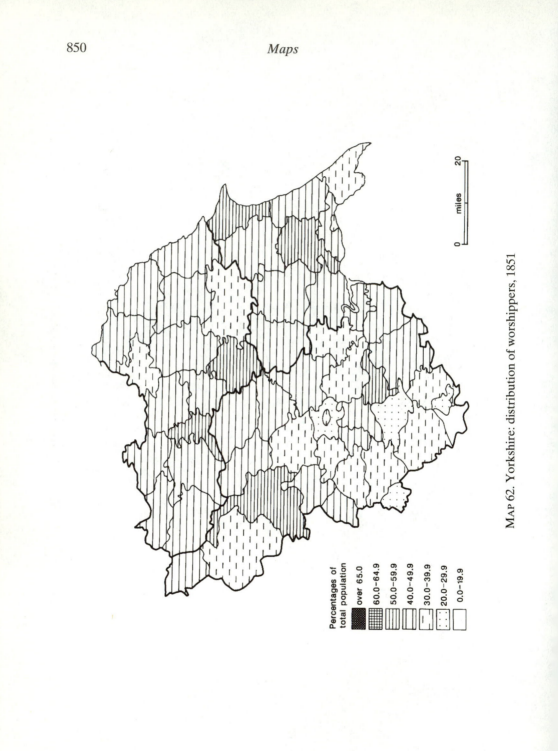

MAP 62. Yorkshire: distribution of worshippers, 1851

Percentages of total population

over 65.0
60.0–64.9
50.0–59.9
40.0–49.9
30.0–39.9
20.0–29.9
0.0–19.9

miles
0   20

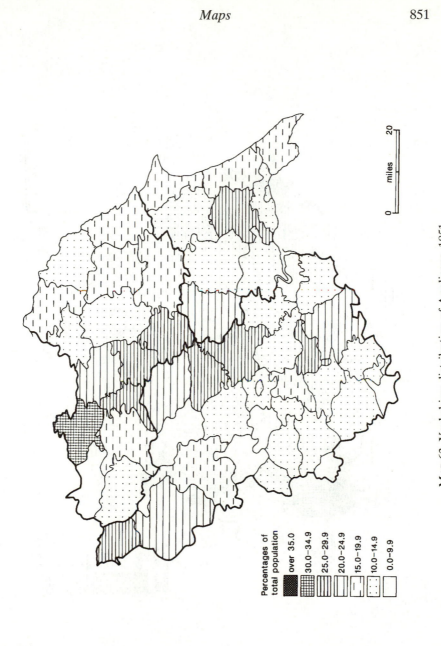

MAP 63. Yorkshire: distribution of Anglicans, 1851

Maps

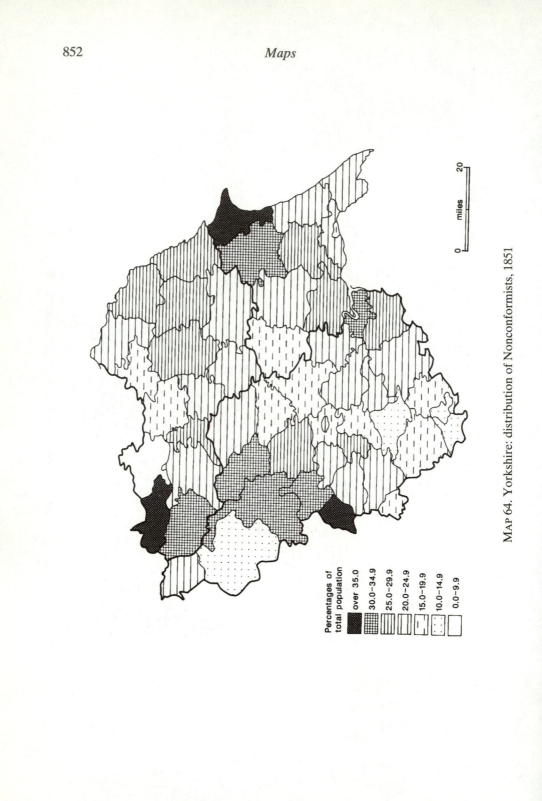

Percentages of
total population

over 35.0
30.0–34.9
25.0–29.9
20.0–24.9
15.0–19.9
10.0–14.9
0.0–9.9

0   miles   20

MAP 64. Yorkshire: distribution of Nonconformists, 1851

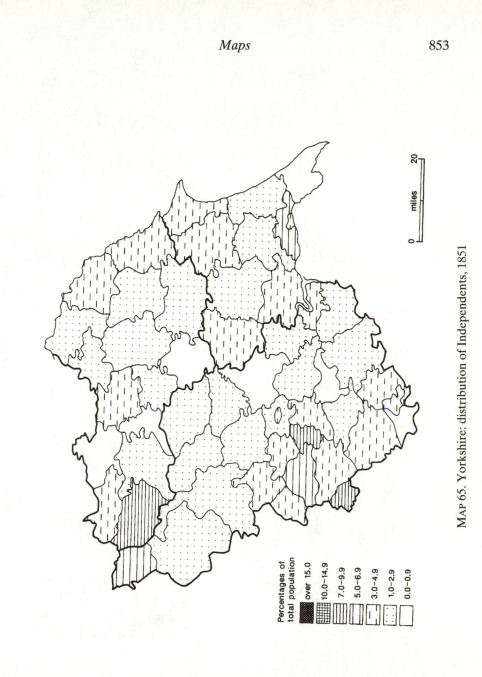

MAP 65. Yorkshire: distribution of Independents, 1851

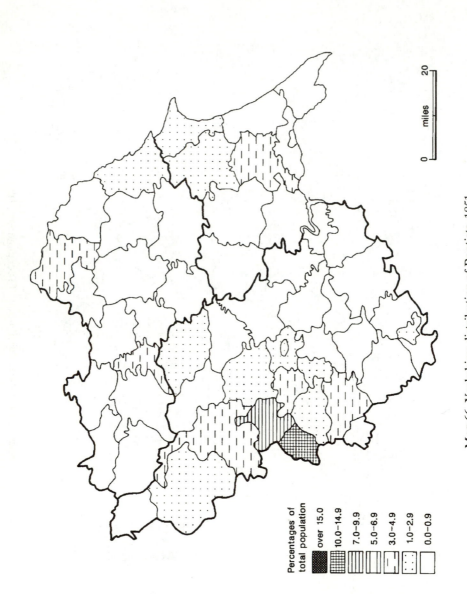

MAP 66. Yorkshire: distribution of Baptists, 1851

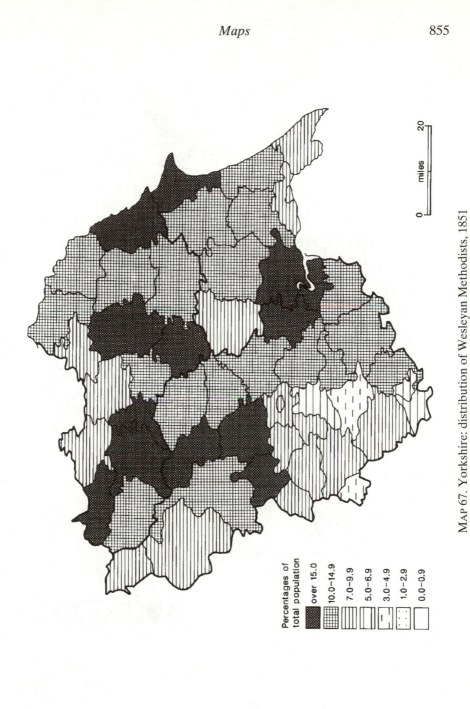

Percentages of
total population

over 15.0
10.0–14.9
7.0–9.9
5.0–6.9
3.0–4.9
1.0–2.9
0.0–0.9

MAP 67. Yorkshire: distribution of Wesleyan Methodists, 1851

0   miles   20

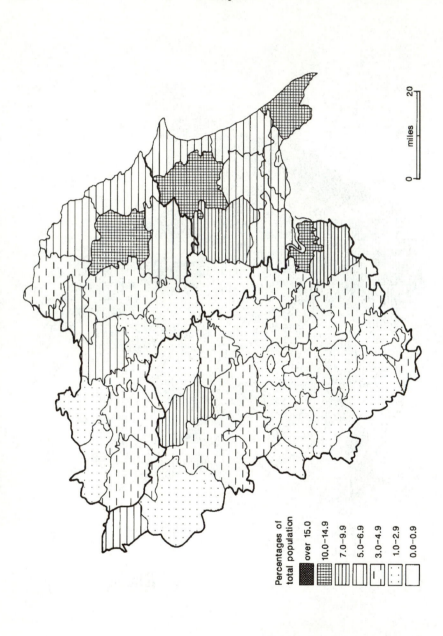

Percentages of
total population

over 15.0

10.0–14.9

7.0–9.9

5.0–6.9

3.0–4.9

1.0–2.9

0.0–0.9

0   miles   20

MAP 68. Yorkshire: distribution of Primitive Methodists, 1851

1 Chester–le–Street
2 Houghton–le–Spring
3 Newcastle

Berwick
Glendale
Belford
Alnwick
Rothbury
Bellingham
Morpeth
Longtown
Castle Ward
Tynemouth
Brampton
Haltwhistle
Hexham
3
South Shields
Carlisle
Gateshead
Sunderland
Wigton
1
Alston
Weardale
Durham
2
Penrith
Easington
Cockermouth
Auckland
Stockton
West Ward
East Ward
Teesdale
Whitehaven
Darlington
Bootle
Kendal

0 miles 20

MAP 69. Northern England: registration districts, 1851

Maps

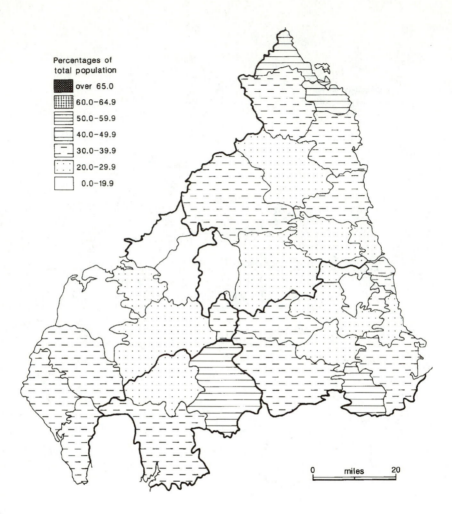

Percentages of
total population

over 65.0

60.0–64.9

50.0–59.9

40.0–49.9

30.0–39.9

20.0–29.9

0.0–19.9

0   miles   20

MAP 70. Northern England: distribution of worshippers, 1851

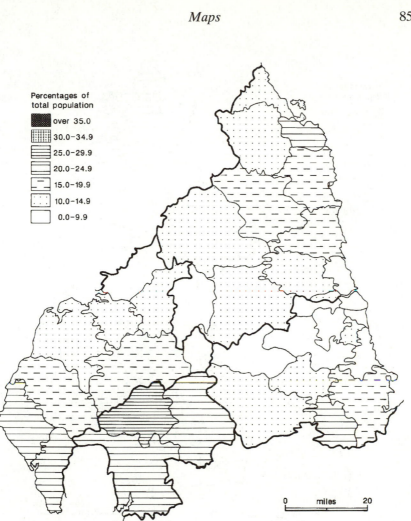

MAP 71. Northern England: distribution of Anglicans, 1851

Maps

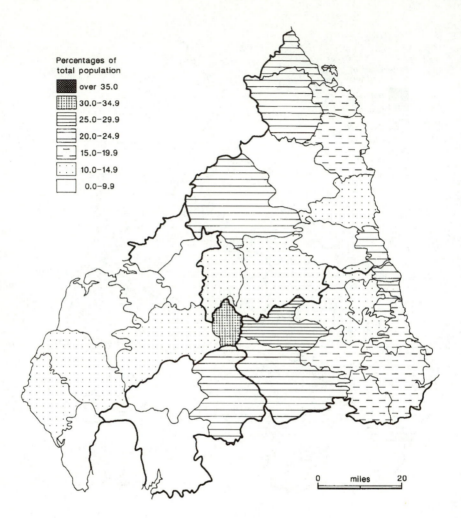

Percentages of
total population

over 35.0

30.0–34.9

25.0–29.9

20.0–24.9

15.0–19.9

10.0–14.9

0.0–9.9

0   miles   20

MAP 72. Northern England: distribution of Nonconformists, 1851

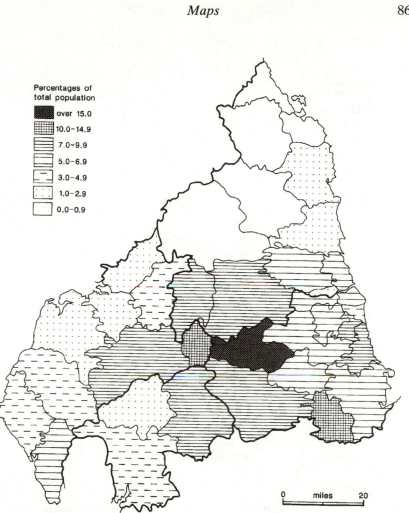

MAP 73. Northern England: distribution of Wesleyan Methodists, 1851

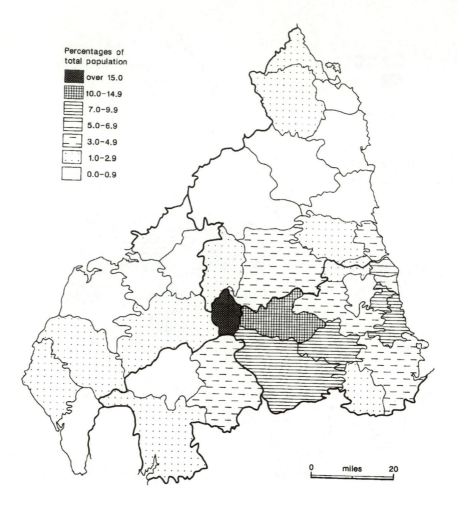

Percentages of
total population

over 15.0

10.0–14.9

7.0–9.9

5.0–6.9

3.0–4.9

1.0–2.9

0.0–0.9

0   miles   20

MAP 74. Northern England: distribution of Primitive Methodists, 1851

MAP 75. Wales: registration districts, 1851

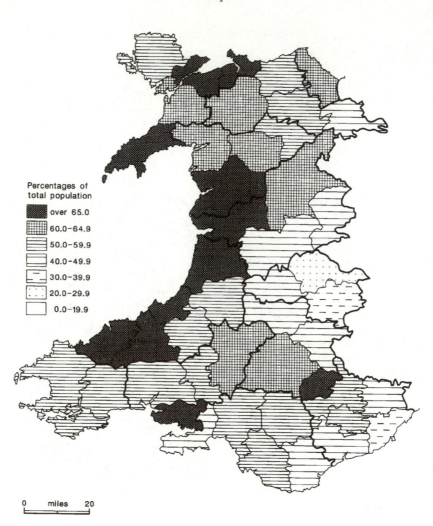

Percentages of
total population

- over 65.0
- 60.0–64.9
- 50.0–59.9
- 40.0–49.9
- 30.0–39.9
- 20.0–29.9
- 0.0–19.9

0   miles   20

MAP 76. Wales: distribution of worshippers, 1851

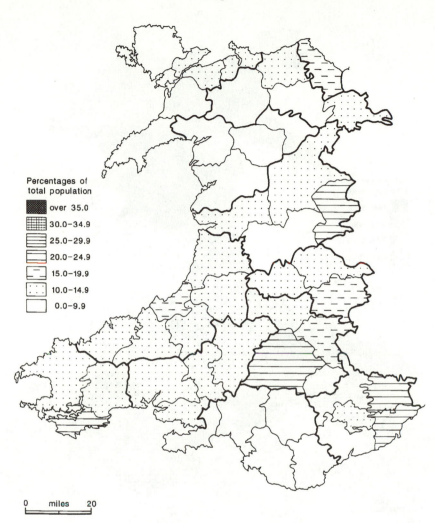

Percentages of
total population

over 35.0

30.0–34.9

25.0–29.9

20.0–24.9

15.0–19.9

10.0–14.9

0.0–9.9

0   miles   20

MAP 77. Wales: distribution of Anglicans, 1851

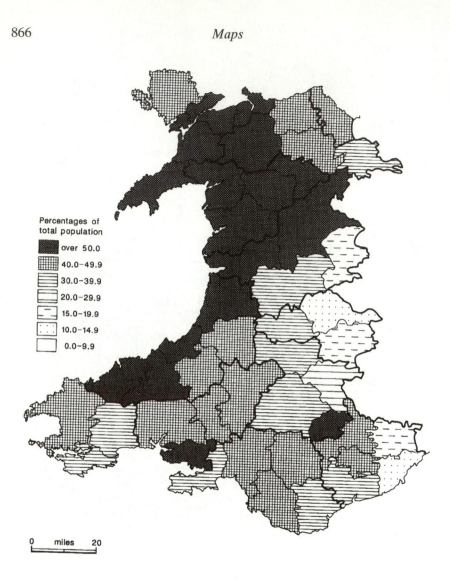

Percentages of
total population

over 50.0

40.0–49.9

30.0–39.9

20.0–29.9

15.0–19.9

10.0–14.9

0.0–9.9

0   miles   20

MAP 78. Wales: distribution of Nonconformists, 1851

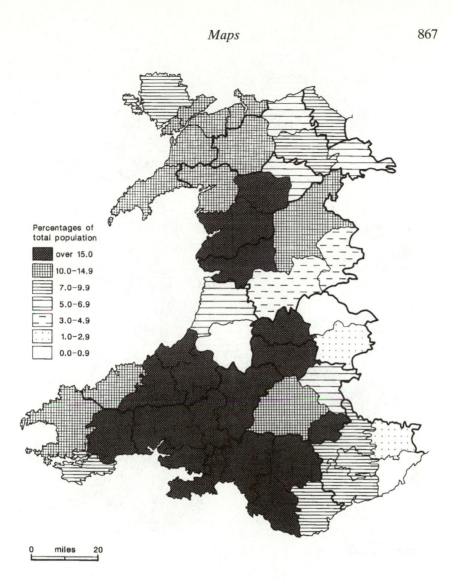

MAP 79. Wales: distribution of Independents, 1851

Maps

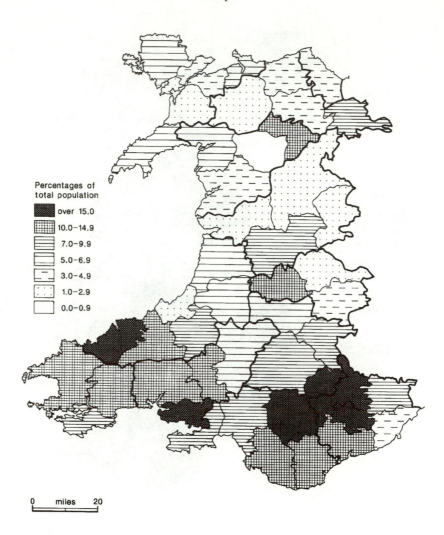

Percentages of
total population

- over 15.0
- 10.0–14.9
- 7.0–9.9
- 5.0–6.9
- 3.0–4.9
- 1.0–2.9
- 0.0–0.9

0   miles   20

MAP 80. Wales: distribution of Baptists, 1851

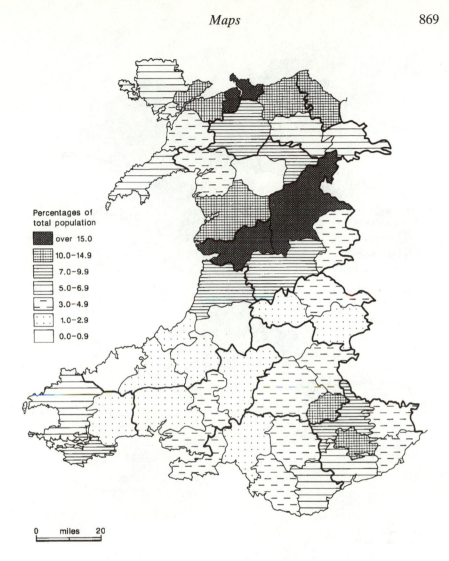

MAP 81. Wales: distribution of Wesleyan Methodists, 1851

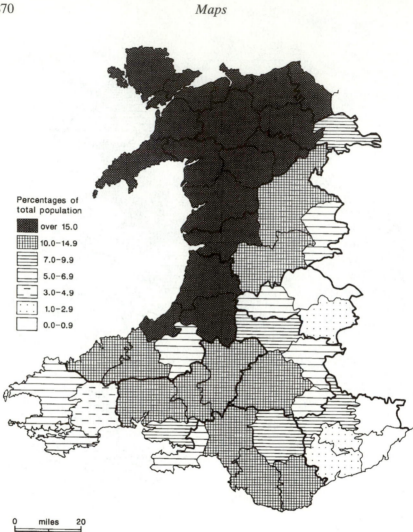

MAP 82. Wales: distribution of Calvinistic Methodists, 1851

Index